GW00838526

Web : www.jainbookagency.com
E-mail : sales@jainbookagency.com

JAIN BOOK AGENCY
1, Aurbindo Place Market, Hauzk...
New Delhi -110016
Tel:- 011 - 41755666, 265670...

Company Law

Company Law

by

Dr Avtar Singh

Advocate

B. Com., LL.M., LL.D., (Luck.),

Vidya Bhushan (Hindi Sansthan, U.P.)

Ex-Visiting Professor of Business Laws, I.I.M., Lucknow

Ex-Reader in Law, Lucknow University

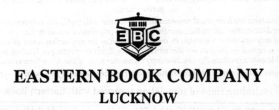

EASTERN BOOK COMPANY
LUCKNOW

EASTERN BOOK COMPANY

Website: www.ebc-india.com
E-mail: sales@ebc-india.com

Lucknow
34, Lalbagh, Lucknow-226 001
Phones: +91-522-4033600 (30 lines)
Fax: +91-522-4033633

Delhi
1267, Kashmere Gate,
Old Hindu College Building,
Delhi-110 006
Phones: +91-11-23917616, +91-9313080904
Telefax: +91-11-23921656

New Delhi
5-B, Atma Ram House, 5th Floor,
1, Tolstoy Marg, Connaught Place,
New Delhi-110 001
Phones: +91-11-45752323, +91-9871197119
Fax: +91-11-41504440

Allahabad
Manav Law House, 8/10, M.G. Marg,
Opp. Bishop Johnson School,
Allahabad-211 001
Phones: +91-532-2560710, 2422023
Fax: +91-532-2623584

Shop online at: www.ebcwebstore.com

Other works of the same author:

An Introduction to the Law of Contract
Company Law (An Introduction)
Elements of Commercial Law
Law of Arbitration and Conciliation
Laws of Banking and Negotiable Instruments
Law of Carriage
Law of Consumer Protection: Principles and Practice
Law of Contract and Specific Relief
Law of Insolvency
Law of Insurance
Law of Monopolies, Restrictive and Unfair Trade Practices
Law of Partnership (Principles, Practice & Taxation)
Law of Partnership (An Introduction)
Negotiable Instruments
Principles of Mercantile Law
Sale of Goods and Hire Purchase
Textbook on Law of Contract

(Ed.) E.E. Jhirad's Law Relating to Private
  Companies
(Ed.) V.M. Shukla's Legal Remedies
Bhagidari Vidhi
Company Vidhi
Company Vidhi (Ek Parichay)
Ekadhikar, Avarodhak Tatha Anuchit
  Vyaparik Vyavahar Vidhi
Madhyastham, Sulah evam Anukalpi Vivad
  Niptan Vidhi
Mal Vikraya Evam Avkraya Vidhi
Parkramya Likhat
Samvida Vidhi
Samvida Vidhi (Ek Parichay)
Upbhokta Sanrakshan Vidhi
Vanijyik Vidhi

First Edition,	1966	Twelfth Edition,	1999
Ninth Edition,	1989	Thirteenth Edition,	2001
Tenth Edition,	1991	Fourteenth Edition,	2004
Eleventh Edition,	1996	Fifteenth Edition,	2007

Reprinted, 2009

Rs 395.00

ISBN: 81-7012-287-2

9 788170 122876

All rights reserved. No part of this work may be copied, reproduced, adapted, abridged or translated, stored in any retrieval system, computer system, photographic or other system or transmitted in any form by any means whether electronic, mechanical, digital, optical, photographic or otherwise without the prior written permission of the copyright holders, Eastern Book Company, Lucknow. Any breach will entail legal action and prosecution without further notice.

While every effort has been made to avoid any mistake or omission, this publication is being sold on the condition and understanding that neither the author nor the publishers or printers would be liable in any manner to any person by reason of any mistake or omission in this publication or for any action taken or omitted to be taken or advice rendered or accepted on the basis of this work. For any defect in printing or binding the publishers will be liable only to replace the defective copy by another copy of this work then available.

All disputes will be subject to jurisdiction of courts, tribunals and forums at Lucknow only.

Copyright © including right of translation reserved with Eastern Book Co., Lucknow

PUBLISHERS: EBC PUBLISHING (P) LTD., 34-A, LALBAGH, LUCKNOW – 226 001
PRINTERS: JIPPY PRINTERS, ALAMBAGH, LUCKNOW – 226 005

To My Father

Gyani Ganga Singh

PREFACE TO THE FIFTEENTH EDITION

The Companies Act was amended twice earlier to the present edition. One of the Amendment Acts brought into the Companies Act a huge new part on producer companies. Going through its provisions, it seems as if an Act within an Act has been implanted. The whole set of provisions is meant to give encouragement to cooperatives by conferring upon them the status and advantages of incorporation. This part has already been brought into force.

The Second Amendment Act, 2002 apart from making other changes, also brought in a new part providing for Revival and Rehabilitation of Sick Industrial Companies. This part has not yet been enforced. Earlier to this Amendment Act, the phenomenon of sick industrial companies was in the care of the Sick Industrial Companies (Special Provisions) Act, 1985 under which the Board of Industrial and Financial Reconstruction was constituted which made its efforts for salvaging of such companies by providing protection from devouring state of liabilities and by adopting schemes of revival. The Legislature in its wisdom thought that the phenomenon of corporate industrial sickness should be encountered through a single Act, namely, the Companies Act, instead of creating duplicity of authorities. The fate of such companies was to be handled by the National Company Law Tribunal. This Tribunal was to make its efforts consistently with the new provisions to provide relief and rehabilitation to sick industrial companies.

The Second Amendment Act of 2002 also made a serious reallocation of the role of different authorities under the Companies Act. The adjudication of company matters was basically going to be done by the National Company Law Tribunal. Appeals from the decisions of this Tribunal were to go to the Appellate Tribunal and further appeals to the Supreme Court. The Company Law Board was going to be abolished. The whole of its jurisdiction was to be transferred to the Tribunal. Apart from that, almost the whole chunk, barring a few matters of jurisdiction of the courts under the Companies Act, was to be vested in the Tribunal. Some part of the jurisdiction of the Central Government was also going to be vested in the Tribunal. Thus, there were to be only two principal authorities under the Act, namely, the Tribunal and the Central Government. The jurisdiction of the Courts was to be marginalised. These provisions lie unenforced.

The Amendment of 2006 has added a few provisions to bring about the requirement that all directors, existing or proposed, should obtain an identification number. The Amendment also enables filing and inspection of documents through electronic media.

There have been significant developments in the judicial front also. Change in ownership of shareholding of a company or its management does not affect its legal status or identity or its residence. What are resembling company names has been judicially construed. The requirement of precision in notice exercising the right of pre-emption has been emphasised. The relief of rectification of registers, etc, has been held to be in the nature of a specific relief and, therefore, bound by the principles of judicial discretion and proper conduct on the part of the seeker of relief. The Company Law Board can deal with matters involving SEBI violations in petitions relating to share transfers. Breach of trust on the part of directors has been found in diversion of funds, secret creation of a new rival company and diverting employees and use of confidential information in diverting a major contract. Removal of the managing director of a Government company and downsizing its employees are in the realm of contract and not writ jurisdiction. Companies have been held liable for their officers' crimes under the doctrine of attribution of criminal intent. There has to be some justification in the conduct of a member who moves out of a meeting just only to render it inquorate. Pledge of shares with voting rights has been held to be valid. Penalty provisions have been held to be not violative of human rights. Courts cannot sanction rectification of accounts. Removal of a private company director may amount to oppression qua member. Advance distribution of surplus assets can be made in the process of winding up.

—AVTAR SINGH

Ghaziabad   (Vidya Bhushan, Hindi Sansthan, U.P.)

SHORT CONTENTS

———

CONTENTS

Chapter			Pages
12. **Dividends, Accounts and Audit** (*contd.*)			
Separate Bank Account for Dividend		..	425
Rule in Lee v Neuchatel	..	..	425
Unrealised appreciation of assets	..	..	427
Statutory Provisions	..	..	428
Depreciation [S. 205]	..	..	428
Compulsory reserves [S. 205]..	..	..	429
Unpaid dividend account [S. 205-A]	..	..	430
Transfer of unpaid dividend to Investor Education and Protection Fund	..	..	430
Investor Education and Protection Fund [S. 205-C]		..	430
Payment to registered holders [Ss. 206 and 206-A]		..	431
Declared dividend a statutory debt	..	..	432
Interim dividend	..	..	432
Mode of Payment [S. 207]	..	..	433
Payment of interest out of capital [S. 208]	..	..	434
Reserve fund	..	..	434
Capitalisation of profits	..	..	435
Bonus shares	..	..	435
Accounts	..	..	437
Books of account or accounting records [S. 209]		..	437
True and fair view	..	..	438
Accrual basis	..	..	439
Balance sheet of holding company [Ss. 212-214]		..	439
Annexure of profit and loss account [S. 216]		..	439
Preservation of account books..	..	..	439
Duty of compliance	..	..	440
Accounts to comply with accounting standards..		..	440
National Advisory Committee on Accounting Standards [S. 210-A]		..	440
Right of inspection [S. 209-A]	..	..	441
Inspection by directors..	..	..	441
Inspection by Registrar, etc	..	..	442
Inspection by members..	..	..	443
Report by way of annual accounts to general meeting [S. 210]	..	..	443
Directors' Responsibility Statement	..	..	445
Form and content of balance sheet, profit and loss account [S. 211]		..	446
Right of members to copies [S. 219]	..	..	446
Authentication of accounts [S. 215]	..	..	447
Annexed and attached documents [S. 216]..		..	447

TABLE OF CASES

TABLE OF STATUTES

1

Corporate Personality

DEFINITION OF 'COMPANY'

"The word 'company' has no strictly technical or legal meaning."[1] In the terms of the Companies Act,[2] a "company means a company formed and registered under" the Companies Act.[3] In common law a company is a "legal person" or "legal entity" separate from, and capable of surviving beyond the lives of, its members.[4] "Like any juristic person, a company is legally an entity apart from its members, capable of rights and duties of its own, and endowed with the potential of perpetual succession."[5] But the "company" is not merely a legal institution. It is rather a legal device for the attainment of any social or economic end and to a large extent publicly and socially responsible. It is, therefore, a combined political, social, economic and legal institution.[6] Thus the term has been variously described. "[It] is a means of co-operation in the conduct of an enterprise...."[7] "Corporate device is one form of associated enterprise."[8] It is "an intricate, centralised, economic administrative structure run by professional managers who hire capital from the investor".[9]

In a practical way, a company means a company of certain persons registered under the Companies Act. Two or more persons who are desirous of carrying on joint business enterprises, have the choice of either forming a company or a partnership. Partnership is a suitable device for a small scale business which can be financed and managed by a small group of partners who take personal interest and there is mutual trust and confidence among them. But where the enterprise requires a rather greater mobilisation of capital which the resources of a few persons cannot provide, the formation of a company is the only choice. Even for a small scale business the choice of a company would be better, as this is the only form of business organisation which offers the privilege of limiting personal liability for business debts. Accordingly, the company has become the most dominant form of business organisation.[10] One of the best assessments in reference to

---

1. BUCKLEY J in *Stanley, Re*, [1906] 1 Ch 131, 134.
2. No 1 of 1956 or under any of the preceding Acts.
3. Section 3 (*i*).
4. *Salomon v Salomon & Co*, [1895-99] All ER Rep 33: 66 LJ Ch 35: 75 LT 426: 13 TLR 46: 1897 AC 22. And *see*, Graff Evans, *What is Company*, (1910) 26 LQR 259.
5. Hahlo's CASEBOOK ON COMPANY LAW, 42 (2nd Edn, by Hahlo and Trebilock).
6. A.A. Berle, Jr. in Foreword to THE CORPORATION IN MODERN SOCIETY, (1959).
7. Woodrow Wilson, THE NEW FREEDOM, 26 (1968) Jaico.
8. FRANKFURTER J in *Nierbo v Bethle Ram Shipping Corpn*, (308) under Ss. 165, 169.
9. Manning, reviewing Livingston's THE AMERICAN STOCKHOLDER, (1958) 67 Yale LJ 1476.
10. *See*, Lee Loevinger, THE LAW OF FREE ENTERPRISE, 59 (1949).

companies in the context of the modern economies is enshrined in the following words:

"[C]ompanies abound in the national economy. Ranging from the small family or partnership concern to the faceless multinational corporation, they provide the structural framework of the modern industrial society."[11]

Evolution

"They [corporations] are not novelties. They are institutions of very ancient date".[12] But the large partnerships from which the modern business company evolved appeared on the English scene during the commercial revolution.

A body corporate during the seventeenth and eighteenth centuries could be brought into existence either by a Royal Charter or by a special Act of Parliament. Both these methods were very expensive and dilatory. Consequently, to meet the growing commercial needs of the nation, large unincorporated partnerships came into existence, trading, however, in corporate form. The membership of each such concern being very large, the management of the business was left to a few trustees. This resulted in separation of ownership from management. Trustees had the opportunity of trading with other people's money. Rules of law applicable to such companies were not yet developed. Consequently, fraudulent promoters had a unique opportunity of exploiting public money. Many spurious companies were created which would appear only to disappear resulting in loss to the investing public. The English Parliament, therefore, passed an Act, known as the Bubbles Act of 1720[13] which, instead of prohibiting the formation of fraudulent companies, made the very business of promoting companies illegal. This proved to be a great setback to the expanding trade and commerce. Yet the Act remained on the statute book for over a century. It was repealed in 1825.[14] But it was only in 1844[15] that registration and incorporation of large partnerships was made compulsory. The Joint Stock Companies Act of 1844 was the first legislative measure which facilitated registration, although the concerns registered under it were still known as partnerships and the principle of unlimited liability was maintained. The right to trade with limited liability was granted in 1855[16] and a year later in 1856 the whole law relating to such companies was consolidated.[17] Since

---

11. Note 5 above at p 69.
12. MARSHAL LJ in *Bank of U.S.* v *Dandridge*, 12 Wheat (25 US 64, 92).
13. Royal Exchange & London Insurance Corporation Act, (6 Geo 1 C 18).
14. By The Bubble Companies, etc., Act, (6 Geo 4, C 91).
15. Joint Stock Companies Act, (7 & 8 Vict C 110).
16. By The Limited Liability Act of that year, (18 Vict C 133).
17. Joint Stock Companies Act, 1856, (19 & 20 Vict C 47).

then Companies Acts have been considerably amended, enlarged and improved upon until we get to the English Acts of 1948 and 1985 and of 1989.[18]

The history of Indian Company Law began with the Joint Stock Companies Act of 1850. Since then the cumulative process of amendment and consolidation has brought us to the most comprehensive and complicated piece of legislation, the Companies Act, 1956.[19] But even so it is not exhaustive of all the modes of incorporating business concerns. Organisations for business or commercial purposes can still be incorporated by special Acts of Parliament. The Life Insurance Corporation of India, for example, has been incorporated for business in life insurance under the Life Insurance Corporation Act of 1956. Institutions so created are better known as "corporations". Business firms, or other institutions incorporated under the Companies Act are known as companies.

The Companies Act has been subjected to a number of amendments. The amendments which came into being up to 2000 were absorbed into the preceding edition. This new edition has absorbed into it both the amendments of 2002. The list of amendments of 2002 and the proposed amendments of 2003 have been presented in the appendix.

The First Amendment of 2002 provides for producer companies. The Second Amendment of 2002 replaces the Company Law Board with National Company Law Tribunal and also creates an Appellate Tribunal. Apart from taking over the jurisdiction of the Company Law Board, the National Company Law Tribunal has been vested with the jurisdiction of the High Courts under the Companies Act. The result is that the jurisdiction of the High Courts has also become reduced to a very few points. Since this amendment has not been enforced, the original Act holds good.

The Companies Act is also not exhaustive of the whole of company law. It only amends and consolidates certain portions of company law. Common law has still a lot of role to play in this field. The duties of corporate directors and their social responsibilities, which is at present one of the most developing aspects of company law, are still largely governed by the principles of common law.

NATURE OF CORPORATE FORM AND ADVANTAGES

Incorporation offers certain advantages to the business community as compared with all other kinds of business organisation.

---

18. The Companies Act, 1948, (11 & 12 Geo 6, C 38) and that of 1985 and 1989 [English].
19. For history of English Company Law, *see* Horrwitz, *Historical Development of Company Law*, (1946) 62 LQR 375; Gower, PRINCIPLES OF MODERN COMPANY LAW, 22-38; (3rd Edn, 1969), Cooke, CORPORATION, TRUST & COMPANY, (1950) Manchester University Press; Clive M. Schmitthoff, *The Origin of the Joint Stock Company*, (1939) 3 Toronto LJ 74-96.

1. Independent corporate existence [S. 34]

The outstanding feature of a company is its independent corporate existence. A partnership has no existence apart from its members. It is nothing but a collection of the partners.[20] A company, on the other hand, is in law a person. It is a distinct legal *persona* existing independent of its members. By incorporation under the Act, the company is vested with a corporate personality which is distinct from the members who compose it. One of the effects of incorporation is stated in Section 34(2) of the Act. It says that upon the issue of the certificate of incorporation, the subscribers to the memorandum and other persons, who may from time to time be the members of the company, shall be a *body corporate*[21] capable forthwith of exercising all the functions of an incorporated company and having perpetual succession and common seal. Thus the company becomes a body corporate which is capable immediately of functioning as an incorporated individual. The enterprise acquires its own entity. It becomes impersonalised. No one can say that he is the owner of the company. The business now belongs to an institution. The entity of the enterprise becomes institutionalised. In the words of Palmer:

"The benefits following from incorporation can hardly be exaggerated. It is because of incorporation that the owner of the business ceases to trade in his own person. The company carries on the business, the liabilities are the company's liabilities and the former owner is under no liability for anything the company does, although, as principal shareholder, he is able to take full advantage of profits which the company makes.[22]

The following further passage from Palmer[23] was cited by WADHWA J:[24]

The principle that, apart from exceptional cases, the company is a

---

20. This basic difference between a company and a partnership has been explained by GHULAM HASAN J in *Bacha F. Guzdar v CIT, Bom*, AIR 1955 SC 74: (1955) 1 SCR 876, 883: (1955) 25 Comp Cas 1.
21. *See* the decision of the Supreme Court in *Ashoka Marketing Ltd v PNB*, (1990) 4 SCC 406, 423-24, for an explanation of the term 'body-corporate' in the context of the modern corporations. The expression is defined in S. 2(7) of the Act as including a company incorporated outside India but does not include a 'corporation sole' (such as King, or President) or a cooperative society. The Government may by notification exclude from the scope of the definition any other body corporate also. Thus the expression 'body corporate' is wider than the term 'company' though every company registered under the Act is a body corporate. This expression would include all corporations created under special Acts of Parliament. An incorporated company is a body corporate but incorporation under the Companies Act is not the only method of creating a body corporate. *Madras Central Urban Bank v Corpn of Madras*, (1932) 2 Comp Cas 328. A registered society under the Societies Registration Act, 1860 has been held to be not a body corporate, *Board of Trustees, Ayurvedic and Unani Tibia College v State of Delhi*, AIR 1962 SC 458.
22. Palmer's PRIVATE COMPANIES, 13 (42nd Edn, 1961).
23. Palmer's COMPANY LAW, para 2, 1523 (25th Edn).
24. In *New Horizons Ltd v UOI*, (1997) 89 Comp Cas 785 at p 802 Del overruled by the Supreme Court on other grounds in *New Horizons Ltd v UOI*, (1995) 1 SCC 478: (1997) 89 Comp Cas 849 SC.

body corporate, distinct from members, lies at the root of many of the most perplexing questions, that beset company law. It is a fundamental or cardinal distinction—a distinction which must be firmly grasped. This principle is thrown into clear relief by contrasting an incorporated company with a partnership, for under English law (though not under Scottish law or that of the most Continental systems) a firm or partnership is not a separate entity from its members.''

A well-known illustration of this principle is the decision of the House of Lords in *Salomon* v *Salomon & Co.*[25]

One Salomon was a boot and shoe manufacturer. His business was in sound condition and there was a substantial surplus of assets over liabilities. He incorporated a company named, Salomon & Co Ltd, for the purpose of taking over and carrying on his business. The seven subscribers to the memorandum were Salomon, his wife, his daughter and four sons and they remained the only members of the company. Salomon, and two of his sons, constituted the board of directors of the company. The business was transferred to the company for £40,000. In payment, Salomon took 20,000 shares of £1 each and debentures worth £10,000. These debentures certified that the company owed Salomon £10,000 and created a charge on the company's assets. One share was given to each remaining member of his family. The company went into liquidation within a year.[26]

On winding up, the state of affairs was broadly something like this: Assets £6,000; Liabilities—Salomon as debenture holder:[27] £10,000 and unsecured creditors: £7,000. Thus after paying off the debenture holder nothing would be left for the unsecured creditors.

The unsecured creditors, therefore, contended that, though incorporated under the Act, the company never had an independent existence; it was in fact Salomon under another name; he was the managing director, the other directors being his sons and under his control. His vast preponderance of shares made him absolute master. The business was solely his, conducted solely for and by him and the company was a mere sham and fraud, in effect entirely contrary to the intent and meaning of the Companies Act. But it was held that Salomon & Co Ltd was a real company fulfilling all the legal requirements. It must be treated as a company, as an entity consisting of certain corporators, but a distinct and independent corporation. Their Lordships of the House of Lords observed:

"When the memorandum is duly signed and registered, though there be only seven shares taken, the subscribers are a body corporate

---

25. [1895-99] All ER Rep 33: 66 LJ Ch 35: 75 LT 426: 13 TLR 46: 1897 AC 22.
26. *Salomon* was not to blame for the liquidation, for it was due to general trade depression.
27. *Salomon* had transferred his debentures to another who had a receiver appointed and started the winding up. *Broderip* v *Salomon*, [1895] Ch 323 CA, reversed, sub nom. *Salomon* v *Salomon & Co*, [1895-99] All ER Rep 33: 66 LJ Ch 35: 75 LT 426: 13 TLR 46: 1897 AC 22.

capable forthwith of exercising all the functions of an incorporated company. It is difficult to understand how a body corporate thus created by statute can lose its individuality by issuing the bulk of its capital to one person. The company is at law a different person altogether from the subscribers of the memorandum; and though it may be that after incorporation the business is precisely the same as before, the same persons are managers, and the same hands receive the profits, the company is not in law their agent or trustee. The statute enacts nothing as to the extent or degree of interest which may be held by each of the seven or as to the proportion of interest, or influence possessed by one or majority of the shareholders over others. There is nothing in the Act requiring that the subscribers to the memorandum should be independent or unconnected, or that they or any of them should take a substantial interest in the undertaking, or that they should have a mind or will of their own, or that there should be anything like a balance of power in the constitution of the company.''[28]

The principle had been recognised in India even before the *Salomon* case. The decision of the Calcutta High Court in *Kondoli Tea Co Ltd, Re*,[29] seems to be the first on the subject.

Certain persons transferred a tea estate to a company and claimed exemptions from *ad valorem* duty on the ground that they themselves were the shareholders in the company and, therefore, it was nothing but a transfer from them in one to themselves under another name.

Rejecting this, the Court observed: ''The company was a separate person, a separate body altogether from the shareholders and the transfer was as much a conveyance, a transfer of the property, as if the shareholders had been totally different persons''.[30]

In reference to one-man companies of the *Salomon* type, the Bombay High Court observed:[31]

''Under the law, an incorporated company is a distinct entity, and although all the shares may be practically controlled by one person, in law a company is a distinct entity and it is not permissible or relevant to enquire whether the directors belonged to the same family or whether it is, as compendiously described a 'one-man company'.''[32]

---

28. For a criticism of this decision *see* O. Kahn Freund, *Some Reflections on Company Law Reforms*, (1944) 7 Mod LR 54; Kiralfy, *Some Unforeseen Consequences of Private Incorporation*, (1949) 65 LQR 231.

29. ILR (1886) 13 Cal 43. For a detailed account of Indian cases on the subject, *see* R. P. Singh, *Corporate Personality in India*, [1968] 1 Comp LJ 9.

30. *See* also *Ram Kanai Singh* v *Mathewson*, AIR 1915 PC 27: 42 IA 97; *J.H. Pattinson* v *Bindhya Debi*, AIR 1933 Pat 196; *Tata Engg & Locomotive Co* v *State of Bihar*, (1964) 6 SCR 885: [1964] 1 Comp LJ 280: (1964) 34 Comp Cas 458: AIR 1965 SC 40.

31. *T.R. Pratt (Bombay) Ltd* v *E.D. Sasoon & Co Ltd*, AIR 1936 Bom 62.

32. See *Praga Tools Corpn* v *Imanual*, (1969) 1 SCC 585: AIR 1969 SC 1306: (1969) 39 Comp Cas 889.

Thus one-man companies exist with the encouragement of the Legislature, and "the great majority of them are as *bona fide* and genuine as in a business sense they are convenient and suitable media for provision and application of capital to industry".[33]

In *Dhulia-Amalner Motor Transport Ltd v R. R. Dharamsi:*[34]

A partnership firm carrying on the business of plying buses having worked for some time, some of the partners formed a private limited company, which they could do under the law even while the partnership continued to be a running concern. Such of the partners who formed the company sold to the company their own buses which were heretofore being used by the firm. The other set of partners who constituted the minority sued the section forming the company for accounts and their share of profits on the ground that in reality the company was not a different entity from the firm and that the business carried on by it was the same as that of the firm.

It was held that the plaintiffs had no legal right to sue for accounts of the business done by the company which was altogether a third person. Buses which the company was plying were the property not of its shareholders, but the property of the company itself. The company was a corporate body whose entity was entirely different from the entities of its shareholders. Motive for becoming shareholders is not a field of enquiry. The law recognises the existence of the company quite irrespective of the motives, intentions, schemes, or conduct of the individual shareholders.[35]

2. Limited liability

The privilege of limiting liability for business debts is one of the principal advantages of doing business under the corporate form of organisation. The company, being a separate person, is the owner of its assets and bound by its liabilities. Members, even as a whole, are neither the owners of the company's undertaking, nor liable for its debts. Where the subscribers exercise the choice of registering the company with limited liability, the members' liability becomes limited or restricted to the nominal value of the

---

33. YOUNGER LJ in *Commr of Inland Revenue v Sansom*, [1921] 2 KB 492: 125 LT 37. Also see *British Thompson & Houston Co v Sterling Accessories Ltd*, [1924] 2 Ch 33: [1924] All ER Rep 294; Warner Fuller, *The Incorporated Individual: A Study of One-man Companies*, (1938) 51 Harv LR 1373.
34. AIR 1952 Bom 337: ILR 1952 Bom 795.
35. *Abdul Haq v Das Mal*, (1910) 19 IC 595, the plaintiff sued for his wages and that of his *chaprasi* employed by him on behalf of the company and in doing so impleaded as defendants, the secretary and managing director of the company and not the company itself. It was held that a suit to recover salary or wages due from a company lies against the company and not against its directors or members; *Flitcroft* case, (1882) 21 Ch D 519; *Restraithblain Estates Ltd* case, (1948) Ch D 228, the members of a company attempted to dissolve it by distributing between themselves the title deeds of the company's assets; B. Errabi, *Problem of Juristic Personality of a Corporation*, 1965 JILI 158. A company was allowed to sue as forma pauperis, *Mamata Papers (P) Ltd v State of Orissa*, (2000) 99 Comp Cas 294 Ori.

shares taken by them or the amount guaranteed by them. No member is bound to contribute anything more than the nominal value of the shares held by him.[36] In a partnership, on the other hand, the liability of the partners for the debts of the business is unlimited. They are bound to meet, without any limit, all the business obligations of the firm. The whole fortune of a partner is at stake, as the creditors can levy execution even on his private property. Speaking of the advantage of trading with limited liability, BUCKLEY J observed:[37]

> "The statutes relating to limited liability have probably done more than any legislation of the last fifty years to further the commercial prosperity of the country. They have, to the advantage of the investor as well as of the public, allowed and encouraged aggregation of small sums into large capitals which have been employed in undertakings of great public utility largely increasing the wealth of the country.
>
> One of the primary and accepted motivations behind incorporating a company is to limit personal risks by obtaining the benefit of limited liability."

3. Perpetual succession

An incorporated company never dies. It is an entity with perpetual succession. *A, B* and *C* are the only members of a company, holding all its shares. Their shares may be transferred to, or inherited by *X, Y* and *Z*, who may, therefore, become the new members and managers of the company. But the company will remain the same entity. In spite of the total change in membership, "the company will be the same entity, with the same privileges and immunities, estates, and possessions".[38] Perpetual succession, therefore, means that the membership of a company may keep changing from time to time, but that does not affect the company's continuity, "in the like manner as the river Thames is still the same river, though the parts which compose it are changing every instant".[39] The death or insolvency of individual members does not, in any way, affect the

---

36. *J.H. Rayner (Mincing Lane) Ltd* v *Deptt of Trade and Industry*, (1989) 3 WLR 969 HL, member-States which created an international company were held not liable to pay its debts. Lord OLIVER observed: "Once given the existence of the *International Tin Council* as a separate legal person and given that it was the contracting party in the transactions upon which the appellants claim, there is no room for any further inquiry as to what type of legal person the contracting party is. The person who can enforce contracts and the person against whom they can be enforced in English law are the parties to the contract and in identifying the parties to the contract there are no gradations of legal personality".
37. *London & Globe Finance Corpn, Re*, [1903] 1 Ch 728, 731.
38. Canfield & Wormser, CASES ON PRIVATE CORPORATIONS, (2nd Edn) 1.
39. Blackstone, COMMENTARIES, quoted by F. Pollock, JURISPRUDENCE AND LEGAL ESSAYS: THE FICTION THEORY OF CORPORATIONS, 219 (1961).

corporate existence of the company.[40] "Members may come and go but the company can go on for ever."[41]

The guarantors of a company's loan could not claim to be relieved of liability by reason of the fact that the company's management had totally changed including the managing director. Such changes do not affect the continuity of the company or its commercial and contractual relations.[42] The identity of a company is not linked with its membership or management. The liability of the company for electricity dues remained the same, though the arrears belonged to a period when the company was in the hands of some other persons.[43]

4. Separate property

A company, being a legal person, is capable of owning, enjoying and disposing of property in its own name. The company becomes the owner of its capital and assets. The shareholders are not the several or joint owners of the company's property. "The company is the real person in which all its property is vested, and by which it is controlled, managed and disposed of".[44] A member does not even have an insurable interest in the property of the company. A person was the holder of nearly all the shares, except one, of a timber company and was also a substantial creditor. He insured the company's timber in his own name. The timber having been destroyed by fire, the insurance company was held not liable to him.[45] "No shareholder has any right to any item of property owned by the company, for he has no legal or equitable interest therein".[46] "In WALTON J's simple truism[47]: 'The

---

40. Gower cited this illustration in a footnote in his book PRINCIPLES OF MODERN COMPANY LAW, 76 (3rd Edn, 1969): "During the war all the members of one private company, while in general meeting, were killed by a bomb. But the company survived; not even a hydrogen bomb could have destroyed it". *Gopalpur Tea Co Ltd* v *Penhok Tea Co Ltd*, (1982) 52 Comp Cas 238 Cal, the whole undertaking of a company was taken over under an Act which purported to extinguish all rights of action against the company, the court held that neither the company was thereby extinguished nor any body's claim against it. W. Jethro Brown, *The Personality of the Corporation and the State*, (1905) 21 LQR 365, 366 and *K/9 Meat Supplies (Guildford) Ltd, Re*, [1967] 1 Comp LJ 37: [1966] 3 All ER 320 (Ch D) the bankruptcy of a member of a private company is no ground for winding up of the company.
41. Gower, 75-76, note 40 above.
42. *Punjab National Bank* v *Lakshmi Industrial & Trading Co (P) Ltd*, AIR 2001 All 26.
43. *Amit Products (India) Ltd* v *Chief Engineer (O & M Circle)*, (2005) 127 Comp Cas 443 SC.
44. *Bacha F. Guzdar* v *CIT, Bombay*, AIR 1955 SC 74: (1955) 1 SCR 876: (1955) 25 Comp Cas 1; *R.T. Perumal* v *John Deavin*, AIR 1960 Mad 43: (1960) 30 Comp Cas 340, where their Lordships observed that "no member can claim himself to be the owner of the company's property during its existence or in its winding up". *Regional Provident Fund Commr* v *Narayani Udyog*, (1993) 1 Raj LR 224, property is that of the company and not of its members, nor directors are the company's employees.
45. *Macaura* v *Northern Assurance Co Ltd*, 1925 AC 619 HL. It has been held in a Canadian decision that a sole shareholder has insurable interest in the company's property, *Kosmopolous* v *Constitution Ins Co*, (1984) 149 DLR (3d) 77.
46. Lord BUCKMASTER in *Macaura* v *Northern Assurance Co Ltd*, 1925 AC 619 at p 625.
47. *See* Murray A. Pickering, *The Company as a Separate Legal Entity*, (1968) 31 Mod LR 497.

property of the company is not the property of the shareholders; it is the property of the company'."[48]

Thus, incorporation helps the property of the company to be clearly distinguished from that of its members. "The property is vested in the company as a body corporate, and no changes of individual membership affect the title. The property, however much, the shareholders may come and go, remains vested in the company, and the company can convey, assign, mortgage, or otherwise deal with it irrespective of these mutations."[49] On the nationalisation of the coal mines of a company, it was found that it had sold an item of its immovable property to the wife of one of its directors. The Court rip open the veil to probe into the genuineness of the transaction and discovered its shamness. The property continued to be that of the company and became vested in the Government.[50] The assets of a company were not allowed to be used for payment of a shareholder's debts.[51] Unless a company's incorporation can be viewed as a sham, its property would fall outside the distribution of matrimonial assets on divorce.[52] In a partnership, on the other hand, the distinction between the joint property of the firm and the private property of the partners is often not clear.

5. Transferable shares

When joint stock companies were established the great object was that their shares should be capable of being easily transferred.[53] Accordingly the Companies Act in Section 82 declares: "The shares or debentures or other interest of any member in a company shall be movable property, transferable in the manner provided by the articles of the company". Thus incorporation enables a member to sell his shares in the open market and to get back his investment without having to withdraw the money from the company. This provides liquidity to the investor and stability to the company.[54] In a partnership, on the other hand, a partner cannot transfer his share in the capital of the firm except with the unanimous consent of all the partners. If a transfer is made against the will of the partners, the transferee does not become a partner, although he has some rights in the dissolution of the firm.[55]

---

48. *Gramophone & Typewriter Co v Stanley*, [1906] 2 KB 856, 869; *Hyderabad Sind Electric Supply Co v UOI*, AIR 1959 Punj 199. *M. V. "Dong Do" v Ramesh Kumar & Co Ltd*, (2002) 109 Comp Cas 450 Cal, assets of company not assets of shareholders, in a maritime claim, it was held that ships belonging to different companies which were all controlled by the Government were not sister ships.
49. Palmer's PRIVATE COMPANIES, 19 (42nd Edn, 1961).
50. *Subhra Mookherjee v Bharat Coking Coal Ltd*, (2000) 3 SCC 312: AIR 2000 SC 1203: [2000] CLC 677: (2000) 101 Comp Cas 257.
51. *H.C. Shashtri v Dolphin Cornpack (P) Ltd*, (1998) 93 Comp Cas 201 Del.
52. *Wilson v Wilson*, [1999] SLT 249 Scotland.
53. Lord BLACKBURN in *Bahia & San Francisco Rly Co, Re*, (1868) LR 3 QB 584: 18 LT 467.
54. Barle and Means, THE MODERN CORPORATION AND PRIVATE PROPERTY, 282 (1932).
55. S. 29 of the Indian Partnership Act, 1932.

6. Capacity to sue and be sued

A company, being a body corporate, can sue and be sued in its own name.[56]

Criminal complaint can be filed by a company but it must be represented by a natural person. It is not necessary that the same person should act as a representative throughout. The complaint by a company is liable to be dismissed because of the absence of the representative in the same way in which an individual complaint is liable to be dismissed for absence of the complainant.[57]

A company has the right to protect its fair name. It can sue for such defamatory remarks against it as are likely to damage its business or property etc. It can be defamatory to a company to allege that its directors allowed the company to continue trading at a time when it ought to have been facing insolvency.[58] A company has a right to seek damages where a defamatory material published about it affects its business. The preparation of a video cassette by the workmen of a company showing their struggle against the company's management and its exhibition could be restrained only on showing that the matter would be defamatory.[59]

The Court of Appeal[60] held that a company can complain under the Broadcasting Act, 1996 about unwarranted infringement of its privacy. The Court said that a company may have activities of a private nature which need protection from unwarranted intrusion. Without such right the company would be disadvantaged as against individuals under a legislation which is designed to encourage and achieve proper standards of conduct in public life. The complaint was about the secret filming of transactions in shops by the BBC and the allegation was that this constituted an infringement of the company's privacy.

7. Professional management

The corporate sector is capable of attracting the growing cadre of professional managers. Young management graduates willingly join companies because of the feeling that they would thereby belong to a

---

56. A company can be allowed to sue in *forma pauperis* under Order 33, Rule 3 of the Civil Procedure Code. *Union Bank of India* v *Khaders International Constructions Ltd*, [1993] 2 Comp LJ 89 Ker. Managing director is not a necessary party to corporate proceedings. *Bank of Maharashtra* v *Racman Auto P Ltd*, (1992) 74 Comp Cas 752 Del.
57. *Associated Cement Co Ltd* v *Keshvanand*, (1998) 1 SCC 687: (1998) 91 Comp Cas 361 SC.
58. *Aspro Travel Ltd* v *Owners Abroad plc*, (1996) 1 WLR 132 (CA).
59. *TVS Employees' Federation* v *TVS & Sons Ltd*, (1996) 87 Comp Cas 37 Mad; *Krishna Exports Industries Ltd* v *DCM Ltd*, (2005) 4 Comp LJ 75 Del, company held not liable for contempt committed by its officer. *Lalit Surajmal Kanodia* v *Office Tiger Database Systems India (P) Ltd*, (2006) 129 Comp Cas 192 Mad, employees of one company not liable for contempt of court committed by another company in the same group though they were common employees.
60. *R* v *Broadcasting Standards Commission*, The Times, Sept 1999 and April 12, 2000.

managerial class. Their independent functioning as managers is assured because of the fact that there is no human employer and the shareholders exercise only a formative control and that also for the sake of name only. Such an atmosphere of independence gives them an opportunity to develop extraordinary managerial capabilities. With the financial backing that companies are able to provide, they are able to develop the business to a considerable extent. "Prudent developments may be made, and new branches established in different places, and other concerns may be acquired. Thus, before very long a great business may be built up which is worthy and capable of absorbing the attention of such a competent manager, assisted by other directors working in harmony with him. Men of this calibre are not to be found everyday, but, when found and supported by capital, they are capable of achieving the very highest success in commercial undertakings".[61]

8. Finances

The company is the only medium of organising business which is given the privilege of raising capital by public subscriptions either by way of shares or debentures. Further, public financial institutions lend their resources more willingly to companies than to other forms of business organisation. The facility of borrowing and giving security by way of a floating charge is also an exclusive privilege of companies. "Capital in many cases is the life-blood of a concern, and it is always a great misfortune where the development of a business is arrested or restricted by want of capital".[62]

DISADVANTAGES

The above advantages of incorporation are by no means inconsiderable and, as compared with them, the disadvantages are, indeed very few. Yet some of them, which are in essence complications arising out of the privilege of trading with limited liability, deserve to be pointed out.

1. Lifting the corporate veil

The chief advantage of incorporation from which all others follow is the separate legal entity of the company. In reality, however, the business of the legal person is always carried on by, and for the benefit of, some individuals. In the ultimate analysis, some human beings are the real beneficiaries of the corporate advantages, "for while, by fiction of law, a corporation is a distinct entity, yet in reality it is an association of persons who are in fact the beneficial owners of all the corporate property".[63] And

---

61. Palmer's PRIVATE COMPANIES, 25-26 (42nd Edn, 1961).
62. *Ibid* at p 24.
63. *Gallaghar* v *Germania Brewing Co*, (1893) 53 Minn: 214 NW 1115, *per* MITCHEL LJ.

what the *Salomon* case decides is that "in questions of property and capacity, of acts done and rights acquired or, liabilities assumed thereby... the personalities of the natural persons who are the company's corporators is to be ignored".[64]

This theory of corporate entity is indeed the basic principle on which the whole law of corporations is based. Instances are not few in which the courts have successfully resisted the temptation to break through the corporate veil. A landlady's bid to regain tenanted premises for self-business could not succeed as the business was in the name of her company.[65] The Supreme Court did not allow a shareholder to sue for the violation of the fundamental rights of his company.[66] Where a company acquires a majority of the shares and also the assets of another company, that does not extinguish the debt of one to the other.[67] The shareholders and creditors of a dissolved company cannot maintain an action for the recovery of its left-over assets.[68] A managing director cannot be compelled in his personal capacity to produce books of which he has custody in official capacity.[69] In *Lee* v *Lee's Air Farming Ltd*,[70] Lee incorporated a company of which he was the managing director. In that capacity he appointed himself as a pilot of the company. While on the business of the company he was lost in a flying accident. His widow recovered compensation under the

---

64. Lord PARKER in *Daimler Co Ltd* v *Continental Tyre & Rubber Co Ltd*, [1916] 2 AC 307: [1916-17] All ER Rep 191, cited by C. A. Masten, *One-man Companies and their Controlling Shareholder*, (1936) 14 Can BR 663.
65. *Tunstall* v *Steigman*, [1962] 2 WLR 1045: [1962] 2 QB 593; *I.K.M. Basheer* v *Lona Chackola*, (2003) 115 Comp Cas 127 Ker, the need for occupation of the premises by the company is something different from the personal need of a director.
66. *Chiranjit Lal* v *UOI*, 1950 SCR 869: AIR 1951 SC 41, 52. The Supreme Court in *R.C. Cooper* v *UOI*, (1970) 1 SCC 248: (1970) 3 SCR 530: (1970) 40 Comp Cas 325 also known as the *Bank Nationalisation* case held that a shareholder, a depositor or a director is not entitled to move a petition for infringement of the rights of the company, unless by the State action impugned by him, his rights are also infringed. The test in determining whether the shareholders' right is impaired is not formal, it is essentially qualitative, if the State action impairs the right of the shareholders as well of the company, the court will not, concentrating merely upon the technical operation of the action, deny to itself jurisdiction to grant relief. In applying this proposition, the court in *Bennett, Coleman & Co* v *UOI*, (1972) 2 SCC 788, 806, extended the rule by stating: "It is now clear that the fundamental rights of citizens are not lost when they associate to form a company. When their fundamental rights as shareholders are impaired by State action their rights as shareholders are protected. The reason is that the shareholders' rights are equally and necessarily affected if the rights of the company are affected". So the company acquires a standing by impleading a shareholder with itself in the action. See also *Godhra Electricity Co* v *State of Gujarat*, (1975) 1 SCC 199, 211-212.
67. *Spencer & Co* v *CWT*, AIR 1969 Mad 359: (1969) 39 Comp Cas 212.
68. *P. Leslie & Co* v *V.O. Wapshare*, AIR 1969 SC 843: (1969) 3 SCR 203: 39 Comp Cas 808: [1969] 2 Comp LJ 113.
69. *S. A. K. Chinnathambi* v *Murgugar*, [1968] 2 Comp LJ 260.
70. 1961 AC 12: [1960] 3 All ER 420 PC, reversing the New Zealand Court of Appeal. An employee cannot bring an action for an unfair dismissal against the majority shareholder of a company which selected him, *Schouls* v *Canadian Meat Processing Corpn*, (1984) 147 DLR (3d) 81.

Workmen's Compensation Act. "In effect the magic of corporate personality enabled him to be master and servant at the same time".[71] Where the total number of directors and shareholders consent to the misuse of the company's money, they can be prosecuted for theft because the consent of the whole number may not be the consent of the company.[72]

But the theory cannot be pushed to unnatural limits. Circumstances must occur which compel the courts to identify a company with its members. "There are situations where the court will lift the veil of incorporation in order to examine the 'realities' which lay behind. Sometimes this is expressly authorised by statute... and sometimes the court will lift of its own volition."[73] A company cannot, for example, be convicted of conspiring with its sole director. In the circumstances, the court said: "where the sole responsible person in the company is the defendant himself, it would not be right to say that there were two persons or two minds".[74] The corporate veil is said to be lifted when the court ignores the company and concerns itself directly with the members or managers.[75] "It is impossible to ascertain the factors which operate to break down the corporate insulation".[76] The matter is largely in the discretion of the courts and will depend upon "the underlying social, economic and moral factors as they operate in and through the corporation".[77] All that can be said is "that adherence to the Salomon principle will not be doggedly followed where

---

71. Gower, PRINCIPLES OF MODERN COMPANY LAW, 202 (3rd Edn, 1969).

72. *Attorney-General's Reference of 1984 (No 2 of 1983)*, (1984) 2 QB 456; *A-G's Ref*, (1984) QB 624; *R* v *Phillipou*, (1989) 5 BCC 33. A director's personal telephone was not allowed to be disconnected for the company's default in payment, *Kailash Prasad Modi* v *GM, Orissa Telecommunications*, AIR 1994 Ori 98. In *Rashtriya Mill Mazdoor Sangh* v *Khatau Makanji Spg & Wvg Co Ltd*, (2000) 100 Comp Cas 33 Bom, a company was directed to pay salary and though the decree could have been executed, the company was held liable to be punished for contempt of court. The human agents through whom the company committed contempt are not absolved from their liability. *Delhi Development Authority* v *Skipper Construction Co (P) Ltd*, (1997) 11 SCC 430: (1997) 89 Comp Cas 362 SC.

73. John P. Lowry, *Lifting the Corporate Veil*, 1993 JBL 41; Ruthren, *Lifting the Veil of Incorporation in Scotland*, (1969) Juridical Review 1.

74. *R* v *McDonnel*, [1966] 1 All ER 193: [1966] 1 QB 233. A company has, however, been held liable for conspiring with its directors where there are at least two of them. *R* v *I.C.R. Haulage Ltd*, 1944 KB 551: [1944] 1 All ER 691. A company cannot be prosecuted for the violation of an Act which provides for compulsory imprisonment. *Modi Industries Ltd* v *B.C. Goel*, (1983) 54 Comp Cas 835 All; *State of Maharashtra* v *Jugmandar Lal*, AIR 1966 SC 940 and *Nanak Chand* v *State of U.P.*, 1971 All LJ 1229; *P.V. Pai* v *R. L. Rinawma*, (1993) 77 Comp Cas 179 Kant. A company cannot be prosecuted for cheating and conspiracy because such offences require *mens rea. Akkhosla* v *T.S. Venketasan*, (1994) 80 Comp Cas 81 Cal. A company cannot be imprisoned for evasion of taxes or any other crime. But penalties can be imposed. *Oswal Vanaspati and Allied Industries* v *State of U.P.*, (1992) 75 Comp Cas 770 All; *Maniam Transports* v *S. Krishna Moorthy*, [1993] 1 Comp LJ 153 Mad.

75. *Veil of Corporate Personality*, (1962) 78 LQR 315.

76. Warner Fuller, *The Incorporated Individual: A Study of One-man Company*, (1938) 51 Harv LR 1373, 1377.

77. *Id* at p 1379. *Tata Engineering Locomotive Co* v *State of Bihar*, (1964) 6 SCR 885: [1964] 1 Comp LJ 280: (1964) 34 Comp Cas 458: AIR 1965 SC 40.

this would cause an unjust result".[78] But the following grounds have become well-established.[79]

(a) Determination of character.—Occasionally it becomes necessary to determine the character of a company, for example, to see whether it is "enemy". In such a case, the courts may in their discretion examine the character of persons in real control of the corporate affairs. *Daimler Co Ltd* v *Continental Tyre & Rubber Co Ltd*[80] is illustrative:

> A company was incorporated in England for the purpose of selling tyres manufactured in Germany by a German company. The German company held the bulk of the shares in the English company. The holders of the remaining shares (except one) and all the directors were Germans, resident in Germany. Thus the real control of the English company was in German hands. During the First War the English company commenced an action to recover a trade debt. And the question was whether the company had become an enemy company and should, therefore, be barred from maintaining the action.

The House of Lords laid down that a company incorporated in the United Kingdom is a legal entity, a creation of law with the status and capacity which the law confers. It is not a natural person with mind or conscience. It can be neither loyal nor disloyal. It can be neither friend nor enemy. But it may assume an enemy character when persons in *de facto* control of its affairs are residents in any enemy country or, wherever resident, are acting under the control of enemies. Accordingly the company was not allowed to proceed with the action. If the action had been allowed the company would have been used as a machinery by which the purpose of giving money to the enemy would be accomplished. That would be monstrous and against public policy.[81]

But where there is no such danger to public interest, the courts may refuse to tear open the corporate veil. The American case, *People's Pleasure Park Co* v *Rohleder*,[82] is an instructive illustration.

> Certain lands were transferred by one person to another perpetually enjoining the transferee from selling the said property to coloured persons. He transferred the property to a company composed exclusively of negroes. An action was commenced for annulment of this conveyance on the ground that all the members of the company being

---

78. John P. Lowry, *Lifting the Corporate Veil*, 1993 JBL 41. A company can be held liable for perjury if false evidence is given by a witness appearing on its behalf, *Odyssey (London) Ltd* v *OIC Run Off Ltd*, (2000) TLR 201 CA, noted in (2000) 116 LQR 527.
79. Such cases have been summed up by Professor Wormser, *Piercing the Veil of Corporate Entity*, (1912) 12 Col LR 496, and by Murray A. Pickering, *Company as a Separate Legal Person*, (1968) 31 Mod LR 481; Mervyn Woods, *Lifting the Corporate Veil in Canada*, (1957) 23 Can B R 1176.
80. [1916] 2 AC 307: [1916-17] All ER Rep 191, considered by James Edward Hogg, *The Personal Character of a Corporation*, (1917) 33 LQR 76.
81. *Sovfracht V/O* v *Van Udens Scheepvaat*, 1943 AC 203.
82. (1908) 109 Va 439: 61 SE 794.

negroes, the property had, in breach of the restriction, passed to the hands of coloured persons.

The court, however, rejected this argument and held that members individually or collectively are not the corporation, which "has a distinct existence—an existence separate from that of its shareholders. It leads its own life... It stands apart as a separate subject and, in contemplation of law, as a stranger to its own members".[83]

The interest of a company in a leasehold property was not affected by the fact that the company admitted new members. The company remains the same entity in spite of the total change in membership.[84]

(*b*) *For benefit of revenue.*—"The court has the power to disregard corporate entity if it is used for tax evasion or to circumvent tax obligation".[85] A clear illustration is *Dinshaw Maneckjee Petit, Re*:[86]

> The assessee was a wealthy man enjoying huge dividend and interest income. He formed four private companies and agreed with each to hold a block of investment as an agent for it. Income received was credited in the accounts of the company but the company handed back the amount to him as a pretended loan. This way he divided his income into four parts in a bid to reduce his tax liability.

But it was held that, "the company was formed by the assessee purely and simply as a means of avoiding super-tax and the company was nothing more than the assessee himself. It did no business, but was created simply as a legal entity to ostensibly receive the dividends and interests and to hand them over to the assessee as pretended loans".

The leading English authority is *Apthorpe* v *Peter Schoenhofen Brewing Co*:[87]

> Aliens were not allowed to hold land in New York. An English company acquired the business and assets of a New York company. But the American company was kept on foot to hold the land. The business was financed and run by the English company.

It was held that the American company had become the agent of the English company and therefore, the whole of its profits were liable to be taxed as the income of the English company.[88]

---

83. *Sunil Kumar* v *Mining & Allied Mach Corpn*, [1968] 1 Comp LJ 214, and *Hyderabad Sind Electric Supply Co* v *UOI*, AIR 1959 Punj 199 where the court held that the fact that a majority of the shareholders of a company had migrated to India did not and could not change the nationality of the company.
84. *Naga Brahma Trust* v *Translanka Air Travels (P) Ltd*, (1997) 88 Comp Cas 136 Mad.
85. *Juggilal* v *CIT*, (1969) 2 SCC 376: AIR 1970 SC 529: (1970) 1 SCR 720. *India Waste Energy Development Ltd* v *Govt of NCT of Delhi*, (2003) 114 Comp Cas 82 Del, lifting corporate veil permissible in cases of tax evasion even in the absence of any statutory provisions.
86. AIR 1927 Bom 371.
87. (1899) 4 TC 41: 80 LT 395 CA.
88. Subsequently, however, the courts have been more cautious. See *Kodak* v *Clark*, [1903] 1 KB 505 CA; *CIT* v *Sri Meenakshi Mills Ltd*, AIR 1967 SC 819: (1967) 1 SCR 934, 941: 63 ITR

Members themselves, however, are not allowed to claim that they should be regarded as economically identical with the company, particularly when this is not in the interest of revenue. In *Bacha F. Guzdar* v *CIT, Bombay*:[89]

> Under the Income Tax Act, then in force, agricultural income was exempt from tax. The income of a tea company was exempt up to 60% as agricultural income and 40% was taxed as income from manufacture and sale of tea. The plaintiff was a member of a tea company. She received a certain amount as dividend in respect of shares held by her in the company and claimed that this dividend income should be regarded as agricultural income up to 60%.

But it was held that although the income in the hands of the company was partly agricultural, yet the same income when received by the shareholders as dividends could not be regarded as agricultural income.

Another attempt by the members of a company to treat themselves at par with the company was frustrated by the Calcutta High Court in *CIT* v *Associated Clothiers Ltd.*[90]

> The assessees, Associated Clothiers, formed a company holding all its shares. They sold certain premises to the new company. The difference between the selling price and the cost of the property in the hands of assessees was assessed as their income.

They contended that this could not be done as there was no commercial sale, but only a transfer from self to self. The court rejected this and held that it was sale from one entity to another and not a trading with oneself.

From this point of view, incorporation sometimes becomes too dear. Shareholders are virtually compelled to pay the price for the advantages of incorporation. Those shareholders who become directors have then to owe duties of fiduciary nature to their own company and they cannot use the assets of the company as if they were their own. In a way they become strangers to their own enterprise.[91] This is one of those situations which go to prove the truth in Professor Kahn-Freund's statement that "sometimes *corporate entity* works like a boomerang and hits the man who was trying to use it".[92]

609; *Firestone Tyre & Rubber Co Ltd* v *Lewellin*, [1957] 1 WLR 464; *McDowell & Co* v *CTO*, (1985) 3 SCC 230; *Jurniss* v *Dawson*, [1984] 1 All ER 530.

89. AIR 1955 SC 74: (1955) 1 SCR 876: (1955) 25 Comp Cas 1.

90. AIR 1963 Cal 629. See also *CIT* v *Sri Meenakshi Mills Ltd*, (1967) 1 SCR 934: AIR 1967 SC 819: 63 ITR 609.

91. See, *George Newman & Co, Re*, [1895] 1 Ch 674: [1895-9] All ER Rep Ext 2161; *E.B.M. Co Ltd* v *Dominion Bank*, [1937] 3 All ER 555 PC.

92. *See* O. Kahn Freund, *Company Law Reform*, 9 Mod LR 235.

(c) *Fraud or improper conduct.*—The corporate entity is wholly incapable of being strained to an illegal or fraudulent purpose. The courts will refuse to uphold the separate existence of the company where it is formed to defeat or circumvent law, to defraud creditors or to avoid legal obligations. One clear illustration is *Gilford Motor Co v Horne.*[93]

Horne was appointed as a managing director of the plaintiff company on the condition that "he shall not at any time while he shall hold the office of a managing director or afterwards, solicit or entice away the customers of the company". His employment was determined under an agreement. Shortly afterwards he opened a business in the name of a company which solicited the plaintiff's customers.

It was held that "the company was a mere cloak or sham for the purpose of enabling the defendant to commit a breach of his covenant against solicitation. Evidence as to the formation of the company and as to the position of its shareholders and directors leads to that inference. The defendant company was a mere channel used by the defendant Horne for the purpose of enabling him, for his own benefit, to obtain the advantage of the customers of the plaintiff company, and that the defendant company ought to be restrained as well as the defendant Horne".

Where a person borrowed money from a company and invested it in shares of three different companies in all of which he and his son were the only members, the lending company was permitted to attach the assets of such companies as they were created only to hoodwink the lending company.[94] Where a company created a subsidiary and transferred its investment holdings to it in a bid to reduce its liability to pay bonus to its workers, the Supreme Court brushed aside the separate existence of the subsidiary company. "It is the duty of the court, in every case where ingenuity is expended to avoid taxing and welfare legislation, to get behind the smokescreen and discover the true state of affairs".[95] The following

93. [1933] 1 Ch 935. Another illustration is *Conners Bros v Conners*, [1974] 4 All ER 179 PC. See also *Delhi Development Authority v Skipper Construction Co (P) Ltd*, (1997) 11 SCC 430: (1997) 89 Comp Cas 362 SC, where the corporate veil to bring to the surface persons who were using the company for defrauding people by luring them into booking for plots and flats.
94. *PNB Finance v Shital Pd Jain*, (1983) 54 Comp Cas 66 Del. Property acquired under fraudulent schemes was allowed to be chased even in the hands of third persons. *SEBI v Libra Plantation Ltd*, (1999) 95 Comp Cas 373 Bom; money collected under fraudulent investment schemes was ordered to be chased in whosoever hands it might be, *Ali Jawad Ameer Hasan Rizvi v Indo French Biotech Enterprises Ltd*, (1999) 95 Comp Cas 373 Bom; *SEBI v Libra Plantations Ltd*, [1999] 1 Comp LJ 294: (1999) 95 Comp Cas 373 Bom; *Dindas Shankar Thange v State of Maharashtra*, (1999) 95 Comp Cas 373 Bom.
95. *Workmen v Associated Rubber Industry Ltd*, (1985) 4 SCC 114, 118-119; *National Dock Labour Board v Pinn and Wheeler Ltd*, 1989 BCLC 647 QBD, where a group of three companies working in the same geographical location of a dock were not allowed to claim that they should be treated as three different companies when their purpose was to avoid the effect of the Dock Labour Scheme; *Chitra Kumar Basu v Property Development Trust Ltd*, (1988) 93 Cal WN 725, evasion of welfare legislation.

statement in the judgment of CHINNAPPA REDDY J shows how the court guessed that evasion was the only purpose:

A new company is created, wholly owned by the principal company, with no assets of its own except those transferred to it by the principal company, with no business or income of its own except receiving dividends from shares transferred to it by the principal company and serving no purpose whatsoever except to reduce the gross profits of the principal company. These facts speak for themselves. There cannot be direct evidence that the second company was formed as a device to reduce the gross profits of the principal company for whatever purpose. An obvious purpose that it served and which stares one in the face is to reduce the amount to be paid by way of bonus to workmen.

This finding was further supported by the fact that the subsidiary was subsequently wound up and amalgamated into the holding company.

A person who had incurred a disqualification, for example, blacklisting as a contractor, was not allowed to hide his disqualification by forming a company and tendering in its name.[96] The Court further held that the experience of the shareholders of a company could not be regarded as that of the company for tendering purposes. This decision was reversed by the Supreme Court.[97] The court said that it was permissible to see through the corporate veil to find out from the shareholders or from the people controlling the company something about the nature of the company. The company was composed of two joint venturers who, among other things contributed their personal expertise. In such circumstances, the court said, the experience of the company can only mean the experience of its constituents. Such experience was ignored by the tender evaluation committee on a wrong hypothesis. This resulted in a disqualification of the tendering company. A legal wrong was caused to it.

A controlling shareholder commenced action against a company for recovery of a loan supposed to have been made by his company to the debtor company. The alleged loan agreement pre-dated the incorporation of the lending company. The action was, therefore, dismissed. Subsequent to this the company commenced an action on the basis of a written loan agreement. This action was dismissed under the principle of *res judicata*. The company was wholly owned and controlled by one person and might have started the action at his behest.[98]

---

96. *New Horizons Ltd* v *UOI*, AIR 1994 Del 126.
97. *New Horizons Ltd* v *UOI*, (1995) 1 SCC 478: (1997) 89 Comp Cas 849 SC.
98. *Barakot Ltd* v *Epiettee Ltd*, (1997) 1 BCLC 303 QBD; *Jai Narain Parasrampuria* v *Pushpa Devi Saraf*, (2006) 133 Comp Cas 794 SC, promoters represented that the property was purchased for the company, the company was shown as the owner in all documents signed by promoters; they were the only shareholders and directors in the company, they were estopped from claiming that the property belonged to them personally, they were using the personality of the company for personal motive, not to be allowed to set up a case contrary to the company's interests.

A director's knowledge that there was a winding up petition against the company was attributed to the company. An *ex parte* order was passed. The director moved for having the order set aside long after. The court refused to condone the delay.[1]

(*d*) *Government companies.*—A company may sometimes be regarded as an agent or trustee of its members or of another company and may, therefore, be deemed to have lost its individuality in favour of its principal. In India this question has frequently arisen in connection with Government companies. A large number of private companies for commercial purposes have been registered under the Companies Act with the President and a few other officers as the shareholders.[2] The obvious advantage of forming a Government company is that it gives the activities of the State "a little of the freedom which was enjoyed by private corporations and [the Government] escaped the rules and principles which hampered action when it was done by a Government department instead of a Government corporation. In other words, it gave the Government some of the robes of the individual".[3] And in order to assure this freedom the Supreme Court has reiterated in a number of cases that a Government company is not a department or an extension of the State.[4] It is not an agent of the State. Accordingly its employees are not civil servants[5] and prerogative writs cannot issue against it.[6] In one of these cases, the court remarked:

"The company being a non-statutory body and one incorporated under the Companies Act there was neither a statutory nor a public duty imposed on it by a statute in respect of which enforcement could be sought by means of a mandamus".[7]

---

1. *Serum Institute of India Ltd* v *V. Yugendra Kumar*, (2006) 133 Comp Cas 135 AP.
2. Shradha Kumari, *Government Companies in India*, (1957) Indian Law Journal 143.
3. Thurman W. Arnold, THE FOLKLORE OF CAPITALISM, 193 (1956).
4. *State Trading Corpn of India Ltd* v *CTO*, AIR 1963 SC 1811: (1963) 33 Comp Cas 1057: (1964) 4 SCR 99; *Sukdev Singh* v *Bhagatram*, (1975) 1 SCC 421: (1975) 45 Comp Cas 285.
5. *Praga Tools Corpn* v *Imanual*, (1969) 1 SCC 585: AIR 1969 SC 1306: (1969) 39 Comp Cas 889; *Abani Bhusan Biswas* v *Hindustan Cables Ltd*, [1968] 2 Comp LJ 197; *Pyarelal Sharma* v *Managing Director, J&K Industrial Ltd*, (1989) 3 SCC 448: [1989] 3 Comp LJ 70: (1990) 67 Comp Cas 195 SC. But otherwise it being an organ of the State, it cannot be permitted to enforce against an employee a contract which is unfair. *Modern Food Industries (India) Ltd* v *M.D. Juvekar*, [1988] 2 LLJ 534 Guj: 1989 Lab IC 224. It is also required to act fairly in trade matters and commercial bargains. *Mahabir Auto Stores* v *IOC*, (1990) 3 SCC 752: (1990) 69 Comp Cas 746 SC, the Supreme Court did not permit the IOC to cancel without proper procedure an 18 year old channel of distribution.
6. *Heavy Engg Mazdoor Union* v *State of Bihar*, (1969) 1 SCC 765: (1969) 39 Comp Cas 905: AIR 1970 SC 82; *R.D. Singh* v *Secy, Bihar State Small Industries Corpn*, (1975) 45 Comp Cas 527 Pat.
7. Cited in *Ram Singh* v *Fertilizer Corpn of India Ltd*, (1980) 50 Comp Cas 553, where the court refused to issue a writ in favour of an employee whose pay had been reduced by the company, the petitioner to pursue his ordinary remedy in the law of contract.

The Madhya Pradesh High Court regarded a Government company to be a separate entity for the purpose of enabling a Development Authority to subject it to development tax.[8] The assets of a Government company were held to be not exempt from payment of non-agricultural assessment under an AP legislation. The exemption enjoyed by the Central Government property from State taxation was not allowed to be claimed by a Government company.[9] The subsidiary of a Government company which also becomes a Government company was not allowed the benefit of the UP Public Money (Recovery of Dues) Act, 1972.[10] Steel Authority of India has been held to be not a department of the State.[11] Similarly, the Court of Appeal in England in *Ebbw Vale UDC* v *S. Wales Traffic Area Licensing Authority*[12] refused to hold that transport services provided by a company all of whose shares were owned by the Transport Commission were services provided "by the Commission or by any person acting as agent for the Commission". A Government company will be regarded as an agent of the State only when it is performing in substance governmental or sovereign and not merely commercial functions.[13]

Ultimately the employees have found some success at the hands of KRISHNA IYER J. The case before the Supreme Court was *Som Prakash Rekhi* v *UOI*.[14] The company in question arose out of the acquisition and vesting in the Central Government of the assets and business of Burmah Shell. The employee, who had certain rights as to provident fund etc., against the former company, claimed them against the Government by means of a writ. His claim was resisted on the ground that the undertaking had been vested in a company registered under the Companies Act and the question of a writ against a private company could not arise. KRISHNA IYER J brushed aside this contention. He laid emphasis upon the fact that the whole undertaking had been vested in the Central Government and, therefore, it became a State undertaking. The learned judge also stressed the fact that the law should not go by the fact whether the company is registered under the Companies Act or otherwise, but by the nature of the functions that the unit was performing. Here the statement of reasons stated that the

---

8. *Bharat Aluminium Co Ltd* v *Special Area Development Authority*, (1981) 51 Comp Cas 184 MP.
9. *Electronics Corpn of India Ltd* v *Secy, Revenue Deptt, Govt of A.P.*, (1999) 4 SCC 458: AIR 1999 SC 1734: (1999) 97 Comp Cas 470. The Food Corporation was held to be not exempt from State taxes. It does not enjoy the status of the Central Government, *Food Corpn of India* v *Municipal Committee*, (1999) 98 Comp Cas 824 SC.
10. *Rewa Gases (P) Ltd* v *State of U.P.*, [1999] 3 Comp LJ 227 All.
11. *Steel Authority of India Ltd* v *Shri Ambica Mills Ltd*, (1998) 92 Comp Cas 120 SC; *Hindustan Steel Works Construction Ltd* v *State of Kerala*, [1998] 2 Comp LJ 383 SC.
12. [1951] 2 KB 366 CA.
13. *Tamlin* v *Hannaford*, [1950] 1 KB 18, 25: [1949] 2 All ER 327 CA.
14. (1981) 1 SCC 449: (1981) 51 Comp Cas 71.

company was being acquired in public interest and thus the new company was created to perform a function of public nature. The court noted the fact that the reason why the State chose to function through companies was not to frustrate employees, but to assure commercial flexibility and freedom from departmental rigidity, slow motion procedures and hierarchy of officers.[15] The learned judge cited the following remark of President Roosevelt:[16]

> Concentration of economic power in all-embracing corporations... represents private enterprise become a kind of private Government which is a power unto itself—a regimentation of other people's money and other people's lives.

Hitting at the reality of the situation, KRISHNA IYER J remarked:

> "The true owner is the State, the real operator is the State and the effective collectorate is the State and the accountability for actions to the community and to Parliament is of the State. Nevertheless a distinct juristic person with a corporate structure conducts the business. Be it remembered though that while the formal ownership is cast in the corporate mould, the reality reaches down to State control.... What we wish to emphasise is that merely because a company or other legal person has functional and jural individuality for certain purposes, it does not necessarily follow that for the effective enforcement of fundamental rights, we should not scan the real character of that entity; and if it is

---

15. There is, however, an equivalent amount of hierarchy of officers in the corporate infrastructure also. The word "State" as defined in Article 12 of the Constitution includes all authorities within the territory of India or under the control of the Government of India. The word "authority" has all along been taken to mean only those authorities whose orders are to be obeyed. The word will accordingly exclude associations registered under the Companies Act. The Allahabad High Court accordingly held in *Noor Mohamad v Phoola Rani*, (1986) 59 Comp Cas 312 All, that the Bengal Chamber of Commerce which is registered under the Companies Act is not an authority within the meaning of Article 12. In *State of Punjab v Raja Ram*, (1982) 52 Comp Cas 104 SC, a statutory corporation, viz., the Food Corporation of India, has been held to be not equivalent to State for the purposes of the Land Acquisition Act. An employee was allowed to proceed against a Government company under writ jurisdiction to question the termination of his services. *H. Purushotam v UOI*, (1997) 14 SCR 191 Cal; *Mysore Papers Ltd v Mysore Paper Mills Officers' Assn*, [1999] 1 Comp LJ 88 Kant. In *Secy, Haryana SEB v Suresh*, (1999) 3 SCC 601: AIR 1999 SC 1160, the Supreme Court observed that although the doctrine of not "lifting of the veil", as enunciated in *Salomon* case, came to be recognised in the corporate jurisprudence but its inapplicability in the present context cannot be doubted, since the law court invariably has to rise up to the occasion to do justice between the parties in a manner as it deems fit. *Kapila Hingorani v State of Bihar*, (2003) 116 Comp Cas 133 SC, the Government not allowed to shelter behind the lack of resources in discharging its obligation to pay wages of the employees of a Government company. *A.K. Bindal v UOI*, (2003) 5 SCC 163: (2003) 114 Comp Cas 590 SC, the Government held not liable to pay the salary of the staff of a Government company. The company was an independent legal person and its staff members were not Government employees.
16. Franklin D. Roosevelt, Acceptance Speech, Democratic National Convention, 27th June, 1936.

found to be a mere agent or surrogate of the State, in fact owned by the State, in truth controlled by the State and in effect an incarnation of the State, Constitutional lawyers must not blink at these facts and frustrate enforcement of fundamental rights despite the inclusive definition of Article 12 that any authority controlled by the Government of India is itself State.''

The Supreme Court refused to hold the Life Insurance Corporation as an instrumentality of the State when it was exercising its ordinary right as a majority shareholder in a company for removing the existing management and reconstituting the board of directors.[17]

Agency or Trust, where no Functioning Autonomy Granted

Thus it appears that it is very difficult to persuade the courts to go behind the corporate entity of a company to determine whether it is really independent or is being used as an agent or a trustee. ''Under the ordinary rules of law'' observes COHEN LJ ''a parent company and a subsidiary company, even a 100 per cent subsidiary company, are distinct legal entities, and in the absence of an agency contract between the two companies one cannot be said to be the agent of the other''.[18] If one company is to be fixed with liability as a principal for the acts of another company, the relationship of agency should be substantively established. The facts of *Smith, Stone & Knight Ltd* v *Birmingham Corpn*[19] revealed a relationship of this kind. A company acquired a partnership concern, registered it as a company, and then continued to carry it on as a subsidiary company. The parent company held all the shares except a few, treated the subsidiary's profits as its own, appointed managers and exercised effectual and constant control. When the business of the subsidiary was acquired by

---

17. *LIC* v *Escorts Ltd*, (1986) 1 SCC 264, 343: (1986) 59 Comp Cas 548: [1986] 1 Comp LJ 91 SC. Employees of nationalised banks have been held to be public servants for the purposes of the Prevention of Corruption Act, 1947, *M.P. Kini* v *State*, (1992) 75 Comp Cas 289 AP. A nationalised insurance company was held to be an instrumentality of the State so as to enable the court to issue directions under writ jurisdiction. *Bholenath Cold Storage* v *National Ins Co Ltd*, (1994) 79 Comp Cas 90 Cal. A company with minimum Government control would not be so regarded. *P. B. Ghayalord* v *Maruti Udyog Ltd*, (1994) 79 Comp Cas 96 Del. A company in which the Government had only 17% shareholding and no control over management, was not held to be a Government company or a State instrumentality, *Nav Bharat Corpn* v *Nagarjuna Fertilizers & Chemicals Ltd*, (1991) 72 Comp Cas 518 AP. *Mysore Paper Mills Ltd* v *Mysore Paper Mills Officers' Assn*, (2002) 2 SCC 167: (2002) SCC L&S 223: (2002) 108 Comp Cas 652 SC, 97% mixed Government holding, appointment of directors required Government concurrence, important duties of public nature were entrusted to the company. The company was regarded as an instrumentality or agency of the State.
18. The court considered this to be clearly established by *Salomon* v *Salomon & Co*, [1895-99] All ER Rep 33: 66 LJ Ch 35: 75 LT 426: 13 TLR 46: 1897 AC 22, and the observations of TOMLIN J in *British Thompson & Houston Co* v *Sterling Accessories Ltd*, [1924] 2 Ch 33: [1924] All ER Rep 294.
19. [1939] 4 All ER 116 KB. A similar claim has again been upheld in *DHN Food Distributors Ltd* v *Tower Hamlets London Borough Council*, [1976] 1 WLR 852.

the defendant corporation the court allowed the parent company, brushing aside the legal distinction between the two companies, to claim compensation in respect of removal and disturbance. The subsidiary company was not operative on its own behalf, but on behalf of the parent company. ATKINSON J first noted the rule that "it is well settled that the mere fact that a man holds all the shares in a company does not make the business carried on by that company his business. It is also well settled that there may be such an arrangement between the shareholders and a company as will constitute the company the shareholders' agent for the purpose of carrying on the business and make it the business of the shareholders". The learned judge then referred to six points which are useful for ascertaining who really was carrying on the business. The first point was: Were the profits treated as the profits of the parent company? Secondly, were the persons conducting the business appointed by the parent company? Thirdly, was the company the head and the brain of the trading company? Fourthly, did the company govern the adventure, decide what should be done and what capital should be embarked on the venture? Fifthly, did the company make the profit by its skill and direction? Was the company in constant and effectual control? After considering the answer to these questions the learned judge concluded that if ever one company could be said to be the agent or employee, or tool or *simulacrum* of another, that was the case here.[20]

Thus exclusive control in all respects and without any other person having any voice in the affairs is the surest indication of agency or trust. The following statement of Lord DENNING, MR pictorially portrays the circumstances in which a company is nothing but the controller himself under another hat.[21]

"It is plain that *W* used many companies, trusts, or other legal entities as if they belonged to him. He was in control of them as much as any "one-man company" is under the control of one who owns all the shares and is the chairman and managing director. He made contracts of enormous magnitude on their behalf on a sheet of note paper without reference to anyone else. I am prepared to accept that the companies... were distinct legal entities... even so they were just the puppets of *W*. He controlled their every movement. Each danced to his bidding. He pulled the strings. No one else got within the reach of them. Transformed into legal language, they were his agents to do as he commanded. He was the principal behind them. I am of the opinion that

---

20. This formula was cited in *Dy Commr, IT* v *Cherian Transport Corpn Ltd*, (1992) 74 Comp Cas 563 Mad, for the guidance of the IT authorities as to when they can club the income of certain companies together for a single assessment.
21. *Wallersteiner* v *Moir*, [1974] 1 WLR 991: [1974] 1 All ER 217 CA.

the court should put aside the corporate veil and treat these concerns as being his creatures for whose doings he should be, and is, responsible.''

For purposes of taxation also the same tests are applicable to see whether a company is not an agent or trustee of another. Lord DENNING MR said in a case:[22]

> ''The doctrine laid down in *Salomon v Salomon & Co* has to be watched very carefully. It has often been supposed to cast a veil over the personality of a limited company through which the courts cannot see. But that is not true. The courts can and often do draw aside the veil. They can, and often do, pull off the mask. They look to see what really lies behind. The legislature has shown the way with group accounts and the rest. And the courts should also follow suit. We should look at the Fork company and see it as it really is—the wholly owned subsidiary of the tax-payers. It is the creature, the puppet of the tax-payers in point of fact, and it should be so regarded in point of law.''

Another illustration is *F. G. (Films) Ltd, Re.*[23]

> An American company produced a film called 'Monsoon' in India technically in the name of a company incorporated in England. The English company had a capital of £100 in £1 shares, 90 of which were held by an American director. The production was financed by the American company. In these circumstances the Board of Trade refused to register it as a British film and their decision was upheld by the court. It would be a mere travesty of the facts to say or to believe that this insignificant company undertook the arrangements for the making of the film. They acted, in so far as they acted at all in the matter, merely as the nominee of, and agent for the American company.

> A group of thirteen companies incorporated abroad separately applied for permission under the Foreign Exchange Regulation Act, 1974 for investment in Indian companies. The Act, on the one hand, encouraged flow of such investment from non-resident Indians, and, on the other, imposed a ceiling so that the privilege may not be used to destabilise Indian companies. It was contended that all the thirteen companies belonged to one family trust and therefore the ceilings were violated. The Supreme Court refused to accept this. This Act itself permits the veil to be lifted for the purpose of knowing whether 60 per cent holding makes the company belong to non-resident Indians. To go further with lifting the veil would be against national interest because it would discourage the flow of non-resident investment.[24]

---

22. *Littlewoods Mail Order Stores Ltd* v *IRC*, [1969] 3 All ER 855 CA: [1969] 1 WLR 1241.
23. [1953] 1 WLR 483.
24. *LIC* v *Escorts Ltd*, (1986) 1 SCC 264, 336-337: (1986) 59 Comp Cas 548: [1986] 1 Comp LJ 91 SC. It is not easy for the creator-controller of a company to get rid of his personal handicaps

Personal Liability of Directors and Members: Statutory provisions

The Act also imposes personal liability on the directors or members of a company in certain cases. Independent existence of the company is maintained and the company may also be liable. But, apart from the liability of the company, those cloaked behind it are also made liable. Following are some such provisions of the Act.

(*a*) *Reduction in Membership*

Section 45 provides:

> If at any time the number of members of a company is reduced, in the case of a public company, below seven, or in the case of a private company, below two and the company carries on business for more than six months while the number is so reduced, every person who is a member of the company.... and is cognizant of the fact.... shall be severally liable for the payment of the whole debts of the company contracted during that time....''

The purpose of the provision is to withdraw the advantages of incorporation when the conditions of incorporation are not maintained.

A member of a company became liable severally and jointly with the company for the debts incurred during the period when he was the sole member of the company. He had himself purchased the shares of the only other member of the company.[25] HOFFMAN J observed:

> "I have considerable sympathy with the appellant, who has fallen into a trap created by an ancient and obsolete rule. Section 24 of the [English] Companies Act, 1985 requires that a company should have at least two members. In default of compliance it strips the remaining member of the protection of limited liability. The rule goes back to Section 48 of the [English] Companies Act, 1862 when the minimum number of members was seven. This reflects the evolution of company law from partnership, but the reason why it has survived through successive Companies Act is obscure. It seems to serve no purpose in protecting the public or anyone else. It is not necessary that the second

---

by operating through a company. Thus in *Canada Enterprises Corpn Ltd* v *MacNab Distilleries Ltd*, [1987] 1 WLR 813, three different debenture-holders of a company transferred their debentures to their self-controlled companies, which demanded repayment of the debentures. The defendant company was granted a stay against them for a counter-claim which the company had against the controlling shareholders for breaches of their vending agreements. They were treated as being identical with their companies, the court considering the substance of the transaction to be more important than the legal form. *Lalit Surajmal Kanodia* v *Office Tiger Database Systems India (P) Ltd*, (2006) 129 Comp Cas 192 Mad, employees of one group company committed contempt of court, employees of other group companies could not be punished.

25. *Nisbet* v *Shepherd*, (1994) BCLC 300: (1995) 19 Corpt LA 234 CA.

member should hold his share or shares beneficially. The appellant could have satisfied the requirement of the Act by transferring a single share to his wife, lawyer or accountant to hold in trust for himself. But he did none of these things. Since 1983, the appellant has been the sole member and is liable accordingly.''

All the remaining members would have to be impleaded as necessary parties, even if the circumstances are such that some of them would not be severally liable.[26]

(b) *Misdescription of Name*

Secondly, where in any act or contract of a company, its name is not fully or properly indicated as required by Section 147 those who have actually done the act or made the contract shall be personally liable for it. Thus the directors were held personally liable on a cheque signed by them in the name of a company stating the company's name as ''L R Agencies Ltd'', the real name being ''L & R Agencies Ltd''[27].

(c) *Fraudulent Conduct of Business*

Thirdly, Section 542 imposes liability for fraudulent conduct of a company's business. According to the section, ''if in the course of winding up of a company, it appears that any business of the company has been carried on with intent to defraud creditors of the company or any other persons, or for any fraudulent purpose'', those who were knowingly parties to such conduct of business may, in the discretion of the Tribunal, be made personally liable for all or any of the debts of the company.[28]

(d) *Holding and Subsidiary Companies* [S. 4]

A company qualifies as a holding company when it has the power to control the composition of the board of directors of another company or holds a majority of its shares. It has been seen that a subsidiary company, even a 100 per cent subsidiary, is a separate legal entity and its creator and controller is not to be held liable for its acts merely because he is the creator and controller. Nor is the subsidiary to be held as an asset of the holding company. The decision of the Delhi High Court in *Freewheels (India) Ltd* v *Dr Veda Mitra*,[29] is an illustration in point:

---

26. *Madanlal* v *Himatlal*, [1997] 1 Comp LJ 399: (2000) 37 CLA 273 MP.
27. *Hendon* v *Adelman*, The Times, June 16, 1973: 1973 New LJ 637.
28. *William C. Leitch Bros Ltd, Re*, [1932] 2 Ch 71: [1932] All ER Rep 892. Nigel L. Mecassey, *Responsibility for Fraudulent Trading*, 1973 New LJ 822.
29. AIR 1969 Del 258: [1969] 1 Comp LJ 138; *Nandh Products Promoters (P) Ltd* v *District Forest Officer*, (2005) 123 Comp Cas 367 Mad, the dues of the company to the Forest Department were not allowed to be adjusted against the Department's dues to a firm only because some of the partners of the firm were also officers of the company.

A fifty-two per cent subsidiary company proposed to issue further capital which, following Section 81, was offered to the existing holders of equity shares. The holding company requested the court that its subsidiary should be restrained from going ahead with the issue as it would deprive its parent of their controlling interest and would also depreciate the value of its shares.

KAPUR J refused to issue the injunction prayed for and said: "Here the parent holds only a nominal majority in the share capital of the subsidiary. With the meagre majority alone I am not prepared to hold, even if it were possible to do so for such a purpose, that the subsidiary company has lost its identity as a separate legal entity".[30]

A holding company was not allowed to interfere in the disinvestment decision of a sub-subsidiary company (subsidiary of subsidiary) even if one of the effects of the disinvestment could have been the loss of position as a holding company.[31] The application of a foreign company for approval for establishing a wholly owned subsidiary company was held to be not an application for establishing a joint venture because a parent company and its subsidiary are usually treated as one economic entity whereas a joint venture presupposes two independent parties.[32] A holding company cannot be made liable for dues of the subsidiary. In this case, the subsidiary owed certain sums to the Employees' Provident Fund. The holding company was held to be not liable in that respect, because it could not be supposed to be the employer of workers of its subsidiary. The subsidiary was not a branch of the holding company.[33]

An English company created a foreign subsidiary for listing and tax advantages. The foreign subsidiary was used for raising money on bonds through financing banks. The money thus raised was loaned to the holding company. When the holding became unable to pay and was put under administration, the financing banks lodged their claims for the money provided by them to the subsidiary and the subsidiary also lodged its claim

---

30. *See* also *State of U.P.* v *Renusagar Power Co*, 1989 Supp (2) SCC 312: AIR 1989 SC 1737: (1991) 70 Comp Cas 127, a subsidiary company was created for the purpose of generating and supplying power only to its parent company and the two were treated as one for excise purposes. *PNB* v *Bareja Knipping Fasteners Ltd*, (2001) 103 Comp Cas 958 P&H, companies in a group are nevertheless distinct juristic personalities with different sets of shareholders. A decree against one company cannot be executed against another company even if they are being managed by the same set of persons.
31. *BDA Breweries* v *Cruickshonk & Co Ltd*, (1996) 85 Comp Cas 325 Bom: (1997) 25 Corpt LA 275.
32. *Mehra (UK)* v *UOI*, (1997) 88 Comp Cas 213 Del.
33. *Industrial Development Corpn, Orissa Ltd* v *Regional PF Commr*, (2002) 112 Comp Cas 527 Ori; *Alembic Glass Industries Ltd* v *Collector of Central Excise & Customs*, (2002) 9 SCC 463: (2002) 112 Comp Cas 379, two public limited companies holding shares in each other, not allowed to be regarded as related persons. The court also said that a shareholder does not have any interest in the business of the company.

for the same money because it provided the loans to the holding company. The financing banks wanted that the claim of the subsidiary should be ignored because it was a part of the same economic entity. The court refused to do so and said that those two companies could not be regarded as one and the same entity. All the companies in a group are separate legal entities and have to be so regarded unless there are compelling circumstances. The court said that even if in certain circumstances the court could go behind the veil to examine the real substance of the transaction, it would still be looking at the legal substance and not the economic substance.[34]

A subsidiary company may, however, lose its separate identity to a certain extent in two cases. Firstly, the Legislature may brush aside the legal forms and require the companies in a group to present a joint picture. Thus, Sections 212-214 contain provisions "designed primarily to give better information of the accounts and financial position of the group as a whole to the creditors, shareholders and public".[35]

Secondly, the court may, on facts of a case, refuse to grant a subsidiary company an independent status. "It may not be possible to put in a straitjacket of judicial definition as to when the subsidiary company can really be treated as a branch, or an agent, or a trustee of the holding company. Circumstances such as the profits of the subsidiary company being treated as those of the parent company, the control and conduct of business of the subsidiary company resting completely in the nominees of the holding company... may indicate that in fact the subsidiary company is only a branch of the holding company".[36] That result followed in the case of a wholly owned subsidiary whose parent company was allowed to recover compensation when the land of its subsidiary on which it was carrying on business was acquired.[37] A change of majority shareholding between two

---

34. *Polly Peck International plc (No 3), Re*, (1996) 1 BCLC 428 Ch D. See also *H (Restraint Order Realisable Property), Re*, (1996) 2 BCLC 500 CA, the corporate structure was used as a device or facade to conceal criminal activities (evasion of taxes).

35. Note 29 (above) at p 142 of Comp LJ. For details about such accounting provisions *see*, Chapter 19. See also *Liability of a Corporation for Acts of a Subsidiary or Affiliate*, (1958) 71 Harv LR 1122.

36. KAPUR J in *Freewheels (India) Ltd v Dr Veda Mitra*, AIR 1969 Del 258: [1969] 1 Comp LJ 138 142-143. See also *Smith, Stone & Knight Ltd v Birmingham Corpn*, [1939] 4 All ER 116 KB where all such cases have been reviewed.

37. *DHN Food Distributors Ltd v Tower Hamlets London Borough Council*, [1976] 1 WLR 852, distinguishing it from the Scottish case of *Woolfsan v Strathelyde Regional Council*, [1978] SLT 157, noted 1977 JBL 250-251, because here the subsidiary was not wholly owned but only one in a group. In *Hackrbridge-Hewittic and Easun Ltd v GEC Distribution Transformers Ltd*, (1992) 74 Comp Cas 543 Mad, a company becoming a subsidiary company for a business right which it had exclusively granted to another company was held to have violated the covenant. In *Fatima Tile Works v Sudarsan Trading Co Ltd*, (1992) 74 Comp Cas 423 Mad, where the subsidiary was a completely controlled company and therefore the subsidiary's use of a trade mark was regarded as that of the holding company so as to show a connection between the goods and the owner of the trade mark.

companies associated with each other being the subsidiaries of the same company, did not have the effect of enabling the statutory tenants of the company's flats to say that the landlord had changed.[38]

Subsidiary of Multinational

That result did not follow in reference to the wholly owned foreign subsidiaries of a multinational corporation. A group of oil companies in the United Kingdom owned and controlled certain oil companies in Rhodesia. The English parent company was called upon to produce certain documents relating to a pipeline contract which were in the possession of its subsidiaries. The court rules empowered the court to require the disclosure of all documents in the "possession, custody or power" of a party. The question was whether the documents in the possession of a foreign subsidiary could be deemed to be in the possession of the "parent". The court of appeal answered the question in the negative.[39] Lord DENNING laid emphasis upon the position of the company in the setting of local laws applicable to it and the degree of freedom from interference by the parent:

"These South African and Rhodesian companies were very much self-controlled. Their directors were local directors—running their own show, operating it with comparatively little interference from London. They were subject, of course, to all local laws and ordinances. That seems to be a different position from the concept of a one-man company, or a 100 per cent company, which is operating in this country with the self-same directors, or a 100 per cent parent with various subsidiaries. It is important to realise that subsidiaries of multinational companies have a great deal of autonomy in the countries concerned."

A learned commentator explains in the following words the value of this decision to the international community:[40]

"The importance of this case lies in the fact that for the first time an English court has held that, if a multinational finds itself in a conflict between the interest of the home and the host country, the interests of the host country will prevail. This rule which was also adopted in

---

38. *Michaels* v *Harley House (Marlebone) Ltd*, [1999] 1 All ER 356 (CA); *Samayanallur Power Investment (P) Ltd* v *Covanta Energy India (Balaji) Ltd*, (2006) 30 Comp Cas 21 Mad, the holding company proposed to sell its entire shareholding in its subsidiary which was holding shares in a joint venture company. This company's articles provided for pre-emptive rights. The holding company became subjected to the clause, but the shareholders, entitled to pre-emptive right had waived it by making a bid for the shares.

39. *Lonrho Ltd* v *Shell Petroleum Co Ltd*, [1980] 2 WLR 367 CA.

40. Clive M. Schmitthoff, *Lifting the Corporate Veil*, 1980 JBL 158. *Tecnion Investments Ltd, Re*, 1985 BCLC 434 CA, a company would be the *alter ego* of an individual so as to regard his company's possession as his possession if the company was under his unfettered control. Merely that he is a dominant figure in running the company's business would not be enough.

France in the *Fruehauf* case[41] should now be regarded as an established principle of international law.''

In a case before the House of Lords,[42] certain South African miners were employed by the local subsidiary of a UK multinational company. They wished to sue the parent company for compensation for industrial diseases contacted while working for the subsidiary. Their Lordships found that there was likely to be greater access to justice under the English law because the English Court was more appropriate forum for a trial for a complex group action. Their Lordships accordingly held in favour of the minors.

Liability for Insolvent Subsidiary

The question whether the parent company should be held liable for the debts of its insolvent subsidiary involves a difficult problem. The difficulty has been indicated in a case which exposes the legal inadequacy and which has been thus presented: [43]

English company law possesses some curious features, which may generate various results. A parent company may spawn a number of subsidiary companies, all controlled directly or indirectly by the shareholders of the parent company. If one of the subsidiary companies turns out to be the runt of the litter and declines into insolvency to the dismay of its creditors, the parent company and the other subsidiary companies may prosper to the joy of the shareholders without any liability for the debts of the insolvent subsidiary. It is not surprising that when a subsidiary collapses, the unsecured creditors wish the finances of the company and its relationship with other members of the group to be narrowly examined, to ensure that no assets of the subsidiary company have leaked away; that no liabilities of the subsidiary company ought to be laid at the door of the other members of the group and that no indemnity from or right of action against any other company, or against any individual is by some mischief overlooked.[44]

Subsidiary Establishments

There is also the power in the Central Government as conferred by Section 8 to declare that any establishment of a company carrying on the

---

41. Clive M. Schmitthoff, *Multinationals in Court*, 1972 JBL 103, 106.
42. *Libbe* v *Cope plc*, [2000] 1 WLR 1545 HL.
43. *Southard & Co Ltd, Re*, [1979] 1 WLR 1198, 1208, TEMPLETON LJ, noted 1908 JBL 160.
44. For comments upon the decision *see*, Clive M. Schmitthoff, *The Wholly Owned and Controlled Subsidiary*, 1979 JBL 218, 226, where it is suggested that the Companies Act, should provide for such liability.

same or substantially the same activity as that carried on by the head office of the company, shall not be treated as a branch office of the company for any of the purposes of the Act.

Where proceedings were initiated against a company at the place of its branch office, it was held that notwithstanding the *Explanation* to Section 20 of the Civil Procedure Code which confers jurisdiction on the courts at the place of the company's branch office, it is also necessary that the cause of action should have arisen there. A charge of interference in management of the complainant's business could be alleged only against the head office of the company and not against the branch office unless it can be shown that the branch office was used for the purpose of committing the wrong.[45]

CONCLUSION

Thus it is abundantly clear that incorporation does not cut off personal liability at all times and in all circumstances.[46] "Honest enterprise, by means of companies is allowed; but the public are protected against kiting and humbuggery".[47] "The sanctity of a separate corporate identity is upheld only in so far as the entity is consonant with the underlying policies which give it life".[48] "Those who enjoy the benefits of the machinery of incorporation have to assure a capital structure adequate to the size of the enterprise. They must not withdraw the corporate assets or mingle their own individual accounts with those of the corporation or represent to third parties that no difference exists between themselves and the company. The courts have at times seized upon these facts as evidence to justify the imposition of liability upon the shareholders".[49]

2. Formality and expense

Another disadvantage of incorporation is its expense and formality. Incorporation is a very expensive affair and requires a number of formalities to be complied with. As compared with it, the formation of a partnership is

---

45. *Bhankerpur Simbhaoli Beverages (P) Ltd* v *Sarabhjit Singh*, (1996) 86 Comp Cas 842 P&H. See also *B.B. Verma* v *National Projects Construction Corpn Ltd*, [1999] 4 Comp LJ 274 Del, the company's project site was regarded as the place where the company was carrying on its business and coincidentally the company also had its subordinate office there.
46. Clive M. Schmitthoff, *Salomon in the Shadow*, 1976 JBL 305, where the learned writer says that if it were otherwise Salomon would have been misunderstood.
47. Cadman, THE CORPORATION IN NEW JERSEY, 353 (1949).
48. *Mull* v *Colt Co*, 31 FRD (1962), quoted in W. Friedman, LEGAL THEORY, 564 (5th Edn, 1967).
49. *Judicial Supervision of One-man Corporation*, 46 Harv LR 1084. Cohen & Simitis, *Lifting the Veil*, (1963) 12 IC LQ 189; Adolfe A. Berle Jr., *The Theory of Corporate Entity*, (1947) 47 Col LR 343; Douglas & Shanks, *Insulation from Liability through Subsidiary Corporation*, (1939) 39 Yale LJ 198.

·very simple. Again, the administration of a company has to be carried on strictly in accordance with the provisions of the Act. General meetings must be held in time; accounts must be prepared and audited and then presented to the shareholders in general meetings; copies of accounts are to be filed with the Registrar; mortgages and charges and certain resolutions have to be registered with the Registrar and in many other ways companies are under Government control and regulation. As many returns have to be filed with the Registrar as there are weeks in a year and every failure is penalised.[50] Accordingly "corporate directors wake up each morning as potential criminals". A partnership firm is comparatively free from all these complications. In the words of a critic who suggests that the formation of a small company should be made much more simple than at present:

> Incorporation of a business as a limited company involves expense, capital duty and stamp duty, printing etc., and recurring expenditure on company registration fees and audit fees and also a not inconsiderable expenditure of time in complying with the provisions of the Companies Act. It also involves disclosure to the public of the company's accounts and various other matters.[51]

3. Company is not citizen

Lastly, it may be added that a company, though a legal person, is not a citizen either under the Constitution of India or under the Citizenship Act. This has been the conclusion of a special bench of the Supreme Court in *State Trading Corpn of India Ltd* v *CTO*.[52]

> "The State Trading Corporation of India is incorporated as a private company under the Companies Act. All the shares are held by the President of India and two secretaries in their official capacities. The question was whether the corporation was a citizen. One of the contentions put forth on behalf of the corporation was that "if the corporate veil is pierced... one sees three persons who are admittedly the citizens of India", and, therefore, the corporation should also be regarded as a citizen."

But it was held that "neither the provisions of the Constitution, Part II, nor of the Citizenship Act, either confer the right of citizenship on, or

---

50. G. Narayanaswamy, *Complexity, Cumbersomeness and Anomalies of Company Law*, [1966] 2 Comp LJ 20, where the learned writer counts 50 items in respect of which returns have to be filed. There are more than 200 offences under the Act. *See*, Tahir Mahmood: *Offences under the Companies Act and the Doctrine of Mens Rea*, [1969] 2 Comp LJ 25. Some more have been added by the subsequent amendments.
51. W.J. Sandars, *Small Business Suggestions for Simplified Forms of Incorporation*, 1979 JBL 14.
52. AIR 1963 SC 1811: (1964) 4 SCR 99: (1963) 33 Comp Cas 1057.

recognise as citizen, any person other than a natural person''. In the striking words of HIDAYATULLAH J (afterwards CJ):

"....if all of them (the members) are citizens of India the company does not become a citizen of India any more than, if all are married the company would be a married person.''

A company is, however, a person in the eyes of law and it can claim the protection of such fundamental rights as are guaranteed to all persons whether citizens or not. A company cannot claim the protection of such fundamental rights as are expressly guaranteed to citizens only. But even so there is no "cause for anxiety about corporations in general and companies in which States hold all or the majority of the shares in particular. They are amply protected under our Constitution. There can be no discrimination, no taxation without authority of law, no curbs involving freedom of trade, commerce or intercourse, and no compulsory acquisition of property. There is sufficient guarantee there and if more is needed then any member (if citizen) is free to invoke Article 19(1)(*f*), (*g*) and there is no doubt that the corporation in most cases will share the benefit. We need not be apprehensive that corporations are at the mercy of State Governments''.

The hardship caused by this pronouncement has, however, been subsequently modified, (though not by conceding in so many words that a company may be a citizen for certain purposes) by holding that a citizen shareholder may petition, proceeding on behalf of the company, against violation of his company's fundamental rights.[53]

Nationality, Domicile and Residence

A company does, however, have a nationality, domicile and residence. Speaking of this MACNAGHTEN J laid down:[54]

"It was suggested that a body corporate has no domicile. It is quite true that a body corporate cannot have a domicile in the same sense as an individual any more than it can have a residence in the same sense as an individual. But by analogy with a natural person, the attributes of residence, domicile and nationality can be given to a body corporate.''

A company incorporated in a particular country has the nationality of that country, though, unlike a natural person, it cannot change its nationality.[55]

The same principles apply to the determination of the residence of a company. Lord LOREBURN stated in a case before the House of Lords[56] that

---

53. See *State of Gujarat v Shri Ambica Mills Ltd*, (1974) 4 SCC 656; *Neptune Assurance Co v UOI*, (1973) 1 SCC 310, 335: (1973) 43 Comp Cas 469, and the *Bank Nationalisation* case, (1970) 1 SCC 248: (1970) 40 Comp Cas 325.
54. *Gasque v Commrs of Inland Revenue*, [1940] 2 KB 80.
55. *See* also *Kuenigl v Donnersmarck*, [1955] 1 QB 515, 535: [1955] 1 All ER 46.
56. *De Beers Consolidated Mines v Howe*, 1906 AC 455.

in applying the concept of residence to a company we ought to proceed as nearly as we can upon the analogy of an individual. "A company cannot eat or sleep, but it can keep house and do business. We ought, therefore, to see where it really keeps house and does business. An individual may be of a foreign nationality and yet reside in the United Kingdom, so may a company. Otherwise it might have its chief seat of management and its centre of trading in England under the protection of English laws, and yet escape the appropriate taxation by the simple expedient of being registered abroad and distributing its dividends abroad. A company resides for purposes of income tax where its real business is carried on. The real business is carried on where the central management and control actually resides".[57]

Ordinarily the residence of the company is at the place where its registered office is situated. This observation occurs in a case in which the company was incorporated in Australia and it also carried on business and personally worked for gain at that place. It filed a case under the Copyright Act in Ernaculam whereas the breach of the copyright had taken place in Chennai. No part of the cause of action had taken place in Ernaculam. The mere fact that the company's power of attorney was residing and doing business there did not confer any jurisdiction on the courts at that place.[58]

---

57. For further study Vaughan Williams and M. Crussachi, *The Nationality of Corporations*, (1933) 49 LQR 334 and E. H. Young, *The Nationality of a Juristic Person*, (1908) 22 Harv LR 10.
58. *Saranya Zaveri v Kamadon Academy (P) Ltd*, (2006) 133 Comp Cas 546 Ker.

2

Registration and Incorporation

Procedure of registration [S. 33]

To obtain the registration of a company an application has to be filed with the Registrar of Companies. The application must be accompanied by the following documents:[1]

1. Memorandum of Association.
2. Articles of Association, if necessary.[2]
3. The agreement, if any, which the company proposes to enter into with any individual for his appointment as its managing or wholetime director or manager.

The documents for registration must be supported by a declaration stating that all the requirements of the Act relating to registration have been complied with. The declaration must be signed by an Advocate of the Supreme Court or of a High Court or an attorney or a pleader entitled to appear before a High Court or a Secretary, or a chartered accountant, in whole-time practice in India who is engaged in the formation of a company or a person named in the articles as a director, manager or secretary of the company. [S. 33(2)]

Section 12, which states the mode of forming an incorporated company, enables any seven persons (two for a private company) to associate for any lawful purpose and to get themselves incorporated into a company with or without limited liability. They can do so by subscribing their names to a memorandum of association and by complying with other requirements.

When the requisite documents are presented for registration, the Registrar has to see whether they answer the requirements of the Act. He may, however, accept the declaration as sufficient evidence of compliance. He then registers the company and other documents and places the name of the company in the Register of Companies.[3] A certificate of incorporation is then issued by the Registrar which certifies "under his hand that the

---

1. S. 33. The application has to be made to the Registrar of the State in which the registered office of the company is stated by the memorandum to be situate.
2. Articles are compulsory only for unlimited companies, companies limited by guarantee, and private companies [S. 26]. The documents have to be in print and computer printing by laser is valid for this purpose, but not xerox. *Selvarajan* v *ROC*, [1986] 3 Comp LJ 275 Mad: (1987) 62 Comp Cas 220.
3. Refusal to register on a ground which is not legitimate can be set right by a court order, e.g. refusal on the ground of an enquiry into the motives on future plans of promoters. *Exclusive Board of the Methodist Church* v *UOI*, (1985) 57 Comp Cas 43 Bom.

company is incorporated and, in the case of a limited company, that the company is limited".[4]

Certificate of incorporation [S. 34]

The certificate of incorporation brings the company into existence as a legal person. Upon its issue the company is born. For the Act provides that "from the date of incorporation such of the subscribers of the memorandum and other persons, as may from time to time be the members of the company, shall be a body corporate,... capable forthwith of exercising all the functions of an incorporated company".[5] The company's life commences from the date mentioned in the certificate of incorporation and the date appearing on it is conclusive, even if wrong.[6]

Certificate as Conclusive Evidence

Not only does the certificate create the company. It also is "the conclusive evidence that all the requirements of this Act have been complied with in respect of registration and matters precedent and incidental thereto and that the association is a company authorised to be registered and duly registered under this Act".[7] In other words, the validity of the certificate cannot be disputed on any grounds whatsoever. This is illustrated by the decision of the Judicial Committee of the Privy Council in *Moosa Goolam Ariff* v *Ebrahim Goolam Ariff*.[8]

The memorandum of association of a company was signed by two adult persons and by a guardian of the other five members, who were minors at the time, the guardian making a separate signature for each of the minors. The Registrar, however, registered the company and issued under his hand a certificate of incorporation. The plaintiff contended that this certificate of incorporation should be declared void.

Lord MACNAGHTEN said:

Their Lordships will assume that the conditions of registration prescribed by the Indian Companies Act were not duly complied with;

---

4. S. 34(1). *Electrical Cable Development Assn* v *Arun Commercial Premises Coop Housing Society Ltd*, (1998) 5 SCC 396: AIR 1998 SC 1998, the conversion of an unregistered association into a company was not successful because the articles of the company which was registered did not carry a clause that the members of the association would become members of the company, nor there was any resolution to that effect. The association and the company remained different entities.

5. S. 34(2). *Link Hire Purchase & Leasing Co (P) Ltd* v *State of Kerala*, (2001) 103 Comp Cas 941 Ker, the company, a person for the purposes of the Kerala Money Lenders Act, bound to obtain licence like an individual. *John Thomas* v *Dr K. Jagadessan*, (2001) 106 Comp Cas 619 SC, in the case of defamation of company, its director is an "aggrieved person", entitled to maintain prosecution under Sections 499-500, IPC.

6. *Ibid*.

7. S. 35.

8. ILR (1913) 40 Cal 1 PC.

that there were no seven subscribers to the memorandum and that the Registrar ought not to have granted the certificate. But the certificate is conclusive for all purposes.

In England the question whether the Registrar's certificate is conclusive was decided so far back as 1867 by Lord CAIRNS.... In *Peel* case [9] after signature and before registration a proposed memorandum of association had been altered without the authority of the subscribers so materially that the "alteration entirely neutralised and annihilated the original execution and signature of the document". The company, however, was registered and the Registrar gave his certificate of incorporation. It was objected that the memorandum of association had not been signed by seven or indeed by any subscribers and that the provisions of the Act had not been complied with. To that proposition Lord CAIRNS assented. But "the certificate of incorporation", he said, "is not merely a *prima facie* answer, but a conclusive answer to such objection.... When once the certificate of incorporation is given nothing is to be inquired into as to the regularity of the prior proceedings". The observations of Lord CHELMSFORD in *Oakes* v *Turquand*[10] are to the same effect. "I think", said his Lordship, "the certificate prevents all recurrence to prior matters essential to registration...and that it is conclusive... that all previous requisites have been complied with.[11]

"Thus the position is firmly established that if a company is born, the only method to get it extinguished is not by assailing its incorporation, but by resorting to the provisions of enactments, which provide for the winding up of the companies". This summary view of the position is to be found in the judgement of CHANDRA REDDY CJ in *T.V. Krishna* v *Andhra Prabha (P) Ltd.*[12]

"In this case the Express Newspapers (P) Ltd were the leading publishers of newspapers and weeklies. The Government adopted certain recommendations of the Wage Board for improvement in the terms of service and salaries of the working journalists. Thereupon the Express Newspapers sold its undertaking to a new company known as Andhra Prabha Private Ltd. It was alleged that the new company was formed for the illegal purpose of evading the new responsibility imposed by the Wage Board and, therefore, the registration of the company should be declared void."

---

9. (1867) 2 Ch App 674: 16 LT 780.
10. (1867) LR 2 HL 325. *See* also *Jubilee Cotton Mills* v *Lewis*, 1924 AC 958.
11. ILR (1913) 40 Cal 1 PC.
12. AIR 1960 AP 123. *Salim Akbarali Nanji* v *UOI*, (2003) 113 Comp Cas 141 Bom, a certificate of incorporation was not allowed to be challenged. The company could have been extinguished only by winding up. A cooperative society which fulfilled the requirements of Part IX for registration as company was registered in this case.

The Court, however, did not assent to the proposition that the purpose for which the company was formed was in any way unlawful or opposed to public policy and, therefore, held that company was validly incorporated. But even if some of the objects were illegal, the legal *persona* of the company could not have been extinguished by cancelling the certificate. Even in such a case the certificate is conclusive and the remedy would be to wind up the company. The illegal objects, however, do not become legal by the issue of the certificate.[13] Section 12 clearly mentions that "persons associated for any lawful purpose may... form an incorporated company".

Judicial Review

In some English cases the courts have explored the possibility of reviewing the Registrar's certificates and have come to the conclusion that they should be open to judicial review. Accordingly, a company which happened to be registered for an unlawful object, was ordered to be struck off.[14]

The Kerala High Court has held that a writ cannot be issued to cancel the registration of a company under the Companies Act.[15]

Pre-incorporation contracts

Company cannot be sued on Pre-incorporation Contract

Sometimes contracts are made on behalf of a company even before it is duly incorporated. But no contract can bind a company before it becomes capable of contracting by incorporation. "Two consenting parties are necessary to a contract, whereas the company, before incorporation, is a non-entity".[16] A company has no status prior to incorporation. It can have no income before incorporation for tax purposes.[17] Shares cannot be acquired in the name of a company before its incorporation. A transfer form is liable to be rejected where the name of a proposed company is entered in

---

13. *Universal Mutual Aid & Poor Houses Assn* v *A. D. Thappa Naidu*, AIR 1933 Mad 16. Registrar can refuse to register a memorandum with unlawful objects and, if per chance, he happens to do so, his certificate is not conclusive as to lawfulness of objects. *Performing Rights Society Ltd* v *London Theatre of Varieties*, [1922] KB 539; *R* v *ROC*, [1931] 2 KB 197.
14. R. R. Drury, *Nullity of Companies in English Law*, (1985) 48 Mod LR 644 considering *R* v *ROC*, (unreported) QBD, Dec 17, 1980. This is so because a company cannot properly be registered for an unlawful purpose. See *More, ex p*, [1931] 2 KB 197, 201; *Brown, ex p*, [1914] 2 KB 1161. The registration may be cancelled by appropriate proceedings. *Bowman* v *Secular Society Ltd*, 1917 AC 406, 438-439: [1916-17] All ER Rep 1. The conclusive presumption may not be raised where, e.g., non-compliance with a material statutory provision leaves the registration an incomplete fact, *Gaiman* v *National Assn of Mental Health*, (1971) 1 Ch 317. The certificate would not be conclusive where a trade union is registered as a company, *British Assn of Glass Bottle Mfg Ltd* v *Nettlefield*, (1911) 27 TLR 27.
15. *Maluk Mohamed* v *Capital Stock Exchange Kerala Ltd*, (1991) 72 Comp Cas 333 Ker.
16. Erle CJ in *Kelner* v *Baxter*, (1866) LR 2 CP 174: 15 LT 213: [1861-73] All ER Rep Ext 2009.
17. *CIT* v *City Mills Distributors (P) Ltd*, (1996) 2 SCC 375.

the column of transferee.[18] Thus, for example, in *English & Colonial Produce Co, Re*:[19]

A solicitor, on the instructions of certain gentlemen, prepared the necessary documents and obtained the registration of a company. He paid the registration fee and incurred the incidental expenses of registration.

But the company was held not bound to pay for those services and expenses. "The company could not be sued in law for those expenses, inasmuch as it was not in existence at the time when the expenses were incurred...and ratification was impossible".

"It is not desirable to saddle the corporation with burdens imposed upon it in advance by overly optimistic promoters."[20]

Company cannot sue on Pre-incorporation Contract

Secondly, the company is also not entitled to sue on a pre-incorporation contract. "A company cannot by adoption or ratification obtain the benefit of a contract purporting to have been made on its behalf before the company came into existence". This was held in *Natal Land & Colonisation Co v Pauline Colliery Syndicate.*[21]

N Co entered into an agreement with one C, who acted on behalf of a proposed syndicate. Under the agreement N Co was to give the syndicate a lease of coal mining rights. The syndicate was then registered and struck a seam of coal and claimed a lease which N Co refused. An action by the syndicate for specific performance of the agreement or in the alternative for damages was held not maintainable as the syndicate was not in existence when the contract was signed.

Ratification of Pre-incorporation Contract

Thus, so far as the company is concerned, it is neither bound by, nor can have the benefit of, a pre-incorporation contract. But this is subject to the provisions of the Specific Relief Act, 1963. Section 15 of the Act provides that where the promoters of a company have made a contract before its incorporation for the purposes of the company, and if the contract is warranted by the terms of incorporation, the company may adopt and enforce it. "Warranted by the terms of incorporation" means within the scope of the company's objects as stated in the memorandum. The contract should be for the purposes of the company. A person, who intended to promote a company, acquired a leasehold interest for it. He held it for

---

18. *Inlec Investment (P) Ltd v Dynamatic Hydraulics Ltd*, [1989] 3 Comp LJ 221, 225 CLB.
19. [1906] 2 Ch 435: 22 TLR 669. In *Clinon's Claim*, (1908) 2 Ch 515 CA, a promoter was not allowed to recover registration fee paid by him. *Rover International Ltd v Cannon Film Sales Ltd*, (1987) 1 WLR 1597, somebody who does not exist cannot contract.
20. Joseph H. Gross, *Pre-incorporation Contracts*, (1971) 87 LQR 367, 368.
21. 89 LT 678: 1904 AC 120: [1900-03] All ER Rep Ext 1050.

sometime for a partnership firm, converted the firm into a company which adopted the lease. The lessor was held bound to the company under the lease.[22]

According to a decision of the Supreme Court, the company has to accept the transaction but it is not necessary that the transaction should be mentioned in the company's articles. The very fact that the company was seeking a declaration of its ownership of the property which the directors had purchased for it before incorporation was sufficient to signify acceptance of the transaction.[23] A contract to allot shares after the company is incorporated is not for the purposes of the company so that the company cannot enforce it against the other party.[24]

Section 19 of the same Act provides that the other party can also enforce the contract if the company has adopted it after incorporation and the contract is within the terms of incorporation.

Personal Right and Liability of Contracting Agent

Now, in reference to contracts which do not fall within the purview of the above provisions, the question arises whether they can be enforced by or against the agent who acted on behalf of the projected corporation? The answer will depend upon the construction of the contract. If the contract is made on behalf of a company not yet in existence, the agent might incur personal liability. For, where a contract is made on behalf of a principal known to both the parties to be non-existent the contract is deemed to have been entered into personally by the actual maker. Similarly, "where a person purports to contract as agent he may nevertheless disclose himself as being in truth a principal, and bring an action in his own name".[25] Thus the agents were held personally liable in *Kelner* v *Baxter*:[26]

The facts were that the plaintiff intended to sell wine to a company which was to be formed, but under the contract he agreed to sell to the proposed directors of the company. The proposed directors intended to buy the wine on behalf of the company, but, as it was not in existence when the contract was made, they personally took delivery. It was held that as they had contracted on behalf of a principal who did not exist, they having received the wine, must pay for it.[27]

---

22. *Vali Pattabhirama Rao* v *Ramanuja Ginning & Rice Factory (P) Ltd*, (1986) 60 Comp Cas 568 AP. A new contract can also be made by the company after incorporation in terms of the earlier contract, *Howard* v *Patent Ivory Mfg Co*, (1888) 38 Ch D 156. An implied contract may arise if the company after incorporation acts on the contract but not when it is under mistaken belief of being bound by the earlier contract, *Northumberland Avenue Hotel Co, Re*, (1986) 33 Ch D 16 CA.

23. *Jai Narain Parasrampuria* v *Pushpa Devi Saraf*, (2006) 133 Comp Cas 794 SC.

24. *Imperial Tea Mfg Co* v *Munchershaw*, (1889) 13 Bom 415.

25. Lord Goddard CJ in *Newborne* v *Sensolid Ltd*, [1953] 1 All ER 708, 709: [1954] 1 QB 45.

26. (1866) LR 2 CP 174: 15 LT 213: [1861-73] All ER Rep Ext 2009.

27. Lord Goddard CJ at p 709 in *Newborne* v *Sensolid Ltd*, [1953] 1 All ER 708, 709. The company had gone into liquidation before paying the plaintiff's bill. By virtue of S. 9(2) of

As against it, in an Australian case, a vendor of land was not allowed to sue for specific performance the directors of a proposed company who contracted to buy something under the name of the company which subsequently refused to adopt the purchase.[28]

Where the contract is purported to be made by the company itself, it cannot be enforced by or against the agent through whom the company contracted, because "the relationship between a company and its directors is not the ordinary one of principal and agent. Where a company contracts, it is the company who contracts and its contract is merely authenticated by the signature of one or more of the directors". And so in *Newborne v Sensolid (GB) Ltd*:[29]

> The plaintiff was a promoter and prospective director of a limited company, named Leopold Newborne (London) Ltd, which at the material time had not been registered. A contract for the supply of goods by the company to the defendants was signed thus: 'Leopold Newborne (London) Ltd'; and the plaintiff's name 'L. N.' was written underneath. In an action for breach of the contract brought by the plaintiff against the defendants it was held that the contract was made, not with the plaintiff whether as agent or as principal, but with a limited company which at the date of the making was non-existent, and, therefore, it was a nullity, and the plaintiff could not adopt it or sue on it as his contract.

To the same effect is the decision of the Bombay High Court in *Ramkumar Potdar v Sholapur Spinning & Weaving Co Ltd.*[30]

> There was a clause in the memorandum of a proposed company under which a certain firm was to be appointed as managing agent of the company. After incorporation the company appointed them, but subsequently, the directors resolved to dismiss them. In an action to restrain the company from committing breach of the contract, it was held that a clause of this kind in the memorandum or articles does not constitute a contract between the company and an outsider. Even if it does constitute an implied contract, yet, "this was a preliminary contract such as the promoters make before incorporation of the company. It is not possible to bring a company into existence under the Act bound by a contract previously made".[31]

the European Communities Act, (S. 36 of the English Companies Act, 1989) an agent of an unformed company becomes personally liable. See *Phonogram Ltd v Lane*, [1981] 3 All ER 182, CA.

28. *Smallwood v Black*, (1965) 39 ALJR 405 HC. Facts borrowed from R. Baxt, *Personal Liability of Agent of Unformed Company*; *Kelner v Baxter Revisited*, (1967) 30 Mod LR 328, *See also* W. E. Davies, *Personal Liability of Directors of Non-Existent Companies*, (1964) 6 Univ. of W. Australia LR 400.
29. [1953] 1 All ER 708: [1954] 1 QB 45.
30. AIR 1934 Bom 427: (1934) 36 Bom LR 907.
31. *Id.* at p 429, see also *B B I Rly Co v District Board, 24 Parganas*, AIR 1946 Cal 23.

Thus it seems that the desire of the courts is to protect the new company from the burden of promoters' promises, for they "are proverbially profuse in their promises, and if the corporation were to be bound by them it would be subject to many unknown, unjust and heavy obligations".[32] With this protection goes some sacrifice also, for a company could not sue a person who before its incorporation had contracted to buy its shares. In some cases persons rendering services before incorporation had to go unremunerated.[33] Here the Courts will as far as possible saddle the promoter with personal liability. Thus, for example, in *Touche v Metropolitan Rly Warehousing Co*[34] under a contract with a promoter services were rendered by a third party to a company before its incorporation. The third party not being able to sue, it was held that the promoter must sue the company as a constructive trustee for the benefit of the third party.

Statutory Reform

Some of these complications have been solved by the European Communities Act, 1972. Section 9(2)[35] provides that when a contract purports to be made by a company, or by a person as agent for a company, at a time when the company has not been formed, then, subject to any agreement to the contrary, the contract shall have effect as a contract entered into by the person purporting to act for the company or as agent for it and he shall be personally liable on the contract accordingly. These provisions have been incorporated into S. 36-C of the [UK] Companies Act, 1989.

A person attempting to incorporate a pop group, obtained financial assistance from a recording company. He was held personally liable to refund the amount on his project failing to materialise.[36]

Commencement of business [S. 149]

A private company can commence business right from the date of its incorporation.[37] But, in the case of a public company, a further certificate

---

32. *Parke v Modern Woodmen*, 181 Ill 214, 234, (SC of Illinois, U.S.A.).
33. See, *Hereford & South Wales Waggon & Engg Co, Re*, (1876) 2 Ch D 621; *Rotherham Alum & Chemical Co, Re*, (1883) 25 Ch D 103; *National Motor Mail-Coach Co, Re*, (1908) 2 Ch 228: [1908-10] All ER Ext Rep 1373.
34. (1871) LR 6 Ch App 671.
35. This provision was incorporated in S. 36(4) of the 1985 Act [English] and re-enacted as S. 36(1) in the 1989 Act. In order to avoid such personal liability the modern practice is to keep a draft-contract ready to be executed by the company after incorporation.
36. *Phonogram Ltd v Lane*, (1981) 3 All ER 182, noted: John McMullen, *Preliminary Contracts by Promoters*, [1982] Camb LJ 47. See also *Catronic (UK) Ltd v Desonite*, (1991) BCLC 721 CA, here also the contracting agent was held liable but that his liability by itself would not give him the right to sue the other party.
37. S. 149(7). This will be so even if the private company is the subsidiary of a public company. The section would not apply to deemed public company also unless the operative category of deeming provisions would require the filing of a statement in lieu of prospectus. The Deptt of Co Affairs (DCA) [File No 44/50 (L-IV/62] is of opinion that the commencement certificate

for the commencement of business has to be obtained. This becomes necessary where a company has issued a prospectus inviting the public to subscribe for its shares. It will be entitled to the certificate subject to the following conditions: [S. 149(1)]

    (*a*) shares payable in cash must have been allotted up to the amount of the minimum subscription;

    (*b*) directors must have paid in cash the application and allotment money in respect of the shares contracted to be taken by them for cash;

    (*c*) no money is liable to become refundable to the applicants by reason of failure to apply for or to obtain permission for shares or debentures to be dealt in on any recognised stock exchange.

A declaration signed by any director of the company or its secretary that the above requirements have been complied with should be filed with the Registrar. A company which has not appointed a secretary, can get the signature of a secretary who is in whole time practice. A company which has not issued a prospectus has only to file a statement in lieu of prospectus and to certify that every director has paid his application and allotment money for shares contracted to be taken by him for cash. [S. 149(2)] When this is done, the Registrar certifies that the company is entitled to commence business. The certificate is conclusive evidence that the company is so entitled.[38]

No public company can commence any business or exercise any borrowing power unless this certificate is obtained.[39] Any contract made before the date at which the company is entitled to commence business shall be provisional only and shall not be binding on the company until the certificate is obtained.[40]

The Amendment Act of 1965 introduced certain new conditions for the commencement of business by a company. It has added two new sub-sections to Section 149. As a result of the amendment of Section 13, the objects clause of a company incorporated after the amendment will have to be divided into two sub-clauses, namely:

(S. 149) and statutory meeting requirement (S. 165) would not apply to a private company converting itself into a public company. Certain internal formalities which would be needed are appointing a chairman, adopting a common seal, opening a bank account, and allotting shares either to raise capital or otherwise to the subscribers. These formalities would require a meeting of directors.

38. S. 149(3). A writ cannot be issued to cancel the certificate of commencement, *Muluk Mohamed v Capital Stock Exchange Kerala Ltd*, (1991) 72 Comp Cas 333 Ker.

39. S. 149(4). *Kodak Ltd v Srinivasan*, (1936) 6 Comp Cas 440 Mad. The company becomes entitled to all kinds of business operations necessary for the attainment of its objects. *Kishangarh Electric Supply Co Ltd v State of Rajasthan*, AIR 1960 Raj 149. Research, explorations, search for markets, mobilisation of resources and other preliminary things can be undertaken even without the certificate.

40. S. 149(6) imposes a penalty for any contravention of these provisions.

1. *Main objects*.—This will state the main objects of the company and the objects incidental or ancillary to the attainment of the main objects.

2. *Other objects*.—This will include a statement of other objects not mentioned in the above clause.[41]

If a company wishes to start a business included in the "other objects" it shall have to obtain the authority of a special resolution of its shareholders. Similarly, when an existing company wants to commence any new business which though included in its objects is not germane to the business which it has been carrying on at the commencement of the Amendment Act, it shall have to obtain the authority of a special resolution.[42] Where, however, a special resolution has not been passed, but the votes cast in favour of the resolution exceed the votes cast against it, the Central Government may, on an application by the Board of directors, allow the company to commence such business.[43]

In both the above cases there must be filed with the Registrar a declaration by the secretary or a director that the requirement as to the resolution has been complied with.[44]

---

41. S. 13(1)(d). The existing companies' memorandum can remain as they are S. 13(1)(e).
42. Explanation and sub-section (2-A). Where the business is not related with the existing business it is not germane. Thus a new and unrelated business would attract these requirements.
43. S. 149(2-B).
44. S. 149(2-A)(ii). A penalty is imposed for contravention of this provision.

3
Memorandum of Association

An important step in the formation of a company is to prepare a document called the memorandum of association. As observed by Palmer:[1] "It is a document of great importance in relation to the proposed company." Its importance lies in the fact that it contains the following fundamental clauses which have often been described as the conditions of the company's incorporation:[2]

1. Name Clause;
2. Registered Office Clause;
3. Objects Clause;
4. Liability Clause; and
5. Capital Clause.

NAME

The first clause of the memorandum is required to state the name of the proposed company. A company, being a legal person, must have a name to establish its identity. "The name of a corporation is the symbol of its personal existence."[3] Any suitable name may be selected subject, however, to the following restrictions.[4]

Legal requirements as to name

Resembling names not allowed [S. 20]

In the first place, no company can be registered with a name which, in the opinion of the Central Government, is undesirable.[5] The Trade Marks

---

1. Palmer's COMPANY LAW, 56 (20th Edn, 1959). The "memorandum" is defined in S. 2(28) as meaning the memorandum of association of a company as originally framed or as altered from time to time. . . . "
2. Section 13 states the requirements with respect to memorandum. Section 14 provides that the form of memorandum should be in such one of the forms in Tables B, C, D and E in Sch. 1, as may be applicable to the company. Section 15 requires that the document should be printed and divided into paragraphs numbered consecutively.
3. JOHNSON J in *Osborn v Bank of U.S.*, 9 Wheat (22 US) 738, 877 borrowed from Percival E. Jackson, THE WISDOM OF THE SUPREME COURT, 79 (1962).
4. For a study of the principles relating to the selection of a name and its importance *see* Emerson, *Corporations and Corporate Name*, (1968) 46 Can BR 488.
5. S. 20(1). Abbreviated names are not allowed at the first instance. An established company may change its name into an abbreviated form by showing that it has become well-known in its field under its abbreviation. [DCA Circular No 4/93 of Mar 31, 1993]. The name should not violate the provisions of the Emblems and Names (Prevention of Improper Use) Act, 1950. The Act prohibits the use of names given in its schedule which is as follows:

   1. The name, emblem or official seal of the United Nations Organization. 2. The name, emblem or official seal of the World Health Organization. 3. The Indian National Flag. 4. The name, emblem or official seal or emblem of the Government of India or of any State or any

Act, 1999 introduced a change into the provisions of the section. Without prejudice to the generality of the provision in sub-s. (1), sub-s. (2) provides:

(1) a name is undesirable if there is a previously registered company bearing that name;

(2) a name is undesirable if it is identical with or too nearly resembles a registered trade mark or the trade mark which is the subject of an application for registration of another person under the Trade Marks Act, 1999.

The Central Government may consult the Registrar of the Trade Marks Act before declaring a name to be undesirable.

The name of the company should not be identical with or should not too nearly resemble, the name of another registered company, for such a name may be declared undesirable by the Central Government.[6] Moreover, the other company can also apply for an injunction to restrain the newcomer from having an identical name.[7] The reason for the rule was explained by LAWRENCE J in *Society of Motor Manufacturers and Traders Ltd* v *Motor Manufacturers and Traders Mutual Insurance Co Ltd*[8]. He said: "Under the Companies Act, a company by registering its name gains a monopoly of the

---

insignia or coat of arms used by any such Government or by a Department of any such Government. 5. The emblems of the St. John's Ambulance Association (India) and the St. John's Ambulance Brigade (India) consisting of the device of a white eight pointed cross embellished in the four principal angles alternatively with a lion passant Quadrant and a Unicorn passant whether or not the device is surrounded or accompanied by concentric circles or other decoration or by lettering. 6. The name, emblem or official seal of the President, Governor, Sadar-i-Riyasat or Republic or Union of India. 7. Any name which may suggest or be calculated to suggest (*i*) the patronage of the Government of India or the Government of State or (*ii*) connection with any local authority or any corporation or body constituted by the Government under any law for the time being in force. 8. The name, emblem or official seal of the United Nations Educational, Scientific and Cultural Organization. 9. The name or pictorial representation of Rashtrapati, Rashtra Bhavan, Rashtrapati Bhavan, Raj Bhawan. (9-a). The name or pictorial representation of Mahatma Gandhi or the Prime Minister of India. 10. The medals, badges or decorations instituted by the Government from time to time or the miniatures or replicas of such medals, badges or decorations or the names of such medals, badges or decorations or the miniatures or replicas thereof. 11. The name, emblem or the official seal of the International Civil Aviation Organization. 12. The word (Interpol) which is an integral part of the International Criminal Police Organization. 13. The name, emblem or official seal of the World Meteorological Organization.

6. S. 20(2).

7. The promoters have to seek an advance approval of the name and once an advance approval is granted to a particular applicant, the Registrar will not make that name available to any other person. This process can be abused so as to pre-empt others from a particular name. In order to prevent such abuses the Registrars have been directed to see that the promoters, as per availability of name and application, are also the subscribers to the memorandum and articles of association of the proposed company at the time of its registration. In the case of any change in the name(s) amongst the subscribers, the changed subscribers are advised to make fresh application for availability of name. The Registrar may, as per existing procedure, allow the same name to any other applicant, if otherwise available, after three months from the date when the name was allowed to the original promoters.

8. [1925] 1 Ch 675: 133 LT 330.

use of that name since no other company can be registered under a name identical with it or so nearly resembling it as to be calculated to deceive".[9] The name of a company is a part of its business reputation and that would definitely be injured if a new company could adopt an allied name.

The resemblance between the two names must be such as to be "calculated to deceive". A name is said to be "calculated to deceive" when it suggests that the corporation adopting it is in some way connected or associated with the existing corporation. In the case referred to above:

> The plaintiff society was incorporated in 1902 under the name: The Society of Motor Manufacturers and Traders Ltd. In 1924 the defendant society was incorporated under the name: Motor Manufacturers and Traders Mutual Insurance Ltd. The plaintiff company brought an action to restrain the use of this name.

It was held that the defendant company's name could not be regarded as one "calculated to deceive". "Anyone who took the trouble to think about the matter would see that the defendant company was an insurance company and that the plaintiff society was a trade protection society and I [LAWRENCE J] do not think that the defendant company is liable to have its business stopped unless it changes its name simply because a thoughtless person might unwarrantedly jump to the conclusion that it is connected with the plaintiff society."[10]

According to a practice direction issued by the Companies' Registrar in England, a name is misleading when the company is with small resources, but the name suggests that it is trading on a great scale or over a wide field. The name must not suggest connection with an unlawful activity or be offensive in form. Two women forming a company for their personalised services were not allowed the name "Prostitutes Ltd."[11] The name 'Air Equipment' was held to be not available name because a comparison of the names 'Air Equipment' and 'Air Component' in the context of all the circumstances in which they were actually used or likely to be used, namely

---

9. [1925] 1 Ch 675, at 686-7.
10. *Id.* See also P. T. Mitchel, *A Practice Note on Company Incorporation*, (1969) 12 Can BJ 292, dealing with similarity of names; *Aerators Ltd* v *Tollitt*, [1902] 2 Ch 319; *Ewing* v *Buttercup Margarine Co*, [1917] 2 Ch 1. The Registrar is under a duty to inquire as to the genuineness of the proposed name. Where the Registrar registered a company under the name the "Methodist Church of India" without inquiry into its credentials, that was held to be wrong. Accordingly when a genuine representative of the Methodist Church sought registration under that name the Bombay HC ordered the Registrar to accept the name. *Methodist Church* v *UOI*, (1985) 57 Comp Cas 43 Bom. *Ewing* v *Buttercup Margarine Co*, (1917) 2 Ch 1, the plaintiff's trade name was *Buttercup Dairy Co*. He was allowed to restrain a new company adopting the name, *Buttercup Margarine Co Ltd*. It was likely to create the impression that new company was connected with his business. But in *Aerators Ltd* v *Tollitt*, (1902) 2 Ch 319, Aerators Ltd, could not prevent the registration under the name, *Automatic Aerators Patents Ltd*, the word "aerator" being a word of language and of common use.
11. *R* v *ROC*, (unreported) QBD, Dec 17, 1980.

the types of products the companies dealt in, the location of the business, the types of customers and the persons involved in the operation of the two companies, suggested an association between the two companies or that they were a part of the same group.[12] The name 'MRJ Contractors Ltd' was held to be as nearly similar to 'MPJ Construction Ltd' as it was possible to be. This effect could not be avoided simply by adopting a stationery of a different style. The get up adopted by a company could be an important element in public awareness or perception of a company but it could not have the effect of allowing a company to rely on its get up to avoid the thrust of the prohibition on similar names.[13]

When a company is directed to change its name, the court cannot directly tell the Registrar to effect the change in the name of the company. It can only direct the company to do so. The company would have to follow the prescribed statutory procedure of special resolution and approval of the Central Government and then filing the documents with the Registrar. The company cannot simply file the court order regarding the change.[14]

Use of the word "Limited" and Publication of Name

Secondly, whatever be the name of the company, if the liability of the members is limited, the last word of the name must be "Limited",[15] and in the case of a private company "Private Limited". This is to ensure that all persons dealing with the company shall have clear notice that the liability of the members is limited. And for the same reason it is further required that such name of the company must be painted on the outside of every place where the business of the company is carried on.[16] Such name, including the address of the registered office, must also be mentioned on all business letters and other official publications, on all negotiable instruments issued or endorsed by the company and on all other orders, receipts, etc. Any default in this respect might involve the officers of the company in most serious consequences. For example, if a bill of exchange is issued by a company on which its name is not properly mentioned or if the word "limited" has been omitted, and if the company fails to pay the bill, the officer who issued or authorised the issue of such a bill would be personally liable under it[17] and will also be punishable with a fine.[18]

---

12. *Recketts* v *Ad Valorem Factors Ltd*, (2004) 1 BCLC 1 (CA).
13. *Archer Structures Ltd* v *Griffiths*, (2004) 1 BCLC 201 (Ch D).
14. *Halifax plc* v *Halifax Repossessions Ltd*, (2004) 2 BCLC 455 (CA).
15. S. 13(1)(*a*). S. 24 authorises the Registrar to add the word "private" to the names of all the existing private limited companies.
16. S. 147, sub-section (2) imposes penalty for default upon "the company and every officer of the company who is in default".
17. *Basudeo Lal* v *Madan Lal*, AIR 1967 Ori 107; *Atken & Co* v *Wardle*, (1889) 58 LJ QB 377.
18. S. 147(4). S. 148 requires that documents issued by the company mentioning its authorised capital must similarly mention the amount actually subscribed and paid-up.

But the omission must be deliberate or of negligent origin and not merely accidental. Thus in *Dermatine Co Ltd* v *Ashworth*:[19]

A bill of exchange was drawn upon a limited company in its proper name and it was accepted by two directors of the company. The word "limited", however, did not appear in acceptance. The reason was that the rubber stamp by which the words of acceptance were impressed on the bill was longer than the paper of the bill, and therefore, the word "limited" overlapped the paper.

On the company's failure to pay the bill it was held that the directors would not be personally liable thereon. "It was an obvious error of most trifling kind and the mischief aimed at by the Act did not here exist."

But in *Nassau Steam Press* v *Tyler*:[20]

The registered name of a company was Bastille Syndicate Ltd. The defendants who were two directors and the secretary of the company accepted a bill of exchange on its behalf giving the name of the company as The Old Paris and Bastille Ltd.

It was held that the name of the company was not mentioned in accordance with the requirements of the Act and that the company not having paid the bill, the defendants were personally liable thereon. The correct name of the company should be inserted. Any omission or addition amounting to misdescription would make the person purporting to sign the bill personally liable.

On the same principle the directors were held personally liable on a cheque signed by them on the company's behalf stating the name as "L R Agencies Ltd", the real name being "L & R Agencies Ltd"[21]. The personal liability imposed by the section is not identical with the liability of the company. Thus where the name of the company was not fully stated on a cheque which was dishonoured and the payee accepted part payment from the company, the liability of the officer was not thereby discharged. The liability arose when the cheque was dishonoured and could not be affected thereafter in the way in which the liability under a contract of guarantee might be affected.[22] Taking note of the modern banking practice to issue to the customers cheque forms showing the name of the customer and his account number, a director who had inserted his bare signature on such

---

19. (1905) 21 TLR 510.
20. (1894) 70 LT 376. No action will be possible where the omission is due to the holder's own conduct; *Durham Fancy Goods* v *Michael Jackson (Fancy Goods) Ltd*, [1968] 2 QB 839: [1968] 2 All ER 987: [1968] 2 Lloyd's Rep 98. Personal liability where the name was not accurately stated. *Londholst Co A/S* v *Fowler*, 1988 BCLC 166 CA; *Blum* v *Oil Repartition SA*, 1988 BCLC 170 CA.
21. *Hendon* v *Adelman*, The Times, June 16, 1973: Noted 1973 New LJ 637.
22. *British Airways Board* v *Parish*, [1979] 2 Lloyd's Rep 361 CA; *See also Maxform SpA* v *Mariani & Goodville*, [1979] 2 Lloyd's Rep 385.

cheques was held to be personally not liable when they were dishonoured.[23] Commenting on this it has been said:[24]

The decision will be welcomed by the business community. As the cheque contained the printed name and account number of the company, the payee could be under no doubt that the cheque was a company cheque. The Draconian imposition of personal liability on a director who signed a company cheque without indicating his representative capacity, has thus lost much of its sting.

Misdescription of name does not, however, affect the validity of the contract. "A limited company has characteristics other than its name by reference to which it can be identified".[25]

Venture Capital Companies

The Department of Economic Affairs of the Finance Ministry has issued this guideline that a company should be allowed to use, as part of its name, expressions like Venture Capital/Venture Capital Company/Venture Capital Fund/Venture Capital Finance Co or such similar expressions only when the company or its promoters have obtained approval from the Department of Economic Affairs or any other nominated authority. This became necessary to properly identify companies which should be entitled to tax benefits on account of its venture capital services.

Licence to drop "Limited" [S. 25]

The Central Government may, by licence, allow a company to drop the word "Limited" from its name.[26] The licence is granted subject to the following conditions:

1. The company should be formed for the promotion of commerce, art, science, religion, charity or any other useful object.
2. The company should apply its income in promoting its objects and must prohibit the payment of dividends to its members.[27]

The licence may be granted "on such conditions and subject to such regulations" as the Central Government thinks fit.[28] The Government may

---

23. *Bondina Ltd* v *Rollaway Blinds Ltd*, The Times, Nov 20, 1985 CA.
24. 1986 JBL 9-10, editorial note. Acceptance in full form of a bill which was drawn on the company in an abbreviated name was held to be alright, *Stacey & Co Ltd* v *Wallis*, (1912) 28 TLR 209. An order for supply of goods placed innocently in the old pad of the company carrying its old name did not make the signor personally liable, *John Wilkes (Footwear) Ltd* v *Lee International (Footwear) Ltd*, (1985) BCLC 444.
25. *Goldsmith (Sicklesmere) Ltd* v *Baxter*, [1969] 3 WLR 522: [1969] 3 All ER 733: [1970] 1 Ch 85: (1970) 40 Comp Cas 809. *See also* Vincent Powell Smith, *Misdescribing a Company*, (1968) 118 New LJ 901.
26. S. 25. The power under the section has been delegated to Regional Directors.
27. S. 25(1) and (3). See *ADRBM Mandal* v *Joint Charity Commr*, (1973) 43 Comp Cas 361 Bom. Western UP Chamber of Commerce & Industry has been granted licence under the section.
28. S. 25(5).

also grant exemption from such of the provisions of Act as may be specified in the order.[29] This exemption is intended to encourage the incorporation of associations and societies of public utility with the members having to incur no liability. And to give further encouragement it is provided especially that "a firm may be a member of any association or company licensed under this section...."[30]

Such companies have been exempted from the requirement of having a minimum amount of share capital as required by the amendment of Section 3 by the Companies Amendment Act, 2000.

The licence is revocable at the discretion of the Central Government. The discretion is unrestricted, but it may be exercised only when the fundamental conditions of the licence are contravened. This should be apparent from sub-section 8(*a*) which prohibits the company from changing its objects "except with the previous approval of the Central Government".[31]

If such a company refuses to accept any person as a member, he cannot proceed under S. 111 for an order that he should be granted membership.[32]

Change of name [S. 21]

A company may change its name by passing a special resolution and with the approval of the Central Government signified in writing.[33] But if a company has been registered with a name which subsequently appears to be undesirable or resembling the name of another company, it may change its name by passing an ordinary resolution and with the approval of the Central Government.[34] In such a case the Central Government can also within twelve months of registration direct the company to rectify its

---

29. S. 25(6).
30. S. 25(4). A Departmental clarification points out that restrictions on inter-corporate loans are applicable to S. 25 companies also. [No 1/6/88, CL Vol dated April 28, 1989]. Many exemptions have been conferred upon such companies including the manner of enrolling members and appointing directors. *Sunil Dev* v *Delhi and District Cricket Assn*, (1994) 80 Comp Cas 174 Del, failure to lay accounts before the AGM did not invalidate the meeting. *K. Leela Kumar* v *Government of India*, (2002) 108 Comp Cas 610 Mad, another privilege is the right to suspend members temporarily in accordance with the company's articles. The articles were approved by the Regional Director. The suspension of the member of a club (registered as S. 25 company), which was intended to protect discipline and fair image of the club was held to be not a public act or involving violation of a statute or a fundamental right and, therefore, writ remedy was not available.
31. Some business companies were allowed to merge into a charitable company. If any violation of S. 25 was involved, the Government could take care of the matter. *Walvis Flour Mills Co P Ltd, Re*, (1993) 76 Comp Cas 376 Bom.
32. *Ramesh H. Bagga* v *Central Circuit Cine Assn*, (2005) 128 Comp Cas 370 CLB; *G.S. Mayawala* v *Motion Picture Assn*, (2006) 132 Comp Cas 388 Del, failed attempt to change articles about reelection of members to office positions.
33. S. 21. The power under the section has been delegated to Regional Directors.
34. S. 22(1)(*a*).

name.[35] If a direction is issued the company must change its name within three months from the date of the direction unless the time is extended. [S. 23] This is known as rectification of name.[36] The new name would also require advance approval of the Central Government. The British Diabetic Society was compelled to change its corporate name to something that would not impinge upon the goodwill of the British Diabetic Association. There was a sufficient similarity between the two names to necessitate a change, even though there was no intention to mislead the public.[37] An injunction was not allowed to prevent the use of an ancestral name (Kirloskar). There is a right to use in a *bona fide* manner one's own name or the name of a place or ancestral name.[38]

The power of the Central Government is being exercised by the Regional Directors to whom it has been delegated. The Gujarat High Court described the power to be of quasi-judicial nature because orders passed in exercise of this power are likely to have civil consequences. Regional Directors must record reasons for their orders.[39]

When a company changes its name, it becomes the duty of the Registrar to enter the new name in the register and to issue a new certificate of

---

35. S. 22(1)(*b*). *See also* sub-section (2) which imposes penalty for default. The court does not have the power to extend the period of 12 months. After the expiry of 12 months, the only remedy which survives is a court action to restrain the use of the name. *Concord International (Mauritius) Ltd v Concord Tourist Guide Agency Ltd*, [1985] LRC (Comm) 751 Mauritius CA; *Sidhvi Constructions India (P) Ltd v ROC*, (1997) 90 Comp Cas 299; *Hope Textiles (P) Ltd v UOI*, 1995 Supp (3) SCC 199: (1994) 205 ITR 508. In counting the period of 12 months, the period covered by a court stay order, if any, would have to be discounted. *Sen & Pandit Electricals Ltd v UOI*, AIR 1999 Cal 289 Cal.

36. Where the Calcutta based "Kilburn" company permitted a Madras based company to use the word Kilburn as a part of its name, the latter was ordered to drop the word from the names of two other companies which it floated, *Kilburn Electricals Ltd v Regional Director*, CLB, (2000) 99 Comp Cas 243 Mad. In *Kalpana Polytech India Ltd v UOI*, (1998) 16 SCR 207 Cal, the company was ordered to drop the word 'Kalpana' from its name. See *Glaxo plc v Glaxo Wellcome Ltd*, (1996) FSR 388 and *Direct Line Group Ltd v Direct Line Estate Agency Ltd*, (1997) FSR 374. Where the court noted and considered it necessary to counter people who get certain some such names registered in advance which real businessmen would like to use and then they sell the readymade registered company in such names to needy people for large sums. *Sen & Pandit Electronics (P) Ltd v UOI*, (2003) 115 Comp Cas 299 Cal, in calculating the time, the period of stay granted by the court is to be excluded. No action was taken by the authority within the prescribed time. The court did not issue any direction to the authority.

37. *British Diabetic Assn v Diabetic Society*, [1995] 4 All ER 812. *Kothari Products Ltd v ROC*, (2001) 103 Comp Cas 841 All, company registered under the name of "*Parage International (KNP) (P) Ltd*". The owner of the trade mark "Parag" obtained an order from the court directing the Registrar to cancel the registration and permitting the company to apply for change of name.

38. *Kirloskar Proprietary Ltd v Kriloskar Dimensions (P) Ltd*, (1999) 96 Comp Cas 726.

39. *Pino Bisazza Glass (P) Ltd v Bisazza India Ltd*, (2003) 114 Comp Cas 165 Guj. The unreasoned order passed in this case was set aside.

incorporation with necessary alterations. Change of name becomes effective only on the issue of such a certificate.[40]

Change of name does not affect the rights and obligations of the company. For Section 23(3) provides:

> The change of name shall not affect any rights or obligations of the company, or render defective any legal proceedings by or against it; and any legal proceedings which might have been continued or commenced by or against the company by its former name may be continued by or against the company by its new name.[41]

The degree of protection afforded by this provision was considered by the Calcutta High Court in *Malhati Tea Syndicate Ltd* v *Revenue Officer*.[42]

> A company had changed its name from "Malhati Tea Syndicate Ltd" to "Malhati Tea and Industries Ltd." It filed a writ petition in its former name.

Declaring the petition to be incompetent, the court said:[43]

> Nothing in this sub-section [S. 23(3)] authorised the company to commence a legal proceeding in its former name at a time when it had acquired its new name which has been put on the register of joint stock companies.

REGISTERED OFFICE

The second clause of the memorandum must specify the State in which the registered office of the company is to be situate.

Within thirty days of incorporation or commencement of business, whichever is earlier, the exact place where the registered office is to be located must be decided and notice of the situation given to the Registrar

---

40. S. 23(1). On the change of an English company's name, it presented the certificate of its Registrar to an Indian company for changing its name in the register of members and on the company's refusal to do so, the CLB ordered rectification of the register of members, *Sulphure Dyes Ltd* v *Hickson & Dadajee Ltd*, (1995) 83 Comp Cas 533 Bom.
41. *Memtec Ltd* v *Lunarmech*, (2001) 103 Comp Cas 1078 Del, change in ownership of company resulting in change of name also was held to be not a ground for dismissing a suit pending against the company. Corporate identity does not change with transfer of shareholding. *Dinesh Gandhi* v *Bayer Diagnostics India Ltd*, (2002) 111 Comp Cas 547 CLB, obligations of the company in pending proceedings continue as before. The change of name necessitates issuing of new share certificates in place of those which were issued bearing the former name. In this case, the company had cancelled the old certificates with effect from certain date under information to the shareholders and the stock exchange.
42. (1973) 43 Comp Cas 337: AIR 1973 Cal 78 DB. A company, which changes its name, is allowed to change the name on pending legal proceedings, S. 115 and Order 6 Rule 17, CPC, *Simbhaoli Sugar Mills Ltd* v *Hindustan Brown Boveri Ltd*, (1994) 23 All LR 259.
43. The court distinguished *D. Srinivasaiah* v *Vellore Varalakshmi Bank Ltd*, ILR 1954 Mad 533: AIR 1954 Mad 802: (1954) 24 Comp Cas 55, where proceedings were commenced in the old name, the court said that it was a misdescription and the suit was maintainable. *Pioneer Protective Glass Fibre* v *Fibre Glass Pilkington*, [1985] 3 Comp LJ 309: 1985 Tax LR 2121 Cal DB.

who is to record the same. [S. 146] All communications to the company must be addressed to its registered office.[44]

Change of registered office situation

A company can shift its registered office from one place to another within the same city, town or village. [S. 146(2)] But if it is proposed to carry the registered office from one city to another within the same State, a special resolution to that effect must be passed.[45] A notice of any such change must be given to the Registrar within thirty days of the change.[46] If the shifting of the registered office has the effect of taking the office from the jurisdiction of one Registrar of Companies to that of another within the same State, permission of the Regional Director must be taken. Application for permission has to be made on a prescribed form. The Regional Directors are required to confirm the company's application and inform it accordingly within a period of 4 weeks.[47] After getting the confirmation of the Regional Director, the company must file a copy of the same with the Registrar of Companies within two months from the date of confirmation together with a copy of the altered memorandum. The Registrars are required to register the same and inform companies within one month from the date of filing. The Registrar's certificate is a conclusive evidence of the fact of alteration and of compliance with requirements [S. 17-A].

Shifting of the registered office from one State to another is a much more complicated affair, as it involves alteration of the memorandum itself. The alteration of the memorandum for this purpose is subject to the provisions of Section 17 which requires, in the first place, a special resolution of the company and, in the second, confirmation by the Company Law Board (CLB) can confirm the alteration only if the shifting of the registered office from one State to another is necessary for any of the

---

44. S. 51, dealing with service of documents on company. A notice of recovery on a company which was received by the company's managing director was held to be a good service. *Maharashtra State Financial Corpn* v *Masvi & Co (P) Ltd*, (1993) 76 Comp Cas 168 Bom. There is uncertainty as to whether S. 51 provides an exclusive mode of service on a company, but there are rulings to the effect that S. 51 prevails over the modes of service recognised by the Civil Procedure Code. *Harendra Nath Ghosal* v *Superfoam (P) Ltd*, (1992) 74 Comp Cas 740 Cal. A service at any other place is not good. *Vyasya Bank Ltd* v *Randhir Steel and Alloys (P) Ltd*, (1993) 76 Comp Cas 244 Bom, distinguishing *Fortune Copper Mining Co, Re*, (1870) LR 10 Eq 390, where the building of the company's registered office was demolished and service at some other place was considered a good service. *T. O. Supplies (London) Ltd* v *Jerry Creighton Ltd*, (1952) 1 KB 42, serving by personally delivering or by post at registered office, registered post not necessary.
45. S. 17-A. It is not necessary that the meeting for such resolution should be held at the registered office. It may be held anywhere allowed by S. 166(2), *Metal Box India Ltd, Re*, [2000] 2 Comp LJ 390 CLB.
46. S. 146(4). There is a penalty for default. The company and every officer of the company who is in default is punishable with fine extending up to Rs 500 for every day of default.
47. Section 17-A, introduced by the Amendment of 2000, has prescribed this procedure.

purposes detailed in Section 17(1). When this condition is fulfilled, the second stage is reached, namely, to consider the objections of a "person or class of persons whose interest will, in the opinion of the CLB, be affected by the alteration".[48] In two cases before the Orissa High Court,[49] shifting of the registered offices of certain companies to places outside Orissa was opposed by the State on several grounds, including the loss of revenue and employment opportunities. The Court declined confirmation in both cases. In one of them BARMAN J based his decision on the ground that in a Federal Constitution every State has got the right to protect its revenue and, therefore, the interests of the State must be taken into account and are of considerable importance in confirming inter-State change of registered office.[50] The Calcutta High Court described this as a "parochial" consideration. In a case before it[51]—

> A company desired to shift its registered office from the State of West Bengal to Bombay. The company's petition was resisted by the State on the ground of loss of revenue.

The Court refused to sustain the contention of the State and allowed the transfer.[52]

> "There is no statutory right of the State, as a State, to intervene in an application made under Section 17 for alteration of the place of the registered office of a company. To hold that the possibility of the loss of revenue is not only relevant, but of persuasive force in regard to the change is to rob the company of the statutory power conferred on it by Section 17. The question of loss of revenue to one State would have to be considered in the total conspectus of revenue for the Republic of India and no parochial considerations should be allowed to turn the scale in regard to change of registered office from one State to another within India."

This decision was indorsed by a Division Bench of the Calcutta High Court in *Rank Film Distributors of India Ltd* v *Registrar of Companies,*

---

48. S. 17(3). Where an objection was raised by a creditor not of the company but that of a company in the same group, the CLB directed that the company should take care of the interests of such a creditor also. *Deutsche Babcock Power Systems Ltd, Re*, (1999) 97 Comp Cas 341 CLB.

49. *Orient Paper Mills Ltd* v *State*, AIR 1957 Ori 232: (1958) 28 Comp Cas 523 and *Orissa Chemicals and Distilleries, Re*, AIR 1961 Ori 162: (1962) 32 Comp Cas 497.

50. For a criticism of this decision *see* Sangal and Ponnuswami, *Inter-State Change of Registered Office of a Company*, [1964] 1 Comp LJ 104 (Journal Section).

51. *Mackinnon Mackenzie & Co, Re*, [1967] 1 Comp LJ 200: (1967) 37 Comp Cas 516. Other rulings to the same effect, *Metal Box India Ltd, Re*, [2000] 2 Comp LJ 390 CLB; *SPML India Ltd, Guwahati, Re*, [2000] 4 Comp LJ 177 CLB; *Metal Box India Ltd, Re*, [2000] 2 Comp LJ 390 CLB, shifting in accordance with BIFR approved scheme, workers' objections were already heard and considered.

52. *Id.* Followed in *Minerva Mills Ltd* v *Govt of Maharashtra*, (1975) 45 Comp Cas 1 Bom.

West Bengal.[53] But the problem does not seem to have ended with it. Capital has a tendency to fly away from areas of labour trouble. Another evidence of this is *Bharat Commerce & Industries Ltd, Re,*[54] also before the same court.

A company resolved and sought confirmation for removing its office from West Bengal to New Delhi. Explaining its reasons the company said that due to disturbances at the registered office caused by two or three employees it had become impossible to manage the branches of the company located at different places. The State of West Bengal having learned its lessons in the earlier cases did not oppose but the employees opposed the confirmation. They felt that the management had taken this course to frustrate the outcome of an industrial dispute.

They fairly well succeeded. For DATTA J held that the decision of the management was *mala fide.* But on appeal to a Division Bench his decision was overruled.[55] The court did not like to decide whether it was open to the court to examine the *bona fides* of the shareholders' resolution for removing their office from one State to another.

The Company Law Board did not hesitate in granting permission to a company to move out of the host State whose actions and policies frustrated the hopes and aspirations of the company and to shift its registered office to any other State which was willing to provide the necessary facilities.[56] Where a company wanted to shift its registered office from New Delhi to Gurgaon, the Company Law Board, confirmed the company's resolution subject to this condition, that Delhi based shareholders, who were willing to attend annual general meetings, must be provided free transport facility.[57] The Company Law Board did not hesitate to permit the shifting of the registered office to a place where majority of the shareholders of the company resided.[58] A company which was taken over by another company was allowed to carry its registered office to the place of the registered office of the other country.[59]

Where some employees objected to the proposed shifting on the ground that they would be prejudiced in respect of their cases pending before labour courts, the CLB permitted the shifting but ordered that the workers'

---

53. AIR 1969 Cal 32: (1968) 38 Comp Cas 487: 72 CWN 384: [1968] 1 Comp LJ 129.
54. (1973) 43 Comp Cas 162 Cal.
55. *Bharat Commerce & Industries Ltd* v *ROC (WB),* (1973) 43 Comp Cas 275 DB Cal.
56. *Paradise Plastic Enterprises Ltd, Re,* [1989] 3 Comp LJ 248, 250 CLB. *See* also *Kalitara Wood Industries Ltd, Re,* [1989] 3 Comp LJ 24, 27 CLB, where the CLB did not approve the policy of the State Financial Corpn and the State Industrial Development Corpn insisting upon shifting of office to their State in order to avail loan facilities.
57. *A.K.G. Acoustics (India) Ltd, Re,* (1996) 3 Comp LJ 355 CLB.
58. *Pal-Peugeot Ltd, Re,* (1997) 89 Comp Cas 808: [1997] 3 Comp LJ 334 CLB.
59. *K.G. Khosla Compressors Ltd, Re,* [1997] 4 Comp LJ 461 CLB.

interests should be safeguarded, and that none of them should be prejudiced either by way of transfer or retrenchment or otherwise and that pending cases before local courts should not be prejudiced.[60] A person who has no stake in the company either as a shareholder or as a creditor was not allowed to raise any objections. He was personal creditor of the managing director. He had no *locus standi*, his criminal proceedings against the managing director notwithstanding.[61]

Where a company had all its manufacturing units in Uttar Pradesh and none in West Bengal, the CLB confirmed its special resolution to shift its registered office from West Bengal to Uttar Pradesh.[62] Where a company had one manufacturing unit in Bihar and the other in Maharashtra and because it had undertaken massive expansion programme in Maharashtra, its desire to carry the registered office to Pune was allowed. Its Bihar unit was to continue as it was.[63] A company was allowed to take away its registered office from Bihar to West Bengal in spite of the fact that the Bihar Government had granted land on lease for the company's factory on the condition that the registered office would not be shifted. The CLB said that the fact of interest-free loans, sales-tax, holidays, concessional electricity and other subsidies had no bearing on the company's right to shift.[64]

Duty and power of Company Law Board [S.17(2)-(7)]

Before confirming the alteration, the CLB must satisfy itself that sufficient notice has been given to every debentureholder or person or class of persons whose interests are likely to be affected.[65] In reference to creditors, the CLB has to feel satisfied that those who have raised objections, their interests have been safeguarded either by paying them out or securing their payment. The CLB may, if necessary, dispense with the requirement of the consent of any such person.

---

60. *J.L. Morrison (India) Ltd, Re,* (1999) 95 Comp Cas 907 CLB.
61. *Seaways Maritime (P) Ltd, Re,* (2000) 39 CLA 49 CLB; *Seaways Maritime P Ltd, Re,* (2002) 111 Comp Cas 78 CLB, allegations of *mala fide* against the managing director were not considered to be anything worthwhile when there were no allegations against the company, shifting was sanctioned.
62. *Upper Ganges Sugar & Industries Ltd, Re,* (2000) 27 SCL 369 CLB.
63. *Neelachal Auto Ltd, Re,* (2000) 38 CLA 217 CLB.
64. *Usha Beltron Ltd, Re,* (2000) 27 SCL 124 CLB; *Reckitt Benckiser (India) Ltd, Re,* (2004) 55 SCL 437 CLB, shifting from West Bengal to National Capital Region allowed, care was taken of the interest of objecting creditors and employees. Shifting was necessary for better business avenues.
65. Publication of notice of the petition in two newspapers inviting objections from any person whose interest is likely to be affected by the proposed alteration of memorandum regarding change of registered office was held to be sufficient notice to "every other person or class of person" within the meaning of Section 17(3)(*a*). *Metal Box India Ltd, In re,* (2001) 105 Comp Cas 939 CLB; *Perfect Refractories Ltd, Re,* (2005) 125 Comp Cas 234 CLB, shareholders cannot object after unanimous resolution.

The CLB has also to see that a notice has been served on the Registrar of the Company to enable him to state his objections, if any. The CLB may make a conditional order of confirmation. Where there are dissenting members, the CLB may formulate a scheme of arrangement under which they will be paid out but not in a manner as to affect the structure of the company's share capital.

OBJECTS AND POWERS

In the third clause, the memorandum must state the objects for which the proposed company is to be established. The Companies (Amendment) Act, 1965, requires that in the case of companies in existence before this amendment, the objects clause has simply to state the objects of the company.[66] But in the case of a company to be registered after the amendment, the objects clause must be divided into three sub-clauses, namely:

(*i*) *Main objects.*—This sub-clause has to state the main objects to be pursued by the company on its incorporation and objects incidental or ancillary to the attainment of the main objects.[67]

(*ii*) *Other objects.*—This sub-clause must state other objects which are not included in the above clause. [S. 13(1)(*d*)]

(*iii*) *States to which objects extend.*—In the case of non-trading companies, whose objects are not confined to one State, this sub-clause has to mention the States to whose territories the objects extend.[68]

Choice of objects lies with the subscribers to the memorandum and their freedom in this respect is almost unrestricted. The only obvious restrictions are that the objects should not go against the law of the land and the provisions of the Companies Act. For example, law prohibits gambling. Obviously, no company can be incorporated for that purpose. Thus, where a company was incorporated for conducting a lottery, it was ordered to be wound up, that object being illegal.[69] Again, for example, the Act provides

---

66. S. 13(1)(*c*). The memorandum and articles of asset management companies (AMCs) require SEBI approval. Such companies are compulsory for organising a mutual fund. [Circular No 4/92 of Sept 4, 1992.] *See* SEBI Guidelines for Asset Management Companies.
67. *Ferrom Electronics (P) Ltd* v *Vijaya Leasing Ltd*, (2002) 109 Comp Cas 467 Kant, the company was not carrying on its main objects, carrying on of ancillary objects was considered to be alright.
68. " 'Trading Corporation' means a trading corporation within the meaning of Entries 43 and 44 in List I in the 7th Sch of the Constitution." [S. 2(42)]. A Public Financial Institution cannot insist that the company seeking loan from it should confine itself to one State. *Kalitara Wood Industries Ltd, Re*, [1989] 3 Comp LJ 24, 27 CLB. The business of *kuries* has been held to be of trading nature, *John* v *Oriental Curries Ltd*, (1994) 2 Ker LT 353.
69. *Universal Mutual Aid & Poor Houses Assn* v *A.D. Thoppa Naidu*, AIR 1933 Mad 16: 139 IC 644; *Bowman* v *Secular Society Ltd*, 1917 AC 406: [1916-17] All ER Rep 1. Section 12 clearly says that the subscribers must assemble for a lawful purpose.

that a company limited by shares cannot, subject to a few exceptions, purchase its own shares. [S. 77] Accordingly, any clause in the memorandum giving the company a power to purchase its own shares will be inoperative.[70]

The English Act has made things more simple by providing that a memorandum may only state that the objects are commercial.

Why objects?

The ownership of the corporate capital is vested in the company itself. But in reality that capital has been contributed by the shareholders and is held by the company as though in trust for them. Such a fund must obviously be dedicated to some defined objects so that the contributors may know the purposes to which it can be lawfully applied. The statement of objects, therefore, gives a very important protection to the shareholders by ensuring that the funds raised for one undertaking are not going to be risked in another.[71]

The objects clause, in the second place, affords a certain degree of protection to the creditors also. The creditors of a company trust the corporation and not the shareholders and they have to seek their repayment only out of the company's assets. The fact that the corporate capital cannot be spent on any project not directly within the terms of the company's objects gives the creditors a feeling of security. Public financial institutions providing loans to companies have to go object-wise because they have their own list of priorities. The objects clause is their only guidance in this respect.

Thirdly, by confining the corporate activities within a defined field, the statement of objects serves the public interest also. It prevents diversification of a company's activities in directions not closely connected with the business for which the company may have been initially established.[72] It also prevents concentration of economic power. Any change of objects would require approval of the Company Law Board thus giving the Board an opportunity to examine whether the proposed plan of diversification would not be against public interest.

Doctrine of ultra vires

Those then are the reasons which explain the necessity of an objects clause. The same reasons require that the company should devote itself only to the objects set out in the memorandum and to no others. It is the function of the memorandum "to delimit and identify the objects in such plain and unambiguous manner as that the reader can identify the field of industry

---

70. *Trevor v Whitworth*, (1887) 12 App Cas 409: [1886-90] All ER Rep 46.
71. *Wamanlal v Scindia Steam Navigation Co*, AIR 1944 Bom 131, 135: (1944) 14 Comp Cas 69.
72. D. L. Mazumdar, TOWARDS A PHILOSOPHY OF THE MODERN CORPORATION, 119 (1967).

within which the corporate activities are to be confined".[73] And it is the function of the courts to see that the company does not move in a direction away from that field.[74] That is where the doctrine of *ultra vires* comes into play in relation to joint stock companies. "*Ultra*" means beyond, "*vires*" means powers. An action outside the memorandum is *ultra vires* the company. Its application to such companies was first demonstrated by the House of Lords in *Ashbury Railway Carriage and Iron Co Ltd* v *Riche*.[75]

The memorandum of association of a company thus defined its objects: "The objects for which the company is established are to make and sell, or lend on hire, railway carriages and wagons and all kinds of railway plants, etc., ...; to carry on the business of mechanical engineers, and general contractors ...." The company entered into a contract with Riche, a firm of railway contractors, to finance the construction of a railway line in Belgium. The company, however, repudiated the contract as one *ultra vires*. And Riche, brought an action for damages for breach of contract. His contentions were that the contract in question came well within the meaning of the words "general contractors" and, was, therefore, within the powers of the company, and, secondly, that the contract was ratified by a majority of the shareholders.

But the House of Lords held that the contract was *ultra vires* and, therefore, null and void. In substance the judgment of Lord CAIRNS LC was this: "The subscribers are to state the objects for which the proposed company is to be established and then the company comes into existence for those objects and those only. Such a statement of objects has a two-fold operation. It states affirmatively the ambit and extent of powers of the company and it states negatively that nothing shall be done beyond that ambit, and that no attempt shall be made to use the corporate life for any other purpose than that which is so specified. The terms "general contractors" must be taken to indicate the making generally of such contracts as are connected with the business of mechanical engineers. If the term "general contractors" is not so interpreted, it would authorise the making of contracts of any and every description, such as, for instance, of fire and marine insurance and the memorandum in place of specifying the particular kind of business, would virtually point to the carrying on of the business of any kind whatsoever and would, therefore, be altogether unmeaning. Hence the contract was entirely beyond the objects in the memorandum of association. If so, it was thereby placed beyond the powers of the company to make the contract. If the company could not make it, much less could it be ratified. If every shareholder of the

---

73. Lord WRENBURY in *Cotman* v *Brougham*, 1918 AC 514 at p 522: [1918-19] All ER Rep 265.
74. PHEAR J in *Port Canning & Land Investment Co, Re*, (1871) 7 Beng LR 583, 598-611, where the learned Judge explains the great mischief, public and private, which might ensue if companies were not held strictly to the terms of their incorporation.
75. (1875) 44 LJ Exch 185: (1875) LR 7 HL 653: [1874-80] All ER Rep Ext 2219.

company had been in the room and had said: "That is a contract which we desire to make, which we authorise the directors to make" the case would not have stood in any different position from that in which it stands now. The shareholders would thereby, by unanimous consent, have been attempting to do the very thing which, by Act of Parliament, they were prohibited from doing."

In the next leading case of *Attorney-General* v *Great Eastern Railway Co*,[76] the House of Lords observed that the doctrine of *ultra vires,* as it was explained in the *Ashbury* case, should be maintained. But it ought to be reasonably and not unreasonably understood and applied and that whatever may be fairly regarded as incidental to the objects authorised ought not to be held as *ultra vires,* unless it is expressly prohibited.

Thus a company may do an act which is: (*a*) necessary for, or (*b*) incidental to, the attainment of its objects, or (*c*) which is otherwise authorised by the Act.

The Companies Act now requires incidental objects also to be stated in the memorandum. [S. 13(1)(*c*)] But even if they are not so stated, they would be allowed by the principle of reasonable construction. Thus a railway company, having authority to keep steam vessels for the purpose of a ferry, may use them for excursion trips to the sea when they are otherwise unemployed.[77] Again a railway company whose railroad is carried over arches may convert the arches into shops,[78] otherwise "it might as reasonably be contended that a railway company are not entitled to sell the hay which grows on their banks so as to make something out of it". A chemical manufacturer was allowed to distribute £1,00,000 to universities and scientific institutions for the furtherance of scientific education and research as it was conducive to the continued progress of the company as chemical manufacturers.[79]

"But no company can devote any part of its funds to an object which is neither essential nor incidental to the fulfilment of its objects, how beneficial so ever that object might seem likely to prove."[80] Accordingly in *London County Council* v *Attorney-General*[81]:

> The Council having statutory power to work tramways was restrained from running omnibuses in connection with the tramways. The court found that the omnibus business was in no way incidental to

---

76. (1880) 5 AC 473: [1874-80] All ER Rep Ext 1459. The Supreme Court of India in *A. Lakshmanaswami Mudaliar* v *LIC*, AIR 1963 SC 1185: (1963) 33 Comp Cas 420, affirmed that an *ultra vires* contract remains *ultra vires* even if all the shareholders agree to it.
77. *Forest* v *Manchester etc., Rly Co*, (1861) 54 ER 803.
78. *Foster* v *London Chatham & Dover Rly Co*, [1895] 1 QB 711.
79. *Evans* v *Brunner, Mond & Co*, [1921] 1 Ch 359: 90 LJ Ch 294.
80. *Eastern Counties Rly Co* v *Hawkes*, (1855) 10 ER 928 at p 934: (1855) 5 HL Cas 331.
81. 1902 AC 165.

the business of working tramways, and, therefore, could not be undertaken although it might have materially contributed to the success of the Council's tramways.

In India the origin of the doctrine dates back to 1866 when the Bombay High Court applied it to a joint stock company and held on the facts of the case before it that "the purchase by the directors of a company, on behalf of the company, of shares in other joint stock companies, unless expressly authorised in the memorandum is *ultra vires*".[82] Since then the rule has been applied and acted upon in a number of cases.[83]

The doctrine has been affirmed by the Supreme Court in its decision in *A. Lakshmanaswami Mudaliar v LIC*.[84]

The directors of a company were authorised "to make payments towards any charitable or any benevolent object, or for any general public, general or useful object". In accordance with a shareholders' resolution the directors paid two lakh rupees to a trust formed for the purpose of promoting technical and business knowledge.

The payment was held to be *ultra vires*. The court said that the directors could not spend the company's money on any charitable or general object which they might choose. They could spend for the promotion of only such charitable objects as would be useful for the attainment of the company's own objects. The company's business having been taken over by the Life Insurance Corporation, it had no business left to promote.

Objects, Powers and Charitable Contributions

The above Supreme Court decision is an authority for two propositions. Firstly, that a company's funds cannot be diverted to every kind of charity even if there is an unrestricted power to that effect in the company's memorandum.[85] Secondly, that objects must be distinguished from powers. The power, for example, to borrow or to make a charity, is not an object. Objects have to be stated in the memorandum, but not powers. Even if powers are stated, they can be used only to effectuate the objects of the company.[86] They do not become independent objects by themselves. Thus in *Introductions Ltd, Re*:[87]

---

82. *Jehangir R. Modi* v *Shamji Ladha*, (1866-67) 4 Bom HCR 185.
83. See *Port Canning & Land Investment Co, Re*, (1871) 7 Beng LR 583; *Ahmed Sait* v *Bank of Mysore*, (1930) 59 MLJ 28; *Imperial Bank of India* v *Bengal National Bank*, AIR 1930 Cal 536: (1931) 1 Comp Cas 63: ILR 57 Cal 328; *Madras Native Permanent Fund, Ltd, Re*, (1931) 60 MLJ 270; *Wamanlal* v *Scindia Steam Navigation Co*, AIR 1944 Bom 131: (1944) 14 Comp Cas 69; *Iron Traders* v *Hiralal Mittal*, AIR 1962 Punj 277: (1962) 32 Comp Cas 1022.
84. AIR 1963 SC 1185: (1963) 33 Comp Cas 420.
85. But according to the report of the Jenkins Committee the power to make donations of any kind should not be allowed to be challenged, though the directors might be liable to account if the amount of such donations is unreasonable. (Comnd 1947), para 52.
86. L. H. Leigh, *Objects, Powers & Ultra Vires*, (1970) 33 Mod LR 81.
87. [1968] 2 Comp LJ 28: [1969] 2 WLR 791: [1969] 1 All ER 887 CA.

A company had an independent clause in its memorandum empowering it to borrow money on debentures. Yet its act of loan for a purpose known to the lender to be outside the scope of its objects was held to be *ultra vires*.

The power to borrow is not an object. It cannot stand on its own, but must be exercised in order to promote the company's objects. But it is for the directors to decide in good faith what is necessary to promote the objects of the company. Thus where under an express power to that effect the directors of a company charged its assets to secure a benefit to another company in the same group, the charge was held to be valid.[88] The contention that it was not made in the interest of the company was not accepted. While the separate interest of a company cannot be sacrificed or ignored, yet the directors are not required to consider the interest of an entity in a group in isolation.

Similarly, a power to make charitable contributions cannot be acted upon to make grants of every kind. According to EVE J in *Lee, Behrens & Co Ltd, Re*,[89] the validity of such grants must be tested by the answer to three pertinent questions:

1. Is the transaction reasonably incidental to the carrying on of the company's business?
2. Is it a *bona fide* transaction?
3. Is it done for the benefit and to promote the prosperity of the company?

Applying these tests to the facts the learned Judge held that the grant of an annual pension of £500 to the widow of a managing director five years after his death was *ultra vires*. "The predominant consideration operating in the minds of the directors was a desire to provide for the applicant (widow), and the question what, if any, benefit would accrue to the company never presented itself to their minds."[90]

---

88. *Charterbridge Corpn v Lloyds Bank Ltd*, [1969] 2 All ER 1185. Considered in L. H. Leigh, *Objects, Powers & Ultra Vires*, [1970] 33 Mod LR 81 and D. Li Morgan, *Corporate Collateral Security*, 1970 JBL 256. Ralph Instone, *Powers and Objects*, (1978) JBL 948. See also *Ridge Securities Ltd v JRC*, [1964] 1 All ER 275: [1964] 1 WLR 479 where the grant of a debenture to the company's parent company at a high rate of interest for the purpose of avoidance of taxes, was held to be a dressed up gift of capital to the parent company and, therefore, *ultra vires*. Similarly in *Halt Garage 1964 Ltd, Re*, [1982] 3 All ER 1016, remuneration of £30 to a non-working shareholder-director was held to be excessive amounting to a dressed-up return of capital. A remuneration of £10 a week has been regarded as reasonable in such cases.

89. [1932] 2 Ch 46: [1932] All ER Rep 889.

90. Where payment of a sum of money was made by the company's managing director by way of bribe to obtain work for the company, the company was allowed to recover the amount from the managing director, it being neither within his authority, nor authorised by the company's shareholders. *E. Hannibal & Co Ltd v Frost*, Times, Oct, 8, 1987.

Similarly, where the directors of a company proposed to distribute the money received on the sale of its assets as compensation to the employees who had lost their jobs, the court restrained the scheme.[91] Their motives may be laudable from the point of view of industrial relations, but the law does not recognise them as a sufficient justification to enable the majority to spend the money of the company. In *Hutton* v *West Cork Rly Co*,[92] BOWMEN LJ explained the judicial attitude:

Charity has no business to sit at boards of directors qua charity. There is, however, a kind of charitable dealing which is for the interest of those who practise it, and to that extent and in that garb, charity may sit at the board, but for no other purpose.

Thus the interests of the company cannot be elbowed out. Charity is allowed only to the extent to which it is necessary in the reasonable management of the affairs of the company. There must be proximate connection between the gift and the company's business interests.[93] Thus "gifts to foster research relevant to the company's activities"[94], *ex gratia* payments to workers to induce them to work hard[95] and "payment to widows of ex-employees on the footing that such payment encouraged persons to enter the employment of the company"[96] have been upheld.[97] Some limit on corporate charity is obviously necessary. But the question whether the limit has been exceeded has to be considered by keeping in mind the fact that "the image of the business corporation is evolving from the nineteenth century one of a heartless exploiter of a wage slave labour, single mindedly bent upon the maximisation of profits to that of the corporate good citizenship of today. Corporations are coming to focus their attention upon their duty to serve mankind. The goal of the enlightened corporation is to provide full employment and high wages for labour, to

---

91. *Hutton* v *West Cork Rly Co*, (1883) 23 Ch D 654; *Parke* v *Daily News Ltd*, (1962) 2 All ER 929.

92. *Id.* at p 673. *Gibson Executor* v *Gibson*, (1980) Scottish LT, where *ex gratia* payment in lieu of pension was not allowed on the eve of liquidation.

93. *A. Lakshmanaswami, Mudaliar* v *LIC*, AIR 1963 SC 1185: (1963) 33 Comp Cas 420. Donation of money by a charitable company to a trust having similar objects was not *ultra vires* and not questionable, *Mohanram Sastri* v *Swadharma*, (1995) 83 Comp Cas 272 Mad.

94. *Evans* v *Brunner, Mond & Co*, [1921] 1 Ch 359: 90 LJ Ch 294.

95. *Hampsons* v *Price's Patent Candle Co*, (1876) 45 LJ Ch 437.

96. *Henderson* v *Bank of Australia*, (1889) 40 Ch D 170. *See also W. & M. Roith Ltd, Re*, [1967] 1 All ER 427, where the attempt of a creator and managing director of two companies to provide pension to his widow after his death from the companies' income was frustrated, it being not reasonably incidental to, nor necessary to promote, the prosperity of the companies. The case is adversely commented upon by Harry Silberberg, *Gratuitous Payments for the Benefit of a Company*, 1968 JBL 213.

97. For a remarkable account of such cases and other interests that corporate directors can consider *see* R. C. Beuthin, *The Range of a Company's Interests*, (1969) 86 SALJ 155; R. Reels, CORPORATION GIVING IN A FREE SOCIETY, 1956; J.A.C. Hetherington, *Corporate Responsibility*, (1969) Stanford LR at pp 278-79.

lower its prices to consumers, to help the needy, to contribute to education and to secure the needs of society generally."[1]

Since the application of the European Community Law in England, the doctrine of *ultra vires* stands restricted to a certain extent. Section 9(1) of the Act provides that "in favour of a person dealing with a company in good faith, any transaction decided on by the directors shall be deemed to be one which it is within the capacity of the company". Thus as against a third person acting in good faith, the company can no longer plead that the act was *ultra vires*.[2]

Main Objects Rule of Construction

The *ultra vires* doctrine confines corporate action within fixed limits. While it handicaps the ambitious manager, it lays a trap for the unwary creditor. That is why there has been a revolt against it almost ever since its inception. The businessman has always endeavoured to evade the limitations imposed by the doctrine on their freedom of action. One of the methods of bypassing *ultra vires* is the practice of registering memoranda containing a profusion of objects and powers.[3]

For example, in *Cotman* v *Brougham*[4] the House of Lords had to consider a memorandum which contained an objects clause with thirty sub-clauses enabling the company to carry on almost every conceivable kind of business which a company could adopt. Such an objects clause naturally defeats the very purpose for which it is there.[5] In a bid to control this tendency the courts adopted the "main objects rule" of construction. The rule owes its origin to the decision in the *Ashbury* case where it was held that the words "general contractors" must be read in connection with the company's main business. *German Date Coffee Co, Re*,[6] is another illustration of its application.

The memorandum of a company stated that it was formed for working a German patent which would be granted for manufacturing

---

1. Loius O. Kelso, *Corporate Benevolence and Welfare Redistribution*, (1960) Business Lawyer 259; D. L. Mazumdar, TOWARDS A PHILOSOPHY OF THE MODERN CORPORATION, (1967); A. Hacker (Ed), THE CORPORATION TAKE-OVER, [1964] and THE CORPORATION IN MODERN SOCIETY, (1959) edited by Mason; D. Cohen, *Gratuitous Payments to Employees and the Ultra Vires Doctrine*, 134 New LJ 716.
2. For comments on the provision *see* 1972 JBL 85; James H. Thompson, *Directors' Powers under the European Communities Act*, 1973 New LJ 593; A.T. Hirtenstein, *European Communities Act*, 1972, 1973 New LJ 312 and (1973) Camb LJ 1. The provision has been incorporated into the [English] Companies Act, 1985 [S. 35]
3. Lord WRENBURY in *Cotman* v *Brougham*, 1918 AC 514 at p 523: [1918-19] All ER Rep 265: 119 LT 162. The main objects rule of construction has been explained by the Bom HC, *Bilasrai Juharmal, Re*, AIR 1962 Bom 133: (1962) 32 Comp Cas 215.
4. 1918 AC 514: [1918-19] All ER Rep 265: 119 LT 162.
5. Sangal, *Ultra Vires and Companies: The Indian Experience*, (1963) 12 ICLQ 967.
6. (1882) 20 Ch D 169: [1881-5] All ER Rep 372. *See* also *Amalgamated Syndicate, Re*, (1897) 2 Ch 600 and P.C. Heerey, *Winding Up on the Just and Equitable Ground*: *Failure of Substratum*, (1973) 47 Aust LJ 718.

coffee from dates; for obtaining other patents for improvements and extension of the said invention; and to acquire and purchase any other invention for similar purposes. The intended German patent was never granted, but the company purchased a Swedish patent, and also established works in Hamburg where they made and sold coffee from dates without any patent.

A petition having been presented by two shareholders, it was held that the main object for which the company was formed had become impossible and, therefore, it was just and equitable that the company should be wound up. The court said: "In construing a memorandum in which there are general words... they must be taken in connection with what are shown by the context to be the dominant or main objects. It will not do under general words to turn a company for manufacturing one thing into a company for importing something else. Taking that as the governing principle, it seems to be plain that the real objects of this company which is called German Date Coffee Co, was to manufacture a substitute for coffee in Germany under a patent. It is what the company was formed for and all the rest is subordinate to that."

This principle will, however, be of no help where a company is formed for general purposes as opposed to a defined subject-matter. Pointing this out in *Kitson & Co Ltd, Re*,[7] the court said: "The impossibility of applying such a construction seems to be manifest when one remembers that business is a thing which changes. It grows or it contracts. It changes; it disposes of the whole of its plant; it moves its factory; it entirely changes its range of products, and so forth. It is more like an organic thing. It must be remembered that in these substratum cases there is every difference between a company which on the true construction of its memorandum is formed for the paramount purpose of dealing with some specific subject-matter and a company which is formed with wider and more comprehensive objects. With regard to a company which is formed to acquire and exploit a mine, when you come to construe its memorandum of association you must construe the language used in reference to the subject-matter, namely, a mine and, accordingly, if the mine cannot be acquired or if the mine turns out to be no mine at all the object of the company is frustrated, because the subject-matter which the company was formed to exploit has ceased to exist.... But when you come to the subject-matter of a totally different kind like the carrying on of a type of business, then, so long as the company can carry on that type of business, it seems that *prima facie* at any rate it is impossible to say that its substratum has gone." The facts of the case were:

A company was incorporated with the object of (*a*) acquiring an existing engineering concern and (*b*) carrying on the business of general

7. [1946] 1 All ER 435 CA.

engineering. Subsequently the company proposed to sell the original business and to embark upon other general engineering activities. Some of the shareholders petitioned for winding up on the ground that the company's substratum had disappeared. The court rejected the petition.[8]

In *Cotman v Brougham*[9] the main objects rule was excluded by a declaration in the objects clause that "every clause should be construed as a substantive clause and not limited or restricted by reference to any other sub-clause or by the name of the company and none of them should be deemed as merely subsidiary or auxiliary". The House of Lords expressed strong disapproval of the inclusion of such a clause, but their Lordships held that it excluded the "main objects rule" of interpretation.

Thus the rule has failed to prevent the evasion of *ultra vires*. And now the decision of the Court of Appeal in *Bell Houses Ltd v City Wall Properties Ltd*[10] has stamped its approval upon another technique of evasion. In this case a company's objects clause authorised it to carry on any other trade or business which in the opinion of the board of directors could be carried on advantageously in connection with the company's general business. The court held the clause to be valid and an act done in *bona fide* exercise of it to be *intra vires*. But a clause of this kind does not state any objects at all. Rather, it leaves the objects to be determined by the directors' *bona fides*.[11]

Consequences of ultra vires transactions

When a company gets involved in an *ultra vires* transaction the question arises as to what are its effects.

1. *Injunction*

In the first place, that members are entitled to hold a registered company to its registered objects has been recognised long since. Hence whenever an *ultra vires* act has been or is about to be undertaken, any member of the company can get an injunction to restrain it from proceeding with it.[12]

---

8. *Ferrom Electronics (P) Ltd v Vijaya Leasing Ltd*, (2002) 109 Comp Cas 467 Kant, the company was not carrying on its main objects, carrying on of ancillary objects, alright.
9. 1918 AC 514: [1918-19] All ER Rep 265: 119 LT 162.
10. [1966] 2 WLR 1323: [1966] 2 All ER 674.
11. *See* R. C. Beuthin, *The Ultra Vires Doctrine: An Obituary Notice*, (1966) 83 SALJ 461; *The Death of Ultra Vires*, (1966) 29 MLR 674; *Ultra Vires or the Directors' Bona Fides*, (1967) 30 Mod LR 566; R. Bank, *Is the Doctrine of Ultra Vires Dead*, 20 ICLQ 301.
12. *Attorney-General v Great Eastern Rly Co*, (1880) 5 AC 473: [1874-80] All ER Rep Ext 1459. *See* an interesting article on *'Personality of Associations'* by H. J. Laski in 29 Harv LR 404; *Jenkin v Pharmaceutical Society of Great Britain*, LR [1921] 1 Ch 392; Avtar Singh, *Injunctions against Ultra Vires Acts of Companies*, 1958 Mad LJ 55; PHEAR J in *Port Canning & Land Investment Co, Re*, (1871) 7 Bengal LR 583 at 598-611, where the learned

2. *Personal liability of directors*

It is one of the duties of directors to see that the corporate capital is used only for the legitimate business of the company. If any part of it has been diverted to purposes foreign to the company's memorandum, the directors will be personally liable to replace it.[13] Thus, for example, the Bombay High Court in *Jehangir R. Modi* v *Shamji Ladha*[14] held that—

A shareholder can maintain an action against the directors to compel them to restore to the company the funds of the company that have by them been employed in transactions that they have no authority to enter into, without making the company a party to the suit.[15]

3. *Breach of warranty of authority*

It is the duty of an agent to act within the scope of his authority. For if he goes beyond he will be personally liable to the third party for breach of warranty of authority. The directors of a company are its agents. As such it is their duty to keep within the limits of the company's powers. If they induce, however innocently, an outsider to contract with the company in a matter in which the company does not have the power to act, they will be personally liable to him for his loss. In *Weeks* v *Propert*:[16]

A railway company invited proposals for a loan on debentures. At the time the advertisement was published the company had issued debentures of the amount of £60,000 being the full amount which it was by its constitution authorised to issue. It had thus exhausted its borrowing powers. The plaintiff offered a loan of £500 upon the footing of that advertisement. The directors accepted it and issued to him a debenture of the company. The loan being *ultra vires* was held to be void. In an action by the plaintiff against the directors, it was held that the directors by inserting the advertisement had warranted that they had

---

Judge explains the great mischief, public and private, which might ensue if companies were not held strictly to the terms of their incorporation. Abolition of the doctrine of *ultra vires* in England by virtue of the provision in S. 35(1) of the 1989 Act nevertheless preserves this right by providing in S. 35(2) that a member may restrain an act which but for S. 35(1) would have been beyond the company's capacity. But such proceedings cannot be allowed in respect of acts to be done in fulfilment of legal obligations arising from a previous act of the company. The company's freedom in altering its objects as now granted and therefore of ratifying unauthorised acts would also be a stumbling block in the right to get an injunction.

13. *Exchange Banking Co, Re, Flitcroft* case, (1882) 21 Ch D 519: 48 LT 86; *George Newman & Co, Re,* [1895] 1 Ch 674: [1895-9] All ER Rep Ext 2161.
14. [1866-67] 4 Bom HCR 185; *Kathiawar Trading Co* v *Virchand,* ILR (1894) 18 Bom 119.
15. In the case of deliberate misapplication, criminal action can also be taken for fraud. See *R* v *Sinclair, Queens-wood, E. W. Smithson,* [1968] 1 WLR 1246. To the same effect is *Aviling Barford Ltd* v *Perion Ltd,* 1989 BCLC 626 Ch D, where it was pointed out that directors who throw away the company's money on unauthorised objects are personally liable to make good the company's loss. Sale of property at half of its price to a shareholder was held to be ultra vires and beyond ratification constituting the recipient as a constructive trustee to the company.
16. (1873) LR 8 CP 427.

the power to borrow which they did not in fact possess. Their warranty consequently was broken and they were personally liable.

It must, however, be remembered that the representation of authority which the directors hold out must be a representation of facts and not of law. For example, whether a company is authorised by its memorandum to borrow is a question of law which every man dealing with the company is supposed to know. But where the memorandum authorises a company to borrow, whether that power has been fully exercised or not becomes a question of fact. A misrepresentation of the former will not, but that of the latter will, give a cause of action against the directors.[17]

4. Ultra vires acquired property

If a company's money has been spent *ultra vires* in purchasing some property, the company's right over that property must be held secure. For, that asset, though wrongly acquired, represents the corporate capital. Thus, for example, the Madras High Court[18] allowed a company to sue on a mortgage to recover the money lent in spite of the fact that the transaction was beyond the powers of the company. The court relied upon the following observation of Brice on the DOCTRINE OF ULTRA VIRES: "Property legally and by formal transfer or conveyance transferred to a corporation is in law duly vested in such corporation, even though the corporation was not empowered to acquire such property."[19]

Similarly in *Selangor United Rubber Estates* v *Cradock (No 3)*,[20] it was held that "the fact that the Companies Act[21] makes it unlawful for a company to give any financial assistance for anyone to purchase any of its shares does not prevent such a person from being held a constructive trustee for the company of such of its money as is unlawfully provided for such purpose".[22] A Canadian court allowed recovery of *ultra vires* payments 43 years after they were made.[23]

---

17. For the consequences of *ultra vires* borrowings, *see* Borrowing Powers, Ch 13 *below*.
18. *Ad Sait* v *Bank of Mysore*, (1930) 59 MLJR 28.
19. The following authorities are cited: *Ayers* v *South Australian Banking Co*, (1871) LR 3 PC 548; *Coltman* v *Coltman*, (1881) 19 Ch D 64; *Turner* v *Bank of Bombay*, ILR (1901) 25 Bom 52, where the court held that the contract is void, and no action can be brought on it, but the company can sue for the recovery of its assets wrongfully delivered under the contract.
20. [1968] 2 All ER 1073: [1968] 1 WLR 1555.
21. S. 54 of the English Act, 1948 (deleted by the 1985 Act and replaced by a new set of provisions on financial assistance in purchasing the company's shares) and S. 77 of the Indian Act, 1956.
22. *See* also *Great Eastern Rly Co* v *Turner*, (1872) 8 Ch App 149, where shares purchased *ultra vires* the company were held in the name of a director, but they could not pass to the assignee of the director.
23. *Canada Trust Co* v *Lloyd*, (1968) 66 DLR (2d) 722.

5. *Ultra vires contracts*

''A contract of a corporation'', observed Justice GRAY, "which is *ultra vires,* that is to say, outside the objects as defined by its memorandum is wholly void and of no legal effect".[24] The objection to an *ultra vires* contract is, not merely that the corporation ought not to have made it, but that it could not make it. The question is not as to the legality of the contract: the question is as to the competency and power of the company to make it. "An *ultra vires* contract, being void *ab initio,* cannot become *intra vires* by reason of estoppel, lapse of time, ratification, acquiescence or delay."[25] "No performance on either side can give the unlawful contract any validity or be the foundation of any right of action upon it."[26] This incapacity of a company occasionally results in manifest injustice. For example, in *Beauforte (Jon) (London) Ltd, Re*:[27]

A company was authorised by its memorandum to carry on the business of costumiers, gown-makers and other activities of allied nature. The company decided to undertake the business of making veneered panels which was admittedly *ultra vires* and for this purpose erected a factory at Bristol. A firm of builders who constructed the factory claimed £2,078 as owing to them. Another firm supplied veneers to the company and had a claim of £1,011. A third firm sought to prove for a simple contract debt of £107 in respect of coke supplied to the factory. None of these applicants had actual knowledge that veneered business was *ultra vires,* yet none of them could make the company liable for his claim.

The reason is that every one dealing with a company is supposed to know its powers. In India there is an even earlier authority on the point.[28]

A company purchased and operated a rice mill beyond its powers. The rice was consigned to certain persons who had paid the price. The consignees had to sell the rice, owing to its inferior quality, at considerable loss. The company gave them drafts promising to pay for the loss. The company went into liquidation and the question about the enforceability of the drafts arose.

---

24. *Central Transportation Co v Pullman's Car Co,* (1890) 139 US 24.
25. Lord CAIRNS LC in *Ashbury Rly Carriage and Iron Co Ltd v Riche,* (1875) 44 LJ Exch 185: [1874-80] All ER Rep 2219.
26. GRAY J in (1890) 139 US 24.
27. [1953] Ch 131, noted 69 LQR 166.
28. *Port Canning and Land Investment Co, Re,* (1871) 7 Beng LR 583. A later illustration of such injustice is *Introductions Ltd, Re,* [1968] 2 Comp LJ 28: [1969] 2 WLR 791: [1969] 1 All ER 887 CA; Criticised by K. W. Wedderburn, *Unreformed Company Law,* (1969) 32 Mod LR 563. *See also* 1969 JBL 4.

The court held that trading in rice was a transaction *ultra vires* the company; the directors, therefore, could not bind the company, and the consignees could not recover.

There is yet another problem concerning *ultra vires* contracts. "Who can plead that a contract is *ultra vires*?" This question has gained importance since the decision of the Queen's Bench in *Anglo-Overseas Agencies Ltd* v *Green*[29], where the defence of *ultra vires* was set up against a company. But the point was not decided as the court found that the contract in question was not *ultra vires*. The question again arose in *Bell Houses Ltd* v *City Wall Properties Ltd.*[30]

> The plaintiff company's principal business was the acquisition of vacant sites and the erection thereon of housing estates. In the course of transacting the business, the chairman acquired knowledge of sources of finance for property development. The company introduced the financier to the defendant company and claimed the agreed fee of £20,000 for the same.

The trial judge held that the contract was *ultra vires* the plaintiff company and, therefore, void. But this was reversed on appeal. The Court of Appeal relied on the clause in the memorandum which authorised the company "to carry on any other trade or business whatsoever which can, in the opinion of the board of directors, be advantageously carried on by the company in connection with its general business", and held that since the directors honestly believed that the transaction could be advantageously carried on as ancillary to the company's main objects, it was not *ultra vires*.[31]

Thus the question whether the defence of *ultra vires* can be set up against a company remains open. But SALMON LJ observed:

> It seems strange that third parties could take advantage of a doctrine, manifestly for the protection of the shareholders, in order to deprive the company of the money which in justice should be paid to it by the third party.[32]

Under the UK Act, a company may only state that its objects are commercial. This minimises the problem of *ultra vires* contracts. The problem may only arise when the contract in question is proved to be non-commercial.

---

29. [1961] 1 QB 1: [1960] 3 All ER 244: [1960] 3 WLR 561. Noted 77 LQR 11.
30. [1966] 2 WLR 1323: [1966] 2 All ER 674: [1966] 2 QB 656. Noted, *Ultra Vires and the Opinion of Directors*, (1966) 32 LQR 463; K. W. Wedderburn, *What is the point of Ultra Vires*, (1966) 29 MLR 171; Firmston, *Who can Plead that a Contract is Ultra Vires*, (1961) 24 MLR 715.
31. This decision has been appreciated in 1966 JBL 346.
32. [1966] 2 WLR 1323, 1345. But the leading text writers on the law of contract believe that the company should not be able to enforce an *ultra vires* contract. *See* Anson's LAW OF CONTRACT, 202 (22nd Edn by Guest, 1964).

6.   Ultra vires torts

The rule of constructive notice of memorandum and articles explains why a company is not liable for an *ultra vires* contract, but that does not solve the problem of injustice involved. Moreover, the rule altogether fails to hold ground when a company is sought to be made liable for a tort committed by a servant of the company while acting beyond the company's powers. Any one dealing with a company may, at the pain of losing the bargain, be required to acquaint himself with the company's memorandum. But that can hardly be expected of a person who has been the victim of an *ultra vires* tort. For example, a company is operating omnibuses—a venture entirely alien to its objects as described in the memorandum. The driver of one such bus negligently injures the plaintiff who sues the company for the tort. It can, no doubt, be contended against him that the driver was not a servant of the company. The company, having no existence outside its corporate sphere, could not have appointed him.[33] But can it be said that the plaintiff ought to have known that fact. Doubtless the plaintiff deserves to be compensated. But the law has not yet clearly declared the justice of his demand.[34] As the law seems to stand at present, to make a company liable for any tort it must be shown that—

(1)   that the activity in the course of which it has been committed falls within the scope of the memorandum, and

(2)   that the servant committed the tort within the course of his employment.

CONCLUSION

This brief study of the nature and consequences of *ultra vires* rule points to some of its inherent complications resulting in occasional injustice. The English Company Law Revision Committee (known as the Cohen Committee, 1945), recommended its abolition. It has to be conceded that the rule of *ultra vires* is not based on any dogmatic concept of a limited liability company.[35] The statement of objects indicates the permissible range of corporate activity. Everything else beyond that is implicitly prohibited so that the corporate capital may be preserved for the benefit of shareholders and creditors. But that protection does not in any way suffer if the memorandum, like articles, is made a contract only between shareholders and the company. Every contract made on behalf of the company whether

---

33. *See* E. H. Warren, *Executory Ultra Vires Transactions*, (1910-11) 24 Harv LR 387.
34. See *Liability of Corporations for the Torts of their Servants*, 10 Camb LJ 419; *Poulton* v *London S. W. Rly Co*, (1867) LR 2 QBD 534; A. L. Goodhart, *Corporate Liability in Tort and the Doctrine of Ultra Vires*, 25 Camb LJ 350; E. H. Waress, *Torts by Corporation in ultra vires undertakings*, [1925] Camb LJ 180; Holdworth, HISTORY OF ENGLAND, 49-62; H. J. Laski, *Personality of Associations*, 29 Harv LR 404.
35. *Company Law Reform and the Doctrine of Ultra Vires*, 62 LQR 66.

within or beyond its powers should be valid. But if it involves a misapplication of corporate capital the directors should be, and already are, bound to replace it.[36]

This reform has been adopted by the European Communities Act, 1972. It was incorporated in Section 35 of the [English] Companies Act of 1985. A company will now be liable to a person acting in good faith for every act decided on by the directors. As a result of the amendment made by the 1989 Act, Section 35(1) of the Act now is as follows: "The validity of an act done by a company shall not be called into question on the ground of lack of capacity by reason of anything in the company's memorandum."

Alteration of objects

Section 17 allows alteration of objects within certain defined limits. "The intention of the Legislature is to prevent too easy an alteration of the conditions contained in the memorandum."[37] The exercise of the power is, therefore, fenced by safeguards which are calculated to protect the interests of creditors and of shareholders.[38] The limits imposed upon the power of alteration are of two kinds, namely, substantive and procedural. The former defines the physical limits of alteration and the latter the procedure by which it can be effected.

1. Substantive limits

Section 17 provides that a company may change its objects only in so far as the alteration is necessary for any of the following purposes:

(*a*) *To enable the company to carry on its business more economically or more efficiently.*—The alteration which is contemplated in this clause seems to be an alteration which will leave the business of the company substantively what it was before, with only such changes in the mode of conducting it as will enable it to be carried on more economically or more efficiently. In *Scientific Poultry Breeders' Assn, Re,*[39] a company was allowed amendment to enable it to pay remuneration to its managers, which was formerly forbidden, being necessary for efficient management. The words of this clause have been liberally interpreted. For example, amendments were allowed under this clause to enable companies to make contributions to political parties as this would enable them to go better with the Government and a healthy relationship leads to business efficiency.[40]

---

36. The Report of Dr Prentice was also in favour of the view that companies with unlimited capacity and without objects clause should be allowed to be registered. For a view of the report, *see* Brenda M Hannigan, *The Reform of the Ultra Vires Rule*, 1987 JBL 173.
37. Lord HENWORTH MR in *Scientific Poultry Breeders' Assn, Re*, 1933 Ch 227 at p 229.
38. WARRINGTON J in *Cyclists' Touring Club, Re*, [1907] 1 Ch 269 at p 275.
39. 1933 Ch 227.
40. See *Straw Products Ltd* v *Registrar of Companies*, [1970] 1 Comp LJ 93: ILR 1968 Cut 964: (1969) 39 Comp Cas 974; *Jayantilal* v *Tata Iron & Steel Co*, AIR 1958 Bom 155; *Indian Iron & Steel Co Ltd, Re*, AIR 1957 Cal 234: (1957) 27 Comp Cas 361.

(*b*) *To enable the company to attain its main purpose by new or improved means.*—This clause is intended to enable companies to take advantage of new scientific discoveries. With the objects remaining the same, only the means of carrying them out are permitted to be changed under this clause.

(*c*) *To enlarge or change the local area of the company's operation.*— This is to enable companies to carry their trades to new quarters of the globe. For example, *Indian Mechanical Gold Extracting Co, Re*,[41] a company was allowed to drop the words from its memorandum which required it to confine business to the "empire of India", subject, of course, to the condition that the word "Indian" was dropped from its name.

(*d*) *To carry on some business which under existing circumstances may conveniently or advantageously be combined with the business of the company.*—This is the only clause which allows a company to undertake any new business having no relation to its existing business except that it must be such as can conveniently or advantageously be combined with the company's existing business. What new business can be so combined must be determined by the persons engaged in the business. Thus a tyre company was allowed to undertake the general business of bankers and financiers.[42] The new business must not, of course, be inconsistent with the existing business. Thus, in *Cyclists' Touring Club, Re*,[43] a club incorporated to protect cyclists on public roads was not allowed to undertake protection of motorists also, as cyclists had to be protected against motorists.

These principles have been largely followed in India also. The choice of new objects must rest with the shareholders of the company and their directors and an alteration will ordinarily be confirmed except when "it is detrimental to, or inconsistent with, the existing business". Thus a company formed originally for "business in jute" has been allowed to include "business in rubber"[44] and a "spinning and weaving company" to manufacture "industrial and power alcohol",[45] a spinning and weaving company, having sold its undertaking, to purchase a running cinema,[46] and a colliery company whose business was nationalised, to adopt new objects.[47] It should not, however, be supposed that the Board's confirmation is a bare

---

41. [1891] 3 Ch 538.
42. *Patent Tyre Co, Re*, [1923] 2 Ch 222.
43. [1907] 1 Ch 269.
44. *Juggilal Kamlapat Jute Mills v ROC*, [1966] 1 Comp LJ 292 All: (1967) 37 Comp·Cas 20.
45. *Modi Spg and Wvg Mills Co Ltd, Re*, (1963) 33 Comp Cas 901 All; *Motilal Padampat Sugar Mills Co, Re*, (1964) 34 Comp Cas 86 All; *Ambala Electric Supply Ltd, Re*, (1963) 33 Comp Cas 585 Punj; *Dalmia Cement Bharat Ltd, Re*, (1964) 34 Comp Cas 729 Mad and *Bhutoria Bros, Re*, AIR 1957 Cal 593: (1958) 28 Comp Cas 122.
46. *New Asarwa Mfg Co Ltd, Re*, (1975) 45 Comp Cas 15: 16 Guj LR 553.
47. *United Collieries Ltd, Re*, (1975) 45 Comp Cas 226 Cal.

formality. The Board has a real discretion, "a discretion to be exercised judicially, in the interest of the members of the company and its creditors, not to confirm the alteration or to confirm the same in whole or in part, or subject to such terms and conditions as it deems fit".[48] Thus the Punjab High Court refused to confirm an alteration as the proposed "new business had nothing to do even remotely with the existing business".[49] Similarly, in a case before the Calcutta High Court, "an alteration to carry on a new business was not confirmed on the ground that it could not by any stretch of language, imagination or business principles or commercial possibilities, be regarded as a business which could conveniently or advantageously be combined with the business of the company in the existing circumstances".[50] But where the company is in sound financial position and the alteration is not objected to by its shareholders and creditors, the Board may take a lenient view and allow any kind of alteration resolved upon by the company.[51] Accordingly, when the business of an insurance company was taken over by the Central Government, the Punjab High Court allowed the company to alter its objects so as "to include business in engineering works, cotton and importing and exporting".[52] And the same court allowed a cable manufacturing company to undertake hoteling services.[53] Similarly, the Madras High Court has held that where a company's assets greatly exceed its liabilities, an expansion of business activities in the light of the company's special resolution should be allowed.[54]

---

48. *Juggilal Kamlapat Jute Mills* v *ROC*, [1966] 1 Comp LJ 292, 299 All: (1967) 37 Comp Cas 20.
49. *Punjab Distilling Industries Ltd* v *ROC*, (1963) 33 Comp Cas 811 Punj. CLB refused to confirm an alteration enabling the company to convert itself into a Nidhi Company within the meaning of S. 620-A because the matter was not coming under any of the clauses. *Lord Mahaveer Gountham Benefit Ltd, Re*, (1994) 1 Comp LJ 301, CLB Mad: (1994) 79 Comp Cas 535.
50. *Bhutoria Bros, Re*, AIR 1957 Cal 593: (1958) 28 Comp Cas 122; *See* also *Indian Iron & Steel Co Ltd, Re*, AIR 1957 Cal 234: (1957) 27 Comp Cas 361; *Bharat Mining Corpn, Re*, (1967) 37 Comp Cas 430: [1967] 1 Comp LJ 119 Cal.
51. For a fuller account of cases under this section, *see* S. P. Tiwari, *Confirmation of Alteration in Objects Clause by Courts under S. 17 of the Companies Act, 1956*, 17 Law Review of the Punjab University Law College, Chandigarh. *Geo Rubber Exports Ltd, Re*, (1991) 72 Comp Cas 713 CLB, a financially sound company allowed to start new business at a time when it was doing no business at all.
52. *New Asiatic Insurance Co Ltd, Re*, [1965] 2 Comp LJ 24 Punj. *Standard General Insurance Co Ltd, Re*, AIR 1965 Cal 16 is to the same effect.
53. *Industrial Cables India Ltd* v *Registrar of Companies*, (1973) 43 Comp Cas 353 P&H; *Delhi Bharat Grain Merchants Assn, Re*, (1974) 44 Comp Cas 214 Del, where a company carrying on forward business in grains was allowed to shift to cotton, grain business having been banned.
54. *Rajendra Industries (P) Ltd, Re*, [1957] 2 Comp LJ 144 Mad. In most of the above cases the applications for confirmation had been opposed by the Registrar of Companies under directions from the Central Government as the latter does not want diversification of objects. For other cases of the same kind see *Straw Products* v *Registrar of Companies*, [1970] 1 Comp LJ 100; *Natesar Spg & Wvg Mills, Re*, AIR 1960 Mad 257.

The Company Law Board permitted a new object (trading at stock exchange) which was sought by the company some eight years after its incorporation, but insisted that it should not be listed among "main objects" because the new business was not being commenced on incorporation. The CLB also observed that a company could not have a negative objects clause. If the stock exchange rules were not permitting certain things they could be dropped from the memorandum.[55]

(*e*) *To restrict or abandon any of the object specified in the memorandum.*

(*f*) *To sell or dispose of the whole, or any part of the undertaking, of the company.*

(*g*) *To amalgamate with any other company or body of persons.*[56]

2. Procedure of alteration

Alteration of Objects

Since the amendment of S. 17 of the Act by the Companies (Amendment) Act, 1996, the prescribed procedure for altering objects is only the requirement of a special resolution and its filing with the Registrar. The requirement of seeking confirmation of the Company Law Board has been dispensed with. The alteration of objects has become an internal matter. No outside confirmation is necessary. The only restraint now is that the special resolution of the company should be within the scope of the permissible range of alteration as outlined in S. 17(1). The matter being wholly internal, only the shareholders can object to any change which is extraneous to the substantive limits stated in S. 17(1). The memorandum is a contract between the company and its members. This contract operates within the framework of the Companies Act. Members can prevent through a civil court action violation of the Companies Act by their company. Lending institutions and creditors would not be able to object. It would, however, be better to inform them and to take their approval because they can think in terms of withdrawing loan facilities where such facilities were extended on the basis of objects as they then stood. They may not like to risk their financial resources in new and adventurous objects.

The Company Law Board was also required to have regard to the rights and interests of the members of the company. If there are any dissentient

---

55. *Servin Securities (P) Ltd, Re,* (1995) 17 Corpt LA 387 Bom.
56. An alteration for the purpose of amalgamation was confirmed in *Nagaisuree Tea Co v Ram Chandra Karnami,* [1966] 2 Comp LJ 208 Cal.

members the Board may order that an arrangement be made for the purchase of the interest of such members.[57]

The Company Law Board had the discretion to refuse to confirm the alteration or to confirm it either wholly or in part or subject to such conditions as may be deemed fit. [S. 17(5)] In a case before the Allahabad High Court, an alteration was confirmed only in part and that too subject to the condition that a separate profit and loss account in respect of the new business should be maintained for a period of five years.[58]

Under the English Act confirmation of the Court was not necessary except when an application had been lodged against the alteration within 21 days of the passing of the special resolution. The application had to be filed by the holders of not less than 15 per cent in nominal value of the company's issued share capital or any class thereof. If the company was limited by shares the application had to be filed by at least fifteen per cent of the company's members. Fifteen per cent of the company's debenture-holders could also proceed under the section. The English procedure saved a good deal of time and expense. The sanction had already become a needless ritual. Alterations were seldom opposed. Explaining the reason why the same had not been adopted in India, a learned judge said:

> It may be that the Indian Parliament in its wisdom might have thought that the shareholders in India have neither the sense of responsibility, nor the maturity of business experience of the English shareholder to be left free to judge by themselves the ultimate desirability of altering so important a feature of the company as the objects clause of the memorandum.[59]

But now, since the above noted amendment of 1996, the procedure in India is also very liberal. No outside approval is necessary. Only the members can restrain their company by civil proceeding from altering objects outside the scope of limits specified in S.17(1).

Alteration of provisions of Memorandum other than Conditions [S. 16]

The above procedure has to be followed only for the alteration of the conditions contained in the memorandum. And only those provisions are regarded as conditions as are required by Section 13 to be stated in the memorandum, namely, its five clauses. Anything else contained in the memorandum can be altered simply by passing a special resolution.[60]

---

57. S. 17(6). In *Sipani Automobiles Ltd, Re*, (1993) 78 Comp Cas 557, the CLB refused its confirmation because there was the probability that new business would be financed out of the depositors' money and not by raising new capital, thereby exposing it to new risks.

58. *Motilal Padampat Sugar Mills Co, Re*, (1964) 34 Comp Cas 86 All.

59. *Bhutoria Bros, Re*, AIR 1957 Cal 593: (1958) 28 Comp Cas 122, *per* MUKHERJI J at p 597.

60. The effect is that any such other provision, including the provision, if any, for the appointment of a managing director or manager, can be altered in the manner of articles. Any

Registration of alteration [S. 18]

In the case of alteration of objects, a copy of the resolution should be filed with the Registrar of Companies within one month from the date of the resolution. In the case of inter-State shifting of the registered office a certified copy of the Central Government's order and a printed copy of the altered memorandum must be filed with the Registrar within three months of the order. The documents have to be filed with the Registrar of the place from where the office is to be shifted and also with the Registrar of place at which the new office is to be established.[61]

Within one month the Registrar will certify the registration. Alteration takes effect when it is so registered.[62] If an application for registration is not made within the above time, the whole proceedings of alteration will lapse.[63] The company may, however, seek from the Central Government an order for the revival of the lapsed proceedings, provided an application is made within the further period of one month and is based upon a sufficient cause. In computing the period of three months the time taken for drawing up of the Central Government's order as well as time taken for obtaining a copy thereof is to be excluded.[64] The Central Government has the power to extend time for registering an alteration when there is sufficient cause to excuse the delay. [S. 18(4)]

LIABILITY

The fourth clause has to state the nature of liability that the members incur. If the company is to be incorporated with limited liability, the clause must state that "the liability of the members shall be limited by shares".[65] This means that no member can be called upon to pay anything more than the nominal value of the shares held by him, or

---

extra provisions in the memorandum are treated as a part of the company's articles. See *Ramkumar Potdar* v *Sholapur Spg & Wvg Co Ltd*, AIR 1934 Bom 427: (1934) 36 Bom LR 907; *Ahmedabad Jubilee Mills* v *Chotta Lal*, (1908) 10 Bom LR 141; *Venkataramana* v *Coimbatore Mercantile Bank*, (1923) 74 IC 966: AIR 1924 Mad 126.

61. See *Ishita Properties Ltd, Re*, (2002) 112 Comp Cas 547 CLB, there was delay in filing the documents at the place to which the office was shifted (delay one month and 18 days), excused, because there was a substantial compliance.

62. S. 19. The Registrar's certificate is conclusive evidence that the requirements as to alteration have been complied with. S. 18(2).

63. S. 19(2). Where the extension of time for filing of documents was sought after sixty days from the expiry of 30 days from the date of the resolution, it was held that the resolution had become void and there was no question of extension of time, *Ganga Textiles Ltd* v *ROC*, (1998) 94 Comp Cas 36 CLB.

64. S. 640-A, and *Saroja Mills Ltd* v *ROC*, (1964) 34 Comp Cas 336: [1964] 1 Comp LJ 103: [1964] 1 Mad LJ 197.

65. S. 13(2). Sections 39 and 40 require that the copies of the document which have to be supplied to members, on demand must be a copy as altered.

so much thereof as remains unpaid; and if his shares be fully paid up his liability is nil.[66] If it is proposed to register the company limited by guarantee, this clause will state the amount which every member undertakes to contribute to the assets of the company in the event of its winding up. The clause will, for example, run like this: "Every member of the company undertakes to contribute to the assets of the company in the event of its being wound up such amounts as may be required, not exceeding one thousand rupees."[67]

CAPITAL

The last clause states the amount of the nominal capital of the company and the number and value of the shares into which it is divided.[68] The Companies Amendment Act, 2000 has, by amending S. 3, prescribed the requirement that a public company must have a minimum paid up capital of five lakh rupees or such higher amount as may be prescribed.[69] A private company is required to have a minimum paid up capital of 1 lakh rupees or such higher amount as may be prescribed by its articles.

SUBSCRIPTION

The memorandum concludes with the subscribers' declaration. The subscribers declare: "We, the several persons whose names and addresses are subscribed, are desirous of being formed into a company, in pursuance of this memorandum of association, and we respectively agree to take the number of shares in the capital of the company set opposite our respective names."[70] The memorandum has to be subscribed by at least seven persons in the case of a public company and by at least two in the case of a private company.[71] Each subscriber must sign the document and must write

---

66. S. 12(2)(*a*).
67. S. 13(3) and 12(2)(*b*).
68. S. 13(4)(*a*). In an unusual case on this point a company sought court permissions for reduction of capital to enable it to state a part of the capital in terms of foreign currencies. The court had no choice but to allow it because all that the section requires is that the memorandum shall state the amount of share capital and the division thereof into shares of fixed amount. It does not prescribe any currency in which the amount has to be stated, nor that it should be stated in a single lump sum. L.S. Sealy in his book on CASES AND MATERIALS IN COMPANY LAW at 329 (4th Edn, 1989) describes the effect of this decision in these words: "HARMAN J ruled that it was in order for a company to have the nominal capital denominated in "mixed basket of currencies".
69. The definition of public company now (after amendment) is that it is a company which is not a private company, which has a minimum paid capital of 5 lakh rupees or higher as may be prescribed or a private company which is the subsidiary of a company which is not a private company.
70. Table B, Schedule I which gives a specimen of the memorandum of a company limited by shares.
71. S. 12.

opposite his name the number of shares he takes.[72] But no subscriber shall take less than one share.[73]

After incorporation no subscriber can withdraw his name on any ground whatsoever. "The subscriber to the memorandum cannot have rescission on the ground that he was induced to become a subscriber by the misrepresentation of an agent of the company".[74] But he may withdraw his name before the memorandum is actually registered as up to that time "there is no contract at all".[75]

---

72. *See* S. 15 which requires that the memorandum shall be printed and divided into paragraphs numbered consecutively and signed by subscribers.
73. S. 13(4)(*b*) and (*c*).
74. BUCKLEY J in *Metal Constituents Ltd, Re, Lord Lurgan* case, [1902] 1 Ch 707 at p 709: (1880) 86 LT 291.
75. *Ibid.* But see *Banwari Lal* v *Kundan Cloth Mills*, AIR 1937 Lah 527, where the court refused a subscriber's attempt to withdraw his name even before the company was duly incorporated by registration of the memorandum.

4
Articles of Association

Articles when compulsory [S. 26]

Articles of association is the second document which has, in the case of some companies, to be registered along with the memorandum. Companies which must have articles of association are:[1]

1. Unlimited companies;
2. Companies limited by guarantee; and
3. Private companies limited by shares.

This document contains rules, regulations and bye-laws for the general administration of the company. Schedule I of the Companies Act, 1956, contains various model forms of memoranda and articles. The Schedule is divided into several Tables. Each Table serves as a model for one kind of company. A company limited by shares may either frame its own set of articles or may adopt all or any of the regulations contained in Table A.[2] But if it does not register any articles, Table A applies; if it does have some regulations, for the rest, as far as applicable, Table A applies, in so far as its regulations are not excluded.[3] Other companies may adopt Table C, D or E.[4] The chief advantage of adopting the appropriate Table is that its provisions are legal beyond all doubt.[5]

Public companies are free to have or not to have articles. But they cannot survive without articles of association because without any rules or regulations they may not be able to hold in harmony the diversity of relations under which they have to function.

Form and signature of articles [S. 30]

If articles are proposed to be registered they must be printed. They should be divided into paragraphs, each consisting generally of one regulation and numbered consecutively. Each subscriber of the memorandum has to sign the

---

1. S. 26 states this requirement. Section 27 requires that the articles of an unlimited liability company shall state the number of members with which the company is to be registered and the amount of its share capital, if any. A guarantee company's articles must state the number of members with which it is to be registered. The articles of a private company which is with share capital must state all the three requirements of a private company and, if it is without share capital, the applicable requirement as to number of members.
2. S. 28(1). S. 24 says that for companies other than those limited by shares, the form of articles shall be such one of the forms as in Table C, D, or E to Sch 1.
3. S. 28(2).
4. S. 29. Such companies may include additional clauses in their articles but they should be consistent with the Table adopted.
5. As explained in *Lock v Queensland Investment and Land Mortgage Co*, [1986] 1 Ch 397.

document in the presence of at least one attesting witness, both of them adding their addresses and occupations.

Contents of articles

Articles of association may prescribe such regulations for the company as the subscribers to the memorandum deem expedient. The Act gives the subscribers a free hand. Any stipulations as to the relations between the company and its members, and between members *inter se* may be inserted in the articles. But everything stated therein is subject to the Companies Act.

The document must not conflict with the provisions of the Act.[6] Any clause which is contrary to the provisions of the Act or of any other law for the time being in force, is simply inoperative and void.[7] Section 439 of the Companies Act, for example, confers the right on a shareholder to petition for winding up of the company in certain circumstances. This right cannot be excluded or limited by the articles.[8] Similarly, the articles cannot sanction something which is forbidden by the Act. Section 205, for example, declares that no dividend shall be paid by a company except out of profits. The force of this section cannot be undone by any provision in the articles of association.

Articles in relation to memorandum

Articles have always been held to be subordinate to the memorandum. If, therefore, the memorandum and articles are inconsistent, the articles must give way. In other words, articles must not contain anything the effect of which is to alter a condition contained in the memorandum or which is contrary to its provisions.[9] "This is so because the object of the memorandum is to state the purposes for which the company has been established, while the articles provide the manner in which the company is to be carried on and its proceedings disposed of."[10] This constitutes the principal difference between the two documents. In the words of Lord CAIRNS, the difference is this:

---

6. S. 9 gives overriding effect to the Act. *Madras Stock Exchange Ltd* v *S&R Rajkumar*, (2003) 116 Comp Cas 214 Mad, the Stock Exchange was a guarantee company, a provision for expulsion of members in the interest of discipline was held to be consistent with the Act and Table C. The member under compulsion was holding office in another company in violation of the company's articles. The provision and forfeiture valid.
7. *See*, for example, *Noble* v *Laygate Investments Ltd*, [1978] 2 All ER 1067, where the provisions of a company's articles had to give way because they were in conflict with the Income and Corporation Taxes Act, 1970 [English]. An article prohibiting members from proceeding against the company would be contrary to public policy and, therefore, void, *St. Johnson Football Club Ltd* v *Scottish Football Assn Ltd*, (1965) Scottish Lt 171 OH.
8. *Peveril Gold Mines Ltd, Re*, [1898] 1 Ch 122.
9. *Baglan Hall Colliery Co, Re*, [1870] 5 Ch App 346.
10. *Bryon* v *Metropolitan Omnibus Co*, (1885) 27 LJ Ch 685 at p 687.

The memorandum is, as it were, the area beyond which the action of the company cannot go; inside that area the shareholders may make such regulations for their own government as they think fit.[11]

In the words of BOWEN LJ:[12]

There is an essential difference between the memorandum and the articles. The memorandum contains the fundamental conditions upon which alone the company is allowed to be incorporated. They are conditions introduced for the benefit of the creditors, and the outside public, as well as of the shareholders. The articles of association are internal regulations of the company.

Some of the conditions of incorporation contained in the memorandum cannot be altered except with the sanction of the CLB. Articles of association, on the other hand, can be altered simply by a special resolution.[13] If the memorandum ever comes to be altered by the same procedure by which articles can be, the difference between these two documents will disappear.[14] The English Companies Act, 1948, made the memorandum alterable by special resolution, sanction of the court being not ordinarily necessary, unless the alteration was challenged within 21 days by a qualified minority of shareholders or creditors.

But, unless the *ultra vires* rule is abolished, the memorandum will always differ from articles in a principal respect. If a company does something beyond the scope of the objects stated in the memorandum it is absolutely void and altogether incapable of ratification. Whereas anything done by a company in contravention of the provisions of its articles is only irregular and can always be confirmed by the shareholders. Now that the objects clause of the memorandum has become alterable by a special resolution only, a company should be in a position to ratify or adopt a transaction by introducing by means of a special resolution suitable or requisite changes in the objects clause. Some of the clauses of the memorandum can be altered only with the sanction of the CLB.[15]

---

11. *Ashbury Rly Carriage and Iron Co Ltd* v *Riche*, [1874-80] All ER Rep Ext 2219: (1875) LR 7 HL 653, 671.
12. *Guinness* v *Land Corporation of Ireland*, (1882) 22 Ch D 349, 381.
13. S. 31.
14. The possibility of disappearance of the dichotomy of memorandum and articles has been explained by Geoffery Hornsey, *Alteration of the Constitution of Companies*, (1949) 61 Jur Rev 263. The amendment of 1996 has allowed objects to be altered in the same manner as articles, namely by passing a special resolution. Now there is only clause of the memorandum, namely, registered office clause, which requires sanction of the Company Law Board for shifting the registered office from one state to another.
15. This is true of the registered office clause. Also capital can not be reduced except with the sanction of the CLB, S. 100.

Lastly, it is suggested in Palmer's COMPANY LAW[16] with the authority of a passage in the judgement of JESSEL MR in *Anderson* case[17], that "though the articles cannot alter or control the memorandum, yet, if there is an ambiguity in the memorandum, the articles registered at the same time may be used to explain it, but not so as to extend the objects". But this rule, as is shown in the above work itself, will not apply to the interpretation "of those portions of the memorandum of association which the Act of Parliament requires to be stated in the memorandum". "In any case" to quote BOWEN LJ again, "it is certain that for any thing which the Act of Parliament says shall be in the memorandum, you must look to the memorandum alone. If the Legislature has said one instrument is to be dominant you cannot turn to another instrument and read it in order to modify the provisions of the dominant instrument".[18]

BINDING FORCE OF MEMORANDUM AND ARTICLES [S. 36]

Section 36 declares:

Subject to the provisions of this Act, the memorandum and articles shall, when registered, bind the company and the members thereof to the same extent as if they respectively had been signed by the company and by each member, and contained covenants on its and his part to observe all the provisions of the memorandum and of the articles.[19]

In reference to the corresponding provision in the English Act Gower observes: "The exact effect of what is now Section 20(1) of the Companies Act has long been one of the most baffling questions in company law."[20]

The section aims to impart contractual force to the memorandum and articles. It is only the exact limits of that effect and the persons it is intended to cover that are somewhat uncertain. The law may be stated in terms of the following propositions:

1. Binding on members in their relation to company

In the first place, the members are bound to the company by the provisions of the articles "just as much as if they had all put their seals to them",[21] and had thus contracted to conform to them. In the words of Lord

---

16. (1959) 20th Edn by Schmitthoff and Curry, 58.
17. [1876-77] 7 Ch D 75. The passage relating to contemporaneous documents occurs at p 90.
18. *Guinness v Land Corpn of Ireland*, (1882) 22 Ch D 349, 381.
19. Knowledge of the documents being necessary for this purpose, S. 39 entitles members to get copies of the memorandum, articles and special resolutions on payment of fee of Re. 1. The company is bound to comply with the request within 7 days or else there is a running penalty for the default. Section 36(2) declares that all money payable by any member to the company under the company's memorandum and articles shall be a debt due from him to the company.
20. *The Contractual Effects of Articles of Assn*, 21 Mod LR 401. For a view of this baffling problem, *see* [1957] Camb LJ 194: [1958] Camb LJ 93.
21. BOWEN LJ in *Imperial Hydropathic Hotel Co v Hampson*, (1882) 23 Ch D 1, 13.

HERSCHELL: "It is quite true that the articles constitute a contract between each member and the company."[22] In *Borland's Trustee* v *Steel Bros & Co Ltd*:[23]

> The articles of association of the defendant company contained clauses to the effect that on the bankruptcy of a member his shares would be sold to a person and at a price fixed by the directors. *B*, a shareholder, was adjudicated bankrupt. His trustee in bankruptcy claimed that he was not bound by these provisions and should be at liberty to sell the shares at their true value. But it was held that "contracts contained in the articles of association is one of the original incidents of the shares. Shares having been purchased on those terms and conditions, it is impossible to say that those terms and conditions are not to be observed".[24]

2. Binding on company in its relation to members

Secondly, just as members are bound to the company, the company is bound to the members to observe and follow the articles. "Each member is entitled to say that there shall be no breach of the articles and he is entitled to an injunction to prevent the breach."[25] This is clear from the section itself which says that "the memorandum and articles shall bind the company". In *Wood* v *Odessa Waterworks Co*:[26]

> The articles of the Waterworks Co, provided that 'the directors may, with the sanction of the company at general meeting, declare a dividend to be paid to the members'. Instead of paying the dividend in cash to the shareholders a resolution was passed to give them debenture bonds. In an action by a member to restrain the directors from acting on the resolution, STIRLING J held: "The question is whether that which is proposed to be done in the present case is in accordance with the articles of association of the company. Those articles provide that the directors may, with the sanction of a general meeting, declare a dividend to be paid to shareholders. Prima facie that means to be paid in cash. The

22. *Welton* v *Saffery*, 1897 AC 299, 315: [1895-9] All ER Rep 567.
23. [1901] 1 Ch 279.
24. *See* also *New London & Brazilian Bank* v *Brocklebank*, (1882) 21 Ch D 302, 308; *Bradford Banking Co* v *Briggs Son & Co*, (1886) 12 App Cas 29: 56 LT 62; *Gan Sin Tuan* v *Chew Kian Kor*, (1957) 24 Malayan LJ 62; *Lyle & Scott* v *Scott's Trustees*, 1959 AC 763. In the exercise of the powers of the Government company under its articles the Government could change the status of a permanent Government servant serving in the company. *Jawahar Lal Sazawal* v *State of J&K*, (2002) 3 SCC 219.
25. BYRNE J in *Peveril Gold Mines Ltd, Re*, [1898] 1 Ch 122.
26. (1889) 42 Ch D 636. *Tony Francis Guiness* v *Indekka Software (P) Ltd*, (2006) 131 Comp Cas 846 Bom, provision in the articles for increasing capital by passing a resolution by consent vote, resolution was passed without consent vote, there was failure to communicate the offer of shares to the complaining shareholder either by registered post or under certificate of posting, directors were restrained from acting on the resolution.

debenture bonds proposed to be issued are not a payment in cash."
Accordingly the directors were restrained from acting on the resolution.

3. But not binding in relation to outsiders

Thus, the articles bind the members to the company and the company to
the members. But neither of them is bound to an outsider to give effect to the
articles. "No article can constitute a contract between the company and a
third person." For example, in *Browne v La Trinidad*:[27]

> The articles of association of a company contained a clause to the
> effect that *B*, should be a director and should not be removable till after
> 1888. He was, however, removed earlier and had brought an action to
> restrain the company from excluding him. It was held that there was no
> contract between *B* and the company. No outsider can enforce articles
> against the company even if they purport to give him certain rights.

Who is an outsider?—Who is an outsider for this purpose? The
expression naturally means a person who is not a member. But even a
member may be an outsider. Section 36 creates an obligation binding on the
company in its dealings with the 'members', but the word 'members' in this
section means members in their capacity as members, that is, excluding any
relationship which does not flow from the membership itself. *Eley v Positive
Government Security Life Assurance Co* is a leading authority.[28]

> The articles of a company contained a clause that the plaintiff (Eley)
> should be the solicitor to the company and should not be removed from
> his office unless there was misconduct. He was a member also. He acted
> as a solicitor to the company for some time, but ultimately the company
> substituted other solicitors for him. He brought an action against the
> company for breach of the contract in not employing him as a solicitor
> on the terms of the articles. His action was dismissed. Even a member
> cannot enforce the provisions of articles for his benefit in some other
> capacity than that of a member.

"The purpose of the memorandum and articles is to define the position of
the shareholder as shareholder, not to bind him in his capacity as an
individual."[29] Thus "a third person who purports to have rights against the
company would be precluded from relying on the articles as a basis of his
claim and must prove a special contract outside the articles".[30] But sometimes
the articles may create an implied contract between the company and a third
person.[31] Where, for example, on the footing of a clause in the articles a
person is employed to serve the company in some capacity, such as a director,
and he accepts the office, the terms of the article are embodied in and form

---

27. (1887) 37 Ch D 1.
28. (1876) Ex D 881.
29. BUCKLEY LJ in *Bisgood v Henderson's Transvaal Estates Ltd*, (1908) 1 Ch 743, 759.
30. *Duraiswami v UIL Assurance Co*, AIR 1956 Mad 316; *Ramkumar Potdar v Sholapur Wvg &
    Spg Co*, AIR 1934 Bom 427: (1934) 36 Bom LR 907.
31. *Issacs* case, (1892) Ch D 158; *Beckwith* case, (1898) 1 Ch D 324.

part of the contract between the company and the director.[32] "Articles do not themselves form a contract, but from them you get the terms upon which the director is serving."[33] Following these principles the Lahore High Court held in a case before it that—

> Where in pursuance of certain articles acted upon by the company, a member was appointed managing director and acted for eleven years in that capacity, the articles constitute an implied contract between the member and the company. If the company removes him from office, he would be entitled to damages for the breach.[34]

4. How far binding between members

Lastly, how far do the articles bind one member to another? Unfortunately, on this point the law has yet to take a final shape. The Companies Act does not purport to settle the rights of members *inter se*. It leaves these to be determined by the articles. Hence articles define the rights and liabilities of members. But whether those rights and liabilities can be enforced by one member against another is the moot point. Lord HERSCHELL said in *Welton* v *Saffery*:[35] "It is quite true that articles constitute a contract between each member and the company, and that there is no contract in terms between individual members of the company; but the articles do not any the less regulate their rights *inter se*. Such rights can only be enforced by or against a member through the company." "Memorandum and articles did not constitute a contract between the members *inter se*, although they regulated their rights which could be enforced through the company and that they only regulated the rights of the members *qua* members for the purposes of the company law."[36] Thus in a case before the Calcutta High Court,[37] a member of a company who had a commercial dispute of private nature with another member could not be compelled to refer the dispute to arbitration in terms of the company's articles. The Court said: "Articles do not affect or regulate the rights arising out of a commercial contract with which the members have no concern, rights completely outside the company relationship."[38]

---

32. *See* WRIGHT J in *New British Iron Co, Re*, [1898] 1 Ch 324: [1895-9] All ER Rep Ext 1655.
33. Lord ESHER MR in *Swabey* v *Port Darwin Gold Mining Co*, (1889) 1 Meg 385 CA.
34. *Sardar Gulab Singh* v *Punjab Zamindara Bank Ltd*, AIR 1942 Lah 47. *See* also *Krishna Rao* v *Anjaneyulu*, AIR 1954 Mad 113; *International Cable Co, Re*, (1892) 66 LT 253; *Sree Meenakshi Mills Ltd* v *Callianjee & Sons*, 1935 Comp Cas 102 Bom. For further study *see*, G.D. Goldberg: *The Enforcement of Outsider Rights*, (1972) 35 Mod LR 362.
35. 1897 AC 299, 315: [1895-99] All ER Rep 567.
36. *Khusiram* v *Hanutmal*, (1948) 53 CWN 505, 520.
37. *Ibid*.
38. Similarly, in *Dale & Plant Ltd, Re*, (1889) 61 LT 206, a secretary working on the terms of articles of association was not allowed to prove a claim for damages for termination of services on account of winding up. In *Beattie* v *Beattie*, [1938] Ch 708, a provision in the articles for arbitration could not be enforced by a director who was sued for wrongs done in

It follows that the extent to which the articles seek to regulate the rights of shareholders as shareholders, they can be directly enforced by one member against another without joining the company as a party. The case of *Rayfields* v *Hands*[39] lends support to this conclusion:

The plaintiff was a shareholder in a company. Clause 11 of the company's articles required him to inform the directors of his intention to transfer his shares in the company and which provided that the directors will take the said shares equally between them at a fair value. In accordance with this provision the plaintiff so notified the directors, who contended that they were not bound to take and pay for the plaintiff's shares. The articles, they said, could impose no such obligation upon them in their capacity as directors. This argument was brushed aside by the court by treating the directors as members. Accordingly the directors were compelled to take the plaintiff's shares at a fair value and it was not considered necessary for the plaintiff to succeed in his action, that he should join the company as a party.[40]

ALTERATION OF ARTICLES [S. 31]

Every company has a clear power to alter its articles of association by a special resolution. It is a statutory power given by Section 31, and, therefore, it cannot be negatived by contract. If, for example, there is a clause in the articles providing that the company would not introduce any change in its original articles, it will be invalid on the ground that it is contrary to the statute. Similarly, a company cannot deprive itself of the power of alteration by a contract with any one.[41]

---

his capacity as a director. All such cases have been considered in G.D. Goldberg, *The Enforcement of Outsider Rights under S. 20(1) of the Companies Act*, (1972) 35 Mod LR 362. *See* also *Hickman* v *Kent or Romeny Marsh Sheep Breeders' Assn, Re*, [1915] 1 Ch 881. *Skypark Builders & Distributors* v *Kerala Police Housing & Construction Co Ltd*, (2003) 114 Comp Cas 425 Ker, the memorandum and articles of a Government company provided that the directors would be competent to refer disputes to arbitration. This was held to be an enabling provision and not a compulsory requirement. No agreement could be inferred from it.

39. [1958] 2 WLR 851: [1960] Ch 1: [1958] 2 All ER 194.
40. L.C.B. Gower welcomes the decision in 21 MLR 101. For another critical appreciation *see* Bastin, *The Enforcement of a Member's Rights*, 1977 JBL 17 at p 25.
41. See *Melson* v *National Ins & Guarantee Co*, [1874] 1 Ch 200; *Walker* v *London Tramways Co*, (1879) 12 Ch 705; *Punt* v *Symons & Co*, [1903] 2 Ch 506: [1900-3] All ER Rep Ext 1040; *All India Rly Men's Benefit Fund* v *Baheshwarnath*, AIR 1945 Nag 187. A provision in the articles depriving the company of its power of alteration would be void, *Malleson* v *National Insurance Corpn* (1894) 1 Ch 200. The court does not have an inherent power to force a company to alter its articles. *Scott* v *Frank F. Scott (London) Ltd*, (1940) 1 All ER 508 CA: (1940) Ch 794 CA. The Company Law Board has the power under Sections 402-404 to force a company to alter its articles if it is necessary for prevention of oppression and mismanagement. An irregular alteration pushed through without observing the requirements of a special resolution can be rectified through court order. The court may not interfere where the alteration had been acted upon for long or was the result of the shareholders'

The altered articles will bind the members just in the same way as did the original articles.[42] But that will not give the alteration a retrospective effect.[43] A transfer of shares when first presented was permissible within the company's articles, but it was rejected because the stamps were not cancelled. Before it could be presented again, the company changed articles excluding such transfers. The alteration was held to be effective against the transfer.[44]

The power of alteration of articles as conferred by Section 31 is almost absolute. It is subject only to two restrictions. In the first place, the alteration must not be in contravention of the provisions of the Act. It should not be an attempt to do something which the Act forbids.[45] Secondly, the power of alteration of articles is subject to the conditions contained in the memorandum of association. The proviso to sub-section (1) says that an alteration which has the effect of converting a public company into a private company would not have any effect unless it is approved by the Central Government.

Alteration against memorandum

Sometimes a change in the articles seems apparently to influence the memorandum. To take, for example, *Hutton v Scarborough Cliff Hotel Co*[46].

A resolution passed at a general meeting of a company altered the articles of association by inserting the power to issue new shares with preferential dividend. No such power existed in the memorandum.

The alteration was held to be inoperative. The issuing of new shares with a preferential dividend was considered to be a variation of the

---

agreement without a formal resolution. *Joseph Michael* v *Travancore Rubber & Tea Co Ltd*, (1986) 59 Comp Cas 898 Ker; *Cane* v *Jones* (1981) 1 All ER 533.
42. S. 31(2). Section 2(2) says that " 'articles' means the articles of association of a company as originally framed or as altered from time to time. . . ." The procedure of special resolution has to be followed for making any change in the articles even if the change is intended only to rectify an error or a mistake, *Scott* v *Frank F. Scott (London) Ltd*, (1940) 1 All ER 508 CA.
43. *Swaminathan M.* v *Chairman*, 1988 Writ LR 41, 51 Mad. Section 40 requires that the alteration shall be noted in every copy of the document subsequently issued. *M. V. Shekaran* v *Jt Registrar of Coop Societies*, (1995) All HC 2798 Ker, alteration of articles retrospectively to enable a company to recover its dues from members was held to be for the benefit of the company and, therefore, valid.
44. *Mathrubhumi Ltd* v *Vardhman Publishers Ltd*, [1992] 1 Comp LJ 234 Ker DB: (1992) 73 Comp Cas 80 Ker overruling on this point *Vardhaman Publishers Ltd* v *Mathrubhumi Ltd*, (1991) 71 Comp Cas 1, 37 Ker. It was observed in *Allen* v *Gold Reefs of West Africa*, (1900) 1 Ch 656 that alteration of articles giving extended lien was not retrospective. It was not made to take effect before the date of alteration. It operated only from and after that date. *M. V. Shekaran* v *Jt Registrar of Coop Societies*, 1995 All HC 2798 Ker, an alteration to enforce recovery of the company's debts, held valid.
45. *See*, for example, *Madhava Ramachandra Kamath* v *Canara Bkg Corpn Ltd*, AIR 1941 Mad 354, where a resolution was passed expelling a member and authorising the directors to register the transfer of his shares without an instrument of transfer. The resolution was held to be invalid as being against the Companies Act.
46. (1865) 62 ER 717: 2 Dr & Sm 521.

constitution of the company as fixed by the memorandum. "The question is", said the Vice-Chancellor, "whether the power given to the general meeting, by special resolution to modify the regulations of the company is unlimited: clearly there must be some limit to the power; otherwise they might alter not only such articles as relate to the management of the company, but they might alter the very nature and constitution of the company."

It must be noted that the memorandum was silent. It neither authorised nor prohibited the issue of preference shares. The court inferred from its silence that it intended equality of status of all the shareholders. But now the courts refuse to draw this inference. The power of alteration of articles is subject only to what is clearly prohibited by the memorandum, expressly or impliedly. This change was brought about by the decision in *Andrews* v *Gas Meter Co Ltd*[47].

By the 5th clause of a company's memorandum it was stated that the nominal capital of the company was £60,000 divided into 600 shares of £ 100 each. Neither in the memorandum nor in the original articles was there any provision as to preference shares. A special resolution was passed authorising the directors to issue shares bearing a preferential dividend, which was accordingly done.

It was held that the issue was valid. "If this had been forbidden by the memorandum, it could not have been done: but as it was not; it was immaterial that the change quite altered the composition of the company."[48]

Alteration of articles to provide for compulsory transfer of shares against the shareholders' wishes was held to be permissible and binding on the shareholders.[49]

Alteration in breach of contract

Sometimes an alteration of articles may operate as a breach of contract with an outsider. To take, for instance, a Madras case.[50] A clause in the articles of a company provided Rs 250 a month as the remuneration of the

---

47. [1897] 1 Ch 361: [1895-99] All ER Rep 1280. The unsoundness of the decision in *Hutton* v *Scarborough, etc.* was distinctly pointed by Lord MACNAGHTEN in *British & American Trustee & Finance Corpn* v *Couper*, 1894 AC 399: [1891-94] All ER Rep 667. His Lordship said at 417: "It seems that the decision in *Hutton* v *Scarborough Cliff Hotel Co*, (1865) 62 ER 717: 2 Dr & Sm 521 was not founded upon a sound view of the Companies Act, 1862 and I respectfully dissent from it. COTTON LJ disapproved of the chief ground on which the decision was based. "In reality it is not by implication from the construction of the memorandum that equality of the shareholders as regards dividends arises, but by the implication which the law raises as between partners unless their contract has provided the contrary. *Guinness* v *Land Corpn of Ireland*, 22 Ch D 349 at p 377. I agree that the equality of shareholders as regards dividend is an implied condition of the memorandum."
48. Topham's summing up of the decision at 44 of his PRINCIPLES OF COMPANY LAW, 12th Edn.
49. *Gothami Solvent Oils Ltd* v *Malline Bharathi Rao*, (2001) 105 Comp Cas 710 AP.
50. *Chithambaram Chettiar* v *Krishna Aiyangar*, ILR 33 Mad 36.

company's secretary. The plaintiff accepted the post upon those terms. Subsequently, the company modified the article and reduced the secretary's pay to Rs 25 a month. Could this be done? The answer depends upon the nature of the contract. If the contract is wholly dependent upon the provisions of the articles, as it was in this case, the alteration would naturally be operative. Articles are subject to the statutory power of alteration. Anyone accepting an appointment purely on the terms of the articles takes the risk of those terms being altered.[51]

But, where apart from the articles, the company has entered into an independent agreement, the company may repudiate it by changing articles, but it will be answerable in damages for the breach. "A company cannot, by altering articles, justify a breach of contract."[52] *Southern Foundries Ltd* v *Shirlaw*[53] is the leading authority.

The plaintiff was a director in the defendant company. In 1933 he was appointed as a managing director for a term of ten years. In 1935 the defendant company was amalgamated with another company and new articles were adopted under which powers were taken to dismiss a director. It was further provided that a managing director's appointment would be subject to determination, ipso facto, if he ceased to be a director. Under these articles the plaintiff was removed from the office of director. He sued for the wrongful repudiation of the contract. It was held that the agreement was unqualified in regard to the term of ten years. The removal was, therefore, a breach of the agreement for which the employer must answer in damages.

The court may even restrain an alteration where it is likely to cause a damage which cannot be adequately compensated in terms of money. The facts of *British Murac Syndicate Ltd* v *Alperton Rubber Co.*[54] involved a situation of this kind.

An agreement provided that so long as the plaintiff syndicate should hold 5,000 shares in the defendant company, it should have the right of nominating two directors on the board of the defendant company. A provision to the same effect was contained in Article 88 of the defendant company's articles. The plaintiff syndicate had nominated two persons as directors whom the defendant company refused to accept. An attempt was then made to cancel Article 88, but an

---

51. *Farrer (T.N.) Ltd, Re*, [1937] 1 Ch 352: 106 LJ Ch 305: (1937) 2 All ER 505.
52. *Baily* v *British Equitable Assurance Co*, [1904] 1 Ch 374; COZENS-HARDY LJ reversed on appeal 1906 AC 35. *Mathrubhumi Ltd* v *Vardhman Publishers Ltd*, (1992) 73 Comp Cas 1, 37 Ker, where the court held that the alteration would be valid in spite of breach of contract.
53. 1940 AC 701: [1940] 2 All ER 445; *Madanlal* v *Changdeo Sugar Mills*, AIR 1958 Bom 250.
54. [1915] 2 Ch 186. An injunction was not issued to prevent the holding of an extraordinary general meeting called for the purpose of changing articles in such wise as could affect seriously the position of the company's managing or wholetime directors, *K.G. Khosla* v *R.C. Kirloskar*, (1997) 24 Corpt LA 30 Del.

injunction was granted to restrain it. "The contract clearly involved as one of its terms that Article 88 was not to be altered, that is, that the plaintiff syndicate so long as it held the stipulated number of shares, was to have a perpetual right of nominating two directors of the company."[55]

In another case, COZENS HARDY LJ said:[56]

It would be dangerous to hold that in a contract of loan or a contract of service or a contract of insurance validly entered into by a company there is any greater power of variation of the rights and liabilities of the parties than would exist if, instead of the company, the contracting party had been an individual.

In a case before the Calcutta High Court[57]—

The plaintiff had taken out a policy of life insurance in the defendant company. He was entitled under the contract to draw from the company a certain sum on a certain date. The company altered its articles by which such sums were made payable out of a special fund. At the time the amount became payable to the assured, that fund was insolvent. The plaintiff sued for his payment under the original contract.

It was held that "the effect of the alteration of articles was that it involved a fundamental breach of contract which the company had previously entered into with the plaintiff and in respect of that contract the (new) article was inapplicable."

Increasing liability of members

An alteration cannot require a member to purchase more shares or increase his liability in any way except with his consent in writing.[58] A person who becomes a member under the protection of limited liability cannot be converted into a member with unlimited liability except with his consent in writing.

Fraud on minority shareholders

Lastly, the alteration must not constitute a "fraud on the minority".[59]

---

55. SARGENT LJ at 194, *ibid.* Thus there can be a provision that articles will not be altered except with the consent of a particular person. Special rights of a shareholder may not be alterable without his consent. *Cumbrian Newspapers Groups Ltd* v *Cumberland & Westmorland Herald Newspaper & Printing Co Ltd*, (1986) 1 WLR 26: (1986) 2 All ER 816: [1987] 2 Comp LJ 39. In the case of a private company specially weighted voting rights may be given to a member-director to safeguard his interest, *Bushell* v *Faith*, (1970) 1 All ER 53 HL.
56. *Baily* v *British Equitable Assurance Co* , [1904] 1 Ch 374; on appeal 1906 AC 35.
57. *Hari Chandana* v *Hindustan Insurance Society*, AIR 1925 Cal 690.
58. S. 38 which, however, permits incorporated clubs and associations to increase the annual subscription of its members.
59. For detailed study of the concept of "fraud on the minority" *see* Chap. 15 below on "MAJORITY POWERS AND MINORITY RIGHTS". The basic requirements are that the power of alteration must be exercised in good faith in the interests of the company and also fairly as

CONSTRUCTIVE NOTICE OF MEMORANDUM
AND ARTICLES OF ASSOCIATION

The memorandum and articles of association of every company are registered with the Registrar of Companies. The office of the Registrar is a public office and consequently the memorandum and articles become public documents. They are open and accessible to all.[60] It is, therefore, the duty of every person dealing with a company to inspect its public documents and make sure that his contract is in conformity with their provisions. But whether a person actually reads them or not, "he is to be in the same position as if he had read them". He will be presumed to know the contents of those documents.[61] This kind of presumed notice is called constructive notice. *Kotla Venkataswamy* v *Rammurthy*[62] shows the practical effects of this rule.

> The articles of association of a company required that all deeds etc., should be signed by the managing director, the secretary and a working director on behalf of the company. The plaintiff accepted a deed of mortgage executed by the secretary and a working director only. It was held that the plaintiff could not claim under this deed. The court observed: "If the plaintiff had consulted the articles she would have discovered that a deed such as she took required execution by three specified officers of the company and she would have refrained from accepting a deed inadequately signed. Notwithstanding, therefore, she may have acted in good faith and her money may have been applied to the purposes of the company, the bond is nevertheless invalid."

Another effect of this rule is that a person dealing with the company is "taken not only to have read those documents but to have understood them according to their proper meaning".[63] He is presumed to have understood not merely the company's powers but also those of its officers.[64] Further, there is constructive notice not merely of the memorandum and articles, but also of all the documents, such as special resolutions[65] and particulars of charges[66] which are required by the Act to be registered with the Registrar.[67] But there is no notice of documents which are filed only for the sake of

---

between different classes of shareholders. *Mutual Life Insurance Co of New York* v *Rank Organisation*, 1995 BCLC 11.

60. The right of inspection, etc., is expressly granted by S. 610 of the Act.
61. *See* Lord HATHERLEY in *Mahony* v *East Holyford Mining Co*, (1875) LR 7 HL 869, 893: [1874-80] All ER Rep 427; Wilberforce, *Law and Economics*, 1966 JBL 301, where the protection afforded by a public register is explained.
62. AIR 1934 Mad 579.
63. Palmer's COMPANY LAW, 243, 20th Edn by Schmitthoff and Curry (1959). *See* also *Oakbank Oil Co* v *Crum*, (1882) 8 AC 65, 71.
64. *Ridley* v *Plymouth Grinding & Baking Co*, (1848) 2 Exch 711.
65. S. 192.
66. S. 125.
67. See *William Twuin* v *Union Bank of Australia*, [1877] 2 AC 366.

record, such as returns and accounts. According to Palmer, the principle applies only to documents which affect the powers of the company.[68] One of the suggested approaches is that all documents which are open to public inspection should be regarded as public documents.[69] This is in keeping with the disclosure philosophy of company law and things which are required to be disclosed in a public office should have public effects and should be usable as instruments of public accountability. In reference to the document containing "particulars of directors" it has been held that it becomes a 'public document'. Persons dealing with the company would be deemed to have constructive notice as to who are the directors of the company, Accordingly, if a document is required to be signed by a director and the person actually signing is not there in the document filed by the company, it would not be a properly signed document. The court said: "...the common law doctrine of constructive notice should apply to the form. To reiterate the form is a public document which contains particulars of directors who are the mind and will of a company, as well as managers and secretaries who are responsible for the day-to-day running of the company. It is a document which affects the powers of the company and its agents. Certainly, its purpose must be more than just to provide information about the company's directors, manager and secretary. Therefore, persons dealing with the company should check with the registrar of companies who its directors, managers and secretaries are at any given time".[70]

Statutory reform of constructive notice [S. 35-A of 1989]

Constructive notice is more or less an unreal doctrine. It does not take notice of the realities of business life. People know a company through its officers and not through its documents. Section 9 of the European Communities Act, 1972 has abrogated this doctrine. The provisions of Section 9 are now incorporated in Section 35 of the Companies Act, 1985 [English]. An example of the impact of the new provisions has been provided by a case[71] where a debenture issued by a company was signed by a solicitor as attorney of a director of the company, but not by the director personally. The articles of the company provided that "every instrument to which the seal shall be affixed shall be signed by a director". Even so the company was held liable. Stating the effect of the new provision, the court said that before this enactment came into force a person dealing with the company was required to look at the memorandum and articles of the company to satisfy himself that the transaction was within the corporate capacity but that Section 9(1) had changed this. The sub-section says that

---

68. Company Law, 243 (20th Edn, 1959).
69. *See* R. Baxt, *Negligent Statements in Company Accounts*, (1973) 36 Mod LR at pp 43-44.
70. *K. L. Engg* v *Arab Malaysia Finance*, (1995) 1 SCR 85 Malaysia.
71. *TCB Ltd* v *Gray*, Financial Times, Nov 27, 1985; 1986 JBL 10, where it is felt that the decision indicated the great change—and a change to the better.

good faith is to be presumed and that the person dealing with the company is not bound to inquire. The expression "a person dealing with a company" has been held not to include a shareholder allottee. The court refused to validate an allotment of bonus shares by using the share premium account without authorisation.[72] The courts in India also do not seem to have taken the rule of constructive notice seriously. For example, in *Dehra Dun Mussoorie Electric Tramway Co* v *Jagmandardas*,[73] the articles of a company expressly provided that the directors could delegate all their powers except the power to borrow. Even so an overdraft taken by the managing agents without approval of the board was held to be binding, the court saying that such temporary loans must be kept outside the purview of the relevant provision. Similarly, the Calcutta High Court enforced a security which was not signed in accordance with the company's articles.[74]

DOCTRINE OF 'INDOOR MANAGEMENT'

Scope of operation

The role of the doctrine of indoor management is opposed to that of the rule of constructive notice. The latter seeks to protect the company against the outsider, the former operates to protect outsiders against the company. The rule of constructive notice is confined to the external position of the company and, therefore, it follows that there is no notice as to how the company's internal machinery is handled by its officers. If the contract is consistent with the public documents, the person contracting will not be prejudiced by irregularities that may beset the indoor working of the company. The rule had its genesis in *Royal British Bank* v *Turquand*.[75]

> The directors of a company borrowed a sum of money from the plaintiff. The company's articles provided that the directors might borrow on bonds such sums as may from time to time be authorised by a resolution passed at a general meeting of the company. The shareholders claimed that there had been no such resolution authorising the loan and, therefore, it was taken without their authority. The company was, however, held bound by the loan. Once it was found that the directors could borrow subject to a resolution, the plaintiff had the right to infer that the necessary resolution must have been passed.

In a subsequent case the rule is thus stated: "If the directors have power and authority to bind the company, but certain preliminaries are required to be gone through on the part of the company before that power can be duly

---

72. *EIC Services Ltd* v *Phipps*, (2004) EWCA 1069: (2005) 1 WLR 1377 (CA).
73. AIR 1932 All 141.
74. *Charnock Collieries Ltd* v *Bholanath*, ILR (1912) 39 Cal 810 and *Probodh Chandra Mitra* v *Road Oils (India) Ltd*, ILR (1929) 57 Cal 1101: AIR 1930 Cal 782.
75. (1856) 119 ER 886.

exercised, then the person contracting with the directors is not bound to see that all these preliminaries have been observed. He is entitled to presume that the directors are acting lawfully in what they do."[76]

The rule is based upon obvious reasons of convenience in business relations. Firstly, the memorandum and articles of association are public documents, open to public inspection. But the details of internal procedure are not thus open to public inspection. Hence an outsider "is presumed to know the constitution of a company; but not what may or may not have taken place within the doors that are closed to him".[77] The wheels of commerce would not go round smoothly if persons dealing with companies were compelled to investigate thoroughly "the internal machinery of a company to see if something is not wrong".[78] People in business would be very shy in dealing with such companies.[79]

Yet another reason is explained by Gower in these words: "The lot of creditors of a limited company is not a particularly happy one; it would be unhappier still if the company could escape liability by denying the authority of the officials to act on its behalf."[80]

The rule is of great practical utility. It has been applied in a great variety of cases involving rights and liabilities. It has been used to cover acts done on behalf of a company by *de facto* directors who have never been appointed,[81] or whose appointment is defective,[82] or who, having been regularly appointed, have exercised an authority which could have been delegated to them under the company's articles, but never has been so delegated,[83] or who have exercised an authority without proper quorum.[84] Thus, where the directors of a company having the power to allot shares only with the consent of the general meeting, allotted them without any such

---

76. *Premier Industrial Bank Ltd* v *Carlton Manufacturing Co Ltd*, [1909] 1 KB 106, citing *Fountaine* v *Carmarthen Rly Co*, (1868) LR 5 Eq 316; *Rajendra Nath Dutta* v *Shibendra Nath Mukherjee*, (1982) 52 Comp Cas 293 Cal.
77. *Pacific Coast Coal Mines Ltd* v *Arbuthnot*, 1917 AC 607.
78. *Dey* v *Pullinger Engg Co*, [1921] 1 KB 77.
79. *Morris* v *Kanssen*, 1946 AC 459: [1946] 1 All ER 586, 592: 174 LT 353.
80. MODERN COMPANY LAW, 153 (3rd Edn, 1969).
81. *Mahony* v *East Holyford Mining Co*, (1875) 33 TLR 338, money withdrawn from company's banking account by *de facto* directors; *Sree Meenakshi Mills Ltd* v *Callianjee & Sons*, AIR 1935 Mad 799; *Duck* v *Tower Galvanizing Co*, [1901] 2 KB 314; *Imperial Oil, Soap & General Mills* v *Wazir Singh*, AIR 1915 Lah 478.
82. *Pudumjee & Co* v *N. H. Moos*, AIR 1926 Bom 28; *Probodh Chandra Mitra* v *Road Oils (India) Ltd*, ILR (1929) 57 Cal 1101: AIR 1930 Cal 782.
83. *Biggerstaff* v *Rowatt's Wharf Ltd*, [1896] 2 Ch 93: [1895-99] All ER Rep Ext 1933; *Premier Industrial Bank Ltd* v *Carlton Mfg Co Ltd*, [1909] 1 KB 106; *Dey* v *Pullinger Engg Co*, [1921] 1 KB 77; *Kishan Rathi* v *Mondal Bros & Co*, [1966] 1 Comp LJ 19 Cal.
84. *County of Gloucester Bank* v *Rudry Merthyr Steam & House Coal Colliery Co*, [1895] 1 Ch 629.

consent;[85] where the managing director of a company granted a lease of the company's properties, something which he could do only with the approval of the board;[86] where the managing agents having the power to borrow with the approval of directors borrowed without any such approval,[87] the company was held bound.[88]

Exceptions

The rule is now more than a century old. In view of the fact that companies having come to occupy the central position in the social and economic life of modern communities, it was expected that its scope would be widened. But the course of decisions has made it subject to the following exceptions:

1. Knowledge of irregularity

The first and the most obvious restrictions is that the rule has no application where the party affected by an irregularity had actual notice of it. "Thus where a transfer of shares was approved by two directors, one of whom within the knowledge of the transferor was disqualified by reason of being the transferee himself and the other was never validly appointed, the transfer was held to be ineffective.[89]

Knowledge of an irregularity may arise from the fact that the person contracting was himself a party to the inside procedure. In *Howard* v *Patent Ivory Manufacturing Co*,[90] for example, the directors could not defend the

---

85. *P.V. Damodara Reddy* v *Indian National Agencies Ltd*, AIR 1946 Mad 35; *Commr of Agricultural IT* v *H. S. Mills*, AIR 1965 Pat 58.
86. *Khulna Loan Co* v *Jahir Goldar*, (1914) 24 IC 20.
87. *Charnock Collieries Ltd* v *Bholanath*, ILR (1912) 39 Cal 810; *Balasaraswathi Ltd* v *A. Parameswara*, AIR 1957 Mad 122; *Varkey* v *Keraleeya Bkg Co*, AIR 1957 Ker 97; *Damodara Reddy* v *Indian National Agencies*, AIR 1964 Mad 35.
88. *See* also *Sree Meenakshi Mills Ltd* v *Callianjee & Sons*, AIR 1935 Mad 799. There are indeed, many illustrations. For example, *Dewan Singh Hira Singh* v *Minerva Films Ltd*, AIR 1959 Punj 106. Under a company's articles the directors had the power to allot only 5,000 'A' class shares. They, however, went much beyond and allotted above 13,000. It was held that "the allottees of shares were contracting in good faith with the company, and they were entitled to assume that the acts of the directors in making allotments to them were within the scope of their powers conferred upon them by the shareholders of the company. They were not bound to inquire whether the acts of the directors which related to internal management had been properly and regularly performed." *Changa Mal* v *Provincial Bank Ltd*, ILR 1914 All 412, an allotment of shares by an irregularly constituted board of directors was held binding on the company. For other illustrations, see *Abdul Rehman Khan* v *Mufassal Bank Ltd*, (1926) 24 ALJ 593; *Ram Baran Singh* v *Mufassal Bank Ltd* (2), AIR 1925 All 206; *D. Pudumjee & Co* v *N. H. Moos*, (1925) 27 Bom LR 1218; *Probodh Chandra Mitra* v *Road Oils (India) Ltd*, ILR (1929) 57 Cal 1101: AIR 1930 Cal 782, where it was held that irregularity in affixing seal on documents required by articles to be under seal is a part of internal machinery. For a detailed account of the cases on the subject *see* P.S. Sangal, *Royal British Bank* v *Turquand & Indian Law*, [1964] 2 Comp LJ 173.
89. *Devi Ditta Mal* v *Standard Bank of India*, (1927) 101 IC 568. All such cases have been reviewed in *A. J. Judah* v *Rampada Gupta*, AIR 1959 Cal 715, 732.
90. (1888) 38 Ch D 156.

issue of debentures to themselves because they should have known that the extent to which they were lending money to the company required the assent of the general meeting which they had not obtained. Similarly, in *Morris* v *Kanssen*[91] a director could not defend an allotment of shares to him as he participated in the meeting which made the allotment. His appointment as a director also fell through because none of the directors appointing him was validly in office. The trend of decisions has been slightly altered by *Hely-Hutchinson* v *Brayhead Ltd*,[92] according to which the mere fact that a person is a director does not mean that he shall be deemed to have knowledge of the irregularities practised by the other directors. A newly appointed director entered into contracts of indemnity and guarantee with the company through a director whom the company had knowingly allowed to hold himself out as having the authority to enter into such transactions, although in fact he had no such authority. The new director had no knowledge of the irregularity. The company was held liable.

But apart from this, the principle is clear that a person who is himself a part of the internal machinery cannot take the advantage of irregularities. Any other rule would "encourage ignorance and condone dereliction from duty".[93]

2. Suspicion of irregularity

The protection of "the *Turquand* rule" is also not available where the circumstances surrounding the contract are suspicious and, therefore, invite inquiry. Suspicion should arise, for example, from the fact that an officer is purporting to act in a manner which is apparently outside the scope of his authority. Where, for example, the plaintiff accepted a transfer of a company's property from its accountant, the transfer was held void. The plaintiff could not have supposed, in the absence of a power of attorney, that the accountant had authority to effect transfer of the company's property.[94] Where a person holding directorship in two companies agreed to apply the money of one company in payment of the debt of the other, the court said that it was something so unusual "that the plaintiffs were put upon inquiry to ascertain whether the persons making the contract had any authority in fact to make it". Any other rule would " place limited companies without any sufficient reasons for so doing, at the mercy of any servant or agent who should purport to contract on their behalf".[95]

---

91. 1946 AC 459: [1946] 1 All ER 586: 174 LT 353.
92. [1967] 3 WLR 1408: [1967] 2 Comp LJ 676: [1967] 2 All ER 14: [1968] 1 QB 549 CA.
93. *Morris* v *Kanssen*, 1946 AC 459: [1946] 1 All ER 586; *Underwood Ltd* v *Bank of Liverpool*, [1924] 1 KB 775: [1924] All ER Rep 230.
94. *Anand Behari Lal* v *Dinshaw & Co*, AIR 1942 Oudh 417. *See* also *T. R. Pratt Ltd* v *M.T. Ltd*, AIR 1938 PC 159.
95. *Houghton & Co* v *Nothard, Lowe & Wills Ltd*, 1928 AC 1: [1927] All ER Rep 97.

3. Forgery

Forgery may in circumstances exclude the *Turquand* rule. The only clear illustration is *Ruben* v *Great Fingall Consolidated.*[96]

> The plaintiff was the transferee of a share certificate issued under the seal of the defendant company. The certificate was issued by the company's secretary, who had affixed the seal of the company and forged the signatures of two directors.

The plaintiff contended that whether the signatures were genuine or forged was a part of the internal management and, therefore, the company should be estopped from denying genuineness of the document. But it was held that the rule has never been extended to cover such a complete forgery. Lord LOREBURN said: "It is quite true that persons dealing with limited liability companies are not bound to inquire into their indoor management and will not be affected by irregularities of which they have no notice. But this doctrine, which is well established, applies to irregularities which otherwise might affect a genuine transaction. It cannot apply to a forgery."[97]

This statement has been regarded as a *dictum*, as the case was decided on the principle that the secretary did not have actual or implied authority to represent that a forged document was genuine and, therefore, there was no estoppel against the company. Hence, a general statement that "the *Turquand* rule" does not apply to forgeries is not exactly warranted by the present authorities. Thus, for example, Andrews R. Thompson,[98] writing in an extensive article on the subject, says: "A company may represent that a forged instrument is genuine. In such a case, it will be estopped from denying that a forged instrument is genuine as against an outsider who has relied to his detriment upon the representation. Also, a company may represent that the forger has authority to execute the forged instrument. In that event it will be bound by the forged instrument as against an outsider who has relied on the apparent authority to execute the instrument."

In a case before the Madras High Court, a document on which a company borrowed a sum of money was executed by the managing director who was the chief functionary of the company and, to comply with the requirements of the articles, the signatures of two other directors were forged, the company was not allowed to eschew liability under the document.[99]

---

96. 1906 AC 439.
97. Another illustration of forgery, *Kleinwort* v *Associated Automatic Machine Corpn Ltd*, (1934) 39 Comp Cas 189.
98. *Company Law Doctrines and the Authority to Contract*, (1955-56) 11 Toronto LJ, 238, 275.
99. *Official Liquidator* v *Commr of Police*, [1969] 1 Comp LJ 5 Mad.

"We hold the company liable as a matter of social and economic policy. The basis of liability is the eminently practical view that if authority is conditioned on facts peculiarly within the agent's knowledge, his representation express or implied should bind the principal."[1]

4. Representation through Articles

This exception deals with the most controversial and highly confusing aspect of "the *Turquand* rule". Articles of association generally contain what is called the "power of delegation". *Lakshmi Ratan Cotton Mills* v *J.K. Jute Mills Co*[2] explains the meaning and effect of a "delegation clause".

> One *G* was a director of a company. The company had managing agents of which also *G* was a director. Articles authorised directors to borrow money and also empowered them to delegate this power to any or more of them. *G* borrowed a sum of money from the plaintiffs. The company refused to be bound by the loan on the ground that there was no resolution of the board delegating the power to borrow to *G*. Yet the company was held bound by the loan. "Even supposing that there was no actual resolution authorising *G* to enter into the transaction, the plaintiff could assume that a power which could have been delegated under the articles must have been actually conferred. The actual delegation being a matter of internal management, the plaintiff was not bound to enter into that."

Power of Delegation in Articles

Thus the effect of a "delegation clause", is "that a person who contracts with an individual director of a company, knowing that the board has power to delegate its authority to such an individual, may assume that the power of delegation has been exercised".[3]

Suppose that the plaintiff when he contracted with an individual director had not consulted the company's articles and, therefore, had no knowledge of the existence of the power of delegation. Could he assume that the power of which he did not know at the time had been exercised? This question arose in *Houghton & Co* v *Nothard, Lowe and Wills Ltd*.[4]

> The defendant company and one P & Co were engaged in fruit trade. One *M L* was a director of both companies. By the articles of the defendant company the directors could "delegate any of their powers to committees consisting of such member or members of their body as

---

1. *The Tort of a Company's Servant*, 13 Can BR 116, where the decision in *Ruben* v *Great Fingall Consolidated*, has been criticised.
2. AIR 1957 All 311.
3. Quoted from the Head Note to *Houghton & Co* v *Nothard, Lowe & Wills Ltd*, [1927] All ER Rep 97: 1928 AC 1.
4. [1927] 1 KB 246: [1927] All ER Rep 97: 1928 AC 1.

they think fit". *M L* acting on behalf of the defendant company, contracted with the plaintiffs, a firm of fruit brokers, that in consideration of the plaintiffs advancing a sum of money to P & Co, the plaintiffs should have the right to sell on commission all the fruit imported by the defendants and P & Co and to retain the sale proceeds belonging to both companies as security for the advance. The plaintiffs required the confirmation of the agreement by the defendant company itself. The secretary of the defendant company accordingly wrote a letter confirming the agreement and then the plaintiffs made the advance. The defendants subsequently repudiated the agreement as made without their authority. In an action for the breach of the agreement, the plaintiffs claimed that *M L* or the secretary had ostensible authority as the board could have delegated their powers to them under the company's articles.

But it was held that the plaintiffs were not entitled to assume that any authority to make the contract had been delegated to them by the board, and this for the following reasons: Firstly, that "the plaintiffs are not entitled to rely on the supposed exercise of a power which was never in fact exercised and of the existence of which they were in ignorance at the date when they contracted, and secondly, that there was something so unusual in an agreement to apply the money of one company in payment of the debt of another that the plaintiffs were put upon inquiry to ascertain whether the persons making the contract had any authority in fact to make it". SARGANT LJ added that "even if the plaintiffs had known of the existence of the express power of delegation, they would not have been entitled to assume that it had been exercised in favour of *M L* or the secretary to any greater extent than was to be inferred from the position that they occupied or were held out by the company as occupying".

Delegated Authority of acting Director

It appears that the unusual nature of the transaction more than anything else was responsible for this result. That this is so becomes clear from the subsequent decision of the same court in *British Thomson Houston Co Ltd* v *Federated European Bank Ltd*[5].

Under a company's articles of association, the directors had power to determine who should be entitled to sign contracts and documents on the company's behalf. One director *NP* describing himself as the chairman and without having been so authorised, executed and gave a guarantee to the plaintiffs in the name of the company.

---

5. [1932] 2 KB 176: [1932] All ER Rep 448. Noted 48 LQR 461.

It was held that "if the outsiders find an officer of the company openly exercising an authority, which the directors have power to confer upon him, they are relieved from the duty of further inquiry and are entitled to assume that the power has been regularly and duly conferred. . . . In the present case we have a director acting in a matter which are normally entrusted to directors. He was permitted to assume the title of the chairman of the board of directors. The plaintiffs were entitled to assume that he was duly authorised to act for the company". Knowledge on the part of the plaintiffs of the contents of the articles was considered to be irrelevant.

Ostensible Position allowed to Directors

Thus the ostensible position allowed to an officer is the most crucial factor. The decision of the Court of Appeal in *Ford Motor Credit Co Ltd* v *Harmack*,[6] is a further evidence of this.

> One *Y* was in control of three companies. He acquired a car on hire-purchase in the name of one company and gave it to the sales manager of the second company and also issued a cheque on the account of the second company for the liquidation of a debt of the third company. The recipient thought that *Y* owned all the three companies and they all seemed to be one company.

Lord DENNING MR said: "Where there was a group of companies all controlled by the same person who was in full control of everything—it had to be supposed that he was the chairman and managing director of each. It seemed that he had not only actual but also ostensible authority."

The decision has been described to be "in harmony with the modern tendency to afford protection to a third party contracting in good faith with a director having ostensible authority".[7]

Contracting party's Knowledge of Articles

The extent to which knowledge of articles is essential was once again in question in *Rama Corpn* v *Proved Tin and General Investment Co.*[8]

> One *T* was the active director of the defendant company. He, purporting to act on behalf of his company, entered into a contract with the plaintiff company under which he took a cheque from the plaintiffs. The company's articles contained a clause providing that "the directors may delegate any of their powers, other than the power to borrow and make calls, to committees consisting of such members of their body as they think fit". The board had not in fact delegated any of their powers

---

6. The Times, July 7, 1972; noted 1972 JBL 226.
7. 1972 JBL 226.
8. [1952] 2 QB 147: [1952] 1 All ER 554.

to *T* and the plaintiffs had not inspected the defendant's articles and, therefore, did not know of the existence of the power to delegate.

It was held that the defendant company was not bound by the agreement. SLADE J was of the opinion that knowledge of articles was essential. "A person who at the time of entering into a contract with a company has no knowledge of the company's articles of association, cannot rely on those articles as conferring ostensible or apparent authority on the agent of the company with whom he dealt." He could have relied on the power of delegation only if he knew that it existed and had acted on the belief that it must have been duly exercised.

Knowledge of articles is considered essential because in the opinion of SLADE J the rule of "indoor management" is based upon the principle of estoppel. Articles of association contain a representation that a particular officer can be invested with certain of the powers of the company. An outsider, with knowledge of the articles, finds that an officer is openly exercising an authority of that kind. He, therefore, contracts with the officer. The company is estopped from alleging that the officer was not in fact so authorised.[9]

This view that knowledge of the contents of articles is essential to create an estoppel against the company has been subjected to great criticism. One point of attack is that everybody is deemed to have constructive notice of the articles. But this suggestion was brushed aside by SLADE J on the ground that the doctrine of constructive notice is a negative one. It operates against the outsider who has not inquired. It cannot be used against the interests of the company.[10] The principal point of criticism, however, is that even if the plaintiffs had read the articles, all that they would see would be that the directors had the power to delegate their authority. They would not yet be able to know whether the directors had actually delegated their authority.[11] Moreover, the company can make a representation of authority even apart from its articles. The company may have held out an officer as possessing an authority. A person believes upon that representation and contracts with him. The company shall naturally be estopped from denying the authority of that officer for dealing on its behalf, irrespective of what the articles provide. Articles would be relevant only if they had contained a restriction on the apparent authority of the officer concerned.[12] Hence, the

---

9. *See* the judgment of the learned Judge at 149, *ibid.*
10. *See* Slade J at p 149 of [1952] 2 QB 147 and I.D. Campbell, *Contracts with Companies*, 75 LQR 469, 479.
11. *See* Lord ATKIN LJ in *Kreditbank Cassel* v *Schenkers Ltd*, [1927] 1 KB 826, 844.
12. Andrews R. Thompson: *Company Law Doctrines and Authority to Contract*, (1955-56) 11 Toronto LJ, 248, 267.

rule of law should be as stated by ATKIN LJ in *Kreditbank Cassel* v *Schenkers Ltd*[13]:

> If you are dealing with a director in a matter in which normally a director would have power to act for the company, you are not obliged to inquire whether or not the formalities required by the articles have been complied with before he exercises that power.[14]

Scope of Authority

In other words, "if the act is one which is ordinarily within the powers of such an officer, then the company cannot dispute the officer's authority to do the act, whether the directors have or have not actually invested him with authority to do it."[15] To refer again to *Lakshmi Ratan Cotton Mills* v *J K Jute Mills Co*[16] where, referring to the ostensible authority of a director who borrowed money on behalf of the company, the Court observed: "The creditor was, therefore, dealing with a person who was armed with such formidable and all embracing powers. There was no reason whatsoever to suspect the propriety or validity of the transaction." The act was within the scope of his apparent authority and it was irrelevant that the plaintiff had not read the articles or that there was no actual resolution authorising him to enter into the transaction. To the same effect is *Mahammed* v *Ravat Bombay House,* reported from South Africa.[17]

The plaintiff sued on two promissory notes signed by one of two directors on behalf of the defendant company. Unknown to the plaintiff the articles of the company provided that documents requiring the signature of the company should be sufficiently signed if signed by two directors unless and until otherwise determined at a meeting of the directors.

The Supreme Court of South Africa held that the plaintiff was entitled to rely on the apparent authority of a single director to bind the company even though no directors' meeting had determined that a single director should have power to bind the company.[18]

---

13. [1927] 1 KB 826 at p 844: [1927] All ER 421.
14. This view of his Lordship has been supported in leading text books. In Palmer's COMPANY LAW, 20th Edn, (1959) it is said: "it is submitted that the wider interpretation of the rule in the *Turquand* case, which ATKIN LJ expounded, is not only salutary and consonant with business principle but is also defensible in law because the true *ratio* of that rule is the principle of construction *Omnia praesumuntur rite,* and not the equitable doctrine of estoppel". (249). Similarly Gower says: "On this point the judgment of ATKIN LJ in the *Schenkers* case is greatly to be preferred." MODERN COMPANY LAW, 152 (2nd Edn, 1957).
15. Adopted from the note by WHG to the case of *British Thomson Houston & Co Ltd* v *Federated European Bank Ltd,* [1932] 2 KB 176: 1932 All ER Rep 448.
16. AIR 1957 All 311.
17. (1958) 4 SALJ 704.
18. Facts collected from (1959) Current Law Year Book, 412. *See also* G. A. Mullingan, *Companies Contracting through Agents,* (1960) 77 SALJ 332.

In *Freeman* v *Buckhurst*[19] WILLMER LJ attempted to reconcile all the previous authorities. The facts of the case may be noted first:

> *K*, who carried on business as a property developer, entered into a contract to purchase an estate. He had not enough money to pay for it and obtained financial assistance from *H*. They formed a limited company with certain capital subscribed equally by *K* and *H* to buy the estate with a view to selling it for development. *K* and *H* with a nominee of each, comprised the board. The quorum of directors was, by the articles of association, four. *H* was at all material times abroad. There was power under the articles to appoint a managing director, but the board did not in fact do so. *K* to the knowledge of the board acted as if he were managing director of the company in relation to finding a purchaser for the estate, and, again without express authority of the board, employed on behalf of the company, a firm of architects and surveyors for the submission of an application for planning permission etc. The firm claimed from the company their fees for work done.

It was held that the company was liable for the fees claimed because *K* throughout acted as managing director to the knowledge of the company and thus was held out by the company as being managing director, and the ostensible authority thus conferred could bind the company since its articles of association in fact provided for there being a managing director of the company. *K*'s act in employing the plaintiffs was within the ordinary ambit of the authority of such a managing director. The fact that the plaintiffs had not examined the company's articles and had not enquired whether *K* was a properly appointed managing director did not prevent them from establishing their claim against the company based on their reliance on *K*'s ostensible authority. Referring to the authorities WILLMER LJ observed:

> "Though I have no doubt that *Rama* case[20] was rightly decided on its own facts, I cannot agree with the view expressed by SLADE J that the previous decisions of this Court were conflicting. I do not think that, when properly understood, the *Houghton* case[21], the *Kreditbank* case[22] and the *Rama* case are in conflict with the decision in the *British Thomson Houston* case[23]. They were all cases of most unusual transactions, which would not be within what would ordinarily be expected to be the scope of the authority of the officer purporting to act on behalf of the company. In none of these cases were the plaintiffs in a position to allege that the person with whom they contracted was acting

---

19. [1964] 1 All ER 630: [1964] 2 Comp LJ 36 CA.
20. [1952] 1 All ER 554: [1952] 2 KB 147.
21. [1927] 1 KB 246.
22. [1927] All ER 421: [1927] 1 KB 826 CA.
23. [1932] All Rep 448, 675: [1932] 2 KB 176.

within the scope of such authority as one in his position would be expected to possess."

In India it does not seem to have been insisted in any of the cases on the subject that knowledge of articles is essential. But as late as 1966, MUKHARJI J observed *obiter* in a decision of the Calcutta High Court[24] that "if a person has not, in fact, knowledge of the existence of the power of delegation contained in the company's articles he cannot rely upon its suggested exercise".[25] The net conclusion, however, to be drawn from this string of authorities is that what matters is not the plaintiff's knowledge of the company's articles, but whether the act in question is within the ostensible authority of the officer through whom he contracted with the company. The lead given by WILLMER LJ in *Freeman* v *Buckhurst*,[26] has been followed by the Court of Queens's Bench in its decision in *Hely-Hutchinson* v *Brayhead Ltd.*[27] In this case a company was held liable upon the contracts of indemnity and guarantee made by a director whom the company had knowingly allowed to hold himself out as having the authority to enter into such transactions. The principle that emerges from these two recent authorities is that once it is shown that the contract in question is within the ostensible authority of the officer through whom it was made, the company cannot escape liability, unless, of course, it can show that under its memorandum or articles of association it had no capacity either to enter into a contract of that kind or to delegate the authority in the matter to the officer. But even this principle has been described "to be too narrow in the modern circumstances of business".[28]

5. Acts outside apparent authority

Lastly, if the act of an officer of a company is one which would ordinarily be beyond the powers of such an officer, the plaintiff cannot claim the protection of "the *Turquand* rule" simply because under the articles power to do the act could have been delegated to him. In such a case the plaintiff cannot sue the company unless the power has, in fact, been delegated to the officer with whom he dealt. A clear illustration is *Anand Behari Lal* v *Dinshaw & Co.*[29]

The plaintiff accepted a transfer of a company's property from its accountant. Since such a transaction is apparently beyond the scope of

---

24. *Kishan Rathi* v *Mondal Bros & Co*, [1966] 1 Comp LJ 19 at p 15 Cal.
25. The company was held liable as the court found that the plaintiff had relied upon the provisions of the articles in giving loan on a hundi to an officer of the company.
26. [1964] 1 All ER 630: [1964] 2 Comp LJ 36 CA.
27. [1967] 2 WLR 1312: [1967] 2 Comp LJ 67: [1967] 2 All ER 14 QBD.
28. Clive M. Schmitthoff, *The Companies Bill and the Company Law Reform*, 1966 JBL 106, 111
29. AIR 1942 Oudh 417.

an accountant's authority, it was void. Not even a 'delegation clause' in the articles could have validated it, unless he was, in fact, authorised.

The well-known English authority is *Kreditbank Cassel* v *Schenkers Ltd.*[30]

The defendant company, by its memorandum, had power to draw and accept bills of exchange and, by its articles, the directors were empowered "to determine who shall be entitled to sign, draw, accept, etc, bills on company's behalf". The defendant's business was that of forwarding agents. They had a branch at Manchester under a branch manager who, without having received any authority from the company, and in fraud, drew seven bills purporting to do so on company's behalf. The company was sued on these bills as drawers.

It was held that having regard to his position, drawing of bills was not within the ostensible authority of this branch manager and, therefore, the company was not bound, unless it had given him actual authority or was otherwise precluded from setting up the want of authority.[31]

————

30. [1927] All ER 421: [1927] 1 KB 826 CA.
31. *See* generally, Andrew R. Thompson, *Company Law Doctrines and Authority to Contract,* (1955-56) 11 Toronto LJ 248; Arthur Stiebel, *Ostensible Powers of Directors,* (1933) 49 LQR 350; J. L. Montrose, *Apparent Authority of an Agent of a Company,* (1934) 50 LQR 224; V Rameshan, *Protection of Contractors with Companies,* [1964] 2 Comp LJ 210; I. D. Campbell, *Contracts with Companies,* (1959) 75 LQR 469 and *Contracts with Companies II. The Indoor Management Rule,* (1960) 76 LQR 115; G. A. Mulligan, *Companies Contracting through Agents,* (1960) 77 SALJ 322; Aharon Barak, *Company Law Doctrines and the Law of Agency in Israel,* (1969) 19 ICLQ 847; L. M. Montrose, *The Basis of Power of an Agent in cases of Actual and Apparent Authority,* (1938) 16 Can BR 757.

5

Prospectus

Statement in lieu of prospectus [S. 70]

One of the great advantages of promoting a company is that the necessary capital for business can be raised from the general public by means of a public issue. This advantage is, however, enjoyed only by a public company which is listed at a recognised stock exchange. "A listed public company means a public company which has any of its securities listed in any recognised stock exchange."[1] A private company is, by its very constitution, prohibited from inviting monetary participation of the public.[2] But even a public company need not necessarily go to the public for money. The promoters may be confident of obtaining the required capital through private contacts. In such a case no prospectus need be issued to the public. The company can remain as an unlisted public company,[3] or even if listed, it can think in terms of managing its financial requirements through private access rather than public issue. In such cases the company is only required to prepare a draft prospectus containing the information required to be disclosed by Schedule III of the Act. This document is known as a "Statement in Lieu of Prospectus". A copy of it must be filed with the Registrar at least three days before any allotment of shares is made.[4] This is intended to preserve an authoritative record of the terms and conditions of the capital issue. If the statement contains any misrepresentation or omission, the liability, civil and criminal, is the same as in the case of an issued prospectus.[5]

The process of issuing securities through a statement in lieu of prospectus is a kind of private placement. The other documents, namely, a copy of the statement in lieu of prospectus and application form, are not issued to the public in general. They are circulated among selected persons for their personal use and with no right to pass them on to others. This method is gradually slipping into the hands of banking and financial institutions. The functioning is in the name of book building process. Orders are collected from investment bankers and larger investors based on an indicative price. SEBI guidelines have been issued.[6] Even in the case of a

---

1. As stated in S. 2(23-A), *inserted* by the Amendment of 2000.
2. S. 3(3)(*c*).
3. Its shares can be traded as unlisted securities at Over the Counter Exchanges.
4. There is a penalty for contravention which may extend up to ten thousand rupees. The liability is that of the company and guilty officers. S. 70(4).
5. Criminal liability for misrepresentation in prospectus is imprisonment up to two years or fine extending up to fifty thousand rupees or both. *See* S. 70(5) and *Blair Open Hearth Furnace Co Ltd, Re*, [1914] 1 Ch 390: (1914) 109 LT 839.
6. Clarification XIII, Dec 12, 1995; Clarification XVII, 9-12-1996 and Clarification XXI, 23-10-1997.

public issue, operation through book building is allowed to the extent to which reservation in issues is permissible. It will be identified separately in the placement portion. Where the issue is above one crore rupees, book building process can be used to the extent of 100%. The process is advantageous because the demand for and value the company's securities is discovered by providing price flexibility and bidding.

Most companies have, however, to issue a public appeal for subscription. This involves the issue of a prospectus. No applications for shares or debentures of a company can be invited unless the appeal is accompanied by a memorandum containing such salient features of a prospectus as may be prescribed, and complying with the requirements of the section.[7]

Definition of prospectus [S. 2(36)]

Prospectus is defined by Section 2(36). "A prospectus means any document described or issued as prospectus and includes any notice, circular, advertisement or other document inviting deposits from the public or inviting offers from the public for the subscription or purchase of any shares in or debentures of a body corporate." In essence, it means that a prospectus is an invitation issued to the public to take shares or debentures of the company or to deposit money with the company.

Application forms to be accompanied with prospectus or abridged prospectus

Any advertisement offering to the public shares or debentures of the company for sale is a prospectus. Application forms for shares or debentures cannot be issued unless they are accompanied by a prospectus. Publication cost of a prospectus had become very expensive and, therefore, the 1988 amendment introduced the concept of an abridged prospectus.[8] It is a memorandum containing such salient features of a prospectus as may be prescribed.[9] Thus the effect is that only a document has to be sent along with application forms showing a brief version of the salient features of the prospectus. One abridged prospectus can carry two application forms.

In a Calcutta case[10] an advertisement was inserted in a newspaper stating: "Some shares are still available for sale according to the terms of the prospectus of the company which can be obtained on application." This

---

7. S. 56(3).
8. Now defined in S. 2(1), *vide* Amendment of 2000.
9. *Substituted* for the requirement of full prospectus by the amendment of S. 56(3) in 1988. A proviso added to clause (*b*) prescribes that a full prospectus would have to be made available to a person who makes a request for it before the closing of the subscription list. Two application forms can be issued with one abridged prospectus. There should be nothing in it which is not there in the full prospectus.
10. *Pramatha Nath Sanyal* v *Kali Kumar Dutt*, AIR 1925 Cal 714: 88 IC 5: 29 CWN 523.

was held to be a prospectus as it invited the public to purchase shares. The directors were accordingly convicted under Section 92(5) [now Section 60(5)] for not complying with the disclosure requirements of the Act.

Public issue

The provisions of the Act relating to prospectus are not attracted unless the prospectus is issued. "Issued" here means issued to the public.[11] What does or does not amount to an issue is a question of fact in each case and is not capable of exact definition. In *Nash* v *Lynd*[12] it was held that "the term 'issue' is not satisfied by a single private communication".

The facts were that a document marked "strictly private and confidential" but in form a prospectus was prepared by the defendant, the managing director of a company. But the document did not contain all the material facts required by the Act to be disclosed. A copy of it along with application forms was sent to a solicitor who in turn sent it to the plaintiff.

It was held that this did not amount to an issue and accordingly the plaintiff's action for compensation for loss sustained by reason of the omissions was dismissed. Viscount SUMNER said:

"It is difficult to think of a prospectus being issued without some measure of publicity, however modest.... Though literally it is true that the issue is not expressly said in the section to be an issue to the public, I think it must be so in substance, otherwise any private letter, written by a person engaged in forming a company and advising his correspondent to take shares... would become an issued prospectus. 'The public' is of course a general word. No particular numbers are prescribed. Anything from two to infinity may serve: perhaps even one, if he is intended to be the first of a series of subscribers, but makes further proceedings needless by himself subscribing the whole. The point is that the offer is such as to be open to anyone who brings his money and applies in due form, whether the prospectus was addressed to him on behalf of the company or not. A private communication is not thus open."

---

11. The Act says in S. 2(22) that "issued generally" means, in relation to a prospectus, issued to persons irrespective of their being existing members or debenture-holders of the body corporate to which the prospectus relates. Section 67 says that no offer or invitation shall be treated as made to the public if it is not calculated to become available to persons other than addressees or is otherwise a domestic concern of the persons making and receiving the offer etc. The Amendment of 2000 has restricted this number to 50 persons. The effect is that any circulation to more than 50 persons would become a public offer.

12. 1929 AC 158: 140 LT 146. *See* also *Sherwell* v *Combined Incandescent Mantles Syndicate Ltd*, (1907) 23 TLR 482; *Baty* v *Keswick*, (1901) 85 LT 18: 17 TLR 664.

Thus the issue need not be made to the public as a whole. An advertisement among a group or a class of persons only would be an issue also. Accordingly, where 3000 copies of a document in the form of a prospectus were sent out and distributed among the members of certain gas companies only, it was held to be an offer of shares to the public.[13] Section 67(1) of the Act also provides that in the context of offering shares or debentures to the public or invitation to the public to subscribe for shares or debentures, the term 'public' includes any section of the public, whether selected as members or debenture-holders of the company concerned or as clients of the person issuing the prospectus or in any other manner.

In the following cases, however, although shares are offered and application forms issued, a prospectus containing all the details is not necessary:

1. Where the offer is made in connection with a *bona fide* invitation to a person to enter into an underwriting agreement with respect to the shares or debentures.
2. Where the shares or debentures are not offered to the public.[14]
3. Where the offer is made only to the existing members or debenture holders of the company.
4. Where the shares or debentures offered are in all respects uniform with shares or debentures already issued and quoted on a recognised stock exchange.[S. 56(5)(*a*) and (*b*)]
5. Where a prospectus is issued as a newspaper advertisement, it is not necessary to specify the contents of the memorandum, or the names etc., of the signatories to the memorandum or the number of shares subscribed for by them.[S. 66]

Contents of prospectus and formalities of issue

"The investor wants a sound concern."[15] Prospectus is one of the means by which he is informed of the soundness of the company's venture.[16] That indeed is the basic function of the prospectus. But this fact also affords an opportunity to directors and promoters to impose a fraud on the public. "The Companies Act accordingly now contains a comprehensive set of regulations intended to protect the investing public from such victimization."[17] The chief

---

13. *South of England Natural Gas and Petroleum Co, Re*, [1911] 1 Ch 573: 104 LT 378.
14. S. 56(3)(*a*) and (*b*). *See* Frank Evans, *Abridged Prospectus*, 27 LQR 286 (1911). Circulation of private and confidential letters for placement of shares to the addressees with right to renounce in favour of others would have the effect of making the offer to the public and would go beyond the scope of this exception. *See* Press Note of 6-7-1992, No 7/921.
15. An observation in *Baty* v *Kiswick*, (1901) 85 LT 18: 17 TLR 664.
16. KINDERSLEY VC in *New Brunswick etc Co* v *Muggeridge*, (1860) 3 LT 651: 30 LJ Ch 242.
17. J. A. Hornby, AN INTRODUCTION TO COMPANY LAW, p 54 (1st Edn, 1957).

aim of the Legislature in making these regulations, is "to secure the fullest disclosure of all material and essential particulars and lay the same in full view of the intending purchasers of shares."[18] The relevant rules and regulations are briefly set out below:

1. *Every prospectus to be dated* [S. 55]

Every prospectus has to be dated. This ensures a *prima facie* evidence of the date of its publication.[19]

2. *Every prospectus to be registered* [S. 60]

A copy of every prospectus has to be registered with the Registrar of Companies. This preserves an authoritative record of the terms and conditions of the capital issue. Registration must be made on or before the publication of the prospectus. The copy sent for registration must be signed by every person who is named in the prospectus as a director or a proposed director of the company. The copy for registration must be accompanied with—

(*a*) if a report of an expert is to be published, consent of the expert; [S. 60(1)(*a*)]

(*b*) a copy of every contract relating to appointment and remuneration of managerial personnel; [S. 60(1)(*b*), Sch II, clause 16]

(*c*) a copy of every material contract, unless it is entered into in the ordinary course of business or two years before the date of the prospectus;[20]

(*d*) a written statement relating to the adjustments, if any, "as respects the figures of any profits or losses or assets and liabilities", dealt with in any report set out in the prospectus in pursuance to Part II of Schedule II. The statement should give reasons for the adjustments and be signed by an expert;[21]

(*e*) the consent in writing of the person, if any, named in the prospectus as the auditor, legal advisor, attorney, solicitor, banker or broker of the company, to act in that capacity. [S. 60(3)]

The prospectus must be issued within ninety days of its registration.[22] The company and every person who knowingly issues a prospectus without

---

18. *Pramatha Nath Sanyal* v *Kali Kumar Dutt*, AIR 1925 Cal 714: 88 IC 5: 29 CWN 523.
19. The date of issue is important to very many things connected with the prospectus, for example, pricing of the issue is related to the value of the proffered securities to the timing of the issue. The date mentioned on the prospectus, unless the contrary is proved, is taken as the date of publication of prospectus. [S. 55]
20. Clause 16(1)(*b*) of Schedule II.
21. S. 60(1)(*b*)(*ii*) and clause 32 of Schedule II.
22. S. 60(4).

registration is punishable with a fine which may extend up to fifty thousand rupees.[23] It must be stated on the face of the prospectus that it has been registered and that the requisite documents, giving names, have been filed. [S. 60(2)(*a*) & (*b*)]

The Registrar is under duty not to register a prospectus which does not comply with the requirements of Sections 55, 56, 57 and 58 and 60(1) and (2) and which does not contain the consent in writing of the person, if any, named in the prospectus as auditor, legal adviser, attorney, solicitor, banker or broker of the company. The consent should be his acceptance to act in that capacity.[24] Section 61 provides that the contracts which are referred to in the prospectus or in a statement in lieu of it, are not to be varied unless the variation is approved by the company in general meeting or made under its authority.[25]

3. *Expert's consent* [S. 58]

If the prospectus includes a statement purporting to be made by an expert, consent in writing of that expert must be obtained and this fact should be stated in the prospectus. The expert should not be one who is himself engaged or interested in the formation, promotion or management of the company.[26] He should be unconnected with the formation or management of the company. "This section enacts a wholesome rule intended to protect an intending investor by making the expert a party to the issue of the prospectus and making him liable for untrue statements."[27]

---

23. S. 60(5). See *Pramatha Nath Sanyal* v *Kali Kumar Dutt*, AIR 1925 Cal 714: 88 IC 5: 29 CWN 523; *Mansukhlal* v *Jupiter Airways Ltd*, (1951) 54 Bom LR 777 and *Superintendent and Remembrance of Legal Affairs, Bengal* v *Bengal Salt Co*, (1936) 40 CWN 320, where a variation between the registered prospectus and its Bangla translation which was issued rendered the promoters liable to conviction.

24. S. 60(3).

25. Where the letters of offer for allotment of shares stated that the money collected from the issue was to be used for the specified purposes, it was held that the shareholders could by a resolution permit the use of money for different purposes. *Kothari Industrial Corpn Ltd* v *Maxwell Dyes and Chemicals (P) Ltd*, (1996) 85 Comp Cas 79: (1995) 18 Corpt LA 22 Mad. This decision of the single judge was affirmed by the Division Bench in *Maxwell Dyes and Chemicals (P) Ltd* v *Kothari Industrial Corpn Ltd*, (1996) 85 Comp Cas 111: (1996) 20 Corpt LA 247 (Mad)(DB). The change over in the deployment of issue proceeds was permitted by all financial and lead institutions and Governmental authorities. Matters relating to violation of this section are not within the jurisdiction of a civil court. They are the subject-matter of a civil suit before any competent civil court, *Poonam Chand Kothari* v *Rajasthan Tubes Mfg Co Ltd*, (1996) 87 Comp Cas 842 Raj. Shifting registered office even before allotment to some place other than that mentioned in the prospectus does not come within the scope of S. 61, *Pal Peugeot Ltd Re*, (1997) 89 Comp Cas 808 CLB.

26. S. 57. *See also* S. 59 which defines "expert". S. 59(2) says that "the expression 'expert' includes an engineer, a valuer, an accountant and any other person whose profession gives authority to a statement made by him".

27. Report of the Company Law Committee, (1952) p 46. The administration of power under the section and S. 57 has been vested in SEBI w.e.f. 13-12-2000.

4. *Disclosures to be made* [S. 56]

Section 56 requires every prospectus to disclose the matters specified in Schedule II of the Act.[28] The Schedule is divided into three parts. Part I contains the matters to be specified, Part II, the reports to be set out, while Part III is explanatory of Parts I and II.

PART I

This part has to disclose some general information, capital structure of the company, terms of the present issue, particulars of the issue, company, management and project, particulars in regard to the company and other listed companies under the same management which made any capital issue during the last three years, information about certain pending litigation, management perception of risk factors e.g., sensitivity to foreign exchange rate fluctuations, difficulty in availability of raw materials, or in marketing of products, cost-time overrun, etc.

PART II

This part has to carry some general information[29] and financial information in terms of reports relating to profits and losses and assets and liabilities of the company. Report must refer to the rates of dividends, if any, paid by the company in respect of each class of shares for each of the five financial years before the issue of the prospectus. The report of the auditors must also state separately the profits and losses of the company's subsidiaries and also combined profits and losses. If the company proposes to acquire any business, a report should be made by an accountant, whose name should be disclosed, upon the profits and losses of the business for five years before the date of the prospectus and assets and liabilities of the business.[30] This part has also to carry disclosures as to utilisation of proceeds of the issue and some statutory and other information.

---

28. S. 56(1). Schedule II was recast in 1991. Non-disclosure is a punishable offence. The power of taking action has been delegated to SEBI [GSR Notification of Nov 24, 1993]. Similar delegation has been made under S. 59.

29. Relating to consent of the concerned parties; changes, if any, in directorship during the last three years; resolutions authorising issue; procedure and time schedule for allotment and names and addresses of the secretary, legal adviser, lead managers, co-managers, auditors, bankers and brokers. *Kothari Orient Finance Ltd* v *Tele Data Informatics Ltd*, (2002) 108 Comp Cas 863 Mad, a prospectus was not restrained on the allegation of the financier that the debt owed to him was not disclosed. The company disclosed the same in a subsequent newspaper advertisement and SEBI which had okayed the issue, did not withdraw its permission even after the complaint.

30. These are the only disclosure requirements which have to be published in the prospectus. Formerly, a licence for public issue had to be obtained from the Controller of Capital Issues. That office was abolished and substituted by Securities and Exchange Board of India (SEBI). It issued guidelines in 1992 as to disclosure requirements for investor protection. SEBI renders the service of vetting the prospectus. For this purpose they need a lot of information for the consumption of their own office by looking at which they can find out whether the

Part III offers some explanations about the contents of Parts I and II.

Shelf Prospectus [S. 60-A]

Filing of a shelf prospectus has been made compulsory for any public financial institution, public sector bank, or a scheduled bank whose main object is financing. The advantage to the filing company is that it shall not have to file a prospectus every time it issues securities within the period of validity of such prospectus. The meaning of a shelf prospectus (like information contained in a file lying on a shelf) is confined to a prospectus issued by financial institutions or banks. A company filing such prospectus is also required to file an information memorandum on all material facts relating to new charges created, changes occurring in the financial position in the period from first offer of securities, previous offer of securities and the succeeding offer within such time as may be prescribed by the Central Government prior to the making of a second or subsequent offer of securities under the shelf prospectus. The information memorandum has to be issued to the public along with the shelf prospectus at the stage of first offer of securities. The prospectus remains valid for one year from the date of opening of the first issue of securities. Where an update of the information is filed every time an offer of securities is made, such memorandum together with the shelf prospectus shall constitute the prospectus. Financing means making loans to or subscribing to the capital of a private industrial enterprise engaged in infrastructure financing or such other company as the Central Government may notify for this purpose.

Information memorandum [S. 60-B]

Consequent upon introduction of a new variety of prospectus, namely, shelf or red-herring prospectus, the concept of "information memorandum" has been defined in Section 2(19-B) by the Amendment Act of 2000. It is as follows:

"Information memorandum means a process undertaken prior to the filing of a prospectus by which a demand for the securities proposed to be issued by a company is elicited, and the price and the terms of issue for such securities are assessed by means of a notice, circular, advertisement or document."

---

prescribed regulations have been followed or not, for example, whether the promoters have taken their requisite quota, pricing norms have been followed, prescribed gaps between two issues have been observed and the like. Preparation of a prospectus through a lead merchant (merchant bankers) and their certificate to the effect that SEBI disclosure requirements have been satisfied amounts to automatic SEBI vetting. Thus prospectus issue has become virtually free. Vetting is also not required where the issuer company has a three-year track record of dividend payment. The administration of powers under the section has been vested in SEBI.

A public company making an issue of securities may circulate an information memorandum to the public prior to the filing of a prospectus. A company which invites subscription by means of an information memorandum has to file a prospectus prior to the opening of the subscription list and the offer as a red-herring prospectus, at least three days before the opening of the offer. The information memorandum and the red-herring prospectus carry the same obligations as are applicable to a conventional prospectus. The issuing company has to highlight any variations between the information memorandum and the red-herring prospectus. For the purposes of the provisions contained in first four sub-sections of Section 60-B a red-herring prospectus means a prospectus which does not offer complete information on the price and the quantum of the securities proposed to be issued. [S. 60-B(4) [*Explanation*]]

Variations must be individually intimated to the persons invited. Where payment has been received in advance by means of drafts, cheques, etc, they shall not be encashed without first individually intimating to the prospective subscribers the fact of the variations and without giving them an opportunity to withdraw their applications. Applications may be withdrawn within seven days of the intimation of the variation. If any allotment is made without complying with this requirement it is void. The applicants shall be entitled to be paid back their subscription money with 15% interest.

On completion of allotment and closing of the offer of securities, a final prospectus has to be prepared completing the information which was missing in the red-herring prospectus, namely, the amount of capital raised whether by way of debt or share capital, the closing price of the securities, etc. Such prospectus has to be filed with SEBI in the case of a listed public company and with the Registrar in other cases.

Issuing houses and deemed prospectus (S. 64)

These requirements show that "provisions relating to prospectus are most stringent and the duty of preparing and filing it in accordance with the law is extremely onerous".[31] But these onerous requirements were often evaded by companies in this way. The whole of the capital of a company was allotted to an intermediary known as an "Issuing House". The "House" then offered the shares to the public by means of an advertisement of its own, which was obviously not a prospectus and thus the requirements of the Act relating to prospectus were evaded. But now every such advertisement sponsored by an "Issuing House" is known as an "offer for sale" and is deemed to be a prospectus issued by the company. The responsibility of the company, its directors and promoters is,

---

31. Quoted from the judgment in *Pramatha Nath Sanyal* v *Kali Kumar Dutt*, AIR 1925 Cal 714: 88 IC 5: 29 CWN 523.

therefore, the same. In addition, the "Issuing House" incurs its own liability. [S. 54(1)]

Now, how is it to be known whether an agreement to allot shares to an "Issuing House" is intended for the shares to be offered to the public. Apart from the express provisions of the agreement, the Act provides in Section 64(2) that the intention to offer shares to the public shall be presumed in the following cases:

1. where the "Issuing House" offers the shares to the public for sale within six months after they were allotted or agreed to be allotted to the House; or

2. where at the date of offer to the public, the whole of the consideration to be received by the company in respect of shares has not been received.

The prospectus issued by an "Issuing House" shall state the following further particulars: [S. 69(3)]

1. net amount of consideration to be received by the company in respect of those shares, and

2. place and time at which relevant contracts may be inspected.

Disclosures should give true and fair view of company's position

Above all, the golden rule as to the framing of prospectus must be observed. The rule was laid down by KINDERSELY VC in *New Brunswick and Canada Rly and Land Co* v *Muggeridge*[32] and was described as a "golden legacy" by PAGE WOOD VC in *Henderson* v *Lacon*.[33] Briefly, the rule is this:

> Those who issue a prospectus hold out to the public great advantages which will accrue to the persons who will take shares in the proposed undertaking. Public is invited to take shares on the faith of the representations contained in the prospectus. The public is at the mercy of company promoters. Everything must, therefore, be stated with strict and scrupulous accuracy. Nothing should be stated as fact which is not so, and no fact should be omitted the existence of which might in any degree affect the nature or quality of the privileges and advantages which the prospectus holds out as inducement to take shares. In a word, the true nature of the company's venture should be disclosed.

This golden legacy has condensed in few words the whole doctrine as to the rule of conduct between shareholders and directors.[34]

---

32. (1860) 3 LT 651: 30 LJ Ch 242.
33. (1867) 17 LT 527: 59 LJ Ch 794: 5 Eq 249.
34. (1867) 17 LT 527: 59 LJ Ch 794: 5 Eq 249. In addition to these requirements of the Companies Act, SEBI's guidelines for disclosures in prospectus have also to be observed. *See* SEBI Guidelines for Disclosure and Investor Protection of 1992. Securities and Exchange

REMEDIES FOR MISREPRESENTATION

These stringent provisions have proved to be very useful. As a result litigation on this subject has already declined. The fear of heavy liability and of criminal sanctions has controlled the directors' tendency of "using extravagant terms and flattering descriptions".[35] The law allows the following remedies for misrepresentation in a prospectus.

1. Damages for deceit

Deceit is a tort. It means fraud. Anyone who has been induced to invest money in a company by a fraudulent statement in a prospectus can sue the persons responsible for issuing it. If his action is successful he recovers full compensation for the loss sustained by him directly as a result of the fraud. But the burden of proof lies on him to establish the following main points of the action. When a claim under the tort of deceit has been established, the amount of damages would not be reduced on the ground of contributory negligence, if any, on the part of the claimant.[36]

Fraudulent misstatement

In the first place, the plaintiff must prove that there was a fraudulent misstatement. "To support an action of deceit", said Lord HERSCHELL[37], "fraud must be proved and nothing less than fraud will do. Fraud is proved when it is shown that false representation has been made—

(*a*) knowingly, or

(*b*) without belief in its truth, or

(*c*) recklessly, carelessly whether it be false or true."

Board of India, with headquarters at Bombay, was established under the SEBI Act, 1992 to take over the supervision of the capital market from the erstwhile Controller of Capital Issues who was functioning under the now repealed Capital Issues Control Act, 1947. SEBI is functioning by sub-dividing its workload into two divisions, one for controlling the primary market, namely issue of securities and the other for controlling the market transactions in securities, the secondary market. For issue of securities it has laid down guidelines as to disclosures in accordance with which prospectus must be prepared for vetting. For transactions in securities markets it has identified a number of market intermediaries who have been subjected to discipline through registration and conduct rules. Section 55-A provides that provisions of Sections 55 to 58, 59 to 84, 108, 109, 110, 112, 113, 116, 117, 118, 119, 120, 121, 122, 206, 206-A, in so far as they relate to issue and transfer of securities and non-payment of dividend are to be administered by SEBI in case of listed public companies and companies intend to get their securities listed on any recognised stock exchange. In other respects, the administration has to be by the Central Government. The *Explanation* to the section says that all powers relating to all other matters including prospectus, statement in lieu of prospectus, return of allotment, issue of shares and redemption of irredeemable preference shares are to be exercised by the Central Government, CLB or the ROCs.

35. Lord CAIRNS in *Peek* v *Gurney*, (1873) 43 LJ Ch 19 at p 40: [1861-73] All ER Rep 116.
36. *Standard Chartered Bank* v *Pakistan National Shipping Corpn (No 2)*, [2000] 1 Lloyds Rep 218 CA.
37. *Derry* v *Peek*, (1889) 14 AC 337: (1886-90) All ER Rep 1: (1889) 5 LQR 410.

In other words, if the directors publish a statement with knowledge that it is false or without any knowledge, whether it is true or false, it is a fraud. "Fraud may be committed by reckless representations without knowing how the matter stands one way or the other".[38] Section 17 of the Indian Contract Act defines "fraud" as including, among other things, the suggestion that a fact is true when it is not so and the person making the suggestion does not believe it to be true and the active concealment of a fact. These definitions show that if the person making the statement honestly believes it to be true, he is not guilty of fraud, even if the statement is not true. *Derry* v *Peek*[39] involved a situation of this kind.

> A special Act incorporating a tramway company provided that carriages might be moved by animal power and, with the consent of the Board of Trade, by steam power. The directors issued a prospectus containing a statement that by their special Act, the company had the right to use steam power instead of horses and that a saving would be effected thereby. No reference was made to the Board of Trade who refused their consent. Consequently, the company had to be wound up. The plaintiff having taken shares on the faith of the statement brought an action of deceit against the directors. But they were held not liable.

The statement was certainly untrue because the power to use steam was stated to be an absolute right, when in truth it was conditional on the approval of the Board of Trade. But the directors honestly believed that once the Act of Parliament had authorised the use of steam the consent of the Board of Trade was practically concluded.

Representation relating to Fact

Secondly, the false representation must relate to some existing facts which are material to the contract of purchasing shares. The purposes for which the new money is going to be used is an important fact. In *Edgington* v *Fitzmaurice*,[40] for example—

> The directors of a company issued a prospectus inviting subscriptions for debentures and stating that the objects of the issue of debentures were to complete alterations in the buildings of the company, to purchase horses and vans and to develop the trade of the company. The real object of the loan, however, was to enable the directors to pay off pressing liabilities. Relying upon the statement the plaintiff advanced money. The company became insolvent and the plaintiff sued the directors for fraud.

---

38. DENMAN LJ in *Edgington* v *Fitzmaurice*, (1885) 29 Ch D 459, 465: (1885) 53 LT 369.
39. (1889) 14 AC 337: (1886-90) All ER Rep 1.
40. (1885) 29 Ch D 459: (1885) 53 LT 369.

The directors argued that the suggestion of possible purposes to which the money might be applied was not a statement of existing facts. But they were held liable. BOWEN LJ said that the directors had misrepresented their state of mind and "the state of a man's mind is as much a fact as the state of his digestion". The statement was also regarded as material to the contract. "A man who lends money reasonably wishes to know for what purpose it is borrowed, and he is more willing to advance it if he knows that it is not wanted to pay off liabilities already incurred."[41]

Remedy of Direct Allottees

Thirdly, the plaintiff should have taken the shares directly from the company by allotment. "Those only who are drawn in by the mis-representation in the prospectus to become allottees can have a remedy against the directors."[42] A purchaser of shares in the open market has no remedy against the company or the promoters though he might have bought on the faith of the representations contained in the prospectus. This rule owes its origin to *Peek* v *Gurney*.[43]

A deceitful prospectus was issued by the defendants on behalf of a company. The plaintiff received a copy of it but did not take any shares originally in the company. The allotment was completed and several months afterwards the plaintiff bought 2000 shares on the stock exchange. His action against the directors for deceit was rejected. "The office of a prospectus", the Court said, "is to invite persons to become allottees, and, the allotment having been completed, such office is exhausted and the liability to allottees does not follow the shares into the hands of subsequent transferees. Directors cannot be made liable *ad infinitum* for all the subsequent dealings which may take place with regard to those shares upon the stock exchange."[44]

Buyers in Secondary Market

But "where the object with which the prospectus of a company is issued is not merely to induce applications for allotment of shares, but also to induce persons to whom it is sent to purchase shares in the market, its function is not exhausted when the company has gone to allotment, and the person issuing the prospectus is responsible for the consequences of false representation contained in it".[45] In other words, "there must be something to connect the directors making the representation with the party

---

41. Another illustration of liability for fraud, *S. Chatterjee* v *T.B. Sarwate*, AIR 1960 MP 322.
42. *Peek* v *Gurney*, (1873) 43 LJ Ch 19: [1861-73] All ER Rep 116: LR 6 HL 377.
43. (1873) 43 LJ Ch 19: [1861-73] All ER Rep 116: LR 6 HL 377.
44. Similar is the position of a person in whose favour shares were renounced. For a criticism of this principle, see *Joseph H. Gross case*, (1973) 36 Mod LR 600.
45. RIGBY LJ in *Andrews* v *Mockford*, (1896) 1 QB 372, 383: (1896) 73 LT 726.

complaining that he has been deceived and injured by it, as, for example, where the fraudulent prospectus is delivered to a person who thereupon becomes a purchaser of shares".[46] This principle found application in *Andrews* v *Mockford*.[47]

The defendants sent to the plaintiff a prospectus of a company which they knew would be a sham or pretended company in order to induce the plaintiff to purchase shares therein. The plaintiff did not then do so. The prospectus, having produced but a scanty subscription for shares, the defendants thereupon fraudulently published a telegram in a newspaper. The plaintiff believing in the truth of the telegram was induced to purchase shares in the open market. The directors were held liable for the systematic fraud. "The function of the prospectus was not exhausted, and the false telegram was brought into play by the defendants to reflect back upon and countenance the false statements in the prospectus."

Further, by reason of the decision of the House of Lords in *Hedley Byrne & Co* v *Heller & Partners Ltd*,[48] a person may become liable for holding out a false statement to anyone whom he knew or ought to have known would act in reliance upon the statement.

Where a prospectus was circulated among the existing shareholders inviting them to subscribe to the company's rights issue and one of them, thinking that the offer was good, not only accepted the rights shares offered to him, but also bought more shares of the category in the market. He was not allowed to hold the directors liable for misleading statements in the prospectus in respect of his market purchases. The court said that there was no sufficient proximity for a duty to be owed to those buying shares in the open market.[49]

Further developments in this respect have been noted in *Possfund Custodian Trustee Ltd* v *Diamond*.[50] The prospectus here was for floatation of securities on the unlisted securities market. A majority of the complainants were original allottees and others were buyers in the open market (after-market purchasers). The company went into receivership. There were actions against the company for false statements in the prospectus. The company applied for striking out the claims of after market purchasers. The court said that such purchasers would have to establish that they had reasonably relied on the representations made in the prospectus

---

46. *Peek* v *Gurney*, (1873) 43 LJ Ch 19 at p 38: [1861-73] All ER Rep 116: LR 6 HL 377. The *Explanation* to S. 19, Indian Contract Act.
47. (1896) 1 QB 372: (1896) 73 LT 726.
48. [1963] 3 WLR 101: [1963] 2 All ER 575: 1964 AC 465.
49. *Al-Nabib Investments (Jersey)* v *Longcroft*, (1991) BCLC 7 Ch D applying *Capro Industries plc* v *Dickman*, [1990] 1 All ER 568: [1990] 2 WLR 358 HL: (1990) BCLC 273 HL.
50. (1996) 2 BCLC 665 Ch D and also *Parr* v *Diamond*, (1996) 2 BCLC 665 Ch D.

and reasonably believed that the representor intended them to act on the statements and that there existed a sufficiently direct connection between the purchaser and the representor to render the imposition of such a duty fair, just and reasonable. The wide publicity of a prospectus would go to show that the intention was to influence not only the first buyers but also subsequent market operations. The issue should, therefore, be tried on merits and was not to be struck out.

Liability of Company

The company may also be sued for damages provided that the fraud was committed by the directors within the scope of their authority. But the action against the company is beset with the limitation laid down by the House of Lords in *Houldsworth* v *City of Glasgow Bank*,[51] that the contract of allotment must first be rescinded. One cannot remain in the company as a shareholder and yet sue it for damages.[52] But the English Misrepresentation Act, 1967 now "entitles the Court to award damages in lieu of rescission".[53] Thus, rescission is no longer necessary as a prerequisite for liability of the company.

2. Compensation under Section 62

The decision of the House of Lords in *Derry* v *Peek*[54] exposed the inadequacy of the tort action of deceit to protect the interest of investors in public companies. The directors in that case had, no doubt, told their falsehood in good faith rather than from corrupt motive.[55] But that would not console the misled investor for he is not concerned with the state of the directors' mind or conscience. His loss is just the same whether the misrepresentation is innocent or fraudulent. Accordingly, within a year of the decision in *Derry* v *Peek* the Directors' Liability Act, 1890 was passed and the directors were made answerable for false statements although they might have believed their assertions to be substantially true. The provisions of this Act have been re-enacted in Section 43 of the English Companies Act, 1948. Section 62 is the corresponding provision in the Indian Act. Following persons are liable under this section:

---

51. (1880) 5 App Cas 317: (1880) 42 LT 194 HL.
52. Followed in *Addlestone Linoleum Co, Re*, (1887) 37 Ch D 191 CA.
53. S. 2(2). *See* GOWER, PRINCIPLES OF MODERN COMPANY LAW, p 316 (3rd Edn, 1969).
54. (1889) 14 AC 337: [1886-90] All ER Rep 1: (1889) 5 LQR 410.
55. *See* Fredrich Pollock, *Derry* v *Peek in the House of Lords*, (1889) 5 LQR 410. The amount of compensation to the misled investor is the value taken from him and the real value of the share. One method of ascertaining such value is to see the difference between the allotment value and the market value of the security, *Smith New Court Securities Ltd* v *Serimgeour Trust Ltd*, (1997) 1 BCLC 350 HL. Here the price which the buyer paid for the share less the price which he realised on resale was allowed by way of compensation. Delay on his part in reselling the share was not taken into account because he has justifiable reasons for the delay.

1. Every person who is a director of the company at the time of the issue of the prospectus.

2. Every person who has authorised himself to be named as a director in the prospectus.

3. Every promoter who was a party to the preparation of the prospectus.[56]

4. Every person who authorised the issue of the prospectus.

They are liable to compensate the investor for any loss sustained by him by reason of any untrue statement contained in the prospectus.[57] A statement is deemed to be untrue if it is false in the form and context in which it is included.[58] Omissions which are calculated to mislead shall also render the prospectus false.[59] An instance of liability under the section is provided by *Greenwood* v *Leather Shod Wheel Co.*[60]

The prospectus issued by a wheel manufacturing company stated: "Orders have already been received (inter alia), from the House of Commons.... Wheels for the trolleys in the House of Commons have been ordered and are now in use." In fact no single order had been obtained except for trial and by way of experiment. It was held that the prospectus contained untrue statement.

The chief advantage of proceeding under this section is that the plaintiff does not have to prove fraud. If the representation is false, the directors cannot escape liability even if they had made it *bona fide* and not with intent to deceive. But they have the following special defences under the section. [S. 62(2)]

(a) *Withdrawal of consent.*—A director will not be liable if he had withdrawn his consent to become a director before the issue of the prospectus and the same was issued without his authority or consent.

(b) *Issue without knowledge.*—Even where a director's name appears in the prospectus he can escape liability by proving that it was issued without his knowledge or consent and on becoming aware he forthwith gave a public notice to that effect.

(c) *Ignorance of untrue statement.*—Sometimes a director may be ignorant of the untruth of the statements made in the prospectus. Such a director can defend himself by showing that, on becoming aware of the untrue statement, he withdrew his consent by a reasonable public notice. Obviously, this must be done before allotment.

---

56. S. 62(a) and (b).
57. The liability is joint and several and the person who becomes liable may recover contribution from others equally guilty of misrepresentation. S. 62(3).
58. S. 65(1)(a).
59. S. 65(1) and (6).
60. [1900] 1 Ch 421: [1900] 81 LT 595.

(d) Reasonable ground for belief.—A director will also be protected if he can show that "he had reasonable ground to believe, and did up to the time of allotment believe the statements to be true". It may be recalled that under the rule in *Derry* v *Peek,* a director having honest belief in the truth of his statement is protected. But under this section it is not enough for him to say that he was honest. He must go further and show that his honest belief was based upon reasonable grounds. And so in *Adams* v *Thrift*:[61]

> An action was brought by the plaintiff to recover compensation from a director of a company in respect of false statements in a prospectus. The director contended that the statements were prepared by the promoters and before issuing he enquired from one of them, "Is everything perfectly alright" and he said "of course, it is". It was held that although the director did honestly believe the statement to be true, he had no reasonable ground to do so. "The promoter is the very last person whose uncorroborated statement ought to be relied upon by an intending director as justification for saying that he had reasonable ground for belief. If they had taken the opinion or obtained a report of competent people as to material facts in the prospectus that might have afforded a reasonable ground for belief."[62]

(e) Statement of expert.—If the untrue statement happens to be contained in the report of an expert, the director sued has to show that he had reasonable ground to believe and did up to the time of allotment believe that the expert was competent, and if it is in some public official document, that it was a correct and fair representation of the document.

3. Rescission for misrepresentation

An allotment of shares can be avoided at the option of the allottee if it was caused by misrepresentation whether innocent or fraudulent.[63] By avoiding the contract he is able to get rid of his shares and claim the money he paid for them.[64] Further under Section 75 of the Contract Act, a person who lawfully rescinds a contract is entitled to compensation for any damage which he has sustained through the non-fulfillment of the contract. The action is against the company to have the subscriber's name removed from the register of shareholders. The essential requisites of the action are as follows:

(a) False representation

In the first place, there must be a false representation in the prospectus. False representation means a positive misstatement,[65] or a concealment of

61. (1915) 2 Ch 21: 113 LT 569 CA.
62. Lord COZENS-HARDY MR, *ibid. See* also *Reese River Silver Mining Co, Re,* (1867) 2 Ch 604.
63. S. 18 of the Indian Contract Act.
64. S. 64, Indian Contract Act, 1872.
65. S. 18(1), *ibid.*

material facts.[66] But, generally speaking, "a mere non-disclosure does not amount to misrepresentation unless the concealment has prevented an adequate appreciation of what was stated".[67] "Everybody knows that sometimes half a truth is no better than a downright falsehood".[68] *R* v *Kylsant (Lord)*[69] illustrates the point.

Lord Kylsant was prosecuted for issuing a prospectus with untrue statements. A table was set out in the prospectus showing that between (1911-1927), the company had paid dividends varying from five to eight per cent, except in 1914, when no dividend was paid and in 1926 when a dividend of 4 per cent was paid. This statement created the impression that the company was in a sound financial position; whereas the truth was that during the seven years preceding the date of the prospectus the company had made substantial trading losses and dividends could be paid only by recourse to funds which had been stored up during the war period. The whole prospectus was held to be false, not because of what it stated, but because of what it did not state.

AVORY J relied upon the following statement of Lord HALSBURY in *Aaron's Reefs Ltd* v *Twiss*:[70] "...taking the whole thing together was there false representation? I do not care by what means it is conveyed—by what trick or device or ambiguous language: all these are expedients by which fraudulent people seem to think that they can escape from the real substance of the transaction. If by a number of statements you intentionally give a false impression and induce a person to act upon it, it is not the less false, although if one takes each statement by itself there may be a difficulty in showing that any specific statement is untrue."[71]

Even if those who issued a prospectus were prompted by innocent motives, the subscriber would be entitled to his remedy.[72] Accordingly, a prospectus stating that "more than half the shares have already been sold", when, in fact, only one promoter of the company had signed documents applying for more than half the shares, but had not paid any money and ultimately he took only two hundred;[73] a prospectus stating that "the directors and their friends have subscribed a large portion of the capital and

---

66. Ss. 18(2), (3) and 17(2), Indian Contract Act.
67. The Explanation to S. 17 of the Indian Contract Act also declares that mere silence is not fraud unless there is duty to speak or silence is, in itself, equivalent to speech. *See* also *Arnison* v *Smith*, (1889) 41 Ch D 348: (1889) 61 LT 63 CA.
68. Lord MACNAGHTEN in *Gluckstein* v *Barnes*, 1900 AC 240, 250: 69 LT Ch 385.
69. [1932] 1 KB 442, followed in *R* v *Bishirgain*, [1936] 1 All ER 586 CA.
70. 1896 AC 273, 281: [1896] 74 LT 794.
71. *See* AVORY, J's judgment at p 448, 1932 KB 442. *See* also *Bentley & Co* v *Black*, (1893) 9 TLR 580 CA, where the court said that the prospectus must be taken as a whole to see whether it conveyed a meaning which amounted to a misstatement of fact, even if each paragraph taken separately contains no misstatement.
72. *Eaglesfield* v *Marquis of Londonderry*, (1876) 4 Ch D 693.
73. *Ross* v *Estates Investment Co*, (1868) 3 Ch App 682: (1868) 19 LT 61.

they now offer to the public remaining shares", the fact being that the directors had subscribed only ten shares each;[74] a prospectus stating that "*B and M*, two leading businessmen of repute, have agreed to become directors of the company", when they had only expressed their willingness to help the company[75] were all held to be misleading, giving the subscribers the right to rescind.

With these may be contrasted the facts of *Shiromani Sugar Mills Ltd* v *Debi Prasad*.[76]

Printed in red ink on the cover of a prospectus was the statement that "the managing agents with their friends, promoters and directors have already promised to subscribe shares worth six lakh rupees". But they had taken much less. Yet it was held that this could not be assailed as a misrepresentation of fact. "The only fact asserted was the existence of promise... and the existence of promise is not falsified by breaking of it."[77]

In the same way where the alleged misrepresentation in a prospectus was the statement that "the company will commence business with six steamships of special tonnage and rate of speed" and at the time of the prospectus the company had no ships and had only contracted for the supply of two ships, this was not a misrepresentation there being nothing to show that the ships of the specified character might not at any time be purchased in the market.[78]

Sometimes an ambiguous statement is put forward bearing two different meanings, one of which is true and the other untrue. A case of this kind is *Smith* v *Chadwick*.[79]

The prospectus of a company which was being formed to take over certain iron works contained the statement that "the present value of the turnover is £1,000,000 sterling per annum". If the statement meant that the works had actually in one year turned out produce worth more than a million, it was untrue. If, on the other hand, it meant that works were capable of turning out that amount of produce, it was true. It was held that "if they put forth a statement which they knew may bear two meanings one of which is false to their knowledge and thereby the plaintiff putting that meaning on it is misled, they cannot escape by saying 'he ought to have put the other'."

A misreading of the prospectus will not, however, entitle a purchaser of shares to rescission.[80]

---

74. *Henderson* v *Lacon*, (1867) 17 LT 527: 59 LJ Ch 794: 5 Eq 249.
75. *Metropolitan Coal Consumers' Assn, Re, Karberge case*, (1892) 3 Ch 1: (1892) 66 LT 700.
76. AIR 1950 All 508: (1950) 20 Comp Cas 296: 1950 ALJ 836.
77. DESAI J at p 512, *ibid*; see also *Bansidhar Durgadatta* v *Tata Power Co*, (1925) 27 Bom LR 330.
78. *Hallows* v *Fernie*, 3 Eq 520: (1868) 3 Ch App 467.
79. (1884) 9 CA 187: [1881-5] All ER Rep 242: 50 LT 697.
80. MACLEOD CJ in *Bansidhar Durgadatta* v *Tata Power Co*, (1925) 27 Bom LR 330 at p 337.

Change of circumstances.—There is often an interval of time between the publication of a prospectus and the allotment of shares. During this interval a statement which was true when made may cease to be so owing to some change of circumstances. For example, in *Rajagopala Iyer* v *South Indian Rubber Works*:[81]

The plaintiff had applied for shares in a company on the basis of a prospectus containing the names of several persons as directors. But before the allotment took place, there were changes in the directorate, some directors having retired. That was held sufficient to entitle the plaintiff to revoke his application as few matters are more important than the names of directors. "Moreover, the persons who applied for shares on the faith of one state of things should have the option of retiring when a totally different state of things came into existence."[82]

(b) Of Facts and not of Law

Secondly, the misrepresentation must be of facts and not of law. If, for example, a prospectus represents that the company's fully paid shares will be issued at half their nominal price, when the Companies Act prohibits the issue of shares at so much discount,[83] it is a misrepresentation of law and a person deceived by it will have no remedy. Again, the facts misrepresented must be material to the contract of taking shares. Materiality of misrepresentation is a question of fact in each case.[84] Generally speaking, a fact is said to be material if it is likely to influence the decision of an average purchaser of shares, that is, if it will urge or induce him to purchase or refrain from purchasing shares. This rule enables the directors to include what are commonly known as 'flourishing or puffing up statements' and make the prospectus attractive, as was done, for example, in *Mckeown* v *Boudard Peveril Gear Co Ltd.*[85]

A company was incorporated for working inventions of one Boudard relating to the driving gear of cycles. Its prospectus stated:

---

81. [1942] 2 MLJ 228: AIR 1942 Mad 656. *See* also *Vankataramayya* v *Indian Industrial Bank*, AIR 1930 Mad 325: 124 IC 193.
82. MALINS VC in *Scottish Petroleum Co, Re, Anderson case*, (1881) 17 Ch D 373, 375.
83. S. 79.
84. For illustrations of material misrepresentation see *Metropolitan Coal Consumers' Assn, Re, Karberge case*, [1892] 3 Ch 1: (1892) 66 LT 700, where LINDLEY LJ said that "few matters are more material than the names of the first directors. What is a prospectus worth without the names of good men upon it"; *Wimbledon Olympia Ltd, Re*, [1910] 1 Ch 630: 102 LT 425, where the omission to disclose the state of previous mortgages was held to be a material misrepresentation; *Coal Economising Gas Co, Re*, (1875) 1 Ch 182, where the meaning of material contracts is explained; *State* v *Red Grande Rubber Estates Ltd*, 1913 AC 853 and *Pacaya Rubber & Produce Co*, [1914] 1 Ch 542, in both of which there were material inaccuracies in reports included in the prospectus; *Russian Vyksounsky Iron Works Co, Re*, (1866) 1 Ch App 574: (1866) 15 LT 817, objects misstated.
85. (1896) LT 310: 65 LJ Ch 735.

"Within a few weeks the following exciting, and at the time unheard of, performances took place." Then the results of various cycle races were set out in all of which the company's cycle was claimed to have bettered the record and the prospectus concluded with these words: "This is the first occasion that a mile has been done under two minutes in England. Every rider to whom speed is an object will be bound to have it. What cycle riders are there who will buy slow machines when one admittedly faster is there in the market." All the records set out in the prospectus were indeed true. But the plaintiff complained on the ground that the prospectus did not disclose that they had already been beaten at the time of the prospectus.

It was held that the omission of later performances which had outdone the records referred to in the prospectus was not material and did not render the prospectus misleading. "It is impossible to suppose that the plaintiff could have been really deceived by such a common quality in the prospectus as puffing or that he was blind to the possibility that the records and the performances set forth might possibly be due not solely to the merits of the gear, but also to the merits and skill of the riders and to the general improvement in cycles."

(c) Reliance and Inducement

It is further necessary that the plaintiff should have acted in reliance on the statements contained in the prospectus. Misrepresentation should be at least one of the inducements for his contract of taking shares. It is for this reason that a purchaser of shares in the open market cannot proceed against the company[86] unless the company had done something to induce him to purchase in the market.[87] For the same reason a person cannot complain of misrepresentation if "he had the means of discovering the truth with ordinary diligence".[88] But a recipient of a prospectus is entitled to rely on it. He is not bound to verify it. Explaining this in a case, the House of Lords observed[89]:

> But the appellants say that even admitting the prospectus to be open to the objections which are made to it, the respondent has no ground of

---

86. *Hyslop v Morel*, (1891) 7 TLR 263; *Peek v Gurney*, (1873) 43 LJ Ch 19: [1861-73] All ER Rep 116: LR 6 HL 377.
87. *Andrews v Mockford*, (1896) 1 QB 372: (1896) 73 LT 726.
88. In *Mohun Lall v Sri Gungaji Cotton Mills Co*, (1900) 4 CWN 369, the prospectus was issued in May and shares were allotted in November. The Court held that between these dates there was ample time and opportunity to find out whether Mr Campbell who was represented to be a provisional director had actually consented to be a director. The Court applied the exception to S. 19 of the Contract Act.
89. *Director of Central Rly Co v Kisch*, (1867) LR 2 HL 99: 36 LJ Ch 849: 16 LT 500.

complaint, because he had an opportunity of ascertaining the truth of the representations contained in it, of which he did not choose to avail himself, that he was told by the prospectus that the "engineer's report together with maps, plans and surveys of the line, might be inspected, and any further information obtained, on application at the temporary offices of the company"; and in his letter of application he agreed to be bound by all the conditions and regulations contained in the memorandum and articles of the company, which, if he had examined, would have given him all the information necessary to correct the errors and omissions in the prospectus.

But it appears that when once it is established that there has been any fraudulent misrepresentation or wilful concealment by which a person has been induced to enter into a contract, it is no answer to his claim to be relieved from it to tell him that he might have known the truth by proper inquiry.

(d) By or on behalf of Company

"A company is not responsible for the statements in a prospectus unless it is shown that the prospectus was issued by the company or by someone with the authority of the company — by the board of directors, for instance,[90] or that the prospectus, having been issued by the promoters was ratified by the company.[91] This becomes particularly important where a representation is made apart from prospectus. Thus where a person was induced to join a company as a shareholder by representations of the secretary of the company, he could not obtain rescission as the secretary has no general authority to make representations.[92] But where shares were applied for on the basis of fraudulent representation made by a person both before and after he had become a director, rescission was allowed.[93]

Limits of recission and loss of right

A contract induced by misrepresentation is valid until it is rescinded. The option to rescind is not an unlimited one. It is lost in the following circumstances.

---

90. Palmer's, COMPANY LAW, p 165 (20th Edn, 1959). See *Metal Constituents Ltd, Re, Lord Lurgan case*, [1902] 1 Ch 707: (1880) 86 LT 291, where a misrepresentation was made before incorporation and the company was held not liable.
91. *National Exchange Co of Glasgow* v *Drew*, (1855) 2 Macg 124: 25 LT SO 223; *Houldsworth* v *City of Glasgow Bank*, (1880) 5 App Cas 317: (1880) 42 LT 194 HL.
92. *Diwan Chand* v *Gujranwala Sugar Mills*, AIR 1937 Lah 644.
93. *Hilo Mfg Co* v *Williamson*, (1911) 28 TLR 164 CA. A stranger, which means a person who has not invested any money in the company on the faith of the prospectus, has no right to start a public interest litigation against the company on the ground that it has published a misleading prospectus. *Kisan Mehta* v *Universal Luggage and Mfg Co*, (1988) 63 Comp Cas 398 Bom.

(a) By Affirmation

If the allottee, with full knowledge of misrepresentation, upholds the contract, he cannot afterwards rescind. Affirmation may be express or implied. An implied affirmation takes place by the shareholder's conduct, where, for example, after discovering his right to rescind, he endeavours to sell his shares, attends meetings of the company, receives dividends or pays calls.[94]

(b) By Unreasonable Delay

"Any man who claims to retire from a company on the ground that he was induced to become a member by misrepresentation, is bound to come at the earliest possible moment after he becomes aware of the misrepresentation."[95] Accordingly in *Christineville Rubber Estates Ltd, Re,*:[96]

> An applicant to whom shares were allotted in a company became fully aware of misrepresentation in the prospectus by the end of July, but in December he moved to have his name removed from the register. It was held that the unexplained delay of five months precluded him from obtaining relief.[97]

(c) By Commencement of Winding Up

The right of rescission is lost on the commencement of winding up of the company. Shareholders cannot be permitted to get rid of their shares after the proceedings for the winding up of the company have been initiated. The names of the shareholders are entered in the register of members and the register is *prima facie* evidence of membership. It is open to public inspection. "The object being that the creditors might form their own opinion as to the person who constituted the shareholders of the company."[98] Creditors might have lent money on the faith of so many good names being there on the register. And if the shareholders can get their names removed from the register even after the winding up is on, the creditors would be seriously misled.[99] "But where a shareholder has started

---

94. *Briggs, ex p*, (1866) LR 4 Ch App 332; *Sharpley v South and East Coast Rly Co*, (1876) 2 Ch D 663; *Scholey v Central Rly*, (1868) LR 9 Eq 266; *Dunlop Truflault Cycle & Tube Mfg Co, Re*, (1896) 66 LJ Ch 25; *Deposit Life Assurance Co v Ayscough*, (1856) 119 ER 1048.
95. *London & Staffordshire Fire Insurance Co, Re*, (1883) 24 Ch D 149: 48 LT 955.
96. (1911) 81 LJ Ch 63: 106 LT 260.
97. *See* also *Madrid Bank, Re*, (1867) 2 Ch App 536; *Jagannath Prasad, Re*, AIR 1938 All 193: 1938 ALJ 94: 174 IC 886; *Shiromani Sugar Mills Ltd v Debi Prasad*, AIR 1950 All 508.
98. *First National Reinsurance Co Ltd v Greenfield*, [1921] 2 KB 260: 1920 All ER Rep Ext 777.
99. LORD CAIRNS in *Cachar Co, Re*, (1867) 2 Ch App 412; *Tennent v City of Glasgow Bank*, (1879) 4 App Cas 615: 40 LT 674: 27 WR 649 HL.

active proceedings to be relieved of his shares, the passing of the winding up order during their pendency would not prevent his getting the relief."[1]

4. Liability under Section 56

Section 56(1) states that a company's prospectus must contain certain particulars and sub-section (3) imposes penalty for its contravention. But the section is silent as to the subscriber's remedy in case all the required particulars are not disclosed. "The section in terms gives no remedy or cause of action; but it is a remedial section for the protection of applicants for shares against wiles of promoters and others."[2] The provision does contemplate a liability in damages on the part of directors and other persons responsible for prospectus, for sub-section (4) exonerates such persons from liability if they can prove certain matters. That is equivalent to saying that they are liable if they cannot prove those defences. Hence an allottee can recover damages from the directors for mere failure to comply with Section 56(1). But the plaintiff who has subscribed for shares on the faith of a prospectus which did not disclose the material particulars required to be disclosed by the section must prove that he has sustained damage. The onus lies on him to show that he has acted on the faith of the prospectus, that is to say, if he had known of the undisclosed matter he would not have become a shareholder.[3] It should be noted that the section does not entitle a shareholder to get rid of his shares by reason merely of the omission of any of the facts required to be disclosed by the section.[4] Where, however, the omission amounts to fraud or misrepresentation within the meaning of Sections 17 and 18 of the Indian Contract Act, an action for rescission will also lie.

A director or other person sued under this section may defend himself by showing—[S. 56(4)]

1. that he had no knowledge of the matter not disclosed;[5]
2. that the contravention arose out of an honest mistake of fact;[6]

---

1. DESAI J in *Shiromani Sugar Mills Ltd* v *Debi Prasad*, AIR 1950 All 508, 513: 1950 ALJ 836: (1950) 20 Comp Cas 296; *See* also *Jagannath Prasad, Re,* AIR 1938 All 193: 1938 ALJ 94.
2. Lord LINDLEY in *Macleay* v *Tait*, 1906 AC 24, 28.
3. *Twycross* v *Grant*, (1877) 2 CPD 469 CA: 46 LJ QB 636: 36 LT 812: 25 WR 701 CA.
4. *Shiromani Sugar Mills Ltd* v *Debi Prasad*, AIR 1950 All 508.
5. For an explanation of the circumstances in which this defence may be resorted to see BYRNE J in *Walts* v *Bucknall*, [1902] 2 Ch 628. *See* also *Twycross* v *Grant*, (1877) 2 CPD 469 CA: 46 LJQB 636: 36 LT 812: 25 WR 701 CA, where it was pointed out that the liability would arise under the section even where an omission has been made under *bona fide* belief that it was unnecessary to specify the matter complained of. *See* also *Hoole* v *Speak*, [1904] 2 Ch 732: 91 LT 183, and the proviso to sub-section (4) which states that there shall be no liability for matters specified in cl. 18 of Sch. II unless there was knowledge of the matters not disclosed.
6. *Macleay* v *Tait*, 1906 AC 24.

3. if, in the opinion of the Court, the matter not disclosed was immaterial or that the person sued ought to be excused.[7]

Criminal liability for misrepresentation [S. 63]

Where a prospectus includes any untrue statement, every person who authorised the issue of the prospectus shall be punishable with imprisonment for a term which may extend to two years, or with fine which may extend up to fifty thousand rupees or with both.[8] A director prosecuted under this section can defend himself by showing that the statement was immaterial or he had reasonable ground to believe and did up to the time of the issue of the prospectus believe that the statement was true.[9] A company's prospectus stated that the company had the experience in its line of business of two and a half decades. The experience was, infact, that of the partners of a firm which had been taken over by the company and not that of the company itself. The court granted relief against any possible liability. There was no *mala fide* intention behind the statement. The management was successful. The statement was not so materially false as to invite prosecution.[10]

Invitation for deposits [S. 58-A]

The Central Government has taken the power by Section 58-A to regulate, in consultation with the Reserve Bank, the acceptance of deposits by companies. Such rules may prescribe for the limits up to which, the manner in which and the terms and conditions on which deposits may be invited or accepted. Apart from the regulations that may be thus prescribed, the section itself contains certain important provisions. Deposits should be invited in accordance with the deposit rules and by an advertisement accompanied by a statement showing the financial position of the company in such form as may be prescribed by the rules.[11] If any deposit is accepted

---

7. *South of England Natural Gas & Petroleum Co, Re*, [1911] 1 Ch 573: 80 LJ Ch 358: 104 LT 378. The administration of the power under this section is vested in SEBI, S. 55-A.
8. *Srinivasan* v *Emperor*, (1944) MWN 312 and *R* v *Kylsant*, [1932] 1 KB 442: 101 LJ KB 97.
9. *See also* sub-section (2) which excludes from liability under the section a person who has given consent under S. 58 or S. 60. See *R* v *Kylsant*, [1932] 1 KB 442: 101 LJ KB 97; *R* v *Bishirgain*, (1936) 1 All ER 586 CA. The power of prosecution under the section has been delegated to the Securities and Exchange Board of India (SEBI).
10. *Progressive Aluminium Ltd* v *Registrar of Cos*, (1997) 89 Comp Cas 147 AP: [1997] 4 Comp LJ 215. *Ramakrishna Raja* v *ROC*, (2005) 123 Comp Cas 319 Mad, a complaint against false representation in prospectus was made after 7 years. S. 468, CrPC, prescribed a period of three years from the date of knowledge of the offence. *British Polysters Ltd, Re*, (2005) 123 Comp Cas 348 CLB, the offence is compoundable under S. 621-A even if a prosecution is pending. *Hafeez Rustom Dalal* v *ROC*, (2005) CLC 625 Gau, notice issued after 10 years of the prospectus, held barred by delay and laches.
11. Private companies cannot advertise for deposits. When a private company accepts deposits from its members or directors, it has to take a declaration from them that they are not making deposit out of borrowed money. *Vijay Kumar Gupta* v *Eagle Paint & Pigment Industries (P) Ltd*, (1997) 26 Corpt LA 236 CLB.

or renewed in contravention of such rules, the company shall repay it within thirty days or within further thirty days if allowed by the Central Government on sufficient cause. Where a deposit is not refunded in accordance with its terms and conditions, the Company Law Board may order repayment. It may do so on its own motion or on the application of the depositor. The Board may extend the schedule for repayment. In *Pure Drinks (New Delhi) Ltd, Re,*[12] the Company Law Board did not authorise reduction in rate of interest. The Board may take into account the interest of the company, that of the depositor and also public interest. The Board may require refund either in full or in part and subject to such conditions and within such time as the order may prescribe. The company and any interested person should be given an opportunity of being heard.[13]

If the deposit is not so refunded the company shall be liable to a fine twice the amount of the deposit not refunded. Out of this amount, when realised, the court pays back the depositor and then the company's liability stands discharged. Officers are punishable with fine and imprisonment not exceeding five years.

Deposits in excess of the limits prescribed by the rules also involve fine on the company to an amount equal to the deposit; for mere invitation the fine may go up to ten lakh rupees, but not less than Rs 50,000. Officers are punishable with fine and imprisonment up to five years.

No company can invite deposits or renew them if it is in default in the repayment of any deposits in full or in part or any interest due on them.[14]

These provisions are not applicable to a banking company, or a company which the Central Government may, in consultation with the Reserve Bank, exempt; any other financial company which the Central Government may similarly exempt, but not from the requirement as to advertisement.[15] The *Explanation* appended to the section defines the term "deposit" as any deposit of money including any amount borrowed by the company, but excluding categories of amounts which may be prescribed by the Central Government in consultation with the Reserve Bank.[16]

---

12. (1995) 83 Comp Cas 174 CLB.
13. Disobedience of the orders of the CLB under S. 58-A(8) is punishable under sub-section (9). *Thapar Agro Mills, Re,* (1997) 25 Corpt LA 102 CLB, rescheduling at 2% higher interest rates.
14. This restriction was introduced by the Companies (Amendment) Act, 1996 (w.e.f. 1-3-1997).
15. Sub-s. (7). The exemption is also there in favour of deposits for booking vehicles, and those accepted by financial companies like hire-purchase, housing, investment, loan-mutual benefit financial companies, an equipment leasing company, a chit fund company, such industrial companies (as may be prescribed) and relief undertakings.
16. *Gopal K. Maheshwari* v *Hawk Multimedia (P) Ltd,* (2005) 126 Comp Cas 76 CLB, an individual loan to the company at 18% interest was held to be not a public deposit, the company had also not issued any deposit receipt.

Acceptance and repayment of deposits

Of late, companies have shown a marked preference for raising funds by inviting fixed deposits from public generally instead of raising capital by means of a prospectus. There is a greater desire to raise loan capital instead of share capital. The craze began for the reason that no sanctions were necessary initially in inviting deposits and no regulations had to be followed in subsequently maintaining them. People were tempted to invest because higher interest rates were offered as compared with banks. Some investors had, however, to face a very sad experience. Unscrupulous companies failed to pay back and the deposit-holders had no effective remedy. There was a wave of public disappointment with companies. The Government intervened. The Companies Act was amended. Sections 58-A and 58-B came into being. They regulate public invitation for deposits, their acceptance and repayment and also provide criminal sanctions for breach of rules. Section 58-B provides that the provisions of the Act relating to prospectus shall, as far as may be, apply to an advertisement for deposits. Every person who at the time of any contravention of the provisions was in responsible position in the company shall be guilty and punishable.[17] The Madras High Court witnessed a case arising out of prosecution under the section.[18] The provisions of the section and the rules framed under it by the Reserve Bank of India prescribe the maximum extent to which a company can receive deposits. There is a criminal sanction against violation of the ceiling. The deposits received by a company were in excess of the permitted amount at the time when the section was enforced. The section required refund of the excess amount within thirty days. The company did not do so but instead renewed such deposits for further periods. This entailed prosecution. The company, its managing director and the directors who were brought on record wanted the proceedings to be quashed till their application to the Central Government for exemption from the operation of the section was disposed of and also on the ground that the section should apply only to the acceptance of fresh deposits and not to the renewal of existing ones, because the word

---

17. See *RBI* v *Dhanlakshmi Funds*, (1987) 60 Comp Cas 439 Mad, where the partners of an erstwhile firm, which was taken over by a company, were held liable for contravention of the provisions; *Chennai Bolting Co* v *Asstt ROC*, (1987) 61 Comp Cas 770 Mad, lenient punishment where deposits were repaid after breach.

18. *Sujani Textiles (P) Ltd* v *Asstt ROC*, (1980) 50 Comp Cas 276 Mad; *Jagjivan Ram Hiralal Doshi* v *ROC*, (1989) 65 Comp Cas 553 Bom: [1989] 2 Comp LJ 315, 328 Bom. The magistrate taking cognisance of an offence under the section also enjoys the power of recalling cognisance and without trying it there it would be premature to apply to the High Court for quashing the proceedings. *Ramakrishna Flour and Besan Mills (P) Ltd* v *Company Registrar, MP*, (1994) 79 Comp Cas 528 MP. Following *K.M. Mathew* v *State of Kerala*, (1992) 1 SCC 217: (1992) 1 Ker LT 1 SC, the court below, if satisfied, had jurisdiction to recall the order of cognisance and to drop proceedings.

"renewal" does not figure in the section. These arguments were not accepted. The prosecution was directed to proceed. The court said:

> "Instead of repaying the excess amount, the petitioners have kept the amount and have issued fresh deposit receipts. This renewal amounts to receiving fresh deposits. The word "renew" also means "to acquire again". Therefore renewal amounts to receiving fresh deposits within the meaning of Section 58-A(4) punishable under Section 58-A(5)(*b*). Since the punishment under the Section is for more than three years, and also fine, the prosecution is not barred by reason of the provisions of Section 468-C of the Criminal Procedure Code."

Whenever new regulations of this kind are brought into being curbing the earlier freedom of action, some default in their implementation may creep in and no punishment is deserved if the default is made good as soon as it is pointed out. The Calcutta High Court adopted this approach in a case where the company readily rectified the default.[19] The company in this case was the famous East India Hotels Ltd. The company's deposits exceeded the prescribed limits. The company applied to the Government of India seeking exemption. The Department of Company Affairs expressed their inability to do so. The company immediately covered the deposits by securing them by creating a trust. The company then prayed for relief against the penal consequences. The Registrar opposed the company. The court allowed relief. The company had made good the default by giving security to the depositors. No depositor had made any complaint against the company which made it reasonable to suppose that they had accepted the security. There was no further violation of Section 58-A and its rules. Thus relief was fully deserved.

One of the rules promulgated by the Government[20], Rule 3-A requires a company to deposit or invest a sum equal to at least 10 per cent of the amount maturing during the year in certain specified accounts in a scheduled bank or in specified securities, which should not be subjected to any charge or lien. Some of the affected companies challenged the validity of the rule. The Supreme Court rejected the petitions.[21] Ten per cent of the

---

19. *East India Hotels Ltd, Re,* (1980) 50 Comp Cas 381 Cal, where a prosecution was commenced under the section for receiving excess deposits at a time when only S. 58(B)(5)(*a*) and (*b*) of the Reserve Bank of India Act, 1934 was in force. The Madras High Court quashed the proceeding because S. 58-A(5)(*a*) and (*b*) of the Companies Act provide for a different and greater punishment. *Sun Paper Mill Ltd* v *Asstt Registrar of Companies,* (1986) 59 Comp Cas 320 Mad.

20. SEBI Guidelines for companies rendering financial services, SEBI Rules and Regulations for Mutual Funds and Asset Management Cos and Rules and Regulations for Portfolio Managers, 1993.

21. *Delhi Cloth and General Mills* v *UOI; Arvind Mills* v *UOI; Madhusudan Veg Products* v *UOI; Modi Spg and Wvg Mills* v *UOI; Goetze (India) Ltd* v *UOI,* (1983) 4 SCC 166: (1983) 54 Comp Cas 674: (1983) Tax LR 2584. The decision of the Madras HC in *P.* Court

amount maturing every year is required to be kept in a free deposit as a measure of protection of the depositors. The deposit will accumulate into a sizable amount. The depositors will be able to get their refund surely. There is nothing inherently wrong with the scheme. The fact that the Government had the power to exempt some companies from the requirement did not make the power arbitrary unless there was arbitrary use of it. The Court, however, conceded that companies have a right to go in for writs against violation of the right to equality or fundamental freedoms as enshrined in Article 19.[22]

In case of default in repayment of deposit money or payment of interest, the Tribunal[23] (formerly CLB) may, on the application of the depositor, order repayment. The Tribunal can do so on its own motion also.

The orders of the Company Law Board (now Tribunal) are enforceable through the civil court in the manner of a court decree.[24]

Duty to small depositors [S. 58-AA]

This new provision has been introduced by the Amendment of 2000. If a company fails to pay back a small depositor, it has to inform the National Company Law Tribunal accordingly. A small depositor means a depositor who has in a financial year deposited with the company not more than Rs 20,000.[25] The information has to be submitted on monthly basis within

---

allowed relief under S. 633(2) by directing the Registrar not to prosecute for violation of S. 58-A because by the time the show-cause notice was given, the directors had already rectified the default. *G. M. Mohan* v *ROC*, (1984) 56 Comp Cas 265. Failure to fulfil this requirement has been held to be one-time offence attracting the six months' bar of limitation under S. 468, CrPC, 1973; failure to repay is a continuing offence, *Sivandhi Adityam* v *Addl ROC*, (1995) 83 Comp Cas 616 Mad.

22. The court was of the view that the judicial attitude has changed since the *Bank Nationalisation case*, (1970) 1 SCC 248: (1970) 40 Comp Cas 325 SC. The offence of non-payment is not of continuing nature. Subsequent directors are not liable for earlier defaults. *Asstt ROC* v *R. Narayanaswamy*, (1985) 57 Comp Cas 787. Fundamental rights are not violated by deposit rules. *A. S. P. Aiyer* v *RBI*, (1984) 56 Comp Cas 352 Mad. The duty to file a return as to deposits continues even after the time for filing the return has expired and the default being of continuing nature, penalty proceedings cannot be barred by limitation. *U.P. Paper Corpn (P) Ltd* v *ROC*, (1987) 61 Comp Cas 728 Cal. It has been held that different ceilings for individuals, firms and companies are not violative of Art. 14 of the Constitution. *Kanta Mehta* v *UOI*, 62 Comp Cas 769 Del. The return must be in reference to the latest audited balance-sheet of the company. *Malayala Manorma Co Ltd* v *ROC*, (1990) 69 Comp Cas 339 Ker. The auditor's remark in his certificate that there was a non-compliance with deposit rules was held to be *prima facie* evidence for framing a charge of violation. *Mohan Lal Rathi* v *Addl ROC*, [1992] 1 Comp LJ 207 Del. *Carrier Savings & Investments India Ltd* v *UOI*, (2002) 110 Comp Cas 631 Raj, the company applied for permission for retaining deposits beyond maturity period. The Government passed an order without considering representation of the depositors. Violation of natural justice. The court ordered for rehearing of the matter.
23. *Substituted* for CLB by the Second Amendment Act, 2002.
24. *Edpuganti Bapanaiah* v *Nagarjuna Finance Ltd*, (2002) 111 Comp Cas 496 CLB.
25. S. 58-AA, *Explanation*. Depositor includes his successors, nominees and legal representatives.

60 days of each default and with all the particulars of the deposit. The default may be for the whole amount or a part of it or in respect of interest. On receipt of such information, the CLB is under a duty to exercise the power under Section 58-A(9) to order the company to pay back the depositor. The CLB may pass such an order of its own motion within 30 days. After such period, it may do so under intimation to the depositor but his presence at the hearing for an order is not necessary.

Such a defaulting company cannot accept any further deposit from small depositors unless it has paid back the whole amount due to each and every such depositor. This disability is not to apply in respect of a deposit which has been renewed by the depositor voluntarily or where repayment could not be made due to the death of the depositor or stay order of a court or some other authority.

The total amount of default in respect of small deposits has to be included in future advertisement and application forms inviting public deposits. Where interest accruing to small depositors has been waived, this fact should also be included in the advertisement and application forms.

Where after acceptance of new deposits, the company has been successful in taking loans for its working capital, before such loan amount is used for any other purpose, it should be applied in repayment of dues on small deposits. Application forms must inform future small depositors of past defaults in repayment of principal or waiver of interest.[26]

On the abolition of the Company Law Board by enforcement of the Second Amendment Act, 2002, the powers of CLB would become vested in National Company Law Tribunal (NCLT) or (Tribunal).

Fraudulently inducing investment of money [S. 68]

It is a punishable offence to fraudulently induce persons to invest money in companies. The penalty of the section is attracted when investment is brought about by knowingly or recklessly making any statement, promise or forecast which is false, deceptive or misleading or by any dishonest concealment of material facts. Liability would be incurred even when one is only attempting to do so. The object of the inducement is to bring about any agreement for acquiring, disposing of or subscribing for or underwriting any shares or debentures or bringing about profit from fluctuations in the value of shares or debentures.[27]

---

26. Default committed knowingly in not complying with the provisions or in carrying out the orders of the Company Law Board entails punishment by way of imprisonment extending to three years or daily fine of not less than Rs 500. Directors and the company are deemed to be guilty. In other respects S. 58-A applies. The offences under the section have been made cognizable when complaint is made by the Central Government or its authorised functionary, S. 58-AAA.
27. Administration of power under the section has been vested in SEBI.

First issue in demat form [S. 68-B]

The Amendment of 2000 has added this new section. It provides that every listed public company, making initial public offer of securities of Rs 10 crore or more, shall issue the same in dematerialised form. For this purpose the requirements of the Depositories Act, 1996 and Regulations made under that Act should be complied with.[28]

Vesting of Powers in SEBI [S. 55-A]

This provision was added by the Amendment of 2000 (w.e.f. 13-12-2000) for vesting of powers in SEBI in respect of the power under the following sections: Ss. 55 to 58; Ss. 59 to 84; 108, 109, 110, 112, 113, 116, 117, 118, 119, 120, 121, 122, 206, 206-A, to the extent to which these provisions relate to issue and transfer of securities, and non-payment of dividend.

The operation of this section is restricted to listed companies and those which are proposed to be listed. In other respects the powers are to be exercised by the Central Government or CLB or the Registrar of Companies, as the case may be.

———

28. *Mukesh Malhotra* v *SEBI*, (2005) 124 Comp Cas 336 SAT, on failure to furnish information.

6

Promoters

Definition and importance

In many company matters, the term "promoter" is of frequent occurrence. The Companies Act itself uses the word at some places for the purpose of imposing liability upon promoters.[1] Yet "it has never been clearly defined either judicially or legislatively".[2] "The difficulties in defining the term led the judges to state that the term 'promoter' is not a term of art, nor a term of law, but of business."[3] The emphasis upon its business implication is quite apparent from the statement of BOWEN LJ that the term is used to sum up "in a single word a number of business operations, familiar to the commercial world, by which a company is generally brought into existence".[4] Most of the definitions are in terms of categories of work that promoters usually perform. "A promoter is a person who brings about the incorporation and organisation of a corporation. He brings together the persons who become interested in the enterprise, aids in procuring subscriptions, and sets in motion the machinery which leads to the formation itself."[5] "A promoter is one who undertakes to form a company with reference to a given project and to set it going, and who takes the necessary steps to accomplish that purpose."[6] The term, therefore, "has no very definite meaning".[7] Whether a person is a promoter or not is a question of fact in each case. Much depends upon the nature of the role played by him in the promotion of business. In *Twycross* v *Grant*,[8] the court said "that the defendants were the promoters of the company from the very beginning can admit of no doubt. They framed the scheme, they not only provisionally formed the company, but were, in fact, to the end its creators, they found the

---

1. For example, Sections 62, 69 and 478 impose liability upon promoters. "Before a company can be formed there must be some persons who have the intention to form a company, and who take the necessary steps to carry that intention into operation. Such persons are called 'promoters'." Charlesworth and Morse, COMPANY LAW, p 98 (14th Edn, 1991).
2. Joseph H. Gross, *Who is a Company Promoter*, (1970) 86 LQR 493.
3. *Id.*, at p 506.
4. *Whaley Bridge Calico Printing Co* v *Green*, (1880) 5 QBD 109: 28 WR 351 : 41 LT 674.
5. *Bosher* v *Richmond Land Co*, 89 Va 455 (16) SE 360 : 37 Am St Rep 879. Collected from Canfield and Wormser, CASES ON PRIVATE CORPORATIONS.
6. COCKBURN CJ in *Twycross* v *Grant*, [1877] 2 CPD 469, 541 : 46 LJ QB 636 : 36 LT 812: 25 WR 701 CA. This definition was adopted by the Mad HC in *Weavers Mills* v *Balkis Ammal*, AIR 1969 Mad 462 at pp 468-69: [1969] 2 MLJ 509: ILR [1969] 1 Mad 433.
7. LINDLEY, J, in *Emma Silver Mining Co* v *Lewis*, (1879) 4 CPD 396, 407: 40 LT 749; followed in *Thiruvenkatachariar National Livestock Registration Bank Ltd* v *A. T. Velu Mudaliar*, ILR 1938 Mad 192: AIR 1938 Mad 154. The advantage of having a flexible definition is that only those would be subjected to the strict duties of a promoter who fulfil the functional concept of the definition. *Jacobus Marler Estates Ltd* v *Marler*, (1913) 85 LJPC 167.
8. (1877) 2 CPD 469 CA: 46 LJQB 636: 36 LT 812: 25 WR 701 CA.

directors, and qualified them, they prepared the prospectus, they paid for printing and advertising, and the expenses incidental to bringing the undertaking before the world." The court added that the functions of promoters come to an end as soon as they hand over the company to a governing body, like a board of directors.[9]

A person who acts in a professional capacity is not a promoter. Thus a solicitor, who prepares on behalf of the promoters the primary documents of the proposed company, is not a promoter.[10] Similarly, an accountant or a valuer who helps the promotion in his professional capacity is not a promoter. The Companies Act, in Section 62, while providing for the liability of a promoter for misrepresentation in prospectus, also excludes such a person from the category.[11] But any such person may become a promoter if he helps the formation of the company by doing an act outside the scope of his professional duty. A person may, for example, help in getting a purchaser for the company's patent, or of shares, or in getting personnel for the company. Any such role may make him a promoter.[12]

DUTY AND LIABILITY

Fiduciary position

The position of promoters in relation to the company was explained by Lord CAIRNS in *Erlanger* v *New Sombrero Phosphate Co*[13] in the following words:

> They stand, in my opinion, undoubtedly in a fiduciary position. They have in their hands the creation and moulding of the company. They have the power of defining how and when, in what shape and under what supervision the company shall start into existence and begin to act as a trading corporation.

---

9. A person may become a promoter even after the formation of the company, for example, by becoming party to share issues or to procuring subscriptions. Section 62 makes liable for misstatements in prospectus every person who is promoter of the company. Stringent provisions of the Companies Act and of the allied Acts have virtually eliminated fraudulent practices in company promotions.

10. A servant or agent of a promoter is not to be regarded as a promoter for that reason alone; also a solicitor doing only legal work, *Great Wheal Polgooth Ltd, Re,* (1883) 53 LJ Ch 42.

11. Sub-section (6) of the section says "For the purpose of this section—(a) the expression 'promoter' means a promoter who was a party to the preparation of the prospectus ... containing the untrue statement, but does not include any person by reason of his acting in a professional capacity for persons engaged in procuring the formation of a company."

12. A person who leaves the task of promotion to others and sits behind to share their profits is likely to be regarded as a promoter. *Emma Silver Mining Co* v *Lewis,* (1879) 4 CPD 396: 40 LT 749 and *Tracy* v *Mandalay,* (1952-53) 88 CLR 215.

13. (1878) 3 App Cas 1218 at p 1236: 48 LJ Ch 73: 39 LT 269: 27 WR 65. The Madras High Court has accepted this position of promoters in *Weavers Mills* v *Balkis Ammal,* AIR 1969 Mad 462: [1969] 2 MLJ 509: ILR [1969] 1 Mad 433. The basic element in the duty is something that needs no saying, namely, their duty is to promote the interests of the company.

The business of promotion thus gives a very advantageous position to the promoter in relation to the proposed company. The courts have, therefore, fixed him with the responsibility of a fiduciary agent. "The promoter is in the situation akin to that of a trustee of the company, and his dealings with it must be open and fair."[14] Thus the first and the foremost duty of a promoter is that if he starts a company for the purpose of buying his property and wants to draw his payment from the money obtained from shareholders, he must faithfully disclose all facts relating to the property. If he conceals any fact in relation to the character or value of the property, or his personal interest in the proposed sale, the company will be entitled to set aside the transaction or recover compensation for its loss. He is guilty of breach of trust if he sells property to the company without informing the company that the property belongs to him or he may commit a breach of trust by accepting a bonus or commission from a person who sells property to the company. In short, the chief duty of the promoter as a fiduciary agent is to disclose to the company his position, his profit and his interest in the property which is the subject of purchase or sale by the company.[15]

The only difficult question is to whom the disclosure is to be made. It was suggested by the House of Lords in *Erlanger* v *New Sombrero Phosphate Co*[16] that it should be made to an independent and competent board of directors. The facts of the case were as follows:

> A group of persons headed by *E* purchased an island containing phosphate mines for £55,000. A company was then incorporated to take over the island and to work the mines. *E* named five persons as directors. Two were abroad. Of the three others, two were persons entirely under *E*'s control. These three directors purchased the island for the company at a price of £1,10,000. A prospectus was then issued. Many persons took shares. The purchase of the island was adopted by the shareholders at their first meeting; but the real circumstances were not disclosed to them. The company failed and the liquidator sued the promoter for refund of the profit.

The only material contention urged on behalf of the promoter was that the company's board of directors had full knowledge of the facts. Rejecting this Lord CAIRNS said:

> If they (promoters) propose to sell their property to the company, it is incumbent upon them to take care that they provide the company with an executive body who shall both be aware that the property which they

---

14. Morawetz, CORPORATION, Section 546. *Omnium Electric Palaces Ltd* v *Baines*, (1914) 1 Ch 332 CA, they are not trustees in the real sense of the word because the company may not be in existence as a legal person. Fiduciary position emerges from agency.
15. There is no duty that the promoter must restrain himself from making any profit whatsoever in the business of promotion. *Omnium Electric Palaces Ltd* v *Baines*, (1914) 1 Ch 332 CA.
16. (1878) 3 App Cas 1218: 48 LJ Ch 73: 39 LT 269: 27 WR 65.

are asked to purchase is the promoter's property and who shall be competent and impartial judges as to whether the purchase ought or ought not to be made. They should sell the property to the company through the medium of a board of directors who can and do exercise an independent and intelligent judgment on the transaction.[17]

Subsequent experience, however, showed that it may not always be possible for the promoters to give to the company an independent board of directors. In the case of a private company, or a public company which, like that of Saloman & Co, consists of only the family members, it is just not possible to constitute an independent board of directors. In such a case the promoter should disclose his interest and profit to the shareholders of the company. But it will not be enough to disclose the truth to the first few shareholders. The disclosure should be made to the whole body of persons who are invited to become the shareholders. This was emphasised by the House of Lords in their well-known decision in *Gluckstein* v *Barnes*.[18]

A syndicate of persons was formed to raise a fund, buy a property, called "Olympia" and resell it to a company. They first bought up some of the charges upon the property for sums below the amount which the charges afterwards realised, and thereby made a profit of £20,000. They bought the property for £1,40,000, formed a limited company and resold the property for £1,80,000 to the company, of which they were first directors. They issued a prospectus inviting applications for shares and disclosing the two prices of £1,40,000 and £ 1,80,000 but not the profit of £20,000. Shares were issued but the company afterwards went into liquidation.

It was held that the promoters ought to have disclosed to the company the profit of £20,000. The defendant, who was one of the promoters, contended that the fact was known to the parties to the transaction. Rejecting this, HALSBURY LC said:

It is too absurd to suggest that a disclosure to the parties to this transaction is a disclosure to the company. They were there by the terms of the agreement to do the work of the syndicate, that is to say, to cheat the shareholders; and this, forsooth, is to be treated as a disclosure to the company, when they were really there to hoodwink the shareholders, and so, far from protecting them, were to obtain from them the money, the produce of their nefarious plans.[19]

---

17. (1878) 3 App Cas 1218: 48 LJ Ch 73: 39 LT 269: 27 WR 65, at p 1223.
18. 1900 AC 240: 69 LJ Ch 385: 82 LT 393: 16 TLR 321: 7 Mans 321.
19. 1900 AC 240 at p 247. *See* also *Postage Stamp Automatic Delivery Co, Re*, [1892] 3 Ch 566: 61 LJ Ch 597: (1892) 67 LT 88; *Promoters Profits: Control by Court & Commission*, (1936) 59 Harv LR 785.

Disclosure is not the most appropriate word to use when a person who plays many parts announces to himself in one character what he has done and is doing in another.[20]

The duty continues even after incorporation until the profits are fully disclosed and fully accounted for.[21]

Where rescission is not possible, that is, the company is not in a position to return the property, it can recover damages for breach of the duty of good faith, though the measure of damages is the profit which the promoter made from the breach of his duty.[22]

The Companies Act now requires through Section 56 the promoters' earnings to be disclosed in the prospectus itself. The disclosure has to be made of the amount paid within the last two years or to be paid to the promoters of the company. The statement has to include any other benefit also. Disclosure has also to be made of any interest of the promoter in the promotion of the company or in any property acquired by the company during the two years or proposed to be acquired.[23]

A leasehold interest was purchased by a promoter for a company which he intended to form. However, he first formed a partnership firm and then converted it into a company. It was held that the interest in the lease became the property of the company without any formality of conveyance. From the very first day of purchase it became in equity the property of the company.[24]

---

20. Lord MACNAGHTEN, *ibid.*

21. *Emma Silver Mining Co* v *Lewis*, (1879) 4 CPD 396: 40 LT 749. Subject to such disclosures, it is quite lawful for a promoter to sell his property to the company at a profit to himself, *Omnium Electric Palaces Ltd* v *Baines*, (1914) 1 Ch 332 CA. He is bound to disclose his profit only minus the expenses in earning the same, *Lydney and Wigpool Iron Ore Co* v *Bird*, (1886) 33 Ch D 85 CA.

22. *Leeds & Hanley Theatres of Varieties Ltd, Re*, [1902] 2 Ch 809: 72 LJ Ch 1: 87 LT 488. *See*, generally, Joseph Gold, *The Liability of Promoters for Secret Profits in English Law*, (1943-44) 5 Toronto LJ 21 and J. H. Cross, COMPANY PROMOTERS, Tiagidim Publishing House, 1972.

23. *See* clause 11 of Part C of Part II of the Second Schedule.

24. *Vali Pattabhirama Rao* v *Ramanuja Ginning and Rice Factory (P) Ltd*, (1986) 60 Comp Cas 568 AP. In addition to all these obligations, the promoters have to comply with SEBI Guidelines, 1992 relating to their contribution to the public issue and lock-in-period.

7
Shares

ALLOTMENT

Offers for shares are made on application forms supplied by the company. When an application is accepted, it is an allotment.[1] "What is termed 'allotment' is generally neither more nor less than the acceptance by the company of the offer to take shares."[2] "Broadly speaking it is an appropriation by the directors... of shares to a particular person."[3] "It is an appropriation out of the previously unappropriated capital of a company."[4] Consequently where forfeited shares are re-issued, it is not the same thing as an allotment.[5]

A valid allotment has to comply with the requirements of the Act and principles of the law of contract relating to acceptance of offers.

Statutory restrictions on allotment

1. *Minimum Subscription and Application Money* [S. 69]

The first requisite of a valid allotment is that of minimum subscription. When shares are offered to the public, the amount of minimum subscription has to be stated in the prospectus. Minimum subscription means the amount which is, in the estimate of the directors, enough to meet the following needs, namely, purchase price of any property to be defrayed partly or wholly out of the proceeds of the issue, preliminary expenses and working capital (not to be less than 90% of the whole issue offered to the public, as now prescribed).[6] No shares can, be allotted unless at least so much amount has been subscribed and the application money, which must not be less than five per cent of the nominal value of the share, has been received in cash.[7]

---

1. See *Sri Gopal Jalan & Co v Calcutta Stock Exchange Assn*, AIR 1964 SC 250, 251: 33 Comp Cas 862. Reaffirmed by the Supreme Court in *Gopal Paper Mills v CIT*, (1970) 2 SCC 80, 86: AIR 1970 SC 1750; *Associated Clothiers v UOI*, ILR [1957] 2 Punj 505, 511-12. The Madras High Court has held in *Shri Ayyanar Spg & Wvg Mills v V.V.V. Rajendran*, (1973) 43 Comp Cas 225 Mad, that an oral application for shares is equally valid. But since S. 41 requires an agreement in writing, no allotment can be made without a written application for allotment. *H. H. Manabendra Shah v Official Liquidator*, (1977) 47 Comp Cas 356.
2. CHITTY J in *Florence Land & Public Works Ltd, Re*, (1885) 29 Ch D 421, 426, adopted by the Supreme Court in *Sri Gopal Jalan & Co v Calcutta Stock Exchange Assn*, AIR 1964 SC 250: 33 Comp Cas 862.
3. STIRLING J in *Spitzel v Chinese Corpn*, (1899) 80 LT 347, 351.
4. SARKAR J in *Sri Gopal Jalan & Co v Calcutta Stock Exchange Assn*, AIR 1964 SC 250: 33 Comp Cas 862.
5. *Ibid.* Allotment has to be an initial issue, *CIT v V.S.S.V. Meenakshi*, (1984) 55 Comp Cas 545. In *Plate Dealers Assn (P) Ltd v Satish Chandra Samwalka*, (2006) 129 Comp Cas 316 Cal, reissue of forfeited shares.
6. S. 69(1) and clause 5 of Schedule II.
7. S. 69(3). Cash means actual cash received whether by means of cheque, draft or otherwise. An application accompanied by cash of more than Rs 20,000 (then permissible Income Tax Act

A number of cases have established that it is a condition precedent to valid allotment that the whole of the application money should have been paid to and received by the company in cash.[8] Any means by which money can be remitted may be used, but remittances must be cleared and actual cash received by the company before proceeding to allotment. An application for shares, if not accompanied by any such payment, does not constitute a valid offer.[9] Further, it has been held that an allotment of shares made without the application money being paid is invalid and the directors are guilty of misfeasance.[10]

The object of these provisions, says Gower, is to prevent the company getting under way until it has raised the capital needed to carry out the objects in which it has invited the public to participate; it would obviously be iniquitous to force an applicant, who has accepted an invitation to participate in a one million issue for the purpose of buying Wembley Stadium, to sink his capital in a company which has only raised enough money to buy a suburban villa. They also afford protection to the creditors by ensuring that a limited company is not able to incur commitments if it is grossly under-capitalised.[11]

If the minimum subscription has not been received within 120 days of the issue of the prospectus, the money received from the applicants must be repaid without interest.[12] If the money is not paid back within 130 days the directors become personally liable for it with interest, unless they can show that the default was not due to any negligence or misconduct on their part.[13] Application money can be appropriated towards allotment or it has to be

---

limit for cash payments) was held to be rightly rejected, the mode of payment being illegal, *Mohd. Rafeek* v *SEBI*, (1999) 98 Comp Cas 802.

8. *See*, for example, *Nears* v *Western Canada Pulp & Paper Co*, [1905] 2 Ch 353; *National Motor Mail-Coach Co, Re*, [1908] 2 Ch 228: [1908-10] All ER Ext Rep 1373; *Malabar Iron & Steel Works Ltd, Re*, AIR 1964 Ker 311. *Universal Incast Ltd* v *SEBI*, (2002) 108 Comp Cas 248 P&H, the application money has to be kept in a separate bank account with the bankers to the issue and not in any bank of the company's choice. The money must remain there till all the mandatory requirements are complied with and the company can proceed to make allotment. Where the company did not do so even after receiving orders from the SEBI (Authority), the Stock Exchange was held to be justified in refusing to list the company's securities.

9. *Ramlalsao Gupta* v *M.E.R. Malak*, AIR 1939 Nag 225: ILR 1941 Nag 567: 183 IC 748.

10. *Indian States Bank Ltd* v *Kunwar Sardar Singh*, AIR 1934 All 855: 154 IC 33.

11. THE PRINCIPLES OF MODERN COMPANY LAW at p 300 (3rd Edn, 1969).

12. S. 69(5). The investors can make use of the new commercial instrument, namely, stock invest scheme under which their application money remains with their own bank and is collected by the company only if some shares are allotted to the applicants. *M.S. Shoes East Ltd* v *MRTPC*, (2005) 128 Comp Cas 945 Del, it is essentially a money claim three years period of limitation becomes applicable.

13. The rate of interest is 6% per annum. A director may, however, defend himself by showing that he was not guilty of any negligence or misconduct. S. 69(5). The minimum subscription prescribed under the rule making power is 90% subscription against the entire issue offered to the public. The applicants cannot waive this right [Sub-sec (6)]. *Rank Industries Ltd* v *ROC*, (2007) 135 Comp Cas 601 AP, there are penalty provisions also. Limitation period for filing complaint commences from the date on which the prosecuting agency comes to know of the offence.

refunded. It cannot be adjusted towards any claim of the company against the applicant.[14]

2. *Statement in lieu of Prospectus* [S. 70]

Where prospectus has not been issued, no allotment shall be made unless at least three days before a statement in lieu of prospectus has been filed with the Registrar.

An allotment made in contravention of the above two rules is voidable at the instance of the applicant, provided he moves within two months of the statutory meeting of the company or where statutory meeting is not required to be held or where the allotment is made after the holding of the statutory meeting, within two months after the date of the allotment.[15] Notice of avoidance given within this time will be sufficient, though actual legal proceedings, if necessary, may be commenced thereafter.[16] It is not necessary that the allottee should commence actual legal proceedings within two months. It is enough for him to give a notice to the company of his intention to revoke the allotment. Such an allotment is voidable even if the company is in the course of winding up. [S. 71(2)]

Where the contravention is wilful, the directors guilty thereof are liable to compensate both the allottee and the company, provided that the party suing has sustained a loss and brings the action within two years of the allotment. [S. 71(3)]

3. *Opening of Subscription list* [S. 72]

Shares cannot be allotted at once after the issue of the prospectus. Section 72 enjoins that no allotment shall be made until the beginning of the 5th day from the date of the issue of the prospectus. This is known as the time of opening of subscription list. The directors may extend this time by a statement to that effect in the prospectus, but it cannot be cut short. The validity of an allotment is not affected by any contravention of this section, although a penalty is imposed on the company and its officers.[17] Applications for shares are not revocable until the end of the 5th day from the opening of the subscription list. [S. 72(5)]

4. *Shares to be dealt in on Stock Exchange* [S. 73]

Every company intending to offer shares or debentures to the public by the issue of a prospectus has to make an application before the issue to any one or more of the recognised stock exchanges for permission for the shares

---

14. *Dhananjay Pande* v *Dr Bais Surgical & Medical Institute (P) Ltd*, (2005) 125 Comp Cas 626 CLB.
15. S. 71(1). *Finance & Issue Ltd* v *Canadian Produce Corpn*, (1905) 1 Ch 37: 73 LJ Ch 751.
16. *National Motor Mail-Coach Co, Re*, (1908) 2 Ch 228: [1908-10] All ER Ext Rep 1373.
17. S. 72(3). Where any person responsible under S. 62 for any statement in the prospectus has given a public notice excluding his liability, 5th day for opening subscription list would be counted from the date of such notice [sub-s.(1) proviso].

or debentures to be dealt with at the exchange. The amendment of 1988 has made an application to a stock exchange compulsory. Formerly it was optional with the company.[18] It is a condition precedent for listing permission that the application money is deposited in a separate bank account.[19]

An allotment shall become void if the permission has not been granted before the expiry of ten weeks from the date of the closing of the subscription list.[20]

If the allotment becomes void under this section, the money received from the applicants shall be forthwith repaid.[21] If it is not refunded within 8 days, the directors will be personally liable to repay it with interest.[22]

The object of Section 73 has been explained by the Supreme Court in *Union of India* v *Allied International Products Ltd.*[23] The object of the provision is to enable shareholders to find a ready market for their shares so that they can convert their investment into cash whenever they like. The Supreme Court held that even if one out of the several stock exchanges applied for and granted recognition it would be sufficient to validate the allotment; the facility of at least one stock exchange would thereby be available. The amendment of 1974 nullified this part of the judgment. Now the position is that if, out of the stock exchanges applied for, a single stock exchange refuses to grant listing, the allotment, if already made, becomes

---

18. This is known as listing. Stock Exchanges charge their fee for listing agreements. Provisions of Securities (Contracts Regulation) Act, 1956 are applicable to the subject. Government guidelines on the subject are also there.
19. S. 69(4) and S. 73(3). *Universal Incast Ltd* v *AA SEBI*, [2000] CLC 948 P&H.
20. Ten weeks are to be reckoned from the closure of the subscription list and not from the date of allotment even if earlier. *Raymond Synthetics Ltd* v *UOI*, (1992) 2 SCC 255: AIR 1992 SC 847: (1992) 73 Comp Cas 1: [1992] 1 Comp LJ 209. The period of ten weeks cannot be extended by the court on the ground of injunction against public issue, *Unjha Formulations Ltd* v *Unjha Pharmacy*, (1996) 2 Guj LH 511.
21. Since the money lies in a separate bank account, it is refundable to allottees even if the company is in winding up. *Nanwa Gold Mines Ltd, Re*, [1955] 1 WLR 1080, 1085. Refund orders are required under Government prescription to be sent by registered post.
22. S. 73(2). The amendment of sub-section (2) in 1988 provides that the company and every officer of the company who is an officer in default shall on and from expiry of the 8th day be jointly and severally liable to repay that money with interest at such rate, not less than 4% and not more than 15% as may be prescribed. The following rates of interest has been prescribed w.e.f. 21-2-1992: The rates of interest, for the purposes of sub-s. (2) and (2-A) shall be 15% per annum. (GSR No 312E of 6-3-92).
    The subscription money has been held to be in the nature of trust money and not a part of the banker's general assets so as to be usable in his insolvency. It is refundable *in specie*. *Reserve Bank of India* v *BCCI (Overseas) Ltd*, (1993) 78 Comp Cas 230 Bom. Misuse of the money may amount to criminal breach of trust and punishable as such under the Indian Penal Code, 1860. Power of prosecution has been delegated to SEBI. *Radhey Shyam Khemka* v *State of Bihar*, (1993) 3 SCC 54: (1993) 77 Comp Cas 356 SC. The offence involved in failure to despatch was held to be wiped out where as soon as the failure was discovered, the default was made good by sending duplicate refund warrants, *Herdillia Unimers Ltd* v *Arun Bansal*, (1999) 96 Comp Cas 521 Raj.
23. (1970) 3 SCC 574: (1971) 41 Comp Cas 127. The advantage of listing is that shares become freely marketable and this enhances their value.

void. The company may appeal to the Central Government. If the appeal is successful, the decision of stock exchange is set aside and the listing would be granted. The allotment would be saved.[24] Where a stock exchange failed to dispose of the company's application and the Central Government, on appeal, ordered listing, the allotment was saved.[25]

The first sub-section of Section 73 was completely changed. The sub-section requires the name of the stock exchange or exchanges to which an application for permission has been made to be specified in the prospectus itself. The second change is that if any such stock exchange has not granted its permission, or has not disposed of the application within ten weeks,[26] the allotment shall become void, even if some other exchanges have granted the permission. The third change is in reference to time. Formerly, an application had to be disposed of within four weeks, which could have been extended by the exchange to seven weeks. Now the time is that of ten weeks from the date of the closing of the subscription list.[27] Where an appeal has been preferred under Section 22 of the Securities Contracts (Regulation) Act, 1956 against the refusal of a stock exchange, the allotment does not become void until the dismissal of the appeal.[28]

Over-subscribed prospectus [S.73(2-A)].—Where the permission of a stock exchange has been granted and, therefore, the allotment completed is valid, the prospectus being over-subscribed, the over-subscribed portion of the money received must be sent back to the applicants forthwith. The margin is only that of eight days from the completion of the allotment. A failure to do so would create a liability which has been thus stated: "The company and every officer of the company who is an officer in default shall, on and from the expiry of the 8th day, be jointly and severally liable to repay that money with interest at such rate not less than 4% and not more than

24. *Rishyashringa Jewellers Ltd* v *Stock Exchange, Bombay*, (1995) 6 SCC 714: AIR 1996 SC 480: (1996) 85 Comp Cas 479; *Rich Paints Ltd* v *Vadodra Stock Exchange Ltd*, (1998) 15 SCL 128 Guj. Followed in *Jaltrang Motels Ltd* v *UOI*, (1999) 95 Comp Cas 339, the refundable money was invested in purchasing land, the court directed attachment of the land and deposit of a sum of money with SEBI.
25. *Urmila Bharuka* v *Coventry Spring and Engg Co Ltd*, (1997) 88 Comp Cas 197 Cal. Another litigation arising out of the same case is *Urmila Bharuka* v *UOI*, (1999) 97 Comp Cas 97 Cal. One of the effects of the refusal is that the Stock Exchange can ask the company to delete its name from the company's prospectus, *Lunkad Mehta & Entertainment Ltd* v *Stock Exchange, Mumbai*, (2000) 39 CLA 267 SAT.
26. S. 73(5).
27. *UOI* v *Allied International Products*, (1971) 41 Comp Cas 116 at pp 120-121.
28. S. 73(1), proviso. The procedure for appeals is prescribed by Appeal to Central Government Rules, 1993. Rules and Regulations have also been prescribed for Registrars to Issue and Transfer Agents. The listing is done in accordance with the rules framed under the Securities (Contracts Regulation) Act, 1956. The rules and requirements of the Stock Exchange have to be complied with. Listing particulars are required to be published in the prospectus. A listing agreement has to be entered into.

　　Brokers at stock exchanges may not accept unlisted securities. For the convenience of investors in new and small companies an Over the Counter Exchange of India (OTCEI) has been established which provides liquidity facilities to such investors.

15%, as may be prescribed, having regard to the period of delay in making the repayment of such money''.[29]

Section 74 provides guidance as to the manner in which the fifth, eighth or the tenth day for the purposes of Sections 72 and 73 are to be reckoned.[30]

General principles

An effective allotment has to comply with the requirements of the law of contract relating to acceptance of an offer.[31]

1. *Allotment by proper authority.*—In the first place, an allotment must be made by a resolution of the board of directors. "Allotment is a duty primarily falling upon the directors", and this duty cannot be delegated except in accordance with the provisions of the articles. Accordingly, an allotment made by a general manager under an improper delegation by the directors was held to be void.[32] But where the articles so provided, an allotment made by secretaries and treasurers was held to be regular.[33]

2. *Within reasonable time.*—Secondly, allotment must be made within a reasonable period of time, otherwise the application lapses. What is reasonable time must remain a question of fact in each case. The interval of about six months between application and allotment has been held to be not reasonable. On the expiry of reasonable time Section 6 of the Contract Act applies and the application must be deemed to have been revoked.[34]

---

29. A flat rate of 15% has been prescribed w.e.f. 21-2-92. According to S. 74 the days specified above have to be exclusive of public holidays. The default under the section has been held to be an offence of a continuing nature. *Ghanshyam Chaturbuj* v *Industrial Ceramics (P) Ltd*, (1990) 68 Comp Cas 36 Mad. The default under S. 73 (2-A) which attracts interest with refund money due has been held by the Supreme Court to be not a penalty but a method of calculating the refundable amount, but the default under sub-s. (2-B) is a penalty. *Raymond Synthetics Ltd* v *UOI*, (1992) 2 SCC 255: AIR 1992 SC 847: (1992) 73 Comp Cas 762 SC: [1992] 1 Comp LJ 209. Management of issues is in the hands of Merchant Bankers. They have to function under SEBI Rules and Regulations for Merchant Banking. No interest is payable if refund is made in time, *J. S. Sodhi* v *C. T. Scan Research Centre (P) Ltd*, (1995) 83 Comp Cas 762 P&H, following *Pritam Singh Batra* v *Deol Agro Oil Ltd*, (1995) 82 Comp Cas 685 P&H. A default under the section is a continuing offence, *Bausch & Lamb India Ltd* v *ROC*, (2000) 38 CLA 13 Del.

30. The section is as follows: Manner of reckoning fifth, eighth and tenth days in Sections 72 and 73.—In reckoning for the purposes of Ss 72 and 73, the fifth day, [or eighth day] after another day, any intervening day which is a public holiday under the Negotiable Instruments Act, 1881 (26 of 1881), shall be disregarded, and if the fifth, [or eighth day] (as so reckoned) is itself such a public holiday, there shall for the said purposes be substituted the first day thereafter which is not such a holiday.

31. S. 72(1)(*b*) specially provides that the provisions of the section will not have the effect of affecting any liability under the general law.

32. *Bank of Peshawar Ltd* v *Madho Ram*, AIR 1919 Lah 351: 51 IC 812.

33. *Pasurala Sanyasi* v *Guntur Cotton, Jute & Paper Mills Co*, AIR 1915 Mad 325: 26 IC 349.

34. *Ramlalsao Gupta* v *M. E. R. Malak*, AIR 1939 Nag 225: ILR 1941 Nag 567: 183 IC 748. Where an application was made in December and accepted in August—allotment was held to be too late. *See* also *Ramsgate Victoria Hotel Co* v *Montefiore*, (1866) 1 Ex 109, application in June, allotment in November, held invalid; *Radhe Shyam Beopur Co Ltd* v *Prabhu Dayal*, AIR 1936 Lah 16; *Indian Coop Navigation & Trading Co Ltd* v *Padamsey Premjit*, (1933) 36 Bom LR 32, in both of which allotment was delayed for a whole year and was held void.

3. *Must be communicated.*—Thirdly, the allotment must be communicated to the applicant. Posting of a properly addressed and stamped letter of allotment is a sufficient communication even if the letter is delayed or lost in the course of post.[35] *Household Fire and Carriage Accident Insurance Co v Grant*[36] is the leading authority.

The defendant *Grant* applied for some shares in the plaintiff company. His application was sent by post and a letter of allotment was despatched by the company soon after. But the letter never reached the applicant. He was nevertheless held liable as a shareholder.

4. *Absolute and unconditional.*—Allotment must be absolute and in accordance with the terms and conditions of the application, if any. Thus where a person applied for 400 shares on the condition that he would be appointed cashier of a new branch of the company, the Bombay High Court[37] held that he was not bound by any allotment unless he was so appointed.[38] A condition which is to operate subsequently to allotment will not affect its validity. An applicant to whom shares were allotted on the condition that he would pay for them only when the company paid dividends was held to be bound even though the company had gone into liquidation before paying any dividend.[39]

The applicant must promptly reject the allotment when shares have been allotted to him without his condition being fulfilled. An acquiescence on his part would amount to a waiver of the condition. Thus where a shareholder accepted or pledged his shares, he was held to have lost his right to insist on the condition in his application.[40]

Certificate of shares [S. 113]

An allottee of shares is entitled to have from the company a document, called share certificate, certifying that he is the holder of the specified number of shares in the company. Accordingly, every company making an allotment of shares or debentures or debenture-stock is obliged to deliver to the allottee a certificate of shares, etc., within three months after the

---

35. *Dunlop v Higgins*, 1 HLC 381. *See* Sections 4, 5 and 6 of the Indian Contract Act, 1872. *Sangramsinh P. Gaekwad v Shantadevi P. Gaekwad*, (2005) 123 Comp Cas 566 SC, The right to get shares fructifies only when the application for shares is accepted by allotment of which information has been given to the applicant. The personal right of a shareholder to be allotted shares is not heritable.
36. (1879) 4 Ex Div 216: 48 LJ Ex 597: 41 LT 298: 27 WR 858. According to the Indian Contract Act, 1872 acceptance becomes binding on the offeror when the letter of acceptance is posted to him so as to be out of power of the acceptor, (S. 4). An application may be withdrawn before the letter of allotment is posted and in that case the applicant will not be bound by the allotment. See *National Savings Bank Assn, Re*, (1867) 4 Eq 9. Allotment letters are required under Government prescription to be sent to allottees by registered post.
37. *Ramanbhai v Ghasiram*, ILR (1918) 42 Bom 595; *Mutual Bank of India v Sohan Singh*, AIR 1936 Lah 790.
38. *See* further *Monarch Insurance Co, Re*, (1873) 8 Ch App 507.
39. *Motilal Chunilal v Thakorlal*, (1912) 14 Bom LR 648.
40. *Hargopal v People's Bank of Northern India Ltd*, AIR 1935 Lah 691.

allotment.[41] In the case of a transfer, the certificate has to be delivered within two months. The CLB may grant an extended period of not more than 9 months. If a company makes a default in this respect, the allottee or transferee may give a notice to the company reminding it of its obligation and, if the default is not made good within ten days of the notice, the allottee can apply to the Central Government for a direction to the company to issue share certificates in accordance with the Act.[42] The delivery must be effected in accordance with Section 53 of the Act. The burden of proof is on the company to show that share certificates have been despatched.[43]

A consequential amendment to the section introduced by the Depositories Act, 1996 provides that where shares are dealt with in a depository, the company has to intimate the details of the allotment to the depository immediately on such allotment. Shares in a depository record would not have to be given their distinctive numbers.

The right of an allottee to get his certificate cannot be defeated by putting up the right of lien for any dues owed by the allottee to the company. Lien is not exercisable against the responsibility to issue certificates to allottees.[44]

A complaint was allowed to be filed at a place other than the company's registered office. The court was of the view that the trade in securities was taking place throughout the country and that trade would be defeated if a complaint could be filed only at one place.[45] The Supreme Court has laid down that a complaint would lie only at the place of the company's

---

41. The section is not applicable to issue of bonds. *Mahanagar Telephone Nigam Ltd, Re*, [1993] 3 Comp LJ 239 CLB. The requirement prescribed by the Department for uniform size certificates has been withdrawn. The prescription was under the Companies (Issue of Share Certificate) Rules, 1960.

42. S. 113(3); sub-section (2) imposes penalty for default. The Calcutta High Court had held in *Asiatic Oxygen Ltd, Re*, (1972) 42 Comp Cas 602: AIR 1972 Cal 50 that the only obligation of the company was to keep the certificates ready for delivery, but the court could not compel the company to actually deliver them. The decision was contrary to *Burdett v Standard Exploration Co*, (1899) 16 TLR 112, on the basis of which it was observed in Palmer's COMPANY LAW at p 307 (20th Edn, 1959) that "the right to a certificate can be enforced by action against the company". The amendment of 1988 has made it a positive duty of the company to deliver. See *PNB Mutual Fund v MS Shoes East Ltd*, (1998) 16 SCL 627 CLB, the company directed to deliver debenture certificates.

43. *Cardiff Chemicals Ltd v Fortune Bio-Tech Ltd*, (2005) 126 Comp Cas 275 CLB, the company did not produce any conclusive proof of despatch, hence, in default.

44. *Trishla Jain v Oswal Agro Mills Ltd*, (1996) 86 Comp Cas 48 CLB.

45. *Ranbaxy Laboratories Ltd v Indra Kala*, (1997) 88 Comp Cas 348 Raj. The company had failed to register a debenture transfer and to issue new certificate. The issue of process against the company and defaulting directors was upheld. *Hindustan Development Corpn Ltd v Kushal Chand Bader*, [1998] 1 Comp LJ 110: (1998) 29 Corpt LA 222 Raj. The mere fact that the company has appointed transfer agents and authorised them to carry out the transfer work does not give immunity to the company from its responsibility. The company, its transfer agents, directors and other officers were allowed to go in for compounding. *Herdilia Unimers Ltd v Renu Jain*, (1995) 4 Comp LJ 45 Raj; *Reliance Industries Ltd, Re*, (1997) 89 Comp Cas 67 and 465 CLB.

registered office.[46] The jurisdiction under the section allows only the recovery of share certificates and not compensation for any losses caused by the delay in getting the certificate.[47]

Object and effect of share certificate [S. 84]

Section 84 speaks in plain language of the object of a share certificate, ''A share certificate under the common seal of the company, specifying any shares held by any member, shall be *prima facie* evidence of the title of the member to such shares.'' Thus, the share certificate being *prima facie* evidence of title, it gives the shareholder the facility of dealing more easily with his shares in the market. It enables him to sell his shares by showing at once a marketable title.[48]

1. *Estoppel as to title.*—A share certificate once issued binds the company in two ways. In the first place, ''it is a declaration by the company to all the world that the person in whose name the certificate is made out, and to whom it is given, is a shareholder in the company.''[49] In other words, the company is estopped from denying his title to the shares.

---

46. *H.V. Jayaram* v *ICICI Ltd*, (2000) 99 Comp Cas 341: (2000) 2 SCC 202: AIR 2000 SC 579. Followed in *Zee Telefilms Ltd* v *State of A.P.*, (2002) 110 Comp Cas 884 AP, which followed another Supreme Court decision to the same effect in *Jayaram (H.V.)* v *ICICI*, (2002) 99 Comp Cas 341 SC. *Hari Kumar Rajah* v *Ashok R. Thakkar*, (2004) 515 SCL 735 Mad.

47. *Harish Kumar Agarwal* v *Punjab Communications Ltd*, (1998) 28 Corpt LA 249 CLB. *Hindustan Development Corpn Ltd* v *Kushal Chand Bader*, (1998) 29 Corpt LA 222 Raj: [1998] 1 Comp LJ 110, the Special Magistrate (Economic Offences) at Jaipur was held to have jurisdiction to entertain a complaint against a Calcutta based company. The complainant purchased debentures in the open market and applied to the company to register him as a debenture holder. The company failed to do so within the statutory period. *Natvarlal A. Jani* v *N. N. Jain*, (1998) 29 Corpt LA 415 Guj, the substitution of the word CLB for court in 1988 has not taken away the jurisdiction of the court to entertain complaints for violation of S. 113. Prosecution for an offence under the section can be launched before a Magistrate and not before the CLB. *Nestle India Ltd* v *State*, [1999] 4 Comp LJ 446 Del, the transferee is an aggrieved person for the purposes of a complaint, the period of limitation commences from the date of the commission of the offence, namely failure to deliver in time. A complaint made after two years after that was held to be time-barred. The Supreme Court held in *Registrar of Companies* v *Rajshree Sugar & Chemicals Ltd*, (2000) 6 SCC 133: (2000) 101 Comp Cas 271: AIR 2000 SC 1643 that the Registrar is an aggrieved person within the meaning of S. 113(2) and, therefore, competent to file a complaint. Followed in *Indian Petro Chemicals Corpn* v *State of Rajasthan*, (2001) 104 Comp Cas 285 Raj, *Dhirubhai H. Ambani* v *Sonia Sethi*, (2001) 106 Comp Cas 486 MP, notice issued to the vice-president of the company, he was bound to honour the court summons and was not allowed to say that he had nothing to do with the offence. *State of Maharashtra* v *Raymonds Woollen Mills Ltd*, (2002) 111 Comp Cas 847 Bom, a complaint against delay in delivering certificates which was filed out of time without application for condonation of delay was not allowed to be entertained. *Jiwatram Kukreja* v *Eastern Mining & Allied Industries Ltd*, (2004) 121 Comp Cas 762 Gau, three years period of limitation is available under Article 47, Limitation Act, 1963; *Surajben Naval Chand Shah* v *Asian Food Products Ltd*, (2006) 131 Comp Cas 565 Bom, contempt of court for not complying with the direction of producing share certificates in original or duplicate.

48. *See* COCKBURN CJ at p 595, in *Bahia & San Francisco Rly Co, Re*, (1868) LR 3 QB 584: 18 LT 467. It is necessary for this presumption of *prima facie* title to operate that the share certificate must have been issued under the company's seal affixed in accordance with the statutory requirements and the company's articles. *Kelapa Sawit* v *Yeoh Kim Leng*, (1991) 1 SCR 415 Malaysia.

49. *Ibid.*

Suppose *A*, by practising fraud on a company, obtains a share certificate in his name as the holder of some shares. He then sells them in the market. *B*, purchasing them in good faith applied to the company to have the shares registered in his name. The company, having discovered the fraud, refuses. The company must compensate *B* for the loss he has sustained by acting on the faith of the share certificate. The measure of damages would be the market price of the shares at that time.

In a case of this kind:[50]

The plaintiff applied for 300 shares in a company. A clerk in the company who owned no shares executed a transfer in favour of the plaintiff. The company without requiring the clerk to produce his certificate registered the transfer and issued a new certificate to the plaintiff. The company was held liable to the plaintiff in damages.

2. *Estoppel as to payment.*—Secondly, if the certificate states that on each of the shares full amount has been paid, the company is estopped, as against a bona fide purchaser of the shares, from alleging that they are not fully paid.[51] Thus in *Bloomenthal* v *Ford*:[52]

B lent £1000 to a company on the security of 10,000 shares which were issued to him as fully paid. In fact nothing had been paid on them. In the winding up of the company, it was held that neither the company nor the liquidator could deny that the shares were fully paid and, therefore, *B* could not be placed on the list of contributors.

Where a person knows that the statements in a certificate are not true, he cannot claim an estoppel against the company.[53] But a *bona fide* transferee from him can claim an estoppel.[54] Where shares were issued as fully paid and there was no fraud in the transaction on the part of the holder, the company was held to be under an estoppel as to payment and was not allowed to question it after a long period of time during which the holder had obtained loans on the security of the shares from financial institutions which acted in good faith.[55]

---

50. *Dixon* v *Kennaway & Co*, [1900] 1 Ch 833: 82 LT 527.
51. *K. Md Farooq Ahmed* v *Fortran Cirkit Electronics (P) Ltd*, (1997) 25 Corpt LA 209 CLB, a company is completely estopped from denying the amount of payment indicated on the share certificate.
52. 1897 AC 156: 76 LT 205.
53. See *Crickmer case*, (1875) 10 Ch App 614: 46 LJ Ch 870; *American Remedies Ltd* v *Prakash Chandra Gupta*, (2002) 111 Comp Cas 777 CLB, allotment made and entry in share register also made under a stock invest scheme which failed to pay. Transferees of such shares were called upon to pay and certificates were to be issued only to those who paid. Rectification of the register of members in respect of shares permitted for deleting the name of the allottee.
54. *Barrow case*, (1880) 14 Ch D 432: 42 LT 891 CA.
55. *K. Md Farooq Ahmed* v *Fortran Cirkit Electronics (P) Ltd*, (1998) 92 Comp Cas 498 CLB.

Duplicate certificate [S. 84(2)]

A shareholder is expected to keep his share certificate in safe custody, for he is not entitled to a duplicate unless he shows that the original has been lost or destroyed, or, having been defaced or mutilated or torn, is surrendered to the company. The articles of the company may further require him to give an indemnity bond.[56] Any other terms and conditions may also be prescribed.[57] Where the share certificates were delivered to the holder's husband but because of matrimonial differences they could not reach her, the Company Law Board ordered issue of duplicate certificates.[58] A civil suit lies for determining ownership of shares and for an order of issue of duplicate share certificates. Civil court jurisdiction becomes barred only in respect of matters for which special jurisdiction has been constituted under the Act.[59] The Company Law Board has no power under Section 113 to give directions for issue of duplicate certificates. The remedy lies under Section 4(3) of the Companies (Issue of Share Certificates) Rules, 1960. The CLB advised the petitioner to approach the company in accordance with the rules.[60]

TRANSFER OF SHARES

"When joint stock companies were established, the great object was that the shares should be capable of being easily transferred."[61] Accordingly, by Section 82 of the Companies Act, it is provided that the shares or debentures or other interest of a member in a company shall be moveable property capable of being transferred in the manner provided by the articles of the company.[62] "The regulations of the company may impose fetters upon the

---

56. *See* clause 8 of Table A in Sch. 1.
57. S. 84(4). Before passing a mandatory injunction against the company for issuing duplicates, the court should insist upon some proof of the title of the claimant to the shares. *S. Sundaram Pillai* v *P. Govindaswami*, (1987) 62 Comp Cas 414 Mad. Precautions necessary for ascertaining whether the original has been lost must be observed. It could not be said that the original was lost when the company was supposed to know that it was under pledge. The purpose of the provision is to safeguard the market from fraudulent dealings in duplicates. *Tracstar Investments Ltd* v *Gordon Woodroffe Ltd*, (1996) 87 Comp Cas 941 CLB. Affirmed in *Shoe Specialities Ltd* v *Tracstar Investments Ltd*, (1997) 88 Comp Cas 471 Mad. The offence committed by directors in issuing duplicates without precautions was compounded in *Reliance Industries Ltd, Re*, (1997) 89 Comp Cas 67 and 465 CLB. *Inter Sales* v *Reliance Industries Ltd*, (1998) 1 Cal LJ 531 Cal, the matters connected with issue of duplicate securities are not within the jurisdiction of company courts. Companies (Issue of Share Certificates) Rules, 1960, Rule 4(3) is not mandatory. *Rameshchandra Mamital Kotia* v *State of Gujarat*, (1998) 2 Guj LR 1222, S. 197, IPC would be attracted if the false share certificate would be admissible in evidence without proof. *Suryakant Gupta* v *Rajaram Corn Products (Punjab) Ltd*, (2002) 108 Comp Cas 133 CLB, in the case of a closely held company, an unnatural stand was taken that shares had been despatched to all members. The company was directed to issue duplicates.
58. *Sujata Khetawat* v *Usha Shree Tea (P) Ltd*, (2006) 133 Comp Cas 943 CLB.
59. *Inter Sales* v *Reliance Industries Ltd*, (2002) 108 Comp Cas 680 Cal.
60. *Ajit Jayantilal Sheth* v *Shriram Transport Finance Co Ltd*, (2006) 133 Comp Cas 604 CLB.
61. BLACKBURN J at p 595, in *Bahia & San Francisco Rly Co, Re*, (1868) LR 3 QB 584: 18 LT 467.
62. The requirements of the articles must be satisfied. Where the articles required that transfer fee and the share certificates must be deposited in the office, court did not compel the company to register a transfer which did not satisfy the requirements and held that depositing them in the

right of transfer. But in the absence of restrictions in the articles the shareholder has by virtue of the statute the right to transfer his shares without the consent of anybody to any transferee, even though he be a man of straw, provided it is a *bona fide* transaction in the sense that it is an out and out disposal of the property without retaining any interest in the shares."[63] A transfer made with the avowed object of escaping liability was held to be valid in *Discoverers Finance Corpn Ltd, Re,*:[64]

> A holder of partly paid shares, being alarmed at the precarious condition of the company and with a view to escape liability on the shares, sold his shares, to a purchaser in Germany for nominal price, which he never received. The transfers were duly lodged and passed by the Board of directors. It was held that, in the absence of any collusion between him and the directors, the transfers were effective.[65]

Restrictions on transfer (Private Companies)

It is open to a company to restrict the right of its members to transfer their shares.[66] The articles of a private company as against those of a public company contain more rigorous restrictions on the right of its members to transfer shares. This is so because "private companies are (no doubt) in law separate entities just as much as are public companies, but from the business and personal point of view they are much more analogous to partnerships than to public corporations". Accordingly, it is to be expected that in the articles of such a company the control of the directors over the

---

court would not do. *Malabar and Pioneer Hosiery (P) Ltd, Re*, (1985) 57 Comp Cas 570 Ker; *P. V. Chandran v Malabar & Pioneer Hosiery Mill Ltd*, (1990) 69 Comp Cas 164 Ker, followed in *Mathrubhumi Ltd v Vardhman Publishers Ltd*, (1992) 73 Comp Cas 80 Ker: [1992] 1 Comp LJ 234 Ker DB. *Rehana Rao v Balaji Fabricators (P) Ltd*, (2004) 122 Comp Cas 804 CLB, the articles required transfer only to a person approved by the Board, transfer without such approval was not possible.

63. BENNET J at p 238 in *Delavenne v Broadhurst*, [1931] 1 Ch 234: 144 LT 342. Disinvestment of shares by the Government in a public sector company, no interference; employees had no right to demand any percentage, price to employees, no interference; the court directed the Government to device a scheme for effective worker participation in its disinvestment. *Babu Mathew (Prof) v UOI*, (1997) 90 Comp Cas 455 Ker.

64. [1910] 1 Ch 207. *Barnicoal v Knight*, (2004) 2 BCLC 464 (Ch D), a transfer of shares by directors was subject to the condition that the purchaser would see to it that the directors paid loans to the company. The transfer was held to be valid and the condition effective against the purchaser to make them liable in the manner of a guarantor.

65. See *Manisha Commercial Ltd v N. R. Dangre*, (2000) 101 Comp Cas 106 Del, the Court refused to stay transfer of shares inspite of the allegation that they were a part of a long-time trust and were, not transferable. The beneficiary of the trust was seeking transfer in his own name.

66. There is no inherent power of rejection. It would have to be acquired by provisions in the company's constitutional documents. *Luxmi Tea Company Ltd v P. K. Sarkar*, 1989 Supp (2) SCC 656: [1989] 3 Comp LJ 285, 288 SC. The power of refusal based on the company's articles (for not accepting odd lot shares) as required also under the listing agreement was held to be not questionable. *Dipak Kumar Jayantilal Shah v Atul Products Ltd*, (1995) 82 Comp Cas 603 CLB not approved in *Atul Products Ltd v Dipak Kumar Jayantilal Shah*, (1997) 88 Comp Cas 876 Guj.

members may be very strict indeed.[67] Moreover, the Act itself requires a private company to impose some restrictions on the right of transfer.[68] Articles requiring that on the insolvency of a member his shares would be transferred at a fair value to a nominee of the directors[69] or that on the death of a member his shares must be offered to the other members have been held to be valid.[70] Articles providing that shares can be transferred to outsiders only if no existing members accept them at face value, are called *pre-emption* clauses. Such a clause does not authorise the directors to refuse to register a transfer so long as it is made to an existing member only.[71] Where no existing member accepts the proposal, transfer in favour of an outsider should be allowed.[72] Articles may contain a clause that the other members will be bound to take shares so offered.[73] The question is in what manner the directors shall exercise this power and to what extent the court or CLB can interfere in its exercise. Some of the principles were laid down in *Smith and Fawcett Ltd, Re*.[74]

A clause in the articles of a private company provided: ''The directors may at any time in their absolute and uncontrolled discretion refuse to register any transfer of shares.'' The issued capital of the company consisted of 8002 shares of which the two directors of the company *S* and *F* held 4001 each. *F* died and his son applied to have the shares registered in his name. But *S*, in the exercise of the above power, refused to consent to the registration. He, however, offered to accept the applicant upto 2001 shares, provided the remaining were sold to him at a fixed price. The plaintiff brought an action contending that *S*'s refusal to register the transfer was on a wrong principle since it was not made for the benefit of the company but was rather to preserve his own dominating position.

---

67. Lord GREENE MR in *Smith & Fawcett Ltd, Re*, 1942 Ch 304, 306: [1942] 1 All ER 542. *S. Bhuneshwari* v *ACJ, (Agro Chemical Industries) Ltd*, (2004) 51 SCL 158 Mad, transfer in violation of a provision in the articles that the transferring member should inform the directors who would offer the shares to other members proportionally. The transfer not valid, *Maharashtra Power Development Corpn Ltd* v *Dabhol Power Co*, (2005) 4 Comp LJ 50 Bom.
68. S. 3(*iii*) provides that ''a private company means a company which by its articles restricts the right to transfer its shares....''
69. *Borland's Trustee* v *Steel Bros & Co Ltd*, 1901 Ch 279.
70. *Jarvis Motors (Harrow) Ltd* v *Carabott*, [1964] 1 WLR 1101, though at the particular moment there was only one other shareholder in the company.
71. *Delavenne* v *Broadhurst*, [1931] 1 Ch 234.
72. *Ocean Coal Co Ltd* v *Powell Duffryn Steam Coal Co*, [1932] 1 Ch 654.
73. See *Rayfield* v *Hands*, (1958) 2 WLR 851: (1958) 2 All ER 194: [1960] Ch 1.
74. [1942] Ch 304: (1942) 1 All ER 542. The principles laid down in this case were cited with approval by the Nagpur High Court in *Balwant Transport Co* v *Y. H. Deshpande*, AIR 1956 Nag 20, where the court refused to interfere with the director's discretion. *See also* the decision of the Supreme Court in *Harinagar Sugar Mills Ltd* v *Shyam Sunder Jhunjhunwala*, AIR 1961 SC 1669: (1961) 31 Comp Cas 387, where all the implications of the power of the Court or that of CLB have been elaborately explained.

It was held that the court would not be justified in interfering in the discretion of the directors. "The directors must exercise their discretion bona fide in what they consider — not what a court may consider — is in the interest of the company." And if they have done that, the court cannot substitute its judgment for theirs.[75]

Judicial or Quasi-Judicial Interference in Transfer Matters

In the following circumstances, however, there can be judicial or quasi-judicial intervention:

1. *Mala fide*

Where it is proved that the directors have not exercised their power of refusal in good faith for the benefit of the company. The power of declining a transfer is vested in the Board of directors for the purpose of protecting the interests of the company. Hence their refusal must appear to have proceeded out of an honest desire to benefit the company. A *mala fide* refusal to register a transfer will not be sustained.[76] The CLB has to decide whether in exercising their power, the directors are acting oppressively, capriciously or corruptly, or in some way *mala fide*.[77]

2. *Inadequacy of reasons*

The practice with the courts was not to ask the directors to supply reasons for their refusal to pass a transfer.[78] But, if they voluntarily disclosed

---

75. Similar sentiments have been expressed in *Tett v Phoenix Property and Investment Co Ltd*, 1984 BCLC 599 at p 621, non-interference if the directors' decision was such that a reasonable board could *bona fide* believe it to be in the interest of the company. *Xavier Joseph v Indo-Scottish Brand (P) Ltd*, (2002) 110 Comp Cas 706 CLB, transmission in the case of a closely held company in favour of the son of a deceased member not allowed because he could have caused disharmony. The directors were required to purchase his shares. *Kulveer Chandhoke v Eastern Linkers (P) Ltd*, (2001) 103 Comp Cas 997 Del, the High Court decided and the Supreme Court affirmed that the applicant had no title to the shares in question, an application for permission for transfer when the company was in winding up was not allowed.

76. *Gresham Life Assurance Society, Re*, [1972] LR 8 Ch App 446, 452: 28 LT 150; *Coalport China Co, Re*, [1895] 2 Ch 404: [1895-9] All ER Rep Ext 2021; *Bell Bros, Re*, (1981) 65 LT 245: 7 TLR 689. Refusal on the ground that it was necessary to protect the interest of directors is not good, their interest is not equal to that of company or on the ground that there was no consideration for transfer, *Jagdishchandra Champaklal Parekh v Deccan Paper Mills Co Ltd*, (1994) 80 Comp Cas 159 CLB. A refusal on the ground that the transferee was a member of a company which was heavily indebted to the company and that transfer of 4% shares would prejudicially affect the balance of power in the company was not accepted, *Vijaya Commercial Credit Co Ltd v T. K. Alwa*, (1994) 79 Comp Cas 656 CLB. As against this an application for 6.84% shares was held to be justifiably refused because it was likely to prejudicially change the composition of the Board of directors. *Gordon Woodroffe Ltd v Trident Investment*, (1994) 79 Comp Cas 764 CLB: [1994] 1 Comp LJ 313. Where, the changes apprehended in the Board of directors had already taken place, refusal on that ground was held to be not good. *Patel Engg Co Ltd v Patel Relators (P) Ltd*, (1992) 74 Comp Cas 395 CLB. These decisions were under S. 22-A of the Securities Contracts (Regulation) Act, 1956. The role of CLB under that Act was explained in *Gammon India Ltd v Hongkong Bank Agency (P) Ltd*, (1992) 74 Comp Cas 123: [1992] 1 Comp LJ 279 CLB.

77. SHAH J in *Harinagar Sugar Mills Ltd v Shyam Sunder Jhunjhunwala*, AIR 1961 SC 1669, 1675: (1961) 31 Comp Cas 387. *See* also *Indian Chemical Products Ltd v State of Orissa*, [1966] 2 Comp LJ 64: (1966) 36 Comp Cas 592: AIR 1967 SC 253.

78. *Mathew Michael v Teekay Rubbers (India) Ltd*, (1983) 54 Comp Cas 88 Ker, the directors had disclosed no reasons and the court expressed its helplessness in the matter.

their reasons, the court had the power to look into them and if they did not seem to be sufficient to justify their decision the court might set it aside.[79] Now, by virtue of the amendment of 1988, it has become compulsory to disclose such reasons. This gives an opportunity to the Company Law Board to examine the relevancy of the reasons and proceed accordingly as the reasons are adequate or inadequate to support the directors' decision.

3. *Irrelevant considerations*

"The directors (in refusing a transfer) must have regard to those considerations and those only, which the articles on their true construction permit them to take into consideration."[80] A refusal based on extraneous considerations will be wrong.[81] The directors have to specify the grounds on which they have declined a transfer.[82] Refusal by directors on the ground of inadequacy of consideration was held to be not proper.[83]

Thus where the directors were empowered to refuse to register a transferee if it was not in the interest of the company that he should be a member, it was held that a refusal on the ground that the shares were transferred singly or in small amounts and to persons who had no interest in shipping was unjustified.[84] In another case[85], the directors had the power to refuse a transfer of partly paid shares to a person of whom they would not approve. In the exercise of this power they rejected a transfer of fully paid shares on the ground that the transferee had bought them, not so much for investment, as for the purpose of acquiring control of the company. This was held to be unwarranted by the articles. Where the directors of a private

---

79. *Ibid. See* also *Mathesan* v *Nath Singh Oil Co Ltd*, 18 JC 481; *Bajaj Auto Ltd* v *Firodia*, (1970) 2 SCC 550: AIR 1971 SC 321: (1971) 41 Comp Cas 1.
80. Lord GREENE MR in *Smith & Fawcett Ltd, Re*, [1942] Ch 304, 306: [1942] 1 All ER 542. Refusal on frivolous grounds is not sustainable. *Techno-Electric and Engg Co Ltd* v *Payal Singh*, [1992] 1 Comp LJ 334 Cal. DCA is of the same view. Circular No. 3 of 1993, March 22, 1993. *Standard Chartered Bank* v *Housing and Urban Development Corpn Ltd*, (1996) 23 Corpt LA 84 CLB, no empowerment in articles for refusing registration of transfer of the company's bonds, innocent buyer cannot be prejudiced by private agreements. *Housing and Urban Development Corpn Ltd* v *Standard Chartered Bank*, (1996) 23 Corpt LA 198 Del, restrictions imposed by the Controller of Capital Issues were meant to be observed by the company and not by allottees. *Volvo Lastvagnar Komponenter AB* v *Morgardshammar (India) Ltd*, (1998) 30 Corpt LA 382 CLB, private agreements, not incorporated in articles, cannot be used for refusing transfers.
81. *Babulal Choukhani* v *Western India Theatres*, (1958) 28 Comp Cas 565: AIR 1957 Cal 709. A refusal on the ground of an agreement between members not contained in the company's article was held to be wrong. *V. B. Rangaraj* v *V.B. Gopalakrishnan*, (1992) 1 SCC 160: AIR 1992 SC 45: (1992) 73 Comp Cas 201 SC: [1992] 1 Comp LJ 11.
82. *Coimbatore Kamala Mills Ltd* v *T. Sundaran*, (1950) 20 Comp Cas 61 Mad. There is now adverse presumption if they do not do so. *Muthapa Chettiar* v *Salem Rajendra Mills*, (1955) 25 Comp Cas 283: [1955] 2 Mad LJ 535.
83. *Vikas Jalan* v *Hyderabad Industries Ltd*, (1997) 88 Comp Cas 551 CLB.
84. *Bede S S Co Ltd, Re*, [1917] 1 Ch 123: 115 LT 580: 33 TLR 13.
85. *Jalpaiguri Cinema Co Ltd* v *Pramatha Nath Mukherjee*, (1971) 41 Comp Cas 678 Del. *See* also *South Indian Bank Ltd* v *Joseph Michael*, (1978) 48 Comp Cas 368.

company refused to accept a transfer in favour of a company whereas they had power to exclude only undesirable persons, the Calcutta High Court[86] held that such blanket ban on admission of companies was beyond their authority. The court pointed out: "Approval of the transferee means approval of the transferee personally as distinguished from laying down a general rule that no corporate body would be allowed to join the company as a shareholder."[87]

Strict Construction of Restrictions

"In construing the relevant provisions in the articles it is to be borne in mind that one of the normal rights of a shareholder is the right to deal freely with his property and to transfer it to whomsoever he pleases, and this right is not to be cut down by uncertain language or doubtful implications."[88] "Any limitation on the right of transfer must be strictly complied with."[89] Moreover, "the directors must exercise their right to decline registration only by passing a resolution to that effect; mere failure, due to a deadlock or something, to pass a resolution is not a formal active exercise of the right to decline, and therefore the applicant will be entitled to be registered as a member of the company".[90] Thus, for example, in *Moodie* v *W&J Shepherd Ltd:*[91]

The directors failed to agree to an application for transfer; one in favour of granting it and the other refused to do so. It was held that the transfer had not been declined and, therefore, the applicant must be registered.

Further, "the power must be exercised within a reasonable time; four months is not a reasonable time". "The period of two months specified in Section 78 of the (English) Companies Act[92] may safely be taken as the outside limit after which there is unnecessary delay. By reason of such delay the power ceases to be capable of being exercised."[93] Similarly, where the directors have the power to veto a transfer they will lose it if it is not exercised within a reasonable time after a transfer application is lodged.[94]

---

86. *Master Silk Mills (P) Ltd* v *D. H. Mehta*, (1980) 50 Comp Cas 365 Guj.
87. *See* further, *V. S. Ratnam* v *Ossar Estates Ltd*, [1989] 3 Comp LJ 355, 359 CLB, where a transfer was rejected on the ground that the transferee was the nominee of another person who was an undesirable person, and the same was held to be not proper.
88. Lord GREENE MR in *Smith & Fawcett Ltd, Re*, (1942) Ch 304, 306: (1942) 1 All ER 542.
89. PENNYCUICK J in *Swaldale Cleaners, Re*, (1968) 1 WLR 1710: [1968] 3 All ER 619 CA.
90. *Moodie* v *W&J Shepherd Ltd*, [1949] 2 All ER 1044.
91. *Ibid.* See also *Ramesh Chandra* v *Jogini Mohan*, 47 Cal 901 and *Mohinuddin case*, AIR 1928 Mad 571; *Babulal Choukhani* v *Western India Theatres*, AIR 1957 Cal 709: (1958) 28 Comp Cas 565.
92. S. 111(2) of the Indian Companies Act prescribes the same period.
93. Following, *Joint Stock Discount Co, Re*, (1886) 3 Eq 77, the Madras High Court in *M. G. Amirthalingam* v *Gudiyatham Textiles (P) Ltd*, (1972) 42 Comp Cas 350, upheld a rejection notified after two and a half months.
94. *Swaldale Cleaners, Re*, [1968] 1 WLR 1710: [1968] 3 All ER 619 CA.

Under the articles of a private company no transfer was possible without the previous sanction of the Board of directors. It was held that this would require a written resolution for sanctioning a proposed transfer.[95]

Scope of interference where power unfettered.—Where, however, the directors have an unfettered discretion, it is difficult for the Company Law Board to interfere.[96] The CLB has to presume, unless the contrary is shown, good faith on the part of the directors. The directors have to disclose their reasons. The first decision on the adequacy of such reasons has to be that of the CLB under Section 111. If subsequently the matter is taken to the court, it can also pronounce upon the adequacy of the reasons. Earlier to the amendment of 1988, disclosure of reasons was not compulsory. The rejected transferee had to make an application to the Central Government under Section 111 as it then stood and the Government had the power to demand a disclosure of the reasons at the pain of adverse presumption. This course proved useful to the transferee in *Bajaj Auto Ltd* v *Firodia*.[97]

The shareholders of a company were divided into two groups. Both bought shares in the open market at exaggerated prices. The purchases effected by the controlling group were registered. Some instalments of the opposite block were also registered, but the rest were suddenly refused. The directors had the unfettered discretion to do so.

Rejected transferees applied to the Central Government under Section 111. The Government demanded reasons. The directors disclosed that they were prompted by the report of the opposite group to the Central Government that the appointment of managing agents was renewed without proper formalities; that if all the purchases were registered it would reduce the majority of the controlling block to less than three-fourth and thus jeopardise the functioning of the company. But both the Government, and on appeal, the Supreme Court, regarded these reasons as absolutely irrelevant to the consideration of the company's best interests. The report was not only in the interest of the company but also in public interest. Any reduction in the strength of the majority cannot by itself mean that the company's business would be paralysed.

---

95. *John Tinson & Co (P) Ltd* v *Surjeet Malhan*, (1997) 9 SCC 651: AIR 1997 SC 1411: (1997) 88 Comp Cas 750: A transfer without any such approval was held to be void.
96. In the case of a public company, listed or otherwise, an absolute power of refusal does not give the directors an unfettered discretion to refuse. The power would have to be exercised in good faith in the interest of the company. *Mathrubhumi Ltd* v *Vardhman Publishers Ltd*, (1992) 73 Comp Cas 80 Ker. A company listed at a recognised stock exchange was fully authorised to reject a transfer which fell in the four point formula of S. 22-A of the Securities (Contracts Regulation) Act, 1956, *Bajaj Tempo Ltd* v *Bajaj Auto Ltd*, (1994) 80 Comp Cas 618 CLB. But now this section has been *omitted*. The only surviving power of rejection is to be found in the provisions of S. 111-A. There cannot be a contrary provision in the articles.
97. (1970) 2 SCC 550: AIR 1971 SC 321: (1971) 41 Comp Cas 1. *See* also *Turner Morrison & Co* v *Shalimar Tar Products*, (1980) 50 Comp Cas 296 Cal, transfer passed in haste.

Thus, it appears that the function of approving or rejecting a transfer is no longer a private affair. However widely drafted the power of rejection may be, its exercise would now have to be justified on objective reasons. This has been re-emphasised by the Supreme Court in *LIC* v *Escorts Ltd*[1] because "discretion implies just and proper consideration of the proposal in the facts and circumstances of the case". The directors refused to register a bulk purchase of shares by a group of foreign companies all operated by a non-resident Indian under a family trust. The directors contended that if the purchases ostensibly effected in the name of 13 companies were regarded as a one-man affair, the ceilings prescribed by the rules under the Foreign Exchange Regulation Act, 1973 [now FEMA] would be violated and further the purchases were effected without the permission of the Reserve Bank. The permission was, however, retrospectively granted. The court advised the directors that they had no right to sit in judgment over the decision of the Reserve Bank or of the Central Government as to retrospective permissions. The FERA did not insist upon prior permission. The court would not lift the corporate veil in this case to see whether all the companies were under the control of one man.[2]

Directors were not allowed to reject a duly executed transfer only on the ground that there was a family dispute between the transferor and his son,[3] or on the ground that the share certificate submitted along with the instrument of transfer was of greater number of shares than those transferred.[4]

Transfers contravening pre-emptive clauses

A company can reject a transfer contravening the provisions of the company's articles,[5] but the company can waive its right and accept a contravening transfer and once it does so, it loses the right to question the validity of the transfer. Hence, a transfer contravening articles is not a nullity,[6] nor void *ab-initio*.[7] A transfer in violation of pre-emptive provision

---

1. (1986) 1 SCC 264 at p 326: [1986] 1 Comp LJ 91 SC: (1986) 59 Comp Cas 548.
2. See further *Bajaj Tempo Ltd* v *Unit Trust of India*, (1992) 73 Comp Cas 451 CLB, the directors' decision to refuse was based on the apprehension that the transferee company would, by reason of its inter-connections, become a monopolistic undertaking was not upheld by the CLB.
3. *M. M. Anandram* v *Mysore Lachia Setty & Sons (P) Ltd*, (1985) 58 Comp Cas 162 Kant.
4. *Kumar Exporters (P) Ltd* v *Naini Oxygen Acetylene and Gas Ltd*, (1985) 85 Comp Cas 97 All. A transferee was not allowed to question the validity of an article empowering directors to decline a transfer of fully paid shares replacing the old article which permitted refusal of only partly paid shares. *Joseph Michael* v *Travancore Rubber and Tea Co Ltd*, (1986) 59 Comp Cas 898 Ker.
5. See *Satyanarayana Rathi* v *Annamalaiar Textiles (P) Ltd*, (1999) 95 Comp Cas 386 CLB, a transfer in violation of pre-emptive clauses.
6. *See* the old case of *Shortridge* v *Bosanquet*, (1852) 16 Beav 97: 51 ER 708.
7. See *Hunter* v *Hunter*, 1936 AC 222 HL, 264; *Coupe* v *J. M. Coupe Publishing Ltd*, [1981] I NZLR 275 CA and *Tett* v *Phoenix Property and Investment Co Ltd*, 1984 BCLC 599.

can be set right by subsequent assent of shareholders or by ratification or even by acquiescence.[8] Further, as between transferor and transferee, the latter does become an equitable owner of the shares and this despite the fact that no specific enforcement can be had against the company because of the contravention of pre-emptive or other provisions.[9] The purchaser is not totally without remedies. The seller is accountable to him for all accretions to the shares, such as bonus and dividend.[10] What has been described as "the most explicit authority" is *Tett v Phoenix Property and Investment Co Ltd*[11] where VINELOTT J "held that despite the disregard of the pre-emptive provisions there had occurred a complete and effective transfer between transferor and transferee in terms of which the equitable title passed to the latter."[12] In this case, the shares in question were sold to an outsider and a transfer deed executed in his favour completely forgetting the pre-emptive clauses. Some shareholders were interested in acquiring the shares but not at a price which *Tett* was prepared to pay. Even so the Court of Appeal held that the company was not compellable to accept the transfer. The decision has been appreciated. "The privacy of a 'close corporation' is more important than the price offered by an outsider. A different decision would have defeated the intention of the incorporators when they formed the company."[13] In *Hunter v Hunter*,[14] shares were mortgaged to a bank. This transaction was viewed as a valid one inspite of the pre-emptive provisions. But the bank having gone to the extent of getting its nominee registered as a holder of those shares, an order was granted for rectification of the register of members by restoring the name of the original shareholder-mortgagor. The bank then transferred the shares to an existing shareholder of the company thus complying with the requirements of the company's articles that the shares could be transferred to existing members only. The original mortgagor's action questioning the validity of the transfer failed.

---

8. See *Hunter v Hunter*, 1936 AC 222 HL; *Coupe v J. M. Coupe Publishing Ltd*, [1981] I NZLR 275 CA and *Tett v Phoenix Property and Investment Co Ltd*, 1984 BCLC 599. A member cannot be denied his proportion under pre-emptive rights out of the shares offered by another member even if there was some irregularity in observing the company's articles which was rectifiable, *Lakshmi Natrajan v Bharatan Publications Ltd*, (1997) 25 Corpt LA 96 CLB.
9. *Pool v Middleton*, (1861) 29 Beav 646: 54 ER 778; *Heron International Ltd v Grade*, 1983 BCLC 244.
10. *Coachcraft Ltd v S.V.P. Fruit Co Ltd*, (1978) 3 ACLR 658.
11. 1984 BCLC 599.
12. As summarised by A Borrowdale, *The Effect of Breach of Share Transfer Restrictions*, 1988 JBL 307. *Hawks v McArthur*, [1951] 1 All ER 22 and *Chinn v Collins*, 1981 AC 533 HL, both recognising the validity of transfer of beneficial interest without formalities and also *D. J. Lal v S. Ganguli*, (1990) 68 Comp Cas 576 Del.
13. *See* the editorial note in 1986 JBL 8-9. To the same effect is *Shanta Genevieve Pommeret v Sakal Papers (P) Ltd*, (1990) 69 Comp Cas 65 Bom.
14. 1936 AC 222 HL. The principle of the *Hunter case* was followed in *Cruickshank Co Ltd v Stridewell Leather (P) Ltd*, (1995) 17 Corpt LA 415 CLB: (1996) 86 Comp Cas 439, where transfer of shares to outsiders was registered by the company and CLB ordered rectification of the register of members by retransferring to the original member.

Where the articles required a member desiring to transfer his shares to inform the company specifying his price and he specified a price which was likely to vary according to certain future events, it was held that the notice had to specify a certain price and the same having not been done, the notice was defective.[15]

The articles of a private company prohibited transfer to non-members. The shares of a member were sold under a court auction. It was held that even such a sale could not knock off the prohibition. The Board of directors were entitled not to accept the transfer.[16]

Private agreement between members

A private agreement between two or more shareholders, which is not incorporated in the company's articles, restricting the right of transfer, does not bind the company. The company can be compelled to register a transfer even if it violates such an agreement.[17]

Listed public companies and pre-emptive clauses

Refusal by a listed public company to register a transfer of shares on the ground of pre-emptive rights of existing shareholders was held to be not justified. Where shares of such companies are subject to pre-emptive clauses, they have to carry a warning on the face of the certificate. There being no such warning in the present case, the company had no right to refuse either under Section 111 or Section 111-A.[18]

Power to refuse registration and appeal against refusal [S. 111]

This section has become confined to private companies only.

A company refusing to register a transfer on any grounds whatsoever is required by Section 111(1) to send within two months a notice of the refusal to both the transferor and the transferee or the person claiming transmission.[19] The company must disclose reasons for such refusal.[20] The

---

15. *BWE International Ltd* v *Jones*, (2004) 1 BCLC 406 (CA).
16. *S. A. Padmanabha Rao* v *Union Theatres (P) Ltd*, (2002) 108 Comp Cas 108 Kant; *Claude Lila Parulekar* v *Sakal Papers (P) Ltd*, (2005) 11 SCC 73: (2005) 124 Comp Cas 685 SC, where no time limit was prescribed in the articles for exercising the right of pre-emption, reasonable time formula was to apply, the directors could not of their own fix a time limit and defeat the right.
17. *Volvo Lastvagnar Kamponenter A. B.* v *Morgard Shammar India Ltd*, (2000) 100 Comp Cas 131; *Mafatlal Industries Ltd* v *Gujarat Gas Co Ltd*, [1998] 4 Comp LJ 112: (1999) 97 Comp Cas 301 Guj.
18. *Pawan Gupta* v *Hicks Thermometers Ltd*, (1999) 98 Comp Cas 814 CLB.
19. An appeal cannot be filed by a person who is neither a transferor nor a transferee. An appeal by an inter-mediator in the transaction of sale of shares between the transferor and transferee was not allowed. *Vinod K. Patel* v *Industrial Finance Corpn of India Ltd*, [1999] 3 Comp LJ 215. *Vinod K. Patel* v *Industrial Finance Corpn of India Ltd*, (2001) 103 Comp Cas 557 Del, a stranger cannot file an appeal.
20. S. 111(2). The CLB has no power to condone delay by a company in accepting or rejecting a transfer of shares. *Carbon Corpn Ltd* v *Abhudaya Properties (P) Ltd*, (1992) 73 Comp Cas 572 CLB.

transferor[21] or the transferee can prefer an appeal to the Company Law Board[22] against the refusal. The appeal must be lodged within two months of either the notice of refusal or where the company has not given any such notice, within 4 months from the date on which the papers were lodged with the company, as the case may be.[23] An opportunity must be afforded to the transferee, transferor and the company to make their representations. If the refusal, on a consideration of the whole case, does not seem to be justified, the CLB will issue an order to the company to register the transfer, which must be done within 10 days of the receipt of the order.[24] The nature and scope of the power of the Central Government, which was inherited by the Company Law Board, was explained by the Supreme Court in *Harinagar Sugar Mills Ltd* v *Shyam Sunder Jhunjhunwala.*[25]

> A company having refused to register a transfer, an appeal was preferred before the Central Government. The latter ordered the company to register the transfer but gave no reasons. The company appealed against the Government's order.

It was held that the power of the Central Government (now CLB) was of a judicial nature and must be exercised subject to the limitations of a judicial tribunal. "The Central Government has to decide whether in exercising their power the directors are acting oppressively, capriciously, or corruptly, on in some way *mala fide.* The decision has manifestly to stand those objective tests, and has not merely to be founded on the subjective satisfaction of the authority deciding the questions."[26] Hence the CLB has to decide the appeal on the basis of the reasons for refusal as they have been submitted by the company. This was not done in the present case and, therefore, the matter was referred back.[27] The power of directors to refuse to

---

21. The "person aggrieved" would include the transferor *S. V. Nagrajan* v *Lakshmi Vilas Bank Ltd*, (1997) 90 Comp Cas 392 CLB. In this case the transferor had lodged the transfer documents.
22. *Substituted* for the CLB by the Second Amendment of 2002.
23. An informal refusal is sufficient to invoke S. 111. Thus where the directors observed in their resolution that the application forms were defective and one member of the board personally informed the transmittee, that was held to be an informal refusal for purposes of S. 111, *Narinder Kumar Sehgal* v *Leader Valves Ltd*, (1993) 77 Comp Cas 393 CLB. Where a company sent the notice of refusal after prolonged correspondence and long delay, it was held that the period of two months started running from the date of the receipt of the letter. *Pushpa Vadhera* v *Thomas Cook (India) Ltd*, (1996) 87 Comp Cas 921 CLB.
24. S. 111(5).
25. AIR 1961 SC 1669: (1961) 31 Comp Cas 387. *See* the judgment of SHAH J (afterwards CJ).
26. *See* the judgment of SHAH J at AIR 1961 SC 1669, 1674-75. Reaffirmed by the Supreme Court in *Bajaj Auto Ltd* v *Firodia*, (1970) 2 SCC 550: AIR 1971 SC 321: (1971) 41 Comp Cas 1; *LIC* v *Escorts Ltd*, (1986) 1 SCC 264 at p 326: (1986) 59 Comp Cas 548. Where reasons were not given, the company should be given an opportunity to state its reasons, if any, *Talayar Tea Co Ltd* v *UOI*, 1992 Supp (3) SCC 38.
27. The Supreme Court advised public financial institutions to keep in mind while considering disinvestment of shares in bulk and transferring them to private hands that such a policy would be against public interest and not congenial to promotion of business. Care should also be taken to see that transferees are proper persons. *N. Parthsarathy* v *Controller of Capital of*

accept a transfer is exercisable whether the transfer is by one member to another or from a member to an outsider.[28]

Time for Exercising Power of Refusal [S. 111(1)]

The period prescribed by the section for refusing an application for transfer is that of two months. This raises the question whether on the expiry of the two months the company loses the right of rejection and the transferee gets a vested right to get himself registered. The section does not speak anything on the point and, if it speaks at all, it only talks of penalty for the default.[29] The Bombay High Court, facing this problem, as it seems to be, for the first time, did not agree with the view either that the company would lose the right of rejection or that the transferee would acquire vested right.[30] The view reflects truism to this extent that in such a case a court order would be necessary and the court would in any case go by merits. But the position as established through cases is that the disposal must be within reasonable time and that the two months' time allowed by the Act is quite reasonable.[31] The transferee has silently to sit through this waiting period because he cannot resort to any proceedings till then.[32] Even if the transferee does not get any vested right, his position becomes stronger because the belated exercise of the power may not carry much conviction. The penalty incurred by the expiry of two months cannot be wiped out by subsequently attending to the application. The intention of the legislature seems to be to confer only a time-bound right of rejection. It is a characteristic of such privileges that they lapse with the expiry of time. The legislature means to say that the transfer shall be registered if not rejected within two months.[33]

Issues, (1991) 3 SCC 153: AIR 1991 SC 1420. An order of the Company Law Board is appealable and, therefore, a writ petition does not lie against the order, *Alaknanda Mfg & Finance Co (P) Ltd v CLB*, (1995) 83 Comp Cas 514 Bom.

28. *Kwality Textiles v Arunchalam Chettiar*, (1991) 1 SCR 140 Malaysia. Though the Company Law Board does not have the power under the section to prevent the company from parting with its estate, the CLB can prescribe its approval for alienation of property where the transferees' shares would become worthless if the property was gone, *A. J. Coelho v S. I. Tea & Coffee Estates Ltd*, (1997) 25 Corpt LA 89 CLB.
29. Sub-s. (12) which punishes default "in complying with any of the provisions of this section".
30. *S. P. Mehta v Calico Dyeing and Printing Mills Ltd*, (1990) 67 Comp Cas 533 Bom. Affirmed by the Supreme Court in *Shailesh Prabhudas Mehta v Calico Dyeing & Printing Mills Ltd*, (1994) 3 SCC 339: (1994) 80 Comp Cas 64 SC.
31. *Sewaldale Cleaners Ltd, Re*, [1968] 1 WLR 1710: [1968] 3 All ER 619 CA. Following this case in *Popley v Planarriye Ltd*, (1997) 1 BCLC 8 Ch D, it was held that it would be enough compliance with the requirement of time if the directors decide the matter within time though they failed to communicate the party of their decision. They may incur personal liability for their failure to the party or the company but there would be no violation of the requirement of time.
32. *Zinotty Properties Ltd, Re*, [1984] 1 WLR 1249: [1984] 3 All ER 754.
33. *Hackney Pavilion Ltd, Re*, 1923 All ER Rep 524: [1924] 1 Ch 276. The Karnataka High Court in *Kamlabai v Vithal Pd Co (P) Ltd*, (1993) 77 Comp Cas 231 Kant, came to the conclusion that a company which did not reject an application for transmission within two months was no longer in a position to do so.

Compensation for delay

A transfer had remained pending for 20 years. During this period the company remained in the hands of rival groups and had also become a public company. For certain periods in between the transferee herself was a part of the management and partly responsible for the delay. She could not get the relief of an order for registering shares in her name and rectifying the register of members accordingly. She was held entitled to compensation for her loss.[34]

Rectification of register [S. 111(4)]

If a person's name appears in the register of members, he is presumed to be the shareholder or member, even if, in fact, he is not so. Contrarily, if a person's name is absent from the register, apparently he is not a member, although he may have done everything to entitle him to become one. Injustice may, therefore, result if a company's register of members is not maintained according to law. It is, therefore, the duty of the company to keep the register up to date so as to give at all times the accurate and correct position as to particulars of shareholding. If the company does not do so, an order can be sought from the Company Law Board in respect of all matters falling within Sections 111 and 111-A.[35] The power to order rectification of the register has, therefore, been conferred on the CLB. An aggrieved person or any member or the company itself can apply for rectification on any of the following grounds:

1. Where a person's name has been entered in the register without sufficient cause. Thus rectification has been ordered on this ground where a person was induced to become a member by misleading prospectus, where allotment was invalid[36], or where a forged transfer has been registered,[37] or where the allotment was subject to shareholders' approval and they did not do so,[38] or where a transfer could be effected only with the approval of the Board of directors and there was no evidence of any such approval.[39]

---

34. *Claude-Lila Parulekar* v *Sakal Papers (P) Ltd*, (2005) 124 Comp Cas 685 SC.
35. *Volvo Lastvagnar Kamponenter A. B.* v *Morgardshammar (India) Ltd*, (2000) 100 Comp Cas 131 CLB.
36. *Indian States Bank Ltd* v *Kunwar Sardar Singh*, AIR 1934 All 855: 154 IC 33; *Bank of Peshawar Ltd* v *Madho Ram*, AIR 1919 Lah 351: 51 IC 812.
37. *Societe Generale de Paris* v *Janet Walker*, (1885) 11 AC 20: 54 LT 389; *People's Insurance Co* v *Wood & Co*, AIR 1960 Punj 388. Where shares were registered in the name of a minor through signatures by the minor's mother as a natural guardian, an application by the minor's father to have the name removed was not allowed. This would require a civil adjudication as to who could act for the minor. *Jonas Hemant Bhutta* v *Surgi Plant Ltd*, (1993) 78 Comp Cas 296 CLB. *Nupur Mitra* v *Basubani (P) Ltd*, (2002) 108 Cri LJ 359 CLB, the CLB can permit rectification of the register of members for the purpose of reduction of capital.
38. *Subhas Ghosh* v *Happy Valley Tea Co Ltd*, (2006) 133 Comp Cas 861 CLB.
39. *Chotoo Sud* v *Bhagwan Finance Corpn (P) Ltd*, (2006) 130 Comp Cas 567 CLB.

2. Where a person's name being in the register has been without sufficient cause deleted.[40]

3. Where a person has fulfilled every requirement of law to enable him to become a member, but the company has defaulted or delayed or caused "unnecessary delay" in placing his name in the register[41] [including refusal to register a transfer within the meaning of sub-section (1)] and where a person has rightly ceased to be a member but his name has not been removed with due promptitude from the register.[42]

---

40. *Navinchandra* v *Gordhandas*, [1967] 1 Comp LJ 82: (1967) 37 Comp Cas 747, a minor's name struck off, rectification ordered. *Jayantilal P. Patrl* v *Gordhandas Desai (P) Ltd*, [1967] 1 Comp LJ 272 Bom: (1968) 38 Comp Cas 405. An appeal to Company Law Board was not stayed where the dispute as to the agreement of transfer was to be adjudicated by international arbitration and the Indian company whose register was sought to be rectified was not a party to the agreement, *Insotex (India) Ltd* v *AEGNGEF Ltd*, (1995) 83 Comp Cas 358 CLB. Affirmed on appeal in *AEG-Atkiengesllscrapt* v *Insotex (India) Ltd*, (1995) 83 Comp Cas 677: AIR 1996 Kant 69, the court further found that many other matters were there before CLB and the balance of convenience was also against stay. The CLB has to record a finding as to how the matter before it is covered by one clause or the other and the power became exercisable. *T. G. Veera Prasad* v *Sree Rayalaseema Alkalies & Allied Chemicals Ltd*, (1999) 98 Comp Cas 806 AP. *S. Siv Kumar* v *Cirlacs Data Systems Ltd*, (2002) 112 Comp Cas 162 CLB, name deleted under allegedly forged transfer documents, criminal court conducting inquiry into the forgery aspects, the CLB, being not proper forum for such inquiry, waiting for the result of the criminal case. *Gopalkrishna Sen Gupta* v *Hindustan Construction Co*, (2002) 112 Comp Cas 166 CLB, the CLB not competent for investigating whether signatures on transfer deeds forged. *W. Gunther* v *Switching Technologies Gunther Ltd*, (2004) 4 Comp LJ 507 CLB, a German company's shares were transferred to another company without any authorisation from the side of the company. *Vipin Aggarwal* v *HCL Infosys Ltd*, (2005) 127 Comp Cas 593 CLB, shares stolen from the petitioner's office, he informed police and also the company with particulars requesting it not to register them in any other person's name. The company did register them but was compelled to restore them to the petitioner's name. *Shree Cement Ltd* v *Power Grid Corpn Ltd*, (2004) 122 Comp Cas 332 CLB, transfer of allotted bonds, refusal on the ground that the original allottee had not paid for them.

41. *H. G. Ariff* v *Surattee Bara Bazar Co*, (1919) 49 IC 288. *See also* the case of *The Indian Specie Bank Ltd, Re*, (1915) 17 Bom LR 342: AIR 1915 Bom 1, where a member had transferred all his shares and applications for registration of the transfer were duly lodged with the company. But the company went into liquidation before the transfer could be registered in the usual course of things. It was held that the transferor was not entitled to rectification of the register of members as he had not shown any unnecessary delay on the part of the company. But see *Babulal* v *New Standard Coal Co*, [1967] 1 Comp LJ 161, where a rectification was ordered in favour of a bona fide purchaser of shares who had fulfilled the requirements of transfer. There is no question of delay where the petitioner has not established his title to the shares. *K. S. Narayana Iyer* v *Talayar Tea Co Ltd*, (1995) 16 Corpt LA 258 Mad.

42. *Dale & Carrington Investments (P) Ltd* v *P. K. Prathapan*, (2002) 111 Comp Cas 410 CLB, permission to hold shares in an Indian Company could be granted *ex post facto*, rectification not to be ordered prematurely for deleting names of foreign investors. Confirmed in appeal to High Court in *P. K. Prathapan* v *Dale & Carrington Investments (P) Ltd*, (2002) 111 Comp Cas 425 Ker; *Rajiv Das (Dr)* v *United Press Ltd*, (2002) 111 Comp Cas 584 CLB, joint shareholding, company has no power to split it. This can be done only through a suit for partition. *SCV Subramanyam Naidu* v *Incablenet Thirupathi (P) Ltd*, (2006) 130 Comp Cas 606 CLB, stamps not cancelled, no proof of delivery of documents to the company, no proof of directors' approval, rectification in favour of the purchaser not ordered.

This is obviously a summary remedy obtained by petition to the CLB.[43] Earlier to 1988 when this power was vested in the court under the now repealed Section 155, the view taken was that a regular suit for rectification could also be filed and this used to be the only appropriate remedy where complicated questions were involved.[44] Although great discretionary powers had been given to the court to "decide all questions which it was necessary or expedient to decide in connection with an application for rectification", yet a petition under this section was not viewed with favour in some cases. For example, in *Jayshree Shantaram* v *Rajkamal Kalamandir (P) Ltd*,[45] the Bombay High Court held that:

> Where discovery and inspection are necessary and complicated questions such as forgery and fabricated documents arise, the summary procedure trial under Section 155 (now Section 111) should not be allowed.[46]

---

43. Relief could be obtained under the section from any civil court. *Joginder Singh* v *Basawa Singh*, (1985) 58 Comp Cas 843 P&H.

44. *See*, for example, *Balwant Singh* v *Krishna Bus Service*, [1967] 1 Comp LJ 137; *Ramesh Chandra* v *Wearwell Cycle Co*, [1966] 1 Comp LJ 248, where all the earlier authorities have been reviewed. Where a matter was pending under S. 155, it was held that no other action would lie elsewhere in respect of the same cause of action, *India Fruits Ltd* v *Mantrad (P) Ltd* (1993) 2 Andh LT 726.

45. AIR 1960 Bom 136: (1960) 30 Comp Cas 141. For some other cases where petitions for rectification of register of members were dismissed, see *People's Insurance Co* v *Wood & Co*, AIR 1960 Punj 388; *Laxminarayan* v *Praga Tools Corpn*, AIR 1953 Hyd 126; *Jagan Nath* v *Gopi Chand*, AIR 1915 Lah 100: 29 IC 770; *Daddy S. Mazda* v *K. R. Irani*, (1977) 47 Comp Cas 39 Cal.

46. Similar opinions were expressed in *Sadashiva* v *Gandhi Sewa Samaj*, AIR 1958 Bom 247: (1958) 28 Comp Cas 137; *Manilal Gangaram* v *W. I. Theatres Ltd*, AIR 1963 Bom 40, where SHAH J explained the objects of the provisions of the Act. See *Mahadeo Lal* v *New Darjeeling Union Tea Co*, AIR 1952 Cal 58; *Dhelakhat Tea Co, Re*, AIR 1957 Cal 476: (1958) 28 Comp Cas 62; *Dewan Singh Hira Singh* v *Minerva Films Ltd*, AIR 1959 Punj 106; *Benarsi Das* v *DD Cement Ltd*, AIR 1959 Punj 232; where a petition was rejected as it involved controversies under several heads; *People's Insurance Co* v *Wood & Co*, AIR 1960 Punj 388. The remedy is not available as of right without the court having discretion to refuse it, *see* at p 390; *Mahendra Kumar Jain* v *Federal Chemical Works*, [1965] 1 Comp LJ 151, where the Allahabad High Court pointed out that the petitioner's title to shares being defective petition under the section was not proper, see also *Somasundram* v *Official Liquidator*, [1967] 1 Comp LJ 257, where a delayed petition for rectification was not allowed. *Public Passenger Service Ltd* v *Khadar*, [1965] 1 Comp LJ 1: AIR 1966 SC 489: (1966) 36 Comp Cas 1, Bachawat J at p 492 P&H; *Puran Devi* v *Gurnam Singh*, (1977) 47 Comp Cas 796, where signature was denied. Where a person challenged the validity of the register long after his name was deleted and that too in circumstances involving voluminous evidence, discretionary remedy of the section was not allowed. *S. Gurucharan Singh Mahant* v *Rattan Sports (P) Ltd*, (1986) 59 Comp Cas 279. Rectification was ordered where a transfer was registered violating the requirement of the articles that shares must be offered first to existing members. *Amrit Kaur Puri* v *Kapurthala Flour, Oil and General Mills Co (P) Ltd*, (1984) 56 Comp Cas 194 P&H. A dispute about genuineness of signature of the transferor, should be relegated to a civil court, *Indian Bank* v *Deepak Fertilizers & Petrochemical Corpn Ltd*, (1999) 35 CLA 389 Bom; *Tarsen Kansil* v *Dey Spinners Ltd*, (2000) 37 CLA 132. The company disputed the validity of the documents which were produced for showing that the removal of the petitioner's name was wrongful, held, matter fit for civil suit, *Bipin K. Jain* v *Savik Vijay Engg (P) Ltd*, (1998) 91 Comp Cas 835; complications arising out of unauthorised sale of shares by a bank to whom the shares were not even pledged and, therefore, had no lien over them, matter fit for civil court trial, *A. Akhilandam* v *Great Eastern Shipping Co Ltd*, [2000] 1 Comp LJ 110. *Nupur Mitra* v *Basubani (P) Ltd*, (2002) 108 Comp Cas 359 CLB,

Similarly, Delhi High Court[47] rejected a petition under the section as it involved ascertainment of a number of facts like the value of imported machinery against which shares were allotted and which required expert opinion and its cross-examination and the Madhya Pradesh High Court did not entertain a petition which required investigation as to whether there was a free consent or one under undue influence or fraud.[48] The Court of Appeal expressed the opinion that the court can deal with, even in this summary nature proceedings of the power of rectification, the matters relating to the petitioner's ownership of shares.[49] Where the question was whether the petitioner was the real transferee and questions of fraud, etc., were not at all involved, the court said that it was not necessary to drive the parties to a civil suit. There should be no hesitation in exercising the jurisdiction where matters are not too complicated and can be sorted out on the basis of evidence produced by the parties.[50] There is no general rule that whenever complicated questions of fact are involved the parties must be relegated to a civil suit.[51] The matter is to be decided by the Company Law Board.[52]

But apart from the case where complicated questions arise, the Supreme Court has laid down that "the jurisdiction created by the section is very

there is no rule of law that in all cases the parties should be called upon to refer complicated questions of fact to a civil suit. *Bharat K. Gajjar* v *Castrol India Ltd*, (2003) 115 Comp Cas 396 CLB, proceedings under the section are in the nature of summary proceedings, serious disputes relating to title cannot be tried in a summary jurisdiction, civil suit is the proper remedy. *Tarsen Kansil* v *Dey Spinners Ltd*, (2001) 103 Comp Cas 835, allegations of fraud, forgery, manipulation, collusion, and misrepresentation, etc, can not be decided in summary jurisdiction. *Pradip Kumar Chetlangia* v *Bajaj Auto Ltd*, (2005) 126 Comp Cas 347 CLB, questions of title. *Beena Toshniwal* v *ITC Ltd*, (2005) 128 Comp Cas 955 CLB, essentially a jurisdiction for rectification of register. *Kantha Devi Agarwal* v *ROC*, (2006) 129 Comp Cas 485 CLB, no jurisdiction to examine orders of Registrar of Companies.

47. *Punjab Distilling Industries* v *B.P.C. Mills Ltd*, (1973) 40 Comp Cas 189 Del. *RDF Power Projects Ltd* v *M. Muralikrishna*, (2005) 124 Comp Cas 277 CLB, rectification is exclusive jurisdiction of CLB but questions of right and title can be decided by the Civil Court. *RDF Power Projects Ltd* v *M. Muralikrishna*, (2005) CLC 234 (AP), stay of proceedings before the CLB not warranted. *Ram Vasant Kotak* v *International Transport & Trading Systems (P) Ltd*, (2005) 59 SCL 181 (CLB) the CLB can go on with the matter even if criminal proceedings have also been initiated.
48. *Kamla Devi Mantri* v *Grasim Industries Ltd*, (1990) 69 Comp Cas 188 MP: [1989] 3 Comp LJ 278. A dispute between joint purchasers of shares. A Full Bench of the Kerala High Court ordered the company to register the respective names in the agreed proportion. The Supreme Court rejected appeal against it. It was a matter of civil court jurisdiction and not of the company court. *K. P. Antony* v *Thandiyode Plantations (P) Ltd*, (1996) 86 Comp Cas 684 Ker (FB). Doubts about the validity of a will cannot be considered under this jurisdiction. *T. G. Veera Prasad* v *Shree Rayalseema Alkalies & Allied Chemicals Ltd*, (1997) 89 Comp Cas 13 CLB; *G. N. Bayra Reddy* v *Arathi Cine Enterprises (P) Ltd*, (1997) 89 Comp Cas 745 CLB. This jurisdiction would include an inquiry into the validity of an allotment of securities, *Shiv Dayal Agarwal* v *Sidhartha Polyester (P) Ltd*, (1996) 88 Comp Cas 705 CLB.
49. *Keene* v *Martin*, [2000] 1 BCLC 194 CA.
50. *V. L. Pahade* v *Vinay L. Deshpande*, (1999) 97 Comp Cas 889 AP. Disputes involving ownership, fraud, forgery can be relegated to a civil suit, *National Insurance Co Ltd* v *Glaxo India Ltd*, (1999) 98 Comp Cas 378 Bom.
51. *Nupur Mitra* v *Basubani (P) Ltd*, (2002) 108 Comp Cas 359 CLB.
52. *Khurshid Alam* v *P. Pagnon Co (P) Ltd*, (2003) 108 Comp Cas 523 CLB.

beneficial and should be liberally exercised".[53] The question whether an allotment of shares is in accordance with the articles of the company has been held by the Patna High Court to be not such a complicated question as cannot be disposed of in a petition for rectification. The court accordingly ordered deletion of names of certain persons to whom shares were allotted in violation of articles.[54] The Gujarat High Court expressed the opinion that a petition under the section is more or less analogous to a suit and, therefore, the court can decide all questions which can be tackled in a regular suit.[55] Where the claimant was not able to produce even a transfer form, the court allowed him to prove his title to the shares, because if he could do so, the execution of the transfer form could be ordered.[56]

---

53. *Indian Chemical Products Ltd* v *State of Orissa*, [1966] 2 Comp LJ 63: (1966) 36 Comp Cas 592: AIR 1967 SC 253. The Court was required by the now repealed S. 156 to order the company to send a copy of the order of rectification to the Registrar within 30 days. *Bhupinder Rai* v *S. M. Kannappa Automobiles (P) Ltd*, (1995) Corpt LA 262 Mad: (1996) 86 Comp Cas 18, further issue of capital and its allotment to a block of shareholders to the exclusion of others is not a matter under S. 111 of the Act. The CLB would not provide the relief of rectification where it would involve reduction of capital because the CLB does not have the jurisdiction in the matter of reduction of capital.
54. *Basudeb Kataruka* v *Dhanbad Automobiles (P) Ltd*, (1977) 47 Comp Cas 68 Pat. No such order could be made in a case where the company never prepared its register of members or filed any return of allotment. *Rajnikant Shah* v *Deccan Farms & Distilleries*, (1978) 48 Comp Cas 322 Bom. Rectification was allowed where allotment of securities was in violation of the company's memorandum of association. *M. V. Sathyanarayana* v *Global Drugs (P) Ltd*, (1999) 95 Comp Cas 595 CLB.
55. *Shri Gulabrai Kalidas Naik* v *Shri Laxmidas Lallubhai Patel*, (1978) 48 Comp Cas 438 Guj. The irregularity, if any, can be challenged within three years from the date of its entry in the register, Article 137 of the Limitation Act, 1963. *Anil Gupta* v *DCM Ltd*, (1983) 54 Comp Cas 301 Del. Any member can challenge an irregularity. *Killick Nixon Ltd* v *Dhanraj Mills (P) Ltd*, (1983) 54 Comp Cas 432 Bom. The same case decided that a company can make changes in the register of members even when it is closed to the public. The reason why every member can question the validity of the register is also explained in *Om Prakash Berlia* v *UTI*, (1983) 54 Comp Cas 469 Bom. Questions of title can now be decided, but earlier the position was different. See *Kamla Devi Mantri* v *Grasim Industries Ltd*, (1990) 69 Comp Cas 138 MP: [1989] 3 Comp LJ 278, question of the validity of a will, not decided under the erstwhile S. 155; *Kalyani Sundaram* v *Shardlow India Ltd*, (1990) 67 Comp Cas 306 Mad, a dispute about a right of pre-emption not taken up; *Kumeran Polty* v *Venad Pharmaceuticals & Chemicals*, (1989) 65 Comp Cas 246 Ker, agreement to convert a loan into capital, not proved; *Vishnu Dayal Jhunjhunwala* v *UOI*, (1989) 66 Comp Cas 684 All. Where the question of the title of a person has to be decided, and if such person is not a party, he must be brought on record, otherwise no order can be passed about his title, *Subhash Chandra* v *Vardhman Spinning & General Mills Ltd*, (1995) 83 Comp Cas 641 CLB.
56. *K.P. Antony* v *Thandiyode Plantations (P) Ltd*, (1987) 62 Comp Cas 553 Ker. The same view has been adopted in *Harnamsingh* v *Bhagwan Singh*, (1992) 74 Comp Cas 726 Del, questions of title; *E. V. Swaminathan* v *K. M. M. A. Industries & Roadways (P) Ltd*, (1993) 76 Comp Cas 1 Mad, the beneficial nature of the jurisdiction would be lost if it were reduced to a summary jurisdiction; *Ammonia Supplies Corpn (P) Ltd* v *Modern Plastic Containers (P) Ltd*, (1994) 79 Comp Cas 163: AIR 1994 Del 155 NOC, the matter can be relegated to a civil suit only in cases of extreme factual complexity. *Abhipara Capital Ltd* v *J.C.T. Electronics Ltd*, (2002) 111 Comp Cas 863 CLB, company refused to accept a transfer on the ground that the signature of the transferor did not tally. The transferee proved that his letter to the transferor came back unserved. Original share certificates were with the transferee. The transferor did not lodge any objection nor asked for duplicates. No other claimant. The company directed to register the transfer.

The words "unnecessary delay" have not been defined in the Act and, therefore, it becomes a question of evidence to be decided on the facts of each case. A failure to register a transfer within one month of the application, which was contrary to the listing agreement, was held to be an unreasonable delay.[57]

Every shareholder has an interest in the proper maintenance of the company's register of members. Any member can make an application without showing any injury or prejudice to him. Personal grievance is not necessary for *locus standi*.[58]

On receiving such appeal against refusal or an application for rectification, the CLB has to hear the parties.[59] It may either dismiss the appeal or reject the application, or may order that the company shall register the transfer or transmission and the company has to comply with the order within 10 days or direct rectification of the register and require the company to compensate the aggrieved person for any loss sustained by him.[60] The CLB has been empowered to make necessary interim orders, orders as to costs and incidental and consequential orders regarding payment of dividends or allotment of bonus or rights shares.[61] The CLB has the power of deciding the applicant's title to the shares in question and of deciding generally any question which it is necessary to decide in connection with the application for rectification.[62] These provisions are applicable to the

---

57. *Joseph Michael* v *Travancore Rubber & Tea Co*, (1989) 66 Comp Cas 136: [1989] 2 Comp LJ 81 Ker.

58. *Om Prakash Berlia* v *Unit Trust of India*, (1983) 54 Comp Cas 136 Bom, reversed on other grounds in *Unit Trust of India* v *Om Prakash Berlia*, (1983) 54 Comp Cas 469 Bom; *Arjan Singh* v *Panipat Woolen & General Mills Co Ltd*, (1963) 33 Comp Cas 534 Punj; *Tracstar Investments Ltd* v *Gordan Woodroffe Ltd*, (1996) 87 Comp Cas 941 CLB, affirmed in *Shoe Specialities Ltd* v *Tracstar Investments Ltd*, (1997) 88 Comp Cas 471 Mad.

59. Where a pledgee of shares was registered as member and on an order of rectification his name was removed, it was not necessary that he should have been heard on the matter. *Malleswara Finance and Investment Co* v *CLB*, (1994) 81 Comp Cas 66: AIR 1994 Mad 341. Pendency of a petition for prevention of oppression and mismanagement is not a ground for refusing an application for rectification. The applicant's name was substituted on the register without any sufficient cause and he was seeking rectification, *Anand Hemant Patel* v *Ornate Club (P) Ltd*, (2000) 99 Comp Cas 318 CLB.

60. S. 111(5). An application for rectification filed by directors who participated in the decision to accept the impinged transfer was not allowed. There was a long delay also. *Mohanram Sastri* v *Swadharma*, (1995) 83 Comp Cas 272 Mad; *S. Seetha* v *Satyam Computer Services Ltd*, (2002) 112 Comp Cas 139 CLB, instead of accepting a duly lodged transfer, the company by negligence issued duplicates to the transferor. The company directed to register the transfer and also to give the transferee the bonus shares and dividend amount to which he became entitled in the meantime.

61. S. 111(6). Where a substantial acquisition of shares was under question, the CLB restrained the company from transferring its assets because otherwise the transferee would ultimately get control over a barren company, *Coetho (AJ)* v *South India Tea & Coffee Estates Ltd*, (1998) 93 Comp Cas 401 CLB.

62. S. 111(7). *Nupur Mitra* v *Basubani (P) Ltd*, (2002) 108 Comp Cas 359 CLB, CLB order of rectification having the effect of reduction of capital was held to be permissible.

rectification of the register of debenture-holders also.[63] An appeal against refusal or an application for rectification has to be in the form of a petition in writing and accompanied by such fee as may be prescribed.[64]

Limitation Act not applicable

This sub-section does not prescribe any period of limitation.[65] Petitions under this sub-section would not be crippled by the periods prescribed by sub-sections (2) and (3). For the purposes of jurisdiction for rectification, sub-section (4) says in clause (b) that it includes refusals under sub-section (1).[66] Though the period of limitation is not applicable, an action which is initiated several years after the cause of action may not be entertained because of inordinate delay and latches.[67] An aggrieved person cannot be prevented from approaching the CLB by reason of delay in exercising his rights, the period of limitation being not applicable.[68] Delay can be condoned. In this case the delay was condoned because it was due to a *bona fide* pursuit of other remedies.[69]

---

63. S. 111(8). Sub-section (9) provides for penalty for default in complying with the orders of the Board.
64. S. 111(10).
65. The CLB is not a court for the purposes of jurisdiction for rectification of register of members. Hence, the periods of limitation as prescribed by the Limitations Act, 1963 are not applicable. The only requirement will be that the petition must not suffer from laches or acquiescence, i.e., there should be no unreasonable delay in seeking relief. *Shiv Dayal Agarwal* v *Sidhartha Polyester (P) Ltd*, (1996) 88 Comp Cas 705 CLB; *ITG Veera Prasad* v *Rayalseema Alkalies*, (1997) 89 Comp Cas 13 CLB, the CLB has the power to ask parties to go to a civil court for sorting out factual complications; *G. N. Bayra Reddy* v *Arathi Cine Enterprises (P) Ltd*, (1997) 89 Comp Cas 745 CLB. An application after two months of refusal was held to be maintainable, *Kana Sen* v *C. K. Sen & Co (P) Ltd*, (1998) 91 Comp Cas 26 CLB. When matters of rectification were in the jurisdiction of courts, three-year period of limitation was applicable. *Bipin Vadilal Mehta* v *Ramesh B. Desai*, (1997) 26 Corpt LA 71 Guj. *Peerless General Finance & Investment Co Ltd* v *Poddar Projects Ltd*, (2007) 136 Comp Cas 160 (Cal), Limitation Act not applicable.
66. *Citi Bank NA* v *Power Grid Corpn of India*, (1995) 17 Corpt LA 25 CLB: (1995) 83 Comp Cas 454. Unauthorised transfers are liable to be struck out, e.g., one executed by the holder of a power of attorney in a surreptitious exercise of his authority. Delay in application will not be a material factor in such a case. *Farhat Sheikh* v *Eseman Metalo Chemical (P) Ltd*, (1991) 71 Comp Cas 88 Cal. *Gurnam Singh Gujral (Cal)* v *Indian Hotels Co Ltd*, (2002) 112 Comp Cas 86 CLB, petition filed 2 years after the name of the original owner was restored to register, held barred by time. Shares in question were a stolen property, transfer deeds were also found to be forged.
67. *C. Mathew* v *Cochin Stock Exchange Ltd*, (1997) 26 Corpt LA 312 CLB.
68. *Mahendra Singh Mewar* v *Lake Palace Hotels & Motels (P) Ltd*, (1997) 27 Corpt LA 229 CLB; *UOI* v *R. C. Bhargava*, (1998) 30 Corpt LA 229 CLB. The time limit specified by the Companies Act would be applicable, but not that of the Limitation Act because the CLB is not a court, and the Limitation Act applies only to courts. *Anil R. Chhabria* v *Finolex Industries Ltd and Finolex Cables Ltd*, (2000) 99 Comp Cas 168. To the same effect *Nupur Mitra* v *Basubani (P) Ltd*, (2002) 108 Comp Cas CLB, unexplained long delay, laches and acquiescence may bar a petition. *Jagjit Rai Maihi* v *Punjab Machinery Works (P) Ltd*, (2001) 103 Comp Cas 979 P&H, allotment and transfer of 1972, petition in 1981 for rectification, too late.
69. *Khurshid Alam* v *P. Pagnon Co (P) Ltd*, (2003) 108 Comp Cas 523 CLB. *Calcutta Security Printers Ltd* v *Calcutta Phototype Co Ltd*, (2002) 112 Comp Cas 434 CLB, the question of limitation viewed liberally where the transfer was based on fraud and forged papers.

Where there was delay in filing an application for transmission of shares, the CLB said that the Limitation Act was applicable and the delay could be condoned because the applicant remained preoccupied with other proceedings relating to the shares.[70]

The discretion in ordering or refusing to order rectification of the register of members is the same as discretion in granting or refusing to grant specific performance of an agreement to allot shares. Prejudicial delay may be one of the causes of refusal. By sitting back and doing nothing for seven years until it suited him to enforce his right, the petitioner had failed to display the need for promptitude which was ordinarily required of a person seeking specific performance. In this case a person had purchased the controlling power in the company thinking that the shares purchased by him represented the whole of the company's issued share capital being totally unaware of the large number of unregistered shares. The court, therefore, held that even if the plaintiff established his right to the allotment of 10,000 shares, the court could refuse to exercise discretion in his favour.[71]

Spot delivery contract

In a spot delivery contract, the consideration was offered much after the date of the sale. The transfer was held to be void and refusal of registration justified.[72]

Directors' power of rectification of entries

It is open to directors to rectify the register of members of their own even where there are no objections and a wrong entry has been detected. There is no need, in such a case, to apply to the Tribunal for an order of rectification. "If there is no dispute, and if the circumstances are such that the tribunal would order rectification," the Board may itself effect the necessary corrections.[73] "An application to the court is only essential when the company disputes the right to rectification. There is no reason why the directors if they *bona fide* agree and that a shareholder has the right to avoid a contract should not thereupon assent to the rescission of the contract and

---

70. *Tommy Mathew Daroflex Ltd, Re*, (2004) 122 Comp Cas 741 CLB. *Vinayak Vasudev Sahasrabudhe v Pentagon Drugs (P) Ltd*, (2005) 128 Comp Cas 122 CLB, the complainant's shares were transferred to another person in 1997 but he came to know only in 2001. His application in 2001 was held to be not time-barred. *A. Devarajan v N.S. Nemura Consultancy India (P) Ltd*, (2006) 130 Comp Cas 407 CLB, petition in 2003, transfer in 1995, petitioner came to know only in 2002 during inspection, petition within 3 years. The company could not produce any documents for the transfer, petitioner's name directed to be restored to the register.
71. *ISIS Factors plc, Re*, (2003) 2 BCLC 411 (Ch D); *Dulat v ISIS Factors plc*, (2003) 2 BCLC 411 (Ch D); *MSDC Radharamanan v Shree Bhatarathi Cotton Mills (P) Ltd*, (2006) 130 Comp Cas 414 CLB, 16 years delay, no condonation.
72. *Bhagwati Developers (P) Ltd v Peerless General Finance & Investment Co Ltd*, (2005) 6 SCC 718: AIR 2005 SC 3345.
73. HALSBURY'S LAWS OF ENGLAND, p 176 [4th Edn, 1996, para 306, Vol 7(1)]; *Pool Firebrick & Blue Clay Co, Hartlay case*, (1875) 10 Ch App 157.

rectify the register in the appropriate manner. An order of the court is not necessary in such cases.''[74] However, the directors have no power to rectify the register by substituting the name of another person in the place of an existing member, except on an application for transfer duly made in compliance with the provisions of Section 108.[75]

Application to private companies

Before its amendment in 1997, Section 111 was applicable to public companies and in a very restricted manner to private companies. After the amendment, the section applies only to private companies. Section 111-A has been *inserted* for public companies.

Grounds of refusal under Securities Contracts Regulation Act, 1956

Section 22-A of the Act permitted a listed public company to refuse to register a transfer only on any of the specified four grounds:[76] This section has been *omitted*. The grounds stated below are no longer applicable. The rulings also belong to the earlier period.

(A) Bad delivery of transfer documents.—A company can refuse to accept a transfer where the instrument of transfer is not properly prepared, not duly stamped, or signed, the certificate of shares under transfer has not been delivered or some other applicable formal or legal requirement has not been complied with.

(B) Contravention of law.—The transfer in question is in contravention of some law, e.g., that the requirements of permission under the Foreign Exchange Regulation Act, 1974 have not been complied with.[77]

(C) Prejudicial to company or public interest.—Where the transfer is of a nature that it is likely to change the composition of the board of directors in such a way as would be prejudicial to the interest of the company or public interest.[78]

---

74. That was decided in *Wright case*, (1871) 7 Ch D 55 and *Ress River Silver Mining Co v Smith*, (1869) 4 HL 64; *Michaels v Harley Harley House Marleybone Ltd*, [1997] 3 All ER 446: [1997] BCLC 166 Ch D.
75. *Jayantilal P. Patel v Gordhandas Desai (P) Ltd*, (1968) 38 Comp Cas 405 Bom.
76. *Surat Electricity Co Ltd v UOI*, AIR 1995 Bom 377: (1995) 4 Bom CR 71 Bom, the purport of SCRA is to regulate buying and selling of securities, prevention of undesirable speculation and to ensure free transferability of securities.
77. *Bharat Petroleum Corpn Ltd v Stock Holding Corpn of India Ltd*, (1995) 82 Comp Cas 539 CLB, refusal by a company to register shares in the name of a company on behalf of mutual funds held justified being violative of S. 49, Companies Act.
78. *Alaknanda Mfg & Finance Co (P) Ltd v CLB*, (1995) 83 Comp Cas 514 Bom, this is a statutory guideline to the directors to consider, firstly, whether the transfer would cause change in the composition of the company's board and, if so, whether that change would be adverse to the company or public interest. If the Company Law Board upholds the directors' refusal, an appeal lies but not a writ petition. The provisions of the section were held to be constitutionally valid. The reasons on which directors refused were found to be justified because it appeared that the transferees intended to change things in a prejudicial manner. The court found that purchases were effected with institutional funds which was something

(D) Stay order.—Where the transfer has been stayed by a court order or by any other authority or tribunal.

Where the refusal is on the basis of the last three grounds, namely, contravention of law, likelihood of prejudicial changes or stay order, the company had to state its reasons and refer the matter to the CLB and inform the parties accordingly. The decision of CLB, unless appealed against, prevailed. For example, if the rejection was on the ground of likelihood of a prejudicial change, the board of directors had to state their reasons for so thinking and the CLB then decided whether the reasoning of the company was sound or not.[79]

Appeals

An appeal lies to the High Court against an order of the Company Law Board on a question of law but not on a question of fact.[80]

By virtue of the consequential amendment of the Companies Act introduced by the Depositories Act, 1996, the provisions of Section 111 are to be confined in their application only to private companies. For companies whose shares are traded at a stock exchange, a new provision, namely, Section 111-A has been introduced. The section says that shares, debentures and any interest in such company shall be freely transferable. Where the securities are transferred through a depository, an appeal will lie to the Company Law Board in connection with any transfer only if it is in contravention of the provisions of the Securities and Exchange Board of India Act, 1992 or any regulations made thereunder or the Sick Industrial Companies (Special Provisions) Act, 1985 (SICA)[81] or any

against public interest and the small shareholders totalling to 46% would have suffered most from change in the complexion of management. A person was already a shareholder to the extent of 9.68% and was working as joint managing director. He purchased further shares to the extent of 3.81% and applied for registration. He was refused. The Company Law Board did not uphold the refusal. In the opinion of the Board, 13% shareholding would not have brought about any such change in the composition of the company's board of directors as would have prejudiced the company or public interest. There were three shareholders blocks and the other two were holding 70%. *Vimal K. Gupta* v *Auto Lamps Ltd*, (1996) 86 Comp Cas 157: [1995] 3 Comp LJ 152. Where the company failed to place before the Company Law Board any material to justify their apprehension that prejudicial changes would be brought about in the composition of the company's board of directors, the company's rejection of the share transfer was held to be not justified. *Surat Electricity Co Ltd* v *UOI*, AIR 1995 Bom 377: (1995) 4 Bom CR 71 Bom.

79. See *Gammon India Ltd* v *Hongkong Bank (Agency) (P) Ltd*, (1992) 74 Comp Cas 123: [1992] 1 Comp LJ 279 CLB; *Patel Engg Co Ltd* v *Patel Relators (P) Ltd*, (1992) 74 Comp Cas 395 CLB; *Gordon Woodroffe Ltd* v *Trident Investment*, (1994) 79 Comp Cas 764 CLB: [1994] 1 Comp LJ 313.

80. The distinct trend of authorities at present is to restrict the scope of refusal to accept a transfer of shares and this trend has been confirmed by the amendment of 1988 by making it compulsory that reasons for refusal must be indicated. *Joseph Michael* v *Travancore Rubber & Tea Co*, (1989) 66 Comp Cas 491: [1989] 2 Comp LJ 81 Ker.

81. Provisions of this Act have been merged into the Companies Act.

other law for the time being in-force.[82] An application under the section can be filed by a depository, by the company itself, or by a participant or an investor. The CLB has been given the discretionary power to make an interim order suspending voting rights in respect of the shares under transfer till the completion of inquiry and making of final orders. The transferee can exercise voting rights unless they are suspended by an order of the CLB. Pending the disposal of the application, any further transfer of the shares in question shall entitle the transferee to exercise voting rights. The provisions of sub-sections (5), (7), (9) and (12) of Section 111 are applicable to proceedings under Section 111-A.

The CLB should not mechanically reject a petition because of some pendency of the same matter before a civil court. The matter should be disposed of on due consideration of affidavits so as to find out whether there is a real possibility of conflicting decisions.[83]

Public Companies: Amendment of Section 111 by Depositories Act [Insertion of S. 111-A]

Section 111 has been amended by the Depositories Act, 1996. Sub-section (14) was added by the amendment. The effect of the amendment is that Section 111 has been confined in its operation to private companies only.

By way of further amendment Section 111-A was inserted by the Depositories Related Laws (Amendment) Act, 1997. This section applies to public companies only. It became necessary because Section 111 having been confined to private companies only, no system of rectification remained available in cases of public companies. The section lays down that subject only to the provisions in the section, the shares or debentures of a listed company shall be freely transferable. Thus, the transfer of securities has been made the subject-matter of a free market independent of the director's discretionary power of refusal. For example, where the refusal to accept a transfer was on ground that the shares were a part of the trust which was of perpetual nature, it was held that the shares being those of a public limited company, they were freely transferable and the company was not concerned with the conditions of the trust.[84] A company was not allowed to refuse a transfer on the ground that the transferees were not the

---

82. *ICICI Venture Funds Management Co Ltd* v *Sofil Information System (P) Ltd*, (2007) 136 Comp Cas 84 CLB, agreement between buyer and seller of shares containing restrictions on transfer not incorporated in the company's articles not binding on the company.
83. *Nupur Mitra* v *Basubani (P) Ltd*, (1999) 35 CLA 97 Cal.
84. *Jose Pulikken* v *Damien Subsidies & Kuries Ltd*, [2000] 4 Comp LJ 421 CLB: (2000) 109 Comp Cas 699. See also *Kamdhenu Chemicals (P) Ltd* v *Advent Computer Services (P) Ltd*, [2000] 4 Comp LJ 424 CLB, another case of unjustified refusal. *Peerless General Finance and Investment Co* v *Poddar Projects Ltd*, (2007) 2 SCC 431: (2007) 136 Comp Cas 160 Cal: (2007) 136 Comp Cas 197, order of rectification for implementing a scheme of amalgamation. The order already implemented. Appeal to Supreme Court infructuous.

natives of the company's State of registration.[85] A company was not allowed to refuse a transfer on the ground that the transferee was an ex employee who was dismissed for irregularities and his admission as a shareholder would not be in the interest of the company.[86]

The CLB cannot look into validity of an allotment of shares by a public company. The powers which it could have exercised under Section 111(4) cannot now be exercised in respect of public companies under Section 111-A.[87] The CLB is no longer in a position to look into title disputes relating to transfers to which the company is not a party. A public listed company is bound to accept a transfer for which all the appropriate papers have been filed. The CLB cannot go into questions as to whether there had been an actual sale or not or whether documents were genuine or forged. All such matters have now to be the subject-matter of a civil suit.[88]

If a company refuses to register a transfer within two months of lodgement and the transferee brings the matter before the CLB, it shall direct the company to register the transfer. Thus, the right of appeal to the Tribunal against the refusal is allowed only to the transferee. The CLB has also been given the power to order rectification of the register of members by the company or by the depository where a transfer is in contravention of the Securities and Exchange Board of India Act, 1992 or any rules or regulations made by SEBI[89] or Sick Industrial Companies (Special Provisions) Act, 1985[90] or any other law for the time being in force. It means that the CLB's power of ordering rectification is in respect of violation of laws.[91] Unlawful transfers are open to rectification. An

---

85. *Namita Gupta* v *Cachar Native Joint Stock Co Ltd*, (1999) 98 Comp Cas 655 CLB. The ground of refusal that the transfer was prejudicial to the interest of the company is no longer applicable. Section 22-A of the Securities Contracts (Regulation) Act, 1956 was scrapped in 1995 by the Depositories Act. *Canara Land Investment Ltd* v *Sea Rock Investment Ltd*, (1999) 35 CLA 209. *Industrial Development Bank of India* v *Rambal Ltd*, (2003) 114 Comp Cas 167 Mad, bank credit facilities given to a company subject to the condition that promoters would not alienate their shares. The company agreed to disinvestment of its shares to the extent of 26% in favour of a foreign company. This being contrary to the loan agreement, the bank was granted an injunction to restrain it.

86. *P. R. Gokhale* v *T.N. Mercantile Bank Ltd*, (2002) 110 Comp Cas 866 CLB.

87. *Gopal Krishna Banga* v *Poona Industrial Hotels (P) Ltd*, (1999) 34 CLA 177 Bom.

88. *Charanjit Singh Ghumman* v *Dr Reddy's Laboratories Ltd*, (1999) 97 Comp Cas 360 CLB. *JRY Investments (P) Ltd* v *Deccan Leafline Services Ltd*, (2004) 121 Comp Cas 12 Bom, transfer was not allowed to be refused on the ground that the consideration for the transaction had failed to materialise.

89. See *SPS International Ltd* v *Vijay Remedies Ltd*, (1998) 93 Comp Cas 547 CLB, where the scope of CLB power was explained and the transfers were found to be in violation of SEBI Guidelines in respect of the promoters' lock-in-period; *Bakhtawar Construction Co (P) Ltd* v *Blossom Breweries Ltd*, (2000) 36 CLA 14 CLB, violation of SEBI Takeover Code. Another similar ruling, *Azzilfi Finlease & Investments (P) Ltd*, [2000] 1 Comp LJ 118 CLB. *Shirish Finance & Investment (P) Ltd* v *M. Sreenivasulu Reddy*, (2002) 109 Comp Cas 913 Bom, acquisition of shares in violation of SEBI Regulations as to limit was held to be void, rectification not allowed.

90. This Act has been repealed and its provisions merged into the Companies Act.

91. *SPS International Ltd* v *Vijay Remedies Ltd*, (1998) 30 Corpt LA 113 CLB, the power has become so confined. It does not extend to inquiry into fraud, forgery, lack of authority,

application for this purpose can be made by a depository, company, participant or investor. This is a *post-registration power*. The proviso to sub-section (2) confers the power to order registration, a *pre-registration power*, of a transfer which has been refused by the company without sufficient cause. The three grounds mentioned in the proviso would constitute a sufficient cause.[92] Two months period is available for this purpose. In the case of a depository, two months run from the date of transfer; in other cases, from the date of delivery of the transfer papers. During the inquiry before the Tribunal, the transfer would remain effective giving the transferee his voting rights unless suspended by the CLB. As a matter of interim relief, the CLB could also suspend exercise of voting rights. This power is, of course, there in the civil court. The power of the civil court in this respect has not been taken away by these provisions. The matters of title and rights are generally raised in civil proceedings.[93] The shares will also remain further transferable with similar effects.

The procedural aspects of Section 111 would apply to the proceedings, under S. 111-A also i.e., powers of the CLB (sub-section 5); decisions as to questions of title (sub-section 7); and penalty for default in implementing orders of CLB (sub-section 12).

The decision of the Company Law Board (Mad) in *Shashi Prakash Khemka* v *NEPC Micon Ltd*[94] shows the extent to which the Company Law

---

procedure etc; *Volvo Lastvagnar Komponenter AB* v *Morgardshammar (India) Ltd*, (1998) 30 Corpt LA 382 CLB, in example of wider jurisdiction earlier. *McDowell & Co Ltd* v *Shaw Wallace & Co Ltd*, (2003) 108 Comp Cas 306 CLB, the word law does not include case-law, transfer in favour of a business rival was not allowed to be refused. *Pratibha Dilip Karnad* v *Satyam Computer Services Ltd*, (2002) 108 Comp Cas 347 CLB, refusal because of a court decree, no interference. The CLB (now Tribunal) has no power to grant compensation because of delay in dematerialisation of shares. *Deccan Cements Ltd* v *Geekay Exim (India) Ltd*, (2002) 112 Comp Cas 616 CLB, shares pledged as security for repayment of loan, on default in repayment, the company was requested to register the shares in the name of the pledgee. The company's refusal was held to be not justified. *Asha Purandare* v *Integrated Controls (P) Ltd*, (2002) 112 Comp Cas 623 CLB, a typographical error in mentioning the number of one of the certificates was held to be not a ground for rejecting the transfer of the whole lot. *Maruti Udyog Ltd* v *Pentamedia Graphics Ltd*, (2002) 111 Comp Cas 56 CLB, rejection of application for transfer of pledged shares not proper even if the pledgor had given notice to the company not to register the transfer. *Shapoorji Pallonji Finance Ltd* v *Mideast India Ltd*, (2002) 110 Comp Cas 868 CLB, transfer of pledged shares could not be refused. *Mani Credit Capital (P) Ltd* v *Reliance Industries Ltd*, (2002) 111 Comp Cas 808 CLB, retransfer of pledged shares to the transferor, rectification ordered.

92. *Estate Investment Co (P) Ltd* v *Eiltap Chemicals Ltd*, (1999) 96 Comp Cas 217 CLB. Where a person claims that shares registered in some other person's name really belong to him, he must have court decision to that effect and then rectification of the register would automatically follow, *Eternit Everest Ltd* v *Neelamani Bhartiya*, [1999] 2 Comp LJ 171 Raj.

93. *Shirish Finance & Investment (P) Ltd* v *M. Sreenivasulu Reddy*, (2002) 109 Comp Cas 913 Bom; *M. Sreenivasulu Reddy* v *Kishore R. Chhabria*, (2002) 109 Comp Cas 18 Bom. *Beena Toshniwal* v *ITC Ltd*, (2005) 5 Comp LJ 134, jurisdiction is only for rectification and not for recovery of the consideration money. *New Millennium Exhibition Ltd* v *New Millennium Experience Co Ltd*, (2004) 1 BCLC 19, creditor's application not maintainable.

94. (1997) 90 Comp Cas 228 CLB-Mad. The jurisdiction of the CLB earlier was wider and included decision on questions of title and all other incidental matters, *Mafatlal Industries Ltd* v *Gujarat Glass Co Ltd*, (1998) 30 Corpt LA 167 Guj. *Indian Bank* v *Kiran Exports Ltd*,

Board has suffered loss of jurisdiction. It will have no jurisdiction under Section 111 in matters of public companies. That section now gives jurisdiction to the CLB only in respect of private companies. In the matter of public companies the CLB will have jurisdiction only in respect of transfers and transmission and that too only to enforce all lawful transfers and to prevent all unlawful transfers. A dispute about shareholding arising in any other manner than involving a transfer is now a matter for a civil suit and not a petition before the CLB even if the matter arose before the jurisdiction of the CLB was thus curtailed.

SEBI Takeover Code

SEBI violations can be taken care of by SEBI itself. When a company's shares have been acquired in violation of SEBI Takeover Code Regulations and entered in the company's register of members, the company itself can apply to the CLB for rectification of the register of members. Notwithstanding the SEBI's powers to rectify the matters, the CLB can look into the petition and pass appropriate orders.[95]

Civil Remedy not Barred

A wrong entry affects the rights of shareholder in so many respects, e.g., the right to dividend, participation in meetings and in further issues, etc., It partakes of the nature of a common law right. Therefore, the right to file a civil suit for rectification of the register has not been taken away by the Act.[96] A petition under the section for declaration of title to certain shares was not allowed. A civil suit is the only appropriate remedy for such relief.[97]

An approach to the Consumer Forum is also not barred. A transferee of shares filed his complaint before a Consumer Forum in the matter of bonus shares which happened to be allotted to the transferor. The Consumer Forum did not permit him to go to any other forum. The CLB did not entertain his petition.[98]

(2001) 104 Comp Cas 320, shares held by a bank under a pledge were allowed, on the failure of the pledger to pay back, to be registered in the name of the bank. *Shyama Prasad Murarka* v *Calcutta Stock Exchange Assn Ltd*, (2002) 108 Comp Cas 203 CLB, Stock Exchange Co not allowed to refuse transfer, refusal communicated 2 years after lodgment was held to be not proper, Stock Exchange had no right to call upon the transferee to deposit the consideration amount in the Stock Exchange.

95. *Aska Investments (P) Ltd* v *Grab Tea Co Ltd*, (2005) 126 Comp Cas 603 CLB. *Kesha Appliances (P) Ltd* v *Royal Holding Services Ltd*, (2006) 130 Comp Cas 227 Bom, the Bombay High Court was of the view that violation of SEBI Takeover Code should be adjudicated only by SEBI Authority [CAT].

96. *M. Sreenivasulu Reddy* v *Kishore R. Chhabria*, (2002) 109 Comp Cas 18 Bom.

97. *Arun Kumar Mallick* v *Hindustan Lever Ltd*, (2002) 112 Comp Cas 464 CLB. *ICICI Venture Funds Management Co Ltd* v *Sofil Information Systems (P) Ltd*, (2007) 136 Comp Cas 84 CLB, questions of law and fact, civil court should itself adjudicate.

98. *Krithika Mullengada* v *Wipro Ltd*, (2004) 121 Comp Cas 676 CLB.

Restriction on extent of shareholding

The articles of a company provided that no member shall hold more than 10% of the company's share capital. It was also provided that a member holding more than 10% would not count for voting in excess of 10%. A member purchased shares in excess of 10%. The rejection of his application for registration was held to be not justified. The provision did not have the effect of a blanket prohibition. The court directed registration of transfer subject to the restriction on voting rights.[1]

Condonation of delay in filing appeals

Section 637-B is a general authorisation to the Central Government to condone delays in making applications to the Central Government. This provision was applicable at a time when appeals under Section 111 were to be filed before the Central Government. But now they have to be filed before the Company Law Board which has been constituted into an independent and autonomous quasi-judicial body. Whether this section would still be applicable is a matter that has to wait for a decision.

It is believed that there is no power vested in the Company Law Board to condone delay. Section 5 of the Limitation Act, 1963 confers power on courts to condone delay in filing applications and appeals if there is a sufficient cause. The Limitation Act is not applicable to the Company Law Board, it being not a court. Where a matter requiring determination of "sufficient cause" was returned by the High Court to the CLB under the remark that the CLB did have the power to condone delay, the CLB looked at the matter again and found that time was lost by the petitioner in his efforts to persuade the directors and he approached for his remedy only after ultimate failure. He had sufficient cause to ask for condonation.[2]

Procedure of transfer [S. 108]

A transfer of shares is completed by registration with the company, or in other words, a transfer is incomplete until registered and the transferor remains legal owner of the shares liable for the unpaid amount, if any.[3] Thus where[4], without any fault or unnecessary delay on the part of the

---

1. *M. Ratnavarma Padival* v *Karnataka Theatres Ltd*, (2002) 109 Comp Cas 461 Kant.
2. *V. K. Gupta* v *Auto Lamps Ltd*, (1999) 96 Comp Cas 555 CLB. *Jinendra Kumar Jain* v *Mangalore Refinery & Petrochemicals Ltd*, (2006) 133 Comp Cas 566 CLB, delay of 10 years, no explanation except that the transferor was ignorant of law, he was aware since 1996 that his shares had been transferred to others by playing a fraud on him, delay not condoned.
3. See *LIC* v *Escorts Ltd*, (1986) 1 SCC 264 at p 327: (1986) 59 Comp Cas 548: [1986] 1 Comp LJ 91 SC. *Martin Castelino* v *Alpha Omega Ship Management (P) Ltd*, (2001) 104 Comp Cas 687, a mere agreement to sell shares does not deprive a member from exercising his rights as a member.
4. *Indian Specie Bank Ltd, Re*, (1915) 17 Bom LR 342.

Shares *[Chap.*

company, duly lodged transfers could not be registered before the commencement of winding up, the transferor could not have his name removed from the list of contributories.[5] But where a transfer was omitted by mistake or oversight, rectification was ordered notwithstanding winding up.[6]

The transferee is the proper person to apply for registration of transfer, but the transferor may also apply.[7] "The transferor is entitled as much as the transferee to enforce registration."[8]

The following conditions must be fulfilled before a company can lawfully register a transfer.[9]

1. The instrument of transfer must be executed both by the transferor and the transferee. The instrument must specify the name, address and occupation, if any, of the transferee. It should also comply with the requirements of the company's articles.[10]

---

5. *See* also *Amraoti Electric Supply Co v R. S. Chandak*, AIR 1954 Nag 293.
6. *Sussex Brick Co, Re*, [1904] 1 Ch 598: [1904-07] All ER Rep 673: 90 LT 426.
7. S. 110(1).
8. Where the application is made by the transferor and relates to partly paid shares, the transfer shall not be registered, unless the company gives notice of the application to the transferee and he makes no objection to the transfer within two weeks from the receipt of the notice. Section 110(2). *See also* sub-section (3).
9. S. 108. Oral transfers are not recognised by the Act. See *Greene v Green*, [1949] Ch 333: [1949] 1 All ER 167. A company cannot lawfully register a transfer unless the requirements of the section are complied with. See *Jayantilal P. Patel v Gordhandas Desai (P) Ltd*, [1967] 1 Comp LJ 272 Bom: (1968) 38 Comp Cas 405 Bom. The same court observed in *Jagdish Mills Ltd, Re*, AIR 1955 Bom 79 "that if a company registers an instrument of transfer which is not duly stamped, it would be doing something which is not lawful". Cf *M.K. Sugar Mills v I.K. Sugar Mills*, (1963) 33 Comp Cas 1142: AIR 1965 All 135. Such registration can be rectified by an order of the Board. *Mahabir Singh v Jai Singh*, (1978) 48 Comp Cas 558 Delhi. Formalities of S. 108 are, however, not necessary where shares have been sold under an order of a court. *Hanuman Mills (P) Ltd, Re*, (1977) 47 Comp Cas 644 and also by Delhi High Court in *CIT v Bharat Nidhi Ltd*, (1982) 52 Comp Cas 80 Del, the court saying that unless the requisite documents are prepared and signed the ownership would not pass because the shares would not be in a deliverable state.
10. For example, the transfer fee prescribed by the articles must be paid to the company itself. Subsequent deposit of the fee in the court will not do. *P. V. Chandran v Malabar and Pioneer Hosiery (P) Ltd*, (1992) 73 Comp Cas 80 Ker; *Mathrubhumi Ltd v Vardhman Publishers Ltd*, (1992) 73 Comp Cas 80 Ker: [1992] 1 Comp LJ 234 Ker DB. Though consideration amount has to be mentioned in the instrument, the company is not concerned with that fact. That is a matter between the transferor and transferee. Though inadequacy of consideration is no defence, where shares and transfer forms were handed over by the husband without the authority or signature of his wife to whom the shares belonged and the consideration amount was also Re 1, the transaction was held to be void. *John Tinson & Co (P) Ltd v Surjeet Malhan*, (1997) 9 SCC 651: (1997) 88 Comp Cas 750: AIR 1997 SC 1411. In *Karnataka Theatres Ltd v Venkatesan*, AIR 1996 Kant 18, the CLB did not approve the rejection of a transfer on the ground that the price paid for the shares was very high. *Mallina Bharathi Rao v Gowthami Solvent Oils Ltd*, (2001) 105 Comp Cas 700 CLB, the articles of the company enabled a director to sign transfer documents as an agent of the expelled shareholder without his consent, the transfer was held to be void. The article was against the mandatory provision of S. 108 which requires that the document must be signed by the transferor or his authorised signatory. *Khushal Jain v Sidharth Tubes Ltd*, (2005) 57 SCL 380 MP, transfer without instrument, the applicant not entitled to declaration of his ownership. *Jacob F. Bothfello v Dr Reddy's Laboratories*, (2006) 133 Comp Cas 561 CLB, refusal by company to register

2. The instrument of transfer should be duly stamped.[11]

3. The instrument should be delivered to the[12] company along with the certificate relating to the shares transferred.[13]

4. The instrument of transfer should be in the prescribed form and, before it is signed by the transferor, and before any entry is made in it, should be presented to the prescribed authority.[14]

The prescribed authority will stamp or otherwise endorse on the instrument the date on which it is so presented. It should then be executed by the transferor and completed in all other respects and should be presented to the company for registration. Presentment to the company should be made, in the case of shares quoted on the recognised stock exchange, before the company closes the register of members in accordance with the provisions of the Act or within twelve months, whichever is later. In other cases, presentment should be made within two months from the date of presentment to the prescribed authority.[15] An instrument of transfer which does not fulfil this requirement shall not be accepted.[16]

because of difference in transferor's signature, the Stock Exchange conducted enquiry and advised the company to accept the transfer if the transferor did not serve a restraint order on the company within a particular time. No such stay order came within the designated time. *Chotoo Sud* v *Bhagwan Finance Corpn (P) Ltd*, (2006) 130 Comp Cas 567 CLB, articles required directors' approval, no proof of any such approval and also no proof of articles' requirement for payment of transfer fee. Transfer ineffective. Register of members rectified.

11. *Claude-Lila Parulekar* v *Sakal Papers (P) Ltd*, (2005) 124 Comp Cas 685 SC, the requirement of stamp is mandatory. *Dove Investment (P) Ltd* v *Gujarat Industrial Investment Corpn Ltd*, (2005) 124 Comp Cas 399 Mad, stamp got endorsed from prescribed authority. Stamps on the transfer form must be defaced or cancelled or else the company can reject it and where a form was resubmitted after cancellation and by that time its validity period had expired, the company was held to have rightfully rejected the same. *A. S. Manvi* v *Kritapur Processing and Ginning Factory Ltd*, [1989] 3 Comp LJ 217, 220 CLB. Where the company changed its articles of association before the rectified instrument was presented again, the alteration would be effective against the transfer. *Mathrubhumi Ltd* v *Vardhman Publishers Ltd*, (1992) 73 Comp Cas 80 Ker; *Muniyamma* v *Aarthi Cine Enterprises (P) Ltd*, (1991) 72 Comp Cas 555 Kant. The Company Law Board did not accept a petition for rectification which was based on transfer form carrying uncancelled stamps. *Bharat Hotels Ltd, Re*, (1994) 81 Comp Cas 897 CLB. Company itself cancelling stamps, registration of the transfer was held to be invalid, *Subhash Chandra* v *Vardhman Spg & General Mills Ltd*, (1995) 83 Comp Cas 641 CLB.

12. These requirements are prescribed by S. 108, a proviso to which provides that where the instrument of transfer has been lost, the company may register the transfer on such terms of indemnity as the board of directors may think fit. S. 108 (1) proviso.

13. If no such certificate is in existence, the letter of allotment should be sent. S. 108(1). See *Amraoti Electric Supply Co* v *R. S. Chandak*, AIR 1954 Nag 293. A company cannot be compelled to register a share purchaser's name unless the certificate for the relevant shares alongwith the instrument of transfer are made available to the company. *Pravin Agarwal* v *Reckitt & Coleman of India Ltd*, (2000) 37 CLA 119 CLB.

14. Who is a person already in the service of the Government. S. 108(1-A) (a).

15. The Central Government has the power to extend time in hard cases. This power has been delegated to Regional Directors. The power is exercisable on the basis of hardship to the applicant and beyond this neither any hearing nor any natural justice are requisite. *Vishnu Dayal Jhunjhunwala* v *UOI*, (1989) 66 Comp Cas 684, 693 All.

16. *See* Sections 108(1-A) and (1-B) as substituted by the Amendment Act of 1966. *See also* sub-sections (1-C) and (1-D) which contain exceptions. Where shares are vested in the State by

The transfer should be approved at a valid meeting of the company's Board of directors.[17]

Blank Transfers

This last mentioned requirement is intended to do away with the evil of blank transfers. A blank transfer form means a form which has been signed by the transferor only and there is no other entry on it. It is given over to the transferee with the right to have himself or any other person registered as a shareholder. Before the provision was enacted, a blank form could remain in circulation for any length of time creating many problems mostly that of evasion of taxes and priority between transferees. But now it can remain in circulation only for twelve months after it is signed by the authority or upto the time when the company closes its register of members.[18]

But, apart from this restriction, a blank transfer form is a valid instrument. The basic principles were restated by the Gujarat High Court in *Pranlal Jayanand Thakar* v *V. R. Shelat*[19]. Firstly, an instrument of transfer which carries no entry except the signature of the transferor is a valid instrument. Secondly, a person to whom such an instrument is delivered along with share scrips gets an implied authority to complete the instrument. Thirdly, the transferee acquires good title to the shares if he has received the documents in good faith and for consideration.[20]

---

operation of law, neither these formalities, nor rectification of the register are necessary. *Doypack Systems (P) Ltd* v *UOI*, (1988) 2 SCC 299, decided under Swadeshi Cotton Mills Co (Acquisition and Transfer of Undertakings) Act, 1986. An instrument of transfer which has been rejected by the company by reason of the efflux of time cannot be presented again under any such thing as a symbolic revalidation by the Registrar of Companies. *Mathew Michael* v *Teekoy Rubber and Tea Co*, (1994) 79 Comp Cas 370: [1993] 3 Comp LJ 449 CLB. *Chandravadan Parikh* v *Krishna Mingranite Ltd*, (2003) 115 Comp Cas 423 CLB, the transferor had signed the papers before his death as a security for a loan, the company was compelled to register the transfer.

17. *Claude-Lila Parulekar* v *Sakal Papers (P) Ltd*, (2005) 124 Comp Cas 685, the meeting was invalid because of deficient notice.
18. As amended in 1988 and enforced with effect from 15-6-1988, GSR 559(E) of 10-6-1988.
19. (1973) 43 Comp Cas 203 Guj.
20. The following cases establish these principles: *Official Assignee, Bombay* v *Madholal Sindhu*, (1946) 48 Bom LR 828: AIR 1947 Bom 217; *Maneckji Pestonji Bharucha* v *Wadilal Sarabhai & Co*, (1926) 28 Bom 771: AIR 1926 PC 38: 53 IA 92; *Arjun Prasad* v *Central Bank of India*, AIR 1956 Pat 32, the transferee got himself registered and that was held to be valid. A blank transfer does not operate in anybody's favour unless the formalities of transfer have been complied with. *Travancore Electro-Chemical Industries Ltd* v *Alogappa Textiles*, (1972) 42 Comp Cas 569 Ker. A blank transfer which is delivered as a pledge and not as transfer does not have this effect. Violation of marketing regulations such as the Securities Contracts (Regulation) Act, 1956 renders the transfer to be ineffective. The transferor remains the owner for purposes of attachment. The above Act applies to shares of non-listed companies as well if they are marketable. *A. K. Menon* v *Fairgrowth Financial Services Ltd*, (1994) 81 Comp Cas 508 (Special Court); *BOI Finance Ltd* v *Custodian*, (1994) 81 Comp Cas 508 (Special Court). The word "law" as used in that Act means the law in force in India and not merely the Companies Act. A transfer form not complying with stamp law is not valid. *Kothari Industrial Corpn Ltd* v *Lazor Detergents (P) Ltd*, [1994] 1 Comp LJ 669 Mad. Where there was no such violation of laws, a pledge of shares-cum-contract to sell, was held

The facts of the case were that the transferee had received the shares under a gift deed from a lady who signed blank transfer forms which, however, could not be registered before her death.

The other heirs having claimed the shares, the court held that the transferee had not acquired a good title to shares as he had received them without consideration. The gift was not complete without registration. But on appeal to the Supreme Court this decision was reversed.[21] In the view of the Supreme Court a complete gift had taken place on delivery of the share scrips and transfer deeds. Registration with the company was a formality which had nothing to do with the completeness of the gift as between the parties.[22]

Transfer contravening Section 108

When requirements of Section 108 are complied with, the company registers the transfer. The name of the transferor is struck off the register of members and that of the transferee substituted. It has been held by the Calcutta High Court that the requirements of Section 108 are directory and not mandatory.[23] The court followed a decision of the Allahabad High Court[24] where it was pointed out that Section 108 does not impose any penalty for, nor indicates any consequences of, its non-observance. It is also not exhaustive of all the modes of transfer. It covers only two. It has no application to other modes of transfer. Hence a company can register a transfer without the original scrips being produced. All that it can require to protect itself is an indemnity against untoward consequences. The court accordingly ordered the company to register a transfer when the transferee was not able to produce the original scrips. But the decision of the Allahabad High Court which the Calcutta High Court purported to follow had been reversed by the Supreme Court in *Mannalal Khetan* v *Kedar Nath Khetan*.[25] RAY CJ laid emphasis upon the words "shall not register" as used in Section 108, which leave no doubt that the provision is mandatory. "The mandatory character is strengthened by the negative form of the language. The prohibition against transfer without complying with the provisions of the Act is emphasised by the negative language. Negative language is worded to emphasise the insistence on compliance with the provisions of the Act." The facts were that on the partition of a family shares were agreed to be transferred in blocks between members and the company registered the transfers on the basis of the partition deed itself

---

to pass property upon delivery of certificate and blank transfer form, *Jagdishchandra Champaklal Parekh* v *Deccan Papers Mills Co Ltd*, (1994) 80 Comp Cas 159 CLB.

21. *Vasudev Ramachandra Shelat* v *Pranlal Jayanand Thakur*, (1974) 2 SCC 323: AIR 1974 SC 1728: (1975) 1 SCR 534: (1975) 45 Comp Cas 43.
22. Reemphasised by the Supreme Court in *LIC* v *Escorts Ltd*, (1986) 1 SCC 264 at pp 323-324.
23. *Jatia Cotton Mills Ltd* v *Ram Prasad Bajoria*, (1975) 45 Comp Cas 686 Cal.
24. *Maheshwari Khetan Sugar Mills* v *Ishwari Khetan Sugar Mills*, (1963) 33 Comp Cas 1142.
25. (1977) 2 SCC 424: (1977) 47 Comp Cas 185.

without any transfer form having been executed. The Supreme Court accordingly held that this transfer should not have been registered.[26]

Where the trustees of the shares passed a resolution authorising one of them to transfer the shares, it was held that the transfer under such authority was not valid. The trustees could not delegate the power to one of them. The transferee could not apply for rectification of the register of members.[27]

Once the necessary formalities have been complied with, the transferee gets the right to be put on the register. Emphasising this fact in *LIC* v *Escorts Ltd*,[28] CHINNAPPA REDDY J of the Supreme Court observed:

> Where the transfer is regulated by a statute, as in the case of a transfer to a non-resident which is regulated by the Foreign Exchange Regulation Act, the permission prescribed by the statute must be obtained. In the absence of the permission, the transfer will not clothe the transferee with the right 'to get on the register'. Where the permission has been obtained, the transferee may ask the company to register the transfer and the company may not refuse except for a bona fide reason, [but] neither arbitrarily nor for any collateral purpose. The paramount consideration is the interest of the company and the general interest of [its] shareholders. Once the permission is obtained it is not open to the company.... to take upon itself.... the task of deciding whether the permission was rightly granted.[29]

Demat transfers

The provisions of this section as to procedure and formalities of transfer are not to apply where both the transferor and transferee are entered as beneficial owners in the records of a depository.[30]

---

26. See further *Shanta Genevieve Pommeret* v *Sakal Papers (P) Ltd*, (1990) 69 Comp Cas 65 Bom, of the four transferors, the signature of one on the transfer from was not there and the form was held to be ineffective as a transfer. *Kothari Industrial Corpn* v *Lazor Detergents (P) Ltd*, [1994] 1 Comp LJ 178 CLB Mad, in the case of a transfer which has already been registered, deficiency in stamps, if any, must be pointed out within one year because otherwise the transferee would be deprived of his opportunity of getting things rectified.
27. *Claude-Lila Parulekar* v *Sakal Papers (P) Ltd*, (2005) 124 Comp Cas 685 SC.
28. (1986) 1 SCC 264 at p 327: (1986) 59 Comp Cas 548: [1986] 1 Comp LJ 91 SC.
29. Citing *Fry, Re*, [1946] 2 All ER 106, the permission of the Treasury was requisite and that being not obtained the company was not compelled to register the transfer. A transfer not approved at a meeting of the Board is not effective and is liable to be struck down. *Tarlok Chand Khanna* v *Raj Kumar Kapoor*, (1983) 54 Comp Cas 12 Del. As between transferor and transferee, transfer becomes complete when the contract is documented and tax authorities are bound to recognise it whether it has been accepted by the company or not. *CIT* v *M. Ramaswamy*, (1985) 57 Comp Cas 7 Mad. Transfer of the right to receive dividends on shares is not the same thing as transfer of the shares themselves. Shares are not ordinary goods. They are a part of a complex web of relations. The principles relating to ordinary goods cannot apply to them in toto *Khadija* v *P. K. Mohd (P) Ltd*, (1985) 58 Comp Cas 543. The right to have the transfer registered arises when it is complete in all respects. *K. N. Narayanan* v *ITO*, (1984) 55 Comp Cas 182 Ker. Where the company did not accept a lodged transfer and continued to deal with the transferor, it was injuncted from preventing the transferor from exercising the normal rights of a shareholder, *Chougle Matrix Hebs Ltd* v *Chowgule & Co Hind (P) Ltd*, [2000] CLC 1830 AP.
30. Consequential amendment made by the Depositories Act, 1996.

Unfair Trade Practices in Securities Market

For prevention of unfair trade practices in the securities market, the Securities and Exchange Board of India (SEBI) has prescribed SEBI (Prohibition of Fraudulent and Unfair Trade Practices relating to the Securities Market) Regulations, 1995. The rules provide for an investigation in respect of the conduct and affairs of any person buying, selling or otherwise dealing in any securities. Persons connected with the securities market would include primary sellers or buyers. Such persons can be proceeded against even if the transaction in question has been carried through a broker or agent. Securities market is not confined to stock exchanges only. SEBI has the power to call for information and documents relevant to an inquiry even from persons against whom an inquiry cannot be or has not been constituted.[31]

Certification of transfer [S. 112]

Ordinarily, the transferor hands over the certificate of shares to the transferee who then lodges it with the company for registration. But where the shares transferred are less than the number of shares included in one certificate, or where they are transferred to different persons, the transferor has to lodge the share certificate with the company. The company then gives him a certificate saying that the shares under transfer have been lodged with the company. This is called "certification of transfer". In effect it is a representation to any person acting on the faith of the certification that the company has received such documents as go to show a *prima facie* title of the transferor, but not that the transferor has any title to the shares. [S. 112(1)] Thus in *Bishop* v *Balkis Consolidated Co*:[32]

> *B* transferred his shares to two persons and lodged the certificate with the company. The company certificated the transfer, but, instead of destroying the original certificate, returned it to the transferor who borrowed money on it.

The company was held not liable to the lender. Even if he had deceived a person to accept the transfer of those shares the company would not have been liable to the transferee. "The reason is that the share certificate is neither a negotiable instrument nor a warranty of title on the part of the company issuing it...."[33]

---

31. *Karnavati Fincap Ltd* v *SEBI*, (1996) 87 Comp Cas 186 Guj. *Chairman, SEBI* v *Shriram Mutual Fund*, (2006) 131 Comp Cas 591 (SC), penalty imposed for excess of transaction through brokers. There is no discretion with the authority about the levy of penalty the same being mandatory, discretion is only about quantum of penalty.
32. (1890) 25 QBD 512 CA.
33. Charlesworth, COMPANY LAW, p 151, 8th Edn, 1965 by T.E. Cain: [p 260, 11th Edn, 1977].

But if a company issues a false certification negligently or deliberately, it would be liable to any person who is deceived by having acted on the faith of the certification. [S. 112(2)] A certification is deemed to be made by the company when it is signed by a person authorised to do so. [S. 112(3)]

Forgery in transfer

Sometimes a forged instrument of transfer may be presented for registration. "The first thing that a company should, therefore, do when a transfer is tendered, is to inquire into its validity."[34] "It has, therefore, become usual, when a transfer is brought, not to register it at once, but, as one precaution, to write to the registered address of the shareholder, and inform him that such a transfer has been lodged, and that if no objection is made before a day specified, it would be registered."[35] But, notwithstanding this precaution, a forged transfer may chance to slip through[36] and the consequences will be:

Firstly, a forged transfer is a nullity and, therefore, the original owner of the shares continues to be the shareholder and the company is bound to restore his name to the register of members.[37]

Secondly, if the company has issued a share certificate to the transferee and he has sold the shares to an innocent purchaser, the company is liable to compensate such a purchaser if it refuses to register him as a shareholder.[38]

Thirdly, if the company has been put to loss by reason of the forged transfer, it may recover indemnity from the person who lodged it.[39]

Relationship between transferor and transferee

A shareholder who has contracted to sell his shares becomes a constructive trustee of the transferee for those shares until the transfer is duly registered. It is, therefore, the duty of the transferor not to sell the shares again; "nor should he prevent or do anything to prevent the company from accepting the purchaser or his nominee".[40] But he is not bound to do

---

34. BLACKBURN J *Bahia & San Francisco Rly Co, Re,* (1868) LR 3 QB 584: 18 LT 467.
35. BLACKBURN J in *Societe Generale de Paris* v *Janet Walker,* (1885) 11 AC 20, 35: 54 LT 389.
36. This was the course pursued in *Swan* v *North Br Australasian Co Ltd,* 7 CBNS 411, but the company's letter was intercepted by the forger. The result of the consequent litigation showed that even after all those precautions the company did suffer from registering the transfer, being obliged in the end to restore shares to *Swan.*
37. *Barton* v *N. Staffordshire Rly,* (1888) 38 Ch D 458: 58 LT 549; *Barton* v *LNW Rly,* (1889) 24 QBD 77: 62 LT 164; *People's Insurance Co* v *Wood & Co,* AIR 1960 Punj 388 at p 390.
38. See *Balkis Consolidated Co Ltd* v *Fredrick Tomkinson,* 1893 AC 396: 69 LT 598; *Dixon* v *Kennaway & Co,* [1900] 1 Ch 833: 82 LT 527.
39. *Sheffield Corpn* v *Barclay,* [1905] AC 392: 93 LT 83. Where the share certificate was sent to a wrong person of the same name and he transferred the shares to a bank, he faced prosecution for impersonation under S. 116, *BPL Sanyo Technologies Ltd* v *Rahul Agarwal,* (1995) 83 Comp Cas 885 Raj.
40. *London Founders Assn* v *Clarke,* (1888) 20 QBD 576: 59 LT 93. Where transfer documents are valid and the same have been registered by the company, their validity cannot be brought

more. And so a transferor who sold his shares on a stock exchange was held not liable when the company, having the power to do so, refused to register the transferee as a member.[41] In such a case the legal title to the shares remains in the vendor, but the beneficial interest is transferred to the purchaser. "The vendor is the trustee of all property annexed to the shares. He is a trustee not only of the *corpus* but also of the income."[42] The transferee is entitled to recover dividend amount or bonus shares that might have been received by the transferor.[43] He must pay the dividends, if any, to the purchaser.[44] The purchaser also has the right to control the exercise by the vendor of the right to vote and he may so control it as to ask the vendor to vote for the alteration of the company's articles so as to procure transfer of shares in his name.[45]

But then how far is the transferor bound to obey the wishes of the transferee? The limits have been explained by the Supreme Court in *R Mathalone* v *Bombay Life Assurance Co.*[46]

A shareholder disposed of a part of his holding, but the company refused to register the transferee as a shareholder. Meanwhile the company increased capital by issuing further shares to the existing shareholders. A number of shares were offered to the transferor, but he applied to take only those few which appertained to his unsold shares. The transferee sought to compel him to apply in his name for the whole of the shares and that for the benefit of the transferee.

But the argument did not find favour with MAHAJAN J of the Supreme Court. He laid down "that as long as a transfer is not registered the

---

into question on account of any dispute between transferor and transferee, such as failure to pay purchase price in full. *K. Kamaraj* v *Mackimalai Tea Estates (P) Ltd*, (1995) 16 Corpt LA 270; *Muniyamma* v *Arathi Cine Enterprises (P) Ltd*, (1991) 72 Comp Cas 555 Kant. Where a person was present as a director in the board meeting which approved a transfer he was not allowed afterwards to question its validity. *Mukundlal Manchanda* v *Prakash Roadlines Ltd*, (1991) 72 Comp Cas 575 Kant. This decision was affirmed in *Suresh Kumar Manchanda* v *Prakash Roadlines Ltd*, (1996) 87 Comp Cas 102 Kant; *Milan Sen* v *Guardian Plasticote Ltd*, (1998) 91 Comp Cas 105 Cal.

41. *Ibid.* But where the transferor obstructs the transfer, he will have to indemnify a person who has suffered by reason of the obstruction. *Hichens, Harrison, Woolston & Co* v *Jackson & Sons*, [1943] AC 266.

42. *E. D. Sasoon & Co Ltd* v *K. A. Patch*, (1943) 45 Bom LR 46; *Wimbush, Re*, [1940] Ch 92: [1940] 1 All ER 229: 162 LT 133.

43. *Vikas Jalan* v *Hyderabad Industries Ltd*, (1997) 88 Comp Cas 551 CLB, transferee's right to dividend.

44. Expressly recognised by the Supreme Court in *CIT* v *India Discount Ltd*, (1969) 2 SCC 514: 75 ITR 191. The beneficial interest of the transferee cannot be attached for claims against the transferor. See *D. J. Lal* v *S. Ganguli*, (1990) 68 Comp Cas 576 Del, where the court permitted review of an order of attachment passed in ignorance of the fact that shares standing in the name of the transferor in the company's records in fact stood transferred to another.

45. *Ibid. See also* the decision of the Supreme Court in *R. Mathalone* v *Bombay Life Assurance Co*, AIR 1953 SC 385: 24 Comp Cas 1; *Hardoon* v *Belilios*, 1901 AC 118: 83 LT 573.

46. AIR 1953 SC 385: 24 Comp Cas 1.

transferor is the trustee of the transferee for the shares — a trustee for the dividends and the right to vote. But he cannot be called upon to incur additional liability. He is not bound to obtain for the benefit of the transferee new shares in the further issue of capital. Nor is the principle of equitable trust extended to cases where the transferee has not taken active steps to get his name registered with due diligence.'' But his Lordship added that if the transferor of his own volition chose to obtain the new shares which appertain to the shares sold by him, he would have to hand over those shares to the transferee on payment of the amount spent.[47]

If the shares are partly paid and the company calls upon the transferor to pay the unpaid balance, the transferee must provide the money or indemnify the transferor against the amount of the call.[48]

A person who gets shares under a gift deed with blank transfer forms and is not able to get them registered until the transferor's death, acquires a good title to them, as against the legal heirs.[49] This was not applied in a situation in which blank transfer forms were handed over not by the owner herself or under her signature but by her husband without her authority.[50]

Bonus shares issued after the transfer were held to be the property of the transferee and not that of the transferor.[51] Where the transfer documents were lost in post and the transfer became delayed because the company did not receive the original documents and in the meantime bonus shares were issued, the transferee was not allowed to sue the company in respect of those shares. His remedy was to proceed against the transferor to whom they were allotted because his name was still there in the register.[52]

Compensation for Misrepresentation as to Value

Any misrepresentation by the transferor as to the value of the shares will make the transferor liable to make good the transferee's loss, if any. Where the transferor told the transferee that according to his forecast the company's earnings would touch a particular figure which turned out to be wrong, the transferor was held liable to pay damages ascertained on the

---

47. Reemphasised by the Supreme Court in *LIC* v *Escorts Ltd*, (1986) 1 SCC 264 at p 323: (1986) 59 Comp Cas 548: [1986] 1 Comp LJ 91 SC. Followed in *Pradip Kumar Sarkar* v *Luxmi Tea Co Ltd*, (1990) 67 Comp Cas 491, 509 Cal. Where the transfer in question was registered by the company and the transferee received the dividend amount and subsequently the transfer was held to be invalid with the result that the shares reverted to the transferor, the transferee was held to be not bound to pay back the dividend amount received by him. *Mathew Michael* v *Teekoy Rubber & Tea Co*, (1994) 79 Comp Cas 370: [1993] 3 Comp LJ 449 CLB.
48. *Spencer* v *Ashworth, Partington & Co*, [1925] 1 KB 589: [1925] All ER Rep 324 CA.
49. *Vasudev Ramachandra Shelat* v *Pranlal Jayanand Thakur*, (1974) 2 SCC 323: AIR 1974 SC 1728: (1975) 1 SCR 534: (1975) 45 Comp Cas 43.
50. *John Tinson & Co (P) Ltd* v *Surjeet Malhan*, (1997) 9 SCC 651: AIR 1997 SC 1411: (1997) 88 Comp Cas 750.
51. *Vikas Jalan* v *Hyderabad Industries Ltd*, (1997) 88 Comp Cas 551 CLB.
52. *Pyariben M. Shah* v *NIIT Ltd*, (2002) 111 Comp Cas 816 CLB.

basis of the difference between the warranted earnings and actual earnings.[53] A founder member signed a blank transfer form to enable the company to increase the membership base of the company by transferring some of his founder member's shares. The company used the shares for other purposes. The aggrieved member was allowed to recover compensation measured by the value of his shares.[54] Where a director is buying from a member there is a fiduciary duty to disclose the truth about the value of the shares. If this duty is not performed the seller member would be entitled to compensation for his loss. The measure of compensation would be the value of his shares at the time of sale. A valuation based on estimated future income stream would be preferable to the one based on the value of net realisable assets. But because of uncertainties in the income position, the assets value was held to be preferable in this case.[55] A clause in a sale agreement excluding liability for breach of warranty about the value of shares would be given narrowest possible meaning against the seller.[56]

Depository scheme

The procedural requirements, as noted above, show that the country's stock markets are functioning under a cumbersome process for effecting transfers of securities. A scheme for establishing depositories has been established to record ownership details in book entry forms.[57] Investors in securities will have the option to continue with the existing system of ownership and transfer through share certificates or to come under the depository mode. Each depository would have to register itself with SEBI and to obtain from it a certificate for commencement of business. Each depository will have its agents to be known as participants. Such agency can be conferred on banks, financial institutions, or large corporate brokerage firms. A shareholder who joins a participant, his shares will be dematerialised. His name will be entered in a book showing him as a beneficial owner. In the company's records the depository will be shown as the registered member. But all the benefits of shareholding will remain vested in the individual shareholders. A shareholder will have the right to withdraw from the scheme after joining it. His share certificate will be restored to him and his name brought back to the register of members.

Transfers are recorded automatically on delivery versus payment basis with constant flow of information to the company's depository.

---

53. *Lion Nathan Ltd* v *CC Bottlers Ltd*, (1996) 2 BCLC 371 PC.
54. *Lloyd* v *Poply*, [2000] 1 BCLC 19 Ch D.
55. *Platt* v *Platt*, [1999] 2 BCLC 745 Ch D.
56. *Dixon Group plc* v *Murray Obodynski*, [2000] 1 BCLC 1 CA.
57. Hindustan Times, Sept 22, 1995, p 19, by means of a Presidential Ordinance.

Other things will remain the same. The duty of the company to accept a transfer and the right of the transferor or transferee to appeal to the Company Law Board against refusal by the company will remain the same.

It is predicted that scores of foreign institutional investors (FIIs) will pump in billions of dollars into Indian Stock Exchanges. Market operations will be very convenient with the elimination of the physical movement of share certificates, etc., and minimisation of forged and other bad deliveries of transfer documents. The system will involve consequential changes in the Companies Act, Stamp Act and the Income Tax Act. The costs of transfer will be minimised because of the elimination of burdensome paper work. [Depositories Act, 1996]

Priority between transferees

Where a shareholder has fraudulently sold his shares to two different transferees, the first purchaser will, on the ground of time alone, be entitled to the shares in priority to the second.[58] A person assigned his property, including some shares, for the benefit of his creditors. The assignee failed to get the share certificate, but gave notice of assignment to the company. The assignor sold the shares to another, who applied for registration. It was held that the assignee's claim was prior in time and, therefore, entitled to registration.[59] Similarly, where a person, holding shares in trust for his wife, mortgaged them, but, before the mortgage could be registered, the wife asserted her claim and was held to have priority.[60] But the second claimant in point of time may displace the original priority of the first purchaser by showing that as against him he has acquired the full status of a shareholder; or, at any rate, that all the formalities have been complied with and that nothing more than some purely ministerial act remains to be done by the company.[61] But the subsequent transferee who gets his name registered with notice of the prior transfer is not entitled to priority.[62]

Specific enforcement of agreement to sell shares

An agreement for dealing in shares is specifically enforceable. A company, having contracted to buy a controlling block of shares, applied for specific enforcement and it was held to be no defence for the other party to say that the company had not yet complied with the requirements of Section 372 to enable it to invest in shares of other companies.[63]

---

58. *Societe Generale de Paris* v *Janet Walker*, (1885) 11 AC 20: 54 LT 389.
59. *Peat* v *Clayton*, [1906] 1 Ch 659: 94 LT 465.
60. *Ireland* v *Hart*, [1902] 1 Ch 522: 86 LT 385.
61. *Moore* v *North Western Bank*, [1891] 2 Ch 599: 64 LT 456.
62. *Coleman* v *London County & Westminster Bank*, [1916] 2 Ch 353.
63. *Brooke Bond India Ltd* v *UB Ltd*, (1994) 79 Comp Cas 346 Bom. Where the purchaser is a joint family, the contract would be enforceable by asking for registration in the name of

Mortgage or pledge of shares

A share in a company is moveable property. It can, therefore, be delivered as a security for raising a loan. Where a share certificate is delivered to the pledgee it will operate as a pledge. The pledgee can only retain possession till his dues are paid.[64] Where not merely possession of share certificates is delivered, but some right or interest is created in favour of the lender, such as, for example, handing over blank transfer forms under the signature of the transferor, it operates as a mortgage. The mortgagee gets a special interest, for he can have himself registered as a shareholder and the same will be effective against the transferor and his representatives. Where the pledging shareholder executed an agreement in favour of the bank authorising it to exercise voting rights and the company was also a party to it, the court said that the bank became entitled to exercise voting rights at a meeting on filing the transfer documents. The entry in the register of members was a mere formality. The validity of the pledge, etc., could not be adjudicated by the chairman under the in-house procedure.[65] Where the lender gets himself registered as a shareholder, it would be a clear cut complete transfer. No residuary interest in the pledged shares would survive in favour of the borrower. His interest is protected by his right of redemption, i.e. his right to recover back the shares on paying back the lender.[66] In a case of this kind before the Patna High Court:[67]

Certain share certificates were delivered to a bank as against a loan. The blank transfer forms in respect of those shares were signed by all the persons whose signatures were necessary and were delivered to the bank. The company subsequently went into winding up and the bank had the scrips registered in its name, which was done by the liquidator with the permission of the court.

It was held that the registration in favour of the bank was valid. DAS J stated the effect of authorities in these words:[68]

Thus where under the articles of the company a transfer of shares may be made by an instrument in writing, the shareholder may sign a

---

the *karta* of the family. *Vickers Systems International Ltd* v *Mahesh P. Keshwani*, (1992) 73 Comp Cas 317 CLB. There is also the decision of the Company Law Board that a company can lawfully refuse to register a transfer of shares which is, in reference to the buying company, void by reason of violation of S. 372. *Gordon Woodroffe Ltd* v *Trident Investment*, (1994) 79 Comp Cas 764 CLB: [1994] 1 Comp LJ 313. An agreement to sell hares was specifically enforced even when there was some delay in delivery caused by the fact that the seller received the share certificate from the company with some delay. *Grant* v *Cigman*, (1996) 2 BCLC 24 Ch D.

64. See *Kunhunni Elaya Nayyar* v *Krishna Pattar*, AIR 1943 Mad 74, where LEACH CJ recognised the validity of a pledge of shares by mere delivery of possession and without the need for any instrument of transfer. The only difference would be that for enforcing the security he would have to resort to a court of law.

65. *Sarvopari Investments (P) Ltd* v *Soma Textiles & Industries Ltd*, (2005) CLC 1302 (Cal).

66. *M. Ratnavarma Padival* v *Karnataka Theatres Ltd*, [2000] CLC 489: 38 CLA 171 Kant.

67. *Arjun Prasad* v *Central Bank of India*, AIR 1956 Pat 32.

68. *Id.*, at p 35.

blank transfer and hand it over to a purchaser or mortgagee with authority to the holder of it for the time being to fill in the name of the transferee, and such a transfer when filled in can be sent in for registration and no objection can be raised by the company to its validity.[69]

Where the original transferee of blank forms further delivers them in blank to another person, the latter will get the rights of the transferor but no better rights. The transfer being in blank, he cannot say that he had received it in good faith.

A simple delivery of share certificates unaccompanied by any transfer forms operates only as a simple mortgage, what is called in English law as an equitable mortgage.

NATURE OF SHARE

A man's movable property is of two kinds, namely, chose-in-possession and chose-in-action. Chose-in-possession means property of which one has actual physical possession, but chose-in-action means property of which one does not have immediate possession, but has a right to it, which can be enforced by a legal action. This right is generally evidenced by a document, for example, a railway receipt. A share in a company is also a chose-in-action and a share certificate is the evidence of it.[70] Section 2(46) defines "shares" as share in the share capital of the company, and includes "stock" except where a distinction between stocks and shares is express or implied.[71] But in India a share is also regarded as "goods".[72] Section 82

---

69. Banks have been directed by the Reserve Bank of India to have the shares pledged to them registered in their names. A pledge under a short term loan was held not to confer that right and, therefore, refusal by the company to register the shares in the name of a bank was held to be justified. *Canara Bank v Ankit Granites Ltd*, (1999) 97 Comp Cas 511 CLB. The bank has the right to get itself registered where the pledge is under a long term cash credit arrangement. The fact that no consideration was mentioned in the transfer form was immaterial because this requirement is for stamp duty and the nationalised banks are exempt from stamp duty. *Indian Bank v Kiran Overseas Exports Ltd*, [2000] 4 Comp LJ 416 CLB. Where a "deed" is requisite for a transfer, mere form will not do beyond serving as an evidence of the parties' intention. *Colonial Bank v Frederick Whinney*, (1886) 11 AC 426. Other cases considered by the court where blank transfers were recognised as conferring right upon the transferee: *Tahiti Cotton Co, Re*, (1874) 17 Eq 273; *Colonial Bank v Cady*, (1890) 15 AC 267; *Fox v Martin*, (1895) 64 LJ Ch 473; *Colonial Bank Ltd v Hepworth*, (1887) 36 Ch D 36; *Harrold v Plenty*, (1901) 2 Ch 314; *Carter v Wake*, (1877) 4 Ch D 605; *London and Midland Bank v Mitchell*, (1899) 2 Ch 161.
70. *VGM Holdings, Re*, [1942] Ch 235, 241. Adopted by the Supreme Court in *Sri Gopal Jalan & Co v Calcutta Stock Exchange Assn*, AIR 1964 SC 250, 252: 33 Comp Cas 862; *Viswanathan v East India Distilleries & Sugar Factories*, AIR 1957 Mad 341: (1957) 27 Comp Cas 175.
71. *LIC v Escorts Ltd*, (1986) 1 SCC 264 at p 320: (1986) 59 Comp Cas 548: [1986] 1 Comp LJ 91 SC, where the nature of a share and the position of shareholder is explained.
72. *Maneckji Pestonji Bharucha v Wadilal Sarabhai & Co*, (1926) 53 IA 92; *Elaya Nayar v Krishna Pattar*, (1942) 2 MLJ 120: AIR 1943 Mad 74; *Arjun Prasad v Central Bank of India*, AIR 1956 Pat 32, in all these cases shares were considered as goods. *Indian Iron & Steel Co v Dalhousie Holdings Ltd*, AIR 1957 Cal 293. It has been held that shares do not mature into goods before issue. Hence an applicant for shares is not a consumer so as to create jurisdiction in a consumer forum to interfere in the matter on the ground of an alleged unfair

of the Companies Act, 1956, provides that shares or other interest of any member in a company shall be movable property. An amendment of Section 82 introduced by the Companies (Amendment) Act, 1999 says that while before this amendment Section 82 confined itself to the "shares or other interest of any member", the statement should now be read as "shares, debentures or any other interest of any member." Section 2 of the Sale of Goods Act defines goods as including every kind of moveable property. Hence shares in a company in India are goods and not mere chose-in-action.[73] The analysis of the "share" in terms of goods has been carried further to some of its natural implications by the Supreme Court in *LIC* v *Escorts Ltd.*[74] If shares are goods, rules relating to passing of ownership in goods would apply. Section 19 of the Sale of Goods Act says that property in the goods sold passes when it is intended to pass. "Shares" are specific goods and Section 20 of the Act says that ownership in specific goods passes when the contract is made. Thus a purchaser of shares becomes the owner of the property in the shares when he contracts to buy them. The inevitable implication of these provisions is that the company cannot deprive him of his ownership by refusing to register him as a shareholder unless there is a genuine reason to do so. But even so shares are not "goods" in the ordinary sense of the word.[75]

Shares are a peculiar kind of movable property which cannot pass from hand to hand like bales of cotton. The property in these shares belonged to the registered shareholders and could not be transferred to another except according to the articles of the company.[76]

Thus the exact nature of a share does not admit of easy explanation, the company being an altogether distinct person from the members composing it. It is universal, though not obligatory, for an incorporated company to have a capital stock. It is equally universal to divide the capital into shares of nominal value. A person who holds such a share is known as the shareholder. Each shareholder, therefore, holds a portion of the capital of the company. "A share means a share in the capital of the company. It is a tangible property."[77] "But shareholders are not, in the eyes of law, part owners of the undertaking. The undertaking is something

trade practice, *Morgan Stanley Mutual Fund* v *Kartick Das*, (1994) 4 SCC 225: (1994) 81 Comp Cas 318 SC.

73. It was held in *Hazarimull Sohanlal* v *Satish Chandra Ghose*, ILR 46 Cal 331, that a share certificate passing from hand to hand with blank transfer deeds does not thereby become a negotiable instrument. Accordingly, a bona fide purchaser of shares from a person, who is in possession of them by fraud, does not acquire a good title to them.
74. (1986) 1 SCC 264 at p 321: (1986) 59 Comp Cas 548: [1986] 1 Comp LJ 91 SC. In an earlier decision of the Delhi High Court, *CIT* v *Bharat Nidhi Ltd*, (1982) 32 Comp Cas 80 it was recognised that unless the requisite documents were prepared and signed, the shares would be unascertained goods and not in a deliverable state.
75. *France* v *Clark*, (1884) 26 Ch D 257.
76. *Vadilal Sarabhai* v *Manekji Pestonji Bharucha*, AIR 1923 Bom 423.
77. *SNDP Yogam, Re*, ILR 1969 Ker 516: [1970] 1 Comp LJ 85.

different from the totality of the shareholdings.''[78] All the assets of the company are vested in the corporate body and not in the individuals composing it. Hence a share does not constitute the holder a part owner of the company's capital.

But shareholders are the owners of certain rights and interests and subject to some liabilities. A shareholder acquires an interest not in a mere chattel, but in the company itself, an interest of a permanent nature. ''A share is the interest of a shareholder in the company measured by a sum of money for the purpose of liability and dividends, in the first place, and of interest, in the second, and also consisting of a series of contract as contained in the articles of association.''[79] ''A share is not a sum of money but an interest measured by a sum of money and made up of various rights and liabilities. A share is an existing bundle of rights.''[80] ''It is well established that shares are simply bundles of intangible rights against the company which had issued them. Share certificates are not valuable property in themselves—they are just evidence of the true property, which are the proportionate interests of the shareholders in the ownership of the company. One *pari passu* share is exactly the same as any other. This was recognised in *Solloway* v *McLaughlin*.[81] Therefore, each share certificate with the depository evidences the same bundle of rights and each bundle of rights can satisfy the client's proprietary interest as any other.''[82] A share, for example, entitles the holder to receive a proportionate part of the profits of the company; to take part in the management of the company's business in accordance with the articles, to receive a proportion of the assets in the event of winding up and all other benefits of membership.[83] A share also carries some liabilities, for example, the liability to pay the full value in winding up. All these rights and liabilities are subject to the terms and conditions contained in the company's article. Rights and liabilities as regulated by articles are of the very essence of a share. ''When, therefore, the owner of the share dies, what passes upon his death and what has to be

---

78. *Short* v *Treasury Commissioners*, [1948] 1 KB 116 at p 122: [1947] 1 All ER 22.
79. *Borland's Trustee* v *Steel Bros & Co Ltd*, [1901] 1 Ch 279, 288. Adopted by the Supreme Court in *Charanjit Lal* v *UOI*, AIR 1951 SC 41 at p 55: (1951) 21 Comp Cas 33.
80. *Pauline, Re*, [1935] 1 KB 26 cited with approval by the Supreme Court in *CIT* v *Standard Vacuum Oil Co*, [1966] 1 Comp LJ 187 at p 192: AIR 1966 SC 1393.
81. [1937] 4 All ER 328: [1938] AC 247.
82. *Pacific Finance Ltd, Re*, [2000] 1 BCLC 494.
83. *See* comment on ''share'' in A DICTIONARY OF ENGLISH LAW. Some of the rights of shareholders have been listed in the judgment of the Supreme Court in *LIC* v *Escorts Ltd*, (1986) 1 SCC 264 at p 326: (1986) 59 Comp Cas 548: [1986] 1 Comp LJ 91 SC. ''The rights of a shareholder are (*i*) to elect directors and thus to participate in management through them; (*ii*) to vote on resolutions at meetings of the company; (*iii*) to enjoy the profits of the company in the shape of dividends; (*iv*) to apply to the court for relief against oppression; (*v*) to apply for relief against mismanagement; (*vi*) to apply for winding up; (*vii*) to share in the surplus on winding up.

valued is nothing more than the totality of his rights and liabilities as they exist under the provisions of the Companies Act and the constitution of the particular company.''[84] ''The act of becoming a member [of a corporation] is something more than a contract; it is entering into a complex and abiding relation.''[85]

A share has become a symbol of "passive property".[86] The "active property" is under the control of the corporate managers. The legal concept of the shareholder is still that of the owner of the enterprise. But in fact his position has receded to that of the "functionless rentier" of capital.[87] Having supplied capital to the enterprise, he does not wish to be bothered except by dividends. His investment confers upon him a claim on income. "What is bought and sold in the market is not productive wealth itself, but income producing prospects. Right to income has become commodity for exchange."[88] "Tersely, the shareholder has a piece of property with an open market value."[89]

RETURN AS TO ALLOTMENT [S. 75]

Within thirty days[90] of allotment of shares, a company is required to send to the Registrar a report, known as the "return as to allotment". It must contain the following particulars:

1. The number and nominal amount of shares allotted; the names, addresses and occupations of the allottees; the amount, if any, paid or payable on each share. No shares should be shown as allotted for cash unless cash has actually been received in respect of the allotment.

2. Contracts in writing[91] under which shares have been allotted for any consideration other than cash, must be produced for examination of the Registrar.

---

84. *Pauline case*, [1935] 1 KB 26, 57. The nature of a share has been fully explained in *Bacha F. Guzdar v CIT*, (1955) 1 SCR 876 at pp 881-82: AIR 1955 SC 74: (1955) 25 Comp Cas 1.
85. HOLMES J in *Modern Woodman v Miner*, 267 US 544, 551.
86. The concepts of "active property" which means control of the corporate wealth and of "passive property" which means the interest of the shareholder in the corporation first coined by Berle and Means in MODERN CORPORATION AND PRIVATE PROPERTY, (1932) at p 279.
87. *See* Mason in his introduction to THE CORPORATION IN MODERN SOCIETY, (1959) and Hatherington, *Corporate Responsibility*, (1969) Stan LR at p 255.
88. Paul P. Harbrecht, *The Modern Corporation*, (1964) 64 Columbia LR 1410 at p 1415.
89. Berle and Means, p 287, note 1 above.
90. The Registrar can extend this period if he is satisfied on an application by the company that it was inadequate for complying with the requirements of the section. Such application may be made before or after the expiry of the period of 30 days [S. 75(3)].
91. S. 75(1)(*b*). Where such a contract is not in writing, the company must submit a document containing the prescribed particulars of the contract. The document must be stamped with the same amount of stamp duty as would have been payable if the contract had been in writing. S. 75(1). *S.K. Services Ltd v Phipps*, (2004) 2 BCLC 589(CA), shares can be paid for in cash

3. Where bonus shares have been issued, the return must show the nominal amount of the shares allotted; names and addresses and occupations of the allottees and a copy of the resolution authorising the issue of such shares.[92]

4. Where the shares have been issued at a discount, the return must include a copy of the resolution authorising such an issue, a copy of the Tribunal's order sanctioning the issue, and, where the rate of discount is more than ten per cent, a copy of the order of the Central Government permitting the issue.[93]

ISSUE OF SHARES AT DISCOUNT [S. 79]

Generally speaking, the Companies Acts have always discouraged issue of shares for a price less than their face value. Allotment of shares at a discount is *ultra vires* and, therefore, the allottees who have been put on the register of members become bound to pay the full value of their shares.[94] But a contract to take shares at a discount is not enforceable.[95]

Law does not tolerate issue of shares at a discount even in an indirect way. Thus where a company issued debentures at a discount, which is allowed by the Act, and gave each debenture-holder the right to convert his debentures into shares, it was held that it was a colourable scheme for issuing shares at a discount and, therefore, was not legal.[96] But, subject to the following strict conditions[97], a company may issue its shares at a discount. In the first place, the shares of the class issued for the first time are not allowed to be sold at a discount. Discount can be allowed only on that class of shares which the company has already once issued before at full value. Secondly, the company contemplating such an issue must have become entitled to commence business at least one year before the date of issue. The procedure to be followed is this. A resolution authorising the issue must be passed. The resolution must specify the rate of discount which must not exceed ten per cent, except with the approval of the Central

---

or by some other consideration. There is no special way in which payment for shares has to be made.

92. S. 75(1)(*c*)(*i*). *Shree Shanti Textile Mills Ltd* v *Siddharth N. Shah*, (2005) 125 Comp Cas 576 (Bom), the return has to show the names of all joint holders. In this case the return showed single owner in respect of certain shares but in the company's record, joint holding was shown, the court said that what was recorded with the Registrar must prevail.

93. S. 75(1)(*c*)(*ii*). Where the period of thirty days is found to be inadequate, the company may apply to the Registrar for extension. S. 75(3). The "return" need not include the allotment of such shares as have been forfeited for non-payment of calls (sub-section (5)). *See also* sub-section (4) which imposes penalty for default. Evidentiary value of the contents of the return is that they are presumed to be true until the contrary is shown. *Om Prakash Berlia* v *Unit Trust of India*, (1983) 54 Comp Cas 136 Bom.

94. *Ooregum Gold Mining Co of India* v *Roper*, 1892 AC 125: 66 LT 427.

95. *Sandys, ex p*, (1889) 42 Ch D 98: 61 LT 94.

96. *Mosely* v *Koffyfontein Mines Ltd*, [1904] 2 Ch 108: 91 LT 266.

97. LINDLEY LJ in *Licensed Victuallers' Mutual Trading Assn, Re*, (1889) 42 Ch D 1 at p 7..

Government.[98] Finally, the sanction of the Central Government must be obtained and the shares issued within two months of the Board's sanction.

Sweat equity shares [S. 79-A]

The Companies (Amendment) Act, 1999 has introduced this section (w.e.f. 31-10-98) enabling companies to issue shares in lieu of services. The shares should be of a class which has already been once issued. The issue should be authorised by a special resolution at a general meeting of the company. The resolution should specify the number of shares and their current market price and also the class or classes of directors or employees to whom they are to be issued and consideration for the sweat equity shares proposed to be issued. At least one year must have elapsed between the commencement of business by the company and the date of such issue. Such shares shall be issued in accordance with SEBI Regulations. Where the shares are not listed at a stock exchange, they can be issued as sweat equity in accordance with the guidelines which may be prescribed.

The first *Explanation* to the section says that for the purposes of the section, the expression "company" means a company incorporated, formed and registered under the Companies Act and includes a subsidiary company incorporated in a country outside India. The second *Explanation* says that the expression "*sweat equity shares*" means equity shares issued at a discount or for consideration other than cash for providing know-how or making available rights in the nature of intellectual property rights or value additions, by whatsoever name called.

Shares issued as sweat equity shares are to be treated for all purposes like other shares and, therefore, all the limitations, restrictions and provisions relating to equity shares will be applicable to them. [S. 79-A(2)]

UNDERWRITING COMMISSION [S. 76]

The second exception is in favour of underwriting commission. Section 76 allows a company to pay commission to any person for his subscribing or agreeing to subscribe for shares or debentures or for procuring or agreeing to procure subscription for shares or debentures of the company. When shares are offered to the public the company would naturally like to ensure success of the issue. The company may, therefore, make an agreement with financial institutions who, in consideration of the commission, agree to subscribe for the shares to the extent to which they are not taken up by the

---

98. In *Mare Steel Castings (P) Ltd, Re*, [1993] 2 Comp LJ 261 CLB Mad, the CLB permitted discount upto 25%, which was feasible and also viable in the interest of the company. The Company Law Board in *Jersey (India) Ltd, Re*, (1997) 88 Comp Cas 854 CLB permitted a discount of more than 10% for issue of non-cumulative convertible preference shares. The issue was in the interest of the company. The conditions imposed were that promoters' holding was not to be increased, converted equity shares were to be listed within ten weeks.

public. The agreement may be limited to a "certain number of shares if and so far as not applied for by the public".[1] Underwriting is now compulsory for the full issue and minimum requirement of 90% subscription of the portion offered to the public is also mandatory for each issue of capital to public.[2]

Underwriting commission can be paid subject to the following conditions:[3]

1. The payment of the commission must be authorised by the articles.

2. The rate of commission should not exceed five per cent of the price at which the shares are issued or any less amount prescribed by the articles. In the case of debentures it should not exceed 2.5%.

3. The rate should be disclosed in the prospectus or statement in lieu of prospectus.

4. The prospectus should also indicate the number of shares or debentures which have been underwritten.

5. A copy of the underwriting contract should be delivered to the Registrar along with the prospectus.[4]

The effect of an underwriting agreement is that it is not merely a guarantee, but also an application for shares which are not taken up by the public. Hence the company can allot shares in terms of the contract without further application.[5]

BROKERAGE

The Act, however, permits such brokerage to be paid as has been lawful for a company to pay.[6] It has been recognised in *Metropolitan Coal Consumers' Assn* v *Scringeour*[7] that reasonable brokerage should always be allowed. In that case a commission of two and a half per cent to brokers was held to be reasonable. Brokerage is different from underwriting

---

1. Lord TOMLIN in *Australian Investment Trust Ltd* v *Strand & Pitt Street Properties Ltd*, 1932 AC 735 at p 745 PC. An underwriter does not guarantee the success of the prospectus. He only agrees to take those shares which would not be taken by the public.

2. *See* Section D of SEBI·Guidelines for Disclosure and Investor Protection, 1992 and SEBI Underwriter Rules and Regulations, 1993. Managers to the issue must satisfy themselves of the net worth of the underwriters. Model underwriting agreements have also been prescribed.

3. S. 76(1).

4. The section now clearly forbids the payment of commission on any shares which are not offered to the public, except where a person has agreed to subscribe for shares before the prospectus is issued. *See* sub-s (4-A). Sub-s (5) imposes penalty for breach of the section.

5. *Pioneer Co* v *Kaithal Cotton & General Mills*, (1970) 40 Comp Cas 562: [1970] 2 Comp LJ 123 P&H. The underwriter may relieve himself of the burden by entering into sub-underwriting contracts on the same basis. The sub-underwriter becomes bound to the company in the same way as the original underwriter.

6. S. 76(3). The business of brokers is now under SEBI; Rules and Regulations for Brokers and Sub-Brokers, 1992 and Guidelines for Foreign Brokers. Brokers who play the role of market makers of companies have to observe SEBI Guidelines for Market Makers.

7. [1895] 2 QB 604: 73 LT 137.

commission. A broker does not undertake to subscribe for shares to the extent of public default. Brokers are professional men, such as "stock-brokers, bankers and the like, who exhibit prospectuses and send them to their customers, and by whose mediation the customers are induced to subscribe".[8] Thus brokerage can be paid only to a person who carries on the profession of a broker and not to a person who has casually induced others to subscribe. Thus in *Andreae v Zinc Mines of Great Britain*:[9]

There was an agreement to pay commission for sale of shares to a lady who was not carrying on any business, the court held: "It cannot be suggested that what was to be paid to the plaintiff was brokerage. She was in no sense a broker. She did not carry on business as a broker, and it was a mere accident that she came into the company's office and was consulted in this matter."

Restraining access to market

A broker who works without registration commits violation of Section 12 of the SEBI Act and Rule 3 of the Broker Rules as well as the provisions of the Code of Conduct of sub-brokers specified under Broker Regulations. The inquiry had found him guilty of trading without registration. SAT is slow to interfere in findings of fact. Punishment was reduced to suitable warning.[10]

An investor indulged in large volumes of trading in a particular scrip creating an artificial market in that security. He offered no plausible explanation. Indulgence of insiders for trading in the scrip could be inferred in the circumstances. Direction by SEBI prohibiting the investor from buying and selling or dealing in securities directly or indirectly for a period of one year was held to be justified.[11]

A broker has to keep the money of his client in a separate account. In this case the money of the client was withdrawn from his account in violation of the conditions of registration. He put the money to his personal use. The certificate of registration of the broker was suspended for a modified period of seven days as against the period of 3 months ordered by SEBI.[12]

There should be parity in imposing penalty otherwise it may entail a charge of discrimination. Where the alleged irregularities were not serious, the debarment of four months was reduced to a simple warning.[13]

---

8. BAILHACHE J in *Andreae v Zinc Mines of Great Britain Ltd*, [1918] 2 KB 454. By agreeing to "place" the company's shares the broker does not become a shareholder. *Monarch Insurance Co, Re*, (1873) 8 Ch App 507.
9. *Ibid.*
10. *Doogar and Associates Securities Ltd v SEBI*, (2005) 2 Comp LJ 502: (2005) 59 SCL 356 (SAT).
11. *Shashikant G. Badani v SEBI*, (2005) 123 Comp Cas 473 SAT.
12. *Kerala Stock Broking Ltd v SEBI*, (2005) 2 Comp LJ 434 SAT.
13. *Chona Financial Services (P) Ltd v SEBI*, (2005) 2 Comp LJ 437 SAT; *Kaynet Capital Ltd v SEBI*, (2005) 3 Comp LJ 531 SAT.

Every opportunity should be given to the broker to rehabilitate himself. The charges in this case were of minor nature. None of them were serious enough to warrant a penalty of suspension. Having regard to other comparable cases, a strong warning was held to be sufficient as against suspension of certificate of registration for 3 months.[14] Where the alleged irregularities were not serious, the SAT reduced the penalty of four months imposed by SEBI to a mere warning. SAT said that punishment should not so harass as to deprive the broker for a long period of his trading rights to his own detriment and also to the detriment of his clients.[15]

ISSUE OF SHARES AT PREMIUM [S. 78]

If the market exists, a company may issue its shares or securities at a price higher than their nominal value. There is no restriction whatever on the sale of shares at a premium. But SEBI Guidelines have to be observed as they indicate when an issue has to be at par and when premium is chargeable.[16] Premium may be received in cash or in kind. Where the value of the assets received by a company as a consideration for allotment is greater than the nominal value of shares, it is in essence an allotment at a premium. An amount equal to the extra value of assets would have to be carried to the share premium account.[17] The Act does regulate the disbursement of the amount collected as premium. It is clearly provided that the amount so received, whether in cash or kind, shall be carried to a separate account to be known as the *The Securities Premium Account*. The amount to the credit of share premium account has to be maintained with the same sanctity as share capital and can be reduced only in the manner of share capital.[18] Liberty is, however, given to use the fund in the following four ways:[19]

---

14. *Shyam Sundar Dalmia v SEBI*, (2005) 2 Comp LJ 452 SAT.
15. *Sanghvi Bros Brokerage Ltd v SEBI*, (2005) 2 Comp LJ 475 SAT.
16. SEBI Guidelines for Disclosure and Investor Protection, Section A.
17. *Head (Henry) & Co Ltd v Ropner Holdings Ltd*, [1952] Ch 124.
18. See, *Thorn EMG plc Case*, 1989 BCLC 812 Ch D; *Tip-Europe Ltd Case*, 1988 BCLC 231 Ch; *Ratners Group plc, Re*, 1988 BCLC 231, all on reduction share premium account. The decision of the Court of Appeal in *Ransames plc Case*, [1999] 2 BCLC 591 CA, affirmed the decision of the court below in sanctioning reduction of share premium account irrespective of irregularities like short notice of meeting, increasing the number of shareholders to assure smooth passage of the resolution and highly abbreviated notice, because the interests of the shareholders were not prejudiced there being otherwise good resources for paying them back in full in case of need. Dividends cannot be paid out of the premium amount, *Drown v Gaumont-British Picture Corpn Ltd*, (1937) Ch 402; *Duffe Settlements, Re*, (1951) Ch 923 CA; *Shearer v Bercain*, (1980) 3 All ER 295; *Head (Henry) & Co Ltd v Ropner Holdings Ltd*, [1952] Ch 124, shares of extra value received on merger, not allowed to be used for being distributed as dividend.

  The amount to the credit of the share premium account has to be shown as a separate item in the Balance-sheet and if it was disposed of, wholly or partly, how it was disposed of (Sch VI, Part I). The DCA is of opinion that the amount of premium cannot be treated as a free reserve as it is in the nature of a capital reserve. Circular No 3/77 of 15-4-1977.
19. S. 78(2). It has been held by the Supreme Court that a company may charge varying premiums in respect of blocks of shares having the same rights issued under different

1. It may be applied to issue to the members as fully paid by way of bonus the unissued shares of the company.[20]
2. It may be used to write off preliminary expenses.
3. It may be used to write off commission or discount account.
4. It may be spent in providing for the premium payable on the redemption of preference shares or debentures of the company.

A reduction of the premium account was allowed under a scheme which experts had approved as fair, just and proper.[21] Reduction of the share premium account for wiping out losses incurred in trading in securities was allowed. The articles of association enabled the company to reduce its share premium account. The reduction of capital did not involve either diminution of liability in respect of unpaid capital or payment to any shareholder of paid up capital. Creditors and shareholders raised no objections.[22]

Bona fide reduction of share premium account

The company proposed to write off accumulated losses by utilising the share premium account and by reducing the face value of its shares. The need and purpose of reduction was duly explained and discussed at an extraordinary general meeting at which a special resolution was unanimously passed. The company had no secured creditors. The unsecured creditors had given their written consent. Nothing was shown to be there either against public interest or against law. The court allowed the proposed reduction.[23] The share premium account is treated as paid up share capital for a limited purpose. But not as a reserve fund. A company can be allowed to write off or adjust a loss against share premium account if there is no diminution of the share capital account and corresponding reduction in the share premium account.[24]

PENALTY FOR FRAUDULENTLY INDUCING INVESTMENT [S. 68]

The provision in Section 68 is as follows:

"**Any person who, either by knowingly or recklessly making any statement, promise or forecast which is false, deceptive or misleading, or by any dishonest concealment of material facts, induces or attempts to induce another person to enter into, or to offer to enter into—**

---

resolutions, and "on principle there is no objection to the charging of varying rate of premium for shares issued under a single resolution, if all the parties concerned agree". *CIT v Standard Vaccum Oil Co*, AIR 1966 SC 1393: [1966] 1 Comp LJ 187, 192.
20. *EIC Services Ltd* v *Phipps*, (2004) 2 BCLC 589 CA: (2005) 126 Comp Cas 454: (2005) 1 WLR 1377, bonus shares were not allowed to be issued by capitalisation of the share premium account without authority of an ordinary resolution of the company and to shareholders whose shares were not fully paid. It could not be regularised by an agreement of the shareholders.
21. *Zee Telefilms Ltd, Re*, (2005) 124 Comp Cas 102 Bom.
22. *Hyderabad Industries Ltd, Re*, 2004 CLC 1385: (2005) 123 Comp Cas 458 AP, DB.
23. *India Infoline Ltd, Re*, (2004) 53 SCL 396 Bom.
24. *Global Trust Bank Ltd, Re*, (2005) 57 SCL 164 AP: 2005 CLC 353: (2005) 127 Comp Cas 604.

    (*a*) any agreement for, or with a view to, acquiring, disposing of, subscribing for, or underwriting shares or debentures; or

    (*b*) any agreement, the purpose or pretended purpose of which is to secure a profit to any of the parties from the yield of shares or debentures, or by reference to fluctuations in the value of shares or debentures;

shall be punishable with imprisonment for a term which may extend to five years, or with fine which may extend to ten thousand rupees, or with both.''

Prospectuses offering securities under concealment of vital facts would be within the mischief of this section.[25]

PERSONATION FOR ACQUISITION OF SHARES [S. 68-A]

This provision has been introduced by the Companies (Amendment) Act, 1965. The purpose of the section is to prevent allotment of shares in fictitious names. Accordingly, no application should be made to a company for acquiring or subscribing for any shares in a fictitious name. Similarly, no one should induce a company to allot, or register any transfer of, shares in a fictitious name. The penalty for this offence is a term of imprisonment which may extend to five years.

Every company which issues a prospectus is required to reproduce prominently the provisions of the section in the prospectus and application forms.

A person who gets shares allotted in a fictitious name becomes liable as a shareholder. Thus where a person carried on business under an assumed name and took shares in that name, his trustee in bankruptcy could not avoid liability.[26]

-----

25. *M. K. Srinivasan, Re*, AIR 1944 Mad 410: (1944) 14 Comp Cas 193. Power of prosecution under the section has been delegated to SEBI. *Sundaram Finance Services Ltd* v *Grand Trust Finance Ltd*, (2002) 112 Comp Cas 361 Mad, a prosecution launched under the section. *A. V. Mohan Rao* v *M. Kishan Rao*, (2002) 6 SCC 174: 2002 SCC Cri 1281: (2002) 111 Comp Cas 390, huge sums of money were collected under a document described as ''project overview'' by NRIs but shares not allotted in the proposed joint venture company instead the money was diverted to some off-shore companies controlled by the accused persons, offence under Sections 60, 63, 68, 68-A, 621 *prima facie* made out.
26. *Central Klondyke Gold Mining Co, Re*, (1899) WN 1.

8

Shareholders and Members

The words "member" and "shareholder" are used interchangeably and, generally speaking, apart from a few exceptional cases, they are synonymous. There are, for example, companies limited by guarantee or unlimited companies, which may not have share capital and, therefore, can have no shareholders, but they do have members. Contrarily, the bearer of a share warrant is a shareholder, but not a member, as his name is struck off the register of members.[1]

Definition of member [S. 41]

Section 2(27) talks of a member in relation to a company and says that the expression does not include a bearer of a share warrant of the company issued in pursuance of Section 114. This is an exclusion clause rather than a definition. The real definition is to be found in the provisions of Section 41 and here the emphasis in both the sub-sections is entry in the register of members. Here is what the section says:

41. *Definition of "Member"*—(1) The subscribers of the memorandum of a company shall be deemed to have agreed to become members of the company, and on its registration, shall be entered as members in its register of members.

(2) Every other person who agrees in writing to become a member of a company and whose name is entered in its register of members, shall be a member of the company.

(3) Every person holding equity share capital of a company and whose name is entered in as beneficial owner in the records of the depository shall be deemed to be a member of the concerned company.

In reference to the subscribers of the memorandum, the section ordains that they shall be entered as members in the register of members and in reference to others the section prescribes that there should be an application in writing[2] and the name should be there in the register of members. The words "agreed in writing" were brought in by the amendment of 1960 so as to prevent in the circumstances of our country a person being surprised by the presence of his name in the register and then facing the burden of a *prima facie* evidence and leading evidence to show that he never agreed to be a member. In either case the section requires as a condition of membership that the name of the person in question is there in the register of members. But even so the courts have ruled that the wider definition of membership in Section 2(27) as excluding only warrant holders, cannot be curtailed by Section 41 and, therefore, a person may be regarded as a

---

1. S. 115(1). The articles of association of a company may provide that in all or some respects the bearer of a share warrant may be deemed to be a member. S. 115(5).
2. *Vijay Kumar Narang* v *Prakash Coachbuilders (P) Ltd*, (2005) 128 Comp Cas 976 CLB, this requirement applies when a person is becoming a member for the first time and not when a person, being already a shareholder, purchases further shares.

member if he has acquired the right of membership though his name is not in the register[3] and a person whose name is in the register may not be regarded as a member if he did not agree to be a member in writing or is not accepting his position as such.[4]

Shares can be held jointly. The principles relating to rights and liabilities under joint promises would apply. Where one joint holder died and the shares were registered in the name of the surviving joint holder, that was held to be justified though the legal heirs were claiming registration in their name.[5]

A consequential amendment of Section 41 made by the Depositories Act provides that a person holding an equity share capital of a company and whose name is entered as a beneficial owner in the records of a depository is a member of the company. Holding equity shares through a depository constitutes the holder into a member [S. 41(3)]. A person who holds shares in a demat form, his name does not appear in the company's register of members.

How to become a member

One may become a shareholder in a company in any one of the following ways:

1. By subscribing to memorandum [S. 41]

In the first place, Section 41 of the Act provides that the subscribers of the memorandum of association shall be deemed to have agreed to become the members of the company, and on its registration shall be entered as members in the register of members. Accordingly, it was held in *Official Liquidator* v *Suleman Bhai*[6] that:

> The subscriber of the memorandum is to be treated as having become a member by the very fact of subscription. Neither application form, nor allotment of, shares is necessary. Even an absence of entry in the register of members cannot deprive him of his status. He acquires, as soon as the company is registered, the full status of a member with all the rights and liabilities.

3. *N. Satyaprasad Rao* v *V. L. N. Sastry*, (1988) 64 Comp Cas 492 AP.
4. *Shri Balaji Textile Mills (P) Ltd* v *Ashok Kavle*, (1989) 66 Comp Cas 654, 661-662 Ker. This is more true of English law where the words "in writing" are not used. See *Nuneaton Borough Assn Football Club Ltd, Re*, 1989 BCLC 454 CA; *National Steel & General Mills* v *Official Liquidator*, [1989] 2 Comp LJ 214 Del: (1990) 69 Comp Cas 416, continuity of membership. *Ram Kishan* v *Kanwar Paper (P) Ltd*, (1990) 69 Comp Cas 209 HP, the name was ordered to be removed from the register because there was no agreement in writing.
5. *Jayalakshmi Acharya* v *Kal Electronics and Consultants (P) Ltd*, (1997) 90 Comp Cas 200; *Kamla Pal* v *Esso Standard Refining Co (P) Ltd*, [1997] 3 Comp LJ 138 CLB.
6. AIR 1955 MB 166.

The facts were that one *S* had subscribed the memorandum of a company for 200 shares. The company was duly registered, but he ultimately took only 20 shares. He was held liable in the winding up of the company to pay for all the 200 shares although they were, in fact, never allotted to him.[7]

2. Qualification shares [S. 266]

Under the Companies Act no person is capable of being appointed a director of a public company unless he takes, or signs and files with the Registrar an undertaking to take, from the company his qualification shares, if any.[8] Such directors who have signed an undertaking to take and pay for their qualification shares are also in the same position as subscribers of the memorandum.[9] They are also deemed to have become members automatically on the registration of the company.[10]

Where, however, a director fails to take his qualification shares and his office falls vacant automatically on the expiry of the prescribed time, his name, in the view of the Bombay High Court, cannot be placed on the list of contributories.[11]

3. By allotment

A person may become a shareholder by agreeing to take shares in the company by allotment.[12]

4. By transfer

One may purchase shares of a company in the open market and then apply to the company to register him as a member. Section 41 which defines "member" says that it includes the subscribers to the memorandum of a company and every other person who agrees in writing to become a member of the company and whose name is entered in its register of members. Thus

---

7. *Evan case*, (1867) 2 Ch App 427, 431; *Migott case*, (1867) LR 4 Eq 238, where it was held that an allotment to the subscriber of fully paid shares belonging to another is not enough. In *Synemodelux Ltd* v *K. Vannamuthu Pillai*, AIR 1939 Mad 498, it was held that an express allotment of shares to the subscriber is necessary to make him liable. It appears that proper authorities were not cited before the Court. If the subscriber pays by transferring assets (non-cash payment) expert valuation report would be needed.
8. S. 266(1)(*b*). Alternatively, he may sign the memorandum for his qualification shares in which case he will become member by subscription. Sub-section 1(*a*)(*i*).
9. S. 266(2).
10. *See also* sub-section (5) which contains exceptions which are that the section will not apply to companies not having a share capital, a private company, or which was private before becoming a public company or the issue of a prospectus one year from the date from which the company was entitled to commence business.
11. *Zamir Ahmed* v *D. R. Banaji*, (1957) 27 Comp Cas 634: AIR 1958 Bom 198: 59 Bom LR 591.
12. For details as to allotment, *see* the preceding Chapter.

it requires two things: (*a*) an agreement in writing to become a member and (*b*) an entry in the register.[13]

5. By transmission

On the death of a member his executor or the person who is entitled under the law to succeed to his estate gets the right to have the shares transmitted to his name in the company's register of members. Transmission is different from transfer. Section 108 which lays down the formalities of transfer specially provides that nothing in the section shall prejudice the power of the company to register as shareholder any person to whom the right to any shares has been transmitted by operation of law.[14] It follows that an instrument of transfer is not necessary. No formalities like transfer deed, execution, attestation and stamp duty are needed. Legal heirs as shown by the succession certificate are aggrieved persons entitled to seek relief against refusal.[15] Provisions relating to formalities of transmission are generally found in the company's articles. Clauses 25 to 28 of Table A contain such provisions. If the company unduly refuses to accept a transmission, the same remedies are available as in the case of a transfer, namely, an appeal to the Company Law Board under Section 111. The refusal by directors to accept a transmission has been held to be appealable to the CLB under Section 111-A(2).[16] A company's refusal to accept a transmission unless a succession certificate is produced has been held to be a refusal enabling the legal heir to file an appeal against it. A succession certificate obtained after death would apply not only to transmission but also to bonus shares, dividend, interest and other benefits accruing to the shares. A fresh certificate is not necessary for such benefits.[17]

---

13. The Kerala High Court emphasised in *Lalithamba Bai* v *Harrisons Malayalam Ltd*, (1988) 63 Comp Cas 622, 666 the importance of the fact of "agreement in writing" by holding that it must be proved and that an agreement for taking over the assets of a company does not have the effect of taking over its shares from its members.

14. S. 108(1), 2nd proviso. It may be necessary to submit a succession certificate, but vesting takes place from the moment of death and not from the date of the grant of certificate. *Margaret T. Desor* v *Worldwide Agencies (P) Ltd*, (1989) 66 Comp Cas 5 Del; the Supreme Court affirmation on other points, *Worldwide Agencies (P) Ltd* v *Margarat*, (1990) 1 SCC 536: 1990 SCC (Tax) 171: (1990) 67 Comp Cas 607 SC: AIR 1990 SC 737: [1990] 1 Comp LJ 208.

15. *Kamlabai* v *Vithal Pd Co (P) Ltd*, (1993) 77 Comp Cas 231 Kant. Succession certificate or letters of administration would be necessary, particularly where there is no agreement among known legal heirs. *Narinder Kumar Sehgal* v *Leader Valves Ltd*, (1993) 77 Comp Cas 393 CLB, relying upon *Kasi Vishwanathan Chettiar* v *Indo Burma Petroleum Co Ltd*, (1936) 6 Comp Cas 42 Rang. Where it was certain that the widow was the sole surviving heir, insistence upon succession certificate was held to be not justified. The shareholding being established otherwise also, production of share scrips may also be not necessary. *Simret Katyal* v *Mahavir Ice Mills (P) Ltd*, (1995) 83 Comp Cas 699 CLB. For effecting a transmission, the procedure prescribed by the Act and the company's articles has to be followed, *Anand Hemant Patel* v *Ornate Club (P) Ltd*, (2000) 99 Comp Cas 318 CLB.

16. *Anil R. Chhabria* v *Finolex Industries Ltd*, (2000) 99 Comp Cas 168.

17. *Arjun Kumar Israni* v *Cipla Ltd*, (2000) 99 Comp Cas 237 CLB-WB. *Khurshid Alam* v *P. Pagnon Co (P) Ltd*, (2003) 108 Comp Cas 523 CLB, shares stood in the name of a deceased

The new provisions relating to transfers are equally applicable to transmissions.[18]

Where the company had accepted transmission in respect of a part of the shares but demanded succession certificate or probated 'will' in respect of the rest of the shares, the CLB held that the company had lost the right to refuse transmission for all the shares. No other person had raised any claim or objection.[19] Thus, for example, in a case before the Supreme Court, the State of Orissa became entitled by devolution to the shares of a *Maharaja*, but the company refused to register the State's representative as a shareholder. BACHAWAT J held that the State became entitled to the shares by operation of law. It was, therefore, a case of transmission and the company was bound to accept the same.[20] A company was not allowed to refuse the registration of transmicon in favour of the legal heir of a deceased member on the ground that he was carrying on a competing business.[21] Among Christians, a letter of probate is not required for succession under a will. The legal heir (son) had established an unopposed will in his favour. The CLB said that the company was not justified in demanding a letter of probate.[22]

Where the succession certificate was produced, but the company objected to non-payment of stamp duty, the CLB directed transmission to be carried out. The matter of stamp duty to be sorted out in the court.[23]

The executor or the successor also has the right to transfer the shares. Section 109 specially enables the legal representative to effect a transfer even if he is not a member himself. Thus he has an option. But he must decide within a reasonable time. The directors may require him by notice to make up his mind within 90 days and if the notice is not complied with, payments due on the shares may be withheld, until the notice is complied with.[24]

Mohammedan, son applied for transmission, he produced his father's will favouring him, other legal heirs did not object, the company was held not justified in insisting upon probate or letters of administration.

18. *Finolex Industries Ltd* v *Anil Ramchand Chhabria*, (2000) 26 SCL 233 Bom, not approving the ruling in *Sashi Prakash Khemka* v *NEPC Micon Ltd*, (1999) 95 Comp Cas 583 CLB.
19. *Nandita Bhardwaj* v *Sapphire Machines (P) Ltd*, [2000] 2 Comp LJ 109 CLB.
20. *Indian Chemical Products Ltd* v *State of Orissa*, [1966] 2 Comp LJ 63: (1966) 36 Comp Cas 592: AIR 1967 SC 253. *See also M. K. Sugar Mills* v *I. K. Sugar Mills*, (1963) 33 Comp Cas 1142: AIR 1965 All 135, where the matters relating to transmission are explained, *see* at p 140.
21. *S. M. Hajee Abdul Sahib* v *KNS Co (P) Ltd*, (1998) 91 Comp Cas 843 CLB. Rectification of register of members was ordered. *Debasish Dutta* v *B. G. Somadder & Sons (P) Ltd*, (2003) 115 Comp Cas 70 CLB, company directed to register legal heirs under transmission.
22. *Ashok Cherian* v *ITC Ltd*, (2005) 122 Comp Cas 857 CLB.
23. *Renn Kana Dutta* v *Gour Nitye Tea and Industries*, (2007) 135 Comp Cas 271 CLB.
24. Clause 20 (proviso), Table A, Schedule 1.

In the above three cases, namely, allotment, transfer and transmission, a person does not become a member unless his name is entered in the company's register of members.[25]

Nomination of shares and debentures [S. 109-A] [Amendment of 1999]

This newly introduced section provides the facility to shareholders, etc., to register the name of any person with the company in whom the shares will be vested on the death of the nominating shareholder. Debenture holders and depositors have also been given similar rights. Nomination can be filed at any time in a manner to be prescribed. Joint holders can also nominate any person for the purpose of vesting of shares in the event of the death of all the joint holders. Such nomination will supersede the law of succession and any 'will' or disposition whether testamentary or otherwise. The shares or debentures will be vested in the nominee to the exclusion of any claimant whether under 'will' or succession. The only process by which any change can be brought about is that the security holder should himself change the nomination. Where the nominee is a minor, the security holder may suggest any other name in the prescribed manner in whom the shares would be vested should the nominee die during his minority.

Transmission of shares under nomination [S. 109-B]

The nominee gets the right on the death of the security holder to register himself as the security holder or transfer the securities. His right of transfer will be subject to the same limits and restrictions as the right of the original security holder was. The Board of directors will have the same right of refusal as would have been there had the securities been transferred by the original holder. Sub-section (7) has been inserted by the Companies (Amendment) Act, 1999 to make it clear that the Board of directors will have no right to decline or suspend registration of transfer in the event of nomination of a shareholder in favour of a nominee. If the nominee wants to register himself as the holder he should send to the company in writing a notice under his signature accompanied by the death certificate. Since this also amounts to a transfer, it will be under the same restrictions which would have been applicable as if the original holder had made a transfer. Even before he gets himself registered, he will be entitled to all the advantages as to dividend, etc., but unless he gets himself registered as a holder, he will have no right in relation to the meetings of the company. If he does not exercise his right of becoming a security holder or of transferring the securities, the Board of

---

25. Section 116 provides penalty for impersonation of shareholder. For a statement of the formalities of a transmission see *UTI* v *Om Prakash Berlia*, (1983) 54 Comp Cas 723 Bom; *Killick Nixon Ltd* v *Dhanraj Mills (P) Ltd*, (1983) 54 Comp Cas 432 Bom.

directors may ask him to regularise the matter. If he does not do so within 90 days of the receipt of notice, the company may deny him the benefit of dividend, bonus or moneys becoming payable in respect of the shares.

Who may be member

Minor

Every person who is competent to contract may become a member. A minor and a person of unsound mind, being incompetent to contract, cannot be members of a company.[26] According to English law, however, a minor may join a company as a member, but the contract is voidable at his option during minority as well as within reasonable time after the attainment of majority.[27] But as long as it is not avoided it is a valid contract.

In India also a minor may be allotted shares. His name may remain on a company's register of members, but during minority he incurs no liability. In *Palaniappa* v *Official Liquidator*:[28]

Shares were allotted to a minor on an application signed on her behalf by her guardian. In the winding up of the company neither the minor nor her guardian were held liable as contributories.

On attaining majority and becoming aware of the presence of his name in the register of members, the minor has the option to repudiate his shares within a reasonable time. Where he does not do so he may safely be taken to have accepted his position. His liability as a shareholder commences. This was laid down by the Bombay High Court in *Fazulbhoy Jaffar* v *Credit Bank of India Ltd*.[29]

An infant was registered as a shareholder. After attaining majority he received dividends from the company. The Court observed: "Under these circumstances it cannot be doubted that he has intentionally permitted the company to believe him to be a shareholder and in that belief to pay him dividends since he attained majority. He is, therefore, estopped now by his conduct from denying that he is a shareholder." The company was in winding up.

The erstwhile Companies Tribunal held in *Navinchandra* v *Gordhandas*[30] that if a minor's name is entered in the register of members as an allottee, the company cannot afterwards *suo motu* delete it and the minor is entitled to rectification if the company does so. The Delhi High Court in *Golcunda Industries Ltd* v *ROC*[31] has held that the Registrar of Companies

---

26. Ss. 10 and 11 of the Indian Contract Act, 1872.
27. *Steinberg* v *Scala (Leeds) Ltd*, [1923] 2 Ch 452: [1923] All ER Rep 239, where the minor was released from further liability but refund of what he had already paid was not allowed.
28. AIR 1942 Mad 470: [1942] 1 MLJ 425: 201 IC 731.
29. AIR 1914 Bom 128: ILR 39 Bom 331: 27 IC 335.
30. [1967] 1 Comp LJ 82: (1967) 37 Comp Cas 747.
31. AIR 1968 Del 170.

cannot refuse to accept a return as to allotment in which a minor is shown as an allottee. The court agreed that the whole law relating to a minor joining a company is still uncertain. There is nothing in the Companies Act prohibiting a minor from becoming the member of a company. Section 41(2) read with Article 19(1) of Table A indicates that the agreement in writing can be made by the guardian on behalf of the minor. It will not be a case of a trust because the minor's name will be entered in the register of members. The shares being fully paid, he would incur no liability.[32]

Others Disqualified

Others disqualified would include, for example, persons of unsound mind and insolvents. The position of a person of unsound mind is akin to that of a minor. So far as an insolvent is concerned, if he was a member before, his name can remain in the register notwithstanding his insolvency, unless the articles provide otherwise. The changes which occur under insolvency laws as to his position as a shareholder are only these that the beneficial interest in the shares would be vested in his assignee, who would also control voting rights. In all other respects he can exercise the normal membership rights, for example, the right of instituting a minority action for redressing corporate wrongs.[33]

Company as Member

A company, being a legal person, may become the member of another company. But a company can invest money in another company only if it is so authorised by its memorandum of association.

A company cannot, however, buy its own shares, except in a limited manner permitted by Section 77. Similarly, subject to a few exceptions given in Section 42, a company cannot buy shares of its holding company. Restrictions on inter-corporate investments are stated in Section 372.

Trade Union

A trade union registered under the Trade Unions Act, can be registered as a member and can hold shares in a company in its own corporate name.[34]

Partnership

A partnership firm, not being a person, cannot buy shares in its own name. It may buy shares as a part of the assets of the firm, though they will have to be held in the name of individual partners. A firm may be a member

---

32. *Gautam R. Palival* v *Karnataka Theatres Ltd*, [2000] CLC 1765 CLB, following *R. Balaraman* v *Buckingham & Carnatic Co Ltd*, [1969] 1 Comp LJ 81 CLB.
33. See *Morgan* v *Gray*, [1953] Ch 83; *Birch* v *Sullivan*, [1957] 1 WLR 1247.
34. *All India Bank Officers Confederation* v *Dhanlakshmi Bank Ltd*, (1997) 90 Comp Cas 225: [1997] 3 Comp LJ 132: (1997) 26 Corpt LA 33 CLB.

of any association or company licensed under Section 25 as a charitable institution, but it shall cease to be a member on its dissolution. [S. 25(4)].

Ceasing to be member

A person may cease to be a member by transfer, death, forfeiture, surrender, on winding up of the company and otherwise in accordance with the provisions of the company's articles of association.

Liability of members

Liability of members depends on the nature of the company. If the company is registered with unlimited liability, every member is liable in full for all the debts of the company contracted during the period of his membership. Where the company is limited by guarantee, each member will be bound to contribute in the event of winding up a sum of money specified in the liability clause of the memorandum of association.[35] Most companies are, however, incorporated with the liability of members limited by shares. Each member is bound to contribute the full nominal value of his shares and his liability ends there.

Calls on shares

The liability of a shareholder to pay the full value of the shares held by him is enforced by making "calls" for payment. Every shareholder is under a statutory liability to pay the full amount of his shares as Section 36(2) declares that "all money payable by any member to the company... shall be a debt due from him to the company". But the liability to pay this debt arises only when a valid call has been made. For example, in *Pabna Dhana Bhandar Co Ltd* v *Foyezud Din Mia*:[36]

> It was held that "a mere demand by a company acquiring the rights of another company in respect of its uncalled capital cannot take the place of a formal call".

However, according to Section 92 a company can accept voluntary payment of the uncalled amount, if it is so authorised by its articles. Voting rights are, however, regulated only by the amount actually called by the company.

An enforceable call shall have to conform to the provisions of the Act and the articles of association of the company. The following are some of the important requisites of a valid call:

---

35. *See* "Guarantee Companies" "unlimited companies" *infra*, Ch. 19 and S. 12(2)(6), and *Stadmed (P) Ltd* v *Kshetra Mohan*, AIR 1968 Cal 572: [1968] 1 Comp LJ 321: 72 CWN 601.
36. AIR 1932 Cal 716: 140 IC 252: 36 CWN 589.

1. *By resolution of board*

In the first place, a call must be made under a resolution of the Board of directors.[37] "In making a call care must be taken that the directors making it are duly appointed, and duly qualified, and that the meeting of the directors has been duly convened, that the proper quorum is present and that the resolution making the call is duly passed."[38] However, every small irregularity should not be taken to render a call invalid. To cover minor discrepancies the articles often provide that the acts of directors would be valid notwithstanding that it should be afterwards discovered that there was some defect in the appointment or qualifications, etc. of such directors. Accordingly, in *Dawson* v *African Consolidated Land & Trading Co*,[39] where a clause of this kind existed, it was held that a call made by a resolution of three directors was valid, although one of them had under the articles of association vacated his office by parting with all his qualification shares for a few days. *Shiromani Sugar Mills Ltd* v *Debi Prasad*[40] is another illustration:

> The directors had by not paying allotment and call moneys disqualified themselves, yet their act in making a call was held to be valid.[41]

Section 92 gives the company the power, if so authorised by its articles, to accept from any member the whole or a part of the amount remaining unpaid on any shares held by him, although no part of that amount has been called up. Such payment will not entitle the member to more voting rights as compared with other members until all have been called upon to pay.[42]

2. *Amount and time of payment*

Secondly, the resolution must state the amount of the call and the time at which it is to be paid, otherwise the call will be invalid. In *E&W Insurance Co Ltd* v *Kamala Mehta*:[43]

> The directors of a company had, by two resolutions, resolved to make a call. But neither resolution specified the date and the amount of

---

37. Accordingly, the High Court of Bombay held in *E&W Insurance Co Ltd* v *Kamala Mehta*, AIR 1956 Bom 537 that "such an important power which is vested in the directors could not be delegated by them to any one and could not be exercised by any one". . . but if they do not wish to do what the articles require them to do and leave the doing of it to someone else, they must clearly resolve to that effect.
38. Palmer's COMPANY LAW, 318 (20th Edn, 1959).
39. [1898] 1 Ch 6: 77 LT 392.
40. AIR 1950 All 508: (1950) 20 Comp Cas 296: 1950 ALJ 836.
41. Ordinarily this should have been regarded a breach of trust and the directors should be compelled to pay as much as other shareholders had paid. See *Alexander* v *Automatic Telephone Co*, [1900] 2 Ch 56: [1900-03] All ER Rep Ext 1755.
42. Where the rate of interest permitted by the articles on such advance payment was 6%, but it could be varied by shareholders in general meeting, 10% interest as resolved by shareholders was considered to be quite reasonable. *Dy CIT* v *Manipal Industries Ltd*, (1997) 12 SCL 15 ITAT.
43. AIR 1956 Bom 537.

payment. The blanks were subsequently filled by the secretary, who sent a notice of call to the defendant. The call notice was held to be invalid.[44]

3. *Bona fide in interest of company*

Thirdly, the capital of a company is a trust fund in the hands of directors. The amount called up must be used scrupulously for the objects of the company and the amount uncalled must be called only when it is necessary for the promotion of those objects. Hence the power to make a call is in the nature of a trust and is to be exercised in the interest of the company. Good faith is lacking where, without paying what is due on their own shares, the directors call upon the other shareholders to pay. In such a case the court would require them to pay as others have paid.[45] Similarly, where the directors paid into the company's account the amount due on their shares and immediately thereafter withdrew it as their fee, it was held that the payment was not for the benefit of the company and they remained liable to pay.[46]

4. *Uniform basis*

Section 71 provides that "calls shall be made on a uniform basis on all shares falling under the same class". Hence a call cannot be made on some of the members only, unless they constitute a separate class of shareholders. Thus where a shareholder paid the first two calls after a great delay and neglected to pay the third call and the directors, being annoyed, called upon him to pay the whole amount due, the call was held to be invalid.[47] But "shares of the same nominal value on which different sums have been paid shall not be deemed, for this purpose, to fall under the same class."[48]

A shareholder on whom a regular call for payment has been served may choose to pay the sum due in respect of only a part of his shares. In the view of the Punjab High Court the debt is not "an entire and indivisible debt", and, therefore, the company may be bound to accept the amount tendered by the shareholder.[49]

---

44. *See* also *Cawley & Co, Re*, (1889) 42 Ch D 209: 61 LT 601, where it was held that in such cases there is no proper call made until the directors pass a second resolution fixing the date of payment. To the same effect is *Major Teja Singh* v *Liquidator of Hindustan Petroleum Co Ltd*, (1961) 31 Comp Cas 573.
45. *Alexander* v *Automatic Telephone Co*, [1900] 2 Ch 56: [1900-03] All ER Rep Ext 1755.
46. *European Central Rail Co, Re*, (1872) LR 13 Eq 255: 26 LT 92.
47. *Galloway* v *Halle Concerts Society*, [1915] 2 Ch 233: [1914-15] All ER Rep 543.
48. *Explanation* to S. 91.
49. *Hind Iron Bank Ltd* v *Raizada Jagan Bali*, (1959) 29 Comp Cas 418. For a detailed account of the subject *see* M. S. Srinivasan, *Calls on Shares in Companies*, [1964] 1 Comp LJ 91.

Payment in kind (*Payment by non-cash consideration*)

Shares may be paid for in cash or kind or in any manner that has the effect of actual cash being received by the company. In *Larocque* v *Beauchemin*:[50]

> A company purchased a paper mill for 35,000 dollars payable in cash. Subsequently, however, the vendors purchased shares in the company and allowed it to retain a part of the sale proceeds in payment of the shares.

It was held that the effect of the agreement was that the shares had been paid in full in cash as it was not necessary that the company should first receive the share money and then hand it back to the vendor in payment of its debt. Similarly, the company may allow a shareholder set-off for the amount due to him against his liability to pay for his shares. Thus payment for shares may be in property, goods or services.[51]

Where shares are allotted for any consideration other than cash, that is to say, for purchase of property or in return for services, the company has to file with the Registrar[52] a copy of the contract in writing showing the title of the allottee or other consideration he gave for the shares.

This is necessary to prevent frauds inherent in a transaction of this kind by overvaluing the assets transferred to the company. Where the consideration is grossly inadequate or illusory or colourable or apparently less than the value of the shares allotted, the agreement is set aside and the allottee is ordered to pay for the shares in full. Thus where a director was given 200 shares of £1 each in return for a loan of £100, it was held to be a colourable transaction to issue shares at a discount.[53] But, in the absence of a fraud in valuation, the court may not interfere only on the ground of inadequacy of consideration.[54] In *Alote Estate* v *R. B. Seth*:[55]

> Shares were allotted in return for sugarcane growing land transferred to the company. In the winding up of the company it was alleged that the

---

50. 1897 AC 358: 76 LT 473.
51. *Ooregum Gold Mining Co of India* v *Roper*, 1892 AC 125: 66 LT 427.
52. Within 30 days of the allotment, S. 75. Where the contract is not in writing, the prescribed particulars of the contract should be filed. Such particulars would be regarded as an instrument within the meaning of the Stamp Act, 1899. It would have to be stamped with the stamp duty as would have been payable if the contract were in writing and the Registrar may require that the duty payable be adjudicated under S. 31 of the Stamp Act.
53. *James Pilkin & Co, Re*, (1916) 85 LJ Ch 318; *Derham & Allen Ltd, Re*, [1946] Ch 31; *Alote Estate* v *R. B. Seth*, (1970) 1 SCC 425, 429: (1970) 40 Comp Cas 1116: AIR 1971 SC 920.
54. *Hong Kong & China Gas Co Ltd* v *Glen*, [1914] 1 Ch 527: [1914-15] All ER 1002; *Wragg Ltd, Re*, [1897] 1 Ch 796: [1895-99] All ER Rep 398; *Punjab Distilling Industries* v *BPC Mills Ltd*, (1973) 43 Comp Cas 189 Del, shares allotted in consideration of out of date foreign machinery.
55. (1970) 1 SCC 425: (1970) 40 Comp Cas 1116: AIR 1971 SC 920.

value of the land was ten times less than the value of the shares allotted. Even so GROVER J of the Supreme Court, refused to interfere. The learned judge said that there was no allegation of fraud. The facts stated related more to inadequacy of price or consideration and not to its being illusory. There should be no inquiry into the question whether the appellants had paid consideration which was inadequate.[56]

It has been held by the Madras High Court that shares cannot be allotted in consideration of promissory notes.[57]

FORFEITURE OF SHARES

If a member, having been called upon to pay, defaults, the company may, of course, bring an action against him. But articles of association often provide that in such a case the company may proceed to forfeit his shares. Shares cannot be forfeited unless there is a clear power to that effect in the articles. Thus in *Madhwa Ramchandra Kamath* v *Canara Bkg Corpn Ltd*:[58]

The articles of a company only authorised it to expel a member. That was held to be not sufficient to enable the company to deprive the expelled member of his shares.

Forfeited shares become the property of the company. To this extent for- feiture involves a reduction of the company's capital. The shares can, however, be re-issued, even at a discount, but that is not the same thing as an allotment.[59]

"The right to forfeit shares must be pursued with the greatest exactness: it must be exercised by the proper parties, that is, by directors properly appointed, and by the requisite number of them and in the proper manner and for the proper cause. The right must be exercised *bona fide* for the purpose for which it is conferred. The power of expulsion is a trust the execution of which will be narrowly scanned by the courts."[60] The proper procedure to be observed in carrying out a forfeiture is as follows:

---

56. Where shares were allotted to directors, on the company becoming a public company, for their past services in establishing the company and its business, they were held liable to pay the price in the company's winding up because past services are no consideration, *Eddystone Marine Ins Co, Re*, [1893] 3 Ch 9: 69 LT 363. An allotment of shares for a future service would be equally without consideration making the allottee liable to pay the price, *National House Property Investment Co Ltd* v *Watson*, 1908 SC 888, Scotland. A company may make immediate payment for hiring future services and then take back the money as consideration for shares, *Gardner* v *Iredale*, (1912) 1 CR 700.

57. *Chokkalingam* v *Official Liquidator*, AIR 1944 Mad 87: [1943] 2 MLJ 499.

58. AIR 1941 Mad 354. Regulations 29 to 35 of Table A provide for the power of forfeiture.

59. *Calcutta Stock Exchange Assn, Re*, AIR 1957 Cal 438. Upon reissue the capital becomes intact. See *Calcutta Stock Exchange Assn* v *Nandy*, ILR 1950 Cal 235.

60. SHADI LAL J (after words, CJ), in *Kanshi Ram* v *Kishore Chand*, AIR 1915 Lah 109. The learned judge added: "It (the power of forfeiture) cannot, for example, be exercised surreptitiously for the purpose of expelling a shareholder, nor by connivance for the purpose of assisting him in getting rid of his shares." *See* also *Esparto Trading Co, Re*, (1879) 12 Ch D 191, where a forfeiture that appeared to have been carried out at the request of a shareholder to

1. In accordance with articles

A forfeiture to be valid must proceed on the grounds specified in the company's articles. It seems to be a principle of English law that shares can be forfeited only for a non-payment of calls.[61] A call which does not fix the time for payment cannot support a valid forfeiture.[62] A forfeiture on any other ground would be an illegal reduction of capital.[63] But the Supreme Court has now held in *Naresh Chandra Sanyal* v *Calcutta Stock Exchange Assn Ltd*[64] that "there is no provision in the Companies Act restricting the exercise of the right to non-payment of calls only".

A stock broker, holding one fully paid share in the Exchange, carried on business on its premises. He had agreed to buy certain shares from a company, but failed to carry out his commitment. The shares were then resold by the company with the authority of the Exchange. The broker was required to pay the difference between the contract and resale prices. On his failure to do so his share was forfeited.

The Supreme Court held the forfeiture to be valid.[65] The Court said:

> [A] company may by its articles lawfully provide for grounds of forfeiture other than non-payment of a call, subject to the qualification that the articles relating to forfeiture do not offend against the general law of the land and in particular the Companies Act, and public policy; that the forfeiture contemplated does not entail or effect a reduction in capital or involve or amount to purchase by the company of its own shares, nor does it amount to trafficking in its own shares.

---

relieve him from liability was set aside. *Abdul Karim* v *Sirpur Paper Mills*, [1969] 1 Comp LJ 144.

61. *See*, for example, *Viswanath Prasad Jallan* v *Holyland Cinetone Ltd*, AIR 1934 All 739: 1939 ALJ 950, where it was held that where certain subscribers had undertaken to purchase a certain number of shares but there was no term in the articles of association by which they were to pay the amount on a particular date, nor was any date fixed by the board of directors, their shares were not liable to forfeiture. Similarly in *Panna Lal* v *Jagatjit D&A Industries*, AIR 1952 Pepsu 47, it was held that where a call for payment is made on the transferee of shares before his name is registered as a member, the call would be invalid and consequently the forfeiture of shares for non-payment of the call money would also be invalid.

62. *Bengal Electric Lamp Works Ltd, Re*, AIR 1942 Cal 516.

63. *See*, for example, *Hopkinson* v *Mortimer Harley & Co Ltd*, [1917] 1 Ch 646, where it was held that a forfeiture for debts due from a member generally as distinct from those due from him as a contributory, would amount to an illegal reduction of capital. This view has been accepted in Palmer's COMPANY LAW, 329 (20th Edn). But Calcutta High Court has held in *Naresh Chandra Sanyal* v *Ramani Kanto Roy*, AIR 1949 Cal 360: 49 CWN 503, that forfeiture is justifiable on any grounds provided for in the company's articles of association. *See also Kotah Transport Co* v *State of Rajasthan*, (1967) 37 Comp Cas 288 Raj, where forfeiture on irrelevant considerations was not allowed.

64. (1971) 1 SCC 50: (1971) 41 Comp Cas 51.

65. For a criticism of this approach *see* K. Ponnuswami, *Forfeiture of Shares*, [1964] 1 Comp LJ 171. For a discussion of the whole of law of forfeiture *see* Srinivasan, *Forfeiture of Shares in Companies*, [1964] 1 Comp LJ 135.

The learned judge then stated that the forfeiture of shares did not result in reduction of capital. The company was under an obligation to dispose of the forfeited share, and could not retain the same. Further, the reissue of a forfeited share was not an allotment, but only a sale, for otherwise the forfeiture, even for non-payment of call, would be invalid as involving an illegal reduction of capital.

Where the buses of a transport company were divided into two groups of shareholders, each group operating them separately, and one of them causing losses, that would not justify forfeiture of their shares.[66]

2.   Notice precedent to forfeiture

A notice under the authority of the Board of directors must be served on the defaulting shareholder.[67] The notice should require him to pay the amount on a day specified which should not be earlier than fourteen days from the date of service. The notice should clearly warn him that in the event of non-payment before the time fixed, the shares would be liable to be forfeited.[68] The notice must also specify the exact amount due from the shareholder. Where, for example, the notice of forfeiture claimed interest from the date of the call instead of the date fixed for its payment, it was held to be a bad notice and the forfeiture invalid.[69] "This seems to be somewhat technical. But in the matter of forfeiture of shares, technicalities must be strictly observed."[70] "A very little inaccuracy is as fatal as the greatest." It has been held by BACHAWAT J in a decision of the Supreme Court,[71] that a notice which does not specify the amount claimed by the company as call money, interest and expenses, is defective. "The defect in the notice, though slight, invalidates it and is fatal to the forfeiture." In a case before the Delhi High Court,[72] shares were forfeited on the basis of a

---

66. *Dilbhajan Singh* v *New Samundri Transport Co (P) Ltd*, (1985) 58 Comp Cas 247 P&H; *K. Md Farooq Ad* v *Portran Cirkit Electronics (P) Ltd*, (1997) 25 Corpt LA 209 CLB, fully paid shares paid, not allowed to be forfeited for the fact that the NRI holder had not obtained RBI approval. Seven years had passed and the allottee had already become a resident.

67. *Sulochana Nathany* v *Hindustan Malleables and Fongings Ltd*, (2002) 110 Comp Cas 874 CLB, notice of forfeiture was not given because the shares were held by a trust and the same should not have been entered in the register of members. The company had been dealing with the trust, issued bonus shares to it and paid dividends. Forfeiture ordered to be cancelled and the name of the trust restored with direction that shares be registered in the names of trustees. *K.B. Modhavan* v *Federal Bank Ltd*, (2007) 135 Comp Cas 235 CLB, notice sent to the NRI's address in India as recorded in India, all other documents were also addressed to the same place, not allowed to say that forfeiture notice should have been sent to his foreign address.

68. *Satish Chandra Sanwalka* v *Tinplate Dealers Assn (P) Ltd*, (2001) 107 Comp Cas 98 CLB, a notice which does not specify that the failure to pay the call would result in the forfeiture being regarded invalid.

69. *Johnson* v *Lyttle's Iron Agency*, (1877) 5 Ch D 687: 36 LT 528.

70. Lord ROMER in *Premila Devi* v *People's Bank of Northern India*, ILR (1939) 20 Lah 1 PC.

71. *Public Passenger Service Ltd* v *Khadar*, [1965] 1 Comp LJ 1: AIR 1966 SC 489: (1966) 36 Comp Cas 1: [1966] 1 MLJ 23.

72. *Promila Bansal* v *Wearwell Cycle Co (India) Ltd*, (1978) 48 Comp Cas 202 Del.

registered acknowledgment due notice which came back as unserved, it was held that the forfeiture was bad, for it was the duty of the company to know whether the address of the member had changed. The fact that forfeited shares had been reallotted to others was held to be no defence and the member was entitled to have her name put back in the register for the same shares which she held before forfeiture. Even laches or delay on the part of the shareholder in protesting against the forfeiture was held to be not sufficient to disentitle her from her remedies.

3. Resolution of forfeiture

The above notice does not by itself operate as a forfeiture. The directors have further to pass a resolution declaring the forfeiture. Thus where the final resolution of forfeiture was not passed the court held[73] that, ''a declared intention to forfeit not carried into effect is no forfeiture at all''.[74] But the notice threatening forfeiture may incorporate the resolution of forfeiture as well. It may state that in the event of default the shares shall be deemed to have been forfeited. In such a case no further resolution is necessary.

4. Good faith

Lastly, ''the object of a power of forfeiture is that the company shall be enabled, for its own benefit, and adversely to the shareholder, to forfeit his shares if he fails to pay his calls. The power cannot be used at the request of the shareholder to relieve him of shares. The power must be exercised in good faith in the interest of the company.''[75]

5. Right and liability after forfeiture

The liability of a member whose shares have been forfeited depends upon the provisions of the articles. The articles may provide that the member should be liable to pay all calls owing upon the shares at the time of the forfeiture. In such a case the members will remain liable as a debtor of the company, but not as a contributory,[76] even if the winding up follows more than one year after the forfeiture. He, however, remains a contributory as a past member for one year from the date of forfeiture.

---

73. *Prayam Prasad* v *Gaya Bank*, AIR 1931 Pat 44. *See also* the case of *Kanshi Ram* v *Kishore Chand*, AIR 1915 Lah 109: 29 IC 567.
74. Lord Lindley on COMPANIES, 738 (6th Edn), "but if everything required to be done is substantially done by the company, and if the shares have been treated both by the company and the shareholder as forfeited, the shareholder will not be a contributory".
75. See *Esparto Trading Co, Re*, (1879) 12 Ch D 191.
76. *Ladies Dress Assn Ltd* v *Pulbrook*, [1900] 2 QB 376 CA. *See* further *Sri Gopal Jalan & Co* v *Calcutta Stock Exchange Assn*, AIR 1964 SC 250: 33 Comp Cas 862; *Calcutta Stock Exchange Assn* v *Nandy*, ILR (1950) Cal 235; *Naresh Chandra Sanyal* v *Ramani Kanto Roy*, AIR 1949 Cal 360: 49 CWN 503.

His right is that when his shares are resold he can collect from the company the surplus of the sale proceeds after deducting the amount due. Thus the Supreme Court in *Naresh Chandra Sanyal* v *Calcutta Stock Exchange Assn Ltd*[77] declared that the articles of the Exchange which allowed it to retain such proceeds were invalid for two reasons: first, it would amount to penalty against the spirit of Section 74 of the Indian Contract Act; secondly, it would also be equivalent to a purchase by the company of its own shares in contravention of Section 77. The case is different from others, for forfeiture is generally carried out for non-payment of calls. Whereas, here, a fully paid share was forfeited. The grounds on which the court ordered refund of surplus may not apply to the case of a forfeiture for non-payment.

A person to whom forfeited shares have been reissued is governed by the terms of reissue. When the reissue is without any stipulation as to the outstanding calls, the new allottee cannot be held liable for the previous calls and interest on the overdue amount and his shares cannot be forfeited on that ground.[78]

Surrender of shares

Every surrender of shares, like forfeiture, amounts to reduction of capital.[79] But, while forfeiture is recognised by the Act, surrender is not. "There is no reference in the Act to surrender of shares; but these have been admitted by the courts, upon the principle, that they have practically the same effect as forfeiture, the main difference being that one is a proceeding *in invitum* and the other a proceeding taken with the assent of the shareholder who is unable to retain and pay future calls on the shares."[80] Hence a company can only accept a surrender under conditions and limitations subject to which shares can be forfeited. A valid call and a default must exist and the directors may, instead of going to the length of forfeiture, in good faith accept a surrender from the shareholder. Surrender should not be used as a device for relieving a shareholder from his liability.[81]

---

77. (1971) 1 SCC 50: (1971) 41 Comp Cas 51.
78. *Satish Chandra Sanwalka* v *Tinplate Dealers Assn (P) Ltd*, (2001) 107 Comp Cas 98 CLB.
79. COZENS-HARDY·J in *Bellerby* v *Rowland & Marwood's Steamship Co*, [1902] 2 Ch 14, 32: [1900-03] All ER Rep Ext 1290.
80. See *Dronfield Silkstone Coal Co, Re*, (1880) 17 Ch D 76.
81. Following cases are illustrations of bad surrender of shares: *Collector of Moradabad* v *Equity Insurance Co*, AIR 1948 Oudh 197. In this case, after the death of a Raja who held several shares in a company, his shares were surrendered to the company and the surrender was accepted by the secretary of the company. It was held that "even if the secretary intended to accept the surrender, the transaction would be *ultra vires*. Under our law it is not open to a shareholder to surrender the shares held by him, or to the company to accept the surrender, unless the act of the company can be brought within the rules relating to forfeiture of shares". Yet another case is *Mangal Sain* v *Indian Merchants Bank, Amritsar*, AIR 1928 Lah 240. The

REGISTER OF MEMBERS [S. 150]

Every company is bound to keep a register of shareholders, which should contain the following particulars: (1) The name and address of each member and his occupation; (2) The number of shares held by each member and the extent to which the shares have been paid up.[82] Each share should be distinguished by its appropriate number; the class of shareholders to which the member belongs should be indicated; (3) The date at which he was entered in the register as a member; and (4) The date at which any person ceased to be a member.[83]

The register may be in the form of a bound book or a computer record. Required particulars should be recorded and adequate precautions should be taken against tampering. Companies with more than fifty members are required to maintain an index of members.[84] The register itself may be kept in the form of an index or a separate card index may be used for the purpose. This is to enable entries relating to a particular member to be readily found. Any change in the register shall be noted on the index within fourteen days.

Register and index of beneficial owners [S. 152-A]

Where shares or debentures are held in the demat form, the register and index of beneficial owners maintained by a depository under S. 11 of the Depositories Act, 1996 is to be deemed as an index and register of members and that of debentureholders, as the case may be.

Foreign register of members [Ss. 157-158]

Where a company has issued shares or debentures to persons resident in another country, the company may, if so authorised by its articles, keep a branch register in that country. It will be known as a "foreign register". The Registrar of the company should be informed within 30 days of the situation of the office where the register is kept. If any change occurs in the situation

---

objector having been placed in the list of contributories in the winding up of a company contended that he had surrendered his shares, and that the directors had, under a clear power in the articles of association, accepted the surrender. It was held that a company can only accept a surrender under conditions and limitations under which shares can be forfeited, which did not exist in the present case. See also *Mirza Ahamad Namazi, Re*, AIR 1924 Mad 703; *Bellerby* v *Rowland & Marwood's Steamship Co*, [1902] 2 Ch 14: [1900-03] All ER Rep Ext 1290. Where old shares are surrendered to get new ones of the same value, that is not a surrender, for it does not involve reduction of capital or of liability. *Rowell* v *John Rowell & Sons Ltd*, [1912] 2 Ch 609: 107 LT 374.

82. This means the amount which has been paid or agreed to be considered as paid. S. 150(1)(*b*).
83. S. 150(2) provides that the "company and every officer of the company who is in default, shall be punishable with fine which may extend to five hundred rupees for every day during which the default continues". Under S. 152 a similar register in respect of the same particulars has to be maintained for the company's debentureholders.
84. S. 151. Company and its officers are punishable for default with a fine extending up to five hundred rupees S. 152(4) for every day of default.

of the register or when the register is discontinued, the Registrar should again be informed within 30 days.

Section 158 supplements the provision by saying that the foreign register shall be a part of the company's home register which shall, in contrast to that, be called the principal register. In respect of closure, copies, extracts, inspection, etc., the foreign register is bound by the same provisions as apply to the principal register. An additional requirement, however, is that an advertisement for closure must also be published in a newspaper circulating in the district where the foreign register is maintained. Entries in the foreign register have to be transmitted to home office and a duplicate register has to be maintained in the home office. Entries in the foreign register should not be reflected in the principal register. But when the foreign register is discontinued, they may be shifted either to some other foreign register or to the principal register. For the rest of the matters, companies can frame their own rules.

Place of keeping, inspection and closure of register [S. 163]

The appropriate place for keeping the register is the registered office of the company.[85] Every member and a debentureholder has the right of inspection without fee but a prescribed fee can be charged from any outsider who wishes to inspect. This is to enable persons dealing with the company to ascertain for themselves the membership of the company. The company may, however, impose reasonable restrictions on the right of inspection, but the register must remain open for at least two business hours each day. The right to inspect also includes the right to make extracts from the register. The company is also bound to supply on demand a copy of the register.[86] Thus in *British India Corporation Ltd* v *Robert Menzies*:[87]

> A member applied for a copy of the register of members. The company received from him a fee of five hundred rupees, but put him off under pretexts of many kinds. On his application to the High Court, the latter ordered the company to supply a copy immediately. The court said: "It is a fundamental principle of legal administration that where the law requires something to be done there must be in existence a court that can directly order it to be done."

---

85. The register may, of course, be kept at any other place within the same city, town or village in which the registered office is situate, provided a special resolution is passed to that effect and a copy of which has been given in advance to the Registrar and advertised for three consecutive days in a local daily. (S. 163).

86. S. 163(3)(*b*) gives this right on the payment of a prescribed amount for every one hundred words or fractional parts thereof required to be copied. For right of debentureholders, *see Narotamdas T. Toprani* v *Bombay Dyeing & Mfg Co Ltd*, [1986] 3 Comp LJ 179 Bom.

87. AIR 1936 All 568: 1936 ALJ 748: 164 IC 387.

Now sub-section (6) of Section 163 has, in very clear words, given power to the Central Government to order the company to allow inspection and to give copies forthwith. The provision says that the Central Government may compel an immediate inspection of the document or supply of extracts.[88]

Where shares are in dematerialised form and the register of members is also in the magnetic form, only the stock holding corporation is shown as a member and not the individual beneficial holders of those shares. Such beneficial holders are not entitled to get a copy of the register. Their names are not there in the register at all.[89]

A company can close the register for 45 days in a year, but not for more than 30 days at any one time. [S. 154] Seven days before the register is closed a notice must be published in a local daily.[90]

Register, prima facie evidence [S. 164]

The register of members is a *prima facie* evidence of the truth of its contents.[91] The contents of the register of members are of decisive importance in determining as to who were the shareholders of the company at the crucial time.[92] Accordingly, if a person's name, to his knowledge, is there in the register, he shall be deemed to be a member and onus lies on him to show that he is not a member.[93] Moreover, he must quickly apply to the court to take his name off the register, failing which the doctrine of holding out comes into play. For example, in *M. F. R. D.'Cruz, Re*:[94]

The plaintiff had applied for 4000 shares in a company. No allotment was, however, made. But, without his application, 4000 shares were transferred to him and his name placed in the register. The plaintiff, knowing that his name was in the register, took no steps to have it rectified. The company collapsed and it was held that his name was rightly placed in the list of contributories. The court said: "When a person knows that his name is included in the register of shareholders and stands by and allows his name to remain, he is holding out to the

88. *Nutech Agro Ltd* v *Ch Mohan Rao*, (2002) 111 Comp Cas 75 AP, a complaint under the section was entertained for the company's failure to comply with the requirements even after the complainant had satisfied all the requirements for getting copies.
89. *HB Stockholdings Ltd* v *Jaiprakash Industries Ltd*, (2003) 116 Comp Cas 29 CLB.
90. The word newspaper must be taken in its popular sense. Consequently, the Daily Official List of Stock Exchange is not a newspaper. *Talayar Tea Co* v *UOI*, [1990] 1 Comp LJ 360 Mad: (1991) 71 Comp Cas 95.
91. S. 164. This presumption, however, applies only to those contents which are required by the Act to be inserted therein.
92. *Ashish Das Gupta* v *Satvinder Singh*, (2000) 37 CLA 104 CLB.
93. *See*, for example, *Amar Singh* v *Khalsa Bank Ltd*, AIR 1933 Lah 108; *Waryam Singh* v *Official Liquidator of Eastern Commercial & Banking Co Ltd*, AIR 1926 Lah 414; *Peninsular Life Assurance Co Ltd, Re*, AIR 1936 Bom 24; *Hans Raj Gupta* v *Asthana*, AIR 1932 PC 240.
94. AIR 1939 Mad 803: (1939) 2 MLJ 122.

public that he is shareholder and thereby he loses his right to have his name removed."[95]

NO NOTICE OF TRUST [S. 153]

Sometimes shares of which *A* is the real owner may be had by him registered in the name of *B*. *A* is the beneficial owner and *B* is the trustee. In other words, *B* holds the shares in trust for *A*. Now, as the company's register of members will only show the name of *B*, therefore, for all purposes of company law, *B* alone is the member entitled to the rights and bound by the liability of membership. The company is not bound to recognise the existence of the trust, for, Section 153 declares in so many words that "no notice of any trust, express, implied or constructive, shall be entered on the register of members". A case from the Calcutta High Court provides a suitable illustration:[96]

S, a lady, was the registered holder of certain shares in a company. The company, on learning that the shares really belonged to her husband, sued him for the unpaid calls on the shares. Holding that the husband was not liable, although he was the real owner, the court said: "Assuming that the registered shareholder is not the real owner but if he is the member in the books of the company, it is he alone who would be entitled to the rights of a shareholder and he alone is liable for share calls and to be put on the list of contributories."

But it is the beneficiary who is ultimately liable for the calls. He has to indemnify the trustee against calls and perhaps the company may directly sue him in the rights of the beneficiary.[97]

The company may, however, take notice of a trust for its own benefit without entering it in the register. In a Madras case:[98]

A managing director's wife, having quarrelled with her husband and to teach him a lesson, brought an action for winding up. All the shares held by her were financed by her husband.

---

95. There are many cases of this nature where a person had the right to have his name removed, but did not in time insist on it and, therefore suffered. *See* for example, *Peninsular Life Assurance Co Ltd, Re*, AIR 1936 Bom 24; *Mohd Akbar Abdulla Fazalbhoy* v *Official Liquidator*, AIR 1950 Bom 217: (1950) 20 Comp Cas 26; *Hans Raj Gupta* v *Asthana*, AIR 1932 PC 240; *Simpson* v *Molson's Bank*, 1895 AC 270, the company was not bound to take notice of the restrictions on transfer in a will under which shares were registered in the name of the present holder and a copy of the will was there with the company.

96. *Murshidabad Loan Office Ltd* v *Satish Chandra Chakarvarty*, AIR 1943 Cal 440: 209 IC 317.

97. *Hardoon* v *Belilios*, 1901 AC 118: 83 LT 573.

98. *S. Parameswari* v *K. M. R. Mills Ltd*, AIR 1971 Mad 293. Shares purchased by a firm of two partners were registered in the name of a minor. The liquidator of the company was not allowed to have the name of the minor substituted with those of the partners. The person on the register was liable whatever be his worth. *National Bank of Wales Ltd, Re*, (1907) 1 CR 582.

The court held that the company could take notice of this fact and present it to the court for the purpose of showing that her petition was not *bona fide* and was brought to exert pressure upon the managing director for settlement of the family dispute.

The articles of a company contained a clause that not more than a given percentage of shares were to be held by non-Bermudians. It was held that this clause was to apply only to registered shareholders and not to the beneficial owners of the shares. The registered holder was a Bermudian company. The provision was accordingly not violated whatever be the characteristic of shareholding in that member company.[1]

Certain bonds were purchased by a mutual fund. They were not allowed to be registered in the name of the trustee of the fund as S. 153 prohibits registration of any relationship of trustee and beneficiary in the register.[2] A shareholder executed a will before his death bequeathing the shares to his bank and constituting it as a trustee of the holding. It was held that S. 153 was not an obstruction to registering the trustee as a shareholder of the company.[3]

Public trustee [Ss. 153-A, 153-B and 187-B]

The provisions of these sections have been deleted by the Amendment Act of 2000. The Amendment says that nothing contained in this section (in all the three sections) shall apply on or after the commencement of the amendment, i.e. Jan 14, 2001.

Declaration of beneficial interest [S. 187-C]

This section and Section 187-B have been deleted by the Companies (Amendment) Act, 2000. The new provision in Section 187-B says that the provisions of this section shall not apply on and after the commencement of the amendment, i.e. Jan 14, 2001. The new provision under Section 187-C says that the provisions of the section shall not apply to the trustee referred to in Section 187-B.

LIEN ON SHARES

"It is eminently fair for a company to provide by its articles, that the shareholders who are indebted to the company should not be permitted to dispose of their shares without paying their debts and that the company should have a lien on the shares for the debts."[4] Lien is the right to retain

---

1. *Bermuda Cablevisions Ltd* v *Calico Trust Co Ltd*, [1998] 2 WLR 82.
2. *Canara Bank* v *NTPC*, (2001) 104 Comp Cas 97 SC.
3. *State Bank of India* v *Business Development Consultants (P) Ltd*, (2005) 128 Comp Cas 557 CLB.
4. *Allen* v *Gold Reefs of West Africa*, [1900] 1 Ch 656 at p 678: [1900-03] All ER Rep 746.

some property for some debt and in the case of a company, lien on a share ultimately means that the member would not be permitted to transfer his shares unless he pays his debt to the company. The right of lien is not inherent, but must be clearly provided for in the articles. It is safer to adopt clauses 9 to 12 of Table A, which provide for this right.[5] The effect of lien on shares may be illustrated with the case of *Amar Nath* v *Karnal Electric Supply Co.*[6]

A company had by its articles the first and paramount lien on the shares of each member for his debts to the company. The company was in liquidation and the plaintiff was a contributory. The liquidator was ordered by the Court to pay back half the value of each share to contributories, but he had not paid this amount to the plaintiff who brought an action to recover it. The liquidator contended that the company had a claim against him for which proceedings under Section 235, 1913 Act were pending and that he was withholding the payment in the exercise of the right of lien. He was held entitled to do so until the company's claim was settled. The mere fact that the claim was disputed could not suspend the lien for otherwise "any shareholder has only to dispute the liability and thereby to defeat the lien".

Postponement and loss of lien

A company's lien will, however, be postponed if the shareholder has mortgaged or pledged his shares before he has incurred any debt to the company and the company has notice of it. Thus where certain shares which were subject to a "first and paramount lien" were given to a bank as security for an overdraft and the bank had given notice to the company, it was held that the bank had priority over the company's claim which arose subsequently.[7] Notice obtained by the directors in the course of business will definitely amount to notice to the company. But if a director knows about the mortgage in his private capacity, will that operate as a notice to the company? The High Court of Allahabad has held that it would. The case is *U.I. Sugar Mills Co Ltd, Re.*[8]

The liquidator of a company had a surplus and he proposed to divide it among the shareholders. The company had lien on shares. The managing director was indebted to the company for a large sum of money but he had mortgaged his shares before the commencement

---

5. Lien is governed strictly by the provisions of the Companies Act and the company's articles and not by those of the Contract Act relating to pledge of goods. *Khadija* v *P. K. Mohd (P) Ltd*, (1985) 58 Comp Cas 543.
6. AIR 1952 Punj 411.
7. *Bradford Banking Co* v *Briggs, Son & Co*, (1886) 12 App Cas 29: 56 LT 62.
8. AIR 1933 All 607: 1933 ALJ 1322: 146 IC 801.

of winding up. Neither he nor the mortgagee had given notice to the company. As against the managing director the company was clearly entitled to exercise its lien on the amount payable to him. But the mortgagee claimed the amount on the ground that as the managing director had himself pledged the shares, his knowledge amounted to notice to the company. The court upheld this contention and said: "The company shall be deemed to have knowledge of such transaction when the managing director who has all powers of the board has himself pledged his shares, although in his private capacity."

The decision amounts to this that knowledge obtained by a managing director in the course of a private transaction of his own amounts to notice to the company. The only case cited as an authority in support of this view is *Rainford* v *James Keith & Blackman Co Ltd*,[9] but in this case the facts were entirely different. A shareholder who was also a servant of the company had informed the directors that his shares were with someone else from which, the court said, the directors should have inferred that they must have been pledged. Even according to the ordinary principles of the law of agency notice to an agent is not deemed to be notice to the principal if the agent fraudulently withholds it from his principal.[10]

Where the holder of shares is a trustee, the company's lien will prevail over the claim of the beneficiary unless he has given notice to the company before any occasion arose for enforcing the lien.[11] A company's claim against the beneficial owner of shares cannot entitle the company to exercise the right of lien against the trustee-holder of those shares.[12] Where the right to exercise the lien has arisen and the shareholder transfers a part of his shares, the transferee can insist that the company should satisfy its claim to the extent possible from the shares remaining in the hands of the shareholder.[13] Lien remains effective even after the death of the shareholder and can be exercised against his executors.[14]

Sale of shares under lien

In order to realise the money due to it the company may take the power to sell the shares held under lien. The transferee of such shares will get a

---

9. [1905] 2 Ch 147.
10. S. 229, Indian Contract Act, 1872, Avtar Singh, LAW OF CONTRACT.
11. *New London & Brazilian Bank* v *Brockle Bank*, (1882) 21 Ch D 302; *Mackereth* v *Wigan Coal Co*, [1916] 2 Ch 293.
12. *Perkins, Re*, (1890) 24 QBD 613 CA.
13. *Gray* v *Stone*, (1893) 69 LT 282.
14. *Allen* v *Gold Reefs of West Africa*, [1900] 1 Ch 656: [1900-03] All ER Rep 746.

good title even if there has been some irregularity in the procedure of transfer as it will be covered by the principle of indoor management.[15]

The present position of a listed public company being that it can no longer reject a transfer on any ground whatsoever, its lien may also become defeated under the doctrine of absolutely free transferability. In this case, the shares held by the managing director were transferred by his legal heirs after his death. The company was directed to accept the transfer and also to pay the amount of dividend which it had withheld under its lien for claims against the managing director.[16]

Time-barred debt

Lien on shares may be exercised even for a time-barred debt, provided that it can be done without resort to a court of law.[17]

ANNUAL RETURNS [Ss. 159-161]

Every company has to file with the Registrar an annual return containing certain particulars. This is to enable the Registrar to record the changes that have occurred in the constitution of the company during the year. Separate kinds of returns are required from companies, those with share capital and those having no share capital. The return of a company having share capital has to contain the particulars specified in Part I of Schedule V regarding—

(a) its registered office,

(b) its register of members,

(c) the register of its debentureholders,

(d) its shares and debentures,

(e) its indebtedness,

(f) its members and debentureholders, past and present, and

(g) its directors, managing directors, managers and secretaries, past and present.

The return of a company having no share capital has to state the following particulars: [S. 160(1)]

(a) the address of the registered office of the company;

(b) the names of members and the respective dates on which they became members and the names of persons who ceased to be members since the date of the annual general meeting of the

15. *Unity Co (P) Ltd v Diamond Sugar Mills*, [1970] 2 Comp LJ 64 Cal.
16. *Ferrom Electronics (P) Ltd v Vijaya Leasing Ltd*, (2000) 36 CLA 327 Kant.
17. *Ferrom Electronics (P) Ltd v Vijaya Leasing Ltd*, (2000) 36 CLA 327 Kant.

immediately preceding year, and the dates on which they so ceased;

(*c*) all such particulars with respect to the persons who, at the date of the return, were the directors of the company, its manager and its secretary as are set out in Section 303;

(*d*) a statement containing the particulars of the total amount of the indebtedness of the company in respect of all charges which are or were required to be registered with the Registrar under the Act. [S. 160(2)]

Where any of the five preceding returns has given the particulars, then the return may only give such of the particulars as relate to persons ceasing to be or becoming members or shares transferred or changes in the holding of a particular member.

The return has to be filed within sixty days from the date of the annual general meeting.[18] It must be signed both by a director and by the manager or secretary of the company, if any, otherwise, by two directors of the company, one of whom shall be the managing director where there is one. [S. 161(1)] The return of a company whose shares are quoted at a stock exchange must also be signed by a secretary in wholetime practice.[19] The return must accompany a certificate signed likewise stating that the return states the facts as they stood on the day of the annual general meeting and that since the date of the last annual return the transfer of all shares and debentures and the issue of all further certificates of shares and debentures have been appropriately recorded in the books maintained for the purpose.[S. 161(2)] In the case of a private company, the certificate must further state that the company has not during the year issued any invitation to the public to subscribe for shares or debentures of the company[20] or for deposits and that its annual turnover has not crossed the prescribed limit.

Although sixty days are reckoned from the date of the annual meeting, it has been held by the Supreme Court in *State of Bombay* v *Bandhan Ram Bhandani*[21] that the obligation to file returns is not excused by any default in calling the meeting, for they can be prepared independently of the annual meeting.[22] The penalty is imposed upon "every officer in default", which

---

18. S. 159(1).
19. A secretary can sign the returns of up to 30 companies. Notification ICSI No 2 of Aug 2, 1989; 1989 Chartered Secy 701.
20. S. 161(2) and (6). *See also* S. 162 which contains provisions about penalty and interpretation.
21. AIR 1961 SC 186: (1961) 1 SCR 801: (1961) 31 Comp Cas 1.
22. Reaffirmed in *State of H.P.* v *Andhra Provincial Potteries Ltd*, (1973) 2 SCC 786: (1973) 43 Comp Cas 514.

according to Section 5 means a person who is knowingly guilty of the default or who knowingly or wilfully permits or authorises such default. Kerala High Court did not allow this penalty to be imposed upon an officer merely on the ground that he should have known that no return was filed from the fact that he did not sign any. It could as well have been signed by others.[23]

Nature of offence, whether continuing

There is a conflict of views between the High Courts as to whether offences punishable under this Section are of a continuing nature. Failure to file the annual return has been held not to be a continuing offence in some cases. The opposite view has been taken in this case.[24]

Evidentiary value

Where the holding of a given percentage of shares is a requisite qualification for exercising certain rights under the Companies Act, entries in the annual returns can serve as evidence for the purpose.[25] The annual return has been held to be not a conclusive evidence of membership. It serves only as a *prima facie* evidence. Its contents can be overthrown by evidence to the contrary.[26]

---

23. *V. M. Thomas* v *ROC*, (1980) 50 Comp Cas 247 Ker. The Calcutta High Court has held that the default is a single offence and not a continuing offence. Prosecution must be commenced within six months from the date of default otherwise it becomes time-barred. *Nripendra Kumar Ghosh* v *ROC*, (1985) 58 Comp Cas 672 Cal, overruling its earlier decision in *Ajit Kumar Sarkar* v *Asstt ROC*, (1979) 49 Comp Cas 909: 83 Cal WN 108 and following *National Cotton Mills* v *Asstt ROC*, (1983) Cal HN 180: (1984) 56 Comp Cas 222. The plea of time-bar should be raised at the trial stage. *Sanjeev Kumar Gupta* v *ROC*, [1990] 2 Comp LJ 70 Del; Members and debenture-holders are entitled to free inspection and Re 1 for 100 words copy; others, Rs 10. Rule 21-A of the Companies (Central Govt's) Rules and Forms, 1956. A director who was not connected with the default, not allowed to be prosecuted, *Registrar of Companies* v *Bipin Bihari Nayak*, (1996) 86 Comp Cas 641 Ori; prosecution quashed where the director in question had ceased to be so on the due date of the return, *Jayesh R. Mor* v *State of Gujarat*, [2000] CLC 486 Guj; *K. Setha Lakshmi* v *ROC*, (2001) 103 Comp Cas 532 Mad, on the demise of the accused director his wife was allowed to be impleaded because she was also a director in her right and was also in a position of being in charge.
24. *Asstt Registrar of Companies* v *Premier Synthetics (P) Ltd*, (1997) 89 Comp Cas 732: (1997) 26 CLA 269 Mad. One serious implication of a continuing offence is that the provisions of Sections 467 to 473 of CrPC relating to periods of limitation for starting proceedings do not apply. S. 472 of the Code says that in the case of continuing offence, a fresh period of limitation begins to run at every moment of the time during which the offence continues. *Pravin Jha* v *State of A.P.*, (2001) 106 Comp Cas 554 All, not a continuing offence, cognizance has to be taken within 6 months from the date of the offence, S. 468, CrPC.
25. *Rashmi Seth* v *Chemon India (P) Ltd*, [1992] 3 Comp LJ 89 CLB: (1995) 82 Comp Cas 563, the petition here was for prevention of oppression and mismanagement.
26. *Chotoo Sud* v *Bhagwan Finance Corpn (P) Ltd*, (2006) 130 Comp Cas 567 CLB.

9

Share Capital

Share capital is not a necessary condition of incorporation, although greater number of companies are registered with it than without it. In case share capital is thought necessary, the memorandum must state the amount of capital with which the company is desired to be registered and the number of shares into which it is to be divided.[1] The meaning of "share capital" was explained by the Kerala High Court in *S. N. D. P. Yogam, Quilon, Re:*[2]

> An application was presented under Section 397 against "Yogam" and the question was whether the company was with or without share capital. According to the memorandum the liability of the members was limited; each member was required to take at least one share, but no authorised capital was mentioned.

The court quoted from Buckley on THE COMPANIES ACTS and from Palmer's COMPANY LAW to find support for the proposition that the words "capital" and "share capital" are synonymous. For a company to have share capital it is necessary that its memorandum should state the amount and its division. Thus share capital is different from membership fee, even if the payment is symbolised by the issue of a share.

The amount stated in the memorandum becomes the *authorised capital* of the company. The whole or any part of it may be issued. Supposing that only half of it is issued, then that is the *issued capital* of the company. If the offer of issue is made to the public the whole of it may not be taken up. That part of the issued capital which has been allotted is the *subscribed capital*. The company need not immediately call up the whole amount. The actual amount received is the *paid-up capital.*

The uncalled capital of a company can be converted into *reserve capital*. By passing a special resolution the company may declare that a portion or whole of its uncalled capital shall not be called except in the event of the company's winding up.[3] Such a capital cannot be called except in winding up; it cannot be converted except with the leave of the court; it cannot be charged by the directors. Thus, where a company issued debentures charging its undertaking including the uncalled capital, it was held that the charge was not operative on the reserve capital.[4]

---

1. S. 13(4). Section 82 says that the share or other interest of a member in the company shall be movable property transferable in the manner provided in the company's articles.
2. (1970) 40 Comp Cas 60: ILR 1969 Ker 516: [1970] 1 Comp LJ 85.
3. S. 98 gives the power to an unlimited company on getting itself registered as a limited company to increase the nominal amount of its share capital by increasing the nominal value of shares provided that the increased amount shall not be called up except for the purposes of winding up. The company can provide that a specified portion of its uncalled capital shall not be capable of being called up except on winding up.
4. *Mayfair Property Ltd, Re*, [1898] 2 Ch 28: [1895-99] All ER Rep 738.

KINDS OF SHARE CAPITAL

Capital must be divided into shares of a fixed amount. All the shares may be of only one class or may be divided into two different classes of securities. For this purpose securities means securities defined in Section 2(*h*) of the Securities Contracts (Regulation) Act, 1956 and includes "hybrids".[5] The Act permitted only two kinds of shares to be issued, namely:[6]

1. Equity share capital, that is, ordinary shares, and

2. Preference shares, which constitute the preference share capital.

Ordinary share capital or 'equity share capital' is defined in the Act as meaning all share capital which is not preference share capital.[S. 85(2)]

The Companies (Amendment) Act, 2000, has substituted Section 86 with new provisions which are that the share capital of a company limited by shares shall be of two kinds only, namely: (*a*) equity share capital (*i*) with voting rights; or (*ii*) with differential rights as to dividend, voting or otherwise in accordance with such rules and subject to such conditions as may be prescribed. (*b*) preference share capital.

The Companies (Amendment) Act, 2000 introduced some other categories of shares:

Derivative

Which has been given the same meaning as in Section 2 of the Securities Contracts (Regulation) Act, 1956.

Hybrid

As defined in Section 2(19-A), it means any security which has the characteristics of more than one type of security, including their derivatives.

Preference share capital [S. 85]

Preference share capital means that part of the share capital of a company which fulfils both the following requirements:[7]

1. During the continuance of the company it must be assured of a preferential dividend. The preferential dividend may consist of a fixed amount (say fifty thousand rupees in one year) payable to preference shareholders before anything is paid to the ordinary shareholders, or the amount payable as preferential dividend may be calculated at a fixed rate, for example, 5 per cent of the nominal value of each share.

---

5. S. 2(45-AA) introduced by the Amendment Act, 2000 (w.e.f. 14-1-2001).
6. S. 86. Each share shall be distinguished by its appropriate number. S. 83. Private companies are exempted and, therefore, they enjoy the freedom of having any other kinds also.
7. *Id.*, sub-section (1). It is not necessary to give any priority to the amount of dividend remaining unpaid up to the commencement of winding up or to any fixed premium or premium on any fixed scale specified in the memorandum or articles of the company. [S. 85(1)(*b*)(*i*) and (*ii*)]

2. On the winding up of the company it must carry a preferential right to be paid, that is, the amount paid up on preference shares must be paid back before anything is paid to the ordinary shareholders. This preference, unless there is an agreement to the contrary, exists only up to amount paid up or deemed to have been paid up on the shares.

Cumulative and non-cumulative preference shares

Preference shares may be either *cumulative* or *non-cumulative*. If there are no profits in one year and the arrears of dividends are to be carried forward and paid out of the profits of subsequent years, the preference shares are said to be cumulative. But if unpaid dividend lapses, the shares are said to be non-cumulative preference shares. Whether they are of one class or the other will depend upon the terms of issue and provisions in the company's articles. But, in the absence of any clear provision to the contrary, preference shares are presumed to be cumulative. *Foster* v *Coles, Foster & Sons Ltd*[8] is an authority:

A company whose memorandum and articles provided for preference shares carrying a "cumulative preferential dividend" was reconstructed and clause 95 of the articles was altered by striking out the word "cumulative" before "preference" so as to read thus: "The net profits from time to time available for distribution as dividend shall be applied first in payment to holders of preference shares of a preference dividend." Even so it was held that the holders of preference shares were entitled to a cumulative preferential dividend. The word "cumulative" was dropped obviously with the intention of converting the preference shares into non-cumulative shares. But unless there was a clear provision in the articles to that effect they were presumed to be cumulative preference shares.

Thus preference shares are always presumed to be cumulative and the accumulation of dividend can be excluded only by a clear provision in the articles of association. As, for example, in *Staples* v *Eastman Photographic Materials Co*:[9]

The provision in the articles of association of a company was like this: "The holders of preference shares shall be entitled out of the net profits of each year to a preference dividend at the rate of 10 per cent per annum." It was held that according to this provision, preference shareholders were not entitled to a cumulative dividend of 10 per cent so as to have the deficiency in one year paid out of the profits of a subsequent year. The provision meant that the profits of each year only were to be paid in that way.

---

8. (1906) 22 TLR 555.
9. [1896] 2 Ch 303. *See* also *Webb* v *Earle*, (1875) LR 20 Eq 556: 44 LJ Ch 608.

Preference shareholders cannot compel the directors to pay dividends, whatever be the amount of accumulation.[10]

Participating preference shares

There is yet another problem concerning preference shares. After the fixed amount of dividend has been paid to the preference shareholders and some amount has by way of dividend been paid to the ordinary shareholders, there may be surplus profits which are proposed to be distributed among the shareholders. The question is whether the preference shareholders are also entitled to take part in the distribution of the surplus. Again, in the winding up of a company, if, after paying back both the preference and ordinary shareholders, there is a surplus, the question will be whether preference shareholders are also entitled to a share in the distribution of the surplus. If they are so entitled they will be known as *participating preference shares*. [S. 185(1) Explanation]

The general principle is that preference shares are presumed to be not participating. The holders of such shares are not entitled to any share in the distribution of any such surplus, unless there is a clear provision in the memorandum, or the terms of issue or the articles conferring upon them the right of participation. This appears from a consideration of the authorities. Reference may be made here to one of them, namely, *Will v United Lanket Plantations Co Ltd*:[11]

> Preference shareholders were entitled to a cumulative preference dividend at the rate of 10 per cent per annum and, it was further provided in the company's articles, that such preference shares ranked both as regards capital and dividend in priority to other shares. It was held that preference shareholders were not entitled in the distribution of the profits to anything more than 10 per cent dividend.

Accordingly, to find out the rights of a special class of shareholders we must look within the four corners of the articles of association of the company and the terms of the issue. If the right to participate in the surplus is not specified in the terms of the issue, preference shares are presumed to be not participating. This was affirmed by the House of Lords in *Scottish Insurance Corpn v Wilsons & Clyde Coal Co*:[12]

> A company intended to go into voluntary liquidation. Meanwhile it proposed to reduce its capital by returning their capital to the holders of the preference stock. Under the articles of the company, in the event of winding up, preference stock ranked before the ordinary to the extent of

---

10. *Buenos Aires Great Southern Rly Co v Preston*, [1947] Ch 384: [1947] 1 All ER 729.
11. [1912] 2 Ch 571: 1914 AC 11: 107 LT 360.
12. 1949 AC 462.

the amount paid thereon. The reduction of capital was opposed by certain preference stockholders on the ground that it deprived them of the right to participate in the liquidation and the division of the company's surplus assets. Thus the question was whether the preference stockholders would be entitled in winding up to a share in the surplus assets or, in other words, to receive more than a return of their paid up capital.

Lord SIMONDS said:

"It is clear from the authorities that subject to any relevant provisions of the general law, the rights *inter se* of the preference and ordinary shareholders must depend on the terms of the instrument which contains the bargain that they have made with the company and each other."

It means that their right to participate in the surplus depends upon the terms of the contract they have made with the company and there is no presumption that they have the right to participate unless it is excluded by the articles. There was nothing in the articles giving them the right to receive anything beyond the amount paid on their shares.

Then again the mere fact that under a company's articles preference shareholders are entitled to participate with the ordinary shareholders in the surplus profits does not entitle them in the company's winding up to participate in the surplus assets also. This was the position taken in *Isle of Thanet Electricity Supply Co, Re*:[13]

A clause in the articles of association of a company defined the rights of shareholders as follows: "The issued preference shares shall confer on the holders the right to a fixed cumulative dividend at the rate of 6 per cent per annum in priority to the ordinary shares and the right to participate *pari passu* with the ordinary shares in the surplus profits which in respect of any year it shall be determined to distribute.... and the preference shares shall confer the right in a winding up of the company to repayment of capital, together with arrears, if any." The company went into voluntary liquidation. Certain arrears of dividend on the preference stock were paid and the capital on both the preference and ordinary stock was repaid. As regards the surplus, it was held that the onus lay on the preference stockholders to show that they were entitled to participate therein; the above provision in the articles must be taken as being exhaustive in defining their rights and, therefore, the onus had not been discharged.[14]

---

13. [1949] 2 All ER 1060: [1950] Ch 161; *W. Foster & Sons Ltd, Re*, [1942] 1 All ER 314.
14. For other cases see *Chatterley-Whitfield Collieries Ltd, Re*, [1948] 2 All ER 593 CA and *Prudential Assurance Co Ltd v Chatterley etc.*, 1949 AC 512: [1949] 1 All ER 1094.

Issue and redemption of preference shares [S. 80]

A company has the power under Section 80 to issue what are known as redeemable preference shares. There must, however be an authority to issue such shares in the articles of the company. The option of redemption lies with the company, that is to say, the company may choose to pay back the holders of such shares. Paying back is called redemption. There are following restrictions in regard to the fund out of which shares can be redeemed. [S. 80(1) Proviso]

Firstly, the shares to be redeemed must be fully paid.

Secondly, shares shall be redeemed only out of profits of the company which would otherwise be available for dividends. The only other method allowed by the Act is to make a fresh issue of shares and utilise the proceeds to carry out the redemption. Again, if any premium is payable on redemption, the amount must have been provided for out of the profits of the company or out of the company's Securities[15] Premium Account.

Lastly, where redemption is made out of profits, a sum equivalent to the amount paid on redemption shall be transferred to a reserve fund to be called, *Capital Redemption Reserve Account*. This amount is to be preserved with the same sanctity as the company's share capital and can be reduced only in the like manner.[16] Redemption of preference shares is not taken as reduction of the company's authorised share capital.[17] The company may issue new shares up to the nominal amount of the shares redeemed and the capital shall not be deemed to have been increased.

The capital redemption reserve account may be applied in paying up un-issued shares of the company to be issued to the members as fully paid bonus shares.[18]

Irredeemable Preference Shares

The amendment of 1988 abolished the category of irredeemable preference shares. Sub-section (5-A), inserted by the amendment, says that no company limited by shares shall issue any preference share which is irredeemable or is redeemable after the expiry of a period of 10 [now 20 years, amendment of 1996] from the date of issue.[19]

---

15. *Substituted* for "shares" by the Companies (Amendment) Act, 1999, w.e.f. from Oct. 31, 1999.
16. S. 80(1)(*d*).
17. S. 80(3).
18. S. 80(5). *See also* sub-section (6) which contains penalty provisions.
19. A new section, S. 80-A, was inserted to provide about the redemption of existing irredeemable preference shares. They had to be redeemed within 5 years from the effective date of the amendment. Shares which were redeemable within ten years had to be redeemed as they fell due, but the period should not be more than ten [now 20 years, amendment of 1996]. If a company was not able to do so, it had to make a petition to the Company Law Board. The Board could permit their renewal under a ten-year scheme and then they were deemed to have been redeemed. A company which did not carry out a redemption as required by the new

Ordinary shares compared with preference shares

Preference shares, particularly redeemable preference shares, are more like debentures than like shares. They are entitled to a fixed rate of dividend even as debentures earn a fixed rate of interest. The company may choose to pay them back,[20] but ordinary shareholders cannot be paid back except under a scheme involving reduction of capital. [S. 100]

Secondly, an ordinary shareholder is entitled to vote on all matters affecting the company. But the right of a preference shareholder to vote is restricted to resolutions which directly affect the rights attached to his preference shares, except when dividend has remained unpaid in which case he may vote on any resolution in respect of preference share capital.[21]

Thirdly, preference shares offer a profitable and safe source of investment. While the fixed rate of income is guaranteed, the risk involved is much less as compared to the risk undertaken by an ordinary shareholder.

Alteration of capital [S. 94]

A limited company with a share capital can alter the capital clause of its memorandum of association in any of the following ways, provided authority to alter is given by the articles:[22]

(*a*) It may increase its capital by issuing new shares.[23]

(*b*) Consolidate the whole or any part of its share capital into shares of larger amount.

(*c*) Convert shares into stock or *vice versa.*

---

provision is restrained from paying dividends up to the time of implementation. In quite a few cases the Company Law Board permitted renewal alongwith accumulated dividend amount. See *Kalyanpur Cements Ltd, Re,* [1993] 3 Comp LJ 109 CLB Cal; *British India Corpn Ltd, Re,* [1993] 3 Comp LJ 445 CLB; *Mangalore Chemicals Ltd, Re,* [1994] 1 Comp LJ 306 CLB: (1994) 79 Comp Cas 551; *Calendonian Jute & Industries Ltd, Re,* (1995) 18 Corpt LA 44: (1996) 85 Comp Cas 180, allotment of new shares to carry arrears of dividend whether due, declared or not. *Auckland Holdings Ltd, Re,* (1995) 17 Corpt LA 154 CLB, the Board did not permit postponement of redemption on grounds like difficulty of liquidity, particularly in view of the fact that the company had reserves and also current profits to meet the costs of redemption. *Rishi Gases (P) Ltd, Re,* (1995) 83 Comp Cas 589 CLB, arrears of dividend, whether declared or not, ordered to be included in the value of the shares to be issued in lieu of redemption. *Jessop & Co Ltd, Re,* (2000) 27 SCL 82 CLB, the CLB did not have the power to extend the period for redemption. *Raja Ram Corn Products (Punjab) Ltd v CLB,* (2003) 113 Comp Cas 33 P&H, the CLB could prescribe the rate of dividend to be attached to new shares.

20. S. 80. This, however, does not mean that the holder of redeemable preference shares can treat himself like a creditor if his shares are not redeemed in time on maturity and take the liberty of filing a creditor's petition for an order of winding up. *Lalchand Surana* v *Hyderabad Vanspati Ltd,* (1990) 69 Comp Cas 415 AP.

21. S. 87(2) (Explanation) and clause (*b*).

22. S. 94(1). Cancellation of shares under clause (*e*) does not amount to reduction of capital for the purposes of the Act [S. 94(3)]. Section 96 provides that where a company having a share capital has converted any shares into stock and notified the Registrar, the provisions of the Act relating to shares shall cease to apply.

23. *Nupur Mitra* v *Basubani (P) Ltd,* (2002) 108 Comp Cas 359 CLB, increase of capital beyond the authorised limit set in the memorandum is *ultra vires.* The capital clause of the memorandum would have to be altered for that purpose.

(*d*) Sub-divide the whole or any part of its share capital into shares of smaller amount.

(*e*) Cancel those shares which have not been taken up and reduce its capital accordingly.

Any of the above things can be done by the company by passing a resolution at a general meeting, but do not require to be confirmed by the National Company Law Tribunal.[24] Within thirty days of alteration notice must be given to the Registrar who will record the same and make necessary alteration in the company's memorandum and articles.[25] Notice to the Registrar has similarly to be given when redeemable preference shares have been redeemed.[26] Similar information is also required to be sent where the capital has been increased beyond the authorised limit, or where a company, being not limited by shares, has increased the number of its members.[27]

REDUCTION OF CAPITAL

A reduction of capital is unlawful except when sanctioned by the court.[28] "Conservation of capital is one of the main principles of company law." The share capital of a company is the only security on which the creditors rely. Any reduction of capital, therefore, diminishes the fund out of which they are to be paid. It is for this reason that companies limited by shares are not allowed to purchase their own shares, because the capital is thereby reduced.[29] For the same reason, the power to forfeit, and to accept a surrender of, shares is strictly guarded.[30] But sometimes there may be a genuine necessity for the reduction of capital. Closely fenced power is, therefore, given by Section 100. Under this section a company limited by shares or a guarantee company having a share capital may reduce its capital in any way. It may, for example:

1. extinguish or reduce the liability on any of its shares;

---

24. S. 94(2). The section requires only an ordinary resolution for increase of capital. *Janaki Printing (P) Ltd v Nadar Press Ltd*, [2000] 3 Comp LJ 283 CLB.
25. S. 95. *See also* sub-section (3) which imposes penalty for default. The default is a continuing offence. Subsequent replacement of the original resolution which remained unnotified did not wipe out the offence, *Amison Foods Ltd v ROC*, [1999] 1 Comp LJ 115 Ker. Another ruling to the same effect is *Amison Foods Ltd v ROC*, (2001) 103 Comp Cas 846 Ker.
26. S. 95(1)(*e*).
27. S. 97. *See* sub-section (3) which imposes penalty for default. See also *Mahalaxmi Mills Co v State*, [1970] 1 Comp LJ 80 Raj.
28. S. 100.
29. S. 77.
30. See *Forfeiture of Shares*, Chapter 8, above. Where rights issue meant for employees was allotted under misrepresentation to employees' relatives, the company was permitted to rectify the register of members by substituting the names of employees but not to cancel them because that would have amounted to reduction of capital. *Polar Latex Ltd v Lakshmi Narayan*, (1995) 18 Corpt LA 7 CLB. Some other provisions founded on the requirement of maintaining the capital are, a subsidiary cannot purchase shares in its holding company, [S. 42]; dividends are not allowed to be paid out of capital, [S. 205]; in England, under EC directives a meriting of members has to be called when the company has lost half or more than half of its share capital.

2. cancel any paid-up share capital which is lost or is unrepresented by any available assets;[31]

3. pay off any paid-up share capital which is in excess of the wants of the company.[32]

Complete details of the procedure to be followed for effecting a reduction are given in the Act itself. Authority to reduce capital must be present in the articles. In pursuance of that authority a special resolution must be passed which should authorise the contemplated reduction of capital.[33] The next stage is to apply, by petition, to the court for an order confirming the reduction.[34]

Duties of Court

The court is burdened with onerous duties. The basic function of the court, however, is to look after the interest of the creditors and different classes of shareholders.

Interest of creditors.—Creditors are likely to be hit only when the reduction diminishes the liability of shareholders to pay the uncalled capital or where the proposed reduction involves payment to any shareholders of any paid-up share capital.[35] In other cases creditors are not entitled to object. Again only such creditors are entitled to object to whom the company owes a debt which would have been provable in the winding up of the company.[36] Of such creditors who are entitled to object the court must settle a list. Should all the creditors not consent to the reduction, the court may dispense with the consent of dissentient creditors provided that their debts are secured to the satisfaction of the court. The court has also been given the discretionary power of dispensing altogether with the consent of creditors, but this the court will do only when it is convinced that they are not in any

---

31. See *Vantech Industry Ltd, Re,* [1999] 2 Comp LJ 47, a company allowed to cancel capital in respect of shares which were allotted to public but which remained unpaid.

32. S. 100(1). For a statement of the ways in which the need for reduction may arise, see *Indian National Press (Indore) Ltd, Re,* (1989) 66 Comp Cas 387, 392 MP. Where a scheme of amalgamation under Ss. 391 to 395 involves reduction of capital, the procedure prescribed for such reduction has to be followed. *Asian Investments Ltd, Re,* (1993) 73 Comp Cas 517 Mad; *Durairajan v Waterfall Estates Ltd,* (1972) 42 Comp Cas 563 Mad.

33. There should be a valid meeting and a valid resolution. See *Jaiton Stock Exchange Assn Ltd, Re,* AIR 1952 Pepsu 114. In *Barry Artist Ltd, Re,* (1985) BCLC 283, the court allowed reduction on the basis of a resolution signed by all the members without a formal meeting. The court, however, issued this warning that the practice should not be repeated. *Birla Global Finance Ltd, Re,* (2005) 126 Comp Cas 647 Bom, redemption of preference share capital amounts to reduction, all formalities were complied with. *Parry's Confectioners Ltd, Re,* (2004) 122 Comp Cas 900 Mad, restructuring of capital by wiping out losses by using the share premium account.

34. S. 101. Where shares were allotted to a lender by mistake and he claimed back his money, it was held that even in such a case the formalities of reduction should be met. *Rupak Ltd v ROC,* (1976) 46 Comp Cas 53 Pat.

35. S. 101(2). Officers of the company concealing the names of creditors are made punishable under S. 105.

36. S. 101(2)(*a*).

way affected.[37] In one of the cases on the subject,[38] a company had issued shares and debentures in equal amount. It lost the bigger part of its capital. A part of the lost capital was recouped out of subsequent profits. The rest was proposed to be written off. The debenture holders were not allowed to raise any objection. Their position remained the same whether with or without reduction. Where certain creditors objected but the company secured their dues and also complied with the direction of the court to keep an amount in fixed deposit in the name of the Registrar of the court, the reduction was confirmed.[39]

Interest of shareholders.—The second duty of the court is to look after the interest of the shareholders. The proposed scheme of reduction must be reasonable and fair between all the classes of shareholders in the company. If the capital of a company consists of only one class of shares and all of them are to bear the reduction proportionately the scheme is obviously fair and must be confirmed. And so in *Marwari Stores Ltd* v *Gouri Shanker Goenka*:[40]

> The defendant company had a capital of Rs 1,92,000 divided into 1920 shares of Rs 100 each. By a special resolution the company resolved to reduce the capital to half, that is, to Rs 96,000 divided into 1920 shares of Rs 50 each. In other words, the paid-up capital was to be cancelled to the extent of Rs 50 on each share. The petitioner, a shareholder, opposed the reduction on the ground that there had been no loss of capital and, therefore, the reduction was unwarranted.

The question was whether a scheme of reduction can be confirmed only on the proof of the fact that there has been a real loss of capital. This fact was, however, proved by the company and, therefore, the court did not hesitate in confirming the scheme but cited with approval the opinion of Lord MACNAGHTEN in *Poole* v *National Bank of China Ltd*,[41] where his Lordship said: "The condition that gives jurisdiction is not proof of loss of capital or

---

37. S. 101(2), clauses (*a*), (*b*) and (*c*) and sub-section (3). *See*, for example, *Lucania Temperance Billiard Halls (London) Ltd, Re*, [1965] 3 All ER 879: [1966] 1 Comp LJ 350: [1966] Ch 98: [1966] 2 WLR 5. Another case in which creditors are not likely to be affected is where a company had to rectify its register of members by removing the names of members of its own parent companies to whom shares had been allotted in violation of the Exchange Control Act, 1947, (English). See *Transatlantic Life Assurance Co Ltd, Re*, [1979] 3 All ER 352. *Essar Steel Ltd, Re*, (2006) 130 Comp Cas 123 Guj, restructuring of capital for improving financial resources not affecting creditors, approved, an objecting shareholder was not present at the meeting and also not representing majority.

38. *Meux's Brewery Co Ltd, Re*, [1919] 1 Ch 28: [1918-19] All ER Rep 1192.

39. *OCL (India) Ltd, Re*, AIR 1998 Ori 153. The court considered *Meux's Brewery Co Ltd, Re*, (1919) 1 Ch 28: [1918-19] All ER Rep 1192 where the debentureholders unsuccessfully objected that the proposed reduction would be prejudicial to their security by enabling the company to pay dividends out of profits instead of such profits being applied in making good the lost capital. No evidence was adduced to show that the lost capital was attributable to circulating capital. *Wesburnt Sugar Refineries Ltd, Re*, [1951] 1 All ER 881, paying off capital can be done otherwise than by payment of money.

40. AIR 1936 Cal 327.

41. 1907 AC 229: [1904-07] All ER Rep 138: 96 LT 889.

proof that capital is unrepresented by any available assets or that capital is in excess of the wants of the company. The jurisdiction arises whenever the company seeking reduction has duly passed a special resolution to that effect."

But a warning was issued in the case of *Caldwell* v *Caldwell & Co:*[42]

....if capital not lost or unrepresented by available assets were cancelled, it might be possible thereafter by some adjustment of the figures in the company's balance sheet to carry the amount so cancelled to the company's profit and loss account and so indirectly return the paid-up capital to shareholders, thus affecting the rights of creditors. It was therefore thought, if not necessary, at any rate wise and prudent to insist on some evidence of the fact of loss of capital.

"The court cannot, however, always so insist for the simple reason that the question of reducing capital is a domestic one for the decision of the majority. The company may reduce the capital of all its shareholders *pro rata,* or may reduce the shares of any individual shareholder or any class of shareholders wholly or in part. Although the court must see that the interests of the minority have been protected and there is no unfairness shown to them, but in doing so the court shall keep in view the consideration that the decision has been arrived at by businessmen who are fully cognizant of their necessities and are the best custodians of their interest and should therefore be slow to interfere."[43] Moreover, lost capital can be written off even where it is still represented by available assets.[44]

The court's job becomes a little more difficult where there are two classes of shareholders enjoying different rights and the proposed resolution for reduction affects them differently. In such a case the court has to see that the scheme of reduction should be fair and equitable as between the ordinary and preference shareholders. But what is fair and equitable must depend upon the circumstances of each case. The decision of the House of Lords in *Scottish Insurance Corpn* v *Wilsons & Clyde Coal Co*[45] is an instructive illustration.

Under an Act the colliery assets of a coal mining company were acquired. The company intended, after receiving compensation, to go into voluntary liquidation. Meanwhile, it proposed to reduce its capital by paying back the preference stock which would be thereby

---

42. [1916] SC (HL) 120: (1966) WN 70 Scotland.
43. The discretionary nature of the court's power has been explained by B. O. Rourke, *Reduction of Share Capital—The Reassertion of Discretionary Power,* (1970) 87 SALJ 161.
44. *Hoare & Co Ltd, Re,* [1904] 2 Ch 208: [1904-07] All ER Rep 635 CA.
45. 1949 AC 462: [1949] 1 All ER 1068. *See* also *Robert Stephen Holdings, Re,* [1968] 1 All ER 195 (Ch D); *Saltdean Estate Co Ltd, Re,* [1968] 1 WLR 1844: [1968] 3 All ER 829; *Holders' Investment Trust Ltd, Re,* [1971] 2 All ER 289. In this case it was held that a cancellation of preference shares by repayment of the capital paid on them and also consistently with the rights attached to those shares did not involve variation of the rights of other shareholders. Followed in *House of Fraser* v *A C G E Investments Ltd,* [1987] BCLC 478 HL.

extinguished. The power to pay off the preferential stock was there in the articles. It was also provided that in the event of winding up the preference stock ranked before the ordinary to the extent of the amount paid thereon. The reduction was opposed by some preference stockholders on the ground (*inter alia*) that it deprived them of the advantage of their investment rather prematurely and, therefore, the proposed reduction was unfair.

It was, however, held that the proposed reduction was not unfair or inequitable, because, even without it, the preference shareholders would not be entitled to anything more than a return of their paid-up capital. Lord SIMONDS said:

> Whether a man lends money to a company at 7 per cent or subscribes for its shares carrying a cumulative preferential dividend at that rate, he cannot complain of unfairness if the company, being in a position lawfully to do so, proposes to pay him off. No doubt, if the company is content not to do so, he may get something he may never have expected but, so long as the company can lawfully repay him, whether it be months or years before a contemplated liquidation, I see no ground for the court refusing its confirmation. Funds being available for payment of the capital, the natural order is to pay off the capital which has priority and I see no glimmer of unfairness in the company doing so at the earliest possible moment.

The Calcutta High Court also faced a problem of this kind in *Hindustan Commercial Bank* v *H. G. E. Corpn.*[46]

> A company, having lost nearly the whole of its capital, proposed a scheme of reduction under which the preference shareholders had to forego their accumulated arrears of dividend and 70 per cent of their capital and ordinary shareholders to forego 80 per cent of their capital. The scheme was approved by necessary majority at a separate meeting of preference shareholders and also at a general meeting of the company.

Some preference shareholders subsequently contended that "*prima facie* the whole of the capital paid-up on the ordinary shares should be cancelled before any part of the capital paid-up on preference shares is cancelled". The court, however, sanctioned the scheme and said that "special circumstances may justify a departure from this *prima facie* rule". And the special circumstances here were that due to the loss of almost the whole of the paid-up capital of the company the only alternative to reduction was winding up in which case neither class of shareholders would have got anything.[47]

---

46. AIR 1960 Cal 637: (1960) 30 Comp Cas 367.
47. The Court relied upon the following authorities: *Credit Assurance and Guarantee Corpn Ltd, Re*, [1902] 2 Ch 601; *Bannatyne* v *Direct Spanish Telegraph Co*, (1886) 34 Ch D 287, 299-300; *Floating Dock Co of St Thomas Ltd, Re*, [1895] 1 Ch 691; *British & American Trustee & Finance Corpn* v *Couper*, [1894] AC 399: [1891-1904] All ER Rep 667. *See also* Surendra Nath, *Reduction of Shares Capital of a Company*, AIR 1969 Journal 7 and 18.

Where reduction involves paying back capital to shareholders, priority must be given to those who would be entitled to prior refund of capital in the winding up.[48]

Where reduction involves variation of class rights, the procedure prescribed by the Act and the company's articles must also be complied with.[49]

If the court is satisfied in all respects it may make an order confirming the reduction on such terms and conditions as it thinks fit.[50] The court may, for example, require the company to add to its name as the last words "*and reduced*" during such period as it thinks proper.[51] The company may also be directed to publish for public information the reasons for the reduction.[52] The company should get the reduction registered with the Registrar.[53]

Where reduction became necessary as a part of a scheme of amalgamation the court passed necessary orders for the purpose without the need for following the special procedure except this that a special resolution which is a mandatory requirement must be observed.[54]

This special procedure is not applicable when reduction of share capital is the result of adjustment of accumulated losses against Capital Redemption Reserve Account and Share Premium Account because in such a case interests of creditors are not affected.[55]

---

48. See *Prudential Assurance Co Ltd* v *Chatterley-Whitfield Collieries Ltd*, 1949 AC 512: [1949] 1 All ER 1094.
49. *Old Silkstone Collieries Ltd case*, [1954] Ch 169 [CA]. Burden of proving unfairness lies on those who oppose the scheme. See *Carruth* v *ICI Ltd*, 1937 AC 707. In a takeover scheme all the ordinary shares were to be transferred to the acquiring company and the scheme was approved by 97% of the shareholders, the court approved the scheme; though the company had some ''B'' shares, a separate meeting of that class was considered to be not necessary. *BTR plc, Re*, [2000] 1 BCLC 740 CA.
50. S. 102(1). The court has to watch the interest of even those shareholders who do not appear. *Indian National Press (Indore) Ltd, Re*, (1989) 66 Comp Cas 387 MP.
51. S. 102(2).
52. S. 102(2)(*b*).
53. S. 103. The detailed procedure of registration is explained in the section. The effective date of reduction is the date of filing the return of reduction with the Registrar. *CIT* v *Industrial Credit & Devt Syndicate Ltd*, [1989] 2 Comp LJ 266 Kant. A certified copy of the court order and the minute of reduction approved by the court should be filed. The Registrar issues a certificate which is conclusive that requirements have been complied with. The minute becomes incorporated in the capital clause of the memorandum.
54. *Novopan India Ltd, Re*, (1997) 88 Comp Cas 596 AP and *Sumitra Pharmaceuticals & Chemicals Ltd, Re*, (1997) 88 Comp Cas 619 AP; *EOC Tailor Made Polymers India (P) Ltd, Re*, (2005) 125 Comp Cas 648 Bom; *Raj Prakash Chemicals Ltd, Re*, (2005) 125 Comp Cas 648 Bom.
55. *Rallis India Ltd, Re*, (2005) 125 Comp Cas 268 Bom; *Essar Steel Ltd, Re*, (2005) 59 SCL 457 Guj, the reduction was confirmed because there was no diminution of liability on unpaid capital or any payment to any shareholders from paid-up capital.

Liability of Members after Reduction [S. 104]

Liability of members in respect of reduced shares is explained in Section 104 of the Act. A member shall be liable to pay the amount deemed to have been unpaid on his shares. His liability is to pay the difference between the amount deemed to have been paid on his shares and the nominal value of the reduced shares.[56] However, the members' liability to pay the original nominal value of the shares can be restored in one case. Sometimes a creditor having the right to object to a reduction may have been left out of the list of creditors because of his ignorance of the proceedings or their effect on his interest and subsequently the company has become unable to pay its debts.[57] The court may, to meet the claim of such a creditor, order the members to pay that amount on their shares which they would have been liable to pay before the reduction.[58]

FURTHER ISSUE OF CAPITAL [S. 81]

Under Section 94 of the Act a company can at any time by passing an ordinary resolution at its general meeting resolve to increase its capital by such amount as it thinks expedient by issuing new shares. The time at which and the persons to whom new shares are to be allotted is an important question in company law. If the directors or the majority of shareholders are allowed to disperse the new issue at their discretion, they would naturally offer it to their nominees, thus adding to their own majority and reducing the strength of the minority. Section 81 partly deals with this problem.

Shareholders' pre-emptive right or rights shares

The section comes into play whenever it is proposed to increase the subscribed capital of the company (within the limit of authorised capital) by allotment of further shares after the expiry of two years from the formation of the company or after the expiry of one year from the first allotment of shares, whichever is earlier.[59]

The new issue must be offered to the existing holders of equity shares in the proportion, as nearly as the circumstances admit, of the shares held by them.[60] "The object of the section obviously is that there should be an

---

56. S. 104(1).
57. S. 105 penalises any officer of the company who conceals information as to creditors.
58. S. 104(1) proviso. Sub-s. (2) says that the rights of the contributories among themselves shall not be affected. *See also* S. 105 which imposes penalty for concealing the name of any creditor.
59. S. 81(1). Section I of SEBI Guidelines for Investor and Creditor Protection, 1992 prescribes the minimum interval of 12 months between two issues. *Ashok V. Doshi* v *Doshi Time Industries (P) Ltd*, (2001) 104 Comp Cas 306 CLB, 2 years had still not passed when the next issue was made. Section not applicable.
60. S. 81(1)(*a*). *Nupur Mitra* v *Basubani (P) Ltd*, (2002) 108 Comp Cas 359 CLB, the provision is mandatory, increase was with the consent of the whole Board of the family company, lawful, though there was absence of minutes and notices to members.

equitable distribution of shares and the holding of shares by each shareholder should not be affected by the issue of new shares."[61]

Offer must be made to the existing holders of equity shares in the company in proportion, as nearly as the circumstances admit, to the capital paid up on those shares. Offer is to be made by giving a notice specifying the number of shares offered.[62] The notice must fix a time which should not be less than fifteen days from the date of the offer within which the offer must be accepted.[63] The notice must also inform the shareholders that if the offer is not accepted within the specified time, it shall be deemed to have been declined. Again, the notice has to inform the shareholders that they have the right to renounce all or any of the shares offered to them in favour of their nominees.

If a shareholder has neither nominated anyone nor accepted the shares himself, the board of directors will get the discretion to dispose of the shares declined in such manner as they think most beneficial to the company.[64] Similarly, if after carrying out proportional allotment as nearly as the circumstances admit, some shares are left, they may be disposed of by the directors in such manner as they think most beneficial to the company.[65]

61. *Nanalal Zaver* v *Bombay Life Assurance Co*, AIR 1949 Bom 56: 50 Bom LR 413; *Sangramsinh P. Gaekwad* v *Shantadevi P. Gaekwad*, (2005) 123 Comp Cas 566 (SC), shareholders who were aware of the decision were not allowed to question the further issue.

62. See *Jadabpore Tea Co Ltd* v *Bengal Dooars National Tea Co*, (1984) 55 Comp Cas 160 Cal, where the notice was under certificate of posting and the Court presumed delivery. *Cotton Corpn of India Ltd* v *Telangana Spg & Wvg Mills Ltd*, (2005) 61 SCL 219 (AP), it was difficult for the court to believe that a very important letter like offer of rights shares should have been sent by ordinary post. Thus there was no *prima facie* evidence of posting of letters. An *ad interim* relief was granted to restrain the person to whom the plaintiff's proportion was allotted. He was restrained from dealing with shares or to exercise any rights in respect of them.

63. The Delhi High Court held in *Shrimati Jain* v *Delhi Flour Mills Co Ltd*, (1974) 44 Comp Cas 228 that a notice posted within Delhi and giving seventeen days' time to accept was a good notice. Such a letter is likely to be delivered the next day and thus leaves a time of fifteen clear days exclusive of the date of posting and of delivery. The court also pointed out that the validity of an allotment under the section cannot be challenged in the absence of the allottee as that would be against the principle of natural justice. *See* at p 250. Letters of offer have to be sent by registered post.

64. S. 81(1)(*d*). *Sangramsinh P. Gaekwad* v *Shantadevi P. Gaekwad*, (2005) 11 SCC 314: AIR 2005 SC 809: (2005) 123 Comp Cas 566 (SC), some of the shareholders did not participate in the issue, directors allotted their proportion to persons of choice, not objectionable. There was no proof that the proportion of the chairman was renounced by him, its allotment to others, not proper. A part of the allotment was transferred by the majority shareholders to their private company. This was held to be not valid because it was in violation of articles, other shareholders could not claim allotment of such shares to them.

65. *V. Shanmugasundaram* v *Emerald Automobiles Ltd*, (2001) 103 Comp Cas 1108 CLB, rights shares first offered to existing shareholders and then to outsiders, allotment valid. *Geeta Kapoor* v *Union of India*, (2005) 5 Comp LJ 13 Del, rights shares can be offered to foreign shareholders either under automatic approval scheme for raising foreign equity or under formal approval. The Government policy applicable at the time of allotment would hold good and not any subsequent revised policy.

Role of Directors' Discretion and Judicial Control

Subject to these restrictions, directors enjoy the full discretion of deciding whether an increase in the capital of the company is necessary or not and at what particular time the capital should be increased. This appears from the decision of the Bombay High Court as affirmed by the Supreme Court in *Nanalal Zaver* v *Bombay Life Assurance Co.*[66]

> Tempted by the soundness of a company, one *S* purchased a majority of its shares in the open market. The directors immediately came out with a further issue of capital and allotted it to the existing members in accordance with Section 105(*c*) (of Act, 1913) [now Section 81]. Two of the shareholders who had sold their interest to *S* objected to the scheme on two grounds, firstly, that the company was in no need of further capital and, therefore, the allotment was not made in the *bona fide* interest of the company, and, secondly, some 272 shares of the total new issue were not offered to the shareholders at all.

Both these contentions were rejected. Regarding the second, it was held that "the legislature did not intend that every one of the shares had to be offered to the members in proportion to the existing shares held by each member. Such shares had to be offered only as nearly as the circumstances admit" and that was done in the present case. As for the first argument, the Bombay High Court, as upheld by the Supreme Court, observed:

> The scheme of the section is fairly clear. It is left to the discretion of directors to decide whether an increase in the capital of the company is necessary or not. It is also left to their discretion to determine at what particular time the capital should be increased.... Once it is established that the company is in need for funds, then, whatever other motives might have actuated the directors, the Court will not interfere with their discretion. However mixed the motives might be, if it is established that in fact the company was in need of funds, then it could not be said that the exercise of their fiduciary powers by the directors was not a *bona fide* exercise. It is only when that discretion is exercised solely for the personal ends of the directors, for their personal aggrandisement, for keeping themselves in power, then undoubtedly that discretion cannot be said to have been exercised *bona fide.*[67]

---

66. AIR 1949 Bom 56: 50 Bom LR 413. The directors' discretion in this connection was emphasised in *Miheer H. Mafatlal* v *Mafatlal Industries Ltd,* (1996) 87 Comp Cas 705 Guj. The court added that an allotment of shares is a contract. If it is made in contravention of a court injunction, would be contrary to public policy and void as between the company and the allottee. If the company is in need of more capital in accordance with director decision, it can make further issue, the only constraints being that the directors should decide the matter in good faith and proceed in accordance with the requirements of S. 81, *Milan Sen* v *Guardian Plasticote Ltd,* (1998) 91 Comp Cas 105 Cal.

67. *See* MAHAJAN J at p 179, AIR 1950 SC 172. Cf. *Percy* v *S Mills & Co Ltd*, [1920] 1 Ch 77; *Hogg* v *Cramphorn Ltd,* [1966] 3 All ER 420: [1967] Ch 254; noted K. W. Wedderburn, *Shareholders' Control of Directors' Powers*, [1967] 30 Mod LR 77. *See also* L. H. Leigh,

Excluding Operation of the Section

The operation of this section can, however, be excluded and the new shares offered to outsiders to the total exclusion of the existing shareholders in the following two cases:[68]

1. If the company has, by passing a special resolution, resolved to allot the new issue in a different manner than that provided in the section, or

2. If an ordinary resolution to that effect has been passed and the Central Government is satisfied, on an application made by the board of directors, that the proposal to offer the shares to outsiders is most beneficial to the company.

The requirement of special resolution was introduced by an amendment in 1960.[69] Before this amendment the right could be excluded by an ordinary resolution. But in either case the question arises whether the exercise of this majority power is governed by the fiduciary principle or whether the majority can act in its personal interest in disregard to that of the company. This in essence was the question before the Supreme Court in *Shanti Prasad Jain* v *Kalinga Tubes Ltd*.[70]

The shares of one private company were held equally by two groups. The petitioner was introduced to provide financial and administrative help. He was allotted shares equal to both the groups and was made chairman of the board of directors. The company's business was successful. In order to avail of the loan facilities provided by the Orissa Government the company was converted into a public company. A substantial increase of capital was proposed. The two groups having majority both in the board and general meeting resolved to offer and allotted the new issue to outsiders selected by them.

Companies Act, 1967, (1968) 31 Mod LR 183, 186, where the learned writer maintains that *Hogg* v *Cramphorn Ltd*, [1966] 3 All ER 420: [1967] Ch 254 shows that "it will be improper to issue shares to management primarily with a view to maintain control, and the directors will have to ensure that an issue is made in the company's interest if litigation is to be avoided". *Vijay M. Shah* v *Flex Industries Ltd*, (2001) 103 Comp Cas 1063 Del, a case filed under S. 81 alleging failure of company to send rights offer in time because of *mala fides*, fraud and oppression, the court said that it was in essence a matter under Ss. 397-398. It should have gone before the CLB (now National Company Law Tribunal).

68. S. 81(I-A). *Janaki Printing (P) Ltd* v *Nadar Press Ltd*, (2001) 103 Comp Cas 546 CLB, ordinary resolution by shareholders who were fully informed, considered to be sufficient for expression of shareholders', will.

69. Companies (Amendment) Act, 1960.

70. [1965] 1 Comp LJ 193: AIR 1965 SC 1535: (1965) 35 Comp Cas 351. Again affirmed by the Supreme Court in *Needle Industries (India) Ltd* v *Needle Industries Newey (India) Holding Ltd*, (1981) 3 SCC 333: AIR 1981 SC 1298: (1981) 51 Comp Cas 743. The court will set aside the allotment where it would appear to have been made only to reduce the strength of a shareholder. *Jadabpore Tea Co Ltd* v *Bengal Dooars National Tea Co*, (1984) 55 Comp Cas 160.

The question was whether the majority power was exercised in good faith in the interest of the company or only to deprive the petitioner of his right under Section 81. If the voting power of the new allottees was utilised by the majority group, seventy-five per cent of the votes would concentrate in their hands. But that, the court held, was not sufficient to show that there was a "combination"[71] to squeeze out the petitioner. WANCHOO J said: "The seven persons to whom the new shares were allotted were respectable persons of independent means and there was nothing to show that they were stooges of the majority groups."

The decision, with due respect, does not seem to take into account the footing on which majority powers stand. For "the majority has the right to control; but when it does so, it occupies a fiduciary relation towards the minority, as much as the corporation itself, or its officers or directors."[72]

Where the Section does not Apply

The above restrictions, however, do not apply to any increase in the subscribed capital caused by the exercise of an option attached to debentures issued or loans raised by the company to convert such debentures or loans into shares or to subscribe for shares in the company.[73] The option to convert must be contained in the terms of issue of the debentures or loan. Again, approval of the Central Government for such terms must have been obtained before the issue was made or it should have been made in conformity with the rules, if any, made by the Central Government. It is also necessary that the terms should have been approved by a special resolution of the company except where the loan is from the Government or any institution specified by it.[74] A private company is also exempt from the provision.[75]

---

71. MISRA J in *Kalinga Tubes Ltd* v *S. P. Jain*, [1964] 1 Comp LJ 117. A similar compulsion was there in *Jacques Taru Lalvani* v *JBA Printing Inks Ltd*, (1997) 88 Comp Cas 759 Bom because a private company's capital had to be increased on the eve of making it a public company. Any incidental benefit to the directors cannot be a decisive factor. *N. Jagan* v *Investment Trust of India Ltd*, (1996) 85 Comp Cas 75 Mad, statutory right of shareholders to exclude pre-emptive rights. The court did not interfere in the shareholders' resolution authorising the directors to allot further issue to the promoters' group. A similar resolution was not interfered with in *Kothari Industrial Corpn Ltd* v *Maxwell Dyes & Chemicals (P) Ltd*, (1996) 85 Comp Cas 79 Mad, where also the shareholders resolved that the further issue be allotted to NRIs, overseas corporate bodies and promoters' group. This decision was affirmed by the Division Bench in *Maxwell Dyes and Chemicals (P) Ltd* v *Kothari Industrial Corpn Ltd*, (1996) 85 Comp Cas 111 Mad.

72. BRANDIES J in *Southern Pacific Rly Co* v *Bogert*, 250 US 483, 492. Many such opinions have been cited by Berle and Means, THE MODERN CORPORATION AND PRIVATE PROPERTY, 258 (1932); Carlos L. Israels, *Are Corporate Powers still held in Trust*, (1964) 64 Col LR 1446.

73. S. 81(3).

74. Proviso to S. 81(3) as *substituted* by the Amendment Act of 1963.

75. S. 81(3)(a). See *Needle Industries (India) Ltd* v *Needle Industries Newey (India) Holding Ltd*, (1981) 3 SCC 333: AIR 1981 SC 1298: (1981) 51 Comp Cas 743. The decision was to the effect that S. 81 would not apply to private companies which have become deemed public companies by virtue of S. 43-A and which have retained the features of a private company. *V. Radha Krishnan* v *P. R. Rama Krishnan*, (1993) 78 Comp Cas 694 Mad: (1995) 17 Corpt LA 63, here the shareholding was that of a company in winding up and it was held that its

The English Companies Act, 1948, does not provide for pre-emptive rights.[76] "England has never adopted this doctrine as a compulsory legal rule.... The only restraint on the directors is that entailed by the rule that they must act as fiduciaries when issuing further capital."[77] One aspect of this fiduciary principle is that the directors must not allot new shares to themselves or their nominees solely for the purpose of maintaining themselves in power. Thus they have been restrained from issuing shares to enable themselves to control the next general meeting,[78] or to pass a special resolution.[79] The fiduciary principle has been reaffirmed in the cases of *Hogg* v *Cramphorn Ltd*[80] and *Bamford* v *Bamford*.[81] In both cases the directors had to face a take-over bid and by way of defence new shares were allotted. In the first case the allotment was made to certain trustees for the benefit of the company's employees, the company providing an interest free loan for the purpose. This helped the directors to regain majority at a general meeting. BUCKLEY J said:

> Assuming that the directors acted in good faith and they believed that the establishment of a trust would benefit the company and that avoidance of take-over would also benefit the company, I must still remember that an essential element of the scheme, and its primary purpose, was to ensure control of the company by the directors and those whom they could confidently regard as their supporters. Was such a manipulation of the voting position a legitimate act on the part of the directors?

The learned Judge held that it was not, unless it was affirmed by a majority of shareholders in general meeting. The decision was accordingly deferred until the wishes of shareholders could be ascertained in a general meeting at which new allottees would not vote.

In the other case the directors took the precaution of having the shareholders' sanction to the allotment. The court held that even assuming

---

proportionate shares ought to have been offered to it.

76. *Abbotsford Hotel Ltd* v *Kingham*, [1909] 101 LTR 917: [1910] 102 LT 118. For American literature on the subject of pre-emptive rights, following articles may be consulted: Henry S. Drinker, Jr., *The Pre-emptive Right of Shareholders*, [1929-30] 43 Harv LR 586; *The Right of Stockholder to New Stock*, [1908-09] 18 Yale LJ 101; Victor Morawetz, *The Pre-emptive Right of Shareholders*, [1928-29] 42 Harv LR 186; Gower, *British & American Corporation Law*, [1956] 69 Harv LR 1369, 1380; *Freezing Out Minority Shareholders*, [1961] 74 Harv LR 1630, 1631-32. *See also* Avtar Singh, *Shareholders' Pre-emptive Right: A Comparative Study*, [1969] Shareholders' Journal 16.
77. Gower, *British and American Corporation Law*, 69 Harv LR 1369, 1380.
78. *Fraser* v *Whalley*, (1864) 2 H & M 10: 71 ER 361: [1861-73] All ER Rep Ext 1456; *Percy* v *S. Mills & Co Ltd*, [1920] 1 Ch 77: [1918-19] All ER Rep 313.
79. *Punt* v *Symons & Co*, [1903] 2 Ch 506: [1900-03] All ER Rep Ext 1040.
80. [1966] 3 All ER 420: 1967 Ch 254: (1967) 30 Mad LR 77. Considered by K. W. Wedderburn, *Shareholders' Control of Directors' Powers: A Judicial Innovation*, (1967) 30 Mod LR 7 and *Going the Whole Hogg* v *Cramphorn Ltd*, (1968) 31 Mod LR 688. *See also* 1964 JBL 51.
81. [1969] 2 WLR 1107: [1969] 1 All ER 969: noted 1969 JBL 49: 1970 Ch 212.

that the allotment was not made in the *bona fide* interest of the company, the members could ratify it, they not being subject to the fiduciary duty of directors to act in the best interest of the company. The Court of Appeal affirmed the decision but on a different ground. It held that according to the articles, the residual power of allotment was with the company and the company exercised it in its own right and not in the right of the board.

Freezing out Techniques

Subject to these considerations, however, issuing new shares with the dominant purpose of diminishing the voting power of the minority shareholder is an abuse of their position by a majority of the shareholders.

A small private company had only two shareholders, the plaintiff holding 45% and her aunt 55%. The aunt was a director along with some others who were not shareholders. A resolution was passed increasing share capital which was to be allotted partly to the directors and partly in trust for employees. The plaintiff's holding would thereby be reduced to half and that of the majority group along with the new shares would be increased to 75%.

The House of Lords restrained the scheme. The dominant purpose was to diminish the voting strength of the minority and the resolution was adopted to serve only that purpose.[82]

One of the results of these cases is the development of the "proper purpose" doctrine which requires directors to use their powers in good faith only for the purpose for which they are meant. A Canadian court found that the directors of a company had issued shares in good faith to a third person in order to wipe off the control by a majority shareholder and held that the proper purpose doctrine was merely an aspect of the broader principle that directors must act *bona fide* and, therefore, there was no breach of duty.[83] But this decision seems to have been not approved by the Privy Council in a case where their Lordships held that the directors were in breach of their proper purpose duty irrespective of their *bona fides*.[84]

Besides this, the stock exchange regulations (effective in England) now require the new issues of quoted securities to "be offered in the first place to the equity shareholders unless those holders have agreed in general meeting to other specific proposals".[85]

---

82. *Clemens* v *Clemens Bros Ltd*, [1976] 2 All ER 268 Ch D.
83. *Teck Corpn* v *Millar*, (1972) 33 DLR (3d) 288 Canada.
84. *Howard Smith* v *Ampol Petroleum*, 1974 AC 821 PC. All the different view points on the subject have been collected and considered by Kenneth C. K. Chow, *Proper Purpose Doctrine and the Companies Bill*, [1979] New LJ 123.
85. *See* Clive M. Schmitthoff, *The Issue of Securities in Great Britain*, 1969 JBL 1, 4.

Private Companies and Convertible Issues

The section does not apply to private companies,[86] or to increase of the subscribed capital of a public company by the exercise of an option attached to debentures issued or loans raised by the company. It is necessary that such scheme of conversion was either approved by the Government or is in accordance with the rules, if any, made by the Government and in the case of conversion of loans or debentures of private holders, that the scheme has been approved by the shareholders of the company by a special resolution.

Employees Stock Option

This expression has been defined in Section 2(15-A) as follows:

> "Employees stock option" means the option given to the wholetime directors, officers or employees of a company, which gives such directors, officers or employees the benefit or right to purchase or to subscribe at a future date, the securities offered by the company at a pre-determined price."[87]

"Option in securities" has been given the same meaning as in Section 2(*h*) of the Securities Contracts (Regulation) Act, 1956.[88]

Power to convert loans into capital [S. 81(4) to (7)]

By the amendment of 1963 the Central Government has taken a new power of converting into shares any debentures issued to or loan taken from the Government by a company. Where a company has issued any debentures to the Government or has taken any loan from it, the Central Government may direct that such debentures or loan (or any part of it) shall be converted into shares in the company. The power is to be exercised only if such conversion appears to be necessary in the public interest. The conversion shall be on such terms and conditions as appear to the Government to be reasonable in the circumstances of a particular case. Regard shall be had to the financial position of the company, the original terms of the issue, the rate of interest, the capital of the company, its liabilities, its reserves, its profits during the preceding five years and the current market value of the company's shares. Further, the Government must exercise the power at a time when it will not cause undue violent fluctuations in the market value of shares. Care has also to be taken to avoid serious imbalance in the ratio of debt to equity capital of the company.

---

86. The section does not apply to private companies including a private company which is subsidiary of a public company. The interests of shareholders of such companies are usually protected by pre-emptive clauses in articles of association. *Ashok Doshi* v *Doshi Time Industries (P) Ltd*, (2000) 38 CLA 278 CLB. Any decision about the applicability of the section to such companies is likely to go wrong if the state of the company's articles is not taken into account, *Jayanthi Detergents (P) Ltd* v *Secy, CLB*, [1999] 3 Comp LJ 237 AP.
87. Introduced by the Amendment Act, 2000.
88. S. 2(31-A) as introduced by the Amendment Act, 2000.

If the terms and conditions proposed by the Government are not acceptable to the company, it may within thirty days prefer an appeal to the court and the decision of the court shall be final. Subject to the decision of the court, the order shall become final and conclusive.[89]

A copy of every order proposed to be issued by the Government is to be laid in draft before each House of Parliament for a total period of thirty days.[90]

A power of this kind opens the door to backdoor nationalisation.[91]

Section 94-A inserted by the Amendment of 1974 provides that where the Government or any public financial institution has converted its debentures or loans into capital, the capital of the company shall thereby stand increased by an equal amount and its memorandum altered accordingly. The Central Government is required to send a copy of the order to the Registrar so that he may effect the necessary alterations in the company's memorandum.

Variation of shareholders' rights or class rights [S. 106]

The share capital of a company can be divided into two different classes of shares, namely, preference shares and ordinary shares. Frequently, and obviously, rights attached to one class of shares may be different from those attached to the other class. A shareholder who was given the right to purchase the shares of the company on a pre-emptive basis was held to constitute a special class distinguishing him from other shareholders who did not have any such right, and consequently, his right was not permitted to be taken away without his consent.[92] If it is proposed to change the rights of any class, certain procedure has to be followed. Firstly, there should be a provision in the memorandum or articles of the company entitling it to vary such class rights or, at any rate, there should be nothing in the terms of issue of the shares of that class prohibiting such a variation.[93] Secondly, the holders of three-fourths of the issued shares of that class must have given their consent in writing or a special resolution sanctioning the variation must have been passed at a separate meeting of the shareholders of that class. Thirdly, the holders of at least ten per cent of the shares of that class who did not consent to or vote in favour of the resolution may apply to the court and then variation shall not take effect unless and until it is confirmed by the court.[94] An application should be made within twenty-one days of the date of consent or resolution.[95] The court shall grant a

---

89. S. 81(7).
90. S. 81(6).
91. *See* 1970 JBL 242, reviewing Avtar Singh's, COMPANY LAW.
92. *Cumbrian Newspapers Group Ltd* v *Cumberland & Westmorland Herald Newspaper & Printing Co Ltd,* [1986] 1 WLR 26: (1986) 2 All ER 816: [1987] 2 Comp LJ 39.
93. S. 106(*a*) and (*b*). See *Sitarama Reddy* v *Bellary Spg & Wvg Co,* (1984) 56 Comp Cas 817 Ker where the resolution was not passed in accordance with the provisions.
94. S. 107(1).
95. S. 107(2).

hearing to the applicant and any other persons who apply to the court to be heard and appear to be interested in the application.[1] If the court, having regard to all the circumstances of the case, is satisfied that the variation would unfairly prejudice the shareholders of that class, it would be disallowed. But if the scheme appears to be reasonable and fair it would be confirmed. The decision of the court is final.[2] The company shall, within thirty days, send a copy of the court's order to the Registrar.[3]

New issue of preference shares ranking *pari passu* with the existing shares does not amount to variation so as to require the consent of preference shareholders.[4] The conversion of the loans of an ex director into shares was held not to violate class rights, although voting power of shareholders was affected. Proper procedure was followed and the scheme was also of *bona fide* nature.[5] Cancellation of shares and reduction of capital also do not amount to variation of class rights.[6]

Share warrants [Ss. 114, 115]

A public company has the right to convert its fully paid-up shares into share warrants,[7] provided, of course, there is an authority to that effect in its articles and the previous approval of the Central Government has been obtained. The advantage of issuing share warrants is that transfer of warrants becomes very easy. A share warrant issued by a company has to be under its seal and must state that the bearer of the warrant is entitled to the specified number of shares. He may transfer the shares comprised in the warrant by simple delivery of the warrant. Registration of transfer with the company is not necessary. Payment of dividends may be made by issuing coupons with warrants or otherwise.

On the issue of a share warrant the company shall strike out from its register of members, the name of the member in respect of the shares

---

1. S. 107(3).
2. S. 107(4).
3. S. 107(5) which also imposes penalty for default.
4. *White* v *Bristol Aeroplane Co*, [1953] 1 All ER 40: [1953] Ch 65: 2 WLR 144. See *PSI Data Systems Ltd, Re*, (1999) 98 Comp Cas 1: AIR 2000 Ker 23, where a company unilaterally and without the participation of preference shareholders decided to redeem their stake, the court said that the scheme would have to satisfy the requirements of S. 80(1) and approved under S. 391.
5. *Girish Kumar Kharia* v *Industrial Forge & Engg Co Ltd*, (2000) CLC 105 Pat. The scheme could not be implemented without the permission of the Board of Industrial & Financial Reconstruction, the company being under a scheme prepared under Sick Industrial Companies (Special Provisions) Act, 1985. *Girish Kumar Kharia* v *Industrial Forge & Engg Co Ltd*, (2001) 103 Comp Cas 150 Pat, a variation which affects enjoyment of rights without affecting the right itself is not actionable, e.g., a valid increase of capital which causes proportional diminution of voting rights.
6. *Essar Steel Ltd, Re*, (2006) 130 Comp Cas 123 Guj.
7. Partly paid-up shares cannot be converted into warrants. *Home & Foreign Investment Co, Re*, [1912] 1 Ch 72: 106 LT 259.

comprised in the warrant just as if he had ceased to be a member. The following particulars shall be entered in the register:

1. The fact of the issue of the warrant.
2. A statement of the shares specified in the warrant, distinguishing each share by its number.
3. The date of issue of the warrant.

The bearer of a share warrant has, subject to the articles of the company, the right to surrender his warrant for cancellation and to have his name entered in the register of members. The articles of a company may provide that the bearer of a share warrant shall be deemed to be a member of the company for all or any purposes defined in the articles.[8]

Purchase by company of its own shares [S. 77]

It is not open to a company to purchase its own shares, for Section 77 declares in so many words that "no company limited by shares, and no company limited by guarantee and having a share capital, shall have power to buy its own shares, unless the consequent reduction of capital is effected and sanctioned in pursuance of Sections 100 to 104 or of Section 402".[9] Buying its own shares by a company involves a permanent reduction of capital without sanction of the court which is "illegitimate" and "in violation of statute law". "The object of the section is to prevent a person from acquiring control of a company and paying for its shares out of the accumulated assets of the company itself, in other words, to prevent a person from plundering the coffers of the company for his own benefit."[10]

For the same reason a subsidiary company is not allowed to purchase the shares of its holding company.

This principle was laid down by the House of Lords as early as 1887 in *Trevor* v *Whitworth*.[11]

The articles of a company contained a clause to the effect that "any share may be purchased by the company from any person willing to sell it, and at such price as the board think reasonable". A director bought on behalf of the company 533 shares from the executors of a shareholder. The company, before paying the whole price, went into liquidation and the executor claimed the money. It was held that "the whole transaction was ultra vires the company". "In my opinion", said Lord WATSON, "the application of the company's funds in furtherance of any such object is

---

8. S. 115(5). Sub-section (*b*) provides penalty for default. The provisions relating to shares cease to apply to so much of the company's capital as has been converted into stock. S. 96.
9. S. 77(1).
10. Paul L. Davies, editing *Fowlie* v *Slater*, (1979) 129 New LJ 465 in 1980 JBL 48.
11. (1887) 12 App Cas 409: [1886-90] All ER Rep 46.

altogether illegitimate because it is foreign to the proper business of the company and in violation of statute law".[12]

The reason for the rule was explained in a subsequent case by JESSEL MR in the following words:

> The creditor. . . gives credit to the company on the faith of the implied representation that the capital shall be applied only for the purposes of the business and has, therefore, a right to say that the corporation shall keep its capital and not return it to the shareholders.[13]

To make the restriction really effective sub-section (2) provides that no public company or its subsidiary private company shall in any way provide money or financial assistance to any person to enable him to buy any shares in the company or in its holding company. Thus an agreement to provide a loan for purchase of the company's own shares is void and a guarantee given for the performance of the agreement is also void.[14]

An agreement between a company and the managing director of group companies under which he was to transfer his shares in one of the companies to his son and the company was to pay him salary, bonus and pension on his retirement was held to be not an agreement to pay for the purchase of the company's shares. The company was to pay him salary etc. for his working and services to the company. Thus there was no reduction in the net assets of the company and no financial assistance in violation of the provisions.[15]

Exceptions.—The sub-section, however, does not prohibit the following kinds of transactions:

1. The lending of money by a banking company in the ordinary course of its business.

2. The provision of money for the purchase of fully paid shares in the company by trustees for and on behalf of the company's employees.[16] (Employee share schemes).

---

12. *See* also *Indian Iron & Steel Co* v *Dalhousie Holdings Ltd*, AIR 1957 Cal 293.
13. *Exchange Banking Co, Re*, (1882) 21 Ch D 519, 533-34: 48 LT 86 CA. *See also* W. Strachan, *Return of Company's Capital to Shareholders*, (1910) 26 LQR 231.
14. *Heald* v *O'Connor*, [1971] 2 All ER 1105. Where a loan was given by a company to a person to enable him to purchase another company's shares and that other company issued a debenture to the lending company for the loan, the arrangement was held to be valid. *Victor Battery Co Ltd* v *Curry's Ltd*, [1946] Ch 242: [1946] 1 All ER 519. This decision was questioned and has not been followed in the subsequent case of *Heald* v *O'Connor*, [1971] 2 All ER 1105: [1971] 1 WLR 477; *Carney* v *Herbert*, 1985 AC 301 PC, where it was held that where the unlawful element in the agreement could be severed from the lawful part, the latter would be enforceable.
15. *Parlett* v *Guppys (Bridport) Ltd*, (1996) 2 BCLC 34 CA.
16. *Hogg* v *Cramphorn Ltd*, [1966] 3 All ER 420: (1967) Ch 254: (1967) 30 Mad 5 LR 77, where a trust for the purchase of a company's shares on behalf of its employees was financed by an interest free loan by the company. Section 153 of the English 1989 Act widened the provision to allow companies to guarantee loans made to such schemes. The new provision adds good-

Purchase by company of its own shares

3. Lending money by a company to its employees to enable them to buy fully paid shares in the company and to hold them by way of beneficial ownership. The amount of loan cannot exceed the employees' salary for a period of six months.[17] The word "employee" for this purpose does not include directors or managers.[18]

The provision in the first exception is to protect banks. They have to make loans in the ordinary course of their business and they can hardly supervise the purpose for which the borrower uses the loan money. Hence if a borrower from a bank uses the money for purchasing the bank's shares, the bank and its officers will be protected from liability. The words "lending in the ordinary course of business" are not defined. An English court held that where money is given for the very purpose of purchasing the bank's shares that would not be lending in the ordinary course of business and the provision would be violated.[19]

Redemption of preference shares constitutes an exception to the restriction contained in the section though redemption is the same thing as a company buying its own shares.[20]

Consequences of illegal financing.—Where the directors provide the company's money for the purchase of its own shares outside the scope of the above exceptions, it is a breach of trust for which they are liable. "The illegality of the transaction could not shield those responsible for the transaction by virtue of their fiduciary position."[21] The transaction is *ultra*

---

faith criteria to such schemes. Assistance can also be given by group companies for trading under the scheme.
17. S. 77(3).
18. S. 77(2)(*c*). *See also* sub-section (4) which imposes penalty for default in this connection. See *Financial Assistance by a Company in the Purchase of its Shares*, (1965) XLIII Can BR 502; Jass B. Murry, *Financial Assistance by a Company in Connection with Purchase of its Shares*, (1960) 3 ALJ 17; *South Western Mineral Water Co Ltd v Ashmore*, [1967] 2 All ER 953: [1967] 1 WLR 1110: noted 1967 JBL 360.
19. *Fowlie v Slater*, (1979) 129 New LJ 465. For details *see* Keith Walmsley, *Lending in the Ordinary Course of Business*, (1979) 129 New LJ 801. The court followed *Steen v Law*, [1964] AC 287 PC, the effect of which is that loans deliberately made for the very purpose of financing the purchase of the company's shares are not in the ordinary course of business. *See also* Keith Walmsley, *Lessons from the Stonehouse Investigation*, [1978] New LJ 252.
20. *Anarkali Sarabhai v CIT*, (1997) 3 SCC 238: (1997) 89 Comp Cas 28 SC. Redemption is different from buyback, *Barclays Bank Plc v British & Commonwealth Holdings Plc*, (1996) 1 BCLC 1 Ch D and CA.
21. *Selangor United Rubber Estates Ltd v Cradock*, [1969] 3 All ER 965. Noted, *Directors' Liability for Breach of Trust*, 1969 JBL 47, 49, where the learned writer supports the decision with reference to the Privy Council case of *Steen v Law*, 1964 AC 287. But whether the money provided by the company to the third party contrary to the section can be recovered is "an open question". But see *Victor Battery Co Ltd v Curry's Ltd*, [1946] Ch 242: [1946] 1 All ER 519 and *Essex Aero Ltd v Cross*, unreported, noted, 1969 JBL 49; *Spink Ltd v Spink*, [1936] Ch 544; *Flap Envelope Co Ltd, Re*, (2004) 1 BCLC 64 (Ch D); *Willmobt v Jenkin*, (2004) 1 BCLC 64 (Ch D), the company lent money to a person for purchasing shares for a director. A figurehead director was appointed for a single day to make the statutory declaration for lending. The declaration was not properly made. The directors were held guilty of breach of a

*vires a*nd incapable of ratification. Any shareholder can sue on behalf of the company for restituting the company to its former position. But may the company abandon its claim? The Court of Chancery Division faced this problem in *Smith v Crofit (No 2).*[22] A 14.5% minority shareholder showed that payments were made to associated companies for purchasing the company's shares, and that the same were illegal. The circumstances as they developed disentitled the company from proceeding against the matter because a great majority of the shareholders, including a financial institution which was independent of the majority block, resolved to abandon or compromise the company's rights and the company thereby having become disentitled from enforcing its rights, it was not open to a minority shareholder to reopen a chapter of closed rights.[23]

A buy-back of shares by the company was held to be invalid where the company did not have the necessary distributable profits as required by Section 160(1)(*a*) of the [English] Companies Act, 1985. The relevant accounts were qualified and auditors' statement that the qualification was not material had not been made and laid before the company in general meeting as required by the Act. The purchase was held to be invalid even though the auditors' believed that the company had sufficient distributable reserves and they could have made a statement to that effect.[24]

The company's bank paid the company's cheque not knowing that the withdrawal was a part of an elaborate arrangement to cause the company's own funds to be used to finance a take-over. The bank was held liable despite its being unaware of the real purpose of the transaction. UNGOED THOMAS J said (in *Selangor No 3*) that the bank paid the cheque out of the company's money in circumstances known to the bank before the payment in which a reasonable banker would have concluded that the payment was to finance the purchase of the stock in the company.[25]

A company's fully paid shares may be transferred to a nominee or trustee of the company for its benefit. There is nothing wrong where the

---

fiduciary duty. The company's net assets had become reduced to the extent of the loan. *Ramesh B. Desai* v *Bipin Vadilal Mehta*, (2006) 5 SCC 638: (2006) 132 Comp Cas 479 any valuable consideration paid out of the company's assets amounts to a transaction of purchase, invalid.

22. [1987] 3 All ER 909 Ch D.

23. For a critical appreciation of the decision, *see* L. S. Sealy, CASES AND MATERIALS IN COMPANY LAW, 486 (4th Edn, 1989).

24. *B. G. D. Roof Bond Ltd* v *Doughlas*, (2000) 1 BCLC 401 Ch D. A buy-back scheme was not restrained because if the shareholders had any grievances, they could resort to proceedings for prevention of oppression etc. *J. K. Puri* v *H. P. State Industrial Development Corpn*, (1998) 93 Comp Cas 491 HP.

25. *Selangor United Rubber Estates* v *Cradock (No 3)*, [1968] 1 WLR 1555: [1968] 2 All ER 1073 and *Karak Rubber Co* v *Burden (No 2)*, [1972] WLR 602. An amendment was held not liable for the fact that his sub-underwriter had carried on the financing of his portion of the shares with the company's money. Knowledge of the misuse of the company's money could not be imputed to him from the fact that his sub-underwriter was the Chief Executive of the company, *Eagle Trust plc* v *SBC Securities Ltd (No 2)*, (1996) 1 BCLC 121 Ch D.

company does not become its own member, or does not have to pay for its own shares or does not reduce its capital. Where shares were allotted to partners of a firm for taking over their business and the allotment happened to exceed the value of assets acquired; allottees returned the extra shares to the company which were taken in the name of a trustee for the benefit of the company, the court could find nothing wrong with it.[26] Similarly, where a shareholder bequests by his will his shares in the company to the company itself, the latter can hold them in the name of a trustee for its benefit.[27] Voting rights on such shares are exercisable by the directors of the company.[28]

Exemption of private company from financial assistance.—Sub-section (2) of Section 77 confines itself to a private company and its subsidiary private companies. This leaves a private company free to provide loans, guarantees or securities for the purpose of financing the purchase of its own shares. Such assistance should be confined to use of funds otherwise available for dividend distribution. If it is to go beyond that, the book value of the net assets of the company must remain untouched. Sections 154-158 of the English 1989 Act prescribe an elaborate procedure for the exercise of this power requiring a statutory declaration of the financial position, auditors' report, special resolution of shareholders and the right of dissenting holders of 10% shares to apply to court.

Buy-back of shares [S. 77-A]

Traditionally, subject only to a few exceptions specified in S. 77, companies were not permitted to purchase their own shares. Section 77-A, brought in by the Companies (Amendment) Act, 1999, has caused this structural change in the theme and philosophy of Company Law that, subject to the restrictions envisaged in the section, a company may buy back its own shares.

Sub-section (1) indicates the fund out of which the exercise of buy back is to be financed. The sources allowed are the company's free reserves, securities premium account, proceeds of an earlier issue. No buy back of any kind of shares or other specified securities can be made out of the earlier proceeds of the same kind of shares or the same kind of other specified securities. The expression "free reserves" has the same meaning as is attached to it in S. 372-A.

---

26. *Kirby* v *Wilkins*, (1929) 2 Ch 444.
27. *Castiglione's Will Trusts*, [1958] CR 549: [1950] 2 WLR 400: [1958] 1 All ER 480.
28. Jenkins Committee has recommended that this should not be allowed as directors can thereby perpetuate themselves. Para 156. *See also* the decision of the House of Lords in *Brady* v *Brady*, [1988] 2 All ER 617 HL, which examines the extent to which financial assistance can be provided in good faith for the larger interests of the company. Sub-section (5) provides that the section shall not affect the right of a company to redeem any shares issued under S. 80. Sub-section (4) provides penalty for default to the company as well as the officers in default.

Sub-section (2) prescribes certain formalities. There should be a provision in the articles authorising buy back of shares. In the exercise of that authority a special resolution at a meeting of the shareholders[29] or a resolution of the Board of directors should be passed. The amount involved in buy-back should be less than 25% of the company's total paid up capital and free resources.[30] After the buy back, the ratio between the debts owed by the company should not be more than twice the capital and free resources of the company.[31] The shares to be bought back should be fully paid. The buy-back should be in accordance with the regulations made by the Securities and Exchange Board of India. This requirement applies to listed securities. In the case of other securities, the buy-back has to be in accordance with guidelines as may be prescribed.

An amendment introduced in 2001[32] provides an exception to the operation of sub-section (2). The requirement of the sub-section is not to apply where the buy-back is 10%, or less than that, of the total paid-up equity capital and free reserves of the company and has been authorised by a resolution of the Board of directors passed at its meetings. No offer of buy-back can be made within one year (365 days) reckoned from the date of the preceding offer of buy-back.

The section permits shares and other specified securities[33] to be bought back. The *Explanation* to sub-section (2) says that "specified securities" would include employees' stock option or other securities as may be notified by the Central Government from time to time.

The notice for convening the meeting of shareholders for passing a special resolution should carry the information prescribed by sub-section (3). The information is (*a*) a full and complete disclosure of all material facts; (*b*) the necessity for the buy-back; (*c*) the class of security intended to be purchased; (*d*) the amount to be invested in buy-back; (*e*) the amount involved and (*f*) time-limit for completion of the transaction. This is subject to the restriction set out in sub-section (4) that every such transaction must be completed within 12 months from the date of the special resolution.

The power may be exercised in buying back the shares from the existing shareholders of the company directly or from the open market or from odd

---

29. *Gujarat Amiya Exports Ltd, Re*, (2004) 118 Comp Cas 265 Guj, scheme of buy-back of shares from small shareholders, approved by majority of such shareholders. The court refused to examine the propriety of every clause of the scheme or to examine the commercial wisdom of shareholders and to reject the scheme merely because a better scheme was also possible.
30. A proviso adds that the buy-back of equity shares in any financial year shall not exceed 25% of the company's total paid-up equity capital in that financial year.
31. A proviso adds that the Central Government may prescribe a higher ratio of the debt than specified under this clause for a class or classes of Companies Debt means secured unsecured debts.
32. Companies (Amendment) Act, 2001, w.e.f. 23-10-2001.
33. Which may be specified by the Central Government from time to time.

lots[34] or from the employees' stock option shares or sweat equity shares.[35]

Declaration of solvency [sub-section (6)]

A declaration of solvency has to be filed with the Registrar and SEBI. This has to be filed before the resolution for buying back is implemented. It has to state that the Board of directors has made a full inquiry into the affairs of the company and have found that it is capable of meeting all its liabilities and will not be rendered insolvent for a period of 12 months from the date of the declaration. It has to be on a prescribed form and verified by an affidavit. It has be to be signed by at least two directors of the company, one of whom should be the managing director, if any. A company whose shares are not listed at a stock exchange has not to file this declaration with SEBI.

Physical destruction of securities [S. 77-A(7)]

Where a company has bought back its securities, it has to extinguish them and physically destroy them. This should be done within 7 days of the last day on which the buy-back process is completed.

Further issue after buy-back [S. 77-A(8)]

Where a company has resorted to the buying back of its securities, it cannot make a further issue of securities within a period of six[36] months. It may, however, make a bonus issue and discharge its existing obligations such as conversion of warrants, stock option schemes, sweat equity or conversion of preference shares or debentures into equity shares. This restriction applies only to the type of securities bought back. The company is free to issue other types of security.

Register of bought back securities [S. 77-A(9)]

A register has to be maintained containing the particulars of the bought back securities, including the consideration paid for them, the date of cancellation and such other particulars as may be prescribed.

Return of buy-back [S. 77-A(10)]

After completing the process of buy-back, the company has to file a return with SEBI and Registrar. The return has to contain the prescribed particulars. It should be filed within 30 days from the date of completion.

---

34. Which means the lot of securities in a listed public company which is smaller than the number of shares which can traded in a particular stock exchange in one transaction. Where the resolution for purchasing the shares of the company in the market did not satisfy the statutory requirements, it was held that the resolution was not of binding nature and was not enforceable against the company or against any one else, *Vision Express (UK) Ltd* v *Wilson (No 2)*, (1998) BCC 173; *Western* v *Righlast Holdings Ltd*, (1989) GWD 23-950 (Scotland). A defective resolution can be rectified before implementation but not afterwards, *R. W. Peak (King Lynn) Ltd, Re*, [1998] BCLC 193: [1998] BCC 596.

35. For meaning of sweat equity *see* S. 79-A.

36. *Substituted* for 24 months by the amendment of 2001.

Penalty [S. 77-A(11)]

A default in complying with the requirements of the section and rules made under it has been made a punishable offence. The company and every officer of the company who is in default will have to face an imprisonment which may extend up to two years or also fine which may extend to Rs 50,000 or both.

Transfer of money to Capital Redemption Reserves Account [S. 77-AA]

Where a company purchases its own shares out of free reserves, then a sum equal to the nominal value of the shares purchased has to be transferred to the Capital Redemption Reserve Account and its details have to be disclosed in the balance-sheet.

Prohibition of buy back in certain circumstances [S. 77-B]

A buy-back exercise has to be done directly and not through the medium of other companies. The section says that buy-back shall not be done through any subsidiary company including the company's own subsidiaries. It should also not be done through any investment company or a group of investment companies. A company shall not resort to buy-back if it is in default in payment of deposits, redemption of debentures or preference shares or repayment of a term loan to any financial institution or a bank.

No company is allowed to purchase its own shares directly or indirectly if the company has not complied with the provisions of Section 159 (annual return), Section 207 (default in paying declared dividend) and Section 211 (filing of annual report or accounts).

10
Directors

"A corporation is an artificial being, invisible, intangible and existing only in contemplation of law."[1] "It has neither a mind nor a body of its own."[2] "A living person has a mind which can have knowledge or intention and he has hands to carry out his intention. A corporation has none of these, it must act through living persons."[3] This makes it necessary that the company's business should be entrusted to some human agents. Hence the necessity of directors. Section 252 of the Act, therefore, requires that "every public company shall have at least three directors and every private company shall have at least two directors".[4] By an amendment of the section by Amendment Act, 2000 it has been provided that a public company having a paid up share capital of rupees five crore or more and one thousand or more small shareholders, should have a director elected by the small shareholders. The manner of such election is to be prescribed. A small shareholder for this purpose means having shares of the nominal value of twenty thousand rupees or less in a public company.

POSITION OF DIRECTORS

The position that the directors occupy in a corporate enterprise is not easy to explain.[5] They are professional men hired by the company to direct its affairs. Yet they are not the servants of the company. They are rather the officers of the company. "A director is not a servant of any master. He cannot be described as a servant of the company or of anyone."[6] "A director is in fact a director or controller of the company's affairs. He is not a servant."[7] A director may, however, work as an employee in a different capacity. For example, in *Lee* v *Lee's Air Farming Ltd*:[8]

The principal controller and a director of a company was also working

---

1. MARSHALL J in *Trustees of Dartmouth College* v *Woodward*, (1819) 17 US 518, 636, cited in Laski, *The Personality of Associations*, 29 Harv LR 404.
2. HALDANE LC in *Lennard's Carrying Co* v *Asiatic Petroleum Co*, 1915 AC 705 at p 713: [1914-15] All ER Rep 280: 113 LT 195.
3. *Tesco Supermarkets Ltd* v *Nattrass*, 1977 AC 153 at p 170, *per* Lord REID.
4. S. 252(2). "Public company", for this purpose, does not include a private company which has become a public company under S. 43-A. As long as the requisite figure is maintained the requirements of the Act are fully satisfied even if all or substantially all the powers are delegated to a single director as long as he is in office. *Whitehouse* v *Carlton Hotel (P) Ltd*, (1987) 70 Australian LR 251, High Court of Australia. Sub-section (3) says that directors collectively are referred to as the "Board of directors" or as "Board".
5. *Ram Chand & Sons Sugar Mills* v *Kanhayalal*, AIR 1966 SC 1899: [1966] 2 Comp LJ 224.
6. *Moriarty* v *Regent's Garage & Engg Co*, [1921] 1 KB 423. LUSH J at p 431.
7. McCARDIE J at 446, *ibid*.
8. [1960] 3 All ER 420 PC: 1961 AC 12.

as its pilot. Following his death while acting as a pilot, his widow recovered compensation under the Workmen's Compensation Act.[9]

The Companies Act makes no effort to define their position. Sub-section (13) of Section 2 only provides that "director includes any person occupying the position of a director, by whatever name called". The Nigerian Act carries a better definition: "Directors of a company registered under this Act[10] are persons duly appointed by the company to direct and manage the business of the company".[11] In the words of BOWEN LJ:[12]

> Directors are described sometimes as agents, sometimes as trustees and sometimes as managing partners. But each of these expressions is used not as exhaustive of their powers and responsibilities, but as indicating useful points of view from which they may for the moment and for the particular purpose be considered.

According to JESSEL MR:[13]

> "Directors have sometimes been called trustees, or commercial trustees, and sometimes they have been called managing partners, it does not matter what you call them so long as you understand what their true position is, which is that they are really commercial men managing a trading concern for the benefit of themselves and of all other shareholders in it."

Directors as agents

It was clearly recognised as early as 1866 in *Ferguson* v *Wilson*,[14] that directors are in the eyes of law, agents of the company. The Court said:

> The company has no person; it can act only through directors and the case is, as regards those directors, merely the ordinary case of principal and agent.

The general principles of agency, therefore, govern the relations of directors with the company and of persons dealing with the company through its directors. Where the directors contract in the name, and on behalf of the company, it is the company which is liable on it and not the directors. Thus where the plaintiff supplied certain goods to a company through its chairman, who promised to issue him a debenture for the price, but never did

---

9. This principle will not apply where no proof of employment apart from being a director is available. Thus in *Parsons* v *Albert J. Parsons Ltd*, [1978] IRC 456: noted 1978 JBL 61, a person who was removed from directorship of a private company was not allowed to recover compensation for unfair dismissal. Though the Employment Appeal Tribunal had allowed his claim, the court of appeal disallowed it.
10. Companies and Allied Matters Act, 1990.
11. *See* Ameze Guobardia, *The Criminal Liability of Directors of Failed Banks in Nigeria*, 1998 JBL 198.
12. In *Imperial Hydropathic Hotel Co* v *Hampson*, (1882) 23 Ch D 1: 49 LT 150. *See* also *A. J. Judah* v *Rampada Gupta*, AIR 1959 Cal 715.
13. *Forest of Dean Coal Mining Co, Re*, (1878) 10 Ch D 450 at pp 451-452.
14. (1866) 2 Ch App 77: 36 LJ Ch 67: 15 LT 230.

so and the company went into liquidation, he was held not liable to the plaintiff.[15] Similarly, where the directors allotted certain shares to the plaintiff, they were held not liable when the company, having exhausted its shares, failed to give effect to the allotment.[16] Just as notice to an agent in the course of business amounts to notice to the principal so it is true of directors in relation to the company.[17] But notice to a director will amount to notice to the company only if the director is, like an agent, bound in the course of his duty to receive the notice and to communicate it to the company. It was held in *Hampshire Land Co, Re,*[18] that where one person is an officer of two companies, his personal knowledge is not necessarily the knowledge of both the companies unless he is under a duty to receive the notice and to communicate it to the other.[19] Like agents, they have to disclose their personal interest, if any, in any transaction of the company. It should, however, be remembered that they are the agents of an institution and not of its individual members, except when that relationship arises due to the special facts of a case.[20]

---

15. *Elkington & Co* v *Hurter*, [1892] 2 Ch 452: 66 LT 764. *Kuriakos* v *PKV Group Industries*, (2002) 111 Comp Cas 826 Ker, a director was held to be not personally liable in a suit against a private chit fund company. Attachment of the property of the managing director was held to be not permissible.

16. *Ferguson* v *Wilson*, (1866) 2 Ch App 77: 36 LJ Ch 67: 15 LT 230. *See* also *Belvedere Fish Guano Co* v *Rainham Chemical Works*, 1921 AC 465, 488; *Hrashikesh Panda* v *Indramani Swain*, (1988) 63 Comp Cas 368 Ori, a director held not personally liable for the debts of the company. *Kundan Singh* v *Moga Transport Co*, (1987) 62 Comp Cas 600 P&H where the court said that there is no provision in the Companies Act or in the Industrial Disputes Act which makes the managing director of a company personally liable for claims against the company; so is true of liability in respect of taxes. *P.C. Agarwal* v *Payment of Wages Inspector*, (2005) 127 Comp Cas 787 SC, overdue wages could not be recovered from the director. There is no such liability unless there is a specific statutory provision to that effect. *Tikam Chand Jain* v *State Govt*, (1987) 62 Comp Cas 601 P&H. A managing director was not allowed to be put under arrest and detention for company's debts, *Maruti Ltd* v *Pan India Plastic (P) Ltd*, (1995) 83 Comp Cas 888 P&H.

17. *See*, for example, S. 229 of the Indian Contract Act, 1872 and *T. R. Pratt Ltd* v *M. T. Ltd*, AIR 1938 PC 159, common directors of three companies in a group were supposed to know that the assets of one company were mortgaged for the loan to another.

18. [1896] 2 Ch 743.

19. Followed in *Sree Meenakshi Mills Ltd* v *Ratilal Thakar*, AIR 1941 Bom 108: 43 BLR 53. Receipt of money by directors from agents known to them for investment in the company when those agents knew that it was misapplied trust money.

20. *See*, for example, *Allen* v *Hyatt*, (1914) 30 TLR 444. It is a matter of evidence in each case whether a director can be regarded as a principal officer or agent for income tax purposes, *Shyam Sundar Jalan* v *State*, (1977) 47 Comp Cas 61 Cal. Directors who issued duplicate share certificates against those which were lying under pledge with the company were held personally liable to the deceived person. The company was not liable because the directors resorted to the tactics to combat a take over bid as a part of their own game plan, *Shoe Specialities Ltd* v *Tracstar Investments Ltd*, (1997) 88 Comp Cas 471 Mad. The company was held liable where its directors in order to promote the company's business gave unfounded estimates to a person to persuade him to accept the company's franchise, *Williams* v *Natural Life Health Foods Ltd*, (1996) 1 BCLC 288, affirmed by the court of appeal, (1997) 1 BCLC 131 CA. *Ray Cylinders & Containers* v *Hindustan General Industries Ltd*, (2001) 103 Comp Cas 161 Del, permission granted to file a suit against a company was not allowed to be treated as a permission against directors as well.

For a loan taken by a company, the directors, who had not given any personal guarantee to the creditor, could not be made liable merely because they were directors.[21]

The articles of association empowered the managing director to represent the company in legal proceedings. It was held that a further authorisation was not necessary to enable him to file a complaint for dishonour of a cheque under S. 138, Negotiable Instruments Act.[22]

As trustees

On the position of directors as trustees, the Nigerian Act contains this provision:[23]

> "Directors are trustees of the company's money, properties and their powers and as such must account for all the moneys over which they exercise control and shall refund any moneys improperly paid away, and shall exercise their powers honestly in the interest of the company and all the shareholders, and not their own sectional interests."

Although directors are not properly speaking trustees, yet they have always been considered and treated as trustees of money which comes to their hands or which is actually under their control; and ever since joint stock companies were invented directors have been held liable to make good moneys which they have misapplied upon the same footing as if they were trustees.[24] In *Ramaswamy Iyer* v *Brahmayya & Co*,[25] the Madras High Court observed that:

> The directors of a company are trustees for the company, and with reference to their power of applying funds of the company and for misuse of the power they could be rendered liable as trustees and on their death, the cause of action survives against their legal representatives.[26]

---

21. *Indian Overseas Bank* v *RM Marketing P Ltd*, (2001) 107 Comp Cas 606 Del.
22. *Sarathi Leasing Finance Ltd* v *B. Narayana Shetty*, (2006) 131 Comp Cas 798 Kant.
23. S. 283 of the Companies and Allied Matters Act, 1990.
24. LINDLEY LJ in *Lands Allotment Co, Re*, [1894] 1 Ch 616 at p 631. *See* also *Sharpe, Re*, [1892] 1 Ch 154: [1891-4] All ER Rep Ext 1974, where directors were held liable to replace capital which was spent by them in paying interest *ultra vires* the company. Some other examples are: *Great Luxembourg Rly Co* v *Sir William Magnay (No 2)*, (1858) 25 Beav 586; *Rose* v *Humbles*, [1970] 1 WLR 1061. *See* also SIR GEORGE JESSEL *Forest of Dean, Coal Mining Co, Re*, (1878) 10 Ch D 450: 40 LT 287 and Lord SELBORNE in *G. E. Rly Co* v *Turner*, (1872) 8 Ch App 149, 152, where his Lordship said: "The directors are mere agents or trustees of the company; trustees of the company's money or property; agents in transactions which they enter into on behalf of the company." *See* also *Selangor United Rubber Estates* v *Cradock (No 3)*, [1968] 2 All ER 1073: [1968] 1 WLR 1555. Where the directors have been held trustees of the money standing to the credit of the company's bank account which they operate.
25. [1966] 1 Comp LJ 107.
26. *See*, the judgment of P. CHANDRA REDDY CJ at pp 130-132, *ibid*, where he discusses all the English authorities on the subject. *See* also *Ekambaram* v *Venkatachalapathi Mills*, [1967] 1 Comp LJ 133: (1967) 37 Comp Cas 693 AP, where for certain loans granted in contravention of S. 86-D(1) of the Act of 1913 and which remained unpaid, the legal representatives of a deceased director were held liable. "Such cause of action *prima facie*

Another reason why directors have been described as trustees is the peculiar nature of their office. "The directors are persons selected to manage the affairs of the company for the benefit of the shareholders. It is an office of trust, which if they undertake, it is their duty to perform fully and entirely."[27] Some of their duties to the company are of the same nature as those of a trustee. For example, they, like trustees, occupy a fiduciary position. Moreover, almost all the powers of directors are powers in trust.[28] The power to make calls,[29] to forfeit shares,[30] to issue further capital,[31] the general powers of management[32] and the power to accept or refuse a transfer of shares, are all powers in trust which have to be exercised in good faith for the benefit of the company as a whole.

Yet directors are not trustees in the real sense of the word. There is nothing in common between a director and "a trustee of a will or of a marriage settlement".[33] Moreover, a trustee is the legal owner of the trust property and contracts in his own name. A director, on the other hand, is a paid agent or officer of the company and contracts for the company.[34] The real truth of the matter is that "directors are commercial men managing a trading concern for the benefit of themselves and of all the shareholders in it".[35]

For whom trustees?.—Directors are trustees of the company and not of individual shareholders. This principle was laid down in 1902 in *Percival* v *Wright*,[36] and still holds ground as a basic proposition.[37] In that case:

Negotiations for the sale of a company's undertaking were on foot and without disclosing this the directors purchased shares from the plaintiff-shareholders. The selling shareholders had written to the company's secretary asking him if he knew anyone willing to purchase their shares. Three directors offered to buy the shares at a price assessed

---

survives the death of such a person liable." The Court considered: *Peerdan Juharmal Bank, Re*, AIR 1958 Mad 583: (1958) 28 Comp Cas 546; *Sankaram Nambiar* v *Kottayam Bank*, AIR 1946 Mad 304.

27. ROMILLY MR in *York & North Midland Rly Co* v *Hudson*, (1853) 61 Beav 485: 22 LJ Ch 529.
28. *See*, for example, Berle, *Corporate Powers as Powers in Trust*, 44 Harv LR, 1949 where the learned writer enlists the powers which have been held as powers in trust.
29. *Alexander* v *Automatic Telephone Co*, [1900] 2 Ch 56: [1900-03] All ER Rep Ext 1755.
30. *Esparto Trading Co, Re*, (1879) 12 Ch D 191.
31. *Nanalal Zaver* v *Bombay Life Assurance Co*, AIR 1950 SC 172: (1950) 20 Comp Cas 179.
32. *Marshall's Valve Gear Co Ltd* v *Manning, Wardley & Co Ltd*, [1909] 1 Ch 267: 100 LT 65.
33. ROMER J in *City Equitable Fire Insurance Co, Re*, [1925] Ch 407: [1924] All ER Rep 485: 133 LT 520.
34. JAMES LJ in *Smith* v *Anderson*, (1880) 15 Ch D 247 at p 275.
35. JESSEL MR *Forest of Dean Coal Mining Co, Re*, (1878) 10 Ch D 450 at pp 451-452: 40 LT 287. Their position is that of constructive trustees. *See* an excellent study by D. W. Fox, *Constructive Trusts in a Company Setting*, 1986 JBL 23.
36. [1902] 2 Ch 421, cited with approval by the Madras High Court in *Ramaswamy Iyer* v *Brahamayya & Co*, [1966] 1 Comp LJ 107.
37. *See*, Louis Loss, *The Fiduciary concept as applied to Trading by Corporate "Insiders" in the U. S.*, (1970) 30 Mod LR 34 at 40-41, where the learned writer says that although abandoned or escaped by importing special circumstances, the *Percival* concept still represents "majority rule".

by an independent valuer but they did not disclose that they were in the process of negotiating the sale of the company at a price per share considerably higher than the amount offered to the shareholders. The negotiations proved to be abortive, but the plaintiffs claimed that the non-disclosure was a breach of the fiduciary duty entitling them to repudiate the sale.

But the court held that there was no such fiduciary duty towards individual shareholders and, therefore, the directors were not bound to disclose negotiations which ultimately proved abortive. The court also pointed out that a premature disclosure of this kind might well be against the best interests of the company.

The principle of the case was reiterated in *Peskin* v *Anderson*.[38] Ordinarily the directors are not agents or trustees of members or shareholders and owe no fiduciary duties to them.

This decision remained unchallenged in common law jurisdictions until the New Zealand decision in *Coleman* v *Myers*.[39]

The case involved a struggle for control of a privately held family company. The company had substantial assets, like cash reserves, valuable lands and buildings. The assets were undervalued in the books of account. They showed the share value to be at $4.10 on a going concern basis. If accounts were taken of the true asset backing of the shares, they were worth $7.75. The dominant majority shareholder formed another company which made a takeover offer at $4.80 per share. The reluctant minority shareholders were given notices of compulsory acquisition of shares. They eventually agreed. They had no access to inside information on the true value of the assets. No information was given to them. When they discovered the true facts they sought setting aside of the sale because of the breach of fiduciary duty.

MAHON J, said that the case could not be distinguished from *Percival* v *Wright* but that, in fact, *Percival* v *Wright* was incorrectly decided and, in the circumstances of the two cases, where directors were buying shares in their own company, a fiduciary duty was owed to shareholders. The Court of Appeal were, however, content to distinguish *Percival* v *Wright* on the special facts of the case. It held that the court will not impose a fiduciary duty automatically upon directors when they enter into transactions with the company's shareholders. Because of the special circumstances of this case, the court did impose a fiduciary duty. The circumstances were:

Face-to-face negotiations in which the members relied upon the directors to disclose all material information; the directors had a high

38. [2000] 2 BCLC 1.
39. [1977] 2 NZLR 225.

degree of inside knowledge; and the directors actively promoted the scheme and advised the shareholders to accept.[40]

The decision in *Percival* v *Wright* left scope for the rule that when negotiations reach a certain stage of maturity a disclosure of the director's profits to the selling shareholders would be necessary, otherwise the directors would be failing in their fiduciary obligation towards them.[41] The principle found application in *Allen* v *Hyatt*.[42]

> The directors of a company represented to the shareholders that their consent was necessary in order to effect an amalgamation and induced the shareholders to give them the option to purchase their shares. They exercised the option, carried out the amalgamation and made a profit.

It was held that the directors were trustees of this profit for the benefit of the shareholders. They cannot always act under the impression that they owe no duty to individual shareholders. No doubt the duty of the directors is primarily one to the company itself. But the facts of the present case showed that the directors had held themselves out to the individual shareholders as acting for them. Now, of course, there is a statutory obligation to disclose any profit of this kind to the shareholders along with the offer by which their shares are proposed to be acquired.[43]

In situations like this where the directors act as agents for the shareholders, the latter would be liable to the purchasers of their shares for any fraudulent misrepresentation made by the directors in the course of negotiations.[44]

Trustees of institution.—The role of the corporation in the modern society is something different from what it was in the previous century. "The modern company should function not simply as an economic machine designed to churn out profits for its shareholders, but rather as an institution which owes social responsibilities to a wide circle of interests."[45] The

---

40. For other cases on the subject see *Clement* v *Walker*, (1983) 1 NZCLC 98, 636, here the shareholder in question was also a director of the company with professional experience and had access to all the information contained in the company's records and *Cottam* v *GUS Properties Ltd*, (1995) 7 NZCLC 260, 821, where the duty was violated.
41. *See*, Robert H Mundheim, *The Texas Gulf Sulphur Complaint*, 1966 JBL 284 which discusses the duty of a corporate insider to disclose information materially enhancing the value of corporate stock before purchasing it.
42. (1914) 30 TLR 444. A decision of the Privy Council on appeal from Ontario.
43. Sections 319-321 of the Companies Act, 1956. *See also* under Duties of Directors, *infra*.
44. It has been so held by the House of Lords in *Briess* v *Woolley*, 1954 AC 333: [1954] 1 All ER 909. *See also* Merrick Dodd, Jr, *For Whom are Corporate Managers Trustees*, (1932) 45 Harv LR 1145, and Duty of Good Faith, *infra*.
45. R. C. Beuthin, *The Range of a Company's Interests*, (1969) 86 SALJ 155, 146. The concept of the company as a social institution is developed in the following works: George Goyder, THE FUTURE OF PRIVATE ENTERPRISE, (1951) and THE RESPONSIBLE COMPANY, (1961); Peter F. Drucker, THE CONCEPTION OF THE CORPORATION; D. L. Mazumdar, TOWARDS A PHILOSOPHY OF THE MODERN CORPORATION, Asia (1967).

Supreme Court has already conferred its recognition upon the "social character" of a company. In *Charanjit Lal* v *Union of India*,[46] MUKHERJEE J observed: "A corporation which is engaged in the production of a commodity vitally essential to the community, has a social character of its own and it must not be regarded as the concern primarily or only of those who invest money in it." Accordingly, the directors become "the administrators of a community system".[47] A business executive once declared: "I am a trustee of the institution and not merely an attorney of the investor."[48] If this position comes to be accepted, the corporation law would become "in substance a branch of the law of trusts".[49] Whether this is so or not, it is widely recognised that the directors have to consider the interests of labour, consumers, the general public and the State.[50] Public responsibility of a company means to take account of outside interests affected by corporate operations. To the extent the directors are bound to consult outside interests, they become the trustees of such interests.[51]

Directors as organs of corporate body

"There was a time when corporations played a very minor part in our business affairs, but now they play the chief part, and most men are the servants of corporations."[52] "There is scarcely any business pursued requiring the expenditure of large capital, or the union of large numbers that is not carried on by corporations. It is not too much to say that the wealth and business of the country are to a great extent controlled by them."[53] This gives the company and its executive an enormous power to affect the lives of labourers and consumers and shareholders.[54] Every position of power implies responsibility.[55] But it often became difficult to hold a company to its responsibilities in view of the artificial nature of its personality. There

---

46. 1950 SCR 869: AIR 1951 SC 41 at p 59: (1951) 21 Comp Cas 33.
47. Joseph L. Weiner, *The Berle-Dodd Dialogue of the Concept of the Corporation*, (1964) 64 Col LR 1458.
48. Cited in the above article.
49. *Id*. See also Carlos L. Israels, *Are Corporate Powers still held in Trust*, (1964) 64 Col LR 1446.
50. *See*, Lord DENNING at the 14th Legal Convention of the Law Council of Australia, cited in (1967) 41 Aust LJ 363-64, and Schmitthoff in 1966 JBL 112-13.
51. *See*, Eugene W. Rostow, *To Whom and For What Ends is the Corporate Management Responsible*, Mason. THE CORPORATION IN MODERN SOCIETY, (1959) 46, and W. H. Ferry, *Irresponsibilities in Metro Corporate America* in Andrews Hacker. THE CORPORATION TAKE-OVER, (1964) 108.
52. Woodrow Wilson, THE NEW FREEDOM, 24 (1967, Jaico).
53. FIELD J in *Pacel* v *Virginia*, 3 Wall (75 US) 168, 181-182; borrowed from Jackson, WISDOM OF THE SUPREME COURT, at 80. This statement is true of every modern democratic society.
54. Dodd, reviewing Dimock & Hyde, BUREAUCRACY AND TRUSTEESHIP IN LARGE CORPORATIONS, (1942) 9 Uni Ch L Rev 538.
55. *Id*. Cited by Joseph L Weiner, *The Berle-Dodd Dialogue of the Concept of the Corporation*, (1964) 64 Col LR 1458. *See also* Adolf A. Berle, *Modern Functions of the Corporate System*, 62 Col LR 433 (1962) and Henry G. Manne, *The Higher Criticism of the Modern Corporation*, 62 Col LR 399.

was a time when a company could not be held responsible for any wrong involving mental element. But today the range of corporate responsibility almost corresponds with that of an individual[56], as "the offending corporation cannot escape from the consequences which would follow in the case of an individual by saying that they are a corporation".[57]

This transformation has been brought about under the influence of the organic theory of corporate life, "a theory which treats certain officials as organs of the company, for whose action the company is to be held liable just as a natural person is for the action of his limbs".[58] Thus "the modern directors are something more than mere agents or trustees. The board is also correctly recognised to be a primary organ of the company."[59] As NEVILLE J put it in *Bath* v *Standard Land Co*:[60]

> The Board of directors are the brain and the only brain of the company, which is the body and the company can and does act only through them.

"When the brain functions the corporation is said to function."[61] Similarly, GREER LJ said in *Fanton* v *Denville*[62] that "a general manager of the business is regarded as the *alter ego* of the company, and it would be responsible for his personal negligence". Likewise, a company was held liable for giving a false warranty without having reason to believe that it was true.[63] The decision of the House of Lords in *Lennard's Carrying Co* v *Asiatic Petroleum Co*[64] gave a further fillip to this development:

> The facts were that the Merchant Shipping Act of 1874 provided that a shipowner would not be liable to make good a loss of or damage to the goods happening without "his actual fault". The shipowner in this

---

56. C. R. N. Winn, *Criminal Liability of Corporations*, (1929) 3 Camb LJ 398. The company would be liable in civil respects where the criminal conduct of those working for the company is either within the range of their authority or in the course of their employment, *Javali (MV)* v *Mahajan Borewell & Co*, (1998) 91 Comp Cas 708 SC.

57. BOWEN LJ in *R* v *Tyler*, [1891] 2 QB 588, 594. Cited by HALLET J in *D. P. P.* v *Kent & Sussex Contractors Ltd*, [1944] KB 146: [1944] 1 All ER 119. A company can be punished by way of fine and not imprisonment. *Oswal Vanaspati and Allied Industries* v *State of U.P.*, (1992) 75 Comp Cas 770 All; *Maniam Transports* v *S. Krishna Moorthy*, [1993] 1 Comp LJ 153 Mad. Where imprisonment is the only punishment prescribed under an Act, a company cannot be prosecuted. *P. V. Pai* v *R. L. Rinawma*, (1993) 77 Comp Cas 179 Kant; *Delhi Municipality* v *J. B. Bottling Co*, (1975) Cri LJ 1148 Del. A company can be held liable for statutory violations like an individual, but it cannot be imprisoned. *M.V. Javali* v *Mahajan Borewell & Co*, (1997) 8 SCC 72: 1997 SCC (Cri) 1239: (1998) 91 Comp Cas 708 SC.

58. TALUKDAR J in *Gopal Khaitan* v *State*, AIR 1969 Cal 132 at p 138: (1969) 39 Comp Cas 150.

59. R. C. Beuthin, *The Range of a Company's Interests*, (1969) 86 SALJ 155, 156.

60. [1910] 2 Ch 408, 416.

61. *State Trading Corpn of India Ltd* v *CTO*, AIR 1963 SC 1811 at p 1832: (1963) 33 Comp Cas 1057: (1964) 4 SCR 99 .

62. [1932] 2 KB 309 at p 329.

63. *Chuter* v *Freeth & Pocock Ltd*, [1911] 2 KB 832.

64. 1915 AC 705: [1914-15] All ER Rep 280: 113 LT 195.

case was an incorporated company and the loss had taken place due to the negligence of a managing director. The company was sued for the loss and its chief defence was that the company, being an artificial person, was incapable of committing "actual fault".

Rejecting this contention, Lord HALDANE in his well-known passage said:[65] "A corporation is an abstraction. It has no mind of its own any more than it has a body of its own; its acting and directing will must, consequently, be sought in the person of somebody who for some purpose may be called an agent, but who is really the directing mind and the will of the corporation. That person may be under the direction of shareholders in general meeting; that person may be the board of directors itself. (His) fault is the fault of somebody who is not merely a servant or agent for whose action the company is liable upon the footing *respondeat superior*, but somebody for whom the company is liable because his action is the very action of the company itself."

The company's intention to occupy a premises for its own business requisite under the Tenancy Acts to evict a tenant, can be known by referring to the directors' conduct irrespective of any formalities.[66] DENNING LJ explained the organic character of the company's life in the following words:[67]

> A company may in many ways be likened to a human body. It has a brain and a nerve centre which controls what it does. It has also hands which hold the tools and act in accordance with directions from the centre. Some of the people in the company are mere servants and agents who are nothing more than hands to do the work, and cannot be said to represent the mind or will. Others are directors and managers who represent the directing mind or will of the company and control what it does. The state of mind of these managers is the state of mind of the company and is treated by the law as such.[68]

"But the courts have not attempted to define the persons whose acts or intentions are to be considered the acts or intentions of the company."[69] It

---

65. *Id.* at pp 713-714. Reaffirmed by the House of Lords in *Tesco Supermarkets Ltd v Nattrass*, [1971] 2 WLR 1166: [1971] 2 All ER 127: 1972 AC 153.

66. *H. L. Bolton (Engg) Co Ltd v T. J. Graham & Sons*, [1956] 3 WLR 804: [1956] 3 All ER 624 CA: [1957] 1 QB 159. For the liability of a company to be evicted, see *V. G. Paneerdas v Swadeshmitran*, [1986] 2 Comp LJ 267 Mad. A director can be held personally liable for the offence of cheating by issuing a cheque if he knew of inadequate funds and also intended to cheat. *Rachna Flour Mills (P) Ltd v Lal Chand Bhangadiya*, (1987) 62 Comp Cas 15 AP.

67. *Id.* See also *C. Evans & Sons Ltd v Spritebrand Ltd*, [1985] 2 All ER 415 CA, a director and his company held liable for infringement of copyright which the director authorised, directed and procured. *Attorney-General Ref No 2 of 1982*, [1984] 2 All ER 216, whether directors depriving the company of its property in connivance with shareholders can be prosecuted for theft.

68. *See also* Lord PARKER in *Daimler Co Ltd v Continental Tyre & Rubber Co Ltd*, [1916] 2 AC 307 at p 235: [1916-17] All ER Rep 191 and DU PARQ LJ in *Triplex Safety Glass v Lancegae Safety Glass*, [1939] 2 KB 395, 408: [1939] 2 All ER 613.

69. TALBOT J in *Wheeler v New Merton Board Mills*, [1933] 2 KB 669.

has, however, been suggested that it would include the company's governing body, directors, managing director[70] or general manager or other persons having authority from the board of directors to conduct the company's business.[71] For certain purposes even the secretary has been recognised as an essential organ. For example, in *Panorama Development (Guildford) v Fidelis Furnishing Fabrics*,[72] a company was held liable for the hire of taxis engaged by the secretary for his personal purposes while operating from the office of the company. Commenting upon the growing importance of the secretary, Lord DENNING MR said:

> A modern secretary is not a mere clerk but an officer of the company with extensive duties and responsibilities and has authority to sign contracts connected with the administrative side of a company's affairs and has ostensible authority to enter into a wide range of contracts. In that respect his position has altered very materially since the 19th century.[73]

Personal Liability of Working Organ

When a tort or some other wrong happens to occur in the working processes of a company, the question would be whether the responsibility for it is to be attributed to the company or it should be borne by the director alone. The applicable principle has been thus stated:

> "The authorities . . . clearly show that a director of a company is not automatically to be identified with his company for the purpose of the law of tort, however small the company may be and however powerful his control over its affairs. Commercial enterprise and adventure is not to be discouraged by subjecting a director to such onerous potential liabilities. In every case where it is sought to make him liable for his company's torts, it is necessary to examine with care what part he played personally in regard to the act or acts complained of."[74]

---

70. *Ashok Kumar v Shingal Land and Finance P Ltd*, (1995) 82 Comp Cas 430 Del, managing director disposing of land of a colonising company under his authority under the articles to act on behalf of the company, held company bound.
71. *See*, the judgements of SCRUTTON and LAWRENCE LJJ in *Rudd v Elder Dempster & Co*, [1933] 1 KB 566 at p 576 and 594; *Moore v I. Bresler Ltd*, [1944] 2 All ER 515; *Tesco Supermarkets Ltd v Nattrass*, (1972) 2 All ER 127 HL where it was held that a branch manager of a shop was not sufficiently senior for the purpose that his default should be regarded as that of the company. He was not the *alter ego* of the company. Such an *ego* would be found amongst directors, managers, secretary or other officers of the company or someone to whom they delegated control and management with full discretionary powers in reference to some part of the company's business. Branch managers have not been regarded as the brain and the mind of the company. The deception practised on a branch manager was not the same thing as deception of the company, *R v Rozeik*, (1996) 1 BCLC 380 CA.
72. [1971] 3 WLR 440: [1971] 3 All ER 16: (1971) 2 QB 711 CA.
73. Noted (1971) 87 LQR 457. Another influence of the organic theory is shown by *Bognor Regis Urban District Council v Campion*, [1972] 2 WLR 983: [1972] 2 All ER 61, where it has been held that a corporation not only has a right to sue for libel affecting its property, but also for one affecting its personal reputation.
74. *Per* SLADE LJ in *C. Evans & Sons Ltd v Spritbrand Ltd*, (1985) BCLC 105 at p 110.

In a *New Zealand* case[75] the director of a one-man company gave advice, through the company, to a client for spraying of an insecticide around fruit trees. The advice was so negligent that fruit trees perished alongwith their parasites. The court did not consider the circumstances to be such as to hoist personal liability on the director. He had made it clear that he was trading through the company and the company was the legal contracting party to be charged with liability. As compared with this, in *Fairline Shipping Corpn* v *Adamson*[76] the director became personally liable for loss of perishable goods from the storage provided by his one-man company. The liability hinged on a letter written by the managing director to the plaintiffs on his own note paper rather than that of the company, an act which the court thought displayed an assumption of personal duty of care. In *Williams* v *Natural Life Health Foods Ltd*,[77] a health food shop was established under a franchise agreement. The franchiser company provided income projections estimates from the shop on which the plaintiff company relied in accepting the franchise. These projections proved inaccurate and after 18 months the plaintiff's business closed with substantial losses. The franchiser company came to be wound up. The plaintiffs sued the promoter-director of the company who had provided the estimate. The Court of Appeal held that in this case the director had acted in a capacity outside that of a mere director and had assumed a personal responsibility to the plaintiffs which was additional to that of the company.[78]

Liability for Bouncing of Cheques

The company would be liable to be prosecuted for the bouncing of a cheque if it was issued under the authority of the company. A complaint which alleged that the cheque was issued by a director who was in charge of and responsible for the day to day administration of the affairs of the company, was not liable to be quashed.[79]

APPOINTMENT OF DIRECTORS

The success of a company depends, to a very large extent, upon the competence and integrity of its directors. It is, therefore, necessary that management of companies should be in proper hands.[80] The appointment of directors is accordingly strictly regulated by the Act. There are now special provisions for preventing management by undesirable persons.

---

75. *Trevor Ivory* v *Anderson*, (1992) 2 NZ LR 517.
76. [1974] 2 All ER 967: [1975] QB 180.
77. [1997] 1 BCLC 131.
78. *See* notes by Jennifer Payne, *Personal Liability of Directors*, and *The Attribution of Tortious Liability between Director and Company*, 1998 JBL 153.
79. *Unico Trading and Chit Funds (India) (P) Ltd* v *Zahoor Hasan*, (1991) 71 Comp Cas 270 Kant; *Voltas Ltd* v *Hiralal Agarwalla*, (1991) 71 Comp Cas 273 Cal. The prosecution is under S. 138 of the Negotiable Instruments Act, 1881.
80. *See*, the judgment of YOUNG J in *Indian States Bank Ltd* v *Kunwar Sardar Singh*, AIR 1934 All 855.

One evil which has been abolished by the Act is that of a company or a firm acting as a director of another company. Now, according to Section 253, only an individual can be the director of a company. No company or firm or association can be appointed as a director.[81] A proviso has been added to the section by the amendments of 2006 which says that no company is to appoint or appoint any individual as a director unless he has been allotted a Director Identification Number under S. 266-B.

First directors [S. 254]

The first directors of a company are to be appointed by the subscribers of the memorandum. They are generally listed in the articles of the company. If they do not appoint any, all the subscribers who are individuals become directors. The very fact of incorporation makes them the first directors of the company. The first directors, howsoever appointed,[82] hold office only up to the date of the first annual general meeting of the company and the subsequent directors must be appointed in accordance with the provisions of Section 255.[83]

Appointment at general meeting [S. 255]

Annual rotation.—"Election of directors is the primary managerial function of stockholders in business corporations, and one that needed careful regulation in their interest."[84] According to Section 255, directors must be appointed by the company in general meetings. In the case of a public company and its subsidiary private company, of the total number of directors, only one-third can be given permanent appointment. The office of the rest of them must be liable to determination by rotation. The articles can provide for all the directors to be rotational. The effect of sub-sections (1) and (2) is that the rotational directors have to be appointed at general meetings except where the Act provides otherwise and other directors of a public and all the directors of a private company which is not subsidiary of a public company have also to be appointed at general meetings subject only to the regulations in the company's articles.

---

81. S. 204 prohibits appointment of firms etc., to any place of profit under the company. *See* the New Zealand case of *Commercial Management Ltd* v *ROC*, [1987] NZLR 744 where it is pointed out that the partners of a firm cannot be collectively appointed as directors. It would be "quite foreign to the concept of the office of directors which calls for individual judgment and responsibility".

82. Such directors have to file with the company their consent to act as a director but they do not have to file their consent with the Registrar. [S. 264].

83. *Usha Chopra (Dr)* v *Chopra Hospital (P) Ltd*, (2006) 130 Comp Cas 483 CLB, two-member, two-director company both of them NRIs, new directors appointed with no record of board meeting or of notice to directors, appointments held to be wrong and oppressive.

84. Cadman, THE CORPORATION IN NEW JERSEY, 302, (1949).

"The provision is designed to eradicate the mischief caused by self-perpetuating managements."[85] At an annual meeting only one-third of such directors shall go out.[86] In the first place those directors will retire who have been longest in office since their last appointment. As between persons who became directors on the same day, retirement is to be determined either by mutual agreement, or, in default, by lot.[87]

It has been held by the Delhi High Court[88] that directors cannot prolong their tenure by not holding a meeting in time. They would automatically retire from office on the expiry of the maximum permissible period within which a meeting ought to have been held. If no *de jure* directors are left in office to call an annual general meeting, the Company Law Board may call a meeting to appoint directors, which will not be an annual meeting, nor conduct the business of such meeting, for the court did not have the power to call an annual meeting. Now both the powers, namely, the power of calling the annual general meeting and that of calling the extraordinary general meeting are vested in the Company Law Board.

Where a director to be rotated out is also holding the office of managing director, the latter office will also go with the former, but expiry of the term of, or removal from managing directorship, does not entail the cessation of his office as a director.[89]

Reappointment (deemed reappointment) [S. 256].—The vacancies thus created should be filled up at the same meeting. But the general meeting may also resolve that the vacancies shall not be filled up. If it has done neither, the meeting shall be deemed to have been adjourned for a week. If at the reassembled meeting also no fresh appointment is made, nor there is a reso-

---

85. *Oriental Metal Pressing Works Ltd* v *Bhaskar Kashinath Thakoor*, (1961) 31 Comp Cas 143: AIR 1961 SC 573: (1960) 63 Bom LR 505. A company not for profit or which prohibits payment of dividend to members may have in its articles its own provisions on the matter [S. 263-A].
86. S. 256(1). If their number is not three or a multiple of three, then the number nearest to one-third shall retire.
87. S. 256(2). This may give rise to serious disputes. *See*, for example, *All India Tea & Trading Co* v *Upendra Narain Sinha*, 42 CWN 774 and *Kailash Chandra Dutt* v *Jogesh Chandra Majumdar*, AIR 1928 Cal 868: 32 CWN 1084, where it was held that "so long as the general meeting is not held in which new directors are to be elected, the directors elected at the previous general meeting would continue to be in office". The Madras High Court in *Ananthalakshmi Ammal* v *IT & I Ltd*, AIR 1953 Mad 467 and the Bombay High Court in *Colaba Land & Mills Co* v *Vasant Investment Corpn*, [1962] 2 Comp LJ 89 have held that the directors retire at a time when the meeting ought to have been held. But cf. *Pasari Flour Mills* v *Kesho Dev*, AIR 1961 MP 340: 1961 Jab LJ 299; *see* also *Karus* v *Lloyd Property Ltd*, 1965 VR 232 (Aust.). The controversy is still going on. A later decision is *Shrimati Jain* v *Delhi Flour Mills Co Ltd*, (1974) 44 Comp Cas 228. The effect of the provisions and of preponderance of authorities is that their office stands vacated on the last day by which the meeting ought to have been held.
88. *B. R. Kundra* v *Motion Pictures Assn*, (1976) 46 Comp Cas 339 Del.
89. *Swapan Das Gupta* v *Navin Chand Suchanti*, (1988) 64 Comp Cas 562: [1988] 3 Comp LJ 76 Cal.

lution against appointment, the retiring directors shall be deemed to have been reappointed, except in the following cases:[90]

1. Where the appointment of a particular director was put to vote, but the resolution was lost.

2. Where the retiring director has, in writing addressed to the company or its board, expressed his unwillingness to continue.

3. Where he is unqualified or has incurred a disqualification.

4. Where a special or ordinary resolution is necessary for his appointment by virtue of any of the provisions of the Act.[91]

5. A motion to appoint two or more persons as directors by a single re-solution, if passed without unanimous consent, being void under Section 363(2), it shall not have the effect of reappointing rotated out directors.

Fresh appointment **[S. 257].**—If it is proposed to appoint a new director in place of a retiring one the procedure prescribed by Section 257 must be followed. A notice in writing for his appointment should be left at the office of the company at least fourteen days before the date of the meeting along with a deposit of Rs 500 which shall be refunded to such person or member, if the candidate gets elected as a director.[92] Notice may be given by the proposed director himself or by anyone intending to propose him. The company is required to inform the members at least seven days before the meeting about the candidature.[93]

---

90. *B. R. Kundra* v *Motion Pictures Assn*, (1976) 46 Comp Cas 339 Del. Clause (*b*) of sub-s. (4); *Lalchand Mangraj* v *Shreeram Mills Ltd*, (1968) 38 Comp Cas 606 Bom. Following this case it was held in *Euro India Investments Ltd* v *Cement Corpn of Gujarat Ltd*, (1993) 76 Comp Cas 691 Guj, that a director, whose reappointment was deferred to the adjourned meeting, but no such meeting was held, nor the matter was put to vote and lost, was deemed to have been reappointed. Directors so reappointed have not to file with the Registrar their consent to act as director. [S. 264]

91. It is also necessary that the meeting must be a validly constituted meeting. *Cardamom Marketing Co* v *N. Krishna Iyer*, (1982) 52 Comp Cas 299 Ker.

92. S. 257(1). Relying upon the section and the decision in *Horbury Bridge Coal, Iron & Waggon Co, Re*, (1879) 11 Ch D 109: 40 LT 353, the Nagpur High Court has held in *Berar Trading Co* v *Gajanan Gopal Rao Dixit*, (1972) 42 Comp Cas 48 Bom that the candidature for directorship need not be seconded and if the Chairman rules it out on this ground that would invalidate all subsequent proceedings. *Oriental Benefit & Deposit Society Ltd* v *Bharat Kumar K. Shah*, (2001) 103 Comp Cas 947 Mad, the section does not prescribe any particular time of the last day for filing of nomination.

93. S. 257(1-D). The information may be given to the members either by personal notices or by publication in two local newspapers of which one must be in English and the other in the regional language. Sub-section (1-A). Where only two directors were retiring under annual rotation, but the company received notices from three persons for appointment and the company informed the members that appointing one more director would increase the number of directors, this was a sufficient compliance with the requirements of the Act. The appointment was valid because the increase was within the maximum stated in the articles. *S. Pazhamalai* v *Aruna Sugars Ltd*, (1984) 55 Comp Cas 500 Mad. It is not necessary for proposing a candidate by a special notice that the requirements of S.188 relating to circulation of members' resolution be complied with. *Gopal Vyas* v *Sinclair Hotels & Transportation Ltd*, AIR 1990 Cal 45: [1990] 1 Comp LJ 388: (1990) 68 Comp Cas 518 distinguishing *Pedley* v *Inland Waterways Assn Ltd*, 1976 JBL 349: [1977] 1 All ER 209. The ruling in *Gopal Vyas* case has been followed in

Appointment by nomination

Section 255(2) leaves scope for appointments to be made in accordance with the company's articles without being routed through the company's general meeting. An agreement among the shareholders may be imbibed in the articles to the effect that every holder of 10% shares shall have the right to nominate a director on the board.[94] Lending institutions also insist on putting upon the company's board of directors some of their nominees for watching their interest. The phenomenon of nominee directors is now a part of the corporate scenario.

Appointment by voting on individual basis [S. 263]

The appointment of every director is required to be made by voting at the general meeting. The candidates cannot be put to vote en bloc. Rather each candidate has to be voted on individually.[95] Wishes of shareholders in relation to each proposed director should be obtained. If two or more persons are appointed directors by a single resolution, the same is void and non-existent in the eyes of law.[96] But if the meeting has unanimously so resolved, more than one person may be elected by a single resolution.[97] A person who has been appointed as a director for the first time is required to submit within thirty days of his appointment a written consent to act as a director to the Registrar of Companies.[98]

Where the candidates are greater in number than the posts, the first appointment will go to the top scorer and further in the descending order from among those in whose favour the number of votes cast are more than those cast against them.[99]

Karnataka Bank Ltd v *A. B. Datar*, (1993) 2 Kar LJ 230: (1994) 79 Comp Cas 417 and *Prakash Road Lines Ltd* v *Vijay Kumar & Narang*, (1993) 4 Kar LJ 561: (1995) 83 Comp Cas 569 Kant. On receiving a notice the company becomes bound to inform the members. It has no discretion in the matter. *See* the first cited case above.

   Namita Gupta v *Cachar Native Joint Stock Co Ltd*, (1999) 98 Comp Cas 655 CLB, non-compliance with the requirements of procedure renders the appointment void. In this case, the members were not informed.

   Section 257 does not apply to a private company which is not a subsidiary of a public company. *Sree Rama Vilas Press and Publications (P) Ltd, Re*, (1992) 73 Comp Cas 275 Ker; *K. Meenakshi Amma* v *Sree Rama Vilas Press and Publications Ltd*, (1992) 73 Comp Cas 285 Ker.

94. *Bharat Bhushan* v *H. B. Portfolio Leasing Ltd*, (1992) 74 Comp Cas 20 Del.
95. S. 263(1). S. 263-A exempts from these provisions a company which does not carry on business for profit or which prohibits the payment of dividend to its members.
96. *Raghunath Swarup Mathur* v *Dr Raghuraj Bahadur*, [1966] 2 Comp LJ 100: (1967) 37 Comp Cas 802 All. But that is not a punishable offence.
97. There should first be an agreement to that effect at the meeting without any vote being given against it.
98. S. 264.
99. *B. Sivaraman* v *Egmore Benefit Society Ltd*, (1992) 75 Comp Cas 198 Mad. A company not for profit or which prohibits payment of dividend to members may have different provisions on the matter in its articles [S. 263-A].

Appointment by Special Resolution [S. 261] (*deleted* by 1969 amendment)

Appointment by proportional representation [S. 265]

It is apparent from the above provisions that the basic method adopted by the Act for the appointment of directors is election by simple majority. All the directors of a company can, therefore, be appointed by a simple majority of shareholders and a substantial minority cannot succeed in placing even a single director on the board. "Section 265 was, therefore, enacted by the Legislature so that the minority may have an opportunity of placing their representative on the board."[1] This section enables a company to provide in its articles the system of voting by proportional representation for the appointment of directors. This system of voting is devised to make minority votes effective. It is thus explained by BALLETINE in his book on CORPORATIONS:

> "Cumulative voting is the privilege, where several directors are to be voted for at the same time, of casting votes of the whole number of shares held, multiplied by the number of directors to be elected, for the candidate, for distributing the votes among part of the vacancies to be filled."[2]

"Cumulative voting is a voting procedure which permits a substantial minority of stockholders to elect one or more directors. A group owning one-seventh of the shares can always elect one-seventh of the directors."[3] Under this system each shareholder's vote is more important than under straight voting. It also facilitates the removal of an inefficient management. "Thus in some cases in the United States companies were salvaged by a single director placed on the board by cumulative voting and who brought out correct information."[4]

Casual vacancies [S. 262]

A casual vacancy occurs when the office of a director is vacated before the expiry of his term. Such a vacancy may be filled in accordance with the procedure prescribed by the articles. In the absence of any such clause in the articles, power is given to the directors to fill the vacancy at a board meeting. Any person so appointed holds office until the expiry of the period for which the outgoing director would have held office.

Additional directors [S. 260]

Additional directors can be appointed by the board if there is a power to that effect in the articles, provided that the total number of directors shall not

---

1. For a remarkable account of the importance of this system *see* Justice P. N. BHAGWATI'S, *Rights of Minority Shareholders*, published in *Current Problems of Corporate Law Management and Practice* of the Indian Law Institute, New Delhi.
2. Para 177 (1946 Edn).
3. John G. Sobieski, *In Support of Cumulative Voting*, 1960 JBL 316.
4. Ved Prakash Juneja, *Proportional Representation on Boards of Companies*, [1969] 2 Comp LJ 29.

exceed the maximum fixed by the articles. Where the strength of directors fell below the legal minimum, the appointment of an additional director by the remaining directors was held to be valid.[5] Such additional directors shall hold office only up to the date of the next annual general meeting.[6] They are exempted by Section 264 from the requirement of filing consent to act as director.

Appointment by Board

While the general power to appoint directors is vested in the general meeting of shareholders, there are at least two cases when the board can also appoint new directors. Firstly, articles may empower the directors to appoint additional directors subject, of course, to the maximum number fixed therein.[7] And, secondly, the Act itself by Section 262 authorises the directors to fill casual vacancies.

This may occasionally result in a conflict between the general meeting and the directorate. This kind of situation developed in *Viswanathan* v *Tiffins B.A. & P. Ltd.*[8]

A clause in the articles of a company authorised the directors to fill casual vacancies and also to increase the number of directors within the maximum number fixed in the articles. Some casual vacancies occurred but they were promptly filled at a general meeting of the shareholders. This was challenged on the ground that once the power to appoint was delegated to the board, it could not have been exercised at a general meeting.

After an extensive review of English authorities, VENKATRAMA IYER J upheld the appointment and said: "The principles can be summed up thus: A company has inherent power to take all steps to ensure its proper working and that, of course, includes the power to appoint directors. It can delegate this power to the board and such delegation will be binding upon it, but if there is no legally constituted board which could function or if there is a board that is unable or unwilling to function then the authority delegated to the board lapses and the members can exercise the right inherent in them of appointing directors."

---

5. *Shailesh Harilal Shah* v *Matushree Textiles Ltd*, AIR 1994 Bom 20. This power of the directors is not to be affected by the provisions of Ss. 255, 258 or 259. The effect seems to be that the requirement approval of Central Govt. under S. 259 for increasing the number of directors would not be applicable. There being no special provision, appointment of additional directors and employees can be questioned in a civil suit, *Vijay Kumar Gupta* v *Ram Naresh Singh*, (2004) 122 Comp Cas 771 Pat.
6. Where the AGM was stayed or deferred at the orders of the CLB, the nominee director remained in office till the stay was vacated and the meeting actually held, *Ador-Samia Ltd* v *Indocan Engg Systems Ltd*, (2000) 100 Comp Cas 370 CLB.
7. S. 260.
8. AIR 1953 Mad 520: [1953] 1 MLJ 346: (1953) 23 Comp Cas 79.

The court found that at the time of the general meeting there was no director validly in office and, therefore, the members had the right to elect.[9]

A similar appointment was upheld by the Privy Council in *Ram Kissendas* v *Satya Charan.*[10] But their Lordships added:

> The articles may, however, be so expressed as to delegate the power of appointing new directors to the board to the exclusion of the general meeting.

It follows, therefore, that the question turns upon the construction of the language used in the articles.

Appointment by Central Government [S. 408]

The Central Government has the power under Section 408 to appoint directors for the purpose of prevention of oppression and mismanagement. This power comes into play when a petition has been made to the National Company Law Tribunal for prevention of oppression and mismanagement.

Appointment by Company Law Board [S. 402]

The Company Law Board has the power to appoint directors for prevention of oppression and mismanagement.

Right to increase number of directors [Ss. 258-259]

A company may increase the number of its directors by passing an ordinary resolution at a general meeting. But the total number of directors must not exceed the limits fixed by the company's articles. However, an increase shall not have any effect unless approved by the Central Government and shall be void so far as it is disapproved. But in the following cases, the sanction of the Central Government is not necessary:

1. In the case of a company in existence on July 21, 1951, for an increase which was within the permissible maximum under its articles as in force on that date.

2. In the case of other companies an increase which is within the permissible maximum under the articles of a company as first registered.

---

9. The authorities reviewed by the learned Judge were: *Blair Open Hearth Furnace Co Ltd* v *Reigart*, (1913) 108 LT 665, which was considered to be of doubtful validity; *Worcester Corsetry Ltd* v *Witting*, [1936] Ch 640 CA; *Ram Kissendas* v *Satya Charan*, AIR 1950 PC 81; *Isle of Wight Rly Co* v *Tahourdin*, (1883) 25 Ch D 320: 50 LT 132; *Barron* v *Potter*, [1914] 1 Ch 895: 110 LT 929.

10. AIR 1950 PC 81. *See* also *Ananthalakshmi Ammal* v *IT & I Ltd*, AIR 1953 Mad 467 and *Srinivasan* v *Subramania*, AIR 1932 Mad 100: 136 IC 193, where the power of appointment vested in the shareholders, having been usurped by the directors, the appointments were held to be void.

3. Where the permissible maximum is twelve or less and the proposed increase does not make the total number of directors more than twelve.[11]

An agreement between groups of shareholders not to increase the number of directors and capital of the company and also not to do anything disturbing the existing pattern of management was held to be not binding on the company so as to prevent it from doing any of those things.[12]

Qualifications of directors

Share qualification [S. 270]

The articles of a company may provide that a certain number of shares will have to be held by each director. Such shares are called qualification shares. Within two months of appointment of a director, he must obtain the required number. No person can be compelled to obtain qualification shares before his appointment as director or within a period shorter than two months of his appointment.[13] The value of qualification shares cannot exceed five thousand rupees except when the nominal value of a single share exceeds that amount. Holding of share warrants does not serve the purpose of the Act. Only shares must be held. A director who fails to acquire his qualification shares within the prescribed period suffers in two ways: firstly, his office falls vacant[14] and, secondly, he becomes liable to a penalty if he continues to act as a director.[15]

The director must hold the shares in his own right.[16] He must not take them as a present from the promoters. If he does so, he will hold such shares in trust for the company.[17] Joint holding and holding by the firm in which he is a partner have been held to be sufficient.[18]

---

11. Not applicable to a private company unless it is a subsidiary of a public company. Increasing the number of directors beyond 12 would require Central Government approval, *Vinod Kumar Mittal v Kaveri Lime Industries Ltd*, [2000] 2 Comp LJ 354 CLB. An increase without such approval would be ineffective, *Registrar of Companies v Bharat Produce Co Ltd*, (1980) 50 Comp Cas 250.

12. *Rolta India (P) Ltd v Venire Industries Ltd*, (2000) 100 Comp Cas 19.

13. S. 270(2). Though the section does not provide as to the time from which the period of two months is to be taken from the time that the director in question should come to know of his appointment as such.

14. *Coal Products v R. A. Jalan*, [1968] 1 Comp LJ 311: (1969) 39 Comp Cas 223 Cal. *See* also *Zamir Ahmad v D.R. Banaji*, (1957) 27 Comp Cas 634: AIR 1958 Bom 198: 59 Bom LR 591, where it was held that when the office falls vacant by reason of failure to acquire qualification shares, the director's name cannot be placed on the list of contributories.

15. Extending up to 500 rupees per day (S. 272). Section 273 saves private companies which are not subsidiaries of public companies from the operation of Ss. 270 and 272.

16. *Boschoek Proprietary Co Ltd v Fuke*, [1906] 1 Ch 148: 94 LT 398 and *Sutton v English & Colonial Produce Co*, [1902] 2 Ch 502: 87 LT 438.

17. *Canadian Oil Works Corpn, Re*, (1875) 10 Ch App 593: 33 LT 466.

18. *Spencer v Kennedy*, [1925] All ER Rep 135: [1926] Ch 125; *Grundy v Briggs*, [1910] 1 Ch 444: 101 LT 901.

Shareholders may, however, insist on some other qualification. It was observed in *S.V.S. Nidhi* v *Daivasigamani*:[19]

> [T]hat to be a director the holding of shares is not a necessary *sine qua non*. The shareholders may well desire to have other qualifications. The matter is left entirely to the discretion and judgment of the share-holders. Hence a special resolution providing for the holding of a fixed deposit of one thousand rupees as an additional qualification for a director is *intra vires* and legal.

Direction Identification Number

Application for allotment of number [S. 266-A]

Existing directors as well as persons seeking to become directors have to apply to the Central Government for allotment of a number. Existing ones have to apply within 60 days from the date of commencement of the Amendment. The application has to be in a prescribed form and has also to be filed in the prescribed manner including electronic filing. Once an application is made, the existing directors can continue in position. The Central Government has to make the allotment within one month [S. 266-B].

Prohibition on more than one Identification number [S. 266-C]

Once a number has been allotted, the individual concerned cannot seek allotment of any other number. The director has then to inform his companies of the number allotted to him. [S. 266-D]

Company to inform Registrar [S. 266-E]

Within one week of the receipt of information about the number, the company has to inform the Registrar or a designated officer. The information has to be furnished by the company in a prescribed form. Any particulars or information concerning a director which has to be furnished by the company under the Act has to specify his identification number. [S. 266-E].

Section 266-G contains penalty provisions.

Disqualifications [S. 274]

Section 274 lays down the minimum eligibility requirements. A person is not capable of being appointed a director in the following cases:

(*a*) Where he is of unsound mind, provided that the fact has been certified by a court of competent jurisdiction and the finding is in force;

---

19. AIR 1951 Mad 520: (1951) 21 Comp Cas 85. See also *Navnitlal Chabildas* v *Scindia Steam Navigation Co Ltd*, AIR 1927 Bom 609: 105 IC 541. The Act, however, does not prescribe any share qualification. See *The People's Bank of Northern India, Re*, AIR 1933 Lah 51. This is, however, subject to the requirements of S. 270 which requires that the amount should not exceed Rs 5000 and those of S. 274 which provides that a public company cannot add any other disqualifications. A qualification in terms of deposit etc., may become necessary where the company is without share capital.

(*b*) Where he is an undischarged insolvent;[20]

(*c*) Where he has applied to be adjudicated as an insolvent;

(*d*) Where he has been sentenced to at least six months of imprisonment for an offence involving moral turpitude and five years have not elapsed from the date of the expiry of the sentence;[21]

(*e*) Where he has not paid for six months any call on his shares;[22]

(*f*) Where he has been disqualified under Section 203 of the Act for the purpose of preventing fraudulent persons from managing companies.

(*g*) Where such person is already a director of a public company,—

    (A) which has not filed the annual accounts and annual returns for any continuous three financial years, (commencing on and after the first day of April, 1999); or

    (B) has failed to repay its deposit or interest on it on due date or redeem its debentures on due date or pay dividend and such failure continues for one year or more. (The person so disqualified shall not be eligible for appointment as director of any other public company for five years from the date of the specified types of failure).[23]

---

20. *Jayesh Ramniklal Doshi* v *Carbon Corpn Ltd*, (1993) 96 Comp Cas 748 Bom. On appeal to the Supreme Court, *Mukul Harkisondass Dalal* v *Jayesh*, 1994 Mah LJ 259 Bom. The Supreme Court discharged the proceedings itself and the director remained qualified for his post.

21. This may be waived by the Central Government in favour of any person by notification in the Official Gazette [sub-section (2)]. Leave can be granted to a person about whom there was no evidence to show that he was misusing the names or assets of the company. *Lightening Electrical Contractors Ltd, Re*, (1996) 2 BCLC 302 Ch D. The period of *de facto* disqualification during the pendency of the proceedings is a relevant consideration for granting leave to a disqualified person. *Secy of State for Trade and Industry* v *Arif*, (1997) 1 BCLC 34 Ch D. Where such conviction is under appeal and there is a prayer for suspending the sentence for the purposes of this disqualification, the court should consider the possible effect of the director continuing in office upon the interests of the company and its shareholders. *Rama Narang* v *Ramesh Narang*, (1995) 2 SCC 513: (1995) 83 Comp Cas 194: (1995) 16 Corpt LA 247 SC. The meaning of the expression "moral turpitude" was traced by the Kerala High Court in *Joy* v *State of Kerala*, (1991) 72 Comp Cas 57. K. T. THOMAS J said: "The expression "moral delinquency" or "moral turpitude" has not been defined. All offences do not necessarily involve moral turpitude, e.g., violation of traffic rules, or non-compliance with certain statutory requirements such as filing of returns. Though the expression is vague, it is generally taken to mean a conduct contrary to justice, honesty, modesty or good morals. It implies depravity and wickedness of character. In BOUVIER'S LAW DICTIONARY it is described as an act of baseness or depravity in private or social duties which a man owes to his fellowmen or to the society in general, contrary to the accepted and customary rule of right and duty between man and man. The offence must be of such a type as would bring the offender into disrepute among the right thinking members of the society."

22. May also be waived. Id. *Ramesh Narang* v *Rama Narang*, (1995) 2 Bom CR 7 Bom, the power of removing disqualification on conviction can be exercised in respect of a director but not a managing director.

23. *Snowcem India Ltd* v *UOI*, (2005) 124 Comp Cas 161, these provisions have been held valid. The circular exempting nominee directors from these provisions, also valid. Also to the same

Provision for Additional Disqualifications

A private company which is not a subsidiary of a public company may add to the above further disqualifications.[24] It has been held by the Supreme Court[25] that this is an indirect way of saying that a public company and its subsidiary private companies cannot increase the disqualifications or add any other qualification, such as, for example, that the candidate should be a graduate.

The restriction on providing for additional disqualifications has been held to be not applicable to a Stock Exchange Public Company. Such a company can increase the grounds of disqualification for the membership of its governing council.[26]

Number of companies [Ss. 275 and 276]

A person cannot hold office of a director in more than 15 companies at the same time.[27] Facts are the only basis on which a director can properly exercise his judgment in the affairs of the company. No man can have the detailed knowledge of the facts of many enterprises. Where a director already holding office in 15 companies is appointed, the appointment shall not take effect and shall become void unless within fifteen days he vacates his office in some companies so as to bring down the number to twenty.[28]

Vacation of office by directors [S. 283]

The office of a director is vacated when he incurs any of the disqualifications mentioned in S. 274 and also on the following additional grounds:

1. he fails to obtain within the time specified in sub-section (1) of Section 270, or at any time thereafter ceases to hold, the share qualification, if any, required of him by the articles of the company;

---

effect, *Saurashtra Cement Ltd* v *Union of India*, (2007) 136 Comp Cas 1 Guj; *Hindustan Club Ltd* v *Pawan Kumar Jain*, (2006) 129 Comp Cas 171 Cal, declaration of disqualification before appointment or nomination. *Pawan Jain* v *Hindustan Club Ltd*, (2005) 5 Comp LJ 1 Cal.

24. S. 274(3).
25. *Cricket Club of India* v *Madhav L. Apte*, (1975) 45 Comp Cas 574 Bom.
26. *Ketan Harkishan Marvadi* v *Saurashtra Kutch Stock Exchange Ltd*, (2002) 109 Comp Cas 269 Guj.
27. S. 275.
28. In computing the number for this purpose the following companies shall be excluded: (1) a private company which is neither a subsidiary nor a holding company of a public company; (2) an unlimited company; (3) an association not carrying on business for profit and which prohibits the payment of dividend to its members; (4) a company in which such a person is only an alternate director and will act only in the absence or incapacity of a director. S. 278. *See also* S. 279 which provides a penalty of Rs 50,000 in respect of each company after the first fifteen companies. Section 277 gives similar choice on the commencement of the Companies (Amendment) Act, 2000.

2. he is found to be of unsound mind by a court of competent jurisdiction;

3. he applies to be adjudicated an insolvent;

4. he is adjudged an insolvent;

5. he is convicted by a court of any offence involving moral turpitude and sentenced in respect thereof to imprisonment for not less than six months;]

6. he fails to pay any call in respect of shares of the company held by him, whether alone or jointly with others, within six months from the last date fixed for the payment of the call [unless the Central Government has, by notification in the Official Gazette, removed the disqualification incurred by such failure;]

7. where he absents himself from three consecutive meetings of the Board or from all meetings of the Board for a period of three months, whichever is longer, without leave of absence from the Board,[29] Three months start running from the date of the first meeting that the director did not attend.[30]

8. Where he takes a loan from the company in contravention of Section 275;

9. Where he makes a contract with the company in contravention of Section 299, that is, without disclosing his interest in the contract;[31]

---

29. See *Devi Talkies (P) Ltd* v *V. R. Partha Sarthi*, (1982) 52 Comp Cas 242 Mad, where the director proved that of the three alleged meetings two were never held and the other was notified late, but even so the court did not reinstate him as he was not re-elected at a subsequent meeting. Though a director may question the fact of a meeting or the fact of notice to him, he is not entitled to an opportunity of being heard before the section is permitted to operate. *Shekhar Mehra* v *Kilpest (P) Ltd*, [1986] 3 Comp LJ 234 MP. *Gautam Kapur* v *Limrose Engg (P) Ltd*, (2005) 128 Comp Cas 237 CLB, no proof that three meetings were actually held. The matter is within the jurisdiction of ordinary civil courts and, therefore, the court can examine on evidence whether the requirements for vacation of office have been made out or not, *Radhakrishnan* v *Thirumani Asphalts and Felts (P) Ltd*, (1997) 27 Comp LA 78: (1997) 91 Comp Cas 31 Mad. Notice of meeting given at a time when the director was known to be abroad and, therefore, unable to attend and there was also no proof of despatch, no automatic vacation, *T. M. Paul (Dr)* v *City Hospitals Ltd*, [2000] 2 Comp LJ 84: (1999) 97 Comp Cas 216 Ker DB; *Atmaram Modi* v *ECL Agrotech*, (1999) 34 CLA 14 CLB, meeting not properly convened; *Puneet Goel* v *Khelgaon Resorts Ltd*, (2000) 38 CLA 259, CLB, also no proof of notices. *S. T. Ganapathi Mudaliar* v *S. G. Pandurangan*, (1999) 96 Comp Cas 919 CLB, notice sent at an address where the director was not residing, failure to attend meeting did not constitute a ground for automatic vacation. *Kamal K. Dutta (Dr)* v *Ruby General Hospital Ltd*, (2000) 36 CLA 214, 231 CLB, notice at local address, when the director was in abroad, served no purpose.

30. *Ajit Singh* v *DSS Enterprises P Ltd*, (2002) 109 Comp Cas 597 CLB. *Dalip Singh Sachar* v *Maa Karni Coal Carriers (P) Ltd*, (2006) 130 Comp Cas 641 CLB, time is not to be computed from calendar month.

31. The matter of the appointment of a director, his qualification and disqualification, vacation of office, etc., are matters of the jurisdiction of ordinary civil courts. *Avanthi Explosives (P) Ltd* v *Principal Subordinate Judge*, (1987) 62 Comp Cas 301 AP. *Suryakant Gupta* v *Rajaram Corn Products (Punjab) Ltd*, (2002) 108 Comp Cas 133 CLB, in the case of a closely held company

10. He becomes disqualified by an order of the court under Section 203, [To restrain fraudulent persons];

11. He is removed in pursuance of Section 284;[32]

12. If he was appointed *ex officio,* he ceases to hold that office in the company.

The provision as to disqualification by non-attendance of meetings was held to be not attracted where four meetings were held within a period of less than three months.[33]

A director is obliged at the pain of penalty to leave office when he incurs any of the above disqualifications.[34]

Where the vacation of office is due to adjudication as insolvent or conviction for an offence or an order of disqualification, it will not take effect for thirty days. If an appeal is preferred against the order within thirty days, it will not take effect until the expiry of seven days from the disposal of the appeal. If a further appeal is preferred, the order will become effective after the disposal of the appeal. [S. 283(2)].

Automatic Operation

The tenor of the section and the penalty provision which becomes effective from the date of disqualification show that the operation of the

---

the dealings of the company with a firm in which the director was interested was known to all the directors. The failure to formally disclose his interest did not invalidate the resolution.

32. See *Vithalrao Narayana Raw Patil* v *Maharashtra State Seeds Corpn Ltd*, (1990) 68 Comp Cas 608 Bom. All matters relating to appointment, disqualification, vacation of office, removal of directors are matters for the jurisdiction of civil courts and not those of company courts. See *Panipat Woollen and General Mills* v *Kaushik*, (1969) 39 Comp Cas 249 P&H, followed in *Prakasam* v *Sree Narayana Dharma Paripalna Yogam*, (1980) 50 Comp Cas 611 Ker; *Avanti Explosives (P) Ltd* v *Coromandal Pharmaceuticals Ltd*, (1997) 89 Comp Cas 270 AP. There is no provision in Companies Act which gives exclusive jurisdiction in all company matters to company courts, *Myalarapu Ramkrishna Rao* v *Mothey Krishna Rao*, (1947) 17 Comp Cas 63 Mad; *Marturi Umamaheshwara Rao* v *Pendayala Venkatarayudu*, (1970) 40 Comp Cas 751: AIR 1970 AP 225; *Marikar Motors* v *Ravikumar*, (1982) 52 Comp Cas 362 Ker; suits for refund of subscription money, *Vatsa Industries Ltd* v *Shankarlal Saraf*, (1996) 87 Comp Cas 918 and relating to forfeiture of shares; *Tej Prakash S. Dangi* v *Coromandal Pharmaceuticals Ltd*, (1997) 89 Comp Cas 270 AP, have been held to be matters of civil court jurisdiction.

33. *Puneet Goel* v *Three ACES Services Ltd*, (2002) 109 Comp Cas 863 CLB. *Ajit Singh* v *DSS Enterprises P Ltd*, (2002) 109 Comp Cas 597 CLB, in the case of a private company leave of absence is normally granted without any written or oral application. Three months start running from the date of the first meeting that the director did not attend.

34. Sub-section (2-A) of S. 283 provides that if a person functions as a director when he knows that the office of director held by him has become vacant on account of any of the disqualifications specified in the several clauses of sub-section (1), he shall be punishable with fine which may extend to five thousand rupees for each day on which he so functions as a director. Where there is no provision in the articles regarding resignation, a director's resignation takes effect from the date of submission. Formality of acceptance by the board is not necessary. He will not be liable for any default happening afterwards, such as failure to file accounts. *T. Murari* v *State*, (1976) 46 Comp Cas 616 Mad. For a study of the liability of such directors *see* L. S. Sealy, DISQUALIFICATION AND PERSONAL LIABILITY OF DIRECTORS, (1987). *K. Venkat Rao* v *Rockwool India Ltd*, (2002) 108 Comp Cas 494 AP, factual matters fall within the jurisdiction of the company court.

section is automatic. The office becomes vacated from the date of disqualification. No formalities, no show-cause notice, no hearing and no decision are necessary. All that is necessary is that there should be proof of the happening of the disqualifying event.[35]

Removal of directors

1. *Removal by shareholders* [S. 284]

Section 284 provides that "a company may, by ordinary resolution, remove a director before the expiration of his period of office". Section 184 of the English Companies Act, after providing the same, adds "notwithstanding anything in its [company's] articles or any agreement between it and him". But despite the absence of these words from the Indian provision, the same effect would follow as any provision in the company's articles or in any agreement between a director and the company by which the director is rendered irremovable by an ordinary resolution would be void, being contrary to the Act. The section is intended to do away with arrangements under which directors were either irremovable or removable only by extraordinary resolutions. "The field over which [the section] operates is thus extensive".[36] But it admits of the following exceptions:

1. It does not apply to the case of a director appointed by the Central Government in pursuance of Section 408. [S. 284(1)].

2. It does not, in the case of a private company, authorise the removal of a director holding office for life on April 1, 1952. [proviso].

3. It does not apply to the case of a company which has adopted the system of electing two-thirds of its directors by the principle of proportional representation. [proviso].[37]

A special notice of a resolution to remove a director is required, that is, notice of the intention to move the resolution should be given to the company not less than fourteen days before the meeting.[38] This is to enable

---

35. *Bharat Bhushan* v *H. B. Portfolio Leasing Ltd*, (1992) 74 Comp Cas 20 Del. If the company's records show despatch of board meeting notices, it would create a presumption under S. 53(2) of proper service. Under S. 264, directors have to file their consent to act as such with the company. Not applicable to directors reappointed after retirement by rotation and those who apply for candidature under S. 257. Directors have also to file within 30 days of appointment a consent letter with the Registrar. Not applicable to reappointment, alternate and additional directors and those named in the articles as first directors. The vacation of office is a matter for civil court jurisdiction and not company court, *K. Radhakrishnan* v *Thirumani Asphalts & Pelts (P) Ltd*, (1998) 91 Comp Cas 31 Mad.

36. Any restriction upon the power of removal would be void. See *Tarlok Chand Khanna* v *Raj Kumar Kapoor*, (1983) 54 Comp Cas 12 Del.

37. The section also does not apply to nominated directors and those of a Government company. The matter of appointment and removal is in the realm of contract and therefore cannot be challenged under writ jurisdiction. *Parrel Putado* v *State of Goa*, (1994) 80 Comp Cas 859 Bom.

38. This privilege of members to propose by special notice the appointment or removal of a director cannot be subjected to the requirement of S.188 relating to circulation of members' resolutions. *Gopal Vyas* v *Sinclair Hotels and Transportation Ltd*, AIR 1990 Cal 45: [1990] 1

the company to inform the members beforehand. As soon as the company receives the notice, it must furnish a copy of it to the director concerned who will have the right to make a representation against the resolution and to be heard at the general meeting. If the director submits a representation and requests the company to circulate it among the members, the company should, if there is time enough to do so, send a copy of the representation to every member of the company to whom notice of the meeting is sent. If this is not possible, the representation may be read out to the members at the meeting.[39]

Where a meeting is requisitioned by the shareholders for the very purpose of removing a director, the Supreme Court laid down that it is not necessary for the requisitionists to state the reasons on which they wish to proceed against the director.[40] Earlier the Bombay High Court had expressed the opinion that a notice of removal which does not mention the grounds would be against the meaning and intent of the Companies Act because it would defeat the director's statutory right of representation in the sense that

---

Comp LJ 388: (1990) 68 Comp Cas 516. Followed in *Karnataka Bank Ltd* v *A. B. Dattar*, (1993) 2 Kar LJ 230: (1994) 79 Comp Cas 417; *Prakash Road Lines Ltd* v *Vijay Kumar Narang*, (1993) 4 Kar LJ 561: (1995) 83 Comp Cas 569 Kant and in *Ernakulam Financiers & Kurries (P) Ltd* v *Joseph Chandy*, (1998) 93 Comp Cas 275 CLB, the company was not entitled to a declaration that the requirements of circulation of a members' resolution should be satisfied. Also to the effect that the requirement of circulation of members' resolution has not to be satisfied is *Karedla Suryanarayana* v *Shri Ramdas Motor Transport Ltd*, (1998) 28 Corpt LA 233 CLB: (1999) 98 Comp Cas 518 CLB. Contrary rulings are *Pedley* v *Inland Waterways Assn Ltd*, (1977) 1 All ER 209 Ch D; *Amar Nath Malhotra* v *MCS Ltd*, (1993)) 76 Comp Cas 469 Del. A resolution passed without special notice would be invalid irrespective of the fact whether the meeting was valid or not. *Queens Kuries and Loans (P) Ltd* v *Sheena Jose*, (1993) 76 Comp Cas 821 Ker.

39. S. 284(2) to (4). The meeting should be a valid meeting in all its aspects. *M. G. Mohanraj* v *Mylapore Hindu Permanent Fund Ltd*, [1990] 1 Comp Cas 87 Mad: [1990] 1 Comp LJ 73 Mad. A resolution without affording the opportunity of making a representation would be null and void. Where there is no evidence of the posting of a letter to the director sought to be removed, it is a denial of opportunity, *Bhankerpur Simbhaoli Beverages (P) Ltd* v *P. R. Pandya*, (1995) 17 Corpt LA 170 P&H: The proviso to sub-s (4) provides that the representation need not be circulated nor read at the meeting where, on application to the Central Government, the latter is satisfied that the rights conferred by the section are being abused for giving needless publicity to defamatory matter. The director may be ordered to pay the costs of the application even if he is not a party to it, see for a discussion on the point, *Jarvis* v *Price Waterhouse Coopers*, [2000] 2 BCLC 368 Ch D. The same considerations apply to the representation of an auditor. *Dankha Devi Agarwal* v *Tara Properties (P) Ltd*, (2006) 7 SCC 382: (2006) 133 Comp Cas 236 SC, if there is no proof of notice of meeting, the meeting as well as removal become invalid.

40. *LIC* v *Escorts Ltd*, (1986) 1 SCC 264: (1986) 59 Comp Cas 548: [1986] 1 Comp LJ 91 SC. Section 284 cannot be used for calling a meeting for a declaration that election of directors at a previous meeting was not valid. *B. Sivaraman* v *Egmore Benefit Society Ltd*, (1992) 75 Comp Cas 198 Mad. Where for the removal of two directors of a banking company a letter was written by the company to the Reserve Bank recommending removal on stated grounds, it was held that a copy of the same letter should have been attached with the notice to the directors concerned, without which the notice was not valid, *B. G. Somayaji* v *Karnataka Bank Ltd*, (1995) 83 Comp Cas 649 Kant. The stay order on the ground of incomplete notice was vacated by the Supreme Court on the condition that a letter containing necessary information be circulated before the meeting, *P. Rajan Rao* v *B. G. Somayaji*, (1995) 83 Comp Cas 662 SC.

it would be impossible to write a representation without proper information. This proposition was not accepted by the Supreme Court. CHINNAPPA REDDY J[41] cited an observation of COTTON LJ:[42]

> Then there is a second object, "To remove, (if deemed necessary or expedient) any of the present directors, and to elect directors to fill any vacancy in the board." The learned judge below thought that too indefinite, but in my opinion a notice to remove "any of the present directors" would justify a resolution for removing all who are directors at the present time; "any" would involve "all". I think a notice in that form is quite sufficient for all practical purposes.

The Court also cited a passage from the speech of FRY LJ:

> The second objection was, that a requisition to call a meeting "to remove (if deemed necessary or expedient) any of the present directors" is too vague. I think that it is not. It appears to me that there is a reasonably sufficient particularity in that statement. It is said that each director does not know whether he is attacked or not. The answer is that all the directors know that they are laid open to attack. I think that any other form of requisition would have been embarrassing, because it is obvious that the meeting might think fit to remove a director or allow him to remain, according to his behaviour and demeanour at the meeting with regard to the proposal made at it.

The Court also pointed out that the company cannot go behind the apparent exercise of a shareholder's statutory right of requisitioning a meeting. The company was accordingly not allowed to say that the LIC in requisitioning the meeting had gone beyond its constitutional competence. That aspect is for the State to take care of.[43] The Company Law Board (now Tribunal) restrained the company from putting the resolution before the meeting where it found that the member sending the notice was not honestly motivated. He had made it a practice of sending such notices to all companies wherein he was a member.[44]

The vacancy thus created may be filled at the same meeting, provided special notice of the proposed appointment was also given. The director so appointed would hold office for the period for which the director removed

---

41. Overruling *Escorts Ltd* v *UOI*, (1985) 57 Comp Cas 241: [1984] 3 Comp LJ 387.
42. (1986) 1 SCC 264 at p 340.
43. The court cannot prevent shareholders from exercising their power. It can only examine whether the procedure prescribed by the Act has been followed or not, *Khetan Industries (P) Ltd* v *Manju Ravindra Prasad*, (1995) 16 Corpt LA 169: AIR 1995 Bom 43, nor entertain a suit for removal of a director.
44. *Dabur India Ltd* v *Anil Kumar Poddar*, (2002) 108 Comp Cas 293 CLB. *House Development Finance Corpn* v *Sureshchandra V. Parekh*, (2002) 112 Comp Cas 650 CLB, another case in which the company was restrained from considering the resolution because the member concerned had made it a practice to send such notices year after year.

would have been in office. If the vacancy is not filled at the meeting, it may be filled by the board as a casual vacancy, provided that the director removed should not be reappointed. [Sub-sections (5) and (6)]

The section, however, does not deprive the person removed of any compensation or damages payable to him on the termination of his appointment.[45]

The powers of management are generally vested in the directors and the shareholders do not, ordinarily, have the right to interfere in the matter. But if they are not agreeable with the policy of a particular director, they can use their power of removal and thus have a greater voice in the administration of the company.[46]

The section applies to private companies as well. But they can evade its operation in the manner shown by the decision of the House of Lords in *Bushell* v *Faith*.[47]

A small private company was composed of three persons, *C, K* and *G,* each holding 100 shares of £1 each. *C* and *G* were directors. Clause 9 of the articles of association provided that when it was proposed to remove a director he would, on a poll, have the right to three votes per share. *C* and *K,* being dissatisfied with *G* as a director, proposed to remove him. He demanded a poll, at which he cast 300 votes for his 100 shares and thus defeated the motion.

The trial judge held that the clause which gave a shareholder treble voting power was invalid as it would make a "mockery" of Section 184. The Court of Appeal, as upheld by a majority of the House of Lords, reversed this decision. The majority found that the clause was consistent with the Act. Lord DONOVAN pointed out that Parliament, being fully aware of the phenomenon of articles of association carrying "weighted votes" made no provision against it and left to companies and their shareholders liberty to allocate voting rights as they pleased.

The decision has been criticised. It has been described as one that defeats "the clear intention of the legislature"; that "contravenes the spirit, if not letter, of Section 184"; that "sanctions evasion of the Companies Act".[48] Its merit,

---

45. S. 280(7)(*a*). Though if the removal is in accordance with the articles or terms of service, no compensation may be payable. *Read* v *Astoria Garage (Streathan) Ltd*, [1952] Ch 637 CA: [1952] 2 All ER 292.
46. Where the directors do not call a meeting on requisition, the requisitioning shareholders can themselves call it. In their notice of meeting the requirements of S. 273 as to explanatory statement is not applicable. The court did not restrain the meeting and also held that S. 284 is not applicable to the removal of a managing director from his managership as distinguished from his directorship. *S. Varadrajan* v *Venkateswara Solvent Extraction (P) Ltd*, (1994) 80 Comp Cas 693 Mad.
47. [1970] 1 All ER 53: [1970] 2 WLR 272: (1970) 86 LQR 155.
48. Clive M. Schmitthoff, *HL Sanction Evasion of the Companies Act*, 1970 JBL 1. *See also* D. Prentice, *Removal of Directors from Office*, (1969) 32 Mod LR 693 and *Bushell* v *Faith,*

however, has not been ignored. "In this particular field it may be highly desirable that 'partners' should be safeguarded in directorships, whether by means of special voting rights or by means of shareholders' voting agreements".[49] In a South African case[50] two shareholders of a company contracted between themselves not to vote on a resolution removing the third from his office of director. They were restrained from voting against the terms of their agreement. Now another remedy that would be available to a director of a small private company who has been successfully removed from office is to apply for winding up on the just and equitable ground. In the words of Lord WILBERFORCE:[51]

> The just and equitable provision nevertheless comes to his assistance if he can point to, and prove, some underlying obligation of his fellow members in good faith, or confidence, that so long as the business continues he shall be entitled to management participation, an obligation so basic that, if broken, the conclusion must be that the association must be dissolved.

In a two-member-director company the attempt of the majority shareholder to remove the minority shareholder (49%) from his office as director was frustrated by the latter by not attending the meeting. The court ordered a meeting to be called and held to consider the motion and that the meeting would be valid even if only one member attended. The quorum provision cannot be used so as to veto the power. The decision highlights the importance of the majority's statutory right to remove a director.[52]

The procedure prescribed by this section is not applicable where a relief sought under Section 402 contemplates en bloc removal of all the directors.[53]

2. *Removal by Central Government* [S. 388-B to 388-E]

A director may also be removed at the initiative of the Central Government. A special Chapter of the Companies Act enables the Central Government to remove managerial personnel from office on the recommendation of the Company Law Board. The Government has the power to make a reference to the CLB against any managerial personnel.[54]

[1970] 1 All ER 53: [1970] 2 WLR 272: (1970) 86 LQR 155; Bernard J. Cartoon, *The Removal of Company Directors*, 1980 JBL 17 where the decision has been supported.

49. R. C. Beuthin, *A Director firmly in the Saddle*, (1969) SALJ 489; noted, *Removal of Directors*, (1970) 75 CAL WN 5 Journal.

50. *Stewart* v *Schwab*, (1956) 4 SA 791; noted (1970) 86 LQR 155.

51. *Westbourne Galleries Ltd, Re*, [1972] 2 All ER 492: 1973 AC 360, 380.

52. *Opera Photography Ltd, Re*, 1989 BCLC 763 Ch D. *Rohit Churamani* v *Disha Research and Marketing Services (P) Ltd*, (2005) 123 Comp Cas 467 CLB, two-member, two-director company, one could not remove the other because latter did not attend meeting, restitution ordered.

53. *Shoe Specialities Ltd* v *Standard Distilleries & Breweries (P) Ltd*, (1997) 90 Comp Cas 1 Mad.

54. *Union of India* v *Premier Automobiles Ltd*, (2005) 128 Comp Cas 383 CLB, reference can be made only by the Central Government, shareholders cannot seek to become interveners.

The power can be exercised where, in the opinion of the Central Government, there are circumstances suggesting:

(*a*) that any managerial personnel is or has been guilty of fraud, misfeasance, persistent negligence or default in carrying out his legal obligations or functions or breach of trust; or

(*b*) that the business of the company has not been conducted in accordance with sound business principles or prudent commercial practices; or

(*c*) that the company has been managed by the person concerned in such manner which has caused or is likely to cause serious injury to the interest of the trade, industry or business to which the company belongs; or

(*d*) that the person concerned has conducted the business with intent to defraud creditors or members or any person or for a fraudulent or unlawful purpose or in a manner prejudicial to public interest.[55]

The reference is made by stating a case against the person with a request that the CLB may inquire into the case and record its decision whether he is a fit or proper person to hold the office of a director or other managerial office.[56] The person against whom a case is presented is joined as a respondent to the application. The application should contain a concise statement of the circumstances and materials necessary for the purpose of the inquiry. The CLB has the power to direct by an interim order that the respondent shall not discharge the duties of his office until further orders. [S. 388-C(1)] The CLB may appoint a suitable person in his place and he shall be deemed to be a public servant.

At the conclusion of the inquiry the CLB has to record its decision. [S. 388-D] If the decision is against the respondent, the Central Government may by order remove him from office. [S. 388-E] But, before making its order, the Government has to give him a reasonable opportunity to show cause against the same. But he cannot raise any matter which has already been decided by the CLB. The person removed is disabled from holding a managerial office for five years, unless the period is remitted. No compensation is payable to him. The company may, with the previous approval of the Central Government, appoint another person to the office. [S. 388 E(5)]

The nature and scope of the power and its constitutional validity have been examined by the Calcutta High Court in *Alak Prakash Jain* v *Union of*

55. *Central Government* v *Premier Automobiles Ltd*, (2005) 125 Comp Cas 508 CLB, reference on the basis of inspector's report on accounts, Govt. bound to disclose the report to affected persons but not the notings on the basis of which the opinion was formulated.
56. See *S. P. Jain* v *UOI*, [1966] 1 Comp LJ 42 Bom.

India.[57] Looking at the charges levelled against the director concerned as substantiated by reports from reliable quarters, the court said:

> It seems to us that in the facts of this case, it cannot be said that there was no material to justify the opinion which the Central Government formed. The charges are sufficiently grave and serious, namely, fraud, misappropriation, manipulation of accounts, diversion of the company's funds, illegal declaration of dividends and unlawful payment of travelling expenses. Full particulars with dates and amounts involved have been furnished.

The court further held that the power of the Central Government is not of discriminatory nature, for the word "may" couples power with duty and, therefore, when the circumstances justify a reference, the Central Government has no choice but to make a reference; that the delegation of the power to the Company Law Board is not invalid as the board functioned subject to the control of the Central Government[58] and that the resignation by the director either before or after the reference does not make it infructuous. The power is not merely to remove from an existing office but is also to restrain future conduct.

3. *Removal by Company Law Board* [S. 402]

When, on an application to the CLB for prevention of oppression or mismanagement, the CLB finds that a relief ought to be granted, it may terminate or set aside any agreement of the company with a director or managing director or other managerial personnel. When the appointment of a director is so terminated he cannot, except with the leave of the CLB, serve any company in a managerial capacity for a period of five years.[59] Neither can he sue the company for damages or compensation for loss of office.[60]

Resignation

In a case before the Madras High Court,[61] of the two directors of a company, one died and the other wanted to resign. There was no provision in the company's articles about resignation. Nor is there anything in the Companies Act as to whether, and by what procedure, a director can resign. The Act, however, indirectly recognises resignation by the provisions in Section 318 one of which is that no director is entitled to compensation if he resigns his office. If there is a provision in the articles, resignation will take

---

57. (1973) 43 Comp Cas 68 Cal. Before the amendment of 1988, a reference under the section had to be made to a High Court. Now this jurisdiction is vested in the Company Law Board.
58. S. 10-F(6).
59. S. 407(1)(*b*).
60. S. 407(1)(*a*). Sub-section (2) contains penalty provisions. Disputes about appointment, removal, qualifications, etc., are matters within the jurisdiction of ordinary civil courts and not that of company courts. *Prakash Road Lines Ltd* v *Vijay Kumar Narang*, (1993) 4 Kar LJ 561: (1995) 83 Comp Cas 569 Kant.
61. *S. S. Lakshmana Pillai* v *ROC*, (1977) 47 Comp Cas 652 Mad.

effect in accordance with such provision and, if there is no provision, resignation will take effect in accordance with its terms. Notice may be written or oral. The court accordingly held that the resignation was effective even when no other director was in office, but added that no resignation can avail a director to evade his obligations by severing his connection with the company.[62]

Once a director has given a notice of resignation of his office, he is not entitled to withdraw that notice, but, if it is withdrawn, it must be by the consent of the company properly exercised by their managers who are the directors of the company.[63]

POWERS OF DIRECTORS

General powers vested in Board [S. 291]

Section 291 declares that "subject to the provisions of the Act, the board of directors of a company shall be entitled to exercise all such powers and to do all such acts and things as the company is authorised to exercise and do".[64] The effect of this section is that subject to the restrictions contained in the Act, and in the memorandum and articles of the company, the powers of directors are co-extensive with those of the company itself. Once elected and in control, the directors have almost total power over the operations of the company, until they are removed. The share market crash highlighted the problem inherent in directors' autonomy over all company affairs. There is no restriction on the appointment of directors. There are, however, two important limitations upon their powers. Firstly, the board is not competent to do what the Act, memorandum and articles require to be done by the shareholders in general meeting and, secondly, in the exercise of their powers the directors are subject to the provisions of the Act, memorandum and articles and other regulations not inconsistent therewith, made by the company in general meeting. "Individual directors have such powers only as are vested in them by the memorandum and articles. It is true that ordinarily the courts do not unsuit a person on account of technicalities. But the question of authority to institute a suit on behalf of a company is not a technical matter. It has far reaching effects. It often affects policy and

---

62. *Mother Care (India) Ltd* v *Ramaswamy P. Aiyar*, (2004) 51 SCL 243 Kant, effective when communicated to the Board. *L. Srinivasan* v *Raxi Nidhi Ltd*, (2005) 124 Comp Cas 140 CLB, after such communication, directors bound to inform Registrar in appropriate form.
63. *Glossop* v *Glossop*, [1907] 2 Ch 370: 97 LT 372. The notice of resignation must be addressed to the company. A letter addressed to a third party has no effect. *Registrar of Companies* v *Orissa Paper Products Ltd*, (1988) 63 Comp Cas 460 Ori. A person appointed to the post of managing director of a Govt. company too has a right to resign though he is appointed by the President to hold office during the pleasure of the President. *Prasanta Chandra Sen* v *UOI*, (1990) 67 Comp Cas 87 Cal.
64. A director, therefore, cannot be deprived of his right by the other directors. *Pulbrook* v *Richmond Consolidated Mining Co*, (1878) 9 Ch D 610. The Board of directors have the power to regulate the working hours of the company's employees, *Metalurgical & Engg Consultants (India) Ltd* v *Mecon Executive Assn*, (1998) 28 Corpt LA 381 MP.

finances of the company. Thus unless the power to institute a suit is specifically conferred on a particular director, he has no authority to institute a suit on behalf of the company... such power can be conferred by the board of directors only by passing a resolution in that regard."[65]

"The Act thus tries to demarcate the area of proper management control and proper shareholder control."[66] But however precise the demarcation may be, there will always be a scope for clash between the two basic organs of the company, namely, shareholders and directors, as to their respective powers. A prototype of the clash which they are likely to pick up is *Automatic Self-Cleansing Filter Syndicate Co Ltd* v *Cuninghame.*[67]

A company had power under its memorandum of association to sell its undertaking to another company having similar objects. By its articles the general management and control of the company were vested in the directors subject to such regulations as might from time to time be made by extraordinary resolution. Particularly important was the provision in the articles by which directors were empowered to sell or otherwise deal with the property of the company on such terms as they thought fit. The shareholders passed a simple resolution for the sale of the company's assets on certain terms and required the directors to carry the sale into effect.

On the director's refusal to do so it was contended by the shareholders that it was a mere question of principal and agent. The shareholders are the principal, and directors, the agents, and it would be an absurd thing if an agent should act like a dictator and manage the principal. But it was held that "directors are agents not of a majority of the shareholders, but of the company, of the whole entity made up of all the shareholders. And if the

---

65. *Al-Amin Seatrans (P) Ltd* v *Owners and Party interested in Vessel M V Loyal Bird,* (1995) 17 Corpt LA 204 Cal, per BABOO LAL JAIN J who unsuited the managing director in his attempt to get possession of a ship because he had no authority of the board of directors to sue. Where the directors by their resolution authorised a particular director and he delegated the power to an officer of the company, an appeal filed by that officer was held to be competent because it was not necessary that for every piece of work a board resolution should be passed. *Hindustan Petroleum Corpn Ltd* v *Sardar Chand,* (1991) 71 Comp Cas 257 P&H. The courts do not interfere in decisions cf corporate bodies made through responsible organs, *U. P. Financial Corpn* v *Naini Oxygen & Acetylene Gas Ltd,* (1995) 2 SCC 754: (1995) 17 Corpt LA 219, the court did not interfere in the decision of a corporation to enforce recovery by disposing of the unit of the borrower and did not accept the argument that more loans should have been provided to keep the unit afloat. *BOC India Ltd* v *Zinc Products & Co (P) Ltd,* (1996) 86 Comp Cas 358 Pat, winding up petition on behalf of company filed by person not authorised, incompetent.
66. *See,* Henry G. Manne, *The Higher Criticism of the Modern Corporation,* (1962) 62 Col LR 399, 408.
67. [1906] 2 Ch 34: 94 LT 651. Followed in India in *M. P. & V. Works* v *M. Murarka,* AIR 1961 Cal 251: (1961) 31 Comp Cas 301, which refers to a large number of decided cases on the point: *A. P. Pothen* v *Hindustan Trading Corpn,* (1967) 37 Comp Cas 266: AIR 1968 Ker 149; *Suburban Bank (P) Ltd* v *Thariath,* [1967] 2 Comp LJ 182: AIR 1968 Ker 206: (1968) 38 Comp Cas 13 Ker, where the members were not allowed to interfere in the directors' discretion.

whole entity of shareholders has entrusted the directors with a particular power a simple majority could not interfere in exercise of it."

In a subsequent case, FARWELL LJ observed:[68] "Even a resolution of a numerical majority at a general meeting cannot impose its will upon the directors when the articles have confided to them the control of the company's affairs." In another leading case[69] GREER LJ explained the principle in the following words:

A company is an entity distinct alike from its shareholders and directors. Some of its powers may, according to articles, be exercised by directors, certain other powers may be reserved for the shareholders in general meeting. If powers of management are vested in the directors, they and they alone can exercise these powers. The only way in which the general body of the shareholders can control the exercise of the powers vested by the articles in directors is by altering their articles, or, if opportunity arises under the articles, by refusing to re-elect the directors of whose action they disapprove. They cannot themselves usurp the powers which by the articles are vested in the directors any more than the directors can usurp the powers vested by the articles in the general body of the shareholders.

This principle was followed in *Scott v Scott*[70] and applied to the case even of a private company. The court observed:

Under the articles of this private company the management of the business and the declaration of the interim dividends were both assigned to the directors. That being so, they were not subject to any control in that respect by the shareholders in general meeting. It is true that if the company in general meeting disapproved of the management or the declaration of an interim dividend, they could remove the directors, but the general meeting could not, as the articles stood, directly interfere by resolution with the management or the declaration of an interim dividend. The division of authority is important even in the case of what may be called family companies and having regard to the liability of directors as occupying a fiduciary position, it is necessary that it should be strictly observed.

Thus the relationship of the board of directors "with the general meeting is more of federation than one of subordinate and superior".[71]

---

68. *Gramophone & Typewriter Ltd* v *Stanley*, [1908] 2 KB 89: 99 LT 39. *See* also *Salmon v Quin & Axtens Ltd*, [1909] 1 Ch 311: 100 LT 161.
69. *John Shaw & Sons (Salford) Ltd* v *Peter Shaw & John Shaw*, [1935] 2 KB 113: [1935] All ER Rep 456 CA.
70. [1943] 1 All ER 582. For an Indian authority see *Srinivasan v Subramania*, AIR 1932 Mad 100: 136 IC 193, where the directors were not allowed to exercise a power expressly vested in the shareholders. Followed in *Pothen v Hindustan Trading Corpn*, [1966] 2 Comp LJ 252: (1967) 37 Comp Cas 266: AIR 1968 Ker 149. *See* also *Murarka Paint and Varnish Works v M. Murarka*, (1960) 65 CWN 32: AIR 1961 Cal 251: (1961) 31 Comp Cas 301, which refers to a large number of decided cases on the point.
71. R. C. Beuthin, *The Range of a Company's Interests*, (1969) 86 SALJ 155, 156.

These principles have been generally followed by the courts in India. For example, in a case before the Kerala High Court,[72] by the articles of a banking company, the power of management was vested in the directors. The shareholders by a resolution pressed the directors to forego a debt. The court held that the directors were entitled to enforce the payment of the debt.[73]

Shareholders' intervention in exceptional cases

"But the fact should not be overlooked that the company is an institution owned and controlled by its shareholders. According to the legal theory the shareholder is the ultimate and final authority within the corporate enterprise."[74] The inherent, residuary and ultimate powers of a company lie with the general meeting of shareholders.[75] Thus the shareholders can interfere in management by replacing the existing management with a new one which would be more responsive to their and the company's interests. This aspect of the relationship between the directorate and shareholders has been highlighted in the decision of the Supreme Court in *LIC* v *Escorts Ltd.*[76] CHINNAPPA REDDY J cited a passage from the speech of COTTON LJ.[77]

It is a very strong thing indeed to prevent shareholders from holding a meeting of the company, when such a meeting is the only way in which they can interfere if the majority of them think that the course taken by the director, in a matter *intra vires* of the directors, is not for the benefit of the company.

---

72. *Suburban Bank (P) Ltd* v *Thariath*, [1967] 2 Comp LJ 182 Ker: AIR 1968 Ker 206: (1968) 38 Comp Cas 13.
73. The directors of a company cannot be restrained from exercising their managerial powers in general, though they can be restrained in reference to some particular act. *Rajapalayam Industrial and Commercial Syndicate Ltd* v *K. A. Vairaprakasam*, [1989] 2 Comp LJ 236: AIR 1989 Mad 13. Unauthorised legal proceedings cannot be ratified. *Breckland Group Holdings Ltd* v *London and Suffolk Properties Ltd*, 1989 BCLC 100 Ch D. A solicitor was not permitted to recover his fee for conducting such proceedings. *Fletcheritunt (Bristol) Ltd, Re*, 1989 BCLC 108 Ch D. The courts may have to face practical difficulties in attempting to review the merits of the board's decision. "The courts have not been slow to acknowledge that their skill is not that of the businessman, and that the so-called business judgment doctrine acknowledges that it is both unfair to review, with the benefit of hindsight, the board's decision, and that the court is ill-placed to judge entrepreneurship." Ross Grantham, *The Content of the Director's Loyalty*, 1993 JBL 149.
74. J. A. C. Hetherington, *Corporate Responsibility*, (1969) Stan LR 248, 251. Sylvie Hebert, *Corporate Governance "French Style"* 2004 JBL 656, explaining how after the Cadbury Committee Report on Corporate Governance, France has focussed on the way in which companies can be better managed and monitored, explaining important topics like transparency in remuneration and auditing. John Birchall, *Duties of Good Fails in Commercial Joint Ventures? Contractual Duties and Shareholder Remedies*, 2005 JBL 269. A Worthington, *Corporate Governance Remedying and Ratifying Directors Breaches*, (2000) 166 LQR 638.
75. *See*, M. A. Pickering, *Shareholders' Voting Rights & Company Control*, (1965) 81 LQR 248.
76. (1986) 1 SCC 264 at pp 340-341: (1986) 59 Comp Cas 548: [1986] 1 Comp LJ 91 SC.
77. *Isle of Wight Rly Co* v *Tahourdin*, (1883) 25 Ch D 320: 50 LT 132.

In the case before the Supreme Court, public financial institutions, including LIC were holding a majority of shares in the company. They requisitioned a meeting to remove nine directors. No reasons were stated. But the background was that the directors had refused to register certain transfers and had engaged the company in a calamitous litigation against the Government and also in a litigation to stay the requisitioned meeting and all this without consulting the principal block of majority shareholders who had so much at stake in the company. The Bombay High Court granted the stay.[78] The Supreme Court vacated it. The shareholders had a right to meet and decide whether the destinies of the company were safe in the hands of the present management. The company had no right to say that the public financial institutions were going beyond their powers in trying to interfere in management, they being constitutionally only investing institutions. They have a right to be vigilant in safeguarding their investment and putting it in the hands of a management which can assure safety and security. In this respect they exercise their elementary right as shareholders. They do not thereby directly undertake to manage the company.

In the following exceptional situations the general meeting is competent to act even in a matter delegated to the board.

1. *Mala fide*

In the words of FAZL ALI J of the Supreme Court:[79] "[O]rdinarily the directors of a company are the only persons who can conduct litigation in the name of the company, but when they are themselves the wrongdoers, and have acted *mala fide*... and their personal interest is in conflict with their duty in such a way that they cannot or will not take steps to seek redress for the wrong done to the company, the majority of the shareholders [may take steps to redress the wrong]." "The duty of supervision on the part of this court will thus be confined to the honesty, integrity and fairness with which the deliberation has been conducted, and will not be extended to the accuracy of the conclusion arrived at."[80] *Marshall's Valve Gear Co Ltd* v *Manning Wardley & Co Ltd*[81] is a case of this kind.

A and three other persons were the four directors of *M Co* and they held substantially the whole of the subscribed capital of the company. *A* was the majority shareholder, but held less than three-fourth. Another company, known as *N Co*, was committing an infringement of *M Co's* trade mark and the other three directors were interested in that company.

---

78. *Escorts Ltd* v *UOI*, [1984] 3 Comp LJ 387: (1985) 57 Comp Cas 241. The court also relied upon *Inderwick* v *Snell*, 42 ER 83 and *Bentley Stevans* v *Jones*, [1974] 2 All ER 653 also involving removal of directors.
79. *Satya Charan* v *Rameshwar Prasad Bajoria*, 20 Comp Cas 39: 1949 FCR 673: AIR 1950 FC 133: 1950 SCR 394.
80. *Beloved Wilke's Charity, Re*, (1851) 3 Mac & G 440.
81. [1909] 1 Ch 267: 100 LT 65.

With the result that at a meeting of the board they declined to sanction any proceeding against *N Co. A,* at a general meeting of the shareholders, resolved and commenced an action to restrain the alleged infringement. The other directors applied for striking down the name of the company on the ground that as the articles had left the powers of management with the board, the shareholders could not interfere by a simple resolution.

It was held that the majority of the shareholders had the right to control the action of the directors in the matter. NEVILLE J explained the reason thus:

> Now it is obvious that in the position in which they (directors) have placed themselves on this question their duty and their interest are in direct conflict. On the one hand, it is their duty as directors to protect the interest of the original patent which is the property of the company; on the other hand, their personal interests are clearly to maintain the validity of the patent which belongs to them. And, therefore, the majority shareholders are entitled to decide whether or not an action in the name of the company shall proceed.

2. *Board incompetent*

Secondly, majority of the shareholders may exercise a power vested in the board when the directors have, for some valid reason, become incompetent to act. One situation would be when all the directors are interested in a transaction of the company. Another illustration is *Viswanathan* v *Tiffins B. A. & P. Ltd,*[82] where the power to fill casual vacancies was delegated to the board, but the appointments made by shareholders in general meeting were held to be valid as at the material time no director was validly in office. Where the circumstances were such that a valid board could not be constituted, it was held that the majority shareholders could act to protect the interests of the company and they could conduct the company's defence in a suit pending against it.[83]

3. *Deadlock*

A third occasion for shareholders to intervene would be when the directors are unwilling to act, or, on account of a deadlock, unable to act. The leading case in line is *Barron* v *Potter.*[84]

> There were only two directors on the board of a company and the one refused to act with the other. There was no provision in the articles

---

82. AIR 1953 Mad 520: [1953] 1 MLJ 346: (1953) 23 Comp Cas 79, the full facts and judgment of the case have been discussed above in connection with appointment of directors. Where the board of directors is validly constituted and whether its meeting should be stayed is a matter for the ordinary civil court and not a company court. *Maharaja Exports* v *Apparels Exports Promotion Council,* (1986) 60 Comp Cas 353.
83. *Glucoseries (P) Ltd* v *Deb Kanta Roy,* (2000) 38 CLA 39 Cal.
84. [1914] 1 Ch 895: 110 LT 929. See also *Foster* v *Foster,* [1916] 1 Ch 532; [1916-17] All ER Rep 856.

enabling the general meeting of the shareholders to increase or reduce the number of directors.

It was held that as there was a deadlock in the administration resulting from the fact that the directors were unwilling to act and exercise their powers, the company had the inherent power to take necessary steps to ensure the working of the company and to appoint additional directors for the purpose.

4. *Residuary powers*

The residuary powers of a company reside in the general meeting of shareholders.[85] Thus it has been held that "where a power to allot shares is conferred by the articles of a company on its directors and they act in excess of that power a residuary inherent power remains in the company to validate the allotment by an ordinary resolution in general meeting".[86]

STATUTORY PROVISIONS: RESTRICTIONS ON POWERS

Powers exercisable by resolution at board meetings [S. 292]

The Act also makes a careful effort to lay down the manner in which certain powers of the company are to be exercised. Section 292 provides that following powers of the company can be exercised only by means of resolutions passed at meetings of the board: The power (1) to make calls; (2) to authorise buy-back referred to in the first proviso to clause (*b*) of Section 77-A(2); (3) to issue debentures; (4) to borrow money; (5) to invest the funds of the company; and (6) to make loans.

The board may by a resolution delegate the power to borrow money to any committee of directors or other principal officers of the company.[87] The resolution should specify the amount up to which moneys may be borrowed by the delegate.[88] Similarly, the power to make investments may be delegated. The resolution should once again specify the extent and nature of investment.[89] In the same way the power to make loans is delegable, but the resolution should specify the total amount up to which loans may be made, the purposes of the loans and the maximum that can be made for a particular purpose.[90] The shareholders in general meeting may place any restrictions on, or otherwise regulate, the exercise of the above powers.[91] Delegation must be by a specific resolution of the board. In a case where a hire purchase agreement was entered into by directors without authorisation, the agreement was held to be not enforceable against the company. Entries in the

---

85. G. D. Goldberg, *Article 80 of Table A of the [English] Companies Act*, 33 Mod LR 177.
86. *Bamford* v *Bamford*, [1968] 3 WLR 317: [1968] 2 All ER 655. Judgment of PLOWMAN J affirmed on appeal on different grounds, [1969] 2 WLR 1107: [1969] 1 All ER 969.
87. S. 292 (proviso).
88. S. 292 (2).
89. S. 292 (3).
90. S. 292 (4).
91. S. 292(5).

company's ledger were not sufficient by themselves to fasten liability on the company.[92]

Powers exercisable with general meeting approval [S. 293]

Further, Section 293 imposes important restrictions on the powers of the board of directors of a public company or any subsidiary of a public company. Following powers can be exercised by the board only with the consent of the company in general meeting:

1. sale or lease of the company's undertaking;[93]
2. extension of the time for payment of a debt due by a director;
3. investment of compensation received on compulsory acquisition in securities other than trust securities;
4. borrowing of money beyond the paid-up capital of the company. This, however, does not include temporary loans obtained from the company's bankers in the ordinary course of business;[94]
5. contributions to any charitable or other funds beyond fifty thousand rupees in one financial year or five per cent of the average net profits during the preceding three financial years, whichever is greater.

92. *Ambala Bus Syndicate (P) Ltd* v *Roop Nagar Credit & Instrument Co (P) Ltd,* (1997) 88 Comp Cas 821 P&H.
93. The sale of one out of the three vessels of the company which was not in use was held to be not a sale of the company's undertaking so as to require shareholders' resolution. The sale was also found to be necessary for raising funds for the company's business. Shareholders were not allowed to question it. *P. S. Offshore Inter Land Services P Ltd* v *Bombay Offshore Suppliers and Services Ltd,* (1992) 75 Comp Cas 583 Bom. A closed or out of function unit of a company may be an undertaking. *Pramod Kumar Mittal* v *Andhra Steel Corpn Ltd,* (1985) 58 Comp Cas 772 Cal; *R.C. Cooper* v *UOI,* (1970) 1 SCC 248: (1970) 3 SCR 530: (1970) 40 Comp Cas 325, "In reality the undertaking is a complete and complex weft and the various types of business and assets are threads which cannot be taken apart from the weft"; *Yallamma Cotton, Woollen and Silk Mills Co, Re,* (1970) 40 Comp Cas 466; *International Cotton Corporation (P) Ltd* v *Bank of Maharashtra,* (1970) 40 Comp Cas 1154. Undertaking means a substantial part of assets. Leasing of the use of premises (slaughter house) during periods of non-use by the company, not a lease of undertaking, *Allana Cold Storage Ltd* v *Goa Meat Complex Ltd,* (1997) 10 Comp Cas 50 Bom: [1997] 4 Comp LJ 225 : (1998) 29 Corpt LA 45. The court said that an agreement of sale etc. would mean a complete and exclusive transfer whereby the transferee gets the right to hold, possess and control the assets. *Mohta Alloys & Steel Works* v *Mohta Finance and Lease Co Ltd,* (1997) 89 Comp Cas 227, no formality was considered necessary to execute a lease on behalf of the company where authority was given by the board under its powers conferred by the articles. *Shoe Specialities Ltd* v *Tracstar Investment Ltd,* (1997) 88 Comp Cas 471 Mad, investment of the company's money in shares was not regarded as a sale of undertaking or even a substantial part of it. *Cochin Malabar Estates & Industries Ltd* v *P. V. Abdul Khader,* (2003) 114 Comp Cas 777 Ker, a single shareholder holding 0.02% shares was not allowed to question the wisdom of disposing of the company's assets under a directors' resolution as confirmed by the company in general meeting.
94. *See,* Explanation II. Any resolution passed by the company in general meeting allowing borrowing beyond this limit or making contributions beyond the specified limit should specify the total amount. (*Explanation I*).

If the directors have in breach of the above restrictions sold or leased the undertaking of the company, the title of the purchaser or lessee will not be affected, provided he acted in good faith and with due care and caution. Thus the purchaser must see that the transaction is executed in accordance with the company's articles, because otherwise it would be ineffective to pass any title to him.[95] This restriction does not apply to the case of a company whose ordinary business is to sell or lease property. Where[96] borrowing has been effected exceeding the amount of the paid-up share capital, the lender may not be able to enforce the loan against the company, unless he can prove that he advanced the loan in good faith and without knowledge that the limit had been exceeded.[97]

The consent of the general meeting may be expressed by means of a formal resolution or informally through conduct as it happened, for example, in *Joint Receivers and Managers of Niltan Carson Ltd* v *Hawthorne*.[98] The hotel premises of the company were handed over to a director of the company under a lease granted by the managing director without the approval of the shareholders. The lessee director had acted with complete honesty and openness and with the agreement of practically all the shareholders who desired that she should run the community home independently of the company. The transaction was held to be not voidable without showing that there was no proper consideration.

Audit Committee [S. 292-A]

A public company with share capital of not less than five crores of rupees is required to constitute a committee of the Board of directors to be known as the Audit Committee. Its membership is not to be of less than three directors and such number of other directors as the Board may determine. Two-thirds of them must be directors other than the managing or wholetime directors. The committee has to act in accordance with the terms of reference to be specified by the Board in writing. The members of the committee have to elect a chairman from amongst themselves.

The auditors, the internal auditors, if any, and the director-in-charge of finance shall attend and participate in meetings of the Audit Committee but shall not have the right to vote. The committee should have discussions with auditors periodically about internal control systems, the scope of audit including the observations of the auditors and review half-yearly and annual financial statements before they are submitted to the Board and also ensure compliance of the internal control systems.

---

95. For a suitable illustration see *U. Ba Din* v *Janki Devi*, AIR 1938 Rang 447.
96. S. 293(2)(*b*).
97. S. 293(5). *See also* sub-section (4).
98. 1988 BCLC 298 QBD. *See also Brady* v *Brady*, [1988] 2 All ER 617 HL.

The Audit Committee would enjoy authority to investigate into any matter relating to the terms specified in the section or referred to it by the Board. The committee shall have for this purpose full access to information contained in the records of the company. It may also take external professional advice, if necessary. The recommendations of the committee on any matter relating to financial management, including the audit report shall be binding on the Board. If the Board does not accept the recommendations of the committee, it shall record its reasons for the same and communicate them to the shareholders.

The chairman of the committee has to attend the annual general meetings of the company to provide any clarifications on matters relating to audit.[1]

Board's sanction when directors interested [S. 297]

Section 297 further restricts the powers of individual directors. Whenever a company has to deal for the sale, purchase or supply of any material or services or for underwriting any shares or debentures with any director or his relative, or with a firm in which such a director or relative is a partner or any other partner in such a firm or with a private company of which such a director is a member or a director, the consent of the board of directors must be obtained.[2] Such an approval of the board is, however, not necessary in the following cases:

1. Where the contract is for cash at the prevailing market prices.
2. Where the contract relates to goods in which the company or the other party trades or does business, but not exceeding the value of five thousand rupees in any year.
3. The transactions of a banking or insurance company.

Such contracts may, however, be made in any emergency and beyond the value of five thousand rupees, provided approval of the board is obtained within three months. If the approval is not obtained or is refused, the contract will be voidable at the option of the board.[3]

---

1. Sub-s. (11) provides that if a default is made in complying with the provisions of the section, every officer who is in default shall be punishable with imprisonment for a term which may extend to one year, or with fine extending to Rs 50,000 or both.
2. A contract of this kind was not permitted to be avoided after the expiry of its term. The contract also otherwise complied with the provisions. The court pointed out that the mere presence of a director at the meeting where the matter of his interest was being considered would not amount to fraud or undue influence. *Mehta Teja Singh & Co* v *Globe Motors Ltd*, (1983) 54 Comp Cas 883 Del.
3. S. 297(3), (4), (5) and (6). *Dintex Dyechem Ltd, Re,* (2001) 104 Comp Cas 735 CLB, failure to take approval of the Central Government for purchase/sale of goods of negligible amount through partnership firms in which some of the directors were interested, the offence against the company and directors was compounded on payment of compounding fee of Rs 75,000.

The amendment of 1974 has extended this restriction to contracts for underwriting the subscription of any shares or debentures of the company.[4] The amendment further provides that in the case of a company having paid-up share capital of rupees one crore or more, contracts of the above kind should not be entered into except with the previous approval of the Central Government.

Power to make political contributions [S. 293-A]

Before the Companies (Amendment) Act, 1985 (35 of 1985) companies were not permitted to make contributions for political purposes. Now this ban has been lifted, except in the case of Government companies and companies which have been in existence for less than three years. Rest of the companies have been permitted to contribute money to any political party or to any person for political purposes. The amount should not exceed 5 per cent of the company's net profits during the three immediately preceding financial years. Contribution should be sanctioned by a resolution of the company's board of directors and that will be sufficient authorisation for all-round validity. Donation given to enable a party to win public support would also be a contribution so also those for publication of a souvenir, brochure, tract, pamphlet or the like.[5] The amount contributed must appear in annual accounts. Defaulting company will be punishable with three times the amount and defaulting officers with fine and imprisonment extending up to three years.

DUTIES OF DIRECTORS

Corporate executives are today possessed of "immense power which must be regulated not only for the public good, but also for the protection of those whose investments are involved."[6] Directorships will always be susceptible to abuse. "Some directors will always be faithless to their trust. They can capitalise their strategic position in the company to serve their own interest."[7] The law, therefore, continues to struggle against their wiles and imposes upon them certain duties which, when properly enforced, will, without driving away from the field competent men, materially reduce the chances of abuse.[8]

---

4. S. 297(1)(*b*).
5. This restriction is not violated where contribution has been made as the cost of advertisement appearing in a party's souvenir. *Graphite India Ltd* v *Dalpat Rai Mehta*, (1978) 48 Comp Cas 683 Cal. But if the consideration is unreal or illusory or a mere pretence for a contribution, different result should follow. J Parkinson, *Political Donations and Companies*, 5 BLR 200. Section 293-B empowers directors and other persons to make contributions to National Defence Fund etc.
6. William C. Douglas, *Directors who do not Direct*, (1934) 47 Harv LR 1305, 1307.
7. *Id.*, at p 1317.
8. For a systematic account of the duties of directors *see* D. N. Hossie, *The Civil Liability of the Directors of a Corporation*, (1952) 30 Can BR 908, and for a broader view of directors'

Fiduciary obligation [Duty of Good faith]

Liability for breach of trust.—Traditionally the duties of directors were non-statutory. They were fashioned out essentially from the common law as developed through the cases. But now company legislation of some countries has made a departure from this tradition. The Nigerian Act contains the following provision on the point:[9]

"A director of a company stands in a fiduciary relationship towards the company and shall observe the utmost good faith towards the company in any transaction with it or on its behalf."

The first and the most obvious obligation of persons in fiduciary position is to act with honesty. "Greatest good faith is expected in the discharge of their duties."[10] Good faith requires that all their endeavours must be directed to the benefit of the company. Thus where a director of a company, being also the member of another company, earned bonuses from the other company by providing some business facility of his company, he was held liable to account for such profits, although the company had itself lost nothing and also could not have earned the bonus.[11] Where a director was aware of the fact that the company's property was being sold for £350,000 when its real value stood at £650,000, this was a breach of the fiduciary duty and since the recipient of the property was aware of this fact, he became a constructive trustee towards the company for his undeserved gain.[12] Where a company's funds were used to buy a house in the name of the wife of the majority shareholder and chairman, it was held that the money so applied was held in trust for the company. An order could be passed for tracing the

---

fiduciary, common law and statutory duties in general as well as their enforcement, covering duties to shareholders and creditors as well as to the company, *see* Robert R. Pennington, Directors' Personal Liability (1987).

9. The Companies and Allied Matters Act, 1990, S. 279.

10. *See*, Patel in *Bank of Poona v Narayandas*, AIR 1961 Bom 252 at p 253: (1961) 31 Comp Cas 364. *See* also *Turner Morrison & Co v Shalimar Tar Products*, (1980) 50 Comp Cas 296 Cal, general statement of duty of good faith.

11. *Boston Deep Sea Fishing & Ice Co v Ansell*, (1888) 39 Ch D 339: [1886-90] All ER Rep 65. A good account of such cases is to be seen in D. W. Fox, *Constructive Trusts in a Company Setting*, 1986 JBL 23.

12. *Aviling Barford Ltd v Perion Ltd*, 1989 BCLC 626 Ch D; *International Sales and Agencies Ltd v Marcus*, [1982] 3 All ER 551, liability for giving away the company's property to an outsider without consideration and without shareholders' consent. This is on the basis of the principle that a person who receives money or property from the hands of a person knowing that the disposal was in breach of trust, would become a constructive trustee. The court applied the principle of the case in *Belmont Finance Corpn v Williams Furniture Ltd*, (1980) 1 All ER 393 CA. Before a person can be held liable as a constructive trustee it has to be shown that he is guilty of something amounting to dishonesty or want of probity. *Eagle Trust plc v SBC Securities Ltd*, 1991 BCLC 438 Ch D; *Agip (Africa) Ltd v Jackson*, (1989) 3 WLR 1367: 1990 Ch 265. Another case in which the recipient became liable because he had knowledge that he was receiving the shareholders' money is *Houghton v Fayers*, [2000] 1 BCLC 511 CA. *Saurashtra Cement & Chemical Industries Ltd v Esma Industries P Ltd*, (2001) 103 Comp Cas 1041 Guj, the main object of the proposal to purchase shares in another company was to fulfil the personal obligation of directors, the proposal was restrained.

money in the properties of the chairman.[13] The directors of a family company were held personally liable to account for the money received by them on the company's behalf. The court conceded that it could look behind the corporate curtain for imposing such liability on directors.[14]

The Managing Director and three other directors of a company devised a secret plan to set up a rival company and to leave jobs to join that company. Initially, the managing director resigned and left. The three others were allowed to continue for the time being. The managing director broke away most of the skilled workers of the company causing closure of the company. When the plot came to light, it was held that the managing director was perfectly free to proceed to set up a company of his own and invite employees from other organisations to join it. But the remaining three directors, who were still on the board, were under a duty to inform the company of what was going on. They were executive directors. They were held liable to the company for its losses for which sums had been assessed.[15]

Directors' personal profits.—In *Hirsche v Simons*,[16] on the eve of issuing a prospectus for additional capital, the assets of the company were revalued by a leading firm of surveyors and revised values were quoted. This brought about an increase in the market price of the company's shares. The directors sold some of their existing shares and obtained the benefit of the market situation. They were held by the House of Lords to be not accountable for this profit. Directors exercising their powers in a normal way are not accountable if the sensitive market is incidentally influenced creating opportunities of beneficial disposal of existing shares. In *Albion Steel and Wire Co v Martin*,[17] a director sold certain goods to his company out of his personal stock but at the market price of the day, but even so he did make a profit because he had obtained the stock earlier at lower rates. He was required by the court to account for his profit.

Business opportunities (Diversion of Business.)—Similarly, a director should not exploit to his own use the corporate opportunities. "The doctrine of corporate opportunity has been described as an act of a director or controlling shareholder in diverting from the benefit of the corporation any enterprise or transaction in which reasonable persons would agree that the corporation had some expectancy or interest."[18] In *Cook v Deeks*[19], for example, the directors of a company diverted a contract opportunity of the

13. *Brackon Properties Ltd v Gutterbridge*, (2004) 1 BCLC 377(CA).
14. *Saurabh Exports v Blaze Finlease & Credits (P) Ltd*, (2006) 133 Comp Cas 495 Del.
15. *British Midland v Midland International Tooling Ltd*, (2003) 2 BCLC 523 (Ch D).
16. 1894 AC 654.
17. (1875) 1 Ch D 580.
18. Jan Houwink, *The American Close Corporation and its Dutch Equivalent*, (1958) Business Lawyer 250.
19. [1916] 1 AC 554: [1916-17] All ER Rep 285.

company to themselves and by their votes as holders of three-fourths majority resolved that the company had no interest in the contract. It was held that the benefits of the contract belonged in equity to the company and the directors could not validly use their voting power to vest it in themselves. Their Lordships observed:

> It is quite right to point out the importance of avoiding the establishment of rules as to directors' duties which would impose upon them burdens so heavy and responsibilities so great that men of good position would hesitate to accept the office. But, on the other hand, men who assume complete control of a company's business must remember that they are not at liberty to sacrifice the interests, which they are bound to protect, and, while ostensibly acting for the company, divert in their own favour business which should properly belong to the company they represent.[20]

On the same principle, where a director is instructed to purchase some property for the company, and he purchases the same for himself and then sells it to the company at a profit, he is clearly liable to account for the profit so made. As he was under an obligation to acquire the property for the company, the same belonged in equity to the company from the moment he purchased it and he could not have made a profit on its resale. Supposing now that he is not under any such direction to purchase for the company, but purchases some property on his own account which is subsequently sold to the company at a profit. Is the company entitled to this profit also? This was precisely the question in *Burland* v *Earle*,[21] which the Judicial Committee answered in the negative. "It is one thing if a director sells a property to the company which in equity as well as at law is his own. It would be quite another thing if the director had originally acquired the property which he sold to the company under circumstances which made it in equity the property of the company."

One Burland was a director of the plaintiff company. He was also a shareholder and creditor of another company known as Burland Lithographic Company, which was being wound up. At a public sale by the liquidator, Burland purchased all the assets of the company in four lots. The price paid by him for lot 1 was £21,564 and he shortly afterwards sold it to the plaintiff company for £60,000. In these circumstances he was ordered by the lower court to pay to the company the sum of £38,436, being the amount of the profit made by him on the resale.

---

20. Other illustrative cases on the right of a company to recover such secret commissions are: *Grant* v *Gold Exploration & Development Syndicate Ltd*, [1900] 1 QB 233; *Salford* v *Lever*, [1891] 1 QB 168 is a case on agency. No duty is breached by merely being a director in a rival company, *London and Mashonaland Exploration Co* v *New Mashonaland Exploration Co*, *Re*, 1891 WN 185.
21. 1902 AC 83: [1900-3] All ER Rep Ext 1452.

Their Lordships of the Judicial Committee of the Privy Council set aside this decision and observed: "There is no evidence whatever of any commission or mandate to Burland to purchase on behalf of the company, or that he was in any sense a trustee for the company for the purchased property. It may be that he had an intention in his own mind to resell it to the company, but it was an intention which he was at liberty to carry out or abandon at his own will."

A similar case is *Thomas Marshall (Exports) Ltd* v *Guinle*.[22] A company was importing foreign goods for resale in U.K. Its managing director formed a new import company and solicited orders on its behalf from the U.K. buyers. He imported goods from those very firms with whom he had established contact while acting for the company. He was restrained from this course of conduct. It was a breach of service contract and also of the fiduciary duty. In *Fine Industrial Commodities Ltd* v *Powling*,[23] the demand for the company's product had fallen. The director in question knew of an alternative product for which there was a demand and he was also aware of the modification of the company's plant and machinery which was necessary for that purpose. But, instead of doing that, he created a new company and obtained a patent of the new product in the name of his new company. He was held accountable for his profits. His knowledge of the product in demand and of the fact that the company's plant and machinery could be modified for that purpose was considered by the court to be the company's knowledge. Another parallel case is *Cranleigh Precision Engineering Ltd* v *Bryant*.[24] Here a director after resigning from directorship, formed a company with another person and embarked upon manufacturing a product which embodied his own earlier invention made by him while working for the company. He and his company were restrained from doing so. In *Heyting* v *Dupont*,[25] the company was not able to undertake a product which required a patent in a specialised sector of engineering, because it lacked resources. Both the directors formed their different companies for that product and both sued each other for mutual restraint on behalf of the original company. Their actions were dismissed.

A director-shareholder had set up a rival company. He diverted a major contract of the company to his new company by using the company's confidential information. The company had to go into receivership. Its trading ceased. It was held that the shareholders of the company were entitled to damages from the defaulting director for the loss of the value of their investment in the company, a reflective loss. The failure of the

---

22. 1979 Ch 227.
23. (1954) 71 RPC 253.
24. [1964] 3 All ER 289.
25. [1964] 2 All ER 273: [1964] 1 WLR 843.

company was a direct and foreseeable consequence flowing from the diversion of its business.[26]

The duty to account for business opportunity arises only if at the time of the opportunity the director in question had genuine fiduciary relationship with the company. This observation was made in a case in which there was a total lack of confidence between two equal shareholding groups owing to *inter se* disputes. The main business of the company was an agency. The principal terminated the agency after notice in accordance with the terms of the agency agreement. The principal clearly stated that it was dealing with only one group. The principal awarded the agency to that group. There was no evidence of any collusion between them. The court said that it was not a case of diversion of business opportunity.[27]

When director may make personal use of company's opportunity.— There are, however, some cases when a director may profit by a corporate opportunity without incurring the liability to account for it. "Where the corporation is insolvent and defunct, its officers are free to act for themselves, since such condition is ascertainable and not easily feigned. Similarly, if the undertaking would be *ultra vires* for the corporation, that fact, being capable of exact determination by the court, should be a complete defence. Where the opportunity is outside the scope of corporate business, or where the corporation has shown no interest in the property, an officer may buy for himself."[28]

Similarly, where a new venture is offered to a company and its directors *bona fide* come to the conclusion that it is not an investment that the company ought to make, the individual directors who subsequently buy the same do not violate any duty to the company even though they have consulted the company's geologist.[29] These are facts of the Canadian case of *Peso Silver Mines Ltd* v *Cropper*[30]. If *Regal (Hastings) Ltd* v *Gulliver*[31] is

---

26. *Giles* v *Rhind*, (2001) 2 BCLC 582, reversed by the Court of Appeal in *Giles* v *Rhind*, (2003) 1 BCLC 1 (CA), the action for reflective loss was held to be allowable. The assessment took place in *Giles* v *Rhind* (No 2), (2004) 1 BCLC 385 (Ch D). *Bhullar* v *Bhullar*, (2003) 2 BCLC 241 (CA), company's opportunity of making a valuable investment was used up by a director, liable. For comments see *The Law on Corporate Opportunities in the Court of Appeal: Re Bhullar Bros Ltd* by Dr Hans C. Hirt, 2005 JBL 669: Payne and Prentice, *The Corporate Opportunity Doctrine*, (2004) 120 LQR 158; *Crown Dilman* v *Sitton*, (2004) 1 BCLC 468 (Ch D), it is no defence to say that the company would not have taken interest in the opportunity. The company has it be made aware of the opportunity and only then it may decide to waive it. The breach of duty commences from the moment of the failure to make a full disclosure.

27. *Vaishnav Shorilal Puri* v *Kishore Kundan Sippy*, (2006) 131 Comp Cas 609 Bom.

28. *Peso Silver Mines Ltd* v *Cropper*, (1966) 58 DLR (2d) 1.

29. *Ibid.* For a learned comment on this case *see* Stanley M. Beck, *Saga of Peso Silver Mines: Corporate Opportunity Revisited*, (1971) 44 Can BR 80.

30. *Ibid. See* further *New Zealand Netherlands Society "Oranje" Inc* v *Kays*, [1973] 2 All ER 1222, where the Judicial Committee look the view that there may be circumstances in which a person in a fiduciary position vis-á-vis the company may hold that position only in respect of a part of his duties.

31. [1942] 1 All ER 378, *see* infra at p 229.

reviewed in this background, it would seem to be an abnormally strict decision. But the English courts are in no mood to relax their standards.[32]

Position on cessation of directorship.—The decision in *Industrial Development Consultants Ltd* v *Cooley*,[33] is a reaffirmation of the belief in the *Regal* standard of honesty.

> The managing director of a company tried to get from the Gas Board a Government contract for the company. But the Gas Board plainly told him that the Government would not allow the contract to the company, but was willing to deal with him personally. He resigned from the company, under the pretence of ill-health and then promptly obtained the contract for himself. Having earned a handsome profit, he had to face an action from the company to account for it.

The court held that the managing director had acted in breach of his duty and, therefore, must account. In the *Peso Silver Mines* case the directors had in good faith rejected the opportunity to acquire adjacent mines and then some directors used the opportunity. Here the company greatly desired the contract and employed Cooley only in a bid to obtain it.[34] But the fact remains that it was the Government, not Cooley, who was to blame for what had happened. The moral of the decision is that either Cooley should have refrained from the contract or executed it at his personal risk and responsibility, but all the time for the benefit of the company.[35]

In *Cranleigh Precision Engg Ltd* v *Bryant*[36] in the course of his work in designing the company's products, a director discovered the existence of a patent which hindered the company from adding a refinement to its product, so as to make them readily marketable. He resigned his directorship and then purchased that patent from its owner. He formed a new company to

---

32. This despite criticism. *See*, for example, C. D. Baker, *Disclosure of Director's Interests in Contracts*, 1975 JBL 181 and John Birds, *The Permissible Scope of Articles excluding the Duties of Company Directors*, (1976) 39 Mod LR 394. Both consider the validity of Article 84 of Table A of the English Act which came into being in response to the decision in *Regal (Hastings)* case and permits reduction of the fiduciary obligation.

33. [1972] 1 WLR 443: [1972] 2 All ER 162.

34. For an appreciation of this decision *see* 1973 LQR 187 and J. G. Collier, *Directors' Duties*, [1972-A] Camb LJ 222; (1973) 35 Mod LR 655.

35. For another similar authority see *Canadian Aero Service Ltd* v *O'Malley*, (1973) 40 DLR (3d) 371, Supreme Court of Canada, where it was held that it is breach of duty on the part of directors to resign their office and to appropriate a chance to their new company which came before the company while they were still in office. *See* further, *Gilbert* case, (1870) 5 Ch App 559, where the payment of a call was postponed only to enable a director to transfer his shares for avoiding liability and he was nevertheless held liable. For the wisdom of a rule which equates the position of an honest director with that of the dishonest, *see* N. A. Bastin, *The Honest Director and Secret Profits*, 1978 New LJ 527.

36. 1964 All ER 289.

manufacture the product with the addition of the patented improvement. He had to account to the company for the profits of his new company.[37]

Fiduciary obligation does not cease with resignation, but on the company exercising its right on full information to accept the resignation or to terminate his services if it so wishes.[38] Where the termination is due to operation of law, the director ceases to hold office immediately and his fiduciary duties terminate forthwith.[39] However, even in such a situation the duty to maintain confidential information survives. The duty of confidence as to business secrets terminates only when the company releases him from the obligation or when the secret information is published or becomes generally known, that is to say, it is converted by the owner into a matter of public knowledge.[40]

Competition by directors

In a decision on the point, the judicial opinion was that there is no breach of duty if a director competes with his company or holds some interest in a rival company or is a director in a competing company.[41] But accountability will chase a director if he uses the company's assets for the benefit of a rival concern and this includes its business connection, goodwill, trade assets and the list of customers.[42] If a company has invested resources in providing some training to a director or special skills, he may be restrained from using such skills for the benefit of a rival concern.[43] A director can also be restrained by

37. This is in contrast to *Nordick Insulin Laboratorium* v *Gorgate Products Ltd*, 1953 Ch 430, in which an agent had made a profit after the termination of his agency and he was held not liable.
38. *Thomas Marshall (Exports) Ltd* v *Guinle*, 1979 Ch 227.
39. *Reid* v *Explosives Co*, (1887) 19 QBD 264; *Measures Bros Ltd* v *Measures*, [1910] 2 Ch 248.
40. *Morison* v *Moat*, (1851) 9 Hare 241; *Merry Weather* v *Moore*, [1892] 2 Ch 518; *Robb* v *Green*, [1895] 2 QB 315; *Franchi* v *Franchi*, [1967] RPC 149. A breach of this duty is illustrated by a plethora of cases involving directors leaving a company and setting up a business in competition. *SSC & Lintas New Zealand Ltd* v *Murphy*, (1981) 1 NZ CLC 98, 348 where the managing director of an advertising agency left taking staff and clients, is one example, *Independent Broadcasting Company Ltd* v *Rob McKay (Media) Ltd*, (1991) 5 NZ CLC 67, 527 where a radio broadcasting executive and director successfully tendered for a broadcasting frequency, and then left the company to operate a new radio station is another. The director's former company was successful in obtaining an interim injunction. Thorp J discussed the corporate opportunity doctrine in the judgment, which requires that "if the corporation has a present interest in the opportunity, then the fiduciary must present it to the corporation prior to exploiting it himself". For a further discussion of the scope of the prohibition on the misuse of confidential information by directors, see Harris, "Fiduciary Duties of Directors under the Companies Act, 1993" [1994] NZLJ 242 at pp 242-243.
41. *London and Mashonaland Exploration Co* v *New Mashonaland Exploration Co*, 1891 WN 185.
42. *Bell* v *Lever Bros Ltd*, 1932 AC 161; *Saltman Engg Co Ltd* v *Campbell Engg Co Ltd*, 1948 PRC 203; *Horeal Ltd* v *Gaitland*, 1984 BCLC 549.
43. *Hivac Ltd* v *Park Scientific Investments Ltd*, 1946 Ch 169: (1948) 18 Comp Cas 16 CA. The position is thus stated in Charlesworth and Cain, COMPANY LAW, 406 (13th Edn 1987): "Under the general law, apart from the case where a director has a service agreement with the company which requires him to serve only the company, there is authority to the effect that he may become a director of a rival company, i.e. in this way he may compete with the first company, provided that he does not disclose to the second company any confidential information obtained by him as a director of the first company, and that what he may do for a

the terms of his appointment from competing with the company or from joining any other concern as a director whatever be its business. A wholetime director has by virtue of the very nature of employment to restrain himself from joining any other company. He can be sued for breach of his contract with the company[44], though not for an account of his profits elsewhere.[45] If his personal influence weakens the company's ability to offer competition to his other concern and thereby suffers loss of business, he will be liable for the company's set back.[46] He will also be liable if he prevents the company's expansion into an area already occupied by the rival concern.[47] The courts have been somewhat liberal in this respect because they recognise, particularly in the case of part-time directors, that too strict an interpretation of directions' duties of loyalty as part of their fiduciary duties could result in a stifling of enterprise and a bottling up of management talent.

Trading in corporate control

A learned writer says:[48] "A director who acquires property while in office will, however, be liable to account for his profit upon resale if two elements are present. He must have acquired property only by reason of the fact that he was a director and in the course of the exercise of the office of director." *Regal (Hastings) Ltd* v *Gulliver*[49] carries the principle to the farthest limit.

> The plaintiff company were the owners of a cinema in Hastings. Its directors were anxious to acquire two other cinemas in Hastings and then to sell the whole property of the company as a going concern. For the purpose of acquiring the new cinemas they formed a subsidiary company with a capital of £5000 divided into shares of £1 each. They were offered a lease of the two cinemas, but the landlord required a guarantee of the rent by the directors unless the paid-up capital of the subsidiary company was £5000. The original intention was that the plaintiff company should hold all the shares in the subsidiary, but it was

---

rival company, he may do for himself or a rival firm. . . .He must not subordinate the interests of the first company to those of the second. . . ." Citing *London and Mashonaland Exploration Co* v *New Mashonaland Exploration Co*, 1891 WN 165; *Bell* v *Lever Bros Ltd*, 1932 AC 161, 165. *Also see* GOWER'S PRINCIPLES OF MODERN COMPANY LAW, 588 (4th Edn).

44. *Sequois Vacuum Systems Inc* v *Stranky*, (1964) 229 Cap App 2d 281.
45. *Whitwood Chemical Co Ltd* v *Hardman*, [1891] 2 Ch 416.
46. *Singer* v *Carlisle*, (1941) 26 NYS 2d 320.
47. *Rosenblum* v *Judson Engg Corpn*, (1954) 99 NH 267.
48. D. N. Hossie, *The Civil Liability of the Directors of a Corporation*, (1952) 30 Can BR 908. Following articles on the subject of corporate control may be consulted: Hill, *Sale of Controlling Shares*, 70 Harv LR 936 (1951); Berle, *Control in Corporate Law*, 58 Col LR 1212 (1958); *Liability of Directors for Taking Corporate Opportunities, using Corporate Facilities or Engaging in a Competing Business*, (1939) 39 Col LR 219; William D. Andrews, *The Stockholders' Right to Equal Opportunity in the Sale of Shares*, (1965) 78 Harv 505. Hornstein, *The Future of Corporate Control*, 63 Harv LR 476: *See also* Louis Loss, SECURITIES REGULATION, (1951).
49. [1942] 1 All ER 378: [1967] 2 AC 134.

unable to provide for more than 2000 shares. The matter was, therefore, rearranged: 2000 shares were allotted to the plaintiff company; 500 shares were taken by each of the three directors, 500 by the solicitor of the company and the remaining 500 were allotted to certain persons found by the chairman of directors. And thus a capital of £5000 was raised. The two cinemas were taken and all the shares in the plaintiff company and the subsidiary company were sold. The 3000 shares allotted to the directors, the solicitor and the chairman were sold at a profit of £2-16s-1d. per share. The action was brought by the plaintiff company to recover this profit.

It was held that in the circumstances the directors, other than the chairman, were in a fiduciary relation to the company and liable, therefore, to repay to it the profit they had made on the shares. The solicitor was not in a fiduciary relationship and was not liable. They acquired these shares only by reason of the fact that they were the directors of the *Regal* and in the course of their execution of that office. Lord MACMILLAN added:[50] "The plaintiff company has to establish two things: first, that what the directors did was so related to the affairs of the company that it can properly be said to have been done in the course of their management and in the utilisation of their opportunities and special knowledge as directors and, secondly, that what they did resulted in a profit to themselves."

The real ground for the decision seems to be that the opportunity to take 5000 shares was the corporate opportunity.[51] The directors, however, took the shares in good faith because the company was financially unable to make use of the opportunity. But if they were permitted to retain the profit, there would be temptation to induce such inability on the part of the company and to profit by it. The liability of the directors to account, therefore, seems to be just and clear. But to hand over this profit to the purchaser shareholders would be to give them the benefit of an undeserved reduction in price which they had willingly paid up. Recovery, therefore, should have been in favour of the old shareholders who had really suffered. This course was preferred in the American case of *Commonwealth Title Insurance & Trust Co v Seltzer.*[52]

Directors of a corporation had agreed to sell to a prospective purchaser the assets of the corporation indirectly by selling all the stock at a stated price. The directors then bought up the whole of the stock from the shareholders at a lower figure and completed the sale. They were held liable to return the profit thus realised not to the corporation

50. *Regal (Hastings) Ltd v Gulliver,* [1942] 1 All ER 378 at pp 391-392.
51. The full implications of the decision have been discussed by Gower, THE PRINCIPLES OF MODERN COMPANY LAW, 535-537 (3rd Edn, 1969.) *See* also *Lindgren* v *L & P Estates Co Ltd,* [1968] 2 WLR 562: [1968] 1 All ER 917; noted 1968 JBL 152; *Parker v Mckenna,* (1874) 10 Ch App 96: 31 LT 739.
52. 227 Pa 410: 76 Atl 77, (1910); discussed in a note on *Fiduciary Duty of Directors not to compete with the Corporation,* (1941) 54 Harv LR 1190.

but to the old shareholders whose stock was bought. "The payment to the corporation would in substance be a return of a part of the purchase price to the buyer who, of course, had no claim to such a windfall."

Still another duty of controlling shareholders is not to make money for themselves from selling their controlling block of shares. According to Berle and Means: "Control power is itself an asset which may not be traded or disposed of without regard to the interest of the corporation or the totality of shareholders."[53] If the price received by the directors for the controlling block of shareholders is greater than the prevailing market price of their shares, the real consideration for the inflated price is the "control" which the purchaser has acquired. The minority shareholders should, therefore, be entitled to a *pro rata* distribution of the price which is attributable to the right of control.[54] But this broad general principle does not yet seem to have been adopted by the courts.[55] On the contrary, it has been frequently pointed out that "shares" are the private property of the shareholder and he may sell them for any price or in any manner he pleases, even if his shares carry the right to control the company.[56] Yet two inroads upon this principle have already been made.

In the first place, any profit obtained through breach of a fiduciary obligation, such as, sale of office or interception of corporate opportunities, has to be shared with the minority shareholders. *Perlman v Feldmann*[57] is the well known illustration.

During the period when steel was in short supply, a small steel company was offered by a syndicate of steel users an interest-free loan for the expansion of its plants in return for commitment for future deliveries. Instead of accepting this offer, the directors sold to the syndicate their controlling block of shares at a price approximately twice their market value and allowed the purchasers to assume control, who then withdrew the offer of free loan.

In an action brought by minority stockholders the court granted *pro rata* recovery in their favour. The directors had tried to make profit from "the ability to allocate steel in the time of short supply", which was a corporate asset.

---

53. THE MODERN CORPORATION AND PRIVATE PROPERTY, (1932) 244. This statement is quoted in William C. Warren, *Adolf A. Berle*, (1964) 64 Col LR 1377. For reasons why corporate control is a valuable asset *see* Henry G. Manne, *Some Theoretical Aspects of Share Voting*, 1964 Col LR 1427. "A controlling block of shares is worth more than a non-controlling block". *See* Leonard J. Connolly, *Perlman v Feldmann & the Sale of Control*, (1971) BL 1259.
54. See *Individual Pro Rata Recovery in Stockholder's Derivative Suit*, (1956) 69 Harv LR 1314.
55. *See* Anthony John Boyle, *The Sale of Controlling Shares*, (1964) 13 ICLQ 185 at p 189, where the learned writer also considers the academic criticism of the view.
56. *Gerdes v Reynolds*, 28 NYS 2nd 622. For a consideration of this and other cases on the subject *see* a note in (1955) 68 Harv LR 1275.
57. (1955) 349 US 952: 219 F 2d 173, from where the facts have been collected.

Secondly, the sellers of the controlling block would be liable if they have "negligently or fraudulently" passed the "control" to a person who would loot the assets of the company.[58] Such purchasers are often tempted by large liquid assets which they afterwards utilise in paying off short-term loans taken to finance the take-over bid.[59] In such cases it is not necessary that the seller should have actual knowledge of the purchaser's design to loot. It will be enough to make him liable that there were circumstances putting him on inquiry, for example, the purchaser's previous history, excessive price offered, liquidity of the corporate assets, etc.[60]

Statutory provisions relating to sale of controlling shares.—Apart from these judicial developments the legislature have also tried to modify the inequitable result of *Regal (Hastings) Ltd* v *Gulliver*. Sections 319 to 321 of the Companies Act are designed to catch any extra payment that may be received by directors in connection with transfer of the undertaking or property or shares of a company. The right to control the management of a company is a valuable asset and it is desirable that if any price is obtained for the sale of this right, the same should be shared by the members in accordance with their rights. The control of a company may pass in several ways. The whole undertaking or property of the company may be sold.[61] In such a case the directors of the company have to retire from office as the purchasers will like to place their nominees on the board. The directors may receive some payment from the company by way of compensation for loss of office or from the transferee as a consideration for retirement. As long as the amount thus received is nothing more than a *bona fide* payment by way of damages for breach of contract or by way of pension in respect of past services, there is hardly anything objectionable in it. This right of directors is, indeed, expressly protected by sub-section (3) of Section 321. But what may happen is that under the cover of compensation for loss of office, they may manage to make money as an inducement to retire and to facilitate the transfer of control. Indeed, they may be getting the money as a price for the right of control. That is why Section 319 provides that any money received from the transferee in connection with the transfer of the company's property or undertaking must be disclosed to the members of the company

---

58. *See* a note in (1955) 68 Harv LR 1275; *Also see* Hill, *Sale of Controlling Shares*, (1957) 70 Harv LR 986 and Janning, (1956) 44 California LR 1.

59. *See* Anthony John Boyle, *The Sale of Controlling Shares*, (1964) 13 ICLQ 185, 187, where the learned writer cites recommendations of the Jenkins Committee, paras 176 to 186 of the Report. Where the funds of a company were diverted to another company to enable the two sons of the managing director to acquire control over that company, the two sons were not allowed to be charged with conspiracy and criminal breach of trust because they were not even the directors of the company at that time, *Ashim K. Roy* v *Bipinbhai Vadilal Mehta*, (1998) 1 SCC 133: (1998) 91 Comp Cas 1: [1998] 1 Comp LJ 1 SC.

60. *Id.*, 192.

61. For a discussion of the various modes of transfer of control and how side-payments are obtained by the majority sellers, *see* Henry G. Manne, *Some Theoretical Aspects of Share Voting*, 1964 Col LR 1427.

and approved by the company in general meeting. Where this is not done, the amount shall be held by the directors in trust for the company.[62]

Another method of acquiring the control of a company is by purchasing its shares.[63] Shares may be purchased:

1. by making an offer to the general body of shareholders;
2. where the purchaser is a company, by inviting the company to become its subsidiary or a subsidiary of its holding company;
3. by making an offer with a view to obtaining the right to control the exercise of one-third of the total voting power;
4. by making any other offer which is conditional on acceptance to a given extent.

Here also those who acquire control will replace the existing management. The outgoing director may be induced on payment of money to facilitate the transfer of control, although outwardly the payment may have been made as compensation for retirement. If the transferee proposes to pay something to the directors, the latter must take reasonable steps to inform the shareholders of the particulars of such payment along with any notice of the offer made for their shares.[64] Where this disclosure is not made to the selling shareholders, the directors may call a meeting of such shareholders and get the proposed payment approved before any transfer is made.[65] But where they do neither, they shall hold the amount in trust for the shareholders who have sold their shares.[66]

The scope of the words "compensation for loss of office" and "consideration for retirement" is considerably widened by Section 321 so that directors may not avoid their obligation to account by apparently separating the transfer of control from payment. This section provides that any payment made by the transferee in pursuance of any arrangement entered into as a part of the agreement for the transfer of shares, or within one year before or two years after the agreement, shall be deemed to have been received as "compensation for loss of office" or "consideration for retirement" and liable to be accounted for.[67] Similarly, if the price paid to a retiring director for his shares in the company is in excess of the price paid to other shareholders or any other valuable consideration has been given to him, it shall also be regarded as "compensation" or "consideration" and must be disclosed to the shareholders.[68]

---

62. S. 319(2).
63. S. 320(1).
64. S. 320(2). *See also* sub-section (3) which imposes penalty for default.
65. S. 320(4).
66. *Ibid.* According to sub-section (5) if at a meeting called for the purpose of approving any payment a quorum is not present and the meeting having been adjourned, a quorum is again not present, the payment shall be deemed to have been approved.
67. S. 321(1).
68. S. 321(2).

These statutory provisions also modify the result of *Percival* v *Wright*.[69] In cases falling within the scope of the above sections, directors become trustees for those individual shareholders who have sold their shares for any profits made by the directors.

The scope of the disclosure obligation has been considerably widened in the United States. The interpretation of Rule 10B-5 of the Securities Exchange Regulations[70] creates a situation where "fiduciary obligations are no longer owed only to the current owners of the corporation, that is, the stockholders, but are also owed to outside non-stockholders. The insider owes a duty not only to refrain from stating falsehoods, or half-truths, but affirmatively to disclose all the material facts of the transaction."[71] The case of *Securities & Exchange Commission* v *Texas Gulf Sulphur Co*[72] has become well known in this connection.

> The Texas Gulf Sulphur Co carried on certain drilling operations and discovered important mineral deposits. Before disclosing this fact to the public, the directors purchased the company's shares in the market and also acquired options to purchase further shares (calls). They also tipped their relatives and friends to purchase the company's shares. Ultimately, when the fact of discovery was made public, the prices of the company's shares soared up.

The SEC brought an action against the insiders to restrain them from purchasing shares unless a full disclosure of the facts was made and to offer restitution to those whose shares they and their "tippees" had purchased. They contended that they had no intent to defraud and had in good faith withheld the information because any disclosure of this kind would have materially affected the prices of adjoining areas thus defeating the company's chances of acquiring the land at reasonable prices. But even so they were held liable. It is no doubt primarily the function of the management to decide when an information is ripe for disclosure, but in the meantime they should not operate in the company's stock market.[73]

Misuse of corporate information.—Exploitation of unpublished and confidential information belonging to the company is a breach of duty and the company can ask the director in question to make good its loss, if any. Any knowledge or information generated by the company is the property of

69. [1902] 2 Ch 421.
70. Federal Securities Exchange Act, 1934.
71. *Scienter and Rule 10B-5*, (1969) Col LR 1057 to 1061. Also see *The National Securities* case; *The Supreme Court and Rule 10B-5*, (1969) Col LR 906, Israels and Loss, *Recent Developments in Securities Regulations*, (1963) 63 Col LR 856, William Henry Navin, *Insiders' Liability under Rule 10B-5 of the Illegal Purchase of Actively Traded Securities*, (1968) 78 Yale LJ 864.
72. 401 F 2d 833 (2d Cir 1968). Considered in *Scienter and Rule 10B-5*, (1969) Col LR 1057.
73. For criticism of this decision *see* Louis Loss, *The Fiduciary Concept as Applied to Trading by Corporate "Insiders" in the U. S.*, (1970) 33 Mod LR 34 and Henry G. Manne, ECONOMIC POLICY AND THE REGULATION OF CORPORATE SECURITIES, (1968). For a view of all the possible aspects of directors' liability, *see* Robert R Pennington, DIRECTORS' PERSONAL LIABILITY (1987).

the company, commonly known as intellectual property. Turnover of business, profit margins, list of customers, future plans, any personal use of such knowledge is equivalent to misappropriation of property.[74] Use of such information can be restrained by means of an injunction.[75] Any gain made by the use of inside information has to be accounted for to the company.

At common law, equity imposes fiduciary duties on directors because of their position of power in, and their relationship of confidence to, the company. In the course of their office, directors often can and do, obtain access to confidential information relating to sensitive transactions of the company. Also, information is acquired in circumstances where the recipient is required to keep it confidential. It is part of each director's fiduciary duty not to misuse this information. Each director owes a duty to the company not to disclose or use confidential information without the company's consent.

SEBI (Insider Trading) Regulations, 1992.—The Securities and Exchange Board of India has formulated Regulations for preventing and punishing the use of price sensitive unpublished inside information in dealings with the company's securities.[76]

Where the directors sold their shares before publishing half-yearly statements and the market went down after the publication because the accounts were not according to expectations, they were held liable to hand over profits to the company.[77] Purchase of company's shares by directors cheaply with the knowledge that soon they were due to issue an offer to buy from willing shareholders at a higher price out of the company's reserves, made them accountable.[78]

Apart from violations of the regulatory framework, directors' dealings in their own company shares are not illegal. It is considered desirable that directors of listed companies should hold the shares of their companies. As a part of remuneration package, directors are often given share options which enable them to acquire shares in their company, which they may afterwards sell. When directors decide to sell their shares however acquired or to buy more shares, their trading comes to be governed by the legislation on insider

---

74. *Boardman v Phipps*, [1967] 2 AC 46; *Exchange Telegraph Co Ltd v Gregory & Co*, [1896] 1 QB 147; *Exchange Telegraph Co v Central News Ltd*, [1897] 2 Ch 48.
75. *Saltman Engg Co Ltd v Campbell Engg Co Ltd*, 1948 PRC 203; *Terrapin Ltd v Builders Supply Co (Hayes) Ltd*, [1960] RPC 128; *Morris Ltd v Gilman (BST) Ltd*, (1943) 60 RPC 20.
76. *DSQ Holdings Ltd v SEBI*, (2005) 60 SCL 156 SAT a promoter group company was held to be an insider within the meaning of Regulation 2(*e*). There was violation of Regulation 3(1) and, therefore, debarment from dealing in securities for 5 years. The information in his possession related to rights issue. *Samir C. Arora v SEBI*, (2005) 125 Comp Cas 409 SAT, the person in question must have access to price sensitive information, which means such unpublished information which when published would affect prices of the company's securities.
77. *Diamond v Oreamuno*, (1969) 24 NY 2d 494.
78. *Brophy v City Service Co*, (1974) 31 Del Ch 341. Insider trading in violation of the law has been held to be an offence connected with the management of a company and is therefore, a ground for disqualification under the [English] Directors' Disqualification Act, 1986 and under S. 203 of the [Indian] Companies Act, 1956, *R v Goodman*, [1992] 2 All ER 789 CA.

trading. They commit an offence if they trade on some specific non-public information about their companies' securities. "For instance, if the director has access to unpublished price sensitive information, such as information on future earnings' figures, security issues, assets disposal and purchases, etc., which if it were made public would have significant effect on the share prices, it is illegal for them to trade on the information. Consequently, directors can trade in the shares of their own company but the trading must not be based on any inside information."[79]

Outsiders dealing in inside information.—A dealer in a company's securities receiving inside information commits an offence under Section 1(3) and (4) of the Companies Securities (Insider Dealing) Act, 1985 (English) whether he procured that information from a primary insider by purpose or came by it without any positive action on his part.[80]

Directors' duty of care, diligence and skill

Liability for negligence

Fidelity alone is not enough. A director has to perform his functions with reasonable care. He has to attend with due diligence and caution the work assigned to him. The Nigerian Act contains a set of provisions on this aspect of directors' duties:

"A director shall act at all times in what he believes to be the best interests of the company as a whole so as to preserve the assets, further its business and promote the purposes for which it was formed, and in such manner as a faithful, diligent, careful and ordinarily skilful director would act in the circumstances."[81]

Another provision runs as follows:[82]

"Every director of a company shall exercise the powers and discharge the duties of his office honestly, in good faith and in the best interests of the company and shall exercise that degree of care, diligence, and skill which a reasonably prudent director would exercise in comparable circumstances."

79. David Hillier and Andrew Marshall, *The Timings of Directors' Trades in the United Kingdom and the Model Code*, 1998 JBL 454; *Patel Investments v SEBI*, (2005) 59 SCL 506 SAT, the managing director created artificial market for the company's shares by effecting purchases through attached brokers.

80. *Attorney-General's Ref No 1 of 1988*, [1989] 1 All ER 321 CA: [1989] 2 WLR 195; 1988 BCLC 193. The same would be the position where the information comes his way without any effort on his part. *Attorney-General's Ref No 1 of 1989*, [1989] 2 All ER 1 HL. For further study, *see* P.St. J. Smart, *Misuse of Confidential Information: The Company and Minority Shareholder's Remedies*, 1987 JBL 464. Tipees are liable to be prosecuted under S. 1(1) if they had knowledge that the information was still unpublished. *See* Charles Rickett and Ross Grantham, ESSAYS ON INSIDER TRADING AND SECURITIES REGULATION, (1997) on the desirability of such regulation and whether inside trading is really objectionable.

81. Section 279(1) of the Companies and Allied Matters Act, 1990.

82. Section 282, *ibid.*

The New Zealand Companies Act, 1993 also provides that a director must exercise his powers for a proper purpose.

The courts have been very liberal in the matter of the expected standards of skill and care. An early example is *Overend Gurney & Co v Gibb*.[83] A company was formed to take over a private bank. Without investigating the value of the bank's assets and the extent of its liabilities and with knowledge that the bank was in a state of insolvency, the directors paid £50,000 for goodwill. Still holding them not liable, the House of Lords laid down that there should be violation of either the Act or the memorandum or the transaction was such that no man of ordinary prudence would have entered into. In another case of overvaluation of assets, acquitting the directors, the court said that in order to make them liable their negligence must be in a business sense culpable and gross.[84] Directors may not know the nature of the company's trade, because all that the law expects from them is that if they know they must use the knowledge for the company's benefit.[85] Accordingly directors were held guilty of negligence when they participated in a transaction without trying to know whether the transaction was really for the purposes of the company or whether they were authorised by the Board in that respect, and it was no defence for any director to show that he believed that he was bound to sign because the other directors wanted it or that he joined under protest or that even without his joining, the other directors were determined to carry out the transaction.[86] Directors were also held liable where they released the company's funds for paying a debt without trying to know whether anything was really due and for purchasing assets without knowing whether there was any real transfer of those assets.[87] Liability for negligence also followed where without any board resolution being properly passed a single member was allowed to manage a part of the company's business and he misconducted himself.[88] A director would also be guilty of negligence where he discovers something wrong and, instead of informing the shareholders, rests content after pointing it out to the directors only.[89]

Beginning with ROMER J's formulation of directors' duties, a constant judicial effort has been maintained in putting some objectivity into the standards of skill and care expected from directors. "His duties will depend upon the nature of the company's business and the manner in which the work of the company is distributed between the directors and other officials of the company. In discharging these duties a director must exercise some degree of skill and

---

83. (1872) LR 5 HL 480. *See* further *Prudential Assurance Co Ltd v Newman Industries Ltd (No 2)*, [1980] 3 WLR 543: [1982] Ch 204, 221: [1980] 2 All ER 841, no liability where assets reduced to less than liabilities.
84. *Lazunas Nitrate Co v Lagunas Syndicate*, [1899] 2 Ch 392.
85. *Brazilian Rubber Plantations and Estates Ltd, Re*, [1911] 1 Ch 425: 103 LT 697.
86. *Land Credit Co of Ireland v Lord Fermoy*, (1869) LR 3 Eq 7: (1870) 5 Ch App 763.
87. *Selangor United Rubber Estates v Cradock (No 3)*, [1968] 2 All ER 1073: [1968] 1 WLR 1555; *Joint Stock Discount Co v Brown*, (1869) 8 Eq 381; *Ramskill v Edwards*, (1885) 31 Ch D 100.
88. *City Equitable Ins Co, Re*, 1925 Ch 407.
89. *Joint Stock Discount Co v Brown*, (1869) 8 Eq 381; *Ramskill v Edwards*, (1885) 31 Ch D 100.

diligence. But he does not owe to his company the duty to take all possible care or to act with best care. Indeed, he need not exhibit in the performance of his duties a greater degree of skill than may reasonably be expected from a person of his knowledge and experience. It is, therefore, perhaps, another way of stating the same proposition that directors are not liable for mere errors of judgment."[90] This is a well-known observation of ROMER J in the celebrated case of *City Equitable Fire Insurance Company, Re.*[91]

> One *B* was a director of the City Equitable Fire Insurance Co. The company was ordered to be wound up. A searching investigation of the affairs of the company was then made and this investigation showed a shortage in the funds which the company should have been possessed of over £12,00,000. The collapse of the company was due to bad investments, bad debts and misappropriation. All the losses were due to *B's* instrumentality. He was accordingly convicted for his frauds.

But the question naturally arose as to whether during the period covered by *B's* nefarious activities the other directors were properly discharging their duties to the company? It was alleged that they were guilty of negligence in not detecting the frauds. But there was an exemption clause in the articles according to which the directors were liable only for gross negligence. The facts of the case did not disclose that degree of negligence and, therefore, the case of the official receiver against *B's* co-directors failed.

***Exclusion of liability now not allowed* [S. 201].**—"This acquittal (in *City Equitable* case) caused such ferment as to lead to legislation abolishing 'contracting out'."[92] Accordingly, the Act now does not allow liability for negligence to be excluded. Section 201 renders void any provision in the company's articles or in any agreement which excludes liability for negligence, default, misfeasance, breach of duty or breach of trust. The company is also not allowed to indemnify its officers against such liability. The only exception is that where an officer has been sued or prosecuted on any of the above charges and the judgment is in his favour or he has been acquitted, or relief has been granted to him under Section 633, the company may indemnify him against costs incurred in defence. An auditor has been held to be an officer of the company for the purposes of such indemnity.[93] But where an auditor is retained only to conduct and carry out an audit function, without appointment as an auditor, he would not be an officer.[94]

---

90. See *Brazilian Rubber Plantations & Estates Ltd, Re*, [1911] 1 Ch 425: 103 LT 697, directors not liable for ignorance of trade practices.
91. [1924] All ER Rep 485: [1925] Ch 407: 133 LT 520. *See also Union Bank of Allahabad, Re*, AIR 1925 All 519: 88 IC 785; *Govind v Rangnath*, 32 Bom LR 232; *Parke v Daily News Ltd*, [1961] 1 WLR 493: [1961] 1 All ER 695.
92. William O. Douglas, *Directors Who do not Direct*, (1934) 47 Harv LR 1305, 1320. *See also* Samuel, SHAREHOLDERS' MONEY, (1933) 125.
93. *Mutual Reinsurance Co Ltd v Post Marwick Mitchell & Co*, (1997) 1 BCLC 1 CA; *R v Shacter*, [1960] 1 All ER 61: (1960) 30 Comp Cas 334 CCA.
94. *Mutual Reinsurance Co Ltd v Post Marwick Mitchell & Co*, (1997) 1 BCLC 1 CA.

Though this provision came into being in reaction to the decision in the *City Equitable* case, its scope is not confined merely to contracting out of the consequences of negligence. Apart from negligence, it renders void any provision in the articles or in an agreement which exempts a director from liability for default, misfeasance, breach of duty or breach of trust.[1]

Standard and degree of care and skill.—Quite apart from this statutory development, the courts have also been trying to reconsider the standard of care expected of directors. ROMER J formulation is largely subjective, as a director has to use only such "skill as may reasonably be expected from a person of his knowledge and experience". The standard of care required of directors at common law has traditionally been light compared with their duties in other areas. Usually it took gross negligence for directors to be liable. But the current trend is towards objectivity.[2] In the words of Justice CARDOZO:

> The diligent director is the one who exhibits in the performance of his trust the same degree of care and prudence that men prompted by self-interest generally exercise on their own affairs.[3]

This standard demands reasonable business prudence from managers. To the same effect is the observation of BUCKLEY J in *Duomatic Ltd, Re*.[4] A director has to act "in the way in which a man of affairs dealing with his own affairs with reasonable care, and circumspection could reasonably be expected to act...." Applying this standard to the case before him, the learned Judge held that payment of £4000, without legal advice, as compensation to a director for retirement when, in fact, he was entitled to no compensation was, an act which could not be regarded as reasonable.[5]

The directors of a company manufacturing car components were held liable because they failed to ensure that their company had established an efficient production system before commencing production and caused loss by paying wages, salaries and general overheads which were not matched by output.[6] Justice HAND said:

> I cannot agree with the language of *Hun v Carey*[7] that in effect a director gives an implied warranty of any special fitness for his position.

---

1 It has been maintained by some eminent authors that this provision still permits diminution of duty apart from exemption from liability. Duty itself may be modified, though liability for breach of duty cannot be excluded. *See* Gore-Browne, COMPANY LAW, 42nd Edn, 778 and Gower, 532 (3rd Edn) COMPANY LAW.

2 *See* M. J. Trebilock, *Liability of Directors for Negligence*, (1969) 32 Mod LR 409.

3 *People v Mancuso*, 255 GY 463, 469. Borrowed from Jackson, WISDOM OF THE SUPREME COURT, 82, (1962).

4 [1969] 2 WLR 114: [1969] 1 All ER 161: [1969] 2 Ch 365.

5 *See* 1967 JBL at 139-40. *See also* J. A. C. Hetherington, *Corporate Responsibility*, (1969) Stan LR 248 at p 257; M. Feuer, PERSONAL LIABILITY OF CORPORATE OFFICERS AND DIRECTORS, (1961).

6. *Barnes v Andrews*, (1924) 298 F 614, USA.

7. (1880) 82 NY 65, USA, where it was stated that directors should possess at least ordinary knowledge and skill.

Directors are not specialists like lawyers or doctors. They must have good sense; perhaps they must have an acquaintance with the affairs; but they need not, indeed, perhaps they should not, have a technical talent. They are the general advisers of the business, and if they have faithfully given such ability as they have to their charge, it would not be lawful to hold them liable.

Directors would decidedly be liable for omitting to do what they could have done in the circumstances. Where the president of an investment company improvidently invested in companies in which he was interested and caused loss, his fellow directors were held liable because they had left the investment of the company's funds to the president's unfettered discretion and exercised no supervision over him.[8] In another similar case, a money lending company had two chartered accountant directors. They left the matter of the negotiations for loans wholly to the discretion of the third professionally unqualified director without supervision and also for making loans without inquiring for what purpose the loans were made, what was the security, if any, and what were the terms of repayment. The company had suffered loss in the transactions. The directors were held liable.[9]

Where the senior executives of a company caused loss because of illegal price fixing agreements, the directors were held not liable when there was no evidence to show that they knew or had reason to believe that such things were being done or that they were negligent in their choice of senior executives.[10]

What seems now to be the leading case on directors' duty of care is the New South Wales Court of Appeal decision in *Daniels v Anderson.*[11] It was observed in this case that the old cases, with their notions of subjective tests and gross negligence have become outdated. "The idea that the shareholders were ultimately responsible for the unwise appointment of directors led to the duty of care, skill and diligence, which a director owed to a company being characterised as remarkably low."[12] The Court said:

"We see no reason why the relationship of a director to a company should not, in accordance with the law as it has been developed since *Hedley Byrne & Co v Heller & Partners Ltd*[13] satisfy the proximity test. One must look to see whether there are reasons of policy for saying that a director does not owe a duty of care to the company."

The court further said:

"In our opinion, the responsibilities of directors require that they take reasonable steps to place themselves in a position to guide and

8. *Kavanangh v Common Wealth Trust Co,* (1918) 233 NY 103 USA.
9. *Dorchester Finance Co Ltd v Stebbings,* 1 Co Lawyers 38 USA.
10. *Graham v Allis Chalmers Mfg Co,* (1963) 41 Del Ch 78.
11. (1995) 16 ACSR 607.
12. *See* S. M. Watson, *Directors Duties in New Zealand,* 1998 JBL 495 at p 502.
13. [1963] 3 WLR 101: [1963] 2 All ER 575: 1964 AC 465.

monitor the management of the company. The courts have recognised that directors must be allowed to make business judgments and business decisions in the spirit of enterprise. Any entrepreneur will rely upon a variety of talents in deciding whether to invest in a business venture. These may include legitimate but ephemeral political insights, a feel for future economic trends, trust in the capacity of other human beings. Great risks may be taken in the hope of commensurate rewards. If such venture fails, how is the undertaking of it to be judged against the allegation of negligence by the entrepreneur? In our opinion, the concept of negligence which depends ultimately upon a general public sentiment of moral wrongdoing for which the offender must pay[14] can adopt to measure appropriately in the given case whether the acts or omission of an entrepreneur are negligent.''

The practical difference that the developments have made between the old and new version of the duty has been spelt out to be this:

"The new duty is therefore in effect not greatly different from the Re Equitable standard. The major differences are first that the focus is on the level of responsibility taken on by directors rather than the director's actual level of expertise of experience, and secondly that it is likely that the courts will continue the line of applying a higher standard of care and attention to business by all directors. The standard required is that to be reasonably expected of someone occupying the office in question.''[15]

The New Zealand Companies Act, 1993 imposes a new duty on directors, not to engage in reckless trading. This expression is defined in the Act as agreeing to cause or allowing conduct likely to create a substantial risk of serious loss to the company's creditors. The duty of directors in this respect has been thus explained:[16]

"The taking of business risks and allowing directors a wide discretion in matters in business judgment requires a sober assessment by directors as to the company's likely future income stream. Given current economic conditions, did the directors make reasonable assumption in their forecasts of future revenue? Creditors are likely to suffer serious losses if future outflows of cash exceed cash inflows for the same period. If there is no profit margin on goods being sold or services provided the company will reach a stage where the shareholders' risk capital has been exhausted and directors are instead using resources otherwise available to meet all creditor's claims. In

---

14. Citing *Donoghue* v *Stevenson*, 1932 AC 562 at p 580.
15. S. M. Watson, *Directors' Duties in New Zealand*, 1998 JBL 495 at p 504.
16. Ross M, *Directors' Liability and Company Insolvencies—the New Companies Act*, [1994] Commerce Clearing House, 98.

those circumstances, the company should have stopped trading. To continue trading is to risk creditor's money.''

Duty of non-executive director

It has been laid down that in the application of the standards of care and skill, no distinction can be made between executive and non-executive directors. On facts, the two non-executive directors were held guilty of negligence inasmuch as they signed blank cheques which enabled the executive director to act at pleasure in completing the cheques. They were held liable to compensate the company for its loss.[17] Summarising the present position of the duty of care and skill, the court crystallised it into the following three points: (1) There ought to be an exhibition of such a degree of skill as may reasonably be expected from a person with the particular director's knowledge and experience; (2) The director has to exercise in the performance of his duty such care as an ordinary man might be expected to do on his own behalf, and (3) All powers vested in directors must be exercised in good faith and in the interest of the company.

"When exercising powers or performing duties, directors are charged with exercising the care, diligence and skill that a reasonable director would exercise in the same circumstances. Despite arguments in its favour and some case law supporting the approach, the extra knowledge and abilities of professional executive directors do not mean there is a higher duty of care specifically imposed on them. Conversely, a director with a lesser level of skill and experience must, on the exercise of his or her power, still reach the level of the mythical reasonable director. Similarly, traditionally non-executive directors owed lower duties to the company at common law. But there were indications of changing attitudes in the courts. In *Morley*,[18] Mrs Morley, who took no active part in a company run by her husband, was still found to be liable to a third party. In *Deloitte Haskins & Sells v National Mutual Life Nominees Ltd*[19] the court did not accept that a lower standard of care should be imposed on a non-executive director than an executive director. The difference from the common law must be more academic than problematic since practically, in most cases, directors will take on responsibilities commensurate with their abilities. If they do not, it is perhaps reasonable they should face liability if they do not reach the requisite standard.[20]

---

17. *Dorchester Finance Co Ltd v Stebbings*, 1 Co Lawyers 38, USA: 1989 BCLC 498 Ch D. *See* E. J. Jacobs, *Non-Executive Directors*, 1987 JBL 269.
18. *Morley v Statewide Tobacco Co Ltd*, (1990) 8 ACLC 933.
19. (1991) 5 NZ CLC 67, 418.
20. S. M. Watson, *Directors' Duties in New Zealand*, 1998 JBL 495 at p 503. For another contribution on the subject see Jones, *Company Law in New Zealand* (Butterworth, 1993, 119-20). *Yeshwant M. Desai v SEBI*, (2005) 59 SCL (SAT); *Chaitanya D. Mehta v SEBI*, (2004) CLC 498 (SAT), orders of disqualification were vacated in reference to non-executive directors. *Equitable Life Assurance Society v Bawley*, (2004) 1 BCLC 180 (QBD): 2004 BCC

Nominee directors

Where the directors failed to carry out directions of the court for arranging payment to the workers of the sick industrial company, the court said that the nominee director representing the BIFR in the company's Board was not to be held liable for contempt of court.[21] Nominated directors do not have control over day-to-day affairs of the company. They are thus entitled to be protected. The court quashed the summons, orders and subsequent proceedings against such directors.[22]

Special statutory protection against liability [S. 633]

The Act, however, in Section 633, extends special protection against a liability that may have been incurred in good faith. Where it appears to the court that the director sued "has acted honestly and reasonably, and that having regard to all the circumstances of the case..., he ought fairly to be excused, the court may relieve him, either wholly or partly from his liability on such terms as it may think fit."[23] Thus three circumstances must be shown to exist. The position must be such that the person to be excused is shown to have acted firstly, honestly, secondly, reasonably, and thirdly having regard to all the circumstances he ought fairly to be excused.[24] A good illustration is *Claridge's Patent Ashphalt Co, Re*.[25]

A company was formed for the production of certain compositions of cement for making roads. Owing to great increase in motor traffic there was a profitable future in making roads and it was proposed that the company should embark upon this new business. After consulting the company's solicitors, who advised that the scheme was not *ultra vires*, the directors applied the company's capital, but the new business proved a failure.

877, the application of a non-executive director for striking out case against him, the court has to consider reasonableness of his conduct, which is in essence a fact sensitive question and cannot be considered in a summary manner, it could not be said that there was no probability of success. *Secy of State* v *Swan and North*, 2004 BCC 877: (2005) EWHC 603, position considered in the context of disqualification proceedings. In a note on the case by the Editor, John P. Lowry, citing Adrian Cadbury as observing in CORPORATE GOVERNANCE AND CHAIRMANSHIP (Oxford) p 57, that the personal qualities needed of a non-executive director are clearly defined by Mills, CONTROLLING COMPANIES (Unwin, London) 1988, p 94, "A good non-executive director needs to have intellect, integrity and courage. Of these qualities, courage is the most important for without it the other two characteristics are useless.

21. *Girni Kamgar Sangharsh Samiti* v *Matulaya Mills Ltd*, 2002 Cri LJ 253 (Bom).
22. *S.K. Sharma and A.K. Mahajan* v *ROC*, (2005) 126 Comp Cas 222 P&H.
23. S. 633(1); a proviso to which declares that in a criminal action for negligence, etc., the Court shall have no power to grant relief from any liability. The word "officer" as used in the section has been held to include an officer whose service has been terminated. *Amrit Lal Chum* v *Devoprasad*, (1988) 2 SCC 269. Relief is allowed only to officers of the company and not to the company itself, *Balwant Singh* v *ROC*, (1995) 2 Punj LR 563.
24. BUCKLEY J in *Duomatic Ltd, Re*, [1969] 1 All ER 161 at p 171: [1969] 2 WLR 114: [1969] 2 Ch 365.
25. [1921] 1 Ch 543: 125 LT 255.

They were sued for misapplication of funds. But the court allowed relief. "They were acting for the benefit of the company and took the best advice." Similarly, in a case before the Orissa High Court,[26] where the annual general meeting of a company could not be held in time on account of the dissolution at the material time of the company's Board of directors by a court order, the court granted relief against liability for default. The Kerala High Court granted relief to a director who had not disclosed that his joint family was carrying on a contract with the company, the same having been entered into by his deceased father eighteen years ago and, he being not an active member of the family, did not know it.[27] Where a statement in the prospectus was that the company had 25 years of experience in its line of business, whereas the experience was that of the partnership which it had taken over and the business was commenced a bit late than what was stated in the prospectus, the directors were held not guilty of misrepresentation. Relief against prosecution was granted.[28] Relief was granted against the consequences of delay in registering a transfer of shares because the directors had acted on the advice of competent legal advisers.[29] Relief was allowed to a managing director because the delay of 24 days in filing the cost audit report was due to labour problems in the company.[30] Relief was allowed to directors who had resigned before the relevant period during which offences were alleged to have been committed and their resignations were registered with the ROC.[31]

The Calcutta High Court refused to grant relief in a case where there was a default in holding five successive meetings.[32] Relief was allowed where the directors could not hold AGMs and file annual returns, the failure being due to the takeover of the company by the Government and the matters being beyond their control.[33] Similarly, where the directors overdrew their remuneration in anticipation of its being voted to them in future, the court held that they could not be said to be acting reasonably and ought not to be excused,[34] or directors who knowingly accepted

26. *S. L. Kapoor* v *ROC*, [1964] 1 Comp LJ 211 Ori; *C. S. Lognathan* v *Registrar*, [1964] 1 Comp LJ 211 Ori. *Tapan Kumar Chowdhury* v *ROC*, (2003) 114 Comp Cas 631 Cal, there was sufficient cause for failure to hold AGM and file statutory documents with Registrar, relief was granted to the petitioning director alone because for the defaults committed by the directors, the directors were individually responsible and liable for conviction, one director could not make the application in a representative capacity for all the directors.

27. *M. O. Varghese* v *Thomas Stephen & Co Ltd*, (1970) 40 Comp Cas 1131 Ker.

28. *Progressive Aluminium Ltd* v *ROC*, (1997) 89 Comp Cas 147 AP: [1997] 4 Comp LJ 215.

29. *G. R. Desai* v *ROC*, (1999) 95 Comp Cas 138 AP; *Narsimha Janardan Ramath* v *ROC*, [1999] 2 Comp LJ 25 Bom.

30. *M. Meyyappan* v *ROC*, (2002) 112 Comp Cas 450 Mad.

31. *G. Ramesh* v *ROC*, (2007) 135 Comp Cas 655 Mad.

32. *Coal Marketing Co of India Ltd, Re*, [1967] 1 Comp LJ 237 Cal.

33. *Gautam Kanoria* v *Asstt ROC*, (2002) 108 Comp Cas 260 Bom.

34. *Duomatic Ltd, Re*, [1969] 1 All ER 161: [1969] 2 WLR 114. The Allahabad High Court has further pointed out in *G. D. Bhargava* v *ROC*, (1970) 40 Comp Cas 664: [1970] 2 Comp LJ 24,

deposits beyond the statutory limits.[35] No relief was allowed to directors who had collected contributions under the Employees' State Insurance Act and the Provident Fund Act but did not pay the employees according as their claims became due.[36] Relief was not allowed where correct returns were not filed and the offence was *prima facie* made out.[37] Relief has been allowed under the section to persons who become directors only for the purpose of rendering some professional or technical services. Such directors may not be aware of what administrative directors have been doing.[38] Relief was allowed in anticipation to two Japanese directors who were not concerned with the day to day management of the company.[39] Part-time directors are not entitled to any special consideration, but they may be more readily relieved where no evidence of their role in management is adduced.[40] The section was applied to relieve a marketing manager,[41] but not to debenture trustees.[42]

The totality of the circumstances have to be examined for considering whether relief is to be allowed or not. In this case, an *ex offico* chairman of a Government enterprise was also the chairman and managing director of a joint venture company. He was not to be exonerated of his duty to take care to see that the provisions of the Act were complied with. The Board had delegated substantial powers of management to another director. There was also a company secretary in the employ of the company. The court said that the chairman-cum-managing director deserved to be relieved of the alleged

---

that relief under the section is not allowed where the offences are so serious as to attract the provisions of the Indian Penal Code relating to forgery or falsification.

35. *Jagjivan Ram Hiralal Doshi* v *ROC*, (1989) 65 Comp Cas 553 Bom: [1989] 2 Comp LJ 315.
36. *Jagannath Pd Jhalani* v *Regional Provident Fund Commr*, (1987) 62 Comp Cas 571 Del. Relief is not allowable for defaults under other Acts. It is confined to defaults under the Companies Act, *Harishchandra Maganlal* v *UOI*, (1991) 71 Comp Cas 69 Bom.
37. *Farouk Irani* v *BIFR*, (2002) 110 Comp Cas 64 Mad.
38. *Om Prakash Khaitan* v *Shree Keshariya Investment Ltd*, (1978) 48 Comp Cas 85 Del.
39. *Kerji Tamaiya, Re*, (1990) 68 Comp Cas 142 Bom. Anticipatory relief was also allowed to directors who apprehended prosecution for defaults in reference to annual accounts though the period of limitation for proceeding against them had expired, the offence being not of continuing nature. *K. K. Mehra* v *ROC*, (1991) 1 Comp Cas 669 Del.
40. *Jagjivan* (supra) followed in *Harishchandra Maganlal* v *UOI*, AIR 1990 Bom 34, 36: [1990] 1 Comp LJ 355 Bom: (1991) 71 Comp Cas 69 Bom, where the court added that "such other person" whom notice of the proceedings under the section had to be given would include shareholders of the company. *S. P. Punj* v *ROC*, (1991) 71 Comp Cas 509 Del, relief was granted where it was doubtful whether deposits had been taken in excess of limits and whether the accused directors were parties to the resolution for inviting further deposits. Relief was allowed to directors of the sick industrial company which was under reference to the Board for Industrial and Financial Re-construction (BIFR). One and a half year period of relief was extended for two years, *Oriental Power Cables Ltd* v *ROC*, (1995) 83 Comp Cas 447 Raj. There cannot be an automatic relief in favour of a director who was appointed for compliance of laws only in a specified respect, though the default did not relate to the specified matter. *Shiv Kumar Dalmia* v *Mangal Chand Hukum Chand*, (1996) 86 Comp Cas 366: [1996] 2 Comp LJ 219 MP.
41. *Ravinder Kumar Sangal* v *Auto Lamps Ltd*, (1984) 55 Comp Cas 742 Del.
42. *Central Bank Executor & Trustee Co Ltd* v *Magna Hard Temp Ltd*, (1997) 89 Comp Cas 40 AP.

statutory violations. A director who was not on the Board at the time of violations was also to be relieved.[43]

The proviso to Section 633(1) declares that in a criminal proceeding under the section the court shall have no power to grant relief from any civil liability.

It has been held by the Court of Appeal in England that although the provision is expressed in wide language, in its context of company law and on its true construction the only proceeding for which relief can be claimed were proceedings against a director by, on behalf of, or for the benefit of his company for breach of his duty to the company as a director.[44]

Duty to attend board meetings

Negligence by non-attendance

Duties of directors are of intermittent nature to be performed at periodical board meetings. In other words, they are not bound to pay continuous attention to the affairs of the company. "They do not undertake to manage the company."[45] A director is not even bound to attend all the meetings of the board, although he is under an obligation to attend whenever in the circumstances he is reasonably able to do so. According to Section 283(*g*) the office of a director will be vacated if he absents himself from three consecutive meetings of the board, or from all meetings of the board for a consecutive period of three months, whichever is longer, without obtaining leave of absence from the board. Moreover, a director's habitual absence from board meetings may, taken in the light of other circumstances, become evidence of negligence on his part. In an early case in which liability was imposed for failure in this respect, the court said: "[I]f some persons are guilty of gross non-attendance, and leave the management entirely to others, they may be guilty by this means if breaches of trust are committed by others."[46]

---

43. *Madhavan Nambiar v ROC*, (2002) 108 Comp Cas 1 Mad.
44. *Customs and Excise Commrs v Hedon Alpha Ltd*, [1981] 2 All ER 697 CA. According to a circular of the Company Law Board, the Registrar should not file a criminal complaint to set at naught the application of a director for relief under S. 633. *P. S. Bedi v ROC*, (1986) 60 Comp Cas 1061 Del. The jurisdiction under the section is not a proper forum for determining the question whether there had been a default or not. *S. Pandit, Re*, (1990) 68 Comp Cas 129: [1990] 2 Comp LJ 170 Bom. Seizure of books was not a sufficient ground for excuse particularly when copies were supplied. Where proceedings have already been launched, relief can be claimed only from the court where the proceedings are pending, *Jyotindra Manhar Lal Vakil, Re*, (1995) 16 Corpt LA 174 Bom.
45. ROMER J in *City Equitable Fire Insurance Co, Re*, [1924] All ER Rep 485: [1925] 1 Ch 407.
46. *Charitable Corpn v Sutton*, (1742) 26 ER 642. The general practice, however, is not to hold a director liable for things that transpire in his absence at a board meeting. See *Cullerne v London & Suburban General Permanent Building Society*, (1890) 25 QBD 485: 63 LT 511.

Duty not to delegate

Liability for co-directors' defaults

Generally, a director has to perform his functions personally. He is bound by the maxim *delegatus non-potest delegare.* Shareholders have appointed him because of their faith in his skill, competence and integrity and they may not have the same faith in another person. The rule is, however, not inflexible. In the following two cases at least delegation is proper and valid. Firstly, a delegation of functions may be made to the extent to which it is authorised by the Act or articles of association of the company.[47] Secondly, there are certain duties which may, having regard to the exigencies of business, properly be left to some other officials. Directors must be able to entrust details of management to subordinates, or else business could not be carried on. A proper degree of delegation and division of responsibility by the Board is permissible but not a total abrogation of responsibility since this would undermine the collegiate or collective responsibility of the Board of directors which is of fundamental importance to corporate governance. A director might be in breach of duty if he left to others the matters for which the Board as a whole had to take responsibility.[48] These two exceptions permit a reasonable distribution of work among all the directors and other officials of the company. Now, if a co-director or other official to whom a function is so delegated commits a fraud and the company suffers a loss, to what extent are the other directors liable. This was the question before the House of Lords in the leading case of *Dovey* v *Cory.*[49]

> A banking company had suffered heavy loses on account of advances of money made to irresponsible persons and without security; and also on account of payment of dividends out of capital. These losses were due to the mechanism of the chairman and the manager who manipulated the accounts and showed a profit. At a meeting of the board, the defendant was ensured of the correctness of the accounts and, therefore, he gave his authority to the payment of a dividend which was obviously paid out of capital.

He was sued for the losses, but was held not liable. Lord HALSBURY observed:

> Each and all of the charges may be disposed of by the proposition that

---

47. *See* S. 292 under "Statutory Provisions" *supra.* The directors, being in control of the company's affairs, they cannot get rid of their managerial responsibility by nominating a person as the occupier of the factory. *J. K. Industries* v *Chief Inspector of Factories,* (1996) 1 SCC 665: (1997) 88 Comp Cas 285 SC. This will not apply to the case of a Government company, the ultimate responsibility being that of the Government, special rules become necessary, *Indian Oil Corpn Ltd* v *Chief Inspector of Factories,* (1998) 5 SCC 738: 1998 SCC (L&S) 1433: (1998) 94 Comp Cas 64.
48. *Landhurst Leasing plc, Re,* [1999] 1 BCLC 286 Ch D.
49. 1901 AC 477: [1895-9] All ER Rep 724. *See* R. K. Goel, *Delegation of Directors' Powers and Duties: A Comparative Analysis,* (1967) 18 ICLQ 152.

Mr Cory was not himself conscious of any one of these things being done. Was he under a duty to probe into and know these things? It cannot be expected of a director that he should be watching the inferior officers or verifying the calculations of auditors. Business of life could not go on if people could not trust those who are put in a position of trust for the express purpose of attending to the details of management. He could have been held liable only if he had some reasonable grounds to suspect the honesty of the other officials.[50]

This principle was followed by the Madras High Court in *D. Doss v C. P. Connell.*[51]

An undischarged insolvent,[52] having been appointed advisory director of a banking company, misappropriated a part of the security money received from the employees of the company which was at his disposal.

The official liquidator could not succeed in his effort to charge his co-directors with the liability. The court said that the respondents had no reason whatsoever to suspect the integrity of the Chairman. "Insolvency does not necessarily mean that a man is a dishonest man."[53] In a subsequent decision, the same court added:[54]

The ordinary directors of a company are entitled to presume in the absence of features arousing their suspicion that the affairs of the company are being properly conducted by the managing director and the managing committee, and unless any mismanagement or other act of misfeasance is brought to the notice of the directors, they cannot be held liable in respect of the same.

On the same principle, directors were held not liable for misappropriation of stores by the stores manager,[55] or for failure to detect cashier's concealment of overdrafts,[56] or for payment of dividends on false accounts declared at a meeting where the director sought to be made liable

---

50. 1901 AC 485. *See also* LINDLEY LJ in *National Bank of Wales Ltd, Re*, [1899] 2 Ch 629 at p 673: [1895-9] All ER Rep 715; *Denham & Co, Re*, (1883) 25 Ch D 752: 50 LT 523. See also *Land Credit Co of Ireland v Lord Fermoy*, (1870) 5 Ch App 763, where a company's board had, in accordance with the company's constitution, quite properly delegated the making of a transaction to a sub-committee, which made illegal loans, the director who was not a member of the sub-committee and who had no reason to suspect the impropriety of the transaction was held not liable for the loss suffered by the company.

51. AIR 1938 Mad 124.

52. S. 202 now prevents an undischarged insolvent from holding any managerial office.

53. Quoting LINDLEY MR in *National Bank of Wales Ltd, Re*, [1899] 2 Ch 629 at p 673: [1895-99] All ER Rep 715.

54. *Ganesan v Brahamayya & Co*, [1946] Comp LJ 262 Mad.

55. *Vijai Laxmi Sugar Mills, Re*, AIR 1963 All 55.

56. *Prefontaine v Grenier*, 1907 AC 101.

was absent,[57] or for allowing, by one of the two directors, the company's premises to be used for gaming purposes without licence, the other director knowing nothing.[58]

"A director is also permitted to rely on professional or expert advice given by reliable competent employees, professional advisors and experts, and other directors. This is provided the reliance is in good faith, after proper inquiry when appropriate, and without knowledge that the reliance was unwarranted. A prudent director aware that he or she lacked expertise in a particular area could avoid potential liability under Section 137 by obtaining the advice of an expert. In common with other provisions in the Act, the best way a director can protect him or herself from later liability is to lay a 'paper trail' before entering into any transaction or carrying out any action."[59]

This, however, does not mean that directors can always throw up their hands and say, "we knew nothing and believed that everything was alright". Sometimes it is their duty to know. These words of Lord SIMONDS in *Morris v Kanssen*,[60] though spoken in a different context, were borrowed by NAIR, J of the Kerala High Court in deciding the typical case of *Palai Central Bank Ltd v Joseph Augusti*:[61]

The accounts of a banking company in liquidation showed that taxes and dividends were paid for as many as twenty-two years (i.e. from 1936-1958) on profits not really earned, but made to appear firstly by fictitious entries, and subsequently by showing interest, which there was no prospect of ever realising, on the bad and irrecoverable advances. The length of time was by itself a sufficient proof of the deliberateness of the falsification.

The court rejected the directors' plea that they had relied on competent staff and auditors who always certified the accounts as true. Referring to the magnitude of the loss involved, which could not be easily explained, the court said:

Not one of them has cared to disclose who were the persons in actual charge of these matters, what exactly were the duties imposed on them, and what scrutiny there was over their work in order to assure that it was properly done. At best the plea of the respondents can only amount to a plea of complete ignorance born of a complete inadvertence to their duties, as directors, a reckless indifference, or, otherwise put, a

57. *Nagendra Prabhu* v *Popular Bank*, (1969) 39 Comp Cas 685: ILR [1969] 1 Ker 340: AIR 1970 Ker 120.
58. *Huckerby* v *Elliott*, [1970] 1 All ER 189. *The City Equitable* principles have been followed in the following Indian cases: *S. C. Mitra* v *Nawab Ali Khan*, AIR 1926 Oudh 153: 92 IC 50; *National Bank of Upper India* v *Dina Nath Sapru*, AIR 1926 Oudh 243: 95 IC 234; *Thinnappa Chettiar* v *Rajagopalan*, AIR 1944 Mad 536: [1944] 2 MLJ 45.
59. S. M. Watson, *Directors' Duties in New Zealand*, 1998 JBL 495 at p 504.
60. 1946 AC 459 at p 476: [1946] 1 All ER 586: 174 LT 353.
61. [1966] 1 Comp LJ 360.

wilful shutting of their eyes.... The deliberate falsification of the books year after year could not have been the handiwork of the staff of the company; it could only have been at the specific instructions of those at the helm of affairs. In a company, the directors are at the helm of affairs, and although the rudder might be in the hands of the managing director, it is their duty to keep an eye on him and see that he steers a proper course.[62]

Similarly, "the position of a managing director or chairman of the board of directors is different. He cannot say that he signed the accounts without understanding the implication of its entries."[63]

Duty to disclose interest [Ss. 299-300]

Conflict of Interests

Every agent occupies a fiduciary position towards his principal. As such it is his duty to see that his personal interest and his duty to his principal do not conflict. For the proper exercise of the functions of a director, it is essential that he be disinterested, that is, be free from any conflicting interest.[64] This conflict invariably arises when a director is personally interested in a transaction of the company. Naturally a man is likely to prefer his personal interest. This principle was established in the leading case, *Aberdeen Railway Ltd* v *Blaikie*.[65] There, Blaikie had a conflict of interest as director and chairman of the company and managing partner of a firm which supplied office furniture to the company. Despite the fact that the price the company paid for the furniture was fair, the company was entitled to set the contract aside. The judge said:

"A corporate body can only act by agents and it is, of course, the duty of those agents so to act as best to promote the interests of the corporation whose affairs they are conducting. Such agents have duties to discharge of a fiduciary nature towards their principal. And it is a rule of universal application that no one, having such duties to discharge shall be allowed to enter into engagements in which he has, or can have, a personal interest conflicting, or which possibly may conflict, with the interests of those whom he is bound to protect."

Blaikie had an interest as a partner in the firm to sell as high as possible but an interest as director, of the company to purchase as low as possible.

---

62. [1966] 1 Comp LJ 381. The learned Judge then cited passages from the speech of Lord DAVEY in *Dovey* v *Cory*, 1901 AC 477: [1895-9] All ER Rep 724 and distinguished the case on the ground that there the defendant faced a searching examination which certified his innocence.
63. *Official Liquidator* v *Shri Krishna Prasad Singh*, [1969] 1 Comp LJ 325; *National Sugar Mills Ltd, Re*, (1978) 48 Comp Cas 339 Cal, where the managing director was held liable for misappropriations but not his co-directors.
64. Jackson, THE WISDOM OF THE SUPREME COURT, 417-18 (1962).
65. (1854) 1 Mcy 461.

The fairness or otherwise of the price was irrelevant; what the court considered was the *possibility* of unfairness.[66]

The Act lays down a special procedure to be followed in such cases.

In the first place, a director who is interested in a transaction of the company is required to disclose his interest to the board.[67] The disclosure must be made at the first meeting of the board held after he has become so interested.[68] If he is a member of a company or of a firm with which the company has to deal he may give a general notice to the board of his interest in that concern. Such notice must be renewed after every year.[69]

Secondly, an interested director is not allowed to take part in the discussion by the board on the matter of his interest. Neither shall he vote nor shall his presence count for the purpose of quorum. If he does vote, his vote shall be void.[70]

As noted above, these provisions are based upon the sound principle that the company is entitled to the unbiased advice of every director upon matters which are brought before the board.

It is possible, of course, that a person may be altruistic and in coming to an arrangement in which he is concerned he will give better terms to the other contracting party than if he had no interest at all, but persons of such disposition are not usually found among the directors of a company and it must be assumed that in the making of an arrangement a man will consider his own interest rather than the interest of the other contracting party.[71]

What constitutes "Interest".—This obviously raises the question as to what constitutes an "interest" within the mischief of the rule. "The interest to be disclosed is that which in a business sense might be regarded as influencing judgment; the essence of the matter being that any kind of personal interest which is material in the sense of not being insignificant

---

66. Under S. 139 of the New Zealand Companies Act, 1993, directors are deemed to be interested in the following circumstances:
   If the director is a party to or will or may derive a material financial benefit from the transaction;
   If the director has a material financial interest in another party to the transaction;
   If the director is a director, officer or trustee of another party or person who will or may derive a material financial benefit from the transaction;
   If the director is the parent, child or spouse of another party or person who will or may derive a material financial benefit from the contract;
   If the director is otherwise directly or indirectly materially interested in the transaction.
67. Ss. 299-300. The object of these provisions is explained by CHAGLA CJ in *Walchandnagar Industries v Ratanchand*, AIR 1953 Bom 285.
68. S. 299(2)(*a*) and (*b*).
69. S. 299(3).
70. *Id., (b)*. See also sub-section (4) which imposes penalty for default; also sub-sections (5) and (6) which contain some exceptions.
71. *Alexander Timber Co, Re*, (1901) 70 LJ Ch 767. *See also Ramaswami Iyer v Madras Times Printing & Publishing Co*, AIR 1915 Mad 1179.

must be revealed."[72] In short, the interest must be such which conflicts with the director's duties towards the company. Thus, for example, where the directors took part in and voted at a meeting of the board which granted debentures to two of them, the resolution was held to be bad.[73]

Only such interest comes within the mischief of the rule and has to be disclosed which is "personal" in the business sense of the word. Thus the appointment of a director as a chairman or as a managing director is not such an interest and the appointment will, therefore, be valid even if the director to be appointed was present at the meeting and voted.[74] But in *V. Ramaswami Iyer* v *Madras Times Printing & Publishing Co*:[75]

Under a company's articles two directors constituted a quorum for a meeting of the board. Two were present and they appointed one of themselves as managing director and co-editor of the paper run by the company. The appointments were held to be invalid as when the vote of the interested director was excluded there was no quorum to make the appointment in each case.

Where Board already aware.—Where the whole body of directors is already aware of the facts, a formal disclosure is not necessary. A very illustrative case is *Venkatachalapathy* v *Guntur Cotton, etc. Mills*.[76]

A mortgage of Rs 1,23,354 was created over the mill property of a company. The loan was advanced by the wife of a director. Thus he was interested in the transaction. But he neither disclosed his interest, nor

---

72. *Coltness Iron Co, Re*, 1951 SC 476 [Scotland]: 1951 SLT 344.
73. *North Eastern Insurance Co Ltd, Re*, [1919] 1 Ch 198: 120 LT 223. This may be compared with *Bank of Poona* v *Narayandas*, AIR 1961 Bom 252: (1961) 31 Comp Cas 364: 63 Bom LR 122, where a resolution allotting shares to a defaulting director in a meeting at which he was present and voted was held not void. *See* also *Public Prosecutor* v *T. P. Khaitan*, [1956] 2 MLJ 590: AIR 1957 Mad 4: (1957) 27 Comp Cas 717; *Mukkattukara Catholic Co Ltd* v *Thomas*, (1995) 4 Comp LJ 311: (1996) 2 Ker LT 173: (1996) 22 CLA 348. the mechanical function of accepting or rejecting transfer of shares at board meetings does not create conflict of duty and interest.
74. See *Foster* v *Foster*, [1916] 1 Ch 532: [1916-17] All ER Rep 856 and *N. W. Transportation Co* v *Beatty*, (1887) 12 AC 589: 57 LT 426. In the case of *Public Prosecutor* v *T. P. Khaitan*, AIR 1957 Mad 4, it was held that a resolution by which a director was authorised to draw cheques on the company's bankers was not bad simply because the director so authorised had participated in the meeting of the board. *Shailesh Harilal Shah* v *Matushree Textiles Ltd*, AIR 1994 Bom 20, appointment of a director's brother as a director in the company was not viewed as a matter of personal interest so as to be vitiated by the director's presence and voting. Such appointment is neither a contract nor arrangement within the meaning of S. 299. The court cited *Madras Tube Co Ltd* v *Hari Kishon Somani*, [1985] 1 Comp LJ 195 Mad where the court in turn relied upon *Foster* v *Foster*, (1916) 1 Ch 532: [1916-17] All ER Rep 856; *T.N.K. Govindaraju Chetty & Co* v *Kadri Mills (CBE) Ltd*, (1998) 30 CLA 49 (CLB), issue of shares or warrants has been held to be not an arrangement or contract within the meaning of Ss. 299-300 so as to require disclosure.
75. AIR 1915 Mad 1179.
76. AIR 1929 Mad 353: 115 IC 486. Where the daughter of the chairman-cum-managing director was to be appointed as vice-president and the whole number of directors were already aware of this fact, its having been disclosed on an earlier occasion, non-disclosure at this occasion was held to be not a failure in duty, *A. Sivasailam* v *ROC*, (1995) 83 Comp Cas 141 CLB.

abstained from voting. In an action by the company to have the mortgage set aside, it was held that as the fact was already known to the directors there was no necessity of a formal disclosure.

It was also contended by the company that his voting on the matter vitiated the contract. The court was, however, of the opinion that mere voting by an interested director could not render the contract void or voidable unless, in the absence of that vote, there would have been no quorum qualified to contract. The mere fact that voting is an offence[77] punishable with fine does not *ipso facto* render the contract void or voidable. The court agreed with the company's argument that an interested director not declaring his interest would be liable to account for secret profit made by him in the transaction, but the present case revealed no such profits. The mortgage was found to be fair and in the interest of the company.

An English ruling on this point was handed down in *Lee Panavision Ltd v Lee Lighting Ltd*.[78] The court said that it would hesitate to find that the failure to formally disclose at a Board meeting an interest common to all members and, *ex hypothesi*, already known to all the members of the Board would be a breach of duty. This ruling was followed in *MacPherson v European Strategic Bureau Ltd*.[79] In this case, the fact of mutual interest was known to all the directors and, therefore, no importance was attached to the lack of a formal disclosure. But the Court of Appeal[80] did not approve the contract because there was the breach of a fiduciary duty in exercising powers of management for their own benefit rather than for the benefit of the company. The distribution of the company's assets was an attempt to effect an informal winding without making a provision for its creditors.

Effect upon transaction.—It has been pointed out by the Supreme Court that there is no ban on a contract in which a director is interested; only that it should be disclosed, *bona fide* and fair.[81] Even where the interest is not disclosed the transaction is only voidable against the interested director and not void.[82] If the company waives the irregularity and affirms the transaction, he becomes bound by it. He cannot insist on the irregularity.[83]

Accountability for profit from transaction.—The director in question is bound to hand over the benefits, if any, that he might have secured under the transaction and he cannot ask for set off for any claim that he may have

---

77. Sub-section (4) of S. 299 and sub-section (4) of S. 300 impose a penalty for the contravention of the provisions which may extend up to fifty thousand rupees. For a critical examination of these provisions *see* P. A. S. Rao, *Law Relating to Directors' Interest*, [1966] 2 Comp LJ 47.
78. [1992] BCLC 22 CA.
79. [1999] 2 BCLC 203 Ch D.
80. *Mac Pherson v European Strategic Bureau Ltd*, The Times, Sept 5, 2000 CA.
81. *P. Leslie & Co v V. O. Wapshare*, AIR 1969 SC 843: [1969] 2 Comp LJ 113: (1969) 39 Comp Cas 808: (1969) 3 SCR 203.
82. *Narayandas v Sangli Bank*, (1965) 35 Comp Cas 596: [1965] 2 Comp LJ 99: AIR 1966 SC 170.
83. *Ibid*. See also *Yuill v Greymouth, etc Rly Co*, [1904] 1 Ch 32, where a director was not allowed to avoid an allotment on the ground that he took part in it.

against the company. This is the grand contribution of the decision of the House of Lords in *Guinness plc* v *Saunders*.[84] The plaintiff company launched a takeover bid for another company. *W* and two other directors formed a committee of the board for the purpose of conducting the bid. A company controlled by *W* submitted a bill for £5.2m by way of remuneration for services rendered in connection with the take-over. The calculation was in terms of a percentage linked with the amount involved in the take-over. *W* claimed that the payment was under an agreement with the company, but, in fact, it was only under an agreement with the committee of directors and the fact that he had become interested in the transaction by linking his remuneration with the takeover amount was also disclosed only to this committee. He was compelled to refund the whole amount to the company. The matter of his interest had to be disclosed at a meeting of the full board of directors duly convened and not merely to a sub-committee of directors. He thus held the money as a constructive trustee and was obliged to account for it irrespective of any cross-claim he might have by way of *quantum meruit* or equitable compensation for services rendered.

General consequences of default.—According to ISSAC J of the Kerala High Court[85] the consequences of default under the section are: (1) liability to be prosecuted under Section 299(4); (2) cessation of the office of directorship under Section 283(1)(*i*)[86]; (3) liability to be prosecuted under Section 283(2-A) for acting as director after incurring a disqualification; and (4) liability to refund remuneration. It is not possible for the court to relieve the director concerned under Section 633 from the cessation of directorship and its consequences.

Exception.—This procedure has not to be followed where the contract is between two companies and a director does not hold more than 2% [or two or more of them together hold not more than 2%] of the paid-up share capital of the company.[87]

Position and liability of nominee director

A nominee director is not supposed to be in charge of a company's affairs. He is not liable for the failures of the company to comply with the Companies Act and other regulatory laws. His duty is to watch the interest of the institution which nominated him. As a member of the Board the only expectation from him is that he should not do anything against the interest of the company. Where a complaint showed that a nominee director wilfully

---

84. [1990] 1 All ER 652 HL: [1990] 2 WLR 324; the decision of the court of appeal is reported in 1988 BCLC 607: [1988] 2 All ER 940 CA: [1988] 4 BCC 377.
85. *M. O. Varghese* v *Thomas Stephen & Co Ltd*, (1970) 40 Comp Cas 1131 Ker.
86. Punishment is by way of fine which may extend to five thousand rupees. *See* further, *Globe Motors Ltd* v *Mehta Teja Singh*, (1984) 55 Comp Cas 445 Del; *K. S. Dhillon* v *Paragaon Utility Financiers*, (1988) 64 Comp Cas 19, 32 P&H, automatic vacation of office of director.
87. S. 299(6). For an account of liabilities of officers and directors of companies, *see* Dr V. Gauri Shanker, [1986] 3 Comp LJ 127 (Journal section).

abetted the making of a false statement under the Income Tax Act, the court refused to quash the complaint against him. His position was to be considered on evidence.[88]

A nominee director suffers from an essential conflict of duty and interest. He owes his duty to the nominator but he is sitting in the board of the denominator. A holding company nominated a majority of the directors in the subsidiary company's board who remained docile and because of their inaction, the holding company suppressed the business of the subsidiary. Without exploring the possibilities of making the nominees liable for destroying the business of the subsidiary, the court allowed the alternative relief of compelling the holding company to refund the minority investment in the subsidiary taken at a value before the repressive policy began. The court observed that nominee directors cannot consider themselves as merely the watchdog of the nominator's interest. No problem arises so long as the interests of both the companies are in harmony. But when their interests are at a conflict, the nominees would be placed in an impossible position.[89]

In a subsequent case[90] the nominator company and its nominees were sued by those who lost their investment because of acting upon quarterly financial statements issued by the nominees on behalf of the denominator company, the statements being false. They were held not liable because shareholders or investors who appoint or nominate directors owe no duty to anybody about their conscientious functioning unless there is some impropriety in the conduct of the nominator. But the judges were agreed that nominee directors are in the same position as other directors and they owe the same duties.[91] The question of nominee directors was again dealt with in the New Zealand case of *Dairy Containers Ltd* v *NZI Bank Ltd*.[92] Three nominee directors of a New Zealand Dairy Board subsidiary stole large amounts of money for that subsidiary. The Court was critical of the Privy Council decision in *Kuwait Asia Bank*[93] but felt obliged to follow it and state that the Dairy Board was not liable for the acts of its nominee directors since it did not exercise direct control over Dairy Containers Ltd.

Tax Liability

Where the bank account of a director of a private company was frozen for recovering income tax dues of the company, it was held that it was for the director to show that the default on the part of the company was not

88. *J. Sethuraman* v *IAC of IT*, (1992) 74 Comp Cas 815 Mad.
89. *Scottish Cooperative Wholesale Society* v *Meyer*, [1958] 3 All ER 66: (1958) 3 WLR 404 HL: 1959 AC 324.
90. *Kuwait Bank EC* v *National Mutual Life Nominees Ltd*, (1990) 3 WLR 297: [1990] 3 All ER 404 PC.
91. See *Selangor United Rubber Estates Ltd* v *Cradock (No 3)*, (1968) 1 WLR 1555 at pp 1613-1614: (1969) 39 Comp Cas 485.
92. (1995) 2 NZLR 30.
93. *Kuwait Asian Bank EC* v *National Mutual Life Nominees Ltd*, (1993) NZLR 513.

attributable to any breach of duty on his part.[1] But apart from any provisions of the taxing statute, arrears of the tax amount are not to be recovered from any director personally.[2]

MEETINGS OF DIRECTORS

Directors of a company have to exercise most of their powers at periodical meetings of the board. It is, therefore, provided in Section 285 that "in the case of every company, a meeting of its board of directors shall be held at least once in every three months; and at least four such meetings shall be held in every year".[3]

Notice

Notice of every board meeting has to be given in writing to every director who is in India.[4] "The Act does not prescribe the form of notice or mode of service and if the directors are duly informed that in future meetings would be held on the first Saturday of every month, it is a sufficient compliance of the statute."[5] Failure to give notice to any director renders the meeting invalid,[6] and the business conducted at it is void.[7] Where the general manager of a company was removed by a meeting of the board in which one director could not participate as he was not informed, the Supreme Court held that the confirmation of the proceedings and of the notice of termination served by the chairman at a subsequently regularly convened meeting of the board validated the termination. It amounted to a ratification.[8] Explaining the role of the chairman in a subsequent case, the Supreme Court said:[9]

"The chairman of the Board of directors is the central figure in holding the meeting and is the controlling factor in the conduct of the

---

1. *Gurudas Hazra* v *P.K. Chowdhury*, (2002) 109 Comp Cas 109 Cal.
2. *Peter J.R. Prabhu* v *Asstt Commr of Commercial Taxes*, (2002) 109 Comp Cas 299 Kant; *Maddi Swarna* v *CTO*, (2002) 109 Comp Cas 308 AP, sales tax arrears could not be recovered from the director except as provided in the winding up, i.e. in the course of winding up.
3. A proviso to the section enables the Central Government to modify the rule in relation to any class of companies. It is a sufficient compliance that a meeting was called within the permissible time though it could not be held for want of quorum. S. 288(2).
4. S. 286(1). Sub-section (2) penalises any officer whose duty is to give notice for any default.
5. *A. Chettiar* v *Kaleeswarar Mills*, AIR 1957 Mad 309, 319.
6. See *Young* v *Ladies' Imperial Club*, [1920] 2 KB 523: [1920] All ER Rep 223, where a person consented to be a member of the committee only on a promise that she would not be troubled, a failure to send notice to her vitiated the meeting. Also see *Portuguese Consolidated Copper Mines Ltd, Re*, (1889) 42 Ch D 160 CA.
7. *Homer District Consolidated Gold Mines, Re*, (1888) 39 Ch D 546: 60 LT 97, subject, of course, to the principle of indoor management.
8. *Parmeshwari Prasad Gupta* v *UOI*, (1973) 2 SCC 543: AIR 1973 SC 2389: (1974) 44 Comp Cas 1; *Hillcrest Realty SDN BHD* v *Hotel Queen Road (P) Ltd*, (2006) 133 Comp Cas 742 CLB, the principle of invalidation because of want of notice to a single director was not applied on the facts of the case because the shares had been allotted to and accepted by the petitioners and their complaint against it would have to be dismissed, their membership being not valid.
9. *Nazir Hoosein* v *Darayus Bhathena*, (2000) 5 SCC 601: AIR 2000 SC 2427: (2000) 37 CLA 414 SC.

meeting. He authenticates the minutes of the meeting and performs such other functions as empowered under the Companies Act. A chairman is always elected by the Board of directors; thus he has the full support of the majority of Directors which helps him in the control of the meeting and recording authenticated minutes.''

The notice need not specify the agenda for the meeting. The agenda may be set out as a matter of prudence, but it is not required.[10] Even where agenda is specified, the directors need not confine themselves to it. Any other business conducted at the meeting would be equally valid. Any other rule "would be extremely embarrassing in the transaction of the business of companies". However, the members of the board should not be taken by surprise particularly over serious matters. A notice convening a meeting was held to be invalid because it did not specify that the meeting was being called to consider and approve the transfer of controlling interest in the private company and that too in violation of the pre-emptive provisions in the company's articles.[11]

The law also does not prescribe any length of notice. "A few minutes' notice may suffice."[12] Even a chance meeting of directors may be resolved into a board meeting. In *Smith v Paringa Mines Ltd*:[13]

A directors' meeting was duly summoned for filling up a vacancy. There were only two directors *T*, and *B*, *B*, being the chairman. *T* did not attend. *B* went to *T's* personal office and met him in the passage outside his office. While standing there *B* proposed *F's* name. *T* objected. *B*, being in the chair, gave his casting vote and declared *F* elected.

The court upheld the election and said: "There is no reason why a meeting should not be held in the passage." As against it, in another case[14] the only two directors of a company were not on speaking terms, for which reason it became necessary to appoint additional directors. One of them, *P*, waited for the other, *C*, at a railway station and finding him alighting from a train proposed three names. *C* remained silent. Thereupon *P* gave his casting vote

---

10. *See* LINDLEY LJ in *La Compagnie de Mayville v Whitley*, [1896] 1 Ch 788 at 796 CA; *Maharashtra Power Development Corpn Ltd v Dahbol Power Co*, (2004) 120 Comp Cas 560 (Bom), not necessary to state agenda.

11. *Shanta Genevieve Pommeret v Sakal Papers (P) Ltd*, (1990) 69 Comp Cas 65 Bom.

12. *Browne v La Trinidad*, (1887) 37 Ch D 1: 58 LT 137 CA. *See* H. Goitein, COMPANY LAW (1960) 129. A few hours' notice has, however, been held to be not sufficient, particularly in view of the fact that those who attended wanted the others opposing them not to attend. See *Homer District Consolidated Gold Mines, Re*, (1888) 39 Ch D 546: 58 LJ Ch 134: 60 LT 97.

13. [1906] 2 Ch 193. Calling meeting at a time when some directors were abroad and, therefore, could not attend and thereby to take advantage of that absence for passing resolutions which it would not have been possible to pass otherwise, this was held to be a fraudulent purpose which vitiated the meeting. The court also held that questioning resolutions and appointment of directors is a matter for civil court jurisdiction. *T. M. Paul (Dr) v City Hospital (P) Ltd*, (1999) 97 Comp Cas 216.

14. *Barron v Potter*, [1914] 1 Ch 895: 110 LT 929.

and declared the three directors as elected. But the court did not uphold these appointments. "A director cannot have a board thrust upon him without his consent and against his will."

In this respect meetings of board are immensely different from those of shareholders which have to be held in an atmosphere of considerable formality.[15]

In the case of a closely held company the proceedings of meetings of the Board of directors used to be very informal. Minutes were signed only by the chairman. Names of directors who attended were not always recorded.

The CLB (now Tribunal) refused to draw the inference of the absence of a director from a meeting only because his signature on the minutes was not there.[16]

Quorum [S. 287]

The quorum for a meeting of the board is one-third of its total strength (any fraction to be rounded off as one) or two directors, whichever is higher. But where this quorum cannot be formed, because of interested directors, then the number of directors who are not interested, being not less than two, shall be the quorum.[17] If a meeting cannot be held for want of a quorum, it stands adjourned till the same day in the next week.[18] If that day is a public holiday, the meeting will be held at the next succeeding day which is not a public holiday. The quorum requirement does not become dispensed with because one out of two directors is abroad. A meeting attended by only one director was held to be not valid.[19]

Where the company's articles provided for a total number of 15 directors but at the material time only 6 directors were in office, it was held that quorum meant 1/3 of the 6 directors and, therefore, a meeting attended by two directors only was valid.[20]

15. *See* Lord TENTERDON in *R v Pulsford*, (1829) 8 B&C 350, cited by LINDLEY LJ in *La Compagnie de Mayville v Whitley*, [1896] 1 Ch 788 at 796 CA.
16. *T. V. Prasadachandran Nair v Anandamandarim Hotels P Ltd*, (2002) 110 Comp Cas 294 CLB.
17. Proviso to S. 287. *See also* sub-section (1) which explains the meaning of "total strength" of directors for this purpose and says that it shall be taken after deducting the number of posts which are lying vacant.
18. S. 288. Business transacted without a quorum being present is void. *See*, for example, *North Eastern Ins Co Ltd, Re*, [1919] 1 Ch 198: 120 LT 223, where allotment of debentures to two directors, being resolved upon with the help of an interested director's vote, was held void. The Calcutta High Court has held that the directors can fix a time for reassembling and no further notice is necessary. *Promod Kumar Mittal v Southern Steel Ltd*, (1980) 50 Comp Cas 555 Cal.
19. *Hood Sailmakers Ltd v Axford*, (1997) 1 BCLC 721 QBD.
20. *Pradeep Kumar Banerjee v UOI*, (2002) 108 Comp Cas 692 Cal.

Proceedings

The manner of conducting the business of the board is something to be provided for in the articles. According to the regulations given in Schedule I of the Act[21] questions arising at any meeting of the board are to be decided by a majority of votes. The chairman may be given a second or casting vote in case of an equality of votes.[22] Matters decided are put in the form of resolutions proposed and approved. A resolution may be passed either at a meeting of the board or by circulation.[23] Section 289 requires that if a resolution is to be passed by circulation it should be circulated in draft, together with all the necessary papers, to all the directors[24] and should be approved by a majority.[25] The resolutions of the board, even if passed by a majority, are binding on all the directors and all of them are bound to help others in carrying them out whether they voted with or against the majority.[26]

Minutes [S. 193]

The proceedings of every meeting of the board or of any of its committees have to be recorded in a minutes book. Explaining the purpose, Lord ESHER said in *Cawley & Co, Re*:[27]

> Minutes of the board meeting are kept in order that shareholders of the company may know exactly what their directors have been doing, why it was done, and when it was done.[28]

REGISTERS

For the information of shareholders, companies are required to maintain certain registers concerning directors.

1. Register of directors [S. 303]

The first important register to be maintained is known as the Register of Directors. Every company has to keep at its registered office a register of its directors, managing director, managing agents, secretaries and treasurers, manager and secretary. The register is to contain the following particulars:

---

21. *See* Regulations 64-81.
22. In the absence of any such provision, the chairman does not have a casting vote, *Weakley* v *Amalgamated Union of Engineering Workers*, THE TIMES, June 12, 1975, noted 1975 JBL 222.
23. The fact that directors should act by "combined wisdom" is satisfied where they give consent with full knowledge though they do not meet at any one place. See *Collie Claim*, (1871) LR 12 Eq 246: 40 LJ Ch 567.
24. Excepting those who are not in India; (S. 289). But the number present must be sufficient to constitute a quorum.
25. Of those who are present in India. S. 289. For a study of few cases on how informal a meeting of the board may be, *See* Goitein, COMPANY LAW, (1966).
26. *Equitycorp International plc, Re*, [1989] 1 WLR 1010; 1989 BCLC 597 Ch D.
27. (1889) 42 Ch D 209 at p 226: 61 LT 601.
28. For further details about the minutes book *see* Minutes of General Meeting, *infra*, as S. 193 applies uniformly to both kinds of meeting.

1. The full name of the director, etc. with father's name and address; if a married woman, her husband's name; nationality of origin; his business or other occupations; particulars of any office held by him in any other company; his date of birth.[29]

2. In case any of the above offices is held by a body corporate,[30] its corporate name and registered office and the details specified in clause (1) [above] of each of its directors; if the same body corporate holds office in some other companies the particulars of each such office.

3. In case any of the above offices is held by a firm,[31] the name of the firm should be given and also the details specified in clause (1) [above] of each partner in the firm; and if the firm holds office in other companies, the particulars of each such office.

4. If any directors have been nominated by a body corporate, the name of such company should be given and the particulars of each of its directors.

5. If any directors have been nominated by a firm, the particulars of such firm should be given.

A duplicate copy in the prescribed form of the contents of the register should be sent to the Registrar within thirty days of the appointment of first directors. When any change occurs in the managerial personnel a notification of the change should be sent within thirty days from the date of the change.[32]

Shareholders have the right to inspect the register without any charge and any member of the public on payment of one rupee for each inspection.[33] The articles or general meeting of shareholders may impose reasonable restrictions on hours of inspection, but they should not be less than two on each day.

Directors have also been obliged at the pain of penalty to inform the company of any change that occurs in their position and which ought to be specified in the register.[34]

---

29. Not applicable to a private company; S. 303(1)(*a*). The register should include details about a person in accordance with whose directions the board is accustomed to act. (Expln. 1).

30. The office of a director cannot now be held by a body corporate. (S. 253).

31. A firm cannot be a director.

32. S. 303(2). In case of default, the company and every officer in default is liable to a fine extending up to five hundred rupees for every day of default. [S. 303(3)]. The Central Government or Tribunal may by order compel an immediate inspection of the register. [S. 304(2)(*b*)].

33. S. 304(1). *See also* sub-section (2) which penalises refusal of inspection.

34. The time given to him is twenty days from the date of change and the penalty for default may extend up to five thousand rupees. (S. 305).

The Registrar of Companies is also under an obligation to maintain registers for recording information in this respect received from different companies. Such register is also open to public inspection on the payment of prescribed fee.[35]

2. Register of directors' shareholdings [S. 307]

Again for the information of shareholders and general public, companies are required to maintain a register of the directors' shareholding. The number of shares or debentures held by each director should be specified showing also his holdings in the company's subsidiaries and the company's holding company and other subsidiaries of the same holding company. The register must also give details of the shares held "in trust for him or of which he has any right to become the holder on payment or not". A director may, however, insist that the nature and extent of his interest over the shares should also be recorded. Where by reason of any transaction entered into by a director, any shares or debentures have to be recorded in the register or omitted from it, the register must show the date of and consideration for the transaction.[36]

The register is open to the inspection of members subject to reasonable restrictions which may be imposed by the company.[37] But during the period of fourteen days before and three days after an annual general meeting the register must remain open to the inspection of shareholders during any business hours not less than two hours in each day. Where the right of inspection is not allowed, the Central Government or Tribunal may by order compel an immediate inspection of the register.

For the purpose of this section the word "director" would include any person in accordance with whose directions the company's board is accustomed to act, and also any other company whose board is accustomed to act according to the directions of a director, or if such director holds one-third of the voting strength in that company.[38] Entries in the register have also to be made about the shareholding of managing agents, secretaries and treasurers and managers, if the company has any.[39] Directors are obliged to make necessary disclosures to enable the company to prepare the register.[40]

---

35. S. 306. See *S.K. Bhattacharya* v *UOI*, (1998) 91 Comp Cas 37 Del, the Government was held not liable for accepting and putting on record particulars filed by one faction of the company's directors and rejecting those filed by the other faction.
36. S. 307(2). *See also* the proviso.
37. S. 307(5).
38. S. 307(10).
39. S. 307(11).
40. S. 308.

3. Register of contracts, companies and firms in which directors are interested [S. 301]

A company has also to maintain a register of such contracts in which a director is interested and of contracts with such companies or firms in which a director is interested. This register is to contain the particulars regarding the date of the contract, the names of parties, important terms and conditions of the contract, the date on which it was put before the board and the names of directors who were neutral or voted for or against the contract.

LOANS TO DIRECTORS [S. 295]

Lending of money by a company to its directors is now strictly regulated by the Act. Indeed, in the following cases loans to directors are not allowed except with the previous approval of the Central Government:

1. Loans to the directors of the company, or to the directors of its holding company or to any partner or relative of any director.

2. Loans to any firm in which such a director or his relative is a partner.

3. Loans to any private company of which any such director is a member or a director.

4. Loans to any body corporate at whose general meeting any such director or directors control twenty-five per cent of voting.

5. Loans to any company whose board or other managers are accustomed to act in accordance with the instructions of the board of directors, any director or directors of the lending company.

The section prohibits not only direct lending of money by a company to its directors but also giving of any guarantee for a loan taken by a director from any other person and providing of any security for any such loan. It also prohibits the providing of any guarantee or security for a loan given by a director to any person.[41] A complaint that salary was paid to a director's wife in advance and that it amounted to a loan was rejected. It was not enough to show that the recipient was a director's wife. It had to be proved that she merited no salary for which advance payment could be made.[42] Sale of a flat of the company to a director who paid half the price at once and the rest was to be paid in instalments was held to be not a loan.[43]

---

41. Any officer of the company who is knowingly a party to the contravention of this section is liable to a penalty of fine and imprisonment. [Sub-s. (4)]. For any violation of the section complaint has to be filed within the period of limitation. The Calcutta HC has held that a magistrate should not grant *ex parte* condonation of the delay. The directors had already paid back the amount. Relief was granted under S. 633. *Hindustan Wire and Metal Products, Re,* (1983) 54 Comp Cas 104 Cal. The proviso to the sub-section says that imprisonment shall not be awarded where the loan has been paid back.

42. *M. R. Electronics Components Ltd* v *Asstt ROC*, [1986] 3 Comp LJ 281 Mad.

43. *Predie Ardeshir Mehta* v *UOI*, (1991) 70 Comp Cas 210 Bom

This restriction, however, does not apply to a private company which is not a subsidiary of a public company and to banking companies. The section also allows loans to be given by a holding company to its subsidiaries. Further a guarantee or security may be given by a holding company for the loans of its subsidiaries.[44]

REMUNERATION OF DIRECTORS [Ss. 198 AND 309]

Regulation of directors' remuneration becomes necessary for several reasons, prominent among them being the prevention of diversion of corporate funds for personal use and the impact which the unduly high executive reward has upon the rest of the society.[45]

Section 309 provides that remuneration payable to directors shall be determined either by the articles of the company or by a resolution of the company in general meeting. The resolution may be ordinary or special, as the articles may require.[46] But whatever amount or mode of payment may be so determined, it shall be subject to the provisions of Sections 198 and 309.

Section 198 lays down the overall maximum of managerial remuneration which can be paid by public company or a subsidiary of a public company. The total managerial remuneration payable to directors, or manager in respect of a financial year shall not exceed eleven per cent of the net profits of the company.[47] But sometimes a company may make no or inadequate profits in a financial year. This does not mean that its directors shall remain unpaid. In such a case, the company may, with the previous approval of the Central Government, pay by way of minimum remuneration any sum as may be authorised.[48]

The Central Government has to exercise its discretion judiciously and not arbitrarily. The Company Law Board refused to sanction minimum remuneration to the ordinary directors of a company under the policy that part-time directors should be paid only when there are profits. The Calcutta High Court held that ordinary directors cannot be described as part-time

---

44. S. 295(2). *See also* S. 296 which provides that the section will apply to any transaction represented by a book debt which was in its inception in the nature of a loan or advance.

45. *See* Livingston, THE AMERICAN STOCKHOLDER, (1958).

46. It has recently been held in *Radhey Shyam* v *Official Liquidator*, AIR 1968 Raj 220: [1968] 2 Comp LJ 77, that unless there is a clear provision to that effect in the articles, the remuneration cannot be determined at a meeting of the directors themselves. *See* SHINGHAL J at p 222-3.

47. Net profits mean profits calculated in the manner laid down in Ss. 349, 350 and 351, except that the remuneration of the directors shall not be deducted from gross profits. S. 198(1).

48. S. 198(4), proviso, as *substituted* by the amendment of 1988. The *substituted* provision is as follows: Notwithstanding anything contained in sub-section (1) to (3) but subject to the provisions of S. 269, read with Sch. XIII, if, in any financial year, a company has no profits or its profits are inadequate, the company shall not pay to its directors, including any managing or wholetime director or manager, by way of remuneration any sum [exclusive of any fees payable to directors under sub-section (2) of S. 309], except with the previous approval of the Central Government. For prescribed figures *see* Pt. II of Sch. XIII. Also *see* under "Remuneration" in the succeeding chapter.

directors. It was an irrelevant label and the Board should have proceeded by taking into account the present and future profitability of the company.[49]

In order to make this limit effective and to prevent directors from drawing more money in the guise of collateral benefits, the explanation to Section 198 provides that the word "remuneration" shall include the following:

1. any expenditure incurred in providing free accommodation and other amenities connected therewith;

2. any expenditure incurred in providing any other amenity either absolutely free or at a concessional rate;

3. any expenditure incurred in providing any obligation or service which, in the absence of provision by the company, would have to be incurred by that person;

4. any expenditure incurred in providing life insurance, pension, annuity or gratuity for any such person, his spouse or child.

Sitting Fee.—The above limit of eleven per cent does not include any fee that may be payable to directors for attending meetings of the board or of committees of the board.[50]

Guarantee Commission

It has been held that payment of guarantee commission to directors on their guarantees for the company's loans is not a part of the remuneration so as to require Government approval.[51]

Payment of commission to officers [S. 199]

Where any commission or other remuneration payable to any officer or employee (other than directors) or a manager of the company is fixed by way of percentage or otherwise based on the net profits of the company, the net profits for this purpose have to be calculated in the manner set out in Sections 349 and 350.

Mode of payment

Subject to this overall limit, remuneration may be paid to directors on monthly basis or by way of fee for each meeting of the board or a committee

---

49. *Hind Ceramics Ltd* v *Company Law Board*, (1972) 42 Comp Cas 610 Cal.
50. S. 198(2). The maximum sitting fee has been prescribed as follows: Rule 10-B, w.e.f. 15-6-1988; GSR 559(E):

Companies with capital up to Rs 50 lakhs	Rs 250
Rs 50 lakh to 5 crore	Rs 500
Rs 5 to 10 crores	Rs 750
Above Rs 10 crores	Rs 1000

The prescribed maximum was revised in 1993 (w.e.f. Aug 27, 1993) to Rs 2000. GSR 581(E) and the rest has been left to companies.
51. *Suessen Textile Bearings Ltd* v *UOI*, (1984) 55 Comp Cas 492 Del. As a result of this decision the Department withdrew its circular expressing the opinion that such commission would be included in remuneration. *Circular No 3 of 16-12-1994.*

of the board attended by him. But fee for attending meetings of the board cannot be paid on a monthly basis.[52]

Ceilings

It had been held by the Delhi High Court in *Upper Doab Sugar Mills Ltd* v *Company Law Board*,[53] that the Government could not by administrative action reduce the ceiling on remuneration fixed by Sections 198 and 309. In that case the Company Law Board granted approval to appointment of a managing director subject to the condition that his salary be reduced to a ceiling below that imposed by the above sections. The court held that the Board could not do so as Section 637-A permits only such conditions to be imposed as are not contrary to the express provisions of the Act. This aspect of the decision was overruled by the Supreme Court.[54] Section 637-AA added in 1974, expressly empowers the Government to impose a lower ceiling on remuneration while approving a candidate for managing directorship.[55] But in reference to other directors the decision of the Delhi High Court still holds good.

A managing or wholetime director may be paid either on a monthly basis or a specified percentage of the net profits of the company or partly by one way and partly by the other. But the amount shall not exceed five per cent of the net profits in favour of one such director or, if there are more than one, ten per cent for all of them put together.[56]

In the case of a director who is neither wholetime nor managing director, remuneration may be paid to him by way of monthly, quarterly or annual payment, but with the approval of the Central Government, or by way of commission if the company by special resolution authorises such payment.[57]

But the amount of payment to all directors of this category should not exceed one per cent of the net profits of the company, if the company, has a

---

52. Ss. 198(3) and 309(2).
53. (1971) 41 Comp Cas 643 Del.
54. *Company Law Board* v *Upper Doab Sugar Mills Ltd*, (1977) 2 SCC 198: (1977) 47 Comp Cas 173.
55. Even in reference to managing directors etc., the decision is of very little value because since the amendment of 1988, normally no approval is required if the appointment is in accordance with Sch. XIII.
56. S. 309(3).
57. S. 309(4). The Central Government by a notification had reduced the administrative ceiling imposed upon directors' remuneration in 1960 from 1.80 lakhs to 1.35 lakhs. The new ceiling on the remuneration payable to managing directors, whole or part-time directors and managers in public limited companies was Rs 90,000 annually or Rs 7500 monthly. This allowed incentive commission of one per cent on net profits subject to a maximum of Rs 45,000 or per cent of the approved salary. Where remuneration was paid by way of commission on net profits, the ceiling was Rs 1.35 lakhs. Perquisites may be allowed up to Rs 30,000 or 1/3 of the remuneration payable. This will not include: (1) contribution to provident or superannuation funds to the extent these are not tenable: (2) reimbursement of medical expenses actually incurred subject to the limit of Rs 5000 or one month's salary whichever is less. These ceilings had been held to be void. See *Upper Doab Sugar Mills Ltd* v *Company Law Board*, (1971) 41 Comp Cas 643 Del.

managing or wholetime director, or manager, and three per cent in other cases. However the company may in general meeting and with approval of the Central Government, sanction more.[58]

Remuneration for professional service [S. 309(1)]

An amendment introduced in 1965 provides that the remuneration payable to a director as determined according to the above rules shall include any remuneration payable to him for services rendered by him in any other capacity. But where the services of a professional nature have been rendered and, in the opinion of the Central Government, the director rendering them possesses the requisite qualifications for the practice of that profession, extra remuneration may be paid for such services.[59]

Increase in Remuneration [S. 310]

In the case of a public company or its subsidiaries, the remuneration of directors cannot be increased in any way without approval of the Central Government.[60] However, the fee payable to directors for attending meetings of the board or a committee thereof may be increased without approval as long as it does not exceed an amount which may be prescribed.

Any increase in the remuneration of directors will have no effect (*a*) in cases where Schedule XIII is applicable, unless such increase is in accordance with the conditions specified in that schedule;[61] (*b*) in any other case, unless it is approved by the Central Government. In the case of a private company which converts itself into a public company or becomes a public company under Section 43-A, any provision as to sitting fee in excess of the prescribed amount would be deemed to be an increase in remuneration.

---

58. Such special resolution shall remain in force only for a period of five years, but may be renewed from time to time by special resolution for further periods of not more than five years at a time, provided that no renewal shall be effected earlier than one year from the date on which it is to come into force. Sub-s. (7) of S. 309.
59. Where in response to a company's inquiry whether an advocate director could be paid remuneration for his services as a legal adviser, the Government expressed positive opinion, it was held that remuneration paid on the basis of this approval was valid. *Ruben Mills Ltd* v *UOI*, (1985) 57 Comp Cas 193. In this respect there is no difference between the services of a legal advisor or those of a chief consultant and those of a civil or mechanical engineer. *Stup Consultant Ltd* v *UOI*, [1986] 3 Comp LJ 260 Del: (1987) 61 Comp Cas 784, highlighting the duty of the Central Govt. to express opinions when its opinion has been sought. These views have been confirmed by the Department of Company Affairs *vide* 3/54/87-CL V of 14-2-1988: 1988 Chartered Secy 731; Form 25-A is prescribed for applications for approval. The Government cannot impose a restriction on the amount of remuneration payable to a professional. Any such restriction would be liable to be set aside. *Sree Gajanana Motor Transport Co Ltd* v *UOI*, (1992) 73 Comp Cas 348 Kant.
60. Since Schedule XIII limits have been removed, increase in remuneration does not require Government approval. *Fenner India Ltd* v *Addl ROC*, (1994) 80 Comp Cas 1 Mad.
61. The original Schedule XIII has been replaced by a new Schedule with effect from February 1, 1994. Now, subject to the overall limit of 5% and 10% of net profits, companies can pay any amount by way of remuneration without any ceiling and, therefore, without Government approval.

Excess Payment [S. 309(5)]

If any director has been paid in excess of the above limits, he shall hold the excess amount in trust for the company and shall be bound to refund it. The company shall not waive the recovery of any such sum. In the case of a shareholder-director who did no other work than merely holding the office of a director, a remuneration of £30 a week was viewed as excessive, the court saying that £10 a week has been considered reasonable in such cases, and that, therefore, the extra payment was *ultra vires* and recoverable by the company.[62]

These restrictions do not apply to a private company, unless it is a subsidiary of a public company.[63]

Prohibition of tax-free payment [S. 200]

Remuneration of a company's employees or officers cannot be made tax-free. Nor shall remuneration be calculated by reference to, or varying with, any tax payable by an officer or employee.

Compensation for loss of office [S. 318]

A company may make payment to a managing director or a director holding the office of manager or in the wholetime employment of the company, by way of compensation for loss of office, or as consideration for retirement from office. No other director is entitled to compensation. Further in the following cases no compensation is payable:

1. Where the director resigns his office in view of the reconstruction or amalgamation of the company and he is appointed in the company resulting from the reconstruction or amalgamation.
2. Where the director otherwise resigns his office.
3. Where the office of the director is vacated by virtue of Section 203 or under Section 283. Section 203 empowers the court to restrain fraudulent persons from managing companies and Section 283 provides the circumstances in which the office of a director is vacated.
4. Where the company is being wound up and the winding up is due to the negligence or default of the director.

---

62. *Halt Garage 1964 Ltd, Re*, [1982] 3 All ER 1016. Payment made for services actually rendered does not fall in the category of excess payment even if the appointment was defective. The company can waive recovery, *C. R. Priyachandra Kumar v Purasawalkam Permanent Fund Ltd*, (1995) 83 Comp Cas 150 Mad. The fact that the resolution for the waiver of recovery was defective was not considered by the court as sufficient to warrant a stay order against its implementation.
63. S. 309(9). If a wholetime director or managing director is receiving any commission from the company, then he shall not receive any commission or remuneration from any subsidiary. S. 309(6).

5. Where the director has been guilty of fraud or breach of trust, or gross negligence or mismanagement in the affairs of the company.

6. Where the director has instigated or has taken part in bringing about the termination of his office.

The amount of compensation should not exceed the remuneration which he would have earned for the unexpired residue of his term or for three years, whichever is shorter. The amount should be calculated on the basis of the average remuneration actually earned by him during a period of three years before the termination, or where he held office for a lesser period, during such a period. The case of a managing director is outside the section. He may be entitled to compensation in the capacity of an employee.[64]

But where the company is in winding up or winding up commences within twelve months after the termination, no compensation shall be paid, if the assets of the company after deducting the expenses are not sufficient to pay to the shareholders the share capital, including the premium, if any, contributed by them.

Directors with unlimited liability [Ss. 322-323]

A limited company may make the liability of any or all of its directors unlimited. Similarly, the liability of a manager may be made unlimited. A provision to that effect will have to be contained in the company's memorandum. But if the original memorandum does not contain any such provision, it may, if so authorised by articles and by a special resolution, be altered so as to render unlimited the liability of any of the above managerial personnel.[65] But any such new provision will become effective against an officer only on the expiry of his existing term, unless he has accorded his consent to it.[66] In case any of the above managerial personnel proposes a person for appointment to any of the above posts, he shall add a statement to the proposal that the liability of the person holding that office will be unlimited. Before that person accepts the office or acts therein, a notice in writing that his liability will be unlimited shall be given to him.[67]

Prevention of management by undesirable persons [Ss. 202 and 203]

It has been seen that a person who is an undischarged insolvent is disqualified from being appointed to any managerial office. If any such person discharges the functions of a director, or manager of any company or takes part in the promotion, formation or management of any company, he is punishable with both fine and imprisonment.

---

64. *Golden Handshake and Shareholders Protection*, (1978) New LJ 205. See *Taupo Totara Timber Co v Rowe*, [1977] 3 All ER 123 PC, where the contracted amount of compensation was allowed to be recovered on resignation on a take over.

65. S. 323(1).

66. S. 323 (2).

67. S. 322 (2). *See also* sub-section (3).

Section 203 further provides for power to restrain fraudulent persons from managing companies. Where a person is convicted of any offence in connection with the promotion, formation, or management of a company or in the course of winding up it appears that a person has been guilty under Section 542 of fraudulent conduct of business or has been guilty of any fraud, misfeasance or breach of duty in the affairs of the company, the court or the Tribunal may make an order that such a person shall not, without the leave of the court, be a director of any company or take part in the promotion, formation, or management of any company. The order may restrain him for any period but not exceeding five years. A person who intends to apply for an order under this section shall have to give ten days' notice to the person against whom the order is sought.[68] An application for this order may be made by the liquidator of a company, or any member or creditor of the company.[69]

An English court restrained a person from being a director for a period of three years because while acting as a director of a group of five companies he did not involve himself with the financial side of the companies' affairs and thus shirked his responsibility as a director by leaving everything to his co-director and had failed to appreciate the duties attendant on conducting business with limited liability. Thus he was not fit to be concerned in the management of a company. His fellow director was restrained for a period of five years with the exception of one company which he was managing very well and for which leave was given because his departure might have jeopardised the company and the jobs of its employees.[70] Trying to find out the policy behind such restraint orders, the court cited the following passage from an earlier case.[71]

> The public is entitled to be protected, not only against the activities of those guilty of more obvious breaches of commercial morality, but also against someone who has shown in his conduct of more than one company... a failure to appreciate or observe duties attendant on the privilege of conducting business with the protection of limited liability.

Errors of judgment, miscalculations, zeal and passion to keep the company alive and also the inability for dispassionate mind by reason of

---

68. S. 203(3).
69. S. 203(4).
70. *Majestic Recording Studios Ltd, Re*, 1989 BCLC 1 Ch D. Other decisions to the same effect are: *J. & B. Lynch (Builders) Ltd, Re*, 1988 BCLC 376 and *Stanford Service Ltd, Re*, 1987 BCLC 607. *See* also *Mathews (DJ) (Joinery Design), Re*, (1988) 4 BCC 513, where a director was restrained on the basis of misconduct in reference to two companies in the past, though he was, having learned his lessons, managing his latest company in a very successful way. The proceedings in England are launched under Company Directors' Disqualification Act, 1986.
71. Last case cited *ibid*. The object and purpose of the provision is to protect the public from activities of unfit directors and make them to recognise their wrongdoing and face the consequences, *Official Receiver v Cooper*, [1999] BCC 115 Ch D.

tough struggle for survival in business life, all these are not to be visited with any disqualification. Thus remaining in business for the purpose of proper realisation of assets towards winding up which may be inevitable has been held to be not a disqualification though it benefited the creditors more than the crown.[72] But where an unprofitable business was carried on with the money collected for the crown by way of taxes, that was held to be a serious error.[73] The judicial approach has been thus described: "A director should only be disqualified where his conduct was dishonest, in breach of standards of commercial morality or grossly incompetent. Commercial misjudgment does not justify disqualification."[74] To this it has been added that "there must be conduct which if not dishonest is at any rate in breach of standards of commercial morality, some really gross incompetence which persuades the court that it would be a danger to the public if he were allowed to continue to be involved in the management of companies, before a disqualification order is made."[75] A director was disqualified for 18 months because he went on incurring debts and receiving remuneration and collecting but not paying excise duties at a time when he was not able to market any product of the company.[76] Where a director improperly allotted shares to himself in order only to defeat the attempt by the rival faction of members, to gain majority control, this was held to be sufficient cause for warranting disqualification.[77] Where the company's transactions were found to constitute a fraudulent preference, a five year disqualification was imposed upon the director who formulated such transactions.[78] Where the directors withdrew more money from the company's already overdrawn overdraft account, they doing so in the hope that Christmas sales would enable them to tide over, but that proved to be a miscalculation, a two year term of disqualification was imposed.[79] A director can be found to be unfit even though no breach of a formal legal duty could be established. The circumstances may show gross incompetence on his part.[80]

---

72. *C.U. Fittings Ltd, Re*, 1989 BCLC 556 Ch D: 1988 BCC 533.
73. *Churchill Hotel (Plymouth) Ltd, Re*, 1988 BCLC 341 Ch D.
74. *McNulty's Interchange Ltd, Re*, 1989 BCLC 709 Ch D.
75. *Dawson Print Group Ltd, Re*, 1987 BCLC 601, 604 see *Lo-Line Electric Motors Ltd, Re*, 1988 BCLC 698; [1988] 2 All ER 692; 1988 Ch D 477; *Douglas Construction Services Ltd, Re*, 1988 BCLC 397, both involving commercial misjudgment; *Bath Glass Ltd, Re*, 1988 BCLC 329 Ch D, the conduct must be of sufficiently serious nature. *A Company (No 004803), Re, The Times, December 2, 1996.* [1997 PALMER IN COMPANY January p 4] once it becomes apparent that the board will pay no attention to a particular director's views, his remaining on the board is dangerous because it may create the impression that his purpose was simply to continue to draw directors' fees.
76. *McNulty's Interchange Ltd, Re*, 1989 BCLC 709 Ch D.
77. *Looe Fish Ltd, Re*, (1995) 16 Corpt LA 290 Ch D.
78. *Funtime Ltd, Re*, [2000] 1 BCLC 247 Ch D.
79. *City Pram & Toy Co Ltd, Re*, [1998] BCC 537 Ch D.
80. *Barrings Ltd, Re, (No 5)*, [2000] 1 BCLC 523 CA.

The importance of maintaining accounting records was noted in *Firedart Ltd, Re*.[81] The court said that the absence of accounting records is one of the most crucial factors in disqualifying a director. Without proper accounting records the directors may go on trading even when the company is insolvent. Proper accounts may give an advance warning as to the real state of affairs and as to proper level of remuneration.[82]

Trading at losses does not necessarily mean that the directors are unfit, but to do so over a protracted period and accumulating huge losses was held to be unjustifiable.[83] Where there was a huge accumulated deficit and a lengthy history of dishonoured cheques and unsatisfied statutory and other demands for payment, it was held that an overdraft in those circumstances amounted to trading with irresponsibility.[84]

A person who is restrained under the section cannot, without leave of the court, be "a director of or in any way, whether directly or indirectly, be concerned or take part in... the management of, a company". The word 'management' for this purpose means activities which influence policy or decisions of managerial nature affecting the company as a whole or substantially as a whole. Thus acting as a management consultant and advising on financial management and restructuring of a company may amount to being concerned in the management of a company.[85] But routine duties of clerical or administrative nature will not be sufficient to prove the contravention of a restraint order.[86]

A restraint order can be passed by the very court which convicts a director for a conduct falling within the meaning of the section.[87] It is not necessary that the offence should be in the field of management. Carrying on insurance business in the form of a company without licence under the Insurance Companies Act, 1982 (English) has been held to be an offence within the meaning of the section.[88] A *de facto* director would also be within the mischief of the section.[89]

---

81. [1994] 2 BCLC 340 Ch D and *Official Receiver* v *Fairall*, [1994] 2 BCLC 340 Ch D.
82. *Deadduck Ltd, Re*, [2000] 1 BCLC 148 Ch D. A director who failed to keep proper books of account was fined and disqualified for one year, *R* v *Victory (Kevin)*, [1999] 2 Cri App Rep (S) 102.
83. *Secy of State* v *Lubrant*, (1997) 2 BCLC 115.
84. *Richborough Furniture Ltd, Re*, (1996) 1 BCLC 507 Ch D, disqualification order; *Secy of State for Trade & Industry* v *Gash*, (1997) 1 BCLC 341 Ch D, no one personally responsible for the insolvency of the company, no disqualification. *Consolidated Insurance Co of London* v *Burrows*, (1997) 1 BCLC 48 Ch D, unfit non-executive director. *Secy of State for Trade and Industry* v *Mc Tighe*, (*No* 2), (1996) 2 BCLC 477 CA, payment to selected creditors, unfit for management.
85. *R* v *Campbell*, (1983) 78 Cr App R 95.
86. *Commr for Corporate Affairs (Vic)* v *Bracht*, 1988 14 ACLR 728.
87. *R* v *Austen*, (1985) 1 BCC 99, where full-term restraint was ordered because of a series of offences involving £300,000.
88. *R* v *Georgian*, (1988) 4 BCC 322; *R* v *Kemp*, 1988 BCLC 217: [1988] 2 WLR 975: 1988 QB 645.
89. *European Maritime Ltd, Re*, 1987 BCC 190; *Lo-Line Electric Motors Ltd, Re*, 1988 Ch 477: [1988] 2 All ER 692 Ch D.

The court has to take a broad brush approach in making its value judgment about a director's fitness. The criteria of competence, discipline in complying with duties regarding records, accounts and returns, and honesty are no doubt highly relevant factors in assessing fitness. The director was in breach of his duty in causing or permitting inter-company payments when he was aware that payments had not been authorised by the Board. Loans to the company were also permitted to be used for purposes other than those for which they had been made.[90]

Position of de facto directors.—The word director for the purposes of the section includes a situation in which a person has acted as a director even though not validly appointed or even if there has been no appointment at all. For a person to be regarded as a *de facto* director, there must be clear evidence to show that he was the sole person directing the affairs of the company or that he acted on equal footing with other directors in managing the affairs of the company.[91] The position of *de facto* directors has been thus stated:[92] "When deciding whether a director should be disqualified[93] the court was required to have regard to his conduct as a director regardless of whether he had been validly appointed or was merely assuming to act as a director without any appointment at all, since the conduct relevant to his future suitability to act as a director depended on his past record as a director irrespective of the circumstances in which he came to act as such. On the facts, the respondent behaved in a commercially culpable manner in trading through limited companies when he knew them to be insolvent and in using unpaid crown debts to finance such trading and he would be disqualified generally from being a director for three years. However, he would in the circumstances be permitted to be a director of two particular companies subject to certain conditions."[94] The court also observed *per curiam* that the use of moneys which should have been paid to the crown to finance the continuation of an insolvent company's business is more culpable than the failure to pay commercial debts.[95]

The Acts of some countries put an extended meaning upon the word director. The Nigerian Decree defines director to include a wife, husband, father, mother, son or daughter of a director. It has been said that "the

---

90. *Secy of State for Trade and Industry* v *Goldberg*, (2004) 1 BCLC 596 (Ch D).
91. *Richborough Furniture Ltd, Re*, (1996) 1 BCLC 507 Ch D, benefit of doubt was given to the person because there was nothing to show in what capacity he was involved with the company. Where a body corporate is the director of a company whether *de facto* or *de jure* or *shadow*, it would not follow as a matter of course that the directors of such a body corporate would *ipso facto* be regarded as the shadow directors of the other company. There must be evidence to show that the directors of such a company were instructing the directors of the other company. *Secy of State for Trade and Industry* v *Laing*, (1996) 2 BCLC 324 CA.
92. *Lo-Line Electric Motors Ltd, Re*, [1988] 2 All ER 692 Ch D: 1988 Ch 477.
93. Under S. 300 of the Act of 1985 [English].
94. Head Note to the report.
95. Dictum of VINELOTT J in *Stanford Services Ltd, Re*, 1987 BCLC 617, followed; *Dewson Print Group Ltd, Re*, 1987 BCLC 605, not followed.

extended meaning is an attempt to catch up with the tendency of some directors or similarly placed persons to use the members of their family as fronts for those transactions that are unethical or in breach of their obligations to their companies. In one such case[1] the court said that a director might not, even if he could contract with the company negotiate such a contract as would put him in a position to profit at the expense of the company.

The category of *de facto* directors has been held not to include a wife who acted in secretarial capacity in a company controlled by her husband. The court found that she was acting merely as a dutiful spouse for the sake of helping her husband. She was not liable to be disqualified as a *de facto* director.[2] In another similar case, a lady manager was not subjected to a disqualification order. The use of the title 'director' did not make her a *de facto* director. She was not in fact directing the company. There was clear evidence of lack of involvement in things financial. She did not form part of the real corporate governance of the company. She was not in a position to permit the company to go on trading against all odds.[3]

Natural Justice

Natural justice requires that a director facing disqualification should know the charge he has to meet and if the official receiver wishes to change the nature of the allegations on which he is going to rely he must give the director prior notice of the new allegation.[4]

It has been observed that this power has begun "to develop into a powerful weapon in the arsenal of the fight against the improper management of companies".[5]

Prohibition of assignment [S. 312]

A director cannot assign his office in favour of anyone else. Any such assignment is void. The Supreme Court has distinguished "assignment" from "nomination" as well as from "appointment".[6]

A person formed a private company and transferred his business to it. He became the first managing director and had a right given to him by the articles to appoint a successor by his will. He died. His nominee assumed office. The other members challenged the appointment. The Bombay High Court held that the word "assignment" should mean "appointment" in this connection. But the Supreme Court expressed a different opinion. It said

---

1. (1968) 5 N SCC 218.
2. *Red Label Fashions Ltd, Re*, (1999) BCC 308 Ch D.
3. *Secy of State for Trade & Industry* v *Tjolle*, [1998] 1 BCLC 333 at 335 Ch D.
4. Supra *Lo-Line*.
5. 1988 JBL 1, editorial note. *See* for a fuller account, Andrew Hicks, *Disqualification of Directors Forty Years On*, 1988 JBL 27.
6. *Oriental Metal Pressing Works Ltd* v *Bhaskar Kashinath Thakoor*, (1960) 63 Bom LR 505: (1961) 31 Comp Cas 143: AIR 1961 SC 573.

that "on a plain reading of the language used in the section, it does not seem possible to hold that the word 'assignment' in it can mean 'appointment'."

First, the section talks of "assignment of his office" by a director. The word "his" would indicate that the office contemplated was one held by the director at the time of assignment. An appointment to an office can be made only if the office is vacant. It is legitimate, therefore, to infer that by using the word "his", the Legislature indicated that an appointment by a director to the office which he previously held but did not hold at the date of the appointment, was not to be included within the word "assignment".

Secondly, Section 225 of the Act permits one-third of the total number of directors of a public company and all the directors of a private company to be appointed otherwise than by the company at a general meeting, if the articles make provision in this regard. The Act, therefore, expressly permits directors to be appointed otherwise than by the company. It follows that within the limit as to the number prescribed by the section, a power of appointment of directors can be legitimately conferred by the articles on any person including one who holds the office of a director. In order, however, that a director may exercise this power, there must be a vacant office of a director. He may himself bring about the vacancy by resignation of his office. The vacancy may also be caused by his death or expiry of the term of his office. There will be nothing illegal if the power is exercised in the case of the death of the director, by an appointment of his will.[7]

Irregular appointment and validity of acts [S. 290]

Section 290 contains provisions for validation of acts of directors. The section says that acts done by a person as a director shall be valid notwithstanding the fact that his appointment was invalid by reason of any defect or disqualification or by reason of the fact that his appointment had become terminated by virtue of any provision of the Act or the company's articles. The provision does not cover acts which have been done after the defect in the appointment or holding of the office has already become known.

The section operates to protect transactions with outsiders as well as members made by a company through its directors. One of the effects of the provision is that persons dealing with a company are entitled to presume that persons acting as directors are validly in office. An example is to be found in *Dawson* v *African Consolidated Land, etc., Co.*[8]

---

7. SARKAR J (afterwards CJ).
8. [1898] 1 Ch 6 CA. A parallel authority in India is *A. J. Judah* v *Rampada Gupta*, AIR 1959 Cal 715, where sale of shares in the exercise of lien by *de facto* directors was held to be protected.

Three persons purporting to act as directors made a call which was resisted by some shareholders on the ground that they were not validly in office. One of them, unknown to the others, had vacated his office by parting with his qualification shares, although he subsequently reacquired his qualification shares and continued to act.

The court held that the provision covered not only the dealings between a company and outsiders but also with members. The call was valid.

The provision has been applied to the act of a person who ceased to be a director after taking over the company's secretaryship, although the fact could have been known from the company's public documents.[9]

A defective or irregular appointment has been distinguished from a situation where there has been no appointment at all. The person purporting to act for the company is nothing but a usurper. This approach dominated the decision of the House of Lords in *Morris* v *Kanssen*.[10]

A person had ceased to be a director. He sat with another, who had never been appointed, to hold a meeting and appointed still another person as a director. Then all three sat together to allot shares to their new appointee.

The obvious conclusion was that the new director-allottee, being a part of the board, should have known that he was being taken in by persons who were themselves nothing but *de facto* directors. The allotment to him was also not valid for the same reason and also for the added reason that he participated in a meeting which conferred an allotment on him.[11]

Thus the section does not cover a case where there is total absence of authority or fraudulent usurpation of authority. Accordingly, the approval of a sale of assets by a director co-opted at a meeting by a person who had no authority and other directors were not even informed of the meeting was held to be of no use. The co-option and the co-optee's work both were held to be invalid.[12]

Section 290 will also not cover a situation where an act done by the incompetent board is such which even a competent board could not have done. Thus where a person not so qualified, was appointed as a managing director, the provision in the section could not be used to cover up the fact that those who sat together to appoint him were themselves not properly in office. Even a regularly constituted board could not have done that.[13]

---

9. *British Asbestos Co Ltd* v *Boyd*, [1903] 2 Ch 439, at p 444.
10. 1946 AC 459.
11. Followed in *Grant* v *John Grant & Sons Ltd*, (1950) 82 CLR 1.
12. *M. Moorthy* v *Drivers and Conductors Bus Service P Ltd*, (1991) 71 Comp Cas 138 Mad.
13. *Craven-Ellis* v *Canons Ltd*, [1936] 2 KB 403 CA, the person so appointed having acted for some time was allowed to recover remuneration on quantum meruit basis. *Shailesh Harilal Shah* v *Matushree Textiles Ltd*, AIR 1994 Bom 20, it was held that the acts of a director were valid, even though his appointment as additional director was questioned. The court, however, found the appointment to be also valid.

Alternate director [S. 313]

If so authorised by the articles or by a resolution of the company, the board of directors may appoint an officiating director if any director is absent for a period of three months or more from the State in which the meetings of the board are ordinarily held. Such a director is called an "alternate director". He holds office only for the period for which the original director would have been in office. He vacates his office on the expiry of such period and also when the original director returns to the State. The provisions relating to reappointment after rotational retirement apply to the original director and not to the alternate director. The provisions of Section 264 relating to filing of consent to act as director do not apply to such a director. Where there is a compelling need for an alternate director, the board of directors can be compelled to make an appointment. An American company was holding 40% interest in an Indian company. It appointed a director to watch its interests. Its appointee was not able to attend meetings of the board and, therefore, requested the board to accept his nominee as an alternate director, which was refused without proper consideration. That was characterised by the court as something wrong. His request should have been seriously considered keeping in mind the interests of the company and those of its shareholders.[14]

Appointment to place of profit [S. 314]

Following persons can be appointed to a place of profit under the company only with the consent of the company accorded by a special resolution:

    1. Any director of the company.

    2.   (*a*) Any partner or relative of such a director.[15]

              (*b*) Any firm in which such a director or relative is a partner.

---

14. *D. Ross Porter* v *Pioneer Steel Co Ltd*, [1989] 2 Comp LJ 89 Del: (1989) 66 Comp Cas 363.
15. The word "relative" is defined in S. 6. Two or more persons are said to be relatives if they are the members of a Hindu undivided family or if they are husband and wife or if one is related to the other in any manner indicated in Sch. 1-A. The list given in the Schedule is as follows:

1. Father	2. Mother, including step-mother
3. Son, including step-son	4. Son's wife
5. Daughter, including step-daughter	6. Father's father
7. Father's mother	8. Mother's mother
9. Mother's father	10. Son's son
11. Son's son's wife	12. Son's daughter
13. Son's daughter's husband	14. Daughter's husband
15. Daughter's son	16. Daughter's son's wife
17. Daughter's daughter	18. Daughter's daughter's husband
19. Brother, including step-brother	20. Brother's wife
21. Sister, including step-sister	22. Sister's husband.

(*c*) Any private company of which such a director is a member or director or any director, or manager of such a private company,[16] if the remuneration is to exceed an amount as may be prescribed.[17] (Not less than Rs 10,000 or more).[18]

An appointment of any such person can, however, be made to the position of managing director, manager, legal or technical adviser, banker or trustee of the debenture-holders either under the company itself or under any of its subsidiaries, except when the remuneration is paid over by him to the company or its holding company. In a case before the Madras High Court,[19] a company appointed two of its directors as technical advisers for the purpose of surveying buildings and properties to find out their value for purposes of loans to be advanced by the company. On the Registrar's enquiry about their qualifications the company disclosed none. It was only in the court that the company stated for the first time that they had experience in the line. The court accordingly quashed the appointment:

It is not open to a company to give the designation of technical adviser to any director and to appoint him as such and thereby avoid the consequences of Section 314. A technical adviser has to be a person with technical qualifications for the job entrusted to him which consists of rendering advice to the company in matters relating to its business.

The approval may be granted either before the appointment or at the first meeting held after the appointment. Where a relative etc. happens to be appointed without the knowledge of the director, approval may be accorded at the first meeting held after the appointment or within three months, whichever is later. Every subsequent appointment to a place of higher remuneration also requires such approval unless the original appointment was on a time scale.[20]

If a relative etc. was appointed before the director became a director of the company, this section will not apply.[21]

An office is deemed to be a place of profit if it will entitle the director in addition to his remuneration as director and in the case of any other individual, any remuneration whether as salary, fees, commission, perquisites, the right to occupy any premises free of rent as a place of residence or otherwise.[22] A person holding the position of a branch manager under the company has been held by the Calcutta High Court to be holding a

16. S. 314(2). See *Firestone Tyre & Rubber Co* v *Synthetics & Chemicals Ltd*, [1970] 2 Comp LJ 200: (1971) 41 Comp Cas 337 Bom.
17. The Madras High Court has held that the prohibition applies not to the relative of an ordinary director but only to the relative of a director holding a place of profit under the company. *A. R. Sudarasanam* v *MPHJS Nidhi Ltd*, (1985) 57 Comp Cas 776.
18. W.e.f. 26-3-92, DCA notification of 1-3-1992.
19. *Madura Hindu Permanent Fund Ltd* v *Govt of India*, (1977) 47 Comp Cas 318 Mad.
20. S. 314(1) (Explanation).
21. S. 314(1-A).
22. S. 314(3).

position of profit under the company. A special resolution was necessary for his appointment.[23]

When an individual, firm or body corporate is so appointed, he or it, is required to make a declaration of his or its connection with a director.[24]

If the appointment is not approved by a special resolution of the general meeting, the office is automatically vacated with a liability to refund the remuneration already received.[25]

By the Companies (Amendment) Act, 1974, a legal or technical adviser, banker or trustee for debenture-holders of the company, has been excluded from the category of persons whose appointment to a place of profit is regulated by Section 314.

The amendment further provides that the appointment of the following persons to a place of profit under the company carrying a total monthly remuneration of such a sum as may be prescribed (not less than Rs 20,000)[26] can be made only by a special resolution and approval of the Central Government:[27]

1. any partner or relative of a director or manager;
2. any firm in which such a director or manager or relative of either is a partner;
3. any private company of which such a director or manager or relative of either is a director or member.[28]

If any such appointment is made without following the above procedure, the appointee will have to refund the benefits of the office to the company and the company cannot waive their recovery unless permitted to do so by the Central Government. [S. 314(2-B) and (2-D)]. His office shall also be deemed to have been vacated from the expiry of six months from the commencement of the Amendment Act.[29]

A person appointed to directorship by the Central Government under Section 408 is exempted from the section. [S. 314(4)].

OTHER MANAGERIAL PERSONNEL

The fundamental principle relating to the administration of a company is that its board of directors, which is the representative body, should direct

---

23. *Gobind Pritamdas Malkani* v *Amarendra Nath*, (1980) 50 Comp Cas 219 Cal.
24. S. 315(2-A).
25. S. 314(3).
26. W.e.f. 1-3-94.
27. This will not include bonus or reimbursement of medical expenses. *Suessen Textiles Bearings Ltd* v *UOI*, (1984) 55 Comp Cas 492 Del.
28. S. 314(1-B).
29. *Niemla Textile Finishing Mills* v *CIT*, (1975) Comp Cas 554 Punj. The application for approval should be in Form 24-B as renewed with effect from 1-8-1990 and contain particulars in full detail about perquisites being also required by the new form. Circular No 19 of 1990: (1990) 68 Comp Cas 97 St.

and control its affairs. But at the same time the Act allows a person to accept directorship in fifteen companies[30] and does not prescribe the time and attention that he should devote to a particular company.[31] The common law excuses him from the consequences of non-attendance generally. Moreover, a board meeting is a very formal affair and cannot be called very frequently, whereas business has to be managed every day. The primary function of the board, therefore, is to lay down the business policies and make a broad, general supervision over their execution. The day-to-day administration has to be delegated to professional management.

Formerly four types of professional management were recognised, namely, managing director, managing agent, secretaries and treasurers, and manager.[32] But with effect from April 3, 1970, management by managing agents and secretaries and treasurers has been banned.[33] Now the choice is between a managing director or manager. A company can have only one or the other but not both of them at the same time.[34]

Managing director, wholetime director, manager

A managing director as defined in the Act[35] means a director who is entrusted with substantial powers of management which would not otherwise be exercisable by him. The term includes a director occupying the position of a managing director, by whatever name called. The 'substantial powers of management' may be conferred upon him by virtue of an agreement with the company, or of a resolution of the company or its board, or by virtue of its memorandum or articles.[36]

The expression 'wholetime director' which has also been used in Section 269 along with the expression 'managing director' has been defined in the *Explanation* to sub-section (1) as including a person who is in the wholetime employment of the company. Thus he is also an employee of the

---

30. S. 275.
31. *See* M.J. Trebilcock, *The Liability of Directors for Negligence*, (1969) 32 MLR 499 at p 504-5.
32. S. 197-A.
33. S. 324-A [as amended in 1969].
34. S. 197-A. *See also* K.P. Khaitan, *Balance of Power in Company Law*, Chapter V of LECTURES ON MERCANTILE LAW, 61 (1961), a publication of the Indian Law Institute. The Department has advised companies not to use expressions like special directors, executive directors, etc. because such designations are likely to mislead the members of the public [Circular No 2 of 1990 of 29-5-1990 published in (1990) 68 Comp Cas 83 St.] Such designations give an impression to the public at large and those dealing with companies and their executives that they are full-fledged directors entitled to act as such on behalf of the companies. If in fact, these executives are not directors on the board, it will be patently wrong on the part of companies.
35. S. 2(26).
36. *Ibid.* The two provisos to the definition provide that delegation of duties of routine nature does not make a director, a managing director, and that a managing director shall act under the superintendence of the board of directors.

company. Like the managing director, he occupies dual capacity, namely, that of a director and of an employee.[37]

A managing director can be appointed only if there is a power to that effect in the company's articles.[38]

The "substantial powers of management" that are conferred upon a managing director may be revoked or reduced or otherwise altered. Where, for example, his powers have arisen by virtue of an agreement with the company's board, the latter may revoke or alter them. The service agreement of a managing director provided that he should exercise his powers in relation to the company's business and any of its subsidiaries as may be resolved by the directors. The directors resolved that he should confine his attention only to one subsidiary. It was held that the directors' action was competent and no action lay for breach of contract.[39] A managing director, being an agent of the board of directors, cannot exercise any power over and above those of the board. He can exercise only such powers as have been delegated to him. A managing director commenced proceedings against the company's secretary to recover from him the money which he had withdrawn from the company's bank account. He commenced the proceedings without any authorisation from the board. The proceedings were struck out.[40]

But revocation of the appointment itself is something different. A managing director is entitled to compensation if his appointment is prematurely determined even if there is a power to that effect in the articles. Thus, where a managing director was appointed to hold office as long as he was a director, retained his qualification shares and worked efficiently, his dismissal while he still fulfilled these qualifications was held unjustified entitling him to damages.[41] Similarly, where the termination is brought about by an alteration of the articles in a manner inconsistent with the terms of appointment, damages would have to be paid.[42] Where the appointment is

---

37. Lord NORMAND, *Anderson v James Sutherland (Peterhead) Ltd*, 1941 SC 230 at p 238, Scotland.
38. SWINFEN EADY J *Boschoek Proprietary Co Ltd v Fuke*, [1906] 1 Ch 148, 159: 94 LT 398.
39. *Harold Holdsworth & Co v Caddies*, [1955] 1 All ER 725; *Caddies v Harold Holdsworth & Co*, 1951 SC HL 27, Scotland.
40. *Mitchell & Hobbs (UK) Ltd v Mill*, (1996) 2 BCLC 102 QBD. Criminal proceedings can be launched only through board authorised person, *CBS Gramophone Records and Tapes (India) Ltd v P. A. Noorudeen*, (1992) 73 Comp Cas 494 Ker, it was a proceeding for dishonour of a cheque; *Swastic Coaters P Ltd v Deepak Bros*, (1997) 89 Comp Cas 564. An authorised representative's complaint was dismissed because of his default in appearing on the day of hearing.
41. *Nelson v James Nelson & Sons Ltd*, [1914] 2 KB 770: [1914-15] All ER Rep 433 CA.
42. *Shindler v Northern Raincoat Co Ltd*, [1960] 1 WLR 1038: [1960] 2 All ER 239; *Southern Foundries Ltd v Shirlaw*, 1940 AC 701: [1940] 2 All ER 445. It has been held by the Delhi High Court in *Shrimati Jain v Delhi Flour Mills Co Ltd*, (1974) 44 Comp Cas 228, that where a person has been appointed managing director for a term of 5 years, but he ceases to be a director before the expiry of the term, the agreement also ceases to be operative.

not for a fixed period, removal at any time may entail no liability in damages. In one of the cases before the Court of Appeal,[43] the duration of appointment was not specified. The managing director was removed on a month's notice, and the directors' action was upheld by the company in general meeting. He sued for damages on the ground that the notice given to him was not reasonable. The articles contained a clause enabling the company to remove a managing director without notice. It was held that in view of this sweeping power, the requirement of reasonable notice could not be read into the contract.

The requirement of good faith or of "proper purpose" can be read even into an absolutely discretionary power. The decision of the board of directors in removing a managing director can be challenged on the ground that they did so not in the interest of the company but to promote their own.[44] While the appointment may require approval of the Central Government, the removal of a managing director does not require to be so approved. The managing director is an agent of the board of directors. He cannot restrain a meeting of the board called to consider his removal. The approval of his appointment by the Central Government does not militate against the board of directors' power to remove him.[45]

Where his appointment is defective within his knowledge, for example, made by directors who have failed to acquire their qualification shares, no remuneration or compensation is payable; but if the company has accepted his work, it must pay him reasonable remuneration on the principle of *quantum meruit*.[46]

A managing director, being a manager, is an employee of the company to that extent.[47] The remuneration payable to him is taxable as salary. This has been so held by the Supreme Court in *Ram Prashad* v *CIT*.[48] The court discussed at great length the distinction between a servant and an agent and concluded that the managing director is more like an agent than a servant, but this does not prevent him from entering into a contract of employment with the company.[49] But he is not a clerk or a servant so as to be entitled to

---

43. *Read* v *Astoria Garage (Streatham) Ltd*, [1952] Ch 637 CA: [1952] 2 All ER 292.
44. *Hindle* v *John Cotton Ltd*, (1919) 56 SLR HL, Scotland.
45. *Pyare Lal Gupta* v *D. P. Agarwal*, (1983) 53 Comp Cas 586 All.
46. *Craven-Ellis* v *Canons Ltd*, [1936] 2 KB 403: [1936] 2 All ER 1066 CA and *see* Evans D. Marshall, *Quantum Meruit & Managing Director*, (1966) 27 Mod LR 608.
47. A managing director occupies the dual capacity of being a director as well as an employee of the company. He can be regarded as a principle employer for the purposes of the ESI Act, 1948, *Employees State Ins Corpn* v *Appex Engg P Ltd*, [1998] 1 Comp LJ 10 SC. He is not a mere servant, he is also an agent of the company with capacity to bind the company in the sphere of management entrusted to him, *Happy Home Builders (Karnataka) P Ltd* v *Delite Enterprises*, (1994) 13 Corpt LA 405 Kar.
48. (1972) 2 SCC 696: (1972) 42 Comp Cas 544.
49. *Id.* at 548/553. He is an officer of the company for tax purposes and, therefore, can be prosecuted for filing false particulars. *M.R. Pratap* v *V.M. Muthukrishnan*, (1992) 3 SCC 384: (1992) 74 Comp Cas 400 SC.

preferential payment.[50] A managing director was held liable when the stock of the company diminished during his tenure and he was not able to give a satisfactory account of the loss. He was also not excusable under Section 633 because he was not honest about the matter.[51]

Appointment when compulsory

Sub-section (1) of Section 269 declares that on and from the commencement of the Companies (Amendment) Act, 1988, (enforced w.e.f. 15-6-1988) every public company and its subsidiaries, whether public or private, having a paid-up share capital of such sum as may be prescribed, shall have a managing or a wholetime director or a manager. The sum of rupees five crores has been prescribed for this purpose.[52]

Procedure of appointment [S. 269]

Appointment can be made in accordance with the company's articles. Usually the articles leave it to the directors to appoint any one of themselves as the managing director. If this power is conferred on the board of directors, the general meeting of shareholders cannot interfere.[53]

Section 269 has been recast by the amendment of 1988. In the case of companies reaching figure of paid-up share capital which may be prescribed,[54] the appointment of a managing director, wholetime director or manager has been made compulsory. The appointment has to correspond with the conditions specified in Parts I and II of Schedule XIII which parts are subject to the provisions of Part III. A return of the appointment in prescribed form must be filed with the Government within 90 days. Approval of the Central Government is not necessary in such cases. But if the appointment does not comply with the Schedule, approval becomes necessary.[55] Application for approval must be made within 90 days. The Central Government would not accord the approval if it is satisfied that the candidate is not a fit and proper person for the post and his appointment is

50. *Newspaper Proprietary Syndicate Ltd, Re*, [1900] 2 Ch 349: 83 LT 341.
51. *T.A. Angappan* v *Coimbatore Mills Ltd*, (1983) 54 Comp Cas 5 Mad. The mill was taken over by the Government of India.
52. As per Rule 10-A of the Companies (Central Govt's) Rules and Forms. The return to be filed with the Registrar and the accompanying certificates shall be in Form 25-C. The prescribed figure of Rs 1 crore was revised by a Press Note issued by the Ministry of Industry, Deptt of Co Affairs, dated Sept 19, 1990. Source: (1990) 60 Comp Cas 47 St; GSR 795(E) of Sept 18, 1990. The reason given is: "This measure will provide operational freedom to companies in managing their own affairs without undue interference from other sources."
53. *Thomas Logan* v *Davis*, (1911) 105 LT 419 CA.
54. Public companies and private companies which are subsidiaries of public companies with a paid-up capital of Rs 5 crores or more. The earlier GSR 794(E) of 10-6-1988 which prescribed the figure of Rs 1 crore has been replaced by GSR 795(E) of Sept 18, 1990, which prescribed the figure of Rs 5 crores.
55. *Central Govt Deptt of Co Affairs* v *Aurofood Ltd*, (2002) 111 Comp Cas 841 CLB, where approval is necessary because of loss bearing company, it was held that the requirement was not applicable where there was a profit in the year of the appointment.

not in public interest and the terms and conditions of the appointment are not fair.

If there is no approval, the appointee should vacate office from the date of the communication of the refusal to the company failing which he incurs a penalty of Rs 5000 for every day of usurpation of the office.[56]

Where the Government *suo motu* or on information received is *prima facie* of opinion that an appointment has been made without approval in contravention of the requirements of the Schedule, the Government shall be competent to refer the matter to the National Company Law Tribunal for decision. The Tribunal has to give notice to the company, the appointee and any other officer of the company who was responsible for compliance of Schedule XIII to show cause why the appointment should not be terminated and the penalty of sub-section (10) imposed. The Tribunal should give appropriate opportunity and then may make an order declaring that there has been a contravention. The declaration will have the following effects:

1. The company is liable to a fine extending up to Rs 50,000;
2. Every officer of the company who is in default is liable to a fine of Rs 1,00,000;
3. The appointment comes to an end and the appointee is liable to a fine of Rs 1,00,000 and is also liable to refund the entire amount of salaries, commission and perquisites received by him up to the date of the order.

Any violation of the order of the Board or any default in meeting its consequences is further punishable under sub-section (*ii*). Every officer of the company who is in default and the managing or wholetime director or the manager, shall be punishable with imprisonment extending up to three years and with fine extending up to Rs 500 for every day of default. Whether such a double penalty amounts to a violation of the doctrine of double jeopardy, only time will tell.

Sub-section (12) provides that the acts of such a person done by him up to the date of the finding that his appointment was void would be valid provided that they were otherwise valid.

The section concludes with an *Explanation* that the word "appointment" includes reappointment and "wholetime director" includes a director in the wholetime employment of the company.

The function to grant or withhold approval is that of the Central Government. The Government has to determine whether the proposee is a fit and proper person and may refuse to grant approval where there is a

---

56. S. 269(6).

pending prosecution against him.[57] The Supreme Court pointed out in *Rampur Distillery & Chemical Co Ltd* v *Company Law Board*[58] that the Government can take into account the entire conduct and actings past and present and the fact that the proposee has been adversely commented upon by an inquiry committee. The court will not interfere in the matter unless the Government's refusal proceeds on facts totally irrelevant to the issue.[59] Further, the Government has the power to make the appointment subject to any conditions that it thinks fit to impose.[60] The utility of this power was demonstrated by the decision of the Delhi High Court in *Raymond Engineering Works* v *Union of India*.[61]

A company's prospectus disclosed that it had purchased its managing agent's property at 6 lakhs of rupees, but did not disclose that the managing agent had himself paid only Rs 3 ½ lakhs for it. In other words, the profit of approximately Rs 3 lakhs was concealed. The company brought no action. It applied to the Central Government for approval of the appointment of the same managing agent as managing director. The Government granted approval subject to the condition that he refunded Rs 2,75,000 to the company, the balance allowed to him as reasonable expenditure.

The Delhi High Court upheld the condition. "The profit may not be illegal. But the Government was entitled to think that it was unconscionable profit."[62]

The Government may reduce the period of appointment proposed by the company.[63] If the approval is granted subject to any alterations, reasons for the same must be stated. The Gujarat High Court struck down an order which stated no reasons.[64] The appointment was for a period of five years; monthly salary Rs 5000; annual increment Rs 500; commission on profits 1% subject to the ceiling of half the annual salary; gratuity, medical benefits and residential accommodation. The Government approved the appointment but reduced the term to two years and also slashed the salary and other

57. *Rampur Distillery & Chemical Co* v *Company Law Board*, [1969] 1 Comp LJ 204 Del; On appeal to the Supreme Court: (1969) 2 SCC 774. A refusal or a partial or conditional approval must carry a statement of reasons for the same otherwise the order would be liable to be quashed. Where in its approval the Government made this alteration that retirement benefits like provident fund and gratuity, would be linked with salary and not commissions, etc., and gave no reasons for the same, the alteration was set aside. *Bennett, Coleman & Co Ltd* v *UOI*, (1993) 78 Comp Cas 666 Del.
58. (1969) 2 SCC 774: AIR 1970 SC 1789: (1970) 40 Comp Cas 916: [1970] 2 Comp LJ 1.
59. *Id.* See also *Canara Workshop Ltd* v *UOI*, (1966) 36 Comp Cas 63 Mys.
60. S. 637-A.
61. AIR 1970 Del 5: [1970] 2 Comp LJ 162
62. RANGARAJAN J: [1970] 2 Comp LJ 162. The learned Judge cited the following authorities: *A.R. Hussain Khan* v *ROC*, AIR 1965 Mad 307; *Rohtas Industries* v *S.D. Agarwal*, (1969) 1 SCC 325: AIR 1969 SC 707: (1969) 39 Comp Cas 781.
63. S. 269(4).
64. *Cibatul Ltd* v *UOI*, (1980) 50 Comp Cas 437 Guj.

benefits, but assigned no reasons. Despite reminders from the parties and the court, the Government refused to make the order a speaking order. The court was left with no choice but to strike it down.[65]

Removal of managing director of Government company

A person was appointed the managing director of a Government company in accordance with its articles. The articles of such a company do not have the effect of a statute. Subsequently he was removed is accordance with the same articles. It was held that he was not entitled to any relief under Article 226 of the Constitution for enforcement of the contract of service.[66]

Disclosure by company of directors' interest [S. 302]

Where a director is in any way, directly or indirectly, concerned or interested in the person who has been appointed as the company's manager or managing director, the company is required to send to members within 21 days of the appointment an abstract of the terms and conditions of the appointment together with a memorandum clearly specifying the nature of the concern or interest of the director in question. A similar procedure has to be followed when the terms and conditions of the appointment are altered. In the case of a managing director, an abstract of the terms and conditions of the appointment or of any variation thereof has to be sent to members whether any director is interested in the matter or not and where any director is interested, a memorandum specifying the nature of the interest has also to be sent. The same procedure has to be complied with where a director acquires an interest subsequent to the appointment. Contracts for the appointment of manager or managing director have to be kept at the registered office of the company. The members have the right to inspect them and to get extracts in the same manner and subject to the same fee as in the case of register of members.

Disqualifications [S. 267]

According to Section 267, a person suffering from any of the following disqualifications cannot be appointed a managing or wholetime director:

1. A person who is an undischarged insolvent, or has at any time been adjudged an insolvent.
2. A person who suspends, or has at any time suspended, payment to his creditors, or makes or has made a composition with them.
3. A person who is or has been convicted by a court of an offence involving moral turpitude.[67]

---

65. Following *Orient Paper Mills* v *UOI*, AIR 1969 SC 48 and *Siemens Co of India* v *UOI*, (1976) 2 SCC 981.
66. *B.M. Varma* v *State of U.P.*, (2005) 58 SCL 52 (All).
67. Where the High Court suspended the sentence, it was held that the conviction still stood and the disqualification made the appointment void, *Rama Narang* v *Ramesh Narang*, (1995) 2

Subject to these disqualifications, any person may be appointed as managing director,[68] provided that he is not holding the office of a managing director or manager in any other company.[69] However, a person holding such office in one other company may be appointed managing director. But this kind of appointment can be made with the approval of a resolution passed at a meeting of the board of directors and with the consent of all the directors present at the meeting. Specific notice of the meeting and of the resolution should be given to all the directors then in India.[70] Again, the Central Government may permit any person to be appointed as a managing director of more than two companies if the Government is satisfied that it is necessary that the companies should, for their proper working, function as a single unit and have a common managing director.[71]

The maximum term of appointment can be five years at a time[72] and a new term cannot be sanctioned earlier than two years from the date on which it is to come into force.[73] No change can be made in the terms of appointment without the approval of the Central Government.[74]

Remuneration

The remuneration of a managing director, in whatever mode paid, cannot exceed 5% of the net profits. But if there are more than one managing directors, the limit is 10% for all of them together.[75] It was held by the Supreme Court in *Company Law Board* v *Upper Doab Sugar Mills Ltd.*[76] that the Company Law Board could reduce this ceiling as part of the conditions of approval for appointment. A public limited company, which had appointed two managing directors for the first time, sought approval of the appointment. The proposed remuneration for each managing director was Rs 5000 per month and 3-1/2% commission on profits. The Board granted the approval subject to the condition that total remuneration from both sources should not exceed Rs 1,20,000 for each such director. This was

---

SCC 513: (1995) 83 Comp Cas 194: (1995) 16 Corpt LA 247 SC.

68. The relative of a managing director can be appointed as a wholetime director without approval. An approval would be necessary only if the remuneration paid to a director was over and above the remuneration to which he would be entitled as managing or wholetime director because up to that point he would not be regarded as holding a place of profit under the company or when the appointment is not in accordance with Sch. XIII. 1989 Chartered Secretary, 525 carries the above clarification. Form 25-A is prescribed for seeking approval. Circular No 10 of 1990 of 28-5-1990; (1990) 69 Comp Cas 83 St.

69. S. 316(1).

70. Proviso to S. 316(2). Because of the changes made in Sch. XIII such approval is not necessary if the appointee opts to draw remuneration from only one of the two companies.

71. S. 316(4).

72. S. 317(1).

73. S. 317(3).

74. S. 268. According to S. 317(4) these restrictions do not apply to a private company which is not a subsidiary of a public company.

75. S. 309(3).

76. (1977) 2 SCC 198: (1977) 47 Comp Cas 173.

a part of the policy adopted by the Board that no individual should be paid remuneration exceeding Rs 1,20,000 per annum or Rs 10,000 per month. The Board cited a large number of instances in which this condition had been imposed. But the argument of other instances which had remained unchallenged did not appeal to the Delhi High Court[77] and the administrative ceiling so imposed was held to be beyond (*ultra vires*) the rule-making power of the Board. The judgment proceeded on the hypothesis that if the Act itself imposes a ceiling, any reduction of that by administrative regulations would conflict with the Act and hence be *ultra vires*. But the judgment was reversed by the Supreme Court.[78]

Any controversy is now of academic interest only. The amendment of 1974 had added Section 637-AA which enables the Central Government while conferring approval to fix a limit on remuneration below the limits specified in the Act. In fixing such limit, the Government was required to have regard to the financial position of the company, the remuneration of the candidate on other grounds from the same company, his remuneration from other companies, his qualifications and public policy relating to removal of income disparities. Each individual case must be considered on its own merits. A company appointed two executive directors and sought approval. The approval was granted on reduced salary. The company was informed that the reduction had been made in accordance with the guidelines provided by the Ministry. The court said that the Government must take a decision in each individual case. The decisive guidelines laid down in general were outside the scope of the power in Section 637-AA and, therefore, *ultra vires*.[79] The remuneration of a managing or wholetime director or manager may be increased, where Schedule XIII is applicable, in accordance with its provisions and in other cases with the approval of the Central Government.[80]

---

77. *Upper Doab Sugar Mills Ltd* v *Company Law Board*, (1971) 41 Comp Cas 643 Del.
78. *Company Law Board* v *Upper Doab Sugar Mills Ltd*, (1977) 2 SCC 198: (1977) 47 Comp Cas 173.
79. *Mahindra and Mahindra Ltd* v *UOI*, (1983) 53 Comp Cas 337 Del.
80. A managerial person shall also be eligible to the following perquisites which shall not be included in the computation of the ceiling on remuneration specified in paragraph 1 of this section:
    (*a*) contribution to provident fund, superannuation fund or annuity fund to the extent these either singly or put together are not taxable under the Income Tax Act, 1961,
    (*b*) gratuity payable at a rate not exceeding half a month's salary for each completed year of service, and
    (*c*) encashment of leave at the end of the tenure.
    In addition to the perquisites specified in paragraph 2 of this section, an ex patriate managerial person (including a non-resident Indian) shall be eligible to the following perquisites which shall not be included in the computation of the ceiling on remuneration specified in paragraph 1 of this section:
    (*a*) **Children's education allowance.**—In case of children studying in or outside India, an allowance limited to a maximum of Rs 5000 per month per child or actual expenses incurred, whichever is less. Such allowance is admissible upto a maximum of two children.

New Schedule XIII.—All these matters as to remuneration have gone into the limbo of history in view of the complete change-over of Schedule XIII. Now there is no longer any statutory ceiling on remuneration except 5-10 % of the profits. Where because of low profits the remuneration exceeds the above-stated percentage, an amount varying from Rs 75,000 to Rs 2,00,000 per month may be paid depending upon the effective capital of the company. Where it exceeds the link with effective capital, there alone Government approval would be needed. The new Schedule [Part II] was made effective from March 2, 2000.[81]

Where a managerial personnel is working in more than one company, he can draw remuneration from one or both companies provided that the total remuneration drawn from the companies does not exceed the higher maximum limit admissible from any one of the companies of which he is a managerial personnel.

Secretaries and Treasurers

"Secretaries and treasurers" means any firm or company (not being the managing agent) which, subject to the superintendence, control and directions of the board of directors, has the management of the whole, or substantially the whole, of the affairs of a company. The expression includes any firm or company which occupies the position of "secretaries and treasurers".[82]

The Companies (Amendment) Act, 1969, which came into force on April 3, 1970, banned the appointment of secretaries and treasurers.

Manager

A 'manager' means an individual who has the management of the whole or substantially the whole of the affairs of a company. He is subject to the control and superintendence of the company's board.[83]

In *Gibson* v *Barton*,[84] BLACKBURN J defined 'manager' "as a person who has the management of the whole of the affairs of the company; not an agent who is to do a particular thing, or a servant who is to obey orders, but a person who is entrusted with power to transact the whole of the affairs of

---

(b) **Holiday passage for children studying outside India/family staying abroad.**—Return holiday passage once in a year by economy class or once in two years by first class to children and to the members of the family from the place of their study or stay abroad to India if they are not residing in India with the managerial person.

(c) **Leave travel concession.**—Return passage for self and family in accordance with the rules specified by the company where it is proposed that the leave be spent in home country instead of anywhere in India.

81. The company may meet travelling expenses to home on expiry of term, DCA Circular No 9 of July 28, 1993.

82. S. 2(44).

83. S. 2(24).

84. (1875) 10 QB 329.

the company".[85] The word does not apply to a person who acts once or twice in a particular capacity; he must be in charge of all the affairs of the company. Accordingly, the manager of a branch of a bank does not come within the meaning of the word "manager".

A managing director, and a manager have this common feature that they have the management of the whole or substantially the whole of the affairs of the company. Yet there is an important difference between the position of a managing director and that of a manager. A managing director is a part of the company's board of directors and not subordinate to it. He is not a servant of the company.[86] A manager, on the other hand, being a paid executive of the company, is subject to the superintendence, control and directions of the board of directors.

The Act prohibits the appointment of any firm, body corporate or association as manager.[87] Further, following persons are disqualified from appointment:

1. A person who is an undischarged insolvent or who has been adjudged insolvent within the preceding five years.

2. A person who suspends or has within the preceding five years suspended payment to his creditors or makes or has made within the above period a composition with them.

3. A person who has within the preceding five years been convicted by a court in India of an offence involving moral turpitude.[88]

The Central Government, however, reserves the right of removing the above disqualifications either generally or in relation to any company or companies.[89]

A person cannot be appointed as manager if he is a manager or managing director in any other company.[90] However, a person holding such office in only one other company may be appointed, provided the appointment is made or approved by a resolution passed at a meeting of the board with the consent of the directors present at the meeting. Specific notice of the meeting and the resolution should have been given to all the directors then in India.[91] But the Central Government may permit a person to be appointed manager of more than two companies where it is necessary

---

85. Adopted by SHADILAL J (afterwards CJ) in *Basant Lal* v *Emperor*, AIR 1918 Lah 170, 171: 43 IC 791.
86. *Newspaper Proprietary Syndicate Ltd, Re*, [1900] 2 Ch 349: 83 LT 341 and *Ram Pershad* v *CIT*, (1972) 2 SCC 696: (1972) 42 Comp Cas 544.
87. S. 384.
88. S. 385(1).
89. S. 385 (2).
90. S. 386(1).
91. S. 386(2).

that the companies should, for their proper working, function as a single unit and have a common manager.[92]

The remuneration of a manager cannot exceed in the aggregate five per cent of the net profits.[93] In other respects, the same restrictions apply as in the case of a managing director.

The procedure of appointment and requirement of approval are now the same as in the case of managing director.[94] The same is true of any increase in remuneration.[95] He cannot assign his office[96] and can be appointed for a term of five years at a time.[97]

Secretary

Definition

Section 2(45) provides that the expression "secretary" means a company secretary within the meaning of Section 2(1)(c) of the Company Secretaries Act, 1980 and includes any other individual possessing the prescribed qualification and appointed to perform the duties which may be performed by a secretary under this Act and any other ministerial or administrative duties. This transformation of the definition has been brought about by the amendment of 1988 which has also introduced the concept of a "secretary in wholetime practice" and defines it by saying that it means a secretary who shall be deemed to be in practice within the meaning of Section 2(2) of the Company Secretaries Act, 1980 and who is not in full-time employment.

When appointment obligatory and who can be appointed

Section 383-A makes it obligatory for a company having such paid-up share capital as may be prescribed (Rs 50 lakhs)[98] to have a wholetime secretary.[99] The section also provides that where the board of directors of a

---

92. S. 386(4).
93. S. 387.
94. S. 388 which makes Ss. 269, 310, 311, 312 and 317 applicable to a manager.
95. Ss. 310 and 311.
96. S. 312.
97. S. 317.
98. *Substituted* for Rs 50,000 by the Companies (Appointment and Qualifications of Secretary) Amendment Rules, 1993.
99. As to the power of the Institute of Company Secretaries to disqualify a qualified secretary, see *Suraj Prakash Oberoi* v *Institute of Company Secretaries of India*, (1986) 60 Comp Cas 536 Del. It cannot reject an application for membership in a discriminatory manner. *Kalyan Kumar Mukherjee* v *Institute of Company Secretaries of India*, (1987) 62 Comp Cas 466 Cal. Sub-s. (1-A) added by the amendment of 1988 provides that the default in compliance with the provision will make the company and every officer in default punishable with a fine of Rs 500 for everyday. But it will be a defence to show that all reasonable steps to comply with the provision were taken or that the financial position of the company was such that it was beyond its capacity to engage a wholetime secretary. *State of Gujarat* v *Coromandal Investment P Ltd*, (1991) 71 Comp Cas 470 Guj, since a person can discharge the duties of a secretary without joining the company as an employee, hence, there is no violation if he is an employee of some other company.

company has only two members, neither of them shall be the secretary of the company. A proviso to sub-section (1) has been inserted by the Companies Amendment Act, 2000 to require the filing of a certificate of compliance. It is as follows:

"Provided that every company not required to employ a wholetime secretary under sub-section (1) and having a paid-up share capital of ten lakh rupees or more shall file with the Registrar a certificate from a secretary in wholetime practice in such form and within such time and subject to such conditions as may be prescribed, as to whether the company has complied with all the provisions of this Act and a copy of such certificate shall be attached with Board's report referred to in Section 217."

No firm or body corporate can hold the office of a secretary, and no individual can be a secretary in more than one company at the same time.

Elevation of status of Secretary: Authority for contracts

The fact that duties of administrative nature can also be assigned to a secretary is a legislative recognition of the fact that the secretary has become an important executive officer of the company.[1] The courts have not lagged behind in this respect. The English Court of Appeal in its decision in *Panorama Development (Guildford)* v *Fidelis Furnishing Fabrics*[2] has

---

1. The appointment should be by a resolution of the board of directors and removal can also be by the appointing authority. The commencement and cessation of office should be reflected in the register of directors required to be maintained under S. 303.
2. [1971] 3 WLR 440: [1971] 3 All ER 16: (1971) 2 QB 711 CA. In India rules as to qualifications and appointments of secretaries have been promulgated by the Companies (Appointment and Qualifications of Secretary) Rules, 1988. A company with a paid-up share capital of not less than Rs 50 lakhs is required to have a wholetime secretary. Members of the Institute of Company Secretaries of India can be appointed as wholetime secretaries. Companies with a capital of less than Rs 50 lakhs can appoint any other person as their secretary, but he too must be qualified under the Act. Rule 4 prescribes the qualifications. It says that no individual is qualified unless he possesses any one or more of the following qualifications:
   1. Membership of the Institute of Company Secretaries.
   2. Pass in the intermediate examination of the Institute and licenced under S. 25 of the Company Secretaries Act, 1980.
   3. Postgraduate degree in commerce or corporate secretaryship granted by any University in India.
   4. Degree in Law granted by any University.
   5. Membership of the Institute of Chartered Accountants.
   6. Membership of the Institute of the Cost & Works Accountants of India constituted under the Act of 1959.
   7. Postgraduate degree or diploma in managerial science granted by any University, or the Institutes of Management, Ahmedabad, Calcutta, Banglore or Lucknow.
   8. Postgraduate diploma in company secretaryship granted by the Institute of Commercial Practice under the Delhi Administration or Diploma in Corporate Laws and Management granted by the Indian Law Institute, New Delhi.
   9. Postgraduate diploma in Company Law and secretarial practice granted by the University of Udaipur.
   10. Membership of the Association of Secretaries and Managers, Calcutta.
   When a company's capital reaches the mark of Rs 50 lakhs, within one year it should appoint a qualified secretary. Published in (1989) 65 Comp Cas 243 st.

declared that a modern secretary is not a mere clerk but an officer of the company with executive duties and responsibilities. He has authority to sign contracts connected with the administrative side of a company's affairs and has ostensible authority to enter into a wide range of contracts. In this respect his position has altered very materially since the previous century. The facts of the case were:

> The plaintiff ran a car-on-hire business. The defendant company's secretary hired cars from the plaintiff ostensibly for the company's business, telling him that the cars were wanted to carry important customers of the company. He wrote on the company's paper ordering the cars, signing himself "Company Secretary". In fact, he used the cars himself and not for the company's purposes.

It was held that the secretary had ostensible authority to enter into contracts for hiring cars for which the company must pay. Lord DENNING MR had to face arguments based on previous decisions. In one of them it was stated that "a company secretary fulfils a very humble role; and that he has no authority to make any contracts or representations on behalf of the company".[3] A statement from a case of 1887 was also cited.[4] "A secretary is a mere servant; his position is that he is to do what he is told, and no person can assume that he has any authority to represent anything at all..." Replying to these arguments, his Lordship said:[5]

> But times have changed. A company secretary is a much more important person nowadays than he was in 1887. He is an officer of the company with extensive duties and responsibilities. This appears not only in the modern Companies Act, but also by the role which he plays in the day-to-day business of companies. He is no longer a mere clerk. He regularly makes representations on behalf of the company and enters into contracts on its behalf which come within the day-to-day running of the company's business. So much so that he may be regarded as held out as having authority to do many things on behalf of the company. He is certainly entitled to sign contracts connected with the administrative side of a company's affairs, such as employing staff, and ordering cars, and so forth. All such matters now come within the ostensible authority of a company's secretary.

SALMON LJ was equally sure of this development in the position of the secretary:

> Whatever the position of company's secretary may have been in 1887, I am quite satisfied that it has altered a great deal from what it was then. At the end of the last century a company secretary still

---

3. Citing Lord MACNAGHTEN in *George Whitechurch Ltd* v *Cavanagh*, 1902 AC 117 at p 124.
4. *Barnett, Hoares & Co* v *South London Tramways Co*, (1887) 18 QBD 815 at p 817: 1902 AC 117. These decisions were supported in *Ruben* v *Great Fingall Consolidated*, 1906 AC 439.
5. [1971] 2 QB 711 at p 716.

occupied a very humble position very little higher, if any, than that of a minor clerk. Today, not only has the status of a company secretary been much enhanced, but the state of affairs has been recognised by the statutes.... I think there can be no doubt that the secretary is the chief administrative officer of the company. As regards matters concerned with administration, the secretary has ostensible authority to sign contracts on behalf of the company. If a company is ordering cars so that its servants may go and meet foreign customers at airports, nothing is more natural than that the company should hire those cars through its secretary. The hiring is part of his administrative function. Whether the secretary would have any authority to sign a contract relating to the commercial management of the company, for example, a contract for the sale or purchase of goods in which the company deals, does not arise for decision in the present case, but contracts such as the present fall within the ambit of administration.

Liability of Company for Secretary's Acts

A company was not held liable for the conduct of the secretary in trapping persons for taking shares in the company[6] and for issuing a forged share certificate.[7] But he is the proper authority for delivery of the certificates which have been properly prepared.[8] The confirmation of a contract by the secretary, which was made by an unauthorised director, was held to be of no effect.[9] He cannot borrow money on behalf of the company. Thus, where a director advanced a sum of money to the company on the request of the secretary, the company was held not liable. Though the transaction was confirmed at a meeting of the board, that meeting was incompetent, there being no quorum when the interested director was not counted.[10] He has no authority for legal proceedings without instructions from responsible organs.[11] Similarly, without proper authority he cannot call meetings, or register transfer of shares[12] or remove any shareholder's name from the register.[13]

---

6. *Barnett, Hoares & Co* v *South London Tramways Co*, (1887) 18 QBD 815: 1902 AC 117.
7. *Ibid.*
8. *Clavering Son & Co* v *Goodwins, Jardine & Co*, 18 R 652.
9. *Houghton & Co* v *Nothard, Lowe & Wills Ltd*, [1927] 1 KB 246: 1928 AC 1: (1927) All ER Rep 97.
10. *Cleadon Trust Ltd, Re*, [1939] Ch 286 CA.
11. *Daimler Co Ltd* v *Continental Tyre & Rubber Co Ltd*, [1916] 2 AC 307; *Edington* v *Dumbar Steam Laundry Co*, (1903) 11 SLT 117 OH, Scotland.
12. *Zinotty Properties Ltd, Re*, [1984] 3 All ER 754: [1984] 1 WLR 1249, where it was held that the act of a company's secretary in transferring the shares of the company personally to one *C* was not effective to make *C* a registered member because the secretary cannot act without the authority of the board of directors which at that time had ceased to exist because of the company's failure to hold successive general meetings.
13. *State of Wyoming Syndicate, Re*, [1901] 2 Ch 431; *Indo-China Steam Navigation Co, Re*, [1917] 2 Ch 100 and *Chida Mines Ltd* v *Anderson*, (1905) 22 TLR 27.

Secretary is included in the list of officers as given in Section 2(30). Thus, he is an officer for all the purposes of the Act and suffers from the same disabilities as do the directors. The provisions relating to loans to directors, contracts with directors, register of directors, etc., will apply. In a case where the board of directors delegated to the managing director their power of appointing and removing all officers, and a question arose whether the secretary of the company, being an "officer" would fall within the spell of the above-mentioned power of removal. The Punjab and Haryana High Court held that this could not be so, for, otherwise, even directors being "officers", would be removable by the managing director. The court felt fortified in its view by the opening words of Section 2 which constitute a preamble to all the definitions, which are: "unless the context otherwise requires", and when the power of removal of officers is handed over to the managing director, the context requires that the "secretary" should be excluded from the scope of the word "officer" for this purpose.[14]

On the footing of an officer, the secretary would be accountable for any secret profit he might derive from his office. To the extent to which his position or authority permits him to deal with the company's money, property or transactions, he would also be regarded as a constructive trustee of the company in those respects.[15] A secretary was held to be personally not liable for misapplication of the company's funds by someone else though he might have known about it. A director might have become liable in a parallel situation.[16] There has also been a judicial observation to the effect that a company secretary owes no fiduciary duty to the company.[17]

Administrative officer

The Calcutta High Court[18] has held that the amendment of 1974 which has elevated the position of the secretary to that of an administrative officer,

---

14. *Haryana Seeds Development Corpn Ltd* v *J. K. Agarwal*, (1989) 65 Comp Cas 95 P&H.
15. See *McKay* case, [1875] 2 Ch D 1, where the view expressed was that when the secretary wrongfully acquired company property, he did so in his capacity as an officer of the company. However, he would now be described as a constructive trustee. For an indication of the modern view of the fiduciary position of the secretary, see *New Zealand Netherlands Society "Oranje" Inc* v *Kays*, [1973] 2 All ER 1222. For other cases, see *Stapleford Colliery Co, Barrow* case, *Re*, (1880) 14 Ch D 432 CA, liability to account for improper commission in the company's transactions, *Morvah Consols Tin Mining Co Ltd, Re*, (1875) 2 Ch D 1: [1874-80] All ER Rep Ext 2212; *Mckay* case, (1875) 2 Ch D 1 AC; *Gulabdas Bhaidas, Re*, (1892) ILR 17 Bom 672.
16. *Joint Stock Discount Co* v *Brown*, (1869) 8 Eq 381, 396.
17. *Brown* v *Bennet*, (1998) 2 BCLC 97 at 106-107 Ch D.
18. *Mohan Lal Mittal* v *Universal Works Ltd*, (1983) 53 Comp Cas 36 Cal. The secretary commenced a proceeding under Ss. 397 and 398. But see *N. Ramachandran* v *Cardamo Marketing Co (Travancore) Ltd*, (1990) 69 Comp Cas 205 Ker, where the secretary who was managing the affairs of the company was held to be competent to verify the plaint of the company because he was acquainted with the facts and it was immaterial that his appointment was still not approved.

has not altered the basic position of the secretary to such an extent as to enable him to undertake serious litigation on behalf of the company without a decision of the company's board. The court cited the following passage from HALSBURY'S LAWS OF ENGLAND:

> He (the secretary) has no power, without the resolution of the directors, to call a meeting of the company or to commence proceedings on behalf of the company, nor can he alter the register of members, but any such act may be ratified by the directors.[19]

After citing more extensively from HALSBURY'S LAWS OF ENGLAND[20] the court suggested:

> From the above summary it is quite clear that the secretary cannot usurp the functions and powers of the board or the company, but due to the enormous growth of company activities he has been empowered to discharge various ministerial and administrative duties on behalf of the company which generally can be performed by an authorised agent. In due course of time the secretary has been given certain statutory powers, like signing the annual returns, etc. But under no circumstances can he discharge the functions of the board or act on behalf of the company in matters of policy or substantive steps which is not administrative or ministerial in nature.

The court cited the following statements from a decision of the Supreme Court:

> Ordinarily the functions of the secretary of the corporation would be ministerial and administrative. As a secretary only, he would have no authority to bind the corporation by entering into contracts or other commitments on its behalf.[21]

Officer who is in default [S. 5]

The word "officer" has been defined to "include any director, manager, or secretary or any person in accordance with whose directions or instructions the Board of directors or any one or more of the directors is or are accustomed to act."[22]

There are many penal provisions in the Act. Almost all of them provide for punishment by way of fine or imprisonment of directors or other principal officers of the company.[23] It is common with companies to grant

---

19. Paras 546-47 (Vol VII, 4th Edn).
20. Paras 546-47 (Vol VII, 4th Edn).
21. *Lakshmiratan Cotton Mills Ltd* v *Aluminium Corpn of India Ltd*, (1971) 1 SCC 67: AIR 1971 SC 1482.
22. As introduced by the Amendment Act, 2000, S. 2(30).
23. S. 2(30) says that the term "officer" includes any director, manager or secretary or any other person in accordance with whose directions or instructions, the board of directors or any one or more of the directors is or are accustomed to act. A person who gives such instructions or directions is called a "shadow director". Section 7 tries to find out the identity of such person.

positions merely for ceremonial purposes. Such persons may not be much concerned with the affairs of the company and, therefore, may not deserve to be punished. In order to ascertain those who really deserve to be punished, the Companies Acts have all along for all serious defaults used the expression "the officer who is in default". In actual practice, however, it was very difficult to find out who was in charge of a particular affair of a company in respect of which a default had been registered so as to hold him liable as an officer in default. Many cases failed for this reason. Section 5, as redrafted by the amendment of 1988, is an attempt to meet this problem.[24] The provision is as follows:

S. 5. Meaning of "officer who is in default".—For the purpose of any provision in this Act which enacts that an officer of the company who is in default shall be liable to any punishment or penalty, whether by way of imprisonment, fine or otherwise the expression "officer who is in default" means all the following officers of the company, namely:

(*a*)   the managing director or managing directors;

(*b*)   the wholetime director or wholetime directors;

(*c*)   the manager;

(*d*)   the secretary;

(*e*)   any person in accordance with whose directions or instructions the Board of directors of the company is accustomed to act;

(*f*)   any person charged by the Board with the responsibility of complying with that provision:

Provided that the person so charged has given his consent in this behalf to the Board;

(*g*)   where any company does not have any of the officers specified in clauses (*a*) to (*c*), any director or directors who may be specified by the Board in this behalf or where no director is so specified, all the directors:

Provided that where the Board exercises any power under clause (*f*) or clause (*g*), it shall, within thirty days of the exercise of such powers, file with the Registrar a return in the prescribed form.

The effect of the new provision is that professional managers, like managing directors, managers, wholetime directors or secretaries, will be regarded as officers in default without any further inquiry.[25] This category will also include those in accordance with whose directions or instructions

It says that except where the Act expressly provides otherwise, a person shall not be deemed to be, within the meaning of the Act, a person in accordance with whose directions or instructions the board of directors of a company is accustomed to act, by reason only that the board acts on advice given by him in a professional capacity. Where a company was in the position of being a shadow director in another company, it was held that by that reason alone its directors would not be regarded as the shadow directors of the other company, *Secy of State for Trade and Industry* v *Laing*, (1996) 2 BCLC 324 CA. In *Kaytech International plc*, (1999) 2 BCLC 351 CA, the Court of Appeal observed that all the factors in the definition would have to be considered. The individual concerned must have assumed the status and functions of a director so as to have openly exercised real influence on the corporate governance of the company. In this case the individual was acting as a director in the camouflage of a secretary.

24. The new provision has been enforced w.e.f. 15-1-1988, GSR 782(E), dated 13-7-1988.

25. *Ravindra Narain* v *ROC*, (1994) 81 Comp Cas 925 Raj, other directors could be prosecuted only when there was no managing director, wholetime director or manager.

the board of directors is accustomed to act. For the rest it would have to be shown that they were under responsibility.[26] The board can specify who would be responsible for the observance of particular provisions. The consent of such a person should be taken and it should be filed with the Registrar within 30 days in the prescribed form.[27] Such a person would then be held liable for the default in question without any further inquiry. Where there is no professional manager like managing or wholetime director or manager and the board has not designated any person in the above manner, then all the directors will be held as officers in default.[28]

A director was not allowed to be prosecuted for violation of the provisions (S. 370) relating to inter-corporate loans committed during the period before he joined as a director.[29] A director was not allowed to be prosecuted for copyright violations where he had resigned before the

---

26. *R. Dhandayyuthapani* v *C.R. Kaleel*, (2004) 118 Comp Cas 167 Mad no liability for default in respect of EPF contribution, the director had resigned before the default and even otherwise he was not under any responsibility for company's affairs. *Visa Television Network Ltd* v *Gemini Television (P) Ltd*, (2005) 125 Comp Cas 815 AP, it was necessary that there should be specific unambiguous allegation against the director sought to be made liable for violation of copyright by the company as to the role played by him. *Krishan Kumar Bangur* v *Director General of Foreign Trade*, (2006) 133 Comp Cas 83 Del, director not liable unless the Authority shares how and to what extent a particular person is liable under the company's arrangement. *Sabitha Ramamurthy* v *RBS Channabasavaradhya*, (2006) 133 Comp Cas 680 SC, no liability for dishonour of the company's cheque where it could not be shown that the director who was being prosecuted was incharge of the company's affairs. *SMS Pharmaceuticals Ltd* v *Neeta Bhalla*, (2007) 136 Comp Cas 268 SC, requirements of the NI Act for liability of director must be proved. *Lachhman P. Uolhani* v *Redington (India) Ltd*, (2006) 133 Comp Cas 855 Mad, Form 32 filed in the office of ROC showed that the director sought to be prosecuted had resigned before the cheque was issued.
27. Form 1-AA has been prescribed for the purpose.
28. It has been laid down in an Australian case that on a complaint against a director of a company for knowingly and wilfully permitting the company to commit a breach of [a provision of the Companies Act] the prosecution must prove beyond reasonable doubt that the director knew of the acts constituting the breach and in the free exercise of his will authorised or permitted them to be carried out. It is not necessary for the prosecution to prove that the directors knew that the acts were unlawful. *Mcl* v *Flavel*, (1986) 45 South Australian States Reports (SASR) 69 SC. Officers who have not been designated can be prosecuted only by showing their connection with management and default on their part. *R. Banerjee* v *H.D. Dubey*, (1992) 2 SCC 552: (1992) 75 Comp Cas 722 SC. It must be alleged in the complaint that the director proceeded against was a director at the material time and knew of the default, *Registrar of Companies* v *Bipini Behari Nayak*, (1995) 83 Comp Cas 95 Ori. A prosecution under the Insecticide Act, 1968 against a company secretary was not allowed to proceed because there was no allegation that the default was due to his neglect, or consent or connivance, *B.B. Nagpal* v *State of Haryana*, (1995) 83 Comp Cas 596 P&H. Where show-cause notice was not given to the director sought to be prosecuted, the proceeding was quashed, *Sivandhi Adityam* v *Addl ROC*, (1995) 83 Comp Cas 616 Mad. *Rajiv Gupta* v *State*, (2001) 104 Comp Cas 26 Del, a company and its directors could not escape from penal liability under S. 138 of the Negotiable Instruments Act, 1881 on the ground that winding up petition had been presented and was pending at the material time. *Orient Syntex Ltd* v *Besant Capital Tech Ltd*, (2001) 104 Comp Cas 669 Bom, dishonour of a cheque issued for repayment of loan made the directors *prima facie* liable because borrowing is their exclusive domain under S. 292. *M.P. Singh* v *State of Punjab*, (2006) 133 Comp Cas 17 P&H, no liability for defective fertiliser of a director not shown to be incharge.
29. *Siva Prasad* v *Registrar of Companies*, (1997) 88 Comp Cas 420 AP.

violation. Form 32 in the ROC's records showed resignation much before the offence.[30]

A company is a person within the meaning of Section 2(1)(*m*) and Section 27 of the Consumer Protection Act, 1986. The company is liable to be punished for dishonouring the decree of a consumer forum. A director of the company who was responsible for causing the disobedience was also liable to be prosecuted.[31]

Company's liability for officer's crimes

A question arose before the Supreme Court[32] as to whether a company can be prosecuted for an offence which carries compulsory corporal punishment like imprisonment. It was contended on the basis of earlier authorities[33] that there could be no such prosecution. The Supreme Court doubted whether that was the effect of the decision and, therefore, the matter was referred to the Constitution Bench. The decision of the Constitution Bench is reported in *ANZ Grindlays Bank Ltd* v *Directorate of Enforcement*[34] The Bench has been of the view that there is no immunity to companies merely because the offence entails mandatory imprisonment. The court can impose the sentence and ignore the corporal punishment.[35]

Sole selling agents [S. 294]

Definition

The expression "sole selling agent" is not defined in the Act. The definition of "agent" as given in Section 182 of the Contract Act should, therefore, apply.[36] When a company gives a person the exclusive right to sell its goods in a particular area, he is called a "sole selling agent". He alone is given the selling right in respect of the goods. Thus, for example, in *Shalagram Jhajharia* v *National Co*:[37]

> A company appointed a "Corporation as its exclusive distributors in USA, its possessions, Canada and Mexico for sale of jute packing cloth..."

30. *Jayanthilal M. Munoth* v *M. Durairajan*, (2006) 132 Comp Cas 797 Mad.
31. *Ravi Kant* v *Consumer Disputes Redressal Commission*, (1997) 89 Comp Cas 471: [1997] 3 Comp LJ 174 Del.
32. *ANZ Grindlays Bank Ltd* v *Directorate of Enforcement*, (2005) 123 Comp Cas 1 SC: (2005) 4 Comp LJ 464 SC.
33. *Asstt Commr* v *Vellappa Textiles Ltd*, (2003) 203 ITR 550 (SC), Reference was also made to *Balram Kumawat* v *Union of India*, (2003) 7 SCC 728.
34. (2005) 4 Comp LJ 464 SC.
35. To the same effect, *Fidelity Industries Ltd* v *State*, (2006) 129 Comp Cas 561 Mad.
36. According to that section an "agent means a person employed to do any act for another or to represent another in dealings with third parties". See *Shalagram Jhajharia* v *National Co*, [1965] 1 Comp LJ 112 at 118 Cal.
37. [1965] 1 Comp LJ 112 Cal.

The Calcutta High Court held the corporation to be a sole selling agent and it made no difference that a subsequent clause in the contract described the corporation as "a buyer on principal to principal basis". "The relationship is to be determined not by name but conduct of the parties and the purport of their dealings."[38] Thus a "sole selling agent" has to be distinguished from "a buyer with the sole right to sell the goods of a particular manufacturer".[39]

Appointment and Terms

Section 294 regulates the appointment and terms of a sole selling agency. The appointment may be made by the board, but it must be "subject to the condition that it shall cease to be valid if it is not approved by the company in the first general meeting" held after the date of appointment.[40] If this condition is not expressly mentioned in an appointment made by the board, the appointment is invalid *ab initio*. "The provision is mandatory, not merely directory."[41] Further if approval is not obtained at the first general meeting held after the appointment, or if it is disapproved there, it ceases to be valid from the date of the meeting.[42] When the appointment has become invalid, it is to be regarded as dead and cannot be resuscitated or revived by ratification at a subsequent meeting.[43]

The appointment can be made for a period of five years only at a time, but the term may be extended from time to time for five years on each occasion.[44]

A managing agent who has ceased to hold his office cannot be appointed as sole selling agent for a period of three years from the date of the termination of the managing agency. Such appointment may, however, be made with the approval of the Central Government.[45]

Investigation of Terms

The Central Government may for some good reason require a company to furnish to it certain information regarding the terms and conditions of the appointment.[46] The purpose is to enable the Central Government to determine whether or not the terms and conditions are prejudicial to the interest of the company. If the company refuses or neglects to furnish the

---

38. [1965] 1 Comp LJ 112 Cal.
39. *See*, for example, *W.T. Lamb & Sons* v *Goring Brick Co*, [1932] 1 KB 710; *Hope Prudhomme & Co* v *Hamel & Horley*, ILR (1925) 49 Mad 1: AIR 1925 PC 161: 88 IC 307.
40. S. 294(2).
41. *Arantee Manufacturing Corpn* v *Bright Bolts Ltd*, [1967] 2 Comp LJ 54: (1967) 37 Comp Cas 758 Cal. The object of the provisions is to protect the interests of the company and to prevent unnecessary expenditure. *Ramesh B. Desai* v *UOI*, AIR 1988 Del 288; *A.V. Kasargod* v *ROC*, (2001) 105 Comp Cas 676 Kant, the condition of approval in the first meeting is mandatory.
42. S. 294(2-A).
43. *Shalagram Jhajharia* v *National Co*, [1965] 1 Comp LJ 112 Cal, BOSE CJ at p 123.
44. S. 294(1) and the proviso.
45. S. 294(4)
46. S. 294(5).

information, the Central Government may appoint a suitable person to investigate and report on the terms and conditions of the appointment. If the terms are found to be prejudicial to the interests of the company, the Central Government may, by order modify them so as to make them harmless to the company. In *Firestone Tyre & Rubber Co* v *Synthetics & Chemicals Ltd*[47] a company manufacturing a commodity of which there was an acute shortage could not pay dividends for five years owing to lack of profits, but during the same period the sole selling agents had drawn a commission of over 84 lakh rupees. The Company Law Board accordingly advised the company that the terms were detrimental to the interest of the company and the commission should be reduced.

The constitutional validity of this power was brought in question before the Bombay High Court in *Nanavati & Co P Ltd* v *R.C. Dutt*.[48] On the application of some of the shareholders of a company, the Central Government demanded information as to the terms and conditions on which the company appointed its sole selling agents. The Central Government found the terms to be prejudicial to the interest of the company and, therefore, in the exercise of its powers[49] the Government modified the terms as follows:

(*i*)   the rebate of 5% payable to the agents was reduced to 3-1/2%,

(*ii*)   the term with regard to 60 days' credit was altered, and

(*iii*)   the provision for rebate on direct sales effected by the company was taken away.

The allegations were that the power was violative of Article 14 of the Constitution as it could be exercised in the case of a particular company, while in many other companies sole selling agents were allowed to work on similar conditions and that the Company Law Board had not adopted any definite policy in selecting companies for varying sole selling agency agreements and finally that the power to vary does not include the power to abrogate. The court rejected all these contentions and held that the power was valid and validly exercised. TULZAPURKAR J explained the effect of the provision in the following words:

It is no doubt true that under clause (*a*) of Section 294(5) it is for the Central Government to decide whether there is a good reason to call for information or not and it is also true that under clause (*c*) it is for the Central Government to form its opinion on the point as to whether the terms and conditions of the appointment of a sole selling agent are prejudicial to the interest of the company or not, but that does not mean that it is open to the Central Government to pick and choose any company it likes at random. The discretion to select is undoubtedly with

---

47. [1970] 2 Comp LJ 200: (1971) 41 Comp Cas 337 Bom.
48. (1967) 37 Comp Cas 171 Bom.
49. Under S. 294(5) read with Government of India Notification dated February 1, 1964.

the Central Government, but the section itself lays down a policy or principle for the guidance of the exercise of such discretion... and that guiding principle is that the terms and conditions of appointment... (are) prejudicial to the interests of the company.[50]

Referring to the contention that the Central Government had completely thrown out one of the terms of the agreement, whereas it had power only to "vary" them, the learned Judge said:

> It appears that the ordinary dictionary meanings of the expressions 'variation' and 'vary' have been given a go-bye and artificial definitions have been introduced by Section 2(50) so as to include the concept of 'abrogation' within the expression 'variation'.

The matter then came before a Bench of the High Court.[51] The Bench upheld the constitutional validity of the provision, but quashed the order of the Government on other points. Though the power of the Company Law Board is of administrative nature, the principle of natural justice should be followed. As the sole selling agents were not given any notice to show cause, the order was bad. The power to vary the terms no doubt includes the power to abrogate them but abrogation of the contract itself would be a different thing. To convert a sole selling agent into an ordinary agent is not a mere variation of a term, but substitution of one kind of contract for another. This is beyond the powers of the Government.

Where a company has more than one selling agent in any area or areas, the Central Government may require similar information, this time for the purpose of determining whether any one of them should be declared as the sole selling agent for any area.[52]

When a person is appointed to investigate the terms and conditions of an appointment, it is the duty of the company and its officers to produce before him relevant books and papers and to give him all assistance in connection with the investigation.[53]

Compensation for loss of office [S. 294-A]

According to Section 294-A "a company shall not pay or be liable to pay to its sole selling agent any compensation for the loss of his office in the following cases":

1. Where the appointment ceases to be valid because it is disapproved of by the company in general meeting.

2. Where he resigns his office in view of the reconstruction or amalgamation of the company and is appointed as the sole selling

---

50. (1967) 37 Comp Cas 171 at 184 Bom.
51. *Nanavati & Co P Ltd* v *R.C. Dutt*, (1975) 45 Comp Cas 91 Bom.
52. S. 294(6).
53. S. 294(7). The company and every officer in default is punishable with fine

agent of the company resulting from the reconstruction or amalgamation.

3. Where he voluntarily resigns his office.

4. Where he has been guilty of fraud or breach of trust or gross negligence in the conduct of his duty as the sole selling agent.

5. Where he has instigated or taken part in bringing about the termination of the agency.

In other cases compensation for loss of office may be paid.

The amount of compensation shall not exceed the remuneration which he would have earned for the unexpired residue of his term, or for three years, whichever is shorter. The amount should be calculated on the basis of the average remuneration actually earned during a period of three years immediately before the termination, or where he held his office for a period lesser than three years, during such period.

The Companies (Amendment) Act, 1974 introduced the following changes.

Where the product of a company has a ready market, sole selling agents become redundant and in order to dispense with them Section 294-AA has been introduced. The section provides that where the Central Government is of the opinion that the demand for goods or services of a certain category is substantially in excess of production and supply and, therefore, the services of sole selling agents are not necessary for creating a market, the Government may by notification in the Official Gazette declare that sole selling agents shall not be appointed in such cases.[54]

A person, firm or company who or which has substantial interest in the company, should not be appointed as sole selling agents except with the previous approval of the Central Government.[55] A company having paid-up share capital of fifty lakh rupees or more can appoint a sole selling agent only with the consent of the company by a special resolution and the approval of the Central Government.[56]

The provisions of sub-sections (5), (6) and (7) of Section 294 (which deal with investigation and modification of terms), have been made applicable to the sole purchasing or buying agents of a company also.[57] The

---

54. S. 294-AA(1).The Central Government under this section can examine the question whether the notice was according to law and whether the shareholders had accorded their consent. It is not a forum for challenging the validity of the meetings or the resolutions passed thereat. That should be done by separate proceedings. *Ramesh B. Desai* v *UOI*, AIR 1988 Del 303; (1990) 69 Comp Cas 33. It is not a judicial function, but just only administrative function of approval. The Government should follow the guidelines issued by it but is free to change those guidelines. Courts do not generally interfere in writ proceedings in executive decisions relating to economic matters.

55. *Id.* (2).

56. *Id.* (3).

57. *Id.* (4).

provisions of Section 294-AA(2), (3) and (8) have been extended to a sole agent for the purchasing and buying of goods on behalf of the company.

Where a company has already made an appointment before the commencement of the Amendment Act, but the appointment is such that if the amendment had been in force it would have required approval of the Central Government, such approval should be obtained within six months, otherwise the appointment shall stand terminated at the expiry of six months [Section 294-AA(6)].

Meaning of "substantial interest"

The Explanation appended to Section 294-AA explains the meaning of substantial interest:

1. In relation to an individual, it means the beneficial interest held by such individual or any of his relatives whether singly or taken together, in the shares of the company.

2. In relation to a firm, it means the beneficial interest held by one or more partners of the firm or any relative of such partner, whether singly or taken together, in the shares of the company.

3. In relation to any body corporate, it means the beneficial interest held by such body corporate or one or more of its directors or any relative of such a director, whether singly or taken together, in the share capital of the company, the aggregate paid-up amount on which exceeds five lakh rupees. or 5% of the paid-up share capital of the company, whichever is less.

Managing agents

The managing agency system was abolished by the Companies (Amendment) Act, 1969.

Company as an undisclosed principal [S. 416]

Whenever an authorised functionary of a company makes a contract on behalf of the company by keeping the company a secret or undisclosed principal, he has to make a memorandum of the contract in writing showing the terms and the parties with whom the contract is made. He should file the memorandum with the company and send a copy of it to each of its directors. The company should lay a copy of the memorandum before the board of directors at its next meeting. If these formalities are not complied with, the contract becomes voidable at the option of the company. The defaulting officers can be punished with fine extending up to Rs 200.

———

11
Meetings

Statutory meeting [S. 165]

The first meeting of the shareholders of a public company is known as the statutory meeting. It has to be called within six months from the date on which the company is entitled to commence business, but it cannot be held within one month from that date, as the requirement of Section 165 is that the meeting should be held "within a period not less than one month or more than six months from the date at which the company is entitled to commence business". In Palmer's COMPANY LAW the importance of statutory meeting is thus explained:[1]

> The obvious purpose of a statutory meeting with its preliminary report is to put the shareholders of the company in possession of all the important facts relating to the new company, what shares have been taken up, what money received, what contracts entered into, what sums spent on preliminary expenses, etc. Furnished with these particulars the shareholders are to have an opportunity of meeting and discussing the whole situation, the management, methods and prospects of the company.

Members are given the liberty to discuss any matter relating to the formation of the company or arising out of the statutory report.[2]

Statutory Report [S. 165(2)]

The shareholders cannot make the best use of this opportunity unless they have the fullest information on important matters. The directors are, therefore, required to prepare and to send to every shareholder a document known as the "statutory report".

This report must be sent to the members at least twenty-one days before the day on which the meeting is to be held.[3] The report should be certified as correct by at least two directors, one of whom should be managing director, if there is any, and must also be certified by the auditors.[4] The report must set out the following particulars:

1. The total number of shares allotted, giving details whether they are fully or partly paid-up and what consideration has been received.

---

1. Pp 455-456, 20th Edn.
2. S. 165(7).
3. *Ibid.* A proviso declares that if the report is not sent within the time so required, it may be condoned by all the members entitled to attend and vote.
4. S. 165(4).

2. The total amount of cash received in respect of all shares allotted.

3. An abstract of receipts, distinctly setting out the sources, and payments made out of that, balance remaining in hand, estimate of preliminary expenses, commission or discount paid or to be paid on issue of shares.

4. Names, addresses and occupations of the directors, manager and secretary and the changes, if any, that have occurred since the date of incorporation.

5. Particulars of any contract to be submitted to the meeting for approval and modifications done or proposed, if any.

6. If the company has entered into underwriting contracts, the extent, if any, to which they have not been carried out and the reasons for the failure.

7. The arrears, if any, due on calls from every director and manager.

8. Particulars of any commission or brokerage paid or agreed to be paid in connection with the issue or sale of shares or debentures to any director or to the manager.

A copy of the above report should be sent to the Registrar also.[5] If any default is made in filing the statutory report or in holding the statutory meeting, those in default are liable to a fine.[6] The delay in sending the statutory report to the shareholders can, however, be condoned by a unanimous vote of the members present at the meeting. Another consequence of not holding the statutory meeting on time is that the court can under Section 433(*b*) order the compulsory winding up of the company.

Annual general meeting [S. 166]

Every company is required to call at least one meeting of its shareholders each year. This meeting is known as the annual general meeting. The first annual general meeting of a company must be held within eighteen months from the date of its incorporation, and then no meeting will be necessary for the year of incorporation and the following year.[7] Thereafter one annual general meeting must be held every year. The gap between one meeting and the next should not be of more than fifteen months. There is no provision in the Act for deferment of the first AGM.[8]

---

5. S. 165(5).
6. S. 165(9). Every director or other officer of the company who is in default is punishable with fine extending upto Rs 5000.
7. An illustration will make this clear. Suppose that a company is incorporated in Jan 1960, its first annual general meeting should be held within eighteen months, that is, up to June 1961 and then no other meeting will be necessary either for 1960 or 1961.
8. *T. V. Mathew* v *Nadukara Agro Processing Co Ltd*, (2002) 108 Comp Cas 130 Ker. A failure in this respect would invite consequences under the Act.

If a company fails to hold this meeting two consequences will follow. Firstly, any member can apply to the CLB and the latter will order the calling of the meeting. An application can be made by any member under Section 167 of the Act.[9] The CLB can give any ancillary or consequential directions which it thinks expedient in relation to the calling and conducting of the meeting. A meeting held in pursuance of this order will be deemed an annual general meeting of the company.[10] The CLB ordered a meeting to be called for carrying out non-controversial annual routine business and call an extraordinary general meeting, if necessary, for facing the controversial matters.[11]

This power has been vested exclusively in the CLB. The court cannot exercise it even under its inherent powers.[12]

Secondly, the failure to call this meeting either generally or in pursuance of the order of the CLB is an offence punishable with fine.[13] The penalty is imposed upon the company as well as every officer "who is in default". Thus, for example, in *Sree Meenakshi Mills Co Ltd* v *Asstt Registrar of Joint Stock Companies*:[14]

> A company was prosecuted for failure to call an annual general meeting. One general meeting was called in December, 1934. This was adjourned to March, 1935 and then held. Subsequent meeting was held in February, 1936. The prosecution was for not holding a meeting in 1935. It

---

9. "It is clear that a member and not the company is competent to invoke the provisions of S. 167. A company cannot seek directions against itself." *Cannanore Whole Body CT Scan & Research Centre (P) Ltd* v *Saibunnisa S .V.*, (1998) 93 Comp Cas 99.

10. S. 167(2). See *Anuradha Mukherjee* v *Incab Industries Ltd*, [1996] 4 Comp LJ 482 CLB, where a meeting was ordered to be held for each of the gap years. *Mukesh Sood* v *Incab Industries Ltd*, (1996) 23 Corpt LA 178 CLB, meeting ordered to be held with nominee of the financial institution to preside. *M. V. Paulose* v *City Hospital (P) Ltd*, (1998) 28 Corpt LA 46 CLB, the order of CLB for holding an AGM had to be kept in abeyance because a dispute about a substantial block of shares was pending before the High Court. The Company Law Board cannot review its own orders. *National Textile Corpn (UP) Ltd* v *Swadeshi Polytex Ltd*, (1998) 28 Corpt LA 238 CLB, default in holding AGM is a condition precedent; no incidental order issued about any person to preside after ordering a meeting.

11. *Taihan Electric Wire Co* v *TDP Copper Ltd*, (1998) 29 Corpt LA 126 CLB: [1998] 2 Comp LJ 351: (1999) 96 Comp Cas 415. The time for holding the meeting had expired. Without the order of the CLB meeting held out of time would not have been valid. The special business proposed in the notice related to a transaction which had become the subject-matter of a litigation. The CLB, therefore, directed that that business should not be taken up at the meeting. *National Dairy Development Board* v *Indian Immunologicals Ltd*, (2002) 108 Comp Cas 909 CLB, a meeting cannot be ordered just only to relieve defaulters from liability, Administrative difficulties were not accepted to be a ground for considering it to be impracticable to call a meeting.

12. *Nungambakkam D. S. Nidhi Ltd* v *ROC*, (1972) 42 Comp Cas 632 Mad; *A. K. Zacharia* v *Majestic Kuries and Loans (P) Ltd*, (1987) 62 Comp Cas 865 Ker, the court cannot appoint a commissioner for calling or holding a meeting.

13. *See* S. 168. The provision is applicable to private companies as well. *Registrar of Companies* v *F. S. Cabral*, (1988) 63 Comp Cas 126 Bom.

14. AIR 1938 Mad 640: [1938] 1 MLJ 856: 39 Cri LJ 907.

was contended on behalf of the company that a meeting was held in that year.

But the court held that the meeting of March, 1935, was the adjourned meeting of 1934. "There should be one meeting per year and as many meetings as there are years." The company was accordingly convicted.

Similarly, in another case,[15] for a failure to hold a meeting it was held to be no defence that on account of a criminal case against the secretary of the company some important books were exhibited in the court and as they had not been released in time, no accounts could be prepared, and no meeting could be held.[16] But in *Kastoor Mal Banthiya* v *State*:[17]

> The accused and his brother were the only two members and directors of a private company. During the period when a meeting should have been held his brother was lying seriously ill and the consequent failure to hold the meeting was not considered to be a wilful default.[18]

Where a managing director has been pressing his colleagues to call the annual meeting but in vain, he cannot, for the purposes of this section, be described to be an "officer in default".[19]

The Registrar has been given the power, for any special reason, to extend the time for holding an annual general meeting for a period of only three months. But the time for holding the first annual general meeting of a company is never extended.[20]

The meeting should be held during business hours, on a day which is not a public holiday and at the registered office of the company or at any

15. *Brahmanberia Loan Co Ltd, Re*, AIR 1934 Cal 624: 151 IC 693. *See* also *Ramchandra & Sons (P) Ltd* v *State*, [1967] 2 Comp LJ 92.
16. See *PSNSA Chettiar & Co* v *ROC*, [1966] 1 Comp LJ 17 Mad; *Nungambakkam D. S. Nidhi Ltd* v *ROC*, (1972) 42 Comp Cas 632 Mad. The meeting must be brought to completion within the statutory period notwithstanding adjournments. *Bejoy Kumar Karnani* v *Asstt ROC*, (1985) 58 Comp Cas 293. *Tapan Kumar Chowdhury* v *ROC*, (2003) 114 Comp Cas 631 Cal, the factory and offices of the company were the victims of industrial unrest and out of reach of the directors and that was held to be a good defence for the default.
17. AIR 1951 Ajm 39.
18. It should be noted that the section requires the annual general meeting to be held "in addition to" any other meeting that may have been held in the year. Before the words "in addition to" were *inserted*, it was doubtful whether an extraordinary general meeting held in a year would exonerate the holding of the annual general meeting for the year. The Allahabad High Court had held in *Lachmi Narain* v *Emperor*, AIR 1920 All 357, that an extraordinary meeting would amount to annual general meeting for the year. But the Bombay High Court had differed in *Emperor* v *Nasurbhai Abdullabhai Lalji*, AIR 1923 Bom 194. *See* also *India Nutriments Ltd* v *Registrar of Companies*, [1964] 1 Comp LJ 56.
19. *S. S. Jhunjhunwala* v *State*, (1970) All WR 814.
20. Proviso to S. 166(1)(c). See *Dalmia Cement (Bharat) Ltd* v *Registrar of Joint Stock Companies*, AIR 1954 Mad 276. The power of extension cannot be exercised by the Central Government, *Nungambakkam D. S. Nidhi Ltd* v *ROC*, (1972) 42 Comp Cas 632 Mad. The Central Government also cannot examine aspects of validity; that is a matter for civil courts. *Ravinder Kumar Jain* v *Punjab Registered (Iron and Steel) Stock Holders Assn*, (1978) 48 Comp Cas 401 P&H.

place within the town where the registered office is situated.[21] The appointment of additional directors was held to be *prima facie* void where the meeting was held at a different place from the place specified in the notice. Individual notices were not given to members and the change of venue of the meeting was not notified.[22]

In the case of revival and rehabilitation of sick industrial companies this power is to be exercised by the National Company Law Tribunal.[23]

Importance of annual general meeting

Annual general meeting is an important institution for the protection of the shareholders of a company. The ultimate control and destiny of a company should be in the hands of its shareholders. It is, therefore, desirable that the shareholders should come together once in a year to review the working of the company. This meeting affords that opportunity. It is at this meeting that some of the directors will retire and come up for re-election[24] and the shareholders will be able to exercise real control by "refusing to re-elect a director of whose action and policy they disapprove".[25] Again, auditors retire at this meeting enabling the shareholders to consider whether they should be re-appointed or replaced.[26] Dividends are declared at this meeting. Chairman delivers a speech listing the advances of the company during the year. Directors have to present annual accounts for the consideration of the shareholders. A failure to present the accounts is a punishable offence.[27] The shareholders can ask any questions relating to the accounts or affairs of the company.

The business to be transacted at the meeting is generally provided for in the articles of the company and that is known as the ordinary business of the meeting. The meeting may take up any other business also and that will be known as special business.

Extraordinary general meeting [S. 169]

Clause 47 of Table A provides that all general meetings other than annual general meetings shall be known as extraordinary general meetings.

---

21. S. 166(2). The Central Government may exempt a company from this sub-section. *See also* the proviso. According to S. 2(38) "public holiday" means a public holiday within the meaning of the Negotiable Instruments Act, 1881: *Provided* that no day declared by the Central Government to be a public holiday shall be deemed to be such a holiday, in relation to any meeting, unless the declaration was notified before the issue of the notice convening the meeting. *Dinkar Rai D. Desai* v *R. P. Bhasin*, [1985] 1 Comp LJ 38: (1986) 60 Comp Cas 14 Del, a direction that the meeting may be simultaneously held at three different places was held to be void. Postal limits can be considered as city limits for this purpose.
22. *Sikkim Bank Ltd* v *R. S. Chowdhury*, (2000) 102 Comp Cas 187 Cal.
23. This provision has been added by the Second Amendment of 2002, [Proviso to S. 167(3)].
24. S. 255.
25. GREER LJ in *Shaw & Sons* v *Shaw*, [1935] 2 KB 113, 134.
26. S. 224.
27. Ss. 219 and 220. Failure to lay accounts before the meeting does not invalidate the meeting. *Sunil Dev* v *Delhi and District Cricket Assn*, (1994) 80 Comp Cas 174 Del.

The board may, whenever it thinks fit, call an extraordinary general meeting. An extraordinary general meeting also becomes necessary on requisition, for Section 169 provides that on requisition of a given number of shareholders the directors must forthwith call a meeting.[28] The requisition must be signed by holders of at least one-tenth paid-up capital having the right to vote on the matter of requisition.[29] If the company has no share capital the requisition must be signed by as many members as have one-tenth of the total voting power.

The requisition must set out the matters for the consideration of which the meeting is to be called.[30] No other business can be done. For example, where certain shareholders requisitioned a meeting for the appointment of three new directors, and subsequently the chairman wanted to add to the agenda the removal of a director also, the meeting was restrained from considering the matter.[31] Only such matters can be taken up at the meeting in respect of which the requisitionists possess the same voting strength as is required to requisition a meeting.

When a requisition is deposited at the registered office of the company the directors should, within twenty-one days, move to call a meeting and the meeting should actually be held within forty-five days from the date of the requisition.[32] If the directors fail to do so, the requisitionists may themselves proceed to call the meeting[33] and claim the necessary expenses from the company. The company can indemnify itself out of the remuneration due to the directors in default.[34] The directors cannot refuse to call a meeting only on the ground that the resolution that the requisitionists propose to put would be contrary to the Act. That is a matter which can be considered by the court subsequently. The requisitionists wanted to add a clause to the articles that if a person had occupied the position of a director for six years,

---

28. S. 169(1). Where the directors did not call a meeting because of irregularity in requisition notice and did not do so even after a rectified notice was given because of the pending contempt proceedings, the CLB ordered that they should call meeting on the dismissal of the contempt proceedings. *Shoe Specialities Ltd* v *Standard Distilleries & Breweries Ltd*, (1997) 90 Comp Cas 1 Mad.

29. S. 169(4)(*a*). Where a meeting was requisitioned by shareholders holding partly paid shares, the meeting and the appointment of directors made thereat were held be invalid. *Kuldip Singh Dhillon* v *Paragaon Utility Financiers (P) Ltd*, (1986) 60 Comp Cas 1075 P&H. Signatures by the requisite number on a draft requisition prepared by one of them is good enough, *B. G. Somayaji* v *Karnataka Bank Ltd*, (1995) 83 Comp Cas 649 Kant.

30. S. 169(2). *Malvika Apparels* v *UOI*, (2002) 112 Comp Cas 335 Del, the notice which the company served on the members in response to the requisition did not include all the items specified by the requisitionists. They went in for a writ. The court told them that they had an alternative remedy under S. 186.

31. *Ball* v *Metal Industries Ltd*, 1957 SLT 124 Scotland.

32. S. 169(6).

33. *See*, for example, *M.R.S. Rathnavelusami* v *M.R.S. Manickavelu Chettiar*, AIR 1951 Mad 542: [1951] 1 MLJ 5: 64 LW 172: (1951) 21 Comp Cas 93; also see *Topandas Mohanlal Advani* v *Yeotmal Electric Supply Co*, AIR 1940 Sind 87. The Board has been held to be justified in refusing to call a meeting when there is a stay order. *A. D. Chaudhary* v *Mysore Mills*, (1976) 46 Comp Cas 548 Kar.

34. S. 169(9).

he should not seek re-election for three years. The court pointed out that such clause would be invalid under Section 274(3) as prescribing additional disqualifications, but even so directors should not refuse to respond to the requisition.[35] Where a meeting is requisitioned for the purpose of removing a bunch of directors, it has been held by the Supreme Court that it is not necessary for the requisitionists to state the reasons for removal.[36] A special notice of the resolution to remove a director has to be given. Where this was not done, it was held that though the meeting was valid, the resolution was not.[37] A meeting cannot be requisitioned for a declaration that the directors appointed at the preceding meeting were not validly elected and that the requisitionists should be appointed as directors in their place.[38]

It is not necessary that an extraordinary general meeting should be held at the registered office of the company. A resolution passed at a meeting held at any other place than the registered office would be equally void.[39]

The Karnataka High Court held that refusal on the part of the directors to call a meeting on requisition does not amount to any offence either under Section 169 or under Sections 628, 629 or 629-A. The requisitionists have their own alternative of calling a meeting by themselves under Section 169(6).[40] The requisitionists cannot approach the Company Law Board under Section 186 for an order calling an extraordinary general meeting without first trying to call a meeting themselves.[41]

---

35. *Cricket Club of India* v *Madhav L. Apte*, (1975) 45 Comp Cas 574 Bom.
36. *LIC* v *Escorts Ltd*, (1986) 1 SCC 264: (1986) 59 Comp Cas 548: [1986] 1 Comp LJ 91 SC, *reversing* Bom HC in [1984] 3 Comp LJ 387 where the High Court had held that if reasons are not stated the directors' right of making a representation against their removal would be defeated because there cannot be a worthwhile representation without knowledge of the reasons. The right of requisitioning a meeting or exercising normal voting rights is not affected by the fact that a receiver in respect of a member's shares has been appointed or the management of the company is with the Government under the Industries (D&R) Act, 1951. *Balkrishna Gupta* v *Swadeshi Polytex Ltd*, (1985) 2 SCC 167: (1985) 58 Comp Cas 563 SC. Followed in *Vijay M. Porwal* v *Pentokey Organy (India) Ltd*, (1996) 87 Comp Cas 331 CLB, neither the requisitionists nor the company is required to give a statement of reasons. To the same effect, *Karedla Suryanarayana* v *Shri Ramdas Motor Transport Ltd*, (1998) 28 Corpt LA 233 CLB: (1999) 98 Comp Cas 518 CLB, the company has not to comply with the requirement of explanatory statement.
37. *Queens Kuries and Loans (P) Ltd* v *Sheena Jose*, (1993) 76 Comp Cas 821 Ker. Followed in *Bhankerpur Simbhaoli Beverages (P) Ltd* v *Sarabhjit Singh*, (1996) 86 Comp Cas 842 P&H, notice not given to the concerned director and the proceedings became invalidated.
38. *B. Sivaraman* v *Egmore Benefit Society Ltd*, (1992) 75 Comp Cas 198 Mad. Where there was no proof of a requisitioned meeting being held at all, appointment of directors at the alleged meeting was held to be not good. *V.G. Balasundaram* v *New Theatre Carnatic Talkies (P) Ltd*, (1993) 77 Comp Cas 324 Mad.
39. *Metal Box India Ltd, In re*, (2001) 105 Comp Cas 939 CLB.
40. *Anantha R. Hegde* v *Captain (Er.) T.S. Gopala Krishna*, [1996] 3 Comp LJ 333 Kant: (1996) 23 Corpt LA 142. The requisition in this case was short of the mandatory requirement. *Anantha R. Hegde* v *Captain T. S. Gopala Krishna*, (1996) 3 Comp LJ 333 Kant: (1996) 23 Corpt LA 142: (1998) 91 Comp Cas 312, directors' default, no offence. The requisitionists' reasonable expenses are to be reimbursed by the company which in its turn can recover indemnity from the defaulting directors.
41. *B. Mohandas* v *A.K.M.N. Cylinders (P) Ltd*, (1998) 93 Comp Cas 532 CLB.

Power of Company Law Board to call meeting [S. 186]

Where the holding of a meeting, other than an annual general meeting, has for any reason become impracticable, the proper course for the company to follow is to apply to the CLB. In such cases the CLB can on its own motion or on the application of a director or a member order a meeting to be called and held in accordance with its directions. The word "impracticable" as construed in a reasonable way must naturally mean that it is not possible to hold a peaceful or useful meeting. "Impracticable" means impracticable from a reasonable point of view.[42] The CLB takes a common sense view of the matter and orders a meeting if it would appear to a prudent man of business that the holding of a useful meeting has become impracticable. In *Indian Spg Mills Ltd* v *His Excellency*:[43]

A person who was not holding the qualification shares of a director was appointed chairman and some directors had transferred shares to him to enable him to fulfil the requirement. This was alleged, by a group of shareholders, to be invalid and was the subject-matter of a suit. It was held that it was impracticable to hold a meeting in these circumstances and the court could intervene.

Similarly, in *Lothian Jute Mills Ltd, Re,*:[44]

There was a dispute between the shareholders of a company as to who were the lawful directors of the company entitled to call a meeting. It was held to be proper that the court should step in and call a meeting "the validity of which is beyond question".

The power of the CLB was invoked to call a meeting where the company had no duly constituted board of directors. A meeting was necessary for putting the company on rails by removing impediments which had arisen in the way of proper functioning.[45]

In a decision on the power of the court, the Calcutta High Court[46] observed that the power "should be used sparingly with caution so that the court does not become either the shareholder or a director of the company trying to participate in the internecine squabbles of the company". The Board should interfere when it is fully satisfied that the application has been

---

42. *Commr, Lucknow Division* v *Dy Commr, Pratapgarh*, (1937) 41 CWN 1072: AIR 1937 PC 240. Adopted by BANERJEE J in, *Malhati Tea Syndicate Ltd, Re*, 55 Cal WN 653. *See* also *Cricket Club of India* v *Madhav L. Apte*, (1975) 45 Comp Cas 574 Bom.
43. AIR 1953 Cal 355: 56 CWN 398.
44. 55 CWN 646. For other cases see, *Malhati Tea Syndicate Ltd, Re*, 55 Cal WN 653; *Bal Krishna Maheshwari* v *Uma Shanker Mehrotra*, AIR 1947 All 361.
45. *Amrit Kaur Puri* v *Kapurthala Flour, Oil and General Mills Co (P) Ltd*, [1997] 1 Comp LJ 147 (CLB-PB).
46. *Ruttonjee & Co Ltd, Re*, [1968] 2 Comp LJ 155, 172 Cal: (1970) 40 Comp Cas 491, where MITRA J reviewed all the leading Indian and English authorities on the subject and stated the fundamental principles in terms of eight propositions; (1970) 40 Comp Cas 491. The Company Law Board may also fix the agenda of the meeting. *Baptist Church Trust Assn* v *CLB*, [1986] 1 Comp LJ 187 Cal.

made *bona fide* in the larger interests of the company for removing a deadlock otherwise irremovable and that there is *prima facie* proof of the fact that a meeting called in the manner in which meetings are ordinarily called under the Act or articles would be invalid. The facts of the Calcutta case were:

> The directors of a company had divided themselves into two groups each claiming that the others were not lawfully directors. But neither made an effort to requisition a meeting. An application was made to the court to order a meeting. But the court advised them that they should first requisition a meeting themselves to see what the other group would do. Until that is known the court cannot intervene.

In a two-member-director company, there was a petition for prevention of unfairly prejudicial conduct (oppression). For that reason, one director would not sit with the other at a meeting. Additional directors could not be appointed for carrying on the management: A meeting for appointment of additional directors was ordered to be held.[47]

Before the amendment of 1974 this power was exercised by the court. Subsequently it was vested in the Company Law Board. Now it has been vested in the Tribunal.[48] The power being of judicial nature, the Tribunal is likely to follow the above-stated principles.[49]

PROCEDURE AND REQUISITES OF VALID MEETING

Meeting should be called by proper authority

The first essential requisite of a valid meeting is that it should be called by a proper authority. Obviously the only proper authority is the board of directors,[50] except when the meeting has, in the event of default by the directors, been called by the requisitionists or by the Company Law Board. Suppose, for example, that the meeting of the board at which it is resolved to call a general meeting is not properly convened or constituted, will it render the general meeting also invalid? It was held in *Browne* v *La Trinidad*[51] that by reason of irregularity of the board meeting the general

---

47. *Sticky Fingers Restaurant Ltd, Re*, [1992] BCLC 84 Ch D. A meeting was ordered in parallel circumstances in *Pucci Dante* v *Rafeeque Ad*, (1999) 95 Comp Cas 566; *Oriental Benefit & Deposit Society Ltd* v *Bharat Kumar K. Shah*, (2001) 103 Comp Cas 947 Mad, where the holding of an AGM was restrained by an injunction, it was a question of fact whether the meeting itself was restrained or only the consideration of a particular transaction.
48. By the Companies (Second Amendment) Act, 2002.
49. There is no power to appoint an independent chairman where the meeting is not called at the orders of CLB. *Kishore Y. Patel* v *Patel Engg Co Ltd*, (1994) 79 Comp Cas 53 Bom.
50. The natural corollary is that the board of directors can also postpone a meeting, *John Y. Chandy* v *Catholic Syrian Bank Ltd*, (1995) 1 Ker LJ 612.
51. (1887) 37 Ch D 1: 158 LT 137 CA. The court does not have the power to give directions for the conduct of a meeting already called by the directors. *R. Rangachari* v *S. Suppiah*, [1975] 2 SCC 605: (1975) 45 Comp Cas 641.

meeting was not incapacitated from acting. But in the case of *Harben* v *Phillip*:[52]

Certain directors held a meeting of the board but they prevented some lawfully constituted directors from attending the meeting. A quorum was, however, present. It was held that as the meeting of the board was unlawful, the notice convening the general meeting also became invalid. Directors have to exercise their discretion and have to fix the time and place or whether the meeting should be held at all.[53]

Notice [Ss. 171-172]

The second requirement of a valid meeting is that a proper notice of the meeting should be given to the members. Notice should be given to every member of the company.[54] Deliberate omission to give notice to a single member may invalidate the meeting,[55] although an accidental omission to give notice to, or non-receipt of it by, a member will not be fatal.[56] This is based upon the theory that the acts of a corporation are those of the major part of the corporators, corporately assembled. By "corporately assembled" it is meant that the meeting shall be one held upon notice which gives every corporator the opportunity of being present.[57] Secondly, notice should be in writing and must be given twenty-one days before the date of the meeting. "Twenty-one days" are to be computed from the date of receipt of the notice by members and the notice shall be deemed to have been received at the expiration of forty-eight hours from the time of posting.[58] *N. V. R. Nagappa Chettiar* v *Madras Race Club*[59] is an illustration in point:

---

52. (1883) 23 Ch D 14: 48 LT 334: 31 WR 173.
53. *See* also *N.V.R. Nagappa Chettiar* v *Madras Race Club*, [1949] 1 MLJ 662, where all such cases were discussed and a meeting was held invalid, because the board which resolved to call it was not properly present. Compare, *Boschoek Proprietary Co Ltd* v *Fuke*, [1906] 1 Ch 148: 94 LT 398.
54. S. 172(2).
55. *Smyth* v *Darley*, (1849) 2 HL Cas 789; *Musselwhite* v *C.H. Musselwhite & Son*, [1962] Ch 964: [1962] 1 All ER 201. *Gajanan Narayan Patil* v *Dattatraya Waman Patil*, (1990) 3 SCC 634: (1990) 69 Comp Cas 1 SC, failure to give notice to nominees of public financial institutions who were co-opted directors, invalidated the meeting of the board of directors of a cooperative society. *R. R. Rajendra Menon* v *Cochin Stock Exchange Ltd*, (1990) 69 Comp Cas 231 Ker, a dispute as to 'notice' is a matter for the jurisdiction of civil courts and not that of company courts. Another *sub nom* case on the same point, (1990) 69 Comp Cas 256 Ker.
56. S. 172(3).
57. *Mayor, etc. of the Staple of England* v *Governor and Company of Bank of England*, (1887) 21 QBD 160: 57 LJQB 418 CA.
58. S. 53(2)(*b*). See *Balwant Singh Sethi* v *Zoarwar Singh*, (1988) 63 Comp Cas 310 Bom, where notices were posted on August 31 and September 1 for a meeting to be held on September 21, and they were held to be not valid. *Somalingappa Shiva Putrappa Mugabasow* v *Shree Renuka Sugars Ltd*, (2002) 110 Comp Cas 371 Kant, notice served through courier and also received by members well before time, an application for stay order just 3 days before meeting, not allowed.
59. (1949) 1 MLJ 662.

Notices were posted on October 16, for a meeting to be held on November 7. The notice was held to be short by one day as in computing the interval of twenty-one days the date of posting and date of meeting should be excluded.[60]

Where notices were posted during a period of postal strike and decidedly would not have been served upon members, the court said that the strike was in itself an evidence of the fact that there would not be effective service and, therefore, the presumption of deemed service was ruled out.[61]

The gap should be of twenty-one clear and whole days.[62] It has been held by the Madras High Court *Self-Help Private Industrial Estates (P) Ltd, Re,*[63] following Section 171, that all the members can, in the case of an annual meeting, voluntarily consent to a shorter notice either before or after the meeting. In the case of any other meeting the consent of the holders of 95% of the paid-up share capital, or the consent of 95% of the total strength of members, would be necessary. Where a special resolution to shift the registered office was passed at a meeting of which shorter notice was given, the court ignored this fact as there was sufficient evidence of ratification by the requisite number.[64] The fact that one of the members is not traceable does not make the consent less unanimous.[65] Similarly, it has been held in *Bailey, Hay & Co Ltd, Re,*[66] that a notice of a resolution for voluntary winding up had become valid through acquiescence of the company's members, all of whom attended the meeting despite the fact that it was defective, being short by a day.[67] The Bombay High Court has been of the view that the requirement as to length of notice is merely directory and not mandatory. Where no prejudice whatsoever was caused to the member who complained of the notice being short by one day, the court refused to invalidate the meeting and its proceedings.[68] The shareholder who participated in the meeting, accepted dividend as well as directorship, was not allowed to question the validity of the meeting on account of short notice.[69]

---

60. Where a member does not have any registered address in India or has not supplied to the company any address for the giving of notices to him, the company may advertise the notice in a newspaper circulating in the neighbourhood of the company's registered office and it will be deemed to have been served on the member on the date of advertisement. (S. 53).

61. *Bradman* v *Trinity Estate Ltd*, 1989 BCLC 753 Ch D.

62. *Pioneer Motors (P) Ltd* v *Municipal Council, Nagercoil*, AIR 1967 SC 684; *Bharat Kumar Dilwali* v *Bharat Carbon & Ribbon Mfg Co Ltd*, (1973) 43 Comp Cas 197 Del.

63. (1972) 42 Comp Cas 605 Mad.

64. *Parikh Engg & Body Building Co, Re*, (1975) 45 Comp Cas 157 Pat.

65. If the heirs of a deceased member do not supply their addresses, the service at the deceased member's address is sufficient. *Canara Bank Ltd* v *Thampi*, (1972) 42 Comp Cas 473 Ker.

66. [1971] 1 WLR 1357: [1971] 3 All ER 693.

67. Where only one member received notice late, though posted in time, meeting valid. *Calcutta Chemical Co Ltd* v *Dhiresh Chandra Roy*, (1985) 58 Comp Cas 275 Cal.

68. *Shailesh Harilal Shah* v *Matushree Textiles Ltd*, AIR 1994 Bom 20.

69. *V. Shanmugasundaram* v *Emerald Automobiles Ltd*, (2001) 103 Comp Cas 1108 CLB.

A notice of a meeting despatched under certificate of posting creates a presumption that it was served at the expiration of 48 hours.[70] The Company Law Board held in a case that notice of meeting under certificate of posting was not a good notice. The meeting was not valid. The company was directed to send notice by registered post.[71] Certificates of posting are notoriously easily available. When relationships between the parties have become embittered and a specific request has been made on payment of cost that notice of board meeting be sent by registered post, service through postal certificate could not be taken to be a conclusive proof of service.[72]

A notice for an extraordinary general meeting was served by fax. This was held to be good service.[73]

A private company's articles may contain its own special provisions as to duration of notice.[74]

Contents of notice [Ss. 172 and 173]

Notice should specify the place and day and hour of the meeting and the meeting to be valid must be held at the place and time specified,[75] except, perhaps, in a situation that arose in *M. R. S. Rathnavelusami* v *M. R. S. Manickavelu Chettiar*:[76]

> On the failure of the directors of a company to call a meeting on a requisition, the requisitionists themselves sent a notice to all the members for a meeting to be held at the registered office of the company. But the managing director locked the premises of the registered office. It was held that a meeting held at some other place and the resolutions passed thereat were valid.

Again, the notice must contain a statement of the business to be transacted at the meeting. Section 173 puts businesses into two categories, namely:

1. *General business.*—At the annual meeting the business of considering accounts and directors' report, the declaration of dividends, the appointment of directors and auditors and fixing their remuneration are regarded as general business.[77]

---

70. *Challa Rajendra Prasad* v *Asian Coffee Ltd*, (1999) 20 SCL 414 AP.
71. *Hardeep Kaur* v *Thinlac Enterprises (P) Ltd*, (2004) 122 Comp Cas 944 CLB.
72. *Sanjiv Kothari* v *Vasant Kumar Chordia*, (2005) 66 CLA 45 CLB.
73. *PNC Telecom Plc* v *Thomas*, (2004) 1 BCLC 88 (Ch D).
74. Section 170 and see *Sree Rama Vilas Press and Publications (P) Ltd, Re*, (1992) 73 Comp Cas 275 Ker.
75. S. 172(1).
76. AIR 1951 Mad 542: [1951] 1 MLJ 5: 64 LW 172: (1951) 21 Comp Cas 93.
77. *Ramji Lal Baisiwala* v *Baiton Cables Ltd*, ILR 1964 Raj 135, 157.

2. *Special business.*—Any other business at an annual meeting and all business at extraordinary general meetings are regarded as special business.[78]

Further issue of capital, being a special business, required to be mentioned in the notice. Not to have done so rendered the meeting, its notice and the further issue to be invalid.[79]

Explanatory statement

If any special business is to be transacted at an annual meeting, a statement to that effect must be annexed to the notice calling the meeting. The statement must set out all the material facts concerning each item of the special business and should also disclose the interest of any director or other managerial personnel in the matter.[80] "Notice must give a sufficiently full and frank disclosure to the shareholders of the facts upon which they are asked to vote." The purpose of the explanatory statement is that the members should be informed of the nature of the business to be transacted at the meeting.[81] To take, for instance, *Narayanlal Bansilal* v *Maneckji Petit Mfg Co Ltd*:[82]

A company had managing agents. It wanted to adopt a new set of articles changing the terms of their appointment. The notice convening a meeting of the shareholders for the purpose set out the proposed special resolutions, but did not give particulars of the important changes to be effected. Accordingly, the resolutions passed on the basis of this notice were held invalid.

Similarly in *Bimal Singh Kothari* v *Muir Mills Co Ltd*:[83]

It was held that where there is a large body of shareholders residing at great distances from the registered office of the company, it would not be fair to leave the proposed articles at the registered office and give the shareholders notice of that fact. Printed copies of the new articles should be sent with the notice. Where this is not done, the notice is not sufficient.

---

78. *Martin Castelino* v *Alpha Omega Ship Management (P) Ltd*, (2001) 104 Comp Cas 687 CLB, the agenda sent with the notice of the meeting did not contain the item of increase of share capital, the notice was held to be not proper.

79. *Claude-Lila Parulekar* v *Sakal Papers (P) Ltd*, (2005) 11 SCC 73: (2005) 124 Comp Cas 685.

80. S. 173(2) *see also* the proviso. Where the notice of a meeting is given by newspaper advertisement, the statement of material facts need not be annexed to it, but it should be mentioned that the same has been forwarded to the members. [S. 172(2) Proviso]. Apart from this exception the requirements of the section are mandatory. *V. G. Balasundaram* v *New Theatre Carnatic Talkies (P) Ltd*, (1993) 77 Comp Cas 324 Mad.

81. *Rajiv Nag* v *Quality Assurance Institute (India) Ltd*, [2000] 4 Comp LJ 385 CLB. The statement is a part of the notice. It cannot be read de hors of it.

82. (1931) 33 Bom LR 556. *See* also *M. R. Goyal* v *Usha International Ltd*, (1997) 27 Corpt LA 187 (Del), explanatory statement not found to be tricky, complainant minimal shareholder, no harm to his small holding.

83. AIR 1952 Cal 645: ILR (1954) 1 Cal 185: 56 CWN 361.

Where a notice calling a meeting stated that the object of the meeting was to adopt an agreement for the sale of one company's undertaking to another, but did not disclose that a substantial sum was payable to the directors of the selling company as compensation for loss of office, the court held that the notice did not fairly disclose the purpose for which the meeting was convened.[84] Where the shareholders' resolution became necessary for selling a unit of the company, the court said that material facts could comprise of the reasons for sale, whether sale would affect the interests of the company, to whom the sale was being effected, the consideration for it, how and by whom the consideration was assessed, whether directors had any interest in the transaction, whether all statutory clearances were obtained. Such material facts would help the shareholders to make a decision on the proposal.[85] The Supreme Court order restraining the company from the sale of its assets has been held to be a material fact. Non-disclosure of such material fact in the notice calling the meeting vitiated the resolution passed at the meeting. An agreement of sale entered into on the basis of such resolution was not enforceable. No action lay for compensation for breach of the contract.[86]

It was pointed out by their Lordships of the Judicial Committee in *Parsuram* v *Tata Industrial Bank Ltd*,[87] that a shareholder who by his conduct shows that he knew the real effect of the work to be transacted at a meeting cannot complain of the notice on the ground of insufficiency.[88]

---

84. *Kaye* v *Croydon Tramways Co*, [1898] 1 Ch 358: 78 LT 237: 67 LJ Ch 222.
85. *Mendonica (BA)* v *Philips India Ltd*, [2000] 3 Comp LJ 129 CLB.
86. *Sunil Mills Ltd* v *Official Liquidator of Shri Ambica Mills Ltd*, [1999] 1 Comp LJ 423 Guj; *Y. S. Spinners Ltd* v *OL, Shri Ambica Mills Ltd*, [1999] 1 Comp LJ 442: (2000) 100 Comp Cas 547 Guj.
87. AIR 1928 PC 180. *See also* MISRA, J of the Orissa High Court in *Kalinga Tubes Ltd* v *Shanti Prasad Jain*, [1964] 1 Comp LJ 117, 138; *Shalagram Jhajharia* v *National Co*, [1965] 1 Comp LJ 112 Cal. The Rajasthan High Court held in *Seth Sobhag Mal Lodha* v *Edward Mills Co*, 1971 Tax LR 178 Raj: (1972) 42 Comp Cas 1, that where a notice proposed one person for managing directorship and the shareholders appointed another, it was good notice. The validity of a notice on account of inadequacy of time not allowed to be questioned by a transferee of shares when his transferor's right to question had become time-barred. *Joseph Michael* v *Travancore Rubber & Tea Co Ltd*, (1986) 59 Comp Cas 898 Ker. A person whose interest in the company was 0.006% was not permitted to question validity. *Gopaldas Gujrati* v *Titagarh Papers Mills Co Ltd*, (1986) 60 Comp Cas 920 Cal.
88. *See* also *European Home Products plc, Re*, 1988 BCLC 690, where the notice for reduction of share premium account carried an inaccuracy and the same was ignored by the court because no shareholder was apparently influenced by it. *Abnash Kaur* v *Lord Krishna Sugar Mills Ltd*, (1974) 44 Comp Cas 390, the business of a meeting can be transacted even without a formal agenda. The same view was endorsed in *Suresh Chandra Marwaha* v *Lauls (P) Ltd*, (1978) 48 Comp Cas 110 P&H, every agenda has a residuary clause which permits consideration of any other matter with the permission of the chairman. *Joginder Singh Palta* v *Time Travels (P) Ltd*, (1984) 56 Comp Cas 103 Cal, even if there are certain irregularities committed, it would not be a proper exercise of discretion in an application under S. 39 Rules 1 and 2 of CPC to restrain a company from acting on a resolution passed at a meeting irregularly convened or conducted. The company can rectify such matters. *Bentley-Stevens* v *Jones*, (1974) 2 All ER 653. Where the complaining shareholder was already aware of the facts, the meeting was not

Private companies

Section 170 enables private companies to adopt their own regulations over matters covered by Sections 171 to 186. The provisions of these sections would apply to private companies only to the extent to which they are not excluded by private company's own articles.[89]

Quorum [S. 174]

Another requirement of a valid meeting is the presence of a quorum. Quorum means the minimum number of members that must be present at the meeting. It is generally for the articles to provide what number of members will constitute a quorum. But Section 174 provides that unless the articles provide for a large number, five members personally present in the case of a public company and two in the case of a private company shall be the quorum for a meeting. If within half an hour from the time of a meeting a quorum is not present the meeting will stand dissolved if it was called upon requisition. But in other cases the meeting is automatically adjourned to re-assemble on the same day in the next week.[90] And if at the re-assembled meeting also a quorum is not present within half an hour, as many members as are actually present shall constitute the quorum. The crucial problem in such a case is that if only one member turns up, will the meeting be valid, or, in other words, whether a meeting attended by only one member can be called a meeting at all. This was the question in *Sharp* v *Dawes*:[91]

> There were several shareholders in a company. A meeting was called for the purpose of making a call. Only one shareholder attended the meeting. He, however, held the proxies of other shareholders. He took the chair and passed a resolution for making a call and then proposed and passed a vote of thanks. In giving judgment in the Court of Appeal, Lord COLERIDGE said: "The word 'meeting' *prima facie* means a coming together of more than one person.... This was not a meeting within the meaning of the Act."

---

invalidated though the requisite particulars were not set out in the notice, *C. R. Priyachandra Kumar* v *Purasawalkam Permanent Fund Ltd*, (1995) 83 Comp Cas 150 Mad.

89. *Sreerama Vilas Press and Publications (P) Ltd, Re*, (1992) 73 Comp Cas 275 Ker; *K. Meenakshi Amma* v *Sreerama Vilas Press and Publications (P) Ltd*, (1992) 73 Comp Cas 275 Ker, the private company's articles carried special provisions on the subject and therefore the requirement of explanatory statement was not applicable.

90. S. 174(4). Joint shareholders count for one member even if all of them are present.

91. (1876) 2 QBD 26: 46 LJQB 104: 36 LT 188. An extraordinary general meeting called by the requisitionists was presided over by a person who was not a member and the minimum of two members were not present with him, it was not a valid meeting, *Bhankerpur Simbhaoli Beverages (P) Ltd* v *P. R. Pandya*, (1995) 17 Corpt LR 170 P&H. *D.K. Chatterji* v *Rapti Supertonics (P) Ltd*, (2003) 114 Comp Cas 265 CLB, a resolution passed without the requisite quorum is void *ipso facto*.

On the analogy of this case it may be said that even in the case of a meeting adjourned for want of a quorum, the attendance of one member only at the re-assembled meeting may not be enough. Moreover, the section also says that "*the members* actually present shall be a quorum". But exceptions will have to be admitted, particularly in a case like *East* v *Bennet Bros Ltd.*[92]

Where all the preference shares in a company were held by one shareholder only, it was held that a meeting of preference shareholders attended by him only was proper.

Secondly, when the Central Government or the Tribunal calls a meeting under Section 167 or 186 respectively it may be directed that one member of the company present in person or by proxy shall be deemed to constitute a meeting.[93] This course was adopted in *L. Opera Photographic Ltd, Re.*[94] In a company consisting of two members with 51:49 holding, the majority shareholder was not able to remove the other from directorship because under the articles a meeting without the other attending was not possible. So the majority applied for a court (here it would be CLB) order that a meeting should be called at which the attendance of one would be the quorum. Since the majority shareholder had a statutory right to remove the other from directorship his right could not be vetoed by quorum requirements and, therefore, the court passed necessary orders. Further, it was held in *Hartley Baird Ltd, Re:*[95]

Where a clause in the articles of a company provided that "no business shall be transacted at any general meeting, unless a quorum is present when the meeting proceeds to business..." that the condition is sufficiently complied with if there is quorum present at the beginning of the meeting when it proceeds to business, and the subsequent departure of a member reducing the meeting below the number required for a quorum does not invalidate the proceedings at the meeting after his departure.

The authority of this statement has been to a certain extent undermined by *London Flats Ltd, Re:*[96]

A meeting was attended by two members. The chairman was the majority shareholder. The other member proposed a name for appointment as liquidator. The chairman moved an amendment and

---

92. [1911] 1 Ch 163: 80 LJ Ch 123: 103 LT 826.
93. S. 167(1) Explanation; S. 186(1) Explanation. *Shankar Sundaram* v *Amalgamations (P) Ltd*, (2002) 108 Comp Cas 885 CLB, such directions can be given only when CLB has itself ordered the holding of a meeting and not when a meeting is convened by the company itself. *See also* an opinion expressed by Ashwin L. Shah in [1968] 1 Comp LJ 27 and the editor's reply. An order of this kind was made in *El Sombrero Ltd, Re*, [1958] Ch D 900: [1958] 3 WLR 349: [1958] 3 All ER 1.
94. 1989 BCLC 763 Ch D.
95. [1954] 3 WLR 964: [1954] 3 All ER 695: [1955] Ch 143.
96. [1969] 2 All ER 744: [1970] 1 Comp LJ 28.

proposed himself. Thereupon the other member left. The chairman by his majority votes confirmed his appointment.

The Court refused to uphold the appointment on the ground that any further proceedings, after the other member had left, were a nullity. The decision is good inasmuch as it provided to the company an independent liquidator, but the reason advanced may lead to wrong results. "Should it be the law that minority shareholders, realising that they cannot defeat a resolution by the constitutional process of voting against it, should be able to frustrate the wishes of the majority by walking out of the meeting?"[1]

A minority shareholder refused to attend a general meeting.[2] The meeting was inquorate without him and the resolution passed was invalid. He sought an order for convening of meeting to enable the invalidly passed resolution to be put before and passed by a properly constituted meeting. Following the principle of the earlier cases[3], the court came to the conclusion that a meeting would be ordered to be called. The section is procedural in nature. It is intended to enable a company business which needed to be conducted at a general meeting to be so conducted. But the court would not allow the procedure to be used to override class rights or substantive rights conferred.[4]

Where the meeting commenced about 1½ hours late because there was no quorum within half hour of the scheduled time, it was held that S. 174 refers only to the presence of the quorum within half an hour and does not talk of the time at which the meeting should be called to order, a delay in the commencement of the meeting did not invalidate it.[5]

Chairman [S. 175]

For the proper conduct of business at a meeting a chairman is necessary. His appointment is usually regulated by the articles of association. But if there is nothing in the articles "the members personally present at the meeting shall elect one of themselves to be the chairman".

Power of adjournment and postponement

The position and powers of a chairman were explained by the Madras High Court in *Narayana Chettiar* v *Kaleeswara Mills*:[6]

---

1. Editor's note on the case in 1969 JBL 2301, *see* also *El Sombrero Ltd, Re*, [1958] Ch D 900: [1958] 3 WLR 349: [1958] 3 All ER 1 where the court upheld the removal of a director by a meeting attended by one member.
2. *Vectone Entertainment Holding Ltd* v *South Entertainment Ltd*, (2004) 2 BCLC 224 (Ch D).
3. *Woven Rugs Ltd, Re*, (2002) 1 BCLC 124; *Union Music Ltd* v *Watson*, (2003) 1 BCLC 453.
4. *Vectone Entertainment Holding Ltd* v *South Entertainment Ltd*, (2004) 2 BCLC 224 (Ch D).
5. *Janaki Printing (P) Ltd* v *Nadar Press Ltd*, (2001) 103 Comp Cas 546 CLB D.
6. AIR 1952 Mad 515: ILR 1952 Mad 218: [1952] 1 MLJ 18. Other powers and privileges of the chairman will become apparent from the discussion on the procedure of voting. For further discussion on the chairman's power to adjourn meetings see *John* v *Rees*, [1969] 2 WLR 1294:

If the chairman unjustly and without the consent of shareholders stops the meeting, it is perfectly within the powers of the meeting to elect another chairman and conduct the remaining unfinished business.[7]

A chairman by himself cannot postpone a meeting. The proper course to adopt is to hold the meeting and then adjourn it to a more convenient date. An adjournment will be within his competence in the case of a disorder but only for no longer than he considers absolutely necessary and his decision should be communicated to the meeting at least to the extent to which it is possible for him to do so. If the chairman adopts any other course, the members who can constitute a quorum may continue with the meeting and lawfully transact the announced business.[8] Where the chairman was a candidate for being appointed as managing director and, on finding that he wouldn't get majority support, dissolved the meeting and left the hall with his supporters, the appointment by the remaining members, being in quorum, of another person, as a managing director was held to be valid.[9]

Contrary opinions have also been expressed. The Calcutta High Court in its decision in *United Bank of India* v *United India Credit and Development Co Ltd*[10] recognised a chairman's right to make a *bona fide* adjournment but immediately added remarks from the authorities to the effect that if the intention and effect were to interrupt and procrastinate the business, such an adjournment would be illegal; if, on the contrary the intention and effects were to forward or facilitate it, and no injurious effects were produced, such an adjournment would be generally supported.[11]

Fresh light has been thrown on this question by the decision of the Court of Appeal in *Bying* v *Rondan Life Assn Ltd.*[12] A meeting was called for

---

[1969] 2 All ER 274, noted 1969 JBL 232; *Seth Sobhag Mal Lodha* v *Edward Mills Co*, (1972) 42 Comp Cas 1: 1971 Tax LR 178 Raj.

7. *PIK Securities Management (P) Ltd* v *United Western Bank Ltd*, (2002) 109 Comp Cas 500 CLB, power and duty only to assure good conduct of meeting, no power to withdraw a resolution, the chairman dissolving meeting before business finished, members could proceed after electing new chairman.

8. These principles were laid down by the Supreme Court in *Chandrakant Khare* v *Shantaram Kale*, (1989) 65 Comp Cas 121 SC, in connection with the meeting of a municipal corporation. *Peerless General Finance & Investment Co Ltd* v *Essar Oil Ltd*, (2006) 129 Comp Cas 353 Guj, the right of meeting to adjourn by simple majority. *See* Horsley's MEETINGS PROCEDURE, LAW AND PRACTICE (2nd Edn by Taggart) it has been observed in Chapter 10 on Adjournment that under the common law a meeting is deemed to be invested with the right to adjourn its proceeding at its own discretion. A meeting has the inherent power to adjourn where it is not possible to transact all the business without adjourning.

9. *Seth Sobhag Mal Lodha* v *Edward Mills Co*, 1971 Tax LR 178 Raj: (1972) 42 Comp Cas 1.

10. (1977) 47 Comp Cas 689 Cal. Frank Shackleton, LAW AND PRACTICE OF MEETINGS, 69 (3rd Edn); *Catesby* v *Burnett*, [1916] 2 Ch 325; *Deodutt Sharma* v *Zahoor Ad*, 1960 RLW 486: AIR 1960 Raj 25; *Nation Dwelling Society* v *Sykes*, [1894] 3 Ch 325; *United Bank of India* v *United India Credit and Development Co Ltd*, (1977) 47 Comp Cas 689 Cal; *Jackson* v *Hamlyn*, [1953] 1 All ER 887 applied.

11. Citing *John* v *Rees*, [1969] 2 WLR 1294: [1969] 2 All ER 274.

12. 1989 BCLC 400: [1989] 1 All ER 560: [1989] 1 WLR 738 CA.

changing the company's memorandum for facilitating an amalgamation. A fairly large number of members wanted to oppose the move. The meeting became overcrowded. The venue proved too small. The members were seated in the adjoining rooms and a sound system was installed to enable them to hear and to participate. That system failed. Then there was a bewildering confusion and in that state of things the chairman arranged for an alternative venue and resolved to adjourn the meeting to meet again in the afternoon at the new venue. There was opposition to this move. The meeting in the evening at the new venue was held to be invalid and the chairman's adjournment of the morning meeting without taking a sense of the meeting was held to be not lawful. The court recognised that it is not necessary that all the members should be present in one room, but that if the members are seated in different rooms there should be an audio-visual link between all the rooms. In this case the system having failed, the gathering could not be constituted into a valid meeting except for the rudimentary purpose of adjourning itself.[13] Under the articles of the company the chairman could adjourn a meeting only with the consent of the meeting. But even so the court was of the view that a residuary power of adjournment would survive because circumstances may develop, as they did in this case, where it is impossible to ascertain the view of the majority. Finally, the court came to the conclusion that the chairman's power of adjournment was not fairly exercised. He failed to take into account the relevant factors, such as, member, attempts at *sine die* adjournment, their objections to the temporary adjournment and that there was no such urgency, the final date of merger being still off. The court said that for testing the reasonableness of the conduct of a chairman, the same test is applicable which is generally applied in all cases of judicial review, namely, whether the chairman reached a conclusion which no reasonable chairman could have reached having regarded to the purpose of his power to adjourn.[14]

---

13. Even in this respect the court had to face authorities like *Harben v Phillip*, (1883) 23 Ch D 14: 48 LT 334: 31 WR 173, where a meeting was invalid by reason of omission to give notice to all members and the same was held to be not even capable of adjourning itself; *Portuguese Consolidated Copper Mines Ltd, Re*, (1889) 42 Ch D 160 CA, a board meeting called on inadequate notice was held to be not capable of adjourning itself; the court also found in its support the New Zealand case of *Hetcher v New Zealand Glue Co Ltd*, (1911) 31 NZ LR 129 SC where an inchoate meeting was held to be valid for approving the annual return and adjournment.

14. The following cases were cited as propounding the test of judicial review: *Associated Provincial Picture Houses Ltd v Wednesbury Corp*, [1947] 2 All ER 680: [1948] 1 KB 223. See further *Second Consolidated Trust Ltd v Ceylon Amalgamated Tea & Rubber Estates Ltd*, [1943] 2 All ER 567: 169 LT 324, where too the chairman had failed to take into account the relevant factors. *Peerless General Finance & Investment Co Ltd v Essar Oil Ltd*, (2006) 129 Comp Cas 353 Guj, meeting to approve a scheme of amalgamation was adjourned frequently because the scheme was not likely to go through, adjournment on minority votes was held to be valid.

Mixed Nature of Duty

Further, it has been held in *Ram Narain* v *Ram Kishen*[15] that:

A chairman who presides over a meeting of a company is neither wholly a ministerial officer nor wholly a judicial officer; his duties are of a mixed nature, and he is not liable to be mulcted in damages, if, acting *bona fide* according to the best of his judgment and without malice, he erroneously excludes a shareholder from voting and declares him to be ineligible as a director of the company. A shareholder who has been wrongfully refused the right of voting or of election as a director, cannot maintain an action of damages against the chairman of the company.

Where a shareholder pledged his shares with a bank with voting rights and the bank lodged the documents with the company for the purpose of exercising voting rights, it was held that the chairman had no power to examine validity of the documents.[16]

Casting Vote

In the case of a tie of votes, the chairman can exercise a casting vote. This right can be exercised by the person who is occupying the chair. It is not necessary that he should be a regularly elected chairman.[17]

Informal Appointment

The shareholders invited a person (claimant) to be the chairman of the company but no resolution was passed appointing him as such. The shareholders could not say that there was no appointment.[18] It has been stated that the ratio of the decision is that where that which has been done informally could, but for an oversight, have been done formally and was assented to by 100% of those who could have participated in the formal act, if the act had been carried out then it would be idle to insist upon formality as a precondition to the validity of the act which all those competent to effect it had agreed should be effected.[19]

Appointment by Court

The court also has the power to appoint an independent chairman to preside over a meeting of a company. Such a chairman is particularly necessary where there are factions among the shareholders and a peaceful meeting under the chairmanship of a person appointed by either faction is improbable.[20]

---

15. (1911) 10 IC 515.
16. *Servopori Investments (P) Ltd* v *Soma Textiles & Industries Ltd*, (2005) CLC 1302 Cal.
17. *T.V. Prasadachandran Nair* v *Anandamandarim Hotels P Ltd*, (2002) 110 Comp Cas 394 CLB.
18. *Pena* v *Dale*, (2004) 2 BCLC 508 (Ch D). The court applied the principle enunciated in *Duomatic Ltd, Re*, (1969) 1 All ER 161 at p 168.
19. *New Cedo Engg Co Ltd, Re*, (1994) 1 BCLC 797 at p 814.
20. *See*, for example, *Ananthalakshmi* v *Tiffin's Barytes Asbestos & Paints Ltd*, AIR 1952 Mad 60;

Voting

The business of a meeting is done in the form of resolutions passed at the meeting. Shareholders have the right to discuss every proposed resolution and to move amendments. If an amendment is reasonably germane to a proposed resolution and is not in substance a negative of it, it must be admitted and put to the meeting. Accordingly, in *T. H. Vakil* v *Bombay Presidency Radio Club*:[21]

> Where at a meeting of a company the chairman wrongfully ruled an amendment out of order, it was held that the subsequent proceedings relating to that particular motion were invalidated.

After a resolution has been discussed it is put to vote. Every holder of equity shares has the right to vote.[22] For, Section 182 now clearly provides that a company cannot prohibit any member from exercising his voting right on the ground that he has not held his shares for any specified period before the meeting or on any other ground.[23] The only ground on which the right to vote may be excluded is non-payment of calls by a member or other sums due against a member or where the company has exercised the right of lien on his shares.[24] Persons who are members on the last date for holding the meeting alone would be entitled to vote. Those who became members thereafter by virtue of a Government order were held to be not entitled to vote even at the postponed meeting.[25]

A provision in the articles of a company introduced by an amendment to the effect that there would be full voting rights in respect of partly paid up shares also was held to be not permissible. It was in violation of the provisions of the Act.[26]

Before the Amendment of 2000 shares with differential voting rights were not permitted to be issued. Such voting rights existed up to the enactment of the 1956 Act. Now they have been brought back by the amendment. Section 2(46-A) provides that shares with differential voting

---

Selvaraj v *Mylapore H. P. Fund*, [1968] 1 Comp LJ 93 Mad. Apart from such extraordinary circumstances the courts do not interfere in the conduct of meetings by appointing a chairman. See *Kishore Y. Patel* v *Patel Engg Co Ltd*, (1994) 79 Comp Cas 53 Bom. Courts also do not interfere with adjournments agreed to by shareholders, *Swadee Chemicals Ltd* v *Kothari Industrial Corpn Ltd*, (1995) 18 Corpt LA 23 Mad.

21. AIR 1945 Bom 475. *See* also *Henderson* v *Bank of Australasia*, (1890) 45 Ch D 330: [1886-90] All ER Rep Ext 1190.

22. S. 87(1).

23. *See*, for example, the case of *Ananthalakshmi* v *H. I. & F. Trust*, AIR 1951 Mad 927 where a provision in the articles of a company that only those shareholders would be entitled to vote whose names have been there on the register for two months before the date of the meeting was held to be in contravention of the Act. Section 182 however does not apply to a private company which is not a subsidiary of a public company. Disproportionate voting rights have been terminated. S. 89.

24. S. 181.

25. *C.M. Varkey Chan* v *T.V. Mathew*, (2002) 108 Comp Cas 159 Ker.

26. *Ajit Singh* v *DSS Enterprises (P) Ltd*, (2002) 109 Comp Cas 597 CLB.

rights means shares which are issued with differential rights in accordance with the provisions Section 86.

The voting rights of preference shareholders are restricted by Section 87(2). A preference shareholder has the right to vote only on resolutions which directly affect the rights attached to his preference shares.

Informal Agreements

A formal resolution is, however, not the only way for a company to act through the general meeting of its shareholders. An agreement unanimously adopted by all the members is sufficient to express the corporate will. Where a meeting was attended by all the five shareholders of a company and two of them having half the voting power supported a resolution for voluntary winding up and the rest holding the other half abstained altogether from voting, the resolution was held to be the unanimous will of all the members.[27] BRIGHTMAN J said: "It is established law that a company is bound in a matter, *intra vires* the company, by the unanimous agreement of all its corporators."[28] He then quoted ASTBURY J as saying: "Where a transaction is *intra vires* the company and honest, the sanction of all the members of the company, however expressed, is sufficient to validate it." Explaining how the agreement was deemed to be unanimous when three out of five members did not vote, the court said: "Admittedly three of the five corporators did not vote in favour of the resolution, but they undoubtedly suffered it to be passed with knowledge of their power to stop it.... If corporators attend a meeting without protest, stand by without protest while their fellows purport to pass a resolution and permit all persons concerned to act for years on the basis that the resolution was duly passed and rule their conduct on the basis that the resolution is an established fact, it is idle for them to contend that they did not assent to the purported resolution."

Some more decisions have been delivered on the validity of informal agreements having the effect of resolutions. The statutory procedural requirements of a shareholders' resolution at a general meeting for the award of a long term contract was taken by the court to be waived where the sole shareholder consented to the agreement. The correct approach is to consider the purpose and underlying rationale of the formality in question. The sole shareholder had given the genuine consent to something which was within the company's powers. The prescribed procedure was intended to ensure that there was a proper opportunity for shareholders to consider the agreement.[29] Where, however, certain additional requirements are prescribed, e.g., special notice of a resolution for removal of a director, it is doubtful whether such procedure can also be waived. Where a charge was created in favour of

---

27. *Bailey, Hay & Co Ltd, Re*, [1971] 1 WLR 1357: [1971] 3 All ER 693.
28. The learned judge cited *Express Engg Works Ltd, Re*, [1920] 1 Ch 466: [1920] All ER Rep Ext 850 and *Parker & Cooper Ltd* v *Reading*, [1926] Ch 975.
29. *Wright* v *Atlas Wright (Europe) Ltd*, [1999] 2 BCLC 301 CA.

debenture holders but the receiver appointed by them could neither find the requisite shareholders' resolution for the creation of the charge, nor there was any evidence of the way in which the concerned group of shareholders had given its consent, the court said that the debenture could not be validated. But the company was not allowed to avoid the transaction because the debenture trustees had acted in good faith.[30]

By show of hands [S. 177]

In the first instance, voting on a resolution takes place by show of hands. On a show of hands, one member has one vote. A declaration by the chairman on a show of hands that a resolution has or has not been carried is conclusive,[31] except when a poll is demanded or when as held by the Calcutta High Court in *Dhakeswari Cotton Mills* v *Nil Kamal Chakravorty*:[32]

A declaration by the chairman would be conclusive only if he does not find by his declaration the figures for or against the resolution. But where the chairman finds the figures and erroneously in point of law holds that a resolution has been duly passed, the resolution cannot be said to have been passed according to law.

Poll [S. 179]

If there is a dissatisfaction about the result of voting by show of hands a poll can be demanded.[33] Taking a poll means recording the number of votes cast for or against a resolution. The "voting right of a member on a poll shall be in proportion to his share of the paid-up equity capital of the company."[34] Shares with disproportionate voting rights were not allowed to be issued.[35] Section 88 which so provided has been omitted by the Amendment of 2000. Section 86, as replaced by the same amendment, permits shares with

---

30. *Torvale Group Ltd, Re*, (1999) 2 BCLC 605 Ch D. Section 35 of the English 1985 Act validates transactions where the other party did not know of the directors' procedural lapses. The court considered the decisions in *Demite Ltd* v *Pratec Health Ltd*, (1998) BCC 638.

31. S. 178. *See*, for example, *E. D. Sasoon United Mills, Re*, AIR 1929 Bom 38. Section 177 (voting by show of hands) does not apply to a company which does not carry on business for profit or prohibits payment of dividends to members. Such a company may have any provision in the articles on the point. [S. 263-A].

32. AIR 1937 Cal 645: 41 CWN 1137.

33. S. 179. A poll may be demanded even before the declaration of the result on a show of hands. A member who participated in voting by show of hands and did not object to the result or demand a poll, was not allowed to question the validity of the resolution. *Jetu Jacques Taru Lalvani* v *J.B.A. Printing Inks Ltd*, (1997) 88 Comp Cas 759 Bom.

34. S. 87(1)(*b*).

35. S. 88. Under S. 99 disproportionate voting rights in existing companies have also been terminated. But sub-section (4) empowers the Central Government to exempt any company from the operation of the section in public interest. An exemption of this kind was quashed by the Delhi High Court in *Mahant Vaishna Das* v *Fakir Chand*, [1967] 2 Comp LJ 171 because it was granted under the mistaken belief that the company was a trust. The court also pointed out that the Government must give a hearing to those shareholders whose rights are affected by the exemption. One could not go on enjoying disproportionate voting rights by paying penalty. *Namita Gupta* v *Cachar Native Joint Stock Co Ltd*, (1999) 98 Comp Cas CLB.

differential rights to be issued. But so long as a company does not have such shares, the regime of equality of voting rights would prevail. So is true of quoted companies in England.[36] But private companies are exempted from the operation of this rule.[37] Thus a clause in the articles of a private company which gave three votes for each equity share to a director when a resolution was proposed for his removal has been held valid.[38] A poll may be ordered by the chairman of his own motion and he will be bound to order a poll when it is demanded—

1. in the case of a public company having a share capital, by any member or members present in person or by proxy and holding shares in the company (*i*) which confer a power to vote on the resolution not being less than one-tenth of the total voting power in respect of the resolution of, or (*ii*) on which an aggregate sum of not less than Rs 50,000 has been paid;

2. in the case of a private company having a share capital, by one member if not more than seven members are present at the meeting and by at least two members when more than seven members are present at the meeting;

3. in the case of any other company, by the holders of one-tenth of the total voting power in respect of the resolution.[39]

When a poll is taken a member is free to split his votes for as well as against the same resolution. He has the right to distribute his votes in any manner he chooses.[40]

The manner of taking a poll is to be decided by the chairman.[41] He appoints two scrutineers (one of whom must be a member if available and willing) to scrutinise the votes given on the poll.[42] A declaration of the chairman that a resolution has or has not been carried is *prima facie*

---

36. *See* Clive M. Schmitthoff, *The Issue of Securities in Great Britain*, 1969 JBL 1.
37. S. 90.
38. *Bushell* v *Faith*, [1969] 2 WLR 1067: [1969] 1 All ER 1002.
39. *Jetu Jacques Taru Lalvani* v *J.B.A. Printing Inks Ltd*, (1997) 88 Comp Cas 759 Bom, the chairman is not bound to hold a poll in every case.
40. Now expressly provided in S. 183. *See also* the observations of the Calcutta High Court in *Mahaliram* v *Fort Gloster Jute Manufacturing Co*, AIR 1955 Cal 132. Section 180 says that a poll demanded on a question of adjournment shall be taken forthwith and a poll demanded on any other question (not being a question relating to the election of a chairman (which is provided for in S. 175) shall be taken at such time not being later than 48 hours from the time when the demand was made, as the chairman may direct. The meeting is deemed to continue upto that time. *Holmes* v *Keys*, [1958] 2 All ER 129 Ch D; *Shaw* v *Tati Concessions Ltd*, [1913] 1 Ch 292; *Jackson* v *Hamlyn*, [1953] 1 All ER 887. A person who was not then present may nevertheless vote on a poll. *Campbell* v *Maund*, [1835-42] All ER Rep 648; a breakdown of poll arrangement would require another effort. *M. K. Srinivasan* v *W. S. Subramania Iyer*, (1932) 32 Comp Cas 147: AIR 1932 Mad 100.
41. S. 185. *Mela Singh (Maj)* v *Jullundur Club Ltd*, [1969] 1 Comp LJ 273 where the chairman ordered open, not secret ballot.
42. S. 184(1), (2) and (3).

evidence of the resolution.[43] The reason for this rule was explained in the case of *Mahaliram* v *Fort Gloster Jute Mfg Co*:[44]

> The validity of a resolution declared passed by the chairman at a poll was questioned on the ground that certain proxies were improperly rejected. The articles of association of the company provided that in such cases "the determination of the chairman made in good faith shall be final". The court observed: "The chairman by virtue of his position and the nature of his duties has to decide on the spot all emergent questions that arise at the meeting and it is not desirable to reduce the *prima facie* authority of his verdict.... Hence the burden of proof lies on the other party to show that the decision of the chairman was wrong."

Where a poll was demanded on a valid basis but was not allowed by the chairman, the Company Law Board held that the business on the agenda for which poll was demanded and which was carried through by show of hands became invalid.[45]

Voting by proxy [S. 176]

A member may vote either in person or by proxy. Articles may allow voting by proxy even on show of hands.[46] But unless the articles otherwise provide, a proxy shall not be allowed to vote except on a poll. The system of voting by proxy has become very popular because of the unwillingness and inability of shareholders to be personally present at meetings:

> It is commonplace to observe that the modern shareholder is a kind of investor and does not think of himself as or like an owner. He hires his capital out to the managers, and they must run it for him; how they do it is their business, not his; and he always votes 'yes' on the proxy.

"A proxy is a person representative of a shareholder at a meeting of the company, who may be described as his agent to carry out a course which the shareholder has himself decided upon."[47] A proxy is not entitled to act contrary to the instructions of the shareholder in the matter. It is the relationship of principal and agent. Where the authorisation of the proxy appointed through power of attorney exceeded the voting rights of the shareholder, it was held that only the votes in excess were void.[48]

A proxy does not have the right to speak.[49]

---

43. S. 195.
44. AIR 1955 Cal 132: 58 CWN 715.
45. *Namita Gupta* v *Cachar Native Joint Stock Co Ltd*, (1999) 98 Comp Cas 655 CLB.
46. S. 176(1)(c). The English cases bearing on the subject of right to vote by proxy are: *Horbury Bridge Coal, Iron & Waggon Co, Re*, (1879) 11 Ch D 109: 40 LT 353; *Bidwell Bros, Re*, [1893] 1 Ch 603: 68 LT 342; *Ernest* v *Loma Gold Mines Ltd*, [1897] 1 Ch D 1: 75 LT 317.
47. Lord HANWORTH MR in *Cousins* v *International Brick Co*, [1913] 2 Ch 90: 1913 All ER Rep 229; cited with approval in *Narayana Chettiar* v *Kaleeswara Mills*, AIR 1952 Mad 515: ILR 1952 Mad 218: [1952] 1 MLJ 18.
48. *Chadra Chemicals Ltd* v *Jer Button Kavasmaneck*, (2006) 129 Comp Cas 643 Bom.
49. S. 176(1).

The instrument appointing a proxy must be in writing and signed by the shareholder,[50] and should be deposited with the company forty-eight hours before the meeting.[51] The Act requires proxy forms to be supplied to members along with the notice for the meeting. The forms should be in blank and should not carry any suggested names. It would be a misuse of privilege to influence voting that way.[52]

"A proxy is always revocable. Even where by its terms it is made irrevocable, the law allows the stockholder to revoke it."[53] Revocation is, of course, subject to the provisions of the articles. Generally it is provided that revocation must be received at the office of the company before the commencement of the meeting. Accordingly, where a revocation was communicated before the poll, but not before the meeting, it was held to be ineffective and the proxy's vote stood.[54] Where, however, there is no provision in the articles, the power of revocation would be unfettered. And so in *Narayana Chettiar* v *Kaleeswara Mills*:[55]

A proxy had exercised his votes in the first poll of a meeting but the proxy was revoked before the final poll was held. In the absence of any provision in the articles, the revocation was held to be effective and the rejection of the revocation by the chairman, was, therefore, untenable.

Proxy forms can be inspected by any member who has a right to vote at the meeting or on any resolution to be proposed at the meeting.[56]

---

50. S. 176(5). If the appointer is a body corporate, the instrument of proxy should be under its seal or be signed by an officer or attorney duly authorised by it. The relevant form is prescribed by Sch IX and it has been held that the members can use this form even if the company had adopted a form of its own. *General Commerce* v *Apparel Export Promotion Council*, [1990] 1 Comp LJ 297 Del.

51. S. 176(3). This sub-section declares that if the articles of a company require a longer period than forty-eight hours that will be inoperative and the shareholders will have the right to deposit proxies forty-eight hours before the meeting. There is no provision of law requiring holidays to be excluded in computing 48 hours and, therefore, forms filed on a Sunday would be valid *K. P. Chackochan* v *Federal Bank*, [1989] 2 Comp LJ 269: (1989) 66 Comp Cas 953 Ker. Proxy forms with uncancelled stamps have been held to be valid. *M. G. Mohanraj* v *Myalapore Hindu Permanent Fund Ltd*, [1990] 1 Comp LJ 87 (Mad). On the question whether a proxy form can be filed through fax, a beginning has been made with a creditors' meetings (S. 500). It has been held that a creditor can attend a meeting through a proxy by sending the proxy nomination by fax. *A Debtor (No 2021 of 1995), ex p, Re*, (1996) 1 BCLC 538 Ch D; *IRC* v *Debtor*, (1996) 1 BCLC 538 Ch D.

52. *Peel* v *London & North Western Rly Co*, [1907] 1 Ch 5: [1904-07] All ER Rep Ext 1201; *Second Consolidated Trust Ltd* v *Ceylon Amalgamated Tea & Rubber Estates Ltd*, [1943] 2 All ER 567: 169 LT 324.

53. Cook on STOCK HOLDERS, S. 610, cited by Jessee W. Lilienthal, *Corporate Voting & Public Policy*, 10 Harv LR 428.

54. *Spiller* v *Mayo Development Co*, [1926] WN 78; *K. P. Chackochan* v *Federal Bank*, [1989] 2 Comp LJ 269: (1989) 66 Comp Cas 953 Ker.

55. AIR 1952 Mad 515: ILR 1952 Mad 218: [1952] 1 MLJ 18. For further details *see* M. S. Srinivasan, *Proxies*, [1965] 1 Comp LJ 64.

56. S. 176 proviso. The High Court of Delhi has held in *Swadeshi Polytex* v *V. K. Goel*, (1988) 63 Comp Cas 688 at p 697 that where a member filed two different proxy forms in favour of two different persons, the Registrar's order for production of the certified copies of the rival forms was valid.

Resolution by postal ballot [S. 192-A]

The Amendment of 2000 has introduced this new section so as to provide for passing of resolutions by postal ballot. This facility has been extended to listed public companies and that too only in respect of a business which the Central Government declares by notification that it shall be conducted only by postal ballot. In such cases the company would have to pass the resolution by postal ballot instead of transacting the business in the general meeting of the company.

The company has to send a notice to all the shareholders alongwith the draft resolution and carrying an explanation of the reasons which necessitated the resolution. The notice should request the shareholders to send their assent or dissent in writing on the postal ballot within the period of thirty days from the date of the posting of the letter.

The notice has to be sent under acknowledgment due registered post or by any other prescribed method (to be prescribed by the Central Government). It has to carry a postage pre-paid envelope. If the resolution is assented to by the requisite majority, (depending upon the nature of the resolution) it shall be deemed to have been passed at a general meeting.

If anybody fraudulently defaces or destroys either the ballot paper as sent in by the shareholders or his identity, such person has been made punishable with imprisonment extending up to six months or with fine or with both.

Electronic Mode.—Postal ballot would include voting by electronic mode.[57]

Representation of companies and Government [Ss. 187 and 187-A]

Where a company or a corporation is a member of another company, it may attend the meetings of the other company through a representative. The representative must be appointed by a resolution of the board of directors or the other governing body. Where the Central Government or a State Government is a member, the President or the Governor of the State, as the case may be, has the power to appoint representatives to attend meetings of the company. The person nominated holds the position of a proxy.[58]

Resolutions

Kinds of Resolution [S. 189].—Resolutions are of two kinds, namely:

1. Ordinary resolution, and

2. Special resolution.

A resolution is said to be ordinary when the votes cast in favour of it at a general meeting of a company exceed the votes, if any, cast against the

---

57. S. 192-A, *Explanation.*
58. Sections 187(2) and 187-A(2). A trust has been created for disposal of old lot shares. *See* Govt Circular of Oct 8, 1993.

resolution. In other words, it means a resolution passed by a simple majority of shareholders.

A special resolution, on the other hand, requires the support of three-fourth majority of shareholders present and entitled to vote at a meeting. The votes cast in favour of the resolution should not be less than three times the number of votes, if any, cast against the resolution. It is also necessary that the intention to propose the resolution as a special resolution should have been specified in the notice calling the general meeting and the notice itself should have been given in accordance with the provisions of the Act.[59] Questions have arisen whether it is necessary for the validity of a special resolution that it should be passed as notified to the members or whether it can be passed with amendments at the meeting. In a case of this kind:[60]

> A notice was circulated of the intention to propose at an extraordinary general meeting a special resolution to cancel the company's share premium account on the ground that the amount credited to the account had been lost. It was subsequently realised that the figure standing to the credit of the account also included a small amount arising from a recent issue which was definitely not lost. At the meeting the form of the resolution had to be altered so as to provide not that the account had been cancelled, but that it had been reduced to a certain amount.

The court did not confirm the resolution as it was not validly passed. The court laid stress upon the requirement of the section, "intention to propose the resolution as a special resolution", which has been taken to mean that the resolution passed at the meeting must be the same as that specified in the notice.[61] In principle, however, the court agreed that a need for amendment may genuinely arise and the same should be allowed within reasonable limits. Correction of grammatical or clerical errors is allowed. Where the need for an amendment of substantive nature is feared, the notice itself should carry a warning that the resolution shall be passed subject to such amendments as may be determined at the meeting. Thus an amendment of even a slight substance would invalidate the resolution.[62]

---

59. The requirements of the section are mandatory. Non-fulfilment would make the resolution ineffective. *Self-Help Private Industrial Estates (P) Ltd, Re*, (1972) 42 Comp Cas 605 Mad; followed in *V.B. Balasundaram v New Theatres Carnatic Societies*, (1993) 77 Comp Cas 605 Mad.
60. *Moorgate Mercantile Holdings Ltd, Re*, [1980] 1 All ER 40, noted 1980 JBL 190.
61. In Palmer's COMPANY LAW it is categorically stated that such resolutions cannot be amended. Vol. 1, para 54-03 and in Gower, PRINCIPLES OF MODERN COMPANY LAW that the position should be the same as that of an ordinary resolution, namely, "would the amendment so alter the nature of the business as to cause any member who had stayed away reasonably to wish he had not." (545-46, 4th Edn). *See* also *Torbock v Lord Westbury*, [1902] 2 Ch 871.
62. See *Pearce Duff & Ltd, Re*, [1960] 1 WLR 1014; *Duomatic Ltd, Re*, [1969] 1 All ER 161: [1969] 2 WLR 114: [1969] 2 Ch 365.

A typed or printed copy of every special resolution must be registered with the registrar within thirty days of its date.[63]

For a decision relating to almost every important matter affecting the constitution, administration and affairs of a company, the Act has prescribed the formality of a special resolution. The support of a three-fourth majority of shareholders being requisite for passing a special resolution, the requirement is able to take care and protect the interests of a substantial group of shareholders.[64]

Where special notice of a resolution is required by the Act or the articles of a company, the intention to propose such a resolution must be notified to the company at least fourteen days before the meeting.[65] Such a resolution is called an ordinary resolution requiring special notice. This is necessary to enable the company to comply with its statutory obligation of informing the members of the resolution. This information has to be served on the members at least seven days before the meeting. Notice of the resolution may be given in the same manner in which notice for a meeting is given. Where that is not practicable, it may be given by advertisement in a newspaper having an appropriate circulation or in any other mode allowed by the articles.[66] Such notice is necessary, for example, for removing a director or an auditor or for proposing the appointment of a new director. Every member has a right to give a special notice of this kind relating to a proposed resolution, but he does not have the right to have the resolution included in the agenda of the meeting unless he is supported by as many members as can requisition a meeting[67] or can ask for circulation[68] of a member's resolution.[69]

Circulation of members' resolutions [S. 188]

Where certain members of a company desire to propose a resolution at the company's next annual general meeting a requisition may be served on the company requiring it to give the members notice of the resolution. The minimum number of members who must sign the requisition is the holders

---

63. S. 192(1).
64. A special resolution is required: to alter the memorandum [S. 17], articles [S. 31]; to issue further shares without pre-emptive rights [S. 81]; to convert uncalled capital into reserve capital [S. 99]; to reduce share capital [S. 100]; to shift registered office from one State to another [S. 146]; to authorise payment of interest out of capital [S. 208]; to request the Government to appoint inspectors for investigation [S. 237]; to sanction the appointment of management's relatives [S. 261]; to authorise a director to hold a place of profit [S. 314]; to make the liability of any managerial personnel unlimited [S. 332]; to make loans or provide guarantees or security to other companies beyond a certain limit [S. 372-A]; to apply to the court for winding up [S. 433]; to wind up the company voluntarily [S. 484], etc.
65. S. 190.
66. S. 190(2).
67. S. 169.
68. S. 188.
69. *Pedley* v *Inland Waterways Assn Ltd*, 1976 JBL 349: [1977] 1 All ER 209.

of one-twentieth of the total voting power of all tne members having a right to vote on the resolution or one hundred members holding shares on which at least a sum of one lakh rupees has been paid.[70] The requisitionists have to deposit at the registered office of the company a copy of the requisition. Where the requisition requires notice of a resolution to be given to the members, it must be deposited six weeks before the meeting, in any other case, two weeks before. They have also to deposit with the requisition a sum reasonably sufficient to meet the expenses of the requisition. When these requirements are complied with, the company becomes bound to notify the members of the intended resolution. The requisition may require the circulation of any statement of not more than one thousand words with respect to the matter referred to in any proposed resolution of any business to be dealt with at the meeting. However, in certain cases, a company is not bound to give effect to any such requisition. In the first place, if, on the application of the company or any other aggrieved person, the Central Government is satisfied that the right is being abused to secure needless publicity for defamatory matter, the court may relieve the company of the burden of this obligation.[71] Secondly, a banking company shall not be bound to circulate any such statement, if in the opinion of its board of directors, the circulation will injure the interests of the company.[72]

Registration of resolutions and agreements [S. 192]

Following resolutions and agreements have to be registered with the Registrar of Companies:[73]

1. special resolutions;
2. resolutions which have been agreed to by all the members of a company, but which, in the absence of such an agreement would have to be passed as special resolutions;
3. any resolution of the board of directors of a company or an agreement executed by a company relating to the appointment of a managing director or variation of its terms;
4. any transaction of the above kind relating to managing agents or secretaries and treasurers;
5. resolutions or agreements which have been approved by all the members of a class of shareholders, but which would have otherwise required to be passed by a particular majority and resolutions or agreements which bind all the members of a class of shareholders though not agreed to by all those members;

---

70. Where the consenting shareholders did not sign as requisitionists and instead gave power to a single shareholder to represent them at the meeting, this was held to be not a sufficient compliance with S. 188. *Naresh Kumar Jain* v *UOI*, (1997) 90 Comp Cas 445 Del.
71. S. 188(5).
72. S. 188(6).
73. S. 192(4).

6. resolutions passed by a company conferring power under Section 293 upon its directors to sell or dispose of the whole or any part of the company's undertaking; or to borrow money beyond the limit of the paid-up capital and free reserves of the company; or to contribute to charities beyond fifty thousand rupees or five per cent of the average net profits;

7. any resolution approving the appointment of sole selling agents under Section 294;

8. resolutions requiring the company to be wound up voluntarily.

Such resolutions or agreements must be filed with the Registrar within thirty days. The copy to be filed must be certified under the signature of an officer of the company.[74]

Minutes [Ss. 193-195]

Every company has to keep a record of the proceedings of its general meetings and the meetings of its board of directors. Such records have to be kept of all the proceedings of every general meeting and of all the proceedings of every meeting of the board of directors or of every committee of the board. Within thirty days of every such meeting, entries of the proceedings must be made in the books kept for the purpose and their pages must be consecutively numbered. Pasting of loose-leaf papers or maintaining minutes in loose-leafs is not allowed.[75] Proceedings have to be recorded in bound books and, therefore, they have to be handwritten. Typed sheets cannot be pasted.[76] These records are known as minutes. Each page of a minutes book which records proceedings of a board meeting must be signed by the chairman of the same meeting or the next succeeding meeting,[77] adding the date on the last page of the record. In the case of a general meeting this is the responsibility of the chairman of the same or of the next succeeding meeting.

The minutes of each meeting must contain a fair and correct summary of the proceedings of the meeting.[78] All appointments of officers made at any

---

74. S. 192(1). *See also* sub-sections (5) and (6) which provide penalty for default.

75. S. 193(1-B).

76. *Anil Kumar Mukherjee* v *Clarion Advertisement Services Ltd*, (1982) 52 Comp Cas 315. The High Court of Delhi accepted evidence of loose-leaf forms, *Edward Keventer Successors (P) Ltd* v *K. K. Sud*, (1968) 38 Comp Cas 507, but the Calcutta High Court did not accept pasted sheets as evidence, *Gluco Series (P) Ltd, Re*, (1987) 61 Comp Cas 227. The Deptt of Co Affairs (DCA) has advised companies maintaining loose-leafs to observe appropriate safeguards against interpolation of leaves, serially numbering them, authentication and safe-custody and to bind them up periodically say in six months. Field officers have been advised not to take action against loose-leaf practice of keeping minutes.

77. S. 193(1-A). It is not necessary that the chairman who signs the minutes at the next meeting should have been present at the preceding meeting. *Karnataka Bank Ltd* v *A.B. Datar*, (1993) 2 Kar LJ 230: (1994) 79 Comp Cas 417 at p 436, citing Shackleton on THE LAW AND PRACTICE OF MEETINGS, 83, (7th Edn).

78. S. 193(2). Any error in the minutes of an earlier meeting may be rectified by the board of

such meeting must be included in the minutes.[79] In the case of a meeting of the board of directors or of a committee of the board the minutes must state the names of the directors present at the meeting and the names of directors dissenting from or not concurring in a resolution passed at the meeting.[80] The chairman may exclude from the minutes, matters which are defamatory, irrelevant or immaterial or which are detrimental to the interests of the company. The discretion of the chairman in respect to the inclusion or exclusion of any such matter is absolute:[81]

Minutes of the board meeting are kept in order that shareholders of the company may know exactly what their directors have been doing, why it was done, and when it was done. If any alteration or addition is called for it should be done by resolution, not by clerical correction.[82]

Minutes kept in accordance with the above provisions are evidence of proceedings recorded in them. Any such meeting of the proceedings[83] of which proper minutes have been maintained is presumed to have been duly called and held. The proceedings at the meeting and the appointments of directors or of liquidators are deemed to be valid.[84] The presumption is rebuttable. Where a controversy is raised, evidence of conclusive nature to establish the points stated in the minute would become necessary. At the interlocutory stage, however, the trial court was held to be not justified in expressing doubts upon the genuineness of the minutes. He could not discard them at that stage.[85]

---

directors. *Gorden Woodroffe Ltd* v *Trident Investment*, (1994) 79 Comp Cas 764 CLB: [1994] 1 Comp LJ 313. The court also noted that minutes constitute good evidence.

79. S. 193(3).

80. S. 193(4).

81. S. 193(5).

82. *See* Lord ESHER MR in *Cawley & Co, Re*, (1889) 42 Ch D 209, 226: 61 LT 601.

83. S. 194. Thus in *Edward Keventer Successors (P) Ltd* v *K.K. Sud*, (1968) 38 Comp Cas 507, a resolution recorded in the minutes book authorising the general manager to file a suit was held to be good evidence of his authority.

84. S. 195. See *Kerr* v *John Mottram Ltd*, [1940] 2 All ER 629: [1940] Ch 657. No such presumption about an appointment was drawn where the minute book was not produced. *V.G. Balasundaram* v *New Theatre Carnatic Talkies (P) Ltd*, (1993) 77 Comp Cas 324 Mad. Burden of proof would lie on those who allege that a particular record was not factually true. *B. Sivaraman* v *Egmore Benefit Society Ltd*, (1992) 75 Comp Cas 199 Mad. The only way to prove that a particular resolution was passed is to produce the minutes book of the company which carries the record of the resolution in question, *Escorts Ltd* v *Sai Autos*, (1991) 72 Comp Cas 485 Del. Anybody challenging the validity of appointment of a director would have to dislodge the presumption of validity arising from recorded minutes, *C. R. Priyachandra Kumar* v *Purasawalkam Permanent Fund Ltd*, (1995) 83 Comp Cas 150 Mad. Where a Chairman was appointed by the court to preside over a meeting because of a conflict between members, it was held that the minutes prepared and approved by him were to be accepted as authentic and not the minutes prepared by the secretary of the company. *Nazir Hoosein* v *Darayus Bhathena*, (2000) 5 SCC 601: AIR 2000 SC 2427: (2000) 37 CLA 414 SC.

85. *B.D.A. Breweries* v *Cruickshank & Co*, (1996) 85 Comp Cas 325, 374 Bom: (1997) 25 Corpt LA 275. This presumption is not applicable to a meeting held on requisition. Where the records of such a meeting showed that two members were present, but evidence showed that only one

The minutes books are to be maintained at the registered office of the company. They are open to the inspection of members during business hours and without charge.[86] Restrictions may be imposed but a minimum of two hours each day must be granted for inspection. Members are also entitled to obtain copies of minutes.[87] Any denial of this right of members is punishable and the Central Government may compel an immediate inspection or supply of copies.[88]

Publication of reports of proceedings [S. 197]

The section requires that no document purporting to be a report of the proceedings of a general meeting shall be circulated or advertised at the cost of the company. Circulation of any such matter can be made if it is such that it is required to be included in the minutes of the proceedings.[89]

Service of documents on members [S. 53]

The mode prescribed by Section 53 for service of documents by a company on its members is that a document may be served either personally or by sending it to him by post. The letter should be sent to his registered address. If he has no registered address, any address, given by him to the company for the purpose of communications may be used. Where post is used as the medium of communication, service shall be deemed to have been effected when a properly addressed and stamped letter of notice is posted.[90] Where a member wants service by registered post or under certificate of posting and he has paid to the company sufficient amount for the purpose, he must be served in the manner prescribed by him. In either case, the service shall be deemed to have been effected, in the case of notice of a meeting, at the expiration of forty-eight hours from the date of posting, and, in any other case, when such letter is likely to be delivered in the ordinary course of post. Such a presumed service was not deemed to have taken place when the company was not able to produce any record of posting and the addressee denied service.[91]

---

was present, evidence prevailed over the presumption, *Bhankerpur Beverages (P) Ltd* v *Sarbhjit Singh*, (1996) 86 Comp Cas 842 P&H.

86. S. 196(1). Rupee 1 has been prescribed as fee for inspection. Rule 21-A of Companies (Central Government's) General Rules and Forms, 1956.

87. S. 196(2).

88. S. 196(3) and (4).

89. S. 197(1), sub-s. (2) provides that defaulting officers shall be punishable with a fine up to Rs 5000.

90. Service of notice by post under postal certificate which was directed by the court was held to be a good service, *National Breweries Ltd, Re*, (1991) 1 Gau LR NOC 44.

91. *Bhankerpur Simbhaoli Beverages (P) Ltd* v *P. R. Pandya*, (1995) 17 Corpt LA 170 P&H. The presumption of service is rebuttable. The burden of proof is on the addressee to show that he did not receive the service. A director who attended both the Board meeting and the general meeting was not heard to say that he did not receive the notice and was only orally informed by others, *R. Khemka* v *Deccan Enterprises (P) Ltd*, [1998] 5 Comp LJ 258 AP.

In the case of a member who has no registered address in India, nor has supplied any address for communication purposes, service shall be taken to have been effected if an advertisement is inserted in a newspaper circulating in the neighbourhood of the registered office of the company.

In case of joint-holders, a document may be served on the first named holder. In the case of death or insolvency of a member, the same rules apply for service of documents upon his representatives.

Where certain documents were sent by the company to the shareholders by registered post but the post was not delivered to the addressee, the court said that the company was not absolved from its responsibility of delivering the documents to the shareholders.[92]

Service of documents on Registrar [S. 52]

A document may be served on a Registrar by sending it to him at his office by post under a certificate of posting or by registered post, or by delivering it to, or leaving it for him at his office.

Service of documents on company [S. 51]

Documents can be served on a company or its officers by sending them to the registered office of the company by post under certificate of posting or by registered post or by leaving them at the registered office of the company. Where the securities are held in a depository, the records of the beneficial ownership may be served by such depository on the company by means of electronic mode or by delivery of floppies or discs.[93]

The service of a High Court writ by posting it on the company's registered office address was held to be a good service.[94] Service of summons at the company's corporate office has been held to be a good service. There is no compulsory requirement that service in all cases should be at the registered office.[95]

The service of notice on a company, for the purpose of filing a suit, by giving it to the office assistant of the company was held to be not a good service.[96]

---

92. *Inter Sales* v *Reliance Industries Ltd*, (1999) 35 CLA 370 Cal.
93. S. 51 (proviso).
94. *Addis Ltd* v *Berkerly Supplies Ltd*, [1964] 2 All ER 753; *T. O. Supplies (London) Ltd* v *Jerry Creighton Ltd*, [1952] 1 KB 42; *Indian Air Gases Ltd* v *Tarwan Sood*, (1999) 33 CLA 157 Del, concurrent finding of good service by post, not interfered with in a writ petition.
95. *Parasrampuria Synthetics Ltd* v *Shankar Prasad*, (2005) 123 Cases 419 (Del), CPC, Order 29, Rule 2.
96. *Nicco Corpn Ltd* v *Cethar Vessels Ltd*, (1998) 92 Comp Cas 748 Mad.

12
Dividends, Accounts and Audit

DIVIDENDS

Dividend means the share of profit that falls to the share of each individual member of a company. It is that portion of the corporate profits which has been set aside and "declared by the company as liable to be distributed among the shareholders".[1] Almost all commercial corporate enterprises are undertaken with the view of making profits for their members. The profits of a company when distributed among its members are called "dividends". No special authority either in the memorandum or in the articles is necessary to enable a company to pay dividends. The power is implied.

The payment of dividends is bound by two fundamental principles. The first is that dividends must never be paid out of capital.[2] It is supplemented by the second that dividends shall be paid only out of profits. The Act allows dividends to be paid out of the following three sources:

1. profits of the company for the year for which dividends are to be paid;
2. undistributed profits of the previous financial years;[3]
3. moneys provided by the Central or a State Government for the payment of dividends in pursuance of a guarantee by the Government concerned.

Payment of dividends out of capital is a breach of trust and the company may require the directors to replace the capital.[4] Thus in the well-known *Flitcroft case*[5] certain bad debts were credited to the accounts and the fictitious profits thus created were paid away as dividends. The directors were held liable. Explaining the reason JESSEL M R said:

"The creditor has no debtor but that impalpable thing the corporation, which has no property except the assets of the business. The

---

1. GHULAM HASSAN J in *Bacha F. Guzdar* v *CIT*, AIR 1955 SC 74: (1955) 1 SCR 876, 882: (1955) 25 Comp Cas 1.
2. S. 205(1).
3. Payment out of reserves has to be in accordance with the Companies (Declaration of Dividend out of Reserves) Rules, 1975. The restriction envisaged is that the rate shall not exceed the average of the rates at which dividend was declared in five preceding years or 10% of the company's paid-up capital, whichever is less. The amount drawn from reserves should first be applied to set off losses of the year and the reserves must not be depleted to below 15% of the company's paid-up capital.
4. *K. Madhava* v *Popular Bank*, (1969) 39 Comp Cas 717: AIR 1970 Ker 131. They may recover indemnity from the shareholders who have received the dividends. *Moxham* v *Grant*, [1900] 1 QB 88.
5. *Exchange Banking Co, Re, Flitcroft case*, (1882) 21 Ch D 519: 48 LT 86.

creditor, therefore, gives credit to that capital, gives credit to the company on the faith of the representation that the capital shall be applied only for the purposes of the business, and he has therefore a right to say that the corporation shall keep its capital and not return it to the shareholders...."

Where dividend was paid in face of the auditor's qualified report, the payment was held to be wrong. The statutory requirements cannot be waived by shareholders' resolution in this respect. The recipient of such dividends were held to be constructive trustees for the amounts received by them.[6]

The law will not tolerate even an indirect attempt to pay back capital by way of dividends. Thus *Walters' Deed of Guarantee, Re:*[7]

> W guaranteed the payment of the preference dividends for a period of three years and the company agreed to pay him any sums that he might pay under the guarantee.

The agreement was held to be void and W could not recover the amounts paid by him in pursuance of the guarantee.

In such cases only that part of the agreement is void by which the company contracts to indemnify the guarantor. But, apart from this, a guarantee for the payment of dividends is valid.[8]

Payment to shareholder-executives

Where the shareholders of a company were also working as its executives and their remuneration for bringing a contract to fruition was paid in circumstances in which dividend distribution would not have been justified, the directors were held to be not guilty of any breach of duty.[9]

Dividend fund

"As dividends can be declared only out of surplus earnings, there must be an exact method of determining whether surplus earnings for that purpose actually exist."[10] But the Act provides no guidance. "There is nothing at all in the Act about how dividends are to be paid, nor how profits are to be reckoned; all that is left and very judiciously and properly left, to the commercial world. It is not a subject for an Act of Parliament to say how

6. *Cleveland Trust plc, Re*, [1991] BCLC 424 Ch D; *Precission Dippings Ltd* v *Precission Dippings Marketing Ltd*, [1985] BCLC 385 CA; *Bairstow v Queens Moat Houses plc*, [2000] 1 BCLC 549 QBD.
7. [1933] Ch 321: [1933] All ER Rep 430: 148 LT 473.
8. *South Llanharren Colliery Co, Re*, (1879) 12 Ch D 503: 41 LT 567; *Menell et Cie Ltd, Re*, [1915] 1 Ch 759.
9. *Mac Pherson v European Strategic Bureau Ltd*, [1999] 2 BCLC 203 Ch D.
10. SHAH J (afterwards CJ) in *CIT v Standard Vacuum Oil Co*, [1966] 1 Comp LJ 187: AIR 1966 SC 1393, 1396, quoting from Fletcher, ENCYCLOPAEDIA ON CORPORATIONS, Vol 19, para 9237.

accounts are to be kept; what is to be put into a capital account, what into an income account, is left to men of business."[11]

The same truth is reflected by the following observations of RAM-ACHANDRA AYYAR, CJ, of the Madras High Court:[12]

"Section 205 of the Act only prescribes that dividend shall be paid out of profits of the company. It does not say further how those profits have to be ascertained. Profits of a year under the mercantile system of accounting only means the excess of receipts for the year over expenses and outgoings during the same year. It is not necessary that such excess should be in the form of cash in the till of the company. It will be open to a company to declare a dividend on the basis of its accounts... where it is based on the estimated profit, which had not actually come in the form of cash to the company; it will be open to it to pay such dividends from out of other cash in their hands or perhaps even to borrow and pay them off. That will not amount to paying dividend out of capital."

Neither have the courts thought it fit to formulate any rigid rules. The judicial attitude is best reflected by the following observation of Lord MACNAGHTEN in *Dovey* v *Cory*:[13]

I do not think it desirable for any tribunal to do what Parliament has abstained from doing, i.e. to formulate rules for the guidance and embarrassment of businessmen in the conduct of business affairs.

"[T]he real question for determination, therefore, is whether there are profits available for distribution, and this is to be answered according to the circumstances of each particular case, the nature of the company, and the evidence of competent witnesses. There is no single definition of the word 'profits' which will fit all cases."[14]

Thus "dividend fund" is a fluid concept. The primary concern of the courts has been that the capital is maintained in the form of assets if not equal to the paid-up capital at least sufficient to go round the creditors.[15] Once this is done, a complete latitude is given to businessmen to pay dividends in good faith so as to keep up their company's reputation.

---

11. LINDLEY LJ in *Lee* v *Neuchatel Asphalt Co*, (1889) 41 Ch D 1: 61 LT 11: [1886-90] All ER Rep 947.
12. *Hariprasad* v *Amalgamated Commercial Traders*, [1964] 1 Comp LJ 339, 349: AIR 1964 Mad 519: (1964) 34 Comp Cas 209, relying upon *Mercantile Trading Co, Re*, (1869) 4 Ch App 475: 20 LT 591.
13. [1895-99] All ER Rep 724: 1901 AC 477; *National Bank of Wales Ltd, Re*, [1899] 2 Ch 629: [1895-99] All ER Rep 715, the only case that was taken to the House of Lords on the matter of dividend; sub nom.
14. FARWELL J in *Bond* v *Barrow Haematite Steel Co*, [1902] 1 Ch 353: [1900-03] All ER Rep 484.
15. *See*, LINDLEY LJ in *Verner* v *General & Commercial Investment Trust Co*, [1894] 2 Ch 239: [1891-94] All ER Rep Ext 1409.

"People put their money into a trading company to give them an income and the sudden stoppage of all dividends would send down the value of their shares to zero and possibly involve its ruin."[16]

Separate Bank Account for Dividend

Three sub-sections have been added to sub-section (1) of Section 205 by the Amendment Act of 2000. Sub-section (1-A) provides that that the Board of directors may declare an interim dividend. The amount of dividend including interim dividend has to be deposited in a separate bank account within 5 days from the date of declaration of such dividend. Sub-section (1-B) provides that the amount of dividend including interim dividend so deposited shall be used for payment of interim dividend. Sub-section (3) declares that the provisions contained in Sections 205, 205-A, 205-C, 206, 206-A and 207 shall, to the extent possible, apply as much to interim dividend as they apply to regular dividend.

Rule in Lee v Neuchatel

The first specimen of this permissiveness is the rule laid down in *Lee* v *Neuchatel Asphalt Co.*[17] The essence of this decision has been thus stated:[18]

"Suppose that a company has a ship costing £3,00,000 and though good for ten years will at the end of that time have to be broken up. There is, therefore, roughly an annual depreciation or wasting of capital to the extent of £30,000. The company need not, in law, make any allowance for this before declaring a dividend."

In that case, the fixed capital of the company was an asphalt deposit which was being reduced from day to day and so became a wasting asset. Dividend was proposed to be paid out of profits shown by the revenue account in a particular year. A shareholder objected. "It was decided that when assets of the company are in the nature of wasting character depreciated by the efflux of time or exhaustion of material, such as mines, patents or leaseholds, if, for the purpose of carrying on the business of the company and getting a profit the annual consumption of that capital is necessary, there is no obligation by law or statute to create a reserve fund out of revenue to recoup the wasting nature of the capital."[19] LINDLEY LJ said: "The Companies Acts do not require capital to be made up if lost."

There was a storm of disapproval against this decision from business quarters.[20] But even so the ruling was re-affirmed in *Bolton* v *Natal Land*

---

16. MACNAGHTEN LC in *Dovey* v *Cory*, 1901 AC 477: [1895-99] All ER Rep 724.
17. (1889) 41 Ch D 1: 61 LT 11: [1886-90] All ER Rep 947.
18. H. Goitein, COMPANY LAW, 189 (1960).
19. *Mellon* v *Mississippi Glass Wi Co, Re*, (1910) 77 NJ Eq 498, cited in Frey, CASES AND MATERIALS ON CORPORATIONS AND PARTNERSHIP, 786 (1951).
20. *See* (1899) 5 LQR 221: (1899) LJ 353. Cristie, *Wasting Assets and Dividends*, (1893) 5 Jurd Rev 2230; Note: *Effect of Depreciation, Depletion and Appreciation of Assets on Payment of Dividends*, (1928) 28 Col LR 231; For another comment *see* (1934) 43 Yale LJ 1336.

and Colonization Co,[21] where the court held that a decline in the value of the land belonging to a company was not relevant to the calculation of dividend fund.[22]

In the next leading case, namely, *Verner v General & Commercial Investment Trust Co*[23] the rule was tightened only to this extent that "circulating capital" must be maintained out of revenue. The facts were:

A company had invested its capital to the extent of £6,00,000 in investments which had depreciated in value to the extent of £2,50,000. The income, however, left a balance of £23,000 after paying all the charges and expenses. The company proposed to pay a dividend.

The court of appeal allowed it. LINDLEY LJ said:

Fixed capital may be sunk and lost, and yet the excess of current receipts over current payments may be divided, but floating or circulating capital must be kept up, as otherwise it will enter into and form part of such excess, in which case to divide such excess without deducting the capital which forms part of it will be contrary to law.[24]

The distinction between "fixed" and "circulating" capital was explained in *Ammonia Soda Co Ltd v Chamberlain*.[25] Fixed capital is that which is invested in assets intended to be retained by the company more or less permanently and used in producing an income. Ordinary examples are buildings and mills, ships and land. Circulating capital is "a portion of the subscribed capital intended to be used by being temporarily parted with and circulated in business, in the form of money, goods or other assets, and which, or the proceeds of which, are intended to return to the company with an increment, and are intended to be used again and again, and to always return with some accretion." But this is not a permanent division. The emphasis is on the purpose for which the capital is used for the time being. Fixed capital may in course of time become floating capital and *vice versa*. Moreover, an item of assets which is, in the case of one company, a fixed capital may be circulating capital in the case of another company. Thus, for example, in *Bond v Barrow Haematite Steel Co*,[26] FARWELL J held that "the money invested in the leasehold mines, furnaces and cottages was in this company (a smelting company) to be regarded as 'circulating capital', and, therefore, should be maintained, such items coming into the accounts before any profit could be said to be earned."

---

21. [1892] 2 Ch 124: 61 LJ Ch 281: 65 LT 786: 8 TLR 148.
22. For a remarkable account of the development of dividend rules *see* Basil S. Yamey, *Aspects of the Law relating to Company Dividends*, (1941) 4 Mod LR 273.
23. [1894] 2 Ch 239: [1891-94] All ER Rep Ext 1409.
24. *Verner v General & Commercial Investment Trust Co*, [1894] 2 Ch 239, 266. *See* also *Kingston Cotton Mill Co, Re*, (1896) 1 Ch 331, where depreciation of the mill property of a company was held not relevant to the calculation of the distributable profits.
25. [1916-17] All ER Rep 708: [1918] 1 Ch 266: 118 LT 48 CA.
26. [1902] 1 Ch 353: [1900-03] All ER Rep 484.

But it is not necessary to make up losses of circulating capital incurred in previous years before paying dividends out of the current year's earnings.[27]

Unrealised appreciation of assets

Unrealised appreciation of the value of fixed assets was in practice distributed as dividends and was also sanctioned by court decisions. Thus in *Ammonia Soda Co Ltd* v *Chamberlain*:[28]

A company's land and building stood at the value of £63,246. The directors in good faith appreciated the value to £83,788. The surplus thus created was used to wipe out a debit balance in the profit and loss account and the trading profits were declared as dividends.

It was held that the dividend was properly declared. Another illustration was *Lubbock* v *British Bank of South America*:[29]

A company's undertaking at Brazil acquired at £5,00,000 was sold for £8,75,000. The company decided not to carry on a similar business. After deducting all expenses, a net surplus of £2,05,000 was allowed to be distributed as dividends.

The appreciated value should not be blindly or arbitrarily fixed. The directors must in good faith exercise an informed judgment. Further, appreciation in the value of an item of assets should not be taken in isolation. The assets as a whole must be considered. Thus, where certain promissory notes declared as bad debts were unexpectedly paid up in full, the court held that this accretion could not be deemed as profits without reference to the whole accounts taken fairly.[30] It is also necessary that the increase should not be due to temporary market fluctuations and the share capital will remain intact after the distribution.[31] This is known as the 'net assets test'. This has to be observed by public companies. Realised profits cannot be distributed if the amount of the net assets is less then the aggregate of called-up capital and undistributable reserves and the amount of the proposed distribution will not lower the amount of those assets to lower than that aggregate. Net assets means the aggregate of assets less the aggregate of liabilities.[32]

---

27. *National Bank of Wales Ltd, Re*, [1899] 2 Ch 629: [1895-99] All ER Rep 715, affirmed sub nom. *Dovey* v *Cory*, [1895-99] All ER Rep 724: 1901 AC 477.
28. [1916-17] All ER Rep 708: [1918] 1 Ch 266: 118 LT 48 CA.
29. [1892] 2 Ch 198: [1891-94] All ER Rep Ext 1753: 67 LT 74.
30. *Foster* v *New Trinidad Lake Asphalt Co*, [1901] 1 Ch 208. Dividend is declared by the company in general meeting on the recommendation of directors. Distribution of profits or assets by the liquidator in the company's winding up is not a dividend. See, *First ITO* v *Short Bros*, [1966] 1 Comp LJ 279; *Kanhaiya Lal Bhargava* v *Official Liquidator*, [1965] 1 Comp LJ 310.
31. *Dimbula Valley (Ceylon) Tea Co* v *Laurie*, [1961] 1 Ch 353: [1961] 1 All ER 769, noted 24 Mod LR 525.
32. Undistributable reserves include share premium account, capital redemption reserve, unrealised profits and any other reserve which cannot be distributed.

Profits gained on realisation or revaluation of assets is known as capital profit or capital gain. The position of law now is that such profits can be distributed by way of dividend only when it has been actually realised. The English Act of 1980 had to adopt this restriction because of EEC directives. The English Act of 1985 provides that whether or not a profit is a realised profit is to be taken according to the generally accepted accounting principles prevailing at the moment.[33]

The status of accounting standards is that of expert opinion on what is a true and fair view. Considering the evidential role of accounting standards, it has been held that while they are not conclusive and also not rigid rules, they are very strong evidence as to what is the proper standard which should be adopted.

Where assets have been revalued but not realised and by reason of the revaluation a greater amount has to be provided for depreciation, such excess can be treated as realised profit and, therefore, can be utilised for distribution.[34]

STATUTORY PROVISIONS

Depreciation [S. 205]

Since the Amendment Act of 1960, it has become obligatory to provide for depreciation as required by Section 205(2). Depreciation must be provided for the current year as well as for arrears since the amendment. The sub-section says that depreciation must be provided to the extent specified in Section 350. This section says that depreciation is to be calculated at the rate specified in Schedule XIV.[35] If this Act makes no

---

33. Sections 262-263, Sch. IV para 9, English Act, 1985.
34. Part II of Sch. VI, Companies Act, 1956 and Guidance Note on *Treatment of Reserve created on Revaluation of Fixed Assets*, Research Committee, ICAL, New Delhi, 1982. The Financial Accounting Standard Board of USA observed that realisation in the most precise sense means the process of converting non-cash resources and rights into money and is most precisely used in accounting and financial reporting to refer to sale of assets for cash or claims to cash. The related terms "realised" and "unrealised" therefore identify revenue or gains or losses on assets sold and unsold respectively.
35. This schedule has been added by the amendment of 1988 which, according to a Govt, clarification has been declared to be effective from April 2, 1987, though the amendment of Ss. 205 and 350 has been enforced w.e.f. June 15, 1988. It has also been clarified that the rates contained in the schedule should be taken as the minimum rates and, therefore, after the applicability of the schedule lower rates cannot be charged on assets purchased after the applicability. However, if on the basis of a *bona fide* technological evaluation, higher rates of depreciation are justified, they may be provided with proper disclosure by way of a note forming part of the annual accounts. The clarification further says that a company must necessarily provide SLM (Straight Line Method) depreciation at the rates specified in the schedule calculating them on the basis of years including fractions of years. It is stated that SLM rates corresponding to the WDV (Written Down Value) rates as specified in Sch XIV can be different than those prescribed provided a company continues to determine the rates as provided under S. 205. Thus against SLM rates prescribed under Sch XIV of 11.3 per cent (triple shift rate for general plant and machinery) a company can charge depreciation at the rate of 10.56% (Circular No 2 of 1989 of March 7, 1989; (1989) 65 Comp Cas 628 St.) Rates of depreciation have been revised with effect from Dec. 16, 1993. *See* DCA Circular No

provision for a particular kind of asset its depreciation may be worked out on a basis approved by the Central Government. Every company has the choice either to adopt the above method, or to work out depreciation "by dividing ninety-five per cent of the original cost of the depreciable asset by the specified period in respect of such asset".

The Act does not require any provision for depletion of a wasting asset. But "if any asset is sold, discarded, demolished or destroyed for any reason before depreciation for such asset has been provided for in full, the excess, if any of the written down value of such asset over its sale proceeds or its scrap value shall be written off in the financial year in which it is sold".[36]

Previous year's losses incurred after the effective date of the Amendment Act of 1960 must also be set off against the profits of any subsequent year or years before any dividend can be paid.[37]

Compulsory reserves [S. 205]

The requirement of creating compulsory reserves has been introduced by the Companies Amendment Act, 1974. Sub-section (2-A) has been added to Section 205. Before any dividend is declared or paid, certain percentage of profits as may be prescribed by the Central Government, but not exceeding 10%, will have to be transferred to the reserves of the company. The company may, however, create greater reserves.[38]

If on account of inadequacy of profits in a particular year, the company has to pay dividends out of the previous years' reserves, it should follow such rules as may be made by the Central Government. A departure from such rules can be made only with the previous approval of the Central Government.[39]

The preference shareholders of a private company called an extraordinary general meeting and passed a resolution complaining that they had not received their dividend for two years. The meeting and resolution were held to be not valid because the company had not yet commenced business. There was no question of profit and its distribution.[40]

14/93 of Dec 16, 1993.

36. Proviso to S. 205.

37. S. 205(1), proviso (*b*). The proviso (*c*) empowers the Central Government to waive in any particular case the requirement of providing for depreciation. The word loss would include depreciation, *Garden Silk Wvg Factory* v *CIT*, (1991) 189 ITR 512 SC. There is no reason to give the word "loss", as used in S. 205 a different meaning from one in which it is ordinarily understood only because it has to be read with S. 115 of the IT Act, 1961. *V. V. Trans-investments (P) Ltd* v *CIT*, [1999] 3 Comp LJ 173 SC.

38. Companies (Transfer of Profits to Reserves) Rules, 1975.

39. S. 205-A(3), *inserted* by the Amendment Act, 1974. Creation of reserves is in the discretion of the board. Shareholders' approval is not necessary. *CIT* v *Oswal Woollens*, (1981) 51 Comp Cas 733 P&H. Companies (Declaration of Dividend out of Reserves) Rules, 1975.

40. *Hillcrest Realty SDN BHD* v *Hotel Queen Road (P) Ltd*, (2006) 133 Comp Cas 742 CLB. A similar matter was before the High Court of Delhi in *Hotel Queen Roads (P) Ltd* v *Hillcrest Realty SDN BHD*, (2006) 130 Comp Cas 59 Del.

Unpaid dividend account [S. 205-A]

A declared dividend has to be paid within thirty days. If this is not done, or the dividend warrant is not claimed by the shareholder within thirty days, the company shall have to open an account in any scheduled bank, to be called, "Unpaid Dividend Account" and transfer the unpaid dividend into it. Dividends which have remained unpaid up to the commencement of the Act, shall also have to be transferred to the account within six months. The amendment of 1988 (Amendment Act, 1999) added this explanation that the expression "dividend which remains unpaid" means any dividend the warrant in respect thereof has not been cashed or which has otherwise not been paid or claimed. The company shall have to pay interest at the rate of 12% for the benefit of the shareholders concerned on any amount of unpaid dividend which is not transferred to the account. [Sub-section (4)]

If the amount remains unclaimed for a period of three years from the date of deposit, the company has to transfer it to the general revenue account of the Central Government. The person entitled to the amount may claim it from the Government.[41] The company has to file the necessary particulars with the Government.

Transfer of unpaid dividend to Investor Education and Protection Fund

Before the Companies (Amendment) Act, 1999 (w.e.f. 31-10-1998), unpaid dividend remained in the company's unpaid dividend account for a period of three years and thereafter it was transferred to the general revenue account of the Government. The amendment has changed this position. The money will remain in the company's account for seven years and will then be transferred to the newly conceived fund known as the Investor Education and Protection Fund.

Investor Education and Protection Fund [S. 205-C]

The Companies (Amendment) Act, 1999 added this new section so as to bring into existence a new fund known as the Investor Education and Protection Fund. The Central Government has to establish this Fund. The following amounts have to be credited to this Fund:

1. the amounts in the unpaid dividend accounts of companies;
2. the application moneys received by companies for allotment of any securities and due for refund;
3. the matured deposits with companies;
4. the matured debentures with companies.

---

41. S. 205-B. An indemnity bond is prescribed [Rule 6(5)] where the amount claimed is more than Rs 2500. Press Note (1989) 65 Comp Cas 573 St. The affected shareholder has to be informed of the fact of the transfer. *See* Rule 4-A of the Central Government Rules, 1978.

These four items will be credited to the fund only when they have remained unclaimed or unpaid for a period of five years from the date when they became due for payment.

5. the interest accruing on the above items.

6. grants and donations given to the Fund by the Central Government, State Governments, companies or other institutions for the purposes of the fund, and

An *Explanation* to Section 205-C provides that no claim shall lie against the fund or the company in respect of individual amounts which were unclaimed and unpaid for a period of seven years from the dates that they first became due for payment and no payment can be made in respect of any such claims.[42]

The Fund has to be utilised for promotion of investor awareness and protection of the interests of investors in accordance with the rules as may be prescribed. The utilisation shall be in accordance with the prescribed rules.[43]

The Central Government has to constitute an organ for the management of the fund by notification in the Official Gazette. The Government will specify an authority or a committee. Such organ will administer the fund and maintain separate accounts and other relevant records in relation to the Fund. The form of administration will be prescribed in consultation with the Comptroller and Auditor General of India.[44] The organ shall be competent to spend the moneys out of the Fund for carrying out the objects with which it has been established.[45]

Payment to registered holders [Ss. 206 and 206-A]

Dividend warrant should be sent to the registered holder of the shares or to his order or to his bankers and where share warrants have been issued, to the bearer of the warrant or his bankers. A dividend paid to the registered transferee of shares cannot be recovered back from him by the transferor even if the transfer has been subsequently struck off on a technical ground

---

42. *Gauray Toshnival* v *Best & Crompton Engg Ltd*, (2004) 120 Comp Cas 451 CLB, the CLB could not issue directions for payment. *J. Satyamarayana* v *Purasawakum Permanent Fund Ltd*, (2005) CLC 509 CLB: (2006) 131 Comp Cas 493, the explanation does not permit any claim of refund, irrespective of the genuineness of reasons put forth by the claimant, depositor had died, no renewal is terms of contract, depositor's nominee laid claim after seven years, thus the company was not in default in not refunding deposit, CLB did not issue direction for repayment.

43. S. 205-C(3). *Pragma Desai* v *National Stock Exchange of India Ltd*, (2006) 132 Comp Cas 909 Bom, a writ petition to get amount awarded in arbitration from the Investor Protection Fund. The court said that proper remedy was enforcement of the award under the relevant statute. Writ petition not maintainable. Also to the same effect, *Saurin J. Parikh* v *Stock Exchange*, (2006) 132 Comp Cas 910 Bom.

44. S. 205-C(4).

45. S. 205-C(5).

like inadequacy or non-cancellation of stamps.[46] Such technical error should be pointed out to the transferee within good time (one year) so as to enable him to rectify, otherwise it would be too late.

Where an instrument of transfer of shares has been lodged with the company, but such transfer has not been registered by the company, the amount of dividend should be transferred to the "Unclaimed Dividend Account" unless the company is authorised by the registered holder to pay it to the transferee. The rights or bonus shares in respect of the shares under transfer must be kept by the company in abeyance until the matter is finally disposed of.[47]

Declared dividend a statutory debt

Once a dividend is declared it becomes a statutory debt from the company to its shareholders. As pointed out by the Supreme Court in *Bacha F. Guzdar* v *CIT*,[48] "the shareholders' right of participation in the profits of the company exists independently of any declaration of dividend by the company. A declaration is necessary only for the enjoyment of profits. It will follow that once a declaration of dividend is made and it becomes payable, it will partake of the nature of a debt due from the company to the shareholder."[49] But a declaration of dividend subject to remittances from Pakistan or subject to some other condition precedent is not a declaration at all because it does not create an immediately payable debt.[50]

A dividend which has been declared, but not paid nor credited, may be revoked with the consent of shareholders.[51] An interim declared dividend may be revoked before payment.[52]

Interim dividend

The expression "interim dividend" has been defined by the Amendment Act, 2000 by providing that "dividend includes any interim dividend".[53] The declaration of an interim dividend does not create a debt against the company. Dividends can be declared only by a resolution of the shareholders in accordance with the directors' recommendation at a general

---

46. *Kothari Industrial Corpn Ltd* v *Lazor Detergents (P) Ltd*, [1994] 1 Comp LJ 178 CLB Mad.
47. Where the documents were rejected by the company, it could not be said that there was a pending application for transfer. There was nothing wrong in sending bonus shares and rights issue to the transferor. *Nagarujan* v *Lakshmi Vilas Bank Ltd*, (1997) 50 Comp Cas 392 CLB.
48. AIR 1955 SC 74: (1955) 1 SCR 876: (1955) 25 Comp Cas 1.
49. The Court relied upon *Severn & Wye & Severn Bridge Rly Co, Re*, LR [1896] 1 Ch 559; *Kitchner, Re*, LR [1929] 2 Ch 121. *See also Godavaribai* v *Amalgamated Commercial Traders*, [1965] 2 Comp LJ 272 Mad.
50. *Jhimi Bajoria* v *CIT*, [1970] 1 Comp LJ 195: 40 Comp Cas 780 Cal.
51. *Kishinchand Chellaram* v *CIT*, (1962) 32 Comp Cas 1046 SC.
52. *Kothari Textiles Ltd* v *CWT*, (1963) 33 Comp Cas 217; Halsbury's LAWS OF ENGLAND 355-56 (4th Edn, Vol 7).
53. S. 2(14-A).

meeting. But, if so permitted by the articles, the directors can declare an interim dividend between two meetings. "It does not create a debt enforceable against the company, for it is open to the directors to rescind the resolution before payment."[54] Shareholders do not get any vested right under a directors' resolution declaring an interim dividend.[55]

Mode of Payment [S. 207]

In order to ensure prompt payment of dividend to shareholders, Section 207 imposes a penalty if a dividend has been declared and is not paid within thirty days from the date of declaration.[56] The provision is sufficiently complied with if the dividend warrant is posted within the above time.

---

54. *See* N. Netar, *Company Dividends: Whether to be declared only at the Annual General Meeting*, 1965 JILI 151. No debt arises until directors fix a date for payment. *Potel v IRC*, [1971] 2 All ER 504 CD. *See* also *Vazir Sultan Tobacco Co v CIT*, (1981) 4 SCC 435, 455, where it has been held that mere recommendation of a dividend by director does not by itself have any effect unless approved by the general meeting. The case had arisen out of a taxation matter, the question being whether recommended dividend and a provision for it be regarded as having become a part of the company's reserves so as to be included in the company's capital computation. The Supreme Court answered the question in the negative. A. N. SEN J expressed dissenting opinion on the ground that a recommended dividend is generally accepted by the shareholders and therefore setting aside a sum of money for payment of such dividend should be treated as a reserve, (1981) 4 SCC 469.
55. *CIT v Express Newspapers Ltd*, [1998] 3 Comp LJ 23 SC, the court was concerned with rebate on dividends under the IT Act, 1961.
56. The penalty is incurred by every director, provided he is knowingly a party to the default. Punishment is simple imprisonment which may extend to three years. Liability in terms of fine is also incurred. The fine is of one thousand rupees for every day during which the default continues. The proviso to the section says that no offence shall be deemed to have been committed within the meaning of the foregoing provision in the following cases, namely:
    (*a*) where the dividend could not be paid by reason of the operation of any law;
    (*b*) where a shareholder has given directions to the company regarding the payment of the dividend and those directions cannot be complied with;
    (*c*) where there is a dispute regarding the right to receive the dividend;
    (*d*) where the dividend has been lawfully adjusted by the company against any sum due to it from the shareholder; or
    (*e*) where, for any other reason, the failure to pay the dividend or to post the warrant within the period aforesaid was not due to any default on the part of the company.
    But no offence is committed where the dividend is not paid by reason of the operation of any law, or where a shareholder's directions cannot be complied with, or where there is a dispute as to the right, or where the dividend has been set off. See, *Hanuman Prasad v Hiralal*, [1966] 3 Comp LJ 136 All; on appeal to the Supreme Court, [1970] 2 Comp LJ 195. The offence is complete at the place of the registered office and, therefore, the courts there would have jurisdiction in the matter, *H. V. Jayaram v ICICI Ltd*, (2000) 99 Comp Cas 341 overruling *Ranbaxy Laboratories Ltd v Indra Kala*, (1997) 88 Comp Cas 348 Raj. A complaint filed one year after the default was held to be time-barred, *NEPC India Ltd v ROC*, (1999) 97 Comp Cas 500 Mad. The company has to prove despatch of the dividend warrant, *Nutech Ltd v Ch Mohan Rao*, [2000] CLC 1284 AP; *Nutech Agro Ltd v Ch Mohan Rao*, (2002) 109 Comp Cas 487 AP, the burden is on the company to show that there was timely payment or transfer to the unpaid dividend account. *SOL Pharmaceuticals Ltd v ROC*, (2002) 111 Comp Cas 845 AP, delay became excusable when it was shown that the company's financial institutions required it not to pay dividend unless overdues under loans were liquidated.

Dividend is to be paid in cash.[57] Payment in respect of any share should be made to the registered holder or to his order or to his banker.[58] In the case of a share warrant, payment should be made to the bearer of the warrant or to his bankers.[59]

The rate of dividend can be regulated, if the articles so permit, according to the amount paid up on each share where more amount has been paid up on some shares than on others.[60]

Payment of interest out of capital [S. 208]

"Interest" should be distinguished from "dividends". Interest on capital can be paid out of capital in certain cases provided for in Section 208. Where shares are issued for raising money to meet the expenses of construction of any work, building or plant which cannot be made profitable for a long period, the company may pay interest on the paid up amount of such capital and charge the same to the capital account as part of the cost of construction. Following conditions have to be fulfilled to enable the company to make such payments:

1. There should be authority to that effect in the company's articles.
2. Previous sanction of the Central Government should be obtained.
3. The Government may at the expense of the company appoint a competent person to make an inquiry into the matter.
4. The Government sanctions the period for which such interest can be paid and it should not go beyond the close of the half year next after the half year during which the work has been completed.
5. The rate of interest is 12 per cent unless the Government changes it by notification.[61]

Such payment does not operate as reduction of capital.

Reserve fund

Article 87 of Table A empowers directors, before recommending any dividend, to set aside out of the profits any sum as a "reserve fund". Such fund is applicable at the discretion of directors for any purposes to which profits may be applied. It may be used to equalise dividends, or it may be invested in business or may be held in the form of other investments. When it is used in business it does not thereby become capitalised.[62]

---

57. S. 205(3). Dividend warrant should be sent by registered post. Registration is compulsory where the nature of the envelope e.g. window envelope, is such that it reveals its contents.
58. S. 206(*a*).
59. S. 206(*b*).
60. S. 93.
61. *Vide* notification GSR 426 of 8-9-1995.
62. *Hoare & Co Ltd, Re*, [1904] 2 Ch 208: [1904-07] All ER Rep 635 CA.

Even where there is no provision of this kind in the articles, a reserve may be created.[63] A compulsory reserve has to be maintained in accordance with Companies (Transfer of Profits to Reserves) Rules, 1975.

Capitalisation of profits

A company may in general meeting, on the recommendation of the board, resolve and convert into capital any sum standing to the credit of profit or loss account or reserve fund account or otherwise available for distribution.[64] As a general rule only such funds can be capitalised as would be available for dividend distribution.[65]

"It has been the generally accepted view of the law of this country that, if the surplus on capital accounts results from a valuation made in good faith by competent valuers, and is not likely to be liable to short term fluctuations, it may properly be capitalised."[66]

When a distributable profit is capitalised, it is in essence a declaration of dividend combined with the application of that dividend on behalf of the shareholders entitled to participate in it in paying up shares to be allotted and issued to them in satisfaction of their rights of participation.[67]

The advantage to the company is two-fold. A self-financing of this kind helps the company to rid itself of market influences.[68] Secondly, it makes available capital to carry on a larger and more profitable business.[69]

There must be a clear authority to capitalise profits in the company's articles, for, otherwise, a shareholder can insist upon payment in cash.[70]

It has been held by the Supreme Court in *Shri Gopal Paper Mills* v *CIT*[71] that the shareholders become the owners of bonus shares from the date of resolution and not from the date on which certificates are issued. The Gujarat High Court has, on the other hand, held in *CIT* v *Chunilal Khushaldas*[72] that bonus shares cannot be said to be acquired or held by a shareholder before they come into existence by allotment and issue. The above-mentioned Supreme Court decision was not cited before the court.

Bonus shares

If the articles so authorise, a company has the "power to convert its accumulated undivided profits into bonus shares".[73] "Directors may

---

63. *Burland* v *Earle*, 1902 AC 83: [1900-03] All ER Rep Ext 1452: 85 LT 553 PC.
64. Article 96 of Table A.
65. BUCKLEY J in *Dimbula Valley (Ceylon) Tea Co* v *Laurie*, [1961] 1 Ch 353: [1961] 1 All ER 769.
66. *Id.* at 372. *See* also *IRC* v *Thornton, Kelly & Co*, [1957] 1 WLR 482: [1957] 1 All ER 650.
67. *Hill* v *Permanent Trustees Co*, 1930 AC 720 PC.
68. Paul P. Harbrecht, *The Modern Corporation*, (1964) 64 Col LR 1410, 1415-16.
69. VISCOUNT FINLAY in *IRC* v *Greenwood*, [1921] 2 AC 171, 193.
70. *Wood* v *Odessa Waterworks Co*, (1889) 42 Ch D 636.
71. (1970) 2 SCC 80: AIR 1970 SC 1750.
72. (1974) 44 Comp Cas 90.
73. *Shri Gopal Paper Mills* v *CIT*, (1970) 2 SCC 80.

capitalise any profits and allot to the ordinary shareholders in respect of the net amount capitalised fully paid-up shares of the company."[74] The amount may also be used in paying up any amounts for the time being unpaid on any shares.[75] The two other sources from which bonus shares may be financed are Share Premium Account,[76] and Capital Redemption Reserve Account.[77]

Issue of bonus shares is a bare machinery for capitalising profits. There is no distribution of profit among shareholders. Where a company used its development rebate fund for issuing bonus shares, there was no disbursement of money and the company remained entitled to development rebate.[78] In the words of the Supreme Court:[79]

"Bonus share is an accretion. A bonus share is issued when the company capitalises its profits by transferring an amount equal to the face value of the share from its reserve to the nominal capital. In other words, the undistributed profit of the company is retained by the company under the head of capital against the issue of further shares to its shareholders. Bonus shares have, therefore, been described as a distribution of capitalised undivided profit. In the case of issue of bonus share there is an increase in the capital of the company by transferring of an amount from its reserve to the capital account and thereby resulting in additional shares being issued to the shareholders. A bonus share is a property which comes into existence with an identity and value of its own and capable of being bought and sold as such."

Utilisation of reserves arising from revaluation of assets for the purpose of issuing fully paid-up bonus shares is permissible in law. The articles of the company authorised it to issue bonus out of reserves arising from revaluation of capital assets. The articles also defined 'dividend' as including bonus.[80]

Bonus shares cannot be issued as a gift.[81]

---

74. VISCOUNT FINLAY in *IRC* v *Greenwood*, [1921] 2 AC 171, 193.
75. Article 96 of Table A.
76. S. 78(2).
77. S. 80(5). *See* Section M of the SEBI Guidelines, 1992 relating to issue of bonus shares. The Department of Company Affairs' advice to unlisted closely held public companies and private companies is that they should not provide for the issue of bonus shares out of revaluation reserves. *Satish Chandra Sanvalka* v *Tinplate Dealers Assn (P) Ltd*, (2001) 107 Comp Cas 98 CLB, issue of bonus shares from revaluation reserves by a company which had adopted Table A was held to be not valid.
78. *Hansur Plywood Works Ltd* v *CIT*, [1998] 1 Comp LJ 22 SC.
79. *Standard Chartered Bank* v *Custodian*, (2000) 6 SCC 427: AIR 2000 SC 1488.
80. *Bhagwati Developers* v *Peerless General Finance & Investment Co*, (2005) 6 SCC 718: AIR 2005 SC 3345.
81. *Eddystone Marine Ins Co, Re*, [1893] 3 Ch 9: 69 LT 363. See, *CIT* v *Khushaldas*, (1974) 44 Comp Cas 90, where BHAGWATI CJ, explains the nature of bonus shares. As to the impact of bonus issue upon value of shares, see *Chandrakant Mulraj* v *TELCO*, (1985) 58 Comp Cas 320 Bom.

A resolution was passed at a meeting of the company for issue of bonus shares to equity shareholders. The directors were authorised to decide the date of issue. A shareholder transferred his shares after the meeting but before the date specified by the directors. It was held that he being no longer a shareholder at the date of the issue, he was not entitled to the bonus shares in respect of the shareholding which he had already transferred.[82]

ACCOUNTS

Books of account or accounting records [S. 209]

Section 209 requires every company to keep at its registered office proper books of account. The first important obligation is to maintain books containing the following disclosures—

- (*a*) all sums of money received and expended by the company and the matter in respect of which the receipt and expenditure has taken place;
- (*b*) all sales and purchase of goods by the company;
- (*c*) all assets and liabilities of the company;
- (*d*) in the case of a company engaged in production, processing, manufacturing or mining activities, particulars relating to utilisation of material or labour or other items of cost as may be prescribed by the Central Government.[83]

A view of what constitutes proper books of account appears from the provisions of Section 541. The company should maintain such books of account as are necessary to exhibit and explain the transactions and financial position of the business of the company, including books containing entries made from day to day, in sufficient detail, of all cash received and cash paid. Where the business of the company involves dealings in goods, the records should contain statements of the annual stocktakings. Where the dealings are not by way of retailing of goods, a record should be maintained of all goods sold and purchased showing the goods, and the buyers and sellers of such goods in such sufficient details as to enable those goods and those buyers and sellers to be identified.[84]

---

82. *Rajiv Nag* v *Quality Assurance Institute (India) Ltd*, (2001) 105 Comp Cas 178 CLB; *Pradip Kumar Chetlongia* v *Bajaj Auto Ltd*, (2005) 59 SCL 372 CLB, no right to bonus unless the claimant's name is present in the register of members.
83. Clause (*d*) of S. 209(1) has been *inserted* by the Companies (Amendment) Act, 1965. This was considered necessary for the purposes of cost accounting and cost auditing. Small scale industrial undertakings have been exempted from this requirement. The definition of such an undertaking is to be found in Industries (Development and Regulation) Act, 1951. Cost Accounting Record Rules have been prescribed by the Central Government.
84. Section 541 is in connection with liability in winding and liability follows if such records are not available for the two-year period preceding winding up. The requirement becomes a matter of universal application because winding up may creep in unpredictably.

Such books may be kept either at the company's registered office or at any other place the board of directors may decide. Within seven days of any such decision, the address of that place must be sent to the Registrar.

Where a company has a branch office, such accounts relating to the branch business must be maintained there and at intervals of three months summarised accounts should be forwarded to the registered office.[85]

True and fair view

Accounts must give a true and fair view of the state of affairs of the company.[86] "A balance sheet must not be a mere inventory. It is supposed to be a pictorial representation of the trading position of the company. To determine whether a statement is false, its effect upon an ordinary investor should be the test. Thus where loans given to an embryonic firm were described as 'other deposits', the accounts were held to be false."[87] That is why sub-section (3) prescribes that proper books of account shall not be deemed to be kept if there are not kept such books as are necessary to give a true and fair view of the state of affairs of the company and if they are not kept on accrual basis according to the double entry system of accounting.[88]

Directors' fiduciary obligations would compel them to make full and frank disclosures so as to help those who are entitled to use the company's accounts for guidance in their decision making. The mode and manner of disclosure must be such as would show the reality of the financial position and working results of the company. Disclosures should be clear and unambiguous and in accordance with fundamental accounting assumptions and the commonly accepted accounting policies.

It has been held under the EEC directives that the requirement of true and fair view was ensured by taking account of all elements (i.e. profits

---

85. S. 209(2).
86. Ss. 209(3) and 211(1) and (5). As to the meaning of "true and fair view" the general feeling is that the standards adopted by the accounting profession should be followed. It has been said that "although Statements of Standard Accounting Practice (SSAP) has no direct legal effect and is simply a rule of professional conduct for accountants, it is likely to have an indirect effect on the content which English courts will give to the "true and fair" concept because it represents an important statement of professional opinion about the standards which may reasonably be expected in accounts which are intended to be true and fair, and because readers of accounts can expect that they will conform to the standards set by the accounting profession". *See*, K.P.E. Lasok and Edmond Grace, *Fair Accounting*, 1988 JBL 235. For a study of further literature on the subject see the joint opinion of Leonard Hoffman QC and Mary Ardon, ACCOUNTING STANDARDS, 178-182 (1984-85) and a review of that opinion by Peter Bird, *What is a True and Fair View*, 1980 JBL 480. For a study of "off balance sheet accounting" see *Off-Balance Sheet Financing: An Accountant's view*, 1988 JBL 398.
87. *Legal Remembrancer, Bengal* v *Akhil Bandhu Guha*, ILR (1937) 1 Cal 328. For liability for false accounts *see* S. 628 and *P. P. Looke* v *N. J. Mathew*, (1967) 37 Comp Cas 790 Ker: [1967] 2 Comp LJ 146.
88. Government companies have been exempted from the requirement of accrual system. GSR 550(E) dated 16-5-1989.

made, liabilities and losses incurred, charges, income) which actually related to the financial year in question.[89]

Accrual basis.—According to the guidance notes[90] there are two basic features of this system of accounting. First, revenue means revenue earned, whether received in cash for the time being or not; second, costs are incurred when they become payable whether actually paid or not. How these methods are to be applied by an enterprise constitutes its accounting policy namely, a method of accounting which reflects the truth so that those for whose information the accounts are meant are able to get a fair view of things. Hence, what is more important is the substance of the financial position of the company and not the forms and formats through which that substance is presented as a true and fair view. Forms and formats are only for guidance. That is why latitude is given to follow as nearly as may be possible under the circumstances of a particular enterprise, with only this obligation that any significant departure from the prescribed method under accounting policy should be disclosed. Schedule VI itself requires disclosure of accounting policy in reference to some items. They are: policy regarding mode of valuation of stock and basis of valuation of investments.

Balance sheet of holding company [Ss. 212-214].— See under "Holding company and subsidiary" in Chapter 19 dealing with "Kinds of Company".

Annexure of profit and loss account [S. 216].—The profit and loss account is required to be annexed to the balance sheet, whereas the auditors' report is only attached to it, including auditors' special, separate or supplementary report. An annexure becomes a part of the thing to which it is annexed. Things attached are only enclosed with or fastened to the main thing. Auditors have to pay attention to all documents which have been given the status of annexure to accounts. They may refer to any particular document which is attached if it is necessary for audit purposes and in that case the document so commented upon will form part of the auditor's report. According to Section 222 the board's report is attached and not annexed. The proviso to the section gives this latitude that the board's report may give information which is required to be given in accounts and in that case the document containing such information shall be annexed to the accounts.

Preservation of account books

Account books for the preceding eight years should be preserved in good condition.[91] Under the SEBI (Registrars to Issue and Share Transfer

---

89. *Tomberger* v *Gebruder Vonder Wettern GmbH*, (1996) 2 BCLC 457 ECJ.
90. ICAI Guidance Note on Accrual Basis of Accounting.
91. S. 208(4-A). Failure on the part of officers listed in sub-section (6) is a punishable offence under S. 209(5). *P. S. Bedi* v *ROC*, (1986) 60 Comp Cas 1061 Del.

Agents) Rules, 1993, the period prescribed for preservation of documents and records is that of three years. Documents relating to a public issue have been held to be a part of the records under the Act. The period of 8 years would prevail over the period prescribed by SEBI.[92]

Duty of compliance

Persons in charge of the company's management have been put under the duty of compliance. They are required to take all reasonable steps to comply with the accounting requirements. If they fail to do so or by their own wilful act cause a default, they become punishable.[93] It would be a defence to show that a competent and reliable person was charged with the duty of compliance and he was in a position to discharge his duty. This liability is incurred by the managing director, manager, all officers and other employees detailed in Section 240,[94] and in the absence of such persons, every director of the company; or any person made in charge of the matter by the managing director, manager or board of directors.

Accounts to comply with accounting standards

The Companies (Amendment) Act, 1999 has prescribed this requirement by amending Section 211 that every profit and loss account and balance sheet shall comply with accounting standards.[95] It is further provided by the amendment[96] that if there is any deviation from the prescribed standards, the annual accounts shall state:

1. the fact that there has been a deviation;
2. the reasons for such deviation; and .
3. the financial implication of the deviation.

It is further provided by the amendment that for the purposes of this section "accounting standards" means such standards of accounting recommended by the Institute of Chartered Accountants of India as may be prescribed by the Central Government in consultation with the National Advisory Committee on Accounting Standards upto such time that the National Advisory Committee is constituted, the standards of accounting specified by the Institute of Chartered Accountants are to be taken as accounting standards.

National Advisory Committee on Accounting Standards [S. 210-A]

This section has been added by the Companies (Amendment) Act, 1999 (w.e.f. 31-10-1998). The object is that of constituting a committee for establishing accounting standards. The National Advisory Committee will

---

92. *Rajesh Gupta* v *SEBI*, (2000) 39 CLA 82 SAT.
93. Imprisonment up to 6 months or fine up to Rs 10,000 or both. S. 209(5).
94. This category would not include bankers, auditors and legal advisers.
95. S. 211(3-A).
96. S. 211(3-B).

constituted by notification in the Official Gazette. It will advise the Central Government on the formulation and laying down of accounting policies and accounting standards for adoption by companies or a class of companies under the Act.

The membership of the Committee has to be as follows:[1]

1. A Chairperson who shall be a person of eminence well versed in accountancy finance, business administration, business law, economics and similar discipline.

2. One member each to be nominated by the Institute of Chartered Accountants of India, Institute of Costs and Works Accountants of India and the Institute of Company Secretaries of India.

3. One representative to be nominated by the Central Government.

4. One representative to be nominated by the Reserve Bank of India.

5. One representative to be nominated by the Comptroller and Auditor General of India.

6. Any person who is or has been holding the office of a professor in any University or deemed University in the field of accountancy, finance, or business management.

7. The Chairman of the Central Board of Direct Taxes or his nominee.

8. Two members to represent the Chamber of Commerce and Industry to be nominated by the Central Government, and

9. One representative to be nominated by the Securities and Exchange Board of India.

The Advisory Committee has to give its recommendations to the Central Government on such matters of accounting policies and standards and auditing as may be referred to it from time to time for advice.[2]

The terms of membership will be determined by the Central Government at the time of appointment and any vacancy will be filled by the Central Government in the manner applicable to the appointment of the member who vacated his office.[3]

The non-official members will be entitled to fees, travelling, conveyance and other allowances as are admissible to the officers of the Central Government of the highest rank.[4]

Right of inspection [S. 209-A]

Inspection by directors.—Every director has the right to inspect the books of account during business hours.[5] Where a director is carrying on a

---

1. S. 210-A(2).
2. S. 210-A(3).
3. S. 210-A(4).
4. S. 210(5).
5. S. 209(4). The words "other books and papers" as used in the section do not include "nomination

personal business of the same kind as that of the company so that if the accounts are thrown open before him, his interest in his personal business and his duty to the company will be in a sharp conflict, the question will be whether his statutory right should prevail over his duty to the company. In a case of this kind before the High Court of Delhi,[6] the court was of the opinion that the matter would have to be decided on a balance of equities. The court accordingly diluted the right of the director and ordered the inspection of only the following books: bank statements; accounts with banks, financial institutions and private parties from whom loans had been taken by the company, and the register of movable assets. Where the directors wanted to exercise their right of inspection accompanied by a chartered accountant, the Company Law Board allowed it subject to the undertaking being given by the chartered accountant that he would not disclose the information to any person other than the directors.[7]

Inspection by Registrar, etc.—Section 209-A was introduced by the Amendment Act, 1974. Sub-section (1) provides that the books of account and other books and papers of every company shall be open to inspection during business hours by the Registrar or by any such officer as may be authorised by the Central Government. Such inspection can be made without giving previous notice to the company. The directors, officers and employees are required to produce before the inspector books of account, etc., which are in their control, and to furnish him with any other information that he may desire and also to give him reasonable assistance. The inspector may make copies or make marks of inspection.[8]

The Amendment of 2000 has also conferred the right of inspection upon SEBI authorised officers. This right of inspection extends only to sections covered in Section 55-A.

The person making the inspection has been vested with the powers of a civil court in respect of the following matters—

1. the discovery and production of books of account and other documents at such place and time as may be prescribed by him;
2. summoning and enforcing the attendance of persons and examining them on oath;

---

paper for directorship". *K. K. Kanagasabapthy* v *Shanmugham*, (1972) 42 Comp Cas 596 Mad.
6. *D. Ross Porter* v *Pioneer Steel Co Ltd*, (1990) 68 Comp Cas 145 Del.
7. *M. L. Thukral* v *Krone Communications Ltd*, (1996) 86 Comp Cas 643 CLB.
8. Where irregularities were found by the Asstt Registrar, who granted time to the directors for rectification, he was not allowed to prosecute them one year after the expiry of the granted time. *State* v *S. Seshmal Pandia*, (1986) 60 Comp Cas 889 Mad. Nobody should be prosecuted under the section unless he has given an opportunity to explain his position. In this case, the notice to the director in question was delayed for more than six months and in the meantime the liquidator took the records into his custody. Prosecution was not allowed. *P. Venkatakrishna Reddy* v *Registrar of Cos*, (1996) 85 Comp Cas 572 Mad.

3. inspection of any books, registers and other documents of the company at any place.

The inspector has to submit his report to the Central Government. Where the inspection is on behalf of SEBI, the report has to be submitted to SEBI. He will have the power of the Registrar under the Companies Act of making inquiries. A director who commits any default under the section and is convicted for it, shall vacate his office from the date of conviction and shall remain disqualified from directorship for five years.[9]

The right of inspection under the section is limited to books of account and other books and papers. The inspectors cannot, under the guise of this right, undertake a roving inquiry into all the affairs of the company. It is different from an investigation of affairs under Section 237.[10]

Inspection by members.—Members do not have the right of inspection. Members of a charitable company under Section 25 have been granted the right of inspection by clause 9 of Annexure 1 to the Companies Regulations, 1956.

Report by way of annual accounts to general meeting [S. 210]

In addition to accounting records the company has to prepare annual accounts showing the results of the company's trading during the relevant period and the company's assets and liabilities at the end of that period. One is known as the profit and loss account and the other as balance sheet.

At every annual general meeting the board of directors have to lay before the meeting the following documents—

1. Balance Sheet.
2. Profit and Loss Account.[11]

---

9. *Indra Prakash Karnani* v *ROC*, (1985) 57 Comp Cas 662 Cal. The court has jurisdiction to order inspection. *M. K. M. Singh* v *Lake Palace Hotels Ltd*, (1985) 58 Comp Cas 805 Raj. The default is also punishable with a fine of Rs 50,000.

10. *Karuppunni* v *Director of Inspection, CLB*, [1986] 3 Comp LJ 225 Ker; *Swadee Chemicals Ltd* v *Kothari Industrial Corpn Ltd*, (1995) 18 Corpt LA 23 Mad, the inspector here wanted to find out the reasons why the company was not implementing a resolution and that was held to be beyond the scope of this power.

11. In the case of a company not carrying on business for profit, an income and expenditure account shall be laid before the company at its annual general meeting instead of a Profit and Loss Account [S. 210(2)]. According to the requirements of S. 216, profit and loss account has to be annexed and auditors' report has to be attached to the balance sheet. The auditors' special or supplementary report, if any, must also be so attached. Section 218 provides that issuing the balance sheet without authentication as required by S. 215 or without the annexures as required by S. 216 is a punishable offence. According to S. 222 the expression "documents annexed to accounts" shall not include board's and auditors' report or any document attached or required to be attached to the accounts. This became necessary so as to exclude them from the auditor's remarks. In the case of the first annual general meeting of the company, the profit and loss account must come up to a period so as not to make a gap of nine months between the last day of the accounting period and the day of the meeting. In other cases such gap should not be of more than six months. The period of accounting is known as the financial year. It may be less then a calendar year. It should not exceed fifteen months.

3. Report by the company's board of directors.[12]

The directors' report should show the following particulars—

1. the state of the company's affairs;

2. the amounts, if any, which it proposes to carry to any reserves in the balance-sheet;

3. the amount, if any, which it recommends should be paid by way of dividend;

4. material changes and commitments, if any, affecting the financial position of the company;

5. the conservation of energy, technology absorption, foreign exchange earnings and outgo in such manner as may be prescribed.

The report should also deal with any changes which have occurred during the financial year in the nature of the company's business, or in the business of its subsidiaries and the classes of business in which the company has interest.[13]

The Amendment Act, 1974 as further amended in 1988 by inserting Section 217(2-A), requires the directors' report to state the following particulars:

1. A statement showing the name of every employee of the company whose remuneration was not less than a sum as may be prescribed during the financial year or, if employed for a part of the year, not less than a sum as may be prescribed in a month.[14]

---

12. S. 217. *P.S. Bedi* v *ROC*, (1986) 60 Comp Cas 1061 Del, failure in compliance. Section 215 requires that the accounts must be authenticated by or on behalf of the board of directors in the case of a banking company as required by the Banking Companies Act, 1949 and in other cases by the manager or secretary, if any, and by not less than two directors one of whom shall be a managing director where there is one. Where only one director is present in India at the material time, he should sign and also append a statement explaining why the requirement could not be complied with. Authentication should be after approval by the Board. Default is punishable under S. 210(5) and (6).

13. Insofar as it is necessary for the proper appreciation of the company's state of affairs and will not, in the opinion of the board, be harmful to the business of the company.[S. 217(2)]. By virtue of S. 221 officers are under a duty to disclose to the company the particulars of any matter pertaining to them which is required to be reflected in the accounts. Non-banking financial companies and non-financial (residuary) deposit taking companies have to furnish in the Board's report certain information prescribed by the RBI Non-banking Financial Companies (Reserve Bank) Directions, 1977; Residuary Non-banking Companies (Reserve Bank) Directions, 1987.

14. The prescribed particulars have to be disclosed in respect of employees who are in receipt of remuneration of not less than Rs 1,44,000 per annum, if employed throughout the financial year and the remuneration of not less than Rs 12,000 per month, if employed for a part of the year. The clarification further says that the limit of Rs 1,44,000 per annum should be considered if the financial year is of 12 months and on *pro rata* basis if the financial year of a company is less or more than 12 months. (Circular No 3 of 1989; (1989) 65 Comp Cas 558, 561 St) which prescribed Rs 72,000 and Rs 1,44,000 has been replaced by GSR 796(E) of Sept 18, 1990 which prescribed the abovementioned new figures. This liberalisation will lead to economy on the part of companies while preparing annual reports. Companies (Particulars of Employees) Rules, 1975. *Amit Kumar Sen* v *K.A. Rao, Dy ROC*, (2006) 132 Comp Cas 675

2. A statement showing whether any such employee is a relative of any director or manager of the company and, if so, the name of such director and any other particulars as may be prescribed.

3. A statement showing the name of every employee of the company who if employed throughout the financial year or part thereof, was in receipt of remuneration in that year which, in the aggregate, or as the case may be, at a rate which, in the aggregate, is in excess of that drawn by the managing director or whole-time director or manager and holds by himself or along with his spouse and dependent children, not less than two per cent of the equity shares of the company.[15]

Sub-section 2-B, inserted by the Amendment Act, 1999 (w.e.f. 31-10-1998) provides that where the company had gone in for a buy-back of shares but could not complete it within the prescribed time, the Board's reports must state the reasons for such failure.

Directors' Responsibility Statement

The Amendment of 2000 has added sub-section (2-AA) to provide for directors' responsibility statement. The new provision is as follows:

"(2-AA) The Board's report shall also include a Directors' Responsibility Statement, indicating therein,—

(*i*) that in the preparation of the annual accounts, the applicable accounting standards had been followed along with proper explanation relating to material departures;

(*ii*) that the directors had selected such accounting policies and applied them consistently and made judgments and estimates that are reasonable and prudent so as to give a true and fair view of the state of affairs of the company at the end of the financial year and of the profit or loss of the company for that period;

(*iii*) that the directors had taken proper and sufficient care for the maintenance of adequate accounting records in accordance with the provisions of this Act for safeguarding the assets of the company and for preventing and detecting fraud and other irregularities;

(*iv*) that the directors had prepared the annual accounts on a going concern basis:"

Accounts are presented to the meeting for the purpose of its adoption. But even if the meeting does not adopt them, further proceedings with

---

Cal, no duty to submit any such details where there was no such employee at the material time.

15. *See*, Companies (Disclosure of Particulars in Report of Board of Directors) Rules, 1988, GSR 1029 of Dec 31, 1988; (1989) 65 Comp Cas 391 St.

reference to them must be conducted as usual. Preparations for the subsequent years' accounts may also continue as usual.[16]

Form and content of balance sheet, profit and loss account [S. 211]

"Balance sheet" is not defined in the Act. But there is a proforma of the balance sheet in Schedule VI which clearly shows its format and its function. It is an endeavour to show the share capital, reserves and liabilities of the company and the manner in which they are distributed over the several type of assets. It is a historical document because it does not show the present realisable value of the assets.[17]

The format of the balance sheet is set out in Part I of Schedule VI. The balance sheet has to be as near thereto as circumstances admit. It may also be in such other form as may be approved by the Central Government either generally or in reference to a particular case. The notes appended to the Part have to be carefully kept in mind in preparing the balance sheet.[18]

The profit and loss account has to be in accordance with Part II of the Schedule. Exemption can be given to any companies in public interest, conditionally or unconditionally. The requirements of the section may also be modified to suit the particular circumstances of a company either on its application or with the consent of its board of directors.[19]

Right of members to copies [S. 219]

A copy of such accounts and the reports must be sent twenty-one days before the meeting to every member of the company,[20] and every trustee for the debentureholders whether he is entitled to the notice of the general meeting or not. The amendment of 1988 provides that in the case of listed companies, it will be enough to send to the members or trustees of debentureholders a copy of the salient features of the accounts and accompanying documents provided that a copy of the accounts is available at the registered office for inspection. The amendment further provides that any member or holder of debentures of a company and any person from whom the company has accepted a sum of money by way of deposit shall, on demand, be entitled to be furnished free of cost, with a copy of the last balance sheet of the company and of every document required by law to be

---

16. ICAI, Compendium of Opinion, Vol 1, 2nd Edn, 1984.
17. Evidence of the Institute of Chartered Accountants before the Cohen Committee cited in *CIT* v *National Industrial Corpn*, (1982) 52 Comp Cas 535: [1983] 1 Comp LJ 118 Del.
18. Companies falling in a special class, such as, insurance, banking, power generation of which the format is prescribed by their respective governing Acts will proceed according to those Acts in making out their balance sheets and profit and loss account. The true and fair formula is applied to such companies also in accordance with the requirements of their governing Acts. [Sub-section (5)].
19. Punishment for failure to comply with the section can be awarded to those very persons and to that very extent as under S. 209.
20. S. 219. The Act permits abridged accounts of which a format has been approved to be sent to members. *See* Form 23-AB.

annexed or attached thereto, including the profit and loss account and the auditors' report. Any such demand can be enforced through an application to the Central Government.[21] If a director fails to take reasonable steps in complying with this requirement, he is punishable under Section 210(5), and it will be no defence to say that on account of the want of a quorum a meeting could not be held and, therefore, the duty of laying accounts before the meeting could not be performed.[22] Three copies of such accounts have to be filed with the Registrar also.[23]

Authentication of accounts [S. 215]

The annual accounts are to be signed by the manager or secretary of the company, if any, and by any two directors one of whom should be a managing director, if there is one. They should be approved by the board of directors before they are so signed on behalf of the board and before they are submitted to the auditors for their report. If there is only one director or managing director in India at the material time, he should sign making a statement of reasons why the requirements have not been fully complied with.

Annexed and attached documents **[S. 216]**.—The profit and loss account should be annexed to the balance sheet and the auditors report, including their separate, special or supplementary report, has to be attached to the balance sheet. Section 222 provides that annexed matter will not include board's report and auditors report except for such information as is required to be given in accounts but is given in the board's report.

Signing of Board's report **[S. 217(4)]**.—The board's report and any addenda is to be signed by the chairman if so authorised by the board and, if not so authorised, it would have to be signed in the same manner as annual accounts.

---

21. Excepting "debentures with ex facie are payable to the bearer thereof". [S. 219]. Further the proviso to the section adds that the section does not require a copy to be sent to a member or holder of debentures who is not entitled to have notices of the general meetings of the company and of whose address the company is unaware. The statement containing the salient features of the accounts has to be in Form 23-AB. The statement should be approved by the board of directors and signed in accordance with S. 215. Such copy should be attached to the documents filed under S. 220. *See* Rule 7-A of the Companies (Central Govt's) General Rules and Forms, 1956.

22. *Registrar of Companies* v *Radhika Prasad*, (1978) 48 Comp Cas 102 Ori; *Registrar of Companies* v *Radhika Prasad*, (1978) 48 Comp Cas 243 Ori; *Registrar of Companies* v *Utkal Distributors*, (1978) 48 Comp Cas 786; *Registrar of Companies* v *Subimal Chandra Mallick*, (1980) 50 Comp Cas 770 Ori; *M. D. Mundhra* v *Asstt ROC*, (1980) 50 Comp Cas 346 Cal; *Harrison and Crossfield (India) Ltd* v *ROC*, (1980) 50 Comp Cas 426 Ker, where relying upon the circular of the Company Law Board, No 35/9/72-C-L-III, dated February 2, 1974, the meeting was postponed only for account taking to a date when the takeover value was ascertained.

23. S. 220. *Karnataka Bank Ltd* v *B. Suresh*, (2001) 105 Comp Cas 110 Kant, the court having jurisdiction at the registered office of the company is competent to try the offence under the section. *Rani Joseph* v *ROC*, (2001) 103 Comp Cas 928 Ker, the offence is of continue nature, not barred by limitation.

Publication of statement in the form in Table F [S. 223]

A limited banking company, an insurance company or a deposit taking company, provident or benefit society, has to make a statement in the form in Table F in Schedule I or in a form as near to that as circumstances admit. This has to be done before the company commences business and has to be repeated on the first Monday in February and August every year during which it remains in business. A copy of the statement along with the last audited balance sheet as laid before the members has to be displayed until it is taken over by the next following statement. The display must be at some conspicuous place in the registered office of the company and in every branch office or place where the business of the company is carried on. Members and creditors are entitled to copies within a week of the demand on paying a fee of eight annas.[24]

Filing of accounts and penalty provisions [S. 220]

The Act imposes a penalty if a default is made in filing the accounts with the Registrar within 30 days after an annual general meeting. "The company and every officer of the company who is in default" are punishable with fine.[25] "These provisions of the Act have been deliberately enacted to protect the shareholders and the general public and they impose a definite duty upon the directors. It is necessary that these duties should be properly carried out and it is necessary that when the directors fail to do so, the penalties provided for in the Act should be imposed. It was never intended that these sections should only be enforced in cases where fraud or dishonesty was suspected or proved."[26] This explanation of the policy of law was given by the Calcutta High Court in *Bhagirath* v *Emperor*:[27]

> Certain directors of a company were prosecuted for failure to submit accounts within the prescribed time. They were convicted by the lower Court and on appeal they argued that they had no real control of the affairs; they were mere figureheads who did not know that the law had not been complied with.

Rejecting this contention, the Court said: "It is perfectly clear that all the directors of a company are responsible to see that the duties imposed upon a company by the Companies Act are properly carried out. It is clearly the

---

24. [Fifty paise]. Default in complying with requirement is a punishable offence. The section exempts from its operation a life insurance company or provident insurance society to which the provisions as to annual statements of the Insurance Act, 1938 are applicable.

25. S. 220(3). A person's position as a director and as an officer in default and whether he has any defence can be decided in the prosecution itself. *Bachraj Baid* v *State of W.B.*, (1992) 74 Comp Cas 809 Cal. The DCA has advised companies to file their accounts latest by Oct 31. Circular of Sept. 22, 1992.

26. *See*, for example, *Registrar of Companies* v *Himprastha Financers (P) Ltd*, (1974) 44 Comp Cas 154, where after stating this policy the court said that the offence cannot be disposed of by warning under S. 3 of Probation of Offenders Act.

27. AIR 1942 Cal 42.

duty of all directors to see that annual returns and the copies of Balance Sheet and Profit and Loss Account are submitted. There is nothing on record to show that these directors made any attempt to see that these duties were carried out. The presumption of law is that these directors knew their duties."

The company is punishable *per se*, that is, by the mere fact of default. Thus where a company in default was acquitted on the ground that the circumstances were beyond its control, but the directors were convicted, the acquittal of the company was quashed.[28]

After a long drawn out controversy between the High Courts, the Supreme Court had held in *State of A.P.* v *Andhra Provincial Potteries Ltd*[29] that if the annual meeting is not held, the obligation to file accounts did not arise and consequently no penalty was incurred under Section 220(3). The court distinguished the case from its own decision in *State of Bombay* v *Bandhan Ram Bhandani,*[30] where in reference to the obligation to file annual returns under Sections 159-161 it had been held that the obligation is not excused by any default in calling the meeting. The difference between the two situations, as pointed out by the Supreme Court, is that while annual returns can be prepared independently of a meeting, the accounts have to be first laid before the meeting and then filed with the Registrar. But now this controversy has been set at rest by the Amendment Act of 1977. The effect of the amendment is that accounts have to be filed with the Registrar within 30 days from the latest day on or before which the annual meeting should have been held in accordance with the provisions of the Act. Thus accounts will have to be filed whether a meeting is held or not or whether the meeting does or does not adopt the accounts or is adjourned without adopting the balance sheet.[31]

It has been held[32] that it would be no defence for a failure to file accounts that the "directors were not legally qualified under the articles of association to act as directors inasmuch as they had no shares at all in the company or the requisite number of shares to qualify them as directors. A person who acts as a director cannot set up in answer to a penalty that he was not legally a director. He cannot protect himself from liability by saying

---

28. *Asstt Registrar of Companies* v *Sudarsan Liners Ltd,* (1988) 63 Comp Cas 747 Mad.
29. (1973) 2 SCC 786: AIR 1973 SC 2429: (1973) 43 Comp Cas 514.
30. AIR 1961 SC 186: (1961) 1 SCR 801: (1961) 31 Comp Cas 1.
31. As further amended in 1988. Thus accounts have to be filed whether a meeting is held or not. *Registrar of Companies* v *Orissa Paper Products Ltd,* (1988) 63 Comp Cas 460 Ori.
32. *Tota Ram* v *Emperor,* AIR 1916 Lah 397: 34 IC 962. In this case the Court cited and discussed the following cases: *Gibson* v *Barton,* (1875) 10 QB 329; *Catholic Life & Fire Assurance & Annuity Institute, Re,* (1883) 48 LT 675 and *R* v *Tyler,* (1891) 2 QB 588, where it was said that penalty was not intended to be the equivalent for the omission to perform the duty, but is of such a nature that the company cannot by paying the penalty continue to neglect to perform the duty. *See* also *Achhuta Pai* v *ROC,* [1966] 1 Comp LJ 104 Ker.

"I am not a director *de jure*".[33] Similarly, it is no defence that the account books were seized by the police in connection with a criminal case[34] or that they were lying in a court.[35]

The period of limitation for making a complaint, which is one year under Section 468(2)(*b*) of CrPC, runs from the date on which the Registrar, in the usual course of things, comes to know of the default.[36] The Kerala High Court held that the offence is of a continuing nature and, therefore, every succeeding day of default would give start to a new period of limitation.[37] The Calcutta High Court had earlier differed. In its view there is only one offence and the period of limitation begins from the last day on which accounts should have been filed,[38] but now it has held that that decision is no longer a good law.[39] According to the Kerala High Court the period of limitation starts running not from the date on which the accounts are filed but from the date on which the Registrar comes to know of the offence.[40]

---

33. Following further cases on the subject may be consulted: *Lakshmana* v *Emperor*, AIR 1932 Mad 497: 138 IC 317; *Ballav Dass* v *Mohan Lal Sadhu*, AIR 1936 Cal 237: 162 IC 282; *Public Prosecutor* v *BVA Lury Co Ltd*, [1941] 2 MLJ 487: AIR 1942 Mad 75; *Sunder Das* v *Emperor*, AIR 1929 Lah 836; *Chabil Das* v *Emperor*, AIR 1914 Lah 125.

34. *Great India Steam Navigation Co* v *State*, (1967) 37 Comp Cas 135 Cal.

35. *Ramchandra & Sons (P) Ltd* v *State*, [1967] 2 Comp LJ 92. For an enlightening view of the economic utility of disclosures *see* Rita Kishope Dixon Foyle, *Company Law and Economic Development in Sierra Leone*, (1970) 19 JCL 447. A director was held to be not entitled to an automatic or mechanical relief for default under the section though his induction into the company was for the limited purpose of the performance of an export contract of the company. *Shiv Kumar Dalmia* v *Mangal Chand Hukum Chand*, (1996) 86 Comp Cas 366: [1996] 2 Comp LJ 219 MP. *Shree Hanuman Steel Rolling Mills* v *Asstt ROC*, (1996) 2 Cal LJ 64, books of account seized by an investigating agency, failure to submit annual accounts not wilful, prosecution not warranted. *Amita Chadha* v *ROC*, (1998) 74 Del LT 537, dispute about access to books.

36. *Sushil Kumar Lahiri* v *ROC*, (1983) 53 Comp Cas 54 Cal. The Assistant Registrar is also competent to file complaints. *Bhaghat Pd Tantia* v *ROC*, (1983) 53 Comp Cas 56 Cal.

37. *Sudarsan Chits (India)* v *ROC*, (1986) 59 Comp Cas 261 Ker, and also *Shivalik, Factory & Cold Storage (P) Ltd* v *ROC*, (1988) 64 Comp Cas 113 P&H. Other decisions to the same effect, *Rani Joseph* v *ROC*, (1995) 1 Ker LJ 14; *Oriental Coal Co* v *U. Roy*, (1991) 1 Cal LJ 418.

38. *National Cotton Mills* v *Asstt ROC*, (1983) CHN 180: (1984) 56 Comp Cas 222. Overruling its own earlier decision in *Ajit Kumar Sarkar* v *Asstt ROC*, (1979) 49 Comp Cas 909: 83 Cal WN 108. The preponderance of opinion is that the offence is of a continuing nature. *Registrar of Companies* v *Orissa Paper Products Ltd*, (1988) 63 Comp Cas 460 Ori. For an explanation of the difference between a continuing and non-continuing offence, see *C. B. Bhandari* v *Provident Fund Inspector*, (1988) 63 Comp Cas 437 Ker, and also *State of Bihar* v *Deokaran Nenshi*, (1972) 2 SCC 890: 1973 SCC (Cri) 114: AIR 1973 SC 908.

39. *Luxmi Printing Works* v *Asstt ROC*, (1990) 69 Comp Cas 442 Cal. The penal provision contained in Section 162 states that the company and every officer of the company, who is in default, shall be punishable with fine which may extend to Rs 50 for every day during which the default continues. Since the default is visited by a day to day fine, this appears to be a continuing offence. The Division Bench of the Calcutta High Court, Madras High Court and Delhi High Court also supported this view. *Asstt ROC* v *Premier Synthetics (P) Ltd*, (1997) 89 Comp Cas 732: (1997) 26 CLA 269 (Mad).

40. *Thomas Philip* v *Asstt Registrar of Companies*, (2006) 131 Comp Cas 842 Ker.

Default in laying accounts before the general meeting has been held to be a one-time offence and being punishable with fine only, Section 482 of CrPC applied. A complaint filed after six months from the date of default was quashed.[41]

Waiver of penalty

The tenor of the provisions relating to penalty shows that the statutory penalty is immediately payable without more on non-compliance. The ambit of the Registrar's discretion is clearly intended to be limited. He may decide not to recover the penalty in those exceptional cases where he considers that such a decision is conducive to achieve the broad object of the legislation of timely compliance of the specific task entrusted to him, namely the economic and efficient application and management of resourses available for recovery of penalties. The scheme of penalties has been held to be not violative of the Human Rights Convention because the penalties are of civil nature and not criminal and are also very modest. They are being imposed as sanctions for non-compliance with vital regulatory requirements to secure public interest.[42]

Rectification of accounts

Where a company after filing original accounts, applied for permission to file revised accounts, the court said that companies are a creature of statute. Their existence and conduct is regulated by statute. There is no general inherent supervisory jurisdiction in the court in relation to the performance by the Registrar of Companies of his duties. There is at most a jurisdiction in the court to require the Registrar to comply with his statutory duties. The company was seeking the removal of extraneous material which the Registrar was not required by the statute to remove. For this purpose it was immaterial whether the extraneous material was contained in the body of the accounts or in the annexed papers. The court could not permit filing of revised accounts.[43]

AUDIT

Appointment of auditors [S. 224]

The auditors of a company are appointed at its annual general meeting. An auditor appointed at one annual general meeting holds office from the conclusion of that meeting until the conclusion of the next annual general

---

41. *Rakesh Kumar* v *ROC*, (1995) 82 Comp Cas 681 P&H. *Jayes R. Mor* v *State of Gujarat*, (2002) 109 Comp Cas 232 Guj, the director in question had resigned before due date and Form 32 had also been filed, he was not regarded as a person in default.
42. *R (on the application of Pow Trust)* v *Chief Executive and Registrar of Companies*, (2003) 2 BCLC 295 (QBD).
43. *A Company, Re (No 007466 of 2003)*, (2004) 121 Comp Cas 695: (2004) 1 WLR 1357: 2004 EWHC 35 (Ch).

meeting. Unless he is a retiring auditor, he should be informed of his appointment within seven days and he should inform the Registrar within thirty days whether he has accepted the appointment or not.[44]

At an annual general meeting a retiring auditor is re-appointed, except in the following cases:[45]

1. when he is not qualified for re-appointment;
2. when he has given to the company notice in writing of his unwillingness to be re-appointed;
3. a resolution has been passed at that meeting appointing somebody instead of him or providing expressly that he shall not be re-appointed; or
4. where notice has been given of an intended resolution to appoint some person or persons in the place of a retiring auditor, and by reason of the death, incapacity or disqualification of that person the resolution cannot be proceeded with.

Where at any such meeting no auditor is appointed or reappointed the Central Government should be informed of the fact within seven days,[46] because the Government, in such a case, gets the right to appoint a person to fill the vacancy.[47]

The first auditors are appointed by the company's board within one month of incorporation and they hold office until the first annual general meeting.[48] If the board fails to do so, the company may in general meeting make an appointment.[49] Moreover, the company may in general meeting replace by another person the auditor appointed by the board.[50] Any casual vacancy may be filled by the board, except when it is due to resignation, in which case it has to be filled by the company in general meeting.[51] Such an appointee holds office until the conclusion of the next annual general meeting.[52]

Restriction of number of auditorships

Two new sub-sections were added to Section 224 by the Amendment Act of 1974, for the purpose of restricting the number of companies in which a

---

44. S. 224(1-A).
45. S. 224(2).
46. S. 224(4). A failure to give this information entails a penalty of fine for the company and every officer in default.
47. S. 224(3).
48. S. 224(5).
49. S. 224(5) proviso (*b*).
50. S. 224(5) proviso (*a*).
51. S. 224(6)(*a*).
52. S. 224(6)(*b*). It has been held that it is the duty of the auditor appointed to ascertain whether the requirements of S. 225 were complied with. *Ajit Kumar Idyya* v *Institute of Chartered Accountants of India*, (1994) 80 Comp Cas 197 Kant.

person can be appointed as an auditor. In the case of a firm of auditors, "specified number of companies" shall be construed as the number of companies per partner of the firm who is not in full time employment elsewhere. If a person is a partner in more than one firm, the number of companies in reference to him should not exceed the specified number.[53] Where any partner of a firm of auditors is also holding office, in his individual capacity, as the auditor of one or more companies, the number of companies which may be taken into account in his case should not exceed the specified number, in the aggregate. A re-appointment is also not to be conferred on a person who is in full-time employment elsewhere.

A proviso added to Section 224(1) requires every company, appointing or re-appointing an auditor, to obtain a certificate from the auditor that the appointment is within specified limits.

If an auditor is holding at the time of the commencement of the Act, more appointments than the specified number, he should intimate within 60 days to the company or companies whose appointment he would not like to accept from the commencement of the new financial year. The names of such companies should be sent to the Registrar also.[54]

According to the first explanation, specified number means,—

1. in case of companies each of which has a paid-up share capital of less than 25 lakh rupees, twenty such companies;
2. in any other case, 20 companies, of which not more than 10 should have paid-up share capital of twenty-five lakh rupees or more.

The second explanation runs as follows:

In computing the specified number, the number of companies in respect of which or any part of which any person or firm has been appointed as an auditor, whether singly or in combination with any other person or firm, shall be taken into account.

It has been further provided by the Amendment of 2000 that private limited companies shall be excluded in reckoning the number of companies which an auditor can audit.

Appointment by special resolution [S. 224-A]

Section 224-A has been introduced by the Amendment Act, 1974, to specify the case in which an auditor can be appointed only by a special resolution. Where 25% or more of the subscribed share capital of a company is held, singly or jointly, by a public financial institution or the Central or State Government, or by any financial or other institution established by any provincial or State Act or in which a State Government holds 51% of the subscribed capital, or by any nationalised bank or an

---

53. S. 224(1-B).
54. S. 224(1-C).

insurance company carrying on general insurance business, the appointment or re-appointment of an auditor can be made only by a special resolution.

If a special resolution has not been passed, it shall be deemed that the appointment has not been made and the Central Government will get the right under Section 224(3) to make an appointment.[55]

Remuneration of auditor

Section 224(8) provides that the remuneration of the auditor of a company may be fixed by the Board of directors, if the appointment has been made by the Board or by the Central Government, if the appointment was made by the Government. Subject to this, the remuneration has to be fixed by the company in general meeting. Where an auditor has been appointed under Section 619 by the Comptroller and Auditor General of India, his remuneration is to be fixed by the company in general meeting or in such manner as the company in general meeting may determine.[56]

Removal of auditors [S. 225]

An auditor can be removed before the expiry of his term by the company in general meeting after obtaining the previous approval of the Central Government.[57] Approval of the Central Government has to be taken before- effecting the removal though the resolution for removal can be passed before hand.[58] At the expiry of his term, the company may in general meeting appoint another person in his place. But a special notice of any such resolution will be necessary.[59] A copy of the resolution should immediately be sent to the retiring auditor as he has the right of making a representation.[60] A copy of the representation, if any, and if so desired by the auditor, should be sent to every member to whom notice of the meeting has

---

55. The *Explanation* to the section says that for the purposes of the section "general insurance business" has the meaning assigned to it in the General Insurance (Emergency Provisions) Act, 1971; "nationalised bank" means a corresponding new bank as defined in Banking Companies (Acquisition and Transfer of Undertakings) Act, 1970 or in the Banking Companies (Acquisition and Transfer of Undertakings) Act, 1980.
56. Clause (*aa*) added to sub-section (8) of S. 224 by the Amendment of 2000.
57. S. 224(7).
58. *Basant Ram & Sons* v *UOI*, [2000] 4 Comp LJ 55 Del, the court is not likely to interfere in the matter without strong legal justification. *Basant Ram & Sons* v *UOI*, (2002) 110 Comp Cas 38 Del, general body approval again necessary after Central Government approval. Removal becomes effective from the date of general body approval.
59. S. 225. It was held in *Pedley* v *Inland Waterways Assn Ltd*, (1977) 1 All ER 209 Ch D that in addition to special notice, the proposed resolution must also satisfy the requirements of circulation of a member's resolution. This was followed in *Amar Nath Malhotra* v *MCS Ltd*, (1993) 76 Comp Cas 469 Del. But other High Courts are of the opinion that the right to propose a resolution with a special notice, e.g. for removing an auditor, is an independent right and should not be whittled down by superimposing upon it the requirement of circulation of a member's resolution. *Gopal Vyas* v *Sinclair Hotels and Transportation Ltd*, AIR 1990 Cal 45: [1990] 1 Comp LJ 388: (1990) 68 Comp Cas 516; *Karnataka Bank Ltd* v *A. B. Datar*, (1993) 2 Kant LJ 230: (1994) 79 Comp Cas 417; *Prakash Road Lines Ltd* v *Vijay Kumar Narang*, (1993) 4 Kant LJ 561: (1995) 83 Comp Cas 569 Kant.
60. S. 225(2) and (3).

been sent and if this is not done, the representation should be read out at the meeting.[61]

Qualifications [S. 226]

A person cannot be appointed as auditor of a company unless he is a chartered accountant.[62] But a firm may be appointed in its firm name provided all its partners are qualified for appointment.[63]

None of the following persons is qualified for appointment:[64]

(*a*) a body corporate;

(*b*) an officer or employee of the company;

(*c*) a person who is a partner, or who is in an employment of an officer or employee of the company;

(*d*) a person who is indebted to the company for an amount exceeding one thousand rupees, or who has given any guarantee or provided any security in connection with indebtedness of any third person to the company for an amount exceeding one thousand rupees;

(*e*) a person holding any security of the company after a period of one year from the date of commencement of the Companies (Amendment) Act, 2000 (w.e.f. Jan 14, 2001).

An explanation appended to the section says that for the purposes of this section ''security'' means any instrument which carries voting rights.

Powers and duties [S. 227]

Every auditor has the right of access to the books and accounts and vouchers of the company. He may require from the officers of the company any information he thinks necessary for the performance of his duties.[65]

The auditor has to submit a report on the accounts of the company to the members of the company.[66] "The scheme of the Act... is that the directors must prepare the accounts; the auditor must make a report to the members on the accounts; the report must contain statements on certain specified matters."[67] The report should state whether the accounts are kept in

---

61. S. 225(3). But the representation need not be sent out to the members or read out at the meeting if, on the application of the company or of any aggrieved person, the Company Law Board is satisfied that the right of representation is being abused to secure needless publicity for defamatory matter.
62. Within the meaning of the Chartered Accountants Act, 1949 (XXXVIII of 1949).
63. S. 226(1) proviso.
64. S. 226(3).
65. S. 227(1). This duty continues even after winding up has commenced and the auditor has been appointed by the Court. *Bhawnagar Vegetable Products, Re*, (1977) 47 Comp Cas 128 Guj.
66. S. 227(2).
67. PENNYCUICK J in *Thomas Gerrard & Son Ltd, Re*, [1967] 2 All ER 525: [1967] 3 WLR 84.

accordance with the provisions of the Act and whether they give a true and fair view of the state of affairs of the company.[68]

By an amendment of Section 227 made by the Companies (Amendment) Ordinance, 1998 it has been made an additional duty of an auditor to report on this fact whether in his opinion the profit and loss account and balance sheet complied with the accounting standards.[69]

The Amendment of 1965 has imposed new duties upon auditors. A new sub-section (1-A) to Section 227 has been introduced which makes it the duty of the auditor to inquire into the following matters—

1. whether loans and advances made by the company on the basis of security have been properly secured and whether the terms are not prejudicial to the interests of the company or its members;

2. whether book-entry transactions are not prejudicial to the interests of the company;

3. where, the company is not an investment, or a banking company, whether any securities have been sold by the company at a price less than that at which they were purchased;

4. whether loans and advances made by the company have been shown as deposits;

5. whether personal expenses have been charged to revenue account;

6. whether cash has actually been received in respect of any shares shown in the books to have been allotted for cash if no cash has been received, whether the position as stated in the books is correct, regular and not misleading.

Sub-section (3) also requires the auditor's report to state:

(a) whether he has obtained all the information and explanations which to the best of his knowledge and belief were necessary for the purposes of his audit;

(b) whether, in his opinion, proper books of account as required by law have been kept by the company so far as appears from his examination of those books, and proper returns adequate for the purposes of his audit have been received from branches not visited by him;

(bb) whether the report on the accounts of any branch office audited under Section 228 by a person other than the company's auditor

---

68. According to S. 227(3) the auditor's report has also to state whether he has obtained all the information and explanations which to the best of his knowledge and belief were necessary for the purpose of the audit; whether the company's final accounts are in agreement with the books of account and returns; whether he has received report on the accounts of any branch office.

69. S. 227(3)(*d*).

has been forwarded to him as required by clause (*c*) of sub-section (3) of that section and how he has dealt with the same in preparing the auditor's report;

(*c*) whether the company's balance sheet and profit and loss account dealt with by the report are in agreement with the books of account and returns;

(*d*) whether, in his opinion, the profit and loss account and balance sheet comply with the accounting standards referred to in sub-section (3-C) of Section 211;

(*e*) in thick type or in italics the observations or comments of the auditors which have any adverse effect on the functioning of the company;

(*f*) whether any director is disqualified from being appointed as director under clause (*g*) of sub-section (1) of Section 274;

(*g*) whether the cess payable under Section 441-A has been paid and, if not, the details of the amount of cess not paid.

The Central Government has also taken the power by inserting sub-section (4-A) to Section 227 to direct that in the case of a class or description of companies, the auditor's report shall also include a statement on such matters as the Government may direct. The Government may consult the Institute of Chartered Accountants of India on the matter.[70]

If a company has branch offices, the accounts of every branch office shall be audited by the company's auditor or the company may appoint any other auditor for the purpose.[71]

The auditors' report has to be read before the company in general meeting and is open to the inspection of any member of the company.[72]

Right of auditor to attend meetings [S. 231]

Notices and communications relating to meetings which have to be sent to members or to which they are entitled have also to be forwarded to the auditors of the company. The auditors are also entitled to attend any general meeting and is also entitled to be heard on any part of the business which concerns him as an auditor.

---

70. *See*, Manufacturing and other Companies (Auditor's Report) Order 1988. GSR 909(E) of September 1988. (1988) 64 Comp Cas 3119-323 St.
71. S. 228(1). Sub-sections (2) to (4) contain further rules relating to audit of branch office accounts. The auditor's report, as required by S. 229, must be signed by the person appointed as an auditor of the company or, in the case of a firm of chartered accounts, by a partner of the firm practising in India. Any other document required by law to be authenticated must also be similarly signed.
72. S. 230.

Penalty [Ss. 232 and 233]

If default is made by a company in complying with any of the provisions contained in Sections 225 to 231, the company and every defaulting officer is punishable with fine extending up to Rs 5000.

Where an auditor's report is made or any document of the company is made or authenticated, otherwise than in conformity with the requirements of Sections 227 and 229, the auditor or any other person who signs or authenticates the report or document and if the default is wilful, is liable to be punished with fine which may extend to Rs 10,000.

Auditors' duty of care

Position of auditors.—Explaining the position of auditors CHAKRAVARTI CJ of the Calcutta High Court said:[73]

> A joint stock company carries on business with capital furnished by persons who buy its shares. The owners of the capital are, however, not in direct control of its application which is left to the executive of the company. In those circumstances, some arrangement is obviously called for by which those who provide the capital know periodically what is being done with their money, how the affairs of the company stand and what the present value of their investment is. The Companies Act, therefore, provides for the employment of an auditor who is the servant of the shareholders and whose duty is to examine the affairs of the company on their behalf at the end of a year and report to them what he has found. That examination by an independent agency such as the auditor is practically the only safeguard which the shareholders have against the enterprise being carried on in an unbusiness like way or their money being misapplied or misappropriated without their knowing anything about it. The Act provides the safeguard in two forms. It makes the duty of the auditor to give an expression of opinion on certain specified matters of a vital character and it makes him liable, along with the directors, for misfeasance, if he fails to perform his duties as required by law and the approved audit procedure.

Thus the auditors owe a number of duties to the company and its shareholders. The foremost among them is to check the accuracy of accounts. But his duty is "not to confine himself merely to the task of verifying the arithmetical accuracy of the balance sheet, but to inquire into its substantial accuracy, and to ascertain that it was properly drawn up, so as to contain a true and correct representation of the state of the company's af-

---

73. *Dy Secretary v S. N. Das Gupta*, (1955) 25 Comp Cas 413: AIR 1956 Cal 414: 60 Cal WN 124.

fairs".[74] They should not act merely as mechanical adder-uppers and subtractors.[75] Thus, where an auditor of a banking company failed to verify the cash balance claimed by the management and the actual cash in hand turned out to be much less than was shown in the books, he was held guilty of neglect of duty.[76] The court said:

> A certificate from the management can obviously be no substitute for such verification. The whole object of an audit is an examination of what the management have done and if the statements of the very persons who constitute the management were to be accepted in all matters, even in matters capable of direct verification, an audit would be an idle farce.[77]

But in certain matters of technical nature, for example, valuation of stock-in-trade, the auditor will have to rely on some skilled person. Accordingly, an auditor could not be held guilty of breach of duty when, in the absence of suspicious circumstances, he relied for this purpose on the manager of a cotton mill.[78]

Where the accountants assisted the directors in connection with the preparation of a circular for rights issue, they were held not liable to shareholders for statements made to the directors in respect of profit forecasts.[79] An action against auditors for negligence could not succeed though the investor relied on the audited accounts and also on informal discussions with the auditors. There was insufficient evidence to show that the accountants had assumed any duty towards the particular investor.[80]

Standard of care and skill.—Secondly, it has always been the law that an auditor must exercise reasonable care and skill in the discharge of his duty.[81] Referring to this duty ROMER J said in *City Equitable Fire Insurance Co, Re*:[82]

> ....He must be honest, i.e., he must not certify what he does not believe to be true and he must take reasonable care and skill before he believes that what he certifies is true. What is reasonable care in any particular case must depend upon the circumstances of that case. Where

---

74. *See*, STIRLING J in *Leeds Estate Co v Shepherd*, (1887) 36 Ch D 787, 802: 57 LT 684. *See also* RIGBY LJ, *London & General Bank, (No 2), Re*, [1895] 2 Ch 673, 692: 73 LT 304: [1895-99] All ER 953.

75. *See*, L DENNING in *Fomento (Sterling Area) Ltd v Selsdon Fountain Pen Co*, [1958] 1 All ER 11, 23.

76. *Dy Secretary v S. N. Das Gupta*, (1955) 25 Comp Cas 413: AIR 1956 Cal 414: 60 Cal WN 124.

77. Quoting ROMER J in *City Equitable Fire Ins Co, Re*, [1924] All ER Rep 485: 133 LT 520: [1925] Ch 407 481.

78. *Kingston Cotton Mill Co, Re*, [1896] 2 Ch 279: 74 LT 568, *see* the judgment of LINDLEY LJ at pp 286-87. Cited *Thomas Gerrard & Son Ltd, Re*, [1967] 2 All ER 525: [1967] 3 WLR 84.

79. *Abbott v Strong*, [1998] 2 BCLC 420 Ch D.

80. *Electra Private Equity Partners v KPMG Peat Marwick*, [1998] PNLR 135.

81. PENNYCUICK J in *Thomas Gerrard & Son Ltd, Re*, [1967] 2 All ER 525: [1967] 3 WLR 84.

82. [1924] All ER Rep 485: 133 LT 520: [1925] Ch 407, 481-82.

there is nothing to excite suspicion very little inquiry will be reasonably sufficient. Where suspicion is aroused more care is obviously necessary; but, still an auditor is not bound to exercise more than reasonable care and skill even in a case of suspicion and he is perfectly justified in acting on the opinion of an expert where special knowledge is required.

In another case LOPES LJ said: "He (the auditor), is a watchdog, but not a bloodhound."[83] "He is not an insurer."[84]

If the company owns securities the auditor should see that they are in proper custody. "He should not be content with a certificate that securities are in the possession of a particular company, firm or person unless the company, etc., is trustworthy, or is respectable and further is one that in the ordinary course of business keeps securities for its customers."[85] Thus, where the stockbrokers of a company certified to its auditors that they were holding the company's securities, when in fact they did not do so and the company suffered loss, the auditors were held guilty of negligence. They should have at once set the matter right or reported it to the shareholders.[86] Similarly, in a case before the Calcutta High Court:[87]

> The auditor of a company found that the accounts presented by the directors showed that selling agency commission was paid to the managing agents in addition to their remuneration, but was not included in remuneration, nor was it shown as an item of expenditure, but was deducted from the sale proceeds of the goods sold by them.

CHAKRAVARTI CJ held that the auditor ought to have required the directors to explain why the selling agency commission was not included in remuneration and whether a special resolution had been passed to authorise the payment of a separate commission. "His failure to ask for such information betrays negligence in the performance of his duties."

An auditor is, however, not concerned with the policy of the company. In the words of LINDLEY LJ:[88]

> It is no part of an auditor's duty to give advice, either to directors or shareholders, as to what they ought to do. An auditor has nothing to do with the prudence or imprudence of making loans with or without security. It is nothing to him whether the business of a company is being conducted prudently or imprudently, profitably or unprofitably. It is nothing to him whether dividends are properly or improperly declared,

---

83. *Kingston Cotton Mill Co, Re*, [1896] 2 Ch 279, 288: 74 LT 568.
84. ROMER J in *City Equitable Fire Insurance Co, Re*, [1924] All ER Rep 485: 133 LT 520: [1925] Ch 407 at p 481.
85. *Ibid.*
86. *City Equitable Fire Insurance Co, Re*, [1924] All ER Rep 485: 133 LT 520: [1925] Ch 407, but the auditors were protected from liability under special provisions of the company's articles.
87. *Ganesan v A. K. Joscelyne*, AIR 1957 Cal 33: [1957] 27 Comp Cas 114.
88. *London & General Bank, (No 2), Re*, [1895] 2 Ch 673, 682: 73 LT 304: [1895-99] All ER 953.

provided he discharges his own duty to the shareholders. His business is to ascertain and state the true financial position of the company at the time of the audit....

On the facts of the case, however, the auditor was held guilty of breach of duty. He presented a confidential report to the directors calling their attention to the insufficiency of the securities on which the capital of the company was invested, and the difficulty of realising them. But his report to the shareholders merely stated that the value of the assets was dependent on realisation. As a result the shareholders were deceived as to the condition of the company and a dividend was declared out of the capital and not out of income. It was held that the auditor was guilty of misfeasance and was liable to make good the amount of dividend paid. But his liability does not end there. He would also be liable for the costs of recovering the extra tax, if any, which has been paid on the basis of the false accounts and also for any of the extra tax which is not recoverable.[89]

Duty to company and to third parties

The traditional concept of auditors' duty has been that they owe their duty to the company and the company only. This concept was fortified by the judgment of CARDOZO CJ in *Ultramares Corpn v Touche*:[90]

The defendants, a firm of public accountants, were employed by a company to prepare and certify a balance sheet of the company. The company, to the knowledge of the accountants, had borrowed large sums of money from banks and other lenders. They also knew that their certified balance sheet would be exhibited to other lenders to induce them to lend money. Accordingly, when the balance sheet was made up, it was shown to the plaintiffs, who, acting on the faith of it, lent and lost huge sums of money.

The court found that there was evidence of negligence by the defendants in making their report but held that this would not make them liable to the plaintiffs. CARDOZO CJ said:

The defendants owed to their employer a duty imposed by law to make their certificate without fraud, and a duty growing out of contract to make it with the care and caution proper to their calling. Fraud includes pretence of knowledge when knowledge there is none. To creditors and investors to whom the employer exhibited the certificate, the defendants owed a like duty to make it without fraud. A different question develops when we ask whether they owed a duty to them to make it without negligence. If liability for negligence exists, a thoughtless slip or blunder; the failure to detect a theft or forgery beneath the cover of deceptive entries, may expose accountants to a

---

89. *Thomas Gerrard & Son Ltd, Re*, [1967] 3 WLR 84: [1967] 2 All ER 525.
90. (1931) 255 NY Rep 170. Reported in Thurston and Seavy, CASES ON TORTS, (1942) 757 and cited in *Candler v Crane, Christmas & Co*, [1951] 2 KB 164: [1951] 1 All ER 426.

liability in an indeterminate amount for an indeterminate time to an indeterminate class.

It means that nothing less than a fraudulent report will make an auditor liable to an outsider who has been deceived by it. Fraud must be proved in the terms of its definition as laid down by LORD HERSCHELL in *Derry* v *Peek*.[91] A negligent misstatement is not the same thing as fraud. This has been pointed out by the court of appeal in *Candler* v *Crane, Christmas & Co*:[92]

> The plaintiff, who desired to invest £2000 in a limited liability company, was put in touch with the company's accountants by the manager. The accountants knew that the plaintiff was a potential investor. They prepared and showed the accounts to the plaintiff and also talked with him. The plaintiff invested his money in the company. The accounts were carelessly prepared, contained numerous false statements and gave a wholly misleading picture of the state of the company, which was wound up within a year, the plaintiff losing the whole of his investment.

Even so it was held by a majority that the accountants were not liable to the plaintiff. Their Lordships said that a false statement, carelessly, as contrasted with fraudulently, made by one person to another, though acted on by that other to his detriment, was not actionable in the absence of any contractual or fiduciary relationship between the parties. DENNING LJ in his dissenting opinion observed:

> I think that the law would fail to serve the best interests of the community if it should hold that accountants and auditors owe a duty to no one but their client....The accountant, who certifies the accounts of his client, is always called on to express his personal opinion as to whether the accounts exhibit a true and correct view of his client's affairs; and he is required to do this, not so much for the satisfaction of his own client, but more for the guidance of shareholders, investors, revenue authorities, and others who have to rely on the accounts in serious matters of business. (Yet) the persons who are misled cannot complain because the accountants owe no duty to them. If such be the law, I think it is to be regretted, for it means that the accountant's certificate, which should be a safeguard, becomes a snare for those who rely on it. In my opinion accountants owe a duty of care not only to their clients, but also to those whom they know will rely on their accounts in the transactions for which those accounts are prepared.

The decision in *Candler* v *Crane, Christmas & Co* has been overruled by the House of Lords in *Hedley Byrne & Co* v *Heller & Partners Ltd*:[93]

---

91. (1889) 14 App Cas 337.
92. [1951] 2 KB 164: [1951] 1 All ER 426.
93. [1963] 3 WLR 101: [1963] 2 All ER 575: 1964 AC 465.

Here a firm of advertising agents had lost a huge sum of money by placing advertising orders for a company. They asked their bankers to inquire into the company's financial stability and their bankers made inquiries of the respondents, who were the company's bankers. The respondents gave favourable reference but stipulated that these were "without responsibility". In reliance on those references the appellants placed orders which resulted in the loss.

The bankers would have been held liable but for the express disclaimer of responsibility. Lord MORRIS explained the principle thus:

I consider that it should now be considered as settled that if someone possessed of a special skill undertakes, quite irrespective of contract, to apply his skill for the assistance of another person who relies upon such skill, a duty of care will arise. Furthermore, if in a sphere in which a person is so placed that others could reasonably rely upon his judgment or his skill or upon his ability to make a careful inquiry or a person takes upon himself to give information or advice to, or allows his information or advice to be passed on to, another person who, as he knows or should know, will place reliance upon it, then a duty of care will arise.

There is a wind of change in the United States also. For example, it was observed in *Texas Tunnelling Co* v *City of Chattanooga*,[94] "that there have been significant changes in the American society during the thirty years that have elapsed since the decision in *Ultramares case*. The continued growth and expansion of industry, the growth of population, the urbanization of society, the growing complexity of business relations and the growing specialization of business functions all require more and more reliance in business transactions upon the representation of specialists."[95]

The principle of the *Hedley Byrne case* has been followed by the Canadian Court in *Haig* v *Bamford*[96] where an auditor, who issued a certificate without verification, was held liable to a person who was misled by the certificate.[97] A similar liability has been imposed upon an auditor who participated in the negotiations for the sale of a company's shares on the basis of the balance sheet audited and certified by him. The value thus

---

94. 204 F Supp 821 (E.D. Tenn 1962), reversed in 329 F 2d 402 (6th cir 1964). Borrowed from 1966 JBL 190.
95. *See*, Edwin J Bradley, *Liability to third Persons for Negligent Audit*, 1966 JBL 190; Seavey, *Candler* v *Crane, Christmas & Co, Negligent Misrepresentation by Accountants*, 67 LQR 466 (1951); *Accountants Liabilities for False and Misleading Statements*, (1967) 67 Columbia Law Rev 1437; Michael Dean, *Hedley Byrne and the Eager Business Man*, (1968) 31 Mod LR 322 and 1967 JBL 359; R. Baxt, *The Modern Company Auditor—A Nineteenth Century Watchdog*, (1970) 33 Mod LR 413 and *True and Fair Accounts—A Legal Anachronism*, (1970) 44 Aust LJ 541.
96. (1972) 32 DLR (3d) 67 Sask Q. B. noted, Current Law, June, 1973.
97. All such cases have been analysed by R. Baxt, *The Liability of Accountants and Auditors for Negligent Statements in Company Accounts*, (1973) 36 Mod LR 42. *See* further *Arenson* v *Casson, Beckman, Rutlay & Co*, [1975] 3 WLR 815 and *Esso Petroleum* v *Mardon*, (1976) 2 WLR 583, noted, 1976 Mod LR 462.

be determined turned out to be unreal because the balance sheet was not satisfactory. The court emphasised that if the auditor had not participated in the negotiations, the result would have been different.[1]

Where an auditor is appointed to check the accounts of the Employees' Provident Fund maintained by a company, he owes his duty not merely to the company, but also to the beneficiaries of the fund and will be responsible to them for professional misconduct if he fails to report that the trustees have allowed irregular loans to the company out of the fund.[2] If this were not so, the accountants and auditors could as well say: "You may inspect the accounts... of X Company Ltd, but do not expect these documents to have been prepared with any degree of skill or care." "It is our view that the auditor or accountant owes a duty of care to the investor, creditor, and others to prepare proper audits or accounts."[3]

A Civil Aviation Authority was refusing to renew the air travel company's licence due to unsatisfactory financial position unless certain confirmations were given by the auditors in their final report as to the finances of the company. The auditors submitted the requisite information to the Authority. The company collapsed. The accounts were negligently prepared. The Authority's claim against the auditors was allowed as they had assumed responsibility towards the Authority for exercising due care and caution in preparing the company's accounts.[4]

Duty in connection with takeover.—A three-point formula has been propounded by the Court of Appeal in England[5] on the auditor's duty to the investing public. The court said that in determining the auditor's duty of care to those relying on accounts audited by him, it must be shown that—

1. It was foreseeable that the persons relying on the accounts would suffer harm if the auditor was negligent;
2. The auditor and the user of the accounts stood in a relationship of sufficient proximity;
3. The circumstances made it just and reasonable to impose such a duty on the auditor.

One company was taking over another company. It relied upon the company's audited accounts and suffered loss because there was a negligent inaccuracy in the accounts. The plaintiff company was a shareholder of the

1. *Diamond Mfg Co Ltd v Hamilton*, [1968] NZLR 705, considered. R. Baxt, *Negligent Statement in Company Accounts*, (1973) 36 Mod LR 47. A similar liability has been imposed in *Arenson v Casson, Beckman, Rutlay & Co*, [1975] 3 WLR 815.
2. *Institute of Chartered Accountants of India v P. K. Mukherjee*, (1968) 2 Comp LJ 211.
3. For liability in respect of financial statements, see *Kuwait Asian Bank EC v National Mutual Life Nominees Ltd*, [1990] 3 All ER 404 PC.
4. *Andrew v Kounnis Freeman*, [1999] 2 BCLC 641 CA.
5. *Caparo Industries plc v Dickman*, 1989 BCLC 154: [1989] 1 All ER 798 CA, on appeal from *Caparo Industries plc v Dickman*, 1988 BCLC 387 QBD.

other company and was also a potential investor. The court readily conceded that it was foreseeable that the shareholders of the company would suffer economic loss if the auditors were negligent in the matter of the company's accounts. Since they stand between the company and the shareholders and make their report to the shareholders, they owe a responsibility to the individual shareholders so as to put the auditors under a duty of care towards them and there was nothing to make it unfair or unreasonable to impose a duty of care on the auditors towards the investing shareholders of the company, but that there was no such duty towards the non-shareholders who relied on audited accounts to buy the shares of the company under takeover.

Stressing this point again in a subsequent case, HOFFMAN J said:[6]

The directors and financial advisers of the target company in a contested takeover bid owe no duty of care to a known takeover bidder regarding the accuracy of profit forecasts, financial statements and defence documents prepared for the purpose of contesting the bid since the reason such documents are prepared is to advise the shareholders of the target company whether to accept the bid and they are not meant for the guidance of bidders. Accordingly, there does not exist sufficient proximity between the directors and financial advisers of the target company and the bidder to give rise to a duty of care.

It was, therefore, held that the defendants did not owe any duty of care to the plaintiff to ensure that pre-bid financial statements and the profit forecast were accurate. At the time that the plaintiff announced the takeover bid for another company, the recently published financial statements of the company were its reports and accounts for the years 1984 and 1985 which had been audited by a firm of accountants and an unaudited interim statement for six months. These statements were cited in all the circulars sent to the shareholders for their guidance. Another circular forecast a 38% increase in profits in the year up to Jan 31, 1986. This document included a letter from the accountants stating that it had been properly compiled in accordance with the company's accounting policies and a letter from the bank expressing the opinion that the forecast had been made after due and careful inquiry. On this basis the shareholders were advised not to accept the proposed bid. The plaintiff then increased the bid- amount and the same was recommended to the shareholders and accepted by them. Subsequently it was discovered that the accounting policy adopted in the pre-bid financial statement and the profit forecast were negligently misleading and had the effect of grossly overstating the profits and that the company was worthless at the time the bid was made with the result that if the plaintiff had known the true facts,

---

6. *Morgan Crucible Co plc* v *Hill Samuel Bank Ltd*, [1990] 3 All ER 331 Ch D.

it would never had made the bid, let alone increased it. But even so those who prepared the statements from the company's side for the guidance of its shareholders were held not liable to the plaintiff.[7]

Where the audit partner of a firm of accountants expressly vouched for a set of accounts which his firm had audited, the firm would be liable in negligence if those accounts were defective. It was a known fact that the bid would not proceed unless this undertaking that the accounts were true and fair was given.[8]

The duty of an auditor of a subsidiary company to its holding company was explained in *Baring plc* v *Cooper & Lybrand*.[9] The court was of the view that there is no legal principle that a holding company is not entitled to recover damages for loss in the value of its subsidiary resulting directly from a breach of duty owed to the company itself as distinct from the duty owed to the subsidiary. The auditors of the subsidiary are supposed to be aware of the fact that their duty to see the true and fair aspect of the subsidiary's accounts and their report on it is the only basis on which the true and fair view of all the companies in the group (consolidated group accounts) would be ensured. Thus the holding company had the direct right of action against the subsidiary's auditors for their failure to detect a dealer's fraud.[10]

Default in disclosing fraud

The auditors of a company discovered that a senior employee had been defrauding the company at a grand scale and that he was in a position to go on doing so. The court said that in such a situation it would be the auditors' duty to report the matter to the company's management and not to postpone it till they submit their report.[11]

Liability for fraudulent misrepresentation

The liability for fraudulent misrepresentation was explained by CARDOZO CJ in these words:[12]

> Accountants may, however, be liable to third parties even where there is lacking deliberate or active fraud. A representation certified as true to the knowledge of the accountants when knowledge there is none,

---

7. The court referred to *Caparo Industries plc* v *Dickman*, [1990] 1 All ER 568: [1990] 2 WLR 358 HL: 1990 BCLC 273. For a further survey of cases on the subject of responsibility for financial statements, see *Kuwait Asian Bank EC* v *National Mutual Life Nominees Ltd*, [1990] 3 All ER 404 PC.
8. *ADT Ltd* v *BDO Binder Hamlyn*, 1996 BCLC 808.
9. (1997) 1 BCLC 427 CA.
10. The court followed the principle laid down in *George Fischer (Great Britain) Ltd* v *Multi Construction Ltd*, (1995) 1 BCLC 260.
11. *Sasea Finance Ltd* v *RMPG*, [2000] 1 All ER 676 CA; *Law Society* v *KPMG Peat Marwick*, [2000] 1 All ER 515.
12. *Ultramares Corpn* v *Touche*, (1931) 235 NY Rep 170.

a reckless misstatement, or an opinion based on grounds so flimsy as to lead to the conclusion that there was no genuine belief in its truth, are all sufficient upon which to base liability. A refusal to see the obvious, a failure to investigate the doubtful if sufficiently gross, may furnish evidence leading to an inference of fraud.[13]

Accountants' lien

It has been held that an accountant, like a solicitor, is not entitled to exercise a lien over the books and documents of a registered company which are required to be kept at a particular place and made available for inspection. The expression "books of account" would include accounting records such as sale and purchase invoices, cheque books, pay in books and bank statements.[14]

Special audit [S. 233-A]

The Central Government has the power in the following cases to direct the special audit of a company's accounts:

1. when the affairs of any company are not being managed in accordance with sound business principles or prudent commercial practice; or
2. when any company is being managed in a manner likely to cause serious injury or damage to the interests of the trade, industry or business to which it pertains; or
3. when the financial position of any company is such as to endanger its solvency.

A prayer for an order of special audit was made in a petition for prevention of oppression and mismanagement. The Company Law Board did not accede to the request because the allegations of low profitability and inflated expenses were not supported by specific facts and figures. The alleged expenses had been approved by the Income Tax Authorities.[15]

The Government may appoint the company's auditor or any other chartered accountant to conduct the audit. Such a special auditor will have the same powers and duties as an auditor of the company, except that he has to submit his report to the Central Government.[16]

On receipt of this report the Central Government may take such action as it considers necessary in accordance with the provisions of the Act or any other law.[17] But where no action is taken within four months, the

---

13. For an account of such liability *see* Jon H. Holyork, *Accountancy and Negligence*, 1986 JBL 120.
14. *DTC (CNC) Ltd* v *Gary Sargeant & Co*, (1996) 1 BCLC 529 Ch D.
15. *Mahendra Singh Mewar* v *Lake Palace Hotels & Motals (P) Ltd*, (1999) 96 Comp Cas 757 CLB.
16. S. 233-A(3).
17. S. 233-A(6).

Government may send the report to the company requiring it to circulate the same to the members or read it to them at the next general meeting.

Power of registrar to call for special information [S. 234]

A company has to submit several documents to the Registrar under the Act. While perusing any such document, the Registrar may form an opinion that any information or explanation is necessary in respect of a matter to which a particular document relates. He may, in such a case, require the company to furnish the same. If the company fails to do so, or submits an inadequate explanation, the Registrar may require the company to produce the necessary books and papers. The company and its officers may be punished for further default. Further, if the information or explanation discloses an unsatisfactory state of affairs or does not disclose a full and fair statement of the matter in question, the Registrar shall report it to the Central Government.[18]

Seizure of documents by Registrar [S. 234-A]

Sometimes the Registrar may have reasonable ground to believe that the books of accounts of a company or of its managerial agencies may be destroyed or falsified or otherwise tampered with. In such a case he may apply to a Magistrate of the First Class or a Presidency Magistrate, who may authorise him to enter and search the place where such books are kept and seize them. The Registrar has to return such books within thirty days, but he may make copies.

Audit of cost accounts [S. 233-B]

Section 209, as amended by the Amendment Act of 1965, provides that a company pertaining to any class of companies engaged in production, processing, manufacturing or mining activities, should keep proper books of account showing such particulars relating to utilisation of material or labour or to other items of cost as may be prescribed, if such class of companies is required by the Central Government to include such particulars in the books of account.

When a company is required to include in its books of account the above particulars, the Central Government may, whenever it is necessary so to do, direct that an audit of cost accounts of the company should be conducted. The conduct of audit will take place in such manner as may be prescribed in the order. The auditor shall be a cost accountant within the meaning of the Cost and Works Accountants Act, 1959. If cost accountants are not available

---

18. S. 234(5) and (6). *See* also *Barium Chemicals Ltd* v *Company Law Board*, [1966] 2 Comp LJ 151: (1966) 36 Comp Cas 639: AIR 1967 SC 295. Where a written petition was filed to find out whether a foreign company had acquired interest in a company without compliance with Foreign Exchange Regulation Act, 1974, the court said that it would have been better to seek information from the affected company under S. 234. *R. Venkataswamy Naidu* v *Enforcement Directorate*, (1993) 78 Comp Cas 87 Mad.

in sufficient numbers the Government may by notification authorise the appointment of chartered accountants.[19] The appointment will be made by the Board of Directors with the previous approval of the Central Government and also subject to the constraints as to the number of audits specified in Section 224(1-B).[20] A person disqualified under Section 226(3) or (4) or who has been appointed as an auditor of the company is disqualified from appointment [Section 233-B(5)]. If a cost auditor becomes disqualified after appointment he should cease to conduct audit from the date of disqualification [Section 233-B(5)(c)]. The company is under an obligation to provide all facility and assistance to the cost auditor [Section 233-B(6)]. He has all the powers of an auditor, but he submits his report to the Company Law Board with a copy to the company [Section 233-B(4)]. If the report carries any reservation or qualification, the company should inform the Central Government within thirty days [Section 233-B(7)]. The Government may demand further information [Section 233-B(8)]. The Government may then take necessary action [Section 233-B(9)]. The Government may direct the company to circulate the report to the members along with the notice calling the next annual meeting.[21]

---

19. Proviso to S. 233-B(*i*) *inserted* by the Amendment Act, 1970.

20. S. 233-B(1) *substituted* by *ibid.* The Government tried to fix 30 cost audits per auditor. Delhi High Court in *R. Nanabhoy* v *UOI*, (1983) 53 Comp Cas 454, struck it down. Cost audit is not a regular or annual affair. It has to wait for an order of the Central Government. The restrictions would have crippled the growth of the profession. A certificate should be taken from the appointee that his case is not covered by the constraints of S. 224(1-B). *Rakesh Singh* v *UOI*, (2002) 110 Comp Cas 624 Del, the power of approval also includes a power to disapprove a particular person. A complaint against the proposed cost auditor was pending before the Institute of Cost and Works Accountants.

21. S. 233-B(10). Sub-section (*ii*) contains penalty provisions. The Andhra Pradesh High Court refused to quash a complaint filed on the ground that despite several reminders, the petitioners, who were "officers in default" failed to apply to the Central Government for appointment of a cost auditor. The petitioners were directors at the material time and they allowed the default to continue. *Bimal Kumar Nopany* v *ROC*, (1990) 68 Comp Cas 567 AP.

13
Borrowing, Lending, Investments and Contracts

BORROWING

A company cannot borrow money unless it is so authorised by its memorandum. In the case of a trading company, it is not, however, necessary that the objects clause of its memorandum should expressly authorise it to borrow. As borrowing is incidental to trading, such a company has implied power to borrow.[1] Other companies must have a borrowing power clearly specified in the memorandum.

Consequences of unauthorised borrowing

Borrowing without express or implied authority is *ultra vires*. The consequences of such a borrowing as worked out in various cases are as follows:

1. *No Loan*

In the first place, an *ultra vires* lender has no legal or equitable debt against the company. Consequently he cannot sue the company to recover his loan.[2] *Ultra vires* borrowings are forbidden on grounds of public policy. To allow such borrowing to be recovered would be an evasion of that policy.[3]

2. *Injunction*

But if the money advanced to the company has not been spent, the lender may by means of an injunction restrain the company from parting with it.[4]

3. *Subrogation*

Where the money of an *ultra vires* lender has been used to pay off lawful debts of the company, he would be subrogated to the position of the debtor paid off and to that extent would have the right to recover his loan from the

---

1. *See* Memorandum of Association, Objects Clause, *ante*, and *Introductions Ltd, Re*, [1968] 2 Comp LJ 28: [1969] 2 WLR 791: [1969] 1 All ER 887 CA.
2. This was so held in *National Permanent Benefit Building Society, Re*, (1869) 5 Ch App 309 and followed by the Madras High Court in *Madras Native Permanent Fund Ltd, Re*, (1931) 60 MLJ 270, where at 273 the court said: "*ultra vires* loans are void and in truth have no existence. They do not create the relationship of creditor and debtor."
3. See *Sinclair v Brougham*, 1914 AC 398: 111 LT 1: [1914-15] All ER Rep 622: 83 LJ Ch 465: 30 TLR 315.
4. The reason for this rule is that the loan is *ultra vires*, the company, therefore, does not become the owner of that money. The lender continues to be the owner and he has the right to take back the property *in specie*.

company.[5] Subrogation is allowed for the simple reason that when a lawful debt has been paid off with an *ultra vires* loan, the total indebtedness of the company remains the same. By subrogating the *ultra vires* lender, the courts are able to protect him from loss, while the debt burden of the company is in no way increased.

But the subrogated creditor will not enjoy the priority of the original creditor. The best illustration is *Wrexham, Mold & Connah's Quay Rly Co Ltd, Re*:[6]

A company had borrowed to the full extent of its powers by issuing three different series of debentures, *A, B* and *C*. *A* had priority over *B* and *B* over *C*. The company took a fresh *ultra vires* loan from the plaintiff to pay interest on *A* debentures. It was held that to the extent to which the plaintiff's money was used to pay off legal debts, he became a legal creditor, but he was not entitled to the priority of *A* debentures.

4. *Identification and Tracing*

Fourthly, as long as the money of the lender is in the hands of the company in its original form or its products are still capable of identification, he may claim that money or its products. But the problem is much more difficult when the lender's money and that of the company have become mixed up. There is only a common fund composed of the lender's money and the company's money, but no part of it is traceable as belonging to one or the other. In such a case the lender may perhaps be helpless. But in the winding up of the company he may claim *pari passu* distribution of the assets with the shareholders. This was done in the complicated case of *Sinclair* v *Brougham*:[7]

A building society started banking business which was *ultra vires* the society. On its winding up the assets appeared to have been composed partly of the shareholders' money and partly of the depositors' money. But it was not possible to trace out which part of the mixed fund belonged to the shareholders or the creditors. Nor were the assets sufficient to pay both in full. It was, therefore, held that the entire remaining amount should be apportioned between the depositors and the shareholders in proportion to the amount paid by them, respectively. Nearest approach practicable to substantial justice would be done.

Regular borrowings

Where, on the other hand, the borrowing is within the powers of the company, the lender would not be prejudiced simply because its officers

---

5. For an illustration of subrogation, see *Neath Building Society* v *Luce*, (1889) 43 Ch 158.

6. [1899] 1 Ch D 440: [1895-9] All ER Rep Ext 1519: 80 LT 130.

7. 1914 AC 398: 111 LT 1: [1914-15] All ER Rep 622: 83 LJ Ch 465: 30 TLR 315.

have applied the loan to unauthorised activities, provided that the lender had no knowledge of the intended misuse.[8] Thus, for example, in *V. K. R. S. T. Firm* v *Oriental Investment Trust Ltd*:[9]

> Under the authority of a company, its managing director borrowed large sums of money and misappropriated them. The company was nevertheless held liable.

But where a lender provides finance for a business which (within his knowledge) is not within the company's objects, the loan is *ultra vires* and the lenders cannot enforce the security.[10]

Another problem that may sometimes arise in this connection is where borrowing is within the company's power but it is beyond the powers of those managing the company. Whether the company would be liable in such a case was the question in *T. R. Pratt (Bom) Ltd* v *E. D. Sasoon & Co Ltd*:[11]

> There was no limit on borrowing for business in the memorandum of a company. But the directors could not borrow beyond the limit of the issued share capital of the company without the sanction of the general meeting. The directors borrowed money from the plaintiff beyond their powers.

It was held that "the money having been borrowed and used for the benefit of the principal either in paying its debts, or for its legitimate business, the company cannot repudiate its liability on the ground that the agent had no authority from the company to borrow. When these facts are established a claim on the footing of money had and received would be maintainable."

But in *Equity Insurance Co Ltd* v *Dinshaw & Co*:[12]

> It was held that "where the managing agent of a company who is not authorised to borrow, has borrowed money which is not necessary, neither bona fide, nor for the benefit of the company, the company is not liable for the amount borrowed."

The Companies Act, in Section 293(1)(*d*), provides that directors should not borrow beyond the paid-up capital of the company and its free reserves. Sub-section (5) further declares that such a loan shall not be valid, "unless the lender proves that he advanced the loan in good faith and without knowledge that the limit had been exceeded".

---

8. *David Payne & Co, Re,* [1904] 2 Ch 608: [1904-7] All ER Rep Ext 1501.
9. AIR 1944 Mad 532.
10. *Introductions Ltd, Re,* [1968] 2 Comp LJ 28: [1969] 2 WLR 791: [1969] 1 All ER 887 CA .
11. AIR 1936 Bom 62. Followed in *Kumar Krishna Rohatgi* v *State Bank of India,* (1980) 50 Comp Cas 722 Pat, where the company used the money. *See* also *C. K. Siva Sankara Panicker* v *Kerala Financial Corpn,* (1980) 50 Comp Cas 217 Ker, where the act of mortgaging the assets of a company for the help of its sister concern, was held to be valid.
12. AIR 1940 Oudh 202.

Where a loan has not been taken in the name of the company it will not be liable even though it may have benefited. An illustration in point is *Suraj Babu* v *Jaitly & Co*:[13]

P & Co were the managing agents of *L & Co* which was in liquidation. *P* was the manager. *P* borrowed a sum of money from *J* in his own name. In one letter to *J* he indicated that the loan was for a requirement of *L & Co* and that company had actually benefited. But it was held that there was no intention to bind *L & Co.* "The mere fact that the company had benefited was not in itself sufficient to bind the company."

Where a promissory note was executed on a paper the top of which bore the rubber stamp of the company and was signed "*Joshi, Treasurer*", an intention to bind the company was held to be clear.[14] But where a note was endorsed in this manner:

"Mitter and Sons,

Managing Agents,

Lister Antiseptic Co Ltd",[15]

it was held that the intention to involve the responsibility of the company was not clear from the endorsement.

MORTGAGES AND CHARGES

Registration of charges [S. 125]

The power to borrow includes the power to mortgage the company's assets or to create a charge upon them. The reason is that lenders always insist on some security and the only security that a company can give is to charge its assets. Any charge or mortgage created on any of the following assets of a company must be registered with the Registrar of Companies under Section 125 of the Act:[16]

1. a charge for the purpose of securing any issue of debentures;
2. a charge on uncalled share capital of the company;
3. a charge on any immovable property, wherever situate or any interest therein;
4. a charge on any book debts of the company;[17]

---

13. AIR 1946 All 372.
14. *Poona Chitrashala Steam Press* v *Gajanan Industrial & Tramway Co*, AIR 1923 Bom 29.
15. *Sreelal Mangatulal* v *Lister Antiseptic Dressing Co Ltd*, AIR 1925 Cal 1062.
16. S. 124 says that in this part, the expression "charge" includes a mortgage. Where the company defaulted in registering the charge, the court, at the instance of the chargee, compelled the company to comply with the requirement of registration. *ICICI Bond Ltd* v *Klen & Marshall Manufacturers & Exporters Ltd*, [2000] 4 Comp LJ 411 CLB.
17. The right of retention contained in a financing agreement is not a charge on book debts so as to require registration, because it is not possible for a charge to be created in favour of debtor over his own indebtedness to a creditor and there is no relevant property capable of forming the subject matter of a charge. *Charge Card Services Ltd, Re*, [1986] 3 All ER 289 Ch D. The

5. a charge, not being a pledge, on any moveable property of the company;

6. a floating charge on the undertaking or any property of the company including stock in trade;

7. a charge on calls made, but not paid;

8. a charge on a ship or any share in a ship;[18]

9. a charge on goodwill, or a patent or a licence under a patent, on a trade-mark, or on a copyright or a licence under a copyright.

The Registrar has to issue a certificate under his hand of the registration of any charges stating the amounts secured. The certificate is conclusive evidence that the requirements as to registration have been complied with.[19]

Registration must be effected within thirty days of the creation of the charge.[20] However, the Registrar may extend the time up to next thirty days. He has to be convinced that there was a sufficient cause for the default. The company has to pay an additional fee as may be required by the Registrar but it should not exceed ten times the amount of fee specified in Schedule X. The advantage of registration is that the charge becomes binding on the company even in its winding up and also on every subsequent purchaser or incumbrancer of the property covered by the charge.[21] The effect of non-registration is that the charge would be void against the liquidator and any creditor of the company.[22] The lender would not have the benefit of the charge, although his loan stands and it shall become immediately repayable.[23] Where the creditor failed to get his charge registered, the court

---

item "cash at bank" is also not a book debt, *Brightlife Ltd, Re*, [1986] 3 All ER 673 Ch D. A charge over all the future book debts has been held to be a floating charge. *Rhodes v Allied Dunlar Pension Services Ltd*, 1988 BCLC 186 Ch D; *Offshore Ventilation Ltd, Re*, 1988 BCLC 186 Ch D; *A company (No 005009 of 1987) Re, ex p Copp*, 1989 BCLC 13 Ch D, where the charge was on the book and other debts from time to time due and owing. A fixed charge on book debts is also possible. *See* Robert A Pearce, *Fixed Charge over Book Debts*, 1987 JBL 18. A charge on book debts and other debts was held to be a floating charge, *Portbase Clothings Ltd, Re*, (1993) 3 All ER 829 Ch D. *Spectrum Plus Ltd, Re*, (2005) 3 WLR 58 (HC): (2005) 128 Comp Cas 280, a charge on book debts was expressed to be by way of specific charge, the book debts charged could not be used prior to collection and the collection was to be in the chargee's account with the bank, though the charger could withdraw the money, held floating charge.

18. A charge on a share in horses has been held to be not a floating charge because they are choses-in-action. *Sugar Properties (Derisley Wood) Ltd, Re*, 1983 BCLC 146 Ch D.

19. S. 132.

20. Registration may be effected either by the company or by any interested party. S. 134. A copy of the charge should be kept at the registered office. S. 136, S. 145 provides that pre-existing charges would also have to be registered if they were not satisfied at the time that the registration requirements came into force.

21. S. 126.

22. *Capital Finance Co v Stokes*, [1968] 3 All ER 625: [1968] 3 WLR 899: [1969] 1 Comp LJ 341: [1969] 1 Ch 261. Noted 1968 JBL 153. A charge cannot be avoided by the liquidator without proving that it was not registered. *Hindustan Forest Co (P) Ltd v United Commercial Bank*, (1994) 79 Comp Cas 669 P&H.

23. In many cases debenture holders could not enforce the security because of non-registration. *See*, for example, *Dinshaw & Co, Bankers Ltd, Re*, AIR 1937 Oudh 62; *Krishna Ayyangar v*

said that he could not be regarded as a secured creditor. A mere statement of account could not be taken as a proof of the charge. The agreement of the SFC with the bank that the corporation should be treated as a secured creditor was held to be no proof of charge.[24]

It has been said that "the section makes void the security, not the debt, nor the cause of action, but the security, and not as against everybody, not as against the company grantor, but against the liquidator and against any creditor, and it leaves the security to stand as against the company while it is a going concern. It does not make the security binding on the liquidator as successor of the company."[25]

A charge on all the products, movable property and book debts of the company was held to be void because the prescribed particulars were not filed with the Registrar within time nor any extension of time was sought for the purpose.[26]

The possessory lien of a warehouse keeper for his charges which included the power to sell the goods to realise the outstanding charges was held as not amounting to a charge on the goods so as to require registration.[27] In a transaction for sale of goodwill and other rights to, the company, it promised to pay the price by instalments. This was held to be not a charge on the assets of the company so as to require registration.[28]

Nallaperumal Pillai, AIR 1920 PC 56; *Maheshwari Bros* v *Official Liquidators of Indra Sugar Works Ltd*, AIR 1942 All 119; *Indus Film Corpn Ltd, Re*, AIR 1939 Sind 100: 181 IC 681; *Ranjit Ray* v *D. A. David*, AIR 1935 Cal 218; *Molton Finance Ltd, Re*, [1967] 3 WLR 1561: [1967] 3 All ER 843; *F. L. E. Holdings Ltd, Re*, [1967] 1 WLR 1409: [1967] 3 All ER 553; *Calcutta National Bank* v *Kangaroo Tea Co*, AIR 1969 Cal 578. A court decree under which any property of a company may be attached is not a charge. *Suryakant Natvarlal Surati* v *Kamani Bros (P) Ltd*, (1985) 58 Comp Cas 121 Bom; *Praga Tools Ltd* v *Official Liquidator*, (1984) 56 Comp Cas 214 Cal. Registration is necessary only when the company's properties are charged, and not those of a director who guaranteed the company's debts. The charge against the director's property was effective though the charge on the company's property was not registered. *Maharashtra State Financial Corpn* v *Masvi & Co (P) Ltd*, (1993) 76 Comp Cas 168 at 193 Bom. As a consequence of winding up a creditor under an unregistered charge becomes an unsecured creditor, *Rajasthan Financial Corpn* v *Official Liquidator, Jaipur Spg and Wvg Mills Ltd*, (1986) 2 Ker 269; *Indian Bank* v *Official Liquidator Chemmeens Exports (P) Ltd*, (1998) 5 SCC 401: AIR 1998 SC 2111, a preliminary decree passed on the basis of an unregistered charge not objected to, nor appeal filed by the official liquidator, the company could not declare the decree to be void at the instance of the Official Liquidator.

24. *A.P. State Financial Corpn* v *Mopeds India Ltd*, (2005) 124 Comp Cas 833 AP; *Rajasthan Financial Corpn* v *Jaipur Spg & Wvg Mills Ltd*, (2006) 133 Comp Cas 1 SC, no priority to the corporation holding unregistered charge. *Kerala State Financial Enterprises Ltd* v *Official Liquidator*, (2006) 133 Comp Cas 915 SC sums owed to the Govt Company, charge not registered, charge void against liquidator and creditors.

25. *Monolithic Building Co, Re*, [1915] 1 Ch 643 CA, per Phillimore J. cited with approval in *Smith* v *Bridgend Country Borough Council*, [2000] 1 BCLC 775 CA.

26. *Deutsche Bank* v *S. P. Kala*, (1999) 98 Comp Cas 841 Bom.

27. *Hamlet International plc, Re*, [1999] BCLC 506 CA.

28. *M. M. Hussain* v *Laminated Package (P) Ltd*, [2000] CLC 330 AP.

An undertaking by a company with the backing of a resolution to create a charge on its assets was held to be not a present charge so as to require registration.[29]

Rectification of Register [S. 141]

By Section 141, the Central Government has been empowered to allow extension of time for filing the particulars of a charge. An extension is allowed only where the omission was accidental, or due to inadvertence, or to some other sufficient cause, or it is not of nature as to prejudice the position of creditors or shareholders of the company or that on other grounds it is just or equitable to grant relief. No extension was allowed where there was an unexplained delay of two years and the only argument offered was that the creditor thought that the company must have obtained the registration.[30] Generally no extension is allowed once the company has gone into liquidation. Accordingly, refusing the relief in *Dinshaw & Co Bankers Ltd, Re,*[31], the court cited with approval the following observation from *Spiral Globe Co Ltd, Re:*[32]

> Upon a winding up the rights of the whole body of creditors intervene and their position would be very much prejudiced if time for registration were unconditionally extended.

In *Radha Kishen Moti Lal Chamaria* v *Ram Narain*[33] an extension was allowed but with due safeguards to the rights acquired by certain persons prior to the actual registration. Similarly it has been held in *Heathstar Properties Ltd, (No 2), Re,*[34] that—

> ...notwithstanding that an action was proceeding in which the validity of the equitable charge was in issue, the Court would, in the exercise of its discretion, extend the time for registering particulars of the charge,...where the risk of injustice to the company by extending the time of registration was far less than the risk of injustice to the chargeholder by refusing to extend the time.[35]

---

29. *ICICI* v *Official Liquidator, Usha Automobiles & Engg Co Ltd*, (2000) 100 Comp Cas 150 CLB.
30. *Reshma Estate (P) Ltd, Re*, (1977) 47 Comp Cas 447 Bom.
31. AIR 1937 Oudh 62.
32. [1902] 1 Ch 396. *See* also *Ehrmann Bros Ltd, Re*, [1906] 2 Ch 697 and *Chandbali Steamer Service Co, Re*, (1955) 60 CWN 278; *Heathstar Properties Ltd, Re*, [1966] 1 All ER 628: [1966] 2 Comp LJ 26; *Kris Cruisers Ltd, Re*, [1948] 2 All ER 1105.
33. AIR 1927 Oudh 300.
34. [1966] 1 All ER 1000: [1966] 2 Comp LJ 246 Ch D: [1966] 1 WLR 993.
35. PLOWMAN J at p 251; *see* also *United Bank of India* v *K. C. Mullick & Sons*, [1966] 2 Comp LJ 255, where the Calcutta High Court held that where a company created a charge in 1954 which was registered and another charge in 1957 in favour of a bank, but was not registered, the former charge would survive against the liquidator of the company. Extension of time was refused where winding up was inevitable and not merely imminent. Administrators had concluded that rescue was not possible and creditors had finalised proposals for sale of assets towards winding up. *Victoria Housing Estates Ltd, Re*, [1982] 3 All ER 665 and *Barrow Borough Transport Ltd, Re*, 1989 BCLC 653 Ch D: [1989] 1 WLR 858.

Rectification of the register was ordered where the registration form happened to mention only the movable property whereas both movable and immovable were to be covered.[36]

A company awaited credit facilities from a bank undertaking to offer the bank a charge on a block of assets after obtaining the consent of the first chargeholders' on those assets. It was held that the charge impliedly came into existence on the day the undertaking was given. The Company Law Board [now Central Government] ordered the charge to be registered within thirty days of the order.[37]

Where the application for rectification was filed after a long lapse of about five years and there was also the imminence of liquidation, the CLB [now Central Government] refused extension as it would have defeated the interest of other creditors.[38] Where due to inadvertence, the particulars relating to immovable property covered by the charge were not included in the form and without that the security was not worthwhile and no objection was received from any quarter, rectification was allowed.[39] Where the memorandum of satisfaction signed both by the company and the lending bank happened to be filed due to oversight while the charge was still subsisting, rectification of the register for restoring the charge was allowed.[40]

Rectification of the register was allowed where the particulars submitted for registration failed to disclose the correct registration number of the company. The registration number was a particular of the mortgagor and not that of the mortgage. The charge was validly registered.[41] A company assigned its interest in its immovable properties to another company but failed to register the assignment as a charge within the meaning of Section 125. An application by the assignee company for extension of time was allowed by the CLB [now Central Government]. The High Court refused to interfere in the matter.[42]

---

36. *Kesaria Tea Co Ltd, Re*, (1998) 91 Comp Cas 407 CLB. The Board can order rectification of omission or misstatements.
37. *Central Bank of India* v *Saraf Textile Industries Ltd*, (1998) 28 Corpt LA 62 CLB.
38. *Ravi Constructions* v *ROC*, [2000] 1 Comp LJ 115; *Karnataka Telecom Ltd* v *Ravi Constructions*, (2000) 23 SCL 14 CLB. No rectification is allowed where the charge is not registrable in its inception. *S. T. Patil* v *ROC*, (1998) 91 Comp Cas 578, here guarantee for payment of consideration for shares was given by the transferee and he understood not to retransfer shares till payment and there being no commitment from the company, hence, there was no charge requiring registration.
39. *R. K. Nutrisnax (India) (P) Ltd, Re*, (2000) 4 Comp LJ 185 CLB.
40. *IFB Finance Industries Ltd, Re*, (2000) 38 CLA 215 CLB. Where the CLB condoned delay but also passed remarks on the merits of the transaction, the High Court directed the Registrar to proceed according to law in rectifying the register without taking any influence of other remarks, *Choudhary Builders (P) Ltd* v *Sanghi Bros (Indore) Ltd*, [2000] 1 Comp LJ 236.
41. *Grove* v *Advantage Health (TIO) Ltd*, [2000] 1 BCLC 661 Ch D.
42. *Chaudhary Builders (P) Ltd* v *Sanghi Bros (Indore) Ltd*, (2000) 37 CLA 341 MP.

The Central Government does not have the power to examine the validity of the charge.[43] It cannot order deletion of a charge which is already entered in the register. There is no power in this jurisdiction to require one creditor to deliver the original title deeds relating to the charge to another creditor.[44] A registration with a defective or incomplete form, (registration form without directors' signatures) could not be accepted as a valid form in the exercise of this statutory power.[45]

The power of rectification is limited to correcting mistakes of omission or commission in the entry of any particular or in a memorandum of satisfaction in the register. It does not extend to mistakes which are not on the register. The fact that an entry in the register indicated that further details could be found in another document, did not make that other document a part of the register. It is a restricted jurisdiction for rectification.[46]

Appeal against Registrar's order

The order of the Registrar under Section 125(1)(proviso) or that of the Central Government under Section 141 is appealable whether it extends the time or rejects the application. The appellate court can take into account fresh evidence, because it is not a rehearing but a fresh exercise of discretion. The words "just and equitable" confer the widest possible discretion on the court and this carries the issue even beyond the matters specified in the section. Imminence of winding up is only one factor and not the final thing. Accordingly, the failure of the bank's solicitor in breach of his duty in getting the charge registered and the promptitude of the bank in taking immediate action on discovering the omission, was held to be a justifiable cause for an extension.[47]

Unregistered charge while company going concern

However, while the company is a going concern, a charge or mortgage, even though not registered under the Act, is valid. This was held in *Aung Ban Zeya* v *CRMA Chettiar Firm*,[48] where the High Court of Rangoon cited with approval the following observation from *Monolithic Building Co, Re*:[49]

---

43. *Mangalore Chemicals & Fertilisers Ltd* v *CLB*, (2005) 126 Comp Cas 261 Kant, merits of charge or satisfaction of charge are not to be gone into, only sufficient cause for condonation of delay is to be seen. *Ingroup Ltd* v *Oewen*, (2004) 2 BCLC 61 Ch D, deletion from the form of unnecessary information is not also within jurisdiction.

44. *Times Bank Ltd* v *Shri Shardaparrameshwari Textiles Ltd*, (2000) 38 CLA 270 CLB; *Saradha Finance* v *Alsa Investment (P) Ltd*, (2002) 110 Comp Cas 713 CLB, the CLB (now Central Government) was approached for a direction to the company to file particulars of charge. The company disputed the creation of a charge and also the grant of credit facility to it. Disputed matters not to be adjudicated upon under this jurisdiction.

45. *Canara Bank* v *Premier Agro Cool Tech (P) Ltd*, (2006) 129 Comp Cas 58 CLB.

46. *Ingroup Ltd* v *Oewen*, (2004) 120 Comp Cas 361: (2004) 1 WLR 451.

47. *Braemar Ltd, Re*, 1988 BCLC 556 Ch D. For further study, *see* Gerard McCormack, *Extension of Times for Registration of Company Charges*, 1986 JBL 282.

48. AIR 1927 Rang 288.

49. [1915] 1 Ch 643: 84 LJ Ch 441: 112 LT 619: [1914-15] All ER Rep 249.

"Of course the deed is not void to all intents and purposes. It is a perfectly good deed against the company as long as it is a going concern."

Thus the purchaser of the assets of a company which were under an unregistered mortgage was held bound by the mortgage.[50]

Even in winding up, an unregistered charge has been allowed to stand where it was comprised in a decree and no objection was raised by the liquidator.[51]

The Oudh High Court enforced an agreement to create a charge even though the company, after making the agreement but before executing the charge, had gone into liquidation.[52] Referring to the section[53] the court said that it applies only when the charge is created by the company, and not when it arises by operation of law. The Bombay High Court, on the other hand, refused to order the specific enforcement of an agreement to create a charge after the commencement of winding up as that would amount to converting an unsecured creditor into a secured one.[54]

Procedure of Registration

Registration is effected by filing with the Registrar particulars of the charge or mortgage. The Registrar shall give a certificate of registration which shall be endorsed by the company on every debenture or certificate or debenture stock. Registration can also be obtained by the creditor himself. All that has to be done is to file the particulars within the prescribed time. Accordingly, it was held by the Allahabad High Court in *Benares Bank Ltd v Bank of Bihar Ltd*[55] that the section was complied with when particulars of the charge were sent within twenty-one days (now thirty days), although the Registrar neglected to register it for two and a half years. Nothing done by the Registrar on his own account after proper documents have been filed can affect the validity of the charge.

---

50. *Marturi Umamaheshwara Rao v Pendayala Venkatarayudu*, (1970) 40 Comp Cas 751: AIR 1970 AP 225.
51. *Presidency Industrial Bank v H. L. Industries*, AIR 1969 Bom 84 at p 89. A purchaser of property subject to an unregistered charge cannot say that he is also free from the charge; *Marturi Umamaheshwara v Pendayala Venkatarayudu*, AIR 1970 AP 225.
52. *Hukam Chand v Pioneer Mills Ltd*, AIR 1927 Oudh 55.
53. S. 109 of the Act of 1913 (now S. 125).
54. *Maneklal Mansukhbhai v Saraspur Mfg Co Ltd*, AIR 1927 Bom 167.
55. AIR 1947 All 117. To the same effect, *State Bank of India v Haryana Rubber Industries (P) Ltd*, (1986) 60 Comp Cas 472 P&H; *State Industrial and Investment Corpn of Maharashtra v Maharashtra State Financial Corpn*, (1988) 64 Comp Cas 102 Bom; *State Bank of India v Depro Foods Ltd*, (1988) 64 Comp Cas 324; *Siva Sankara Panicker v Kerala Financial Corpn*, (1980) 50 Comp Cas 817 Ker; *N. Babu Janardhanam v Official Liquidator, Golden Cine Studios (P) Ltd*, (1993) 78 Comp Cas 490 Mad, where the documents were filed within time, but actual registration was done some eight months later when a winding up petition was pending and the registration was held to be effective.

Pledge

A pledge of movable property does not require to be registered. Pledge is characterised by delivery of possession of the goods pledged to the creditor. Once the goods pass into the control of the creditor, the company does not enjoy a free use of them. This prevents the company from charging the goods over again. Hence no registration is necessary in such a case.[56]

Acquisition of Property Subject to Charge

If a company acquires a property which is subject to a subsisting charge, such a charge must also be registered in the same manner as if it were a charge created by the company itself. The registration must be effected within thirty days after the date of acquisition.[57]

Series of Debentures

Where a charge is created by virtue of a series of debentures issued by a company which entitle the debenture-holders to a *pari passu* distribution of the assets charged, the application for registration will have to indicate the following particulars:[58]

(*a*) the total amount secured by the whole series;

(*b*) date of the resolution authorising the issue and the date of the deed;

(*c*) a general description of the property charged; and

(*d*) the names of the trustees, if any, for the debenture-holders.

A copy of the deed containing the charge has to be filed or, if there is no such deed, a copy of one of the debentures.

Payment of Commissions etc.

If any commission or allowance is paid to a person for subscribing or procuring subscription for debentures, the rate thereof must be indicated.[59] However, an omission to comply with this minor detail will not affect the validity of the charge.

Certificate of Registration

The Registrar gives a certificate of registration which indicates the amount secured. The certificate is conclusive evidence that the requirements as to registration have been complied with and that the mortgage or charge is

---

56. S. 125. Registration is necessary for non-possessory securities. For illustrations see *R. Radhakrishnan Chettiar* v *Official Liquidator of Madras, Peoples Bank Ltd*, AIR 1943 Mad 73; *F. D. Jones & Co Ltd* v *Ranjit Roy*, AIR 1927 Cal 782; *Bank of Baroda* v *H. B. Shivdasani*, AIR 1926 Bom 427: 96 IC 417; *Tansukhrai M. Karundia* v *Official Liquidator of Andhra Paper Mills Ltd*, [1949] 2 MLJ 66.

57. S. 127. A penalty of Rs 5000 is leviable for default in complying with the requirements of the section.

58. S. 128.

59. S. 129. S. 142 contains penalty provisions for defaults.

properly registered, even though the particulars put forward are incomplete and the entry on the Registrar's register is defective.[60] Thus where a company demised its factory including chattels but in the application for registration the fact of chattels being included was not mentioned and the Registrar registered accordingly, it was held that the charge was nonetheless effective against the chattels.[61] The principle has been applied to other cases including where a wrong date was mentioned apparently to keep the application for registration within 21 days (now 30);[62] where the Registrar effected registration after the expiry of time without condoning the delay[63] and where the certificate was issued without putting the charge on the register.[64] In such cases the Registrar's decision is open to judicial review. Where the original proforma submitted for registration carried no date on it, the Registrar returned it for re-submission and then registered it from the earlier date, the Court of Appeal held that the Registrar's decision was open to judicial review.[65]

But the rule will not allow a person to take the advantage of his own wrong. Thus where a banker's solicitor, having omitted to register a charge for quite a few months, ultimately got it registered under a wrong description, and winding up having followed within a few days, the Court held that the certificate was not conclusive.[66] If a person intentionally abstains from mentioning a part of his security, he cannot rely on the conclusiveness of the certificate as against a person who has been misled by the partial registration.[67]

A copy of the certificate has to be endorsed on every debenture.[68] Any alteration in the terms and conditions of the charge must be intimated to the Registrar,[69] otherwise the modification would be ineffective. In a case before the Madras High Court,[70] a company increased the rate of interest in consideration of the lender not enforcing the security for sometime, but did not inform the Registrar, it was held that the agreement had become void

60. The certificate of registration was held to be effective even where no other record of registration was available. *Maharashtra State Financial Corpn v Masvi & Co (P) Ltd*, (1993) 76 Comp Cas 168 Bom.
61. *See* ATKIN LJ in *National Provincial & Union Bank of England v Charnley*, [1924] 1 KB 431, 452: 130 LT 465. His Lordship relied upon *Yolland, Husson & Birkett Ltd, Re*, [1908] 1 Ch 152.
62. *Eric Holmes (Property) Ltd, Re*, [1965] 2 All ER 333: [1965] Ch 1052: [1966] 1 Comp LJ 19: *Mechanisations (Eaglescliffe) Ltd, Re*, [1964] 3 All ER 840: [1965] 2 WLR 702: [1966] Ch 20.
63. *Desraj, Voluntary Liquidator v Punjab Financial Corpn*, (1970) 40 Comp Cas 551 P&H.
64. *Bank of Maharashtra v Official Liquidator*, (1973) 43 Comp Cas 505 Mys.
65. *R v ROC, ex p, Central Bank of India*, [1986] 1 All ER 105 CA; *R v ROC*, [1985] 2 All ER 79 QBD.
66. *C. L. Nye Ltd, Re*, [1969] 2 All ER 587; Affirmed on appeal, [1970] 3 WLR 158.
67. An *obiter* observation of ATKIN LJ in *Charnley case*, [1924] 1 KB 431 at p 454.
68. S. 133. A default in complying with the requirements of the section is punishable with fine up to Rs 10,000.
69. S. 135.
70. *Official Liquidator v Bharatpur Princess Trust, Mysore*, (1971) 41 Comp Cas 978 Mad.

after the commencement of winding up, but that the increased interest already paid was not recoverable.[71] The Registrar must again be intimated when the charge is satisfied or paid off.[72] On the receipt of this intimation the Registrar informs the chargeholder and if he raises no objection, a *memorandum of satisfaction* is entered in the register of charges.[73] If any objection is raised, the Registrar records the same and informs the company accordingly.[74] The Registrar may enter such a *memorandum of satisfaction* even when no such intimation has been received from the company provided he is satisfied on evidence that the charge has been paid off or the property has been cleared of it. But he must inform the company.[75]

Register of charges

A register of charges has to be maintained both by the Registrar[76] and the company.[77] The Registrar has to keep in respect of each company a register containing the particulars of all the charges requiring registration. The company is under a duty to forward to the Registrar the necessary particulars in such form and on payment of such fee as may be prescribed. The Registrar's register has to show the particulars relating to the charge such as the date of a charge, the amount secured, the property covered and the persons entitled to the charge and if a property already under a charge has been purchased, the date of purchase. The same particulars have to be shown by the company's register. The instruments creating charges and the register of charges are open to the inspection of any creditor or member without fee and to any other person on payment of such fee as may be prescribed.[78]

---

71. Relying upon its own decision in *Tyagrajan* v *Official Liquidator*, (1960) 30 Comp Cas 381: [1959] 2 MLJ 294.
72. S. 138. Satisfaction (payment of the debt) of the charge has to be brought on the Registrar's record within 30 days of payment. As a matter of practice, a letter of satisfaction from the chargeholder is filed. Where the bank delayed in giving to the company its letter and consequently the company also delayed filing of satisfaction, the CLB condoned the delay on the part of the company because the company had relied on a circular of the Deptt of Company Affairs. *Swaraj Mazda Ltd, Re,* (1992) 73 Comp Cas 569 CLB. The matter is also clarified in the Deptt's Circular No 26/91 and No 10/91.
73. S. 138(3). Where the Registrar entered the memorandum of satisfaction before the expiry of the time allowed to the chargeholder for stating his objection, the entry was struck down. See *Walford Transport Ltd* v *ROC*, (1980) 50 Comp Cas 600 Gau.
74. S. 138(4).
75. S. 139.
76. S. 130. S. 131 requires the Registrar to keep the register in chronological index, in the prescribed form and with prescribed particulars relating to the charges registered with him.
77. S. 143. There are penalty provisions in the section.
78. S. 144. Particulars have to be filed with the Registrar in Form 13 with a fee of Rs 10. Form 13 has to be accompanied with Form 8, 10 or 17 as the case may be (Rule 6). The register is open to inspection by any person on payment of fee of Rs 10 for each inspection. [Rule 6-A, Companies (Central Government's) General Rules and Forms, 1956]. Delay in filing the form would require condonation of the CLB under S. 141. Deptt of Co Affairs, No 3123/89 CLV of 21-3-1990; 1990 Chartered Secy 294. The company's register and instruments can be inspected on payment of Rs

Rights of chargee

Chargee's rights depend upon the terms and conditions agreed upon by the parties. To such express rights, a new kind of right by implication has been added by a decision of the English Court of Appeal.[79] A colonising company's progress of work, which was financed through a bank, was very slow so that the funds were exhausted and interest accumulated. The bank agreed to provide more money if the architects who were the cause of delay, were changed by a more respectable firm. That was accordingly done. The firm so removed sued the bank for the tort of inducing breach of contract. It was held that a charge-holder becomes so closely identified with the project that he gets the right to bring about suitable changes in the staff.

Loans to companies [S. 370]

[Provisions stated here were changed by the Companies (Amendment) Ordinance, 1999. *See* under Section 372-A]

INVESTMENTS

Investment in other companies [S. 372]

[Provisions stated here were changed by the Companies (Amendment) Ordinance, 1999. *See* under Section 372-A]

Inter-corporate Loans and Investments [S. 372-A][80]

By an amendment introduced by the Companies (Amendment) Act, 1999, the provisions of Section 370 relating to inter-corporate loans and those of Section 372 relating to inter-corporate investments have been revised by abrogating them first and then substituting them by a single section, namely, Section 372-A. The amendment has the effect of saying that the provisions of Sections 370 and 372 shall not apply and those of Section 372-A will take over the matter of such loans and investments. The main and the most primary change is that the requirement of the Central Government approval has been dispensed with. Companies are now thus free from the shackles of control on inter-corporate loans and investments. The only control mechanism now is wholly internal. The Board of directors can invest or advance up to 60% of their own decision and beyond that with the special resolution of the shareholders.

The new provisions are as follows:

A company can advance loans to other companies or invest in the securities of other companies up to 60% of the paid-up share capital and free

---

10. Rule 21-A of the Companies (Central Government's) General Rules and Forms, 1956. There are penalty provisions in the section.
79. *Edwin Hill & Partners* v *First National Finance Corpn*, 1989 BCLC 89 CA.
80. The Ordinance was first promulgated in Oct 1998 and made effective from Oct 31, 1998. It was subsequently converted into a Bill with some changes. The Bill became an Act in 1999, enforcement date remaining the same.

reserves or up to 100% of free reserves, which is more. The transactions covered under the provision are:

(*a*) loans to any body corporate;

(*b*) guarantee or security for any loan given or taken by a body corporate;

(*c*) acquiring, by way of subscription, purchase or otherwise the securities of any body corporate.

The notice of a meeting of shareholders called for the purpose of giving previous approval of loans and investment beyond 60% must disclose clearly the specific limits, the particulars of the body corporate in which the investment is proposed to be made or loan or security or guarantee to be given, the purpose of the investment, etc, specific sources of funding and other allied details.

The Board of directors can give a guarantee without the authority of a special resolution:

(*a*) if the Board is so authorised by its own resolution to give the guarantee in accordance with the provisions of the section;

(*b*) if some exceptional circumstances are preventing the process of obtaining a special resolution;

(*c*) if the resolution of the Board is confirmed at a general meeting within 12 months or at the annual general meeting held after the guarantee whichever is earlier.

The requirements of sub-sections (1) and (2) are not to apply to any loan made by a holding company to its wholly-owned subsidiary; any guarantee given on any security provided by a holding company in respect of loans made to its wholly-owned subsidiary; or acquisition by a holding company, by way of subscription, purchases or otherwise, the securities of its wholly owned subsidiary.

A company which has defaulted in making payment of fixed deposits or interest due on them cannot, during the period of such default, make any loans, investments or provide any guarantee.

The rate of interest to be charged on loans must not be less than the prevailing bank rate of interest, which shall mean the standard rate made public under Section 49 of the RBI Act, 1934.

The decision of the Board of directors must be at a meeting sanctioning the transaction by a resolution passed with the consent of all the directors present at the meeting and also prior approval of any such public financial institution must be taken whose term loan with the company is subsisting. Prior approval of a financial institution is not required where the 60% limit is not to be exceeded and there are no defaults in payments towards the institution.

Register of investments-loans [S. 372-A(5)].—The company has to keep a register showing the particulars about investments, loans, guarantees and securities:

1. the name of the body corporate;
2. the amount, terms and purpose of the investment or loan or security or guarantee;
3. the date on which the investment or loan has been made;
4. the date on which a guarantee or security has been provided in connection with a loan.

The particulars should be entered in the register chronologically within seven days of the making of loans or investment, etc.

This register has to be kept at the registered office of the company. It should be available for inspection to members who may also take extracts and may demand copies on a similar fee as is applicable in respect of the register of members.[81]

Rule-making power.—The Central Government may prescribe regulations for the purposes of this section.[82]

Exceptions.—The provisions of the section do not apply in respect of the following transactions:[83]

1. a banking company, insurance company or a housing finance company for transactions made in the ordinary course of business, a company established with the sole object of financing industrial enterprises or for providing infrastructural facilities;
2. a company whose principal business is the acquisition of shares, stock, debentures or other securities;
3. a private company, unless it is the subsidiary of a public company;

Sub-section (8) exempts subscription of shares pursuant to Section 81(1)(*a*) (further issue of capital) from compliance with the provisions.

Penalty provisions [S. 372-A(9)].—Two kinds of default have been identified and given different treatment, one is the violation of the main provision and the second is default in maintaining the register. A very light penalty is provided in the matter of the register. The company and every officer of the company who is in default is punishable with fine extending to Rs 5000 and also with a further fine up to Rs 500 for every day during which the default continues.

For failure to comply with the main provisions of the section, the company and every officer of the company who is in default is liable to be punished with fine extending to fifty thousand rupees or imprisonment

---

81. Provisions of S. 163 would apply. Sub-s. (6).
82. S. 372-A(7).
83. S. 372-A(8).

which may extend to two years. Where any loan or investment made in violation of the section has been recovered, the punishment by way of imprisonment is not to be inflicted and where recovery is only partial, the term of imprisonment is to be appropriately reduced.

Where the company suffers any loss because of the contravention, as for example, loans have become irrecoverable, the investment has been lost, or the security has been attached by the security holder or payment under guarantee has been enforced, all the persons who were knowingly a party to the contravention would be jointly as well as severally liable to make good the company's loss.

Loans.—The *Explanation* to the section says that for the purposes of the section "loan" includes debentures or any deposit of money made by one company with another company, except where the depositee company is a banking company.

Free reserves.—"Free reserves" means those reserves which, as per the latest audited balance sheet of the company, are free for distribution as dividend. It also includes the amount of premium received on issue of securities but does not include share application money.[84]

Investments in own name [S. 49]

Section 49 requires that "all investments made by a company on its own behalf shall be made and held by it in its own name". If the company's nominee or director becomes on its behalf a director in another company and is required to hold qualification shares, they may be held jointly in the name of the company and such person.[85] Where a company advances money to another company by way of a loan to enable the borrowing company to make investment in its shares, that does not amount to investment in shares by the lending company in another company's name.[86]

The section recognises a few exceptions also. Firstly, the section does not apply to investments made by a company whose principal business consists of buying and selling of shares or securities.[87] Secondly, a company may hold shares in its subsidiary company in the name of one or more nominees if it is necessary to ensure the number of members from going below the statutory minimum.[88] Thirdly, a company may deposit with its bankers, shares or securities for collection of dividends or to facilitate their transfer.[89] If the transfer is not effected within six months, they shall be held

---

84. *Explanation* (*b*).
85. S. 49(2). Company's shares held jointly with a director did not constitute him into exclusive owner for exercising ownership rights of his own. *Exchange Travel (Holdings) Ltd, Re*, (1991) BCLC 728 Ch D.
86. *Hemangini Finance & Leasing (P) Ltd* v *T.N. Mercantile Bank Ltd*, (1996) 86 Comp Cas 875 CLB.
87. S. 49(4).
88. S. 49(3).
89. S. 49(5).

back by the company in its own name.[90] Fourthly, a company may transfer its shares or securities to another person as a security for a loan or the performance of an obligation.[91]

A further exception has been added under the consequential amendment of the section by the Depositories Act, 1996. A company can hold investments in the name of a depository when such investments are in the form of securities held by the company as a beneficial owner. All such exceptional transactions have to be entered in a register so as to enable their identification and the name in which they are held.

Form of contracts [S. 46]

The brief purpose of the section is to declare that contracts of a company can be made in the same manner in which they can be made by an individual whether they be written or oral. Accordingly, the section says that a written contract can be made on behalf of a company by any person acting under its authority, whether express or implied. An oral contract can also be made in the same manner. Where a debenture was signed not by the director of a company but by the person to whom the director had given his power of attorney, the company was not permitted to question the validity. Section 9(1) of the European Communities Act, 1972 presumes good faith in favour of a person dealing with a company and he is not bound to inquire either into the limitations on the powers of directors or the capacity of the company.[92] (New provisions in the 1989 Act [English] are in Sections 35-A and 35-B).

No personal liability arises under contracts signed for the company. A clause in the contract providing for personal liability of the signatory would be ineffective unless both sides understand that the contract is being on the basis of personal liability.[93]

Execution of deeds and use of seal [S. 48]

Formal deeds can be executed only through a power of attorney. Section 48 accordingly provides that a company may, by writing under its common seal, appoint any person as its attorney and he may, in the exercise of his power, execute deeds on behalf of the company. Such a deed binds the company to the same effect as if it were under the company's common seal.[94] The seal is a method of making a physical impression upon the

---

90. S. 49(5), proviso.
91. S. 49(5)(*b*).
92. *TCB Ltd* v *Gray*, [1986] 1 All ER 587 Ch D 7.
93. *Montogomery Litho Ltd* v *Maxwell*, [2000] Scot Cases 56, HL—Scotland.
94. For documents to be executed outside India, S. 50 lays down the procedural requirements. It says that a company whose business requires transactions outside India, it may, in accordance with its articles, have a seal in that territory, which shall be facsimile of the common seal of the company, mentioning in addition the name of the place where it is going to be used. A person should be authorised in writing to use that seal in that area. Authority of any such person shall remain effective during the specified period, if any, or until revoked. The person using the seal must mention the date and place.

documents of the company, of its name etc. The seal can be used by the authority of the directors or of a committee of directors authorised by directors.[95] The directors may determine who shall sign any instrument to which the seal is affixed, otherwise such a document has to be signed by a director and by the secretary. A company transacting business in foreign countries may have in accordance with its articles its official seal in a foreign country, which is a facsimile of the company's common seal and should include the name of the place where it is to be used.

The requirement of common seal has been dispensed with under Section 36-A(3) of the English Companies Act, 1985. Hence, it is no longer necessary for authenticating the company's formal documents. The Supreme Court held in a case against the company for specific performance that the absence of seal on the contract signed by the directors or absence of a formal resolution authorising the directors to enter into the contract did not vitiate the contract.[96]

Section 48 comes into play when a person wants to enforce obligations against a company arising out of a contract and the company denies the contract or disputes its liability. The section cannot be used where the proceeding is by the company. The validity of the appointment of a person as an adviser of the company was not allowed to be questioned by the appointee because of the lack of any formality. The company had not denied its obligation under the appointment.[97]

Authentication of documents and proceedings [S. 54]

Documents or proceedings which require to be authenticated by the company, may be signed by any director, or manager, or secretary or by any other authorised officer of the company. Common seal would not be necessary in such a case. A representation signed on behalf of a company by a duly authorised agent acting within the scope of his authority or by an officer or employee of the company acting in the course of his duties in the business of the company constitutes a representation made by the company and signed by it.[98]

A suit for recovery of insurance money was filed by the managing director of the claimant company. He could not produce any authentic document showing his authority to proceed on behalf of the company. The suit was not allowed.[99] A criminal complaint on behalf of the company

---

95. *G. Subba Rao* v *Rasmi Die Castings Ltd,* AIR 1998 AP 95, memorandum of understanding signed about a debt by the MD of the company but not indicating that he was signing for and on behalf of company he was also not authorised to affix common seal, company not bound.

96. *Panchanan Dhara* v *Monmatha Nath Maity,* (2006) 131 Comp Cas 577 SC.

97. *Sociedade de Fomento Industrial Ltd* v *Ravindranath Subraya Kamar,* AIR 1999 Bom 158.

98. *UBAF Ltd* v *European American Bkg Corpn,* [1984] 2 All ER 226 CA.

99. *H.P. Horticultural Produce Marketing & Processing Corpn Ltd* v *United India Ass Co Ltd,* AIR 2000 HP 11; *Rajendra Paper Mills* v *Indian Security Press,* (2000) CLC 1438 Del, no proof that the director who filed the suit was duly authorised.

which was the payee of a cheque must be filed with the authority of the
Board of directors or in accordance with the company's article or rules
governing the management of the company's affairs. A complaint filed by
the manager was held to be not competent because he had nothing to show
his authority for institution of proceedings.[1]

A writ petition filed with no material to show that the person signing the
petition was authorised by the Board of directors was held to be not
competent.[2]

Bill of exchange and promissory note [S. 47]

In the case of legal persons, who cannot act by themselves, and who can
act only through representatives, the mode of authentication also becomes
very important. The signature must be that of an authorised person and the
name of the company has to be mentioned in such a manner as to make the
intention to bind the company quite explicit. Section 47 of the Companies
Act, 1956 declares:

A bill of exchange, hundi or promissory note shall be deemed to
have been made, accepted, drawn or endorsed on behalf of a company if
drawn, accepted, made or endorsed in the name of, or on behalf of, or on
account of, the company by any person acting under its authority,
express or implied.

Whether the person signing is actually authorised or not depends upon the
arrangements of the company with its officers, as examined in the light of
principles of the law of agency, but the mode of signature is an external
matter. Where a promissory note was executed on a paper the top of which
bore the rubber stamp of the company and was signed: "*Joshi, Treasurer*", an
intention to bind the company was held to be clear.[3] But where a note was
endorsed in this manner:

"Mitter & Sons,

Managing Agents,

Lister Antiseptic Co Ltd.",

it was held that the intention to involve the responsibility of the company was
not clear from the endorsement.[4] Misdescription of the name of the company
may not, however, affect the liability of the company. "A limited company

---

1. *Nayagam Lourds Prakash* v *Standard Chartered Bank*, (2003) 115 Comp Cas 161 AP.
2. *Klen & Marshalls Manufacturers & Exporters Ltd* v *State of J&K*, (2000) 100 Comp Cas 180 Kant.
3. *Poona Chitrashala Steam Press* v *Gajanan Industrial & Tramway Co*, AIR 1923 Bom 29. See also *P. Rangaswami Reddiar* v *R. K. Reddiar*, (1973) 43 Comp Cas 232 Mad. *Kirlampudi Sugar Mills Ltd* v *G. Venkata Rao*, (2003) 114 Comp Cas 563 AP, promissory note for borrowing money signed by the chief executive on behalf of the company made the company liable though the borrowing was not reflected by the company's account books.
4. *Sreelal Mangatulal* v *Lister Antiseptic Dressing Co Ltd*, AIR 1925 Cal 1062.

has characteristics other than its name by reference to which it can be identified."[5] Those signing, however, do incur personal liability when they misdescribe the name of the company.[6]

Where cheques were drawn on behalf of a company without using the formal word "for" or "on behalf of", and were paid by the bank because the persons signing were duly authorised and the intention to operate the company's account was also clear, the bank was held to be discharged from its liability.[7]

Where a promissory note was executed by the chief executive of the company for the money borrowed for the purposes of the company on which the company's seal was affixed, it was held that the new management of the company could not deny the execution of the note and was liable as a successor-in-interest.[8]

Liability for dishonour

The company, every person who was incharge of the company's affairs at the time of the issue of the cheque and every other officer whose connivance or negligence brought about the debacle can be prosecuted under Section 138 of the Negotiable Instruments Act, 1881 for dishonour of the company's cheque.[9] A prosecution was not quashed although the director in question asserted that he was not participating the company's affairs. He was however, exempted from personal attendance.[10] The managing director and secretary of the company are liable to be prosecuted by virtue of their office without any further proof.[11] A notice sent to the managing director, who was the signatory of the cheques, at the company's address was held to be good notice for prosecuting him.[12] A cheque was issued on behalf of the company by a director and the same director also issued notice to the bank not to pay the cheque. The court refused to consider the question at the initial stage that the director could not be prosecuted on facts.[13]

---

5. *Goldsmith (Sicklesmere) Ltd* v *Baxter*, [1969] 3 WLR 522: [1969] 3 All ER 733: [1970] 1 Ch 85: (1970) 40 Comp Cas 809.
6. *Hendon* v *Adelman*, The Times, June 16, 1973; (1973) New LJ 637 and S. 147 of the Companies Act.
7. *B. M. Bank* v *Oriol Industries*, AIR 1956 Bom 57; on appeal to the Supreme Court, *Oriol Industries* v *B. M. Bank*, AIR 1961 SC 993.
8. *Kirlampudi Sugar Mills Ltd* v *G. Venkata Rao*, (2003) 114 Comp Cas 563 AP.
9. *Anil Hada* v *Indian Acrylic Ltd*, (2000) 99 Comp Cas 56 SC. *S.N. Bangur* v *Klen & Marshalls Mfg (P) Ltd*, (2004) 119 Comp Cas 238 Mad, consent or connivance could not be inferred without any material. *B. Venkat Narendra Prasad* v *State of A.P.*, (2005) 124 Comp Cas 621 AP, a director who had resigned before the cheque was issued, not liable.
10. *V. K. Jain* v *UOI*, (2000) 100 Comp Cas 827 SC.
11. *S.M.S. Pharmaceuticals* v *Neeta Bhalla*, (2005) 127 Comp Cas 563 SC.
12. *Bilakchand Gyanchand & Co* v *A. Chinnaswami*, (1999) 98 Comp Cas 573.
13. *Cref Finance Ltd* v *Shree Shanthi Homes (P) Ltd*, (2005) 127 Comp Cas 311 SC.

EMPLOYEES' SECURITIES AND PROVIDENT FUNDS

Deposit of employees' securities [S. 417]

Money received from employees by way of security deposit must be deposited in the manner prescribed by the section within 15 days from the date of receipt. The openings for depositing the money which are allowed are a Post Office account or a special account with the State Bank or a Scheduled Bank or, where the company itself is a Scheduled Bank, in a special account to be opened by the company in itself, or in the State Bank or any Scheduled Bank.

The money or securities so received are not to be used for any purposes except those agreed to in the contract of service. A receipt granted for money deposited with the company is not a security for the purposes of this section and, therefore, ought to be treated as money received. Any other way of handling such money may amount to breach of trust.[14]

Provident funds of employees [S. 418]

A company constituting a provident fund for its employees or any section of them must deposit contributions from both sides and accruals within 15 days in a Post Office account or in a special account in the State Bank or any Scheduled Bank. But where the company itself is a Scheduled Bank, it may keep the amount with itself in a special account or in the State Bank or any Scheduled Bank. Alternatively, the amount may be invested in trust securities as enumerated in clauses (*a*) to (*e*) of Section 20 of the Indian Trusts Act, 1882. The interest yielded by the investment is the maximum that an employee can claim even if the rules governing the fund or the contract with the employees contain different provisions.

Where the fund becomes a recognised fund within the meaning of clause (*a*) of Section 58-A of the Indian Income Tax Act, 1922 or where the rules of the fund contain provisions corresponding to Rules 4 to 9 of the Indian Income Tax (Provident Fund Relief) Rules, an employee shall have the right to withdraw the sum standing to the credit of his account or take advances from it.

Where a trust has been created of such a fund, the money must be given to the trustees within 15 days. Other things will remain the same except that instead of the company, it shall be the responsibility of trustees to administer the fund.[15]

Employees or their trustees have the right to look at the bank receipts.[16] Section 420 spells out penalties for contravention.

---

14. See *Satpal Bakshi* v *Durgadas*, [1988] 1 Comp LJ 77 Del, where, however, the prosecution failed owing to lack of proper proofs.
15. See *Anil Mohan Banerjee* v *ROC*, (1979) 49 Comp Cas 338 Cal.
16. S. 419. The word "employee" means present employee and not a past one whether retired or removed. *State* v *Gridharilal Bajaj*, AIR 1962 Bom 130: (1962) 32 Comp Cas 1114.

14
Debentures

Definition

Companies have frequently to borrow large sums of money. The loan requirement of a company may not, therefore, be met by a single lender. The loan may have to be split into several units. One very convenient method of doing so is to borrow by issuing debentures. Suppose, for example, the sum to be borrowed is one lakh rupees. It may be divided into one thousand units each of the value of hundred rupees. A lender may purchase as many units as he pleases. The company will certify the number of units he holds and that is the concept of a debenture. A debenture is, therefore, a certificate of loan issued by a company. It is a type of security.[1]

The term "debenture" has, however, been found to be something very difficult to define. The Act in Section 2(12) contains only this definition: "Debenture includes debenture stock, bonds and any other securities of a company whether constituting a charge on the company's assets or not." CHITTY J defined it in these words: "Debenture means a document which either creates a debt or acknowledges it, and any document which fulfils either of these conditions is a debenture."[2] According to Topham: "Debenture is a document given by a company as evidence of a debt to the holder usually arising out of a loan and most commonly secured by charge."[3]

As a matter of fact, the term does not have any precise legal meaning. The term as used in the modern commercial parlance is of extremely elastic character.[4] Indeed no definition can help in all cases to know whether a particular document issued by a company is a debenture or not. "We must look at the substance of the instrument itself and without the assistance of any precise legal definition, form the best opinion we can whether the

---

1. A company may issue debentures convertible into shares either fully (FCDs) or partly (PCDs). For rules and regulations to be observed in this connection *see* Section F of SEBI Guidelines for Disclosure and Investor Protection on issue of convertible and non-convertible debentures.
2. In *Levy v Abercorris Slate & Slab Co*, (1887) 37 Ch D 260, 264.
3. Topham's COMPANY LAW 168 (12th Edn). *See also* speech of Viscount MAUGHAM in *Knightsbridge Estates Ltd, Re*, 1940 AC 613, where all the important definitions have been considered. *See also* VYAS J in *Madanlal v Changdeo Sugar Mills*, AIR 1958 Bom 491, 496.
4. *Chief Controlling Revenue Authority v State Bank of Mysore*, AIR 1988 Kant 1: (1989) 65 Comp Cas 427 FB. A detailed discussion about the nature of a debenture is to be found in *Narendra Kumar Maheshwari v UOI*, [1989] 2 Comp LJ 95.

instrument is or is not a debenture."[5] The Bombay High Court appears to have acted on this principle in deciding *Laxman Bharamji* v *Emperor*:[6]

The main business of a private company was to sell what were called "Patron Bonds" and to invest the money realised by the sale of those bonds. The form of the bond bore a serial number. It acknowledged a debt; it was one of a series; it bore the company's seal; it provided for the payment of interest by determining the lucky numbers. The court observed: "The main features which in our opinion tend conclusively to show that these 'Patron Bonds' are debentures are the acknowledgement of debt, the promise to return it, the fact that they form a series bearing consecutive numbers."

Usual Features

As it appears from the above case the usual features of a debenture are as follows:

In the first place, a debenture is usually in the form of a certificate issued under the seal of the company.[7] Secondly, the certificate is generally an acknowledgement of indebtedness. In the striking words of POLLOCK MR:[8]

But whatever be the characteristics which you would expect to find in debentures, the root meaning of the word is indebtedness; that it does record an indebtedness.

"Further, a debenture usually provides for the payment of a specified principal sum at a specified date." But that is not essential. A company may issue perpetual debentures with no undertaking to pay. For Section 120 provides that debentures, are not invalid simply because "they are made irredeemable or redeemable only on the happening of a contingency, however remote, or on the expiration of a period, however long".[9] Then again a debenture usually provides for payment of interest until the principal sum is paid back. But this again is not essential. Interest may be made payable subject to contingencies of uncertain nature.[10]

Thirdly, a debenture is as a rule one of a series, yet a single debenture is not uncommon. "There may be a single debenture issued to one man." Lastly, a debenture generally creates a charge on the undertaking of the company, or on some class of its assets or on some part of its profits.

---

5. CHITTY J in *Levy* v *Abercorris*, supra, fn 2, cited in *Laxman Bharmaji* v *Emperor*, AIR 1946 Bom 18: 223 IC 110.
6. *Supra.* S. 122 says that a contract to subscribe for the company's debentures may be specifically enforced.
7. The case of *British India Steam Navigation Co* v *Commissioners*, (1881) 7 QBD 165, however, shows that a seal is not necessary. There, a debenture certificate which was merely signed by two directors and did not bear the company's seal was held valid.
8. In *Lemon* v *Austin Friars Investment Trust*, [1926] Ch 1: 133 LT 790.
9. *See* also *Knightsbridge Estates Ltd* v *Byrne*, 1940 AC 613: 109 LJ Ch 200: 162 LT 388: 56 TLR 652: [1940] 2 All ER 401 HL.
10. *Lemon* v *Austin Friars Investment Trust*, [1926] Ch 1: 133 LT 790.

Again this is not an essential element. A debenture which creates no such charge is perfectly valid.[11]

FLOATING CHARGE

It is usual, though not essential, for debentures to create a charge on the company's assets. The charges which a company may create on its assets are of two kinds, namely:

1. Fixed charge, and
2. Floating charge.[12]

The normal concept of a mortgage is that it is created on some definite or specific assets. Such a mortgage is suitable for property which is more or less fixed. But it is quite impracticable where the assets to be charged are of circulating or liquid nature. Such assets keep changing and a fresh charge would have to be created every time they were turned over in the course of business. This would hinder business. Hence there was the necessity of a charge which would not paralyse the company's business and, at the same time, give a safe security to the moneylender. In the words of Gower:[13]

> The ingenuity of equity practitioners led to the evolution of an unusual but highly beneficial type of security known as the floating charge.

A simple illustration will explain this:

> A company borrows money on the security of its stock in trade. The charge created, though present and immediate, will not, however, get fixed on the stock. Rather it will keep floating over the changing stock in trade. And when the time comes for the lender to enforce his security he will do so by seizing whatever stock is then in the company's hands. When this happens, the floating charge becomes fixed or crystallised.

The validity of such a charge was clearly recognised in *Panama New Zealand & Australia Royal Mail Co, Re*:[14]

> A steamship company having power to do so issued mortgage debentures, charging the "undertaking and all sums of money arising therefrom", with repayment at a specified time of the money borrowed with interest in the meantime. Before the debentures became due the company was wound up. The debenture-holders wanted to enforce their security. The unsecured creditors disputed the validity of the charge on a

---

11. S. 2(12). S. 122 provides that a contract with a company to take up and pay for any debentures in the company may be enforced by a decree for specific performance. This provision became necessary because otherwise money lending transactions are not so enforceable. *Sewa Singh* v *Mukha Singh*, ILR 17 Lah 270: AIR 1936 Lah 727.
12. S. 124 provides that the word "charge" includes "mortgage".
13. THE PRINCIPLES OF MODERN COMPANY LAW, 78 (3rd Edn, 1969). *See also* Robert R. Pennington, *The Genesis of the Floating Charge*, (1960) 23 Mod LR 630.
14. (1870) 5 Ch App 318: 22 LT 424.

fluid thing like the "undertaking of the company". But it was held that "the word 'undertaking' had reference to all the property of the company, not only which existed at the date of the debenture, but which might afterwards become property of the company. Debenture-holders, therefore, have a charge upon all the property of the company, past and future."

Thus, floating charge is a charge of ambulatory nature, floating with the property it is intended to cover. "It attaches to the subject charged in the varying conditions in which it happens to be from time to time."[15] "It is a charge which floats like a cloud over the whole assets from time to time falling within a generic description....."[16] It does not get attached to any specific property until it crystallises. In the meantime the company can use the assets charged in the ordinary course of its business.

Characteristics of Floating Charge

The chief characteristics of a floating charge which distinguish it from a fixed charge were explained with remarkable clarity by ROMER J in *Yorkshire Woolcombers' Assn Ltd, Re*:[17]

"A mortgage or charge by a company which contains the three following characteristics is a floating charge:

1. It should be a charge upon a class of assets both present and future.
2. The class of assets charged must be one which in the ordinary course of business of the company would be changing from time to time.[18]
3. It should be contemplated by the charge that until some step is taken by the mortgagee, the company shall have the right to use the assets comprised in the charge in the ordinary course of its business."

In *Indus Film Corpn Ltd, Re*:[19]

A film company borrowed a sum of money and declared a lien "on all our assets, including machinery, etc., now lying or that may be bought hereafter until repayment". This was held to be a floating charge as it covered assets, present and future, of extremely fluctuating nature and imposed no restriction on the use of them.

---

15. Lord MACNAGHTEN in *Govt's Stock Investment Co v Manila Rly Co*, [1897] AC 81, at 86: 75 LT 553.
16. Gower, THE PRINCIPLES OF MODERN COMPANY LAW, 78 (3rd Edn, 1969).
17. [1903] 2 Ch 284: 88 LT 811.
18. Where a charge was created on "fixed plant and machinery" which would have been a fixed charge, but since the company had no firmly fixed machinery, the charge was held to be in the nature of a floating charge. *Hi Fi Equipment (Cabinets) Ltd*, 1988 BCLC 65 Ch D. A construction company's washing machine which was in use at the site, being one fixed item and not likely to change, a charge on it was held to be a fixed charge. *Cosslett (Contractors) Ltd, Re*, (1996) 1 BCLC 407 Ch D.
19. AIR 1939 Sind 100: 181 IC 681.

As against it, in *F. D. Jones & Co Ltd* v *Ranjit Roy*:[20]

> By a deed a company had charged all its machinery, stock in trade and moveable effects, present and future. The deed provided that the "properties shall be in the lender's possession" which was actually given to him. This was held to be no floating charge as it took away the company's right to use the assets charged in the ordinary course of its business.

If the assets are withdrawn from the business and transferred to the lender's possession, there is, indeed, nothing over which the charge is to float. It immediately gets fixed on those assets.[21] A charge on book debts was held to be floating charge where the company had the right to collect the debts and use the proceeds in the ordinary course of its business. The charged book debts were not under the control of the chargee to make it a fixed charge.[22] One distinguishing feature of a fixed charge from a floating charge is the degree of control over the property which the charge-holder exercises.[23]

Whether a charge is fixed or floating, its identification is a two stage process. The first stage involves construction of the instrument of charge. This is necessary to gather the intention of the parties from the language used. The second stage is one of categorisation, a matter of law. This does

---

20. AIR 1927 Cal 782: 103 IC 648. Whether a charge is of one kind or the other does not depend upon the labels attached by the parties. A charge over funds lodged in a bank described by the parties as a fixed charge was found indeed to operate as a floating charge, *ASRS Establishment Ltd, Re*, affirmed by the Court of Appeal, July 20, 2000: (2000) 1 BCLC 727. The courts do not go by description of the parties. A charge on premises described as a fixed charge was found in substance to be a floating charge, *Westmaze Ltd, Re*, The Times, July 15, 1998 Ch D, following *Royal Trust Bank plc* v *National Westminster Bank*, [1996] BCC 613.

21. The following two cases are further illustrations. One is *Bank of Baroda* v *H. B. Shivdasani*, AIR 1926 Bom 427: 96 IC 417 A company gave to a bank as security for loan all its liquid assets including stock in process present and future stored in a godown the keys of which were delivered to the bank. The goods could be taken out under the bank's supervision, but the company was to maintain the goods at a value of 33-½ per cent above the amount due. This was held to be a mortgage of specific assets with a licence to the mortgagor to dispose of them in the course of its business subject to prescribed conditions.

    The other case is *Tansukhrai M. Karundia* v *Official Liquidator of Andhra Paper Mills Ltd*, (1949) 2 MLJ 66. A creditor was given possession of the movables pledged to him and it was provided that as and when other properties were acquired, they would also stand pledged to him. The security was stated to be a continuing one. On default of payment, the lender had the right to sell. Though the debtor company was allowed to run its business, it was only run by the creditor as an agent under an irrevocable power of attorney. This was held to be no floating charge. The element of possession made it something wholly inconsistent with the concept of a floating charge. Looking at the degree of protection that a floating charge is capable of affording the Supreme Court emphasised in *Narendra Kumar Maheshwari* v *UOI*, [1989] 2 Comp LJ 95 that it affords a real protection. It is not illusory or an eyewash.

22. *Burmark Investments Ltd, Re*, [2000] 1 BCLC 353 NZCA; *Double Sprinters Ltd, Re*, [1999] 1 BCLC 220, here also the charge on book debts did not give the chargee the requisite degree of control over the charged items, the charge was a floating charge. To the same effect is *Agnew* v *Commr of Inland Revenue*, (2001) 3 WLR 454: (2002) 109 Comp Cas 184 PC, a charge on book debts was held to be a floating charge though described in the terms of charge as fixed. The charger company had complete control over the debts.

23. *Ibid.*

not depend upon the intention of the parties. If the intention properly construed is to grant the company rights in respect of the charged assets which are inconsistent with the nature of a fixed charge, then the charge cannot be a fixed charge however they may have chosen to describe it. To constitute a charge on book debts a fixed charge, it is sufficient to prohibit the company from realising debts itself, whether by assignment or collection. A restriction on disposition which nevertheless allows collection and free use of proceeds is inconsistent with the fixed nature of a charge.[24]

In a subsequent case on the point, a charge which was described as a "specific charge", was created by a debenture which required that the book debts charged could not be disposed of prior to collection and that on collection the proceeds were to be paid into an account with the chargee bank. This was held to be a fixed charge regardless of the extent of the charger's contractual right to draw out sums equivalent to the amount paid in.[25] This decision was reversed by the House of Lords. The charge was held to be a floating charge.[26]

Subsequent Mortgages or Charges

A floating charge also leaves the company at liberty to create subsequent specific mortgages of the same assets and ranking in priority to the floating charge.[27] Even if the creditor who takes subsequent specific mortgage has knowledge of the floating charge, he may have priority.[28] The company, may, however, be prohibited from creating subsequent specific mortgages. In such a case a creditor who takes a subsequent specific mortgage with notice of the prohibition shall not have priority over the floating charge.[29] Registration of the charge with the Registrar amounts to constructive notice of the charge under Section 126 of the Companies Act.

The decision of the Andhra Pradesh High Court in *State of A.P.* v *Sri Raja Ram Janardhana*[30] is an illustration of the difference in the effects of a fixed and a floating charge.

Certain mortgage debenture-holders had a specific charge on all the properties of a company. The company made a subsequent mortgage in

24. *Richard Dale Agency* v *Commr of Inland Revenue*, (2005) 2 Comp LJ 345 (PC) (New Zealand CA).
25. *Westminster Bank plc* v *Spectrum Plus Ltd*, (2004) 3 WLR 503: (2005) 123 Comp Cas 803 CA. For a study *see* Alan Berg, *Charges Over Book Debts: The Spectrum Case in the Court of Appeal*, 2004 JBL 581.
26. *Spectrum Plus Ltd, Re*, (2005) 3 WLR 58 (HL): (2005) 128 Comp Cas 280: (2005) 2 AC 680 .
27. *Wheatley* v *Silkstone Co Ltd*, (1885) 29 Ch D 715: 52 LT 798; *Florence, Land and Public Works Co, Re*, (1878) 10 Ch D 530; *Borax, Re*, [1901] 1 Ch 326. *Narendra Kumar Maheshwari* v *UOI*, [1989] 2 Comp LJ 95, *see* observations at p 137.
28. *Hamilton, Re*, (1879) 12 Ch D 707.
29. *English & Scottish Mercantile Investment Co* v *Brunton*, [1892] 2 QB 700; *Wilson* v *Kelland*, [1910] 2 Ch 306: 103 LT 17; *Connolly Bros, Re*, [1912] 2 Ch 25: 106 LT 738; *Valletort, etc., Re*, [1903] 2 Ch 654: 89 LT 60.
30. [1965] 2 Comp LJ 222.

favour of the State to secure a loan advanced under the State Aid to Industries Act. In the winding up of the company the question arose as to the priority between the two mortgages. Holding that the debenture-holders were entitled to priority in preference to the claims of the Government, the Court said: "Where a particular property of the company is specifically charged in favour of the debenture-holders the company cannot dispose of it unencumbered by the charge without having obtained the consent of the holders of the charge. In the case of a debenture secured solely by a floating charge, the company may dispose of the property on which the charge exists unencumbered without consulting the holders of the charge until an event happens on which the floating charge, according to its terms, 'crystallises' i.e. becomes a fixed charge. Before crystallisation the company has a free hand to deal with and dispose of the property charged in the ordinary course of the business of the company."

Statutory Restrictions

Section 539 imposes an important condition for the validity of a floating charge. It provides that a floating charge created within twelve months immediately preceding the commencement of winding up shall be invalid, except in the following cases:

(*a*) if the company immediately after the creation of the charge was solvent;

(*b*) to the extent to which any cash was paid to the company under the charge.

Eric Holmes Property Ltd, Re,[31] is an illustration of the utility of this provision :

A company created a charge in favour of a creditor who advanced £400 in cash at the time. Winding up having followed within a year, the charge was held to be void as a fraudulent preference over other creditors save to the extent of £400.

Further, Section 123 provides that if the debenture-holders seek to get their payment by enforcing the charge, the preferential payments as detailed in Section 530 shall have priority over them. Thus, in *IRC* v *Goldblatt*[32] it was held that a receiver would be personally liable if he pays debenture-holders with knowledge that there are unpaid preferential creditors.

Apart from this, there is another category of persons, as established by common law, which is not affected by the floating charge. Such persons include a landlord who has levied for rent due his distress before the crystallisation of the charge;[33] a creditor who has obtained a decree and has

---

31. [1965] 2 All ER 333: [1965] Ch 1052: [1966] 1 Comp LJ 19.
32. [1972] 2 WLR 333: [1972] 2 All ER 202.
33. *Roundwood Colliery Co, Re,* [1897] 1 Ch 373 CA.

got certain goods of the company sold in the execution of the decree[34] or whom the company has paid to avoid an execution sale[35] or who has obtained an absolute (as opposed to a temporary or *nisi*) garnishee order attaching the property of the company,[36] provided all these things take place before crystallisation of the charge; and, a person who has supplied goods to the company under a hire purchase agreement, the goods being still his property.[37]

Crystallisation of floating charge

Debentures generally contain an undertaking to pay the principal sum at a specified date with interest in the meantime. When the company makes a default or when it comes to be wound up, the debenture-holders should take steps to enforce their security by seizing the assets over which the charge was until then floating. When they do this the charge is said to crystallise. But even after the default the charge keeps floating until the debenture-holders intervene. This was laid down in *Government Stock and Other Securities Investment Co Ltd v Manila Railway Co Ltd.*[38]

A company issued debentures by which it undertook to pay the principal at a distant day and interest on fixed days half-yearly and charged by way of floating security all its property present and future. The company reserved the right in the course, and for the purpose of its business, to sell or otherwise deal with its property until the company made a default in payment of interest for three months after the same should have become due. After an instalment of interest had been due more than three months but before the debenture-holders had taken any steps to enforce their security, the company mortgaged its assets.

This mortgage was held to be valid because real crystallisation takes place not on default, but on intervention by debenture-holders after the default. Lord MACNAGHTEN observed: "It is of the essence of a floating charge that it remains dormant until the undertaking charged ceases to be a going concern, or until the person in whose favour the charge is created intervenes. As long as he does not intervene the business will be carried on, not as of right, but by the sufferance of the debenture-holders and at their mercy."[39] Thus a floating charge crystallises when the company ceases to be a going concern, or when it comes to be wound up or when the charge-

---

34. *Standard Mfg Co, Re*, [1891] 1 Ch 627 (CA).
35. *Heaton & Dugard Ltd v Cutting Bros*, [1925] 1 KB 655.
36. *Evans v Rival Granite Quarries Ltd*, [1910] 2 KB 979 CA.
37. *Morrison, Jones & Taylor Ltd, Re*, [1914] 1 Ch 50 CA.
38. 1897 AC 81: 75 LT 553. *See* M. J. Robble and C. P. Gill, *Fixed and Floating Charges: A New Look at the Bank's Position*, 1981 JBL 95.
39. *Id.*, at pp 86-87.

holders intervene on the happening of default[40] by giving notice to that effect.[41]

In another case, where a demand and default took place in accordance with the terms and since this had happened before the appointment of the receiver, it was held that the charge had already become crystallised and was no longer floating at the time of the appointment and, therefore, the money in the company's banking account was to be handed over to the charge-holder.[42]

Debenture trust deed [Ss. 118-119]

Where the debenture-holders do not have the time to look after their interest in the properties mortgaged or charged to them, they may appoint some of themselves as trustees for the supervision of their common interest. A trust deed is made under which some of them are appointed as trustees. Properties of the company are mortgaged or charged to the trustee in favour of the debenture-holders. The deed also contains provisions defining the rights of the debenture-holders and the company. The advantage of this arrangement is that it becomes the function of the trustees to watch the interest of debenture-holders. They are bound to act with the same degree of honesty, care and diligence as is required of all trustees. Any clause in the trust deed which exempts them from liability for breach of their duty as trustees or which indemnifies them against liability is void.[43] Another advantage is that if and when the company makes a default, they can take action for enforcing the security on behalf of all the debenture-holders. Section 118 entitles every debenture-holder and member to demand from the company a copy of the debenture trust deed.[44]

---

40. *See* J Farrar, *World Economic Stagnation puts the Floating Charge on Trial*, 1 Co Law 83.

41. *Brightlife Ltd, Re*, [1986] 3 All ER 673 Ch D, the charge-holder gave notice before commencement of winding up, held, effective crystallisation for the purpose of defeating preferential payments except as provided in the Act.

42. *Permanent Houses (Holdings) Ltd, Re*, 1980 BCLC 563 Ch D. *See* also *Brightlife Ltd*, the Times, Aug 9, 1986, Financial Times, Aug 13, 1986, giving liberty to the charge-holder to convert by notice the floating charge into a fixed charge, and when that notice was given before winding up, the charge became a fixed mortgage. *See* note "*Automatic Crystallisation of Floating Charge*", 1986 JBL 350.

43. S. 119(1). *See also* sub-sections (2) and (3) which allow the trustees in certain circumstances to be released from liability. A debenture trust deed is not in itself a mortgage or a bond. It is only a document expressing the faith of the shareholders upon their chosen trustee and has, therefore, to be stamped as a deed only. *Chief Controlling Revenue Authority v State Bank of Mysore*, AIR 1988 Kant 1, 7-10; (1989) 65 Comp Cas 427 FB, following *Murugharajendra Co v Chief Controlling Revenue Authority*, AIR 1974 Kant 60 FB and *United Bank of India Ltd v Lekharam Sonaram & Co*, AIR 1965 SC 1591. A debenture trustee is not an officer of the company and, therefore, he is not entitled to relief under S. 633 against any apprehended proceedings for negligence, breach of trust etc. *Central Bank Executor & Trustee Co Ltd v Magna Hard Temp Ltd*, (1997) 89 Comp Cas 40 AP.

44. S. 118(1). The trust deed is also open to the members or debenture-holders in the like manner as the register of members, S. 118(4). Sub-section (2) makes denial of this right a punishable offence and sub-section (3) empowers the Court to direct copies to be given.

The rights of a debenture-holder were examined by SUJATA MANOHAR J of the Bombay High Court in *Narotamdas T. Toprani* v *Bombay Dyeing & Mfg Co Ltd.*[45]

A company proposed to issue a new series of debentures. Of the company's present debentures 96% were held by institutions, which permitted the new series; of the remaining 4% which were held by individuals, one questioned the validity of the proposal and wanted the Bombay High Court to stay it till he was able to examine the ratio between the assets and liabilities of the company. The company refused to permit him such access to its assets and stock registers.

The High Court agreed with the company in holding that he had no right to go beyond the declared accounts and allowed the company to go ahead with its debenture-issue subject only to this that if the aggrieved shareholder wanted payment, he should be paid out in cash. The court asserted that it can examine the motive of a petitioner like the present so as to see whether he is really concerned with the interests of the debenture-holders or has something up his sleeves. The court pointed out that the right of a debenture-holder of inspecting the company's records is extremely limited. Under Section 118 he can inspect the debenture-trust deed and obtain a copy of it. Under Section 163 he can inspect and obtain copies of the register of members and of debenture-holders, annual reports and copies of certificates and documents annexed thereto. He may also have the right to copies of annual accounts. But he does not have the right of detailed inspection of the record and registers and books of account and no adverse inference can be drawn if the company does not permit it.[46]

The Companies Amendment Act, 2000 has brought in a set of provisions about debenture trust deeds.

Section 117-A contains three provisions:

Form of trust deed.—The deed has to be in such form and executed within such time as may be prescribed.

Supply of copies and inspection.—A copy of the deed should be available for inspection to members and debenture-holders. They are also entitled to get copies on payment of prescribed fees.

---

45. [1986] 3 Comp LJ 179 Bom.
46. The Supreme Court took opportunity in *Narendra Kumar Maheshwari* v *UOI*, [1989] 2 Comp LJ 95 to explain the value of guidelines issued by the Government of India from time to time on company matters including in this case on the ways in which debenture-holders are to be protected by maintaining among other things the debt-equity ratio. The court may overlook deviations from guidelines if the deviation is justifiable keeping in mind the public interest sought to be served by the State. This is because guidelines by their very nature, do not fall into the category of legislation, direct, subordinate or ancillary. They have only an advisory role to play and non-adherence to or deviation from them is necessarily and implicitly permissible if the circumstances so warrant. *See* Section N of SEBI Guidelines for Disclosure and Investor "Protection on Protection of Interest of Debenture-holders".

Penalty.—If a copy of the trust deed is not made available for inspection or is not given to any member or debenture-holder, every officer of the company who is in default shall be punishable with fine extending up to Rs 500 for every day of default.

Appointment of debenture trustees and their duties [S. 117-B]

Appointment of debenture trustees has to be made before making a debenture issue and the fact of the appointment and their consent to act as such has to be mentioned on the face of the prospectus or letters of offer.

Persons not qualified.—Following persons cannot be appointed as debenture trustees:

1. a beneficial holder of shares in the company;
2. a person who is beneficially entitled to the money which is to be paid by the company to the debenture trustee;
3. a person who has entered into a guarantee in respect of principal debts secured by debentures or interest thereon.

Functions.—The functions of debenture trustees are generally to protect the interests of holders of debentures, to bring about the creation of securities within the stipulated time and to redress grievances of debenture-holders.

Duties.—The particular duties are:

1. to ensure that the assets of the company issuing debentures and of the guarantors are sufficient to discharge the principal amount at all time;
2. to satisfy himself that the prospectus or the letter of offer does not contain anything inconsistent with the terms of the debentures or debenture trust deed;
3. to ensure that the company does not commit any breach of the covenants and provisions of the debenture trust deed;
4. to take reasonable steps against any breach of the covenants or terms of issue;
5. to take care to call meetings of debenture-holders as and when it is required to be held.[47]

Petition to CLB.—Where at any time the debenture trustee comes to the conclusion that the assets of the company are insufficient or are likely to become insufficient to discharge the principal amount as and when it becomes due, he should file a petition before the CLB. The CLB may hear the company or any other interested person. It may then impose restrictions

---

47. A proviso introduced by the Second Amendment Act of 2002 says that in the case of revival and rehabilitation of a sick industrial company under Part VI-A, the provisions of this section shall have effect as if for the word Central Government the word Tribunal had been substituted.

on the company in the matter of incurring further liabilities to safeguard the interests of debenture-holders.[48]

Responsibility of company to create security and debenture redemption reserve [S. 117-C]

The company issuing debentures has to create a debenture redemption reserve. Adequate amounts have to be transferred to the fund every year from the profits of the company till the debentures are redeemed.

The amounts so credited cannot be used for any other purpose. The company is under a duty to go on paying interest and to redeem debentures in accordance with the terms and condition of the issue.

On failure of the company to do so, the debenture-holders or any one of them can apply to the CLB. The CLB, after hearing the parties, may direct the company to pay off interest and principal amount and redeem the debentures. If the orders of the CLB are not carried out, the defaulting'' officers are liable to punishment by way of imprisonment extending to three years and a fine extending to Rs 500 for every day of default.

Remedies of debenture-holders

The remedies of debenture-holders depend upon the terms of their agreement with the company. A debenture-holder who wishes to realise his security and get back his money may exercise remedies given by the debenture trust deed or resort to legal proceedings to enforce his rights.[49] If money due on a debenture is payable on demand the debtor company is entitled, once demand is made, to reasonable time to implement the mechanics of payment, but it is not entitled to any time to raise the money if it was not at hand. A demand under a debenture need not specify the amount due.[50] It is not necessary to allow time to the borrowing company to enable it to engage in a commercial transaction for the purpose of raising funds for redemption of debentures.[51] But one of the remedies which is always open to them as mortgagees under the Transfer of Property Act is to bring the property charged to sale.[52]

Receiver

Secondly, they may appoint a receiver to take charge of the assets subjected to the charge. If they do not have this power under the terms of their debentures they may have a receiver appointed by the court. In either

---

48. *Indian Overseas Bank* v *Essar Machine Works Ltd*, (2002) 112 Comp Cas 557 CLB, the company denied creation of the charge in favour of the bank. The matter was being examined by the Debt Recovery Tribunal. The CLB refused to adjudicate.

49. *Lloyds Bank plc* v *Lampert*, [1999] BCC 507.

50. *Bank of Baroda* v *Panessar*, [1986] 3 All ER 751 Ch D.

51. *Lloyds Bank plc* v *Lampert*, [1999] BCC 507.

52. See *Narain Singh & Co* v *U.P. Oil Industries Ltd*, [1964] 1 Comp LJ 225 All; following *Union of India* v *Official Liquidator*, AIR 1964 AP 555; *Govinda* v *Khan Saheb Abdul Kadir*, AIR 1923 Nag 150.

case the fact of appointment must be brought to the notice of the Registrar within thirty days, whose duty is to enter the same in the register of charges.[53] A similar notice has to be given by the receiver when he ceases to act.[54] When the receiver takes possession of the assets comprised in the charge, he has to maintain proper accounts of his receipts and payments and to submit an abstract with the Registrar once in every half year.[55] If he is appointed under a debenture as an agent of the company, he is under a duty to keep full accounts of the company's affairs, i.e., fuller than abstracts of receipts and payments and to produce them to the company when required to do so.[56] The fact of the receiver's appointment should also be mentioned on every invoice, order for goods, or business letter issued on behalf of the company.[57] Where a company which had gone into liquidation was facing an action and the receiver took over the responsibility of defending the company against the action, it was held that the Court could order that any costs awarded to the plaintiff should be paid by the receiver and that such costs should be treated as expenses of receivership.[58]

A receiver's primary duty is to bring about a situation in which the secured creditor would stand paid. He is entitled to sell the property like a mortgagee in the condition in which it is and without waiting for or effecting any increase in the value of the property. A receiver is not obliged before sale to spend money on repairs or to make the property more attractive before marketing it. He is free to proceed with an immediate sale of the mortgaged property.[59]

Manager

When the receiver has taken possession of the company's assets, obviously they cannot be used by the company for business. Yet sometimes it may be necessary to carry on business for beneficial winding up. In such a case the debenture-holders may appoint a manager also or have him appointed under an order of the court. The above provisions relating to a receiver also apply to a manager.[60]

---

53. S. 137(1). This he does on payment of the prescribed fee. The notice has to be given by the person who appoints or obtains appointment.
54. S. 137(2). Sub-section (3) imposes penalty upto Rs 500 for every day of default.
55. S. 421.
56. *Smiths* v *Middleton*, [1979] 3 All ER 842. The court explained here the duty of the receiver to preserve the security in good faith for the benefit of his mortgagee as well as the company and other encumbrancers. Followed in *Downsview Nominees Ltd* v *First City Corpn Ltd*, (1993) 3 All ER 626 PC: [1994] 1 Comp LJ 31.
57. S. 422. *See also* S. 423 which contains penalty provisions. The section says that if default is made in complying with the requirements of S. 421 (Filing of accounts of receivers) and S. 422 (Invoices, etc. to refer to receiver if there is one) the company and defaulting officer are punishable with fine extending up to Rs 2000. For the purposes of this section the receiver is deemed to be an officer of the company.
58. *Anderson* v *Hyde*, (1996) 2 BCLC 144 CA.
59. *Silven Properties Ltd* v *Royal Bank of Scotland*, (2004) 1 BCLC 352 Ch D.
60. S. 424.

It has been held that a receiver or manager is not an "officer" of the company for the purposes of the Companies Act, nor a "manager" of the company and consequently he cannot be subjected to public examination.[61] He functions as manager, not of the company, but of the assets subject to the charge, and not for the benefit of the company, but for the purpose of realising the security for the benefit of the charge-holders. He is an agent of the company for that purpose so that he may effectively deal with third parties. That is the whole purpose of his appointment and of powers which are conferred upon him.

Though misfeasance proceedings and public examination may not be available, he will definitely be liable for any breach of duty, for he is a trustee of the assets which he is appointed to realise.[62] Thus where he damaged the interest of a subsidiary of the company, the court ordered the Government to appoint an inspector to investigate the affairs of the company.[63] His contention that his conduct cannot be regarded as the affairs of the company was rejected. The court said:

"What the receiver and manager does may in a narrow sense be his affair, but it is also the affair of the company in the broad and natural meaning of the phrase, 'its affairs'. He acts in the name of the company — what he does may ruin its shareholders or leave them with some prospect of future recovery. Under clause (2) of the debenture it is the undertaking of the company which is confided to him and it is its business that he is managing and he is its agent and it is made responsible for his acts or defaults.

There is a clear authority for the proposition that where a receiver or manager is appointed by the court his function as manager confers a duty on him to preserve the goodwill and property of the company, both in the interests of the mortgagee and of the mortgagor."[64]

A receiver's duty to provide accounts or other information to a debtor company is not restricted to his statutory obligations. The extent of the receiver's obligation to provide additional information is to be deducted from the nature of the receivership and a company's right to such information depends on the showing that the information is needed to enable the board of directors to exercise its residual powers or to perform its duties. The right if any, which the company has to obtain information from the receiver is qualified by the receiver's primary responsibility to the deben-

---

61. *B. Johnson & Co, Re*, 1955 Ch 634 CA. A receiver was held to be not personally liable to the employees whose services he continued, *Leyland DAF Ltd case*, (1994) 4 All ER 300 Ch D.
62. *Moss Steamship Co Ltd* v *Whinney*, 1912 AC 254 HL.
63. *R* v *Board of Trade*, [1965] 1 QB 603.
64. The same duty is cast upon a mortgagee of shares. *Bishop* v *Bonhama*, 1988 BCLC 656 CA; *Westminster Corpn* v *Haste*, 1950 Ch 442, dealing with company property in an unwarranted manner. *American Express International Bkg Corpn* v *Hurley*, [1985] 3 All ER 564, the bankers as debenture-holders controlling the actions of the receiver, held liable for the receiver's negligence.

ture-holder so that he can withhold the information if he thinks that the disclosure would be contrary to the debenture-holder's interest.[65]

A receiver has a right to have the documents of the company produced from the custody of the company's solicitors and they cannot refuse on account of their lien because their lien is against the company and the receiver is a third person and not the company for this purpose.[66]

The same should hold good when a receiver and manager is appointed by the debenture-holders.

Kinds of debenture

1. *Redeemable Debentures*

Debentures are generally redeemable. This means that on expiry of the term of the loan the company has the right to pay back the debenture-holders and have its properties released from the mortgage or charge. This is called redemption of debentures. Redeemed debentures can be re-issued. This power is expressly given by Section 121. According to this section if there is no provision to the contrary in the articles, or in the conditions of the issue or if there is no resolution showing an intention to cancel the redeemed debentures, the company shall have the power to keep the debentures alive for the purpose of re-issue. The company may re-issue the same debentures or other debentures in their place. Upon such re-issue the person entitled to the debentures has the same rights and priorities as if the debentures had never been redeemed.[67]

2. *Perpetual Debentures*

A debenture which contains no clause as to payment or which contains a clause that it shall not be paid back is known as a *perpetual or irredeemable debenture*. Section 120 provides that a "condition contained in any debenture . . . shall not be invalid by reason only that thereby, the debentures are made irredeemable, or redeemable only on the happening of a contingency, however remote, or on the expiration of a period, however long."

3. *Debentures to Registered Holder and Bearer Debentures*

A company which has issued debentures will obviously maintain a register of its debenture-holders, as Section 152 provides that every company shall keep a register of the holders of its debentures. The name of the holder is placed both on the debenture certificate and on the company's register. Such a holder is known as the registered holder. He can transfer his debentures in the open market in just the same way as shares are transferred.[68] Transfer will have to be registered with the company. The

---

65. *Gomba Holdings U.K. Ltd* v *Homan*, [1986] 3 All ER 94 Ch D; *Gomba Holdings U.K. Ltd* v *Minories Finance Ltd*, [1988] 1 All ER 261, receiver's duty to return documents.
66. *Aveling Barford Ltd, Re*, [1988] 3 All ER 1019 Ch D.
67. S. 121(2).
68. S. 108.

transferee's title will be subject to all equities between the transferor and the company.[69] Registration of transfer can be avoided only by issuing debentures payable to bearer, as the company has not to maintain a register of such debenture-holders.[70] Such debentures are transferable, like negotiable instruments, by simple delivery and are called debentures payable to bearer. It has been held by the Calcutta High Court in *Calcutta Safe Deposit Co Ltd* v *Ranjit Mathuradas Sampat,*[71] that a person to whom a bearer debenture is transferred becomes its holder and is as such entitled to recover the principal and interest when due. If the same is not paid to him, he can also apply for winding up and, if the petition is otherwise competent, the company cannot ask him to explain how he came by the debenture or why he did not collect the interest for a long time. The court pointed out that Section 118 of the Negotiable Instruments Act applies and, therefore, every holder of a bearer debenture is presumed to be a holder in due course unless the contrary is shown.[72]

Register of debenture-holders [S. 152]

A company issuing debentures has to maintain a register of debenture-holders showing the following particulars:

1. the name, address and occupation of each debenture-holder;
2. the debentures held by each holder, showing numbers and the amount actually paid or deemed to be paid;
3. the date at which each person was entered as a debenture-holder; and
4. the date at which any person ceased to be a debenture-holder.

Index

Where the number of debenture-holders exceeds fifty, an index should be maintained which should enable the entries relating to a debenture-holder to be readily found. Any change in the particulars of the register should be reflected by the index within fourteen days.

Shareholder compared with debenture-holder

In many respects debentures are similar to shares. In the words of Gower: "The company's securities fall into two classes which legal theory tries to keep rigidly separated but which in economic reality merge into each other. The first of these classes is described as shares; the second as debentures."[73] Some of the resemblances between the two are that both the shareholder and the debenture- holder have invested their money in the company; both get some return on the investment, although one gets it by

---

69. *Natal Investment Co, Re*, (1868) 3 Ch App 355: 18 LT 171.
70. S. 152(4).
71. (1971) 41 Comp Cas 1063 Cal.
72. *See* at p 1070 of (1971) 41 Comp Cas 1063.
73. THE PRINCIPLES OF MODERN COMPANY LAW, 343 (3rd Edn, 1969).

way of dividend and the other by way of interest; perpetual or irredeemable debentures, like shares, are not generally paid back; debentures, like shares, are transferable; and where debentures carry a charge, the lot of debenture-holders, like that of shareholders depends upon the assets of the company. Moreover, redeemable preference shares and debentures have many common features. The company can pay back both such securities.[74] The position of the shareholder is undergoing serious transformation. "Indeed, it may be questioned whether shareholders should remain in their present position as owners of the business or be converted into some form of creditors of the business."[75] There are suggestions to the effect that companies should issue participating debentures so as to provide the small saver with adequate return of interest plus a participation in the profits.[76]

The following points of difference are, however, also quite apparent.

In the first place, the basic difference is that while a shareholder is a member of the company and enjoys all the rights of membership, a debenture-holder is simply a creditor of the company. A shareholder, for example, has the right to vote, whereas Section 117 declares that "no company shall issue any debentures carrying voting rights at any meeting of the company, whether generally or in respect of particular classes of business".

Secondly, the debenture-holders are entitled to a fixed rate of interest which the company must pay whether there are profits or not. But they do not have any right to interfere with the business of the company unless, on the company's default, they step in to enforce their security. Shareholders, on the other hand, have the full right of control and the ultimate destiny of the company is in their hands. Of course, they are entitled to get dividends only out of profits, but the rate of dividend may be much higher than the rate of interest.

Thirdly, unless the debentures are perpetual, the company can pay back the debenture-holders but the shareholders cannot be paid back as long as the company is a going concern.[77]

Lastly, in the winding up, debenture-holders, being secured creditors, are paid in priority. Whereas shareholders are paid back only after all other claims have been satisfied.[78]

---

74. *See* Lord SIMONS in *Scottish Insurance Corpn* v *Wilson & Clyde Coal Co*, 1949 AC 462: [1949] 1 All ER 1068.
75. R. S. Nock, *The Ford Foundation Workshop on Company Law, July 1969*, (1970) 11 Journal of the Society of Public Teachers of Law, at 10.
76. 1976 JBL 2.
77. A company may, however, pay back redeemable preference shares, (S. 80), or generally under a scheme involving reduction of capital.
78. The provisions of the Act relating to transfer of shares, remedies against refusal to register a transfer, issue of certificates, etc., are also applicable to debentures. *See* Sections 108, 111 and 113.

15

Majority Powers and Minority Rights

"The protection of the minority shareholders within the domain of corporate activity constitutes one of the most difficult problems facing modern company law. The aim must be to strike a balance between the effective control of the company and the interests of the small individual shareholders."[1] Similarly, in the words of Palmer: "A proper balance of the rights of majority and minority shareholders is essential for the smooth functioning of the company."[2] The modern Companies Acts, therefore, contain a large number of provisions for the protection of the interests of investors in companies. The aim of these provisions is to require those who control the affairs of a company to exercise their powers according to certain principles of natural justice and fair play.[3]

RULE IN FOSS v HARBOTTLE

The basic principle relating to the administration of the affairs of a company is that "the courts will not, in general, intervene at the instance of shareholders in matters of internal administration; and will not interfere with the management of a company by its directors so long as they are acting within the powers conferred on them under the articles of the company".[4] "Nothing connected with the internal disputes between the shareholders is to be made the subject of an action by a shareholder."[5] This rule was laid down as early as 1843 in the celebrated case of *Foss* v *Harbottle*:[6]

> In this case the action was by two shareholders in a company against the directors charging them with concerting and effecting various fraudulent and illegal transactions whereby the property of the company was misapplied and wasted, and praying that the defendants might be decreed to make good to the company the losses. The action was rejected in respect of those transactions which a majority of the shareholders had the power to confirm. Briefly, the opinion of the Court was this: "The conduct with which the defendants are charged is an injury not to the plaintiffs exclusively, it is an injury to the whole

---

1. N. A. Bastin, *Minority Protection in Company Law*, 1968 JBL 320.
2. Palmer's COMPANY LAW, 492 (20th Edn, Ed. by Clive M Schmitthoff and Curry, 1959) on Majority and Minority Rights.
3. These principles are briefly summed up by K. W. Wedderburn, *Going the Whole Hogg* v *Cramphorn Ltd*, (1968) 31 Mod LR 688. *See also* by the same writer, *Unreformed Company Law*, (1969) 32 Mod LR 563.
4. VENKATARAMA AYYER J in *Rajahmundry Electric Supply Corpn* v *A. Nageshwara Rao*, AIR 1956 SC 213, 217: (1956) 26 Comp Cas 91.
5. JAMES LJ in *MacDougall* v *Gardiner*, (1875) 1 Ch D 13: [1874-80] All ER Rep Ext 2248.
6. (1843) 67 ER 189: (1843) 2 Hare 461.

[509]

corporation. In such cases the rule is that the corporation should sue in its own name and in its corporate character. It is not a matter of course for any individual members of a corporation thus to assume to themselves the right of suing in the name of the corporation. In law the corporation and the aggregate of members of the corporation are not the same thing for purposes like this."

The rule was applied in *MacDougall* v *Gardiner*,[7] where MELLISH LJ stated it thus:

> In my opinion, if the thing complained is a thing which, in substance, the majority of the company are entitled to do, or something has been done irregularly which the majority of the company are entitled to do regularly, or if something has been done illegally which the majority of the company are entitled to do legally, there can be no use in having litigation about it, the ultimate end of which is only that a meeting has to be called, and then ultimately the majority gets its wishes.

The rule was restated in the following terms by JENKINS LJ in *Edwards* v *Halliwell*:[8]

> The rule in *Foss* v *Harbottle* comes to no more than this. First, the proper plaintiff in respect of a wrong alleged to be done to a company is prima facie the company itself. Secondly, where the alleged wrong is a transaction which might be made binding on the company by a simple majority of members, no individual member of the company is allowed to maintain an action in respect of that matter for the simple reason that, if a mere majority of the members of the company is in favour of what has been done, then *cadet quaestio*.

An illustration of the working of the rule is to be found in *Bhajekar* v *Shinkar*:[9]

> The directors of a company resolved to appoint a company as its managing agents. Some of the shareholders objected but the appointment was confirmed at two general meetings of the company. An action was then commenced by certain shareholders to restrain the managing agents from acting on the ground that the managing agents' company was a dummy company and it was against the company's interest to appoint them. The Court ordered a general meeting to be held under the supervision of a chairman appointed by it. The chairman put a resolution to the meeting to the effect: "whether the company is willing to maintain the suit and proceed with it." He reported that the resolution

---

7. (1875) 1 Ch D 13: [1874-80] All ER Rep Ext 2248; *P.S. Offshore Inter Land Services (P) Ltd* v *Bombay Offshore Suppliers and Services Ltd*, (1992) 75 Comp Cas 583 Bom, the advocate appearing for the company must have the authority of the board of directors or principal officer of the company and not merely the backing of majority shareholders.

8. [1950] 2 All ER 1064, 1066.

9. AIR 1934 Bom 243.

was lost. "Under these circumstances", the court held, "it is difficult to see how a few shareholders who represent a minority are entitled to maintain the suit and ask the Court to interfere on the question as to who should be the managing agents of the company."[10]

The briefest possible statement of the rule occurs in the observation of Justice CARDOZO that for erring directors there may be absolution if all the shareholders are satisfied.[11] Two English cases *Hogg* v *Cramphorn Ltd*[12] and *Bomford* v *Bomford*[13] bear witness to this absolving power of the majority of shareholders. In either case there was the disposal by the directors of the unissued capital of the company as a tactical move in a battle for control of the company. The court conceded that the power to allot shares was exercised for an improper motive and the directors were guilty of a misfeasance,[14] but held that it is a common place in company law that the directors can by making a full and frank disclosure and calling together the general body of the shareholders, obtain absolution and forgiveness of their sins.[15]

A 50% shareholder brought an action against a director to hold him liable for misappropriation of the company's assets. The court did not allow it. Such loss is recoverable only by the company. It is not recoverable by a shareholder because he does not suffer any distinct loss from that suffered by all the shareholders.[16]

EXCEPTIONS

The majority supremacy, however, does not prevail in all situations. The operative field of the rule in *Foss* v *Harbottle* extends to cases in which the corporations are competent to ratify managerial sins. But there are certain

---

10. *See also Jhajharia Bros Ltd* v *Sholapur Spg & Wvg Co Ltd*, AIR 1941 Cal 174: 195 IC 36 and *Heyting* v *Dupont*, [1964] 1 WLR 843: [1964] 2 All ER 273; *Normandy* v *Ind Coope & Co Ltd*, [1908] 1 Ch 84, where a shareholder was not allowed to maintain an action against directors' increasing their remuneration without the sanction of the general meeting. He must appeal to the general meeting.
11. *McCandless* v *Furland*, 296 US 140, 157.
12. (1968) 31 Mod LR 688.
13. [1969] 2 WLR 1107.
14. *See* RUSSEL LJ at p 1114.
15. *See* HARMAN LJ at 1111. *See* C. J. H. Thomson, *Share Issues and the Rule in Foss* v *Harbottle*, (1975) Aust LJ 134; where a company accepted an order of the Court, a few shareholders were not permitted to file an appeal on behalf of the company. *Bennett, Coleman & Co* v *UOI*, (1977) 47 Comp Cas 92 Bom; *Rajendra Nath Dutta* v *Shibendra Nath Mukherjee*, (1982) 52 Comp Cas 293 Cal, where the managing director was not permitted to challenge a transaction of the company in his personal capacity; *Vivek Goenka* v *Manoj Santhalia*, (1995) 83 Comp Cas 897 Mad, no interference in board managed company or in appointment of directors by directors or of executive directors; grievance, if any, should be sorted out under S. 397; *Bisch* v *Sullivan*, [1958] 1 All ER 841, where the directors appropriated the assets of the company, action was allowed but no action was allowed in *Paulides* v *Jenen*, (1956) Ch 565 where the allegation was that the company's assets were sold at an undervalue.
16. *Stein* v *Blake (No 2)*, [1998] 1 BCLC 573: [1998] 1 All ER 724 CA.

acts which no majority of shareholders can approve or affirm. In such cases each and every shareholder may sue to enforce obligations owed to the company. He brings the actions as a representative of the corporate interest. In the American literature a representative action of this kind is called the "derivative action".[17] The relief goes to the company.[18] Similarly, a shareholder may sue to recover *ultra vires* spent money from the company's officers responsible for the transaction.

1. Acts ultra vires

A shareholder is entitled to bring an action against the company and its officers in respect of matters which are *ultra vires* the company and which no majority of shareholders can sanction. The rule in *Foss* v *Harbottle* applies only as long as the company is acting within its powers. The facts of *Bharat Insurance Co Ltd* v *Kanhaiya Lal*[19] provide a suitable illustration:

> The plaintiff was a shareholder of the respondent company. One of the objects of the company was: "To advance money at interest on the security of land, houses, machinery and other property situated in India...." The plaintiff complained that "several investments have been made by the company without adequate security and contrary to the provisions of the memorandum and therefore prayed for a perpetual injunction to restrain it from making such investments".

The court observed as follows:

> The broad rule in such cases is no doubt that in all matters of internal management of a company, the company itself is the best judge of its affairs and the court should not interfere. But application of the assets of a company is not a matter of mere internal management. It is alleged that directors are acting ultra vires in their application of the funds of the company. Under these circumstances a single member can maintain a suit for a declaration as to the true construction of the article in question.

The plaintiff's own conduct in the circumstances must be proper. Since the minority shareholder's action in which the plaintiff shareholder sues on behalf of the company is a procedural device for the purpose of doing justice for the benefit of the company where it is controlled by miscreant directors or shareholders, the court is entitled to look at the conduct of the

---

17. *See* A. J. Boyle, *The Derivative Action in Company Law*, 1969 JBL 120.
18. For the right of the petitioning shareholder for indemnity, A. J. Boyle, *Indemnifying the Minority Shareholder*, 1976 JBL 18.
19. AIR 1935 Lah 792: 160 IC 24. *See* also *Nagappa Chettiar* v *Madras Race Club*, [1949] 1 MLJ 662: ILR 1949 Mad 808. The action is for recovery of money in favour of the company where it has already been paid over. It must be shown that there was some reason why the company could not sue. Where the independent shareholders of a company in a majority resolved that no recovery should be made of over payment to directors, the court attached importance to this fact and dismissed the minority shareholder's action. *Smith* v *Croft (No 2)*, [1987] 3 All ER 909 Ch D.

plaintiff to satisfy itself that the plaintiff is a proper person to bring the action. Thus, if the plaintiff's conduct was so tainted as to bar equitable relief or if there was an unacceptable delay in bringing the action, the plaintiff might well be held not to be a proper person to bring the action. In this case the action was by the wife, a minority shareholder, against the wrongdoings of her husband as a director. In a matrimonial proceeding between them she came to know of the improper profits made by the husband and such profits were even taken into consideration in preparing the award, it was held that she was not a proper plaintiff for a derivative action.[20]

Where it was proved that the funds of the company were diverted to extraneous purposes, it was held that the court had jurisdiction to pass an order for repayment to the company not only against the guilty members and directors but also against third persons who had knowingly received such money or improperly assisted the wrongful diversion.[21]

2. Fraud on minority

The conduct of a majority of shareholders can also be impeached if it constitutes a "fraud on the minority". The meaning of this phrase is not very clear. But, speaking very briefly, it means a discriminatory action. EVERSHED MR said in *Greenhalgh* v *Arderone Cinemas Ltd*[22], that "a special resolution would be liable to be impeached if the effect of it were to discriminate between the majority shareholders and minority shareholders, so as to give to the former an advantage of which the latter were deprived".

The concept of "fraud on the minority" can best be understood with reference to the line of cases in which it has been developed and applied. The first important case seems to be *Menier* v *Hooper's Telegraph Works*:[23]

> Two companies *A* and *B* were in rivalry. The majority of the members of company *A* were also the members of company *B*. Company *A* had commenced an action against company *B*. At a meeting of company *A*, the majority passed a resolution to compromise the action in a manner favourable to company *B* and unfavourable to *A*. Thus they attempted to deprive the company of the benefits which could have been recovered from company *B*. Consequently, in an action by the minority, the resolution was held invalid. "It would be a shocking thing", the Court observed, "if that could be done, because the majority have put something into their pockets at the expense of the minority."

---

20. *Narcombe* v *Narcombe*, [1985] 1 All ER 65 CA.
21. *Lowe* v *Fahey*, (1996) 1 BCLC 262 Ch D.
22. [1950] 2 All ER 1120: [1951] Ch 286.
23. [1874] 9 Ch App 350.

It follows that the court will interfere to protect the minority where the majority of a company propose to benefit themselves at the expense of the minority. The principle was again applied in *Cook* v *Deeks*:[24]

> Where the directors of a company holding three quarters of the capital obtained a contract in their own names to the exclusion of the company, Lord BUCKMASTER observed: "If, as their Lordships find on the facts, the contract in question was entered into under such circumstances that the directors could not retain the benefit of it for themselves, then it belonged in equity to the company and ought to have been dealt with as an asset of the company. Even supposing it to be not ultra vires of a company to make a present to its directors, it appears that directors holding majority of votes would not be permitted to make a present to themselves. This would be to allow a majority to oppress the minority".

Secondly, just as majority cannot appropriate to themselves the property of the company, similarly they are not allowed to expropriate the interest of minority shareholders. *Brown* v *British Abrasive Wheel Co*[25] is a case of this kind:

> A company was in great need of further capital. The majority representing 98% of the shares, were willing to provide this capital if they could buy up the 2% minority. Having failed to do this by agreement, they proposed to pass an article enabling them to purchase the minority shares compulsorily on certain terms. The plaintiff refused to surrender and brought an action to test the validity of the majority resolution. He succeeded. The question, in the view of the Court, was whether the proposed new article was "for the benefit of the company as a whole. As it was neither just nor equitable, nor for the benefit of the company as a whole to purchase the shares of a minority compulsorily", the resolution was held void.

The decision, therefore, means to suggest that majority powers must be exercised in good faith for the benefit of the company as a whole. If they have not been so exercised there is a "fraud on the minority". The phrase "benefit of the company as a whole" seems to have been borrowed from the judgment of LINDLEY MR in *Allen* v *Gold Reefs of West Africa*[26], where he said:

> The power of altering articles must, like all other powers, be exercised subject to those general principles of law and equity which are applicable to all powers conferred on majorities and enabling them to bind minorities. It must be exercised ... bona fide for the benefit of the company as a whole....

---

24. [1916] 1 AC 554: [1916-17] All ER Rep 285.
25. [1919] 1 Ch 290.
26. [1900] 1 Ch 656, 671: [1900-03] All ER Rep 746. *See* further on this point, *Mutual Life Insurance Co of New York* v *Rank Orgn*, (1995) BCLC 11.

Now, what is meant by the phrase "the company as a whole"? Does it mean the company as distinct from the members or as the whole body of corporators? This question was raised in *Sidebottom* v *Kershaw, Leese & Co*:[27]

> The plaintiffs who were in minority in the defendant company carried on a competing business. The majority of the shares were held by the directors, who passed a special resolution altering the company's articles and introducing a power for the directors to require any shareholder who competed with the company's business to transfer his shares at their full value to nominees of the directors. The validity of this resolution was challenged on the ground that it was not for the benefit of the company as a whole. "If the company as a whole means the whole body of corporators and every individual corporator, and if one of them has detriment occasioned to him by the alteration, it cannot be for the benefit of the company as a whole."

> The court rejected the suggestion and held that it was very much for the benefit of the company to get rid of the members who were in competing business, as such members have the unique opportunity of exploiting the company's business secrets against its very interest.

"Individual interest may be sacrificed to the economic exigencies of the enterprise and the judgment of directors as to this must prevail."[28]

But in doing so no more damage should be done to the individual shareholder than is absolutely necessary for protecting the company's interest. The limits were exceeded in *Dafen, Tinplate Co Ltd* v *Llanelly Steel Co Ltd*:[29]

> There was no power in the original articles of the defendant company for compulsory acquisition of a member's interest. A special resolution was passed altering articles and introducing a power enabling the majority of the shareholders to determine that the shares of any member may be offered for sale by the directors to such persons as they should think fit at the fair value to be fixed. The defendant company was formed with the object that all its shareholders were to take their tinplates from the company. The plaintiff company refused to do so and the defendant company resolved to acquire the plaintiff company's shares. But it was held that the resolutions in conferring an unrestricted and unlimited power on the majority to expropriate any shareholder they might think proper at their will or pleasure went much further than was necessary for the protection of the company.

27. [1920] 1 Ch 154.
28. Berle & Means, THE MODERN CORPORATION AND PRIVATE PROPERTY, 277 (1932).
29. [1920] 2 Ch 124.

Hence, "the question in each case is whether the alteration is genuinely for the benefit of the company, or was the alteration made for the benefit of some section of the company."[30] Now who shall be the ultimate judge of the fact whether a particular line of action adopted by the majority is genuinely for the benefit of the company. Obviously the shareholders are the best judge. The courts cannot manage the affairs of the company for the shareholders. The only restraint upon the majority powers, therefore, is that whatever the majority may decide, they must do so in good faith as reasonable businessmen. This approach was initiated by SCRUTTON LJ in *Shuttleworth* v *Cox Bros & Co*:[31]

When persons, honestly endeavouring to decide what will be for the benefit of the company, decide upon a particular course then, provided, there are grounds on which reasonable businessmen would come to the same conclusion, it does not matter whether the Court would not come to the same decision. It is not the business of the courts to interfere or to manage the affairs of the company, this is for the shareholders and directors. The absence of any reasonable grounds for deciding that a certain course of action is conducive to the benefit of the company may be a ground, for finding that the shareholders with the best motives, have not considered the matters which they ought to have considered.

Finally, in *Greenhalgh* v *Arderone Cinemas Ltd*,[32] EVERSHED MR, explained the concept in the following words:

"In the first place, it is now plain that 'bona fide for the benefit of the company as a whole' means not two things but one thing. It means that the shareholder must proceed on what, in his honest opinion, is for the benefit of the company as a whole. Secondly, the phrase 'the company as a whole' does not... mean the company as a commercial entity as distinct from the corporators. It means the corporators as a general body. That is to say, you may take the case of an individual hypothetical member and ask whether what is proposed is, in the honest opinion of those who voted in its favour, for that person's benefit. I think the thing can, in practice, be more accurately and precisely stated by looking at the converse and by saying that a special resolution of this kind would be liable to be impeached if the effect of it were to discriminate between the majority shareholders and the minority shareholders so as to give the former an advantage of which the latter were deprived. When the cases are examined where the resolution has been successfully attached, it is on that ground that it has fallen down."

---

30. See *Peters American Delicacy Co Ltd* v *Health*, (1939) 61 CLR 457, 481. The judgment in this case contains an elaborate discussion of cases on this subject. A decision of the High Court of Australia.
31. [1927] 2 KB 9.
32. [1950] 2 All ER 1120, 1126: 1951 Ch 286.

Thus the phrase ''corporators as a general body'' means both the present and future members of the company.[33]

But all this is subject to the principle which still holds ground that the right to vote is the private property of a shareholder and, therefore, "a shareholder may vote as he pleases even when his interests are different from or opposed to those of the company. Shareholders are not trustees for the company or for one another and the relations between them cannot be identified with relations between partners."[34] Shareholders often vote in their own selfish interest. They cannot always be required to have only the benefit of the company in view. For example, in *Jhajharia Bros Ltd* v *Sholapur Spg & Wvg Co Ltd*:[35]

The plaintiffs Jhajharias, were the managing and the sole selling agents of the defendant company. They also held minority interests in the company. The company dismissed them from both the offices. They owed certain sums to the company for which a good number of their shares were forfeited and allotted to the new managing agents. The new agents, with the help of these votes combined with those of directors and some shareholders managed to pass a resolution for further increase of capital which was underwritten by them. They thus placed themselves in a position of safe majority. The court could find no ground to interfere. "There is no inherent wrong in that. A majority can increase its own majority, generally speaking, unless there be an element of expropriation or coercion. Proof of party feeling or animosity by itself would not be enough."

Thus the fundamental question is as to who should control the company. From the administrative point of view the company is a collection of the members and, therefore, should be under their control. In the case of any conflict between the interest of the organisation and that of a member, the individual interest is sacrificed. But what often happens is that the majority tends to identify its own interest with that of the company and if the right to vote is their personal property they can use it to fortify their interests. In such cases the rule should be as suggested by Professor Aharan Barack:[36]

"It should be recognised that the shareholder, particularly one with a controlling interest, is not a 'stranger' to the company, but owes it a fiduciary duty and a duty of care, requiring him to act in good faith for the good of the company as a whole. If this approach were to be recognised then the power to ratify would be given only to

---

33. *Gaiman* v *National Assn of Mental Health,* (1971) 1 Ch 317, per MAGARRY J at p 330. His Lordship also added that principles of natural justice are not applicable in this field.
34. See *North-West Transportation Co* v *Beatty*, (1887) 12 App Cas 589; *Public Trustee* v *Rajeshwar Tyagi*, (1973) 43 Comp Cas 371 Del.
35. AIR 1941 Cal 174: 195 SC 36.
36. *A Comparative look at the Protection of Shareholders' Interests: Variations of the Derivative Suit,* (1971) 19 ICLQ 22.

'independent' shareholders, i.e., to those who had not colluded in a breach of duty by the directors, and who were not subject to their control.''[37]

The present trend is towards a principle that any breach of duty which causes loss to the company should be regarded as a fraud on the minority. In an English case[38] the sale of a company's property below its natural market value was held to be a fraud. Welcoming this decision[39], it has been observed that "in view of the inactivity of the legislature in the area of minority protection, it is welcome that the courts have taken it upon themselves to extend that area and to enable minorities more frequently than before to have their grievances ventilated in court". It has been added in a subsequent case that an action should lie whenever directors are guilty of a breach of duty to the company (including their duty to exercise proper care) and as a result of that breach they obtain some benefit.[40] Opinions have been expressed that action should be allowed under this category whenever the justice of the case demands and that the whole doctrine should be adapted to prevent a wrongdoing without a redress.[41] For example, the test of benefit of the company as a whole will fail to apply where class rights are involved and, therefore, in such cases the only requirement could be that the minority should not be made the victim of fraud or oppression.[42]

3. Acts requiring special majority

There are certain acts which can only be done by passing a special resolution at a general meeting of shareholders. Accordingly, if the majority purport to do any such act by passing only an ordinary resolution or without passing special resolution in the manner required by law, any member or members can bring an action to restrain the majority. Such actions were allowed in *Dhakeswari Cotton Mills* v *Nil Kamal Chakravarty*[43] and *Nagappa Chettiar* v *Madras Race Club*[44].

4. Wrongdoers in control

Sometimes an obvious wrong may have been done to the company, but the controlling shareholders would not permit an action to be brought

---

37. *A Comparative look at the Protection of Shareholders' Interests: Variations of the Derivative Suit,* (1971) 19 ICLQ 22 at p 34.
38. *Daniels* v *Daniels*, The Times, July 26, 1977: (1977) New LJ 938.
39. 1976 JBL 347.
40. *See* VINELOTT J in *Prudential Assurance Co Ltd* v *Newman Industries Ltd, (No 2)*, [1980] 2 All ER 841, 869: [1980] 3 WLR 543: [1982] Ch 204.
41. *Estmanco (Kilner House) Ltd* v *Greater London Council*, (1982) 1 WLR 2 at p 11: [1982] 1 All ER 437.
42. *Peter's American Delicacy Co Ltd* v *Health*, (1939) 61 CLR 457 (High Court of Australia). For further developments in this aspect of shareholders' duty of proper exercise of their powers *see* Robert Flannigan, *Fiduciary Duties of Shareholders and Directors*, 2004 JBL 277.
43. AIR 1937 Cal 645: 41 CWN 1137.
44. [1949] 1 MLJ 662: ILR 1949 Mad 808.

against the wrongdoer. In such cases, to safeguard the interest of the company, any member or members may bring an action in the name of the company.[45] This was recognised in *Foss* v *Harbottle* itself:

> If a case should arise of injury to a corporation by some of its members, for which no adequate remedy remained, except that of a suit by individual corporators in their private characters, and asking in such character the protection of these rights to which in their corporate character they were entitled, one cannot but think that the principle so forcefully laid down by Lord Cottenham in *Wallworth* v *Holt*[46], and other cases would apply, and the claims of justice would be found superior to any difficulties arising out of technical rules respecting the mode in which corporations are required to sue.

The principle has now found a suitable illustration in the facts of *Glass* v *Atkin*[47], a decision of the Ontario High Court:

> A company was controlled equally by the two defendants and the two plaintiffs. An action arose alleging that the two defendants had fraudulently converted the company's assets to their own use.

Allowing the action the Court said:

> While the general principle was for the company itself to bring an action where it had an interest, it was appropriate for the two plaintiffs here to bring an action on behalf of the company since the two defendants controlled the company in the sense that they could prevent the company from taking action.

The word "control" for this purpose means majority control. But it has now been recognised that control can exist without majority power. It has been held that "control exists if it would be futile to call a general meeting because the wrongdoers would directly or indirectly exercise a decisive influence over the result. This exception to *Foss* v *Harbottle* applies whenever the defendants are shown to be able by means of any manipulation of their position in the company to ensure that the action is not brought by the company."[48]

It has been suggested that the principle should extend to this extent that "when a director is in breach of fiduciary duty, every shareholder may be regarded an authorised organ to bring the action".[49]

---

45. *V. P. Singh* v *Chairman, Metropolitan Council*, AIR 1969 Delhi 295.

46. 4 Mycle & Cr 635. *See* also *Marshall's Valve Gear Co Ltd* v *Manning Wardley & Co Ltd*, [1909] 1 Ch 267: 100 LT 65, *supra* Chap. 9.

47. (1967) 65 DLR (2d) 501. *See* also *Satya Charan* v *Rameshwar Prasad Bajoria*, 1949 FCR 673: AIR 1950 FC 133: 20 Comp Cas 39: 1950 SCR 394 where FAZL ALI J restates all the cases in which a shareholder can take steps to redress a wrong done to the company.

48. *See* note on *Derivative Actions and Foss* v *Harbottle*, in (1981) 44 Mod LR 202 reviewing the decision of VINELOTT J in *Prudential Assurance Co Ltd* v *Newman Industries Ltd, (No 2)*, [1980] 2 All ER 841: [1980] 3 WLR 543: [1982] Ch 204.

49. *Id.* at p 30. For a statement of principles and indemnity as to costs see *Wallersteiner* v *Moir (No 2)*, [1975] 1 All ER 849 CA.

5. Individual membership rights

Lastly, every shareholder has, vested in him, certain personal rights against the company and his co-shareholders. A large number of such rights have been conferred upon shareholders by the Act itself, but they may also arise out of articles of association. Such rights are commonly known as "individual membership rights" and respecting them the rule of majority simply does not operate. In the words of Palmer, "if such a right is in question, a single shareholder can, on principle, defy a majority consisting of all the other shareholders".[50] For example in *Nagappa Chettiar* v *Madras Race Club*[51], the court observed: "A shareholder is entitled to enforce his individual rights against the company, such as his right to vote, the right to have his vote recorded, or his right to stand as a director of a company at an election." *Pender* v *Lushington*[52] is another authority.

A shareholder who had the right to vote, but whose vote was rejected, brought an action to compel the directors to record his vote. JESSEL MR observed: "He is a member of the company and whether he votes with the majority or the minority he is entitled to have his vote recorded — an individual right in respect of which he has a right to sue. That has nothing to do with the question like that raised in *Foss* v *Harbottle* and that line of cases.[53] He has a right to say 'whether I vote in the majority or minority, you shall record my vote, as that is a right of property belonging to my interest in this company, and if you refuse to record my vote, I will institute legal proceedings against you to compel you'.[54]"

This principle was applied by the Kerala High Court in deciding *Joseph* v *Jos*.[55]

At a meeting of a company it was proposed to elect some directors by separate elections. The plaintiff was a candidate and he contested the election, but was defeated. He was proposed as a candidate again to fill up the second vacancy. But the chairman, on account of his previous defeat, disqualified him.

In his action against this ruling, the court held that he was entitled to a declaration that the proceedings of the meeting as regards the election of directors were null and void. "An individual membership right implies that

---

50. Palmer on COMPANY LAW, 492 (20th Edn).
51. [1949] 1 MLJ 662, 667: ILR 1949 Mad 808.
52. [1877] 6 Ch D 70.
53. *Id*. at pp 80-81.
54. His Lordship also observed at 75-76 that "it is no ground for rejecting a shareholder's vote that he has voted against the interest of the company. There is no obligation on a shareholder of a company to give his vote merely with a view to what other persons may consider the interests of the company at large. He has a right, if he thinks fit, to give his votes from motives or promptings of what he considers his own individual interest." There is a useful list of such rights at 493-96 in Palmer's COMPANY LAW, 20th Edn (1959).
55. [1964] 1 Comp LJ 105. Also see *Srinivasan* v *Subramania*, AIR 1932 Mad 100: 136 IC 193.

the individual shareholders can insist on strict observance of the legal rules, statutory provisions and the provisions in the memorandum and articles which cannot be waived by a bare majority of shareholder. Every shareholder can assert such a right in his own name."[56]

Similarly, in *Karus v Lloyd Property Ltd*:[57]

A director refused to retire in accordance with the articles and invalidly continued in office. The plaintiff shareholder was held entitled to bring an action on the ground that "the individual rights of the plaintiff as a member have been invaded."[58]

The plaintiff, in still another case, was allowed to assert that new articles adopted by the company by a resolution were not binding because when the resolution was being considered, the chairman had wrongly rejected his right to propose an amendment.[59]

6. Oppression and mismanagement

Lastly, it has been stated by SINHA J of the Calcutta High Court in *Kanika Mukherji v Rameshwar Dayal Dubey*[60] that the principle embodied in Sections 397 and 398 of the Indian Companies Act which provide for prevention of oppression and mismanagement, is an exception to the rule in *Foss v Harbottle* which lays down the sanctity of the majority rule.[61]

---

56. Following articles on the subject may be consulted: *Minority Shareholders' Action—Rule in Foss v Harbottle*, (1964) Camb LJ 39; A. J. Boyle, *Minority Shareholder in the Nineteenth Century*, 28 Mod LR 317 (1965); K. W. Wedderburn, *Shareholders' Right and the Rule in Foss v Harbottle*, (1957) Camb LJ 194 and (1958) Camb LJ 93; *Freezing out Minority Shareholders*, 74 Har LR 1630; *Acquisition of Minority Shares*, 1960 LQR 314; *A Liberal Approach to Foss v Harbottle*, 27 Mod LR 603 (1964); G. R. Bretten, *Alteration of Articles and Protection of Minorities*, 1970 JBL 185.
57. 1965 VR 232(Aust.); noted 30 Mod LR 78. *See* also *Berar Trading Co v Gajanan Gopal Rao Dixit*, (1972) 42 Comp Cas 48 Bom.
58. HUDSON J at p 236. *See* K. W. Wedderburn, *Shareholders' Control of Directors' Powers: A Judicial Innovation*, (1967) 30 Mod LR 77, 78.
59. *Henderson v Bank of Australasia*, (1890) 45 Ch D 330: [1886-90] All ER Rep Ext 1190.
60. [1966] 1 Comp LJ 65 Cal. A petition under these sections cannot be stayed under S. 10, CPC, *Rijush K. Guha v W.B. Pharmaceuticals Phyto Commercial Corpn Ltd*, [1982] 1 Comp LJ 199: AIR 1982 Cal 94.
61. This forms the subject-matter of the next chapter. The vulnerable position of the minority shareholder and how he can be protected by expanding the scope of the fiduciary responsibilities of majority shareholders has been explained in the recent American case, *Jones v H. F. Ahman Son & Co*, decision of the Supreme Court of California, Cal 3d 93: 81 Calf Report 592, and is commented upon in a note: *Jones v Ahman Son: The Fiduciary Obligations of Majority Shareholder*, (1970) 70 Col LR 1079.

16

Prevention of Oppression and Mismanagement

In addition to the protection afforded to the minority by the exceptions to the rule of the supremacy of majority, the modern Companies Acts contain special provisions for prevention of oppression and mismanagement. The aim of such provisions, now contained in Chapter VI of Part VI of the Companies Act, 1956, is to safeguard the interest of investors in companies and also to protect the public interest. The rights conferred on shareholders by this chapter are also known as qualified minority rights.[1] The chapter provides for judicial as well as administrative remedies.

PREVENTION OF OPPRESSION

Who can apply (S. 399)

The first remedy in the hands of an oppressed minority is to move the Company Law Board. Whenever "the affairs of a company are being conducted in a manner oppressive to any member or members or prejudicial to public interest", an application can be made to the Company Law Board under Section 397. The requisite number of members who must sign the application is given in Section 399. Where the company is with a share capital, the application must be signed by at least 100 members of the company or by one-tenth of the total number of its members, whichever is less, or by any member or members holding one-tenth of the issued share capital of the company.[2] If the company is without share capital, the application has to be signed by one-fifth of the total number of its members.[3]

---

1. *See* Palmer's COMPANY LAW, Chap. 51 at p 505 (1959) 20th Edn.
2. T. N. K. Govindaraju Chetty & Co v Kadri Mills (CBE) Ltd, (1998) 30 Corpt LA 49 CLB, the percentage is to be taken on the basis of the position before the increase of capital which has been questioned and which has reduced the percentage of the petitioner. Mega Resources v Bombay Dyeing and Mfg Co Ltd, (2003) 116 Comp Cas 205 CLB, a portion of the holding was in violation of SEBI Takeover Code and without it, 10% shareholding was not there with the petitioner. S. Palaniappan v Tirupur Cotton Spg & Wvg Mills Ltd, (2005) 128 Comp Cas 536 CLB, a person holding less than 10% cannot apply. L. Chandramurthy v K.L. Kapsi, (2005) 48 SCL 294 CLB, a person who had disposed of his shares was not allowed to apply. Aska Investments (P) Ltd v Grab Tea Co (P) Ltd, (2005) 126 Comp Cas 603 CLB, excess holding in violation of SEBI limits not qualified to apply.
3. This being a statutory right, cannot be taken away by contrary provisions in the articles or by an arbitration clause. *Kare (P) Ltd, Re*, (1977) 47 Comp Cas 276 Del; *O. P. Gupta v Shiv General Finance (P) Ltd*, (1977) 47 Comp Cas 279 Del. All the consenting members together have to hold the requisite number and not every one of them individually. *Kuttanad Rubber Co Ltd v K.T. Ittiyavirah*, [1993] 3 Comp LJ 39 Ker. Consent through a general power of attorney is valid for this purpose. *P. Punniah v Jeypore Sugar Co Ltd*, (1994) 4 SCC 341: (1994) 81 Comp Cas 2

However, the Central Government may, on application, allow any member or members to sue "if in its opinion circumstances exist which make it just and equitable to do so".[4]

Once the consent of the requisite number is obtained, the application may be made by one or more of them on behalf and for the benefit of all of them.[5] The term "consent" for this purpose means, as defined in Section 13 of the Contract Act, an agreement upon the same thing in the same sense. Accordingly, the Madras High Court[6] rejected a petition because the consenting members were only told that their signatures were needed for requisitioning a meeting. The signatories must be told of the specific facts which are alleged to be as constituting an oppression. "There cannot be a blanket consent."[7] It has been held by the Supreme Court in *Rajahmundry Electric Supply Corpn* v *A. Nageshwara Rao*[8] that if some of the consenting members have, subsequent to the presentation of the application, withdrawn their consent, it would not affect the right of the applicant to proceed with the application.[9] By holding that where a petition has been properly presented, it does not cease to be maintainable merely because three of the applicants have transferred their shares and ceased to be shareholders of the

---

SC. A petition cannot be filed by a general power of attorney. He must be specifically authorised. *Shri Kiran M. Lulla* v *Vikron Fashions (P) Ltd*, (1994) 81 Comp Cas 566 CLB where a company was a member and aggrieved of oppression, an unauthorised director was not allowed to proceed. He needed a decision of the company or its board. Consent of members to a draft petition was not a good consent. There was nothing to show that the petition was based on the grounds noted in the draft. *K. N. Sankarnarayanan* v *Shree Consultations & Services (P) Ltd*, (1994) 80 Comp Cas 558 Mad.

4. S. 399(4). The Government may demand security for costs as a safeguard against vexatious litigation. *See* sub-section (4).

5. The requirement as to minimum shareholding is applicable only at the time of filing. The petition can continue even if after filing some shareholders cease to be members. *S. Varadrajan* v *Venkateswara Solvent Extractions (P) Ltd*, (1994) 80 Comp Cas 693 Mad.

6. *M. C. Duraiswami* v *Sakthi Sugars Ltd*, (1980) 50 Comp Cas 154 Mad.

7. The court considered *Bengal Luxmi Cotton Mills, Re*, (1965) 35 Comp Cas 187 Cal, and *Makhan Lal Jain* v *Amrit Banaspati Co Ltd*, (1953) 23 Comp Cas 100. For another case of consent by misrepresentation see *Naranjan Singh* v *Edwardganj Pub Welfare Assn*, (1983) 54 Comp Cas 330 P&H. Consent to proceedings on the general ground of mismanagement or oppression will not do. *Omni India Ltd* v *Balbir Singh*, [1989] 2 Comp LJ 229: (1989) 66 Comp Cas 903 Del; *K. P. Chackochan* v *Federal Bank*, [1989] 2 Comp LJ 269: (1989) 66 Comp Cas 953 Ker. Consent taken without informing shareholders of the specific grounds so as to give them an opportunity for application of mind will render the petition invalid. See *P. S. Nanawati* v *Jaipur Metals and Electricals Ltd*, (1990) 69 Comp Cas 769 Raj. Preliminary issues relating to maintainability and procedural requirements under CPC and court rules should be decided in the context of the grounds raised. *Saurashtra Cement and Chemical Industries Ltd* v *Essma Industries (P) Ltd*, (1990) 69 Comp Cas 372.

8. AIR 1956 SC 213: (1956) 26 Comp Cas 91.

9. *Kilpest (P) Ltd* v *Shekhar Mehra*, (1987) 62 Comp Cas 717, the court also pointing out that the petition cannot be converted into one for winding up. The Punjab High Court has gone a little further in *Jagdish Chandra Mehra* v *New India Embroidery Mills*, [1964] 1 Comp LJ 291 by holding that even if the petitioning member disposes of his shares, the petition remains competent. *V. Shanker* v *South Indian Concerns Ltd*, (1997) 24 Corpt LA 54 CLB, the petitioner not competent himself in shareholding, consents filed by him did not inspire confidence, petition not entertained.

company. "The validity of the petition must be judged on the facts as they are at the time of its presentation. Neither the right of the applicant to proceed with the application, nor the jurisdiction of the court to dispose of it on its own merits, can be affected by events happening subsequent to the presentation."[10]

All the material facts should be set out in the petition itself. Allegations of fraud, *mala fide*, etc, must be supported with particulars. Supporting facts cannot be brought in subsequently.[11]

Similarly, in a petition against a transport company, the Madras High Court refused to take into account the subsequent conduct of the majority in disposing of all the buses of the company.[12] "The petitioner is not entitled to take advantage of a circumstance that happened after the presentation of the petition."

Where a person has obtained a decree for rectification of his company's register of members so as to have his name entered in it, he may apply for relief under the section although the decree has not yet been enforced and the register does not show his name.[13] Similarly, in *Bayswater Trading Co, Re*,[14] and again in *Jermyn Street Turkish Baths Ltd, Re*,[15] Section 210 of the (English) Companies Act, which provided for relief against oppression, was interpreted to include the representatives of a deceased shareholder.[16] But it seems probable that a purchaser of shares

---

10. Where the transferee was an already registered shareholder and, therefore, his petition was entertained, the removal of his name by the company subsequently from the register on the ground that the transfer deeds carried uncancelled stamps was held to be not a material fact and the petition remained competent. *Sayedabad Tea Co Ltd v Samarendra Nath Ghattak*, (1995) 83 Comp Cas 504 Cal.

11. *P. S. Offshore Inter Land Services (P) Ltd v Bombay Offshore Suppliers and Services Ltd*, (1992) 75 Comp Cas 583 Bom; *M. M. Dua v Indian Dairy and Allied Services (P) Ltd*, (1996) 86 Comp Cas 657 CLB; *Karedla Suryanarayana v Shri Ramdas Motor Transport Ltd*, (1998) 28 Corpt LA 233 CLB, matters of subsequent occurrence and amendment of pleadings. *Subhash Chand Agarwal v Associated Limestone Ltd*, (1998) 29 Corpt LA 190 CLB, an amendment cannot be allowed to set up a new case which was not set out in the original petition. *Srihari Rao v P. K. Majumdar*, (1998) 30 Corpt LA 373 CLB, burden of proof on the petitioner.

12. *C. P. Gnanasambandam v Tamilnadu Transports (P) Ltd*, (1971) 41 Comp Cas 26 Mad.

13. *Stadmed (P) Ltd v Kshetra Mohan*, AIR 1968 Cal 572: [1968] 1 Comp LJ 321: 72 CWN 601. See RAY J (as he then was) at 579. Where a pledgee of shares was registered as shareholder and exercised membership rights, it was held that on the removal of his name from the register under an order of the Company Law Board, he ceased to be member for the purposes of a petition under the section. *Malleswara Finance and Investment Co v CLB*, (1994) 81 Comp Cas 66: AIR 1994 Mad 341.

14. [1970] 1 All ER 608: [1970] 1 WLR 343: (1970) 40 Comp Cas 1196.

15. [1970] 3 All ER 57.

16. A similar view has been adopted under the Companies Act so as to enable the legal representatives to apply. See *Worldwide Agencies (P) Ltd v Margaret*, (1990) 1 SCC 536: 1990 SCC (Tax) 171: (1990) 67 Comp Cas 607 SC: AIR 1990 SC 737: [1990] 1 Comp LJ 208, affirming *Margaret T. Desor v Worldwide Agencies (P) Ltd*, (1989) 66 Comp Cas 5 Del. In the event of the death of one of the respondents, it is not necessary to bring his legal heirs on the record. *Rajender Nath Bhaskar v Bhaskar Stoneware Pipes (P) Ltd*, [1990] 1 Comp LJ 351: (1990) 68 Comp Cas 256 Del. A person who has become entitled to be a member has a right to apply. *Shri Balaji Textile Mills (P) Ltd v Ashok Kavle*, (1989) 66 Comp Cas 654 Ker;

who is not yet registered may not be allowed relief under the section against the oppression caused by the company's refusal to register his name.[17] A person who was entitled to an allotment of shares against his application money was regarded as competent to apply though he had subsequently withdrawn his application money.[18] The petition of a nominee shareholder was not struck out.[19] A trustee holder of shares whom the company was refusing to register was allowed to file petition.[20] The Bombay High Court did not allow a derivative action to be filed by a director of the company who was not its shareholder. Order 1, Rule 1 of CPC would not permit a person to join a proceeding in which he has the right to relief. A person whose name is not borne out by the company's register of members has no *locus standi* to say that a wrong has been done to his company. The court would not lift the veil of incorporation at his instance so as to enable him to show his beneficial interest in the company through a chain of inter-corporate investments.[21] A member whose shares had been forfeited without any authority but whose name was still there in the Register of Members had *locus standi* to apply.[22] Even when the original petitioning member withdraws from the foray and does not want to continue the petition, he cannot compel dismissal of the petition. A representative action of this kind can still be considered on its merits. Any willing member may be substituted as a petitioner even if he is holding less than the requisite number of shares. Share qualification is relevant only to the time of filing and not to the continuance of the petition.[23]

Srikanta Datta Narsimahraja Wadiyar v Venkateshwar Real Estates Enterprises (P) Ltd, (1990) 68 Comp Cas 216; *N. Satyaprasad Rao v V. L. N. Sastry,* (1988) 64 Comp Cas 492 AP, share certificates issued. *Radhey Shyam Gupta v Kamal Oil & Allied Industries Ltd,* (2006) 133 Comp Cas 90 Del petitioner died, refiling after substitution of legal heirs, sufficient cause shown explaining delay in refiling, leniency should be shown. *K.S. Mothilal v K.S. Kasimaris Ceramique (P) Ltd,* (2007) 135 Comp Cas 609 CLB, legal heirs entitled to be registered on probate or will, entitled to apply.

17. This view is expressed in Gower's PRINCIPLES OF MODERN COMPANY LAW, 600, (3rd Edn 1969). A person whose name has been struck off the register also cannot apply unless he first gets the register rectified so as to include his name. *Gulabrai Kalidas Naik v Lakshmidas Lallubhai Patel,* (1977) 47 Comp Cas 151. *See* further *Killick Nixon Ltd v Bank of India,* (1985) 57 Comp Cas 831 Bom, where the court held that a shareholder, who has transferred his shares but the same has not been registered by the company, is entitled to petition and also that the right to petition can be delegated to an agent. A person whose name was there in the register and was unlawfully removed under unauthorised signatures was allowed to file petition, *Rashmi Seth v Tillsoil Farms (P) Ltd,* [1992] 3 Comp LJ 126 CLB: (1995) 82 Comp Cas 409 CLB.

18. *Dhananjay Pande v Dr Bais Surgical & Medical Institute (P) Ltd,* (2005) 125 Comp Cas 626 CLB.

19. *Allasview Ltd v Brightview Ltd,* (2004) 2 BCLC 191 Ch D.

20. *State Bank of India v Business Developments Consultants (P) Ltd,* (2005) 128 Comp Cas 557.

21. *BSN (UK) Ltd v Janardan Mohandas Rajan Pillai,* (1996) 86 Comp Cas 371 Bom; *Radhey Shyam Gupta v Kamal Oil & Allied Industries Ltd,* (2001) 103 Comp Cas 337 Del, those persons whose names are borne by the register of members and annual returns as shareholders are *prima facie* entitled to file petition. *Shankar Sundaram v Amalgamations Ltd,* (2001) 104 Comp Cas 635 CLB, shareholders of holding company cannot apply in respect of oppression or mismanagement in a subsidiary. The subsidiary may be impleaded, if necessary.

22. *N. Kuberan v Monarch Steels (India) Ltd,* (2006) 130 Comp Cas 109 CLB.

23. *LRMK Narayan v Pudhuthotam Estates Ltd,* (1992) 74 Comp Cas 30 Mad. The CLB may be approached even where the matter is pending before a High Court. Proceedings before CLB

A person who was not a shareholder of the company but had a grievance about the value of shares at which they were being allotted, could file a civil suit. The value was fixed by a majority of the shareholders and was approved by the Reserve Bank under the Foreign Exchange Regulation Act, 1973. The court refused to interfere.[24]

The Central Government also has the power to apply for relief under the section.[25] The Government also has the discretionary power to permit a lesser number of members to proceed under the section.[26]

The employees of a company, however much they may be treated like members, or are members also, cannot get any relief under this jurisdiction in their capacity as employees.[27]

Section 400 requires the CLB to give notice of every application made to it under Section 397 or 398 to the Central Government. The CLB has to take into consideration any representation made by the Central Government in connection with a particular application.

Once entertained, a petition under the section can be compromised or withdrawn only with the sanction of the CLB. The compromise should be in the best interest of the company and its shareholders.[28]

"This ingenious remedy has not only permitted redress of many abuses, but its mere availability has had a deterrent effect upon management."[29]

---

are not liable to be stayed for that reason. A representative of the petitioning group of shareholders was appointed by the CLB on the company's board by way of interim relief and was authorised to function as an independent chairman. *Mrunalini Deve Puar of Dhar (Dr)* v *Gaekwar Investment Corpn (P) Ltd*, [1993] 1 Comp LJ 89 CLB: (1995) 82 Comp Cas 899; *Rashmi Seth* v *Chemon (India) (P) Ltd*, [1992] 3 Comp LJ 89 CLB: (1995) 82 Comp Cas 563.

24. *Geeta Kapoor* v *Union of India*, (2006) 132 Comp Cas 369 Del.
25. S. 401. A secretary cannot present a petition by himself. He requires authority of the board of directors. *Mohan Lal Mittal* v *Universal Works Ltd*, (1983) 53 Comp Cas 36 Cal; *Union of India* v *CRB Resources (P) Ltd*, (2005) 128 Comp Cas 766 CLB Central Govt petition not entertained because no public interest was shown to be involved.
26. *Efficient Publicities (P) Ltd, Re*, [1989] 1 Comp LJ 208 CLB where the permission was refused because the alleged facts were not true. *Edwardganj Public Welfare Assn, Re*, (1990) 69 Comp Cas 787 P&H, a petition by a single member in a company without share capital rejected.
27. *Jaber* v *Science and Information Technology Ltd*, (1992) BCLC 764 Ch D; *Alchema Ltd, Re*, [1998] BCC 964 Ch D; *French* v *Mason*, [1998] CLY Feb, para 96.
28. *Kelly and Henderson (P) Ltd, Re*, (1980) 50 Comp Cas 646 Bom, where the court refused to sanction a compromise which was tilted in favour of the person against whom the grievances were alleged. Following, *Syed Mohd Ali* v *R. Sundaramurthy*, (1958) 28 Comp Cas 554: AIR 1958 Mad 587; *Jacob Cherian* v *K. K. Cherian*, (1973) 43 Comp Cas 235 Mad. See *Kumar Exporters (P) Ltd* v *Naini Oxygen*, (1986) 60 Comp Cas 984, 990, where a decree was passed in terms of compromise. All the material facts affecting the matter must be disclosed in the petition itself. Allegations of fraud, *mala fide*, etc, if any, must be supported by particulars. *P. S. Offshore Inter Land Services (P) Ltd* v *Bombay Offshore Suppliers and Services Ltd*, (1992) 75 Comp Cas 583 Bom. The CLB will not stand in the way of withdrawal if there is nothing against public or company's interests, *V. Sundarajan* v *R. R. Spinning Mills Ltd*, (1998) 30 Corpt LA 35 CLB. A compromise cannot be recalled or altered because the CLB has no power to review its own decisions. An order also cannot be modified unless all the parties agree or it is established that the parties did not understand the nature and purport of the compromise (lack of consensus-ad-idem) or it was not voluntary, *Michelle Jawad-Al-Fahoum* v *Indo Sandi (Travels) (P) Ltd*, (1991) 71 Comp Cas 300 Cal: (1998) CLA 42 CLB.

Company itself cannot apply

The company cannot by itself be an applicant for any relief under this jurisdiction.[30]

Conditions of relief [S. 397]

There are certain preliminary conditions which must be satisfied to entitle a shareholder to some relief under the section.[31] These conditions are inbuilt in the language of the section itself. The section comes into play when (1) the company's affairs are being conducted in a manner, (2) prejudicial to public interest or oppressive to any member or members, (3) which would make it just and equitable to wind up the company, but, (4) winding up would unfairly prejudice such member or members.

Oppression

If an oppression of this kind is established, the CLB will, "with a view to bringing to an end the matters complained of, make such an order as it thinks fit". Before this section was enacted the only effective remedy against oppression was a winding up order under the just and equitable clause of Section 433. But this remedy was often worse than the disease.[32] And now the CLB has been given the powers to impose upon the parties whatever solution the CLB considers just and equitable in the circumstances. Thus, instead of forcing a sound business concern to winding up, an effort is made to salvage it.[33]

The meaning of the term "oppression" as explained by Lord COOPER in the Scottish case of *Elder* v *Elder & Watson Ltd*[34], was cited with approval by WANCHOO J (afterwards CJ) of the Supreme Court of India in *Shanti Prasad Jain* v *Kalinga Tubes Ltd.*[35] "The essence of the matter seems to be that the conduct complained of should at the lowest involve a visible departure from the standards of fair dealing, and a violation of the conditions of fair play on which every shareholder who entrusts his money to the company is entitled to rely." The complaining shareholder must be under a burden which is unjust or

---

29. George H. Hornstein, *The Future of Corporate Control*, (1950) 63 Harv LR 476.
30. *Ultrafilter (India) (P) Ltd* v *Ultrafilter GmbH*, (2002) 112 Comp Cas 93 CLB.
31. For the meaning of the word "satisfaction" see *Peerless General Finance & Investment Co Ltd* v *UOI*, [1989] 1 Comp LJ 56 Cal: (1991) 71 Comp Cas 300 Cal.
32. The remedy was introduced in S. 210 of the English Companies Act, 1948, as a result of the recommendations of the Cohen Committee, 1945. The Committee had suggested that: "The remedy of winding up to eliminate oppression is worse than the disease because it generally means that the business of the company would pass into the hands of the majority who would ordinarily be the only available purchaser and the break up value of the assets may be small." See SINHA J in *Kanika Mukherji* v *Rameshwar Dayal Dubey*, [1966] 1 Comp LJ 65 at 77 Cal.
33. *See*, for example, *K. R. S. Narayana Iyengar* v *T. A. Mani*, AIR 1960 Mad 338, 339; Cohen Committee's Report, 30-95.
34. 1952 SC 49 Scotland.
35. [1965] 1 Comp LJ 193, 204: AIR 1965 SC 1535: (1965) 35 Comp Cas 351.

harsh or tyrannical.[36] "A persistent and persisting course of unjust conduct must be shown."[37] In the above-mentioned Scottish case the allegations were that the petitioners, who were two shareholders in a small family company, were removed by the majority from directorship and also from their employment as secretary and factory manager. The petition failed because they had not suffered as shareholders but in different capacities.

"The result of applications under Section 210[38] in different cases must depend on the particular facts of each case, the circumstances in which oppression may arise being so infinitely various that it is impossible to define them with precision."[39]

An attempt to force new and more risky objects upon an unwilling minority may in circumstances amount to oppression. This kind of situation developed in *Hindustan Coop Insurance Society Ltd, Re:*[40]

> The life insurance business of a company was acquired in 1956 by the Life Insurance Corporation of India on payment of compensation. The directors, who had the majority voting power, refused to distribute this amount among the shareholders. Rather they passed a special resolution changing the objects of the company and to utilise the compensation money for the new objects. This was held to be an "oppression". The Court observed: "The majority exercised their authority wrongfully, in a manner burdensome, harsh and wrongful. They attempted to force the minority shareholders to invest their money in a different kind of business against their will. The minority had invested their money in a life insurance business with all its safeguards and statutory protections. But they were being forced to invest where there would be no such protections or safeguards."

Similarly, an attempt to deprive a member of his ordinary membership rights is an "oppression". This is shown by *Mohan Lal Chandumall v Punjab Co Ltd:*[41]

> A public company doing forward contract business amended its articles of association under a statutory direction in such a manner as to

---

36. *See* Lord SIMONDS in *Scottish Coop Wholesale Society* v *Meyer*, [1958] 3 All ER 66: (1958) 3 WLR 404 HL: 1959 AC 324 at p 342. His Lordship said that the dictionary meaning of the term is "burdensome, harsh and wrongful." Referring to this Professor Gower says: "difficulty has been experienced in tracing the dictionary from which he took it . . . it appears to be an adaptation of the SOED's unjustly burdensome, harsh or merciless". PRINCIPLES OF MODERN COMPANY LAW, p 602 (3rd Edn, 1969).

37. See *H. R. Harmer Ltd, Re*, [1958] 3 All ER 689: [1959] 1 WLR 62.

38. Of the English Companies Act, 1948, on which S. 397 of the Indian Companies Act has been based. This section of the English Act was replaced by S. 459 of the 1985 English Act substituting the words "unfair prejudice" for the word "oppression".

39. *H. R. Harmer Ltd, Re*, fn 37, *supra*, adopted by WANCHOO J (afterwards CJ) in *Shanti Prasad Jain* v *Kalinga Tubes Ltd*, fn 35, *supra*. The judicial definitions have been collected by D. Prentice, *Protection of Minority Shareholders*, (1952) Current Legal Problems 122 at p 137.

40. AIR 1961 Cal 443: 65 CWN 68: (1961) 31 Comp Cas 193.

41. AIR 1961 Punj 485.

deprive its non-trading members of their right to vote, to call meetings, to elect directors and to receive dividends. The Court held that "the company in doing so trampled upon the valuable rights of such members by unjust exercise of its authority and power and it amounted to oppression within Section 377". "I cannot conceive of a worse oppression", said MAHAJAN J "than the denial of a voting right to a shareholder.... To take away the right of partaking in dividends is not merely oppressive but even confiscatory."

But as the amendments were in accordance with the requirements of an Act which provided that such companies should consist of only trading members, the court directed the company to purchase the shares of the complaining members to enable them to walk out of the company with such capital as they had invested.

A similar relief was allowed by the House of Lords in *Scottish Coop Wholesale Society* v *Meyer.*[42]

The society created a subsidiary company to enable it to enter the rayon industry. Subsequently, when the need for the subsidiary ceased to exist, the society adopted a policy of running down its business which depressed the value of its shares.

The two petitioners who were managing directors and minority shareholders in the subsidiary successfully pleaded "oppression". The court ordered the society to purchase the minority shares at the value at which they stood before the oppressive policy started.

Similarly, in *Harmer Ltd, Re,*[43] the Court of Appeal allowed relief in circumstances where a majority controller persistently flouted the decisions of the board, committed the company to new business without proper procedure and procured the appointment of dummy directors. Where the chairman of a company, who owed his allegiance to a corporation which had underwritten the shares of the company, tried to oust the managing director of the company at a time when, as a result of the managing director's efforts, the company had brought up its factory and was only waiting for further loans to enter into production, that was held to be an "oppressive policy", which was also against public interest.[44] "Public interest" in this connection means that the company should function for public good or for general welfare of the community and not in a manner detrimental to public good. There was sufficient evidence to show that if the company had gone into production, it would have earned foreign exchange for the country. Those who were causing delay must be held to be guilty of working against public as well as company's interests.

---

42. [1958] 3 All ER 66: (1958) 3 WLR 404 HL: 1959 AC 324.
43. [1958] 3 All ER 689: [1959] 1 WLR 62.
44. *N. R. Murty* v *I. D. Corpn of Orissa Ltd*, (1977) 47 Comp Cas 389 Ori.

Suppressing notices of meetings to some of the members is an act of oppression towards them. Casual omissions may not be, but systematic elimination of notices to some of the members is a serious deprivation of their most important right.[45]

Minor acts of mismanagement, however, are not to be regarded as oppression. As far as possible shareholders should try to resolve their differences by mutual readjustment. Moreover, the courts will not allow these special remedies to become a vexatious source of litigation. For example, in *Lalita Rajya Lakshmi* v *Indian Motor Co*:[46]

> The petitioner alleged that the board of directors were guilty of certain acts detrimental to the minority of the shareholders. The allegations were that the income of the company was deliberately shown less by excessive expenditure; that passengers travelling without ticket on the company's buses were not checked; that petrol consumption was not properly checked; that second hand buses of the company have been disposed of at low cost, that dividends were being declared at too low a figure. It was held that even if each of these allegations were proved to the satisfaction of the court, there would have been no oppression.

The court further observed that "to attempt to get a majority by lawful means is not a fact or circumstance which justifies winding up of the company. If any authority is needed for that proposition, one need only refer to the Privy Council decision in *Ripon Press & Sugar Mills Co Ltd* v *Gopal Chetty*[47], where LORD BLANESBURGH made this significant observation: "The fact that Venkata Rao had a preponderating voice in the company by reason of his owning or controlling a large number of shares was of itself no reason for winding up of the company."[48] An unreasonable refusal to accept a transfer or transmission of shares has been held sufficient to warrant an order under the section.[49] Refusal to allot shares under a rights issue to a

---

45. *Shantidevi Pratap Singh Gaekwad* v *Sangram Singh P. Gaekwad*, [1996] 1 Comp LJ 72 Guj; *Farhat Sheikh* v *Esemen Metalo Chemicals (P) Ltd*, (1995) 16 Corpt LA 147 CLB: (1996) 87 Comp Cas 290 CLB; *Farhat Sheikh* v *Detinners (P) Ltd*, (1996) 87 Comp Cas 290 CLB.

46. AIR 1962 Cal 127: (1962) 32 Comp Cas 207; *A. Ravisankar Prasad* v *Prasad Productions (P) Ltd*, (2007) 135 Comp Cas 416 CLB, the decision of directors to write off bad debts being a business decision, no interference, so was the decision of removing a director which caused no loss to the company.

47. 58 IA 416: AIR 1932 PC 1.

48. *See* also, for example, *Bellador Silk Ltd, Re*, [1965] 1 All ER 667: [1965] 2 Comp LJ 30 where it was held that the petitioner was not entitled to relief under S. 210 of the English Companies Act, 1948 (corresponding to S. 397 of the Indian Act), because the presentation of the petition in order to bring pressure to bear to achieve a collateral purpose was an abuse of the process of the court and on the facts the contributories had no tangible interest in a liquidation, with the consequence that a contributory would not be entitled to a winding up order on the just and equitable ground, and, thus S. 210(2)(*b*) [Ss. 459-461 of the Act of 1985] was inapplicable.

49. *Gajarabai* v *Patni Transport (P) Ltd*, [1965] 2 Comp LJ 234. *See* also the decision of the Calcutta High Court in *Satish Chandra* v *Bengal Laxmi Cotton Mills Ltd*, [1965] 1 Comp LJ

particular shareholder in order to prevent him from becoming qualified to file a petition was held to be oppressive.[50] The removal of a director who had been there in the company for 20 years and denying him access to the company's premises just only to prevent him from having access to the company's records was held to be an oppressive conduct.[51] Shareholders' resolutions cannot be the subject of judicial review but their timings and the conduct of the majority in passing them can be taken into account for deciding whether the conduct of affairs is in an oppressive manner.[52]

"There must be an unfair abuse of the powers and impairment of confidence in the probity with which the company's affairs are being conducted as distinguished from mere resentment on the part of a minority at being outvoted on some issue of domestic policy." "It is not lack of confidence between the shareholders *per se* that brings the section into play... oppression involves at least an element of lack of probity or fair dealing to member in the matter of his proprietary right as a shareholder. Persons concerned with the management of the company's affairs must in connection therewith be guilty of fraud, misfeasance or misconduct towards the members. It does not include mere domestic disputes between directors and members or lack of confidence between one section of members and another section in the matter of policy or administration. Much less it covers

---

45, where MITRA J observed: "The fact that the directors are accused of an offence or that investigation is being made or even if there was a conviction on a criminal complaint would be no ground for taking action under Ss. 397 and 398. Those matters are entirely foreign to company law and administration and beyond the ambit of the jurisdiction the Company Court exercises.... In the instant case there is no deadlock, the application is not one for winding up, nor is the company a private company. It is a public company in which outsiders hold a substantial block of shares and so the principle, that lack of confidence among the directors in a private company resulting in a deadlock is a ground for a winding up order on the just and equitable ground, cannot be applied herein where the special discretionary jurisdiction of the Court (now CLB) under Ss. 397 and 398 has been invoked."

Another important decision is *Rights and Issues Investment Trust Ltd* v *Stylo Shoes Ltd*, [1964] 3 All ER 628: [1965] 1 Comp LJ 234, where PENNYCUICK J observed: "... as there was no principle of law that prevented the members of a company from altering the voting rights attached to shares provided that the alteration was sanctioned by the members in accordance with the constitution of the company, in good faith and for the benefit of the company as a whole, the Court would not grant interlocutory injunction sought." This was a petition under S. 210 of the [English] Companies Act, 1948 (now Ss. 459-461 of the Act of 1985).

See also *New Standard Coal Co (P) Ltd, Re*, [1964] 2 Comp LJ 184, Cal; *Lundie Bros, Re*, [1965] 2 All ER 692: [1966] 1 Comp LJ 30; *Mehta Bros (P) Ltd* v *Calcutta Landing & Shipping Co*, (1970) 40 Comp Cas 119 Cal, a catalogue of vague charges. The shifting of the registered office of a company from Calcutta to Hyderabad at the instance of A. P. State Financial Corpn was not an oppression. The company had its factory in A. P. *Pramod Kumar Mittal* v *Southern Steel Ltd*, (1980) 50 Comp Cas 555 Cal. *K.G. Raghavan* v *Foreword Advertising and Marketing (P) Ltd*, (2002) 111 Comp Cas 784 CLB, default in holding meetings and filing accounts, not acts of oppression, relief available under other sections.

50. *Shri Ramdas Motor Transport Ltd* v *Karedla Suryanarayana*, (2002) 110 Comp Cas 193 AP.

51. *Ibid.* Majority approval of such conduct is not a justification. Those in control can be directed to furnish information to which the shareholders have a legitimate right.

52. *Ibid.* Fabricated resolutions would be oppressive and contrary to public interest. *Pushpa Katoch* v *Manu Maharani Hotels Ltd*, (2002) 110 Comp Cas 584 CLB, preferential allotment without general body approval of the public company, oppression.

mere private animosity between members and directors."[53] This statement has been cited with approval in *Kalinga Tubes Ltd v Shanti Prasad Jain*,[54] where MISRA J of the Orissa High Court dismissed a petition under the section and his decision was affirmed by the Supreme Court in *Shanti Prasad Jain v Kalinga Tubes Ltd.*[55]

A private company consisted of three groups of shareholders, the petitioner and the two respondents holding shares in equal proportion and with equal representation on the board. They had agreed in writing to maintain this equilibrium. But no such agreement was incorporated in the articles of the company. Subsequently, in order to obtain certain loan facilities, the company was converted into a public company and it was proposed to issue 39,000 more shares. Ordinarily, according to Section 81 such new shares should have been offered to the existing shareholders. But the majority of the shareholders consisting of the two respondents' groups passed a resolution to offer these shares to outsiders, which was accordingly done. The petitioner contended that the allottees were friends of the majority group and the allotment had been made purposely to them with the mala fide intention to increase their voting strength and to squeeze out the petitioner.

This, he contended, was oppression within the meaning of Section 397. He relied upon an observation in *Piercy v S. Mills and Co Ltd*,[56] to the effect that "if shares were issued to the public with the immediate object of controlling the greater number of shares in the company and of obtaining the necessary statutory majority for passing a special resolution, then it will not be a valid *bona fide* exercise of the powers."[57] The question, therefore,

---

53. See *Kalinga Tubes Ltd v Shanti Prasad Jain*, [1964] 1 Comp LJ 117, where this statement of law has been cited by MISRA J of the Orissa High Court, at pp 146-147 from *Scottish Coop Wholesale Society v Meyer*, [1958] 3 All ER 66: 1959 AC 324 and *H. R. Harmer Ltd, Re*, [1958] 3 All ER 689: [1959] 1 WLR 62; *Devaraj Dhanram v Firebricks and Potteries (P) Ltd*, (1991) 4 Kant LJ 148, allegations bald, not proved; mere lack of confidence. *Desein (P) Ltd v Elecktrim India Ltd*, (2003) 116 Comp Cas 341 CLB, no proof was there of diversion of funds, not even when a new company was formed.
54. [1964] 1 Comp LJ 117.
55. [1965] 1 Comp LJ 193: AIR 1965 SC 1535: (1965) 35 Comp Cas 351. *See also V. M. Rao v Rajeshwari Balkrishan*, [1986] 1 Comp LJ 1 Mad.
56. [1920] 1 Ch 77.
57. *See also Hogg v Cramphorn Ltd*, [1966] 3 All ER 420: [1967] Ch 254; noted (1967) 30 Mod LR 77 and *Bamford v Bamford*, [1969] 2 WLR 1107: [1969] 1 All ER 969: [1970] Ch 212 and further still *Clemens v Clemens Bros Ltd*, [1976] 2 All ER 268 Ch D. Increasing majority by 95% by changing articles was held to be oppression in the circumstances, *Akbarali v Konkan Chemicals (P) Ltd*, (1997) 88 Comp Cas 245 CLB. The act and policy of materially reducing the voting strength of the petitioners by making a new issue and allotting it to the controlling family was held to be an oppressive conduct; the company was in no need of further capital, *Farhat Sheikh v Esemen Metalo Chemicals (P) Ltd*, (1995) 16 Corpt LA 147 CLB: (1996) 87 Comp Cas 290 CLB; *Farhat Sheikh v Detinners (P) Ltd*, (1996) 87 Comp Cas 290 CLB. *Pearson Education Inc v Prentice-Hall of India (P) Ltd*, (2007) 136 Comp Cas 211 CLB, increase of capital not for any *bona fide* reason, set aside, further issue, notice not sent at the correct address registered with the company, unfair and oppressive, grievance about non-receipt of notice, cannot be made after a long period of time.

was whether the resolution offering the shares to the outsiders was passed in good faith for the benefit of the company or merely to capture an absolute majority and to squeeze out the petitioner.

BARMAN J held that this conduct of the majority amounted to an act of oppression of the minority. But, on appeal, his judgment was reversed. MISRA J of the Orissa High Court who delivered the leading judgment, was of the opinion that "the private agreement between the parties to maintain the equilibrium was not binding on the company". "The fact that the affairs of the company were managed with holding of shares in equal proportion amongst the three groups for a period of four years by itself cannot create a right in favour of the petitioner that it must continue in the same manner even when the company becomes public. To compel the majority shareholders, in these circumstances, to offer the new shares only to the existing shareholders would, far from being an oppression of the minority, amount to depriving the majority of a right conferred upon them by Section 81 entitling them to direct free issue of shares. It would also not be compatible with dynamic concept of industrial expansion. For instance, the expansion scheme would require large capital in crores and any one of the groups may not be in a position to subscribe its proportionate shares as any one or both or residual groups can do. The balance is bound to be disturbed and equilibrium lost even if the affairs of the company would be conducted wholly *bona fide*."[58] The issue of rights shares has become a well known technique for manipulating internal positions. When rights shares are issued simply for manipulative purposes, they can rightly be described, as has been done by a commentator, as "Wrongful Issues."[59] The courts have not been

---

58. At p 134. S. 81 was amended in 1960. Now to exclude the right of pre-emption of the existing shareholders, a special resolution is necessary and if only an ordinary resolution has been passed, prior approval of the Central Government must be obtained.

For a criticism of this decision *see* P. S. Sangal, *Abuse of Authority by a Majority of Shareholders in a Company*, Journal of the Indian Law Institute, Vol 10, (1964) 381 at 394-409. Also *see*, B. H. Macpherson, *Oppression of Minority Shareholders, Part I: Common Law Relief*, 36 Australian Law Journal 404, *Part II: Statuory Relief*, at 427; K.S.N. Murthy, *Minority Protection under Company Law*, [1964] 1 Comp LJ 113 (Journal Section); series of three lectures by Professor Louis Loss on "*The Protection of Investors*", delivered at the University of Witwaterstand, Johannesburg and published in (1963) LXXX South African Law Journal. They are entitled: *The Role of the Government*, 53; *The Role of the Accountant and The Role of the Courts*, 372; M. B. Rao: *Oppression of Minorities and Mismanagement*, [1965] 2 Comp LJ 43 (Journal Section); S. R. Chowdhary: *Freezeout Problems in Corporation Law*, CURRENT PROBLEMS OF CORPORATE LAW, MANAGEMENT AND PRACTICE, Indian Law Institute, (1964) 273.

59. Susan J Burridge, *Wrongful Rights Issues*, (1981) 44 Mod LR 40. Where the capital of a private company was increased without any explanation whatsoever and also in violation of articles, the court agreed with the petitioner that the purpose was to increase numerical strength and to reduce the petitioner to minority and the court ordered the most appropriate relief of requiring the new issue to be offered to existing shareholders, *Rashmi Seth* v *Chemon (India) (P) Ltd*, [1992] 3 Comp LJ 89 CLB: (1995) 82 Comp Cas 563; *Ashok V. Doshi* v *Doshi Time Industries (P) Ltd*, (2001) 104 Comp Cas 306 CLB. Non-allotment of agreed shares to the petitioner in the joint venture company in the nature of a quasi-partnership in which the petitioner had made an equal contribution, amounted to oppression.

able to come to the rescue of the affected shareholder because they are often not able to isolate the manipulative intention from the ostensibly declared purpose of the "*bona fide* interest of the company". It has, therefore, been suggested that:

> The question which arises is sometimes not a question of the interests of the company at all, but a question of what is fair as between different classes of shareholders. Where such a case arises some other test than that of interests of the company must be applied.[60]

The Supreme Court has suggested a way out by providing compensation to the injured shareholder. The case before the court was *Needle Industries (India) Ltd* v *Needle Industries Newey (India) Holding Ltd.*[61]

> The articles of a private company contained a clause that when the directors decided to increase the capital of the company by the issue of new shares the same should be offered to the shareholders proportionately and, if they failed to take, they may be offered to others in such manner as may be most beneficial to the company. The company was a wholly owned subsidiary of an English company. Government of India adopted a policy of diluting foreign holdings. The company accordingly issued new shares to its employees and relatives reducing the foreign holding to sixty per cent. When Section 43-A came into operation, the company became a deemed public company because more than 25% of its share capital was held by a body corporate. The company, however, chose to remain a private company for all other purposes. The leader of the Indian 40% holding was the chief executive and the managing director of the company. The company was further required to reduce its foreign holding to 40%. At this stage the English and Indian blocks developed a difference. The English block wanted that the 20% reduction of their holding should be allotted to one of the Indian companies in which they had substantial interest. A meeting of the company's board of directors, on the contrary, adopted the policy of issuing new rights shares to the existing members, which the English

---

60. See *ibid*, citing LATHAM CJ in *Mills* v *Mills*, 60 Com LR 150, 164. Asking members to buy more shares is not oppression in itself, unless there was some oblique motive, *Jacques Taru Lalvani* v *JBA Printing Inks Ltd*, (1997) 88 Comp Cas 759 Bom and then offering new shares to others on the members' failure to take them is also not oppression in itself. *Shantidevi Pratap Singh Gaekwad* v *Sangram Singh P. Gaekwad*, [1996] 1 Comp LJ 72 Guj. Offering new allotment to promoters at less premium and charging more premium from other members was not allowed to be questioned by those who participated in the process and took their proportion, *N. Jagan* v *Investment Trust of India Ltd*, (1996) 85 Comp Cas 75 Mad. All issues must be attended to, validity of rights issue and if certain investments were involved here, *Kaushiklal Parikh* v *Mafatlal Industries Ltd*, (1995) 17 Corpt LA 102 Guj; *Shrihari Rao* v *Gopal Automotive Ltd*, (1998) 30 Corpt LA 373 CLB, directors to decide on corporate needs of more capital and also matters of dividend distribution.

61. (1981) 3 SCC 333: (1981) 51 Comp Cas 743: AIR 1981 SC 1298; *Vijay M. Shah* v *Flex Industries Ltd*, (1996) 61 Del LT 378, matters of mismanagement in rights issue should be questioned under Ss. 397, 398.

company would not be able to subscribe and thereby its holding would be reduced to 40%. Under the resolution 16 days' time had to be given to the members to take their proportion. The letter offering its proportion to the holding company was sent only 4 days before the last date and it received the letter after the date for exercising the option had already expired. Similarly, the notice of the meeting of directors for completing the allotment was sent to them with so short a gap of time that they received it in England only on the day on which the meeting was being held in India. Neither was it able to exercise the option of buying its block of rights shares nor was it able to attend the crucial meeting of the board. Its block of shares was allotted to Indian shareholders.

The holding company complained of oppression on these facts. But the court was not convinced that there was any such thing as a continuous policy of oppression. The ultimate purpose of the scheme was Indianisation to the extent of 60%. This could be achieved either by buying the excess holding of the English company or by increasing the Indian shareholding. The latter course was adopted in the interests of the company as it would make available to the company extra capital. The fact that proper notice was not given, no doubt, deprived the English company of its opportunity of participating in the rights issue. But the facts were such that even if proper notice was given, the English company could neither have subscribed for its proportion nor renounced it to anyone else. There was no right in the company's articles in favour of any member enabling him to renounce his rights shares in favour of others. In the case of a private company there simply cannot be the right of renouncing rights shares in favour of nominees because that would make it impossible for the company to restrict the number of members. The real loss suffered by the holding company was the loss in terms of the market value of the shares which fell to its share. The market value of the shares was much higher than their nominal value. The allotment was at nominal value. The loss of the holding company was the "unjust enrichment" of those whom the block of rights shares was allotted which, but for the policy restriction, belonged to that company. The Supreme Court accordingly held that the Indian allottees of those shares must compensate the holding company to the extent to which the market value was in excess of the nominal value.[62]

---

62. Increasing capital without any need may amount to an oppressive technique. Where this was so, the Company Law Board ordered the appointment of an interim administration in supersession of the board of directors. *R. N. Jalan* v *Deccan Enterprises (P) Ltd*, (1992) 75 Comp Cas 417 AP; *Rashmi Seth* v *Chemon (India) (P) Ltd*, [1992] 3 Comp LJ 89 CLB: (1995) 82 Comp Cas 563, rights issue allotted in violation of the company's articles, set aside. *Rashmi Seth* v *Tillsoil Farms (P) Ltd*, [1992] 3 Comp LJ 126 CLB: (1995) 82 Comp Cas 409 CLB, increasing majority by fabrication, set aside. Where the company was in genuine need of more capital and the requirements of S. 81 for excluding present shareholders were also satisfied, a complaint by the petitioning shareholder that his holding was thereby diminished was held to be not sustainable. *Standard Industries Ltd* v *Mafatlal Services Ltd*, [1992] 2 Comp LJ 113 CLB. Three warring

Dealing with the argument that the illegal nature of the board meeting should itself be an indication of the repressive policy, CHANDRACHUD CJ said:[63]

> The question sometimes arises as to whether an action in contravention of law is *per se* oppressive. It is said, as was done by one of us, BHAGWATI J in a decision of the Gujarat High Court[64] that "a resolution passed by the directors may be perfectly legal and yet oppressive, and conversely a resolution which is in contravention of the law may be in the interests of the shareholders and the company."

Two English cases, namely, *Five Minute Car Wash Service Ltd, Re,*[65] and *Jermyn Street Turkish Baths Ltd, Re,*[66] have further narrowed down the scope of relief under the section. *Five Minute Car Wash, Re,* the catalogue of charges was: (1) valid debts had not been paid, highly questionable debts had been paid; (2) the company failed to carry out its undertakings with petrol suppliers forcing them to refuse supplies to the company; (3) inefficient staff was being maintained; and (4) car washing machinery was ordered without testing. The court conceded that these charges showed that the majority shareholder was "unwise, inefficient and careless in the performance of his duties",[67] but these things did not establish that he was oppressive towards any particular members. In the *Turkish Baths* case the story was like this:

> A private company consisted of only two shareholders holding equal shares. One of them transferred his shares to one Mrs *P* and the other died. The condition of the company was precarious. But Mrs *P* brought

---

members of a company were brothers, nobody was prepared to sell out, one of them made further issue of capital allotting the whole to himself thus increasing his majority, the CLB said that such an act is oppressive but because all of them were interlocked in a civil suit where the same issues were involved, it would not intervene, *Binod Kumar Agarwal* v *Ringtong Tea Co Ltd,* (1995) 16 Corpt LA 128 CLB. *Shankar Sundaram* v *Amalgamated Ltd,* (2002) 111 Comp Cas 252 Mad, orders can be passed against a subsidiary company though the petition was only against the holding company.

63. (1981) 3 SCC 333 at p 367. The mere illegality of an act is not by itself an act of oppression. *Allianz Securities Ltd* v *Regal Industries Ltd,* (2000) 25 SCL 349 CLB. A conduct in breach of the principles of company law is not itself causative of unfair prejudice, *Anderson* v *Hogg,* [2000] SLT 634 Scotland.

64. *Sheth Mohan Lal Ganpatram* v *Sayaji Jubilee Cotton & Jute Mills Ltd,* (1964) 34 Comp Cas 777: (1964) 5 Guj LR 804: AIR 1965 Guj 96. Followed in *Kaushiklal Parikh* v *Mafatlal Industries Ltd,* (1995) 17 Corpt LA 102 Guj where a civil suit was allowed to test the validity of a board resolution though it was oppressive to shareholders for which special jurisdiction of CLB is prescribed. *Jayanthi R. Padukone* v *ICDS Ltd,* AIR 1994 Kant 354, right of shareholders to approach a civil court for the purpose of removing the chairman of the company cannot be taken away by the fact that the matter also involves things in the nature of oppression and mismanagement for which there is special jurisdiction.

65. [1966] 1 WLR 745: [1966] 1 All ER 242.

66. [1971] 3 All ER 184 CA.

67. See BUCKLEY J's judgment at p 752. For criticism *see* H. Rajak, *Oppression of Minority Shareholders,* (1972) 35 Mod LR 156.

back the company on its feet through further investments for which some shares and a debenture were allotted to her. The personal representatives of the deceased shareholder alleged oppression on the following grounds: (1) allotment of shares was a breach of duty; (2) directors' remuneration was fixed by the board and not by the shareholders as provided in the company's article; (3) notice of meetings was not given to the representatives; (4) excessive remuneration was paid to Mrs *P*; and (5) no dividends were ever declared.

Theoretically these charges showed serious irregularities, but the court could not have ignored the practical side of Mrs *P*'s successes. Commenting on the case D. Prentice observes:

> Mrs *P* had nursed the company from bankruptcy to comfortable profitability, she had devoted all her time to its affairs, and she had loaned capital to it at a time when the estate of *L* (the deceased shareholder) refused to do so. *L*'s representatives also enjoyed the benefits of her efforts as the market value of their shares was thereby increased.[68]

Where in the case of a private company the understanding was that parity of shareholding was to be maintained, it was held that the attempt of one group to take over the company by increasing its shares would entitle the affected members to proceed under the section as also under Section 433 for a winding up order.[69]

Where one of the director-member was excluded from the new allotment, the CLB ordered for proportionate allotment to him.[70] Transfer of shares within the same group without violation of any terms in the articles

---

68. D. Prentice, *Protection of Minority Shareholders: S. 210 of the Companies Act, 1948*, (1952) CURRENT LEGAL PROBLEMS, 124 at p 143.

69. *Bhaskar Stoneware Pipes (P) Ltd* v *R. N. Bhaskar*, (1988) 63 Comp Cas 184 Del; *Rajender Nath Bhaskar* v *Bhaskar Stoneware Pipes (P) Ltd*, [1990] 1 Comp LJ 351: (1990) 68 Comp Cas 256 Del; followed in *Margaret T. Desor* v *World Wide Agencies (P) Ltd*, (1989) 66 Comp Cas 5 Del, on appeal to Supreme Court *World Wide Agencies (P) Ltd* v *Margaret*, (1990) 1 SCC 536: 1990 SCC (Tax) 171: (1990) 67 Comp Cas 607 SC: AIR 1990 SC 737: [1990] 1 Comp LJ 208. An attempt to appoint one more director in the case of a private company without fulfilling the requirements of the company's articles which prescribed a special resolution was held to be oppressive of the minority shareholder, *V. B. Balasundaram* v *New Theatre Carnatic Talkies (P) Ltd*, (1993) 77 Comp Cas 324 Mad; *Farhat Sheikh* v *Esemen Metalo Chemicals (P) Ltd*, (1996) 87 Comp Cas 290 CLB, inadequate notice of shareholders' meeting; *Allianz Securities Ltd* v *Regal Industries Ltd*, (2000) 37 CLA 250, importune notice of Board meeting when a director was abroad. *Dipak G. Mehta* v *Anupar Chemicals (India) Ltd*, (1999) 98 Comp Cas 575 CLB, further issue and allotment of shares for the benefit of a group of shareholders, held oppression. *Praful M. Patel* v *Wonderworld Electrodes (P) Ltd*, (2003) 115 Comp Cas 377 CLB, issues of further capital exclusively to the minority, oppressive, filing of winding up petition not a bar to a petition under S. 397. *Kshounish Chowdhury* v *Kero Rajendra Monolithics Ltd*, (2002) 110 Comp Cas 441 CLB, another case of manipulated increase of shareholding to the disadvantage of the minority group.

70. *Hillcrest Realty SDN BHD* v *Hotel Queen Road (P) Ltd*, (2006) 133 Comp Cas 742 CLB. The allotment was otherwise valid because the company was in need of funds.

of association was held to be no oppression.[71] An allotment of shares to one group giving it time to pay application money and to the other group by using the amount lying with the company to their credit and refunding the balance amount without any demand was held to be not a *bona fide* exercise of power. The allotment was set aside.[72] Preference shareholders cannot complain of oppression by reason of allotment of shares to equity shareholders.[73]

Existence of Alternative Relief

Where there were allegations of violation of foreign exchange regulations and improper accounting, the alternative relief of appointing inspectors under Section 209-A was provided.[74] In this case there was the further allegation that auditors were not appointed at the general meeting. No relief was allowed under these sections because this was a matter to be brought to the notice of the Central Government which alone could take care of it. The complaining shareholders-directors had not raised any objection at the meeting itself and the same auditors were reappointed at a subsequent meeting.[75] It was further held in this case that the orders of investigation are not generally passed under these sections particularly when it is the matter of a closely held company.[76] Another matter which was directed to be referred to the Central Government was that of appointment of managing director in another company which had to be passed at a meeting of the Board was dealt with by a resolution passed by circulation.[77] An objection of over-drawing of remuneration by the managing director which should have been raised at the meeting itself was not so raised. No relief was allowed on this point under this jurisdiction.[78]

Oppression of Majority

It should not, however, be supposed that these special remedies against oppression or mismanagement are available only to minorities. "In an appropriate case, if the court is satisfied about the acts of oppression or mismanagement, relief can be granted even if the application is made by a majority, who have been rendered completely ineffective by the wrongful acts of a minority group." A petition is not liable to be struck out as showing no reasonable cause of action just only because it is filed by a majority

71. *Hillcrest Realty SDN BHD* v *Hotel Queen Road (P) Ltd*, (2006) 133 Comp Cas 742 CLB; see also *N. Kuberan* v *Monarch Steels (India) Ltd*, (2006) 130 Comp Cas 109 CLB, persons wrongfully inducted as directors restrained from acting as such.
72. *A. Ravishankar Prasad* v *Prasad Productions (P) Ltd*, (2007) 135 Comp Cas 416 CLB.
73. *Hillcrest Realty SDN BHD* v *Hotel Queen Road (P) Ltd*, (2006) 133 Comp Cas 742 CLB.
74. *Desein (P) Ltd* v *Elecktrim India Ltd*, (2003) 116 Comp Cas 341 CLB.
75. *Ibid.*
76. *Ibid.*
77. *Ibid.*
78. *Ibid.*

shareholder.[79] Accordingly, a relief under the section was allowed to a majority group by MITRA J of the Calcutta High Court in *Sindri Iron Foundry (P) Ltd, Re.*[80] The learned judge observed that "if the court finds that the company's interest is being seriously prejudiced by the activities of one or the other group of shareholders, that two different registered offices at two different addresses have been set up, that two rival boards are holding meetings, that the company's business, property and assets have passed to the hands of unauthorised persons who have taken wrongful possession and who claim to be the shareholders and directors, there is no reason why the court should not make appropriate orders to put an end to such matters."

The same fact-situation was presented before a bench of the Calcutta High Court in *Ramashankar Prasad v Sindri Iron Foundry (P) Ltd.*[81] Referring to the argument that the right to apply under Section 397 or 398 must be confined to cases where the complaint is by a minority against the majority and not *vice versa*, MITTER J said:

"Section 399 is a code by itself as to the qualification necessary for application under Sections 399 and 398. I see no reason for holding that Section 399 was only aimed at finding the lower limit of qualification of any shareholder or group of shareholders complaining of oppression and mismanagement. If the Legislature has fixed a lower limit but no upper limit and if the object of the section be to prevent mischief, I see no reason why an upper limit should be implied so as to bring the section in line with the English section.[82] If the section is of a remedial nature, its proper construction should be to give the words their widest amplitude."

Referring to the argument that the majority could always call a meeting and put things in order by passing resolutions, the learned Judge said:

"The facts in this case show very clearly, that there is no chance of redress in the domestic forum of the company. If a board meeting was

---

79. *Baltic Real Estate Ltd (No 1), Re,* (1993) BCLC 498 Ch D; *Baltic Real Estate Ltd (No 2), Re,* (1993) BCLC 503 Ch D, the court adding that things like removing a director from office, which can be set right by using majority power, should better be accomplished at that level.

80. (1963) 69 CWN 118. *See* further, *Sebastian v City Hospital (P) Ltd,* (1985) 57 Comp Cas 453 Ker; *Laxmi Film Lab & Studio (P) Ltd,* (1984) 56 Comp Cas 110 Guj.

81. [1966] 1 Comp LJ 310.

82. S. 210 of the (English) Companies Act, 1948, appears under the heading *Minorities,* but the word "minority" is nowhere mentioned in the text of the section. Professor Gower's opinion, as expressly adopted in some cases, is that "the draftsman has rightly recognised that oppression may be exercised by those in control even though they lack in majority holding and that the section affords protection in such cases". PRINCIPLES OF MODERN COMPANY LAW, 599 (3rd Edn 1969). The relevant foot note cites the following authorities: *Associated Tool Industries Ltd, Re,* [1964] ALR 73 at p 82 (Australia); *Benjamin v Elysium Investments (P) Ltd,* [1960] 3 SA 467 (South Africa); *H. R. Harmer Ltd, Re,* [1958] 3 All ER 689: [1959] 1 WLR 62. It was, therefore, futile to have argued on the basis of the heading of the English section that relief was intended to be confined to minorities. Now Ss. 459-461 of the (English) Act of 1985 use the expression "unfair prejudice".

to be called, one group would contend that there were five directors, whereas the other group would urge that there were seven. If a meeting of the shareholders was to be convened, according to one group there would be only sixteen shareholders, while according to the other the number would exceed twenty-five.... There would be complete chaos and confusion....[83]"

Even where the whole number of members is suffering, relief may be allowed to the complaining member because some members may suffer more than others may do. Where the complaint was on the basis of an unfairly low dividend and though all members may suffer alike, the court said that the word "interests" is a wider term than "rights" and that the members of a company may have varying interests though their right might be the same. A course of conduct may affect all the members equally and all may be prejudiced, yet some of them only may be prejudiced unfairly. Low dividends may cause extraordinary prejudice to some members only.[84]

In exceptional cases legitimate expectations might arise on the part of the petitioner outside the terms of formal agreements entered into between the parties.[85] An agreement to conduct the affairs of the company in a particular manner may be outside the articles. It will support a petition if the agreement is broken by those conducting the affairs of the company.[86]

Even where majority shareholders are suffering at the hands of the minority, the Courts are usually very reluctant in ordering the majority to sell out to the minority. Such an order may be passed only exceptionally.[87] Generally, the minority shareholders will be required to sell to the majority.[88]

---

83. *See* also *Albert David Ltd, Re*, (1964) 68 CWN 163 where it was observed that "it is against the principles of company law that the minority should carry on the management without any election as provided in the Act and the majority of the shareholders should be kept out of the management". *Combust Technic (P) Ltd, Re*, [1993] 1 Comp LJ 61 Cal, though it is unusual to ask the majority to sell itself to the minority, a petition by the majority is maintainable. *See* the contrary observation of the Delhi High Court in *Suresh Kumar Sanghi* v *Supreme Motors Ltd*, (1983) 54 Comp Cas 235 Del.

84. *Abbey Leisure Ltd, Re*, 1989 BCLC 619 Ch D, not following *A Company, Re, (No 00370 of 1987)*, [1988] 1 WLR 1068, where an amendment was not allowed to add the fact of low dividends to the petition. *Ashoka Betelnut Co (P) Ltd* v *Chandrakanth (MK)*, (1997) 88 Comp Cas 274 Mad: (1997) 25 Corpt LA 146 Mad, continuous losses and therefore no dividends, minority's dissatisfaction, unsubstantiated allegations of financial propriety, further issue of shares for business needs and no ulterior motive, no relief under S. 397.

85. *A Company, (002015 of 1996), Re*, (1997) 2 BCLC 61.

86. *Anderson* v *Hogg*, [2000] SLT 634 (Scotland).

87. *Deepak Lohia* v *Kamrup Developers (P) Ltd*, (2003) 116 Comp Cas 188 CLB, a private memorandum of agreement not enshrined in the company's articles not taken to be binding but could provide some help in moulding relief, manipulations had become irretrievably deep to be cured and, therefore, directions were issued for purchase of shares of majority group by minority group.

88. *Mahabir Pd Jalan* v *Bajrang Pd Jalan*, [1999] 2 Comp LJ 71 Cal.

"Oppression qua Members"

The complaining member must show that he is suffering from oppression in his capacity as member and not in any other capacity. For example, in *Lundie Bros, Re*,[89] a minority shareholder of a private company was removed from his position as a working director. As an ordinary shareholder he would have gained nothing as the company had never paid any dividend, directors' remuneration being the only return on investment. Yet he could not complain of it because he had suffered as a director and not as a member. This result has been criticised as being unrealistic.[90] Directorship is one of the privileges of membership. Any deprivation of this privilege is a kind of oppression as member.[91]

Removing a member from directorship is often a symbol of breakdown of relation of which the only possible solution is that one faction should move out of the company and the other should pay it out. It will then be a question not so much of deprivation from directorship or from any other place of profit as of which faction should move out and what shall be the procedure of valuation.[92] A member, however, will not be permitted to take advantage of his own misconduct first in inducing breakdown and then of forcing the other to buy him out.[93] The member who has lost directorship and, therefore, control

---

89. [1965] 2 All ER 692: [1966] 1 Comp LJ 30. *Jaladhar Chakraborty* v *Power Tools & Appliances Co Ltd*, (1994) 79 Comp Cas 505, low dividend which did not affect the value of the petitioner's shares, neither oppression nor mismanagement.

90. *See* D. Prentice, *Protection of Minority Shareholders, S. 210 of the Companies Act*, 1948, (1972) CURRENT LEGAL PROBLEMS 124, 131-132. *A Company, Re, ex p Schwarcz (No 2)*, 1989 BCLC 427 Ch D, where the total strength of the minority (father and son) shareholders was only 5.5%, refusal of directorship was held to be not unfairly prejudicial because they had no vested right to be directors.

91. *Quinlan* v *Essex Hinge Co Ltd*, (1996) 2 BCLC 47 Ch D, a shareholder-cum-director was summarily dismissed from production directorship without any justification. The majority shareholder was ordered to purchase his shares without any discount because of the minority shareholding. In the context of a small private company, the expectations of shareholders are not necessarily confined to the constitution of the company. *Kilpest (P) Ltd* v *Shekhar Mehra*, (1996) 10 SCC 696: (1996) 87 Comp Cas 615 and *Vijay Krishna Jaidka* v *Jaidka Motor Co Ltd*, (1996) 23 Corpt LA 289 CLB, partnership principles become applicable, breakdown of confidence and deadlock may make out a case for relief. See further, *Karedla Suryanarayana* v *R. M. Transport Ltd*, (1999) 98 Comp Cas 518 CLB, selection of dealers for the company's products cannot be a cause of complaint in itself unless favouritism could be shown due to other factors, which were not proved here. *Dalip Singh Sachar* v *Maa Karni Coal Carriers (P) Ltd*, (2006) 130 Comp Cas 641 CLB, only membership rights can be agitated, but where company is in essence a partnership, equal participation in management becomes a membership right, removing director without justification (unproved non-attendance of meetings), petition lies for relief. *Pearson Education Inc* v *Prentice Hall of India (P) Ltd*, (2007) 136 Comp Cas 211 CLB, contractual rights cannot be agitated.

92. An apprehension on the part of a director that his distributorship of the company's products was likely to be terminated was held to be not a matter coming within the special jurisdiction for prevention of oppression. Even otherwise the court cannot interfere in the matter of appointment and termination of distributorship, *M. L. Thukral* v *Krone Communications Ltd*, (1996) 86 Comp Cas 648 Kant.

93. *A Company, Re, (No 004475 of 1982)*, 1983 Ch 178; *A Company, Re, (No 007623 of 1984)*, 1986 BCLC 362; *A Company, Re, (No 004377 of 1986)*, [1987] 1 WLR 102. For a view of

to the extent that he has to seek the help of law, the legal choice would be to ask him to take his satisfaction and move out. A minority member cannot be given the privilege of driving out the majority shareholder.[94] The only question will be that of regulating the valuation of shares.

In a small private company where the principles relating to quasi-partnership apply, there was an understanding for equal participation in management. The articles of the company stipulated quorum of three directors at board meetings. A director was removed when one director had left and the meeting was without quorum. This was held to be an oppressive conduct to the member-director.[95]

The questions of rights and interests of members as members can be made the subject-matter of a proceeding under the section and not matters arising out of commercial relations of a member with the company.[96]

Oppression in Conduct of Affairs

The legitimate expectations with which a person joins a company as a member and denial of which may amount to oppression must relate to the affairs of the company. The expectation that shares would be allowed to be transferred in breach of agreement or articles has not been held to be a legitimate expectation. The compulsion that shares must be transferred within the framework of the articles is not an oppression.[97] Where the objects of the company were defeated by a highhanded majority by shifting from construction and hoteling to film making the court said that it was an act straight against the expectations of the shareholders in joining the company. It amounted to oppression. The court ordered the majority group to buy out the minority at a value which was fixed by the court by reference to the cost inflation index issued by the Central Government for computation of capital gains.[98]

---

recent trends on the subject, *see* D. W. Fox, *Compulsory Purchase of Shares in a Private Company Some Recent Developments*, 1987 JBL 276.

94. *A Company, Re, (No 006834 of 1988)*, (1988) 5 BCLC 218. *Synchron Machine Tools (P) Ltd* v *U. M. Suresh Rao*, (1994) 79 Comp Cas 868, outster from directorship, the court directed majority to buy out minority. *Farhat Sheikh* v *Esemen Metalo Chemicals (P) Ltd*, (1995) 16 Corpt LA 147 CLB: (1996) 87 Comp Cas 290 CLB, direction to buy out minority shareholders at a price to be determined by accountant.

95. *Badri Nath Galhotra* v *Aanaam (P) Ltd*, (2007) 135 Comp Cas 534 CLB.

96. *Anil Gupta* v *Mirai Auto Industries (P) Ltd*, (2003) 113 Comp Cas 63 CLB, the subject-matter of the dispute was the termination of the petitioners sole selling agency.

97. *Leeds United Holdings plc, Re*, (1996) 2 BCLC 545 Ch D.

98. *C. N. Shetty* v *Hillock Hotel (P) Ltd*, (1996) 87 Comp Cas 1 AP; *D.K. Chatterji* v *Rapti Supertonics (P) Ltd*, (2003) 114 Comp Cas 265 CLB, payment shown in the account books to a proprietary concern whose business was taken over by the company was held to be not a siphoning of funds. In this case, the lenders were not able to prove that they had asked the company for converting their loans into equity. There could be no finding of oppression on that ground. *C.N. Shetty* v *Hillock Hotels Ltd*, (2001) 104 Comp Cas 722 AP, raising capital through allotment of shares excluding an equal shareholder and that too for an *ultra vires* purpose, oppressive.

Private Agreement amongst Members as to Share Transfer

A private agreement between members of a family as to share transfers which was not incorporated in the company articles was held to have no binding force on the company and members in their relations with the company.[1]

Facts must Justify Winding Up

The facts alleged in the petition must justify a winding up order under the "just and equitable" clause of Section 433.[2] The petitioner cannot seek the relief of an order of winding up in the same petition.[3] A need for an order of winding up can arise when there is a deadlock on account of more or less equal shareholding or when there is lack of probity or no hope or possibility of smooth and efficient running. Where there is not so, no remedy under Section 397 would be available. Events subsequent to the petition cannot be taken into account for this purpose.[4]

This link with desirability of winding up may prevent relief in some deserving cases. This is so because winding up on the "just and equitable" ground itself is beset with many technical requirements. For example, in *Bellador Silk Ltd, Re,*[5] the petition failed because the petitioner could not prove that there would be sufficient assets left with the company for distribution among shareholders after paying off the creditors.[6] The difficulty of obtaining a winding up order is shown by cases like *Westbourne Galleries Ltd, Re,*[7] where a director of a private company which was very much like an incorporated partnership, was deprived by the majority of his directorship, thus making his existence in the company quite

---

1. *Pushpa Katoch* v *Manu Maharani Hotels Ltd*, (2006) 131 Comp Cas 42 Del.
2. *Hanuman Prasad Bagri* v *Bagress Cereals (P) Ltd*, (2001) 4 SCC 420: AIR 2001 SC 1416, the petitioner must make out a case of winding up on just and equitable ground. The High Court's view that the termination of directorship of the petitioner was not such a ground was upheld. Misappropriation of funds by directors may not permit the extreme remedy of winding up and so no relief under the category of oppression or mismanagement. *Palghat Exports (P) Ltd* v *T. V. Chandran*, (1994) 79 Comp Cas 213 Ker. The Supreme Court has emphasised that normally the winding up of the concerned company should not be ordered in the exercise of these powers. *Kilpest (P) Ltd* v *Shekhar Mehra*, (1996) 10 SCC 696: (1996) 87 Comp Cas 615. *Senthil Kumar* v *Sudha Mills (P) Ltd*, (1996) AIHC 5230 Mad, consideration of a winding up petition should be deferred till petition under Ss. 397-398 pending before CLB; but it is not a bar to winding up proceedings, *A. K. Puri* v *Devi Dass, Gopal Kishan Ltd*, (1995) 17 Corpt LA 1 J&K.
3. *D.K. Chatterji* v *Rapti Supertonics (P) Ltd*, (2003) 114 Comp Cas 265 CLB.
4. *Ashoka Betelnut Co (P) Ltd* v *Chandrakanth (MK)*, (1997) 88 Comp Cas 274 Mad.
5. [1965] 1 All ER 667: [1965] 2 Comp LJ 30.
6. A situation of this kind is not likely to arise in India as S. 439(3) has dispensed with this requirement. The English Companies Act, 1985, has also dropped the requirement of desirability of winding up.
7. [1971] 1 All ER 56 CA; *Ruby General Hospital Ltd* v *Dr Kamal Kumar Gupta*, (2006) 129 Comp Cas 1 Cal, allegations of removal from directorship and allotment of shares altering majority, not sufficient to justify winding up. A separate civil suit lies from wrongful removal from directorship.

useless for him and even so the court finding it to be not just and equitable to wind up the company. The decision was, however, reversed by the House of Lords.

Unfair Prejudice

The requirement that facts must justify winding up on the just and equitable ground had made the remedy "virtually useless in practice".[8] Accordingly, the requirement was dropped in England in 1980 and the amendment has been maintained through the Act of 1985. "The key concept is now 'unfair prejudice'. This expression has never caused practitioners or the courts any difficulty. 'Prejudice' denotes detriment of some kind, but because it must qualify as 'unfair' it must be a form of detriment which would strike a man of business as unjust and inequitable. The role of the non-controlling shareholder is that of an investor. No doubt the 'prejudice' will usually take the form of a diminution in the value of the petitioner's shareholding. A scenario which is clearly actionable under Section 459 [of the English Companies Act] though no devaluation of the petitioner's shareholding occurs is a history of unjustifiably low dividends without commercial reason.[9]

Deprivation of shareholders' legitimate expectations was regarded as unfair prejudice in *Saul D Harrison & Sons plc, Re.*[10] The Court said that it would usually be considered unjust, inequitable or unfair for a majority to use their voting power to exclude a member from participation in the management without giving him an opportunity to remove his capital upon reasonable terms. The House of Lords in *O'Neill* v *Philips*[11] have laid this restriction upon the scope of the words ''legitimate expectation'' that this expression cannot be given the status of an independent rule. Such expectations must be founded somewhere. An unfounded expectation cannot support the plea of unfair prejudice. The only foundation which is possible is that there should be something in the articles or promises outside the articles to support the expectation. In this case the allegations were that the majority shareholder terminated the agreement for equal profit-sharing with the minority shareholder and also the agreement for allotment of more shares to the latter. The petition was not allowed because the majority shareholder had not given any such commitments. Their Lordships attached considerable importance to the fact that he had offered to purchase shares at a fair value.

It was held in the case of a quasi-partnership company that the summary removal of a director and his removal as an employee without any cause and

---

8. *See* Ralph Instone, *Unfair Prejudice: An Interim Report,* 1988 JBL 20.
9. *Ibid* at pp 21-22 citing *R. A. Noble (Clothing) Ltd,* 1983 BCLC 273, 290-291 and *Bovey Hotel Ventures Ltd, Re,* 1981, cited *ibid.*
10. (1995) 1 BCLC 14 at p 19.
11. [1999] 2 All ER 961: (1999) 97 Comp Cas 807: [1999] 1 WLR 1092.

with no offer to purchase his shares was an unfair prejudice to his position. The court ordered the purchase of his shares at a price to be calculated on the basis of the company as a going concern and multiple of earnings.[12] The removal of a director in the exercise of majority power and also passing of a resolution authorising excess remuneration and rights issue were held to be unfairly prejudicial to the minority shareholder because he was being virtually forced to leave the company. The majority shareholder was ordered to buy him out at a fair value.[13]

"Oppression" and "Unfair prejudice", difference

The Indian Companies Act still retains the expression "oppression". There is a difference between the two as to scope of possible relief, "oppression" would require some kind of injury to the proprietary interest of the complaining shareholder. This explanation was offered in a case in which the company was running an agency. It became divided between two equally strong shareholder groups. The company, whose agency it was running, was dealing with only one group. It terminated the agency exercising its rights under the agreement and awarded the agency to that group. The other group was not allowed to complain of this as an act of oppression.[14]

Oppression of Continuing Nature

The facts alleged must reveal an oppression of a continuing nature. Isolated acts of oppression will not do. This is apparent from the words of the section itself which says that the affairs of the company must be conducted in an oppressive "manner". This requirement would also prevent cognizance of past oppressive behaviour. For example, in *Raghunath Swarup Mathur* v *Har Swarup Mathur*,[15] M.H. BEG J observed that "whatever may have been the position in the past, the company was carrying on a profitable business, and, even if some bungling had taken place in the keeping of accounts in the past, it may not justify a winding up order where the company is a sound profit-making concern". Past acts are relevant if they constitute a continuing whole with the present facts or if the single past act complained of is capable of unleashing a continuing

---

12. *Pakinson* v. *Eurofinance Group Ltd*, [2000] All ER (D) 826.
13. *Regional Airports Ltd, Re,* (1999) 2 BCLC 30 Ch D; *S. Ranganathan* v *Shyamala Pictures & Hotels (P) Ltd,* (2002) 108 Comp Cas 880 CLB, where shareholding was never equal between members, a complaint was not entertained because of unequal shareholding. *Neelu Kohli* v *Nikhil Rubber (P) Ltd,* (2002) 108 Comp Cas 422 CLB, converting a majority shareholder into a minority in a manner which is not necessary for mobilisation of funds for the company was held to be oppressive.
14. *Vaishnav Shorilal Puri* v *Kishore Kundan Sippy,* (2006) 131 Comp Cas 609 Bom.
15. (1970) 40 Comp Cas 282 All; *Palghat Exports (P) Ltd* v *T. V. Chandaran,* (1994) 79 Comp Cas 213 Ker, past acts which had ceased to exist, petition rejected.

oppression.[16] Events subsequent to the date of the petition are also not to be taken into account.[17] The mere fact of business losses does not by itself show either oppression or mismanagement.[18] The fact of low rate of dividend even when were high profits can be taken into account even if it is a subsequent event and has been brought on record by an amendment of the pleadings.[19]

A single act of issuing additional capital can have a continuing effect and was held to be capable of constituting oppression. There can be no time bar for seeking relief in such cases. The issue had the effect of converting in the family company the majority into minority. Though the petitioning group had a knowledge of the fact, directions were issued to the effect that control be handed over to them.[20] Termination of an agreement between a group of family companies about the use of family trade mark and logo by giving notice to one family company owned by a minority shareholder was held to be an act having far reaching consequences. It, therefore, amounted to an oppression of the minority shareholder.[21]

Fairness of Petitioner's Conduct

There should be fairness in the conduct of the petitioner. There can be factors which would disentitle him though the others might be in the wrong. Accordingly where a reasonable offer is made to him before the petition is heard, the court will restrain further proceedings so as to maintain the status quo between the parties.[22] The majority had offered a fair price for

---

16. *Surinder Singh Bindra* v *Hindustan Fastners Ltd*, [1989] 2 Comp LJ 216: AIR 1990 Del 32: (1990) 69 Comp Cas 718 Del.
17. *Ashoka Betelnut Co (P) Ltd* v *Chandrakanth (MK)*, (1997) 80 Comp Cas 274 Mad: (1997) 25 Corpt LA 146 Mad.
18. *Ibid.*
19. *Jer Rulton Ravasmaneck* v *Gharda Chemicals Ltd*, [2000] 2 Bom LR 56 Bom.
20. *Ashok Kumar Oswal* v *Panchsheel Textile Mfg & Trading Co (P) Ltd*, (2002) 110 Comp Cas 800 CLB. In a subsequent litigation between the same parties, *Ashok Kumar Oswal* v *Panchsheel Textile Mfg & Trading Co (P) Ltd*, (2002) 110 Comp Cas 825 CLB, order issued earlier was not modified because the party seeking modification had knowledge of the fact but suppressed it. *Pearson Education Inc* v *Prentice Hall of India (P) Ltd*, (2007) 136 Comp Cas 211 CLB, single act of issuing shares, continuing effect. *Dayaram Agarwal* v *Ashok Industries (P) Ltd*, (2006) 130 Comp Cas 172 CLB, transfer of shares and further issue of capital in violation of memorandum and articles of association, held to be oppressive.
21. *Vijay R. Kirloskar* v *Kirloskar Proprietary Ltd*, (2006) 130 Comp Cas 139 CLB ; *Nagin M. Doshi* v *Echjay Forgings (P) Ltd*, (2007) 136 Comp Cas 75 CLB, failure to discharge obligations under family settlement, petition maintainable.
22. *Abbey Leisure Ltd, Re*, (1989) BCLC 619 Ch D. Where the minority shareholders who were complaining were given the offer to purchase shares of the majority and it was on their failure only that the shares were sold to outsiders which was not a violation of articles and hence there was no occasion for complaint. *Devaraj Dhanram* v *Firebricks & Potteries (P) Ltd*, (1994) 79 Comp Cas 722 Kant. Where an 85 year old minority shareholder, who had not taken any interest in the company for the last four years, was offered fair price by the majority to be worked out by an accountant and a solicitor, his conduct in continuing the petition with the prayer that he should be permitted to buy out the majority was held to be unfair, *A Company (No 00836 of 1995) Re*, (1996) 2 BCLC 192 Ch D. *See* also on this point *Yashovardhan Saboo* v *Groz Beekeri Saboo Ltd*, (1995) 83 Comp Cas 371 CLB and *Brenfield*

purchasing the complaining members' shares. Similarly, where the articles of the company prescribe a fair procedure of valuation to enable the aggrieved minority to move out, the court may not entertain a petition unless a fair trial is given to that procedure.[23]

The following observation on the facts of case is worthy of being noted:

> In this case, we have the spectacle of two distinguished directors who had themselves been participants in various acts of mismanagement alleged figuring with injured innocence as complainants before the court. This circumstance itself to a large extent demolishes the bona fides of the allegations put forward.[24]

An 85 year old minority shareholder who had not taken any interest in the company for the last four years, was not allowed to claim that he should be permitted to buy out the majority, which majority had offered him a fair price. It was held that it was an abuse of the process of the court for him to continue with the petition. There was no effective way available to him to prevent unfair treatment except that he should take a fair value of the shares and that whatever risk factor was there in working out a fair value was minimised because an independent accountant with the assistance of a solicitor was arranged for the purpose of valuation.[25]

Where the minority group had control over the Board of directors, and using that power, started promoting the interests of a rival company, it was held that this showed lack of *bona fides* and, therefore, in a petition

---

Squash Racquets Club Ltd, Re, (1996) 2 BCLC 184 Ch D, where the majority controllers mixed up the affairs of two group companies and became indebted to one of them. They being not able to pay their debt had to sell their shares under the articles to other members. Thus the minority group became entitled to buy their shares. As a general rule the court would be ready to strike out a petition where it amounted to a serious abuse such as where there is some improper purpose behind it. The same applies where the respondent suffers prejudice by reason of the abuse. *A Company (No 002015 of 1996), Re*, (1997) 2 BCLC 1 Ch D.

23. *A Company, Re, ex p Kremer*, 1989 BCLC 365 Ch D. A motivated petition to pressurise payment is liable to be rejected. *Palghat Exports (P) Ltd v T. V. Chandran*, (1994) 79 Comp Cas 213 Ker.

24. *Joseph (KMI) v Kuttanad Rubber Co Ltd*, (1984) 56 Comp Cas 284 Ker. Another case where the conduct of the petitioner being not fair disentitled him to relief is *Srikanta Datta v Sri Venkateswara Real Estates*, (1991) 72 Comp Cas 211 Kant. *Anugraha Jewellers Ltd v K.R.S. Mani*, (2002) 111 Comp Cas 501 Mad, the petitioner was himself a party to siphoning of funds, not allowed to claim relief. *Amalgamations Ltd v Shankar Sundaram*, (2002) 111 Comp Cas 280 Mad, the petitioner had acquiesced in decisions of which he was complaining, his motive was to exert pressure on company to give him a place of profit.

25. *A Company (No 00836 of 1995), Re*, (1996) 2 BCLC 192 Ch D. *K.N. Bhargava v Trackparts of India Ltd*, (2001) 104 Comp Cas 611 CLB, both factions in management, both guilty of acts of oppression against each other, the company was ordered to be divided between them.

by the majority group, the latter were directed to buy out the minority group.[26]

Effect of Arbitration Clause

Where a dispute arose amongst members concerning the breach of an agreement between them and the agreement contained an *arbitration clause*, the CLB (now Tribunal) said that such disputes were to be referred to arbitration under Section 8 of the Arbitration and Conciliation Act.[27]

A party was not allowed to seek reference to arbitration where it had already filed a full-fledged reply to the petition.[28]

PREVENTION OF MISMANAGEMENT [S. 398]

Section 398 provides for relief in cases of mismanagement. For a petition under this section to succeed, it must be established that the affairs of the company are being conducted in a manner prejudicial to the interest of the company or public interest, or that, by reason of any change in the management or control of the company, it is likely that the affairs of the company will be conducted in that manner. If the CLB is so convinced, it may, with a view to bringing to an end or preventing the matter complained of or apprehended, make such order as it thinks fit. A very clear illustration of mismanagement contemplated by the section is *Rajahmundry Electric Supply Corpn v A. Nageshwara Rao.*[29]

A petition was brought against a company by certain shareholders on the ground of mismanagement by directors. The court found that the Vice-Chairman grossly mismanaged the affairs of the company and had drawn considerable amounts for his personal purposes, that large amounts were owing to the Government for charges for supply of electricity, that machinery was in a state of disrepair, that the directorate had become greatly attenuated and "a powerful local junta was ruling the roost" and that the shareholders outside the group of the Chairman were powerless to set matters right. This was held to be sufficient evidence of mismanagement. The court accordingly appointed two administrators for the management of the company for a period of six months vesting in them all the powers of the directorate.

A similar management was provided to a company by the Calcutta High Court in *Richardson & Cruddas Ltd v Haridas Mundra.*[30]

---

26. *Ultrafilter (India) (P) Ltd* v *Ultrafilter GmbH*, (2002) 112 Comp Cas 93 CLB. *Pokhran Investment (P) Ltd* v *Dadha Estates (P) Ltd*, (2006) 132 Comp Cas 324 CLB, a director who did not call meetings, or perform his duties under articles was not allowed to seek relief.
27. *Pinaki Das Gupta* v *Madhyam Advertising (P) Ltd*, (2003) 114 Comp Cas 346 CLB.
28. *V L S Finance Ltd* v *Sumair Hotels Ltd*, (2002) 111 Comp Cas 403 CLB.
29. AIR 1956 SC 213: (1956) 26 Comp Cas 91.
30. (1959) 29 Comp Cas 549 Cal. Where the group in power was conspiring to defraud members, mismanagement was held to be established. *Hemant D. Vakil* v *RDI Print and Publishing (P) Ltd*, [1993] 2 Comp LJ 113 CLB Del. Where there were only two directors in a private

There should be present and continuing mismanagement. The charges of mismanagement in the past, even if proved, are not enough to establish an existing injury to the interest of the company or public interest.[31] Where directors preferred objects of their liking and made a huge allotment of shares for a consideration other than cash, this was held to be a mismanagement of affairs.[32] Misuse and misapplication of the company's finances by three brothers out of four who were operating the company was held sufficient to invite an order of CLB for readjustment of accounts so as to prevent extraneous use of funds outside the company's business and the shareholders' agreement.[33] Where the company was incurring losses and there were allegations of diversion of funds to sister concerns and banks were refusing funds, the CLB directed the willing faction to takeover the company and pay out the faction indulging in mismanagement.[34]

A probe into the affairs of a company for finding out the fact of mismanagement may include an inquiry into the company's subsidiaries.[35] Where a set of properly appointed directors were not permitted to join and function as directors, their complaint was taken to be indicative of a symptom of mismanagement and was accordingly entertained.[36]

---

company and one was keeping the other totally in the dark about the affairs of the company, mismanagement was held to have been established. *V.G. Balasundram* v *New Theatre Carnatic Talkies (P) Ltd,* (1993) 77 Comp Cas 324 Mad. A State Government cannot take over the undertaking of a company on the ground that the company has been the victim of mismanagement. The provisions of the Companies Act are sufficient in themselves to remedy situations like that whether at the instance of the affected persons or State agencies, *K. R. Lakshmanan* v *State of T.N.,* (1996) 2 SCC 226: (1996) 86 Comp Cas 66 SC.

31. *R. S. Mathur* v *H. S. Mathur,* [1970] 1 Comp LJ 35 All. Losses by themselves cannot support a plea of mismanagement, or that the directors are still drawing their salary or that they have called upon the petitioner to pay Rs 80,000 being the amount unpaid on his shares. *Chennabasappa* v *Multiplast Industries,* (1985) 57 Comp Cas 541 Kant. Where a company had no records, registers etc. whatsoever, it was held to be a fit case for the appointment of an administrator. *Bhajirao* v *Bom Docking,* (1984) 56 Comp Cas 428 Bom; where the newly appointed directors had not even taken charge, the petition was dismissed because it was too early to say as to how they would conduct themselves. *Rai Saheb Vishwamitra* v *Amar Nath Mehrotra,* (1986) 59 Comp Cas 854 All.

32. *Akbarali* v *Konkan Chemicals (P) Ltd,* (1997) 88 Comp Cas 245 CLB.

33. *Narain Das* v *Bristol Grill (P) Ltd,* (1997) 90 Comp Cas 79: [1997] 3 Comp LJ 32 CLB. The advances out of the company's funds made by the controller to his sister concerns were not regarded as mismanagement because of satisfactory explanation and no detriment to the lending company. *Boiron* v *SBL Ltd,* (1998) 30 Corpt LA 21 CLB. Where the complaint was based on misappropriation of funds and property of the company and it could be taken care of under S. 543 by way of misfeasance proceedings, a separate petition under S. 398 was considered to be not necessary, *Sanjeev Kumar Bhardwaj* v *Ghanshyam Dass,* (1999) 34 CLA 370: (2001) 103 Comp Cas 447 Del.

34. *Ram Nath Gupta* v *Phoel Industries Ltd,* (2006) 129 Comp Cas 164 CLB; *Pearson Education Inc* v *Prentice Hall of India (P) Ltd,* (2007) 136 Cas 211 CLB, increasing remuneration proportionately to the profits of the company, no mismanagement.

35. *LIC of India* v *Haridas Mundra,* (1966) 36 Comp Cas 371 All; *Bajrang Pd Jalan* v *Mahabir Pd Jalan,* AIR 1999 Cal 156.

36. *Ador Samia Ltd* v *Indocan Engg Systems Ltd,* (1999) 35 CLA 224 CLB.

"Relief against mismanagement runs in favour of the company and not to any particular member or members."[37] Secondly: "It is not necessary for the court to find cause for winding up in cases of mismanagement in order to grant relief." Proof of prejudice to the public interest or to the interests of the company is enough. Thirdly, the section enables the court to take into consideration outside interests affected by corporate operations. Thus, the Calcutta High Court refused to order the winding up of a grossly mismanaged company and appointed special officers to manage it because the company was engaged in special industries necessary for the implementation of the country's plans.[38] Under Section 397 the power is of discretionary nature which enables the Company Law Board to make an order as it thinks fit with a view to bringing to an end the matters complained of, as distinct from the power granted under Section 398 which enables the Company Law Board to pass an order with a view to bringing to an end or preventing the matter complained of or apprehended.[39]

Powers of Company Law Board [S. 402]

Powers of the CLB under Sections 397 and 398 are fairly wide.[40] "In fact, the Board may make any order for the regulation of the conduct of the company's affairs upon such terms and conditions as may, in the opinion of the Board, be just and equitable in all the circumstances of the case."[41] Apparently the only limitation seems to be the overall objective of the sections and, therefore, the order must be directed to bringing to an end the matters complained of. The CLB can grant relief against a respondent who is no longer a member and such relief can possibly extend to requiring him to purchase the company's shares.[42] However, an attempt is made under Section 402 to define the powers of the CLB. This section provides that, without prejudice to the generality of the powers of the CLB, any order under Section 397 or 398 may provide for:

---

37. *See* Mathew J. Kust, FOREIGN ENTERPRISE IN INDIA, 293 (1964).
38. *Richardson & Cruddas Ltd v Haridas Mundra*, (1959) 29 Comp Cas 549 Cal.
39. *Palghat Exports (P) Ltd v T. V. Chandran*, (1994) 79 Comp Cas 213 Ker. Where the warring group would not come to terms, the court may hand over management to workers under some arrangement for competent guidance, *Kripal Ispat Ltd v Dalip Singh Majithia*, (1992) 20 All LR 34 (Summary of Cases). *Thakur Savadekar & Co v S. S. Thakur*, (1996) 22 Corpt LA 170 Bom, proceedings before CLB are not to be stopped because of an appeal against dismissal of winding up petition.
40. The Company Law Board has to be satisfied that the conditions of relief exists presently and not in reference to some possible conduct in the future. *Peerless General Finance & Investment Co Ltd v Union of India*, [1989] 1 Comp LJ 56 Cal: (1991) 71 Comp Cas 300 Cal.
41. *See*, for example, *Lord Krishna Sugar Mills Ltd v Abnash Kaur*, (1974) 44 Comp Cas 210 Del, where the court, having constituted an interim board of management for a company, held that it had power under S. 402 to give directions and instructions from time to time so as to resolve the problems of the interim board. *See* also *Gokul Chand Morarka v Company Law Board*, (1974) 44 Comp Cas 173 Del.
42. *A Company, Re*, [1986] 2 All ER 253 Ch D.

1. The regulation of the conduct of the company's affairs in future. Thus, for example, in *LIC* v *Haridas Mundra*,[43] the court appointed a special officer with an advisory board to the total exclusion of the shareholders of a company to function subject to the terms and conditions laid down in the order. In *Bennett, Coleman & Co* v *UOI*,[44] the Bombay High Court ordered a new article into the articles of association providing that all the shareholders' directors will retire every year and held that the clause was valid even if it was against the provisions of Section 255.[45]

2. The purchase of the shares or interest of any members of the company by other members or by the company. This kind of relief was provided in *Mohanlal* v *Punjab Co Ltd*,[46] and *H. R. Harmer Ltd, Re*,[47] and also in *Suresh Kumar Sanghi* v *Supreme Motors Ltd*,[48] where the group in actual control was given the opportunity to buy out the other at a value to be fixed by a judge.

---

43. 63 CWN 439: AIR 1959 Cal 695: (1959) 29 Comp Cas 549. *P. Muniswamappa Sonnegowda* v *Mysore Lighting Works (P) Ltd*, (2007) 136 Comp Cas 138 CLB, interim relief by appointing independent chairman not provided because of the company's financial weakness, adequate measures provided for assuring proper management.
44. (1977) 47 Comp Cas 92 Bom.
45. *See* also *Debi Jhora Tea Co Ltd* v *Barendra Krishna Bhowmick*, (1980) 50 Comp Cas 771, where the Calcutta High Court appointed a chairman to preside over the company's shareholders' as well as directors' meetings. *Combust Technic (P) Ltd, Re*, (1986) 60 Comp Cas 872 Cal where a special officer was appointed pending the constitution of a new board. The court may take over the management into its own hands or appoint a receiver or special officer to do so even if the directors who are in office enjoy majority support. *Pradip Kumar Sarkar* v *Luxmi Tea Co Ltd*, (1990) 67 Comp Cas 491 Cal. The power of removing a director can be exercised only when it is established that he acted in a fraudulent manner or used his fiduciary position to the detriment of the company or its shareholders or in a manner prejudicial to public interest. In this case the only alleged irregularity was letting out of the company's premises in a manner not permitted by the articles. But that had been going on for 20 years to the full knowledge of the shareholders and also to the advantage of the company. The CLB directed the matter to be referred to a meeting of the shareholders, *Arjun S. Kalra* v *Shree Madhu Industrial Estates Ltd*, [1997] 1 Comp LJ 318 CLB. In a situation of relentless oppression, the CLB reconstituted the Board of directors and directed it to hold meetings and allot shares to members from whom share money had been taken for further issue, *Shri Anupam Chemical India (P) Ltd* v *Dipak G. Mehta*, [1999] 4 Comp LJ 474 Bom.
46. AIR 1961 Punj 485; *P.K. Prathapan* v *Dale & Carrington Investments (P) Ltd*, (2003) 111 Comp Cas 425 Ker, setting aside of all capital issues made after the initial allotment and consequential rectification of the register of members.
47. [1958] 3 All ER 689: [1959] 1 WLR 62.
48. (1983) 54 Comp Cas 235 Del. *See* also *Surinder Singh Bindra* v *Hindustan Fastners (P) Ltd*, [1989] 2 Comp LJ 216: AIR 1990 Del 32: (1990) 69 Comp Cas 718 Del, where one group of shareholders was installed in power and directions were issued for taking over the shares of the other block. It is unusual to ask the majority to sell itself to the minority. Ordinarily, it would be the other way round. *Yashovardhan Saboo* v *Groz-Beckert Saboo Ltd*, [1993] 1 Comp LJ 20 CLB. Direction to one faction to buy out the other and on their failure to do so, order of winding up, *Nalam Satya Prasada Rao* v *V. L. N. Sastry*, (1991) 70 Comp Cas 303 AP.

3. In the case of a purchase by the company, of its shares the consequent reduction of its share capital.[49]

4. The termination, setting aside or modification of an agreement between the company and managing director, or any other director, the managing agent, the secretaries and treasurers and the manager.

5. The termination, setting aside or modification of any agreement with any person, provided due notice has been given to him and his consent obtained.

6. Setting aside of any fraudulent preferences made within three months before the date of the application.[50]

7. Any other matter for which, in the opinion of the court, it is just and equitable that provision should be made.[51]

In situations of irreconciliable disputes, the usual approach of the CLB has been to order the rival groups to part ways in the interests of the company and those of the public financial institutions having large stakes in

---

49. *Vijay Krishna Jaidka* v *Jaidka Motor Co Ltd*, (1996) 23 Corpt LA 289 CLB, equitable in case of family funds gripping company.

50. Setting aside a transfer under this clause in *Roshan Lal Agarwal* v *Sheoram Bubna*, (1980) 50 Comp Cas 243 Pat, the Patna High Court held that there should be a net period of three months between the date of transfer and that of application. The court excluded the date of transfer in computing the period of three months.

51. *See* as an illustration, *Gajarabai* v *Patni Transport (P) Ltd*, [1965] 2 Comp LJ 234, a decision of the Andhra Pradesh High Court. The facts were that one of the directors died leaving behind a will bequeathing the shares in the company to his second wife and sons who were already the shareholders of the company and the petitioners. The directors on account of their private dispute with the petitioners, acted in a high-handed manner and unreasonably refused to transfer a part of the shares bequeathed under the will, while transferring some shares in favour of them as provided under the will. They made certain improper transfers also. The petitioners applied under Ss. 397 and 398 of the Companies Act for removal of one of the directors from the Board, and for the appointment of a committee of shareholders to manage the affairs of the company. But the court held that "proper order to make, in the circumstances, is to direct the directors to transfer the shares to the petitioners in accordance with the terms of the will". *See* also *Jhambu Kumar Raniwala* v *Edward Mill Co*, [1970] 2 Comp LJ 43, where directions were issued regulating the conduct of directors. *Shoe Specialities Ltd* v *Standard Distilleries and Breweries Ltd*, (1997) 90 Comp Cas 1 Mad, majority was reduced to minority, relief allowed. The CLB has power to exercise control over the implementation of its order. In *All India Shaw Wallace Employees Federation* v *Shaw Wallace & Co Ltd*, [1997] 1 Comp LJ 304 at p 306, the directors of a company unanimously resolved to sell the company's undertaking because of financial crisis. Workers opposed it because of the seizure of the premises by Government agencies to investigate serious financial irregularities. The Company Law Board was approached for sanctioning sale. The CLB appointed two nominee directors to sit with others at a meeting for reviewing the proposal and to formulate specific recommendations. *M.M. Subramanyam* v *Gulf Olfines (P) Ltd*, (2003) 116 Comp Cas 115 CLB, meeting not held, shares allotted discriminately, CLB (now Tribunal) ordered proportional allotment to aggrieved members and their induction back into the Board of directors. *Shri Ramdas Motor Transport Ltd* v *Karedla Suryanarayana*, (2002) 110 Camp Cas 193 AP, the power is wide enough to allow relief even when the fact of oppression is not made out.

it. The CLB can direct the partition of the assets of even a listed company and reducing the capital of the company to that extent.[52]

If the Company Law Board orders any alteration of the memorandum or articles of the company, the company shall not be at liberty to introduce any provision inconsistent with the order.[53] If the order sets aside or modifies any agreement with any managerial personnel, it will not give rise to any claim for damages or compensation for loss of office.[54] Further any managerial personnel whose appointment is so set aside shall not be capable of serving the company in any managerial capacity for a period of five years except with the leave of the Board.[55]

Under Section 406 misfeasance proceedings can also be commenced against guilty officers even though the company is not being wound up. The Gujarat High Court in *Colaba Land & Mills Co* v *J. Pilani*,[56] gave retrospective effect to the provision and allowed proceedings in respect of offences committed before these remedies were introduced by the Companies Act, 1956.

The powers under these provisions are not affected by the existence of an *arbitration clause*. The court may, however, in its discretion refer the matter to arbitration in terms of the parties' agreement and exercise any powers only thereafter.[57] The court cannot make any such direction in respect of matters which are outside the scope of the arbitration clause.[58] There are authorities to the effect that the CLB, being a judicial authority, is bound under Section 8 of the Arbitration and Conciliation Act, 1996 to direct the parties to go in for arbitration within the framework of the arbitration agreement.[59]

Where the shares of a private company were transferred and the method of valuation was under question, the court said that for the purpose of valuing the shares of a private company as a going concern when the company has high returns and little or no assets, the value of the company is the capitalised sum representing the future profits after making an allowance for risks.[60] The point emphasised was that the worth of the

---

52. *K. N. Bhargava* v *Trackparts of India Ltd*, (2000) 36 CLA 291 CLB.
53. S. 404(1). *See* also sub-sections (2), (3) and (4).
54. S. 407(1)(*a*).
55. S. 407(1)(*b*). The prohibition applies to any person who becomes his associate [sub-section (1)]. *See* also sub-s. (3). S. 403 empowers the Board to make any interim order and S. 405 to implead persons who should have been impleaded.
56. (1971) 41 Comp Cas 1078 Guj.
57. *Gurvir Singh Gill* v *Saz International (P) Ltd*, (1987) 62 Comp Cas 197 Del.
58. *Khandwala Securities Ltd* v *Kowa Spg Ltd*, (1999) 97 Comp Cas 632 CLB.
59. *Twentieth Century Finance Corpn Ltd* v *R. F. B. Latex Ltd*, (1999) 97 Comp Cas 636 CLB. *Altek Lammertz Needles Ltd* v *Lammertz Industrienadel GmbH*, (2006) 129 Comp Cas 108 CLB, refusal to refer to arbitration grievances relating to rights and benefits under the Act and articles of association.
60. *Buckingham* v *Francis*, [1986] 2 All ER 738 QBD.

company as a whole must be calculated on the basis of the company as a going concern.[61] The "maintainable level of profits" plays a dominant role as a method of evaluation of the company's net worth. The asset base is another method of valuation. The methodology would vary with the features and nature of the company's business. Where two groups worked together for decades and then fell apart, it was held that each group was entitled to have the proportionate worth of the business.[62]

The Company Law Board can itself do the valuation. In one such case the CLB took into account the financial position of the company and the petitioner's stake in it and fixed the value at which one should pay out the other and, if they failed to do so, the matter should be referred to the statutory auditors for appropriate valuation.[63]

The CLB can provide relief by prescribing a better method of a valuation where the articles of the company provide for an arbitrary or artificial method of valuation.[64] Where some stratagem has been attempted, for example, by delaying tactics for suppressing the value of shares, relief may be provided against it by taking valuation at a time before the suppressing tactics began.[65] Relief may also be provided where the valuer is a person who is not likely to be wholly independent.[66] Where the 40% holding of the complaining member was reduced by oppressing tactics to 4%, the court directed that valuation should be on the basis of 40% strength.[67]

The CLB may pass an order which is contrary to the provisions of the company's articles of association and may also modify contractual arrangements if it is just and equitable to do so in the circumstances of the case. The company concerned may also be directed to change its name.[68]

The powers of CLB continue even after passing of an order till at least such time that its orders are implemented so as to put an end to the matters complained of. Regulation 44 of the CLB Regulations, 1991 is akin to Section 151 of CPC. It confers inherent powers on the CLB. The Board does not become *functus officio* after the passing of an order. Where a CLB order

---

61. Again emphasised in *Bird Precision Bellows Ltd, Re,* (1984) 3 All ER 444 Ch D: [1985] 3 All ER 523 CA.
62. *Rakhra Sports (P) Ltd v Khraitilal Rakhra,* (1993) 76 Comp Cas 545 Kar.
63. *Solitaire Hotels (P) Ltd, Re,* [1992] 3 Comp LJ 119 CLB.
64. *A Company, Re, (No 004377 of 1986),* [1987] 1 WLR 102. A similar approach was adopted in *Lloyd's Bank plc v Duker,* [1987] 1 WLR 1324. Here out of a total of 999 shares, 574 fell to the share of the executor of the deceased shareholder. The court ordered all the shares to be sold in the open market giving the executor the right to purchase any or all because that way the real value of the shares which carried the controlling power would be better ascertained.
65. *A Company, Re, (No 006834 of 1988),* (1988) 5 BCC 218; *A Company, Re, (No 003843 of 1986),* 1987 BCLC 562; *McGuiness v Bremner plc,* 1988 BCLC 673.
66. *Boxwell & Co (Steels) Ltd, Re,* (1988) 5 BCC 145.
67. *A Company, Harris, Re, ex p,* 1989 BCLC 383 Ch D.
68. *Pearson Education Inc v Prentice Hall India (P) Ltd,* (2007) 136 Comp Cas 294 Del.

setting aside an allotment of shares by which an undeserved majority shareholding was created was stayed by the High Court and the stay order was subsequently vacated. Further necessary orders were passed for implementation of the original order.[69]

Compromise

The parties can enter into a compromise and consent orders can be passed on that basis. The compromise was held to be binding on the parties. When they picked up a dispute again over valuation of shares, they were not permitted to question the validity of the compromise by saying that the petition was not maintainable at its initial stage.[70] Where the parties agreed among themselves in terms of their memorandum of understanding, it was held that the CLB had no power to enforce such agreement.[71]

Date of Valuation

The court has discretion to fix the date of valuation which may not necessarily correspond with the date of the court order. It may correspond with the date of the petition.[72]

Central Government's power to appoint directors on CLB's order [S. 408]

The Central Government has the power to appoint such number of persons, known as Government directors, on the Board of directors of a company as the Company Law Board may direct. The CLB can take up the matter for such direction on a reference by the Central Government[73], or on an application by not less than 100 members of the company or of those holding not less than 10% of the total voting power. The Board makes such inquiry as it deems fit in order to find out whether such appointment is necessary to prevent the affairs of the company being conducted in a manner which is oppressive to any members of the company or which is prejudicial to the company's or public interest. The Board has to indicate

---

69. *Shoe Specialities Ltd* v *Standard Distilleries and Breweries Ltd*, (1997) 90 Comp Cas 1 Mad; *Tiruppur Karur Transports (P) Ltd* v *T.V. Raju Naidu*, (2006) 133 Comp Cas 64 CLB, court cannot stay proceedings before CLB. Only CLB can do so.
70. *K. K. Framji* v *Consulting Engg Services (India) Ltd*, (2002) 110 Comp Cas 482 CLB.
71. *Ramesh Chand Goyal* v *Himalaya Communications Ltd*, (2006) 129 Comp Cas 297 HP, the CLB also has no power to review its orders.
72. *Profinance Trust Ltd, SA* v *Gladstone*, [2000] 2 BCLC 516 Ch D. The date of petition was ordered to be the date of valuation in this case.
73. It is not necessary for the exercise of this power that the Central Government should inform the company beforehand by a show-cause notice as to why a reference should not made. The Government should, however, have some cogent material before it at the time of the reference. *Skipper Construction Co (P) Ltd* v *Union of India*, [1992] 3 Comp LJ 160 Del following *Colgate Palmolive (India) Ltd* v *Union of India*, (1980) 50 Comp Cas 456 Del; *Urban Improvement Co (P) Ltd, In re*, (1995) 18 Corpt LA 10 CLB, directions to Government that in appointing directors due representation to be given to those members who were not able to make houses due to managerial non-functioning.

the period for which such an appointment may be made, but the same should not exceed three years on any one occasion.[74] Where the members of a housing company out of sheer frustration abandoned their company to its own fate, the Central Government approached the CLB. The latter ordered appointment by the Central Government of five directors whom two should be from among plot holders, who would carry further the business of the company.[75]

In lieu of such appointment, the CLB may order the company to amend its articles, by including Section 265 and to appoint fresh directors by proportional representation within such time as the CLB may specify. In the meantime the Board may ask the Central Government to put certain additional directors on the company's Board of directors. Any director so appointed shall not have to hold qualification shares, if any. Nor shall he be liable to retire by rotation. The Government may, however, remove or replace him. After such appointment any change in the Board of directors can only be made with the consent of the CLB.

The term of appointment may be extended after the expiry of the first term. It would be necessary for an extension to be valid that the original circumstances of oppression or mismanagement must subsist. For this purpose the company would have to be given an opportunity to explain its present position. If the original circumstances have ceased to exist, the term of appointment should not be extended unless there is a clear possibility of recurrence if the appointment is not renewed.[76]

If this power is exercised in reference to any company, the Government will get the right to issue such directions to the company as it may consider

---

74. The Board has to be satisfied that the prejudicial circumstances are there presently and not in reference to some possible future conduct. *Peerless General Finance & Investment Co Ltd* v *Union of India*, [1989] 1 Comp LJ 56 Cal: (1991) 71 Comp Cas 300 Cal. The court also added that the power under the section is not available for regulating the financial schemes of the company and that the provisions of the section must be construed strictly. The powers under the section cannot be used to regulate the financial scheme of the company because that is the domain of the RBI.

75. *Urban Housing Development Co (P) Ltd, Re,* (1996) 85 Comp Cas 758 CLB; *Urban Improvement Co (P) Ltd,* (1996) 85 Comp Cas 758; *Union of India* v *Everyday Industries Ltd,* (2006) 132 Comp Cas 894 CLB, Central Govt directed to appoint inspectors where there was misuse of large sums of money without approval of directors. *Union of India* v *Morepen Laboratories Ltd,* (2006) 130 Comp Cas 43 CLB, failure to repay public deposits, failure to comply with CLB scheme, Govt directors to be appointed to build public confidence. *Union of India Ministry of Company Affairs* v *Padmini Technologies Ltd,* (2006) 130 Comp Cas 585 CLB, company incurred losses, no reasons pointed out, Act violated, prejudice to company and public interest, Govt directed to appoint two directors. *Khandwala Securities Ltd* v *Kowa Spinning Ltd,* (2006) 132 Comp Cas 318 CLB, alleged diversion of funds, chartered accountants' report verified it. The statement of account not produced despite orders. The Central Govt directed to conduct inspection of books of account u/S 209-A.

76. *Vinod Kumar* v *Union of India,* (1981) Tax LR 2517 Del: (1982) 52 Comp Cas 211. Followed in *Shakti Trading Co Ltd* v *Union of India,* (1985) 57 Comp Cas 789 Del. Where 5 out of 9 directors were appointed to make sure that proceedings commenced against directors' malpractices were not frustrated.

necessary or appropriate in regard to its affairs.[77] The Government can also require the person appointed to report to the Government from time to time with regard to the affairs of the company.[78] Such directions may include an order to remove an auditor already appointed and to appoint another auditor in his place or to alter the articles of the company. Such removal, appointment or alteration shall have effect as if the relevant requirements of the Act have been complied with.

The Central Government can make an application under this section even when shareholders have petitioned for relief against oppression. The jurisdiction under one section does not become barred by an application under another section. The petitions can be heard analogously.[79]

Power to prevent change in Board of directors [Section 409]

Further, under Section 409, the Central Government has the power to prevent any proposed change in the board of directors or membership of the company, if it is likely to affect the company prejudicially. This power can be exercised on a complaint by the managing director, or any other director or manager of the company. The CLB can intervene only if the alleged prejudicial change in the composition of the Board of directors is an actual or likely result of a change in the character of the company's shareholding. This power cannot be used for preventing majority of shareholders from a management of their choice. Normal changes in the composition of the board of directors by a realignment among membership cannot constitute a ground for exercise of this power.[80] The CLB can restrain any resolution from taking effect whether passed or likely to be passed for a change in the

---

77. S. 408(6).
78. S. 408(7). If the circumstances are made out, the choice of directors is with the Government. *Sakthi Trading Co (P) Ltd v Union of India*, (1985) 57 Comp Cas 789 Del. Such directors have the usual powers. Sale of a unit of the company, being not a sale of the undertaking, procedure of S. 293 was not necessary, *Pramod Kumar Mittal v Andhra Steel Corpn Ltd*, (1985) 58 Comp Cas 772 Cal. They do not automatically cease to function as such by efflux of time, *Union of India v S. C. Sugar Mills*, (1984) 55 Comp Cas 42 Bom.
79. *Manohar Rajaram Chhabaria v Union of India*, (2002) 110 Comp Cas 162 Cal. *S. Ashok v T.N. Mercantile Bank Ltd*, (2005) 127 Comp Cas 351 Mad, appointments for prevention of oppression and mismanagement. *Central Govt v Caraws Pharmaceuticals Ltd*, (2004) 121 Comp Cas 238 CLB, appointment of Government directors for putting an end to mismanagement. *Central Govt v Sterling Holiday Resorts (India) Ltd*, (2006) 131 Comp Cas 6 CLB, auditors', report showed that affairs were being conducted in a prejudicial and oppressive manner and against public interest, huge liabilities, good case for appointment of Government directors.
80. *B. Baba Chandersekhar v V.R. Textiles Ltd*, [1992] 2 Comp LJ 103 CLB. *P.H. Rao v Skycell Communication Ltd*, (2002) 110 Comp Cas 734 CLB, 40.5 acquisition of shares which was not likely to affect the existing management. *Ashok Kumar Oswal v S.P. Oswal*, (2002) 110 Comp Cas 747 CLB, change of ownership in shares not in favour of an outsider but within the group in power. No interference necessary. *Union of India v Vikas WSP Ltd*, (2005) 124 Comp Cas 781 CLB, the Central Govt was directed to appoint directors to end financial irregularities. *Central Govt v DSQ Software Ltd*, (2006) 131 Comp Cas 72 CLB, Central Government permitted to appoint directors where inspection of books of account showed losses, dwindling number of employees, and inability to meet statutory obligations.

Board of directors unless it is confirmed by the CLB. Interim orders can also be passed.

The section does not apply to a private company which is not the subsidiary of a public company.

Transfer of powers to Company Law Board

By virtue of the amendment of 1988, the power of the court under Sections 397 and 398 for prevention of oppression and mismanagement; the powers of the court under Section 402 and that under Section 403 to pass interim orders,[81] the power of approval of an alteration in articles or memorandum under Section 404 and that of the Central Government under Section 409 to prevent prejudicial changes in the composition of the board of directors, had been transferred to the Company Law Board.

Civil suit

The members of a family company were already locked in a civil suit for partition of family assets. The matters in issue in a petition for relief against oppression were not substantially the same. Proceedings were also not between the same parties and their representatives. It was held that the civil court had no jurisdiction to grant relief claimed in the company petition. The Company Law Board alone had jurisdiction in the matter.[82]

Where a civil suit was pending between legal heirs, the CLB said that their respective rights could be decided in the suit because otherwise there could be conflict of decisions.[83]

Transfer of powers to Tribunal

The Company Law Board was proposed to be abolished by the Companies (Second Amendment) Act, 2002. A new Tribunal, called National Company Law Tribunal (Tribunal) was to be constituted in its place. The jurisdiction for prevention of oppression and mismanagement was to be vested in the Tribunal. But this amendment has not been enforced.

---

81. *Medical Institutes (P) Ltd* v *Dhananjay Pande*, (2005) 128 Comp Cas 273 Bom an interim arrangement which was not prejudicial to the company was not approved.
82. *Tiruppur Transports (P) Ltd* v *P. Narayanaswamy*, (2006) 133 Comp Cas 416 CLB; *Saravana Stores (P) Ltd* v *S. Yogarathinam*, (2007) 136 Comp Cas 200 CLB.
83. *K.S. Mothilal* v *K.S. Kasimaris Ceramique (P) Ltd*, (2007) 135 Comp Cas 609 CLB.

17
Investigations, Company Law Board and Company Courts

National and individual savings constitute the chief source of capital formation in a democratic country, and is, therefore, vital to economic growth.[1] Incorporated enterprise is one of the methods of allocating and channelling limited capital resources.[2] The proper functioning, that is to say, a performance that will ensure adequate return on capital, is ultimately the best protection of those who provide capital.[3] "Efficient functioning" can be assured by preventing corporate abuses and wrongs.

Corporate managements are today free from many of the former restraints. For example, the doctrine of *ultra vires* is no longer any significant check upon corporate spending.[4] Again, the powers of management are vested in the board to the total exclusion of shareholders.[5]

The shareholder has become an investor, separated in time and understanding, insulated by distance and the proxy machinery from the business activities of the enterprise. The reality of the internal corporate structure has changed from democratic to bureaucratic.[6]

Hence the shareholder is no longer available as an adequate field of responsibility.[7] "Due to great diffusion of stock, shareholders become indifferent to voting and controlling."[8] It is an "illusion that anything like an effective control of the shareholders over the management of a big company can be re-established. The divorce between financial interest and power of management is a fact."[9] "Further the shareholders are ill-equipped to challenge the wisdom and expertise of officers."[10]

Accordingly any remedies against corporate abuses that have to depend for their effectiveness upon shareholder initiative are not likely to be very

---

1. *See* Hsiu-Kwang Wu, *An Economist Looks at S. 16 of the Securities Exchange Act, 1934,* (1968) Col LR 250 at p 269.
2. *Ibid.*
3. Louis Loss, *The Fiduciary Concept as Applied to Trading by Corporate Insiders,* (1970) 33 Mod LR 34.
4. *See* R. C. Beuthin, *The Ultra Vires Doctrine — An Obituary Notice,* (1966) 83 SALJ 461; James William Hurst, *The Legitimacy of the Business Corporation in the Law of United States,* 1780-1970, (1970) Col LR 1317, 1318.
5. *See* Powers of Directors, *Ante.*
6. Abraham Chayes, *The Modern Corporation and the Rule of Law,* in E. S. Mason (Edn), THE CORPORATION IN MODERN SOCIETY, 25, 40 (1959). *See* also J. A. Livingstone, THE AMERICAN STOCKHOLDER, at p 38, where the learned writer says: "The stockholders are investors, who for the most part, do not wish to be bothered except by dividends."
7. A. A. Berle, THE 20TH CENTURY CAPITALIST REVOLUTION (1954).
8. Henry G. Manne, *The Higher Criticism of the Modern Corporation,* (1962) 62 Col LR 399. *See* also Emerson and Latchem, SHAREHOLDER DEMOCRACY, (1954).
9. O. K. Freund, *Company Law Reform,* (1946) 9 Mod LR 235 at p 245.
10. A. A. Berle Jr, *Legal Problems of Economic Power,* (1960) 60 Col LR 4.

successful. "The law suit against management is an uncertain road, open only in relatively extreme cases of perfidy and subject to heavy toll charges in the form of lawyer's fee."[11] Remedies afforded by the exceptions to the rule in *Foss* v *Harbottle*[12] and Sections 397 and 398 for prevention of oppression and mismanagement are beset with a variety of procedural and financial hurdles.[13]

"The reality of control can only be found in the action of public opinion and in the organised supervision exercised by Government agencies. Hence the importance of investigations."[14]

"There is no doubt that few shareholders have the means or ability to act against the management. It would furthermore be difficult for the shareholders to find out the facts leading to the poor financial condition of a company. The Government thought it right to take power to step in where there was reason to suspect that the management may not have been acting in the interests of the shareholders....and to take steps for the protection of such interests (the Act) gives the exploratory power."[15]

Powers of investigation

"Sections 235 to 251 provide for investigation of the affairs of a company."[16] The power is split into two sets, one containing mandatory and the other permissive provisions.

Mandatory Provisions

Under the first part of Section 237 the Government is bound to appoint inspectors to investigate the affairs of a company in the following two cases:

1. When the company by a special resolution demands an investigation, and
2. When the court, by order, declares that the affairs ought to be investigated by an inspector appointed by the Central Government.

There is no guidance in the Act as to who can seek the order of the court for this purpose. The Gujarat High Court has held in *Alembic Glass Industries Ltd, Re*,[17] that the power of the court is not subject to the provisions of Section 235 or 237(*b*):

The Legislature in its wisdom has not put any such condition before the court can make an order, though the court may in its

---

11. J. A. Livingstone, THE AMERICAN STOCKHOLDER, quoted at 1483 of (1958) 67 Yale LJ 1476. The problem of expenses and the possible solutions therefor are discussed in A. J. Boyle, *Indemnifying the Minority Shareholder*, 1976 JBL 18.
12. (1843) 67 ER 189: (1843) 2 Hare 461.
13. Henry G. Manne, *The Higher Criticism of the Modern Corporation*, (1962) Col LR 399, 410.
14. O. K. Freund, *supra*, fn 9, p 246.
15. MUDHOLKAR J in *Barium Chemicals Ltd* v *Company Law Board*, [1966] 2 Comp LJ 151, 161: (1966) 36 Comp Cas 639: AIR 1967 SC 295.
16. *Ibid.*, HIDAYATULLAH J (afterwards CJ) at 164.
17. (1972) 42 Comp Cas 63 Guj.

wisdom expect *prima facie* proof of some of these conditions. While conferring jurisdiction on the court to direct the Central Government to appoint an inspector, the Legislature have not thought fit to circumscribe the discretion or jurisdiction in any manner. It would, therefore, be utterly inappropriate to curtail or circumscribe or fetter the jurisdiction of the court by reading into the section something which is not there.[18]

Even so it seems that the courts would insist upon "solid factual base for the appellant's suspicions, rather than a mere feeling that something is wrong".[19] The material placed before the Company Law Board must be such as to justify an order for deeper probe into the affairs of the company.[20] In *Miles Aircraft Ltd, Re, (No 2)*[21] a company, having suffered a loss of nearly one million pounds in a year, declared 7-½ per cent dividend. This was held to be sufficient to warrant an order for investigation.[22] Delhi High Court[23] has expressed the opinion that the person seeking an order must be able to show some manner of interest in the concern. It would not be correct to read the section as authorising any man in the street to seek an order for investigation. The court accordingly rejected the application of the landlord of the company who wanted investigation on the grounds that he had paid a sum of money to the managing director to induce him to vacate the premises and he misappropriated the money, or that he was using his political contacts for promoting business or that he had misappropriated the money borrowed by the company from banks. Citing a passage from a decision of the House of Lords[24] the court said that the section should be so interpreted as to enable relief to be obtained only by some person whose rights have been affected by the manner in which the affairs of the company have

---

18. D. A. DESAI J at p 68, *ibid.*
19. R. D. Fraser, *Administrative Power of Investigation into Companies*, (1971) 34 Mod LR 260, 261. Observations in management audit report without any corroborative evidence cannot be taken up for seeking an order of the Company Law Board for investigation of the affairs of the company. *A.P. State Civil Supply Corpn Ltd* v *Delta Oils & Fats Ltd*, [1997] 3 Comp LJ 146 CLB-PB; *Rohinton Mazda* v *Hypaids India (P) Ltd*, (2004) 121 Comp Cas 729 CLB, investigation not to be ordered on mere suspicion. There was the allegation of substantial expenditure and siphoning of funds. But there was no conclusive evidence that this had in fact happened.
20. *A.P. State Civil Supply Corpn Ltd* v *Delta Oils & Fats Ltd*, [1997] 3 Comp LJ 146 (CLB-PB).
21. [1948] WN 178.
22. *Id.* at pp 260-61.
23. *V. V. Purie* v *E. M. C. Steel Ltd*, (1980) 50 Comp Cas 127 Del.
24. *Gouriet* v *Attorney General*, [1977] 3 WLR 300. *See* further *Kumarunni Mathrubhumi Printing & Publishing Co, Re*, (1983) 53 Comp Cas 370 Ker; *P. Srinivasan* v *Y. S. A. & Sons*, (1983) 53 Comp Cas 485 Ker; *U. A. Sumathi* v *Dig Vijay Chit*, (1983) 53 Comp Cas 493 Ker.

been conducted or accounts maintained and has, therefore, a grievance in the eyes of law.[25]

Discretionary or Permissive Provisions

Such provisions are to be found partly in Section 235 and partly in Section 237(*b*).

Section 235 enables the Central Government and the Company Law Board to appoint inspectors for investigation in the following cases:

1. *On Members' Application*

    (*a*) On the application of two hundred members, or members holding one-tenth of the total voting power.

    (*b*) Where the company is without share-capital, on the application of one-fifth of the members.[26]

"When members apply they must support their application by evidence and the Company Law Board may ask them to give security for costs of investigations."[27] The evidence must show "that the applicants have good reason for requiring the investigation". The amendment of 1988 has made this alteration that application under this part of Section 235 has to be made to the Company Law Board. The CLB will give an opportunity to the parties of being heard. The CLB may then declare that the affairs of the company ought to be investigated. On such declaration being made, the Central Government has to appoint one or more competent inspectors to investigate the affairs of the company and to submit a report thereon in such a manner as the Government may direct.[28]

---

25. No interim relief can be provided in such orders. Such relief is in the nature of a step-in-aid and, therefore, can be allowed only when the court is required to make a final adjudication. An investigation is only a fact-finding mission. *Ilunet India Ltd* v *ICRAO*, (1995) 17 Corpt LA 192 AP. The power of the High Court and that of the Company Law Board being concurrent, it has been held that the statutory remedy of approaching the Company Law Board should be exercised before asking the High Court to exercise its discretionary power. The court also said that directors against whom there are allegations of mismanagement should be parties. *Safia Usman* v *UOI*, 22 SCL 372 Ker.

26. As shown by the company's register of members, S. 235(*b*).

27. Not exceeding Rs 1000. The power can be exercised by the Central Government after a proper preliminary enquiry. It cannot be exercised simply on the basis of allegations. *Ramesh Motor Transport Ltd* v *Tadi Adinarayana Reddy*, (1997) 25 Corpt LA 177: (1997) 90 Comp Cas 383 SC. The party in this case had gone directly under writ jurisdiction which was not allowed. *Tadi Adinarayana Reddy* v *UOI*, (1997) 90 Comp Cas 376 affirmed in *Tadi Adinarayana Reddy* v *UOI*, (1997) 90 Comp Cas 376. Thus the power under S. 235 or S. 237 can be exercised either through the Company Law Board or the Central Government but not directly under writ jurisdiction. The jurisdiction cannot be diverted to the High Court even if some matters of public interest are involved. The Company Law Board is competent for the purpose. The Department of Company Affairs is supposed to be an expert body in company law matters. Therefore the standard under S. 237(*b*) has to be that of an expert. The Company Law Board jurisdiction is of exclusive nature. Consumer Protection Forums are also excluded. *Chandrika Prasad Sinha* v *Bata India Ltd*, (1997) 88 Comp Cas 81 CLB. The conduct of the petitioning shareholder is not relevant to this power. The petitioner had made out a case for investigation, his conduct, good or bad was irrelevant.

28. S. 236.

2. *On Report by Registrar under Section 234*

This section confers on the Registrar the jurisdiction to call for information or explanation in relation to any document submitted to him.[29] If the information or explanation is not furnished or is unsatisfactory the Registrar can make a report to the Central Government for necessary action.[30] Secondly, if a contributory or creditor, or other person interested, places materials before the Registrar: (*a*) that the business of the company is being carried on in fraud of its creditors or of persons dealing with the company or (*b*) otherwise for a fraudulent or unlawful purpose, the Registrar can, after hearing the company, call upon it to furnish any information or explanation.[31]

"A further power is conferred on the Registrar, who may, after being authorised by a Presidency Magistrate or a First Class Magistrate, enter any place, search or seize any document relating to the company, or its managerial personnel, if he has reason to believe that it may be destroyed or tampered with."[32] On receiving a report from the Registrar the Central Government may appoint inspectors.

3. *On discretion of Company Law Board*

Section 237(*b*) lays down three cases in which the Company Law Board can appoint inspectors on its own motion. The section empowers the Company Law Board to ask the Government to act if there are circumstances suggesting the following:

(*a*) *Fraud, Oppression or Illegality*

That the business of the company is being conducted with intent to defraud creditors, members or any other person, or for a fraudulent or unlawful purpose, or in a manner oppressive to certain members, or that the company was formed for any fraudulent or unlawful purpose. The CLB ordered under this clause, with a view to end oppression, the oppressing group of shareholders to purchase the shares of the complaining group.[33]

(*b*) *Fraud, Misfeasance or Misconduct*

That the persons concerned with the formation of the company or management of its affairs have been in connection therewith, guilty of

---

29. S. 234(1). The information or explanation is required to be submitted on the pain of penalties. *See* sub-section (4).
30. S. 234(6).
31. HIDAYATULLAH J (afterwards CJ), in *Barium Chemicals Ltd* v *Company Law Board*, [1966] 2 Comp LJ 151, 164: (1966) 36 Comp Cas 639: AIR 1967 SC 295.
32. *Ibid.*
33. *Kuki Leather (P) Ltd* v *T.N.K. Govindaraju Chettiar & Co*, (2002) 110 Comp Cas 474 Mad. The Civil Procedure Code, being not wholly applicable, a compromise between the parties was held to be effective though not signed as required by CPC.

fraud, misfeasance or other misconduct towards the company or towards any of its members.[34]

(c) Inadequate Information

That the members of the company have not been given all the information with respect to its affairs which they might reasonably expect including information as to commission payable to the managing director or manager.[35]

The concepts emphasised by the provision are nothing new to company law. The phrase "intent to defraud creditors" has already been judicially construed under Section 542 which imposes liability for fraudulent conduct of business.[36] The word "oppressive" has been construed in a number of cases under Section 397 including the decision of the Supreme Court in *Shanti Prasad Jain* v *Kalinga Tubes Ltd*[37] and the same meaning is likely to be attached here.

Referring to the words "fraud, misfeasance or other misconduct" a learned commentator says:

> These seem to be words of very wide import; in *Selangor United Rubber Estates Ltd* v *Cradock*[38] Goff J held, withdrawing some of his dicta in an earlier case,[39] that "other misconduct" is not to be construed *ejusdem generis* with "fraud" and "misfeasance" and that the statutory wording quoted above does not include "moral turpitude". In view of this, it seems that [the] section... [would] extend to what was called in *B. Johnson & Co, Re*,[40] "common law negligence". The Board of Trade, however, are of opinion that this head does not include mere managerial inefficiency.[41]

Observations in a management audit report which were not substantiated by any evidence could not be taken up for seeking an order of

---

34. *Incab Industries Ltd, Re*, (1996) 23 Corpt LA 245 CLB, diversion of funds and project money, laxity in collection of loans, payment of commission without justification, wasteful expenses, investigation ordered. *A.P. Civil Supplies Corpn Ltd* v *Delta Oils & Fats Ltd*, (2007) 136 Comp Cas 172 AP, statutory and management audit report showed irregularities causing loss to company and benefiting persons in management, Central Government directed to appoint inspectors for deep and elaborate investigation.

35. Where the allegations related to reservation in issues in favour of foreign investors and the same was approved by the shareholders and the Government bodies at various stages and all the approvals were obtained with total transparency, an order of investigation could not be made. *Chandrika Prasad Sinha* v *Bata India Ltd*, (1997) 88 Comp Cas 81 CLB.

36. See *William C. Leitch Bros Ltd, Re*, [1932] 2 Ch 71: [1932] All ER Rep 892; *Nagendra Prabhu* v *Popular Bank*, (1969) 39 Comp Cas 685: ILR [1969] 1 Ker 340: AIR 1970 Ker 120 and *Maidstone Buildings Provisions Ltd, Re*, [1971] 1 WLR 1085.

37. [1965] 1 Comp LJ 193: AIR 1965 SC 1535: (1965) 35 Comp Cas 351.

38. [1967] 1 WLR 1168.

39. *S. B. A. Properties Ltd* v *Cradock*, [1967] 1 WLR 716: [1967] 2 All ER 610.

40. 1955 Ch 634, 648, Lord EVERSHED MR.

41. Minutes of Evidence to the Jenkins Committee, para 6946. The learned commentator is R. D. Fraser, *Administrative Power of Investigation into Companies*, (1971) 34 Mod LR 260 at p 262.

investigation.[42] Failure in finalisation of accounts for over five years has been held sufficient evidence for supporting an order of investigation.[43]

The power is only to make a declaration that the affairs of the company ought to be investigated and not to direct an investigation.[44]

Manner of exercising Discretion

"These grounds limit the jurisdiction of the Central Government."[45] The Government (now Company Law Board) does not have "a general discretion to go on a fishing expedition to find evidence".[46] An order for investigation can be justified only if the circumstances exist which suggest an inference of the enumerated kind. Explaining the scope of the Government's power in *Barium Chemicals Ltd* v *Company Law Board*, HIDAYATULLAH J (afterwards CJ) said:[47]

No doubt the formation of opinion is subjective... (but) the existence of "circumstances" is a condition fundamental to the making of an opinion, the existence of circumstances, if questioned, has to be proved at least *prima facie*. It is not sufficient to assert that the circumstances exist and give no clue to what they are because the circumstances must be such as to lead to conclusions of certain definiteness. The conclusion must relate to an intent to defraud, a fraudulent or unlawful purpose, fraud or misconduct or the withholding of information of a particular kind. We have to see whether the Chairman[48] in his affidavit has shown the existence of circumstances leading to such tentative conclusions. If he has, his action cannot be questioned because the inference is to be drawn subjectively and even if this Court would not have drawn a similar inference that fact would be irrelevant. But if the circumstances pointed out are such that no inference of the kind stated in Section 237(*b*) can at all be drawn the action would be *ultra vires* the Act and void.

The facts of the case were as follows:

The Secretary of the Company Law Board issued an order on behalf of the Board under Section 237(*b*) appointing four persons as inspectors

---

42. *A.P. State Civil Supply Corpn Ltd* v *Delta Oils & Fats Ltd*, (1999) 96 Comp Cas 303: [1997] 2 Comp LJ 146 CLB.
43. *Essar Usha Corpn* v *Richmen Silks Ltd*, (1999) 21 SCL 137: (1999) 34 CLA 336 CLB.
44. *Safia Usman* v *UOI*, (2002) 110 Comp Cas 710 Ker.
45. HIDAYATULLAH J (afterwards CJ) in *Barium Chemicals Ltd* v *Company Law Board*, [1966] 2 Comp LJ 151, 167: (1966) 36 Comp Cas 639: AIR 1967 SC 295.
46. *Ibid*
47. *Id.* at p 168.
48. The Chairman of the Company Law Board. "The Board was constituted on February 1, 1964, by a notification and by a notification of even date in the exercise of the powers conferred by clause (*a*) of sub-s. (1) of S. 637, read with sub-section (1) of S. 10-E of the Companies Act, the Central Government delegated its powers and function to the Board under S. 237(*b*) among others." See HIDAYATULLAH J (afterwards CJ), *ibid*, 165.

to investigate the affairs of the appellant company. The order was challenged on several grounds. Two of the grounds were that the order was *mala fide* and that the Board had acted on materials extraneous to Section 237(*b*). The Chairman in his affidavit alleged that there was delay, bungling and faulty planning of the project entailing double expenditure, continuous losses resulting in one-third of the share capital being wiped out, shares being quoted at half their face value and severance of their connection by some eminent persons.[49]

The Supreme Court held that these circumstances "cannot by themselves suggest an 'intent to defraud or fraudulent management.... Mere bungling or faulty planning cannot constitute either misfeasance or misconduct."[50]

Similarly, where the management of a company acquired the shares of its subsidiary of Rs 10 each at a premium of Rs 100 and offered them to the members in lieu of cash dividends and 99% of them opted for the shares; made a loan of a huge sum to its subsidiary at 2%, though it was not justified by commercial expediency; these were held to be not suggestive of fraud as to warrant an order of investigation.[51]

In another case the allegations that there had not been adequate and proper audit of accounts, as the auditor's reports were based on defective information and that the auditors were not independent, were held insufficient to found an order,[52] particularly when it appeared that knowledge of these facts was acquired after making the order. Similarly, where it was alleged that shares were sold for inadequate consideration, an order for investigation failed as it appeared that no prior effort had been made to ascertain the market value of the shares and to compare it with the value obtained by the company.[53] The Court said: "The fact that one of the directors (though influential) was suspect is irrelevant." The statement of the Government that general meetings were not properly held, excess of application money was not refunded, refundable money placed in some other bank, money not used for purposes stated in the prospectus were held to be making out a ground for investigation.[54]

This line of cases shows that the courts have taken rather a strict view of the power conferred by Section 237. Explaining the reasons, HEGDE J

---

49. See the judgment of SHELAT J at p 188-189.
50. *Ibid.*
51. *Jiyajee Rao Cotton Mills* v *Company Law Board,* [1969] 2 Comp LJ 380 MP; *Ashoka Marketing Ltd* v *UOI,* (1981) 51 Comp Cas 634 Del, involving similar charges.
52. *New Central Jute Mills* v *UOI,* [1969] 2 Comp LJ 32: AIR 1970 Cal 183: (1970) 40 Comp Cas 102.
53. *Rohtas Industries* v *S.D. Agarwal,* (1969) 1 SCC 325: (1969) 39 Comp Cas 781: [1969] 1 Comp LJ 350. Loss of some share certificates in the office of the company and irregularity in issuing duplicates has been held not sufficient, *Charanjit Singh Ghuman* v *Dr Reddy Laboratories Ltd,* (1997) 25 Corpt LA 204 CLB.
54. *Premier Plantations Ltd* v *M. Ebrahim Kutty,* (2002) 110 Comp Cas 721 Ker.

said:[55] "In interpreting Section 237(*b*) we cannot ignore the adverse effect of the investigation on the company.... We must also remember that the section in question is an inroad on the power of the company to carry on its trade or business and thereby an infraction of the fundamental rights guaranteed to its shareholders under Article 19(1)(*g*)." The court may not order an inquiry into the economic functioning of the company. In a case before the Delhi High Court[56] the alleged grounds were a successive fall in profits, directors' relatives were appointed to high positions and on high salaries, creation of a subsidiary company with mainly the directors' relatives and employees and loans to the subsidiary on which no interest had been realised. The court dismissed the petition with the remark that even if all these facts were supposed to be true, the truth was floating on the surface and, therefore, what was to be investigated? "An investigation is necessary to discover something which is not apparently visible to the naked eye."

But subject to these considerations the "order of the Company Law Board under Section 237(*b*) is not justiciable when it is reasonably made *bona fide* even though the reasons given do not appeal to a court of law."[57] Thus where the Central Government came to hold the opinion that the working results and the rates of dividend declared were incompatible, an order for investigation was held to be justified.[58]

The Company Law Board should not hold back from the court the circumstances which suggested the necessity for an investigation. An order cannot be upheld if the circumstances are not disclosed particularly where no privilege is claimed in respect of such materials.[59] In one of the cases,[60] an inspector, having been appointed on allegations of fraud, could

---

55. *Rohtas Industries* v *S.D. Agarwal*, (1969) 1 SCC 325: AIR 1969 SC 707: (1969) 39 Comp Cas 781: [1969] 1 Comp LJ 350.
56. *Delhi Flour Mills Ltd, Re*, (1975) 45 Comp Cas 33 Del.
57. *See* the judgment of the Calcutta High Court in *Ashoka Marketing Ltd* v *UOI*, [1966] 1 Comp LJ 267 and the judgment of SHELAT J in the *Barium Chemical* case.
58. *Ibid.* See also *New Central Jute Mills* v *Dy Secy, Ministry of Finance*, [1964] 2 Comp LJ 152; *Raja.Narayanalal Bansilal* v *Manick Phiroze Mistry*, (1960) 30 Comp Cas 644: AIR 1961 SC 29; *Patrakala Tea Co Ltd, Re*, [1966] 2 Comp LJ 177 Cal; *Ashoka Marketing Ltd* v *Company Law Board*, [1968] Comp LJ 190: (1968) 38 Comp Cas 519 Cal. *See* also *Norwest Holst Ltd* v *DTI*, The Times, February 2, 1978, noted 1978 JBL 179.

   The appointment of inspectors puts the company's management under a cloud. Even so natural justice is not applicable. Lord DENNING, MR said that individual shareholders often in practice had little control over the company's affairs, the directors were often a self perpetuating hierarchy. The Department's power to appoint inspectors should be seen as a substitute for inadequate shareholder control, and consequently courts should not fetter investigations that might be the only machinery available for keeping the public interest intact and seeing that companies were properly conducted, even if this machinery might be slightly unfair to individuals. The court refused to review the Minister's decision on the grounds that, by refusing to state his reasons, the Minister must be assumed to have no good reasons. So long as the Minister acted in good faith, he need not disclose his reasons.

   The duty of inspectors to act fairly should not be elaborated so as to turn a basically inquisitorial procedure into an accusational procedure.
59. *Govt of India* v *Sahu Jain Ltd*, [1969] 1 Comp LJ 231.
60. *Dy Secy, Ministry of Finance* v *Sahu Jain Ltd*, (1970) 40 Comp Cas 83 Cal.

not complete his work even after securing three extensions. He was then relieved by two new inspectors and the investigation was continued for nearly 15 months. When the order was challenged, the Government failed to disclose any facts on which they had proceeded. Their attitude was best described by MITRA J's words:

> The appellants closed and bolted the door. They drew the veil tightly around them, and they thought that the veil can neither be pierced nor lifted to see if materials exist which the statute requires as to be a precondition to the making of an order.

Where a Government corporation had majority in the company's Board of directors and, therefore, it could have carried out a special audit and adopted remedial measures, if necessary, an order of investigation into affairs was considered to be not necessary.[61]

Powers of inspectors [S. 240]

Where an inspector investigating the affairs of a company thinks it necessary to investigate the affairs of another company in the same management or group, he is empowered to do so. However, in some cases mentioned in Section 239(2), he has to obtain prior approval of the Central Government for that purpose.[62] Section 240 has been amended by the Amendment of 2000. Sub-section (1) was substituted. The new sub-section provides that it shall be the duty of all officers and other employees and agents of the company and those of any other body corporate whose affairs are being investigated under Section 239:

(*a*) to preserve and to produce to an inspector or any person authorised by him in this behalf with the previous approval of the Central Government, all books and papers of or relating to, the company or, as the case may be, of or relating to the other body corporate, which are in their custody or power; and

(*b*) otherwise to give to the inspector all assistance in connection with the investigation which they are reasonably able to give.

For facilitating the task of the inspector, it is the duty of all officers in charge of the management of the company to produce to the inspector all books and papers of the company which are in their custody and power and to give to the inspector all assistance in connection with the investigation which they are reasonably able to give.[63] The inspector may examine on

---

61. *Punjab Agro Industries Corpn Ltd* v *Superior Genetics (India) Ltd*, (2002) 108 Comp Cas 349 CLB.

62. *Sahu Jain Ltd* v *Dy Secy, Ministry of Finance*, [1965] 2 Comp LJ 145. S. 238 provides that no firm, body corporate or other association shall be appointed as an inspector under Ss. 235 and 237. *S.P. Gupta* v *State (NCT of Delhi)*, (2006) 132 Comp Cas 402 Del, where a police report had been filed about the dishonour of a cheque, these provisions could not be used to prevent police investigation.

63. S. 240. This duty is imposed upon all officers and other employees and agents of the company, and where the company is or was managed by a managing agent, or secretaries and

oath any such person and for this purpose require his personal attendance.[64] If a person required to appear or produce books, makes a default, that is a punishable offence.[65] Where an inspector finds that a person, whom he has no power to examine on oath, ought to be so examined the inspector may do so with the previous approval of the Central Government. Notes of any such examination are to be taken in writing and signed by the person examined and may be used in evidence against him.[66] A refusal to answer questions is also punishable. For example, in *Pergamon Press Ltd, Re*,[67] the company was engaged in a litigation in a foreign country. Its officers felt that any information given by them might pass to the foreign party and adversely affect their case. So they refused to give any information unless an assurance was given to them that it would not be published without being shown to them. Even so they were held guilty of contempt.

In an English case,[68] an Inspector of Companies was not allowed to be questioned or cross-examined as to why he caused an examination of the company's books and what he considered to be the public interest that made it expedient that the company be wound up. The power is of subjective nature and its exercise could only be challenged on an allegation of bad faith or if the inspector could be shown to have taken into account extraneous material or had otherwise misdirected himself as to the nature of his power,[69] or has been shown to be making an unfair exercise of his power. The principle of bias does not apply to an investigation where the officers are exercising a policing function. The court's powers of review are, however, not limited to cases where it could be shown that the officers had not acted *bona fide*. The ground of unfairness does apply.[70]

In reference to the report, it has been held in some English cases that it "being a statutory report made by persons in a statutory fact-finding

---

     treasurers, upon all officers and agents of any such concern, or, where the affairs of any other company, managing agent, or secretaries, treasurers are investigated under S. 239, upon all officers and agents of such company, etc., or where it is a firm, upon all its partners.

64. S. 240(2).

65. S. 240(3).

66. S. 40(5). See *R. v Harris (Richard)*, [1970] 1 WLR 1252: [1970] 3 All ER 746 (CCA), evidence admitted in criminal proceedings.

67. [1970] 3 WLR 792: [1970] 3 All ER 535 CA. *See* also *Armuent, Re*, [1975] 3 All ER 441, where it was held that the report of inspectors was *prima facie* evidence admissible for founding a winding up order. *See* further *An Inquiry under the Company Securities (Insider Dealings) Act, 1985, Re*, 1988 BCLC 153 HL: [1988] 1 All ER 203, where the House of Lords consider the privilege of a financial journalist not to disclose his sources of information about a take-over; *Lonrho plc v Secy of State for Trade and Industry*, [1989] 2 All ER 609, where refusal to publish the report was considered by the House of Lords as justified because publication would have prejudiced further proceedings in the matter. *London United Investments plc, Re*, [1992] 2 All ER 842 CA, the privilege against self-incrimination is not available in answering questions on which the inspector is seeking information. Also on the same point, *Bishopgate Investment Management Ltd v Maxwell*, [1992] 2 All ER 856 CA.

68. *Golden Chemical Products Ltd, Re*, The Times, December 10, 1976: 1976 JBL 55.

69. *See* further *London & County Securities Ltd v Nicholson*, [1980] 1 WLR 948, question of privilege.

70. *R. v Secy of State for Trade, ex p Perestello*, (1979) 124 SJ 63.

capacity, the court must be entitled to look at it and act upon it, unless it is challenged on behalf of the company."[71]

In still another English case,[72] in the course of his report, the inspector found that the sum of approximately £44,000 had been taken away from the resources of the company. The report also noted the manner of misappropriation and the officers involved. Relying upon an earlier decision[73] the court held that the function of the inspector is to make an inquiry and report and not to come to a judicial decision and, therefore, it is not a proceeding of such a nature that prohibition can lie in respect of it either to the Board of Trade or to the inspector.

Where the report of an inspector was highly critical of the conduct of the chairman and chief executive of the company and the latter challenged its fairness on the ground that the inspector had violated rules of natural justice by not giving him a chance of explaining matters before signing his report, the court allowed him no relief.[74] The court pointed out that the report of the inspector is not evidence in the real sense of the word and, therefore, the persons hit by the report have every chance to disprove its contents. But without doing so they cannot ask the court not to act on it.

Seizure of books [S. 240-A]

Where the inspector has reasonable grounds to believe that relevant books or papers may be destroyed or falsified, he may make an application to a Magistrate and obtain an order for the seizure of such books and papers. The order may authorise him to enter the place where such books and papers are kept, to search the place and to seize them. At the conclusion of the investigation the inspector must return the documents.

Report [S. 241]

The inspector has to prepare and submit a report to the Central Government. The Government is bound to forward a copy of the report to the company at its registered office and also to any company, managing agent, secretaries or treasurers or associates dealt with in the report by virtue of Section 239. Where the inspector was appointed on the application of the members, a copy has to be sent to them also if they request for it and where he was appointed on the court's order, a copy must be sent to the court also. Where an inspector is appointed at the instance of the CLB, a copy of the report should be sent to it. Other interested persons may obtain the report on

71. *Travel and Holiday Clubs Ltd, Re*, [1967] 2 All ER 606: [1970] 1 WLR 711. The report is an evidence only for the purposes of being used as a material for winding up or proceedings against persons commented upon. *Savings and Investment Bank Ltd* v *Gas Co*, [1984] 1 All ER 296 Ch D.
72. *SBA Properties Ltd, Re*, (1967) 1 WLR 799: [1967] 2 All ER 615.
73. *Grosvenor and West End Railway Terminus Hotel Co, Re*, [1897] 76 LT 337: [1895-9] All ER Rep Ext 1836.
74. *Maxwell* v *Deptt of Trade*, [1974] 2 All ER 122 CA.

payment of prescribed fee and the Government may also cause the report to be published.

If the report shows that any person has committed any offence for which he is criminally liable, the Government may prosecute him for the offence. Further, the Government may, on the basis of the report, apply to the court for the winding up of the company or make an application for an order under Sections 397 and 398 for prevention of oppression and mismanagement.

Where it appears from the report that a fraud or misappropriation of property has been committed and the company is, therefore, entitled to bring an action for damages for the misconduct or for the recovery of any property which has been misapplied or wrongfully retained, the Central Government may itself bring proceedings for that purpose in the name of the company. In any such proceeding the report shall be admissible as evidence of the opinion of the inspector in relation to any matter contained in the report.[75]

The expenses of investigation are to be defrayed in the first instance by the Central Government. But the Government is entitled to be reimbursed by any person who has been convicted on a prosecution instituted in pursuance of the report or required to pay damages as a result of the report. The company in whose name proceedings are brought is also bound to reimburse the Government. Reimbursements can also be recovered from any managerial personnel dealt with by the report and from the applicants.[76]

Investigation of ownership of company [S. 247]

Public interest may sometimes require the Central Government to know the persons who are financially interested in a company and who control its policy or materially influence it. For this reason, Section 247 provides that where there is good reason to do so, the Government may appoint one or more inspectors to investigate and report on the membership of the company and other matters relating to it. The amendment of 1988 empowers the CLB, while dealing with any proceedings before it, to declare by an order that the affairs of the company ought to be investigated as regards the ownership for the purpose of determining as to who are or have been financially interested in the success or failure, whether real or apparent of the company or able to control or materially influence the policy of the company. In such a case, the Government becomes bound to appoint inspectors. Subject to the restrictions imposed by the Government, the

---

75. S. 246. The report has to be filed in proceedings initiated on its basis, but otherwise it is a privileged document. The court may order its production in a proceeding for production of privileged documents. *Saden v Burns*, (1996) 2 BCLC 636 Ch D; *R. v Secy of State for Trade and Industry*, (1996) 2 BCLC 636 Ch D.
76. S. 245.

inspector shall have the power to investigate any circumstances which suggest that there is some arrangement or understanding which, though not legally binding has been or is likely to be observed by the company in practice.[77] If the company is or was being managed by a managing agent, secretaries and treasurers, the powers of the inspector will extend to investigate the ownership and control of shares, where such managing agent or secretaries and treasurers is a company, and where it is a firm, the inspector shall have the power to find out the persons who manage or control its affairs as partners. Further, he shall also have the power to know the persons who share or shared the remuneration of such managing agent or secretaries and treasurers.[78]

An inspector appointed for this purpose shall have the same powers with regard to production and seizure of documents and evidence as are enjoyed by an inspector appointed for investigation under Section 235.[79]

After the conclusion of the investigation, the inspector submits a report to the Central Government. The Government, however, in this case is not bound to furnish a copy of the report to the company or any other person, if it is of opinion that there is good reason for not divulging the contents of the report. But the Central Government shall have to keep with the Registrar a copy of such parts of the report as need not be that confidential.[80]

The expenses of this investigation are to be defrayed by Government out of money provided by Parliament. But the Government may order recovery of the expenses from persons on whose application the investigation was ordered.[81]

Investigation of ownership of shares [S. 248]

This section was omitted by the Amendment Act of 2000.[82]

---

77. S. 247(3). *Birla Corpn Ltd, Re*, (2006) 133 Comp Cas 515 Cal, death of a shareholder, held to be not a ground of investigation, the application was based on unfounded apprehensions.
78. S. 247(4).
79. S. 247(5).
80. S. 247(5), proviso.
81. S. 247(6).
82. Where persons in management were also holding controlling interest in the company, their attempt to have the ownership of an insignificant percentage of shares investigated did not succeed. *Bakhtawar Construction Co (P) Ltd v Blossom Breweries Ltd*, (1997) 88 Comp Cas 859 CLB-PB. Cancellation of shares allotted to a managing director on his ceasing to be so and allotting them to another person by creating duplicates was held to be a matter not requiring investigation, *Abani Bhushan Bhattacharya v Ericson India (P) Ltd*, [1997] 4 Comp LJ 473 CLB. Statement of facts appearing in management report showing irregularities, held not sufficient to invite investigation, *A.P. State Civil Supply Corpn Ltd v Delta Oils & Fats Ltd*, [1997] 3 Comp LJ 146 CLB-PB. Where it is necessary to do so, an order of investigation can be made at the instance of even a small shareholder. *Padma Taparia v Assam Brook Ltd*, (1997) 88 Comp Cas 838 CLB. An investigation under the section can be ordered only in a proceeding pending before the CLB. *Bakhtawar Construction Co (P) Ltd v Blossom Breweries Ltd*, (1998) 91 Comp Cas 744 CLB.

Restrictions upon shares and debentures [S. 250]

If as a result of any one of the above types of investigations or otherwise, it appears to the CLB that there is good reason to find out full facts about any shares in a company, the CLB may, if it is necessary for the purpose, impose the following restrictions on the shares:

(a) Any transfer of those shares shall be void.

(b) Where those shares are to be issued, they shall not be issued and any issue shall be void.

(c) No voting right shall be exercisable in respect of those shares.

(d) No further shares shall be issued in the right of those shares.

(e) Except in a liquidation, no payment shall be made of any sums due from the company on those shares whether in respect of dividend, capital or otherwise.[83]

These restrictions may be imposed for any period, but not exceeding three years.

Another power of the CLB under this section is that where as a result of any transfer of shares a change is likely to take place in the composition of the company's Board of directors, and if such change would be prejudicial to the public interest, the CLB may restrain such change from taking place unless the change is confirmed by it and may direct that voting rights on those shares shall not be exercisable for any period not exceeding three years.[84]

Where any transfer of shares involving any of the above changes is likely to take place, the CLB may restrain the transfer for any period not exceeding three years.[85] A restriction of this kind is likely to have a telling effect upon the image of the company and prejudicing the interests of many individual and institutional investors who may not be a party to anything wrong. This fact has to be kept in mind by the CLB before passing any restraint order. For example, no such order was passed in an English case in which an investor being called upon to give information about the nature of his interest in the company's shares, gave wrong information, but soon thereafter acknowledged

---

83. S. 250(2).
84. S. 250(3). Where transfer of shares and changes in the composition of the board of directors had already taken place and that too with the approval of the Company Law Board, the preventive powers under the section were not exercisable. *Alakananda Mfg and Finance Co (P) Ltd* v *Bahubali Services Ltd,* [1993] 3 Comp LJ CLB New Delhi. An investment in the shares of a company to the extent of only 10% of the share capital of the company has been held to be not so substantial as can make prejudicial changes in the management and require an order of investigation for imposing restrictions on shares. *Padma Taparia* v *Assambroke Ltd,* (1997) 88 Comp Cas 838 CLB.
85. S. 250(4). *Bakhtawar Construction Co (P) Ltd* v *Blossom Breweries Ltd,* (1999) 95 Comp Cas 35 CLB, promoters restrained from transferring shares out of their promoters' quota till the final disposal of the petition.

and rectified his errors and also gave an undertaking that he would not dispose of his interest in the shares unless permitted.[86] A restraint order was held to be justified where the nominee shareholders did not attach any importance and gave no response to a notice under the section.[87] In another case arising in connection with the same group of companies,[88] HARMAN J explained the matter in these words:

> Although a company has a *prima facie* right to know who owns its shares, the Act makes it a matter for the discretion of the court whether or not a freezing order under the section should be imposed or continued. On the facts, the failure to release shares from the freezing order could have the effect of preventing a take-over bid from going ahead and this could prejudice those shareholders who wanted to accept the bid.

The CLB will refuse an order or vacate it, where it was sought not in the interests of the company but to enable the directors to defend their position.

As long as the order is in force, any pending transactions can be finalised only with the leave of the CLB.[89]

Section 250-A provides that an investigation may be initiated even when an application for prevention of oppression or mismanagement is pending or the company has passed a special resolution for voluntary winding up. Similarly, an investigation which is in progress will not be stopped or suspended by reason of the fact that an application for prevention of oppression or mismanagement has been made or a special resolution for winding up has been passed.[90]

A Central Government can use the power under this section to make a reference only in connection with an investigation under Sections 247, 248 or 249. Hence, for the purpose of entertaining a petition under S. 250 the grounds specified in any of the above sections must be satisfied. Section 250(1) is only facilitative in nature. It facilitates investigations under the abovementioned sections.[91]

86. *Lonrho plc (No 3), Re,* 1989 BCLC 480 Ch D. A similar case is, *Ricardo Group plc, Re,* 1989 BCLC 566 Ch D where the restraint order was vacated as soon as the correct information was provided.
87. *Ricardo Group plc (No 2), Re,* 1989 BCLC 771 Ch D.
88. *Ricardo Group plc (No 3), Re,* 1989 BCLC 771 Ch D.
89. *Geers Gross plc, Re,* 1988 BCLC 140 CA; [1988] 1 All ER 224 CA; *T. R. Technology Investment Trust, Re,* 1988 BCLC 256 Ch D.
90. Employees are protected by S. 635-B by providing that Government must be informed of any action against an employee. *Ashoka Marketing Co v Addl ROC,* (1985) 57 Comp Cas 117 Cal.
91. *Bakhtawar Construction Co P Ltd v Blossom Breweries Ltd,* (1997) 88 Comp Cas 859 CLB-PB.

Position of legal advisers and bankers

On this point Section 251 provides as follows:

S. 251. Saving For Legal Advisers and Bankers.—Nothing in Sections 234 to 247 and Section 250 shall require the disclosure to the Registrar or to the Central Government or Tribunal or to an inspector appointed by the Government—

(*a*) by a legal adviser, of any privileged communication made to him in that capacity, except as respects, the name and address of his client; or

(*b*) by the bankers of any company, body corporate, [* * *] or other person, referred to in the sections aforesaid, as such bankers, of any information as to the affairs of any of their customers other than such company, body corporate, [* * *] or person.

COMPANY LAW BOARD [S. 10-E]

Proposed Abolition of Company Law Board

As and when the Companies (Second Amendment) Act, 2002 is enforced, the Company Law Board would cease to exist. Its powers and functions would become vested in the National Company Law Tribunal (Tribunal) and appeals from its decisions will be heard by the Appellate Tribunal and a further appeal would lie before the Supreme Court.

Constitution and powers [S. 10-E]

Establishment of the Board of Company Law Administration is one of the important effects of the Amendment Act of 1963. Section 10-E authorised the Central Government to constitute the Board. The amendment of 1988 renewed the power of the Central Government and also effected certain other changes in the section.[92] The function of the Board is to exercise the powers and discharge the functions as may be conferred on it under the Act or under any other law and has also to exercise and discharge such other powers and functions of the Central Government under the Act or any other law as may be conferred on it by the Central Government.

The Board is to consist of such number of members, not exceeding nine, as the Central Government deems fit. One of the members is appointed by the Government as the chairman of the Board. The Board may delegate any of its powers to the chairman or any member or its principal officer.[93] This power was conferred on the Board by S. 10-E (4-A) introduced by the Amendment Act of 1965, and as further amended in 1988.

The members of the Board shall possess such qualifications and experience as may be prescribed.[94] Acts done by the Board cannot be called

---

92. The amendment has been enforced w.e.f. 4-8-1989, GSR 139(E) of 4-8-1989.

93. S. 10-E(6). See *Alak Prakash Jain* v *UOI*, (1973) 43 Comp Cas 68, 99-100 Cal.

94. Qualifications have been prescribed under CLB (Qualifications, Experience and other Conditions of Service of Members) Rules, 1993 (w.e.f. 28-4-1993) and the same have been

in question only on the grounds of any defect in the constitution of the Board.

The composition of the Board was increased from five to nine members. This became necessary to enable the Board to deal with the new business which is being transferred to it under the Amendment Acts. The power of the court under Section 17 to confirm alterations in memoranda, to sanction under Section 73 issue of shares at a discount, to call a general meeting under Section 186, to order rectification of the register of charges, to order rectification of register of members under Section 111 and to provide relief against oppression and mismanagement under Sections 397-409 have been transferred to the Board. The Board is also to share the power of the Central Government under Section 637-A to grant approvals, etc.

Three new sub-sections have been added to Section 10-E to facilitate the handling of the new business. Sub-section (4-B) empowers the Board, to form one or more Benches to exercise special functions. Any act of a Bench shall be deemed to be an act of the Board.

Most of the powers transferred to the Board being of judicial nature, sub-section (4-C) provides that every bench shall have the powers of the court under the Civil Procedure Code, 1908, in respect of the following matters:

1. discovery and inspection of documents or other material objects produced as evidence;
2. enforcing the attendance of witnesses and requiring the deposit of their expenses;
3. compelling the production of documents or other material objects producible as evidence and impounding the same;
4. examining witnesses on oath;
5. granting adjournments;
6. reception of evidence on affidavits.

Sub-section (4-D) further declares that every Bench shall be deemed to be a civil court (for the purpose of Section 195 of Chapter 35 of the Criminal Procedure Code) and every proceeding before it shall be a judicial proceeding. This will enable the Board to punish any person for its contempt.

By the amendment of 1977 the Board has been given the power of an execution court; Section 634-A has been added for the purpose. The section authorises the Board to execute or enforce its orders in the same manner as

---

found to be constitutionally valid. *Satish Chandra* v *UOI*, (1994) 5 SCC 495: (1994) 81 Comp Cas 482 SC: AIR 1995 SC 142. The matters relating to disqualifications of members is under the jurisdiction of the Central Administrative Tribunal, *A.K. Doshi (Dr)* v *Central Administrative Tribunal*, [2000] CLC 1428 Del.

if it were a decree issued by a court; where the Board is not able to execute an order, it may send the order to the court within whose jurisdiction the company's office falls or the individual against whom the order is issued resides or works.

The amendment of 1988 declares that the Company Law Board shall, in the exercise of its powers and discharge of its functions under the Act or under any other law, be guided by the principles of natural justice and shall act in its discretion. The amendment also provides that subject to the provisions of the section, the Board shall have the power to regulate its own procedure.[95]

The CLB has to act in accordance with the principles of natural justice and also its own Regulations. The provisions of the Indian Evidence Act, 1872 and those of the Code of Civil Procedure do not apply to the proceedings before the Board.[96]

The Company Law Board does not have the power to review its own decisions under the existing provisions of the Companies Act.[97] An appeal was held to be maintainable to challenge the jurisdiction of the Company Law Board to pass consent orders.[98]

Where an Act, constituting special courts for trying cases arising out of securities scam relating to transfer of securities, excluded the jurisdiction of all other courts, it was held that the jurisdiction of the Company Law Board was not thereby affected because it is neither a court nor a civil court.[99] This decision of the Company Law Board was reversed

---

95. CLB Regulations, 1991. The constitutional validity of Ss. 10-E and 10-F was upheld by the Madras High Court in *V. Balachandran v UOI*, (1993) 76 Comp Cas 67 Mad. The right of appeal against the decisions of the Board as also under writ jurisdiction are sufficient checks upon the powers of the Board. *Shri Ramdas Motor Transport Ltd v Karedla Suryanarayana*, (2002) 110 Comp Cas 193 AP, the procedure must satisfy the requirements of natural justice.

96. *Rajinder Kumar Malhotra v Harbans Lal Malhotra & Sons Ltd*, (1996) 87 Comp Cas 146 CLB.

97. *Paulose (MV) v City Hospital (P) Ltd*, (1998) 28 Corpt LA 46 CLB. In exceptional cases, it may use its inherent powers, for example, in this case, restoring a petition which was dismissed earlier under mistake of facts, or of law. *Shree Cement Ltd v Power Grid Corpn Ltd*, (1999) 93 Comp Cas 854. The Supreme Court observed in *United India Insurance v Rajendra Singh*, (2000) 37 CLA 405 at p 409 that the remedy to move for recalling an order on the basis of newly discovered facts which showed fraud cannot be foreclosed. No court or tribunal can be regarded as powerless to recall its own order if the order was wangled through fraud or misrepresentation.

98. *Prakash Timbers (P) Ltd v Sushma Singla*, AIR 1995 All 320.

99. *Canara Bank v Nuclear Power Corpn of India*, (1995) 84 Comp Cas 62 CLB, Special Court (Trial of Offences relating to Transactions in Securities) Act, 1992. The Company Law Board is not a court for all purposes. *Prakash Timbers (P) Ltd v Sushma Singla*, AIR 1996 All 262: (1997) 89 Comp Cas 770. The court picked up passages as to the trappings of a court from *Shell Company of Australia v Federal Commr of Taxation*, 1931 AC 275.

on appeal to the High Court of Delhi. The High Court was of the view that the very purpose of the special courts is such that the jurisdiction of all courts and tribunals over the same subject-matter is necessarily excluded.[1]

The CLB has no exclusive jurisdiction on every matter relating to companies. It has jurisdiction only in respect of matters specially provided by the Act. The CLB is a tribunal and not a court. The proceedings before it are not in the nature of a suit. A suit was filed for an order to restrain interference in the functioning of the managing director. A separate petition before the CLB was filed for relief against oppression and mismanagement and for rectification of register of members. Thus the proceedings before the two forums were independent and distinct of each other. Proceeding before the CLB were not stayed.[2] On appeal, the High Court said that though the CLB has some of the trappings of a court, taking into account its scope and functions, special jurisdiction conferred upon it and control of the Central Government over it, it cannot be regarded as a court.

Appeals against orders of CLB [S. 10-F]

The amendment of 1988 introduced a new section to provide about appeals. Since the Board has been taken out of the controlling hand of the State and has been made independent and its powers and functions have been enlarged by conferring upon it jurisdiction in many company matters which was being exercised by the High Courts, an express provision as to appeals became necessary. Section 10-F provides that any person aggrieved by any decision or order of the Company Law Board may file an appeal to the High Court on any question of law arising out of such order.[3] Thus there can be no appeal on a question of fact.[4] The Board has become the final authority so far as questions of fact are concerned. Since facts are discovered by appreciation of evidence and if the appreciation has gone

---

1. *ABN Amro Bank* v *Indian Rly Finance Corpn Ltd*, (1996) 85 Comp Cas 716 Del.
2. *ADF Power Projects Ltd* v *M. Muralikrishna*, (2005) 124 Comp Cas 184. On appeal before A.P. High Court (2005) 59 SCL 313 AP.
3. *Mohd Zafar* v *Nahar Industrial Enterprises Ltd*, [1997] 4 Comp LJ 201 Del: (1998) 28 Corpt LA 251: (1998) 93 Comp Cas 717, where a question of law was neither raised before the CLB nor taken up by the CLB, it could not be said to be question arising out of CLB order. Another decision of the same kind *Gordan Woodroffes & Co Ltd UK* v *Gordan Woodroffe Ltd*, (1999) 97 Comp Cas 582, where the court also added that it is a limited jurisdiction and, therefore, the appellate court cannot go into the validity of a transfer which requires consideration of evidence including examination of witnesses. *Mineria National Limitada* v *Sociedade De Fomento Industrial (P) Ltd*, (2007) 136 Comp Cas 290 Bom, appeal lies before Single Judge and not before a Division Bench.
4. *Bhagwati Developments (P) Ltd* v *Peerless General Finance & Investment Co Ltd*, (2004) 51 SCL 204 Cal; *Micromerities Engineers (P) Ltd* v *Munusamy*, (2004) 122 Comp Cas 150 Mad, finding of fact that notices for the meeting were not issued and no shareholder was present, not disturbed in appeal. *PPN Power Generating Co Ltd* v *Peerless General Finance & Investment Co Ltd*, (2005) CLC 1 Mad DB, appellate court not to reassess facts. *Balaji Fabricators (P) Ltd* v *S. Rehana Rao*, (2006) 120 Comp Cas 97 CLB, order of CLB in setting aside a transfer because of violation of articles was not allowed to be reviewed because there was no apparent error on record.

wrong, factual matters can also be reopened in appeal.[5] A finding of fact which is based on no evidence or based on surmises, conjectures or assumptions, amounts to a finding without evidence. It becomes a question of law, and as such appealable.[6]

In the exercise of its inherent powers, the CLB can take notice of subsequent events lest it may fail to do justice between the parties.[7]

The phrase "arising out of" in Section 10-F would include questions of law arising out of facts found by the CLB.[8] An order as to joinder of parties is a question of law and, therefore, appealable. Consent orders are appealable.[9] If there is a doubt about genuineness of the consent.[10] A dispute as to shareholding pattern was resolved by the Company Law Board under a consent order. There was no grievance as to the genuineness of the consent. The court did not interfere with the order in appeal.[11]

Where in a petition for prevention of oppression and mismanagement, the finding of fact by the CLB was that the preliminary requirements were not satisfied, the Court refused to interfere as it found that the finding was based on the evidence on record. The court said that the section does not permit investigation into a question of fact even where additional evidence is tendered to question the finding of fact.[12] There can be no appeal on a finding of fact even if the appellate court might have differed.[13] The words "any decision or order" would include an order which does finally decide the rights of the parties. In a petition by a director who was taken to have vacated his office by reason of non-attendance, the new appointee in his place was not impleaded and without any information to him an order was passed for the management of the company by the first directors. This order

5. A finding of fact based upon proven facts is not a question of law. A finding that the requirement of S. 84 for issuing duplicate share certificates was not satisfied was held to be a finding of fact, *Shoe Specialities Ltd v Tracstar Investments Ltd*, (1997) 88 Comp Cas 471 Mad. Maintainability of a petition is not a pure question of law, it being mixed up with facts involved, a decision on maintainability was held to be not appealable, *Saroj Goenka v Nariman Point Building Services and Trading (P) Ltd*, (1997) 90 Comp Cas 205 Mad. The question whether the notice of a meeting was late was not raised before the Company Law Board and, therefore, not decided by it, could not be the subject-matter of appeal, *Mohd Jafar v Nahar Industrial Enterprises Ltd*, [1997] 4 Comp LJ 201 Del.
6. *Scientific Instruments Co Ltd v R. P. Gupta*, (1999) 34 CLA 36 All.
7. *Rajendra Kumar Malhotra v Harbans Lal Mehrotra & Sons Ltd*, (1999) 34 CLA 360 Cal.
8. *Nupur Mitra v Basubani (P) Ltd*, (1999) 35 CLA 97 Cal.
9. *Prakash Timbers (P) Ltd v Sushma Singla*, AIR 1995 All 320.
10. *Gillette International v R.K. Malhotra*, (1998) 31 CLA 73 Cal.
11. *Subhash Mohan Dev v Santosh Mohan Dev*, [2000] CLC 1151 Gau: (2001) 104 Comp Cas 405 Gau. An order on consent terms not appealable.
12. *J. P. Srivastava & Sons (Rampur) (P) Ltd v Gwalior Sugar Co Ltd*, [2000] CLC 1792 MP.
13. *Chand Mall Pincha v Hathi Mall Pincha*, (1999) 95 Comp Cas 368 Gau. See also *Boiron v SBLP Ltd*, (1999) 33 CLA 51 Del, where the finding of fact was that a ground for an order of investigation was made out, the court refused to interfere. *T.G. Veera Prasad v Sree Rayalaseema Alkalies & Allied Chemicals Ltd*, (1999) 98 Comp Cas 806 AP. No appeal was allowed against an order for appointment of an administrator, *C. Sri Hari Rao v Sri Ram Das Motor Transport (P) Ltd*, (1999) 97 Comp Cas 685.

was held to be appealable. The order was set aside because it violated natural justice.[14]

The appellate court can interfere in the order of the CLB only if the discretionary or inherent power has been exercised arbitrarily or capriciously or perversely, or where the CLB has ignored the settled principles of law in granting an interlocutory injunction. The court can also interfere with orders if it can come to the conclusion that the CLB has not exercised its power in granting an injunction in spite of the availability of facts established by overwhelming evidence to the *prima facie* extent or the material available on record justifies the grant of injunction and the refusal has caused failure of justice leading to irreparably injury to the party seeking the remedy.[15]

The time for filing appeals has been fixed to be 60 days which are to be counted from the date of the communication of an order or decision to the appellant. The High Court has been empowered on sufficient cause to extend the time for a further period of 60 days.

The provisions of the Civil Procedure Code have to be followed to the extent applicable. Accordingly, the memorandum of appeal should be accompanied by a certified copy of the order appealed against or at least of the operative portion of the order.[16]

An appeal would lie before the High Court where the registered office of the company is situate and not at the place where a decision of the Company Law Board or any of its Benches was delivered.[17]

Advisory Committee [S. 410]

The Companies (Amendment) Act, 1965, abolished the Advisory Commission. Instead, we now have an Advisory Committee. The Amendment says that "in the heading of Chapter VII" of Part VI for the words "Advisory Commission", the words "Advisory Committee", shall be *substituted.* All the sections of this Chapter were repealed and only one section remained, namely, Section 410. This section reads: "For the purpose of advising the Central Government and the CLB on such matters arising out of the administration of this Act as may be referred to it by that Government or CLB, the Central Government may constitute an Advisory Committee consisting of not more than five persons with suitable qualifications." Thus the Advisory Committee has the dual function of advising the Central Government and the CLB on the matters referred to it for advice.

---

14. *Gharib Ram Sharma* v *Daulat Ram Kashyap*, (1994) 80 Comp Cas 267 Raj.
15. *PPN Power Generating Co Ltd* v *PPN (Mauritius) Co*, 2005 CLC 1 Mad DB.
16. *Manohar Rajaram Chhabaria* v *Union of India*, (2002) 110 Comp Cas 162 Cal.
17. *Stridewell Leathers (P) Ltd* v *Bhankerpur Simbhaoli Beverages (P) Ltd*, (1994) 1 SCC 34: (1994) 79 Comp Cas 139 SC, reversing Delhi High Court in *Bhankerpur Simbhaoli Beverages (P) Ltd* v *CLB*, (1994) 1 SCC 34: (1994) 79 Comp Cas 139 SC.

The Advisory Committee differs in important respects from its predecessor, the Advisory Commission. The function of the Advisory Committee is to advise the Government and this was also the function of the Commission. But the Commission had the duty and power to inquire into matters enumerated in the now repealed Section 411. Further the Commission had, under Section 413 (now repealed) the powers of a court for the production of evidence and witnesses whenever necessary for the purpose of an inquiry. Such powers have not been conferred on the Advisory Committee.

Company Courts [S. 10]

Section 10 indicates the jurisdiction of company courts. The section says that the court having jurisdiction under the Act means the High Court of the area in which the registered office of the company is situate, except to the extent to which jurisdiction has been conferred on any District Courts or District Courts subordinate to that High Court. Such District Court functions as a company court in respect of companies having their registered office in the District. The subject-matter of the jurisdiction shall be as may be conferred by the Central Government. Such jurisdiction cannot, however, be conferred in respect of matters specified in Sections 237 (investigation), 391, 394, 395 (reconstruction, compromise, arrangement, amalgamation, etc.), 397 to 407 (prevention of oppression and mismanagement). Such jurisdiction cannot also be conferred in respect of matters relating to winding up except in reference to companies with paid-up share capital of less than one lakh of rupees.[18]

For the purposes of jurisdiction to wind up companies, the expression "registered office" of a company means a place which has longest been the registered office of a company during the six months immediately preceding the presentation of the petition for winding up. The jurisdiction to entertain a winding up petition is in the court in whose jurisdiction, the registered office of the company is situate. Such jurisdiction cannot be ousted or vested in any other court by agreement, acquiescence or understanding. Participation in proceedings in a wrong court would not prevent the party from approaching the right court.[19]

---

18. *Subramanian Swamy* v *Union of India*, (2004) 118 Comp Cas 126 Del, at least a part of the cause of action should arise within the jurisdiction of the court to enable it to take cognizance of an offence.

19. *Data Computer Services* v *Northern Digital Exchanges Ltd*, (1998) 92 Comp Cas 362 P&H; *G.T.C. Industries Ltd* v *Parasrampuria Trading & Finance (P) Ltd*, (1999) 34 CLA 350 All; *J. G. Finance Ltd* v *Jamna Auto Industries*, (1999) 34 CLA 382 P&H. *Punjab State Industrial Development Corpn Ltd* v *PNFC Karamchari Sangh*, (2006) 131 Comp Cas 113 SC, it was not permissible to the company court on the bidding of the State Government to direct the State Financial Corpn to release funds for workers' wages belonging to the company promoted by the Corporation. There is no jurisdiction to direct any third party to make such payment.

Civil Courts

Jurisdiction in respect of the following matters has been conferred upon the District Courts:[20]

Termination of disproportionately excessive voting rights. (S. 89)

Issue of certificates. (S. 113) [Initial application to Central Government]

Right to inspect company's register of charges and copies of instruments creating charges. (S. 144) [Initial application to Central Government]

Place of keeping and inspection of registers and returns. (S. 163) [Initial application to Central Government]

Inspection of minutes-book of general meetings. (S. 196) [Initial application to Central Government]

Right of members to copies of balance-sheet and auditor's report. (S. 219) [Initial application to Central Government]

Power of Registrar to call for information or explanation. (S. 234)

Register of Directors, shareholdings. (S. 307) [Initial application to Central Government]

The Companies Amendment Act of 1988 had vested the jurisdiction under the above sections, excepting that under Section 234, in the Company Law Board. The 2nd Amendment of 2002 has vested these powers in the Central Government.

In matters other than those so handed over to the care of special jurisdictions, the ordinary civil courts have jurisdiction to provide remedies. In other words, the jurisdiction of ordinary civil courts is applicable except to the extent to which it has been excluded.[21]

---

20. Except those of Jammu and Kashmir and for the State of Orissa and the Union Territory of Himachal Pradesh, where the jurisdiction shall be as may be conferred by the High Court. GSR 663 of 19-5-1959.
21. See *Dhulabhai v State of M.P.*, AIR 1969 SC 78 and *Union of India v Tara Chand Gupta*, (1971) 1 SCC 486: AIR 1971 SC 1558, as to exclusion of jurisdiction of ordinary civil courts. *Thiruvalu etc P Ltd v M. K. Seethai Achi*, [1987] 3 Comp LJ 129 Mad, action for accounts by managing director, matter for civil courts; *Prakasam v Sree Narayana Dharma Paripalna Yogam*, (1980) 50 Comp Cas 611 Ker, validity of a general meeting, not a matter for company courts; *M. G. Doshit v Reliance Petrochemicals*, (1994) 79 Comp Cas 830 Guj; breach of provisions at AGM, High Court had no jurisdiction. *Orissa State Financial Corpn v Kaliga Textile Ltd*, ILR 1973 Cal 38 Ori, dispute about an underwriting agreement, a civil matter; *T. L. Arora v Ganga Ram Agarwal*, [1987] 1 Comp LJ 241 Del, election to directorship, a civil matter; *Maharaja Exports v Apparels Exports Promotion Council*, (1986) 60 Comp Cas 353, a general survey of case-law; *Niranjan Singh v Edward Ganj Public Welfare Assn Ltd*, (1977) 47 Comp Cas 285 P&H, election to directorship and validity of notice calling a meeting; *Ravinder Kumar Jain v Punjab Registered (Iron and Steel) Stocks Holders Assn*, (1978) 48 Comp Cas 401 P&H, questioning the validity of a meeting. *B. Sivaraman v Egmore Benefit Society Ltd*, (1992) 75 Comp Cas 198 Mad, questioning the validity of appointment as director and seeking his removal. *Patel Roadways Ltd v Prasad Trading Co*, (1991) 4 SCC 270: (1992) 74 Comp Cas 11 SC, action lies at the place according to the provisions of S. 20 CPC because the word "corporation" as used there includes company. *Kaushiklal Parikh v*

Where a company court ordered the transfer of shares but made it subject to the result in the pending proceeding under Ss. 397 and 398, it was held that the court could modify its orders from time to time finding that the order is affecting adversely one party or the other.[22]

Questioning the validity of meetings and of resolutions passed at meetings,[23] have been held to be matters for civil court jurisdiction.[24] A director who is affected by a disqualification provision can move the company court for adjudication on the operation of the provision.[25]

The effect of passing consent orders was examined by the Supreme Court in *Nazir Hoosein* v *Darayus Bhathena*[26]. The validity of the replacement of the chairman by means of a resolution was questioned in a suit. The appointment of 12 additional directors was also under question. A consent order was passed by the court for a new meeting under the chairmanship of the court nominated person for reconsideration of the whole agenda.

It was held that by virtue of the consent order what was resolved in the earlier meeting was wiped off and became non est. Consequently, without any fresh authority, the earlier Chairman could not preside over any meeting of the Board of directors as his authority was only through the earlier resolutions and as there was nothing to show that the Board of directors had elected him to function as Chairman in any meeting. When in accordance with the consent order, a meeting was held under chairmanship of *S* wherein it was resolved not to appoint 12 additional directors, then any resolution taking a contrary stand could not be sustained. Further, when in a subsequent meeting presided over by the earlier chairman a resolution was passed inducting 57 new life members, since this meeting was not conducted in proper perspective and it also suffered from procedural irregularities the business done was not valid. However, in order to protect the interest of the life members so inducted, their cases were directed to be

---

Mafatlal Industries Ltd, (1995) 1 Corpt LA 102 Guj, questioning the validity of a resolution whether at board or company meeting in spite of the special provisions as to jurisdiction for petition against oppression and mismanagement because a resolution of the Board of directors can be attacked as invalid in a suit though it might not be oppressive to the minority shareholders or prejudicial to the company, while a resolution which may be valid in law might yet be oppressive to the minority shareholders. Following *Sheth Mohan Lal Ganpatram* v *Sayaji Jubilee Cotton & Jute Mills Ltd*, (1964) 34 Comp Cas 777: AIR 1965 Guj 96: (1964) 5 Guj LR 804.

22. *Ratan Chand Jain* v *Uberoi Ltd*, [1992] 2 Comp LJ 202 Del.
23. *T. M. Paul (Dr)* v *City Hospital (P) Ltd*, (1999) 97 Comp Cas 216 Ker, meeting was called at a time when some directors were unable to attend, resolutions passed at such meetings were held to be void.
24. *Allahabad Bank* v *Canara Bank*, (2000) 101 Comp Cas 64 SC, exclusive jurisdiction of Debt Recovery Tribunal.
25. *K. Venkat Rao* v *Rockwool (India) Ltd*, (2002) 108 Comp Cas 494 AP, FB, for example, a decision as to whether any of the disqualifying clauses of S. 283 have operated.
26. (2000) 5 SCC 601: AIR 2000 SC 2427.

placed before the next annual general meeting to be held for its consideration.

There is no provision in the Companies Act conferring jurisdiction on the High Courts to entertain applications relating to forfeiture of shares.[27]

Powers of Securities and Exchange Board of India [S. 55-A]

The new provision as to the powers of SEBI under the Companies Act as inserted by the amendment of 2000 (Jan 14, 2001) is as follows:

"**S. 55-A. Powers of Securities and Exchange Board of India.**—The provisions contained in Sections 55 to 58, 59 to 84, 108, 109, 110, 112, 113, 116, 117, 118, 119, 120, 121, 122, 206, 206-A, 207, so far as they relate to issue and transfer of securities and non-payment of dividend shall,—

(*a*) in case of listed public companies;

(*b*) in case of those public companies which intend to get their securities listed on any recognised stock exchange in India,

be administered by the Securities and Exchange Board of India; and

(*c*) in any other case, be administered by the Central Government.

Explanation.—For removal of doubts, it is hereby declared that all powers relating to all other matters including the matters relating to prospectus, statement in lieu of prospectus, return of allotment, issue of shares and redemption of irredeemable preference shares shall be exercised by the Central Government, Company Law Board or the Registrar of Companies, as the case may be."

These provisions relate to financial aspects and they have been handed over to SEBI's jurisdiction.

---

27. *Tej Prakash S. Dangi* v *Coramandal Pharmaceuticals Ltd*, (2002) 100 Comp Cas 546 AP.

18
Kinds of Company

UNLIMITED COMPANIES

One of the main purposes of the Companies Act is to confer upon the business community the privilege of trading with limited liability. Yet the promoters of a company have the choice to form the company with unlimited liability. Section 12 provides that "seven or more persons or where the company to be formed will be a private company, any two or more persons may form an incorporated company with or without limited liability". "The right of limited liability is desirable, but not a necessary adjunct to incorporation."[1] A company not having any limit on the liability of its members is termed an unlimited company.[2]

Companies with unlimited liability are rarely formed now. But such a company is definitely a suitable choice in cases where heavy liabilities are not likely to be incurred and the other advantages of separate corporate personality are desired.

An unlimited company must have articles of association stating the number of members with which the company is to be registered and if the company has a share capital, the amount of share capital with which it is to be registered.[2]

The obvious disadvantage of an unlimited company is that its members are liable, like the partners of a firm, for all its trade debts without any limit. But this does not mean that the creditors of an unlimited company can directly sue the members. Even in this case, the creditors have, if the company fails to pay, to resort to winding up and the liquidator will call upon the members to contribute to the assets of the company so as to enable him to meet the debts and the expenses of winding up.

There are certain advantages also. For example, an unlimited company need not have any share capital. And if it has, it may increase or reduce its capital without any restriction. And, what is more, it may purchase its own shares, as Section 77 does not apply to the case of an unlimited company.[3]

An unlimited company can get itself re-registered as a limited liability company under Section 32 of the Act. The conversion will not affect any debts, liabilities, obligations or contracts of the company existing at the time

---

1. Leonard W. Hein, *British Business Corporation: Its Origin and Control*, (1963-64) 15 Toronto Law Journal 134.
2. S. 27(1).
3. S. 77 contains restriction on purchase by a limited company of its own or its holding company's shares. *See* Chap 9.

of conversion and such debts etc. will become enforceable under Part IX of the Act.[4]

GUARANTEE COMPANIES

Where it is proposed to register a company with limited liability, the choice is to limit liability by shares or by guarantee. The liability of the members of a guarantee company is limited by a fixed sum which is specified in the memorandum and beyond which they cannot be called upon to contribute. Section 13(3) provides that "the memorandum of a company limited by guarantee shall... state that each member undertakes to contribute to the assets of the company in the event of its being wound up, for payment of the debts and liabilities of the company, such amount as may be required not exceeding a specified amount." Further, the articles of association of the company shall state the number of members with which the company is to be registered.[5]

It is not necessary for a guarantee company to have any share capital. But if it has share capital, it is subject to the same restriction as to reductions as the capital of a company limited by shares.[6] It does not also have the liberty to purchase its own shares.[7]

Any provision in the memorandum or articles of the guarantee company or any resolution which purports to give to any person other than a member the right to participate in the divisible profits of the company shall be void.[8]

Any division of the undertaking of the company into shares or interests is regarded as a provision for share capital even if the nominal amount or the number of shares is not specified.[9]

The Supreme Court has emphasised that the right of a guarantee company to refuse to accept the transfer by a member of his interest in the company is on a different footing than that of a company limited by shares. A guarantee company was running a stock exchange. The right of an existing member to transfer his interest to another person would involve the question of that person's admission to the membership of the organisation. Such membership may carry privileges much different from those of ordinary shareholders. The Supreme Court characterised the decision of the High Court that the same principles were applicable as much to transfer of

---

4. S. 32(3).
5. S. 27(2). *Rajeev Kwatra* v *Sunil Khanna*, (2006) 129 Comp Cas 373 CLB, petition for prevention of oppression filed by reason of induction of new members in contravention of articles.
6. S. 100.
7. S. 77.
8. This applies to companies registered after April 1, 1914. S. 37(1).
9. S. 27(2).

membership as to shares, as wrong. The matter was remitted for reconsideration.[10]

PRIVATE COMPANIES

A private company is a very suitable device for carrying on the business of family and small scale concerns, as the minimum number of members required to form a private company is only two.[11] A private company is defined in Section 3(1)(*iii*). It means a company which in its articles of association contains the following restrictions:

1. *Minimum Paid-up Capital*

The company has a minimum paid up capital of one lakh rupees or such higher amount as may be prescribed by its articles.[12]

2. *Restriction on Transferability of Shares*

There must be some restriction on the right of its members to transfer their shares in the company. Any restriction which will enable the directors to maintain the maximum limit of fifty members will serve the purpose of the Act.[13] This restriction is not necessary in the case of a private company not being limited by shares.[14]

3. *Restriction on Number of Members*

The number of its members must be limited to fifty, which shall be exclusive of members who are or were in the employment of the company. Joint holders of shares shall be treated as a single member.

4. *Prohibition on Issue of Prospectus*

The company must prohibit any invitation to the public to subscribe for any shares in or debentures of the company. The Amendment of 2000 requires that the company should prohibit any invitation or acceptance of deposits from persons other than its members, directors or their relatives.

Existing private companies have to increase the capital to one lakh rupees within two years.[15] The amendment further provides that if a company fails to do so, it would be liable to be struck off the Register of Companies in the manner of a defunct company.

A private company is compulsorily required to have articles of association. They are necessary, if not for anything else, to embody the above restrictions.

---

10. *Narendra Kumar Agarwal* v *Saroj Maloo*, (1995) 6 SCC 114: (1995) 10 Corpt LA 137: [1995] 5 Comp LJ 34 SC: (1996) 85 Comp Cas 172. The Court noted the difference in the set of articles in Sch. I which are applicable to guarantee companies and companies limited by share.
11. S. 12.
12. New requirement introduced by the Companies Amendment Act, 2000.
13. *See* Palmer's COMPANY LAW, p 37 (20th Edn, 1959).
14. S. 27(3).
15. To be computed from the enforcement date of the Amendment Act, 2000, w.e.f. Jan 14, 2001.

Advantages of a private company

The Act applies to private companies in all respects,[16] except where they are expressly exempted from its operation. These exemptions are commonly known as the privileges or advantages of a private company.

It is by virtue of these exemptions that a private company has been described as "an incorporated partnership, combining the advantages of both elements — the privacy of partnership and the permanence and origin of the corporate constitution. Ordinary companies are like bees working in a glass-hive. Private companies can keep their affairs to themselves."[17] Private companies exist with the sanction and encouragement of the Legislature.[18] They enjoy the benediction of the Legislature. Some of the advantages may be mentioned here:

1. *Subscription*

The formation of a private company requires only a minimum of two subscribers to the memorandum of association.[19] This, to a large extent, facilitates the formation and harmonious functioning of a private company and makes the choice of such a company most suitable for family or friendly concerns.

2. *Exemption from Prospectus-Provisions*

Public participation by issuing a prospectus is prohibited.[20] A private company is, therefore, exempt from all the requirements of the Act relating to the prospectus. For example, it has not to file a statement in lieu of prospectus;[21] it can proceed to allot shares without having to wait for any such thing as a minimum subscription.[22] It can commence business immediately on incorporation, as it has not to wait to obtain a certificate for commencement of business.[23]

3. *Directors*

Regarding the appointment of directors a private company is entitled to certain beneficial exemptions. For example, it is required to have only two directors.[24] All its directors can be permanent life directors; the requirement

---

16. Private companies are legal entities as much as public companies. They cannot be called a property of the joint Hindu family, *Vikas Jalan v Nucon Industries (P) Ltd*, (2001) 103 Comp Cas 343 AP.
17. Edward Manson, *The Evolution of the Private Company*, (1910) 26 LQR 11.
18. *See* YOUNGER LJ in *Commr of Indian Revenue v Sansom*, [1921] 2 KB 492: 125 LT 37.
19. S. 12.
20. S. 3(1)(*iii*).
21. S. 70(3).
22. This is so because S. 69 which contains prohibition on allotment unless minimum subscription is received applies only to the case of a company which has offered shares to the public for subscription, something a private company is prohibited from doing.
23. S. 149(7).
24. S. 252(2).

of retirement by rotation does not apply.[25] All the directors can be appointed *en bloc* by a single resolution. The special fourteen days' notice required by Section 257(1) for the appointment of a new director in place of a retiring one does not apply to the case of a private company.[26] Again, a public company cannot increase the number of its directors beyond the permissible maximum under its articles as first registered.[27] This restriction does not apply to the case of a private company. No director of a public company can act as a director,[28] unless he has within thirty days of his first appointment signed and filed with the Registrar his consent in writing to act as such a director. This provision of the Act does not apply to a private company.[29] Similarly the provision of Section 266(1)(*b*) requiring directors of public companies either to sign memorandum for taking qualification shares or to file with the Registrar an undertaking to take them does not apply to the case of a private company.[30] Restriction as to remuneration also do not apply.[31]

4. *Statutory Meeting*

A private company is exempted from the requirement of holding statutory meeting and filing statutory report.[32]

5. *Further Issue of Capital*

Under Section 81 a public company proposing to increase its subscribed capital by allotment of further shares, must, in certain cases, offer them to the existing members. But the section does not apply to a private company which is, therefore, free to allot new issues to outsiders.[33]

6. *Company an Undisclosed Principal*

According to Section 416 if any agent of a company makes a contract on behalf of the company but keeping the company as an undisclosed principal, he has to make a memorandum in writing of the terms of the contract and specifying the other party to the contract. He has also to deliver the memorandum to the company and send copies to each of the directors so that it may be laid before the board at its next meeting. Private companies are exempted from these requirements.

7. *Disclosure of Interest*

Another important exemption is in Section 300. As has already been seen, this section excludes an interested director from participating in

---

25. S. 255(1).
26. S. 257(2).
27. S. 259(*a*)(*b*).
28. Other than a director appointed after retirement by rotation. S. 264(2).
29. S. 264(3).
30. S. 266(5)(*b*).
31. S. 198.
32. S. 165.
33. S. 81(3).

voting at board's proceedings. But, as a private company is exempted from the operation of this section, an interested director is under no obligation to retire from a meeting of the board at which the subject-matter of his interest is discussed. He may participate in the proceeding and exercise his vote.[34]

Conversion of private company into public company

1. *Conversion by Default*

These privileges and exemptions can be enjoyed by a private company only as long as it does comply with the requirements of its definition as detailed in Section 3(1)(*iii*). "When a default is made in complying with any of those provisions, the company shall cease to be entitled to the privileges and exemptions conferred by or under the Act."[35] The whole of the Act would then apply to the company as if it were not a private company. However, discretion is given to the court to grant relief to the company from such consequences where the court is satisfied that the failure to comply with the conditions was accidental or due to inadvertence or to some other sufficient cause, or that on other grounds it is just and equitable to grant relief.[36] The order of relief is made on the application of the company or any other person interested and on such terms and conditions as seem to the court just and equitable.

2. *Conversion by Operation of Law* [S. 43-A]

Section 43-A has been omitted by the Companies Amendment Act, 2000. It was brought into being for converting compulsorily private companies into deemed public companies in certain circumstances like the amount of turnover and holding of capital to a certain percentage by other public companies, or by the private company in public companies or issue of advertisement for deposits. These provisions having been scrapped, the concept of deemed public company under Section 43-A has disappeared.

The only provision that survives in Section 43-A is sub-section (2-A) inserted by the Amendment of 2000. It became necessary to take care of the fact that a good lot of companies that had become deemed public companies would lapse back into private companies and a provision had to be given for the same. The provision says that when a deemed public company becomes a private company after the Amendment of 2000 (Jan 14, 2001), the company has to inform the Registrar and the latter would make necessary changes in his records such as the company's memorandum of association

---

34. S. 300(2).
35. S. 43.
36. Proviso to S. 43. *See*, for example, *Laxman Bharmaji* v *Emperor*, AIR 1946 Bom 18: 223 IC 110, where a private company issued debentures to the public and therefore, became a public company. Its officers were penalised for failure to file Profit and Loss Account and Balance-Sheet with the Registrar.

and certificate of incorporation. He had to carry out this process within 4 weeks from the date of the company's application.

3. *Conversion by Choice* [S. 44]

Apart from the above provisions of the Act, a private company may of its own choice become a public company. It may at any time pass a special resolution deleting from its articles the requirements of Section 3(1)(*iii*) and then, from the date of alteration, it becomes a public company.[37] Within thirty days a prospectus or a statement in lieu of a prospectus must be filed with the Registrar,[38] and all other requirements of the Act should be complied with, such as, increasing the number of shareholders and directors to the statutory minimum.

Conversion of public company into private company

A public company can also be converted into a private company. For this purpose it will be necessary to pass a special resolution by which the articles of the company shall be changed so as to include the requirements of a private company as prescribed in Section 3(1)(*iii*). But Section 31(1) provides that "no alteration made in the articles which has the effect of converting a public into a private company shall have effect unless such alteration has been approved by the Central Government". But confirmation of the court is not necessary.[39]

The conversion of a company from private to public or *vice versa,* does not change the identity of the company.[40]

FOREIGN COMPANIES

A foreign company means a company incorporated outside India. But for the purpose of Section 591, it means a company, which, though incorporated outside India, has a place of business in India. The meaning of the expression "place of business" has been judicially construed. The court considered the extent of business which has to be carried on to make "a place of business" for the purpose, in that case, to establish a sufficient presence within the jurisdiction for service of process.[41] A Canadian railway company's four directors were in England who formed a London Committee for the purpose of raising loans for the construction of the

---

37. S. 44(1).
38. S. 44(1)(*b*). See *Hindustan Lever* v *Bombay Soda Factory*, AIR 1964 Mys 173. A failure in this respect would entail a daily fine of Rs 500 for all defaulting officers till the default is made good. If the statement in lieu of prospectus which has to be filed carries a misleading statement, the guilty officers would be punishable with imprisonment up to 2 years or fine up to Rs 50,000 or both.
39. *Radiant Chemical Co, Re,* AIR 1943 Pat 278.
40. *All India Reporter Ltd* v *Ramchandra*, AIR 1961 Bom 29: ILR 1961 Bom 257. Legal proceedings instituted before conversion can continue, *Solver Oils and Fertilisers* v *Bhandari Cross-fields*, (1978) 48 Comp Cas 260 P&H.
41. *A.S. Dampskib 'Hercules'* v *Grand Trunk Pacific Rly Co*, [1912] 1 KB 222.

railway in Canada. They were using the office of another company without rent and transacted no other business than that of raising loans. The Court of Appeal held that the defendants were carrying on their business in the office used by the London Committee and could therefore be properly served with a writ. In the pictorial words of BUCKLEY LJ:[42]

> We have only to see whether the corporation is "here"; if it is, it can be served. The best test is to ascertain whether the business is carried on here and at a defined place. In the present case the company has a paramount, and also a subsidiary object: its paramount object is to make and run a railway in Canada, to do which a great many things must first happen: it has a subsidiary object, namely, the raising of money to carry out its paramount object. The raising of this loan capital is part of the company's business, and it is done here by a London Committee constituted of the directors resident in England.

Similarly, where an overseas bank hired premises in England, had some staff there for the purpose of conducting external trade and financial relations, that was held to be a place of business, though no actual banking transaction was taken up there.[43] A company established no office in England, but enlisted 5000 residents in the UK as members of its Titan Business Club so as to enable them to earn by chain system. This was held to be sufficient to give jurisdiction to the English courts to entertain a petition for winding up a foreign company. The company's employees were restrained from remitting any funds to Germany.[44] But where a foreign company posted a representative in India only for the purpose of eliciting orders from the company's customers, that was held to be not establishing a place of business in India. The court said that there should be a fixed and definite place where the business-like operations are carried on for a reasonably long period of time.[45]

What has to be shown in every case is that the business which was carried on at the relevant location was the business of the company itself.[46]

If a winding up order is passed, the court would get jurisdiction to restrain any act which would not be lawful. The court restrained recovery under a foreign decree from the company's business in England on a finding that the decree holder was not entitled to the sum awarded to him by a US Court.[47] Where the principal liquidation of the company was in Australia but ancillary

---

42. At p 223, *ibid.*
43. *South India Shipping Corpn Ltd* v *Export Import Bank of Korea*, [1985] 2 All ER 219 Ch D.
44. *Senator Hanseatische Verwattungsgesllseschaft*, (1996) 2 BCLC 562. The money could thus be captured for the purpose of paying back the contributors, *One Life Ltd* v *Roy*, (1996) 2 BCLC 608 Ch D. *Deflin International (SA) Ltd, Re*, [2000] 2 BCLC 71 Ch D, scheme found to be lottery, winding up ordered.
45. *P. J. Johnson* v *Astrofiel Armadorn*, [1989] 3 Comp LJ 5, 10 Ker.
46. *Matchnet plc* v *Williams Blair & Co LLC*, (2003) 2 BCLC 195 Ch D.
47. *Mitchell* v *Carter*, (1997) 1 BCLC 673 Ch D and CA.

liquidation was to be in England and Wales, and the Australian law departed from the general *pari passu* principle, it was held that the *pari passu* principle being a mandatory provision, the English Court had no jurisdiction to order transfer of assets to Australia, unless it could be assured that the distribution in Australia would be subject to the English *pari passu* principle.[48]

A foreign company has to furnish to the Registrar the following documents[49] within thirty days:

1. A certified copy of the charter, statutes or memorandum and articles or any instrument containing the constitution of the company. If the instrument is not in English language, a certified translation of it will have to be filed.

2. The full address of the registered or principal office of the company abroad.

3. A list of the directors of the company. In the case of an individual director, his name in full, his usual residential address, his nationality of origin, his business, occupation and particulars of other directorships held by him should be given. If a body corporate is a director, its corporate name and registered or principal office; and the full name, address, nationality of origin, if different from the nationality, of each of its directors must be specified. If the secretary is an individual, his present name and his usual residential address should be indicated and in the case of a body corporate, its corporate name and registered or principal office.[50]

4. A similar information about the secretary of the company.

5. The name and address or the names and addresses of some one or more persons resident in India, authorised to accept on behalf of the company service of process and any notices or other documents required to be served on the company. Any document, etc, served on such a person shall be deemed to have been served on the company. Where no such person is designated the service may be left at the company's principal place of business.[51]

6. The full address of the office of the company in India which is to be deemed its principal place of business in India.[52]

---

48. *HIH Casualty & General Insurance Ltd Re, Mc Mohon* v *Mc Grath*, (2006) 2 All ER 671 (Ch D).
49. S. 592. A foreign company cannot be sued in India for a cause of action which has arisen wholly outside India even if it has a place of business in India. So held by the Bombay High Court in *Partap Singh* v *Bank of America*, (1976) 46 Comp Cas 532 Bom. Residence in India in not established by merely posting a representative hired for seeking orders. *P. J. Johnson* v *Astrofiel Armadorn*, [1989] 3 Comp LJ 5, 10 Ker.
50. S. 592(2).
51. S. 596. Service of notices of a writ on persons whose names were recorded in the Registrar's files was held to be sufficient though the company had closed its foreign branch and the employees had left for India. See *Rome* v *PNB*, (*No 2*), [1990] 1 All ER 59 CA.
52. Where the writ to be served on the company was not addressed to the person named for

When any change occurs in the above particulars the Registrar must be notified accordingly.[53]

Such documents have to be filed at two places, first, with the Registrar of the State where the principal place of business is situate and, second, with the Registrar at New Delhi.[54]

If the company establishes any branch or branches of its business in India, no further information need be given, except that with the annual accounts the company should deliver three copies of a list of all its places of business in India and with reference to which the accounts are made out.[55]

A foreign company is further bound by the following obligations:

1. The company shall conspicuously exhibit on the outside of every office or place of business its name and the country of incorporation in English characters and in the regional language. The statement must also show whether the liability of the members is limited.

2. The name and the country of incorporation should also appear in English on all business letters, bill-heads and letter papers and on all notices and other official publications of the company. The statement must also indicate whether the liability of the members is limited.

A failure to comply with the above provisions does not affect the validity of any contract made by a foreign company, but "the company shall not be entitled to bring any suit, claim any set-off, make any counter-claim or institute any legal proceeding in respect of any such contract until it has complied with all the provisions of the Act relating to foreign companies".[56]

Accounts of Foreign Company

The obligations of a foreign company in respect of accounts are almost the same as those of a company registered under the Indian Act, for Section 594 provides that "every foreign company shall in every calendar year make out a balance-sheet and profit and loss account in such form, containing such particulars, including such documents (in particular, documents relating to every subsidiary of the foreign company) as, under

---

service of the company, service was held to be not effected in accordance with the legal requirements. But because the writ was posted to the right address and it was also served, the court, in its discretion, held the service to be good, *Boocock* v *Hilton International Co*, [1993] 4 All ER 19 CA.

53. S. 593.

54. S. 597. Non-compliance with the Act is punishable under S. 598 with a fine extending up to Rs 10,000, and, in the case of a continuing offence, with an additional fine which may extend up to Rs 1000 for every day during which the default continues.

55. S. 594(3).

56. S. 599. If the Indian branch of a foreign company changes its objects, the court in whose jurisdiction its place of business is located will have jurisdiction to try shareholders' objections. *F. R. Paymaster* v *British Burmah Petroleum Co*, (1976) 46 Comp Cas 587 Bom.

the provisions of this Act it would, if it had been a company within the meaning of this Act, have been required to make out and lay before the company in a general meeting and deliver three copies of these documents to the Registrar". Separate balance-sheet and profit and loss account in respect of the company's Indian business should be prepared and submitted along with a copy of the company's world business. Three copies of the accounts have to be filed with the Registrar. However, the Central Government has the discretion to exempt a foreign company from this obligation.[57]

Further, Section 600(3) requires a foreign company to maintain books of account referred to in Section 209[58] "with respect to moneys received and expended, sales and purchases made and liabilities in the course of, or in relation to its business in India."

Prospectus of Foreign Company

A foreign company may, even if it has no place of business in India, issue a prospectus offering shares or debentures for subscription. The prospectus shall have to comply with the provisions of the Act relating to prospectus.[59] For instance, it shall have to state the matters specified in Part 1 of Schedule II; the report set out in Part 2 of that Schedule, subject to the provisions of Part 3.[60] It must also be registered with the Registrar before it is issued.[61] The liability for misstatements is also the same as in the case of a prospectus issued by an Indian company.[62] In addition, however, to the general requirements of the Act, the prospectus of a foreign company has to contain particulars with respect to the following matters:[63]

(a) the instrument containing or defining the constitution of the company;

(b) the provision of law under which the company was incorporated;

(c) an address in India where the above instrument and the provisions of law may be inspected. If they are not in the English language, a certified English copy should be made available;

---

57. Proviso to sub-section (1) of S. 594.
58. *See* Chapter on Audit and Accounts. S. 601 gives some guidance about fee payable and S. 602 as to the meaning of some terms.
59. Ss. 603 to 608. Section 606 contain penalty for contravention of Sections 603, 604 and 605 and is as follows:
   "Any person who is knowingly responsible—
   (a) for the issue, circulation or distribution of a prospectus; or
   (b) for the issue of a form of application for shares or debentures or Indian Depository Receipt;
   in contravention of any of the provisions of Sections 603, 604, 605 and 605-A, shall be punishable with imprisonment for a term which may extend to six months, or with fine which may extend to [*fifty thousand rupees*], or with both."
60. S. 603(*i*)(*b*).
61. S. 605.
62. S. 607.
63. S. 603(*i*)(*a*).

    (*d*) the date and the country of incorporation;[64]

    (*e*) whether the company has established a place of business in India and, if so, the address of its principal office in India.

The Companies (Amendment) Act, 1974, reduced Section 591 into Section 591(1) and inserted sub-section (2). The effect of the amendment is that in the case of a foreign company having a place of business in India, if 51% of the paid-up share capital, whether preference or equity is in Indian hands, it shall have to comply with such of the provisions of the Act as may be prescribed as if it were a company incorporated in India.

By an amendment of Section 600, the provisions of Section 159 have been extended to foreign companies subject to such modifications and adaptations as may be made by rules drafted under the Act. Section 159 requires filing of annual returns. Similarly, the provisions of Sections 209-A, 233-B and 234 to 246 have been made applicable to the Indian business of a foreign company. Section 209-A contains provisions about inspection of accounts. Section 233-A empowers the Government to direct special audit, and Section 233-B, audit of cost accounts. Sections 234 to 246 provide for investigations.[65]

Offer of Indian Depository Receipts [S. 605-A]

The Central Government has been authorised by the section to make rules applicable for

    (*a*) the offer of Indian Depository Receipts;

    (*b*) the requirement of disclosures in prospectus or letter of offer issued in connection with Indian Depository Receipts;

    (*c*) the manner in which the Indian Depository Receipts shall be dealt in a depository mode and by custodian and underwriters;

    (*d*) the manner of sale, transfer or transmission of Indian Depository Receipts,

by a company incorporated, or to be incorporated outside India, whether the company has or has not been established or, will or will not establish any place of business in India.

---

64. *See also* S. 595(*a*).
65. For income tax purposes, it has been held by the Calcutta High Court in *Hunger Ford Investment Trust Ltd* v *ITO*, (1977) 47 Comp Cas 181, that a director functioning in India may be regarded as a principal officer. For purposes of liability in the host State as to when a foreign company is to be regarded as an instrumentality of the foreign State so as to require Government permission under S. 86 of the Civil Procedure Code before instituting proceedings, the court said that the Government should examine the question objectively and permit proceedings in civil matters of contractual or tortuous nature. *Veb Deut Nackt Seereederi Roetech* v *New Central Jute Mills*, [1994] 1 Comp LJ 138 SC. All the activities of a government company are not to be held as those of an instrumentality of the State, *Panchra Mayurakshi Cotton Mill Employees* v *State of W.B.*, (1993) 2 Cal LJ 176.

GOVERNMENT COMPANIES[66] [S. 617]

A Government company is thus defined in Section 617:

For the purposes of this Act, Government company means any company in which not less than fifty-one per cent of the paid-up share capital is held by the Central Government, or by any State Government or Governments or partly by the Central Government and partly by one or more State Governments and includes a company which is the subsidiary of a company as thus defined.[67]

Takeover of the management of a company by the Central Government under the provisions of the Industries Development and Regulation Act, 1951 does not have the effect of converting the company into a Government company.[68]

Following are the special provisions of the Act relating to Government companies:

"The auditor of a Government company shall be appointed or re-appointed by the Comptroller and Auditor General of India",[69] who will also have the power to direct the manner in which the accounts of the company shall be audited and give the auditor instructions in regard to any matter relating to the performance of his functions. The Comptroller and Auditor General is also given the power to conduct a supplementary or test audit of the company's accounts by such person or persons as he may authorise in this behalf,[70] and to require information for the purpose of such audit.[71] The

---

66. For a study relating to Government companies, *see* Shradha Kumari, *Government Companies in India*, (1957) ILJ 143.
67. A Government company is not an extension of the State. It is as much bound by the tax structure as any other company. See *Bharat Aluminium Co Ltd v Special Area Development Authority*, (1981) 51 Comp Cas 184 MP; *K. M. Thomas v Cochin Refineries Ltd*, (1985) 58 Comp Cas 48 Ker. But a Government company is growingly being regarded as an instrumentality of the State and as such amenable to writ jurisdiction even in the matter of its commercial bargains because it has to act fairly in trade matters also. See *Mahabir Auto Stores v Indian Oil Corpn*, (1990) 3 SCC 752: (1990) 69 Comp Cas 646 SC, where the IOC was prevented by means of a writ from cancelling without proper procedure an 18-year old distributing agency. Shareholding to the extent of 50% only would not make a Government company. The Govt. otherwise also had no control over the functioning of the company. Writ against termination of employee's services not allowed. *T. M. Devassy v Periyar Latex (P) Ltd*, (1994) 81 Comp Cas 560 Ker. *Balco Employees' Union v Union of India*, (2002) 108 Comp Cas 193 SC, no interference in the policy of disinvestment unless some illegality or *mala fides* shown. Employees also cannot complain. In a subsequent ruling in the context of *Hindustan Petroleum*, the Supreme Court revised its approach to such cases and emphasised that Parliament must be taken into confidence. *Amar Alcohol Ltd v Sicom Ltd*, (2005) 128 Comp Cas 63 SC, a fully owned State Financial Corpn was directed to take over a borrower company. The order was held to be valid though Government was thereby reduced to less than 50%.
68. *Kulbir Singh v Union of India*, (1997) 88 Comp Cas 586 Del. *Phoenix Neuro Relaxation Service Ltd v Estate Officer*, (1996) 2 CHN 440 Cal, a Government company (in this case ITDC) is within the category of Government for eviction under Public Premises (Eviction of Unauthorised Occupants) Act, 1971.
69. S. 619(2).
70. S. 619(3).
71. S. 619(3)(*b*).

auditor is required to submit a copy of his audit report to the Comptroller and Auditor General of India who shall have the right to comment upon or supplement the audit report.[72] Any such comments or supplements shall be placed before the annual general meeting of the company along with the audit report.[73] Where the Central Government is a member of a Government company, it is the duty of the Central Government to prepare an annual report on the working and affairs of the company. The report must be ready within three months of the company's annual general meeting before which the audit report is placed.

The report is to be laid before both Houses of Parliament together with a copy of the audit report and the comments, if any, of the Comptroller and Auditor General of India.[74] Where, in addition to the Central Government, a State Government is also a member of the company, the State Government shall lay the same report before the State Legislature.[75] But where the Central Government is not a member, every State Government which is a member shall have to prepare an annual report within the same time and then, as soon as may be, lay it before the State Legislature.[76]

Section 619-A(4), introduced by the Amendment of 1988, provides that the provisions of the section (regarding annual report on Government Companies) shall also apply to a Government company in liquidation.

Section 620 gives the power to the Central Government to declare by notification in the Official Gazette that any of the provisions of the Act shall not apply to any Government company or which provisions shall apply to any such company. The notification shall be effective to the extent to which it is approved of by Parliament.[77]

In the absence of any such exemption, the whole Act applies to Government companies.[78] The position is explained by the Calcutta High Court in its decision in *River Steam Navigation Co Ltd, Re*[79]. The River Steam Navigation Co was incorporated in England and was carrying on river transport between Calcutta and Assam. Its business suffered a severe

---

72. S. 619(4).
73. S. 619(5).
74. S. 619-A(*i*).
75. S. 619-A(2).
76. S. 619-A(3). For an account of the restrictions on the functioning of a Government company, see *S.K. Debnath* v *Mining & Allied Machinery Corpn*, [1968] 1 Comp LJ 214.
77. S. 620(2) as amended by the Amendment Act of 1977 now provides that a copy of every such notification shall be laid before each House of Parliament for 30 days and if both Houses agree in disapproving or modifying the notification, then it shall not be issued or issued as modified.
78. Thus a Government company was held bound by the provisions of its articles according to which the President had the power to give a binding advice to the company. *G. D. Zalani* v *Union of India*, 1995 Supp (2) SCC 512: (1995) 84 Comp Cas 40 SC. The court did not interfere in a business decision of the managing director in selecting a collaborator because the presumption of good faith was borne out by the facts.
79. [1967] 2 Comp LJ 106 Cal.

setback in the Indo-Pak conflict. The Government considered the service to be of strategic importance and, therefore, backed the company with financial assistance. The company also borrowed from its bankers. But even then it was not able to stand on its own feet. The Government, in order to assure the continuity of the service, acquired a majority of its shares. But even this massive backing was not equal to the debt burden of the company. Schemes of compromise and arrangement were then drawn up which were supported by all the parties concerned except one creditor who had applied for a winding up order. The company applied for the court's sanction to the schemes. P. B. MUKHARJI J had to deal with a number of technical objections. When a majority of the shares of a foreign company are acquired by the Government, does it become a Government company? The learned Judge found that the company, as it stood, satisfied the definitions both of a Government company, under Section 617 and of a foreign company under Section 591, so that it was, at the same time, a Government as well as a foreign company. Since this ruling would have created many absurdities, the court held that the company must be considered as a Government company.[80]

The second technical objection related to the jurisdiction of the Calcutta High Court. The company was not registered in India. It had no registered office in India. It should, therefore, have no right to apply under Section 391. The court overruled this objection by holding that such a company falls within the definition of "unregistered company" under Section 582(*b*), and Section 583(2) provides that for the purpose of jurisdiction the company shall be deemed to be registered in the State where its principal place of business is situate. Explaining the same the learned Judge said:

> If a Government company is incorporated and registered outside India, such a Government company comes within the definition of an "unregistered company" under Section 582(*b*) and all the provisions of Part X consisting of Sections 582 to 590 shall apply *mutatis mutandis* to such a Government company which do not militate against any special provisions for Government companies in Sections 617, 618, 619, 619-A and 620 of the Companies Act.

The next argument was that a Government company should not be permitted to float a scheme of compromise under Section 391 and this for two reasons, firstly, that such schemes originated as an alternative to winding up and a Government company cannot be wound up by the court and secondly, the Government can at any time set at naught the jurisdiction of the court by a notification that Government companies are exempt from

---

80. The court pierced the veil of incorporation for this purpose and finding that majority shares were in the hands of the State regarded the company as a Government company. *See* at p 119, *Ibid.*

the operation of Section 391. The court could not obviously approve of these objections. At the date of the scheme the Government had not issued any such notification and *minus* such exemptions the whole of the Companies Act is applicable to Government companies.

Referring to the argument that a Government company cannot be wound up, the learned Judge said:

> When the Government engages in trading ventures and particularly as Government companies under the Company Law, it does not do so as a political State but it does so, in garb and essence, as a company. The Government company, therefore, is a class of company and is not to be placed on the same pedestal as a State or Government....

> A Government company may have to tide over certain difficulties as a trading institution under the Company Law or it may be required to be wound up for distribution of its assets in certain contingencies. There is, therefore, no justification for holding that a Government company because it is a Government company cannot work under a scheme in an appropriate context. To wind up a Government company or to work a Government company under a scheme is not to wind up the Government but a Government institution trading under the Company Law.

Continuing further, the learned Judge added, that—

> ...to subscribe to the view that a Government company cannot be wound up or work under a scheme would mean that it is a kind of a perpetual company and once established can neither be extinguished nor work under an arrangement with its members and creditors.

Once the technical considerations were overcome, the only thing that the court had to consider was the fairness of the scheme and as to this it had no doubt:

> Balancing all the interests and considerations involved this is the picture which emerges. A large majority of the creditors, secured and unsecured, and the members want the scheme to be accepted. Public and national interest, as well as the interest of the labour and staff demand that a scheme should be evolved to work out the equities between different groups. Except the solitary unsecured creditor, J.S. Desai & Co, every interest represented before me considers that liquidation on such facts will be highly detrimental and prejudicial to all concerned.

The Amendment Act, 1974, has enlarged the concept of "Government company" for the purposes of audit. Section 619-B has been inserted for this purpose. This section says that the provisions of Section 619 (which deals with audit of Government companies) shall apply to a company in which at least 51% of the paid-up share capital is held by the following or any combination thereof:

1. the Central Government and one or more Government companies;

2. any State Government or Governments and one or more Government companies;

3. the Central Government, one or more State Governments and one or more Government companies;

4. the Central Government and one or more corporations owned or controlled by the Central Government;

5. the Central Government, one or more State Governments and one or more corporations owned or controlled by the Central Government;

6. one or more corporations owned or controlled by the Central Government or any State Government;[81]

7. more than one Government company.

Downsizing employees

The directors of a Government company decided to reduce the number of employees and applied the principle of 'last come, first go'. This was held to be not a violation of Article 14 or 16 of the Constitution.[82]

Removal of the managing director in accordance with Articles was held to be not questionable under writ jurisdiction. It belonged to the realm of contract.[83]

Where it was not shown that the Government company was an instrumentality of the State, a writ petition for enforcement of labour rights was not allowed.[84]

Holding company and subsidiary [S. 4]

Where one company has control over another, it is known as the holding company and the company over which control is exercised is called the subsidiary company. This control of one company over another may, within the meaning of Section 4, be held in one of the following three ways.

Firstly, where one company controls the composition of the Board of directors of another, the latter becomes the subsidiary of the former.[85] The

---

81. Corporations of this kind are included within the meaning of the expression "public financial institutions" of which the first list is given in S. 4-A but many more have been added to the list by exercising the power conferred under the section. The disinvestment policy of a Government company cannot be questioned by employees even if it would have the effect of converting the company into a private sector company. The employees would remain the employees of the same company as before. *Southern Structurals Staff Union* v *Management of Southern Structurals Ltd*, (1994) 81 Comp Cas 389 Mad.

82. *Irrigation Development Employees Assn* v *Govt of A.P.*, (2004) 55 SCL 459: (2005) 66 CLA 115 AP.

83. *B.M. Varma* v *State of U.P.*, (2005) 58 SCL 52 All: (2005) 128 Comp Cas 860 All; *A.S. Gill* v *State of Punjab*, (2006) 132 Comp Cas 799 P&H.

84. *R.V. Dnyansagar* v *Maharashtra Industrial and Technical Consultancy Organisation Ltd*, (2005) 128 Comp Cas 520 Bom.

85. The fact that the majority of directors will remain on the Board only upto the next annual meeting is not material. The relationship of holding and subsidiary is established at least for

composition of the Board of directors of a company shall be deemed to be controlled by another if the latter has the power, without the consent or concurrence of any other person, to appoint or remove the holders of all or a majority of the directorships. And a company shall be deemed to have the power to appoint to a directorship in the following three cases:

1. If a person cannot be appointed to a directorship without the exercise in his favour of the power of appointment held by the company.

2. If a person's appointment to directorship follows necessarily from his appointment as director, managing agent, secretaries and treasurers or manager or to any other office or employment in the company.

3. If the directorship is held by an individual nominated by the company or by any of its subsidiaries.

Secondly, where one company holds the majority of shares in another company, the latter becomes the subsidiary of the former. In ordinary cases, "majority shareholding" means holding more than half in nominal value of the equity share capital of a company. But where a company has preference shareholders who had, before the commencement of the Act of 1956 and, therefore, still have, "the same voting rights in all respects as the holders of equity shares", it will be necessary, for the purpose of becoming a majority shareholder, to exercise or control more than half of the total voting power of such a company.

Thirdly, where one company is subsidiary of another, which is itself a subsidiary of some other company, the first mentioned company shall also become the subsidiary of the last mentioned company. For example the section contains this illustration:

> Company 'B' is a subsidiary of Company 'A', and Company 'C' is a subsidiary of Company 'B'. Company 'C' is a subsidiary of Company 'A'. If Company 'D' is a subsidiary of Company 'C', Company 'D' will be subsidiary of Company 'B' and consequently also of Company 'A' and so on.

The above conditions will be deemed to have been satisfied, even if the majority of shares are held or the power of appointment to directorship is exercisable by any person as a nominee of the holding company or as a nominee of any of its subsidiaries. But the section provides that in determining whether one company is a subsidiary of another, shares held or power exercisable in the following three cases shall be disregarded:

---

the time being. See *M. Velayudhan* v *Registrar of Companies*, (1980) 50 Comp Cas 33 Ker. On the holding company's power of appointing directors see *Oriental Industrial Investment Corporation Ltd* v *Union of India*, (1981) 51 Comp Cas 487 Del.

1. Where the shares are held or the power is exercisable by the company in a fiduciary capacity.
2. Where the shares are held or the power is exercisable by any person by virtue of the provisions of any debentures or of a trust deed for securing any issue of such debentures.
3. Where the shares are held or the power is exercisable by a lending company by way of security and only for purposes of a transaction entered into in the ordinary course of business.

Involvement of S. 372-A

Investment by one company in the shares of another company to the extent of majority shareholding comes into conflict with the restrictions on inter-corporate investments envisaged under S. 372-A. That is why S. 372-A(8)(c), (d) and (e) exempts a holding company from the operation of the section and makes it free to invest any amount in the shares of its subsidiary. But at the time when first investment takes place beyond the limits of S. 372-A, the investee company is not a subsidiary. It would become subsidiary only after the investment. If the investment is within the limits of S. 372-A and that investment itself gives a majority status to the investing company, the formalities and approvals prescribed by S. 372-A would not apply. Where the investment goes beyond those limits, a special resolution would be necessary. After thus gaining the status of a holding company, Section 372-A would not apply on further investments in the subsidiary. The exemption from the operation of S. 372-A is not available to a Board-controlled subsidiary. The 1988 amendment withdrew this privilege. It was being abused by establishing a temporary control over the Board of directors and then enjoying the freedom of investment to any amount, and thus by-passing S. 372 as it was before the Amendment of 2000.

Accounts of Holding Company

Sections 212 to 214 contain special provisions about holding and subsidiary companies. Section 212(1) provides that "there shall be attached to the balance-sheet of a holding company the following documents in respect of each subsidiary":

1. A copy of the balance-sheet of the subsidiary. The balance-sheet must be made out in accordance with the requirements of the Act as at the end of the financial year of the subsidiary, where such financial year coincides with the financial year of the holding company. But where they do not coincide, the balance-sheet must be prepared as at the end of the financial year of the subsidiary last before that of the holding company. But the gap between the two financial years must not exceed six months.[86]

---

86. S. 212(2).

2. A copy of the profit and loss account of the subsidiary prepared in accordance with the provisions of the Act for the same period.[87]

3. A copy of the report of its board of directors made out in accordance with the requirements of the Act and for the period referred to above.[88]

4. A copy of the report of its auditors.[89]

5. A statement of the holding company's interest in the subsidiary at the end of the financial year.[90] The statement shall specify the net aggregate of the subsidiary's profits after deducting its losses at the end of the financial year and also for the financial years since it became a subsidiary, but only so far as it concerns the members of the holding company and is not dealt with in the company's accounts. If the profits of the subsidiary are dealt within the holding company's accounts or a provision is made for any losses, the net aggregate amount of the same must be disclosed. This will be necessary only for such profits and losses of the subsidiary which may properly be treated in the holding company's accounts as revenue profits or losses. Profits or losses attributable to any shares held in the subsidiary company and arising before the shares were acquired by the holding company need not be so treated, except where the holding company is itself the subsidiary of another body corporate and the shares were acquired from that body corporate or a subsidiary of it.[91]

6. If, for any reason, the board of directors of the holding company is unable to obtain information on any of the above matters, a report in writing to that effect must be attached to the balance-sheet of the holding company.[92]

7. Where the financial year of the subsidiary does not coincide with the financial year of the holding company a statement has to be attached showing any change in the holding company's interest in the subsidiary taking place between the gap of the two companies' financial years. The statement must disclose the details of the material changes in the subsidiary's fixed assets, its investments, the moneys lent by it, the moneys borrowed by it for any purpose other than that of meeting current liabilities.[93]

---

87. S. 212(1)(*b*) and (2)(*b*).
88. S. 212 (l)(*c*).
89. S. 212(1)(*d*).
90. S. 212(1)(*c*).
91. S. 212(4).
92. S. 212(6).
93. A holding company and its subsidiaries may be regarded as one group for bonus purposes. See *K.C.P. Ltd* v *K.C.P. Employees Assn*, AIR 1969 Mad 370: 18 FLR 52: 1969 Lab IC 1310.

Inspection of Subsidiary's Books of Account

Section 214 provides that "a holding company may, by resolution, authorise representatives named in the resolution to inspect books of account kept by any of its subsidiaries; and the books... shall be open to inspection by those representatives at any time during business hours".[94]

Investment in Holding Company [S. 42]

A subsidiary company is not allowed to acquire membership of its holding company. Consequently, "any allotment or transfer of shares in a company to its subsidiary shall be void". If the holding company is a guarantee or unlimited company, the above restriction will apply to whatever interest the subsidiary company has in it, whether it is in the form of shares or not.[95] The prohibition also extends up to the nominees of the subsidiary company.[96]

The prohibition does not apply to the case of a subsidiary company which already had shares in its holding company at the commencement of the Act or before becoming a subsidiary of the holding company.[97] The section does not apply to the following cases:[98]

1. Where the subsidiary is concerned as a legal representative of a deceased member of the holding company.

2. Where the subsidiary is concerned as a trustee. This exception will not apply where the holding company itself or any of its other subsidiaries is beneficially interested under the trust, except when its interest is only for the purpose of a security for a transaction, including lending of money, entered into in the ordinary course of business.

A subsidiary can buy shares in its holding company where it is a part of a scheme of amalgamation sanctioned by the court.[99]

ILLEGAL ASSOCIATIONS [S. 11]

When Registration Compulsory

An important aim of the Companies Act is to eliminate the evils caused by large partnerships trading in unincorporated form. A business association consisting of a large number of members, unless incorporated as a company, leads to inevitable confusion and uncertainty concerning the rights and liabilities of members *inter se* and their relations with others. It is, therefore, necessary to provide that every business association having a certain number

---

94. Sub-section (5); *see* also S. 213 which gives the Central Government the power to adjust the financial years of holding and subsidiary companies.
95. S. 42(5).
96. S. 42(4).
97. S. 42(3).
98. S. 42(2).
99. *Himachal Telematics Ltd* v *Himachal Futuristic Communications Ltd*, (1996) 86 Comp Cas 325 Del.

of members must be registered as a company, failing which it shall be regarded as an illegal association. Accordingly, Section 11(2) declares that no company, association or partnership consisting of more than twenty persons[1] (ten in the case of banking business) shall be formed for the purpose of carrying on any business that has for its objects the acquisition of gain for itself or for its members unless it is registered as a company under the Companies Act or is formed in pursuance of some other Indian law.[2] If it is not so registered it becomes an illegal association. The conditions of illegality under the section are:

1. the membership of the association must be more than twenty (or ten in the case of banking business);
2. the association must have been formed for the purpose of carrying on a business;
3. the object of the association must be to acquire profits (gain) for itself or for its members;[3] and
4. the association must not have been registered as a company under the Companies Act, nor must it have been formed in pursuance of some other Indian law.[4]

Thus, for example, a stock exchange has been held to be not in the purview of the section as it is not formed for the purpose of carrying on any business much less a business which has for its objects the acquisition of gain.[5]

The section, however, does not apply to a joint Hindu family carrying on business.[6] Where a business is carried on by two or more joint Hindu families, in computing the number of members for the purposes of this section, minor members must be excluded.[7]

---

1. The word "person" would include a company or a corporate person also, though a company joining an association would count only as one person. The confusion caused by the earlier judicial opinion that the word "person" would include only individuals and not bodies of individuals was lifted by subsequent decisions. *Senaji Kapurchand* v *Pannaji Devichand*, AIR 1930 PC 300: 34 Cal WN 1107: 59 Mad LJ 435; *Sri Murugan Oil Industries (P) Ltd* v *A. V. Suryanarayanan Chettiar*, (1963) 33 Comp Cas 833: [1963] 1 Comp LJ 158 Mad.
2. This would also include associations recognised by Indian laws. *Ilfracombe Permanent Mutual Benefit Building Society, Re*, [1901] 1 Ch 102.
3. The disabilities inflicted by the section are restricted to associations of commercial or business nature. Associations for charity, advancement of religion, education, research, literature or recreation clubs would be outside the scope of the section. *IRC* v *Korean Syndicate Ltd*, [1920] 1 KB 598, on appeal [1921] 3 KB 258; *Armour* v *Corpn of Liverpool*, [1939] 1 All ER 363 Ch D; *Tan Waing* v *Bottein*, AIR 1932 Rang 167 : (1933) 3 Comp Cas 112 ; *Dayal Singh* v *Desraj*, [1963] 1 Comp LJ 100 Punj.
4. These essential points have been explained by MODY J in *V. V. Ruia* v *S. Dalmia*, AIR 1968 Bom 347, 350: [1968] 1 Comp LJ 226: (1968) 38 Comp Cas 572.
5. *V. V. Ruia* v *S. Dalmia*, AIR 1968 Bom 347 : [1968] 1 Comp LJ 226 : (1968) 38 Comp Cas 572.
6. Members of a family carrying on business as partners would be covered by the section. *Syamlal Roy* v *Madhusudan Roy*, AIR 1959 Cal 380.
7. S. 11(3). *Agarwal & Co* v *CIT*, (1990) 77 ITR 10.

Consequences of Illegality

Following are some of the consequences of illegality:

Firstly, according to sub-section (4) every member of such an association shall be personally liable for all liabilities incurred in the business.[8] Apart from this unlimited personal liability, members are punishable with a fine which may extend up to ten thousand rupees.[9]

Secondly, the members of an illegal company cannot maintain an action in respect of any contract made by it. For example, the price of any goods sold by the association cannot be recovered.[10]

Thirdly, it cannot be wound up under the Act even under the provisions relating to winding up of unregistered companies.[11]

Lastly, can there be a suit between members for partition or dissolution or taking of accounts of an illegal company? This question arose before the High Court of Allahabad in *Mewa Ram v Ram Gopal*[12]:

> The suit was in respect of a partnership concerned with certain ginning factories. There were more than twenty partners and, therefore, the partnership was illegal. The plaintiff, claiming an eighth share in the partnership, brought an action for a declaration that the partnership was invalid and prayed for a refund of his subscription out of the proceeds realised by an auction sale of the factories or for a division of the properties of the factories.

The case was first heard by a Division Bench consisting of SULAIMAN J (afterwards CJ) and MUKHERJI J. The learned Judges differed. SULAIMAN J was of the opinion that the prayer for a refund of the original subscription could not be granted because the plaintiff had been participating in the profits of the illegal partnership for several years. But he held that the plaintiff was entitled to a partition of the properties.

MUKHERJI J on the other hand, held that the plaintiff was not entitled to any relief, because partition would involve realisation of the assets of the company and payment of its debts, the very things which would be done in a suit for dissolution of partnership or winding up of a company. The case was therefore referred to WALSH J who agreed with MUKHERJI J that a decree for partition would be in substance a direction for winding up or a

---

8. See *Kumaraswami Chettiar v M. S. M.Chinnathambi Chettiar*, [1950] 2 Mad LJ 453 : (1950) 20 Comp Cas 286: AIR 1951 Mad 291.
9. For the purpose of penalty whether the association should be illegal in its inception or whether those also would be covered who subsequently become so, on a minor member becoming major, see *Niraban v Lalit*, ILR [1938] 2 Cal 368: AIR 1939 Cal 187.
10. Nor any other property can be recovered. *Jennings v Hammond*, (1882) 9 QBD 225.
11. Nor it can be sued, though individual members can be sued for anything received by them on behalf of the association. *Padstow Total Loss and Collusion Assurance Assn, Re*, (1882) 20 Ch D 137; *Greenburg v Cooperstein, Re*, [1926] 1 Ch 657. By registration under the Act, the association can rid itself of disabilities. *Thomas Poppleton, Re*, (1884) 14 QBD 379.
12. ILR (1926) 48 All 735.

decree for dissolution of accounts. He added that when such a precedent was once established there was nothing to prevent the formation of an unlimited number of such associations consisting of more than twenty persons carrying on trade for the purpose of gain, any one of the members of which could come to the court and ask for relief in a suit, in the nature of a winding up, for partition of the assets of the association. The result would be to give such associations under another guise the cloak of legality although the statute has forbidden it.

This opinion was followed in *Kumaraswami Chettiar* v *M.S.M. Chinnathambi Chettiar*[13] where the court added that "it is well established that the consequence of the illegality of a partnership is that its members have no remedy against each other for contribution or apportionment in respect of partnership dealings and transactions".

The position was clarified by the Supreme Court in *Badri Prasad* v *Nagarmal*[14]:

> The case arose out of a suit for recovering the contribution made to an illegal association[15] and also for accounts. It was contended that the objects of the association were not illegal and the same, being dissolved, recovery should be allowed in the manner of realisation of the assets of a dissolved firm.

> The court held that "such a claim is clearly untenable. The only course for the courts to pursue is to say that he is not entitled to any relief as the courts cannot adjudicate in respect of contracts which the law declares to be illegal."[16]

The partnership analogy was also rejected. "An unregistered firm is not illegal."[17]

Individual members will be entitled to recover their subscriptions and to have the assets realised for this purpose. This would not advance illegality. It would rather terminate an illegal gathering and would also prevent grabbing of assets and subscriptions by the member in whose hands they perchance fall.[18]

---

13. [1950] 2 MLJ 453.
14. AIR 1959 SC 559 : (1959) 29 Comp Cas 229.
15. The association was illegal under S. 4(2) of the Rewa State Companies Act, 1935, parallel to the present S. 11.
16. Relying upon *Senaji Kapurchand* v *Pannaji Devichand*, AIR 1930 PC 300.
17. The subscribers of a chit fund do not fall within the section because they do not constitute an association, *G. K. Naidu* v *G. K. Mouleswar*, AIR 1962 AP 406.
18. *Seth Badri Prasad* v *Seth Nagar Mal*, AIR 1959 SC 559: (1959) 29 Comp Cas 229 SC.

19

Reconstruction and Amalgamation

Compromises and Arrangements

A "compromise" presupposes the existence of a dispute, for, "there can be no compromise unless there is some dispute".[1]

The dispute may then be resolved by drawing up a scheme of compromise. Even when there is a dispute, but the scheme is such that the members have to give up their rights entirely, it will not be a compromise or arrangement.[2] Surrender of rights without any compensation or any measure of accommodation on both sides cannot be regarded as a compromise. BOWEN LJ observed in a case:[3]

> Everybody will agree that a compromise or arrangement which has to be sanctioned by the court must be reasonable, and that no arrangement or compromise can be said to be reasonable in which you can get nothing and give up everything. A reasonable compromise must be a compromise which can, by reasonable people conversant with the subject, be regarded as beneficial to those on both sides who are making it.... It would be improper for the court to allow an arrangement to be forced on any class of creditors, if the arrangement cannot reasonably be supposed by sensible business people to be for the benefit of that class as such, otherwise the sanction of the court would be a sanction to what would be a scheme of confiscation. The object of this section is not confiscation. It is not that one person should be a victim, and that the rest of the body should feast upon his rights. Its object is to enable compromises to be made which are for the common benefit of the creditors, or a class of creditors as such.

But "arrangement" is a term of wider connotation. A re-arrangement of rights or of liabilities is possible without the existence of any dispute. Thus, where under a scheme each shareholder of a company had to transfer some of his shares to another company and some to its shareholders the court refused to uphold the scheme as there was no dispute which the scheme purported to resolve. But the Court of Appeal held that the word "arrangement" should not be taken to mean the same thing as a compromise.[4]

When a company has a dispute with a member or a class of members or with a creditor or a class of them, a scheme of compromise may be drawn up.

---

1. See *Sneath v Valley Gold Ltd*, [1893] 1 Ch 477 : 68 LT 602, where the word "compromise" appearing in a trust deed was given this meaning.
2. *N.F.U. Development Trust, Re*, [1972] 1 WLR 1548.
3. *Alabama, New Orleans, Texas and Pacific Junction Rly Co, Re*, 64 LT 127 : 7 TLR 171 : [1886-90] All ER Rep Ext 1143: [1891] 1 Ch 213.
4. *Guardian Assurance Co, Re*, [1917] 1 Ch 431 : 116 LT 193. *See also Mercantile Investment & General Trust Co v International Co of Mexico*, [1893] 1 Ch 484, 491 : 68 LT 603.

Where there is no dispute but even so there is need for re-adjusting the rights or liabilities of a member or a class of them or of a creditor or a class of them, the company may resort to a scheme of arrangement with them. Section 390 itself provides that "the expression 'arrangement' includes a reorganization of the share capital of the company by the consolidation of shares of different classes, or by the division of shares into shares of different classes, or by both those methods". The provisions of Sections 391 and 393 show that a compromise or arrangement can be proposed between a company and its creditors or between a company and its members. Such a compromise would also cover any scheme of amalgamation or merger of one company with another.[5]

A company can enter into schemes even where no power has been specifically given by the memorandum of association because Chapter V of the Companies Act gives power to companies to apply for sanction of arrangement, compromise or amalgamation.[6]

Sanction of Court [S. 391]

The company, or its liquidator (if it is in winding up), or any member or creditor may make an application to the Court. An application can be made only by a member or creditor of the class which is affected by the compromise or arrangement proposed by the company.[7] The company has to place different interests in separate classes. Classification of members or creditors in a scheme is necessary only when different members or creditors are affected differently under the scheme.[8] Thus where in a scheme of arrangement, persons with dissimilar interests were put in a single class the court refused to sanction the scheme[9] and said:

---

5. *Miheer H. Mafatlal* v *Mafatlal Industries Ltd*, (1996) 87 Comp Cas 792: (1997) 1 SCC 579.
6. *Aimco Pesticides Ltd, In re,* (2001) 103 Comp Cas 463 Bom. *Liqui Box India (P) Ltd, Re,* (2006) 131 Comp Cas 645 P&H, the scheme required alteration of the company's memorandum, the special provisions applicable to alteration need not be followed, sufficient powers in the court for this purpose.
7. An application was allowed to be made by two persons (one of whom was a managing director) who agreed to provide funds, the court telling the official liquidator of the company to treat them as members for the shares that they had agreed to buy and as creditors in place of those who were going to be paid off with their money. *A. K. Mishra* v *Wearwell Cycle Co (India) Ltd,* (1993) 78 Comp Cas 252 Del. The winding up order was cancelled. *Wearwell Cycle Co (India) Ltd* v *A. K. Mishra,* (1994) Comp Cas 219 Del. An application by a person who was neither a shareholder nor a member was not allowed. His contention that he was a successor to his deceased mother's shares was also doubtful because he had no good papers with him and he never tried to get the shares transmitted to his name. *N. K. Mohapatra* v *State of Orissa,* AIR 1994 Ori 301: (1995) 16 Corpt LA 295. The court also said that a petition under these sections cannot subsequently be converted into one under Ss. 397 and 398. *Bank Muscat SAOG, Re,* (2004) 122 Comp Cas 340, a foreign company incorporated in India by registration with ROC, Del, but with principal place of business at Bangalore, that was deemed to be the place of registered office. The Karnataka High Court had jurisdiction.
8. *Jaypee Cement Ltd, Re,* (2004) 122 Comp Cas 854 All.
9. *Sovereign Life Insurance Co* v *Dodd,* [1892] 2 QB 573 : [1891-94] All ER Rep 246 : 67 LT 396. Members whose shares are paid up in advance constitute a different class from those

It seems plain that we must give a meaning to the term 'class' as it will prevent the section being so worked as to result in confiscation and injustice and that it must be confined to those persons whose rights are not so dissimilar as to make it impossible for them to consult together with a view to their common interest.

In a case before the Allahabad High Court, *Premier Motors (P) Ltd* v *Ashok Tandon*,[10] a scheme of compromise with the company's depositors placed all the depositors in one class, although the deposits of some of them had, and those of others had not, matured. M.H. BEG J found nothing wrong with the classification. He said:

In the case before me, the interests of all the unsecured creditors irrespective of the time when their debts matured appear to be identical. The company alleges inability to pay any of its unsecured creditors according to contracts of the same kind with identically similar terms.... The interests of every one of the whole of this class of creditors required a consideration of the question whether a scheme for repayment of all debts is not more advantageous to each one of them than to wind up the company. In a winding up, the interests of this whole class would have to be dealt with on the same footing. Hence, their interests are common irrespective of the time when their debts mature for repayment.

All the unsecured creditors do not always constitute a single class. Where fixed deposit holders, lenders of money, holders of hundis and suppliers of material were all herded in a single class without ascertaining what representation of these categories was there at the meeting, it was held that the requirements of the section were not satisfied and that a fresh attempt should be made to reclassify creditors and their consent obtained at separate meetings.[11]

It has been held that a wholly owned subsidiary is also a "class" for the purpose of a scheme of arrangement.[12] An unsecured creditor holding a decree has been held to be not a class different from other unsecured creditors. A creditor having only a one time transaction with the company is not a separate class of creditors.[13] Creditors of a public institution, like UTI,

---

whose shares are not so paid up. See *United Provident Assurance Co, Re*, [1910] 2 Ch 477 : 103 LT 531.

10. (1971) 41 Comp Cas 656 All.

11. *D. A. Swamy* v *India Meters Ltd*, (1994) 79 Comp Cas 27 Mad. *State Bank of India* v *Alstom Power Boilers Ltd*, (2003) 116 Comp Cas 1 Bom, classification of creditors into unsecured and secured creditors, no further classification necessary. *Wipro Finance Ltd* v *Suman Motels Ltd*, (2002) 108 Comp Cas 549 Bom, a creditor who was entitled only to rental of the machinery supplied on lease was not allowed to be treated as a separate class of creditors.

12. *Hellenic and General Trust Ltd, Re*, [1975] 3 All ER 382: [1976] 1 WLR 123. The Supreme Court held in *Miheer H. Mafatlal* v *Mafatlal Industries Ltd*, (1997) 1 SCC 579: (1996) 87 Comp Cas 792, that where the whole number of equity shareholders were offered a uniform scheme, it was not necessary to sub-divide them into classes and call separate meetings.

13. *Sharp Industries Ltd, Re*, (2006) 131 Comp Cas 535 Bom; *Pharmaceutical Products of India Ltd, Re*, (2006) 131 Comp Cas 747 Bom.

holding public monies are not a separate class.[14] A scheme proposed restructuring of debts of specified unsecured creditors. They were either banks or financial institutions. The classification was held to be proper. The other unsecured creditors could not say that they were being marginalized. The company had promised to them a separate scheme for their dues.[15]

If an application is properly made, the court may order a meeting of the class of creditors or members to be called, which shall be held and conducted in the manner directed by the court.[16] A single joint application by all companies involved in a scheme for convening of meetings and for sanction has been held to be permissible.[17] An application can be entertained even when proceedings against the company are pending before the Appellate Authority under the Sick Industrial Companies (Special Provisions) Act, 1985.[18]

A statement of the terms of the compromise or arrangement and its effects has to be sent with every notice calling the meeting. The power of the Court being of judicial nature, it is necessary for its proper exercise that notice should be given to all the interested parties including the shareholders and the Central Government.[19] The role of the Government is that of an impartial observer. The statement should explain in particular any material interest of the directors, managing director, managing agents, secretaries and treasurers or manager of the company and the effect of the compromise on their interests in so far as that effect is different from the effect on like interests of other persons.[20] "The extent of disclosure

---

14. *Pharmaceutical Products of India Ltd, Re,* (2006) 131 Comp Cas 747 Bom.
15. *Ibid.*
16. S. 391(1)(*a*) and (*b*). Where a scheme could not be approved by the members because there was no quorum at the meeting, the court refused to move further. *Suri and Nayar Ltd, Re,* (1983) 54 Comp Cas 868 Kant. Under sub-section (6) the court is empowered to stay the commencement or continuation of any suit or proceeding against the company till the final disposal of the application. In *Arvindbhai V. Patel v State of Gujarat,* (1995) 83 Comp Cas 508 Guj, the courts refused to stay prosecution of the manager of the company; he was not a director.
17. *Chembra Orchard Produce Ltd, Re,* (2004) 120 Comp Cas 1 Kant.
18. *Sharp Industries Ltd, Re,* (2006) 131 Comp Cas 535 Bom; *Pharmaceutical Products of India Ltd, Re,* (2006) 131 Comp Cas 747 Bom.
19. *Hind Auto Industries Ltd v Premier Motors (P) Ltd,* (1969) 39 Comp Cas 137: [1969] 1 Comp LJ 258: AIR 1970 All 165. *Maneckchowk & Ahmedabad Mfg Co, Re,* (1970) 40 Comp Cas 819 Guj. Where the requisite meetings of shareholders and creditors was not called and the latest financial position of the company was not laid before the court, sanction to the proposed amalgamation was refused, *Bharat Synthetics Ltd v Bank of India,* (1995) 82 Comp Cas 437: (1995) 17 Corpt LA 152 Bom. An accidental omission or non-delivery of notice, just in the case of an ordinary meeting, would not have the effect of invalidating the meeting. *Maknam Investments Ltd, Re,* (1995) 87 Comp Cas 689 Cal: (1995) 1 CHN 368. It was also held in this case that a person who objects to the scheme would have the right to inspect the company's register of members and also to get copies on payment of fee. The proper procedure of exercising this right would have to be followed.
20. S. 393(1)(*a*). *Gujarat Lease Financing Ltd, Re,* (2003) 115 Comp Cas 136 Guj, an arrangement with debentureholders, notice need not mention bank recovery proceedings or winding up proceedings. Court's sanction would not have affected others. Duties of debenture trustees depend upon provisions of trust deed, adequacy of majority representation depends upon the provision of the company's articles and terms of issue.

required must depend on the nature of the scheme." Thus, where certain information which was exempt from disclosure in the company's accounts was deliberately withheld, the court held that this was not fatal to the arrangement as the proposed compensation was fair and the disclosure of exempt information would have resulted in damage to all the shareholders.[21] But where proper information is not given, the Court will refuse to sanction the scheme even if it has been approved by the requisite majority. Thus:[22]

A circular sent to debentureholders stated that the scheme has been approved by the trustees, but failed to disclose that the trustees were the company's bankers and therefore interested in the scheme and that the assets had been revalued, but did not give the amount of revaluation, the Court refused to sanction the scheme being based on inadequate disclosures.

If the notice calling the meeting is given by advertisement, the statement should be included in the advertisement or the advertisement should indicate the place at which or the manner in which copies of such a statement may be obtained.[23] When a member or creditor entitled to receive a copy applies for it, the company shall be bound to supply him one free of charge. [S. 393(3)]

Every officer of the company is required to give notice to the company of such matters relating to himself as may be necessary for the purposes of the scheme.[24]

If the scheme is approved by a majority representing three-fourths in value of the creditors or members, as the case may be, it may then be sanctioned by the Court.[25] This requirement has been held to be directory,

---

21. *National Bank Ltd, Re*, [1966] 1 All ER 1006 Ch D : [1966] 2 Comp LJ 193.
22. *Dorman, Long & Co, Re*, [1934] Ch 635.
23. S. 393(1)(*b*). *Pharmaceutical Products of India Ltd, Re*, (2006) 131 Comp Cas 747 Bom, in a scheme with secured creditors, there was no mention of any scheme with unsecured creditors, held, not a failure to disclose material facts.
24. S. 393(5). The sub-section imposes a penalty of fine for default in giving the required information. Further, S. 393(4) provides that where a default is made in complying with any of the requirements of the section, every officer who is in default is punishable with fine. The liquidator of the company and trustee for debentureholders are deemed to be officers for this purpose. Criminal proceedings may be commenced or continued, notwithstanding that proceedings have been initiated under S. 390 for sanction of the court. *Uma Investment (P) Ltd, Re*, (1977) 47 Comp Cas 242 Bom.
25. Where a composite scheme has been rejected by the secured creditors and approved by the unsecured, it cannot be said to have been approved by the creditors so as to merit the sanction of the court. *Auto Steering India (P) Ltd, Re*, (1977) 47 Comp Cas 257 Del. Where a powerful creditor, a public financial institution in this case, refused to approve the scheme and without it the statutory majority was not found, the court can neither approve the scheme nor conduct an inquiry into the motives of the creditor. *M. M. Sehgal v Sehgal Papers Ltd*, [1966] 1 Comp LJ 192 P&H. The court cannot accept a scheme when the company is being taken over under the Industries (D&R) Act, 1951. *Gujarat State Textile Corpn v N. J. V. Mills Co*, (1985) 58 Comp Cas 768 Guj; *Manekchowk & Ahmedabad Mfg Co, Re*, (1985) 58 Comp Cas 729 Guj. Power of court to substitute the sponsor. *Bhavnagar Veg Products Ltd, Re*, (1984) 55 Comp Cas 107 Guj. Perfectly reasonable and fair scheme approved by the court in *Mehta*

not mandatory. Where a scheme was not approved by the appropriate majority of creditors at their meeting, but subsequently the creditors to the extent of requisite majority filed individual affidavits before the court, that was held to be a sufficient compliance with the statutory requirements.[26]

Jurisdiction

The transferor company was under the jurisdiction of the principal seat of the High Court. The transferee company fell into the jurisdiction of a Bench of the High Court. It was held that separate applications must be filed at both the jurisdictions.[27]

Duties and Powers of Court

The matters which the Court has to consider in giving its sanction were thus explained by ASTBURY J in *Anglo Continental Supply Co, Re*[28].

First, that the provisions of the statute have been complied with. Secondly, that the class was fairly represented by those who attended the meeting and that the statutory majority are acting *bona fide* and are not coercing the minority in order to promote interests adveyrse to those of the class whom they purport to represent; and, thirdly, that the arrangement is such as a man of business would reasonably approve.

Compliance with statutory provisions.—The first condition enables the court to decline its sanction to a scheme which is *ultra vires* or is otherwise not in compliance with the Act. Thus where a scheme involved reduction of capital, the court refused to uphold it and allowed the

Investments (P) Ltd, Re, [1990] 1 Comp LJ 285 Del; *Indo Continental Hotels and Resorts Ltd, Re*, (1990) 69 Comp Cas 93 Raj; *Hotel Pink City (P) Ltd, Re*, (1990) 69 Comp Cas 93 Raj. *Vidiani Engineers Ltd, Re*, (2003) 115 Comp Cas 389 All, only 10% of the creditors filed affidavits to approve the scheme, the application of the company for sanction was dismissed. *Motorol India Ltd, Re*, (2001) 103 Comp Cas 389 Guj, the court refused to entertain an application where the scheme was opposed by a majority of the creditors who sought winding up.

26. *S.M. Holding & Finance Ltd* v *Mysore Machinery Manufacturers Ltd*, (1993) 78 Comp Cas 432 Kant. The approval was expedient also for the reason that it had become necessary to pull the company out of its standstillness in the interest of workers and machinery. Where meetings of creditors and members were not held and the secured creditors of both the companies which were their respective banks objected justifiably that their claims would be prejudiced because liabilities of both companies exceeded their assets, the court refused sanction. *Bharat Synthetics Ltd* v *Bank of India*, (1995) 17 Corpt LA 152 Bom: (1995) 82 Comp Cas 437. An approval by overwhelming majority is a symbol of the soundness of the scheme. The court would not interfere. It cannot substitute with its wisdom the collective wisdom of the shareholders. *Cetex Petrochemicals Ltd, Re*, (1992) 73 Comp Cas 298 Mad. Rejection by a sole secured creditor amounted to rejection by 100% secured creditors, hence no approval, *Komal Plastic Industries* v *Roxy Enterprises (P) Ltd*, (1991) 72 Comp Cas 61 Del.

27. *Jaipur Polyspin Ltd* v *Rajasthan Spg & Wvg Mills Ltd*, (2006) 130 Comp Cas 694 Raj.

28. [1922] 2 Ch 723, 736. *See* also *Bengal Bank* v *Suresh*, AIR 1952 Cal 133. The court can interfere only when the scheme is manifestly unfair or is adopted as a device to defraud some shareholders, *Makhnam Investments (P) Ltd, Re*, (1996) 87 Comp Cas 689 Cal. Where the scheme was approved by the relevant quarters, objections of persons other than shareholders were ignored, *Malvika Madan Sehgal* v *M.M. Sehgal Ltd*, (1997) 91 Comp Cas 133 Del.

application to stand over to enable the company to comply with the normal procedure of capital reduction.[29] But the court has the power to grant such sanction in the same proceedings. Thus, in *Maneckchowk and Ahmedabad Manufacturing Co, Re,*[30] the Gujarat High Court accorded a separate sanction for reduction of capital and said:

> Section 391 provides a complete code of putting through a scheme of compromise and arrangement, which may even include reorganisation of share capital subject to the well-recognised exception that if reorganisation includes reduction, the proper procedure for effecting the same may be gone through.

In the opinion of the Calcutta High Court it is not necessary for the validity of a scheme of amalgamation that the company should have an express power of amalgamation in the memorandum. Sections 391-395 confer on every company a statutory power for the purpose.[31]

Where the terms of a scheme provided for sale of the company's properties but they ran counter to the Reserve Bank orders of restraint on alienation and refund of deposits, the court sanctioned the scheme saying that its order could override such regulatory requirements.[32]

In the case of listed company, consent of the Stock Exchange has to be obtained before presenting the scheme for sanction of the court. One month before this, the scheme has to be filed before the Stock Exchange for its consent. Such filing is enough, because its approval is not a mandatory requirement.[33]

---

29. *Cooper* v *Johnson*, [1902] WN 199. *See* also *Oceanic Steam Navigation, Re*, [1939] Ch 41. Minor irregularities are, however, ignored. *See* Palmer's COMPANY LAW, p 669 (1959).

30. (1970) 40 Comp Cas 819.

31. *Marybong and Kyel Tea Estates Ltd, Re*, (1977) 47 Comp Cas 802 Cal. Formerly by virtue of the provisions against monopolies in the Monopolies and Restrictive Trade Practices Act, 1969 permission of the MRTP Commission had to be taken. These provisions of the MRTP Act have been repealed. Monopolies Commission can now examine only this aspect whether the merger would be anti-competitive or would establish monopolistic trade practices. *Maharashtra General Kamgar Union* v *Hindustan Lever Ltd*, (1994) 81 Comp Cas 784 MRTPC. The fact that the affected company's name would have to be changed was considered to be no obstruction because it could be done even afterwards in view of the provisions of S. 23 to the effect that change of name does not affect the rights and liabilities of the company, *Hipolin Products Ltd, Re*, [1996] 2 Comp LJ 61 Guj; *Novapan India Ltd, Re*, (1997) 88 Comp Cas 596 AP: (1997) 25 Corpt LA 224 AP; *G.V.K. Hotels Ltd, Re*, (1997) 88 Comp Cas 596 AP. It is not necessary that the transferee company should be converted into a public company before sanction because its membership was to increase after the transfer. Such formalities could be observed afterwards also, *Winfiled Agro Services (P) Ltd, Re*, (1996) 86 Comp Cas 587: AIR 1996 AP 230; *Hindustan Antipests P Ltd, Re*, (1996) 86 Comp Cas 587: AIR 1996 AP 230. Where alteration of objects was necessary, the court could sanction it, *Rangkala Investments Ltd, Re*, (1997) 89 Comp Cas 754 Guj; *Gujarat Organics Ltd, Re*, (1997) 89 Comp Cas 754 Guj. Now the companies have a free hand in alteration of objects by just passing a special resolution. *Hindhivac (P) Ltd* v *Hind High Vacuum Co (P) Ltd*, (2005) 128 Comp Cas 226 Kant, scheme sanctioned though no power in the memorandum or articles.

32. *Maharashtra Apex Corpn Ltd, Re*, (2005) 124 Comp Cas 637 Kant.

33. *Compart Power Sources (P) Ltd, Re*, (2005) 125 Comp Cas 289 AP; *HBL Nife Power Systems Ltd, Re*, (2005) 125 Comp Cas 289 AP.

Bona fide exercise of majority power.—The second condition enables the court to see that the majority power has been exercised in good faith for the benefit of the class as a whole.[34] If it appears to the court that "the majority was composed of persons who had not really the interest of that class at stake", the scheme may not be sanctioned.[35] Thus majority approval obtained by improper inducements will be ineffective.[36] It is not, however, necessary that the meeting should be attended by a majority of the total number of members or creditors. It is enough that the requisite majority is obtained at the meeting.[37]

Reasonableness of scheme.—The last condition enables the court to examine the reasonableness of the scheme. The scheme should be fair and equitable. The approval of the scheme by the statutory majority is a strong evidence of its reasonableness. If the scheme is otherwise fair, the court will not go into its commercial merits.[38] But if the scheme is illusory, the court may refuse its sanction, even if it has been approved by the requisite majority. A scheme of this kind was before the Allahabad High Court in *Premier Motors (P) Ltd* v *Ashok Tandon*[39]:

> Two companies had taken deposits from the public on 12% interest. Most of the depositors were women and aged, of lower middle classes who had invested their life-long savings to make provision for their dependants. When the deposits began to mature, the depositors were told that the companies were running at a loss, one of them remaining out of business for two years. A scheme was drawn up which envisaged full payment to depositors at less interest but gave no date by which they would be fully repaid. At a meeting of depositors held under the court's order the scheme was approved by the statutory majority and the company petitioned for the court's sanction.

M. H. BEG J refused to sanction the scheme. The scheme was not only illusory but was also intended to hoodwink the poor depositors. Its aim was to evade contractual obligations as and when they arose. The majority approval was obtained on inadequate information.

---

34. All majority powers are subject to this principle. *See* LINDLEY MR in *Allen* v *Gold Reefs of West Africa*, [1900] 1 Ch 656, 671: [1900-03] All ER Rep 746.
35. BOWEN LJ in *Alabama etc Rly, Re*, [1891] 1 Ch 213, 244.
36. *British America Nickel Corpn* v *O'Brien Ltd*, 1927 AC 369 PC. *Apurva J. Parekh* v *Essen Computers Ltd*, (2006) 129 Comp Cas 121 Guj, statutory violations, scheme devised not for protecting the company's interests, but to cover up the misdeeds of promoters and directors, sanction refused.
37. *Bessemer Steel Co, Re*, (1876) 1 Ch D 251.
38. *London Chartered Bank of Australia, Re*, [1893] 3 Ch 540. *See also* MAUGHAM J in *Dorman Long & Co, Re*, 1934 Ch 635, 657. *State Bank of India* v *Alstom Power Boilers Ltd*, (2003) 116 Comp Cas 1 Bom, no interference in commercial wisdom of shareholders and their management. *Sharp Industries Ltd, Re*, (2006) 131 Comp Cas 535 Bom, a creditor holding a decree for principal and interest, could be paid only the principal keeping in mind payment to workers, scheme was held to be fair.
39. (1971) 41 Comp Cas 656 All.

As our law stands today, the initial duty of satisfying the court, that all relevant materials, including the latest financial position of the company and the latest auditors' reports and accounts of the company concerned have been placed before the court so as to enable it to judge where the interests of creditors lie, rests upon the supporters of the scheme. If the court cannot be satisfied that all relevant materials have been placed before the court, it could not be said that such material could be or was actually placed before the unsecured creditors on whose behalf decisions were taken by proxies.... The material placed before the court actually indicates that a winding up in each of the two cases is more advantageous to the creditors than the illusory scheme put forward, only to gain time and to prevent further investigation into the way losses have occurred.

Burden of proving unfairness.—Once a scheme has been approved of by a class, the burden of proving that it is unfair is on those who oppose it.[40] Where a scheme offered an option to the transferor company's shareholders either to accept shares in the transferee company, or in case of dissent, cash and the cash was less by about 24% than the value of the shares offered, the court held that spot cash, though less, may still be fair, but it should not be less to that extent. Anything between 15 to 20% less would have been fair.[41] A company which was carrying on two separate businesses, namely, tea broking and property dealing, devised a scheme for transferring the property business to a wholly owned subsidiary. The scheme was approved by all the affected quarters, but was opposed by the Company Law Board on several grounds including this that the property was being transferred at a very nominal cost and this involved evasion of capital gains tax, stamp duty etc, and that the scheme was also intended to avoid obtaining the sanction of the Urban Land Ceiling Authority which would have been necessary otherwise. The Calcutta High Court held that the company had the legal right to split its undertaking and nobody can be deprived of his legal rights merely because the exercise of it involves certain incidental consequences.[42]

Disclosure of material facts.—The Act now specifically provides that the court shall not sanction any scheme unless it is satisfied that the company or the applicant has disclosed to the court by affidavit or otherwise, all material facts relating to the company, such as its latest

---

40. *Holders' Investment Trust Ltd, Re*, [1971] 1 WLR 583: [1971] 2 All ER 289. Technical viability of the scheme is for the companies' experts to consider. *Mafatlal Industries Ltd, Re*, (1995) 17 Corpt LA 249 Guj : (1995) 84 Comp Cas 230.
41. *Dena Bank Ltd, Re*, (1976) 46 Comp Cas 541 Bom. *See also United Bank of India v United India Credit and Development Co Ltd*, (1977) 47 Comp Cas 689 Cal.
42. *A. W. Figgis & Co (P) Ltd, Re*; *Queens Park Property Co (P) Ltd, Re*, (1980) 50 Comp Cas 95 Cal.

financial position,[43] the latest auditors' report, the pendency of any investigation proceedings, *etc*, and the like. Schemes involving cancellation of arrears of accumulated preference dividends,[44] or requiring debentureholders to accept shares in place of debentures,[45] or to accept as their debtor a company to which the assets of their company are transferred, have been approved under the section.[46]

Interest of creditors.—There is nothing in the Act requiring notice of a scheme to be sent to the creditors also. The Delhi High Court has pointed out that this is a lacuna in the Act which should be remedied.[47] But even so there is no special cause of concern because the court can, in the exercise of its discretionary power, refuse to sanction a scheme unless the interest of creditors is taken care of. The court may even call a meeting of the creditors for this purpose. In the instant case, however, no such order was considered necessary because it was the creditor company itself which was taking over the debtor company. The court does not have the power to prevent a secured creditor from enforcing his security. The Bombay High Court refused to issue an injunction to prevent a mortgagee from bringing the company's factory to sale or to resort to any legal proceeding for that purpose.[48]

In a proposal for arrangement with secured creditors and specified unsecured creditors, it was held that other unsecured creditors were entitled to appear before the court and present their objections.[49]

No power to stay criminal proceedings

There is no power in the court under these provisions to stay a criminal prosecution against the company and its directors and guarantors.[50]

Advantages of Court's Sanction

The court's sanction is advantageous from several points of view. In the first place the scheme becomes binding upon all the parties to it[51] including

---

43. *Jaypee Cement Ltd, Re,* (2004) 122 Comp Cas 854 (All), the company filed its latest balance sheet and there was no change in the position of the company up to the date of hearing. *Deepika Leasing & Finance Ltd v Deepika Chit Fund (P) Ltd,* (2005) 3 Comp LJ 51 AP, the court must be satisfied of the financial soundness of the companies involved.
44. *Balmenach Glenlivit Distillery, Re,* [1916] SC 639 Scotland.
45. *Empire Mining Co, Re,* (1890) 44 Ch D 402.
46. *Brown Guild Property Society, Re,* [1898] WN 80. *Creditors of Bedrock Ltd v Bedrock Ltd,* (1998) 2 Bom LR 5 Bom, a petition for compromise and arrangement was dismissed because the petitioners had not stated the relevant facts correctly and candidly either in the petition or in the affidavits. That alone showed that the scheme was not bona fide. *Gujarat Kamdar Sahkari Mandli Ltd v Ahmedabad Shree Ramkrishna Mills Co Ltd,* (1996) 2 Guj CD 317 Guj, bona fide scheme proposed by workers, ordered to be considered by calling meetings.
47. *Union of India v Asia Udyog (P) Ltd,* (1974) 44 Comp Cas 359 Del, and again in *Ansal Properties and Industries Ltd, Re,* (1978) 48 Comp Cas 184 Del.
48. *Sakamari Steel & Alloys Ltd, Re,* (1981) 51 Comp Cas 266 Bom. *LG Electronics System India Ltd, Re,* (2003) 116 Comp Cas 48 Del, a secured creditor whose entire claim has been paid out, has no right to a notice or to appear before the Tribunal to raise any objections.
49. *Pharmaceutical Products of India Ltd, Re,* (2006) 131 Comp Cas 747 Bom.
50. *Sharp Industries Ltd, Re,* (2006) 131 Comp Cas 535 Bom.
51. S. 391(2). See *Punjab National Bank Ltd v Shri Vikram Cotton Mills,* (1970) 1 SCC 60:

the shareholders, the company and creditors.[52] The word 'creditor' includes all kinds of creditors and also the State to which some sales tax is due. If, for example, the scheme envisages the payment of four annas in the rupee "in full and final settlement" of the claim of every unsecured creditor, the State can also recover only ¼th of the tax due. It cannot proceed to recover the entire amount due even if the final assessment was completed after the scheme was sanctioned.[53]

Firstly, this way the majority of a class of members of creditors can bind the minority. Where one of the merging companies was at Bombay and the other in Gujarat and a director of the transferor company at Bombay did not raise any objection when the Bombay High Court granted its approval, he became bound and was precluded from raising any objection while the transferee company sought the approval of the Gujarat High Court.[54] Secondly, the company is rescued from its financial straits. The trouble and expense of winding up and of forming a new company are saved. Thirdly, the court sanctioning the scheme has the power to supervise its implementation.[55]

An appeal can be preferred against the scheme to the next higher court.[56] The order of the court takes effect when a certified copy has been filed with the Registrar.[57]

Power of enforcement and supervision [S. 392]

The Court which has sanctioned a scheme of compromise or arrangement has the power to supervise the carrying out of the scheme. The

---

(1970) 40 Comp Cas 927; *Delhi Flour Mills Ltd* v *Indian Hardware Industries*, (1983) 53 Comp Cas 814 Del. A scheme sanctioned by the court became binding on the landlord of the premises of which the company was the lessee, *Ajit Kumar Bose* v *State of W.B.*, (1998) 20 Corpt LA 222 Cal.

52. But a managing director cannot take the benefit of it. Pending decrees against the company would be superseded, but not the one which was against the company and the managing director jointly. *B. K. Muthukrishna* v *S. Mills Ltd*, (1976) 46 Comp Cas 274 Mad. The effective date of the scheme is the date of the court's order. *CIT* v *Swastik Rubber Products*, (1983) 53 Comp Cas 392 Cal; *Flex Industries Ltd, Re*, [1989] 3 Comp LJ 28 Del; *Mehta Investments (P) Ltd, Re*, [1990] 1 Comp LJ 285 Del, schemes with all round approval.

53. *Seksaria Cotton Mills Ltd* v *A. E. Naik*, (1967) 37 Comp Cas 656 Bom. The court has the power to stay pending civil and criminal proceedings if that be necessary for implementation of the scheme. *Harish C. Raskapoor Jaferbhai Mohamedbhai Chhatpar*, (1989) 65 Comp Cas 163 Guj.

54. *Mafatlal Industries Ltd, Re*, (1995) 17 Corpt LA 249 Guj: (1995) 84 Comp Cas 230. The scheme becomes universally binding from its effective date, namely, date of approval of the parties and not that of the sanction of the court. Where a creditor obtained a decree against the company he could not enforce it in the meantime, *Raghubar Dayal* v *Bank of Upper India Ltd*, AIR 1919 PC 9: 46 IA 135: 23 CWN 697, relied on; approved by the Supreme Court in *Marshall Sons & Co (India) Ltd* v *ITO*, (1997) 2 SCC 302: (1997) 88 Comp Cas 528 SC.

55. S. 392(1)(*a*).

56. S. 391(7).

57. S. 391(3). A copy of the order is also required to be annexed to every copy of the memorandum issued subsequent to the filing of the copy with the Registrar. S. 391(4). Sub-section (5) is a penalty provision. This power includes the fixing of a time-limit up to which proposals would be received. See *Sidhpur Mills Co Ltd, Re*, (1980) 50 Comp Cas 7 Guj.

Court may introduce any modifications necessary for the proper working of the scheme.[58] The Court can pass an order of modification by itself and need not wait for an application.[59] The Court may order an extraordinary meeting of the shareholders of the company if it is necessary for constituting a new board of directors for revival of the company. The exercise of this power would not be affected by the exclusive power of the Court under S. 186 for calling an extraordinary general meeting. The shareholders did not raise any objections at the meeting. The meeting was held to be valid.[60] Where some members failed to execute instruments of transfer of their shares under the scheme, the court appointed two officers of the transferee company to execute transfers on behalf of the defaulting shareholders.[61] If the court finds that the scheme cannot be worked satisfactorily, it may make an order for compulsory winding up of the company. The court may do so on its own motion or on the application of any person interested in the company's affairs.[62]

"The effect of a scheme between a company and its creditors is that so long as it is carried out by the company by regular payments in terms of the scheme, a creditor who is bound by it cannot maintain a petition for winding up. But if the company commits a default there is a debt presently due and a petition for winding up can be sustained."[63] Thus, for example, in *New Kaiser-i-Hind Spinning and Weaving Co, Re*[64]:

A and B, two groups of shareholders were contending for the control of a company. They agreed that A should transfer the controlling shares to B at a nominal value and B should provide finance for running the company's mills, and when the company stabilised, to execute a second mortgage in favour of A for debts. The scheme was confirmed at shareholders' and creditors' respective meetings and sanctioned by the court. Subsequently B failed to provide the necessary finance.

---

58. S. 392(1)(*b*). See *Punjab National Bank Ltd* v *Shri Vikram Cotton Mills*, (1970) 1 SCC 60 : (1970) 40 Comp Cas 927; *Mansukh Lal* v *M. V. Shah, OL*, (1976) 46 Comp Cas 279 Guj.
59. *Ram Lal Anand* v *Bank of Baroda*, (1976) 46 Comp Cas 307 Del; *Ved Mitra* v *Globe Motors Ltd*, (1978) 48 Comp Cas 64 Del. The court cannot be called upon to modify a scheme which was never approved by it. *Nathumal Lal Chand* v *Bharat Jute Mills Ltd*, (1983) 53 Comp Cas 382 Cal.
60. *Sree Rama Vilas Press and Publications (P) Ltd, Re*, (1992) 73 Comp Cas 275 Ker; *K. Meenakshi Amma* v *Sreerama Vilas Press and Publications (P) Ltd*, (1992) 73 Comp Cas 285 Ker. A person who was not able to show himself to be a continuing member of the company was not allowed to raise any objections qua member, *Vayaz Indian Pesticides (P) Ltd, Re*, (1999) 35 CLA 386 Bom.
61. *Bank of Baroda Ltd* v *Mahindra Ugine Steel Co*, (1976) 46 Comp Cas 328 Guj.
62. S. 392(2).
63. *J. K. (Bombay) (P) Ltd* v *New Kaiser-i-Hind Spinning and Weaving Co Ltd*, AIR 1970 SC 1041 : (1970) 40 Comp Cas 689: [1970] 1 Comp LJ 151 SC. *See* also *D. S. Venkataraman* v *Gujarat Industries*, (1977) 47 Comp Cas 352. Where payments were not made in accordance with the terms of the scheme, the court ordered payment of interest for the period of default, *Mysore Electro Chemical Works Ltd* v *G.K. Parmashty*, (1996) 86 Comp Cas 571 Kant.
64. [1968] 2 Comp LJ 225.

The court held that the inability to provide finance in terms of the scheme and the consequent inability of the company to carry on business at a profit makes the scheme unworkable and, therefore, winding up should follow.

Where a scheme for rehabilitation of a company was formulated by the Government and approved by the Supreme Court but the IDBI was raising objections in releasing funds to promoters, the Supreme Court directed the financial institution to implement the scheme and reminded it of its duty to ensure the economic growth of the country.[65] Sanction may be granted subject to modifications by the court as to phases of payment and insertion of default clauses.[66]

There is no power in the court to examine validity of transactions such as whether the transfer of shares was in violation of an injunction of the civil court. That would be in excess of jurisdiction.[67] There is no power in the court of scaling down the guarantor's liabilities.[68]

Interests of Employees and Workers

The Tribunal cannot be called upon to sanction a scheme which is unworkable on the face of it.[69] Where a scheme demanded of the workers to waive their claim to compensation under the Industrial Disputes Act, and also notice money and gratuity, the proposal being unfair, the court refused an order for calling a meeting of the creditors for consideration of the scheme.[70] Where full care was taken of the interest of employees under a commitment by the transferee company that it would honour all the promises of the transferor company to its employees, the court said that the workmen's objections were liable to be overruled.[71] Where, on the other hand, a scheme involved heavy sacrifices on the part of all including workers to restart a textile mill, the scheme was approved by all concerned and the court sanctioned it. It was not considered necessary that the sponsor should disclose the sources of his finance.[72] Kerala High Court approved a scheme proposed by the workers of the company under which they were to take over the management. The members and creditors of the company had agreed to give them a chance.[73]

---

65. *Ashok Paper Mills Kamgar Union* v *UOI*, (1997) 10 SCC 113: (1997) 89 Comp Cas 658 SC.
66. *Sharp Industries Ltd, Re*, (2006) 131 Comp Cas 535 Bom.
67. *National Organic Chemical Industries Ltd* v *Miheer H. Mafatlal*, (2004) 121 Comp Cas 519 SC.
68. *Pharmaceutical Products of India Ltd, Re*, (2006) 131 Comp Cas 747 Bom.
69. As between the workers who prayed that the company should be handed over to them and a cooperative society which also made a similar prayer, the court preferred the former because the cooperative society lacked where-withal and experience. *Rajiv Cotton Traders* v *Official Liquidator*, (1992) 73 Comp Cas 51 Guj.
70. *Krishnakumar Mills Ltd, Re*, (1975) 45 Comp Cas 248 Guj.
71. *Tata Oil Mills Co Ltd* v *Hindustan Lever Ltd*, (1994) 81 Comp Cas 754 Bom; *Hindustan Lever Employees' Union* v *Hindustan Lever Ltd*, 1995 Supp (1) SCC 499: AIR 1995 SC 470: (1995) 83 Comp Cas 30.
72. *Hathisingh Mfg Co Ltd, Re*, (1976) 46 Comp Cas 59 Guj.
73. *Star Tile Works, Re*, (1980) 50 Comp Cas 286 Ker. The employees may refuse to go to the transferee company, but they cannot stand in the way of the scheme being sanctioned.

The mere fact that the company has not paid the claim of a former employee is not sufficient to show that the scheme is unworkable.[74]

Reconsideration of sanctioned scheme

The court has the power to set aside a sanctioned scheme if the court's sanction was obtained by fraud. But no such drastic step was taken because the scheme had been acted on for over ten years. The beneficiaries of the scheme were given the opportunity to reconsider the applicant's claim.[75] An English Court held that it would not set aside a judgment obtained by fraud if satisfied that the result would have been the same even if the fraud had not been practiced. The order in this case was based on wrong facts but even so it turned out to be the right decision in the light of the true facts.[76] The Supreme Court set aside an approved scheme because legal requirements were not complied with. The sanction of the court is not an empty formality and, therefore, the court has to observe the proper procedure. In this case the provisions of the Act were not specified under which the scheme was formulated or vacant land of the company was proposed to be sold. Notice to the Central Government was not given, no other publicity was made, latest financial position and chances of revival were not considered.[77]

Reconstruction and amalgamation [S. 394]

Reconstruction.—"There is 'reconstruction' of a company when that company's business and undertaking are transferred to another company formed for that purpose, so that as regards the new company substantially the same business is carried on and the same persons are interested in it as in the case of the old company."[78] A reconstruction may become necessary for several purposes. A court (now Tribunal) may not, for example, sanction a radical change of objects. New objects can then be adopted only by the process of reconstruction.[79] A reconstruction may also become necessary to

---

Bengal Tea Industries v *Union of India*, (1988-89) 93 Cal WR 542 and *John Wyeth (India) Ltd, Re*, (1988) 63 Comp Cas 233 Bom. It was also pointed out in the above-mentioned first scheme that as the creditors were given the same protection which they had in their debtor company they should not object. *Regional Fund Commr* v *Raj Kumar Nemani*, (1995) 1 Cal LJ 89 Cal: (1995) 16 Corpt LA 405, members of the Committee of Management constituted by the court do not become court officers. The anxiety of the court should be to protect workers and not to obstruct development and growth. *Hindustan Lever Employees' Union* v *Hindustan Lever Ltd*, 1995 Supp (1) SCC 499: AIR 1995 SC 470: (1995) 83 Comp Cas 30; *All India Blue Star Employees' Federation* v *Blue Star Ltd*, (2000) 37 CLA 157 Bom; reaffirmed by DB, (2000) 27 SCL 265 Bom DB, the court did not find any prejudice to the rights of workers.

74. *Chaugule* v *New Kaiser-i-Hind Spinning and Weaving Co*, [1968] 2 Comp LJ 28 Bom.
75. *Central Bank of India* v *Ambalal Sarabhai Enterprises Ltd*, [1999] 3 Comp LJ 98 Guj.
76. *Fletcher* v *Royal Automobile Club Ltd*, [2000] 1 BCLC 31 CA.
77. *State of W.B.* v *Pronab Kumar Sur*, (2003) 9 SCC 490: (2003) 114 Comp Cas 664 SC.
78. J. A. Hornby, AN INTRODUCTION TO COMPANY LAW, p 174 (1957).
79. *North of England Protecting & Indemnity Assn, Re*, (1929) 45 TLR 296.

cause material alterations of the rights of a class of shareholders or creditors.[80]

Amalgamation.—"Amalgamation occurs when two or more companies are joined to form a third entity or one is absorbed into or blended with another."[81] The effect is to wipe out the merging companies and to fuse them all into the new one created. The new company comes into existence having all the property, rights and powers and subject to all the duties and obligations, of both the constituent companies. Explaining the object of an amalgamation and the scheme of the statutory provisions, the Madras High Court observed in *W. A. Beardsell & Co. (P) Ltd, Re*:[82]

> The word 'amalgamation' has not been defined in the Act. The ordinary dictionary meaning of the expression is 'combination'. Judging from the context and from the marginal note of Section 394 which appears in Chapter V relating to arbitration, compromises, arrangements and reconstructions, the primary object of amalgamation of one company with another is to facilitate reconstruction of the amalgamating companies and this is a matter which is entirely left to the body of shareholders, (and) essentially an affair relating to the internal administration of the transferor company. The decision of the body of the shareholders ought not to be lightly interfered with.

Power of amalgamation.—There should be power in the company's memorandum to amalgamate. If it is not there it should be acquired by altering the memorandum.[83] It is not necessary that the company adopting a

---

80. See *Bank of India Ltd* v *Ahmedabad Mfg & Calico Printing Co*, (1972) 42 Comp Cas 211 Bom. Where the companies are situated in two different jurisdictions, the sanction of both the courts would be necessary to give to the scheme an all-round binding efficacy. *Industrial Credit & Investment Corpn of India* v *Financial and Management Services Ltd*, AIR 1998 Bom 305. The supervisory jurisdiction of the court was also stressed in this case.

81. *Somayajula* v *Hope Prudhomme & Co Ltd*, [1963] 2 Comp LJ 61. It is necessary that the transferee company should be in existence at the "appointed day" though not at the time of the preparation of the scheme. *HCL Ltd, Re*, (1994) 80 Comp Cas 228 Del. It is not necessary that both companies should have common objects. *PMP Auto Industries Ltd, Re*, (1994) 80 Comp Cas 289 Bom. The court can authorise necessary alterations in the memorandum after inviting the CLB to state its objections, if any. *Rangkala Investments Ltd, Re*, (1995) 16 Corpt LA 280 Guj ; *Gujarat Organics Ltd, Re*, (1995) 16 Corpt LA 280 Guj.

82. (1968) 38 Comp Cas 197, 204 Mad. See also *Reliance Jute Industries Ltd, Re*, (1983) 53 Comp Cas 591 Cal, where a holding company absorbed its subsidiary and objections under S. 372 [now S. 372-A] were not sustained. The transferor company which is going to be amalgamated can be a foreign company, *Bombay Gas Co (P) Ltd* v *Central Govt*, (1997) 89 Comp Cas 195 Bom. The court followed the decision to the same effect in *Khandelwal Udyog Ltd & ACME Mfg Co Ltd, Re*, (1977) 47 Comp Cas 503, 511. *Banaras Breads Ltd, Re*, (2006) 132 Comp Cas 548 (All), in a scheme of amalgamation, the arbitration award directed convening of a meeting for approval of the scheme. Certain applications alleging oppression and mismanagement were pending before CLB. The court said that the petition for confirmation of the scheme could not be kept pending till CLB decisions.

83. *Hari Krishna Lohia* v *Hoolungooree Tea Co*, (1970) 40 Comp Cas 458, 463 Cal. A separate petition to CLB for alteration of memorandum is not necessary. The CLB (now Tribunal) can be invited to express its objections in the same petition so that a single window clearance can be provided for all matters. *PMP Auto Industries Ltd, Re*, (1994) 80 Comp Cas 289 Bom.

scheme should be in financial difficulties or that it should not be an affluent company. The expression "any company liable to be wound up under this Act" does not mean a company which is insolvent, but any company registered under the Act, every such company being subject to the winding up provisions of the Act.[84]

Forms of reconstruction and amalgamation.—A reconstruction or amalgamation may take any of the following forms:

1. By sale of shares.[85]
2. By sale of undertaking.
3. By sale and dissolution.[86]
4. By a scheme of arrangement.[87]

Sale of shares is the simplest process of amalgamation or takeover. Shares are sold and registered in the name of the purchasing company. The selling shareholders receive either compensation or shares in the acquiring company. If nine-tenths of the holders of a class have approved the terms, shares of the rest can be acquired under Section 395.

The second method involves a sale of the whole of the undertaking of the transferor company as a going concern.[88]

Section 394 applies to every scheme which involves transfer of the whole or any part of the undertaking or liability of a company to another company.[89] Section 391, therefore, applies and an application may be made to the court by any person entitled to move the court under that section. The court may sanction the scheme and make necessary orders.[90] Such an order

---

According to S. 376 conditions prohibiting reconstruction or amalgamation are void. The section is as follows:

"**S. 376. *Conditions prohibiting reconstruction or amalgamation of company.***—Where any provision in the memorandum or articles of a company, or in any resolution passed in general meeting by, or by the Board of directors of the company, or in an agreement between the company and any other person, whether made before or after the commencement of this Act, prohibits the reconstruction of the company or its amalgamation with any body corporate or bodies corporate, either absolutely or except on the condition that the managing director or manager of the company is appointed or reappointed as managing director or manager of the reconstructed company or of the body resulting from amalgamation, as the case may be, shall become void with effect from the commencement of this Act, or be void, as the case may be.".

84. *Khandelwal Udyog Ltd & ACME Mfg Co Ltd, Re*, (1977) 47 Comp Cas 503 Bom.
85. Allotment of shares on preferential basis to the holding company of the transferee company so as to maintain the majority stake was held to be a fair basis of allotment of shares in the transferee company to the members of the transferor company. *Hindustan Lever Ltd, Re; Tata Oil Mills Co Ltd, Re*, (1994) 81 Comp Cas 754 Bom.
86. This is considered in connection with voluntary winding-up.
87. This has already been considered.
88. Amalgamation by outright purchase of the transferor company by the transferee company is recognised by the Accounting Standards of the Institute of Chartered Accountants. A petition is maintainable for the approval of such a scheme, *SPS Pharma Ltd, Re*, (1997) 88 Comp Cas 774 AP; *Targof Pure Drugs Ltd, Re*, (1997) 88 Comp Cas 774 AP.
89. S. 394(1)(*a*) and (*b*). Amalgamation of a company dealing in shares with a transport company, there is no power to prevent it, *Eita India Ltd, Re*, (1997) 24 Corpt LA 37 Cal.
90. The court can examine the bonafides of the person making an objection. Very unusually, the court permitted a transfer of shares which had already been registered to be questioned when

may make provisions for any of the following matters:[91]

(*i*) transfer of the undertaking, property, liabilities of one company to the other;

(*ii*) the allotment or appropriation by the transferee company of any shares, debentures, or other like interests which have to be allotted or appropriated under the contract;[92]

(*iii*) the continuation by or against the transferee company of any legal proceeding pending by or against the transferor company;

(*iv*) the dissolution, without winding up, of the transferor company;

(*v*) the provision to be made for any person who dissents from the scheme;

(*vi*) such incidental, consequential and supplemental matters as are necessary to secure that the reconstruction or amalgamation is fully and effectively carried out.[93]

The order of the Court can provide for matters like violation of Section 42 (subsidiary buying the shares of its holding) or Section 77 (a company buying its own shares) if such processes are involved in the scheme. The Court can also order dissolution without winding up of the transferor company.[94] Section 394 confers wide powers on the Court to be exercised for such purposes so that there are no obstructions to the implementation of a scheme.[95]

In an amalgamation of holding and subsidiary companies, the rights of members and creditors of the transferee (holding) company were not affected and there was going to be no new issue of shares by or reorganisation of share capital of the transferor company, it was held that the transferee company need not file a separate application.[96]

Every company in relation to which the order is made has to file within thirty days a copy of the order with the Registrar for registration.[97]

it was shown that the shareholder was given that position only for the purpose of using him to raise objections. *Piccadilly Radio plc, Re*, 1989 BCLC 683 Ch D. *New Vision Laser Centres (Raj Koti) (P) Ltd, Re*, (2002) 111 Comp Cas 756 Guj, merger of holding and subsidiary allowed. Powers under S. 391 not subordinate to Sections 42 and 77.

91. S. 394(1)(*a*) and (*b*). *Grierson Oldham & Adams Ltd, Re*, [1967] 1 WLR 385: [1968] Ch 17: [1967] 1 All ER 192.

92. *Glofame Cotspin Industries Ltd, Re*, (2006) 130 Comp Cas 334 Guj, the transferee company undertaking to redeem all preference shares issued by the transferor company as they fell due, scheme sanctioned.

93. S. 394(1).

94. *CIT* v *Dalmia Magnesite Corpn*, (1999) 96 Comp Cas 792 SC.

95. *Himachal Telematics Ltd* v *Himachal Futuristic Communications Ltd*, (1996) 86 Comp Cas 325 Del. *Walves Flour Mills Co (P) Ltd, Re*, (1996) 23 Corpt LA 104 Bom, the court at the registered office of the company would not refuse sanction of amalgamation with a Bombay company when the court at Bombay has granted sanction. *State Bank of India* v *Alstom Power Boilers Ltd*, (2003) 116 Comp Cas 1 Bom, when a sick industrial company comes out of sickness and there is a BIFR declaration to that effect, a scheme proposed thereafter does not require sanction of the BIFR.

96. *Vibank Housing Finance Ltd, Re*, (2006) 130 Comp Cas 705 Kant.

97. S. 394(3). The sub-section imposes penalty for default.

Official reports.—An amendment introduced in 1965 provides that a compromise or arrangement in connection with the amalgamation of a company in winding up with any other company or companies shall not be sanctioned unless the court has received a report from the Tribunal or Registrar that the affairs of the company have not been conducted in a manner prejudicial to the interest of the members or to public interest. Similarly, an order for the dissolution of the transferor company shall not be made unless the official liquidator makes a report that its affairs have not been conducted in a manner prejudicial to the interest of members or to public interest.[1] The Gujarat High Court found in a case[2] that the only purpose for which the transferor company was created was to facilitate the transfer of a building to the transferee company without attracting the capital gains tax and the dissolution of the transferor company was sought without winding up. The court refused to sanction the scheme. In another case where a similar report was submitted by the official liquidator, the court sanctioned the scheme but issued directions which formed part of the scheme which were that instruments of conveyance with payment of stamp duty must be executed, that unassignable rights would not be available to the assignee company, that the sanction would not excuse payment of overdue taxes and that the directors would not be absolved from their liability for violations of law, if any.[3] The official liquidator cannot question or object to the share exchange ratio. That is not the function of the official report.[4]

The power of the Court is discretionary. It has been expressly authorised to pay full attention to public interest. The expression "public interest", the court said, "takes its colour from the context in which it is used and will depend upon the object which the legislation wants to promote or the mischief which it seeks to suppress."[5] The philosophy behind taxes being to promote public interests, it cannot be said that a scheme which is designed to avoid taxes is not prejudicial to public interest.[6] The report of the official

---

1. Proviso to S. 395(1) *added* by the Companies Amendment Act, 1965.
2. *Wood Polymer Ltd, Re*, (1977) 47 Comp Cas 597.
3. *Kriti Plastics (P) Ltd, Re*, (1993) 78 Comp Cas 138 MP.
4. *Nav Chrome Ltd, Re*, (1997) 89 Comp Cas 285 AP; *Nava Bharat Ferro Alloys Ltd, Re*, (1997) 89 Comp Cas 285 AP. It was also held in this case that where in spite of wide publicity, no creditor objected, subsequent objections were not to be entertained. Even otherwise the creditors were getting a financially stronger company as their debtor.
5. The court cited *State of Bihar* v *Maharajadhiraja*, 1952 SCR 889, 994: AIR 1952 SC 252. *Bengal Tea Industries* v *Union of India*, (1988-89) 93 Cal WR 542. *Navyug Investments Ltd, Re*, [1993] 3 Comp LJ 305 Del, merger of six sister companies carrying on the same business and operating from the same place.
6. Where an amalgamation was in the interest of the company as also of its creditors, the report of the official liquidator that the transferee company's tax liability was going to be reduced was ignored. Such matters are not within the function of the official liquidator's report. *Shankar Narayana Hotels (P) Ltd* v *Official Liquidator*, (1992) 74 Comp Cas 290 Kant. A scheme was not permitted to be revised twelve years after the original order of merger just only because at that time no provision had been made for payment of taxes. *Union of India* v *Asia Udyog (P) Ltd*, (1993) 78 Comp Cas 468 Del. The transferor

liquidator is necessary only when the court has to pass an order of dissolution. Amalgamation does not necessarily involve dissolution of the transferor company.[7] In other cases a report of the Registrar is sufficient.[8]

Where the latest auditors' report is necessary for working out the exchange ratio, it would be the report which is available at the time of the application, namely report on the preceding year's accounts.[9]

Notice to Central Government: Fairness of Exchange Ratio [S. 394]

The Court has also to give notice of every application to the Central Government and has to take into account the representation, if any, made by the Government before sanctioning the scheme.[10] The extent to which the Central Government can intervene was explained by the Calcutta High Court in *Associated Hotels of India Ltd, Re*[11]:

> A merger of three hotels was approved by overwhelming majority of creditors and shareholders of all the companies and, it was accordingly sanctioned by the court. But the Central Government raised the objection that the mode of valuation of assets was not fair and prayed for appointment of independent valuers.

It was held that there cannot be any interference in the valuation made by experts unless there has been a mistake which defeats justice. For example,

---

company would cease to be a tax payer only when it ceases to exist. *Marshall Sons & Co (India) Ltd* v *ITO*, [1991] 3 Comp LJ 117 Mad: (1992) 74 Comp Cas 236. The company ceases to exist from the date the scheme is sanctioned by the court or such other date as may be specified in the order, *Marshall Sons & Co (India) Ltd* v *ITO*, (1997) 2 SCC 302: (1997) 88 Comp Cas 528 SC. The Supreme Court held that an Income tax notice sent to the company after that date was not legally warranted.

7. *Mathew Philip* v *Malayalam Plantation (India) Ltd*, (1994) 81 Comp Cas 38 Ker FB, not approving on this point, *Official Liquidator* v *Madura Co (P) Ltd*, 1975 Ker LT 562 and citing *Malayalam Plantation India Ltd* v *Harisons and Crossfield (India) Ltd*, [1985] 2 Comp LJ 409 Ker, an example of amalgamation without dissolution; *General Radio and Appliances Co Ltd* v *M. A. Khader*, (1986) 2 SCC 656: [1986] 2 Comp LJ 249 SC: (1986) 60 Comp Cas 1013 and *Saraswati Industrial Syndicate Ltd* v *CIT*, 1990 Supp SCC 657: AIR 1991 SC 70, explaining the effect of amalgamation in general terms. But see *Webb's Farm Mechanisations (P) Ltd* v *Official Liquidator*, (1996) 85 Comp Cas 146: AIR 1996 Kant 65, where it was held that an amalgamation being not possible without the dissolution of the transferor company, the report of the official liquidator becomes necessary in all cases.

8. *Marybong and Kyel Tea Estate Ltd, Re*, (1977) 47 Comp Cas 802 Cal. There is no requirement that Income tax office should be notified. In this case there was not even a suggestion that the scheme was intended for tax evasion, *Anand Crown and Seal (P) Ltd, Re*, (1996) 87 Comp Cas 266 AP. The loss of company's paid up capital and accumulation of liabilities four times to the remaining capital does not prevent amalgamation of such a company with a sound and healthy company. Public interest was also not compromised because the company took over all obligations, *Shree Sai Baba Castings (P) Ltd, Re*, (1997) 27 Corpt LA 72 Bom.

9. *All India Blue Star Employees' Fedn* v *Blue Star Ltd*, (2000) 27 SCL 265 Bom.

10. S. 394-A. *Jindal India Ltd, Re*, (1993) 76 Comp Cas 443 Del.

11. [1968] 2 Comp LJ 292 Cal. Where the exchange ratio was fixed on the basis of the break-up value as recommended by two independent experts, the court considered the ratio to be a fair one though the report of one of them was sketchy and not based upon proper evaluation, that of the other expert was a well considered report, *Mafatlal Industries Ltd, Re*, (1995) 17 Corpt LA 249 Guj: (1995) 84 Comp Cas 230.

if the court finds that the appreciated value of the landed property of one of the companies or loans made by it to its directors have not been taken into account, it will be reluctant to grant its sanction.

In *Cotton Agents* v *Vijay Laxmi Trading Co*[12] the court held that the Central Government cannot interfere in the matter of valuation unless there is allegation of fraud or undue influence or that the books of account are unreliable or that different or discriminatory methods of valuation have been adopted.

In another case,[13] the Central Government raised the objection that the shareholders of the transferor company were to get two shares in the transferee company for every five shares and that this was not reasonable and fair to the shareholders of the transferor company. The court overruled this objection. Two respectable firms of chartered accountants had stated that they had examined the accounts, annual reports, working and financial position of the two companies and also considered the net intrinsic value and came to the conclusion that the ratio of 5:2 was fair and reasonable. The court drew further support from the fact that the scheme of amalgamation had been widely advertised and unanimously approved by the meetings of the shareholders of the two companies and no objection at all had been raised by any of the shareholders or creditors.[14] Calculation of share value by taking net asset value (NAV) on

---

12. [1968] 2 Comp LJ 7 Raj. *See* also *Shahibag Entrepreneur (P) Ltd, Re*, (1976) 46 Comp Cas 642 Guj. *Hindustan Investments Ltd, Re*, (1988) 64 Comp Cas 116 P&H, Regional Director's objection as to exchange ratio overruled. Valuation on the basis of net value of the company's assets and fixation of exchange ratio was held to be fair and not to be interfered on the objections of the Registrar. *Sanghi Industries Ltd, Re*, (1993) 3 Andh LT 719. Objections against exchange ratio worked out by Chartered Accountants not allowed, *Maknam Investments Ltd, Re*, (1995) 87 Comp Cas 689 Cal: (1995) 1 Cal HCN 368. In an amalgamation of two closely-held private companies, the Central Government's objection as to exchange ratio and small capital base of one of them was overruled, *Mahavir Weaves (P) Ltd, Re*, (1995) 83 Comp Cas 180 Guj: (1997) 24 Corpt LA 11 Guj.
13. *M. G. Investment & Industrial Co Ltd* v *New Shorrock Spinning & Manufacturing Co Ltd*, (1912) 42 Comp Cas 145.
14. Non-disclosure of the valuation report is not sufficient to prevent sanction. S. 393(1)(a) does not require all the material facts to be disclosed. *Khandelwal Udyog Ltd & ACME Mfg Co Ltd, Re*, (1977) 47 Comp Cas 503 Bom. Thus the trend of judicial opinion is to attach great weight to the approval by shareholders. Proceeding on this philosophy the Bombay High Court sanctioned a scheme despite the objection from the Government quarters that the quoted company, which was taking over an unquoted company had not made proper valuation of the shares of the latter company. See *Piramal Spinning & Weaving Mills Ltd, Re*, (1980) 50 Comp Cas 514 Bom. The Madras and AP High Courts followed the same principle in *Coimbatore Cotton Mills Ltd & Lakshmi Cotton Mills Co Ltd, Re*, (1980) 50 Comp Cas 623 Mad; *Vijaya Durga Cotton Trading Ltd, Re*, (1980) 50 Comp Cas 785 AP; *Vasant Investment Corpn* v *OL, Colaba Land etc.*, (1981) 51 Comp Cas 20 Bom, winding up stayed on sanctioning a scheme; *Indian Hardware Industries Ltd* v *S. K. Gupta*, (1981) 51 Comp Cas 51 Del, power to call meetings; *Mehtab Chand Golcha* v *OL*, (1981) 51 Comp Cas 103 Raj, power to make modifications for adjustment of tax claims; *Tata Oil Mills Co Ltd, Re*, (1994) 81 Comp Cas 754 Bom; *Hindustan Lever Ltd, Re*, (1994) 81 Comp Cas 754 Bom, fixing the value of an asset by another group company was held to be not proper. Apart from this the valuation rate of share exchange ratio was found to be proper; *Hindustan Lever Employees' Union* v *Hindustan Lever Ltd*, 1995 Supp (1) SCC 499: AIR 1995 SC 470: (1995) 83 Comp Cas 30, approval of valuation by more than 95% of shareholders was not to be interfered

the basis of book value can be accepted as a proper mode of valuation.[15] The date of valuation should be proximate to the date of petition. No balance-sheet was in existence as of that date. The earlier balancesheet nearest to the date of petition should be taken into account.[16]

In another case, the exchange ratio was worked out by independent auditors, who had followed the proper methods and considered all the financial aspects. The calculation could not be questioned only because one of the auditors was the statutory auditor of the transferee company.[17] Where the share-exchange ratio was approved by the requisite majority and no defect was pointed and it was worked out by three chartered accountants by adopting the three applicable methods, the court also approved it. The value of the shares of the transferee company was higher than that of the transferor company's shares. The transferee company also had a good market potential. The court refused to regard the scheme as unfair only because there was a fear in the minds of some shareholders that there would be a big reduction in dividend income.[18]

Where share-exchange ratio was found by the valuers to be fair and equitable and the shareholders of the transferor company also approved the scheme, it was held that the objecting shareholder could not seek direction to the company to provide details of calculation of the ratio.[19]

---

with. The court has jurisdiction to stay recovery of taxes. See *Byford Ltd* v *STO*, (1981) 51 Comp Cas 561 Del. Valuation of shares done by respectable firms of chartered accountants on the well-known methods of valuation was presumed to be fair, *Sumitra Pharmaceuticals and Chemicals Ltd, Re*, (1997) 88 Comp Cas 619 AP; *Miheer H. Mafatlal* v *Mafatlal Industries Ltd*, (1997) 1 SCC 579: (1996) 87 Comp Cas 792. Where the ratio was worked out by taking into account the rise in the value of assets and there were no allegations of fraud or *mala fides* against the valuer, the exchange ratio was held to be fair and reasonable. High valuation of the transferor company's assets for alleged purpose of piloting the public issue of the newly formed private company, was held not to be a manipulation of share prices at that stage, *APCO Electricals (P) Ltd, Re*, (1996) 86 Comp Cas 457 Guj. Private companies, intermingled affairs, share exchange ratio seemed reasonable and also approved by shareholders, *Mahavir Weaves (P) Ltd, Re*, (1997) 24 Corpt LA 11 Guj. Valuation on net asset value basis accepted by both companies and their unanimous shareholders, valuation beyond question, *Jindal India Ltd* v *Cold Rollings India (P) Ltd*, (1998) 28 Corpt LA 255 Del. *Aradhana Beverages & Foods Co Ltd, Re*, (1998) 74 Del LT 276, share exchange ratio by experts, shareholders satisfied, no interference at the instance of Regional Director. *M.M. Sehgal Ltd* v *Sanmati Trading Investments Ltd*, (1997) 65 Del LT 53, frivolous objections by applicants who were not members, rejected, scheme approved.

15. *KMA Ltd* v *Union of India*, (1996) 86 Comp Cas 728: [1997] 1 Comp LJ 343 Del.
16. *Nikhil Rubbers (P) Ltd, Re*, (2002) 108 Comp Cas 438 CLB.
17. *Asian Coffee Ltd, Re*, [2000] CLC 17 affirmed in *Vadalamuddi Rama Rao* v *Asian Coffee Ltd*, [2000] 3 Comp LJ 110 at p 119. *Shiva Texyarn Ltd* v *Annamallai Finance Ltd*, (2003) 114 Comp Cas 55 Mad, the scheme provided for issue of shares at a premium, valuation approved by experts and by requisite majority of shareholders. The scheme was sanctioned.
18. *American Remedies Ltd, Re*, (2003) 113 Comp Cas 114 Mad. *Pan Atlantic Insurance Co Ltd, Re*, (2003) 2 BCLC 678 (Ch D), no violation of human rights by reason of finality of valuation done by an independent adjudicator. *Avcoy Overseas (P) Ltd, Re*, (2006) 129 Comp Cas 332 Guj, amalgamation of two companies under the same management group, valuation by chartered accountants, objection of the Regional Director that separate valuation was not done, not substantial.
19. *Challa Rajendra Prasad* v *Asian Coffee Ltd*, (2001) 103 Comp Cas 17 AP. *Alfa Quartz Ltd* v *Cymex Time Ltd*, (2001) 104 Comp Cas 71 Guj, approval by both the transferor and transferee

The Regional Director, who acts for the Central Government in this respect, raised the objection that the surplus arising out of the scheme was a reserve of capital nature and, therefore, could not be considered as a general reserve for distribution among shareholders. But the shareholders had not raised any such objection and approved the scheme unanimously. The court overruled the objection.[20]

Notice to the Central Government has to be given at the stage of sanction and not at the stage of application for a direction for calling of a meeting.[21] Notice to the Central Government, having been once given at the stage of sanction, is not required to be given at any subsequent stages, like the stage for an order of the dissolution of the transferor company.[22]

Some Instances

Where at a meeting called by the court a scheme of amalgamation was approved by 648 shareholders holding 84,753 shares as against 11 shareholders holding only 48 shares and the dissenting shareholders did not at all appear at the hearing to present their objections, if any, the court accordingly observed:[23]

> If the opposition was legitimate and founded on some material ground, the court would have examined the scheme critically. After examining the scheme from the point of the petitioner, that is, the transferee company, it must be said, without the least fear of being contradicted, that the scheme of amalgamation, by which a huge sum of Rs 14.70 crores with its accumulated interest would be available to the petitioner both for its expansion as well as for its liquid finances, would undoubtedly be a scheme which is such as a man of business applying his commercial judgment, from his own narrow personal angle, would approve.

---

company, the court could not be called upon to say that the exchange ratio was prejudicial to their interests. *Gujarat Ambuja Cotspin Ltd, Re*, (2001) 104 Comp Cas 397 Guj, valuation done by experts was not interfered with. *Blue Star Ltd, Re*, (2001) 104 Comp Cas 371; exchange ratio worked out by recognised firm of chartered accountants and assets were valued by a Government approved valuer, objection by Regional Director of Company Affairs was not accepted, *H.K. Dave (P) Ltd, In re*, (2001) 104 Comp Cas 550 Guj. *Covelong Beach Hotels (India) Ltd, Re*, (2002) 112 Comp Cas 17 Mad, objection and amendment proposed by a shareholder defeated at the meeting, not material, inspection of accounts by ROC also not relevant to the scheme. *Alstom Power Boilers Ltd v SBI*, (2002) 112 Comp Cas 674 Bom, the court did not question the commercial wisdom of shareholders, objectors who did not attend meetings not entitled to raise objections before the court. Objections to classification should have been made after notice of meeting.

20. *Sutlej Industries Ltd, Re*, (2007) 135 Comp Cas 394 Raj.
21. *YLM Holdings (P) Ltd, Re*, (2001) 105 Comp Cas 249 Del.
22. *Vikram Organics (P) Ltd v Anirox Pigments Ltd*, (1997) 88 Comp Cas 804: [1997] 3 Comp LJ 193 Cal.
23. *Ahmedabad Mfg & Calico Printing Co v Bank of India*, (1972) 42 Comp Cas 493 Guj. A lone shareholder holding microscopic minority interest objected to amalgamation, ruled out; an accidental omission to give him notice of the meeting was also not fatal, *Maknam Investments Ltd, Re*, (1995) 1 CHN 368.

In another case[24] arising out of the same facts, the Bombay High Court restated the distinction between "compromise" and "arrangement". The court came to the conclusion that if a scheme of amalgamation involves variation of members' rights that amounts to reorganisation of capital making the sanction of the court necessary and where shares of a different nature, such as bonds convertible into shares, are proposed to be issued that is definitely a reorganisation.

Where a scheme of amalgamation was approved by all the members of the transferee company but no formal meeting was held, the court said that all that was necessary was that the sanction should be put off till a meeting was held and the fact reported to the court.[25]

Vesting of Rights and Transfer of Obligations

All the rights and obligations of the amalgamated company become vested in the amalgamating company.[26] A company taking over another was allowed to continue eviction proceedings. A formal transfer or substitution was not necessary. Where the transfer of property takes place in terms of an order under Section 394, the right to continue the proceedings arises automatically. Where the whole undertaking is taken over, all the rights pass whether mentioned in a schedule or not.[27] The company which emerges from the amalgamation becomes the new tenant because the property rights which pass to the transferee company include tenancy rights also.[28] The

---

24. *Bank of India Ltd* v *Ahmedabad Mfg & Calico Printing Co*, (1972) 42 Comp Cas 211 Bom. In *Gwalior Strips Ltd, Re*, [1993] 2 Comp LJ 377 and *Spring Steels Ltd, Re*, [1993] 2 Comp LJ 377 MP, the court ignored the objection of the Central Government that the liability of transferor company for violation of the Companies Act was going to be wiped only. The alleged liability was for breaches of Ss. 67 and 68.
25. *Union Services (P) Ltd, Re*, (1975) 45 Comp Cas 146 Mad. Sanction of a scheme enjoying all round approval, *Hindustan Coca Cola Bottling S W (P) Ltd Re*, [1999] 4 Comp LJ 442 Del. Amalgamation of two cement companies under a scheme which appeared to be just, fair and reasonable from the point of view of a prudent man of business, sanction granted, *Rassi Cement Ltd, Re*, (1999) 98 Comp Cas 835 AP. *Andhra Bank Housing Finance Ltd, Re*, (2004) 118 Comp Cas 295 AP, amalgamation of 100% banking subsidiary company with its holding with RBI approval sanctioned, holding company not required to call a separate meeting or to make a separate application for sanction.
26. See *Nilinta Chemicals Ltd, Re*, (1997) 26 Corpt LA 347 MP, the court order provided that there would be no prejudice to the tax liability for capital gains and directors' liability for anything wrong and to the need for executing formal documents wherever necessary. *United Breweries Ltd* v *Commr of Excise*, (2001) 105 Comp Cas 71 Bom, the shareholders of both the companies being the same, it did not mean that there was no transfer of ownership after amalgamation.
27. *L. Mullick & Co* v *Benani Properties (P) Ltd*, (1983) 53 Comp Cas 693 Cal.
28. *Telesound (India) Ltd, Re*, (1983) 53 Comp Cas 926 Del. Where, however, care was not taken to comply with the State Rent Act and terms and conditions of the rent agreement were not maintained, the transfer of tenancy was ineffective. *General Radio and Appliances Co Ltd* v *M. A. Khader*, (1986) 2 SCC 656: [1986] 2 Comp LJ 249 SC : (1986) 60 Comp Cas 1013. The shareholders of one company cannot restrain another company from adopting a resolution for taking over the company. *Centron Industrial Alliances Ltd* v *Pravin Kantilal Vakil*, (1985) 57 Comp Cas 12 Bom. Where the scheme did not involve diminution of liability in respect of

supplier of electricity has to take the emerging company as its consumer and cannot say that there has been a transfer of the connection.[29] Where the premises held by the transferor company on lease and licence were found to be not transferable and were, therefore not included in valuation, a failure to mention them in the particulars of the scheme was not fatal to the scheme.[30] Where the circumstances were such that the scheme of revival could not be implemented unless the tenants on the company's premises were evicted, the court passed necessary orders for the purpose.[31]

The transfer of assets of the transferor company to the transferee company takes place under a sanctioned scheme by virtue of the provisions of S. 394(1)(2), and, therefore, it does not fall in the definition of 'conveyance' or 'instrument' as defined in S. 2(14) of the Stamp Act, 1899. There is no liability to pay stamp duty.[32]

The vesting takes place from the *effective date* of the scheme which is either specified in the order of sanction or it is the date of approval of the scheme.[33]

Reduction of Capital in Amalgamation.—Where a scheme of amalgamation involves the merger of two companies into a new company, and the merging companies are to be dissolved without winding up, the fact that the preference shareholders of the merging companies are to be paid back under the scheme does not amount to reduction of capital. This has been so held by the Madras High Court in *T. Durairajan* v *Waterfall Estates Ltd.*[34] The court pointed out "that the scheme of Sections 101 and 102 of the Companies Act clearly envisages reduction in capital in the context of an existing or continuing company, whereas in the present case, both companies had to go out of existence". The court further pointed out

---

unpaid share capital, the procedure for reduction of capital had not to be followed. *HCL Ltd, Re*, (1994) 80 Comp Cas 228 Del.

29. *Gujarat Ambuja Exports Ltd* v *Gujarat Electricity Board*, (2002) 112 Comp Cas 188 Guj.
30. *Tata Oil Mills Co Ltd & Hindustan Lever Ltd, Re*, (1994) 81 Comp Cas 754 Bom. The court also said that since TOMCO was to be dissolved and it was a part of the Tata group, its trademarks which belonged to the group, would have to be given up by the transferee company by absorbing the products into its own marks system.
31. *Hotel Kandath International (P) Ltd* v *Official Liquidator*, (1997) 27 Corpt LA 224 Kant.
32. *Madhu Intra Ltd* v *ROC*, (2006) 130 Comp Cas 510 Cal.
33. *Bombay Gas Co (P) Ltd* v *Central Govt*, (1997) 89 Comp Cas 195 Bom. *Gemini Silk Ltd* v *Gemini Overseas Ltd*, (2003) 114 Comp Cas 92 Cal, transfer of assets and liabilities in terms of the order is a conveyance in consideration of allotment of shares, liable to stamp duty except to the extent of exemption, if any. *Glofame Cotspin Industries Ltd, Re*, (2006) 130 Comp Cas 334 Guj, the matter of stamp duty which was under final adjudication could not prevent sanction of the court. There could be no objection to retransfer of such assets from transferor to transferee company which had earlier been transferred to the transferor company by the transferee company under a court order. *M.N. Chhaya* v *PRS Mani*, (2005) 127 Comp Cas 863 Bom, effective date as may be specified in the order of sanction or the date of sanction.
34. (1972) 42 Comp Cas 563 Mad. The court can sanction reduction of capital also if there is a substantial compliance with the requirements of reduction, *Novapan India Ltd, Re*, (1997) 88 Comp Cas 596 AP: (1997) 25 Corpt LA 224 AP.

that the object of requiring sanction of the court for reduction of capital is to safeguard the interest of the creditors of the company. In the present case the new company had undertaken to pay all the debts of the merging companies and, therefore, the procedure for reduction of capital as laid down in Sections 100, 101 and 102 was not applicable.[35]

There is no prohibition or legal impediment on reduction of share capital when it is a part of a scheme of amalgamation. The only thing is that the procedure required for reduction of capital has to be complied with. A similar procedure has to be observed where the reduction is that of the share premium account and the scheme is not covered by the permitted range of utilisation of such account. The shareholders and creditors had approved the scheme by requisite majority. The auditors report was that the affairs of the company had not been conducted in a manner prejudicial to members' or public interest.[36]

Increase of authorised share capital.—Where the scheme of amalgamation involved an increase of the authorised capital of the transferee company, the court said that the procedure prescribed for such increase would have to be observed without any exemption in this respect. The transferee company was bound to carry out the requirements of the scheme.[37]

Change of name.—There is no automatic change of name of the company involved in an amalgamation. Proceedings for change of name would have to be followed. A term in the scheme providing for change of name on the sanction of amalgamation was ordered to be deleted.[38]

Amalgamation of banking companies

Section 44-A of the Banking Regulation Act, 1949 is a complete, self-contained code on amalgamation of banking companies. Under S. 44-A, the power to grant approval to the scheme of merger of banking companies is with the Reserve Bank of India (instead of Tribunal) and the RBI is also empowered to determine market-value of shares of the objecting shareholder who voted against the scheme as well as to direct payment of the value of the shares to the dissenting shareholder.[39]

---

35. See also *Rassi Cement Ltd, Re*, (1999) 98 Comp Cas 835, scheme involving reduction of capital approved, confirming the resolution for reduction. *Jaypee Cement Ltd, Re*, (2004) 122 Comp Cas 854 (All), a scheme of amalgamation of holding and subsidiary involved reduction of capital, but there was no outflow of cash to shareholders. Reduction was sanctioned along with the scheme.
36. *Comat Infoscribe (P) Ltd, Re*, (2004) 53 SCL 41 Kant: 2004 CLC 851: (2005) 128 CC 152.
37. *Anmol Trading Co Ltd v Shaily Engg Plastics Ltd*, (2003) 113 Comp Cas 107 Bom.
38. *Govind Rubber Ltd, Re*, (1995) 83 Comp Cas 556; *Pavan Tyres Ltd, Re*, (1995) 83 Comp Cas 536 Bom. *Jaypee Cement Ltd, Re*, (2004) 122 Comp Cas 854 All, requirements of the Act for change of name were all complied with, scheme sanctioned alongwith change of name. *Search Chem Industries Ltd, Re*, (2006) 129 Comp Cas 471 Guj, in a scheme of demerger, the transferee company's name and objects had to be changed. The court said that all approvals should be granted in a single window clearance.
39. *Bank of Madura Shareholders Welfare Assn v Governor, Reserve Bank of India*, (2001) 105 Comp Cas 663 Mad.

Demerger

A scheme of sub-division of an enterprise into smaller units or splitting up the unit into more than one parts or separating one or more units from the main enterprise and constituting them into separate units is called demerger. Some of the shareholders would be allotted shares in the demerged unit in exchange of their holding in the original unit. Fair exchange ratio becomes necessary in such schemes also. Same considerations apply as in the case of mergers.[40]

Take-over and Acquisition of Minority Interest [S. 395]

If any of the above schemes involve acquisition of the shares of one company by another company, it may do so by making an offer to the transferor company, so that the scheme or contract may be placed before the shareholders of the company.[41] The shareholders have the option to approve the offer within four months. Approval must be accorded by at least nine-tenths in value of the shares whose transfer is involved. This number must be exclusive of any shares already held by the transferee company or by its nominees or by its subsidiary. Once the approval by nine-tenth majority is accorded, the transferee company gets the right to acquire the shares of the dissenting shareholders, if any. Within two months, after the expiry of the above four months, the transferee company should give a notice to such shareholders that it desires to acquire their shares. Within one month from the date of the notice, the dissenting shareholders may apply to the Court. But if no application is made, the transferee company gets the final right and also becomes bound to acquire those shares on the terms on which the shares of other shareholders are to be transferred.[42]

Fairness of Takeover Bids

Section 395 confers a very wide discretion on the Court to sanction or disallow the attempt to acquire.[43] The two guiding principles are that the scheme should be fair and that onus lies to show its unfairness upon the dissenter.[44] The Court will infer fairness from the very fact that the scheme has been approved by 90% of the members.[45] But the burden to prove

---

40. *Alembic Ltd* v *Dipak Kumar J. Shah*, (2002) 112 Comp Cas 64 Guj.
41. S. 395(1). See *Bihari Mills Ltd, Re*, (1985) 58 Comp Cas 6 Guj.
42. *Waste Recycling Group plc, Re*, (2004) 1 BCLC 352 (Ch D), such compulsory acquisition is not violative of Human Rights and Fundamental Freedoms, 1952.
43. See H. Rajak, *Minority Rights and the Take-over bid*, (1970) 87 SALJ 12; D. D. Prentice, *Take-over bid : The Compulsory Acquisition of Dissenting Shares*, (1972) 35 Mod LR 73, considering *Carlton Holdings Ltd, Re*, [1971] 1 WLR 918 : [1971] 2 All ER 1082, where differential treatment was given. Frank Wooldrige, *Compulsory Acquisition of Shares on Take-over*, 1986 JBL 300.
44. *Hoare & Co Ltd, Re*, (1933) 150 LT 374 : [1933] All ER Rep 105; *Bugle Press Ltd, Re*, [1960] 3 WLR 956 : [1960] 3 All ER 791 CA: [1961] Ch 270.
45. *Grierson Oldham & Adams Ltd, Re*, [1967] 1 All ER 192 : [1967] 1 WLR 385: [1968] Ch 17, 32. *See* also the judgment of MAUGHAM J in *Dorman, Long & Co, Re*, 1934 Ch 635, where at

unfairness may be reversed where the Court finds that the take-over bidder and the accepting majority are the same parties. This was the position in *Bugle Press Ltd, Re*[46].

Here the scheme of take-over was adopted to get rid of a minority. The ninety per cent majority formed a new company which made the offer and it was approved by them. They then attempted to acquire the minority interest in the terms of the scheme.

It was held that the burden of proving fairness lay on them and the mere fact that the compensation was fair was not sufficient to discharge the burden.

Similarly, an attempt to impose new liability on a minority without their consent will be foiled. A well-known authority is *Bisgood* v *Henderson's Transvaal Estates Ltd*[47]:

A company had issued fully paid £1 shares. A scheme of reconstruction was approved by the requisite majority under which the company's undertaking was to be transferred to a new company. Each shareholder was to receive an equal number of shares in the new company but only 17 sh. 6d. credited as paid.

The court granted an injunction on the application of the minority shareholders as the scheme would have enabled the new company to extract more capital from holders of fully paid shares.

Take-over Offer to be from Single Company

It has been held by the Privy Council in *Blue Metal Industries Ltd* v *Dilley*[48] that the power of acquisition can be exercised only when the offer of take-over is made by a single company. Lord MORRIS said:

The significance of the 90% figure is, on this view, that once a company has become so nearly a total power or parent of another company as a shareholding of 90% would represent, it should not be prevented from converting the other company into a wholly owned subsidiary by so small a dissenting minority as 10% or less, but should be entitled to acquire the holding of that minority. Their Lordships consider it important to bear in mind that the statutory procedure is one that involves the acquisition by a private interest of the property of another — an exceptional interference with the rights of individual ownership. It leads almost inevitably to the consequence

---

p 657 the learned Judge said that the proposal must be "such that an intelligent and honest man, a member of the class concerned and acting in respect of his interest, might reasonably approve".

46. [1960] 3 WLR 956: [1960] 3 All ER 791 CA: [1961] Ch 270.
47. [1908] 1 Ch 743 : [1908-10] All ER Rep 744 : 98 LT 809.
48. [1969] 3 All ER 437: 1970 AC 827.

that the powers of the section can only be invoked by a single company, for the objective is to allow a 90% owned subsidiary to be converted into a 100% subsidiary, that pre-supposes a single parent.

Adequacy of Information

Inadequacy of information may be another ground for the Tribunal to withhold its sanction. In one of the cases, however, the court refused to help a minority shareholder although it believed with him that the information given to him was too meagre.[49] Now the Central Government has the power to prescribe the information that ought to be given in an offer of take-over.[50]

---

49. *Evertite Locknuts, Re*, [1945] Ch 220.
50. S. 395(4-A), which has been *added* by the Amendment Act, 1965 runs as follows:

"(4-A) (*a*) The following provisions shall apply in relation to every offer of a scheme or contract involving the transfer of shares or any class of shares in the transferor company to the transferee company, namely:

    (*i*) every such offer or every circular containing such offer or every recommendation to the members of the transferor company by its directors to accept such offer shall be accompanied by such information as may be prescribed;

    (*ii*) every such offer shall contain a statement by or on behalf of the transferee company, disclosing the steps it has taken to ensure that necessary cash will be available;

    (*iii*) every circular containing, or recommending acceptance of, such offer shall be presented to the Registrar for registration and no such circular shall be issued until it is so registered;

    (*iv*) the Registrar may refuse to register any such circular which does not contain the information required to be given under sub-clause (*i*) or which sets out such information in a manner likely to give a false impression; and

    (*v*) an appeal shall lie to the Court against an order of the Registrar refusing to register any such circular.

(*b*) Whoever issues a circular referred to in sub-clause (*iii*) of clause (*a*), which has not been registered, shall be punishable with fine which may extend to five hundred rupees."

Apart from the statutory duty the directors owe no duty to shareholders as sellers of shares. They have only to consider the interest of such shareholders in the discharge of their duty to the company. Where, however, the directors play the independent role of advising the shareholders, that role being outside their position as directors, they have to do so in good faith. They would then be responsible if they mislead the shareholders whether intelligently or negligently. *Dawson International plc* v *Coats Paton plc*, 1989 BCLC 233 CA. The court also pointed out that it is not *ultra vires* for a company for the protection of its own interests to enter into an agreement with a take-over bidder that the company will not cooperate with the rival bidders. Where currency was given to false statements with a view to prevent a rival bidder's take-over bid from succeeding, the court said that the latter's tort action for damages for wrongful interference with trade or business should be given trial on merits and not summarily dismissed. *Lonhro plc* v *Fayed*, 1989 BCLC 485 CA, affirmed, (1991) BCLC 779 HL : [1993] 3 Comp LJ 241. For a study of the working rules of the English Take-over Panel and the scope of judicial review, see *R* v *Panel on Take-Overs and Mergers, ex p Guinness plc*, 1989 BCLC 255 CA. There is also the SEBI Take-over Code (Securities and Exchange Board of India Substantial Acquisition of Shares and Take-overs) Regulations 1994. Regulations 6, 9 and 13 were considered by the securities Appellate Tribunal Mumbai in *Sharad Doshi* v *Adjudicating Officer*, (1998) 29 Corpt LA 383 SAT, time-limit for public announcement, non-compliance is not merely technical lapse so as to warrant a leniency; ignorance of the regulations or their import is also no excuse. *Chowgule & Co Ltd* v *SEBI*, (2006) 130 Comp Cas 87 SAT, exemption from making public offer if certain disclosures are made but no order of exemption was passed, public offer by the acquirer became mandatory, for delay in payment to shareholders the

Offering same Terms to those whose Shares are to be Acquired

Where the class of shares which are to be transferred are already held by the transferee company to a value greater than one-tenth of the aggregate of the values of all the shares in the company of such class, the transferee company will not get the right to acquire the shares of the dissenting shareholders unless the same terms are offered to all holders of the shares of that class and the holders who approve the scheme should be nine-tenths in value of the shares to be transferred (excluding those already held) and should also be three-fourths in number of the holders of those shares.

Notice of Acquisition

When, in pursuance of any scheme or contract of this kind, shares or shares of a class in a company, have been transferred to another company or its nominee, and those shares together with other shares or any other shares of the same class are already held of the transferee company or its nominee company or its subsidiary to the extent of nine-tenths in value of the shares or the shares of that class, the transferee company is required to give a notice of the fact to the holders of the remaining shares who have not assented to the scheme. The notice must be given within one month from the date of the transfer, except when a notice has been given in pursuance of the scheme. Any such holder may, within three months from the giving of the notice to him, require the transferee company to acquire the shares in question. The transferee company then becomes entitled as well as bound to acquire those shares on the same terms on which the shares of approving shereholders were transferred or on such terms as the court may, on the application of the shareholder or transferee company, think fit to order.

Amalgamation in National Interest [S. 396]

Where the Central Government is satisfied that an amalgamation of two or more companies is essential in the public interest, then, the Government may by order notified in the Official Gazette provide for the amalgamation of those companies into a single company. The amalgamated company shall have such constitution, property, powers, rights, interests, authorities and privileges and shall be with such liabilities, duties and obligations as may be

---

acquirer was ordered to pay 10% interest. *Swedish Match AB* v *SEBI*, (2004) 11 SCC 641: (2004) 122 Comp Cas 83 SC, public announcement is necessary to enable shareholders to decide whether they should quit the company. *Jaypee Cement Ltd, Re*, (2004) 122 Comp Cas 854 All, when acquirers can be said to be acting in concert making SEBI inquiry necessary. *Aska Investments (P) Ltd* v *Grab Tea Co (P) Ltd*, (2005) 126 Comp Cas 663, acquisition beyond 5% has to be disclosed whether by a single individual or individuals acting in concert and acquisition would lead to control over the company or not. *Hitachi Home Life Solutions Inc* v *SEBI*, (2006) 129 Comp Cas 247 SAT two groups acting in concert can be said to cease only when they actually do so and not when they declare to do so.

specified in the Government's order. The order may also contain consequential, incidental and supplementary provisions.

Every member or creditor of each of the companies before the amalgamation shall have, as nearly as may be, the same rights and interests in the amalgamated company as he had in the company of which he was originally a member or creditor. But if his rights in the amalgamated company are less than those, he shall be entitled to compensation. The Government may prescribe some authority for the assessment of compensation and it will be paid by the company resulting from the amalgamation.[51]

Before making any order of amalgamation, the Central Government is required to send a copy of the proposed order in draft to each of the companies concerned. This is necessary to enable such companies to file their objections and suggestions. The period for filing objections shall be fixed by the Government, but should not be less than two months. The Government may modify the draft order in the light of any suggestions so received.

Copies of every such order have to be laid before both Houses of Parliament at the earliest convenience.

Preservation of Books and Papers of Amalgamated Company [S. 396-A]

Where a company has been amalgamated with another company under any of the above provisions of the Act, or whose shares have been acquired by another company, the books and papers of such a company shall not be disposed of without the prior permission of the Central Government. Before granting such permission, the Government may appoint a person to examine the books and papers for the purpose of ascertaining whether they contain any evidence of the commission of an offence in connection with the promotion or formation of or the management of the affairs of the company.

------

51. See *Boiron* v *SBL Ltd*, (1998) 30 Corpt LA 21 CLB, foreign collaborator holding 30% as against 60% Indian promoter, expansion of capital base for amalgamation, the promoter resolved for rights issue, collaborator preferred Government loans, promoter to reconsider his decision, amalgamation in national interest could be ordered.

20
Defunct Companies

A defunct company means a company which is not carrying on any business or which is not in operation. In such a case the Registrar will send a preliminary notice to the company inquiring whether the company is still in operation.[1] If no answer is received within one month, the Registrar will within fourteen days send another letter reminding the company of the first letter and informing it that if within one month no answer is received to the second letter, a notice will be published in the Official Gazette with a view to striking the name of the company off the register.[2] If no answer is received within one month or the answer received shows that the company is carrying on no business, he may publish in the Official Gazette and also intimate the company that on the expiry of three months its name will be struck off. The company may, however, in the meantime show cause why it should not be dissolved.[3] When the name is actually struck off, the fact must be published in the Official Gazette and the company shall stand dissolved. The same procedure has to be adopted where a company is being wound up and the Registrar has reasonable cause to believe that no liquidator is acting or that the affairs of the company have been completely wound up, but returns have not been filed.[4] The capacity of the company ceases on becoming defunct. Where the date on which a suit was filed in the name of the company it had been struck off the Register as being defunct, the proceeding was held to be not valid.[5]

But the liability, if any, of every director, or other officer who was exercising any power of management and of every member of the company shall continue and may be enforced as if the company had not been dissolved.[6] "This only means that the existing liability of any director or member prior to the dissolution of the company will continue in spite of the dissolution. If the directors are not personally liable for the plaintiff's claim prior to the dissolution of the company, they will not be liable after the dissolution." And so in *Sri Krishna Dhoot* v *Kamlapurkar*[7]:

The plaintiff, who had deposited certain notes with the Hyderabad Bullion Exchange Ltd, as membership security, instituted a suit against the company, its directors and members of its sub-committee for the

---

1. S. 560(1). A copy of the letter is required to be sent to the Income Tax Authorities also. (Government Order of 1959).
2. *Id.* Sub-section (2).
3. S. 560(3).
4. S. 560(4).
5. *Floating Services Ltd* v *M.V. San Franscesco*, (2004) 25 SCL 762 Guj.
6. S. 560(5). *See* L.J. Hall, *Restoration of Companies to Register*, 120 New LJ 789.
7. [1965] 1 Comp LJ 233 : (1965) 35 Comp Cas 913 AP.

recovery of the value of the notes when the company had become defunct and was dissolved by the Registrar by removing it from the register. Where the company had not been able to raise the requisite capital, its name was allowed to be struck off.[8]

The directors and other officers were, however, held not liable as there would have been no claim against them prior to the dissolution of the company. As for the liability of the company, the court held that a suit against a company which is struck off the register and, therefore, stands dissolved, is not maintainable.

Directors are also not liable for their failure to maintain the routine of a company which to the knowledge of the Registrar is already defunct though actual striking off had been postponed for one reason or another.[9] The court may order the winding up of the company without it being restored to the register.[10]

Restoration

The proper procedure in such cases is to apply to the court for restoration of the company's name. For, Section 560(6) provides that if a company, or any member or creditor feels aggrieved, he may within twenty years move the court. If it is found that the company was actually carrying on business or it is otherwise just to do so, the court may order the name of the company to be restored to the register. Accordingly, in *Bhogilal* v *Registrar of Joint Stock Companies:*[11]

The creditor of a defunct company filed a petition for restoration of its name. The petitioner alleged that he had obtained a decree against the company a day before the publication of the notification. The directors of the company on being asked by the Registrar misinformed him that the company was not in operation. It was also found that the entire share capital of the company was not called up and that the uncalled capital was sufficient to satisfy the decree. Holding that it was just and equitable to restore the name of the company to the register, the court observed: ''No steps were taken to discharge the liability which the company owed to the petitioner. The

---

8. *Khushi Exports (P) Ltd* v *State of Gujarat*, (2005) CLC 613 Guj. The Government has announced a simplified exit scheme, 2005, General Circular No 2/2005. The date of the scheme has expired.

9. *Cambridge Coffee Room Assn, Re*, [1952] 1 All ER 112. An order of winding up may be passed without vacating the order of dissolution, *Seth Kundan Lal* v *Hanuman Chamber of Commerce Ltd*, (1966) 36 Comp Cas 231 Punj ; *Morning Star (P) Ltd, In re*, (1970) 40 Comp Cas 29 Ker : [1970] 1 Comp LJ 46.

10. *Calculating and Business Machines P Ltd* v *State of Bihar*, (1983) 54 Comp Cas 100 Pat. *See* also *Narmada Choudhury* v *Motor Accidents Claims Tribunal*, (1985) 58 Comp Cas 596, directors held not personally liable.

11. AIR 1954 MB 70. *Vijayawada Chamber of Commerce and Industry* v *Registrar of Non-Trading Companies*, (2004) 122 Comp Cas 796 AP, the Company was actually functioning, only its returns had been delayed. The striking off was set aside.

effect of the order of removal would be to make it difficult for the petitioner to obtain the fruits of his decree. Had the Registrar known that the company was actually defending a suit, it is extremely unlikely that he would have ordered the name of the company to be removed from the register."[12]

Thus the provision relating to restoration "seems primarily intended for companies which were active at the moment of their mortal wound".[13] But discovery of outstanding assets of the company is, of course, one of the reasons why restoration is sought. That is why a period of twenty years is allowed. The company may have unknown assets which do not come to light until many years after the company has been struck off and so dissolved.

A contingent or prospective creditor is entitled to a petition for restoration.[14] An income tax officer is a creditor for this purpose and can apply for restoration.[14] So is a person entitled to claim damages under the Fatal Accidents Act.[15] The company which has been struck off may itself apply for restoration, though the court would not order restoration unless there is sufficient evidence of likely benefit to creditors or members.[16]

An officer of the company who was instrumental in getting the company struck off was held to have *locus standi*. He was not aggrieved when he activated the process of striking off. He could become aggrieved subsequently. The Act requires the applicant to be aggrieved at the time of his application.[17]

Restoration operates retrospectively.[18] It produces "as you were position".[19] An illustration of retrospective operation is *Box Co Ltd, Re*[20]:

---

12. Following authorities were cited in the case : *Outlay Assurance Society, Re*, (1887) 34 Ch D 479 : 56 LT 477; *Carpenter's Patent Davit Boat Lowering & Detaching Gear Co, Re*, (1888) 1 Meg 26. *See* also *Umedbhai* v *Moreshwar*, AIR 1954 MB 146. Where a person had a claim against the company for personal injuries but the company was dissolved before the period of limitation for his claim expired, it was held that the company ought to be put back to the register, *Workvale Ltd, Re*, [1992] 2 All ER 627 CA.

13. *Test Holdings, (Clifton) Ltd, Re*, [1969] 3 All ER 517. The court has power to pass an order of restoration subject to certain conditions. See *Purushotamdass* v *ROC*, (1986) 60 Comp Cas 154 Bom; *Bombay Gas Authority P Ltd* v *Central Govt*, (1996) 3 Bom CR 312, transfer of assets by company after struck off becomes valid if it is subsequently restored.

14. *Harvest Lane Motor Bodies Co, Re*, [1968] 2 All ER 1012 : (1969) 39 Comp Cas 961.

15. *ITO (Companies Circle), Re*, [1970] 1 Comp LJ 46.

16. *Belmont M & Co Ltd, Re*, [1951] 2 All ER 898; *Test Holdings (Clifton) Ltd*, [1969] 3 All ER 517; *Rai Saheb UN Mandal's Estate, Re*, AIR 1959 Cal 493 : (1960) 30 Comp Cas 172. A person who inherits the rights of a creditor or member may apply but not a person who acquires such rights, *New Timbiqui Gold Mines, Re*, [1961] 1 All ER 865 ; *Bayswater Trading Co, Re*, [1970] 1 All ER 608 : [1970] 1 WLR 343: (1970) 40 Comp Cas 1196.

17. *Contt* v *Uebersee Bank AG*, [2000] BCC 172 Scotland.

18. *Lindsay Bowman Ltd, Re*, [1969] 1 WLR 1443 : [1969] 3 All ER 601. All that is necessary is that they should be creditors at the time of striking off. *Aga Estate Agencies Ltd, Re*, 1986 BCLC 346.

19. *Bombay Gas Co P Ltd* v *Central Govt*, (1997) 89 Comp Cas 195 Bom.

20. [1970] 2 WLR 959 : [1970] 2 All ER 183.

A company, in ignorance of the fact that it has been struck off the register, created a legal charge on two of its properties. On an application by the company the court restored it to the register and gave the order retrospective effect so as to validate the charges and their registration.

The effects of restoration have been thus stated in a case:[21]

It is clear from the section that on the restoration of a company back to the register after its being struck off the consequence is as though it had never been struck off the register. The company will be deemed to have had its existence althrough. Another consequence is that the rights of all parties would be as though there had been no cessation or interruption in the existence of the company on account of the striking off and the subsequent restoration.

Sub-section (5) also preserves the power of the Court to wind up a company the name of which has been struck off the register. This is so because striking off is different from winding up. In winding up the assets of the company are applied in payment of its debts. "But, if the name of a company is struck off the register, its undisposed property is not appropriated towards its liabilities. It vests in the Crown as *bona vacantia*."[22] Thus the liability of the directors of a wound up private company to pay outstanding income tax under Section 179 of the Income Tax Act, 1961 will not arise if the company is merely struck off. The department may apply for restoration.[23]

Simplified exit scheme

A simplified exit scheme has been introduced by the Central Government.[24]

---

21. *Pazaniappa Chettiar* v *South Indian Planting and Industrial Co Ltd*, AIR 1953 TC 161. Rights and liabilities of the company remain the same as before as if there had been no interruption in the life of the company. *Purushottamdas* v *ROC*, (1986) 60 Comp Cas 154 Bom; *Lakshmana Chettiar* v *S. I. Planting Co*, (1953) 23 Comp Cas 246.
22. *Yeshwant Raghunath Bhide* v *ITO*, (1974) 44 Comp Cas 293, citing Gower, PRINCIPLES OF MODERN COMPANY LAW 652 (3rd Edn, 1969) and *U. N. Mandal's Estate P Ltd, Re*, AIR 1959 Cal 493 : 30 Comp Cas 172.
23. *Ibid.*
24. A case under the scheme, *Khushi Exports (P) Ltd* v *State of Gujarat*, (2006) 130 Comp Cas 457 Guj. A pending criminal case against a company for its failure to increase capital was quashed because it was no use prosecuting a company which had ceased to exist under the scheme. After decision to strike off the name of the company a notification to that effect had been published and after that the company had become dissolved. *Gummadi Aruna* v *Gummadi Construction Ltd*, (2007) 136 Comp Cas 81 CLB, newspaper publication for striking off had yet to be made. The process of striking off was not complete, company not dissolved, directed to accept transmission.

21
Winding Up

Winding up is the second method of putting an end to the life of a company. In the words of Professor Gower: "[W]inding up of a company is the process whereby its life is ended and its property administered for the benefit of its creditors and members. An administrator, called a liquidator, is appointed and he takes control of the company, collects its assets, pays its debts and finally distributes any surplus among the members in accordance with their rights."[1] Winding up of a company differs from the insolvency of an individual inasmuch as a company cannot be made insolvent under the insolvency laws. Moreover, a perfectly solvent company may be wound up.

The company is not dissolved immediately at the commencement of winding up. Its corporate status and powers continue.[2] "Winding up precedes dissolution."[3]

Types of winding up [S. 425]

The Act provides for two kinds of winding up:

1. Compulsory winding up under the order of the Tribunal.
2. Voluntary winding up, which itself is of two kinds, namely: (a) Members' voluntary winding up and (b) Creditors' voluntary winding up.

WINDING UP BY COURT

A company may be wound up at an order of the court. This is also called compulsory winding up. The cases in which a company may be wound up are given in Section 433. They are as follows:

1. Special resolution

If the company has, by special resolution, resolved that it be wound up by the court.[4] The court is, however, not bound to order winding up simply

---

1. THE PRINCIPLES OF MODERN COMPANY LAW, 647 (3rd Edn, 1969).
2. Company remains a tax payer until dissolved by order of court. *Gannon Dunkerley & Co v Asstt Commr, Urban Land Tax*, (1992) 73 Comp Cas 168 Mad. Where the contention was that there was no use winding up the company because all the assets of the company had already been sold, the court ordered winding up, *Syndicate Bank v Printersall (P) Ltd*, (1991) 71 Comp Cas 215 Kant.
3. BACHAWAT J in *Pierce Leslie & Co v Wapshare*, (1969) 2 SCA 378, 389. The order of winding up does not change the character of the company as an industrial concern for the purposes of the State Financial Corpn Act, 1951, *International Coach Builders Ltd v Karnataka State Financial Corpn*, (1994) 81 Comp Cas 19 Kant.
4. S. 433(a). Where the company itself was the petitioner and the financial position of the company was eroded, the court ordered winding up in public interest. *Bombay Metropolitan Transport Corpn Ltd v Employees*, (1991) 71 Comp Cas 473 Bom. The company's right to apply for winding up cannot be taken away by the fact that the company applied for closure

because the company has so resolved. The power is discretionary and may not be exercised where winding up would be opposed to the public or company's interests.

2. Default in holding statutory meeting

If a company has made a default in delivering the statutory report to the Registrar or in holding the statutory meeting, it may be ordered to be wound up.[5] The petition for winding up on this ground can be presented either by the Registrar or by a contributory. If it is brought by any other person e.g., a creditor, it must be filed before the expiration of fourteen days after the last day on which the statutory meeting ought to have been held.[6] The power of the Tribunal is discretionary and instead of making a winding up order the Tribunal may direct that the statutory report shall be delivered or that the meeting shall be held.[7]

3. Failure to commence business or suspension of business

If a company does not commence its business within a year from its incorporation or has suspended business for a whole year, it may be ordered to be wound up.[8] Here again the power is discretionary and will be exercised only when there is a fair indication that there is no intention to carry on business. If the suspension is satisfactorily accounted for and appears to be due to temporary causes, the order may be refused. An illustration is the decision of the Calcutta High Court in *Murlidhar* v *Bengal Steamship Co.*[9]

To carry on its business, a company employed a steamer and two flats. The flats were acquired by the Government during the First World War and the company was not able to replace them immediately in view of the rise in prices. This resulted in suspension of business for more than a year. In a petition to wind up the company, it was held that "the suspension of business for a whole year is sufficiently accounted for and does not furnish an indication that there is no intention to carry on the business".[10]

---

under S. 25-O of the Industrial Disputes Act and its application was dismissed, even if winding up may lead to closure of business.

5. S. 433(*b*).

6. S. 439(7).

7. S. 443(3). This does not apply to private companies since they are not required to hold such a meeting, *S. R. Subramaniam* v *Drivers' & Conductors' Bus Service*, (1978) 48 Comp Cas 672 Mad.

8. S. 433(*c*).

9. AIR 1920 Cal 722: 59 IC 542. *See* also *Bengal Flying Club, Re*, [1966] 2 Comp LJ 213, where the assets of a club were acquired, but it carried on other activities and so an order to wind up was refused.

10. *See* also *Mohanlal Saraf* v *Cuttack Electric Supply Co*, [1964] 1 Comp LJ 58 Ori, where suspension of business due to acquisition was held not sufficient to found winding up order; *O. P. Basra* v *Kaithal Cotton Mills*, AIR 1962 Punj 151; *Malabar Iron & Steel Works* v *ROC*, AIR 1965 Ker 35; *Registrar of Companies* v *Jaipur Stock Exchange Ltd*, (1987) 62 Comp Cas 459 Raj, where also the company was making its due efforts; *Registrar of Companies* v *Jai*

Where, however, there was failure to resume business for five years and the prospects also seemed gloomy, winding up was ordered.[11] Similarly, where a company's business had remained suspended for ten years, its capital having been lost in misappropriation and the Orissa Government, which was the major contributory, having refused further help,[12] and where a company could not commence business for three years after incorporation, its main business having been acquired, where a private company did not commence any business inspite of loans by a financial institution which had taken over and disposed of the company's property, membership was reduced to less than the statutory minimum, all directors but one were reported to be absconding and the only available director filed a petition,[13] the court ordered winding up.[14] Where the company ceased to do any business and also did not offer any proof of the fact that it had resolved upon to resume business and was seeking the permission of ROC, for that purpose, the court declared that the company ought to be wound up.[15] Where the business of a private company which was a family concern remained suspended for many years for want of a quota of wires, the company had no creditors, the Registrar's attempt to put it on winding up on account of suspension of business and perpetuity of losses did not succeed. A family company, having no creditors, should not concern the public whether it is running in profits or losses. Where of the several business units of a company, the business of only one unit was closed with a proposal to dispose it off and to use the proceeds in the exploitation of other objects, the court did not agree that it was a ground for winding up. The court said that even if the business in all the units of the company was suspended, it would still be open to the court to examine whether it would be possible for the company to resume its business.[16]

Agro Industries, (1987) 62 Comp Cas 358 Raj, business suspended for more than a year but otherwise the company in sound state.

11. *Rupa Bharati Ltd* v *ROC*, [1969] 1 Comp LJ 296.

12. *Orissa Trunks & Enamel Works Ltd, Re,* (1973) 43 Comp Cas 503 Ori.

13. *Surendra Kumar Pareek* v *Shree Guru Nanak Oils (P) Ltd,* (1995) 82 Comp Cas 642; *Biraj Kumar Barua* v *Barua and Barua Drugs (P) Ltd,* (2003) 114 Comp Cas 191 Gau, no business commenced, promoters did not pay for their shares, no meetings held, the court (now Tribunal) said that no useful purpose would be served in keeping the company alive. *S. Palaniappan* v *Tirupur Cotton Spg & Wvg Mills Ltd,* (2003) 114 Comp Cas 288 Mad, no proof that business was not commenced for one year.

14. *Registrar of Companies* v *Chouhan Bros Industries (P) Ltd,* (1973) 43 Comp Cas 525 Pat. Winding up was ordered where because of heavy indebtedness the company's assets were under creditors' possession and no business could be done for more than a year, *Karnataka Rubber Ltd* v *Karnataka SFC,* [1999] 3 Comp LJ 231 Kant also where the persons connected with the company totally disappeared from the scene. *Bhartiya Gramin Vikas Vitta Nigam Ltd, Re,* (2000) 27 SCL 249 All. Another case of heavy indebtedness, *Bajaj Organics Ltd* v *Sprolac Laboratories (P) Ltd,* [1999] 3 Comp LJ 234 AP. Where the project of a hotel company became delayed because of administrative uncertainties, winding up was not ordered, *Bikkina Gopalkrishna Rao* v *Seavalley Resorts (P) Ltd,* [2000] 2 Comp LJ 65 AP.

15. *Anil Arora* v *Arora Aluminium and Allied Works (P) Ltd,* (2006) 132 Comp Cas 221 All.

16. *Paramjit Lal Bhadwar* v *Prem Spg and Wvg Mills,* (1986) 60 Comp Cas 420 All. Where a company's subsidiaries were functioning, winding up was not ordered though the company

After ordering winding up on this ground, the court can direct the liquidator to take care of the interests of the financial institutions which had advanced large sums of money to the company and also to investigate whether a secured creditor bank had sold the company's assets at prices lower than their real value.[17]

4. Reduction in membership

If the number of members is reduced, in the case of a public company, below seven, and in the case of a private company, below two, the company may be ordered to be wound up.[18]

5. Inability to pay debts

A company may be ordered to be wound up if it is unable to pay its debts.[19] Inability to pay debts is explained in Section 434. According to this section a company shall be deemed to be unable to pay its debts in the following three cases:

(a) Statutory Notice

Firstly, if a creditor to whom the company owes a sum exceeding one lakh rupees has served on the company, a demand for payment and the company has for three weeks neglected to pay or otherwise satisfy him.[20]

---

itself had ceased to function. *Eastern Telegraph Co Ltd, Re*, [1947] 2 All ER 104: (1948) 18 Comp Cas 46. Where suspension of business was backed by the shareholders' resolution for winding up passed at a meeting called by the court, winding up was ordered. It was not necessary to keep the company alive for booking guilty officers. Remedies are available in the state of winding up also. *A. Sreedharan Nair v Union Hardwares (P) Ltd*, (1997) 89 Comp Cas 37 Ker; *Mohan Lal Ghosh v East India Wires Ltd*, (2004) 118 Comp Cas 322, the company established on the land of one of the promoters but business could not be commenced because of a dispute about a land between promoters, winding up not to be ordered till dispute settled.

17. *Karnataka Rubbers Ltd v Karnataka SF*, (1999) 33 CLA 472 Kant.
18. S. 433(*d*).
19. S. 433(*e*).
20. *See*, for example, *Babu Ram v Krishna Bharadwaj Cold Stores & General Mills Co (P) Ltd*, [1962] 2 Comp LJ 215 All, where neglect to pay a supplier of goods was held to be sufficient although the assets of the company were more than the debts. *Kundremukh Iron Ore Co v Rooky Roadways (P) Ltd*, (1986) 60 Comp Cas 1069 Kant, a person claiming from a carrier compensation for short delivery is not a creditor; reversed in *sub nom.*, (1990) 69 Comp Cas 178 Kant. Where the dispute is a *bona fide* dispute and yet the company makes a conditional offer to pay, it is not a neglect to pay, *Suresh Shenoy v Cochin Stock Exchange Ltd*, (1989) 65 Comp Cas 240 Ker. Where a financially sound company disputed the claim on *bona fide* grounds, that was held to be not a neglect to pay. *New Era Furnishers (P) Ltd v Indo-Continental Hotels & Resorts Ltd*, (1990) 68 Comp Cas 208 Raj. The presumption of deemed inability arises where there is due service of notice and not where there is no proof of notice. *Kalra Iron Stores v Faridabad Fabricators (P) Ltd (No 2)*, (1992) 73 Comp Cas 337 Del. The notice need not carry the warning of winding up, *Devendra Kumar Jain v Polar Forgings & Tools Ltd*, [1993] 1 Comp LJ 184 Del: (1993) 1 Punj LR 67; *United Contractors v Orissa Minerals Development Co Ltd*, (1995) 2 Cal LJ 309 Cal, demand notice is a step in aid, it is not a precondition for bringing the whole claim of the plaintiff in a subsequent suit. *S. N. Enterprises (P) Ltd v Sanpaolo Hambro Nicco Fin Ltd*, (1997) 2 Cal LT 60, arbitration clause no bar to winding up proceedings. *Associated Design Planning Group (P) Ltd v Prodosh Kumar Mullick*, (1995) 18 Corpt LA 14: (1995) 1 Cal LT 54, loan by director, winding up

Where there was no 21 days notice, the defect was held to be not curable even by a subsequent notice during the pendency of the proceedings.[21] The expression "neglects to pay the sum demanded" in Section 434(1)(*a*) is not equivalent to the word 'omitted'. Neglect to pay a debt on demand is omission to pay without reasonable cause. Failure to pay in spite of several communications including service of statutory notice was held to be evidence of neglect and inability.[22]

"The debt must be presently payable and the title of the petitioner demanding it should be complete."[23] The debt must be really due.[24] Where a company guaranteed another man's debt and the liability under it had become established which the company failed to pay, winding up was ordered.[25] Winding up shall be refused if there is a *bona fide* and reasonable dispute as to a substantial part of the debt on which the petition is based,[26] because "when a debtor company believes even wrongly that it is justified in law to refuse to pay, such a refusal cannot be regarded as neglect to pay".[27] "Where the object of a petition to wind up a company is to bring

proceedings is not a method of recovery. *Parimahal Holdings (P) Ltd* v *LKP Merchant Financing Ltd*, (2003) 114 Comp Cas 121 Bom, the debt must be quantified. There cannot be a presumption that the claim of interest must have gone beyond Rs 500 (now Rs 1,00,000). *Uniplas India Ltd* v *State (Govt of NCT of Delhi)*, (2001) 6 SCC 8: AIR 2001 SC 2625: (2001) 106 Comp Cas 669. Notice under Sections 433(*e*) and 434(*a*) containing a demand for payment of the amount covered by a dishonoured cheque, if issued within the statutory period contained in proviso (*b*) to Section 138 of Negotiable Instruments Act, held, would be good enough for the purpose of that section as well.

21. *Manganese Ore (India) Ltd* v *Sandur Manganese & Iron Ores Ltd*, (1999) 98 Comp Cas 755 Kant; *Electron Industries Ltd* v *Soham Polymers (P) Ltd*, (2006) 133 Comp Cas 3 SC, no payment after notice, no denial, debt acknowledged in balance sheet, admission of petition and direction for advertisement were held proper.

22. *Arrow Electronics International Inc* v *Niful Data Systems (P) Ltd*, (1997) 88 Comp Cas 234 Del. Where statutory notice was given by the underwriter of the company's shares for his dues and the company neither replied to it nor raised any defence, but paid half of the amount claimed, the petition was admitted, *Mehta Integrated Finance Ltd* v *Bharat Parentals Ltd*, (1999) 98 Comp Cas 791 Guj.

23. *Jumbad Coal Syndicate Ltd, Re*, AIR 1936 Cal 628: 163 IC 845. An unliquidated claim, such as a right to recover damages is not a debt for this purpose. *Newfinds* v *Vorion Chemicals & Distilleries Ltd*, (1976) 46 Comp Cas 87 Mad. Where a company guaranteed a debt and the principal debtor having failed to pay, the company also did not pay, the amount due was held to be a debt due from the company enabling the creditor to file a petition for winding up. *Ram Bahadur Thakur* v *Sahu Jain Ltd*, (1981) 51 Comp Cas 301 Del. Where loans were given to the company indirectly through the medium of another person, the company was not a debtor. *New India Corpn* v *N. M. T. Assn*, (1983) 54 Comp Cas 32 Kant. *Indian Oil Corpn Ltd* v *NEPC (India) Ltd*, (2003) 114 Comp Cas 207 Mad, the existence of the debt was established, the company could not show that the security in the hands of the petitioning creditor was sufficient for his claim, petition maintainable.

24. *Mohd Amin Bros Ltd* v *Dominion of India*, (1949) 54 CWN 514. Where the sum due was admitted but there was no provision in the contract about interest, the court admitted the petition to fix interest liability and to order winding up if not paid, *Devendra Kumar Jain* v *Polar Forgings & Tools Ltd*, (1993) 1 Comp LJ 184 Del: (1993) 1 Punj LR 67.

25. *S. Kantilal & Co* v *Rajaram Bandekar (Sirigao) Mines (P) Ltd*, (1993) 76 Comp Cas 800 Bom.

26. *The Co* v *Rameshwar Singh*, AIR 1920 Cal 1004: 23 CWN 844: 58 IC 561.

27. *British India Bkg Corpn* v *Sylhet Commercial Bank*, AIR 1949 Ass 45; *Standard Dyer Ltd* v *Parshotham & Bros*, [1967] 1 Comp LJ 6, where the relationship of creditor and debtor between the petitioner and the company was found not to exist.

pressure upon the company in order to make it pay the petitioner cheaply and expeditiously when the company desires to dispute the debt in the civil court, the petition is an abuse of the process of the court and is liable to be dismissed."[28] "Petition for winding up is not to be sought for as a short cut and cheap device to coerce payment and stifle contest."[29] The true rule, which has existed for many years is that the court would not allow a winding up petition to be used for the purpose of deciding a dispute as to a debt which is raised *bona fide* on substantial grounds.[30] Thus where a cricket match, being insured, had to be abandoned on account of rains, the insurance company appointed a surveyor to determine whether this type of loss was covered by the terms of the policy, it could not be said that the company had neglected to pay.[31] MAJITHIA J of Punjab and Haryana High

---

28. *P. Satyarazu* v *Guntur Cotton, Jute & Paper Mills*, AIR 1925 Mad 199: 85 IC 333; *Tulsi Das Lallubhai* v *Bharat Khand Cotton Mills Ltd*, 16 Bom LR 692. The remedy cannot be used as an alternative to a civil suit. Accordingly, a petition was rejected when the petitioner had already resorted to a civil suit. *State Trading Corpn of India Ltd* v *Punjab Tanneries Ltd*, (1989) 66 Comp Cas 634 P&H; *T. Srinivasa* v *Flemming (India) Apothek (P) Ltd*, (1990) 68 Comp Cas 506 Kar.

29. *Chellaradh & Co* v *Sundaram*, AIR 1955 Mys 122; *See also Bharat Vegetable Products Ltd, Re*, 56 CWN 29; *Godavaribai* v *Amalgamated Commercial Traders*, [1965] 2 Comp LJ 272; *Amber Flour Mills Ltd* v *Vimal Chand Jain*, (1991) 70 Comp Cas 561 Del, jurisdiction not available as a substitute for recovery; *Karamchand Thapar & Bros (Coal Sales) Ltd* v *ACME Paper Ltd*, (1994) 1 Comp LJ 274 Del. A petition against a Govt Financial Corporation just because it did not provide further loans was held to be abuse. *PICUP* v *North India Petro*, (1994) 3 SCC 348: [1994] 79 Comp Cas 835 SC.

30. *A Company (No 006685 of 1996), Re*, (1997) 1 BCLC 639 Ch D. The court cannot be dragged into disputed questions of fact which cannot be sorted out without evidence, *Rohtak & Hissar Districts Electricity Supply Co (P) Ltd* v *Amausi Textile Mills (P) Ltd*, (1999) 19 SCL 541. A petition was not allowed where a civil suit was pending over the same claim, *Sir Shadilal Enterprises* v *Cooperative Co Ltd*, (2001) 103 Comp Cas 863 All. In *Deccan Enterprises (P) Ltd* v *Deccan Syntex Ltd*, [2000] 1 Comp LJ 189 AP, parties relegated to a civil suit because of complications. *Rediffusion, Young & Rubicam (P) Ltd* v *Solidaire India Ltd*, (2003) 114 Comp Cas 721 Mad, *bona fide* dispute. *ICDS Ltd* v *Asha Latex and Allied Industries (P) Ltd*, (2003) 114 Comp Cas 581 Bom, petitioner resorted to arbitration proceedings, suppressing this fact, filed a winding up petition, debt also disputed, for these reasons petition dismissed.

31. *British India General Insurance Co, Re*, (1970) 40 Comp Cas 554: AIR 1971 Bom 102. *See also British Burmah Petroleum Co* v *Kohinoor Mills*, (1980) 50 Comp Cas 544 Bom, where the debt was evidenced by two letters of doubtful authenticity; *Yashodan Chit Fund (P) Ltd*, (1980) 50 Comp Cas 356, Bom, non-payment of rent pending fixation of standard rent; *Ronaq Singh* v *Ambala Bus Syndicate*, (1980) 50 Comp Cas 349 P&H, agreement to receive payment in instalments; *Premier Vegetable Products Ltd* v *United Asian Bank*, (1980) 50 Comp Cas 680 Raj, a company receiving goods but not accepting bill of exchange, not allowed to say that there was no debt because the bill had not been accepted; *Maharashtra Small Scale Industries Corpn* v *Trawlers (P) Ltd*, (1980) 50 Comp Cas 674 Bom, inability to pay workmen; *U. V. Shenoy* v *Karnataka Engg Products*, (1981) 51 Comp Cas 116 Kant, company allowed to defend dishonour of cheques on the ground that the goods supplied were of inferior quality. *Fred Hausman* v *Bio-Solar (P) Ltd*, (1987) 61 Comp Cas 714 Del, machinery delivered in damaged state, claim for price, disputed debt. Where the company showed liability only to the extent of one-fourth of the amount claimed and the petitioner showed nothing, the petition was dismissed. *Gangadhar Narsinghdass Agarwal* v *Timble (P) Ltd*, (1992) 74 Comp Cas 246 Bom. Where the company paid the amount which was due and disputed the rest of the claim, the petition was dismissed. *SN Steel Corpn* v *Dany Dairy and Food Engineers*, (1992) 73 Comp Cas 357 All. The company has to substantiate the defence of payment. *M. V. Paulose* v *City Hospital (P) Ltd*, (1992) 73 Comp Cas 362 Ker. No privity

Court captured the working principles in terms of the following propositions:[32]

The principles on which the company court acts are: (1) that the defence of the company is in good faith and one of substance; (2) the defence is likely to succeed in point of law; and (3) the company produces *prima facie* proof of the facts on which the defence depends.[33]

However, where the dispute is not real, but is put forward by the company as a cloak to hide its inability to pay its debts, the application for winding up would be allowed. Thus, for example, in *Vanaspati Industries Ltd* v *Firm Prabhu Dayal*:[34]

The petitioner claimed to be a creditor of the defendant company. The company never disputed that the amount claimed was wrong. They

---

of contract with the company, hence no right to sue, *B. Vishwanathan* v *Seshayee Paper & Boards Ltd*, (1992) 73 Comp Cas 136 Mad. The existence of an arbitration agreement does not take away the right of petition. *Goetz India Ltd* v *Pure Drinks (New Delhi) Ltd*, (1994) 80 Comp Cas 340, 363 P&H.

32. *Kripal Singh* v *Sutlej Land Finance (P) Ltd*, (1989) 66 Comp Cas 841, 844. See *R. P. Bansal* v *Bansal & Co*, AIR 1995 Del 234, claimant did not indicate the state of account and the company submitted a detailed counter-claim ruling out the petitioner; *Tata Davy Ltd* v *Steel Strips Ltd*, AIR 1995 P&H 1, nothing of the claim was left after deduction of amounts for poor quality of goods supplied. *Elmeh India* v *Hi-Sound Corder (P) Ltd*, (1995) 83 Comp Cas 135 Mad, deposit account not produced.

33. The Supreme Court in *Amalgamated Commercial Traders (P) Ltd* v *ACR Krishnaswami*, (1965) 35 Comp Cas 456, laid down that conditional declaration of dividend does not create a debt and the company could dispute its liability. Following this in *Sharma Enterprises* v *J. N. Hotels (P) Ltd*, (1994) 1 Bihar LJR 576, it was held that where in a pending money suit against the company, the latter raised a good counter-claim, a petition for winding up for that very debt was not sustainable. Another decision emphasising that the company's counter-claim should be *prima facie* valid and put-up *bona fide* is *Federal Chemical Works Ltd, Re*, (1964) 34 Comp Cas 963; *Trilok Chand* v *Swastika Strips (P) Ltd*, (1995) 82 Comp Cas 423 P&H, liability to pay on take-over, goodwill overvalued, genuine dispute. *Trend Designs Ltd, Re*, (1998) 29 Corpt LA 135 Ker, a company cannot be said to be unable to pay its debts if it has substantial profits and current assets; a company cannot be expected to discharge a debt which it does not admit on *bona fide* grounds.

34. AIR 1950 EP 142; *K. S. Trivedi & Co* v *Ashok Leyland Ltd*, [1989] 3 Comp LJ 351, neither the amount nor due date given with certainty; *Hindustan Sanitary and Hardware Store* v *J. C.T. Electronics Ltd*, (1990) 67 Comp Cas 585 Punj, where the company paid off a major part of the claim and secured the balance by a bank guarantee; *Ultimate Advertising and Marketing Co* v *G.B. Laboratories*, (1990) 66 Comp Cas 232 All, where the principal paid off and only interest amount disputed, order not granted, here the court also added that winding up is in the discretion of the court and the same may be refused even if all the grounds are made out; *Goyal Electro Steel, Re*, 67 Comp Cas 305 Raj, goods received in damaged state; *Joti Prasad Bala Prasad* v *ACT Developers (P) Ltd*, (1990) 68 Comp Cas 601 Del, *bona fide* disputes about goods supplied to the company; *Aluminum Extrusions and Industrial Components (P) Ltd* v *Central Paints Ltd*, (1990) 68 Comp Cas 477 MP, vague plea of dispute. Debts arising out of settlement of accounts in a family company. Hence *bona fide* defence ruled out. *Deepa Anant Bandekar* v *Rajaram Bandekar (Sirigao) Mines Ltd*, (1992) 74 Comp Cas 42 Bom. The company did not pay rent from day one and replied to the petition saying that it had applied for fixation of standard rent, held not *bona fide* in *Sharda Bhandari* v *Ananya Electronics Ltd*, (1993) 78 Comp Cas 167 Del. Payment of arrears of lease money due on premises taken over by the company, allowed to be raised before the company court, *Devendra Kumar Jain* v *Polar Forgings and Tools Ltd*, (1993) 1 Comp LJ 184 Del: (1993) 1 Punj LR 67.

only said that they had some kind of a counter-claim, which the court found to be of a very nebulous character. All they said was that the accounts required scrutiny and that the petitioner was not presently entitled to the sum claimed, but why, it was not clearly stated. The court, therefore, held that there was no *bona fide* dispute with regard to the sum due.

Similarly, in *Harinagar Sugar Mills Co* v *Pradhan*,[35] Subba Rao J (afterwards CJ) allowed a petition as "the alleged dispute as to the liability of the company to the joint family was not *bona fide* but was only a part of a scheme of collusion between the company and the *karta* of the family".[36]

It is also necessary that the creditor should have delivered a demand under his hand at the registered office of the company.[37] "Statutory notice is a highly formal and important document and it would appear to follow that the provision of the Act as to its service upon the company must be strictly observed."[38] Thus, where the amount due was incorrectly stated in the notice, the petition failed.[39] Notice should be served at the company's registered office. Where the registered office was not functioning and a different address was being given for correspondence, a service at that address, and not at the registered office, was held to be not a good service

35. [1966] 2 Comp LJ 17.
36. Where a company had accepted a number of bills of exchange and in defence the company only said that the acceptances were conditional, but offered no proof of such conditions, it was held that winding up could not be refused. *United Western Bank Ltd, In re,* (1978) 48 Comp Cas 378; *Universal Consortium of Engineers Ltd, Re,* (1983) 54 Comp Cas 33 Cal, no proof of debt offered; *Madan Debi Kundalla* v *Alpine Dairy Ltd,* (1983) 54 Comp Cas 41 Cal, defence of defective goods raised a long time after the supply, not tenable. Where the company first acknowledge the debt and disputed it for the first time at the hearing, that was not the symptom of a *bona fide* dispute. *Bajrangbali Engg Co Ltd, Re,* AIR 1989 Cal 356: [1990] 1 Comp LJ 243. A claim which required to be substantiated by evidence is fit for a civil suit, *Malhotra Steel Syndicate* v *Punjab Chemi Plants,* (1989) 65 Comp Cas 546 P&H. Company paying half the debt, petition allowed because the other half was of more than Rs 500, *United Asian Bank* v *Jaipur Oil Products Ltd,* (1989) 66 Comp Cas 438; *Surendra Packers* v *Punjab Land Development and Reclamation Corpn Ltd,* (1989) 66 Comp Cas 883 P&H, company raising no points.
37. S. 434(2).
38. See Rankin CJ in *Japan Cotton Trading Co* v *Jajodia Cotton Mills,* AIR 1927 Cal 625, and *see* also *Janbazar Manna Estate Ltd, Re,* AIR 1931 Cal 692: 133 IC 321; *Laxmi Sugar Mills* v *National Industrial Corpn,* [1968] 1 Comp LJ 292 Punj. Where the particulars of the notice changed because of payments to creditors, the notice became technically incompetent, a new petition was not allowed to be founded on such notice, *Shantilal Khushaldas* v *Jayabala,* (1994) Mh LJ 432.
39. *Ofu Lynx Ltd* v *Simon Carves India Ltd,* (1971) 41 Comp Cas 174: AIR 1973 Cal 413. A time-barred claim cannot be the basis of a petition, but where the company acknowledged the debt in its balance-sheet that was held to be sufficient both as a proof of the debt and as an extension of the period. *Pandam Tea Co* v *Darjeeling Commercial Co,* (1977) 47 Comp Cas 15 Cal. Where the notice did not mention the date within which payment should be made or mentions a period less than 21 days, it may still be a valid notice, because the Act gives the company a 21 day waiting period. See *Sytron (India) Ltd, Re,* (1990) 69 Comp Cas 767 Cal; *N. K. Gossain & Co (P) Ltd* v *Dytron (India) Ltd,* (1990) 69 Comp Cas 757 Cal.

for the purposes of a winding up petition.[40] Notice sent to the administrative office of the company instead of the registered office was held to be not effective service.[41] But there are contrary rulings.[42] Where a company contested the claim on the ground that the documents in question were not signed in accordance with the articles and, therefore, the company was not liable, that was held to be a *bona fide* dispute disentitling the claimant from winding up order.[43] It may not be necessary to specify in the notice any particular section of the Act, but the notice must give some indication that in the event of non-compliance, steps would be taken for an order of winding up. Where the petitioner had not mentioned in his notice the period within which he must be paid and only asked for payment at an early date, it was not considered to be a valid notice for winding up order.[44]

Once the requirements of a creditor's petition are fulfilled and there is a non-compliance with the statutory notice, winding up may be ordered and

---

40. *Vysya Bank Ltd v Randhir Steel and Alloys (P) Ltd*, (1991) Mah LJ 1578: (1993) 76 Comp Cas 244 Bom, distinguishing *Fortune Copper Mining Co, Re*, (1870) LR 10 Eq 390, where the registered office of the company was pulled down and service elsewhere was held to be sufficient.

41. *N. L. Mehta Cinema Enterprises (P) Ltd v Pravin Chandra P. Mehta*, (1991) 70 Comp Cas 31 Bom. A notice served on the company's administrative office would have been regarded as good if it were not short in terms of time, *Manganese Ore (India) Ltd v Sandur Manganese & Iron Ores Ltd*, (1999) 98 Comp Cas 755 Kant; *Indian Oil Corpn Ltd v NEPC (India) Ltd*, (2003) 114 Comp Cas 207 Mad, notice sent at address shown on the company's letterhead as regd. office, good, even if the office had been shifted, the claimant not knowing it. Service at administrative office has been recognised as valid service. *Laxmi Industrial Greases (P) Ltd v Punjab Chemi Plant International Ltd*, (2001) 103 Comp Cas 429 P&H, notice served on and received by the managing director, substantial compliance. Services at the company's registered office is not merely a technical formality, it has to be strictly complied with, *P. S. V. P. Vittal Rao v Progressive Construction (P) Ltd*, [1999] 2 Comp LJ 228 AP. The notice coming back with the postal remark 'refused' was held to be good service, *Raj Kumar v Organic Chem Oils Ltd*, (1998) 93 Comp Cas 386 P&H. A notice to the managing director has been held to be no good, *N. Gopalkrishnan v Asianet Satellite Communications Ltd*, [2000] 1 Comp LJ 285. Notice sent by Legal Aid & Advice Board on its own behalf and not on behalf of a creditor was held to be incompetent, *Bichitrananda Panda v Orissa Construction Ltd*, (1999) 97 Comp Cas 345 Ori. Service of notice by registered post followed by publication in newspapers was held to be sufficient compliance with Rule 32 of the Companies (Court) Rules, 1956, *Doshi Leather Cloth Mfg Co Ltd, Re*, [2000] 23 SCL 225 Bom.

42. See the rulings cited in the note above.

43. *Softsule (P) Ltd, Re*, (1977) 47 Comp Cas 438 Bom; *Aar Bee Enterprises (P) Ltd v Gyan Security Press Ltd*, (2006) 133 Comp Cas 25 All, principal amount paid, claim of interest *bona fide* disputed, to be settled by Civil Court; *Hindustan Organic Chemicals Ltd v Appollo Trade Ltd*, (2006) 133 Comp Cas 877 Bom, principal amount paid as full and final payment, claim of interest, *bona fide* dispute, petition not admitted. *Mysore Sales International Ltd v United Breweries Ltd*, (2006) 133 Comp Cas 191, claim for commission on business done during pendency of dispute, claim disputed. *Tubecon Products (P) Ltd v Arjun Technologies (I) Ltd*, (2006) 133 Comp Cas 277 Mad, claim for commission on equipment supplied, no proof, *bona fide* dispute. *Superfine Meat Suppliers v Bharat Hotels Ltd*, (2006) 133 Comp Cas 253 Del, claim of enhanced rates after contract, disputed, required adjudication, petition not admitted. *Bhattacherjee Engineers (P) Ltd v Santilal Jaiswal*, (2006) 129 Comp Cas 29 Cal, Confirmation of debt on incorrect representation and authenticity of signature, disputed matter.

44. *Paramjit Lal Bhadwar v Prem Spg and Wvg Mills*, (1986) 60 Comp Cas 420 All.

the company will not be heard to say that the petitioner is acting *mala fides,* or that he has an alternative remedy or that the company is solvent or that the majority of the creditors are opposed to winding up[45] or that the petition was presented only to save the period of limitation.[46]

But even so the power of the court is discretionary. The utility of this discretion is amply illustrated by the decision of the Bombay High Court in *Asnew Drums Co Ltd, Re.*[47] A company's indebtedness aggregated to over Rs 78 lakhs of which the petitioner had a claim of only Rs 11,350. He fulfilled the requirements of the statutory notice. The company prayed for time so as to enable it to draw a scheme of compromise with all its creditors. The court stayed the petition to enable the company to call a meeting of its creditors, but subject to the condition that the company shall not deal with or dispose of its assets in the meantime.[48]

The discretion of the court has been revitalised by the Supreme Court in *M. Gordhandas & Co* v *Madhu Woollen Industries (P) Ltd.*[49] The court found that the debts were not only disputed, but were also falsely shown in the accounts by the petitioners when they were themselves the directors.

---

45. *Advent Corpn Ltd, Re,* [1969] 2 Comp LJ 71; *Seksaria Cotton Mills, Re,* [1969] 2 Comp LJ 155 Bom.
46. *V. K. Jain* v *Richa Laboratories (P) Ltd,* (1993) 78 Comp Cas 283 Del: [1994] 1 Comp LJ 270; *UCO Bank* v *Achal Alloys (P) Ltd,* [1993] 3 Comp LJ 43 MP, defenceless indebtedness to bank. *Sharda Bhandari* v *Ananya Electronics Ltd,* (1993) 78 Comp Cas 167 Del, an application for fixation of standard rent is not a defence to the liability to pay the outstanding rent. *Devendra Kumar Jain* v *Polar Forgings & Tools Ltd,* [1993] 1 Comp LJ 184 Del: (1993) 1 Punj LR 67, the company paying the principal but not the interest allowed by the company judge, a good ground of winding up. *S. Kantilal & Co* v *Rajaram Bandekar (Sirigao) Mines (P) Ltd,* (1993) 76 Comp Cas 800 Bom, debt due under a guarantee. *Haryana Telecom Ltd* v *Haryana Futuristic Corpn Ltd,* (2006) 133 Comp Cas 351 HP, dispute in respect of a purchase contract, cannot be resolved in winding up jurisdiction. *Jagdamba Polymers Ltd* v *Neo-Sack Co,* (2006) 129 Comp Cas 160 MP, *bona fide* dispute about debt, other remedies available, matter fit for civil court.
47. (1968) 38 Comp Cas 287 Bom; *see also Nagree* v *Asnew Drums,* (1967) 2 Comp LJ 289.
48. *See also Kudremukh Iron Ore Co Ltd* v *Kooky Roadways (P) Ltd,* (1990) 69 Comp Cas 178 Kant, where a carrier had become liable for short delivery of goods and the claim was held to be capable of sustaining a petition though its amount was not yet ascertained. Another example of grant of time was in *Rishi Enterprises, Re,* (1992) 73 Comp Cas 271 Guj, the company was in temporary difficulties and the employment of 500 persons was at stake, the company was also doing well in business. *Star Straw Board Mfg Co* v *Mahalaxmi Sugar Mills Co,* (1991) 2 Punj LR 128, company paying undisputed part of the claim, for the balance one-month allowed at 18% interest.
49. (1971) 3 SCC 632: AIR 1971 SC 2600: (1972) 42 Comp Cas 125; *Garodia Hardware Store* v *Nimodia Plantations and Industries (P) Ltd,* AIR 1998 Gau 18, winding up ordered because of inability to pay debts. The agreement for sale of property of the company was not specifically enforced because that way only one person would have got all the benefit. *Tolani Shipping Co Ltd* v *Saw Pipes Ltd,* (1998) 28 Corpt LA 160 Del, complicated and disputed claims not to be accepted as the basis of a petition. *Larsen and Toubro Ltd* v *Prime Displays (P) Ltd,* (2003) 114 Comp Cas 141 Bom, privileged documents were not permitted to be used in proof of debt. The documents had come into being during discussions between the company and its professional legal advisors as to the matters in dispute.

The other creditors were opposed to winding up. Explaining the weight that ought to be attached to this fact Ray J (later CJ) said:[50]

The wishes of the creditors will be tested on the ground whether the case of the persons opposing the winding up is reasonable, secondly, whether there are matters which should be inquired into and investigated if a winding up order is made. It is also well-settled that a winding up order will not be made on a creditor's petition if it would not benefit him or the company's creditors generally.

A time-barred claim cannot sustain a winding up petition.[51] Money paid for allotment of shares and no shares being allotted, nor money refunded, the applicants' petition for winding up filed at a time when the claim to refund had become time-barred was held to be not maintainable.[52] For refund of money lost because of misrepresentations in the prospectus adequate remedies are available under Section 62 of the Companies Act. It is hardly necessary for the allottee to come in under jurisdiction for winding up.[53]

An arbitrator's award can be the basis of a petition even if it has not been made a rule of the court.[54] There have been contrary decisions also.[55] Where there was a pending petition against an award for its setting aside, it was held that the petition for winding up should wait for the outcome of the petition against the award.[56] The court can take up the petition again after

---

50. At p 132. Followed by the Bombay High Court in *Focus Advertising (P) Ltd* v *Ahoora Block (P) Ltd*, (1975) 45 Comp Cas 534 Bom, where though all the conditions of a creditor's petition were satisfied, the bulk of creditors were opposed to it.

51. *K. C. Pangunni* v *Official Liquidator Wandoor Jupiter Chits*, (1981) 51 Comp Cas 453 Ker. Acknowledgement extends time and the fact of a debt being mentioned in the company's balance- sheet amounts to acknowledgment. *Darjeeling Commercial Co Ltd* v *Pandam Tea Co Ltd*, (1983) 54 Comp Cas 814 Cal. Land sold by company under deception and taking advance, refusing to refund, held inability; limitation from the date of final refusal. *Ajai Johri* v *Shingal Land & Finance Ltd*, (1985) 58 Comp Cas 350 Del. Debt becoming time barred by the time of the order does not matter. *Modern Dekor Painting Contracts (P) Ltd* v *Jenson & Nicholson India Ltd*, (1985) 58 Comp Cas 255 Bom. Where the balance confirmation letters were signed by the responsible executive of the company for three consecutive years, the question of time-bar did not arise, *Electro-Flame Ltd* v *Mittal Iron Foundry Ltd*, AIR 1998 AP 203; *Karnataka Leasing & Commercial Corpn Ltd*, (in liquidation) v *N.R. Kini*, (2007) 136 Comp Cas 192 Kant, payment of a promissory note after it had become time-barred did not have the effect of extending the period of limitation.

52. *Ashok Kumar* v *Shinghal Land & Finance (P) Ltd*, (1995) 17 Corpt LA 111 Del: (1995) 82 Comp Cas 430, the court could as well have taken the view, which would have been more consistent with authorities, that application money is in the nature of trust deposit. *See* notes under "Allotment of shares" *supra;* see also *Sham Lal Gupta* v *Hamco Industries (P) Ltd*, AIR 1995 P&H 6, another decision on the same set of facts.

53. *Prashant Khusalchand Shah* v *Rinku Polychem Ltd*, AIR 1998 Bom 203.

54. *Dalhousie Jute Co Ltd* v *Mulchand*, (1983) 53 Comp Cas 607 Cal; *Kalyani Spg Mills* v *Shiva Trading Co*, (1983) 53 Comp Cas 632 Cal. See also *C. A. Galiakotwala Co (P) Ltd, Re*, (1984) 55 Comp Cas 746 Bom, counter-awards.

55. *Punjab Recorders Ltd* v *Magnetic Information Technology Ltd*, AIR 1995 P&H 29, petition not allowed on the basis of an award not made rule of the court.

56. *Civicons Engineers & Contractors* v *Auro Foods Ltd*, (1999) 22 SCL 370 Mad.

the award becomes an evidence of an established debt.[57] An arbitrator has no jurisdiction to order winding up.[58] The existence of an *arbitration agreement* does not oust the jurisdiction of the court.[59]

An employee's claim for compensation for premature termination of employment is not a debt unless it is first ascertained by a court and converted into a decree.[60] Where an incentive or bonus for the preceding year had been calculated and paid and an equal amount of working and calculation was necessary for determining the rate for the subsequent year and accounting being again necessary, it was held that this could appropriately and properly be conducted not under the summary procedure of Section 433, but in a regular suit.[61] Where the Industrial Tribunal directed the company to pay an amount to the dismissed employee by way of an interim relief but the company did not pay, and he filed a petition for winding up, the court directed the company to pay instead of ordering winding up.[62]

A declared dividend which has not been paid has been held to be a 'debt'. The company made payment during pendency of the petition. The court ordered 12% interest for the period of delay.[63]

(b) Decreed Debt

Secondly, a company shall be deemed to be unable to pay its debts if execution or other process issued on a decree or order of any Court in favour of a creditor of the company is returned unsatisfied in whole or in part.[64]

Even in the case of a decretal debt, question of *bona fide* dispute may be raised and the Court may, instead of passing winding up order, allow the petition to stand over on an undertaking by the company to file a suit for setting aside the decree.[65] Thus, for example, in *Steel Equipment & Construction Co, Re*:[66] A company, having been sued on a debt, agreed to

57. *Haryana Telecom Ltd* v *Sterlite Industries (India) Ltd*, (1999) 97 Comp Cas 675 P&H.
58. *Haryana Telecom Ltd* v *Sterlite Industries (India) Ltd*, (1999) 99 Comp Cas 683 SC.
59. *J.G. Finance Co Ltd* v *Jamna Auto Industries Ltd*, [2000] 1 Comp LJ 139 P&H; *Prime Century City Development (P) Ltd* v *Ansal Buildwell Ltd*, (2003) 113 Comp Cas 68 Del, the court can exercise its jurisdiction according to its discretion in spite of the fact that its jurisdiction has been ousted by the arbitration agreement. The court said that there was no actual possibility of clash of jurisdictions. Another similar decision is *Hewlett Packard India Ltd* v *BPL Net Com Ltd*, (2002) 110 Comp Cas 575 Kant.
60. *B. R. Somashkarappa* v *Vignam Industries Ltd*, (1990) 68 Comp Cas 264 Kant.
61. *Sanjay Khanna* v *Discovery Communications India*, (2003) 114 Comp Cas 229 Del.
62. *Karam Chand Thaper* v *Amar Nath De*, (2002) 108 Comp Cas 581 Cal.
63. *SBI Mutual Fund* v *Vikas WSP Ltd*, (2006) 133 Comp Cas 542 P&H.
64. S. 434(*b*).
65. *Bows* v *Hope Life Insurance Guarantee Co*, (1865) 11 HL Cases 389: 13 WR 790, cited by the Calcutta High Court in *O. P. Mehta* v *Steel Equipment & Construction Co*, [1967] 1 Comp LJ 172, 182. A winding up court has a larger power to go behind a decree *Bajrangbali Engineering Co Ltd, Re*, AIR 1989 Cal 356: [1990] 1 Comp LJ 243.
66. (1963) 38 Comp Cas 82: [1967] 1 Comp LJ 172.

a consent decree but failed to satisfy it. In a winding up petition presented on that ground, the company claimed that the debt comprised in the decree was *ultra vires* and had already filed a suit to set aside the decree. The Calcutta High Court held that "the petition shall be adjourned till the disposal of the suit".

Where the decree-holders were the executors of the deceased owner and the real beneficiaries of the decree were not before the court and thus there was a chance of payment not passing over to them and raising of claims against the company over again, the court refused winding up order at the instance of such decree holders.[67]

In the case of a consent decree and the failure of the company to pay according to the decree, the creditor becomes entitled to an order *ex debito justitiae*. The question of company having any defence and the question of examining the solvency of the company are ruled out.[68]

Subject to these considerations a decree-holder is entitled to press for winding up as a legitimate mode for the execution of his decree and is not bound first to resort to execution proceedings.[69]

(c) Commercial Insolvency

Lastly, if it is proved to the satisfaction of the court that the company is unable to pay its debts.[70] In reference to the concept of "unable to pay debts" it has been observed that though it is not necessary that there should be a statutory demand or any demand at all, the court would not be easily satisfied that a company is unable to pay its debts from the mere non-payment of a debt which was never demanded of it.[71] In determining this the court shall take into account the contingent and prospective liabilities of the company. "What has to be ascertained is not whether if all assets were converted into cash, the company would be able to discharge its debts, but whether in a commercial sense the company is solvent." A perusal of the balance-sheet of the company must show that its assets are sufficient to meet its liabilities. If it is not so, the company may be regarded as commercially insolvent. The expression "commercial insolvency" was explained by SIR JAMES in *European Life Assurance Society, Re*.[72] "Not in any technical sense but plainly and commercially

---

67. *Bajrangbali Engg Co Ltd v Amar Nath Sircar*, (1995) 83 Comp Cas 435 Cal.
68. *Bandedker (S.R.) v R. Bandekar (Sirigao) Mines (P) Ltd*, (1997) 88 Comp Cas 673 Bom.
69. *All India General Transport Corpn Ltd v Raj Kumar Mittal*, (1978) 48 Comp Cas 604; *Tube Investment of India Ltd v Everest Cycles Ltd*, (1984) 55 Comp Cas 165 Gau. Commercial insolvency may be presumed from the company's silence in spite of statutory notice, *Associated Forest Products (P) Ltd v KTC (Singapore) plc*, (1993) 1 Cal LJ 382.
70. S. 434(*c*). Particulars of the debt must be given and there should be an averment that the company was unable to pay its debts, *Kalra Iron Stores v Faridabad Fabricators (P) Ltd (No 2)*, (1992) 73 Comp Cas 337 Del.
71. *A Company (No 0067980 of 1995), Re*, (1996) 2 BCLC 48 Ch D.
72. 9 Eq 122 (1869) at 128. Followed in India in *Cine Industries & Recording Co Ltd, Re*, AIR 1942 Bom 231: 44 Bom LR 387; *Vanaspati Industries Ltd v Firm Prabhu Dayal*, AIR 1950 EP 142; *State of A.P. v Hyderabad Vegetable Products*, AIR 1963 AP 243; *Gujarat State*

insolvent that is to say, that its assets are such and existing liabilities are such, as to make it reasonably certain—as to make the court feel satisfied—that the existing and probable assets would be insufficient to meet the existing liabilities." Thus in *Coimbatore Transport Ltd* v *Governor General in Council*,[73] a company was ordered to be wound up as it was unable to pay its taxes in spite of demands, nor was it able to furnish security. Where the assets of a company were taken over by the State and in reply to the creditors' claims and petitions, the company was only telling them that it was trying to retrieve those assets and there was nothing to show any benefit to the creditors in the continuity of the company, the court ordered winding up.[74] Another illustration is *Sree Shanmaugar Mills* v *Dharmaraja Nadar*:[75]

> A company resisted a petition on the ground that while its liabilities amounted only to Rs 8,72,414, its assets were of the value of Rs 10,79,130. It was found that these assets included building and machinery, excluding which only a sum of Rs 3,00,000 would be available to discharge the debts.

The court held that the value of such assets without which the company could not carry on business, should not be taken into account. The proper test is whether in a commercial sense the existing liability would be paid by it while it continued to carry on as a company. However, the company is entitled to regard its uncalled capital as money available for the discharge of its debts. Moreover, "where at the relevant time there is reasonable hope of tiding over the difficulty and emerging into a region in which the company might reasonably expect to carry on at a profit", it may not be ordered to be wound up on this ground.[76]

Financial Services Ltd v *Megabyte Consultancy Services (P) Ltd*, (2003) 115 Comp Cas 165, the burden is on the petitioner to show such a state of the company.

73. AIR 1949 Mad 73. *See* also *Bachharaj Factories* v *Hirjee Mills*, AIR 1955 Bom 355, where as against liabilities of Rs 1,41,50,000 assets were only Rs 60,00,000 the Court declared the company to be not only commercially but hopelessly insolvent; *Netravali* v *Chitale Agri Pro Ltd*, [1968] 1 Comp LJ 212 and *Globe New Patent Iron & Steel Co, Re*, (1875) 20 Eq 337, where failure to pay a bill of exchange on maturity was held as evidence of insolvency. *State Bank of India* v *Hegde and Golay Ltd*, (1987) 62 Comp Cas 239 Kant, bank loans and interest remaining unpaid.

74. *Shree Laxmi Traders Ltd, Re*, (1987) 62 Comp Cas 49 Bom. The possibility of a company being able to realise by the sale of its assets an amount exceeding its liabilities is not sufficient to hold that the company is commercially solvent. The test is whether the company shall be able to meet its current liabilities and whether the existing assets would be sufficient to meet the future demands which the company remains a going concern. *Alliance Credit and Investments Ltd* v *Khaitan Hostambe Spinels Ltd*, (1997) 3 Comp LJ 200 All. A cheque was issued by the company by way of repayment of a deposit. The cheque bounced. The company admitted liability and asked for one month time, which was granted but even then could not pay. It was held that the circumstances created a presumption of inability to pay debts, making the company liable to be wound up. *Arvind Investment Consultant* v *Presto Finance Ltd*, (1997) 14 SCL 256 Guj.

75. AIR 1970 Mad 203. Putting off a creditor under one pretence or the other is a sign of insolvency. *John Paterson & Co* v *Pramod Kumar Jalan*, (1983) 53 Comp Cas 255 Cal.

76. *Sudhiya* v *Bihar National Insurance Co*, AIR 1941 Pat 603. *See* also *Bukhtiarpur Bihar Light Rly Co Ltd* v *Union of India*, AIR 1954 Cal 499; *Bengal Luxmi Cotton Mills Ltd* v

Thus, where past losses were not yet fully wiped out, but the company had made some profit during the year of the petition,[77] and where the company's losses were decreasing every year and it was on the way to make profits, winding up order was refused.[78]

Even where assets are less than liabilities, it does not necessarily follow that the company is insolvent. Where a company was not only able to, but also did meet its claims as and when they arose, winding up was not allowed, although its assets were only worth 6 lakhs as against liabilities of 8.5 lakhs.[79]

The court can also take into account the public interest. The Bombay High Court had to face a case[80] in which a company's business came to a standstill owing to paucity of working capital. The court explained the extent to which public interest has entered into the management of companies and thought it improper to destroy a company which had worked for nearly 87 years and had acquired experience and expertise in the manufacture of structurals, boat building and ship repairing, and held that the best order to make is to appoint a special officer to collect, realise, preserve and maintain the assets of the company and also to make the necessary investigations.

The section thus splits the concept of inability to pay debts into three points. The Madras High Court has expressed the opinion that these sub-grounds are not mutually exclusive. Consequently, if a creditor has obtained a decree he can claim winding up on any of the points and need not confine himself to the category of decree-holders only.[81]

Mahalakshmi Cotton Mills Ltd, AIR 1955 Cal 273; *J. D. Swain Ltd, Re*, [1961] 1 Comp LJ 37: [1965] 2 All ER 761. *See* also *Steel Equipment & Construction Co, Re*, (1963) 38 Comp Cas 82: [1967] 1 Comp LJ 172, where the Calcutta High Court held that the mere fact that a disputed decree has remained unsatisfied is not a proof of insolvency. "The burden of proof for proving insolvency is on the applicant." *See* also *Krishnaswami* v *Stressed Concrete Construction*, AIR 1964 Mad 191; *Anant Sadashiv Netravali* v *Chitale Agri Products Ltd*, (1968) 38 Comp Cas 292, an insolvent company not heard to say that it had a case pending before the SC.

77. *Cinco Laboratories (P) Ltd, Re*, (1973) 43 Comp Cas 550 Pat.

78. *Registrar of Companies* v *Suraj Bachat Yojna*, (1973) 43 Comp Cas 343 P&H.

79. *Registrar of Companies* v *Janta Lucky Scheme & Investment Co*, (1973) 43 Comp Cas 314 P&H; *Rishi Enterprises, Re*, (1992) 73 Comp Cas 271 Guj, the court allowed the company time to pay. Where there was a complicated dispute between parties which involved a detailed analysis of the financial liability (if any) of the company, a petition to wind up the company was held to be not proper. *Amadues Trading Ltd, Re, The Times*, April 1, 1997: 1997 Palmer in Company, May, p 4.

80. *Bhalchandra Dharmajee Makaji* v *Alcock, Ashdown & Co Ltd*, (1972) 42 Comp Cas 190 Bom.

81. See *Thai Mills Ltd* v *N. Perumalsamy*, (1980) 50 Comp Cas 422 Mad. *See* also *Shree Ram Chemicals (P) Ltd, Re*, (1983) 53 Comp Cas 729 AP, where a creditor's petition was converted into a scheme of compromise; *Sarabhai Machinery* v *Haryana Detergents*, [1986] 1 Comp LJ 246 P&H, where the company deposited the principal amount in the court but not the interest due on it, the court nevertheless ordered winding up. *Delhi Cloth & General Mills Co* v *Stepan Chemicals Ltd*, (1986) 60 Comp Cas 1046 P&H. The

Advertisement of petition

A petition is not normally to be advertised on its *ex parte* admission. The company in this case was a working and running concern. The advertisement of the petition on its admission might seriously prejudice the goodwill of the company and its day to day working. The *ex parte* order was set aside. The matter was remitted for fresh consideration.[82]

6. Just and equitable

The last ground on which the court can order the winding up of a company is when "the court is of opinion that it is just and equitable that the company should be wound up".[83] This gives the court a very wide discretionary power to order winding up whenever it appears to be desirable. The court may give due weight to the interest of the company, its employees, creditors and shareholders and general public interest should also be considered.[84] "Though the court is not bound to construe this clause *(ejusdem generis)* as only covering grounds of a like nature with those specified in clauses 1 to 5, yet it will require grounds of a like magnitude before acting under the clause."[85] "For a long period *ejusdem generis* dominated interpretations of the just and equitable provision. But the rule has been entirely abandoned and the words are to be treated as conferring a discretionary power which is of the widest character and the courts are left to work out for themselves the principles on which such orders should be granted.[86] There must be a really strong ground for liquidating a company. Moreover, the Court may refuse to make an order of winding up, if it is of the opinion that some other remedy is available to the petitioner and he is acting unreasonably in seeking to have the company wound up, instead of pursuing that other remedy.[87]

---

mentioning of a debt in a company's balance-sheet is an acknowledgment for the purposes of this right and also for the period of limitation. *Dainik Finance* v *Agriculture Industries*, (1986) 60 Comp Cas 180 P&H; *Krishko International* v *Adwait Steel & Metals (P) Ltd*, (1993) 76 Comp Cas 328 Del, pending criminal proceedings, the company not showing that its defence would be prejudiced if winding up proceeding was not stayed, no stay granted. Following, *Star Paper Mills Ltd* v *Behari Lal*, AIR 1990 Del 241; *Sheriff* v *State of Madras*, AIR 1954 SC 397.

82. *Mansukh Bhai Industries Ltd* v *Shakti Agencies*, (2006) 133 Comp Cas 525 Raj.

83. S. 433(*f*). It is also a remedy of the last resort. *Gadadhar Dixit* v *Utkal Flour Mills (P) Ltd*, (1989) 66 Comp Cas 188 Ori.

84. *See*, for example, *Veeramachineni Seethiah* v *Venkatasubbiah*, AIR 1949 Mad 675; *Cine Industries & Recording Co Ltd, Re*, AIR 1942 Bom 231: 44 Bom LR 387.

85. *Cowasjee* v *Nath Singh Oil Co Ltd*, (1921) 59 IC 524.

86. B. H. McPherson, *Winding up on the Just and Equitable Ground*, (1964) 27 MLR 288. Followed in *Jivabhai M. Patel* v *Extrusion Processes (P) Ltd*, [1966] 2 Comp LJ 74.

87. S. 443(2). See *Jivabhai M. Patel* v *Extrusion Processes (P) Ltd*, supra, where though the petition was allowed, the Bombay High Court explained this principle. *Lokenath Gupta* v *Credits (P) Ltd*, (1968) 38 Comp Cas 599 Cal where despite serious allegations, the court refused this remedy because the alternative remedies were not exhausted. Winding up being a remedy of last resort, compelling circumstances would be needed for the power to be exercised. *Daulat Makanmal Luthria* v *Solitaire Hotels*, (1993) 76 Comp Cas 215 Bom, a

The role of courts discretion is to consider all the affected interests and not merely those of creditors.[88]

It is not desirable nor possible to categorise facts that render it just and equitable to wind up a company. "The tendency to create categories or headings is wrong; the general words of the sub-section should remain general and not be reduced to the sum of particular instances."[89] But the circumstances in which the courts have in the past dissolved companies on this ground can be resolved into general categories. And they are as follows:

(i) Deadlock

Firstly, when there is a deadlock in the management of a company, it is just and equitable to order winding up. The well-known illustration is *Yenidje Tobacco Co Ltd, Re:*[90]

W and R, who traded separately as cigarette manufacturers, agreed to amalgamate their business and formed a private limited company of which they were the shareholders and the only directors. They had equal voting rights and, therefore, the articles provided that any dispute would be resolved by arbitration, but one of them dissented from the award. Both then became so hostile that neither of them would speak to the other except through the secretary. Thus there was a complete deadlock and consequently the company was ordered to be wound up although its business was flourishing.[91]

"But the 'just and equitable' clause should not be invoked in cases where the only difficulty is the difference of view between the majority directorate and those representing the minority."[92] The Madras High Court observed on the facts of a case that "where nine or ten directors belonging to different communities unanimously and solidly take one view as

---

tourism company not ordered to be wound up because inspite of difficulties it was at the threshold of commencing business operations.

88. *Ramdeo Ranglal* v *Ghooronia Tea Co (P) Ltd*, (2005) 60 SCL 449 Guj, the company was in the process of revival and employment of hundreds of workers was at stake.
89. D. D. Prentice, *Winding Up on the Just and Equitable Ground: The Partnership Analogy*, (1973) 89 LQR 107, 108, quoting Lord WILBERFORCE in *Ebrahimi* v *Westbourne Galleries Ltd*, [1972] 2 WLR 1289: [1972] 2 All ER 492, 496.
90. [1916] 2 Ch 426: [1916-17] All ER Rep 1050.
91. Expressly approved by the Privy Council in *Loch* v *John Blackwood Ltd*, 1924 AC 783: [1924] All ER Rep 200 PC; applied: *Davis & Collett Ltd, Re*, [1935] All ER Rep 315: 1935 Ch 693: 5 Comp Cas 467 Ch D; *Lundie Bros, Re*, [1965] 2 All ER 692: [1966] 1 Comp LJ 30; *Expanded Plugs Ltd, Re*, [1966] 1 All ER 877: [1966] 2 Comp LJ 115. Considered: *Jivabhai M. Patel* v *Extrusion Processes (P) Ltd*, [1966] 2 Comp LJ 74. *See* also *Raghunath Prasad* v *Hind Overseas (P) Ltd*, [1970] 1 Comp LJ 213 where the Calcutta High Court held that if a company can be described as a partnership in the guise of a private company, there is no escape from the proposition that the grounds proposition for the dissolution of a partnership shall apply. *Chua Kien How* v *Goodwealth Trading (P) Ltd*, (1993) 1 SCR 486 Malaysia, the only two directors could not agree with each other and could not overrule each other either and the dispute between them as to who was the majority shareholder was the deadlock between them as to the management of the company.
92. *Veeramachineni Seethiah* v *Venkatasubbiah*, AIR 1949 Mad 675.

against the minority of three holding another view and the company has been earning profits and has accumulated a goodwill, the mere incompatibility of good relations between the rival factions in the directorate is not sufficient for ordering winding up".[93] Similarly, the Calcutta High Court has held that "winding up cannot be ordered on the grounds of friction and disputes between directors; the scramble for power is at the bottom of it all".[94] The courts, however, do not insist on a paralysing deadlock. Indeed, it has been said that "the authorities show that there need not be a deadlock".[95] A justifiable lack of confidence resting on a lack of probity in the conduct of a company's affairs is sufficient to found a winding up order.[96]

The allegation in a private company that there was a loss of mutual trust and confidence among shareholders particularly about apportionment in construction activity and accounting was held to be not a ground for winding up of the company.[97]

(ii) *Loss of Substratum*

Secondly, it is just and equitable to wind up a company when its main object has failed to materialise or it has lost its substratum. A good illustration is *German Date Coffee Co, Re*:[98]

> A company was formed for the purpose of manufacturing coffee from dates under a patent which was to be granted by the Government of Germany and also for working other patents of similar kind. The German patent was never granted and the company embarked upon other patents. But, on the petition of a shareholder, it was held that "the substratum of the company had failed, and it was impossible to carry out the objects for which it was formed; and, therefore, it was just and equitable that the company should be wound up".[99]

---

93. Ibid. *Vasant Holiday Homes (P) Ltd v Madan V. Prabhu*, (2003) 116 Comp Cas 172 Bom, where disputes amongst directors had affected their rights and the company was also running at a loss, this was held to be not sufficient to establish a right to seek a winding up order which is a remedy of the last resort. *Cochin Malabar Estates & Industries Ltd v P.V. Abdul Khader*, (2003) 114 Comp Cas 777, company not shown to be commercially insolvent, 0.02% shareholder could have sought his redressal elsewhere.

94. A. N. RAY J (as he then was) in *Hind Overseas Ltd, Re*, [1968] 2 Comp LJ 95, where the learned Judge makes an exhaustive review of all English and Indian authorities.

95. See *J. M. Patel v Extrusion Processes Ltd*, [1966] 2 Comp LJ 74, at p 78.

96. LORD SHAW OF DUNFERMLINE in *Loch v John Blackwood Ltd*, 1924 AC 783: [1924] All ER Rep 200 PC.

97. *Laijuk v Brick Bond Builders (P) Ltd*, (2006) 133 Comp Cas 583 Ker; *Rameshbhai Ramanlal Patel v Shree Bansidhar (P) Ltd*, (2006) 133 Comp Cas 599 Guj, alleged mismanagement and loss of substratum, petition based on *mala fide* intention and vengeance, not a proper ground.

98. (1882) 20 Ch D 169: [1881-5] All ER Rep 372.

99. *See* also *Haven Gold Mining Co, Re*, (1882) 20 Ch D 151: [1881-5] All ER Rep 585, where a company failed to acquire gold mines it was formed to work.

Similarly, where a company's business had come to a standstill owing to a banker having seized and sold all its assets in the execution of a decree,[1] and where the company's main business of supplying electricity in a particular area was taken over by the State and the company had put the compensation money in fixed deposits and did no business for seventeen long years, although it had a long list of objects,[2] winding up was ordered in either case.[3] Where after the filing of the petition on the ground of loss of the main business, the company had embarked upon other subsidiary objects mentioned in its memorandum, the court ordered winding up, because subsequent developments, cannot be taken into account.[4]

However, a temporary difficulty which does not knock out the company's bottom should not be permitted to become a ground for liquidation. For example, in *Steam Navigation Co, Re:*[5]

> A steamship company was incorporated with the principal object of acquiring a firm's business of plying steamers. This business was acquired, but very soon afterwards grave differences arose between the company and the firm. As a result the company had to return seven out of nine steamers acquired from the firm. Subsequently losses were also incurred, yet an application for winding up on the ground of failure of substratum was rejected, as the original objects had not become impossible to attain. The company had bought other steamers and there was nothing to prevent further purchases.[6]

Thus, it is a question of fact in each case whether the substratum of the company is gone or not. In *Seth Mohan Lal* v *Grain Chambers Ltd*,[7] SHAH J (later CJ) of the Supreme Court observed:

> The substratum of a company can be said to have disappeared only when the object for which it was incorporated has substantially failed, or when it is impossible to carry on the business of the company except at a loss, or the existing and possible assets are insufficient to meet the existing liabilities.

---

1. *Davco Products Ltd* v *Rameshwarla*, AIR 1954 Cal 195; *S. Sundaresan* v *Plast-o-Fibre Industries (P) Ltd*, (1993) 76 Comp Cas 38 Mad, a complete failure. *Chua Kien How* v *Goodwealth Trading (P) Ltd*, (1993) 1 SCR 486 Malaysia, the place which the company wanted to develop as its restaurant was lost, it dispensed with restaurant staff which showed that it had no intention to carry on the restaurant business in general nor had done anything in the last six months to secure any premises.
2. *A. Ramachandran* v *Narasaraopet Electric Corpn Ltd*, (1972) 42 Comp Cas 182 AP.
3. *See* also *Lawang Tahang* v *Goenka Commercial Bank Ltd*, (1960) 64 CWN 828.
4. *Rajan Nagindas Doshi* v *British Burma Petroleum Co*, (1972) 42 Comp Cas 197 Bom.
5. (1901) 10 Bom LR 107.
6. *See* also *Murlidhar* v *Bengal Steamship Co*, AIR 1920 Cal 722: 59 IC 542; *Bukhtiarpur Bihar Light Rly Co Ltd* v *Union of India*, AIR 1954 Cal 499.
7. [1968] Comp LJ 275, 285: AIR 1968 SC 772: (1968) 38 Comp Cas 543. *See* also *Bilasrai Juharmal, Re*, AIR 1962 Bom 133: (1962) 32 Comp Cas 215.

In that case owing to a long drawn out litigation the business of a company had come to a standstill and a part of its business was banned by legislation, SHAH J (later CJ) held that "we cannot on that ground direct that the company be wound up. The company could always restart business with assets it possessed."[8] Similarly, in a case before the Calcutta High Court:[9]

By reason of the acquisition of its assets, a club could not carry on its normal activities.

The court refused a winding up order on the petition of a creditor as it appeared that other club activities were going on. Even where a company had lost its business through nationalisation, the court refused an order on the ground that negotiations for compensation could be better conducted by the directors than by the liquidator.[10] Where the railway business of a company was taken over by the Central Government and with the compensation money and in accordance with its memorandum the company started the business of transporting goods, the Registrar's petition to have it wound up on the ground of loss of substratum was rejected. The Calcutta High Court advised the Registrar that he should have taken into consideration the facts that the company had no creditors, that the shareholders had expressed the intention that the business should be continued and that the company had at its disposal an enormous amount of capital.[11] Where, on the other hand, a substantial minority of shareholders was opposed to the employment of the compensation money to other objects, the court ordered winding up so as to enable the shareholders to walk away with the compensation money which may fall to their share.[12]

---

8. *Ibid.*, at p 286. *See* also LORD CAIRNS, LJ in *Suburban Hotel Co, Re*, (1866-67) 2 Ch App 737 at p 750 *See* also *Virendra Singh* v *Nandlal & Sons*, (1980) 50 Comp Cas 54 MP, where the company being insolvent, its directors were busy transferring property to themselves without proper valuation. The court ordered winding up on the ground of loss of substratum; *Bombay Gas Co* v *Hindustan Mercantile Bank Ltd*, (1980) 50 Comp Cas 202 Bom, receiving compensation on merger. *See* also *Syndicate Bank* v *Printersall (P) Ltd*, (1981) 51 Comp Cas 5 Kant, nobody left to take interest in the company.

9. *Bengal Flying Club, Re*, [1966] 2 Comp LJ 213; *Mridula Bhaskar* v *Ishwar Industries Ltd*, (1985) 58 Comp Cas 442 Del, the court refused winding up order only on account of family disputes.

10. *Eastern Telegraph Co Ltd, Re*, [1947] 2 All ER 104: (1948) 18 Comp Cas 46. *See* also *Bukhtiarpur Bihar Light Rly Co Ltd* v *Union of India*, AIR 1954 Cal 499; *Lokenath Gupta* v *Credits (P) Ltd*, [1968] 1 Comp LJ 253, at p 255, where the court also pointed out that "mere mismanagement or misconduct or even misappropriation on the part of directors is no ground for winding up."; *George* v *Athmimattam Rubber*, AIR 1968 SC 772. The mere sale of a company's main plantations does not amount to knocking out the substratum. *Malabar Industrial Co* v *A. J. Anthrapper*, (1985) 57 Comp Cas 717 Ker.

11. *K. G. Ananthakrishnan* v *Burdwan Kutwa Rly Co*, (1978) 48 Comp Cas 211 Cal. Winding up being a remedy of last resort was refused where the company was of socio-economic importance (tourism) and was picking up from its debris. *Daulat Makanmal Luthria* v *Solitaire Hotels*, (1993) 76 Comp Cas 215 Bom.

12. *Nagavararpu Krishna Pd* v *Andhra Bank Ltd*, (1983) 53 Comp Cas 73 AP. Where a company was being operated in total violation of the provisions of the Companies Act, it was ordered to be wound up, *Harikumar Rajah* v *Sovereign Dairy Industries Ltd*, (1999) 32 CLA 335 Mad; *Bharat Steel Tubes Ltd, Re*, (2004) 118 Comp Cas 69 Del, recommendation of the

(iii) *Losses*

Thirdly, it is considered just and equitable to wind up a company when it cannot carry on business except at losses. It will be needless, indeed, for a company to carry on business when there is no hope of achieving the object of trading at a profit.[13] But a mere apprehension on the part of some shareholders that the assets of the company will be frittered away and that loss instead of gain will result has been held to be no ground.[14] Similarly, the Bombay High Court observed in *Shah Steamship Navigation Co, Re*[15] that "the Court will not be justified in making a winding up order merely on the ground that the company has made losses; and is likely to make further losses."

(iv) *Oppression of Minority*

Fourthly, it is just and equitable to wind up a company where the principal shareholders have adopted an aggressive or oppressive or squeezing policy towards the minority. The decision of the Madras High Court in *R. Sabapathi Rao* v *Sabapathi Press Ltd,*[16] is an illustration in point. The Court observed:

> Where the directors of a company were able to exercise a dominating influence on the management of the company and the managing director was able to outvote the minority of the shareholders and retain the profits of the business between members of the family and there were several complaints that the shareholders did not receive a copy of the balance-sheet, nor was the auditor's report read at the general meeting, dividends were not regularly paid and the rate was diminishing, that constituted sufficient ground for winding up.

Similarly, where more than seventy per cent of a company's funds were being used for objects wholly removed from anything within the memorandum and ninety-three per cent of the shareholders wished to dissociate themselves from the new objects, the company was ordered to be wound up.[17] In *Loch* v *John Blackwood Ltd,*[18] the Privy Council ordered the

---

Board of Industrial and Financial Reconstruction that the company be wound up because it was not capable of being revived, given due consideration as showing loss of substratum. *A. Rama Goud* v *Omnitrode Aditya Electrodes (P) Ltd*, (2004) 118 Comp Cas 154 AP recommendation of BIFR not binding on court; it is only a basis for continuation of proceedings, rest of the proceedings have to be in accordance with the Companies Act.

13. A winding up on this ground was ordered in *Bachharaj Factories* v *Hirjee Mills*, AIR 1955 Bom 355. *See* also *Bristol Joint Stock Bank, Re*, (1890) 44 Ch D 703; *Davis & Co* v *Burnswick*, [1936] 1 All ER 299; *Registrar of Companies* v *M. K. Bros Ltd*, (1977) 47 Comp Cas 314 All, where the whole of the capital had been wiped out in losses, the Registrar's petition succeeded.
14. See *Mahanmandai Shastra Prakashik Samiti Ltd, Re*, (1917) 15 All LJ 193.
15. (1901) 10 Bom LR 107.
16. AIR 1925 Mad 489. *See* also *Sabapathi Press Ltd* v *Sabapathi Rao*, AIR 1930 Mad 240.
17. *Tivoli Free, Re*, [1972] VR 445; Current Law, Sept. 1972, D 30.
18. 1924 AC 783: [1924] All ER Rep 200 PC.

winding up of a company because the managing director refused to hold meetings or to pay dividends, perhaps, with a view to squeezing out the minority by purchasing their shares at an under value.

(v) *Fraudulent Purpose*

It is just and equitable to wind up a company if it has been conceived and brought forth in fraud or for illegal purposes. Thus in *Universal Mutual Aid and Poor Houses Assn v A.D. Thoppa Naidu*[19] the Madras High Court observed:

> Where the main object of a company is the conduct of a lottery, the mere fact that some of its objects were philanthropic will not prevent the company from being ordered to be wound up as being one formed for an illegal purpose.

But "the mere fact of there having been a fraud in promotion, or fraudulent misrepresentation in the prospectus, will not be sufficient to found a winding up order, for the majority of shareholders may waive the fraud".[20] Similarly, a fraud against third parties would not provide a ground for winding up.[21]

(vi) *Incorporated or Quasi-Partnership*

It has been observed that "there is little in common between the giant corporation and the family or one-man company. To apply the same legal requirements to such different organisations is productive of inconvenience and injustice."[22] In order to avoid such "inconvenience and injustice" the Act treats them differently in several respects. But even in matters in which the Act treats them alike, the courts have had to distinguish them. One such matter is the interpretation of the "just and equitable" clause in reference to the winding up of a small private company. The principle that seems to emerge from a long line of cases culminating in the House of Lords' decision in *Ebrahimi v Westbourne Galleries Ltd*,[23] is that where a private company is in essence or substance a partnership, it may be ordered to be wound up under the just and equitable clause as interpreted in accordance with the partnership principles.[24] The underlying mutual duties and rights of

---

19. AIR 1933 Mad 16: 139 IC 644.

20. *Oriental Navigation Co v Bhanaram Agarwala*, AIR 1922 Cal 365: 69 IC 241; *S. Palaniappan v Tirupur Cotton Spg & Wvg Mills Ltd*, (2003) 114 Comp Cas 288 Mad, allegations of fraud in sale of the company's assets and issue of further capital, the court said that the CLB (now court) could have been approached for remedy against such conduct. Winding up is not ordered unless an equally effective alternative remedy is exhausted.

21. *Haven Gold Mining Co, Re*, (1882) 20 Ch D 151: [1881-5] All ER Rep 585.

22. R. S. Nock, *The Ford Foundation Workshop on Company Law, July 1969*, (1970) 11. The Journal of the Society of Public Teachers of Law, 1, 7.

23. [1972] 2 WLR 1289: [1972] 2 All ER 492.

24. The decision has provoked a lot of favourable academic discussion. *See*, in particular, M. R. Chesterman, *The "Just and Equitable" Winding up of Small Private Companies*, (1973) 36

co-partners survive even when they become co-members. As Lord WILBERFORCE observed:[25]

> There is room in company law for recognition of the fact that behind the company, or amongst it, there are individuals, with rights, expectations and obligations *inter se* which are not strictly submerged in the company structure.

Yenidje Tobacco Co Ltd, Re,[26] is itself an application of the partnership principles, for the company in that case was ordered to be wound up not merely because of the deadlock between the two member-directors, but because they had forfeited mutual confidence beyond repair.

According to Lord WILBERFORCE[27] a private company can be treated as an incorporated partnership if it possesses one or probably more of the following elements:

> (*i*) An association formed or continued on the basis of a personal relationship, involving mutual confidence—this element will often be found where a pre-existing partnership has been converted into a limited company; (*ii*) an agreement, or understanding, that all, or some (for there must be sleeping members) of the shareholders shall participate in the conduct of the business; and (*iii*) restriction on the transfer of the members' interest in the company—so that if confidence is lost, or one member is removed from management, he cannot take out his stake and go elsewhere.[28]

"To this there might be also added the characteristics that the company's profits will be distributed in the form of salaries rather than 'the financially extravagant method of paying dividends'."[29] In *Atul Drug*

Mod LR 127; D. D. Prentice, *Winding Up on the Just and Equitable Ground: The Partnership Analogy*, (1973) 89 LQR 107; *Minority Shareholder's Oppression*, (1973) 89 LQR 338; N. A. Bastin, *Minority Protection in Private Companies*, (1973) New LJ 473; Trebilock, *A New Concern for the Minority Shareholder*, (1973) 17 McGILL LJ 106; L. H. Leigh, *Just and Equitable Winding Up*, (1972) 88 LQR 468; Kenneth Polak, *Companies Winding Up on Just and Equitable Ground*, 1972 Comp LJ 225.

25. [1972] 2 WLR 1289, 1294: [1972] 2 All ER 492; adopted by the Supreme Court in *Needle Industries (India) Ltd v Needle Industries Newey (India) Holding Ltd*, (1981) 3 SCC 333 at 366: AIR 1981 SC 1298: (1981) 51 Comp Cas 743.

26. [1916] 2 Ch 426: [1916-17] All ER Rep 1050.

27. *Ebrahimi v Westbourne Galleries Ltd*, [1972] 2 WLR 1289: [1972] 2 All ER 492, 500.

28. The articles of the company must carry provisions which speak of the parties' intention to maintain a structure of relations analogous to those of a partnership. *Gadadhar Dixit v Utkal Flour Mills (P) Ltd*, [1988] 2 Comp LJ 45 Ori: (1989) 66 Comp Cas 188. A whimsical conduct cannot be permitted to be used as a ground for wrecking a company. *B. V. S. S. Mani v Kowtha Business Syndicate (P) Ltd*, (1989) 65 Comp Cas 305 AP.

29. D. D. Prentice, *Winding Up on the Just and Equitable Ground: The Partnership Analogy*, (1973) 89 LQR 107, 114. The in-quote is from PLOWMAN J in *Westbourne Galleries, Re*, [1971] Ch 799, 808: [1971] 1 All ER 561. Where a company was in the nature of a partnership and was formed on the basis that a certain person would be a director, his removal from his position as a director was held to be a ground for winding up. *S. Sundaresan v Plast-o-Fibre Industries (P) Ltd*, (1993) 76 Comp Cas 38 Mad. The company was otherwise also in

House Ltd, Re[30], the Gujarat High Court suggested that the partnership analogy will apply only when a private company is a domestic concern. The court accordingly refused to apply the analogy to a private company whose shares were held by two different families. The decision seems to be somewhat unreal, for even a partnership may consist of different families.[31] A Division Bench of the Calcutta High Court in *Ragunath Prasad Jhunjhunwala* v *Hind Overseas (P) Ltd*,[32] ordered the winding up of a private company consisting of two groups. The court found that the original idea was to start a partnership venture. This was shown by their correspondence and a banking account opened by them. The shareholding of the two groups was not equal, but it was clear that the members of one group were functioning as working partners and those of the other as financial. But on appeal to the Supreme Court this decision was reversed.[33] The court laid emphasis upon the fact that the *Ebrahimi* principle would apply when the company is in substance a partnership. In this case, on the other hand, the idea of forming a partnership was abandoned at the very initial stage. The concern came into existence directly as a company. It had divergent interests in it and not merely the interests of a family or two. The exclusion from directorship in such cases cannot be a proper ground for putting the company to an end.

Once it is proved that a private company is analogous to partnership, it may be ordered to be wound up when there is an abuse of power or breach of good faith which partners owe to each other.[34] Breach of articles will be sufficient to lead to a dissolution. For example, in *American Pioneer Leather Co, Re*:[35]

> The articles of a small private company, consisting of only three members two of whom were directors, provided that any member willing to withdraw would offer his interest to the other members and in the event of their refusal to purchase, would be entitled to have the company wound up. The company was accordingly ordered to be wound up when the other members refused to purchase the shares of the petitioner.

---

a state of hopelessness. The court distinguished the matter from *G. Kasturi* v *N. Murali*, (1992) 74 Comp Cas 661, it was a family dispute between the directors and editors of the "Hindu" which had wider public representation.

30. (1971) 41 Comp Cas 352 Guj. The principle of this case was applied in *Kiran Sandhu* v *Saraya Sugar Mills*, (1998) 91 Comp Cas 146 All.

31. Re-affirmed, *Navnitlal M. Shah* v *Atul Drug Houses Ltd*, (1977) 47 Comp Cas 136 Guj.

32. (1971) 41 Comp Cas 308 Cal. Overruling the decision of A. N. RAY J (as he then was), (1971) 41 Comp Cas 279. The learned Judge reviews all the English authorities at pp 290-303. *See* also *Fildes Bros Ltd, Re*, [1970] 1 WLR 592, 596-597: [1970] 1 All ER 923.

33. *Hind Overseas (P) Ltd* v *R. P. Jhunjhunwala*, (1976) 3 SCC 259: (1976) 2 SCR 226: AIR 1976 SC 565: (1976) 46 Comp Cas 91.

34. *See* Lindley, ON PARTNERSHIP, p 588-589 (13th Edn, 1971).

35. [1918] 1 Ch 556: 118 LT 695.

Partners have the right to participate in the management of the business. If this right is denied to any director of an incorporated partnership, it would afford a ground for dissolution.[36] Entitlement to management participation in a small private company is an obligation so basic that if it is broken, the association must be dissolved. Three shareholders of a company had an equal holding with power to nominate directors. One of them sought to change his nominee which was not accepted by the others. It was held to be just and equitable to dissolve the company.[37]

Where the conduct of those in control is in accordance with the company's articles, the court would be slow to interfere. *Cuthbert Cooper & Sons Ltd, Re*[38] is an illustration of a situation of this kind, though after the decision of the House of Lords in *Ebrahimi* v *Westbourne Galleries Ltd,*[39] it seems to have lost its authority. The facts were:

> Half of the capital of a private company belonged to a father and the other half to his two elder sons. His three younger sons were employed in the company. The father died bequeathing his shares equally between his younger sons. The senior ones not only refused to accept the juniors as members, but also removed them from the company's employment and refused to supply them with copies of the company's accounts.

Even so it was held that the circumstances did not warrant an order for dissolution. "The conduct complained of ... was in all respects in accordance with the company's articles and was not shown to be *mala fide*."[40]

This decision has been adversely commented upon by the House of Lords in *Ebrahimi* v *Westbourne Galleries Ltd.*[41] It failed to take account of the fact that co-partners can have rights, expectations and obligations apart from articles and "which are not necessarily merged in the company structure". Secondly, there are circumstances in which even the exercise of legal rights as laid down in the articles may amount to breach of faith, for it may go "outside what can fairly be regarded as having been in the contemplation of the parties when they became members of the company".[42] "Articles are not the whole story; if something done in accordance therewith infringes some extraneous agreement or understanding between the parties of the quasi-partnership company, it may provide grounds for a winding up."[43] The recognition of this fact is the chief contribution of the decision of

---

36. *Davis & Collett Ltd, Re*, [1935] All ER Rep 315: 1935 Ch 693: 5 Comp Cas 467 Ch D; *Zinotty Properties Ltd, Re*, [1984] 1 WLR 1249: [1984] 3 All ER 754, where not only there was exclusion from directorship, the member was kept deprived of any information about the vital matters of the company, which was founded on their mutual trust.
37. *A & BC Chewing Gum, Re*, [1975] 1 WLR 579: [1975] 1 All ER 1017.
38. [1937] Ch 392.
39. [1972] 2 WLR 1289: [1972] 2 All ER 492.
40. M. R. Chesterman, *'Just and Equitable' Winding Up*, (1973) 36 Mod LR at p 135.
41. (1972) 2 WLR 1289: [1972] 2 All ER 492.
42. *Wondoflex Textiles (P) Ltd, Re*, [1951] VLR 458.
43. M. R. Chesterton, (1973) 36 Mod LR at p 135.

the House of Lords in the *Westbourne Galleries* case.[44] Even before this, PLOWMAN J in *Lundie Bros Ltd, Re,* ordered the winding up of a private company when a member was removed from his post as a working director. *Westbourne Galleries Ltd, Re,*[45] again presented the same kind of story before PLOWMAN J:

> *E* and *N* started business together as dealers in Persian and other carpets. *N* provided the greater part of the capital. Subsequently they incorporated a private company, holding equal shares. Still subsequently, *N's* son joined the company taking equal number of shares both from *E* and *N*. All the three were wholetime directors. They received remuneration as directors rather than dividends as members. *N* did not treat *E* as his equal. *E* complained that *N* imported carpets from Persia and sold them to the company at artificially high prices and that the company was paying for his antique business. *N* and his son, acting as majority shareholders, removed *E* from directorship. Thus his investment became useless as he could neither transfer it nor receive any dividends on it.

Even so PLOWMAN J held that he was not entitled to any relief against oppression, because he had suffered as a director and not as a member. The learned Judge, however, held that the conduct of the majority in excluding him from participation in the management only because he was perpetually complaining was an abuse of power and a breach of good faith, which entitled him to a winding up order. The Court of Appeal reversed that aspect of the decision but the House of Lords restored it. Lord WILBERFORCE, who delivered the leading speech, was of the opinion that the principles in this area should be developed as part of company law and not that of partnership law. Such principles may be parallel to those of partnership law and may be applied to private companies possessing partnership features.[46]

---

44. (1972) 2 WLR 1289.
45. [1970] 1 WLR 1378: [1970] 3 All ER 374. See *S. S. Rajakumar v Perfect Castings Ltd,* (1968) 38 Comp Cas 187 Mad, where the court refused to order winding up when a director was removed from office even though the members of the small private company had orally agreed that the company would function as a partnership.
46. Serious disputes between members making it impossible for business to be carried on could have the same effect. *R. P. Shah v Engineers' Enterprises (P) Ltd,* (1977) 47 Comp Cas 294 Bom. Henry E. Markson, *Winding Up: The Partnership Analogy,* 1978 New Law Journal 115; *See* also *A & BC Chewing Gum, Re,* [1975] 1 WLR 579, 590-91: [1975] 1 All ER 1017, breach of agreement. Where the relations registered an irretrievable breakdown, the court ordered winding up giving the option to one family group to buy out the other. *Krishan Lal Ahuja v Suresh Kumar Ahuja,* (1983) 53 Comp Cas 60 Del; *Moti Films (P) Ltd v Harish Bansal,* (1983) 54 Comp Cas 856 Del, where also the court found no evidence of mutual cooperation between family members. *S. Sundaresan v Plast-o-Fibre Industries (P) Ltd,* (1993) 76 Comp Cas 38 Mad, removal of a director of a private company in breach of understanding, held a good ground. This would not be so where the company is a big one, *G. Kasturi v N. Murali,* (1992) 74 Comp Cas 661. Providing directorship to the daughter of the deceased managing director of the company, not wrong in the circumstances, *Anisha K. Shah v Fostenex (P) Ltd,* (1995) 17 Corpt LA 5 Mad: AIR 1995 Mad 67: (1995) 82 Comp Cas 514.

Following this case, the High Court of Delhi has pointed out that what matters is not whether a member has been expelled or not, but whether there has been breach of mutual understanding. Thus where the understanding was that parity of shareholding was to be maintained, it was held that an attempt by one group to take-over the company by increasing its shares would enable the court to exercise its powers.[47]

Public Interest

Winding up can also be ordered under this section when public interest demands it. A type of conduct which comes in conflict with public interest is indicated in a Court of Appeal decision in England.[48] The company in question had no proper records; it pretended to be an impartial adviser in matters of investment when, in fact, it was only a share-vending company; the American companies in which the clients were advised to invest their moneys were such whose shares could not be easily traded and the company was also violating its investment agreement. The court was of the view that public interest demanded winding up of a company which was wasting the capital resources of the country. It was not material that the company had already suspended its business, because, if the company was permitted to remain alive, it may again start befooling small investors.[49] Where the company's business was unlawful because of lack of authorisation under the Financial Services Act, 1986 [English] and there was no evidence of the possibility of grant of such authorisation in the future, the court ordered winding up.[50] Another company was ordered to be wound up in public interest because the company posed danger to the investing public and was also technically insolvent.[51] In another case, winding up was found to be desirable because of many undesirable practices such as false invoicing.[52]

The sanction of winding up being too severe was not inflicted on a company which had committed inadvertent breaches of Air Traffic

---

47. *Bhaskar Stoneware Pipes (P) Ltd* v *R. N. Bhaskar*, (1988) 63 Comp Cas 184 Del. Above all, the matter being entirely in the discretion of the court, an order may be passed where neither the one group of shareholders nor the other have been guilty of any prejudicial conduct, if it is otherwise in the fitness of things. *A Company, Re, (No 00370 of 1987)*, [1988] 1 WLR 1068. See the Supreme Court decisions in *Industrial Credit and Investment Corpn of India* v *Srinivas Agencies*, (1996) 4 SCC 165: (1996) 86 Comp Cas 255 SC, where the factors governing the grant of leave to a secured creditor have been recounted. See *Kiran Sandhu* v *Saraya Sugar Mills Ltd*, (1998) 91 Comp Cas 146 All, where none of the just and equitable grounds were available.
48. *Walter L Jacob & Co Ltd, Re*, 1989 BCLC 345 CA.
49. Another example of the same kind, *A Company, Re, (No 001951 of 1987)*, 1988 BCLC 182 CLD.
50. *Market Wizard Systems Ltd, Re*, [1998] 2 BCLC 282 Ch D.
51. *Secy of State for Trade and Industry* v *Metric Components plc*, Feb 17, 2000 Palmer in company, June 2000 at p 5.
52. *Millennium Advanced Technology Ltd, Re*, (2004) 2 BCLC 77 Ch D.

Licencing Regulations. The court said that even deliberate breaches might not have justified the extreme penalty of winding up.[53]

An order of winding up may be refused when it would operate against public interest. Where a company was running profitably and had a muster-roll of 700 workers who opposed winding up, a creditor's petition for winding up was rejected.[54]

Whether a petition is based on insolvency or on the just and equitable ground, there is a requirement that a creditor should be petitioning by pursuing his private interest attributable to his status as a creditor. This requirement has to be satisfied if the petition is not to be an abuse of the process. The desire on the part of the creditor essentially collateral to his status as such to achieve a public interest in bringing about winding up of a company which had appropriated public funds for private gain, is not an alternative justification. The court found that the principal motive of the creditor's petition was not protection of public interest. There could be discerned within the petition a sufficient private interest as a contingent or prospective creditor in having the company wound up. The assertion in the petition of public interest reasons for winding up did not render the proceedings as a whole an abuse of process.[55]

Existence of Alternative Remedy

The remedy of winding up is a remedy of last resort. It may not be allowed where an equally effective alternative remedy is available. Allegations of misuse of funds, fraudulent transactions, removal of a director under a forged resignation, failure to supply essential documents to shareholders, increase in remuneration of directors without general body approval, illegal allotments of shares, could have been taken care of by a petition under Section 398 against mismanagement of the company's affairs. A petition for winding up was not entertained.[56]

---

53. *A Company, Re*, (*No 5669 of 1998*), [2000] 1 BCLC 427 Ch D, affirmed by the Court of Appeal in *Time Travel (UK) Ltd, Re*, March 2000, CA.
54. *Manjulabai* v *Jayant Vitamins Ltd*, (1991) 71 Comp Cas 443 MP.
55. *Millennium Advanced Technology Ltd, Re*, (2004) 1 WLR 2177: (2005) 123 Comp Cas 170 Ch D.
56. *M. Mohan Babu* v *Heritage Foods India Ltd*, (2002) 108 Comp Cas 771 AP; *K. Mohan Babu* v *Heritage Foods India Ltd*, (2002) 108 Comp Cas 793 AP, internal squabbles among directors, not a ground for winding up. It could have been resolved through other forums. The petitioner must show that he had exhausted other remedies or that the other remedies would not have been helpful. *Takshila Hospital* v *Jagmohan Mathur*, (2003) 115 Comp Cas 343 Raj, need for resorting to alternative mechanism emphasised. *K. Venkateswara Rao* v *Phoenix Share & Stock Brokers (P) Ltd*, (2003) 115 Comp Cas 818 Bom, no proof of allegations of lack of probity, etc. *Rameshbhai Ramanbhai Patel* v *Shree Bansidhar (P) Ltd*, (2005) 58 SCL 396: (2005) 127 Comp Cas 806 Guj, alternative remedy for prevention of oppression available; *Jagdamba Polymers Ltd* v *Neo-Sack Co*, (2006) 129 Comp Cas 160 MP, the company disputed the debt and the petitioner had other remedies.

Who can apply [S. 439]

An application to the court for the winding up of a company is made by a petition.[57] A petition may be presented by any one of the following:

1. *Petition by Company*

The company may itself present a petition for winding up. Petition by the company will be particularly necessary when the only ground for winding up is that the company has passed a special resolution to that effect. There must be a valid resolution to enable the company to take this step. Thus, where a judge passed an order for winding up on the ground that the majority of the shareholders at a meeting were in favour of winding up, it was held that that was not, in the absence of a valid special resolution, a sufficient ground for compulsory winding up.[58] Again, the petition must be presented by the company itself. Where, for example, in *Patiala Banaspati Co, Re:*[59]

An application for winding up of a company was made by the managing director of the company. Rejecting the petition the court said, "the petition by the company must have behind it the decision of the general meeting. The managing director or directors cannot constitute the company for the purpose."

Where a winding up petition was filed on behalf of the company by a person who was not authorised by the board of directors, the petition was held to be incompetent.[60]

2. *Creditor's Petition* [S. 439(2)]

A creditor may apply for winding up.[61] The word "creditor" includes a secured creditor, debenture-holder[62] and a trustee for debenture-holders. Accordingly "a secured creditor is as much entitled as of right to file a petition as an unsecured creditor".[63] "Winding up is equally good whether it is obtained by a secured creditor or an unsecured creditor."[64] It is not even

---

57. A petition can be filed through a special power of attorney and not through a general power. *Shantilal Khushaldas & Bros (P) Ltd* v *C. S. Shah*, (1993) 77 Comp Cas 253 Bom. Petition would lie in the Bench of the High Court in whose jurisdiction the registered office of the company is situate and not in the Principal Bench of the High Court, *Vimal Kumar* v *Bhilwara Wooltax Ltd*, (1993) 1 Raj LW 554: (1993) 2 Raj LR 289; *Registrar of Companies* v *Kamal Infosys Ltd*, (2006) 133 Comp Cas 455.
58. *Oriental Navigation Co* v *Bhanaram Agarwala*, AIR 1922 Cal 365: 69 IC 241.
59. AIR 1953 Pepsu 195.
60. *BOC India Ltd* v *Zinc Products & Co (P) Ltd*, (1996) 86 Comp Cas 358 Pat.
61. A joint petition by several creditors paying single court fee has been held to be valid, *A. V. Krishna* v *Karnataka Leasing & Commercial Corpn Ltd*, (1995) 83 Comp Cas 764 Kant.
62. For the right of the debenture-holder, see *Narotamdas T. Toprani* v *Bombay Dyeing and Mfg Co Ltd*, [1986] 3 Comp LJ 179 Bom.
63. *Karnataka Vegetable Oils & Refineries Ltd* v *Madras Industrial Investment Corpn*, AIR 1955 Mad 582.
64. JESSEL MR in *Moor* v *Anglo-Italian Bank*, (1897) 10 Ch D 681. Where a part of the claim of the secured creditor was satisfied out of the sale proceeds of the security (goods pledged), he

necessary for a secured creditor to apply that he should give up his security.[65] But where a petition is brought by a contingent or prospective creditor, it shall not be admitted unless the leave of the court is obtained for its admission. Such leave is not to be granted unless the court is satisfied that there is a *prima facie* case for winding up the company and reasonable security for costs has been given.[66] The Calcutta High Court has observed that a creditor would not ordinarily be heard to urge that winding up order should be made because the substratum of the company was gone, not for the reason that he was technically and as a matter of law barred from taking that ground at all, but for the reason that it was not proper ground for the creditor to urge except in very special circumstances.[67] Sometimes a creditor's petition is opposed by other creditors. In such cases the court may ascertain the wishes of the majority of the creditors. But their opinion does not bind the court. The question will ultimately depend upon the state of the company. If the company is commercially insolvent and the object of trading at a profit cannot be attained, winding up order would follow as a matter of course *(ex debito justitiae)*.[68]

A creditor who is pursuing his ordinary remedy of a civil suit for the enforcement of his claim can also make the same claim as a ground for winding up. The court may order the stay of his suit but cannot disqualify him on that ground.[69] The pendency of an application filed by the creditor before the Debt Recovery Tribunal did not affect the jurisdiction of the court to admit the creditor's petition for winding up.[70]

A foreign creditor can also apply for winding up. A company did not pay its foreign commission agent. He asked for winding up. The company's defence that Reserve Bank permission was necessary did not appeal to the court. It was a part of the company's duty to make necessary arrangements.[71] A foreign arbitration award can be a good ground for

---

was allowed to file a petition, being still a creditor. *Vyasa Bank Ltd* v *Universal Investment Trust Ltd*, [1990] 1 Comp LJ 353 Del.

65. *India Electric Works, Re*, [1969] 2 Comp LJ 169.

66. S. 439(8). Where a contingent creditor's petition, filed after obtaining leave was dismissed on a technical ground, he was allowed to proceed again without having to obtain a fresh leave. *Pioneer Tubwell Industries (P) Ltd* v *SIP Resins Ltd*, [1990] 1 Comp LJ 110 Cal.

67. *Bengal Flying Club, Re*, [1966] 2 Comp LJ 213, following *Bukhtiarpur Bihar Light Rly Co Ltd* v *Union of India*, AIR 1954 Cal 499. A shareholder of a private company, who broke out from the only other shareholder, was incidentally a lender to the company also and filed a creditor's petition for winding up on the ground of breakdown of relations and the same was not allowed. *A Company (No 003028 of 1987), Re*, 1988 BCLC 282 CLD.

68. *Ibid*. This ruling of the Calcutta High Court is opposed to that of the Madras High Court in *Karnataka Vegetable Oils & Refineries Ltd* v *Madras Industrial Investment Corpn*, AIR 1955 Mad 582 which followed the English authority of *Moor* v *Anglo-Italian Bank*, (1879) 10 Ch D 681.

69. *Central Bank of India* v *Sukhani Mining Industries*, (1977) 47 Comp Cas 1 Pat; *Vivek Hire Purchase & Leasing Ltd* v *Paisa Power Com (P) Ltd*, (2006) 129 Comp Cas 343 Mad, Civil suit for recovery, no bar.

70. *Viral Filaments Ltd* v *Indus Ind Bank Ltd*, (2003) 113 Comp Cas 85 Bom.

71. *Eurometal Ltd* v *Aluminium Cables and Conductors (P) Ltd*, (1983) 53 Comp Cas 744 Cal.

winding up when it has been declared by the competent jurisdiction to be enforceable in India under Section 49 of the Arbitration and Conciliation Act, 1996.[72] A guarantor is a prospective creditor and has a right to apply for winding up.[73] An individual note holder holding beneficially through a depository was held to be a creditor for the purpose of filing a petition.[74] The court also added that "securities" for the purposes of the Act need not only be those which are marketable in India.

Where the claim of a creditor is enforceable at the time of the petition, it does not matter if it ceases to be enforceable by the time of the order.[75]

An unpaid worker is not a creditor for this purpose. The union of workers has also no *locus standi* to file a petition because there are alternative remedies under industrial laws.[76]

An unregistered firm, being not competent to file a suit, was not allowed to file a petition unless the partners also joined it.[77]

The Karnataka High Court has held differently. To the extent to which a company is indebted to its worker or employee for wages or salary, he has a right to apply and his petition can be entertained. Such a petition is as much subject to the discretion of the court as any other petition. This has nothing to do with the ranking of workers' claims under Section 529-A.[78]

A petition by erstwhile directors of the company for recovery of their dues was held to be not maintainable.[79]

---

72. *Marina World Shipping Corpn* v *Jindal Exports (P) Ltd*, (2004) 122 Comp Cas 399 Del; *Vinayak Oil & Fats (P) Ltd* v *Andre (Caymon Islands) Trading Co Ltd*, (2005) CLC 588 (Cal), a foreign award should first be tested for its validity under Ss. 47, 48, 49 of the Arbitration and Conciliation Act, 1996.

73. *Kermeen Foods (P) Ltd, Re*, (1985) 58 Comp Cas 156 Guj.

74. *Essar Steel Ltd* v *G. Emerging Market Fund*, (2003) 116 Comp Cas 248 Guj.

75. *Diwan Chand Kapoor* v *New Rialto Cinema (P) Ltd*, (1987) 62 Comp Cas 810 Del; *Anil Pratap Singh* v *Onida Sawak Ltd*, (2002) 112 Comp Cas 701 Del, time-barred debt, petition not allowed. *Associated Journals Ltd* v *Mysore Paper Mills Ltd*, (2006) 132 Comp Cas 470 (SC), some errors in the supporting affidavit were allowed to be corrected, nothing wrong.

76. *Mumbai Labour Union* v *Indo French Industries Ltd*, (2002) 110 Comp Cas 408 Bom. Also to the same effect, *Khimjibhai Sanabhai Parmar* v *Sevalia Cement Works*, (2005) 60 SCL 496 (All).

77. *Deb Paints (P) Ltd* v *Universal Lime Industries*, (2002) 110 Comp Cas 429 Cal. *Everett Travel Service* v *ASM Shipping Ltd*, (2004) 118 Comp Cas 209 Bom, the petitioning creditor was paid off by the company and he was seeking withdrawal of his petition when another creditor applied that he be substituted for continuation of the petition. The court has to see whether such creditor had the right to file a petition if he had done so originally, in this case the company admitted his claim, the court allowed substitution.

78. *Ashok Mahajan* v *Kaindi India (P) Ltd*, 2004 CLC 1642: (2005) 60 SCL 548 (Kant); *P.K. Passi* v *NEPC India Ltd*, (2006) 131 Comp Cas 176 Mad, arrears of salary not a debt, remedy under Industrial Disputes Act; *Vans Gopal Singh* v *Jaipur Udyog*, (2006) 130 Comp Cas 697 Raj.

79. *Gopal Krishna Sharma* v *Shahibi General Finance & Investments Ltd*, (2005) 125 Comp Cas 96 Raj. To the same effect, *Argha Sen* v *Interra Information Technologies (India) Ltd*, (2006) 133 Comp Cas 49 Del. Apart from being regarded as creditors, workers have no *locus standi*. There was acknowledgement by managing director by e-mail. Limitation started from the date of e-mail.

Where the petition is to be filed through an agent, he must be specifically authorised for the purposes of petition. A general authorisation for suits and proceedings against the company is not going to be sufficient. A power of attorney which was not bearing any date or place of execution was held to be invalid.[80] Where a petition was filed by a power of attorney holder more than eleven years after the disappearance of the person who granted the power, the petition was held to be incompetent unless the attorney proved that his grantor was still alive.[81]

3. *Contributory's Petition*

On the commencement of the winding up of a company, its shareholders are called contributories.[82] Any contributory or contributories may present a petition for winding up.[83] Where the ground of winding up is the reduction in membership below the statutory minimum, any contributory or contributories may apply.[84] But when the application is founded on any other ground, it will be requisite that the shares in respect of which the petitioner is contributory were originally allotted to him or he has been the registered holder[85] for at least six months during the eighteen months immediately before the commencement of the winding up, or the shares have devolved on him through the death of a former holder. In a case on the point :[86]

A transfer had been executed, stamped and dated in June 1967; the company did not register it until October, 1968. A petition presented by

80. *Vimal C. Sodhani* v *Parag Fans & Cooling Systems Ltd*, (2006) 133 Comp Cas 286 MP.
81. *Parbati Dasgupta* v *Official Liquidator*, (2006) 130 Comp Cas 427 Cal.
82. S. 426. *Naresh Kumar Agarwal* v *Davender Kumar Mittal*, (1996) 62 Del LT 595, the court will not go into inquiring whether the petitioner was shareholder to a certain extent. *Shakuntala Bali* v *Eastern Linkers (P) Ltd*, (1995) 60 Del LT 497, established shareholding through legal decision, cannot be reopened. *Anil Arora* v *Arora Aluminium & Allied Works (P) Ltd*, (2006) 132 Comp Cas 221 All, on the death of the contributory his son was substituted. It was not necessary that he should have been holding shares for a particular length of time.
83. S. 439(1) *(c)*. Where a joint petition was filed by a contributory and a creditor, only the latter petition was taken up; contributory-director was not able to establish a cause by the fact that he was removed from membership. *B. P. Gupta* v *Standard Enamel Works (P) Ltd*, (1987) 62 Comp Cas 36 Del.
84. S. 439(4)*(a)*.
85. S. 439(4)*(b)*. Shares must be registered in the contributory's name. The Mad HC in *Nagoslakshmi* v *Mannar Guddi Transports*, [1968] 1 Comp LJ, declined an applicant on whom shares had only devolved and had not been registered in his name.
86. *Gattopardo Ltd, Re*, [1969] 2 All ER 344: [1969] 1 WLR 619. *Vasant Holiday Homes (P) Ltd* v *Madan V. Prabhu*, (2003) 116 Comp Cas 172 Bom, where this requirement was not proved by the contributory who petitioned for winding up. *Naranbhai R. Patel* v *OL, Gujarat State Textile Corpn Ltd*, (2003) 114 Comp Cas 642 Guj, claim for advocate's fee filed after six years, not entertained. *Chloro Controls (India) (P) Ltd* v *Seven Trent Water Purification Inc*, (2006) 131 Comp Cas 501 Bom, transferee company in amalgamation whose name does not appear in the register of members of the transferor company is not contributory by operation of law.

the shareholder in December, 1968 for winding up was held demurrable as she had not held her shares for six months as required by the Act.

But where a company had been ordered to allot shares and had failed to do so, it was held that the person in whose favour the order had been made was qualified to apply.[87]

A question in this connection used to concern the courts in the past. Suppose, there is a contributory holding fully paid-up shares so that his liability is nil. Similarly, suppose, the company has no or insufficient assets so that the contributories will get no return of capital in the winding up. In such circumstances, a contributory's petition would be rejected. The rule was that "if he presents a petition, he must allege and prove, at least to the extent of a *prima facie* case, that there are assets of such amount as that in the winding up he will have a tangible interest".[88] The rule was followed by some High Courts in India also.[89] But now there is a clear provision in the Act which declares that "a contributory shall be entitled to present a petition for winding up, notwithstanding that he may be the holder of fully paid-up shares or that the company may have no assets at all, or may have no surplus assets left for distribution among the shareholders after the satisfaction of its liabilities".[90] Hence, at present, "want of assets may be an element in determining whether the petition is *bona fide,* but, except to that extent, it will not be a relevant consideration for determining whether winding up should be ordered or not".[91]

But in England the rule has been re-affirmed by BUCKLEY J in a case,[92] where he said:

> In my judgment it remains a rule of this court that where a fully paid shareholder petitions for compulsory winding up he must show, on the fact of his petition, a *prima facie* probability that there will be assets available for distribution amongst the shareholders.

---

87. *Patent Steam Engine Co, Re*, (1878) 8 Ch D 464.
88. Buckley on COMPANIES ACTS, 9th Edn, p 321. For English authorities, see *The Patent Artificial Stone Co, Re*, 34 LJ Ch 330; *Lancashire Brick & Tile Co, Re*, 34 LJ Ch 331; *Rica Gold Washing Cò, Re*, (1879) LR 11 Ch D 36; *Diamond Fuel Co, Re*, (1879) 13 Ch D 400; *Iron Colliery Co, Re*, (1882) 20 Ch D 442. For a criticism of this rule *see* Gwyneth Pitt, *Winding Up on the Just and Equitable Ground*, (1977) New Law Journal 619 discussing *Chesterfield Catering Co Ltd, Re*, [1976] 3 All ER 294, where the petition of the executors of the deceased shareholder was rejected only on the ground that there would be no surplus assets, though the company which ran a club was for all intents and purposes dead and though the executor stated that he was not able to administer the estate unless the affairs of the moribund company were sorted out.
89. *See*, for example, *Bharat Bank v Lajpat Rai Sawhney*, AIR 1950 EP 328; *Imperial Oil Soap & General Mills Ltd v Ram Chand*, AIR 1916 Lah 78(2).
90. S. 439(3).
91. For authorities see *Sri Nataraja Textile Mills Ltd v S. V. Angidi Chettair*, [1954] 1 MLJ 468; *Cine Industries & Recording Co Ltd, Re*, AIR 1942 Bom 231: 44 Bom LR 387.
92. *Othery Construction Co, Re*, [1966] 1 All ER 145, 147: [1966] 2 Comp LJ 46

Following this, PLOWMAN J rejected a contributory's petition on the ground that the company was "hopelessly insolvent".[93]

A shareholder filed a petition for a winding up order on the ground that he had been misled by representations in the company's prospectus. The court returned his petition with the remark that an alternative remedy was available to him under Section 62 of the Act.[94]

4. *Registrar's Petition* [S. 439(5)]

The Registrar of Companies is also entitled to present a petition for winding up on any of the grounds of winding up by the court, except the first, namely, that the company has passed a special resolution. But he shall not present a petition on the ground of the company's inability to pay its debts "unless it appears to him either from the financial condition of the company as disclosed in its balance-sheet[95] or from the report of a special auditor appointed under Section 233-A or an inspector appointed under Section 235 or 237, that the company is unable to pay its debts". In all cases, however, the Registrar has to obtain sanction of the Central Government to the presentation of a petition and the latter shall not grant the sanction unless the company has been afforded an opportunity to make its representation, if any.[96]

5. *Central Government's Petition*

The Central Government is also authorised by the Act, in certain cases, to present a petition for winding up. Section 243 enables the Government to petition for winding up where it appears from the report of inspectors appointed to investigate the affairs of a company under Section 235 that the business of the company has been conducted for fraudulent or unlawful purposes as explained in sub-clauses (*i*) and (*ii*) of clause (*b*) of Section 237.[97] The Government may authorise any person to act on its behalf for the purpose.[98]

6. *Central Government or State Government's petition*

If a case falls under Section 433(*h*) (anti-national acts), the Central Government or the State Government may apply to the court for winding up of a company [S. 439(1)(*g*)].[99]

---

93. *Expanded Plugs Ltd, Re*, [1966] 1 All ER 877: [1966] 2 Comp LJ 115.
94. *Prashant Kushalchand Shah* v *Rinku Polychem Ltd*, (2000) 100 Comp Cas 170 Bom.
95. Such condition was evident in *Registrar of Companies* v *Navjivan Trading & Finance (P) Ltd*, (1978) 48 Comp Cas 402 Guj.
96. S. 439 (6). It has been held by the Calcutta High Court in *Standard Brands Ltd, Re*, (1980) 50 Comp Cas 75 Cal, that the petition must be presented within three years from the date of sanction, otherwise it would become time-barred, S. 137 of the Limitation Act being applicable.
97. S. 439(1) (*f*). See under INVESTIGATION, *ante*.
98. S. 243.
99. Companies (Second Amendment) Act, 2002 has inserted a new clause (*g*) in S. 439(1).

Petition where company under voluntary winding up [S. 440]

Conversion of Voluntary Winding Up into Winding Up by Court

A petition for an order of winding up by the court may be presented where the company is already under voluntary liquidation. Such a petition may be presented by any one of those specified in Section 439 or by the Official Liquidator. The court will make such an order only when convinced that the liquidation already under process cannot be continued with due regard to the interests of creditors or contributories or both. In a case of this kind, the court found that the conduct of the creditors' meeting was totally unsatisfactory. The manner of appointment of liquidator justified serious complaints by creditors. The applicant might have a genuine sense of injustice if the voluntary liquidator continued to function. The need of investigation of the affairs of the company could have been better fulfilled by the official liquidator. Winding up by court was ordered.[1]

Powers of Court [S. 443]

After hearing a winding up petition,[2] the court may dismiss it with or without costs:[3] or adjourn the hearing[4] or make any interim order[5] or make an order for winding up[6] or any other order it thinks fit.[7] The court can also

---

1. *Inside Sport Ltd, Re*, [2000] 1 BCLC 302 Ch D.
2. The Supreme Court held by a majority in *National Textile Workers' Union v Ramakrishnan*, (1983) 1 SCC 228: (1983) 53 Comp Cas 184 that the workers have a right to be heard and file appeals. They may not be served with a notice to appear, but they may appear of their own motion. The court would be very slow to order winding up and would explore all possible avenues of keeping the company alive, where winding up would throw a large number of workers out of employment. *Indian Turpentine & Resin Co v Pioneer Consolidated Co of India Ltd*, (1988) 64 Comp Cas 169 Del. Disputes about ownership may also be examined if they are not so mixed up with the propriety of exclusion from management that they cannot be isolated. *A Company, Re, ex p, SP*, 1989 BCLC 579 CLD.
3. See *A Company (No 0067980 of 1995), Re*, (1996) 2 BCLC 48 Ch D, a solicitor who filed a petition without belief that the company was unable to pay its debts, was ordered to pay the whole of wasted costs incurred by the company.
4. *Central Bank of India v Maekenzies Ltd*, (1977) 47 Comp Cas 306 Bom, where many adjournments were allowed. *National Transport and General Co (P) Ltd, Re*, (1990) 69 Comp Cas 791 P&H where an order staying proceedings was withdrawn because it was being abused.
5. Which would necessarily include the appointment of a receiver, *State Bank of India v Poddar Mills Ltd*, [1989] 2 Comp LJ 189 Bom.
6. S. 443(1). The court may put off proceedings but no such order was made only on the ground that a petition under Ss. 397 and 398 was pending for prevention of oppression and mismanagement. *A. K. Puri v Devi Dass Gopal Kishan Ltd*, (1995) 17 Corpt LA 1: AIR 1995 J&K 24. The company sought an adjournment of the petition presented by the Secretary of State in public interest. The company wanted to adduce fresh evidence. The court granted it on strict conditions as to costs. *A Company, Re (005445 of 1996)*, [1998] 1 BCLC 98.
7. Exercising this power in the case of a family private company (father and two sons) where a son died and his shares were transmitted to his widow's name who neither received any dividend nor was given remuneration by making her a member of the board of directors, the court, on her petition for winding up, directed that she should be made a director in her husband's position and given like remuneration, *Anisha K. Shah v Fostenex (P) Ltd*, (1995) 17 Corpt LA 5 Mad: AIR 1995 Mad 67: (1995) 82 Comp Cas 514; *Altos India Ltd v Bharat*

issue a conditional order of winding up. In a case before the Orissa High Court,[8] a company could not pay its creditors for over two years in spite of statutory notices, the reasons being that the business had suffered closure on account of adverse circumstances. The company was, however, making sincere efforts, to revive itself. The court ordered winding up but stayed the operation of the order for six months to enable the company to pay the petitioner, if it could, failing which the order would come into force. In a similar case before the Calcutta High Court,[9] keeping in view the improving industrial climate in the State and the future prospects of the company, winding up was stayed enabling the company to pay the decreed debt by instalments and to relapse to winding up in case of default. The court may conduct an inquiry into the solvency of the company before ordering admission and advertisement of the petition.[10]

The court passed a decree in favour of the creditor on consent terms, the managing director guaranteeing the payment. It was not a fraudulent preference within the meaning of Section 531. Neither the company nor the managing director could pay. The creditor could proceed against the managing director.[11]

Where the allegations made by the petitioners regarding the policy of low dividends and high directors' remuneration constituted a conduct of the three companies' affairs that was unfairly prejudicial to the non-director shareholders, the court said that by far the most likely form of relief they would obtain from the court would be an order that the respondents purchase the petitioners' shares in the companies. The making of a winding up order on a contributories' petition invoking the just and equitable ground was a remedy of last resort. Since the court would set a fair price for the petitioners' shares.[12]

While passing a winding up order, the court may direct that workers' grievances should be redressed.[13]

Telecom Ltd, (2001) 103 Comp Cas 6 P&H, order of sale of the company's assets in the interest of all concerned even before an order of winding up was passed.

8. *Misrilal Dharma Chand (P) Ltd* v *B. Patnaik Mines (P) Ltd*, (1978) 48 Comp Cas 494 Ori.
9. *Unique Cardboard Box Mfg Co, Re*, (1978) 48 Comp Cas 599 Cal. *See* also *Bombay Metropolitan Transport Corpn Ltd* v *Employees*, (1990) 69 Comp Cas 465, winding up order against a public utility company refused. *Maharashtra General Kamgar Union-Intervenor, Ibid.*
10. *Air Wings (P) Ltd* v *Victoria Air Cargo*, (1995) 17 Corpt LA 114: AIR 1995 Kant 69. Advertisement is compulsory; where two petitions are pending both must be advertised. An order without advertisement is liable to be set aside. *Falcon Gulf Ceramics Ltd* v *Industrial Designs Bureau*, AIR 1994 Raj 120. The court postponed order of advertisement and allowed time to company to raise funds, *Karnataka Leasing and Commercial Corpn Ltd* v *Lalitha Holla*, (1995) 83 Comp Cas 127 Kant; *NEPC Agro Food Ltd* v *Hindustan Thompson Associates Ltd*, (2002) 111 Comp Cas 169 Mad, the court appointed a chartered accountant for ascertaining the amount due to the petitioning creditors.
11. *Pratibha Inderjit Kapur* v *Nilesh Lalit Parekh*, (2002) 111 Comp Cas 177 Bom.
12. *A Company (No 004415 of 1996), Re*, (1997) 1 BCLC 479 Ch D.
13. *Maharashtra State Financial Corpn* v *Orkay Industries Ltd*, [1999] 1 Comp LJ 388 Bom.

A winding up petition is maintainable only in the court having jurisdiction over the place where the registered office of the company is situate.[14] Where the agreement provided for jurisdiction at California courts and the courts there had jurisdiction otherwise, other courts became excluded.[15]

Commencement of Winding Up [S. 441]

Winding up commences not from the date of the order, it shall be deemed to commence from the time of the presentation of the petition.[16] But where, before the presentation of the petition, a resolution has been passed by the company for winding up, the winding up shall be deemed to have commenced at the time of the passing of the resolution.[17] Where there were more than one petitions, winding up was deemed to have commenced from the date of the earliest of the creditor's petition. The agreement to sell the company's property executed after that date became void.[18] The principle of relation back does not apply to the passing to the Tribunal the custody of the company's property. Such custody is reckoned from its actual date.[19] The process of winding up takes effect from the date of the order.[20]

Rescission of Order [S. 443]

The court has power under Section 443 to rescind any of its orders including a winding up order. A company was wound up by mistake caused by similarity of names. The company was allowed to seek rescission of the order and removal of the order from the Registrar's Register of Companies.[21] In a similar earlier case where a wrong address was mentioned by the petitioner company and a winding up order was passed against a company who was completely unaware of the proceedings, the

---

14. *Anil Cold Tyres Retreaders* v *Rungta Projects Ltd,* (2004) 56 SCL 42 Raj.
15. *Yokogawa Blue Star Ltd* v *Soffia Software Ltd,* (2004) 119 Comp Cas 929 Mad.
16. S. 441(2). *Administrator, MCC Finance Ltd* v *Ramesh Gandhi,* (2005) 127 Comp Cas 85 Mad, where two petitions were filed one by a creditor and the other by the Reserve Bank, it was held that winding up commenced from the date of the first petition though that petition was dismissed.
17. S. 441(1). Vesting of property in the court, however, does not relate back. *Arya Varta Plywood* v *Rajasthan State J & J Corpn,* [1990] 1 Comp LJ 222 Del, under S. 435 the High Court ordering a winding-up can transfer the proceedings to a District Court subordinate to it, or according to convenience, from one District Court to another [S. 436]. Proceedings commenced in a wrong District Court may be ordered to be continued. [S. 437] These powers can be exercised at any stage of the proceedings. [S. 438]
18. *Y. S. Spinners Ltd* v *Official Liquidator, Shri Ambica Mills Ltd,* (2000) 100 Comp Cas 547 Guj.
19. *Aryavrata Plywood* v *Rajasthan State I&I Corpn,* (1991) 72 Comp Cas 5 Del.
20. *Vasantha Ramanan* v *Official Liquidator,* (2003) 114 Comp Cas 747 Mad.
21. *Calmex Ltd, Re,* [1989] 1 All ER 485 CLD. The exercise of this power would depend upon circumstances. *G.T. Swamy* v *Goodluck Agencies,* [1989] 1 Comp LJ 215, following *Sudarshan Chits (India) Ltd* v *O. Sukumaran Pillai,* (1985) 58 Comp Cas 633 SC. A winding up order was readily recalled where the debt of the petitioning creditor was paid off and no other creditor either asked for winding or opposed the recalling of the order. *G.T. Swamy* v *Goodluck Agencies,* (1990) 69 Comp Cas 819 Kant.

order was set aside, but the company's action against the petitioning company for compensation for loss caused was not allowed. The court said, after reviewing a number of cases on the neighbourhood principle, that there was no duty owed to a litigant to give his correct address.[22] Where the merits of the case became ignored because the company's application for amendment of its pleadings was not allowed, the order of winding up was set aside.[23] The order of winding up was also revoked where the company paid off the petitioner and efforts were on for revival of the company.[24]

The court may revoke the order of admission of a petition where there is an extraordinary situation like abuse of the process, but not when the company is asking for it on the ground of a bona fide dispute. That can be taken up at the hearing.[25]

Stay of Proceedings before Order [S. 442]

Even before any order is made by the court, the company, any creditor or contributory may ask the court that proceedings against the company pending before the Supreme Court or any High Court should be stayed or those pending before any other court should be restrained, the court may pass an order as it thinks fit. The power of the court is extensive and covers all kinds of proceedings, whether of civil, criminal or revenue nature. But it will be used only in circumstances of real need.[26] The proceedings of secured creditors pending before the Bombay High Court were ordered to be transferred to the Gujarat High Court, where a winding up petition was pending, this being necessary for the court to salvage the company after getting a complete view of its affairs.[27] The power under this section is effective up to the winding up order. Thereafter Section 446 takes over the matter. The court does not have the power under the section to stay proceedings before the Debt Recovery Tribunal.[28] The company's application for stay of a creditor's suit was not allowed though he had also filed an appeal against the dismissal of his winding up petition.[29]

---

22. The cases surveyed included: *Donoghue* v *Stevenson*, 1932 AC 562; *Anns* v *Merton London Borough Council*, 1978 AC 728, 751; *Governors of Peabody Donation Fund* v *Sir Lindsay Parkinson*, 1985 AC 210, 239; *Dorset Yatch Co Ltd* v *Home Office*, 1978 AC 1004, 1027; *Leigh & Sullivan Ltd* v *Aliakmon Shipping Co Ltd*, 1986 AC 785, 815; *Yuen Kun Yeu* v *Attorney-General of Hong Kong*, [1987] 3 WLR 776.
23. *Indian Express Newspapers (Bom) Ltd* v *Henkel Chemicals India Ltd*, (1999) 20 SCL 333 Bom.
24. *Someswara Cements & Chemicals Ltd* v *Power Mak Industries*, [2000] 1 Comp LJ 173 AP.
25. *Sree Arvind Steel (P) Ltd* v *Trichy Steel Rolling Mills Ltd*, (1992) 73 Comp Cas 607 Mad.
26. *Official Liquidator, Golcha Properties Ltd* v *Dharti Dhan (P) Ltd*, (1977) 47 Comp Cas 420 SC; *Vocation (Foreign), Re*, [1932] 2 Ch 196; *J. Burrows (Leeds) Ltd, Re*, [1982] 2 All ER 882 Ch D, proceedings before a magistrate restrained.
27. *Vallabh Glass Works* v *ICI Corpn*, (1987) 62 Comp Cas 101 SC.
28. Constituted under the Recovery of Debts due to Banks and Financial Institutions Act, 1993. *Allahabad Bank* v *Canara Bank*, [2000] 2 Comp LJ 170 SC. Criminal proceedings cannot also be stayed, *Bombay Leasing (P) Ltd* v *Gresoil (India) Ltd*, (2000) 103 Comp Cas 666 Bom.
29. *Ranbaxy Laboratories Ltd* v *Jerath Electronics & Allied Industries (P) Ltd*, (2003) 114 Comp Cas 638 HP. *Baranagar Jute Factory plc* v *Laxmi Narayan*, (2006) 133 Comp Cas 115 Cal,

Appointment of Provisional Liquidator [S. 450]

After the presentation of a petition but before the winding up order the Tribunal may appoint the Official Liquidator to be the provisional liquidator of the company. He becomes the Official Liquidator as soon as the winding up order is passed. Before making such appointment the Tribunal should inform the company so as to enable it to make its representation. This is necessary because the appointment of a provisional liquidator is likely to cause a serious setback to the name of the company and its business, if ultimately, the Tribunal does not pass a winding up order.[30] Where, however, the circumstances too obviously demand protection of the company's property, the Tribunal may record its reasons in writing and appoint a provisional liquidator without giving an opportunity to the company to explain its position.[31] The business of a *nidhi* company came to a standstill. It was unable to collect any more deposits, nor able to pay back the existing deposits. A straight away order of winding up would have caused panic among depositors. The court (now Tribunal) appointed a provisional liquidator without formally ordering winding up thinking that he would effectively realise assets for paying back depositors.[32]

The object of appointment is protection and preservation of the company's assets. But the power is not limited to that contingency alone. The Tribunal may make an appointment in any proper case.[33]

The Tribunal can appoint the official receiver as a provisional liquidator in respect of a company that is already in the process of voluntary winding up if such an appointment is necessary to ensure that a full investigation is carried out of the company's affairs in order to protect the public. The official receiver has wider reach than voluntary liquidators when it comes to matters of investigation.[34]

---

company registered outside India, workers seeking revival of company and sought stay of winding up, matter to be considered by the company judge. *Modi Rubber Ltd* v *Madura Coats Ltd*, (2006) 130 Comp Cas 32 All appeal against winding up order, reference to BIFR after order, winding up order put in abeyance till proceedings before SICA authorities pending.

30. Provisional liquidator was not appointed where the company was trading profitably. *Sree Aravind Steel (P) Ltd* v *Trichy Steel Rolling Mills Ltd*, (1992) 73 Comp Cas 607 Mad; Additional provisional liquidator was not appointed because he would have been a needless burden on resources, *BCCI (SA), Re*, (1992) BCLC 579 Ch D. Provisional liquidator was refused where in a group of family companies due care was taken of the interest of the widow of one member of the family who was a managing director in one company and director in others by giving her parallel position in the companies on the same remuneration, *Anisha K. Shah* v *Fostenex (P) Ltd*, (1995) 17 Corpt LA 5 Mad: AIR 1995 Mad 67: (1995) 82 Comp Cas 514.
31. *Brunton and Co Engineers Ltd, Re*, (1988) 63 Comp Cas 299 Ker.
32. *St Marys' Finance Ltd* v *R. G. Jayaprakash*, (2000) 37 CLA 170 Ker.
33. *Pundra Investment & Leasing Co (P) Ltd* v *Petron Mechanical Industries (P) Ltd*, (2000) 23 SCL 220 Bom.
34. *A Company (No 007070 of 1996), Re*, (1997) 2 BCLC 139.

Consequences of winding up order

The court has forthwith to cause intimation of the winding up order to be sent to the Official Liquidator and the Registrar.[35] It is also the duty of the petitioner and of the company to file with the Registrar, within thirty days, a certified copy of the order.[36] The Registrar should then make minutes of the order in his books relating to the company and notify in the Official Gazette that such an order has been made.[37]

Secondly, winding up order is deemed to be a notice of discharge to the officers and employees of the company, except when the business of the company is continued.[38] Thirdly, the order operates in favour of all the creditors and of all the contributories of the company.[39] The winding up order in India of a foreign company registered in the United Kingdom was held to have effect only upon the company's business dealings in India.[40]

Fourthly, on a winding up order being made in respect of a company, the Official Liquidator, by virtue of his office, becomes the liquidator of the company.[41]

---

35. S. 444. This has to be done in a period not exceeding two weeks.
36. S. 445. In computing the period of one month, the time requisite for obtaining a certified copy of the order shall be excluded. There is penalty for default.
37. S. 445(2). Under S. 448 the Central Government attaches Official Liquidators to High Courts. S. 452 permits them to function under the style of Official Liquidator of the particular company.
38. S. 445(3). The employment being conditional on the continued existence of the company, it ceases when the company is wound up. *T. N. Farrer Ltd, Re*, [1937] Ch 352: [1937] 2 All ER 505; *National Transport and General Co (P) Ltd, Re*, (1990) 69 Comp Cas 791 P&H, directors exercising the power of issuing further capital was held to be a nullity so that the allottees of such shares could not be regarded as contributories. *Mehtab Chand Golcha v Official Liquidator*, (1981) 51 Comp Cas 103 Raj. Business continued by order, no appeal. Liability to compensate employees may remain because this is not discharge due to unavoidable circumstances within the meaning of S. 25-FFF of the Industrial Disputes Act, 1947. *K. Shanmugham v Official Liquidator*, (1992) 75 Comp Cas 181 Mad, not agreeing with *Palai Central Bank Employee' Union v Official Liquidator, Palai Central Bank*, (1965) 35 Comp Cas 279: (1965) 2 Comp LJ 110 where winding up order was held to be an unavoidable circumstance. *Textile Labour Assn v OL of Amruta Mills Ltd*, (2005) 58 SCL 452, duty to vacate company's premises on automatic termination of employment.
39. S. 447. The company can immediately recover its dues from its debtors. *Official Liquidator v Bhagwat Singh*, (2004) 55 SCL 613 Raj, decree in favour of OL against person indebted to the company. *Mysore Tools Ltd v Dominion Hardware Stores*, (2005) 128 Comp Cas 376 Kant, recovery of amount due on invoices. *Swastic Filaments Corpn v Swami Marine Products (P) Ltd*, (2006) 32 Comp Cas 840 Ori, the company was taken over by a State Financial Corpn, the debt was admitted liability, the company ordered to be wound up because of inability to pay debts, the corporation restrained from charging assets or dealing with them otherwise.
40. *Baranagar Jute Factory plc v Laxmi Narayan Taparia*, 2005 CLC 500 Cal.
41. S. 449. S. 453 provides that a receiver cannot be appointed of assets in the hands of a liquidator except by or with the leave of the Tribunal. Expenses incurred by him with the leave of the court are a charge on the income in his hands. *Wandoor Jupiter Chits (P) Ltd, Re*, (1992) 74 Comp Cas 215 : [1992] 2 Comp LJ 101 Ker. The object of the section is to avoid any competition between the receiver appointed by the Civil Court and the official liquidator appointed by the company court. The latter cannot be replaced by any one else in his possession of the company's assets. *ICICI v Sidco Leathers Ltd*, (1999) 96 Comp Cas 527.

Legal Proceedings [S. 446]

Lastly, after the order, no suit or legal proceeding can be commenced against the company except by leave of the court and subject to such terms as the court may impose.[42] If a suit or proceeding is pending at the date of the order, it shall not be proceeded with except with the leave of the court.[43] The suit is taken to be filed from the date of leave and not from the date of original filing.[44] This is necessary for the purpose of preserving the limited assets of the company in the best way for distribution among all the persons who have claims on them. "The object of winding up provisions is to put all unsecured creditors upon an equality and pay them *pari passu*;[45] and to prevent the assets of the company from being frittered away in vexatious litigation.[46]

The expression "legal proceedings" in Section 446 means only those proceedings which have a bearing on the assets of a company in winding up or some relationship with the issues in winding up. It does not mean each and every civil proceeding which has no bearing on the winding up proceeding or criminal offences where the company was liable to be prosecuted.[47]

The court in granting leave considers all the circumstances of the case and decides as to whether leave to sue the company should not be granted so that the assets of the company may be preserved for the benefit of the

---

42. S. 446. The provision is mandatory and also applies to attachment proceedings. *Tarubala Saha v Nath Bank Ltd*, (1972) 42 Comp Cas 588 Cal.
43. S. 446(1). See *G. S. Setty & Sons v Y. C. W. Mills*, [1970] 1 Comp LJ 184. Once a leave is granted, no further leave for execution of decree will be necessary. *Shri Ram Saran Sharma v Bank of India*, (1990) 69 Comp Cas 544 P&H. *See* also *Bareja Knipping Fastners Ltd v Swastika Trading Co*, (1990) 69 Comp Cas 552 P&H, suit for price of goods delivered. *Devassy v Official Liquidator*, (1997) 2 Ker LT 80, managing director issued cheques which bounced, trial under S. 138 of the Negotiable Instruments Act, 1881 cannot be stayed and transferred to company court. *Orkay Industries Ltd v State of Maharashtra*, (1998) Vol 100 (2) Bom LR 158 Bom, where the company is in winding up, the provisions of S. 138 to 142 of the Negotiable Instruments Act, 1881 as to liability of the company for dishonoured cheques cannot take precedence over the provisions of the Companies Act. *Harihar Nath v State Bank of India*, (2006) 131 Comp Cas 119 (SC), as long as the stay is effective, there is no question of limitation, a party can apply at any time for leave to continue the proceeding.
44. *State of J&K v UCO Bank*, (2006) 129 Comp Cas 239 SC.
45. The amount realised by a creditor during the pendency of winding up had to be repaid to the liquidator. *Bombay Castwell Engg (P) Ltd, Re*, (1984) 55 Comp Cas 75 Bom.
46. *H. Lal Sharma v Chemical Vessels Fabricators*, (1989) 65 Comp Cas 506; following *Joshi Trading Co (P) Ltd v Essa Ismail Sait*, (1980) 50 Comp Cas 801 Ker. *Vasantha Ramanan v Official Liquidator*, (2003) 114 Comp Cas 747 Mad, proceedings without leave are of no effect, execution of an arbitrator's award requires leave. Leave granted by the Registrar of the court is of no effect. It has to be that of the winding up court.
47. *Ion Exchange Finance Ltd v Firth India Steel Co Ltd (In Liquidation)*, (2001) 103 Comp Cas 666 Bom. *Rajinder Steels Ltd, Re*, (2006) 132 Comp Cas 310 All, directors can be prosecuted for dishonour of the company's cheques under S. 138 of the Negotiable Instruments Act. On the facts however leave was granted. *Counter Point Advt (P) Ltd v Haritha Finance Ltd*, (2006) 133 Comp Cas 435 Mad, criminal liability for dishonour not affected.

creditors."[48] For example, the attachment of the property of a company in winding up effected on behalf of the Provident Fund Commissioner has been held to be ineffective.[49] Similarly, property attached in execution of decree obtained before, but actually sold after winding up order without leave of the court, the sale being void, the liquidator was allowed to recover the sale proceeds.[50] As interpleader suit by a person indebted to the company for an order whether he should pay to the company or to the other claimant, has been held to be a proceeding for which sanction of the court is necessary.[51] Kerala High Court held that eviction proceedings are not covered by the expressions used by Section 446. They are completely unrelated to winding up and, therefore, leave of the court is not necessary.[52] Where the property was with the company under hire-purchase and the ownership had not passed to it, the owner was allowed to withdraw the property.[53] There are, however, rulings to the effect that leave of the court may be necessary where proceedings are for the eviction of a tenant.[54] Where the debt of a company was guaranteed by the managing director, and the action was against both the company and the managing director, it was held that the action could go on against the managing director, but as against the company, leave was necessary.[55] Where the company is bound by an agreement to refer a dispute to arbitration, the court would have the discretion to say whether the matter should be decided by arbitration or otherwise.[56] A secured creditor being outside winding up, his proceedings to enforce his security are not affected.[57]

48. *Suresh Chand* v *The Bank of Calcutta Ltd*, (1950) 54 CWN 832. For instances of cases on the subject see *Palghat Warrier Bank* v *Padmanabhan*, AIR 1951 Mad 348; *Jiwan Lal* v *Radha Nathdas*, AIR 1971 Oudh 322; *Maneklal Mansukhbai* v *Saraspur Mfg Co Ltd*, AIR 1927 Bom 167; *Hansraj* v *Official Liquidators, Dehra Dun Mussoorie Electric Tramway Co*, AIR 1929 All 353; *Hukumchand* v *Radhakissen*, AIR 1925 Cal 916; *South Indian Mills* v *Shivlal Motilal*, AIR 1917 Mad 260; *Rawat Raj Kumar Singh* v *Benares Bank Ltd*, AIR 1941 All 154; *Sunil Chandra Banerjee* v *Krishna Chandra Nath*, AIR 1949 Cal 689. Leave may be obtained before or after the institution of proceedings, *Vyasa Bank Ltd* v *Official Liquidator, Sreeniwas Cotton Mills Ltd*, (1992) Mah LJ 1239.
49. *Ananta Mills Ltd* v *City Deputy Collector, Ahmedabad*, (1972) 42 Comp Cas 476 Guj.
50. *R. Ranganathan* v *Veerakumar Trading Chit Funds*, (1976) 46 Comp Cas 637 Mad. *Reserve Bank of India* v *JVG Finance Ltd*, (2006) 130 Comp Cas 316 Del, the company's property was sold under a suit filed before the Bombay High Court after winding up order sale without leave of the court, the purchaser was directed to deliver possession to the official liquidator.
51. *Televista Electronics (P) Ltd* v *Mass Communications & Marketing (P) Ltd*, (1980) 50 Comp Cas 1 Del. See also *United India General Finance (P) Ltd, Re*, (1980) 50 Comp Cas 847 Del.
52. *Joshi Trading Co (P) Ltd* v *Essa Ismail Sait*, (1980) 50 Comp Cas 801 Ker; *H. Lal Sharma* v *Chemical Vessels Fabricators*, (1989) 65 Comp Cas 506.
53. *Gujarat Lease Financing Ltd* v *OL of Aryan Punjab Ltd*, (2004) 122 Comp Cas 433 Guj.
54. *Nirmala R. Bafna* v *Khandesh Spg and Wvg Mills Ltd*, (1992) 2 SCC 322: (1992) 74 Comp Cas 1 SC ; *Faizabad Distilleries (P) Ltd* v *Salim Tailor*, (1993) 76 Comp Cas 127 All. *Shivkaran Budhia* v *Official Liquidator*, (2006) 130 Comp Cas 592 Raj, company being no longer in need of tenanted premises, was directed to handover premises to the landlord.
55. *Ramanlal Amratlal* v *ESL*, (1981) 51 Comp Cas 1 Guj.
56. *Maruti Ltd* v *B. G. Shirke & Co*, (1981) 51 Comp Cas 11 P&H. See also *Timber (P) Ltd, Re*, (1981) 51 Comp Cas 18 P&H, arbitration proceeding transferred to winding up court.
57. *Maksudpur Refrigeration Industries, Re*, (1977) 47 Comp Cas 67 Pat. No stay may be allowed where it is demanded as a part of delaying tactics. *Official Liquidator* v *Dharti Dhan (P) Ltd,*

A secured creditor has the right to proceed against the company or the guarantor of the company's debts or against both. The Supreme Court held that it was not proper to order that the guarantor should be proceeded against first instead of the company, their liability being co-equal.[58] A creditor who obtains a court decree for recovery and attaches property does not become a secured creditor.[59]

The Supreme Court held in *Kondaskar* v *ITO (Companies Circle), Bombay*[60] that an income-tax officer can commence assessment proceedings without leave of the court.[61] But leave would be necessary for effecting recovering even of the amount of tax deducted by the company at source, which was still lying with the company.[62] Where a sum of money is due to the company, the payer cannot deduct tax at source without leave.[63] If any suit or proceeding is pending in any court that may be transferred to and disposed of by the winding up court.[64] The provision, however, does not apply to appeals and cases pending before the Supreme Court or a High Court.[65] The Madras High Court refused to grant permission to a worker to file his claim before a labour court, for that would waste the time of the liquidator in having to defend suits at so many places.[66] The Calcutta High Court faced a case in which 23 suits were filed by DGSD on behalf of the

---

(1977) 2 SCC 66: (1977) 47 Comp Cas 420. The court may in its discretion require even a secured creditor to pass through the leave of the court particularly where there are complications like *pari passu* claims of others. *Cotton Corpn of India* v *Radhakrishna Mills*, (1993) 76 Comp Cas 637 Mad, or where he has instituted proceedings at an inconvenient place, *Central Bank of India* v *Elmot Engg Co (P) Ltd*, (1994) 4 SCC 519: (1994) 81 Comp Cas 11 Bom. The court ordered the transfer of proceedings to Bombay which was set aside by the SC on appeal, *Central Bank of India* v *Elmot Engg Co*, (1994) 4 SCC 519: (1994) 81 Comp Cas 13 SC : AIR 1994 SC 2358. A secured creditor was permitted to continue the realisation proceedings in another High Court subject to the condition that he would pay workmen's dues after realisation. *Industrial Credit & Investment Corpn of India* v *Hyderabad District Coop Central Bank*, (1995) 16 Corpt LA 227 AP. *Khalid Mukhtar* v *Bucheye Batteries (P) Ltd*, (2003) 114 Comp Cas 70 All, the proceedings for recovery against a guarantor of the company, being not a part of the company's winding up, were allowed, leave was not necessary.

58. *Haripar Nath* v *State Bank of India*, (2006) 131 Comp Cas 119 SC.
59. *Kerala State Financial Corpn Ltd* v *Official Liquidator*, (2006) 4 CCC 346 (SC).
60. (1972) 1 SCC 438 : (1972) 42 Comp Cas 168 : AIR 1972 SC 878.
61. Overruling *Colaba Land & Mills Co Ltd, Re*, (1968) 38 Comp Cas 26 Bom.
62. *ITO* v *Official Liquidator, National Conduits (P) Ltd*, (1981) 51 Comp Cas 174 Del. The court cannot conduct a probe into the assessment proceedings. *State of Kerala* v *Palai Central Bank*, (1987) 62 Comp Cas 742 Ker.
63. *Haryana State* v *Maruti Ltd*, (1992) 75 Comp Cas 663 P&H.
64. S. 446(3). If a suit pending in another court is continued without leave of the winding up court and a decree is passed, it is voidable at the option of the liquidator. See *Bhagwati Devi* v *Dhanraj Mills*, [1970] 1 Comp LJ 71. Also see *Punjab National Bank* v *Punjab Finance (P) Ltd*, (1973) 43 Comp Cas 350 Punj.
65. S. 446(4) and see *Punjab Finance (P) Ltd* v *Malhara Singh*, (1975) 45 Comp Cas 361 Punj.
66. *R. Chidambaranathan* v *Gannon Dunkerly & Co*, (1973) 43 Comp Cas 500 Mad. Consent decree against a company can be challenged only by the company itself and not by a shareholder or director personally. *Vivek Kumar* v *Pearl Cycle Industries*, (1983) 54 Comp Cas 77 Del. Leave was refused where the claim against the company was waived and that against the guarantor was time-barred. *Syndicate Bank* v *Panchkula Malt Co*, (1990) 67 Comp Cas 472 P&H.

Union of India. The Calcutta High Court ordered their transfer to the winding up court. The balance of convenience lay in bringing all those chronic type of cases before the winding up court.[67]

Where a State Financial Corporation wanted to stay outside winding up and applied for permission to dispose of the company's assets held by it by way of security, the Supreme Court said:

> "that realisation and distribution of proceeds are to take place only, in association with the liquidator and under supervision of the company court. The Debt Recovery Tribunal and the District Court under the State Financial Corporation Act is to issue notice to the official liquidator while ordering sale of properties of the debtor company. Otherwise the secured creditors can approach company court."[68]

The creditor standing outside winding up has to submit a valuation report to the court before disposing of the property.[69] The court would not confirm the sale without such report.

Even for proceeding under Section 13 of the Securitisation etc. Act, prior permission of the court was held to be necessary.[70]

It would not be necessary to obtain sanction of the court for prosecuting the company's officers under the Employees' Provident Fund Act.[71] Leave would be necessary for prosecuting the company under Section 58-C for violating rules relating to acceptance of deposits.[72] The court can have even criminal matters transferred before it.[73] The court has jurisdiction to decide—

---

67. *United Provinces Commercial Corpn, Re*, (1983) 53 Comp Cas 441 Cal. *Lok Vikas Urban Coop Bank Ltd* v *Lok Vikas Finance Corpn Ltd*, (2003) 114 Comp Cas 355 Raj, secured creditor's application to remain outside winding up for sale of assets, other creditors and contributories not likely to be affected, sale of assets permitted subject to certain conditions and also subject to confirmation. *Shivalik Agro Poly Products Ltd* v *Disco Electronics Ltd*, (2003) 114 Comp Cas 398 Del, sale by the secured creditor (corporation) not affected by the restraint order or appointment of provisional liquidator in winding up proceedings to which it was not a party.

68. *Rajasthan Financial Corpn* v *Official Liquidator*, (2005) 128 Comp Cas 387 SC.

69. *A.P. State Financial Corpn* v *Professional Grade Components Ltd*, (2005) 125 Comp Cas 345, 365.

70. *State Bank of India* v *Volvo Steel Ltd*, (2004) 122 Comp Cas 440 Guj; *Hotel Rajahmsa International* v *IOB*, (2005) 128 Comp Cas 431 AP.

71. *Manekchowk & Ahmedabad Mfg Co, Re*, (1983) 53 Comp Cas 519 Guj.

72. *B. N. Chikarmane* v *Swashraya Benefit (P) Ltd*, (1983) 53 Comp Cases 519 Guj. The managing director against whom an arrest warrant had been issued by a District Forum in connection with a company offence was held entitled to seek his protection under S. 446. *Narayanakutty* v *Official Liquidator*, (1998) 30 Corpt LA 146 Ker.

73. *Khosla Fans (India) (P) Ltd, Re*, (1983) 53 Comp Cas 858 P&H. Leave was not granted where tenants instead of vacating, as ordered, were trying to involve the liquidator into litigation. *United Provinces Commercial Corpn, Re*, (1986) 59 Comp Cas 362 Cal. Eviction proceedings against company require leave. *LIC* v *Asia Udyog*, (1984) 55 Comp Cas 187 Del. Leave not necessary for executing a decree obtained with leave. *Janta Works (P) Ltd, Re*, (1984) 56 Comp Cas 229 Bom.

1. any suit or proceeding by or against the company;[74]
2. any claim made by or against the company;[75]
3. any application made for compromise or arrangement with creditors under Section 391;
4. any question of priorities or any question whatsoever, whether of law or fact, which may relate to, or arise in the course of the winding up.[76]

---

74. See *Official Liquidator* v *Kerala SEB*, (1990) 67 Comp Cas 577 Ker, claim against the company for compensation for loss caused by an employee's conduct. *See* also *Maruti Ltd* v *H.M. Tractor and Automobiles Corpn*, (1990) 69 Comp Cas 59 P&H, where entries in the books of the company showing the respondent to be indebted to the company, affirmed by officers on oath and not controverted by the respondent were held to be good evidence of the indebtedness. Summary eviction proceedings against trespassers on the company's premises were allowed, *Pushpa Devi Jhunjhunwala* v *Official Liquidator*, (1993) 1 Cal LJ 447. Squatters were not allowed to claim possession by adverse title, the official liquidator is deemed to be in possession, *Yogamaya Ghosh* v *Official Liquidator*, (1993) 1 Cal LJ 485.
75. A claim for goods supplied can be so decided. *Star Engg Works* v *Official Liquidator*, (1977) 47 Comp Cas 30 Guj. Whether a person in occupation of the company's premises is a trespasser and, if so, liable to be evicted, can be decided under S. 446, *Vidyadhar Upadhaya* v *Shri Shri Madan Gopal Jew*, (1990) 67 Comp Cas 394 Cal. Tenancy matters pending before special tribunals can be left to be decided by such tribunals. *S. P. Bhargava (Dr)* v *Haryana Electric Steel Co*, (1994) 2 Punj LR 406; *Deutsche Bank* v *S. P. Kala*, (1992) 74 Comp Cas 577 Bom, court competent under S. 446 to pass orders against guarantor of the company's debts, *MS Fashions Ltd* v *BCC sa (No 2)*, (1993) 3 All ER 769 CA leave to proceed against the debtor where the guarantor could not pay the whole amount due. *Beni Carbon Co Ltd* v *Raj Kumar Goel*, (1993) 2 Punj LR 681, eviction with leave of court, execution of decree not allowed to be resisted on the grounds rejected by the Rent Controller. *UCO Bank* v *Concost Products Ltd*, (1996) 23 Corpt LA 256 Cal, recovery proceedings before Debt Recovery Tribunal have to be transferred to the winding up court. The company court can pass necessary orders for transfer or otherwise after considering all the interests which S. 446 is designed to safeguard. See *Mayur Syntex Ltd* v *Punjab & Sind Bank*, (1997) 27 Corpt LA 206 Del. A Bombay based secured creditor was allowed to continue his proceedings in Bombay though the company was being wound up in AP, *Industrial Credit & Investment Corpn of India Ltd* v *Hyderabad District Coop Central Bank*, (1997) 27 Corpt LA 244 AP. After the winding up order, the assets of the company become vested in the company court and, therefore, the court's permission under S. 446 is necessary for initiating proceedings under the Debts Recovery Act. The permission can also be taken after initiation of proceedings. *Industrial Finance Corpn of India* v *Rama Fibres Ltd*, (1998) 29 Corpt LA 362 P&H. *State Bank of Hyderabad* v *Pennar Paterson Ltd*, (2003) 114 Comp Cas 66 SC, Debt Recovery Tribunal directed the liquidator to cooperate with the Commission appointed by it in the matter of recovery of a bank loan, no leave necessary. *Bank of Nova Scotia* v *RPG Transmission Ltd*, (2003) 114 Comp Cas 764 Del, case before Debt Recovery Tribunal, no interference.
76. S. 446(2). The executing court is subject to the jurisdiction of the winding up court. *Faqir Chand Gupta* v *Tanwar Finance (P) Ltd*, (1981) 51 Comp Cas 60 Del. The period of limitation for the purposes of S. 446 begins to run from the date of the order or the appointment of the provisional liquidator. *K. P. Ulahaman* v *Wandoor Jupiter Chits (P) Ltd*, AIR 1989 Ker 41: (1989) 65 Comp Cas 178; *Maruti Ltd* v *Parry & Co Ltd*, (1990) 66 Comp Cas 309: [1989] 3 Comp LJ 384 P&H; *Maruti Ltd* v *P. R. Sasidharan*, (1990) 68 Comp Cas 5 P&H. The proper mode of realisation of the security by a secured creditor can be prescribed by the court at the application of the official liquidator. *Sushum Overseas Marketing (P) Ltd* v *ROC*, [1990] 1 Comp LJ 293 Del; *O. Narayanan Kutty* v *Official Liquidator, Kerala*, AIR 1998 Ker 278, proceedings against the promoter and subsequently managing director commenced before consumer forum stayed for disposal by company court. *KTC Tyres (India) Ltd* v *Kavitha Auto Parts*, (1997) 2 Ker LT 705, the official liquidator can only enforce those claims which are not barred at the commencement of winding up proceedings. *Anand Finance (P) Ltd* v *Amrit Dasarat Kakade*, (1996) 61 Del LT 305: (1997) 90 Comp Cas 350 Del, payment order under

Debt Recovery Tribunal

After coming into force of Recovery of Debts Due to Banks and Financial Institutions Act, 1993 and the establishment of the Debts Recovery Tribunal (DRT) and in view of the clear provisions of Sections 17, 18 and 34 of that Act, neither it is necessary to apply for leave to prosecute the suits transferred to DRT in terms of Section 446(1) of the Companies Act nor it is open to the company court to transfer the suit to itself for trial in winding up proceedings in terms of Section 446(2) of that Act.[77] A winding up petition is maintainable even if a recovery suit against the company has been filed before the Debt Recovery Tribunal.[78]

PROCEDURE OF WINDING UP BY COURT

Appointment of liquidator [S. 448]

As soon as the winding up order is passed, the Official Liquidator attached to the High Court or District Court becomes the liquidator of the company.

The official liquidator conducts winding up and performs such other duties as the Tribunal may impose.[79]

Provisional liquidator

The court may also appoint a provisional liquidator after a petition is presented but before making a winding up order.[80] Before making such appointment, the court should give reasonable opportunity to the company to make its representation.[81]

The appointment of a provisional liquidator is made before the order of winding up. Supposing that an order of winding up is not ultimately passed, such an appointment even then would be capable of causing a great damage to the company. It may put others on their guard and shake up their confidence in the company. Therefore, that part of the proceedings in which the need for the appointment is debated should better be conducted *in camera*. But as soon as the proceedings cross that sensitive stage, they should be brought back to the open Tribunal.[82] The power of the court is discretionary and is generally exercised when

---

S. 446(2) has the effect of a decree. It can be enforced by filing a certified copy before the proper officer.

77. *Rohtas Industries Ltd (In Liquidation), In re,* (2001) 103 Comp Cas 383 Pat. *AVI Exports (India) Ltd* v *Industrial Finance Corpn of India Ltd,* (2006) 133 Comp Cas 736 P&H, company court cannot stay proceedings before DRT, sale of property would be subject to *pari passu* claim for workers' dues.
78. *Bank of Nova Scotia* v *RBG Transmission Ltd,* (2006) 133 Comp Cas 172 Del.
79. S. 451(3).
80. S. 450(1) and (2).
81. Where no such opportunity is afforded, reasons in writing should be recorded. S. 450(2).
82. *Rondon and Norw Rich Investment Services Ltd, Re,* 1988 BCLC 226 CLD.

liquidation is more or less certain.[83] The precautions which have to be observed were pictorially stated by ROMILLY MR in the following words:[84]

Where there is no apposition to the winding up, I appoint a provisional liquidator as a matter of course on the presentation of the petition. But where there is an opposition to it, I never do, because I might paralyse all the affairs of the company and afterwards refuse to make a winding up order at all.

Where the company's assets are in danger of being diverted or misapplied,[85] or where the company was in a state of non functioning and the debts were accumulating,[86] a provisional liquidator can be justifiably appointed, but not where a winding up petition is nothing but a part of the family struggle for power.[87]

The powers of the provisional liquidator are the same as those of the official liquidator unless restricted by the court appointing him.[88] It becomes the duty of the Official Liquidator to conduct the proceedings in winding up the company and perform such duties as the court may impose.[89] The acts of a liquidator shall be valid notwithstanding any defect in his appointment or qualifications that may afterwards be discovered.[90]

Statement of Affairs [S. 454]

Within twenty-one days[91] of the date of the winding up order or where a provisional liquidator is appointed, from the date of that appointment, a statement as to the affairs of the company has to be submitted to the Official Liquidator.[92] The statement has to be submitted and verified by the director,

---

83. *High Field Commodities Ltd, Re*, [1984] 3 All ER 884.
84. Reproduced in *Kailash Pd Mishra* v *Madwin Laboratories (P) Ltd*, [1986] 1 Comp LJ 291: (1988) 63 Comp Cas 810.
85. *Waryam Singh* v *Bhatinda Transport Co Ltd*, (1963) 33 Comp Cas 897: [1963] 1 Comp LJ 17 Punj; *Darshan Anilkumar Patel* v *Gitaneel Hotels (P) Ltd*, (1994) 81 Comp Cas 805 Bom. *Namco UK Ltd, Re*, (2003) 2 BCLC 78 Ch D, assets not in danger, no appointment made.
86. *Brunton & Co Engineers Ltd, Re*, (1988) 63 Comp Cas 299 Ker.
87. *Mridula Bhaskar* v *Ishwar Industries Ltd*, (1985) 58 Comp Cas 442 Del.
88. *K. Subhakar Rao* v *Monetreck Computers*, (2004) 50 SCL 723 AP.
89. S. 451(1).
90. S. 451(3). But this does not validate acts done by a liquidator after his appointment has been shown to be invalid. [Proviso to S. 451(3)]
91. Time may be extended up to three months by the Official Liquidator or the Tribunal.
92. S. 454(1). Default is punishable. See *Official Liquidator* v *Jagannath Das*, (1968) 2 Comp LJ 12. Where the director who was sought to be prosecuted was not in office at the relevant date, the court said that it was the duty of the official liquidator to lay before the court some material which would show that he was in a position to make the statement. That was not done. The complaint was discharged. *Official Liquidator* v *Koganti Krishna Kumar*, (1993) 3 Andh LT 542: (1997) 89 Comp Cas 672 AP. The time-limit applies only to persons who were the directors of the company at the relevant date. It does not apply when ex-directors

manager, secretary or other chief officer of the company or such persons as the Official Liquidator, subject to the direction of the court, may require.[93] The statement should show the following particulars:[94]

    (*a*) the assets of the company, showing separately cash in hand and at bank and negotiable securities;

    (*b*) its debts and liabilities;

---

are being called upon to submit the statement, *Official Liquidator, AP* v *Koganti Krishna Kumar*, (1997) 89 Comp Cas 672 AP.

93. S. 454(2). See *Registrar of Companies* v *Orissa China Clay Refinery Co*, [1968] 38 Comp Cas 205 Ori, where the seizure of books by the vigilance police was held to be an extenuating circumstance in imposing penalty upon guilty officers. Where winding up followed about ten years after the directors had lawfully retired and had no books to prepare the statement that was held to be a sufficient cause justifying the default. *Official Liquidator* v *K. K. Nair*, (1975) 45 Comp Cas 278 Ker, where some books are available the statement should be prepared out of them to the extent possible. *Official Liquidator* v *Nihal Singh*, (1977) 47 Comp Cas 254 Del. Persons who have retired from directorship more than a year before the commencement of winding up can be ordered by the court to submit the statement. *Official Liquidator* v *B K Modi*, (2007) 2 All LJ 183 (All) Officer includes director. *Sipso Agencies (P) Ltd* v *Gajraj Singh*, (1978) 48 Comp Cas 30 Del, so also those who have resigned. *Registrar of Companies* v *Bihar Investment Trust Ltd*, (1978) 48 Comp Cas 579 Pat; *Lakshmi Narayan Arora* v *ROC*, (1980) 50 Comp Cas 536 Pat; not allowed to be demanded from a person who retired some eight years before winding up, though the court agreed that he was within the range of persons who could be called upon to prepare the statement; *Devinder Kishore Mehra* v *Official Liquidator*, (1980) 50 Comp Cas 699 Del, a person ousted from management some eight years before. The prosecution has to prove that the officer in question was in a position to prepare the statement but did not do so. Where the books were with the Revenue Authorities and though they had returned some of them to the official liquidator, he did not inform the directors. The benefit of doubt was given to them. *Official Liquidator* v *Indira*, (1983) 54 Comp Cas 644 Ker. A director cannot defend himself by showing that he was only a nominal director. *Kothari (Mad) Ltd* v *Myleaf Tobacco Development Co Ltd*, (1985) 57 Comp Cas 690; *Official Liquidator* v *Agro Chemicals Ltd*, (1984) 56 Comp Cas 380 Guj, the position of absentee director. *Globe Associates (P) Ltd, Re*, (1987) 61 Comp Cas 814 Del, the default in filing the statement is of continuing nature and, therefore, the offence is not wiped out by the expiry of any period of limitation. The directors are under a statutory duty to submit the statement without any notice and therefore failure can attract penalty proceedings straightaway on failure. *Official Liquidator* v *Ved Prakash Gupta*, (1994) 80 Comp Cas 675 P&H. Where the directors sought to be prosecuted showed that the assets of the company had already been taken over by a financial corporation and already sold, this was a reasonable excuse for not being able to file the statement, *Official Liquidator* v *Surjit Singh*, (1995) 2 Punj LR 447. Theft of account books for which first information report had been launched was held to be a good excuse, *Pawanta Sahib Cement Works* v *Anil Saini*, (1994) 2 Punj LR 303. *Official Liquidator of Essen Computers Ltd* v *Rajendra A. Shah*, (2002) 108 Comp Cas 559 Guj, the director who had to file the statement showed that records were not available and the company's banks caused delay in furnishing accounts. This was held to be a reasonable excuse. The fine imposed upon the director was reduced. Sub-s. (4) provides that reasonable expenses may be allowed to the person called upon to submit the statement.

94. S. 454(1). *D.D. Sinha* v *OL, Rajasthan Commercial and Industrial Finance (India) Ltd*, (2004) 118 Comp Cas 112 Raj, any inquiries and objections by directors called upon to file the statement could be considered at the trial for their default. *Official Liquidator* v *S. Haridas*, (2006) 133 Comp Cas 5 AP, liability for failure to file inspite of extension of time. *S. Haridas* v *Official Liquidator*, (2006) 133 Comp Cas 34 AP, appeal to DB against the decision of the single judge was held to be not maintainable.

(c) names and addresses of the company's creditors indicating the amount of secure or unsecured debts;

(d) the debts due to the company and the names and addresses of the persons from whom they are due and the amount likely to be realised;

(e) such other information as may be required.

Report by Official Liquidator [S. 455]

As soon as practicable after receiving this statement, but within six months[95] of the order, the Official Liquidator is required to submit a preliminary report to the Tribunal showing—

1. the amount of issued and paid-up capital and the estimated amount of assets and liabilities;

2. if the company has failed, the causes of the failure; and

3. whether, in his opinion, further inquiry is desirable as to any matter relating to the promotion, formation or failure of the company or the conduct of its business.

The report is a privileged document as regards its contents.[96]

Custody of company's property [S. 456]

The liquidator, including the provisional liquidator, has to take into his custody or under his control all the property,[97] effects and actionable claims[98] to which the company is or appears to be entitled. Such property can be recovered with the order of Chief Presidency Magistrate or District Magistrate. What steps or what force would be necessary lies in the judgment of the Magistrate. The property is supposed to be in the deemed custody of the Court. Machinery taken on lease is not the company's property. It is the lessor's property and he has the right to take it away before or during winding up.[99] A lease became determined under a clause in lease deed that it would be terminated on winding up. It was held that the purchaser of assets is court auction sale had no automatic right to seek renewal. But in the interest of workers, the court ordered renewal in favour

---

95. The court may extend this time or may order that no statement need be submitted. S. 455(1).

96. *Bottomley* v *Brougham*, [1908] 1 KB 584.

97. *Rohtas Industries Ltd* v *OL, High Court of Patna*, (2005) 128 Comp Cas 421, eviction of tenant and recovery of the company's property. *Lave Narendra Sinhji* v *OL, Kalol Mills Ltd*, (2005) 60 SCL 24 Guj, property on which the company had lease rights. *Sri Vishnupriya Industries Ltd* v *Supdt of Central Excise & Customs*, (2005) 60 SCL 311 AP, recovery of goods seized by the Customs.

98. *Maheshwari Proteins Ltd, Re*, (2004) 52 SCR 339 MP, bank directed to pay FDR proceeds to the liquidator even if they were attached in a labour dispute. *Gas Authority of India* v *Official Liquidator*, (2004) 53 SCL 209 Bom, invocation of bank guarantee in favour of the company.

99. *Foremost Industries India* v *Credit Capital Finance Corpn Ltd*, (1997) 89 Comp Cas 670 Del.

of the purchaser not at original rates but at the currently prevailing rates.[1] Property taken on hire-purchase is not the property of the company till the last instalment of the hire money is paid.[2]

Where in case of a company under liquidation the Debt Recovery Tribunal (DRT) exercised its power under Section 19(18)(*e*) of the Recovery of Debts Due to Banks and Financial Institutions Act, 1993 and appointed a Commissioner for preparation of an inventory of properties of the company in liquidation, prior permission of the Company Judge was held to be not necessary.[3]

Powers of Liquidator [S. 457]

The liquidator shall have powers, with the sanction of the court—

1. to institute or defend any suit, prosecution or other legal proceeding, civil or criminal, in the name and on behalf of the company;[4]

2. to carry on the business of the company so far as may be necessary for the beneficial winding up of the company;[5]

3. to sell the immovable and moveable property and actionable claims of the company; he may make the sale by public auction or by private contract and shall have the power to transfer the whole in one lot or in parcels;[6]

---

1. *Board of Trustees, Port of Calcutta* v *Efclon Tie-up (P) Ltd*, (2006) 131 Comp Cas 357 SC; *Board of Trustees, Port of Kolkata* v *OL*, (2006) 130 Comp Cas 595 Gau.
2. *Model Financial Corpn Ltd* v *Montana International Ltd*, [2000] 2 Comp LJ 229 AP.
3. *State Bank of Hyderabad* v *Pennar Patterson Ltd*, (2003) 114 Comp Cas 66 SC.
4. In computing the period of limitation for suits on behalf of the company, the period from the date of the commencement of winding up to the date of the order and one year from the date of such order is excluded [S. 458-A]. The extension is available only for suits on behalf of the company and not on behalf of secured creditor. *Gleitlager (India) (P) Ltd* v *Killick Nixon Ltd*, (1977) 47 Comp Cas 79 Bom.
5. This has been held to include the power to ratify acts which, when in being, the company would have had power to perform. Summons for the arrest of a ship on behalf of a company which was without directors at the time, were ratified by the liquidator. The ratification was held to be binding. *Alexander Ward & Co* v *Samyang Navigation Co*, [1975] 1 WLR 673 HL.
6. *Industrial Finance Corpn* v *Official Liquidator, High Court, Calcutta*, (1993) 3 SCC 40: [1993] 77 Comp Cas 305 SC : (1993) 3 Comp LJ 137, instructions of court as to sale ; *United Bank of India* v *Bharat Electrical Industries Ltd*, (1993) 76 Comp Cas 317 Cal, confirmation of sale at a low price as against the original reserve price ; *N. Babu Janardhanam* v *Golden Films (P) Ltd*, (1993) 78 Comp Cas 455 Mad, confirmation of court necessary even when the sale is with the approval of the court. *Virendra Singh Bhandari* v *Nandlal Bhandari & Sons (P) Ltd*, (1995) 17 Corpt LA 226 MP, the official liquidator can lease out the premises of the company only with the approval of the court. *Haryana Electro Steel Ltd* v *Haryana Financial Corpn*, AIR 1995 P&H 37, applying for permission to sell property under wrong the S. 446 instead of S. 457—did not make a difference in substance ; limitation for setting aside sale is three years and a director has no locus standi to apply for setting aside, only the liquidator can apply. *Industrial Credit and Investment Corpn of India* v *Official Liquidator*, 1994 Supp (2) SCC 721 : AIR 1994 SC 167, court supervision of terms of auction by official liquidator; *Syndicate Bank* v *Field Star Cycle Industries (P) Ltd*, (1995) 83 Comp Cas 687 Kant, for court confirmation of sale, the petitioning creditor must be notified. *Narendra Kumar Nikhat* v *Nandi Hasbai Textile Mills*, (1998) 7 SCC 673: AIR 1998 SC 1988, sale by auction not

3(*i*). to sell whole of the undertaking of the company as a going concern;[7]

4. to raise on the security of the assets of the company any money requisite;

5. to do all such other things as may be necessary for winding up the affairs for the company and distributing its assets.

---

confirmed, bidder's earnest money forfeited, balance allowed to be refunded. *A.P. State Financial Corpn* v *Nagarjuna Paper Mills Ltd*, (1997) 89 Comp Cas 557 AP, advertisement for sale without indicating the advantageous features of the property, readvertisement ordered. *Babulal M Kapadia* v *Bank of India*, (1997) 88 Comp Cas 515 Bom, a guarantor of a company's debts was held to have *locus standi* to challenge the validity of sale of assets by the receiver though the sale was with court's sanction. On facts, however, he was not allowed to do so because he participated in the proceedings throughout from the appointment of the receiver till actual sale. *Ayala Holdings Ltd, (No 2), Re*, (1996) 2 BCLC 467 Ch D, a creditor of the company has the right to question the validity of an assignment of assets made by the liquidator. The assignment was set aside because the liquidator had failed to endeavour to negotiate better terms with other firms interested in the matter and proceeded with the assignment even after an objection had been made. The liquidator was also removed and the matter of renegotiations was left to the new liquidator. *Vaz Forwarding Ltd* v *State Bank of India*, (1996) 85 Comp Cas 603 Bom, property under lease is heritable and remains under the company's right even during winding up. In this case the lease carried the right of assignment also. The assignment made by the liquidator was held to be valid. *Nani Gopal Paul* v *T. Prasad Singh*, (1995) 3 SCC 579: (1995) 2 Comp LJ 408 SC; *Lica (P) Ltd* v *Official Liquidator, (No 2)*, (1996) 85 Comp Cas 792 SC, duty of the liquidator to realise proper value and power of the court to set aside if the price realised is not natural. *Jainsons Exports India* v *Binatone Electronics Ltd*, (1996) 22 Corpt LA 239 Del, company court has inherent power to recall an order for sale of property which was obtained by misrepresentation. *Bengal Potteries Ltd, Re*, (1996) 1 Cal WN 71, unless a sale is confirmed, the court retains the discretion to order a fresh auction; the successful bidder in an unconfirmed sale acquires no vested right. *Glovanola Binny, Re*, (1996) 2 Ker LT 828, even in the absence of fraud or irregularity, it is open to the company judge to exercise his discretion in cases where the court comes to the conclusion that there is every possibility of getting higher price. *Sahajanand Cotton Traders* v *Official Liquidator of Shri Yamuna Mills Co Ltd*, (2000) 26 SCL 110 Guj, resale ordered after new advertisement, *A.P. State Financial Corpn* v *Emgee Rubber (P) Industries*, [2000] 1 Comp LJ 175 AP, the secured creditor directed to keep the liquidator about sale process; *Allahabad Bank* v *A. R. C. Holdings Ltd*, (2000) CLC 1780, SC, one more chance given to the company to be sold as a going concern. *Divya Mfg Co (P) Ltd* v *Union Bank of India*, (2000) 6 SCC 69: AIR 2000 SC 2346: 2000 JT (SC) 524: (2000) 38 CLA 206 SC, sale set aside, resale ordered, there was proof of underbidding. *Union Bank of India* v *Official Liquidator*, (2000) 3 SCC 274: (2000) 101 Comp Cas 317 SC, court as the custodian of the company's interests exercises protective discretion. *Allahabad Bank* v *Bengal Paper Mills Co Ltd*, (1999) 4 SCC 383: AIR 1999 SC 1715: (1999) 96 Comp Cas 804 SC, recovery of property already sold ordered, and direction for resale. *Allahabad Bank* v *Bengal Paper Mills Co Ltd*, (1999) 96 Comp Cas 804 SC, confirmed sale set aside. *Bhadohi Woollens Ltd, Re*, AIR 2001 All 18, earnest money of auction-purchaser of the company's property, allowed to be forfeited on default in payment even of the instalment. His defence that the property was under encroachments was not allowed because he had purchased the property after due inspection on as it is basis. *Bysana Anjaneyulu* v *Trilinga Technical & Management Consultant (P) Ltd*, (2003) 114 Comp Cas 37 AP, confirmed sale set aside because of a subsequent higher bid. The court said that the highest price available must be accepted at any stage of the proceedings. *Winsome Yarn Ltd* v *Punjab Wireless Systems Ltd*, (2006) 129 Comp Cas 41 (P&H), offer of the intervener was only marginally higher; no reason to disturb sale, workmen have no right to be associated in the process of sale, fraud in sale could not be inferred from the fact that sister concerns of the purchaser also participates in the auction.

7. New sub-clause (*ca*) added to the Section 457(1) by the Companies (Second Amendment) Act, 2002.

The court may, by order, provide that the liquidator may exercise these powers without its sanction.[8]

Then there are certain powers which he can exercise without the sanction of the court. Section 457(2) provides that the liquidator shall have power—

1. to do all acts in the name and on behalf of the company and to execute all deeds, receipts and other documents and for that purpose he may use, when necessary, the company's seal;

2. to inspect the records and returns of the company or the files of the Registrar without payment of any fee;

3. to prove and claim in the insolvency of any contributory for any balance against his estate and to receive dividends in the insolvency;

4. to draw, accept and endorse any negotiable instruments on behalf of the company;

5. to take out, in his official name, letters of administration to any deceased contributory and to do, in his official name, any other act necessary for obtaining payment of any money due from a contributory or his estate;

6. to appoint an agent to do any business which the liquidator is unable to do himself.[9]

The liquidator can issue a notice to the persons detailed in S. 454(2) requiring them to submit a verified statement of affairs. He can take the help of the court for this purpose.

The liquidator may call any person for recording any statement for investigating the affairs of the company being wound up and it shall be the duty of every such person to give all the information and answer all such questions relating to winding up of the company as the liquidator may require.

The liquidator will have to maintain a separate bank account for each company for depositing the sale proceeds of the assets and recovery of debts and also will have to maintain proper books of accounts in respect of all receipts and payments and submit half yearly returns to the Court. [Sub-section (2-G)].

The exercise of all the above powers is subject to the control of the court and any creditor or contributory may apply to the court with respect to

---

8. S. 458, but the exercise of the powers shall be subject to the control of the court.

9. Official Liquidator, being a principal officer of the company can be called upon to file income-tax returns. *ITO* v *Official Liquidator*, (1977) 47 Comp Cas 54 AP. S. 459 contains provisions for legal assistance to liquidator. It says that the liquidator may, with the sanction of the court, appoint an advocate, attorney or pleader entitled to appear before the court to assist him in the performance of his duties. He should better have the fees and charges of the liquidator fixed by the court while sanctioning the appointment. See *Regional Edward Negus, Re*, (1989) Comp Cas 443 : [1989] 2 Comp LJ 170, 175 Bom.

the exercise of any power.[10] The liquidator may also apply to the court for directions in relation to any particular matter arising in the winding up.[11] He should have regard to any directions which may be given by resolutions of creditors or contributories.[12] And for this purpose he may summon general meetings of the creditors or contributories.[13] He shall, however, be bound to summon such meetings as the creditors or contributories may by resolution direct or when one-tenth in value of the creditors or contributories request him to do so.[14] A person aggrieved by an act or decision of the liquidator may apply to the court.[15]

The liquidator has to present to the court twice a year an account of his receipts and payments as liquidator.[16] The moneys received by him as liquidator have to be paid into the public account of India in the Reserve Bank.[17] The court gets the accounts to be audited.[18] The liquidator has to send a copy of the printed accounts to every creditor and contributory.[19] A copy is also filed with the Registrar.[20] Where the liquidation is that of a Government company, a copy must be sent to the Central Government if it is a member or to any State Government if that is a member or to both where both are members.[21]

The Central Government has the power to take cognizance of the conduct of liquidators of companies.[22] If it appears that a liquidator is not faithfully performing his duties or is not observing the requirements of the Act or if any complaint has been made by any creditor or contributory, the Central Government shall inquire into the matter and take necessary action.[23] The Central Government may require him to answer any inquiry or

---

10. S. 457(3). Tenancy rights are not a property of the company for the purposes of winding up. The company remains a tenant until its dissolution, *Nirmala R. Bafna* v *Khandesh Spg and Wvg Mills Ltd*, (1992) 2 SCC 332: (1992) 74 Comp Cas 1 SC. An application can be made by a creditor or contributory but not by a person who, for example, says that he was denied an opportunity to purchase the property of the company. *Mahomed* v *Mortis*, [2000] 2 BCLC 536 CA.

11. S. 460(4). *Remu Pipes Ltd* v *Industrial Finance Corpn of India*, (2002) 108 Comp Cas 385 AP, the property of the company is vested in the court and not in the liquidator. The liquidator can be directed to take possession of property and to organise its sale. The liquidator may even be directed to undertake private negotiations for sale.

12. S. 460(1).
13. S. 460(3).
14. S. 460(3)(*b*).
15. S. 460(6).
16. S. 462(1).
17. S. 552, as prescribed by official liquidator's Account Rules and Companies (Court) Rules; rules 287 to 291 and 293 to 297.
18. S. 462(3).
19. S. 462(5).
20. S. 462(4).
21. S. 462 (4A).
22. S. 463.
23. S. 463(1).

may apply to the court to examine him on oath,[24] and may also direct a local examination to be made of the books and vouchers of the liquidator.[25]

Committee of inspection [S. 464]

The Court may order the appointment of a committee of inspection to act with the liquidator. The liquidator has then, within two months, to summon a meeting of the creditors for determining the membership of the committee. Within fourteen days of the creditors' meeting he shall call a meeting of the contributories to consider the creditors' suggestions with respect to the membership of the committee. In case there is a conflict of opinion, the liquidator should apply to the court for a final decision.

The committee shall not consist of more than twelve members.[26] It shall have the right to inspect the liquidator's accounts.[27] The quorum for a meeting of the committee shall be one-third of the total number of its members, or two, whichever is higher.[28] A member may resign by notice in writing delivered to the liquidator.[29] His office shall become vacant if he is adjudged an insolvent, or compounds or arranges with his creditors or is absent from five consecutive meetings of the committee without leave of absence.[30] The vacancy is then filled at a meeting of the creditors or contributories, as the case may be.[31]

The committee may meet at such times as it may from time to time appoint. The liquidator or any member of the committee may call a meeting as and when he thinks necessary.[32]

General powers of Court

Power to Stay Winding Up [S. 466]

Even after making a winding up order the Court can stay the proceedings either altogether or for a limited time and on such terms and conditions as may be thought fit. An application for this purpose can be made by the liquidator or any creditor or contributory. The application must show a sufficient cause for the purpose. The Court can exercise this power even when the company is in voluntary liquidation.[33] Certain persons took

---

24. S. 463(2).
25. S. 463(3).
26. S. 465(1).
27. S. 465(2).
28. S. 465(4). The committee acts by a majority of its members. *See* S. 455(5).
29. S. 465(6).
30. S. 465(8).
31. S. 465(9).
32. S. 465(3).
33. *Voluntary Liquidator, Dimples (P) Ltd*, v *ROC*, (1978) 48 Comp Cas 98 Del; *V. B. Purohit* v *Gadag*, (1984) 56 Comp Cas 360 Kant. See *Richa Jain* v *ROC*, (1990) 69 Comp Cas 248 Raj, the court approved a reasonable scheme of arrangement suspending winding up proceedings,

over the management without leave of the court, but at a point of time when the company was adrift without any helmsmen. They had done so at the request of the workers who had no alternative but to face unemployment and starvation. The management was making serious efforts to revive the company. It was held that the management was entitled to be recognized by the company judge for granting permanent stay of winding for revival of the company.[34] Where a scheme was prepared for revival of a company by the Industrial Development Bank of India and all the financial institutions consented to it, the court rescinded the winding up order after considering the scheme in detail. Since the company had remained closed for many years, there was no evidence of any existing employee whose interest had to be taken care of.[35]

Settlement of List of Contributories [S. 467]

The Court's has the power to cause the assets of the company to be collected and applied in discharge of its liabilities. For this purpose, the Court's has the power to make a list of such shareholders (called 'contributories') as are liable to contribute to the assets of the company. If this requires rectification of the register of members, the court may do so in all cases where rectification is required in pursuance of the Act. The Tribunal may, after ascertaining the sufficiency of the company's assets, proceed to make calls on all or any of the contributories requiring them, within the limits of their liability, to pay any money which the court considers necessary to satisfy the debts and liabilities of the company, and the expenses of winding up and for the adjustment of the rights of the contributories.[36] The Court's order, subject to any right of appeal, is conclusive evidence of the money due from the contributory.

Adjustment of Rights of Contributories [S. 475]

The Court has the power to adjust the rights of the contributories among themselves and distribute any surplus among the persons who are entitled to it.

National Steel and General Mills v *Official Liquidator*, [1989] 2 Comp LJ 214 Del: (1990) 69 Comp Cas 416, members can apply to court under S. 391 for sanctioning the scheme. Members do not cease to be members for all purposes. *Nilkanta Kolay* v *Official Liquidator*, (1996) 22 Corpt LA 30 Cal, winding up order and sale of factory not set aside, purchaser had made huge investments to restart factory, application was made by the managing director after long delay and was apparently lacking bona fide.

34. *Baranagar Jute Factory plc* v *Laxmi Narayan Taparia*, (2005) CLC 500 Cal; *Dhankari Investments Ltd* v *Official Liquidator*, (2006) 132 Comp Cas 749 All, company became solvent earning profits again, sufficient assets to fulfil objects no secured creditors, members rescinded the resolution for winding up. The court stayed winding and directed the liquidator to handover the charge to directors.

35. *Union of India* v *Shivalik Cellulose (P) Ltd*, (1991) 72 Comp Cas 545 Del.

36. S. 460.

Power to Arrest Absconding Contributory [S. 479]

After making a winding up order and on proof of a probable cause to believe that a contributory, in order to evade payment of calls or to avoid examination respecting the affairs of the company, is about to quit India or otherwise to abscond or to conceal his books or property the Tribunal may order his arrest and detention until such time as is necessary, or the seizure of his books, papers or property until such time as may be necessary.

Saving of Existing Powers [S. 480]

The powers conferred by the Companies Act on the court are in addition to the already regular and existing powers of instituting proceedings against any contributory or debtor of the company or the estate of any contributory or debtor for the recovery of any call or other sums.

The right of Set-off [S. 469]

Where, apart from his liability as a shareholder, any other money is due from a contributory to the company, the court may order him to pay the same. Suppose the company also owes some money to such a contributory. Does he have the right to claim that the two debts should be mutually set off? Not in all cases, but a limited right to set-off is given by the Act in the following cases:[37]

1. In the case of an unlimited company, a contributory may set off his debt against any money due to him from the company on any independent dealing or contract with the company. But no set-off is allowed for any money due to him as a member of the company in respect of any dividend or profit.

2. If, in the case of a limited company, there is any director, managing agent, secretaries and treasurers or manager whose liability is unlimited, he shall have the same right of set-off, as is described in point(1) above.

3. In the case of any company, whether limited or unlimited, when all the creditors have been paid in full, any money due on any account whatever to a contributory from the company may be allowed to him by set-off against any subsequent call. This is the one case where set-off is allowed for money due on a call.[38]

---

37. S. 473.
38. S. 469(3). See *T. N. Bank Subsidiary Co, Re*, AIR 1940 Mad 266; *Official Liquidator of Industrial Bank of India Ltd* v *Kesho Das*, AIR 1919 Lah 242. Set-off is, however, always allowed to debtors. See *Official Liquidator* v *Lakshmikutty*, (1975) 45 Comp Cas 679 Kant. The maker of a promissory note who had already made part payment was obliged to pay only the balance. *Efficient Financiers (P) Ltd, Re*, (1976) 46 Comp Cas 411 Kant and *Gokul Chit Funds* v *Vareed*, (1977) 47 Comp Cas 264 Ker. *A Company, Re, (No 1641 of 2003)*, (2004) 1 BCLC 210 Ch D, no set off was allowed where there was no evidence and none before the Registrar to prove the factual foundation of the set off claim and the liabilities arose only after presentation of the petition.

Where a director was found liable to contribute to the assets of the company, he was not allowed to set off that liability against any debt owed to him by the company.[39]

Delivery of Property [S. 468]

If any contributory, trustee, receiver, banker, agent, officer or other employee of the company is in possession of any money, property, books or papers of the company, the court may require him to deliver the same to the liquidator. The purpose is to provide a summary procedure for quick collection of the company's assets avoiding expensive and dilatory litigation. Hence, the court can in its discretion order restoration of the company's property on the basis of evidence showing prima-facie title and need not embark into detailed enquiry.[40] Certain movable property (goods) of the company was attached before judgment and subsequently an order was passed that the property be returned after taking security. On a State Financial Corporation's application the creditor was ordered to handover to the official liquidator the company's goods lying with him failing which he would open himself up to legal consequences.[41] The court may also summon before it any officer of the company or person known or suspected to have in his possession any such property of the company, or known or suspected to be indebted to the company or any person whom the court deems capable of giving information concerning the promotion, formation, trade, property or other affairs of the company.[42] Any such person may be examined on oath.[43] This is called "private examination". He cannot refuse to answer

---

39. *Anglo-French Coop Society, Re*, (1882) 21 Ch D 492 followed in *Manson v Smith*, (1997) 2 BCLC 161 CA.

40. *Bala Financiers (P) Ltd v Vjir Singh*, (1989) 65 Comp Cas 651, 653 P&H. *See* also *Maruti Ltd v P. R. Sasidharn*, (1990) 68 Comp Cas 5 P&H salaries paid to employees in good faith were not permitted to be recovered, though they were not sanctioned by the board of directors. The purpose of the section is to enable the liquidator to get maximum possible information about the assets of the company and, therefore, the court permitted the liquidator to share that information with the company's subsidiaries though he had obtained the same from the main creditor, PNB, under a promise of secrecy. *Esal (Commodities) Ltd, Re*, 1989 BCLC 59 CA; *Rome v PNB (No 2)*, [1990] 1 All ER 59 CA.

41. *Karnataka State Financial Corpn v Span Projects (P) Ltd*, (2005) 57 SCL 351 Kant; *Textile Labour Assn v OL of Amruta Mills Ltd*, (2005) 126 Comp Cas 469 Guj, order passed for delivery of property under S. 477 so that the liquidator may not have to resort to any proceedings.

42. S. 477(1).

43. S. 477(2). Where the directors did not submit the statement of affairs and the information with the liquidator was not sufficient to enable him to take action for realising the assets of the company and recovering debts due to it, private examination of the directors was ordered, *Official Liquidator v Ganesh Narain Podar*, (1991) 70 Comp Cas 588 Raj. It has been held that any honest person who finds himself to be involved, however innocently, in a major fraud, which had catastrophic effects for thousands of depositors, naturally was expected to cooperate with those whose duty it was to investigate the matter. Where it was possible that the respondents might be potential defendants although the liquidators had not made even a tentative decision to bring proceedings against them. The court ordered that the respondents should provide the requisite information, *Bank of Credit and Commerce International SA (In Liq.) (No. 2)*, (1997) 1 BCLC 526 Ch D.

questions only on the ground that the information given by him might be used against him in the pending misfeasance proceedings.[44] He may, however, refuse to answer incriminating questions. The court has the power to order examination on the application not only of the liquidator, but also of any creditor or contributory.[45] The court may require him to produce any books and papers in his custody relating to the company. If he claims any lien on them, the production shall be without prejudice to the lien and the court shall have the power to decide the question.[46] Where he fails to appear before the court, it may cause him to be apprehended and brought before it for examination.[47] If, on examination, he admits that he is indebted to the company or has any property in his possession, the court may order him to pay the amount or deliver the property to the liquidator.[48]

Recovery of a debt cannot be ordered under this section. A regular civil suit would have to be filed. The debtor was also disputing liability in this case.[49]

Power to order Deposit in Reserve Bank [S. 471]

The court has the power to require any contributory, purchaser or other person from whom any money is due to the company to pay the money into the public account of India in the Reserve Bank instead of the liquidator. Section 472 then declares that all moneys, bills, hundis, notes or other securities paid or delivered into the Reserve Bank in the course of winding up of a company by the Tribunal are to be in all respects subject to the orders of the court.

Power to Exclude Creditors [S. 474]

The court has the power to fix time or times within which creditors are to prove their debts or claims or to be excluded from the benefit of any distribution made before these debts or claims are proved.

Public Examination [S. 478]

Where the Official Liquidator has made a report to the court stating that in his opinion a fraud has been committed by any person in the promotion or formation of the company, or by any officer of the company since its formation, the court may direct that the person or officer may appear before

---

44. *Pravin Shankarchand Shah* v *D. B. Dalal*, (1967) 37 Comp Cas 317 Bom.
45. *Shankarlal Agarwalla* v *Satya Narayan Jugal Kishore*, (1967) 37 Comp Cas 146 Cal.
46. S. 477(3).
47. S. 477(4).
48. S. 477(5)(*b*). *See* also sub-sections (8) and (9). The orders of the court under this section are executable in the same manner as a decree for payment of money or delivery of property. An order so executed operates as a discharge from liability unless the court orders otherwise. *State of J&K* v *Hindustan Forests Co (P) Ltd*, (1997) 88 Comp Cas 21 and 54 P&H.
49. *Shivalik Chit fund and Machine Tools (P) Ltd* v *Agricultural Industries*, (1997) 89 Comp Cas 62: AIR 1996 HP 83.

it and be publicly examined.[50] Examination shall relate to the promotion or formation of the company, or to the conduct of its business or the person's conduct and dealings as an officer.[51] The necessary conditions for exercising the power to order public examination are—

1. that the Official Liquidator has made a further report;
2. that such report contains a finding of fraud;
3. the finding of fraud must be against the person whose examination is sought;
4. the individual must be one who has taken part in the promotion or formation of the company or who has been an officer of the company.[52]

Thus even where the report of an Official Liquidator contains allegations of fraud, such as over-borrowing by the company on forged documents, the court will not order the examination of an officer unless the report attributes to him some specific acts of fraud.[53] If the allegations are of specific nature, it will not be necessary for the liquidator to offer any proof. A public examination would not have been necessary if proofs were already available. There could have been a direct action in that case. In a Delhi case[54], the allegations were that no receipts had been obtained for certain payments, that certain others were not at all shown in books of account and that there were also overpayments. It was held that these allegations were sufficiently specific to justify an order of public examination of the managing director. Where a director was not charged with fraud in the liquidator's report, but he filed an affidavit assuming

---

50. A receiver appointed by debenture-holders is an officer for this purpose and can be examined. *Hiralal Kalyanmalji Seth* v *Gendalal Mills Ltd*, (1975) 2 SCC 516: (1976) 46 Comp Cas 142. The SEB, taking over an electricity supply company also collected its outstanding bills. The SEB was directed by the court to hand over the amount to the liquidator of the company. *Benaras Electric Light & Power Co* v *UPSEB*, (1983) 53 Comp Cas 597 Cal. The tenancy rights of the company taken over by the Board were held to have become vested in the Board. Where the whole undertaking has not been taken over, nor the company wants to remain in business, tenancy would have to be surrendered to the landlord. *Ravindra Ishwardas Sethna* v *Official Liquidator*, (1983) 4 SCC 269: (1983) 54 Comp Cas 702. For another case on delivery of property see *Inderbir Kaur* v *Satbir Singh*, (1983) 53 Comp Cas 768 Del. *Casterbridge Properties Ltd, Re, Jeeves* v *Official Liquidator*, (2004) 1 BCLC 96 (CA), no order was granted where there was no proper question to be put to the examinee. But an order of examination was passed under the section because the questions to be asked could be identified at the examination. An appeal against the order was dismissed.
51. S. 478(1).
52. See Buckley, ON COMPANIES, 13th Edn 65. Adopted by the Calcutta High Court in *Lohar Valley Tea Co, Re*, (1964) 68 CWN 938. *See* also the Supreme Court decision in *Official Liquidator* v *K. Madhava Naik*, [1965] 1 Comp LJ 161 SC.
53. *Official Liquidator* v *C. V. Raman*, [1966] 2 Comp LJ 124 Mad. *Official Liquidator* v *T. Sundaram*, (2003) 116 Comp Cas 88 Mad, an order of examination was considered not necessary where the directors had not controverted the report of the liquidator.
54. *Shiv Dayal* v *Liberty Finance (P) Ltd*, (1980) 50 Comp Cas 529 Del.

responsibility for the act constituting the fraud, the court ordered him to stand public examination.[55]

"Public examination under the provisions of the Act does not amount to accusation and is not prohibited under Article 20(3) of the Constitution of India."[56]

The Official Liquidator has to take part in the examination.[57] The court may put such questions to the person examined as it thinks fit.[58] The examination shall be on oath and he shall answer all questions as the court may put or allow to be put to him.[59] However, he should be given the opportunity to be heard and present his objections, if any, before any order for his examination is made.[60] He may apply to the court to be exculpated from any charges made or suggested against him. If he does so the Official Liquidator shall appear on the hearing of the application and call the court attention to relevant matters.[61]

Dissolution of company [S. 481]

When the affairs of the company have been completely wound up or when, for want of funds, the liquidator cannot proceed with the winding up or if it is just and reasonable to do so, the Tribunal shall make an order that the company be dissolved from the date of the order, and the company shall stand dissolved. Within thirty days, the liquidator should file a copy of the order with the Registrar.[62]

ENFORCEMENT OF ORDERS AND APPEALS

Enforcement of orders [S. 482]

An order of a winding up court is enforceable throughout the country through courts having jurisdiction in the area where an

---

55. *Central Tipperah Tea Co Ltd, Re*, [1966] 2 Comp LJ 82 Cal. Following *George Stapylton, ex p*, 1896 AC 146 and *Lohar Valley Tea Co, Re*, (1964) 68 CWN 938. *See* also GAJENDRAGADKAR CJ in *K. Joseph Augusthi* v *M. A. Narayanan*, (1963) 34 Comp Cas 546: AIR 1964 SC 1552 at p 1557.

56. *Narayanlal* v *M. P. Mistry*, (1960) 30 Comp Cas 644: AIR 1961 SC 29. Followed : *Official Liquidator* v *Raman*, [1966] 2 Comp LJ 124 and *Official Liquidator* v *Haridas Mundra*, [1970] 2 Comp LJ 46.

57. S. 478(2) and (3).

58. S. 478(4).

59. S. 478(5).

60. See *Lohar Valley Tea Co, Re*, (1964) 68 CWN 938.

61. S. 478(7).

62. The power can be exercised only after the affairs have been completely wound up. *Biswanath Khan* v *Prafulla Kumar Khan*, (1989) 66 Comp Cas 452 Cal: [1989] 3 Comp LJ 208 Cal. The power of the court is extensive enough to cover an order of dissolution without winding up. Accordingly, where the company had no assets left and there was no point in winding up, the court ordered direct dissolution, *Sarmon (P) Ltd* v *Sidha Syntex Ltd*, (1994) 2 Crimes 257.

enforcement is sought to the same extent as if it were an order made by that particular court and the registered office of the company was situate in that jurisdiction. But that court cannot interfere with the order. If anybody is aggrieved with the merits of the order, his proceedings against the order must be in that very court which passed it.[63] The court through which an enforcement is sought must itself be a court having jurisdiction in company matters within the meaning of Section 2(H).[64]

Appeals from orders [S. 483]

Appeals from orders or decisions in the matter of winding up can be filed in the same court which passed or delivered them. A winding up petition often sounds the death knell of the company. It is unlikely that a liquidator would pursue the company's counter-claims with the same diligence and efficiency as the directors would do. The company's appeal against a winding up order was allowed on this ground.[65]

The manner of filing appeals and the conditions subject to which they can be filed are to be the same as in other cases within its ordinary jurisdiction. Where a winding up petition or other petitions under Sections 397 and 398 are pending before the company court, and an interim injunction is passed in any other proceedings, the order is "in the matter of winding up" within the meaning of Section 483 and is, therefore, appealable. The words "in the matter of winding up" mean that the order or decision must be one pertaining to or within the scope of winding up jurisdiction. Every order which may reasonably be considered a judicial order, as distinguished from a merely administrative order, is appealable under the section.[66] A decision upon the right or liability of parties in the exercise of judicial discretion would be appealable.[67] Where during the pendency of a petition under Section 397 or 398 for relief against mismanagement or oppression, an interim injunction was granted and the appointment of a receiver was ordered, this was held to be appealable.[68] An order enabling the parties to compromise was held to be not appealable.[69] The transfer of

63. *Raghbir Singh* v *Distt Magistrate, Delhi*, [1963] 2 Comp LJ 230 : (1964) 34 Comp Cas 25 Punj.
64. *Eastern Investment Co Ltd, Re*, [1905] 1 Ch 352.
65. *Bayoil SA, Re*, [1999] 1 All ER 374 CA. An order of winding up has serious civil consequences. An appeal against such order becomes maintainable. *Bangalore Turf Club Ltd* v *N. Sundaraswamy*, (2005) 124 Comp Cas 373 Kant.
66. The distinction between an administrative and a judicial order was developed by the Supreme Court in *Shankerlal Agarwala* v *Shankerlal Poddar*, (1965) 35 Comp Cas 1 SC: AIR 1965 SC 507. Following this the Supreme Court held in *Shah Babulal Khimji* v *Jayaben D. Kania*, (1981) 4 SCC 8: AIR 1981 SC 1786 that an order refusing the appointment of a receiver for the suit property was appealable.
67. *Manohar* v *TR Mills (P) Ltd*, (1994) 3 Kar LJ 306, interlocutory order, held not appealable.
68. *C. S. Joseph Rev* v *L. J. Thomas*, (1987) 62 Comp Cas 504 Ker.
69. *Ashok Kumar Gupta* v *Metal Goods (P) Ltd*, (1992) 20 All LR 72 Summary: (1993) 76 Comp Cas 23 All, relying upon *Notified Area Committee* v *Sri Ram Singhasan*, AIR 1970

a pending suit to the winding up court[70] and the disposal of a pending suit have been held to be appealable.[71] An order simply admitting a petition for winding up without order advertisement was held to be not appealable.[72]

Where a secured creditor brought the assets of the company to sale and the sale was confirmed in favour of the highest bidder, and after all this, a nominee of the company came out with a higher bid and preferred an appeal against the confirmation, the court set aside the confirmation and remanded the case to the Company Judge with the remark that the highest price available must be accepted at any stage of the proceedings.[73] Where the highest bidder proposed to take away the property to his State, that was held to be no ground for not accepting his bid. The interest of the local State is not a relevant factor in confirmation of sale.[74]

All 561 where it was held that a special appeal lies only against a judgment finally deciding the case.
70. *B. P. Gupta* v *State Bank of India*, (1993) 78 Comp Cas 766.
71. *Ibid.*
72. *Miland Exports (P) Ltd* v *A. V. Venkatnarayana*, (1995) 83 Comp Cas 585 Kant. An appeal does not lie against an order admitting a winding up petition. *Achal Alloys* v *UCO Bank*, (1996) 1 Comp LJ 287 MP.
73. *Bysani Anjaneyulu* v *Trilinga Technical & Management Consultant (P) Ltd*, (2003) 114 Comp Cas 37 AP.
74. *Imperial Fasteners (P) Ltd* v *Industrial Development Corpn Ltd*, (2005) 59 SCL 647 Ori.

22
Voluntary Winding Up

A company may be wound up voluntarily in the following two ways:

1. *By ordinary resolution*

A company may be wound up voluntarily by passing an ordinary resolution when the period, if any, fixed for the duration of the company by the articles, has expired. Similarly, when the event, if any, has occurred, on the occurrence of which the articles provide that the company is to be dissolved, the company may, by passing an ordinary resolution to that effect, commence its voluntary winding up.[1]

2. *By special resolution*

A company may at any time pass a special resolution providing that the company be wound up voluntarily.[2]

Winding up commences at the time when the resolution is passed.[3]

Within fourteen days of the passing of the resolution, the company shall give notice of the resolution by advertisement in the Official Gazette and also in some newspaper circulating in the district of the registered office of the company.[4]

The corporate state and powers of the company shall continue until the company is dissolved, but it shall stop its business, except so far as may be necessary for beneficial winding up.[5]

Declaration of solvency [S. 488]

Voluntary winding up is of two kinds, namely:

1. Members' voluntary winding up, and
2. Creditors' voluntary winding up.

If a declaration of solvency is made in accordance with the provisions of the Act, it will be a members' voluntary winding up and if it is not made, it becomes creditors' voluntary winding up. The declaration has to be made by a majority of the directors at a meeting of the board and verified by an

---

1. S. 484(1)(*a*).
2. S. 484(1)(*b*). See *Neptune Assurance Co* v *UOI*, (1973) 1 SCC 310, RAY J (later CJ) at p 331 : (1973) 43 Comp Cas 469.
3. S. 486.
4. S. 485(1). Sub-section (2) provides that if a default is made in publishing the resolution, the company and every defaulting officer shall be punishable with a fine extending up to 500 rupees for every day of the default.
5. S. 487. See *Hari Prasad Jayantilal & Co* v *ITO, Ahmedabad*, AIR 1966 SC 1481: (1966) 2 SCR 732: [1966] 1 Comp LJ 230. Retrenchment compensation to employees becomes payable from the date of the resolution unless the employees are retained for continuation of business. *P. N. Ganesan (P) Ltd* v *CIT*, (1992) 74 Comp Cas 780 Mad.

affidavit. They have to declare that they have made a full inquiry into the affairs of the company and have formed the opinion that the company has no debts or that it will be able to pay its debts in full within a certain period, not exceeding three years, from the commencement of winding up. The declaration, to be effective, must be made within the five weeks immediately before the date of the resolution and should be delivered to the Registrar for registration before that date. It should also be accompanied by a copy of the report of the auditors on the profit and loss account and the balance sheet of the company prepared up to the date of the declaration and should embody a statement of the company's assets and liabilities as at that date.[6] There is a penalty for making the declaration without having reasonable grounds for the opinion that the company will be able to pay its debts within the specified period.[7] If the company fails to pay the debts within that period, it will be presumed that reasonable grounds for making the declaration did not exist.[8] The liquidator should forthwith call a meeting of the creditors, because the winding up has then to proceed as if it were creditors' winding up.[9]

Members' voluntary winding up [S. 489]

A liquidator is appointed and his remuneration fixed by the company in general meeting of the shareholders.[10] The remuneration so fixed is not to be increased in any circumstances whatsoever, with or without the sanction of the court.[11] 'The liquidator is not to take charge unless his remuneration is so fixed.[12] Within ten days of the appointment, the company should give a notice to the Registrar.[13] The liquidator within 30 days of his appointment, has to publish in the Official Gazette, and deliver to the Registrar for registration, a notice of his appointment in the prescribed form.[14] If a vacancy occurs, the company may in general meeting fill the vacancy[15] and again, within ten days, a notice of the change must be given to the Registrar.

---

6. S. 488(2). *Surat Dyes* v *Arya Sieh Mills (P) Ltd*, (2005) 125 Comp Cas 212 Guj, the condition is mandatory. A declaration filed after the date of resolution and accompanied only by the statement of directors as to assets and liabilities was held to be not a compliance. The winding up was not treated as members' winding up. *New Millennium Experiences Ltd, Re*, (2004) 1 BCLC 19 (Ch D), errors and inaccuracies in the statement did not affect its validity because the statement was not incorrect to the extent of being false.

7. S. 488(3).

8. S. 488(4).

9. S. 495.

10. S. 490(1). In an exceptional case the court allowed the liquidator to recover his remuneration from the trust property which he was safeguarding as a part of his duty, the company having no means to pay him *Berkery Applegate Ltd, Re*, [1988] 3 All ER 71 Ch D.

11. S. 490(2).

12. S. 490(3).

13. S. 493.

14. S. 516. Failure to do so is punishable with fine extending up to Rs 500 for every day of default.

15. S. 492.

The liquidator has also to inform the Registrar of his appointment within thirty days and publish the fact in the Official Gazette.

On the appointment of the liquidator all the powers of the board of directors shall come to an end except when the company or the liquidator sanctions them to continue.[16]

Reconstruction in Winding Up [S. 494]

Where the company in liquidation proposes to sell its business or property to another company, the liquidator may, with the sanction of a special resolution of the company, receive as a consideration for the transfer, shares or other like interest in the transferee company for distribution among the members of the transferor company. Also he may enter into any other arrangement under which the members of the transferor company may, instead of, or in addition to, receiving cash, shares, *etc.*, participate in the profits or other benefits of the transferee company. The interest of a dissenting member, if any, can be purchased by the liquidator at a price to be determined by agreement or by arbitration.[17]

Duty to call Creditors' Meeting

If the company has not been able to, or, in the opinion of the liquidator will not be able to pay its debts in full within the period stated in the declaration of solvency, he should immediately summon a meeting of the creditors and lay before them a statement of the assets and liabilities of the company[18] and, thereafter, the winding up shall proceed in the manner of creditors' voluntary winding up.[19]

Where the liquidation continues for more than a year the liquidator has to call a general meeting of the company at the end of the first year and at the end of each subsequent year.[20] He should lay before the meeting an account of his acts and dealings and the progress of the winding up during the year.[21]

---

16. S. 491. The meeting is to be held in accordance with the provisions of the Act or as the Tribunal may require on application. *Majid Ahmedbhai Oomerbhoy* v *Rashid Sattar Oomerbhoy*, (2006) 132 Comp Cas 382 Bom, directors continue to be directors until orders of winding up be passed. Hence continuing to occupy company premises under arrangement of gratuitous licence which was not terminated remained valid till order of winding up. There was no liability to pay compensation up to that day.
17. Where the company defaulted in paying the amount settled in a scheme, and the court, which had approved the scheme, ordered sale of assets, it was held that Order 34 of CPC for setting aside the sale was not applicable as the sale was not in the execution of a decree, but under an order of the court under its power of supervision. *Bank of Baroda* v *Anand Finance Ltd*, (1980) 50 Comp Cas 279 Del.
18. S. 495(1). Sub-s. (2) provides a penalty for default extending up to five thousand rupees.
19. S. 498.
20. S. 496(1). The meeting must be held within three months from the end of each year or such longer period as the Central Government may allow.
21. A default shall entail punishment extending up to one thousand rupees. S. 496(2). He has also to file audited statements in terms of S. 551.

Final Meeting and Dissolution [S. 497]

When the affairs of the company are fully wound up, the liquidator makes an account of the winding up showing how the winding up has been conducted and the property of the company disposed of. He then calls a general meeting of the company for the purpose of laying before it the accounts of the winding up. The meeting is to be called by advertisement in the Official Gazette and a local newspaper specifying the time, place and object of the meeting. Within a week after the meeting the liquidator sends a copy of the accounts and a return of the meeting to the Registrar and the Official Liquidator.[22] If no quorum was present at the meeting, he makes a return stating the fact.[23]

The Registrar, on receipt of the accounts and the return, registers the documents. The Official Liquidator, to whom also a copy of the accounts and return is sent, is required to make a scrutiny of the books and papers of the company. The liquidator of the company and its past and present officers are under a duty to give the Official Liquidator all reasonable facility for the purpose.[24] The Official Liquidator reports to the Tribunal the result of his scrutiny. If the report shows that the affairs of the company were not conducted in a manner prejudicial to the interest of its members or to public interest, then from the date of the submission of the report to the Tribunal, the company shall be deemed to be dissolved.

If the report reveals that the affairs were conducted in a manner prejudicial to the interests of the members or to public interest, the court shall direct the Official Liquidator to make further investigation into the affairs of the company.[25] The court may invest him with such powers as may be necessary for the purpose. When the court receives the report on further investigation, it may declare that the company stands dissolved or make such order as the circumstances discovered by the report may warrant.[26]

Creditors' voluntary winding up [S. 499]

The company calls a meeting of its creditors. The meeting may be held either on the same day on which a resolution for voluntary winding up is passed or the next day following that day. Notices of the meeting of creditors have to be sent by post to the creditors simultaneously with the

22. The official liquidator referred to in S. 448(1)(*c*), who may be a wholetime or part-time officer appointed by the Central Government.
23. S. 497(4).
24. S. 497(6).
25. S. 497(6-A).
26. S. 497(5), (6), (6-A) and (6-B) as amended by the Amendment of 1965. The unclaimed property of the company, if any, becomes vested in the State and cannot be made the subject-matter of litigation without impleading the State. *Biswanath Khan* v *Prafulla Kumar Khan*, (1989) 66 Comp Cas 452 Cal: [1989] 3 Comp LJ 208 Cal.

sending of the notices of the meeting of the company.[27] Notice of the meeting should also be advertised in the Official Gazette and in two newspapers circulating in the district of the registered office or principal place of business of the company.[28] The board of directors have to lay before the meeting a full statement of the position of the company's affairs and a list of the creditors of the company and the estimated amount of their claims.[29] A copy of any resolution passed at the creditors' meeting must be filed with the Registrar.[30]

Appointment of liquidator is made by nomination both by the members and creditors at their respective meetings.[31] If they nominate different persons, ordinarily, the creditors' nominee shall be the liquidator.[32] But any director, member or creditor may apply to the Tribunal for an order that the company's nominee or the official liquidator or some other person should be appointed. If no person is nominated by the creditors, the members' nominee shall be the liquidator. Likewise, if no nomination is made by the members, the creditors' nominee shall be the liquidator.[33]

The creditors may appoint a committee of inspection consisting of five persons.[34] The company may also add five members to the committee.[35] If the creditors do not accept the company's nominees, an application may be made to the court for settlement.[36] The committee of inspection, or, where there is no such committee, the creditors shall fix the remuneration of the liquidator, failing which, it shall be determined by the court.[37] On the appointment of the liquidator the powers of the board come to an end.[38] The procedure to be followed by the liquidator is just the same as in the case of members' voluntary winding up, except that in addition to the meetings of the members, the liquidator has also to call meetings of the creditors.[39]

---

27. S. 500(1). A creditor can attend in person or through proxy. It has been held that message of proxy received through fax and signed by the creditor or by someone authorised by him would be a proper proxy form and the creditor would have the right to attend the creditors meeting through such a proxy. *A Debtor (No 2021 of 1995), ex p, Re*, (1996) 1 BCLC 538 Ch D; *IRC* v *The Debtor*, (1996) 1 BCLC 538 Ch D.
28. S. 500(2).
29. S. 500(3).
30. S. 501(1). *See* also sub-section (2).
31. S. 502(1).
32. S. 502(2).
33. S. 502(1), (2), (3), and (4). Within twenty-one days, the liquidator should get his appointment published in the Official Gazette and send a notice to the Registrar. S. 506 provides that except where appointed by the court, any vacancy in the office of the liquidator may be filled by the creditors.
34. S. 503(1).
35. S. 503(2).
36. *Ibid.*, proviso and *see* sub-sections (3), (4) and (5).
37. S. 504(1) and (2).
38. But the committee of inspection or the creditors may sanction the board's power to continue. S. 505.
39. *See* Ss. 507, 508 and 509.

Provisions applicable to every voluntary winding up [S. 510]

Statement of Affairs [S. 511-A]

A statement as to the affairs of the company has to be submitted to the liquidator. The statement has to be submitted and verified by the directors, manager, secretary or other chief officers of the company. The statement should show the following particulars:

1. the assets of the company, showing separately cash in hand and at bank and negotiable securities;

2. the debts and liabilities of the company;

3. names and addresses of the company's creditors, indicating the amount of secured or unsecured debts;

4. the debts due to the company and the names and addresses of the persons from whom they are due and the amount likely to be realised;

5. such other information as may be required.

Powers of Liquidator [S. 512]

The powers of the liquidator in voluntary winding up are just the same as those of the official liquidator in a winding up by the Tribunal.[40] There is, however, this difference that in cases where the official liquidator has to obtain the sanction of the Tribunal, the liquidator in voluntary winding up shall have to obtain the sanction of the company, and in the case of creditors' voluntary winding up, he shall have to obtain the sanction of the Tribunal, or of the committee of inspection, or, in its absence, of the creditors. In addition to those powers, the liquidator shall have the following powers:

1. The power of the court of settling the list of contributories.[41]

2. The power of the court of making calls.[42] Sanction of the court is not necessary. His right to make a call is also not affected by the fact that the company had itself made a call which had become time-barred.[43]

3. The power of calling general meetings of the company.[44]

A voluntary liquidator is not, speaking strictly, an officer of the company, but even so he is in the position of an officer because he takes

---

40. Accordingly he has the power to initiate legal proceedings on behalf of the company with the sanction of shareholders or creditors as the case may be, *State of W.B.* v *Arun Kumar Bose,* (1993) 2 Cal LJ 56.

41. *See* S. 467.

42. *See* S. 470.

43. *T. M. Mathew* v *Industrial Bank Ltd,* (1972) 42 Comp Cas 55 Ker.

44. S. 512(1)(*e*).

over the management of the company from its directors. He is, thus, entitled to a relief under Section 633 if the conditions are satisfied.

Advance distribution of surplus assets

A company in voluntary winding up had contingent creditors who had claims arising out of product liability to consumers. The court said that it was clear that it had jurisdiction to authorise a distribution of assets in members' voluntary winding up not withstanding the risk of any future claims which may emerge. The court had, in this case, to balance that risk against the inconvenience to the French parent company if no distribution was made. The court passed the necessary order with the direction that a sufficient reserve was retained to cover the risk of future contingent claims.[45]

Arrangement when Binding [S. 517]

Any arrangement entered into by a company about to be or being wound up and its creditors becomes binding upon the parties provided that it has been sanctioned by a special resolution of the company and acceded to by three-fourths in number and value of the creditors. Any creditor or contributory can prefer an appeal within three weeks and then the arrangement will be approved, varied or discarded depending upon the discretion of the Tribunal and the merits of the scheme.[46]

Costs of Voluntary Winding Up [S. 520]

All costs, charges and expenses properly incurred in the winding up, including the remuneration of the liquidator, are, subject to the rights of secured creditors, payable out of the assets of the company in priority to all other claims. Rents paid for premises which were necessary for winding up are expenses properly incurred, but not accumulated lease money for property which was retained out of sheer inaction.[47] The expenses incurred by the liquidator in proceedings against directors for preferential payments and wrongful trading were held to be costs, charges and other expenses incurred in the course of winding up. They had priority over preferential creditors irrespective of the success or failure of the proceedings.[48]

---

45. *Tombs v Moulinex SA*, (2004) 2 BCLC 397 (Ch D).
46. See *Inland Revenue Commissioners v Adams & Partners Ltd*, [1999] 2 BCLC 730 Ch D, on appeal Daily Telegraph, Oct 31, 2000 CA, a scheme which proposed no dividend to unsecured creditors was held to be a valid scheme of arrangement, but not of compromise. It was sanctioned because it was approved by requisite majority.
47. *Massey, Freehold Land & Brickmaking Co, Re*, 1870 LR 9 EQ 367; *Linda Marie Ltd, Re*, 1989 BCLC 46 Ch D.
48. *Floor Fourteen Ltd, Re*, [1999] 2 BCLC 666 Ch D.

Removal of Liquidator [S. 515]

In the exercise of his powers, the liquidator shall be subject to the control of the Tribunal.[49] Any creditor or contributory may apply to the Tribunal with respect to any exercise or proposed exercise of the liquidator's powers. If the Tribunal finds that, from any cause whatever, no liquidator is functioning the Tribunal may appoint the official liquidator or any other person as the liquidator of the company. The Tribunal also has the power, on cause shown, to remove a liquidator and appoint some other person in his place.[50] In *Dr Hardit Singh* v *ROC*,[51] the Delhi High Court ordered the removal of a voluntary liquidator on the grounds that he had not deposited certain amounts as required by Section 553 of the Act, that he had been uncooperative and defiant regarding the recovery of the company's claims and that the process of liquidation was a collusive affair between the ex-managing director and the liquidator. The Madras High Court[52] rejected an application for removal as the move was not *bona fide,* but was motivated by malice on account of certain actions which were taken against the applicant by the liquidator and because the applicant was apprehensive that the liquidator would pursue the action to the finish. "The courts are loathe to interfere with the scheme of self determination by the members of a company. Vague allegations are not sufficient to secure the removal of a liquidator.[53] Where the liquidator made no response to a creditor's claim and proofs, nor even replied to his letters enquiring about the matter, this was held to be dereliction of duty sufficient to merit removal.[54]

A liquidator is not removable only on the ground that he was a shareholder or director or because the creditors or members in majority demand it.[55]

The following statement occurs in a judgment of Astbury J[56] as to the meaning of the expression "on cause shown".

The words "on cause shown" have not quite the effect of "if the court shall think fit." Jessel MR said in *Sir John Moore Gold Mining Co, Re,*[57] "they point to some unfitness of the person—it may be from personal character, or from his connection with other parties, or from

49. *Registrar of Companies* v *Rowe & Pal*, (1972) 42 Comp Cas 188 Ori.
50. S. 515.
51. (1972) 42 Comp Cas 256 Del.
52. *Rangaswami* v *Mandhi Viswa Brahmana Sarvajana Sahaya Nidhi Ltd*, (1967) 37 Comp Cas 730 Mad.
53. *Registrar of Companies* v *Hardit Singh Giani*, (1978) 48 Comp Cas 152 Del.
54. *Amar Nath Krishan Lal* v *Hindustan Forest Co Ltd*, (1993) 77 Comp Cas 128 P&H.
55. *See* Charlesworth & Cain, COMPANY LAW, 606 (11th Edn, 1977), citing *M. Knight & Co Ltd* v *Montgomerie*, (1892) 19 R 501 and *Ker, Petitioner*, (1897) 5 SLT 126 OH.
56. *Rubber and Produce Investment Trust*, [1915] 1 Ch 382 at p 387.
57. (1879) 12 Ch D 325, 331.

circumstances in which he is mixed up — some unfitness in a wide sense of the term." But, as pointed out by the Court of Appeal in *Adam Eyton Ltd, Re*,[58] this definition was not intended to be exhaustive, and if the court is satisfied on the evidence that it is desirable in the interest of all those interested in the assets that a particular person shall not manage the assets, the court has power to remove him, without there being shown any personal misconduct or unfitness.

The liquidator or any contributory or creditor may apply to the Tribunal to determine any question arising in the winding up of the company or to exercise all or any of the powers which the Tribunal may exercise if the company were being wound by the Tribunal.[59] In the exercise of this power the Tribunal stayed a voluntary winding up because the company was producing a socially needed commodity, cement; it had resources, both raw material and finance and the shareholders wanted to revive their company.[60]

The liquidator may make a report to the Tribunal stating that in his opinion a fraud has been committed by any person in the promotion or formation of the company or by any officer after the formation of the company. The Tribunal may then direct the person to appear for public examination.[61]

Position of liquidator: duties and liability

In a winding up by the court, the liquidator is an officer of the court, and not an agent of the parties concerned.[62] In a voluntary winding up, he is not an officer of the court. He owes his appointment to the company in general meeting. In any case, the duties of liquidators of both kind are more or less of the same nature. In the conduct of winding up they have to perform basically the same functions. They have to take into their custody the property of the company;[63] to keep proper books for recording

58. (1887) 36 Ch D 299 CA.
59. S. 518. The court attaches great weight to the demand of the liquidator for public examination than in other cases. The application of a contributory was rejected when it appeared that his only purpose was to know his own position as a guarantor of the company's debts. *Embassy Art Products Ltd, Re*, 1988 BCLC 1 Ch D.
60. *V. B. Purohit* v *Gadag*, (1984) 56 Comp Cas 360 Kant.
61. S. 519(1). The provisions of sub-ss. (2) to (11) of S. 478 shall apply in relation to any such examination. See *Satish Churn Law* v *H. K. Ganguly*, AIR 1962 SC 806 : (1962) 32 Comp Cas 97.
62. *Rolls Razor Ltd, (No 2), Re*, [1970] Ch 576, 586.
63. S. 456. He can get the orders of a magistrate under this section to recover possession of the company's property. A landlord seized the godown of the company. The goods disappeared from the godown. The landlord was forced to pay to the liquidator the value of the goods lost. *Dalbir Singh* v *Sakaw Industries (P) Ltd*, (1983) 54 Comp Cas 359 Cal. Where a property has been delivered by way of security the liquidator can demand from the security holder the surplus proceeds of the property. *Maharashtra SEB* v *Official Liquidator, Ernakulam*, (1982) 3 SCC 358 : (1983) 53 Comp Cas 248; *India Electric Works Ltd, Re*, (1983) 53 Comp Cas 573 Cal. Where the property of the company was in the nature of shares in another company and that other company made a rights issue without offering its proportion to the company,

proceedings at meetings;[64] to have their accounts audited;[65] to call meetings of committees of inspection;[66] to call meetings of members and creditors.[67] They are to keep the moneys received by him as such in a special account in any Scheduled Bank to be entitled "the Liquidation A/C of...." The Court may, however, permit a liquidator to open any other account and to operate the same as directed for beneficial winding up. He should not hold the money for more than 10 days in his hands because he has then to pay interest @12% and incidental expenses and also take the risk of losing office. The bank in which such an account is opened becomes liable if through negligence any loss takes place to the liquidation account.[68]

The liability of a liquidator for breach of his duties involves the application of agency principles. Functionally, the liquidator is an agent of the company and not a trustee for shareholders or creditors. An individual shareholder or creditor cannot sue him for damages for delaying payments unless it is due to some deliberate misconduct towards a particular person. The proper remedy is to seek an order of the court in reference to his conduct.[69] Where, however, the failure to perform a statutory duty causes loss to an individual claimant, the liquidator may be held liable to him. For example, where the liquidator failed to contact a creditor whose name appeared in the books and the company was dissolved without paying him, the liquidator was held liable for his loss. The creditor could not submit his claim because he did not come to know of the winding up. The general advertisement inserted by the liquidator was considered by the court to be not sufficient.[70]

About the standard of care which the liquidator is expected to use, there is this comment by MAUGHAM J:[71]

> [O]bservations of the learned judges[72] certainly do not encourage the proposition that the liquidator is a mere agent, liable only if negligence of a gross kind is established. I should hesitate a long while

---

the liquidator can proceed to recover the company's due. *V. Radha Krishnan v P. R. Rama Krishnan*, (1993) 78 Comp Cas 694 Mad: (1995) 17 Corpt LA 63.

64. S. 461.
65. S. 462.
66. S. 464.
67. Ss. 495-497 and 508.
68. S. 553 and see *Madras Provincial Coop Bank v South Indian Match Factory*, [1944] 2 MLJ 295. S. 554 enjoins the liquidator not to keep the money in any private banking account. A liquidator defaulting in his functions can be directed by the court under S. 556 to make good the default.
69. *Knowles v Scott*, [1891] 1 Ch 717.
70. *Plusford v Devenish*, [1903] 2 Ch 625.
71. In *Home & Colonial Insurance Co, Re*, [1929] All ER Rep 231: [1930] 1 Ch 103, 124-125.
72. In *Windsor Steam Coal Co, Re*, [1929] 1 Ch 151, where negligence on the part of the liquidator was clearly established.

before deciding that a voluntary liquidator is personally liable, if notwithstanding every care on his part he admits a claim which is ill-founded. The statutory duties cast upon him involve the getting in of the property and applying such property in satisfaction of the liabilities *pari passu,* and subject thereto the distribution of the balance among the members.... The winding up rules recognise that the liquidator, who has to examine every proof of debt lodged with him and the grounds of the debts, may be wrong. The claim of the creditor may be based upon disputable matters of fact, as well as difficult questions of law. Moreover the duty of getting in the property of the company cannot be an absolute duty, since such property may be irrecoverable. I do not, therefore, accept the view that the liquidator in the matter of admitting proof is practically in the same position as an insurer so that, in any event, and under all circumstances, he is liable if a debt is subsequently shown to have been wrongly admitted.

On the other hand, I think there can be no doubt that, in the circumstances of the case, a high standard of care and diligence is required from a liquidator in a voluntary winding up. He is of course paid for his services; he is able to obtain wherever it is expedient the assistance of solicitors and counsel, and, which is a most important consideration; he is entitled, in every case of serious doubt or difficulty in relation to the performance of his statutory duties, to submit the matter to the court, and to obtain its guidance.

Applying these principles to the facts of the case, the court held the liquidator to be liable because he had admitted and paid a very big claim without proper precautions and legal advice. The company had entered into an agreement for re-insuring marine risks with another company. The liquidator paid a large sum of money to that other company which he supposed to be due under the agreement but which subsequently turned out to be void. The dissolution was annulled on that ground. The liquidator was not allowed to recover back the payment from the other company and, therefore, he was held personally liable for the company's loss. He did not fulfil his duty of investigating the claim. He did not take legal advice. The articles of a company cannot give any protection to a liquidator. They do not constitute any contract between him and the company.

Body Corporate cannot be Liquidator [S. 513]

A body corporate is not qualified to be appointed as a liquidator of a company in a voluntary winding up. Such an appointment is void. A body corporate which acts as a liquidator and its every director or manager is punishable with fine extending up to Rs 10,000.

A proviso has been added by the Second Amendment of 2002 to the following effect:

Provided that, notwithstanding anything contained in any other law for the time being in force a body corporate consisting of such professionals as may be approved by the Central Government from time to time, shall be qualified for appointment as Official Liquidator under Section 448.

Corrupt Inducement for becoming Liquidator [S. 514]

A person giving any gratification to any creditor or member for the purpose of becoming liquidator or preventing a person from becoming a liquidator is punishable with fine extending up to Rs 10,000.

WINDING UP SUBJECT TO SUPERVISION OF COURT [S. 522]

When a company has passed a resolution for voluntary winding up, the court may make an order that winding up shall proceed subject to its supervision. The advantages of this are: *Firstly*, the court may appoint an additional liquidator and remove a liquidator according to exigencies. *Secondly*, the court gets the same powers as it has in the case of winding up by the court. *Thirdly*, any creditor contributory or person may apply to the court for determining any question connected with the winding up. [Ss. 522-526]. This method of winding up would become abolished as soon as the second amendment of 2002 is enforced.

23
Conduct of Winding Up

Whether a winding up is by the Tribunal or voluntary, in many respects it is conducted in accordance with uniform rules. The Act contains a number of provisions applicable to every mode of winding up.[1]

One of the foremost duties of a liquidator is to get in the company's assets for the purpose of satisfying its debts and liabilities. If any property of the company is in the custody of some person, the liquidator can, through an application to the Tribunal, recover possession of that property.[2] An important asset which is available for winding up is the uncalled capital, if any, of the company.

Contributories [S. 428]

To realise the uncalled residue of the company's capital, the liquidator has to call upon the shareholders, who are then called contributories, to pay the unpaid balance. A "contributory means a person liable to contribute to the assets of a company in the event of winding up and includes the holders of any shares which are fully paid up".[3] The liability extends to an amount which would be sufficient for payment of the company's debts and liabilities and the costs, charges and expenses of winding up and for adjustment of the rights of contributories among themselves. The extent of each member's liability is to pay the unpaid amount on his shares. In the case of a guarantee company, apart from the guarantee amount, if a member is a shareholder also, he would be liable to pay the unpaid amount on his shares. Where any sum is owing by the company to a member in his capacity as a member such as dividend, it will not give him the rank of a creditor as against other unpaid creditors [even if they are members] of the company. [S. 426] Of such persons the liquidator has to make two lists. *List A* which is for present members and *List B* for past members.

Nature of Liability [S. 429]

List A is drawn up from the company's register of members. Every person whose name appears in the register on the commencement of winding up is placed on the list. When a person knows that his name is entered in a company's register of shareholders and continues to have it there up to the commencement of winding up, he will be estopped from going against the register and disowning liability. The liability of a member

---

1. Chapter V of Part VII.
2. *See* powers of the Tribunal in 'Compulsory Winding Up'. [S. 468].
3. S. 428. The liability of the fully paid shareholder is nil. He is placed on the list for the purpose of distribution of assets and for other procedural purposes. *Alote Estate* v *R. B. Seth*, (1970) 1 SCC 425: (1970) 40 Comp Cas 1116: AIR 1971 SC 920.

of a company to be included in the list of contributories is not *ex contractu,* that is, it does not arise by virtue of his contract to take shares. His liability is *ex lege* which means that it arises by reason of the fact that his name appears on the register of members of the company. It is, therefore, no answer for the contributory against the claims of the company to say that, although his name appears on the register, he is not liable because the allotment to him was void."[4] The total absence of a contract is however, different from the contract being violable. Where shares were allotted to a person without any application from him, the liquidator was not permitted to place his name in the list of contributories.[5]

It should, however, be noted that "a contributory is not liable to pay one farthing of the uncalled share money until the Tribunal has made such an order and a call notice has then been served upon the contributory in accordance with the Tribunal's order".[6] The Tribunal will authorise a call to be made only when it is satisfied that the financial condition of the company is such that a call is necessary to discharge the liabilities of the company.[7] In the case of voluntary winding up a call can be made by the liquidator without sanction of the Tribunal.

But once a call has been made, the liability of the contributory to pay it becomes a statutory debt. A new liability to pay the unpaid balance commences. "It is settled in a long course of decisions that the members of a company in liquidation are liable in respect of unpaid calls even though the calls were made by the company before it went into liquidation and the suit of the company for its realization had become barred by time. The principle of these decisions is that Section 429 creates a new liability on the shareholders in respect of such calls, which is distinct from and independent of the rights which the company had against them before the winding up."[8]

---

4. See *R. Lakshmi Narasa Reddi* v *Official Receiver, Sree Films Ltd,* AIR 1951 Mad 890; *Yamuna Das Kanoujia* v *Behar Engineer & Contractors Ltd,* AIR 1944 Pat 226; *Peninsular Life Assurance Co Ltd, Re,* AIR 1936 Bom 24. In this case a contributory's defence that out of 250 shares shown against his name in the company's register, 200 shares were held by him as nominee of one of the directors, was rejected. *See* also *Hakim Rai* v *Official Liquidator of Peshawar Bank Ltd,* AIR 1915 Lah 320; *Samasundaran Pillai* v *Official Liquidator,* [1967] 2 Comp LJ 257 Mad.

5. *H. H. Manabendra Shah* v *Official Liquidator,* (1977) 47 Comp Cas 356.

6. See *Sonardih Coal Co Ltd, Re,* AIR 1930 All 617. Section 426(1) provides that the section shall not invalidate any provision in a policy of insurance or other contract under which the liability of the individual member on the policy or contract is restricted or only the funds of the company are made liable.

7. S. 470. See *Mohd Akbar* v *Associated Banking Corpn of India,* AIR 1950 Bom 386.

8. *Pokhar Mal* v *Flour & Oil Mills Co Ltd,* AIR 1934 Lah 1015. *See* also *East Bengal Sugar Mills Ltd, Re,* AIR 1941 Cal 143; *P. P. Ramabhadran* v *T. S. Manickam,* AIR 1941 Mad 565; *L. Gupta* v *V. B. Sarvate,* AIR 1956 Nag 204; *Pudukkottai Ceramics Ltd* v *Sethu,* AIR 1956 Mad 448; *S. P. Subbiah* v *Peria Karuppan Chettiar,* [1967] 1 Comp LJ 168. The liquidator cannot claim interest from the date of the company's time-barred call, but only from the date of the court's order. *S. P. Subbiah* v *Peria Karuppan Chettiar,* [1967] 1 Comp LJ 168.

If a person's name is not included in the list, he can call upon the liquidator to make good the default and if the liquidator does not do so within 14 days, the court can under Section 556 issue necessary directions. A notice given six years before the date of application to the court cannot be acted upon.[9]

If a contributory dies during winding up, his liability automatically falls on his legal representatives.[10] "Where a contributory dies before his name is entered in the list of contributories and an order is made by the court for payment of the balance, such balance is recoverable from his legal representatives and heirs. But in such a case, the proper procedure for the company or liquidator to enforce payment is to adopt proceedings for administration of the estate of the deceased and not seek an order for payment personally against the representative."[11] Where a contributory is adjudged insolvent, his assignee in insolvency shall take his place.[12] Where the contributory is a company which is ordered to be wound up, its liquidator shall become the contributory.[13]

Liability of past members [S. 426]

Past members are also liable as contributories in certain circumstances. The liability of a past member is subject to the following qualifications as laid down in Section 426:

1. A past member is not liable to contribute if he has ceased to be a member for one year or upwards before the commencement of the winding up.

2. A past member is not liable to contribute in respect of any debt or liability of the company contracted after he ceased to be a member. In other words, his liability is only for the liabilities incurred up to the date of his membership.

3. No past member is liable to contribute unless it appears to the Tribunal that the present members are unable to satisfy the contribution. The primary liability is that of the present shareholders to pay the unpaid balance. They should be required to pay in the first place and on their default the past members become liable to pay.

In *Paras Ram Brij Kishore* v *Jagraon Trading Syndicate*:[14]

The liquidator of a company called upon the defendant to pay the uncalled amount on his shares. His shares had been forfeited before the

---

9. *Gulzarilal Bhargava* v *Official Liquidator*, (1972) 42 Comp Cas 401, 405-406 Del.
10. *Sumitra Kuer* v *Sitamarhi Sugar Works Ltd*, AIR 1938 Pat 287.
11. S. 430. See *British India Banking & Industrial Corpn Ltd* v *Shiva Chedumbaria*, AIR 1934 Bom 469; *P. K. Krishnaswami, Re*, AIR 1948 Mad 162.
12. S. 431.
13. S. 432.
14. AIR 1936 Lah 226.

winding up and, therefore, he was on *B List*. But the existing members had not been called upon to contribute to the full extent of the unpaid amount of their share money. It was held "that in the circumstances a past member cannot be liable to contribute till *List A* is exhausted".

A person whose shares have been forfeited is also liable as a past member, provided the liquidation commences within one year of the date of forfeiture and the above conditions are fulfilled.[15]

Officers with unlimited liability [S. 427]

Section 322 allows every limited company to provide by its memorandum that the liability of any of its directors or managers shall be unlimited. Any such managerial personnel is liable, in the winding up of the company, in addition to his liability as a shareholder, "to make further contribution as if he were a member of an unlimited company". The liability attaches to both present and past officers. But a past officer is not liable if he ceased to be an officer for a year or more before the commencement of the winding up, or for a debt incurred after he ceased to be an officer or where the Tribunal does not deem it necessary to require further contribution.

Set off

A debtor of the company may set off for any amount which is due to him from the company. The right applies where the cross-claims are mutual. The counter-claims must exist between the same parties in the same right. Set off was allowed to a landlord from whom refund of security was demanded because he had deposited the security money with interest and the company was not able to refund his deposit.[16] Neither a joint claim can be set off against individual liability, nor a set off is allowed where it would result in a preference of one creditor over another. A director who was liable to make good the company's losses was not allowed to claim set off against the money which was due to him from the company.[17] Set off cannot be allowed for a claim which is already time-barred.[18] Set off was not allowed in respect of the claim of the creditor against the holding company.[19]

Payment of liabilities [Ss. 528, 529, 529-A]

Another important duty of the liquidator is to pay off the company's liabilities. All persons who are entitled to receive money from the company have the right to claim their respective amounts from the liquidator. Indeed, Section 528 declares so clearly that "in every winding up.... all debts

---

15. *Mirza Ahamad Namazi, Re*, AIR 1924 Mad 703.
16. *CRB Capital Markets Ltd v Bimla Devi Sawhney*, (2006) 132 Comp Cas 788 Del.
17. *Manson v Smith*, (1997) 2 BCLC 161 CA; *Bank of Credit and Commerce International (No 8), Re*, (1996) 2 BCLC 254 CA.
18. *Maruti Udyog Ltd v Blue Star Ltd*, (1999) 95 Comp Cas 108 P&H.
19. *MCC Finance Ltd v Reserve Bank of India*, (2002) 110 Comp Cas 645 Mad.

payable on a contingency, and all claims against the company, present or future, certain or contingent, ascertained or sounding only in damages shall be admissible to proof against the company." A just estimate shall have to be made, so far as possible, of the value of such debts or claims as are subject to any contingency, or may sound only in damages, or for some other reason may not bear a certain value. But where the company in liquidation is insolvent, insolvency rules will apply and only such claims shall be provable against the company as are provable against an insolvent person.[20] According to the present law of insolvency, demands in the nature of unliquidated damages arising other than by reason of a contract or breach of trust[21] and debts and liabilities which are incapable of being fairly estimated[22] a claim for damages for misrepresentation in purchase of shares,[23] are not provable in insolvency. One of the principles of insolvency laws, as stated in Section 46 of the Provincial Insolvency Act, 1920, is that where there have been mutual dealings between a debtor and the insolvent, only the net amount due after giving him the set off can be recovered from the debtor. The same will be the position of a debtor of an insolvent company notwithstanding Section 530 which provides for preferential payments.[24]

A decree holder is not a secured creditor. Even the judgment of the Supreme Court in favour of a claimant does not have the effect of creating a security. A security has to be created by the parties or under an Act and registered with the ROC. Otherwise, a decree holder ranks as an ordinary creditor and, therefore, cannot claim any priority. There was no general or particular lien also.[25]

A secured creditor need not come in the winding up. He has the right to realize his security, but he shall be liable to pay the expenses incurred by the

---

20. S. 529. See *Gujarat Electricity Board* v *Rajratan Naranbhai Mills*, (1974) 44 Comp Cas 127 Guj. All claimants are put on equality and are entitled to *pari passu* payment including the landlord for his rent. *S. S. Chawla* v *Globe Motors Ltd*, (1987) 62 Comp Cas 815 Del. Claims have to be filed before the liquidator and not consumer forum even if the cause of action was such that if the company had been a going concern, a consumer forum would have had jurisdiction. *Sudarsan Chits India Ltd* v *Official Liquidator*, (1992) 1 Comp LJ 34 Mad.
21. S. 46(1) of the Presidency Towns Insolvency Act and S. 34(1) of the Provincial Insolvency Act.
22. S. 46(4) of the Presidency Town Insolvency Act and S. 34(1) of the Provincial Insolvency Act. *Soden* v *British and Commonwealth Holdings plc*, (1996) 2 BCLC 207 CA, claim for damages for misrepresentation and breach of contract.
23. *Soden* v *British & Commonwealth Holdings plc*, [1997] 1 BCLC 501 HL.
24. Expressly so laid down by the Supreme Court in *Official Liquidator* v *V. Lakshmikutty*, (1981) 3 SCC 32: (1981) 51 Comp Cas 566 SC; *Textile Labour Assn* v *OL, Star of Gujarat Mills Co Ltd*, (2004) 118 Comp Cas 133 Guj, realisations from company's movables, first distribution proportionately among workers and creditors. *Canara Bank* v *Mopeds India Ltd*, (2006) 132 Comp Cas 812 AP, creditor could not appeal against the liquidator's fixation of amount due to workmen, but if the workmen appealed, the creditor could intervene.
25. *Oil and Natural Gas Corpn* v *Ambica Mills Co Ltd*, (2005) 2 Comp LJ 81 Guj: (2006) 132 Comp Cas 579 Guj.

liquidator for the preservation of the security before its realization by the creditor.[26] However, he has the option of relinquishing his security and to prove the amount due to him as if he were an unsecured creditor. Under this scheme a secured creditor was able to rule out all other claims including claims of workmen. This has now been changed. Changes have been introduced in the scheme of Section 529 by the Amendment Act of 1985. Workers' claims have been equated with those of secured creditors by providing that the security of every creditor shall be subject to a *pari passu* charge in favour of workmen. If the secured creditor enforces his security, the liquidator will have the power to represent the workmen to enforce the charge deemed in their favour. For this purpose Section 529-A has also been added to the Act.[27] The section says that workmen's dues as equated with those of secured creditors shall be paid in priority to all other debts. If the

---

26. S. 529(2), proviso. *New Swadeshi Mills of Ahmedabad Ltd, Re*, (1985) 58 Comp Cas 86 Guj. Followed in *Punjab United Forge Ltd* v *Punjab Financial Corpn*, (1993) 76 Comp Cas 660 P&H, claim for contribution towards salaries of watch and ward. *Travancore Ogale Glass Mfg Co Ltd, Re*, (1997) 88 Comp Cas 179 Ker, where the secured creditor realised 1.5 crore rupees less than what was being offered by other bidders and though such offers were received after the completion of the sale, the gap being too big, the sale was set aside in the interest of other creditors. *Karnataka State Industrial Investment and Development Corpn Ltd* v *Intermodel Transport Technology Systems*, AIR 1998 Kant 195, sale under orders of BIFR would also require leave of court. The State Financial Corporation have also to make their contribution towards the costs of preservation of their security but not required to make its contribution to the expenses of winding up order including those of advertisement of the petition. *BIFR* v *Advasi Paper Mills Ltd*, (2000) 100 Comp Cas 794 DB; *Darshan Forgings (P) Ltd* v *Punjab Financial Corpn*, [2000] 1 Comp LJ 53 P&H, corporation required to pay monthly sums for salary of watch and ward; the creditor would be entitled to indemnity from sale proceeds for such contributions. *Accumeasure Punjab Ltd* v *Punjab Wireless Systems Ltd*, [2000] 1 Comp LJ 55 P&H. *ICICI Bank Ltd* v *Shivmoni Steel Tubes Ltd*, (2005) 126 Comp Cas 645. Under the State Financial Corpn Act, the corporation, as a secured creditor, can dispose of its security outside winding up but has to bring the amount into the winding up court, because distribution has to be in accordance with the provisions of Sections 529-A and 530. The corporation has to notify its claim to the liquidator. *Shivmoni Steel Tubes Employees' Assn, Re*, (2005) 126 Comp Cas 522; *S.K. Bhargava* v *Official Liquidator*, (2005) 128 Comp Cas 143 Raj, the bank a secured creditor, obtained a decree from DRT, entered into settlement with debtor company and asked the liquidator to pay. The latter refused because it was not in the interest of shareholders, creditors and companies. *Divya Chemicals Ltd, Re*, (2005) 127 Comp Cas 853 Bom, the effect of a DRT decree in favour of a bank and a financial institution is that the liquidator is not to dispose of the assets and has to wait for orders of the winding up court.

27. *Indian Bank* v *V. S. Perumal Raja*, [1992] 1 Comp LJ 327: (1993) 76 Comp Cas 787 Mad, *pari passu* payment to workers. *State Bank of India* v *Podar Mills Ltd*, (1992) 74 Comp Cas 710 Bom, workers are not a necessary party to the proceeding. All the securities which remained unrealised at the time of the amendment would become subject to the workmen's deemed charge. *UCO Bank* v *Official Liquidator, Bom*, (1994) 5 SCC 1: (1994) 81 Comp Cas 780 SC. There are decisions to the effect that by virtue of the overriding effect under the State Financial Corpns Acts, a corporation can enforce its security without the intervention of the winding up court. *Boolani Engg Corpn* v *Asup Synthetics & Chemicals*, (1994) 81 Comp Cas 872 Raj. Execution of decree would also require leave of the court, *Industrial Finance Corpn* v *Century Mills Ltd*, (1992) 73 Comp Cas 630 Del. It has been held that by virtue of S. 29 of the State Financial Corpn Act, 1951 which gives a direct power of sale of the industrial concern, the right of the corporation cannot be defeated or subjected to S. 529-A, *F. S. Chhajerah* v *Kerala Financial Corpn*, (1995) 82 Comp Cas 1 Ker; *State Bank of India* v *Spinter Tubes and Constructions Ltd*, (1995) 82 Comp Cas Raj, a portion of the proceeds to be earmarked for payment of workers; *Maharashtra State Finance Corpn* v *Official Liquidator, Bombay HC*, (1995) 82 Comp Cas 342 Bom.

assets are not sufficient to meet them they shall abate in equal proportion. The concept of workmen's dues for the purposes of Section 530 has also been made more broad-based. Preferential payments listed in Section 530 are now subject to the provisions of Section 529-A.[28]

The court is the custodian of the property of the company on behalf of secured and unsecured creditors and workmen. It is the obligation of the official liquidator to associate workmen in the process of sale of assets. They have the right to be treated *pari passu* with the claims of secured creditors.[29]

Participation by the secured creditor in proceedings for sale of the company's assets by the court for facilitating realisation of assets does not amount to relinquishing the security. Relinquishment requires a positive act. There is no right in workmen to claim distribution of entire sale proceeds in payment of their claims in priority to all other claims. The court directed *pari passu* distribution between workers and the secured creditor.[30] The provision for overriding preferential payments to bring about *pari passu*

28. See *Govindla Binny Brighton & Co, Re*, [1990] 1 Comp LJ 102, 108: (1990) 67 Comp Cas 441, showing overriding effect of the section. *Pryavarta Plywood v Rajasthan State I & I Corpn*, [1990] 1 Comp LJ 222 Del; *Gendalal Bhaggaji v Shri Sujjan Mills Ltd*, (1989) 65 Comp Cas 480 MP. Claim to interest ceases to run from the date of winding up unless surplus is available after meeting claims of workmen and other creditors. *Haryana Financial Corpn v PNB Auto Ancillary (India) Ltd*, (1994) 81 Comp Cas 588 Del. Since the property of the company is deemed to be in the custody of the official liquidator, a secured creditor can recover possession of such property only with the order of the court. *Indian Textiles v Gujarat State Finance Corpn*, (1994) 81 Comp Cas 599. Where assets of the company were insufficient to meet all the claims, the sale proceeds in the hands of the corporation were ordered to be made available for discharge of other *pari passu* claims. The court said that financial corporations could not use S. 29 of the State Financial Corporations Act, 1951 for defeating the claims of other secured creditors. *A.P. State Financial Corpn v Electrothermic (P) Ltd*, (1996) 86 Comp Cas 402 AP. The Gujarat High Court has differed from the view that workers become secured creditors, see *Gujarat State Financial Corpn v Official Liquidator*, (1996) 87 Comp Cas 658 Guj; *Peerless General Finance & Investment Co Ltd v Majestic Apparels (P) Ltd*, (1997) 24 Corpt LA 44 Del; *Polyolefins Industries Ltd v Kosmek Plastics Mfg Co Ltd*, (1998) 28 Corpt LA 266 Bom; *National Textiles Corpn Ltd v Textile Workers' Union*, (1995) 1 CHN 522 Cal, advance of loans after takeover of management under IDRA, 1951, does not enable the Government to supersede the preferential status of employees in the matters of payment of claims. *UCO Bank v Official Liquidator, High Court*, (1994) 5 SCC 1: (1994) 81 Comp Cas 780 SC. Workers secured creditors alongwith other security-holders. The *non obstante* clause in S. 29 of the State Financial Corporations Act, 1951 would have to yield before that of S. 529-A of the Companies Act, 1956 because it was brought in by an amendment of 1985 and being later in time would prevail over the earlier in time, *A.P. State Financial Corpn v Official Liquidator*, (2000) 7 SCC 291: AIR 2000 SC 2642: (2000) 38 CLA 315 SC. The court said that the object of the new section was to protect workmen in respect of their dues. *International Coach Builders Ltd v Karnataka State Corpn*, (2003) 114 Comp Cas 614 SC, directions sought from the court for working out proper proportions of the claim of the secured creditor and *pari passu* charge in favour of workers. *KTC Tyres (India) Ltd, Re*, (2003) 114 Comp Cas 185 Ker, tax claims of all variety come subsequent to the priority of secured creditors and workmen's dues. *India Maize & Chemicals Ltd v Official Liquidator, UP*, (2002) 108 Comp Cas 401 All, workman cannot be paid in priority to secured creditors.
29. *Punjab Wireless Systems Ltd v Indian Overseas Bank*, (2005) 126 Comp Cas 554 P&H; *Regional Director, ESI Corpn v OL of Prasad Mills Ltd.*, (2006) 131 Comp Cas 652 Guj, sums deducted from employees' wages for contribution, company mortgaged property, realisation from the security to be either kept in separate account to enable the liquidator to pay the ESI portion first, otherwise the procedure under Sections 529-A and 530 to be followed.
30. *Gujarat Steel Tubes Employees Union v Official liquidator*, (2006) 131 Comp Cas 410 Guj.

participation of workers with secured creditors does not have the effect of obliterating creditor's *inter se* priorities. Such priorities are governed by the Transfer of Property Act, 1881. The first charge holder has priority over the next such holder.[31]

Where the secured creditor gave up his security, it was held that the proceeds were to be distributed *pro rata* under Section 529-A.[32]

When the list of claimants is settled, the liquidator may start making payments out of the available assets of the company.

Preferential payments [S. 530]

The first payments to be made are called "preferential payments". They have to be paid in priority to all other debts. Such payments are listed below:

1. All revenues, taxes, cesses and rates due to the Central or a State Government or to a local authority. The amount should have become due and payable within twelve months before the winding up.[33]

2. All wages or salary of any employee, in respect of services rendered to the company and due for a period of four months only

---

31. *ICICI Bank Ltd v Sidco Leathers Ltd*, (2006) 131 Comp Cas 451 SC.

32. *IFCI Ltd v Sidco Leathers Ltd*, (2006) 131 Comp Cas 429 All, the Companies Act prevails over the insolvency legislation.

33. The State is not entitled to preference in respect of any other claims, for example, the cost of machinery supplied. *Union of India v J. R. & Sons*, AIR 1962 Punj 528 or charges for services rendered, *Kerala Water Transport Corpn, Re*, (1967) 37 Comp Cas 538 Ker; *IDC of Orissa Ltd v Snehadhara Industries Ltd*, (2006) 132 Comp Cas 875 Ori, dues under mining lease, claim to be raised in accordance with the normal procedure of winding up. There is no preference for previous years' arrears. *STO v Official Liquidator*, (1968) 38 Comp Cas 430 All. Penalties are not preferential claims unless they are part of the tax due. *STO v R. N. Mills*, (1974) 44 Comp Cas 65 Guj. The winding up is deemed to commence for this purpose from the date of the appointment of the first provisional liquidator, or if no such appointment was made, from the date of winding up order. In the case of voluntary liquidation, the relevant time means the date of the passing of the special resolution for winding up. S. 530(8)(*c*). Tax becomes due for this purpose when it is assessed and demanded. *Baroda Board & Paper Mills Ltd v ITO*, (1976) 102 ITR 153: (1976) 46 Comp Cas 25 Guj. It has been held by the Andhra Pradesh High Court in *ITO v Official Liquidator; ITO v Swaraj Motors*, (1978) 48 Comp Cas 11 Ker, that interest due on unpaid taxes cannot be claimed as a preferential payment. A special order of the court would be necessary because ordinarily interest cannot be claimed from a company after the commencement of winding up. *Official Liquidator v ITO*, (1978) 48 Comp Cas 59 Ker; *ITO v Official Liquidator*, (1985) 58 Comp Cas 590 Ker; *Rajratna Naranbhaw Mills Co v STO*, (1991) 3 SCC 283, relevant period of 12 months. The decision in *Imperial Chit Funds (P) Ltd v Income Tax Deptt*, (1979) 49 Comp Cas 58: AIR 1979 Ker 23 FB was approved by the Supreme Court in *Imperial Chit Funds (P) Ltd v ITO*, (1996) 8 SCC 303: (1996) 86 Comp Cas 555 at 564 (SC), where it was observed that on a total view of the provisions, the IT Deptt is treated as a secured creditor and the amount set aside by the official liquidator is marked off as outside the area of winding up proceedings and jurisdiction of the winding up court. But the company court can decide the matter as to the validity of the claim and its protected amount, see *CIT v Official Liquidator, Golcha Properties (P) Ltd*, (1974) 44 Comp Cas 445 Raj; *K. Ramachandra Rao v Ranks Cables Ltd*, (2004) 118 Comp Cas 122 AP, an auction purchaser of the company's property was not allowed to seek directions to the liquidator that he should be required to pay taxes due in respect of the property of which he was aware when he purchased the property. *Anchor Health & Beauty Care Ltd v M.C. of Greater Bombay*, (2006) 132 Comp Cas 689 Bom, auction purchaser is liable to pay property tax only from the date of purchase. Tax prior to sale to be claimed from the liquidator.

within twelve months before the winding up and any compensation payable to any workman under Chapter V-A of the Industrial Disputes Act, 1947. The amount is not to exceed such sum as may be prescribed in the case of any one claimant.[34]

3. All secured holiday remuneration becoming payable to any employee on the termination of his employment before, or by the effect of the winding up.

4. All amount due in respect of contributions payable during the twelve months before the winding up under the Employees' State Insurance Act, 1948 or any other law.[35]

5. All amounts due in respect of any compensation or liability for compensation under the Workmen's Compensation Act, 1923 in respect of death or disablement of any employee of the company.[36]

6. All sums due to any employee from a provident fund, a pension fund, a gratuity fund or any other fund for the welfare of the employees, maintained by the company.[37]

7. The expenses of any investigation held in pursuance of Section 235 or 237 in so far as they are payable by the company.

After retaining sums necessary for meeting the costs and expenses of winding up,[38] the above debts have to be discharged forthwith so far as assets

---

34. Provided that where a claimant is a labourer in a husbandry who has entered into a contract for the payment of a portion of his wages in a lump sum at the end of the year of hiring, he shall have priority in respect of the whole of such a sum, or a part thereof, as the court may decide to be due under the contract, proportionate to the time of service. S. 530(2). Amounts payable under the Act on the closure of an undertaking are also entitled to preference. See *R. Srinivasan* v *Official Liquidator*, (1967) 37 Comp Cas 544. The amount presently prescribed by notification w.e.f. March 1, 1997 is Rs 20,000 per claimant.

35. This does not apply when the company is being wound up voluntarily merely for the purpose of reconstruction or amalgamation with another company. S. 530(1)(*d*). *Official Liquidator, Golcha Properties (P) Ltd* v *ITO, Jaipur*, (1974) 44 Comp Cas 144 Raj; *National Conduits (P) Ltd, Re*, (1974) 44 Comp Cas 219 Del.

36. This priority also has no application in the above noted case and also when the company has, under such a contract with insurers as is mentioned in S. 14 of the Workmen's Compensation Act, 1923, rights capable of being transferred to and vested in the workmen, S. 530(1)(*e*).

37. *RPF Commr* v *Official Liquidator*, [1968] 2 Comp LJ 15; *S. K. Bhudiraja* v *State of Haryana* (1993) 1 Punj LR 313, duty to pay dues under Employees Provident Fund and Miscellaneous Provisions Act, 1951.

38. S. 476 empowers the court, where the assets are insufficient, to order payment out of the assets for costs, charges and expenses of winding up in such priority as the court thinks just. In the case of a voluntary winding up, S. 520 provides that subject to the claims of secured creditors, if any, the costs of winding up shall be paid in priority to all other claims. The Calcutta High Court has held in *Shadhra (Delhi) Saharanpur Light Rly Co* v *ITO*, (1988) 63 Comp Cas 627 that the court cannot under these sections interfere with assessment proceedings, except that it may hear an appeal after assessment. *Govindla Binny Brighton & Co, Re*, [1990] 1 Comp LJ 102: (1990) 67 Comp Cas 441, capital gains tax on the company's property mortgaged to others is not an expense of winding up. Debts incurred and rents paid for the purposes of winding up are expenses of winding and are payable in priority to all other claims. *Sanitary Burial Assn, Re*, [1990] 2 LCH 289; *Massey Freehold Land and Brickmaking Co, Re*, (1870) LR 9 EQ 367. Improperly incurred expenses do not enjoy this priority; *Linda Marie Ltd, Re*, 1989 BCLC 46 Ch D, rent incurred for premises needlessly retained. *Portbase Clothing Ltd, Re*, (1993) 3 All ER 829 Ch D, priority of expenses of liquidation over preferential creditors and floating charge holders. *Mohinder Singh* v *Indian Overseas Bank*,

are sufficient to meet them.[39] Section 511 provides that the assets of the company shall be applied in satisfaction of its liabilities *pari passu*. The remaining assets have to be distributed among the members according to their rights and interests in the company unless the articles provide otherwise.[40] Where the liquidator carries on business for beneficial winding up, the taxes that become due on the profits are expenses of winding up.[41] The fee payable to a chartered accountant for preparing the statement of affairs is also an expense of winding up.[42] The preferential claims rank equally among themselves and have to be paid in full. But when the assets are insufficient to meet them, they shall abate in equal proportion.[43] By virtue of the provision in Section 178 of the Income Tax Act, 1961, the income tax authorities have been claiming preference over other preferential payments. But the courts have always held that there is nothing in the Income Tax Act which interferes with or abrogates the provisions for priority of debts laid down in Section 530(1)(*a*) of the Companies Act.[44]

(1996) 86 Comp Cas 110 P&H, even a secured creditor might be ordered to pay costs when the company was not in a position to meet the watch and ward expenses for protecting the property. *Grey Martin Ltd, Re*, [1999] 4 All ER 429: (2000) CLC 1258 Ch D, tax liability was incurred as a result of proper performance of the provisional liquidator's duties, the liability was held to be an expense properly incurred. The company continued trading during provisional liquidation. Other similar decisions are: *Toshoko Finance (UK) plc, Re*, [2000] 1 BCLC 683 CA on appeal from [1999] 2 BCLC 777 Ch D. The amount of interest accruing on loans during the period of winding up has been held to be not an expense of winding up, *Kohn v IRC*: sub nom *Toshoko Finance (UK) plc*, [1999] STC 922 Ch D.

39. S. 530(6). The House of Lords in *Buchler v Talbot*, (2004) 2 WLR 582 (HL): (2004) 120 Comp Cas 756. Held that when a company was both in receivership and liquidation, the company's assets were comprised in two quite separate funds namely, proceeds of free assets and those of assests comprised in the floating charge. Each fund has to bear the costs of its own administration and neither being required to bear the costs of administering the other and that, accordingly, none of the costs and expenses of winding up the company were payable out of the assets subject to the floating charge until the whole of the principal and interest therein has been paid. *Buchler v Talbot*, (2004) 2 WLR 582 (HL): (2004) 2 AC 298, assets not sufficient to meet costs and expenses of winding up. Proceeds of the crystallised floating charge not allowed to be used for meeting costs and expenses.

40. Rule 200 of the Companies (Court) Rules provides that payment up to Rs 500 can be made to the legal heirs of a deceased member without succession certificate. *Mittal Steel Re-Rolling & Allied Industries Ltd, Re*, (1999) 33 CLA 44 3610 Ker.

41. *M. R. Agarwal v Official Liquidator*, (1973) 43 Comp Cas 423 Raj.

42. *Barleycorn Enterprises Ltd, Re*, [1970] 2 All ER 155. But when business is not continued there is no question of any business expenditure. Even salaries to staff would not fall in that category. Money earned from fixed deposits would also not be income from business, *Vijay Laxmi Sugar Mills Ltd v CIT*, 1991 Supp (2) SCC 331: (1991) 72 Comp Cas 740 SC.

43. S. 530(5). Where the assets of the company available for payment of general creditors are insufficient to meet them, the preferential payments will have priority over the claims of debenture-holders under any floating charge created by the company and be paid accordingly out of any property covered by the charge.

44. *See*, for example, *Baroda Board & Paper Mills Ltd v ITO*, (1976) 102 ITR 153: (1976) 46 Comp Cas 25 Guj; *ITO v Official Liquidator, National Conduits (P) Ltd*, (1981) 51 Comp Cas 174 Del; *ITO v Official Liquidator*, (1967) 63 ITR 810: (1967) 37 Comp Cas 114 Mys. Contrary views have been expressed in *ITO v Official Liquidator*, (1975) 101 ITR 470: (1976) 46 Comp Cas 46 AP; *Steel Sons (P) Ltd v ROC*, C. P. No 14/1969 Ker. The provision of S. 178 of the Income Tax Act is that when the ITO informs the O. L. the amount of taxes due from the company, the latter must keep in his hands an amount equal to that.

Preferential payments to rank *pari passu* with workers' dues

Workmen's dues have priority over all other dues, even over decrees. There was a Supreme Court order to the official liquidator to pay the dues of ONGC in priority over all other creditors. The workmen sought review of this order. The court said that the order was to be read subject to overriding preferential charge in favour of workmen.[45] The sale has to be subject to the protection of *pari passu* charge of workmen's dues. The sale was conducted by a State Financial Corpn.[46] Workmen's dues do not take priority over secured creditors. Their rights rank *pari passu* with those of secured creditors.[47] The Debt Recovery Tribunal is competent to adjudicate workers' claims.[48]

Insolvency Laws and Preferential Payments

When a company is being wound up on account of its insolvency, Section 529 comes into play. It provides for the application of insolvency laws to the payment of the debts of an insolvent company. One of the principles of insolvency laws provides for cancellation of cross claims where there have been mutual dealings.[49] A question arose before the Supreme Court[50] whether a person having mutual dealings with the company can claim set-off in winding up or whether he should pay what is due from him to the company and then rank as one of the claimants after preferential payments. The Supreme Court ruled that such a debtor-cum-creditor must be given the benefit of set-off. BHAGWATI J tried to reconcile the apparent clash between Sections 529 and 530:[51]

> It is true that Section 530 provides for preferential payments, but the provision cannot in any way detract from full effect being given to Section 529 and in fact the only way in which these two sections can be reconciled is by reading them together so as to provide that whenever any creditor seeks to prove his debt, the rule enacted in Section 46 of the Provincial Insolvency Act would apply and only that amount which is ultimately found due from him at the foot of the account in respect of mutual dealings should be recoverable from him and not that the amount due from him should be recovered fully while the amount due to him should rank in payment after the preferential payments. We find that the same view has been taken by the English courts on the interpretation of the corresponding provisions of the English Companies Act, 1948, and since our Companies Act is modelled largely on the

---

45. *Textile Labour Assn* v *Official Liquidator*, (2004) 9 SCC 741: (2004) 120 Comp Cas 505: 2004 CLC 741: (2004) 2 Comp LJ 409: (2005) 51 SCL 791 SC.
46. *Sneh Contractor's (P) Ltd* v *Tara Cements (P) Ltd*, (2005) 128 Comp Cas 908 Del.
47. *Allahabad Bank* v *Canara Bank*, (2000) 101 Comp Cas 64 SC.
48. *Pandurang Keshew Gorwalkar* v *Paper and Pulp Conversions Ltd*, 2005 CLC 97.
49. S. 46 of the Provincial Insolvency Act, 1920.
50. *Official Liquidator* v *V. Lakshmikutty*, (1981) 3 SCC 32: (1981) 51 Comp Cas 566 SC.
51. *Id.*, at p 570.

English Companies Act, we do not see any reason why we should take a different view, particularly when that view appears to be fair and just.[52]

Where the guarantor claimed to be the beneficial owner of the money held by the insolvent, set-off in respect of such money was not allowed. The court said: "The right to set-off mutual debts and credits is confined within narrow limits, particularly by the requirement of mutuality, because the effect of a set-off is to prefer one creditor over the general body of creditors. The requirement of mutuality cannot be satisfied unless a person's beneficial interest in a bank account in the insolvent bank can be established without any further inquiry. Things were not that clear in this case.[53]

Deposits on Trust

The property divisible among creditors does not include the property held by the company in trust. In a case before the Madras High Court[54] a sum of Rs 40,000 was given to a company for the specific purpose of depositing it with a mill and thereby to secure an agency of the mill. A sum of Rs 30,000 was, in fact, so deposited. The company went into liquidation and, therefore, the agency did not materialise. The deposit was refunded by the mill to the company. The court held that the deposit being in the nature of a constructive trust was refundable to the depositor. The court distinguished the case from the decision of the Supreme Court in *Seth Jissa Ram Fatehchand* v *Om Narain*,[55] where a sum of money deposited by a person with a company to obtain its agency was held to be not a deposit on trust because it was not earmarked for any special purpose and the company had the liberty to put it to any use. Similarly, where vehicles are purchased on hire-purchase finance basis, they belong to the financier and he is entitled to their sale proceeds as though they

---

52. The learned judge cited from Gore-Browne's, COMPANY LAW (43rd Edn) a statement to the effect that: "Indeed, all claims provable in the winding up may be subject to set off, provided that there is mutuality". Observations of the House of Lords in *National Westminster Bank Ltd* v *Halesowen Presswork & Assemblies Ltd*, [1972] 1 All ER 641, 659 are also to the same effect. English law on the subject is now to be found in the Insolvency Act 1986, S. 323, Rule 490. See *Bank of Credit and Commerce International SA (No 8), Re*, (1994) 3 All ER 565 Ch D where the deposits of a third person were lying in the bank and he charged them as a security for the amount due from the principle debtor, the latter was not allowed a set off for the amount of such deposits, the arrangement imposed no personal liability on the third party depositor. Accordingly, where the guarantor accepted liability as principal debtor, deposit amount lying with them was taken to have reduced his liability pro tanto, *MS Fashions Ltd* v *BCCI sa (No 2)*, (1993) 3 All ER 769 CA.

53. *Bank of Credit and Commerce Investment SA* v *Al-Saud*, (1997) 1 BCLC 457 CA. Money lying in an ordinary banking account has not been given the status of a deposit in trust. The account holder can rank as an unsecured creditor of the insolvent company. Payment to the account holders was recovered back as fraudulent preference. *Exchange Travel Holdings (No 3), Re*, (1996) 2 BCLC 524 Ch D. Money of the participants in a holiday promotion scheme which was a part of the general fund was held to be not a trust money, *Holiday Promotions (Europe) Ltd, Re*, (1996) 2 BCLC 618 Ch D.

54. *Mansuba & Co (P) Ltd, Re*, (1973) 43 Comp Cas 244 Mad.

55. AIR 1967 SC 1162: (1967) Comp Cas 204.

were held in trust for him.[56] Margin money deposited in a bank for the purpose of securing a bank guarantee and letter of credit has been held to be trust deposit refundable to the depositor outside of the bank's winding up.[57] Subscription money for shares *etc.* in the hands of the company is also in the same category.[58] Security deposit made by a tenant[59] was held to be not in the nature of a trust deposit.

Employees' Provident Fund is held by the company in trust. The amount is payable out of the sale proceeds of the company's securities by a secured creditor.[60]

The corpus of loans given by a workers' cooperative to the employer company in winding up out of the fund constituted from deductions from wages was held to be a trust property. It could not be included in the assets of the company. The workers' credit society could make a preferential claim.[61]

Employees' Provident Fund

Employees' Provident Fund is maintained by the employer under a statutory duty. The Provident Fund Authorities could effect recovery from the employer without the permission of the BIFR.[62]

Recovery of employees' dues

Suspension of legal proceedings does not bar grant of interim relief to workmen pending writ petition against the award of a labour court.[63]

Donations

Donations were received by a charitable company during the period of winding up but before its final dissolution. The liquidator sought court directions as to whether the amount could be used for paying off the creditors. The court said that donations took effect according to their terms. There was no indication in their terms that they were meant to be used only for charitable purposes.[64]

---

56. *Official Liquidator of Mansuba & Co Ltd* v *Commr of Police*, (1968) 38 Comp Cas 884 Mad. The amount deducted from employees' wages for their co-operative society is in the same category. *Baroda S. & W. Mills* v *B. S. & W. Coop*, (1976) 46 Comp Cas 1 Guj; *Eastern Capital Futures Ltd, Re*, 1989 BCLC 371 Ch D, money belonging to clients held by the company in trust for investment purposes.
57. *RBI* v *BCCI (Overseas) Ltd*, (1993) 78 Comp Cas 207 Bom, following the Supreme Court decision in *Shanti Pd Jain* v *Director of Enforcement*, (1962) 2 SCR 297: (1963) 33 Comp Cas 231.
58. *RBI* v *BCCI (Overseas) Ltd (No 2)*, (1993) 78 Comp Cas 230 Bom.
59. *Nimesh R. Thakkar* v *Official Liquidator*, (1991) 70 Comp Cas 257, the deposit did not carry any terms showing hallmark of trust.
60. *Central Bank of India* v *Recovery Mamlatdar*, (1996) 23 Corpt LA 167 Guj.
61. *Nutan Mills Employees Coop Credit Society Ltd* v *Official Liquidator, Nutan Mills Ltd*, (2001) 104 Comp Cas 439 Guj.
62. *Sarvaraya Textiles Ltd* v *Commr, EPF*, (2002) 108 Comp Cas 406 AP.
63. *Mideast India Ltd* v *K.M. Unni*, (2003) 115 Comp Cas 184 Del.
64. *ARMS (Multiple Sclerosis Research) Ltd* v *Attorney-General*, (1997) 1 BCLC 157 Ch D.

General Creditors and Shareholders

Next the liquidator has to pay the general creditors of the company.[65] The surplus, if any, is then used to pay back the shareholders in accordance with their rights. Preference shareholders are paid first. Where the articles provide that in the event of winding up the preference shareholders would be entitled to their arrears of dividend whether earned, declared or not, it has been held by the Delhi High Court, that this would enable them to claim their arrears even if the company never commenced business or made any profits.[66] Dividends paid to members are not their income, but refund of capital. This will be so even if the dividends include some profits earned by the liquidator. This well-known principle of English Law has now been ratified by the Supreme Court in *CIT* v *M. V. Murugappan*.[67] SHAH J (later CJ) laid down that payments made by the liquidator after the commencement of winding up are not dividends, but return of capital, from whatever source they may be made. This principle applies to the earnings of the whole of the financial year in which winding up commences. The learned Judge quoted the following observation of POLLOCK MR in *CIR* v *George Burrel*:[68]

....[I]t is a misapprehension, after the liquidator has assumed his duties, to continue the distinction between surplus profits and capital.

Unclaimed dividends [S. 555]

Dividends which have not been claimed by any creditor or contributory for a period of six months have to be deposited in the Reserve Bank, which may then be claimed by the person concerned with an order of the Tribunal. If they are not claimed for 15 years they merge in the general revenue of the Central Government.[69] In the meantime they belong to the contributory and cannot be claimed back by the liquidator or the company which has been revived under a scheme of compromise etc.[70]

---

65. Where the general creditor was the landlord of the company, his arrears of rent were paid after deducting the company's security deposit with him. *Mohan Pyari Sethi* v *Official Liquidator*, (1991) 71 Comp Cas 77 Del.
66. *Globe Motors Ltd* v *Globe United Engg & Foundry Co Ltd*, (1975) 45 Comp Cas 429 Del. In all the matters relating to winding up the court has the supplementary power under S. 557 to call meetings of creditors and contributories to ascertain their wishes and prescribe the manner of conducting the meeting.
67. (1970) 2 SCC 145: (1970) 40 Comp Cas 994.
68. [1924] 2 KB 52, 63 CA.
69. The amount so deposited into the company's liquidation account remains available for payment of liabilities, for example, income tax dues which are subsequently confirmed or discovered. *Union of India* v *Hindu Bank Karur Ltd*, (1977) 47 Comp Cas 224 Mad.
70. *Colaba Land and Mills Co Ltd* v *Union of India*, (1985) 58 Comp Cas 513 Bom: (1989) 66 Comp Cas 610; *E. M.C. Golcha* v *Official Liquidator*, (1990) 67 Comp Cas 302 Raj.

ANTECEDENT AND OTHER TRANSACTIONS

Fraudulent preference [S. 531]

The power under the section has been transferred to the Tribunal.

The expression "fraudulent preference" is borrowed from the law of insolvency. According to that law any transfer of property or payment made by a person who is unable to pay his debts in favour of a creditor with a view to giving him a preference over other creditors is regarded as fraudulent preference, if within three months an insolvency petition is presented against him and he is adjudicated insolvent, the transaction becomes invalid. Any such transaction entered into by a company within six months before the commencement of its winding up is deemed a fraudulent preference of its creditors and invalid accordingly.[71]

The facts of *Eric Holmes (Property) Ltd, Re*,[72] furnish a suitable illustration:

A company carried on the business of purchasing land and erecting buildings thereon. *R,* a shareholder, provided finance for the purpose. In each case the company promised to hold the title deeds to his order and to execute a formal charge on demand. When the company became unable to pay its debts, *R*, had the charges formally executed and registered. Winding up followed within two months.

The liquidator applied for a declaration that the charges were void on the ground of fraudulent preference. PENNYCUICK J considered the authorities and said that the principle may perhaps be restated in these terms:

Where a creditor making an advance takes from the debtor a promise to execute a charge at the request of the creditor, the court will in the absence of any other circumstances, readily infer that the purpose of the parties... was to give the creditor the right to be preferred at request. Such an arrangement although for value, is fraudulent and unenforceable.

A creditor of this kind who does not have the security executed and registered commits a fraud on the other creditors by giving them the impression that the company's property is free from encumbrances.[73]

---

71. As to jurisdiction see *Barclays Bank plc* v *Horman*, (1993) BCLC 680 Ch D. Here the holding company was in winding up in London and its US based subsidiary was sold to pay a local bank there and the question arose as to jurisdiction for proceedings for fraudulent preference. The court said that normally the foreign court would be convenient but proceedings there would be restrained if they would be vexatious or oppressive to one party or the other. *Official Liquidator of Piramal Financial Services Ltd* v *RBI*, (2004) 118 Comp Cas 27 Guj, transfer of flats of the company to creditor in adjustment of his claims against the company. The price charged was below the cost of acquisition. The company also made some additional cash payment, to there creditors, the company expressed inability stating that it would take 5 years to clear their dues. The transaction was within a period of 6 months before the petition, held fraudulent preference.
72. [1965] 2 All ER 333: [1965] Ch 1052: [1966] 1 Comp LJ 19.
73. *See* BUCKLEY J in *Jackson & Bassford Ltd, Re*, [1960] 2 Ch D 467, 477, 479: 95 LT 292.

But where a company under pressure of litigation and threat of attachment of its properties, makes payment to a creditor, the same cannot be regarded as a fraudulent preference, provided, of course, the money is really due. This has been held by the Andhra Pradesh High Court in *Official Liquidator* v *Venkataratnam*:[74]

> A Motor Transport Co was sued for a debt and attachment before judgment of its buses. The court passed a compromise decree under which three of the company's buses were given to the creditor. A few days later the company went into liquidation.

The liquidator claimed that the transaction was a fraudulent preference. Rejecting his stand CHANDRA REDDY CJ said: "If a debtor prefers one creditor to another on account of pressure that is put upon him, the payment cannot be regarded as a fraudulent preference... Persons in charge of the management thought that it is profitable to discharge the debts by allotting some of the buses to the creditors."[75]

Thus, it appears that whether a transaction is a "fraudulent preference" or not does not depend on its result but on the "intention" of the debtor. The words "with a *view* to giving him a preference" mean "with the *intention* of giving preference".[76] In the words of PENNYCUICK J in *F. L. E. Holdings Ltd, Re*:[77]

> There is no fraudulent preference when a debtor's dominant intention is to benefit himself rather than to confer an advantage on his creditor.

The facts were:

> A bank took a deposit of title deeds to secure a company's overdraft, but failed to register the deposit as a charge under the Companies Act. Subsequently when the company got into financial straits and when one creditor had served a statutory notice and another obtained a judgment against the company, the bank got the company to execute a legal charge without either exercising any pressure on the company or promising to increase its overdraft.

Winding up having followed within less than six months, it was held that though the charge was void for want of registration, there had been no fraudulent preference, since the dominant intention of the company in effecting the legal charge was not to prefer the bank to other creditors but to

---

74. [1966] 1 Comp LJ 243 AP.
75. *Ibid.*, p 246. *See* also *Jayanti Bai* v *Popular Bank Ltd*, [1966] 2 Comp LJ 36 Ker.
76. See *T. W. Cutts, Re*, (1956) 2 All ER 537 and PENNYCUICK J in *Eric Holmes (Property) Ltd, Re*, [1965] 2 All ER 333: [1965] Ch 1052: [1966] 1 Comp LJ 19, 25. *See* also *Tansukharai M. Karundia* v *Official Liquidator*, AIR 1952 Mad 595.
77. [1967] 1 WLR 1409: [1967] 3 All ER 553; noted 1968 JBL 154.

benefit the company by keeping on good terms with the bank in the hope of keeping the company a going concern.[78]

Payment to directors with knowledge of the company's financial state created the presumption of preference. The directors were not able to justify the payment. They had to pay back the company's loss.[79] Where a security was provided to a creditor at a time when the company was in insolvent circumstances and the directors were unable to rebut the desire to prefer, they were held to be guilty of committing fraudulent preference.[80]

Where payments were made to directors to enable them to clear their loan accounts shortly before the company ceased trading, it was held to be preference over other creditors whose claims were also then due for payment. The court said that in considering whether the creditor of an insolvent company has received preference, the court has to consider the state of mind of the director at the time of the payment so as to see whether there was an overriding intention to prefer one particular creditor.[81]

The recipient of a fraudulent preference becomes a constructive trustee towards the company for the benefits received and is, as such, bound to restore them to the company.[82]

Section 533 provides that if the property was comprised in a charge or mortgage and it goes into the hands of a fraudulently preferred person, the latter would be personally liable as a surety to the extent of the interest of the security-holder.

Further, any transfer or assignment by a company of all its property to trustees for the benefit of all its creditors shall be void.[83]

---

78. An orally created charge may be valid and may not be fraudulent preference. *Sushil Prasad* v *Official Liquidator*, (1984) 55 Comp Cas 52 Del. Where the machinery of the company had been pledged before winding up in the ordinary course of business, no fraudulent preference. *Official Liquidator* v *P. Viswanathan*, (1984) 56 Comp Cas 435 Kant; *Monark Enterprises* v *Kishan Tulpule*, [1992] 74 Comp Cas 89: (1992) 1 Comp LJ 288 where also payment was made under a compromise to save the company from execution of a decree. The liquidator has to prove that the transferor and the transferee joined hands to defraud creditors. It is not enough to show that the company was under some financial strains. Some kind of connivance between the company and the transferee has to be shown. Liquidator has to prove this fact. *Maruti Ltd* v *Laxmi Patel Traders*, (1998) 91 Comp Cas 632 P&H. *Hindustan Development Corpn Ltd* v *Shaw Wallace & Co Ltd*, (2001) 107 Comp Cas 30 Cal, payment directed to be made by court, not a case of fraudulent preference.
79. *Exchange Travel Holdings Ltd (No 4), Re*, [1999] BCC 291 CA; *Katz* v *Nc Nally (Recovery of Preferences)*, [1999] BCC 291 CA.
80. *Transworld Trading, Re*, (1999) BPIR 628 Ch D; *Mills* v *ED, ICT Ltd*, (1999) BPIR 391 Ch D.
81. *Wills* v *Corfe Joinery Ltd*, [1998] 2 BCLC 75 Ch D; *Brain D Pierson (Contractors) Ltd, Re*, [1999] BCC 26 Ch D.
82. *Clasper Group Services Ltd, Re*, 1989 BCLC 143 Ch D where, however, the recipient of a sum of money by way of remuneration, being a minor, no recovery was allowed.
83. S. 532.

Avoidance of voluntary transfer [S. 531-A]

The power under the section has been vested in the Tribunal.

A transfer of immovable or movable property or any delivery of goods made by a company within a period of one year before the presentation of a winding up petition or the passing of a resolution for voluntary winding up, is void against the liquidator.[84] But the following transactions are protected from the operation of this rule:

1. a transfer or delivery of property made in the ordinary course of the business of the company, and

2. a transfer or delivery of property in favour of a purchaser or encumbrancer in good faith and for valuable consideration.[85]

Where money was collected from members by means of a false prospectus and payments were made out of that money lying in the company's banking account and a validation order was sought for such payments, the court refused to pass such order. Even if the company is perfectly solvent, the winding up petition being presented on the ground of public interest, the court cannot sanction a payment to be made at the cost of members. The ultimate end of the payment, in the event of winding up would be preference of the beneficiary of the payment over others.[86]

The payment into the bank account of the company which was overdrawn was held to be a disposition of the company's property in favour of the bank. The payment was void unless sanctioned by the court. Payment to the bank as a creditor in full at the cost of other creditors, like customs, was not for the benefit of creditors as a whole. The evidence produced showed that the bank was attempting to gain a personal advantage by the transaction in question.[87]

About the payment of long standing arrears of rent due under a lease which was made to obtain the lessor's permission for assignment of the lease, the court said that it could not be regarded as made in the ordinary

---

84. It is in the discretion of the liquidator to avoid or not. An income tax officer's direction could not prevail in the matter. *K. N. Narayanan Iyer v CIT*, (1993) 78 Comp Cas 156 Ker.

85. See *S. Sabapathi Rao v Sabapathi Press Co*, AIR 1930 Mad 1012. In this case a winding up petition was presented against a company in 1922 and the order was passed in 1927. During this period the company contracted to purchase certain goods and actually took delivery of them. As the goods were purchased in good faith in the ordinary course of business the transaction was confirmed. *Sugar Properties (Derisley Wood) Ltd, Re*, 1983 BCLC 146 Ch D, where it is emphasised that the exceptions enable the court to protect the transactions of the company which might be for the benefit of those who are interested in the company's property. *Monark Enterprises v Kishan Tulpule*, (1992) 74 Comp Cas 89: [1992] 1 Comp LJ 288, transfer of leasehold premises for payment of price of goods, valid, following *N. Subramania Iyer v Official Receiver*, AIR 1958 SC 1.

86. *A Company, Re, (No 007130 of 1998)*, [2000] 1 BCLC 528 Ch D.

87. *Tain Construction Co, Rose v AIB Group (UK) plc*, (2003) 1 WLR 279 (Ch D): (2003) 2 BCLC 374: (2004) 120 Comp Cas 163.

course of business. It was a disposal of a part of the company's assets.[88] The shares of a company were sold, before it went into insolvent liquidation, at an undervalue, the court said that the person who acquired the shares was to account for the unpaid value together with interest on it.[89]

The sale of the company's mortgaged property to the mortgagee and hypothecated property to the hypothecatee were held to be not so unusual transactions as to be hit by Section 531-A. The transaction was necessary in good faith in the interest of the company and was also made before the commencement of winding up.[90] An agreement between company and its employees for transfer of quarters to them was not validated. Employees were not allowed to sue for specific performance. The directors were aware of the company's financial condition. Employees were allowed to seek refund of their advance.[91]

Avoidance of transfer of shares and disposition of property [S. 536]

In the case of voluntary winding up, any transfer of shares in the company and any alteration in the status of the members of the company, made after the commencement of winding up, is void. But a transfer made to, or with the sanction of the liquidator is valid. In the case of winding up by the court, any disposition of the company's property, and transfer of shares, or alteration in the status of its members made after the commencement of the winding up is void, except when the court orders otherwise. The sanction of the court may be obtained either before or after the transfer is made. Complete discretion has been given to the court to do whatever it may think just in a matter of this kind.[92] Similarly, in the last mentioned case any attachment, distress or execution put in force without

---

88. *Countrywide Banking Corpn Ltd* v *Dean*, [1998] 1 BCLC 306.
89. *Philips* v *Brewin Dolphin Bell Lawrie Ltd*, [1999] 1 BCLC 714 CA.
90. *Official Liquidator, A.P. High Court* v *APSE Corpn Ltd*, [2000] 2 Comp LJ 71 AP. *Percept Advertising Ltd* v *M. Ravindran, Administrator, Anubhav Plantations Ltd*, (2003) 114 Comp Cas 652 SC, orders of avoidance of transfer and dispossession and other incidental orders as to lease etc.
91. *V.R. Mazumdar* v *Mysore Kriloskar Ltd*, (2006) 133 Comp Cas 468 Kant.
92. S. 536. See *Bir Chand* v *John Bros*, AIR 1934 All 161: 1934 ALJ 195; *Transport Corpn of India Ltd* v *Haryana State Industrial Development Corpn*, (1992) 74 Comp Cas 800 P&H, transfer of shares which was the result of a compromise not allowed to be enforced after the commencement of winding up. *ICICI Venture Funds Marketing Ltd* v *Neptune Inflatabler Ltd*, (2005) 127 Comp Cas 1 Mad, loan transaction before the date of winding up petition, the company defaulted in payment. The bank disposed of the mortgaged property before the date of winding up order; lender *bona fide*, transaction validated. *ICICI Ltd* v *Ahmedabad Mfg & Calico Printing Co Ltd*, (2005) 123 Comp Cas 132 SC, application for validation of transactions four years after commencement of winding up, not allowed. In the meantime the company had gone into industrial sickness, wound up as such, the liquidator was holding proceeds. *Reserve Bank of India* v *Crystal Credit Corpn Ltd*, (2006) 132 Comp Cas 363 Del, a *bona fide* purchaser of property applied for confirmation, the property fetched good price, no infirmity in procedure, sale confirmed.

leave of the court, against the estate or effects of the company or any sale held of any property or effects of the company shall be void.[93] The court refused to validate the transfer of the company's leasehold interest for a price so small that it would not have helped the company in any way.[94] The court did not interfere where the transfer of some of the properties of the company to its subsidiary was made in the interest of business expediency and as a part of a scheme of restructuring. The sole objecting creditor was not able to show any prejudice to the creditors' interests.[95]

The payment of a dishonoured cheque does not come within the catch of the section. The section cannot be used to ward off liability under Section 138 of the Negotiable Instruments Act, 1881.[96]

Avoidance of attachments, executions, etc. [S. 537]

The provision applies to companies which are being wound up by the court. Any attachment, distress or execution put in force, against the effects or estate of the company, or any sale held of any of the properties or effects of the company, without leave of the court, after commencement of winding up, can be avoided. The guarantor of a company's bank loans has been allowed to invoke the jurisdiction of the court under this section.[97]

---

93. S. 537. For the effect of winding up on a floating charge *see* S. 534. *See* also *Navjivan Mills Ltd, Re*, (1986) 59 Comp Cas 201 Guj, where the operation of the section was stayed in the interest of the company. *Travancore Rayons Ltd v ROC*, (1988) 64 Comp Cas 819: [1989] Comp LJ 77 Ker, the court ordered the assets to be disposed of in the interest of getting financial support from financial institutions. *Rushvi Estate & Investments (P) Ltd v Official Liquidator of Shri Ambica Mills Ltd*, (2001) 105 Comp Cas 828 Guj, a sale made in violation of Supreme Orders was avoided.

94. *India Maize & Chemicals, Ltd Re*, (1998) 94 Comp Cas 762 All; *Bengal Food Produce (P) Ltd v Official Liquidator*, (1999) 94 Comp Cas 762 All.

95. *K & Co v Aruna Sugars & Enterprises Ltd*, AIR 1999 Mad 45.

96. *Okay Industries Ltd v State of Maharashtra*, [1999] 4 Comp LJ 491 Bom; affirmed by the Supreme Court in *Pankaj Mehra v State of Maharashtra*, (2000) 2 SCC 756: AIR 2000 SC 1953: (2000) 100 Comp Cas 417 SC and followed in *Stephen Aranha v Jindal Leasefin Ltd*, (2000) 28 SCL 170 Del.

97. *K.S. Shivapaa v State Bank of Mysore*, (1988) 63 Comp Cas 229 Kant. A secured creditor would also be within the catch of the section if he has to effectuate his remedies through the court process. Leave of the court would then be necessary, *Gujarat State Financial Corpn v Official Liquidator*, (1996) 87 Comp Cas 658 Guj. The provisions of the Limitation Act are not applicable to an application for setting aside a transaction under the section, *Travancore Ogale Glass Mfg Co Ltd, Re*, (1997) 88 Comp Cas 179 Ker. *Kerala State Financial Enterprises Ltd v Official Liquidator*, (2006) 133 Comp Cas 912, 915 Ker, mortgage in favour of the company was not registered with ROC, the creditor was treated as unsecured, attachment order prior to commencement of winding up but within retrospective period, stayed, attachment does not create a charge, not a case of recovery of tax or duty, dues of Government company covered by the Companies Act, recovery proceedings not allowed.

One of the effects of the doctrine of relation back of the winding up order is shown by *Rajratna Naranbhai Mills* v *New Quality Bobbin Works*.[1] A creditor filed a suit against a company to recover a sum of money due to him and on the same day got some shares of the company attached. Then a winding up petition was presented against the company. After this, but before the winding up order, a consent decree was passed and the attached shares were sold in the execution of the decree. Then came the winding up order. The liquidator applied for a declaration that the sale was void and for recovery of the sale proceeds. Under Section 537(1) any attachment or sale of a company's property after the commencement of winding up without the sanction of the court is void and under Section 441(2) winding up by the court is deemed to commence at the time of the presentation of the petition. Thus, the court had no choice but to hold that the sale, having taken place after the presentation of the petition, was void and the liquidator was entitled to recover the sale proceeds. It was not necessary for him to bring a civil suit for this purpose. The winding up court had sufficient power under Section 446(2) to entertain the summons.

Disclaimer of onerous property [S. 535]

The liquidator may abandon onerous properties belonging to the company. Following kinds of properties are regarded as onerous for purposes of Section 535—

1. land of any tenure, burdened with covenants;
2. shares or stock in companies;
3. any other property which is unsaleable or is not readily saleable by reason of the fact that it requires the possessor to perform certain acts or pay a sum of money;
4. unprofitable contracts.

The liquidator may with the leave of the court disclaim any such property. It is the duty of the court to help the liquidator to get rid of "onerous and burdensome contracts" whenever it is necessary to safeguard in full the interests of the body of creditors and the shareholders of the company.[2] Thus in *Raka Corpn (P) Ltd, Re*:[3]

---

1. (1973) 43 Comp Cas 131 Guj. *See also State Industrial and Investment Corpn of Maharashtra v Maharashtra State Financial Corpn*, (1988) 64 Comp Cas 102 Bom. The section does not apply to a secured creditor realising the security by disposing of the assets. *Aryavarta Plywood v Rajasthan State I & I Corpn*, [1990] 1 Comp LJ 222 Del, distinguishing *Mysore Surgical Cotton (P) Ltd v KSFC*, [1988] 1 Comp LJ 63 Kant. The liquidator was not allowed to question a decree obtained by a secured creditor for recovery by sale of mortgaged property and hypothecated goods, *Hindustan Forest Co (P) Ltd v United Commercial Bank*, (1994) 79 Comp Cas 669 P&H.
2. *West Bengal Small Industries Development Corpn Ltd v Official Liquidator*, (2006) 133 Comp Cas 717 Cal, disclaimer of 99 year lease. It is the duty of the court to hear all parties including the mortgagee of the lease hold right.
3. [1968] 1 Comp LJ 220: (1968) 38 Comp Cas 329. The court did not permit leasehold premises to be disclaimed. The asset in question was of high value to the company. *Union Bank of India v Official Liquidator*, [1993] 3 Comp LJ 414 SC. The court may by order vest the property in any

A company in winding up was called upon to pay Rs 46,052 being the amount of the first call on equity shares held by it in a company. The liquidator asked for time to enable himself to examine the position. He found that the financial position of the company in which the shares were held was not sound and there was no prospect of getting any return on the investment.

He, therefore, applied for leave to disclaim the shares. He was opposed on the ground that by asking for time he had adopted the transaction. The court, finding that the burdensome shares would only hamper the course of the liquidator, granted leave to disclaim.

The term "contract" in this section has been held not to include "lease".[4] The outstanding contracts do not *ipso facto* become inoperative on the commencement of winding up. They remain binding unless disclaimed or rescinded as allowed by the section.[5]

A waste management licence under the Environment Protection Act, 1990 (UK) for management and disposal of wastes has been held to be a disclaimable property. The court said that the licence remains in force until the Authority revokes it or accepts its surrender. This factor does not preclude disclaimer. The court also found that there was a market in which people were prepared to pay for the transfer of the licence.[6] On dissolution of the company the licence would cease to exist and not vest in the Crown as *bona vacantia*.[7]

The disclaimer should be in writing signed by the liquidator. It has to be made within twelve months after the commencement of the winding up or such extended period as the court may allow. Where, however, the liquidator does not come to know of the existence of an onerous property within one month of the commencement of the winding up, the above period of twelve months shall begin to run from the date of his knowledge.[8]

The disclaimer determines in respect of the property disclaimed, the rights, interests and liabilities of the company.[9] It releases the company and the property from liability. But it does not affect the rights or liabilities of

---

person having legitimate claim to such property. *Shree Cement Ltd* v *Official Liquidator*, AIR 1994 Cal 90.

4. *ABC Coupler Engg Co Ltd, Re*, (*No 3*), [1970] 1 All ER 650 at p 669: (1970) 40 Comp Cas 952.

5. *Southern Automotive Corporation (P) Ltd*, (*No 3*), *Re*, AIR 1960 Mad 223: (1960) 30 Comp Cas 119. For the effects of disclaimer in favour of the purchaser on the rights in property see *Capital Prime Properties plc* v *Worthgate Ltd*, [2000] 1 BCLC 647 Ch D.

6. *Celtic Extraction Ltd, Re*, [1999] 4 All ER 684; *Bluestone Chemicals Ltd, Re*, [1999] 4 All ER 684 on appeal from *Mineral Resources Ltd, Re*, [1999] 1 All ER 746; applied in *Swift* v *Dairywise Farms Ltd*, [2000] 1 BCLC 632 Ch D.

7. *Wilmott Trading 1 and 2*, [1999] 2 BCLC 541 Ch D.

8. S. 535(1) and proviso.

9. S. 535(2). Where the sub-lessee of a lease disclaimed by the liquidator did not want to be included in the matter and the court allotted the lease to another person, the right of the sub-lessee became determined. *A. E. Realisations, Re*, [1987] 3 All ER 83 Ch D.

any other person in respect of that property. The court may, before granting the disclaimer, require notices to be given to persons interested in the property.[10] The landlord of the premises who is affected by the disclaimer becomes a creditor for his loss of rent etc.[11]

Sometimes a person interested in any such property may have required the liquidator, to decide whether he will or will not disclaim the property. In such a case the liquidator should, within twenty-eight days,[12] give notice to the applicant that he intends to apply to the court for leave to disclaim. If he does not do so, he shall not be entitled to disclaim the property and where the property is a contract which he has not disclaimed within the above time he shall be deemed to have adopted it.[13]

The landlord sought orders for payment of rent, future rent and delivery of possession of premises. The liquidator pleaded that sophisticated equipment of the company was lying in the premises and shifting it would cause depreciation in value to the detriment of creditors and workmen. But the liquidator neither made any inventory of the property, nor tried to sell it off. The premises was being used only for storage of goods and not for any business. The liquidator was directed to disclaim the tenancy and move to some other premises.[14]

PROCEEDINGS AGAINST DELINQUENT OFFICERS

Liability for fraudulent conduct of business [S. 542]

The power under the section has been vested in the Tribunal.

Sometimes it may appear in the course of winding up that the business of the company has been carried on with intent to defraud creditors of the company or any other persons or for any fraudulent purpose. In such a case the court, on the application of the liquidator or any creditor or contributory of the company, may declare that the persons who were parties to such business shall be personally responsible for such debts of the company as the court may direct. Besides, every person who was knowingly a party to

---

10. S. 535(3).
11. *Park Air Services plc, Re*, (1996) 1 BCLC 547 Ch D; affirmed by the House of Lords in *Park Air Services plc, Re*, [1999] 2 WLR 396 HL, as to how the landlord's loss is to be calculated. *Christopher Moran Holdings Ltd* v *Bairstow*, (1996) 1 BCLC 547 Ch D; *Hindcastle Ltd* v *Barbara Associates Ltd*, (1996) 2 BCLC 234 HL.
12. Or such extended period as may be allowed by the court. S. 534(4).
13. S. 535(4). Where a disclaimer is effected on the orders of the court under rule 268 of the Companies (Court) Rules 1959, which the liquidator is bound to carry out, it is necessary for him to file a copy of the disclaimer in the court. *Ritz Continental Hotels Ltd, Re*, (1986) 60 Comp Cas 526 Cal.
14. *Kaushalya Aggarwal* v *Punwire Paging Services Ltd*, (2004) 121 Comp Cas 431 P&H: 2004 CLC 906

such conduct of business, is punishable with imprisonment or fine or both.[15] A well-known illustration is *William C. Leitch Bros Ltd, Re*:[16]

One *A* transferred his business to a company promoted by himself. He took shares and debentures for the price, the latter creating a charge upon the company's assets. The company came to be indebted up to £6500 for goods supplied and was unable to pay. Even so *A*, the managing director, ordered goods worth £6000 on credit, which became subject to the charge. The company became insolvent and *A* received payments in lieu of the charge. The court held him liable to pay £3000 to the liquidator. WILLIAM MAUGHAM J said: "If a company continues to carry on business and to incur debt at a time when there is, to the knowledge of the directors, no reasonable prospect of the creditors ever receiving payment of those debts, it is in general a proper inference that the company is carrying on business with intent to defraud creditors."

This statement has been cited with approval by the Kerala High Court in *Nagendra Prabhu* v *Popular Bank*.[17] The court added:

Although the section leaves the court with a discretion to make a declaration of liability in relation to "all or any of the debts or other liability of the company", the order would in general be limited to the amount of the debts of those creditors who have been defrauded. Thus, there must be some nexus between the fraudulent trading or purpose and the extent of liability.

Further, this liability arises only when the company is in winding up and for offences committed before or during winding up.[18] "Fraudulent trading connotes real dishonesty—according to current notions of fair trading among commercial men, real moral blame."[19] In this respect it is different from "fraudulent preference" which does not require moral turpitude. In *Patrick & Lyon Ltd, Re*[20], a company remained in business only to save certain debentures which otherwise would have become invalid. The court held that this did not amount to an intention to defraud creditors. Similarly, no responsibility comes under the section to an auditor or the secretary of

---

15. The term of imprisonment may extend to two years and the fine may extend to fifty thousand rupees. [S. 543(3)]. There must be specific allegations and positive evidence, otherwise proceedings would be liable to be dropped. *Security and Finance (P) Ltd* v *B. K. Bedi*, (1991) 71 Comp Cas 101 Del.
16. [1932] Ch 261: [1932] All ER Rep 897: 148 LT 108.
17. ILR [1969] 1 Ker 340: AIR 1970 Ker 120.
18. *Regina* v *Rollafson*, [1969] 1 WLR 815 and the House of Lords in *D. P. P.* v *Schild Kamp*, [1969] 3 All ER 1640. *See* also '*Criminal Liability for Fraudulent Trading*', 1969 JBL 302. *Hypine Carbons Ltd* v *J.C. Bhatia*, (2001) 103 Comp Cas 422 HP, mere failure on the part of the directors-respondents to initiate legal steps against the debtors would not bring the case within the ambit of S. 542 of the Act.
19. MAUGHAM J in *Patrick & Lyon Ltd, Re*, [1933] Ch 786: [1933] All ER Rep 590: 149 LT 231.
20. *Ibid.*

the company for mere failure to report.[21] The same is the position of a person who only provides finance.[22] The directors of a company persuaded a wealthy investor to join as a director and to provide investment capital. But he failed to provide sufficient funds to enable the company to avoid going into insolvent liquidation. It was held that the directors were not liable for payments made up to the time that they had the genuine belief that he would be providing funds.[23] Where a fraud was committed upon a single creditor in a single transaction, it was held that the section was not attracted. A solitary instance could not be taken to mean that the business was being carried on to defraud creditors. Officers guilty of filing false purchase tax returns have been held liable. LORD DENNING MR said:[24] "The section is deliberately framed in wide terms so as to enable the court to bring fraudulent persons to book."[25] The basis of decisions under the section has recently been explained in an Australian case in the following words:[26]

> There is nothing wrong in the fact that directors incur credit at a time when, to their knowledge, the company is not liable to meet all its liabilities as they fall due. What is manifestly wrong is if directors allow a company to incur credit at a time when the business is being carried on in such circumstances that it is clear that the company will never be able to satisfy its creditors. However, there is nothing wrong to say that directors who genuinely believe that the clouds may roll away and the sunshine of prosperity will shine upon them again and disperse the fog

---

21. *Maidstone Buildings Provisions Ltd, Re*, [1971] 3 All ER 363: [1971] 1 WLR 1085, though in view of the extended meaning given to the position of the secretary in *Panorama Development (Guildford)* v *Fidelis Furnishing Fabrics*, [1971] 3 WLR 440: [1971] 3 All ER 16: (1971) 2 QB 711 CA, the case may not sound to be a good law.
22. *Maidstone Buildings Provisions Ltd, Re*, [1971] 3 All ER 363: [1971] 1 WLR 1085. *Official Liquidator, Shield Shoe Co (P) Ltd* v *Fateh Chand Pahwa*, (2007) 135 Comp Cas 467 Raj, Commercial officer appointed for taking care of books of account and bank transactions, etc, was held to be not an officer for the purposes of the section. There were also no specific allegations.
23. *Rod Gunner Organisation Ltd* v *Gunner*, (2004) 2 BCLC 110 (Ch D).
24. *Cyona Distributors Ltd, Re*, [1967] 1 All ER 281: [1967] Ch 889. *Bank of Credit & Commerce International, SA (No. 15), Re, Morris* v *Bank of India*, (2004) 2 BCLC 279 (Ch D), the Chief Manager had knowledge or atleast suspicion that the transactions were being entered into for a fraudulent purpose yet he turned a blind eye to them and regarded them as a matter of routine. This knowledge was attributed to the bank. The court applied the principles in *Produce Marketing Consortium No. 2, Re*, (1989) BCLC 520. *Bank of Credit & Commerce International, Re, Morris* v *State Bank of India*, (2004) 2 BCLC 236 (Ch D), the State Bank remained protected from liability because there were assuring circumstances like guarantees by BCCI for loans advanced. *Official Liquidator of Shubh Laxmi Savings & Fin (P) Ltd* v *Brij Mohan Gorna*, (2007) 135 Comp Cas 547 Raj no cogent material and specific allegation against the director.
25. All such recent cases have been considered by Nigel L. Macassey, *Responsibility for Fraudulent Trading*, [1973] New LJ 822. R. Williams, *Liability for Reckless Trading by Companies: The South African Experience*, 33 IC LQ 684.
26. *White & Osmond (Parkstone) Ltd, Re*, [Unreported]; noted 1976 JBL 225, J. H. Farrar, CORPORATE INSOLVENCY AND THE LAW.

of their depression are not entitled to incur credit to help them to get over the bad time.[27]

Where a person who takes part in the management of a company's affairs obtains credit or further credit for the company when he knows that there is no reason for thinking that funds will become available to pay the debt when it becomes due or shortly thereafter, he may be found guilty of the offence of carrying on the company's affairs with intent to defraud creditors. It is not necessary for the prosecution to prove that there was no reasonable prospect of the company's creditors ever receiving payment of their debts.[28] Heavy withdrawals of money by directors from the company's account under pretended loans knowing fully well that the company was in losses and would not be able to pay its creditors would be sufficient to charge them with liability even if they were only nominal directors and not incharge of the company's affairs.[29]

Where the declaration of liability under Section 542 or 543 is against a firm or a body corporate, Section 544 gives this power to the court that it may make a similar declaration against any person who is a partner in that firm or a director in that body corporate.

Proceedings were allowed to be instituted in an English court though the fraud in question was practised in a cross-country banking transaction through electronic media. Excepting for crediting the money in a New York bank account, everything else was done in England and the fraudster and his victims were both in England.[30]

Falsification of books [S. 539]

If any officer or contributory of a company has, with intent to defraud or deceive any person, destroyed, mutilated, altered, falsified or secreted any books, papers or securities of the company, he is punishable with imprisonment and fine. A person who is privy to such acts is also punishable. There is similar penalty for making any false or fraudulent entry in any book or register or document of the company.[31]

---

27. *See* also *Shiwalik Transport Co* v *Thakur Ajit Singh*, (1978) 48 Comp Cas 465 Punj, where it was held that the liability survives the death of the director concerned, though his legal representatives will be bound to pay only out of the director's estate.

28. *R* v *Grantham*, [1984] 3 All ER 166 CA. In a subsequent case the Court of Appeal pointed out that it is not necessary to bring in the names of any creditors who might have been affected by fraudulent conduct of business. *R* v *Kemp*, 1988 BCLC 217: [1988] 2 WLR 975: 1988 QB 645.

29. *Official Liquidator* v *Ram Swarup*, (1997) 88 Comp Cas 569: AIR 1997 All 72; *Shivmoni Steel Tubes Ltd* v *A. Murali*, (2002) 108 Comp Cas 584 Kant, a person who was sought to be made liable was appointed after the company was placed before the BIFR, no transactions taking place since then till the date of winding up order. The court (now Tribunal) said he could not be held guilty of misfeasance.

30. *R* v *Smith*, (1996) 2 BCLC 109 CA.

31. *P. P. Looke* v *N. J. Mathew*, (1967) 37 Comp Cas 790 Ker: [1967] 2 Comp LJ 146.

Frauds by officers [S. 540]

The section provides a penalty for any of the following acts done by any officer of a company which subsequently goes into liquidation:

1. Where he has, by fraud or false pretences, induced any person to give credit to the company.

2. Where he has, with intent to defraud creditors of the company, made any gift or transfer of any property of the company or has created a charge on, or caused the levying of any execution against any property of the company.

3. Where he has, with intent to defraud creditors of the company, concealed or removed any property of the company within two months before, or since the date of any judgment for payment against the company.

Liability where proper accounts not kept (S. 541)

If it is shown in the case of a company being wound up that proper books of account were not kept by the company throughout the period of 2 years immediately preceding the commencement of the winding up, or the period between the incorporation of the company and the commencement of winding up whichever is shorter, every officer of the company who is in default will be liable unless he shows that he acted honestly and that in the circumstances in which the business of the company was carried on, the default was excusable. Where the auditor who audited the accounts of the company merely stated that at the time the books of account were made available to him the accounts were not complete. There was nothing in the statement of the auditor to show that such books of account were incomplete throughout for a period of two years immediately preceding the commencement of winding up. It was held that in the absence of any averment or evidence no case under S. 541 could be made out.[32]

Offences by officers [S. 538]

Section 538 contains a long list of offences for which officers of a company in winding up are made punishable with imprisonment or fine. Following offences are covered by the section:

1. Failure to discover to the liquidator to the best of knowledge, fully and truly, all the property of the company and how and to whom and for what consideration the company disposed of any property. This does not include dispositions made in the ordinary course of business.[33]

---

32. *Hypine Carbons Ltd* v *J.C. Bhatia*, (2001) 103 Comp Cas 422 HP.
33. See *Official Liquidator, Golcha Properties* v *P. C. Dhadda*, (1980) 50 Comp Cas 175 Raj, where the three officers incharge were not able to account for the money which they had sent to the main office of the company and they were ordered to pay.

2. Failure on the part of an officer to deliver up to the liquidator any property of the company in his custody or control and which he is required by law to deliver up.

3. Failure on the part of an officer to deliver up to the liquidator, books and papers of the company in his custody or control and which he is required by law to deliver up.

4. If any officer, within twelve months before winding up, conceals any property of the company of the value of one hundred rupees or upwards or conceals any debt due to or from the company.

5. Within twelve months before winding up or at any time thereafter, any officer fraudulently removes any property of the company of the value of one hundred rupees or upwards.

6. If any officer makes any material omission in any statement relating to the affairs of the company.

7. If an officer knows or believes that a false debt has been proved by any person under the winding up, but fails within one month to inform the liquidator.

8. After the commencement of winding up, any officer prevents the production of any book or paper affecting or relating to the property or affairs of the company.

9. Within 12 months before or at any time after the commencement of winding up, an officer conceals, destroys, mutilates or falsifies any book or paper relating to the property or the affairs of the company. The next clause, namely, (*f*) covers the making of false entries in books and clause (*k*) punishes fraudulent parting with books and papers of the company.

10. After the commencement of winding up or at any meeting of the creditors within the twelve months before winding up, any officer attempts to account for any part of the property of the company by fictitious losses or expenses.

11. Within the twelve months next before the commencement of winding up or at any time thereafter, any officer by false representation or other fraud, obtains on credit on behalf of the company any property which the company does not subsequently pay for.

12. Under the similar circumstances as above, any officer, under the false pretence that the company is carrying on its business, obtains on credit on behalf of the company, any property which the company does not subsequently pay for.

13. Within the same time as above, any officer pawns, pledges, or disposes of any property of the company which has been obtained

on credit and has not been paid for, except when it is done in the ordinary course of the business of the company.

14. Any officer is guilty of any false representation or other fraud for the purpose of obtaining the consent of the creditors of the company to an agreement with reference to the affairs of the company or the winding up.

Directors owe a continuing duty to produce to the liquidator all the books, property and assets of the company. They have not to wait for this purpose for a request from the liquidator. This duty of cooperation further extends on a continuing basis to passing on to the liquidator any information relating to the company.[34]

Misfeasance proceedings [S. 543]

Section 543 empowers the court to assess damages and requires the delinquent officer to pay the amount to the company. Permitting the company's claims to become time-barred by sheer inaction[35] and transferring from the company's account, while it was in a state of insolvency, to a creditor's account with a view to relieving the director in question from his guarantee for the debt amounting to fraudulent preference, have been held to be misfeasance and the directors in question were accordingly compelled to make good the company's loss.[36] This power of the court comes into play when, in the course of winding up, it appears that any person who has taken part in the promotion or formation of the company or any past or present director or manager, liquidator or officer of the company has misapplied or retained or become liable for any money or property of the company or has been guilty of misfeasance or breach of trust in relation to the company.[37] The liquidator, or any creditor or contributory may apply to the court for action against the delinquent officer.[38] The court shall examine his conduct.[39] If he is found guilty he may be required to repay or restore the money or property of the company or to contribute such

---

34. *R v Mc Credle*, [2000] 2 BCLC 438 CA.
35. *Smart Advertising Com (P) Ltd v Ramesh K. Nanchahal*, (1989) 65 Comp Cas 92 P&H.
36. *West Mercia Safetywear Ltd v Dodd*, 1988 BCLC 250 CA. The proceedings are of quasi-criminal nature. They are not affected by the fact that the person proceeded against may be liable for any offence which may be brought to the surface by the proceeding. *Chamundi Chemicals v M. C. Cherian*, (1993) 77 Comp Cas 1, 18 Kant.
37. *Paras Rampuria Trading & Finance Co Ltd, Re*, (2006) 131 Comp Cas 834 All, *prima facie* proof of fraudulent conduct of business in violation of the provisions of the Act, sufficient ground to maintain application, erstwhile directors to be proceeded against.
38. This application is filed by the liquidator or the relevant party in his own name and not in company's name and therefore the benefit of the additional period of limitation under S. 458-A is not available. *B. Patnaik Mines (P) Ltd v Bijoyananda Pattnaik*, (1994) 80 Comp Cas 237 Ori. The AP High Court allowed the benefit of extended period under S. 458-A because the proceedings are in essence for the benefit of the company. *Official Liquidator v T. J. Swamy*, (1992) 73 Comp Cas 583 AP.
39. The liquidator has only to prove a *prima facie* case. *Supreme Bank of India Ltd, Re*, (1967) 37 Comp Cas 392 Mys.

sum to the assets of the company by way of compensation as the court thinks just. The jurisdiction under Section 468 to secure delivery of property to the liquidator is exercisable "at any time after making a winding up order" and is not barred by any length of time. Thus where a company's agent received money without authority in 1956, the court ordered its delivery to the company in 1964, the company having gone into liquidation in 1959.[40]

The misfeasance proceedings against officers of the company are capable of covering the full range of duties owed by a director to his company and are not restricted to ethical or fiduciary duties.[41]

An application under this section has to be made within five years from the date of the order of winding up or of the first appointment of the liquidator or of the alleged offence, whichever is longer.[42] The period of five years begins to run from the date of the first appointment of the liquidator. Time does not start afresh every time a new liquidator is appointed.[43] To this, the period of one year has to be added under S. 458-A.[44]

There is no such distinct wrongful act known to law as "misfeasance". The section does not create any new right or offence, but only provides a summary and cheap remedy for enforcing such rights as are otherwise enforceable by law. There are two conditions of liability under the section, *i.e.* an act in the nature of breach of trust, and an act which results in loss to the company.[45] The act may be that of commission or omission. Gross negligence on the part of a director which gives opportunity to others to misappropriate would be misfeasance.[46] Misfeasance was held to be inferable where large sums of money were withdrawn by the director at a time when the company was grinding in losses.[47] Where the money of the

---

40. *Bharat Traders Ltd* v *Sadhu Singh*, (1968) 38 Comp Cas 537 P&H.
41. *Westlowe Storage & Distribution Ltd, Re*, [2000] 2 BCLC 590 Ch D.
42. *J.V.V. Singh* v *Shyam Sunder*, AIR 1970 Raj 91.
43. *Punjab Commerce Bank Ltd* v *Ram Narain Virmani*, (1973) 43 Comp Cas 323 Punj.
44. *Ganesh Narain Podar* v *Official Liquidator*, (2006) 133 Comp Cas 843 Raj.
45. *Official Liquidator* v *Dr Shailendra Nath Sinha*, (1973) 43 Comp Cas 107 Cal. The burden of proof is on the applicant liquidator. *Sandal Chit Fund & Financiers (P) Ltd* v *Narinder Kumar Sharma*, (1994) 79 Comp Cas 25 P&H, where the liquidator could not even name any creditor remaining unpaid. *Chamundi Chemicals* v *M. C. Cherian*, (1993) 77 Comp Cas 1 Kant, bona fide decisions of directors are not questionable. *Official Liquidator, Aryodaya Ginning and Mfg Mills Ltd* v *Gulabchand Chandalia*, (2003) 114 Comp Cas 654 Guj, a mere error or mistake in an accounting practice, no loss to company shown, creditors and depositors alleged to be misled by suppression of losses and enhancing the value of assets, held, no misfeasance.
46. *Official Liquidator* v *Ashok Kumar*, (1976) 46 Comp Cas 572 Pat; *Official Liquidator, Janhitkari Alap Bachat Rindayatri Sansthan (P) Ltd* v *Vishnu Kumar Pradhan*, (2001) 103 Comp Cas 1026 Raj, it is not necessary to fix liability under Section 543 that a director should be a shareholder or that he should have actually participated in the management.
47. *Official Liquidator* v *Ram Swarup*, (1997) 88 Comp Cas 569: AIR 1997 All 72; *MDA Investment Management Ltd, Re*, (2004) 1 BCLC 217, diversion of consideration received on

company was lent to a third party in contravention of the company's objects, both the directors (one of them through legal representative since deceased), were responsible for it and were held to be jointly and severally liable to replace the company's money.[48] No liability arose under the section for the sums which were refundable from Income Tax Department, but having not been claimed within time became time-barred because the director in question had sent several reminders to Income Tax Department for refund and subsequently all the records and papers were handed over to the liquidator. Similarly, no liability arose for the sums due to the company from certain parties because the company had itself written off those claims as bad debts and also for stock spoiled and destroyed and written off by the company.[49] Mere vague and general accusations will not be sufficient to found a liability under the section. The Karnataka High Court[50] refused to entertain a proceeding against the managing director on general accusations like this that there was unaccounted cash balance, that proper books of account were not maintained and that the stock-in-trade was in the possession of a bank and its sale was delayed.

There must be specific allegation against each director or officer alongwith a quantification of loss. Mere allegations against former directors were held not sufficient for maintaining an application under the section.[51]

It is a misfeasance on the part of directors to make gifts of the company's property for no proper trading purpose. Disposal of the plant and machinery of the company without any justification was also held to be misfeasance. The directors were required to pay the sums involved with interest.[52] Where no steps were taken by the directors to enforce the

---

sale of company's business which money would otherwise have been available to meet the creditors' claims.

48. *Babubhai Chandulal Mody* v *Official Liquidator, Atlas Import & Export Co (P) Ltd*, (1996) 86 Comp Cas 580 Mad.

49. *Ibid*.

50. *Official Liquidator* v *R. C. Marathe*, (1980) 50 Comp Cas 562 Kant. *Hypine Carbons Ltd* v *J.C. Bhatia*, (2001) 103 Comp Cas 422 HP, allegation of misappropriation of furniture belonging to the company but no specific evidence as to which item was in possession and control of a particular director was given, no case was made out for fastening liability. *Official Liquidator, Dhavalgiri Paper Mills (P) Ltd* v *Chinubhai Khilachand*, (2002) 114 Comp Cas 277 Guj. It is necessary for official liquidator to make specific allegation against each director or officer, mere allegation against former directors is not sufficient.

51. *Official Liquidator, Dhavalgiri Paper Mills (P) Ltd* v *Chinubhai Khilachand*, (2003) 114 Comp Cas 277 Guj. *Ashoka Auto and General Industries (P) Ltd* v *Inder Mohan Puri*, (2005) 124 Comp Cas 423 Del; *Official Liquidator* v *R.B. Sangare*, (2006) 133 Comp Cas 258 Bom allegation of mismanagement relating to travel and legal expenses, custody of stocks, remuneration, etc but no allegation of fraud or breach of trust and no specific allegation and positive evidence. *Sajida Book Shop* v *Kamudi Exporters (P) Ltd*, (2007) 135 Comp Cas 273 Ker, no allegation that the director in question had personally misapplied the security, roving inquiry not to be ordered.

52. *Barton Mfg Co Ltd, Re*, [1999] 1 BCLC 740 Ch D, gratuitous payments were made to one of the directors and his wife.

company's claims and consequently they became time-barred, the directors were held liable to compensate the company for its loss with interest at 12% from the date of winding up till payment.[53]

Failure to take proper care of assets and consequential loss to the company is a ground for misfeasance proceedings. But where the assets were in the possession of a bank for over seven years and with the liquidator for two years, the directors could not be held to be guilty of improper care of assets.[54] The directors were held liable for the loss of the company's diamonds while on a foreign trip without insurance cover. A person who was working as a shadow director was not excused. There were circumstances of gross negligence.[55]

Nominee directors (nominated by a financial institution in this case) can also be held liable depending upon the role which they played in the conduct of affairs, i.e., whether they performed their statutory duties in good faith.[56] They were not permitted to defend themselves against liability just by saying that they only knew that the directors were withdrawing heavy amounts from the company free of interest. The company was led to financial starvation and heavy losses. Their silence gave rise to an inference of complexity.[57]

The principles relating to misfeasance proceedings were restated by the Supreme Court in *Official Liquidator, Supreme Bank Ltd* v *P. A. Tendulkar.*[58] While the proceedings were pending before the Mysore High Court, the chairman of the board and another director died. BEG J laid down that the liability would devolve upon the legal representatives, but would be "confined to the assets or estate left by the deceased in the hands of the successors".[59] Referring to the position taken by one of the directors, BEG J said:

> A director may be shown to be so placed and to have been so closely associated personally with the management of the company that

53. *Xpo Xpert (P) Ltd* v *Jai Gopal Angrish*, [1998] 3 Comp LJ 438 P&H; *Kainth Finance (P) Ltd* v *Shri Karam Singh Kainth*, (1999) 98 Comp Cases 131 P&H.
54. *Official Liquidator, AutoElectricals (India) (P) Ltd* v *D. P. Gupta*, (1999) 98 Comp Cas 59 Raj.
55. *Simmon Box (Diamonds) Ltd, Re*, 2000 BCC 275.
56. *A Stock & Co* v *Dilip Kumar Chakraborti*, (1996) 87 Comp Cas 139 Cal.
57. *Official Liquidator* v *Ram Swarup*, (1997) 88 Comp Cas 569: AIR 1997 All 72. It was not necessary to implead the legal heirs of a legal heir who had also died, there being other legal heirs on record.
58. (1973) 1 SCC 602: (1973) 43 Comp Cas 382; and again in *Official Liquidator* v *Parthasarathi Sinha*, (1983) 1 SCC 538: (1983) 53 Comp Cas 163.
59. The Calcutta High Court did not allow substitution of legal heirs in place of a delinquent director upon his death. *Parthasarathi Sinha* v *Official Liquidator*, (1976) 46 Comp Cas 555 Cal. No decree can be passed against a deceased director until his representatives are brought on record. *Modern Transporters (P) Ltd* v *J. Mehta*, (1977) 47 Comp Cas 302 P&H. *Ennen Castings (P) Ltd* v *M.M. Sundaresh*, (2003) 114 Comp Cas 541 Kant, a director accused other directors of misfeasance, held, the other directors would have to be given the right to cross-examine him.

he will be deemed to be not merely cognizant of but liable for fraud in the conduct of the business of the company even though no specific act of dishonesty is proved against him personally. He cannot shut his eyes to what must be obvious to everyone who examines the affairs of the company even superficially. If he does so he could be held liable for dereliction of duties undertaken by him and compelled to make good the losses incurred by the company due to his neglect even if he is not shown to be guilty of participating in the commission of fraud. It is enough if his negligence is of such a character as to enable frauds to be committed and losses thereby incurred by the company.

The Karnataka High Court[60] stated that though liability for misfeasance will survive the death of the officer, it is necessary that it should have been ascertained during his lifetime, so that he was in a position to defend himself. His legal representatives are not likely to be acquainted with his conduct in the company and, therefore, they cannot be put on the defensive.[61]

Non-joinder of the legal heirs of a deceased director does not affect the proceedings against the others. Where the company fails to bring the representatives of the deceased director on record, the surviving director cannot claim to be relieved of his liability, the liability being joint and several.[62]

The section does not give the court power to fine a director for misconduct. It also does not apply to cases in which the claim is for simple contract debt, or is an ordinary claim for unliquidated damages.[63]

The conduct of a receiver or manager appointed by debenture-holders cannot be examined under the section,[64] he being not an officer of the company. But an auditor is an officer for this purpose. Thus, an auditor was held liable under the section for certifying false accounts whereby dividends were paid out of capital.[65] A liquidator who had negligently admitted claims was held liable under the section.[66] A liquidator who continued trading on

---

60. *Official Liquidator* v *Maganlal Hirachand Shah*, (1980) 50 Comp Cas 762 Kant.
61. Proceedings against legal representatives were not allowed for this reason in *Chamundi Chemicals* v *M.C. Cherian*, (1993) 77 Comp Cas 1 Kant, following *Joseline* v *Official Liquidator*, (1979) 49 Comp Cas 170. But the proceedings do not abate by reason of death, *N.S. Rajagopal* v *Official Liquidator, PNSS Nidhi Ltd*, (1993) 78 Comp Cas 687 Mad. Legal heirs were not allowed to be impleaded seven years after the death of the director, being out of time, *Official Liquidator, Bombay* v *Taru Jethmal Lalvani*, AIR 1994 Bom 74.
62. *Babubhai Chandulal Mody* v *Official Liquidator, Atlas Import & Export Co (P) Ltd*, (1996) 86 Comp Cas 580 Mad. Legal heirs who are not brought on record could not be held liable. Even otherwise the affair was thirty years old and all the creditors had been paid in full, *Official Liquidator* v *Taru Jethmalani Lalvani*, (1997) 88 Comp Cas 834 Bom.
63. *Supreme Bank of India Ltd, Re*, (1967) 37 Comp Cas 392 Mys; *B. Johnson & Co, Re*, [1955] Ch 634 CA.
64. *Ibid.*
65. *Kingston Cotton Mills Co, Re*, [1896] 2 Ch 279: 74 LT 568.
66. *Home & Colonial Insurance Co, Re*, [1929] All ER Rep 231: [1930] 1 Ch 102; *National Sugar Mills Ltd, Re*, (1978) 48 Comp Cas 339 Cal, managing director held liable for

behalf of the company without obtaining sanction of the court or of the committee and increased the deficiency of the company towards creditors was held liable in misfeasance.[67] The Kerala High Court has held that an official liquidator cannot be proceeded against under the section.[68]

Liability of Partners and Directors of Body Corporate [S. 544]

The power under the section has been vested in the court.

Where the declaration of liability is against a firm or a body corporate, the court may further declare that any partner in that firm or director in that body corporate shall also be liable.

Prosecution of delinquent officers and members [S. 545]

Section 545 provides that if it appears to the Tribunal, in the course of a compulsory winding up, that any past or present officer or member of the company has been guilty of any offence in relation to the company, the court may direct the liquidator either himself to prosecute the offender or to refer the matter to the Registrar. The Registrar may, if he thinks fit, refer the matter to the Central Government for further investigation. If the Registrar finds that the case is not one in which proceedings ought to be taken by him, he shall inform the liquidator accordingly. The liquidator may then with the sanction of the court himself take proceedings against the offender. Where the liquidator does not make any report to the Registrar, but an offence appears to the Tribunal to have been committed, it may direct the liquidator to make such a report.

Wrongful withholding of property [S. 630]

If an officer[69] wrongfully obtains possession of a company's property, or, being already in possession wrongfully refuses to deliver it to the company, a complaint can be made to a magistrate by the company or by any creditor or contributory. The magistrate can award punishment in terms of the section[70] and can also order the officer in possession to deliver the

---

misappropriations. It is not necessary for this liability to arise that the loss should be exactly calculated beforehand or that there should be shortfall in assets as against liabilities. *Official Liquidator of Milan Chit Fund* v *Joginder Singh Kohli*, (1978) 48 Comp Cas 357 Del. Misfeasance proceedings cannot be taken against sales agent of the company: *Voluntary Liquidator, Bharat Traders Ltd* v *Rattan Singh*, (1978) 48 Comp Cas 427. Liability survives the death of the director concerned and passes on to his legal representatives though they will be liable to pay only out of the estate of the deceased director. *F. & Co Osler (India) Ltd, Re*, (1978) 48 Comp Cas 698 Cal.

67. *Central Crest Engg Ltd, Re*, [2000] BCC 727.
68. *L. K. Prabhu* v *S. M. Ameerul Millath*, AIR 1997 Ker 347.
69. The word "officer" has been held to include the president of the company, *M. Gopal Krishnan* v *Leafin India Ltd*, (1995) 83 Comp Cas 351 Mad; *Prahladbhai Rajaram Mehta* v *Popatbhai Haribhai Patel*, (1996) 1 Guj CD 564 Guj: (1996) 67 Comp Cas 557 Guj, two remedies for eviction, S. 630 and also Bombay Rents, Hotel and Lodging House Rates Control Act, 1947.
70. Punishment is with fine extending to Rs 10,000.

property to the company. A flat was allotted to an officer. He refused to vacate it on retirement. It was held that he was not entitled to the protection of tenancy laws and could be ordered under Section 630 to vacate the premises of the company.[71] Proceedings can be launched against heirs of an officer or employee who has died and whose heirs are withholding the property.[72] Such people who refuse to hand over vacant possession cause hardship to the company and also to the successive allottees without having any right to cling to possession. A retired officer was refusing to vacate premises at Cochin. A complaint before a magistrate at Calcutta, where the company had its registered office, was held to be competent.[73] A subsequent decision of the same High Court went against this proposition. The complaint in the court where the company had its headquarters was quashed because the premises in question were situated elsewhere.[74]

Where the ingredients for attracting the application of Section 630 are made out, the right of the company to the possession of the property becomes established. There is then no scope for exercising any mercy power in favour of the employee.[75] An employee to whom a flat was given for a

71. *Krishan Avtar Bahadur v Co. Irwin Extross,* (1986) 59 Comp Cas 417 Bom. Proceedings were allowed when the premises in the possession of the company were under a tenancy and the employee surrendered the possession directly to the landlord. *Arvind Kotecha v Mahash Kumar,* (1994) 79 Comp Cas 338 Bom, or where the employee purchased the tenanted premises from the landlord, *Kannan Kandi Gopal Krishna Nair v Prakash Chander Juneja,* (1994) 81 Comp Cas 104 Bom. Proceedings against a director not allowed where the withholding was by the company, *M. K. Chandrakanta v Kannan,* (1994) 20 Comp Cas 307 Mad. Proceedings against a dismissed employee cannot be stopped because of reference under the Industrial Disputes Act, 1947. *Antony (R.) v Renusagar Power Co Ltd,* 1996 LLR 152 All. *Bishan Singh v State of U.P.,* (2006) 132 Comp Cas 887 All, liability to vacate on retirement. *Tatineni Venkata Krishna Rao v KCP Sugar & Industries Corpn Ltd,* (2006) 133 Comp Cas 422 AP, termination of employment due to participation in illegal strike, liability to vacate premises.

72. *Abhilash Vinodkumar Jain v Cox and King's (India) Ltd,* (1995) 3 SCC 732: (1995) 17 Corpt LA 90 SC: (1995) 84 Comp Cas 28 SC. "Officer" includes employees also and also both present and past, *Gokak Patel Volkart Ltd v Dundayya Gurushiddaiah Hiremath,* (1991) 2 SCC 141: (1991) 71 Comp Cas 403 SC; *Yogesh Kumar Kanlilal Shah v Gujarat Steel Tubes,* (1993) 2 Guj LH 1039. *Lalita Jalan v Bombay Gas Co Ltd,* (2003) 114 Comp Cas 515 SC, the legal heirs of deceased employee who were in possession only through the employee and who were refusing to vacate were held liable to be prosecuted.

73. *T. S. Satyanath v Thomas & Co,* (1985) 57 Comp Cas 648 Cal. The Bombay High Court has disagreed with it and did not permit proceeding at Bombay for a property which was being wrongfully withheld at Jamshedpur. *Hirak Ghosh v Amarendra Nath Sinha,* [1989] 1 Bom CR 400: (1991) 70 Comp Cas 324. The default is an offence of continuing nature. *Arun Kumar Das v State,* (1990) 68 Comp Cas 482 Cal; The High Court of Delhi did not allow proceedings to be launched there (company's headquarter) for a withholding committed in the Punjab (company's factory), *Ramesh G. Bhatia v J. M. Malik,* (1994) 79 Comp Cas 44. *TNV Nanjappa Chettiar v Devi Films (P) Ltd,* (1993) 76 Comp Cas 875 Mad. The proceeding under the section is of criminal nature; it cannot be stayed under an order of a civil court. *S. Palaniswamy v Sree Janardhana Mills Ltd,* (1993) 76 Comp Cas 323 Mad; *Texmaco Ltd v Ram Dayal,* (1993) 78 Comp Cas 518 Del.

74. *Vijay Kapur v Guest Keen Williams Ltd,* (1995) 83 Comp Cas 339 Cal. A Bombay decision has also been to the same effect. See *ibid.*

75. *Amrut Lal Pranlal Panchal v Prahladbhai Rajaram Mehta,* (1997) 26 Corpt LA 102 Guj. It is very difficult for an employee to establish that he was put into the premises as a tenant,

specified period was held bound to return it at the expiry of that period irrespective of the fact that the period did not correspond with his retirement.[76] A director was required to return the company's property and documents on his ceasing to be a director by reason of failure to attend meetings. He had filed a civil suit questioning the validity of the proceedings by which his office became vacated. The court did not go into the merits of the matter in a proceeding under Section 630.[77]

A complaint under this section is maintainable against the legal heirs of the deceased employee or officer for retrieval of the company's property wrongfully withheld by them after the demise of the employee concerned.[78] However, the family members of the employee living with him while he was alive cannot be prosecuted.[79]

The machinery of this section will not be available where there is a *bona fide* dispute between an employee and the company as to the title or rights to the property.[80]

Prahladbhai Rajaram Mehta v *Popatbhai Haribhai Patel*, (1996) 1 Guj CD 564 Guj: (1996) 67 Comp Cas 557 Guj; *Bimal Chand* v *DCM Ltd*, (1997) 27 CLA 304 P&H. The accused person can be given the benefit of doubt because it is a criminal matter. A conviction under the section was set aside because the company did nothing to initiate prosecution for two years during which the employee was constantly asserting that he was a tenant, *Chhatrasingh Nathusing Vaghela* v *State of Gujarat*, (1998) 29 Corpt LA 470 Guj. *Tata Tea Ltd* v *Fazlur Rehman*, (2001) 104 Comp Cas 718 Cal, an order can be passed against an employee under S. 630(2) for restoring the property even before the magistrate trying the case under S. 630(1) formally disposes of the criminal case against him. *Lalita Jalan* v *Bombay Gas Co Ltd*, (2003) 114 Comp Cas 515 SC, the court directed the officer or employee to deliver or refund the property within the fixed period but the order was not complied with, the court can awarded a sentence of two years. Earlier to this in *Lalita Jalan* v *Bombay Gas Co Ltd*, (2002) 7 SCC 37 on the question whether a past officer or employee or his legal heir would be included, the matter was referred to a larger Bench.

76. *Tariq Razi Azmi* v *Tata Hydro Electric Supply Co*, [2000] 5 Bom CR 211 Bom.
77. *K. Radhakrishnan* v *Thirumal Asphalts and Phelts (P) Ltd*, (1999) 97 Comp Cas 658 Mad. *Maratt Rubber Ltd* v *J.K. Marattukalam*, (2001) 104 Comp Cas 1 SC. Once the allegations made in the complaint make out an offence of which cognizance had been taken, an application cannot be filed under S. 245 of the Code of Criminal Procedure. Mere pendency of a civil proceeding would not be a ground for quashing the criminal proceedings.
78. *Gajra Gears Ltd* v *Smt Ashadevi*, (2001) 103 Comp Cas 489 MP. *Shubhshanti Services Ltd* v *Manjula Agarwalla*, (2005) 125 Comp Cas 477 SC: (2005) 4 Comp LJ 417, possession of the company's flat with legal heirs, they could not retain it because grounds raised by them were not found to be tenable.
79. *J.K. (Bombay) Ltd* v *Bharti Matha Mishra*, (2001) 104 Comp Cas 424 SC; *Lalita Jalan* v *Bombay Gas Co Ltd*, (2003) 114 Comp Cas 515 SC.
80. *Damodar Das Jain* v *Krishna Charan Chakraborti*, (1985) 57 Comp Cas 115 Bom. Where an ex-officer continuously assured the company that he would vacate and then the period of limitation expired, it was held to be a fit case of extension of time. *B. R. Herman & Mohatta* v *Ashok Raj*, (1984) 55 Comp Cas 61 Del; *Govind T. Jagtiani* v *S. S. Razi*, (1984) 56 Comp Cas 329 Bom, power not excluded by rent laws. "Property" includes both movable and immovable. The offence is of continuing nature. Hence, no period of limitation, *Beguram* v *Jaipur Udhyog Ltd*, (1987) 61 Comp Cas 744 Raj, order for vacation of quarters and punishment for withholding possession; *Baldev Krishna Sahi* v *Shipping Corpn of India*, (1987) 4 SCC 361: 1987 SCC (Cri) 750: (1988) 63 Comp Cas 1 SC, the provision is applicable to past employees. The purpose of the provision is to enable the company to get quick delivery of property from defaulting employees, *Atul Mathur* v *Atul*

The offence is of continuing nature. It continues till the possession is surrendered. Till then every day gives a new period of limitation.[81]

The provision as to prosecution under the section has been described by the Supreme Court to be not strictly speaking a penal provision.[82]

Kabra, (1989) 4 SCC 514: 1989 SCC (Cri) 761: [1989] 3 Comp LJ 127, 131: (1990) 68 Comp Cas 324 SC. It is not necessary that the property should belong to the company. *P.V. George v Jayems Engg Co (P) Ltd*, [1990] 2 Comp LJ 62 Mad. The section examines the employee's conduct. *Narayanana K. v L. V. Subramanian*, [1988] 2 Comp LJ 181 Mad. Disputes of civil nature cannot be examined by the court under this section. *Damodar Das Jain v Krishna Charan Chakraborti*, (1989) 4 SCC 531: (1990) 67 Comp Cas 564 SC: 1991 SCC (Cri) 420. Mere denial of the company's right is not a dispute. *Atul Mathur*, noted above, mere fact that an employee has questioned the validity of his removal under the Industrial Disputes Act, 1948 does not postpone the remedy of the company. *P.V. George v Jayems Engg Co (P) Ltd*, [1990] 2 Comp LJ 62 Mad. the period of limitation for proceedings under the section is to be found in S. 468(2)(c) of the Criminal Procedure Code, 1973. *Herman B.R. and Mohatta Ltd v Ashok Rai*, (1984) 55 Comp Cas 61 Del. *Ganesh Roy v State of Jharkhand*, (2004) 55 SCL 662 (Jhar), challenge to termination before Labour Court immaterial. It was held to be not a *bona fide* dispute that the managing director had agreed to sell the flat to the employee but the board of directors refused. There was no agreement to sell. *Indian Hotels Co Ltd v Bhaskar Moreshwar Karve*, (1994) 81 Comp Cas 132 Bom. It was also held to be not a bona fide dispute that the employee was claiming himself to be tenant without there being any signs and symbols of tenancy, *Texmaco Ltd v Arun Kumar Sharma*, (1991) 20 Comp Cas 287 Del, or that he was claiming himself to be a part owner only on the ground that rent deduction from salary was stopped from date of his promotion, *Airfreight Ltd v K. Kothawala*, (1995) 2 Mh LJ 17: (1995) 4 Bom CR 109 Bom. Remedy under the section was not allowed where the employee was found to be a direct tenant of the owner of the premises, *V.M. Shah v State of Maharashtra*, (1995) 5 SCC 767: 1985 SCC (Cri) 1077: AIR 1996 SC 339. The court cannot go into the merits of the dispute as to the rights of the employee over the property, *Minoo P. Bulsara v Hindustan Petroleum Corpn*, (1996) 23 Corpt LA 120 Bom. The employee's defence that the company had orally agreed to sell the flat to him could not be considered in the summary jurisdiction under S. 630, *Jolly Durga Pd v Goodricks Group Ltd*, (1998) 28 Corpt LA 335 Cal. Conviction of the employee is not a condition to the order of handing over possession to the company. *Metal Box (India) Ltd v State of W.B.*, (1997) 27 Corpt LA 359 Cal; *Airfreight Ltd v K. Kothawala*, (1995) 2 Mh LJ 17: (1995) 4 Bom CR 109 Bom, any claim of the employee to some superior title should be determined only after taking evidence. *Abhilash Vinodkumar Jain v Cox & Kings (India) Ltd*, (1995) 84 Comp Cas 1, legal heirs affected by section. *DCM Ltd v Lt Governor*, (1998) 71 Del LT 70 (DB), approval of closure of mill and settlement with workers, does not convert the workers into statutory tenant, receiver directed to get quarters vacated. *Petlad Bulakhidas Mills Co Ltd v State of Gujarat*, (1998) 2 Guj CD 1213 Guj, continuing offence, no period of limitation. *Mannath Balchandran v Forbes Forbes Campell & Co Ltd*, (1996) 2 Mah LJ 302, subsequent sale of the premises by the company is not material, the court has to see whether offence constituted at the time of complaint. *Jagdish Chandra Nijhawan v S.K. Saraf*, (1999) 1 SCC 119: (1999) 95 Comp Cas 48: (1999) 1 LLJ 295, the agreement had certain requirements for eviction of the employee-tenant, whether they were fulfilled was viewed by the Supreme Court as a dispute of civil nature. *Mohd Zameel Hussain v Asstt Labour Commr*, [2000] 1 Comp LJ 238, the fact that the removal of the employee is under challenge under the Industrial Disputes Act, 1947, is not a ground for withholding order of eviction, *J.K. (Bombay) Ltd v Bharti Matha Mishra*, (2001) 2 SCC 700: AIR 2001 SC 649, the legal heirs of a deceased employee can be proceeded against but not other members of the family.

81. *Gokak Patel Volkart Ltd v Dundayya Gurusiddaiah Hiremath*, (1991) 2 SCC 141: (1991) 71 Comp Cas 403 SC; *Nanjappa Chettiar v Devi Films (P) Ltd*, (1993) 76 Comp Cas 875 Mad; *Kannan Kandi Gopal Krishna Nair v Prakash Chander Juneja*, (1994) 81 Comp Cas 104 Bom.
82. *Shubh Shanti Services Ltd v Majula's Agarwalla*, (2005) 125 Comp Cas 477 (SC): (2005) 4

Annulment of dissolution [S. 559]

After a company has been dissolved in pursuance of any of the provisions of the Act, it is open to the court to declare the dissolution to have been void. But this can be done only within two years of the dissolution and on an application by the liquidator or any other person who appears to the court to be interested. A person entitled to claim damages for negligence from the company is a person "interested" for this purpose, but not his lawyer.[83] The court's order may be subject to such terms as it thinks fit to impose. Any proceedings may then be taken as might have been taken if the company had not been dissolved.

The person on whose application the order is passed should within thirty days or such further time as the Tribunal may allow, file a certified copy of the order with the Registrar.

Disposal of books [S. 550]

The section lays down the manner in which the books and papers of a dissolved company shall be disposed of. It says that when the affairs have been completely wound up and the company is about to be dissolved, the books and papers shall be disposed of in the following manner:

    (*a*) When the winding up is by the court, in such manner as the court may direct.

    (*b*) In the case of members' winding up, in such manner as the company by special resolution directs.

    (*c*) In the case of creditors' winding up, in such manner as the committee of inspection, or the creditors, where there is no committee, may direct.

If the books and papers were committed to the custody of the company, or the liquidator or any other person, no liability will come to it or him after the expiry of five years if he is not able to produce them. In other words, he is accountable only up to five years.

The Central Government is authorised to make rules in the behalf, which may prevent destruction of books and papers for a period not exceeding five years. The rules may enable any creditor or contributory to make a representation to the Government in this matter and appeal to the court against the Government order.

Any contravention of the rules or of any Government order entails punishment up to six months of imprisonment or fine up to Rs 50,000.

Comp LJ 417: (2005) SCL 280: 2005 CLC 657; on appeal from 2004 CLC 1438 Bom, wrongful possession of the family members of the managing director was not established.

83. *Roehampton Swimming Pool Ltd, Re,* [1968] 3 All ER 661.

Winding up of unregistered company

Meaning of Unregistered Company [S. 582]

The expression includes any partnership, association or company consisting of more than seven members[84] at the time of the petition, but does not include—

(1) a railway company incorporated by an Act of Parliament or other Indian law or any Act of the British Parliament;

(2) a company registered under the Companies Act;

(3) a company registered under any previous company law, excepting those having registered office in Burma, Aden or Pakistan before their separation from India.

It has been held that "the word 'association' has to be understood in its general sense and not with reference to the provisions in Section 11 of the Act". Thus, construed, there would be no bar to the winding up of the Ex-servicemen's Rehabilitation Association, registered under the Societies Registration Act, as an unregistered company, though its membership was more than that of 20 persons.[85] Save as stated above, an unregistered company includes any partnership, association or company consisting of more than seven members [at the time when the petition for winding up the partnership, association or company, as the case may be, is presented before the court.

A partnership firm which was not registered under the Partnership Act, 1932 was allowed to be wound up under this jurisdiction. The bar of S. 69 of the Partnership Act was not applicable because a petition for winding up is not a suit nor it is an action based on contract.[86]

---

84. A certificate from the Registrar of Firms that the firm had seven members on his record was held to be a sufficient proof of this requirement despite allegations that the firm had only five members. *Makhan Singh Devinder Pal Singh* v *Roja Oil Mills*, (1999) 98 Comp Cas 190 (P&H), here it could not be shown that the partnership had seven or more members, a petition for order of winding up not sustained. *R. Saraswathi* v *Shakthi Beneficial Corpn*, (1980) 50 Comp Cas 193 Kant. The right to apply for winding up accrues from the date of dissolution of the partnership. Under Article 137 of the Limitation Act, 1963, only three years would be available from that date. In this case the petition was late by a year, *Malini Rao* v *Hotel Dwarka*, (1997) 90 Comp Cas 179 AP.

85. *B. T. Industries* v *Madras Sapper Ex Servicemen's Rehabilitation Assn*, (1988) 63 Comp Cas 733 Kant. Under S. 665 of the English Act of 1985 it has been held that an international society consisting of States as members was not liable to be wound up as an unregistered company. *International Tin Council, Re*, [1987] 1 All ER 890 Ch D; followed in *Maclaine Watson* v *Deptt of Trade*, [1988] 3 All ER 257 CA.

86. *Shree Balaji Steels* v *Countermann-Peippers (India) Ltd*, (2003) 114 Comp Cas 193 Cal.

Winding Up [S. 583]

Such a company can be wound up under the Act and with some exceptions all the provisions of the Act relating to winding up are applicable.[87] Such a company can be wound up only by the Tribunal, not voluntarily.[88] The company may be wound up in the following circumstances:

(1) if the company has been dissolved, or has ceased to carry on business, or is carrying on business only for the purpose of winding up;[89]

(2) if the company is unable to pay its debts;

(3) if the Tribunal is of the opinion that it is just and equitable to wind up the company.[90]

The company is said to be unable to pay its debts in the following cases:[91]

(1) where a creditor to whom the company is indebted for more than Rs 500 has served a notice, but the company has not settled with him for three weeks;

(2) if any case has been filed against a member for a debt due from the company or from the member in his character as member, and the company has not within ten days settled the demand or procured the case to be stayed or indemnified the member against the sum due and the expenses *etc*;

(3) if any execution or other process has been returned unsatisfied in whole or in part;

(4) if it is otherwise proved to the satisfaction of the Tribunal that the company is unable to pay its debts.

---

87. The jurisdiction of the company court to order the winding up of an unregistered company cannot be ousted either by the dissolution of the firm by the partners or under an arbitration clause. *M. V. Parsvarthavardhana* v *M. V. Ganesh Pd*, (1999) 35 CLA 318 Ker.

88. S. 583(3). Proceedings under the section are not in the nature of a civil suit and, therefore, not affected by S. 34 of the Arbitration Act. See *M. Vinoda Rao* v *M. Janardhana Rao*, (1988) 64 Comp Cas 167 Kant. Where the dispute was about profits and capital of the firm, a petition for winding up was not allowed. The partners were already locked up in a civil suit for accounts and partition of family assets. *K. N. Eswara Rao* v *K. H. Shama Rao and Sons*, (2000) CLC 408 Kant. Registered partnerships are not excluded from the definition of unregistered company, *Polaroid India (P) Ltd* v *Naw Nirman Co (No 2)*, (2001) 105 Comp Cas Bom; petition for winding up is not a "suit" for the purposes of S. 69(2) of the Partnership Act, 1932 which bars the institution of a suit to enforce a right arising from a contract by a firm against any third party, *Shree Balaji Steels* v *Gontermann-Peipers (India) Ltd*, (2002) 114 Comp Cas 193 Cal.

89. This clause will cover cases where the partnership firm has already been dissolved; clauses (*b*) and (*c*) apply to cases where the firm is subsisting, *Malini Rao* v *Hotel Dwarka, Hyderabad*, (1994) 1 Andh LT 36.

90. S. 582(4). *K.N. Eswara Rao* v *K.H. Shama Rao and Sons*, (2001) 103 Comp Cas 306 Kant. The dispute regarding profit between partners of a firm is not a sufficient ground for winding up under S. 583 of the Act.

91. S. 582(5).

Winding Up of Foreign Companies [S. 584]

Where a foreign company, having had a place of business in India, has ceased to carry on its business, it may be ordered to be wound up as an unregistered company even if it has already been dissolved in its mother country.[92]

Contributories [S. 585]

A contributory for this purpose means a person who is liable to contribute to the payment of any debt of the company or for adjustment of their mutual rights or the costs *etc.*, of winding up.

These provisions are additional to the rest of the provisions of the Act relating to winding up, all of which are also applicable.[93]

These provisions do not exclude the operation of the Partnership Act relating to dissolution even if the firm in question is likely to fall in the definition of an "unregistered company".[94]

Period of limitation [S. 458-A]

In computing the period of limitation for the purposes of the claims of a company in winding up, the period from the date of the petition to the date of the order of winding up (both inclusive) and the period of one year immediately following the winding up order is to be excluded. Thus, the company in winding up has the benefit of an additional period covering the time from the commencement of the proceeding to the date of the order and one more year from the date of the order.[95] Where leave of the court had to be obtained for filing the company's claim, the time lost in obtaining the

---

92. See *Rajan Nagindas Doshi v British Burma Petroleum Co*, (1972) 42 Comp Cas 197 Bom; *Inland Revenue v Highland Engg Co, Scotland*, (1975) SLT 203: 1976 JBL 51; *RBI v BCCI (Overseas) Ltd, (No 1)*, (1993) 78 Comp Cas 207 Bom; *RBI v BCCI (Overseas) Ltd, (No 2)*, (1993) 78 Comp Cas 230 Bom.

93. S. 589.

94. *Vasantrao v Shyamrao*, (1977) 4 SCC 9: (1977) 47 Comp Cas 666; *G.P. Ganapaiah v M. T. R. Associates*, (1986) 59 Comp Cas 359 Kant; *Navjeevan Enterprises (P) Ltd v T. N. Ramalingaiah*, (1985) 58 Comp Cas 217 Kant; *Deutsche Dampschiffshrts v Bharat Aluminium Co*, (1984) 55 Comp Cas 727 Cal. The provisions of the Act relating to stay or restraint of proceedings are also applicable and on the passing of a winding up order suits or legal proceedings become stayed unless permitted by the court [Ss. 586-587]. Stay of proceedings against the company does not extinguish the liability of individuals, neither does it operate as a stay of proceedings against them, *Venkoba Rao v B.K. Shreenivasa Iyengar*, (1997) 88 Comp Cas 383 Kant.

95. See *Punjab Finance (P) Ltd, Re*, (1978) 48 Comp Cas 271 Punj; *Official Liquidator, Security & Finance (P) Ltd v Pushpa Wati Puri*, (1978) 48 Comp Cas 385 Del. *Karnataka Steel & Wire Products v Kohinoor Rolling Shutters & Engg Works*, (2003) 1 SCC 76. This provision has been brought in to enable the official liquidator to file a claim on behalf of the company, which was legally enforceable on the date of winding up, after excluding the period u/S. 458-A so that the company or its shareholders would not suffer any loss. *Jagdish Parshad Gupta v Youngmen Benefit Chit (P) Ltd*, (1981) 51 Comp Cas 201 Del; *Pushpa Wati Puri v Official Liquidator*, (1984) 56 Comp Cas 88 Del. The period of limitation depends upon the nature of the proceedings. *Official Liquidator v Southern Screws (P) Ltd*, (1988) 63 Comp Cas 749 Mad.

leave, the period between the date of petition and winding up order was excluded and one more year was added.[1] The claim of the company should be alive at the time of the winding up petition.[2] If the company's claim is alive on the date of the petition for winding up, the right to sue accrues to the official liquidator on order of winding up. Three years time plus one more year would be available.[3] Where the company's debt had already become time-barred before presentation of the winding up petition it could not be revived under S. 458-A.[4]

Article 137 of the Limitation Act, 1963 applies to proceedings under Section 446. The period of limitation commences for the purposes of that section from the date of the winding up order or appointment of a provisional liquidator.[5]

Abuse of Legal Process

It is a settled principle of law that a petition for winding up cannot be permitted to be used as an ordinary mode of recovery of claims and counter-claims. The jurisdiction of the company court while entertaining and deciding the company petition was a limited one and the company court normally was reluctant to go into disputed questions of facts requiring detailed evidence and investigation and more so when such claims were based upon the alleged breach of terms of an agreement. The High Court of the area in which the company's registered office is situated can entertain the petition for the winding up of the company and all the powers of the winding up have been given to the High Courts.

Information as to pending liquidations [S. 551]

If the winding up of a company is not completed within one year of commencement, the liquidator has to prepare a statement in the prescribed

---

1. *Sudarsan Chits (India) Ltd* v *Uma Sharma*, (1992) 73 Comp Cas 381 Ker; *Sudarsan Chits (India) Ltd* v *Madlam Narasimhulu Chetty*, [1993] 3 Comp LJ 96 Ker.
2. *Karnataka Steel and Wire Products Ltd* v *Kohinoor Rolling Shutters*, (1993) 78 Comp Cas 96 Kant (FB). The starting point depends upon the right of the company and the nature of its claim to which is added the benefit of this section, *Best and Crompton Engg Ltd* v *Official Liquidator*, AIR 1995 Mad 20: (1995) 82 Comp Cas 77.
3. *Unico Trading and Chit Funds (India) (P) Ltd* v *Zahaor Hasan*, (1991) 71 Comp Cas 270 Kant. Followed in *Unico Trading and Chit Funds (India) (P) Ltd* v *S.H. Lohati*, (1982) 52 Comp Cas 340 Kant; *United Hire-Purchase & Land Finance (P) Ltd*, (1996) 87 Comp Cas 246 P&H.
4. *Karnataka Steel & Wire Products* v *Kohinoor Rolling Shutters & Engg Works*, (2002) 112 Comp Cas 606 SC. *Shivmoni Steel Tubes Ltd* v *Durgapur Steel Plant*, (2006) 132 Comp Cas 684 Kant.
5. See *K.P. Ulahaman* v *Wandoor Jupiter Chits (P) Ltd*, AIR 1989 Ker 41: (1989) 65 Comp Cas 178, winding up order passed on Dec 20, 1973 and a claim was filed on Feb 28, 1978 and the same was held to be within time. The period between the filing of the petition and the winding up order was excluded and one more year was added. For other decisions to the same effect, see *Maruti Ltd* v *Parry & Co Ltd*, (1989) 66 Comp Cas 309: [1989] 3 Comp LJ 384 P&H and *New Kerala Roadways (P) Ltd* v *K. K. Nandal*, [1988] 3 Comp LJ 35 Ker: (1989) 66 Comp Cas 715.

form containing the prescribed particulars and duly audited by a person who is qualified to be a company auditor. The statement must be filed within two months of the expiry of the first year and thereafter each year. If the winding up is by the Tribunal, it should be filed in the Tribunal (a copy with the Registrar), and in the case of voluntary winding up, with the Registrar. Auditing of the statement is not necessary where the liquidator has to get his accounts audited under Section 462. In the case of the liquidation of a Government company, a copy has to be sent to the Central Government or States which are its members. Creditors and contributories are entitled to copies and inspection on prescribed fee. Any default by the liquidator in complying with the requirements and any person falsely claiming himself to be a creditor or contributory, are punishable.

Any person stating himself to be a creditor or contributory in writing, shall have the right of inspecting the documents and a person falsely claiming to be so is liable to punishment under Section 182 of the Indian Penal Code, 1860.

Liquidator's miscellaneous powers [S. 546]

The powers specified below may be exercised by the liquidator with the sanction of the Tribunal where the winding up is by the Tribunal or with the sanction of a special resolution where the winding up is voluntary:

1. The payment of a class or classes of creditors in full;
2. Compromise or arrangement with creditors, the word "creditors" for this purpose including persons claiming to be creditors or having or alleging themselves to have any claim, present or future, certain or contingent, ascertained or sounding only in damages, against the company or whereby the company may be rendered liable;
3. Compromising any call, or liability to call, debt and any claim, present or future, certain or contingent, ascertained or sounding only in damages, subsisting or alleged to subsist between the company and a contributory or alleged contributory or other debtor or person apprehending liability to the company; settling all questions relating to or affecting the assets of the company or its winding up; he may do so on such terms as may be mutually agreeable and take any security for the discharge of the call, debt, liability or claim and give a complete discharge for the same.

In the case of winding up by the Tribunal, the Supreme Court is empowered to make rules in respect of the exercise by the liquidator of any of the above powers and then the power shall be exercisable subject to such conditions, restrictions and limitations as may be specified in those rules.[6]

---

6. S. 546 (1-A).

In the case of voluntary winding up the exercise of the above powers shall be subject to the control of the Tribunal and for this purpose any contributory or creditor may apply to the Tribunal.[7]

This section will not authorise any compromise to be imposed upon any unwilling creditors which is quite possible under S. 391.[8] The sanction of a special resolution or that of the Tribunal is necessary for the sanctity of the transaction.[9] The power of the liquidator is very wide. The Tribunal will act with great caution before putting upon a transaction the stamp of its approval.[10]

Notification of liquidation [S. 547]

When a company is in winding up either voluntarily or by the Tribunal, all its invoices, orders for goods or business letters shall contain a statement that the company is being wound up, failing which the defaulting officer, liquidator, receiver or manager is liable to a fine up to Rs 5000.

Books and papers to be evidence [S. 548]

Where a company is being wound up, all the books and papers of the company shall, as between the contributories of the company, be *prima facie* evidence of the truth of all matters purporting to be stated in them. A *prima facie* evidence creates only a presumption of truth and thereby shifts the burden to the contributory to disprove the inference of truth.[11]

Inspection of books and papers [S. 549]

Subject to the restrictions contained in the Supreme Court Rules, after an order of winding up by the Tribunal, creditors and contributories have the right to inspect the books and papers of the company. The Tribunal may allow inspection if the right is not going to be abused[12] and even to a person who is facing misfeasance proceedings.[13] A provision for secrecy in the Articles may not prevent inspection[14] except where the winding up is for purposes of reconstruction.[15]

Enforcement of duty of liquidator to make returns, etc. [S. 556]

The liquidator has to deliver or file some documents in the performance of his functions and also to give notices, *etc*. This section provides the

---

7. S. 546 (2) and (3).
8. *Albert Life Assurance Co Ltd, Re*, (1871) 6 Ch App 381.
9. *Union Bank* v *Gobind Singh*, ILR 4 Lah 283, but compare with *Cyclemakers Coop Supply Co* v *Sims*, [1903] 1 KB 477.
10. *Bank of Hindustan, China & Japan* v *Eastern Financial Assn Ltd*, (1869) 3 Moore's IA 15, PC.
11. *Great Northern Salt & Chemical Works, Re*, (1887) 36 Ch D 702; *Kesar Singh* v *Joint Official Liquidator of Radheysham Beopar Co*, AIR 1937 Lah 61.
12. *People's Bank of Northern India, Re*, AIR 1937 Lah 821.
13. *Subramaiah Setty* v *Official Liquidator*, (1985) 57 Comp Cas 626: [1985] 2 Comp LJ 205 Kant.
14. *London & Yorshire Bank* v *Cooper*, (1885) 15 QBD 83.
15. *Glamorganshire Bkg Co, Re; Morgan case*, (1884) 28 Ch D 620.

procedure consequent upon a default. It says that if the liquidator does not make good the default within 14 days after the service on him of a notice, the court may make an order directing the liquidator to make good the default within such time as may be specified in the order. An application for this purpose may be made by any creditor or contributory or the Registrar. The order of the court may provide that all costs of and incidental to the application shall be borne by the liquidator.

Meetings to ascertain wishes of creditors or contributories [S. 557]

This section empowers the court in all matters relating to winding up to have regard to the wishes of creditors or contributories and for this purpose to call their meetings and appoint a person as the chairman of a meeting. The court may give due weight to the value of a creditor's debt, and the number of votes that may be cast by each contributory.

Courts or persons before whom affidavits may be sworn [S. 558]

Affidavits required by the Act may be sworn in India before any court or the Tribunal, judge or person lawfully authorised to take and receive affidavits and, in any other country, either before any court, judge or person lawfully authorised to take or receive affidavits in that country or before any Indian Consul or Vice-Consul. All courts, judges, justices, commissioners and person acting judicially in India are required to take judicial notice of the seal, stamp or signature, of the functionaries described above in reference to affidavits or other documents to be used for the purposes of the Companies Act.[16]

COMPANIES AUTHORISED TO BE REGISTERED

PART IX

Companies capable of being registered (S. 565)

Following types of company have been recognised for the purposes of registration and re-registration under the Act:

1. Any company consisting of seven or more members which was in existence on May 1, 1882 including companies registered under the Acts of 1857 and 1860 or any law corresponding to those Acts which was in force in Part-B states.

2. Any company consisting of seven or more members formed before or after the commencement of the present Companies Act, 1956 under any other Act of Parliament or Act of Parliament of UK or Letters Patent in force in India or is otherwise duly constituted according to law. The section provides that the registration is not

---

16. *K. K. Roy (P) Ltd, Re*, [1967] 1 Comp LJ 216: (1967) 37 Comp Cas 737 Cal, an affidavit sworn before a notary in a foreign country accepted though it would not have been evidence under Indian laws.

to be regarded as invalid even if the registration has been brought about for the purpose of getting the company wound up under the Act.

Vesting of property [S. 575]

This section provides that on registration under this part, all property, movable and immovable (including actionable claims) belonging to the company at the date of its registration pass to and vest in the company. A partnership was converted into a private limited company. One of the effects was that the property of the partnership became vested in the company on registration. Copyrights of the partnership also became vested in the company. No separate transfer was necessary for this purpose. An assignment deed was not necessary.[17]

---

17. *LKS Gold Palace* v *LKS Gold House Ltd*, (2004) 122 Com Cas 896 Mad.

24

Miscellaneous

REGISTRATION OFFICES, OFFICERS AND FEES

Registration offices [S. 609]

The Central Government can open registration offices at places it thinks fit. The Government may appoint Registrars, Additional, Deputy and Assistant Registrars and may make regulations as to their duties; fix their salaries; authorise making of seals for authentification of documents.

Inspection, production, and evidence of documents kept by the Registrar [S. 610]

The section confers upon the members of the public the right of inspection and of obtaining copies of documents filed with the Registrar. The inspection shall be in accordance with the rules made under the Declaration of Records Act, 1917. The right extends to any documents kept by the Registrar, being documents filed or registered by him in pursuance of the Companies Act or making a record of any fact required or authorised to be recorded or registered in pursuance of the Act. The right of inspection can be exercised on payment of prescribed fees.

The Registrar can also be asked on payment of prescribed fee to give a certified copy of a company's certificate of incorporation or a copy or extract of any other document or any part thereof.

The prospectus of a company and other papers and documents filed along with it can be inspected within 14 days of the date of the publication of the prospectus and at other times with the permission of the Central Government. Documents in connection with the prospectus which have to be registered under S. 605 can be inspected within 14 days of the date of publication and at other times with the permission of the Central Government.

A process for production of any document by the Registrar has to issue from the Court. The Process should bear a statement on its face that it is issued with the leave of the Board.

Certified copies issued by the Registrar are admissible in evidence in all legal proceedings as of equal validity with the original document.

Documents which have to be filed or registered within a fixed period of time, may be registered after the expiry of that period on payment of additional prescribed fees.

The Amendment of 1996 (S. 610-A) permits the filing of documents in micro films, facsimile copies of documents, computer printouts and documents on computer media.

Filing and inspection through electronic form [S. 610-B]

The Central Government has been authorised to make Rules for bringing about the facility of filing requisite documents in an electronic form and also that of inspection of document in electronic form. Sections 610-B, 610-D, and 610-E, have been inserted into the Act for this purpose by the Amendment of 2006.

Enforcement of duty of company to make returns etc. to Registrar [S. 614]

If a company fails to file requisite papers with the Registrar, the latter should give a 14 day notice to the company to make good the default. In case of further default, any creditor or member or the Registrar can get an order from the court. The order may provide that the costs shall be borne by the company or by any officer who is responsible for the default.

The Registrar is an administrative officer and not a court or an adjudicating authority. He is bound to follow guidelines and instructions provided by Government circulars. Where two rival factions in a company filed two different returns, it was the Registrar's duty to take both of them to the company's file in accordance with Government guidelines and not to accept one and to reject the other.[1]

The procedure prescribed by the section has to be followed for compelling a company to make good its default in filing documents for registration of charges under Section 125 of the Act.[2]

Power of court trying offences to direct filing of documents [S. 614-A]

Where the court is trying an offence arising out of a default in filing documents with the Registrar, the court may, irrespective of the result of the trial, order the officer or any employee of the company to make good the default within such time as may be allowed.

Power of Central Government to direct companies to furnish information or statistics [S. 615]

The Central Government can require a company to furnish information or statistics on any matter in connection with its constitution or working and within a time that may be specified in the order. Such an order has to be published in the Official Gazette. The date of publication is the date of demand. When the order is on an individual company, it should be served on the company in the manner laid down in Section 51. For ascertaining the correctness and completeness of the particulars furnished, the Government may demand more information and require the

---

1. *S.R. Bhattacharya* v *Union of India*, (1998) 91 Comp Cas 37 Del.
2. *ICICI Bank Ltd* v *Klen & Marshall Manufacturers & Exporters Ltd*, (2000) 28 SCL 123 CLB.

production of relevant records or documents. The Government may even constitute an inquiry by a named person. There is a punishment for submitting wrong or incomplete information. An information can also be demanded from an officer of the company but he cannot be punished unless the court is convinced that he was in a position to comply with the order. The provision is applicable to foreign companies carrying on business in India.

Fee in Schedule X to be paid [S. 611]

Schedule X carries a tariff of fees which is payable to the Registrar for the purpose of getting a company registered. It also indicates the structure of fees payable for filing of documents. In the case of delay in filing documents, the Registrar is authorised to receive the document on payment of such an additional fee not exceeding ten times the amount of the original fee as the Registrar may require.[3]

Section 612 provides that all such fee as is collected under the Act shall be paid into the public account of India in the Reserve Bank.

Section 613 empowers the Central Government to reduce the fee, charges etc., which are otherwise payable under the Act.

OFFENCES

Cognizance of offences under the Act [S. 621]

Any violations of the Act which constitute an offence are cognizable only on a complaint by the Registrar, Government or a shareholder of the company. The only exception specified in the section is a prosecution of delinquent officers and members of a company under Section 545. In such cases a complaint can be filed by any person who is interested in the winding up of the company. The word ''shareholder'' would include a person who has purchased the shares of a company and has applied to the company for registering him as a shareholder.[4] A proviso to the section added by the Amendment Act of 2000 says that the court may take cognizance of offence relating to issue and transfer of securities and non-payment of dividend on a complaint in writing by a person authorised by SEBI.

---

3. When a document filed by a company is defective, the Registrar is empowered by Regulation 17 of the Companies Regulations, 1956 to bring the defect to the notice of the company giving it 15 days' time to rectify the defect. If the company still fails to do so, the Registrar will take the defective document on record without prejudice to his powers to take action. Press Note No 12/92 of Dec 12, 1992.

4. *Federal Bank Ltd* v *Sarala Devi Rathi*, (1997) 88 Comp Cas 323 Raj. A complainant, who did not aver in his complaint that he was a shareholder and also concealed that an order of CLB in his favour was stayed by the High Court, had to face dismissal, *V.M. Modi* v *State of Gujarat*, (1997) 88 Comp Cas 871: [1997] 3 Comp LJ 244 Guj; *S. C. Bhatia* v *P. C. Wadhawa*, (1998) 30 Corpt LA 135 P&H.

The bar of the section does not apply to a prosecution by the company of any of its officers and also to any action taken by the liquidator of a company in respect of any offence alleged to have been committed in respect of any of the matters included in Part VII (Ss. 425-560) or in any other provision of this Act relating to the winding up of companies. For the purposes of this provision, a liquidator of a company shall not be deemed to be an officer of the company.

Where a complaint is made by the Registrar or by a representative of the Central Government, then, notwithstanding anything contained in the Criminal Procedure Code, the personal attendance of the complainant in the court shall not be necessary, unless the court for reasons to be recorded in writing requires personal attendance.

A complaint was allowed to be filed at the place of the transaction. The court was of the view that trade in securities was a country-wide phenomenon. The policy behind the penalty provisions would be defeated if a complaint against a company could lie only at the place of its registered office.[5]

Composition of certain offences [S. 621-A]

This section was inserted by the amendment of 1988. The provision became necessary because the concept of an "officer who is in default" has been so defined in Section 5 (also by the amendment of 1988) that a director who is there only ceremonially and who may have no control or grip over the affairs of or even contact with, the company, is also likely to be covered. Such a person may have to pay the price for being merely a director though he may not be responsible for the default in question. Now the facility of compounding an offence has been given so that anyone can get rid of the default by paying composition money and save himself from the torture of a punishment by way of fine.[6] The provision does not apply to offences which are punishable with imprisonment only or with imprisonment and fine. Where the amount of fine does not exceed Rs 50,000 it can be compounded by the Regional Director and, in other cases, by the Central Government. Quite obviously, the compromised amount of fine cannot exceed the amount which would have been otherwise leviable. Where the default has been made good by paying additional fee under Section 611, the amount of such fee can go towards reduction of the fine money which the compromise may bring about.

Where an offence has been repeated within a period of three years from the date of the last similar offence, it cannot be compromised. Where an

---

5. *Ranbaxy Laboratories Ltd* v *Indra Kala*, (1997) 88 Comp Cas 348 Raj.
6. Failure to deliver debenture certificates within the time delimited by S. 113 or even within the extended time has been held to be a compoundable offence, *Vikrant Tyres Ltd, Re*, (1995) 17 Corpt LA 100 CLB Mad : (1995) 83 Comp Cas 210, it was compounded on payment of Rs 5000.

offence was compounded and three years thereafter has been repeated, the repeated offence should be taken to be the first offence.

Regional directors have to work under the supervision and control of the Central Government. An application for composition has to be presented to the Registrar who will forward it to the Regional Director or the Central Government, as the case may be. The fact that an offence has been compounded must be brought to the notice of the Registrar within seven days whether the compounding was before or after the institution of any prosecution. After the compounding of an offence, prosecution proceedings for the same cannot be launched. Where the compounding was done after a prosecution had already been taken up, the composition should be brought to the notice of the Registrar who will inform the court in which the prosecution is pending and thereafter the court shall discharge the company or the officer in question.

While dealing with an application for compounding an offence which arises out of default in filing documents *etc.*, with the Registrar, the defaulting company or officer may be ordered to file the documents on payment of additional fee leviable under Section 611 within a specified time.[7] An employee of the company or officer so ordered will have to suffer a penalty for his default in complying with the order which may extend to an imprisonment for six months or fine up to fifty thousand rupees.

An offence which is punishable with fine or imprisonment or both can be compounded only with the permission of the court in accordance with the provisions of the Criminal Procedure Code. An offence which is punishable with imprisonment only or with imprisonment and fine cannot be compounded.[8]

Jurisdiction to try offences [S. 622]

There is a categorical declaration in the section that no court inferior to that of a Presidency Magistrate or a Magistrate of the first class shall try an offence under this Act.

---

7. An application for compounding was rejected where the company had not made good the default yet, *General Produce Co Ltd, Re,* (1994) 81 Comp Cas 570 CLB.
8. *See* Circular No 5/93 of April 28, 1993 issued by DCA as to matters connected with this power. A default of technical nature (misdescription of a head of account: deposits being described as secured loans) was allowed to be compounded at a nominal fine of Rs 100 for the company and Rs 10 for secretary and each director. The compounding power of the CLB was not affected by the pending appeal in the High Court for quashing of proceedings, *Usha India Ltd, Re,* (1996) 85 Comp Cas 581 CLB. For procedural guidance see *Reliance Industries Ltd, Re,* (1997) 89 Comp Cas 67 and 465 CLB. Permission of the court under the Criminal Procedure Code is not required for compounding under the section, *Hoffland Finance Ltd, Re,* (1997) 90 Comp Cas 38: [1997] 3 Comp LJ 341 CLB. *Ritesh Polysters Ltd, Re,* (2004) CLC 1628 CLB, prosecution after 8 years, compounding allowed because there was no chance of adverse consequences in any way whatsoever.

An offence punishable with fine only which is committed by a person within a Presidency Town may be tried summarily and punished by the Presidency Magistrate.[9]

Offences under the Act are non-cognizable.[10] Prosecutors are appointed by the Central Government.[11]

In the case of an acquittal by any court other than a High Court, the Central Government may authorise the filing of an appeal against such acquittal and it will be a valid appeal notwithstanding anything contained in the Criminal Procedure Code.[12]

Section 625 provides about payment of compensation in cases of frivolous or vexatious prosecution.[13]

Application of fines [S. 626]

A court, imposing any fine under this Act may direct that the whole or any part thereof shall be applied in or towards payments of the costs of the proceedings or rewarding of the person on whose information or at whose instance the fine is recovered.

Production and Inspection of books where offence committed [S. 627]

Where an application is made to a High Court Judge in chambers by the Public Prosecutor of the State or by the Central Government or by a company prosecutor appointed under Section 624-A, there is a reasonable cause to believe that any person while an officer of the company committed an offence in connection with the management of the company's affairs and that evidence of the company, an order may be passed authorising any person to inspect the books and papers for the purpose of investigating and obtaining evidence of the commissions of the offence and requiring the manager of the company or officer of the company named in the order to produce the books and papers to a person, place and time mentioned in the order. The power extends to banking companies also subject to due modifications that its exercise will be confined only to the affairs of the company and the second type of order requiring any officer to produce books etc, will not be passed.[14]

The orders under the section are not appealable.

---

9. S. 623.
10. S. 624.
11. S. 624-A.
12. S. 624-B.
13. *Ratansi Morarji (P) Ltd* v *Kiriti D. Morarji,* (2004) 55 SCL 310 Bom damages to company allowed because of filing of false case against it.
14. The aid of the section is not available in the case of a shareholder seeking to prosecute the company's directors, *Kishan Rao* v *P. Santha Reddy,* [2000] CLC 1911 AP.

Penalty for false statements [S. 628]

Many statements have to be prepared under the Act relating to the affairs of the company. The section requires that statements which are required by the Companies Act to be prepared should not carry any particular which is false in a material respect. Hence, if any person makes a statement which he knows to be false in any material particular or which omits any particular knowing it to be material and, if no punishment is otherwise provided in the Act in that respect, he is punishable with imprisonment extending up to two years and is also liable to a fine. A prosecution under this section for the offence of fabrication of a document coming under S. 75 was allowed.[15] The court said that the period of limitation for a complaint begins from the date on which the complainant acquired knowledge of the commission of the offence and not the date on which the documents (annual accounts in this case) were filed in the office of the Registrar.[16]

The Government appointed a special judge for trial of offences punishable under the Companies Act. The Government order was held to be not quashable by a court exercising jurisdiction under S. 482, CrPC.[17]

Penalty for false evidence [S. 629]

Intentionally giving false evidence in any examination upon oath or solemn affirmation authorised under the Act or in any affidavit, deposition or solemn affirmation, in or about the winding up of any company under the Act or otherwise in or about any matter arising under the Act, is punishable with imprisonment extending up to seven years and shall also be punishable with a fine.

Penalty where no specific penalty provided [S. 629-A]

Any default in complying with the regulatory requirements of the Act is generally punishable under a penalty provision in the section itself. But even so there are many sections which prescribe one thing or the other but which do not carry any penalty provision. This section is intended to deal with such contradictions. This section also applies to defaults in complying with the conditions, restrictions *etc.*, subject to which an approval was granted. The penalty provided is fine extending up to Rs 5000 and, in the case of a continuing default, Rs 500 for every day of default. The Karnataka High Court held that on directors' failure to call a meeting on a requisition received by them, Section 169(*b*) gives an

---

15. *G. Ravi Kumar Reddy* v *Murali Krishna*, (2005) 127 Comp Cas 653 AP.
16. *Thomas Philip* v *Asstt ROC*, 2005 CLC 975 Ker.
17. *G. Ravi Kumar Reddy* v *Murali Krishna*, (2005) 127 Comp Cas 653 AP.

alternative remedy to requisitionists to call a meeting by themselves and therefore directors' failure would not attract Section 629-A.[18]

Form and procedure of certain applications [S. 640-B]

The section deals with applications to the Central Government under Sections 259, 268, 310, 311 and empowers to prescribe forms.

Power to alter Schedules [S. 641]

The section authorises the Government to alter schedules. The Government cannot widen or constrict the scope of the Act or its policy.[19]

Power of Central Government to make Rules [S. 642]

The Central Government has the power to make rules in respect of all the matters which have to be prescribed by it and generally to carry out the purposes of the Act. The rules so promulgated may provide that contraventions will be punishable with a fine extending up to Rs 5000 and in case of a continuing default, with a fine extending up to Rs 500 for every day of default. Rules framed in the exercise of this power have to be laid before each House of Parliament while it is in session for a total period of 30 days. At the end of the session during which the 30-day period is completed, the rules become effective either as originally framed or subject to any modifications or annulment, made by the Parliament. Anything already done on the basis of the original rules will not be prejudiced by any such modification or annulment.[20] The Companies (Amendment) Act, 1999 (w.e.f. 31-10-1998) has added sub-section (4) of the section prescribing the same requirement of Parliamentary approval for Regulations made by SEBI.

Power of Central Government to make Rules relating to winding up [S. 643]

The Central Government is required to make rules providing for all matters relating to the winding up of companies which are to be prescribed under the Act and may also make rules on matters as may be prescribed.

The Central Government is also empowered to make rules, consistent with the Code of Civil Procedure, 1908 on the following matters: (1) as to mode of proceedings to be had for winding up a company in High Courts and in Courts subordinate to High Courts; (2) for the voluntary winding up of companies, whether by members or by creditors; (3) for the holding

---

18. *Anantha R. Hegde* v *Captain T.S. Gopalakrishna*, [1996] 3 Comp LJ 333 Kant: (1996) 23 Corpt LA 142: (1998) 91 Comp Cas 312 Kant.
19. *J. K. Industries Ltd* v *ROC*, (1997) 27 Corpt LA 195.
20. *See* The Companies (Central Government) General Rules and Forms, 1956. *See* further the Central Government's power to alter Schedules as conferred by S. 641 and to lay down Forms and Rules as conferred by S. 640-B.

of meetings of creditors and members in connection with proceedings under Section 391 (compromise and arrangements); (4) for giving effect to the provisions of the Act for reduction of capital; (5) generally for all applications to be made to the court under the provisions of this Act; (6) holding and conducting of meetings to ascertain the wishes of creditors and contributors; (7) the settling of the list of contributors and rectification of the register of members where required and collecting and applying the assets; (8) the payment, delivery, conveyance, surrender, or transfer of money, property, books or papers to the liquidator; (9) the making of calls; and (10) the fixing of time within which debts and claims shall be proved.[21]

Annual report on working of Act [S. 638]

The Central Government is under a duty to cause a general annual report on the working and administration of the Companies Act to be prepared and laid before both Houses of Parliament within one year of the close of the year to which the report relates.

Condoning of delays in certain cases [S. 637-B]

A number of provisions of the Act prescribe a time-limit for filing of applications. This section gives power to the Central Government to condone the delay in filing an application. Reasons for condoning delays must be recorded in writing. A similar power of condonation exists in reference to delays in filing documents with the Registrar. Here again reasons for condonation have to be recorded in writing.

Delegation by Central Government of its powers [S. 637]

The Central Government is empowered by this section to delegate any of its functions or powers to such authority or officer as may be specified in the notification. The delegation can be subject to such conditions, restrictions and limitations as may be specified in the notification: The section clearly says that the prior to appoint a person as a public trustee under Section 153-A and the power to make rules cannot be delegated.

The powers and functions which cannot be delegated under this section are those conferred by or mentioned in the following sections:

Section 10 [Jurisdiction of Courts]; Section 81 [Further Issue of Capital]; Section 89(4) [Termination of disproportionally excessive voting rights]; Section 213 [Financial year of holding company and subsidiary]; Sections 235 and 237 [Investigation of affairs]; Sections 241-245 [Powers

---

21. Section 637-A empowers the Central Government or the Tribunal to accord approval in certain cases specified in the section subject to certain conditions and payment of prescribed fee.

after investigation of affairs]; Section 247 [Investigation of ownership of company]; Section 372 [inter-corporate investments]; Section 396 [Amalgamation in national interest]; Section 399(4) and (5) [Right to apply under Section 397 or 398]; Section 401 [Right of Central Government to apply under Section 397 or 398]; Section 408 [Power of Central Government to prevent oppression or mismanagement]; Section 410 [Appointment of Advisory Committee]; Section 448 [Appointment of official Liquidator]; Section 609 [Registration offices]; Section 620 [Power to modify Act in relation to Government companies]; Section 638 [Annual report by Central Government]; Section 641 [Power to alter Schedules]; and Section 642 [Power of Central Government to make rules].

Enforcement of orders of one court by other courts [S. 635]

An order of one court can be enforced by another court. A copy of the order should be produced to the proper officer of the court required to enforce the order. A certified copy of the order shall be a sufficient evidence of the order. It then becomes the duty of the court to enforce the order. A similar procedure has to be followed when the orders of the Company Law Board or Tribunal have to be enforced through a court.[22] The procedure to be followed in the matter of execution of an order made by the company court is different from that laid down in the Code of Civil Procedure. It is sufficient to produce to the executing court a certified copy of the order sought to be executed.[23]

Protection of acts done in good faith [S. 635-A]

Acts done by the Government or any officer of the Government or any other person in pursuance of the Act and in good faith cannot be the subject-matter of any prosecution or other legal proceeding. The same protection is available in respect of the publication by or under the authority of the Government or such officer of any report, paper or proceedings.

Protection of employees [S. 635-B]

The section provides for protection of employees during investigation by an inspector and pendency of proceedings before courts against any person concerned in the conduct and management of the affairs of a company.

---

22. A certified copy of the order is sent to the court which has to enforce the order and it is not necessary that the matter should be transferred to the executing court in the manner of a decree under CPC. *Sindhu Chits and Trading (P) Ltd* v *Khayirunnissa*, (1993) 76 Comp Cas 878 Kant.

23. *Anand Finance (P) Ltd* v *Amrit Dasarat Kakade*, (1996) 61 Del LT 305: (1997) 90 Comp Cas 350 Del.

Non-disclosure of information in certain cases [S. 635-AA]

The Registrar, any officer of the Government or any other person is not compellable to disclose to any court, tribunal or other authority as to whence he got any information which led the Central Government to direct a special audit or an investigation and which is material in that connection.

Enforcement of orders of court [S. 634]

Orders of court under the Companies Act are enforceable in the same manner as a decree made by a court in a suit pending before it.[24]

Enforcement of orders of Company Law Board [S. 634-A]

The Company Law Board can enforce its orders in the same manner as if it were a decree made by a court in a suit pending before it. If the CLB is unable to do so, it may send the order for execution to the court which has jurisdiction over the party against whom the order is to be enforced. A consent order would be enforceable in the same manner.[25] An amicable settlement order has been held to be enforceable.[26]

Till the date of hearing, in this case, the company had not complied with directions of rectification of register of members contained in the CLB order. The prayer of the petitioner for enforcement was granted. Further time was given to the company to ensure compliance failing which a Bench officer was to visit the office of the company and rectify the register by inserting the name of the petitioner and also to authenticate the entry and also share certificates.[27]

Power to require security for costs [S. 632]

In a suit or proceeding instituted by a limited liability company, if the Tribunal has a reason to believe that the company will not be able to pay the costs of the defendant, should he win, the Tribunal may require sufficient

---

24. An order against the director of a company in winding up calling upon him to pay the debt of the company which he guaranteed was enforced under this section. *Deutsche Bank v S. P. Kala*, (1992) 74 Comp Cas 577 Bom. An order under S. 397 was held to be enforceable under this section as a decree, *Hungerford Investment Trust Ltd v Turner, Morrison Co Ltd*, (1994) 1 Cal LJ 500. *Coastal Roadways Ltd v Kanoi Plantation (P) Ltd*, (2006) 132 Comp Cas 503 Cal, the decree of a company court cannot be executed by the High Court in the exercise of its original civil jurisdiction. It could be executed by the company court alone.
25. *TNK Gonvidaraju Chettiar & Co Ltd v Kuki Leather (P) Ltd*, (2000) 28 SCL 267 CLB.
26. *Betrand Faure v IFB Automotive Seating Systems Ltd*, (1999) 34 CLA 277 CLB. *Gujarat Industrial Investment Corpn v Sterling Holiday Resorts (India) Ltd*, (2006) 133 Comp Cas 795 CLB order for registering transfer of shares enforceable in the manner of a court decree.
27. *Deccan Cements Ltd v Geekay Exim (India) Ltd*, (2005) 5 Comp LJ 169 CLB: (2005) 126 Com Cases 894; *Manish Mohan Sharma v Ram Bahadur Thakur Ltd*, (2006) 131 Comp Cas 149 SC, the CLB ordered arrangement and directed parties to execute documents within specified time. The order being a preliminary decree, was directed to be implemented in the manner of a court decree. *Kamdhenu Commercials (P) Ltd v Advent Computer Services Ltd*, (2007) Comp Cas 208 CLB, failing compliance, Bench Officer to endorse the transfer.

security to be given for those costs and may stay all proceedings until the security is given.[28]

A person who is seeking an order for costs can simultaneously ask the Tribunal for striking out the proceedings.[29] The security for costs can be ordered only by the Tribunal and not by any other Authority like Controller of Patents.[30]

The Tribunal may hesitate in ordering a security for costs where the litigation started by the company involves a point of general public importance.[31]

Penalty for improper use of "Limited" or "Private Limited" [S. 631]

A fine extending up to Rs 500 for every day of default is leviable when the words "limited" or "Private Limited" are used without proper authorisation for anybody's trade or business.

---

28. There should be reason to believe that the company would not be able to pay costs. All the circumstances must be considered to arrive at a decision, *Keary Developments Ltd* v *Tarmac Construction*, [1995] 3 All ER 534. There should be credible evidence for a reason to believe that the company would not be able to pay the defendant's costs, should he win, *Europa Holdings Ltd* v *Circle Industries (UK) plc*, (1993) BCLC 320 CA.
29. *Orsank SA* v *Spencer Associates*, The Times, Feb 19, 1998 CA.
30. *Abdullayoglu's Patent Application*, [2000] RPC 18.
31. *Lancefort Ltd* v *An Bord Pleanala Ireland*, [1998] 2 IR 511 Ireland.

APPENDIX I

Changes made by the Companies (Amendment) Act, 2002 (First)

Producer Companies

This Amendment Act added a new chapter, namely Chapter IX-A to the Act. The chapter contains a complete set of provisions dealing with producer companies. It runs from S. 581-A to 581-ZT.

Objects and Reasons

The statement of objects and reasons appended to the Bill proceeded as follows:

During the last decade, changes have taken place in the Indian economy, in the communication and transportation infrastructures, as well as in the method of commerce, banking and international trade. Liberalisation of the economy is in the process of changing the terms of trade between rural and urban, labour and industry, finance and commerce. Biotechnology, the information revolution, computerisation can all be used to raise the standard of living of the rural masses and ultimately link this economy with regional, national and global demand. Institutions are needed to link the rural economy with the emerging new opportunities. Rural producers are at a potential disadvantage given their generally limited assets, resources, education and access to advanced technology. In the present competitive scenario, if cooperative enterprises are to continue to serve rural producers, they require an alternative to the institutional form presently available under Law.

Keeping all this in view the Government constituted a Committee consisting of experts led by Dr Y.K. Alagh, economist, former Union Minister, to examine and make recommendations with regard to (*a*) framing a legislation which would enable incorporation of cooperatives as companies and conversion of existing cooperatives into companies and (*b*) ensuring that the proposed legislation accommodates the unique elements of cooperative business within a regulatory framework similar to that of companies. The Committee had a series of meeting during which it interacted with, and received responses from various cooperatives, institutes and individuals.

On the basis of the recommendations of the Committee the present Bill has been prepared with the main objective of facilitating formation of cooperative business as companies and to convert existing business into companies. The salient features of the Bill are:

    (*i*) to offer a statutory and regulatory framework that creates the potential for producer-owned enterprises to compete with other enterprises on a competitive footing. The Companies Act envisages and provides for various forms of companies including private limited, public limited, trusteeship companies and *nidhis,* each with specific and appropriate provisions applicable to them;

(*ii*) to provide for the formation and registration of producer companies which include the mutual assistance and cooperative principles within the more liberal regulatory framework afforded by the Company Law with suitable adaptations;

(*iii*) to provide an opportunity to cooperative institutions to voluntarily transform themselves into the new form of producer companies;

(*iv*) Under the Bill conversion of cooperatives to producer companies is purely voluntary;

(*v*) Member equity may not be publicly traded, but may only be transferred, with the approval of the producer company's Board of Directors. Producer companies would not be vulnerable to the takeover by multinationals or other companies;

(*vi*) The conversion option by cooperative society to producer company can be exercised only if two-thirds of the members of the concerned society vote in favour of a resolution to that effect;

(*vii*) The new form of company is designated as "producer company" to indicate that only certain categories of persons can participate in the ownership of such companies. The members of the Producer Company have necessarily to be "primary producers", that is persons engaged in an activity connected with, or relatable to, primary produce;

(*viii*) The objects of a producer company have been defined to include, among other things, production, processing, manufacture and sale of primary produce as well as allied matters.

———

APPENDIX II

The Companies (Amendment) Act, 2006[1]

[NO 23 OF 2006]

An Act further to amend the Companies Act, 1956

Be it enacted by Parliament in the Fifty-seventh Year of the Republic of India as follows:—

Prefatory Note.—Statement of Objects and Reasons.—In context of the rapid developments witnessed in technology, the Ministry of Company Affairs decided to enable the operations carried out by the Ministry and its field offices to be performed more efficiently and effectively through the use of contemporary information technology and computers. It was felt that the earlier efforts at computerisation had not yielded the desired efficiency in operation of the system and an operating system that took into account contemporary technology was necessary. Therefore, it was decided to implement a comprehensive e-Governance system and programme to achieve the above objective.

2. The Ministry of Company Affairs on the recommendations of Department of Information Technology, is implementing an e-Governance initiative through a project named as "MCA-21". This project will provide the public, corporate entities and others an easy and secure online access to the corporate information, including filing of documents and public access to the Information required to be in the public domain under the statute, at any time and from anywhere. This would also result in efficiency in statutory supervision of corporate processes and efficient professional services under the Companies Act, 1956 (the Act).

3. The filing and registration of documents is a statutory requirement under the Act. At present, the Act lays down the procedures for filing of various documents in physical form and the processes associated therewith. While, the broad enabling framework for such an initiative is available under the Information Technology Act, 2000 read with Companies Act, 1956, enabling provisions would still be required to support certain online electronic processes which have since become available due to technological advancement for various detailed procedural requirements under the Companies Act, 1956.

4. It is therefore, proposed to insert new Sections 610-B, 610-C, 610-D and 610-E in the Companies Act, 1956 so as to make provision for electronic filing system and for payment of fees through electronic form under the said Act which the said Act which are essential for the successful implementation of the MCA-21 Project. After the proposed amendments to the Companies Act, 1956 have been enacted, the documents in electronic form duly authenticated with digital signatures shall be accepted under the provisions of the Act. The proposed electronic system also provides for multiple modes of payment of statutory fees.

5. The provisions of the Companies Act, 1956 allow an individual to be a director of up to fifteen companies and such companies can be located in the jurisdiction in any of the Registrars of Companies. There is a need for individual identity of persons intending to be directors of companies to be established. This would also facilitate effective legal action against the directors of such companies under the law, keeping in

---

1. Received the assent of the President on May 29, 2006 and published in the Gazette of India, Extra., Part II, Section 1.

view the possibility of fraud by companies and the phenomenon of companies that raise funds from the public and vanish thereafter. It is, therefore, proposed to insert new Sections 266-A, 266-B, 266-C, 266-E, 266-F and 266-G in the Companies Act, 1956 so as to, *inter alia*, provide for allotment of a unique Director Identification Number to any individual, intending to be appointed as a director in a company or to any existing director of a company, for the purpose of his identification as such, through electronic or other form and to provide for penalty for any violation in this regard.

6. This Bill seeks to achieve the above objectives.

1. Short title and commencement.—(1) This Act may be called the Companies (Amendment) Act, 2006.

(2) It shall come into force on such date as the Central Government may, be notification, appoint and different dates may be appointed for different provisions of this Act.

2. Amendment of Section 253.—In Section 253 of the Companies Act, 1956 (1 of 1956) (hereinafter referred to as the principal Act), the following proviso shall be *inserted*, namely:—

"Provided that no company shall appoint or re-appoint any individual as director of the company unless he has been allotted a Director Identification Number under Section 266-B."

3. Insertion of new Sections 266-A, 266-B, 266-C, 266-D, 266-E, 266-F and 266-G.—After Section 266 of the principal Act, the following sections shall be *inserted*, namely:—

"Director Identification Number"

266-A. *Application for allotment of Director Identification Number.*—Every—

(*a*) individual, intending to be appointed as director of a company; or

(*b*) director of a company appointed before the commencement of the Companies (Amendment) Act, 2006

shall make an application for allotment of Director Identification Number to the Central Government in such form, and manner (including electronic form) along with such fee, as may be prescribed:

Provided that every director, appointed before the commencement of the Companies (Amendment) Act, 2006, shall make, within sixty days of the commencement of the said Act, such application to the Central Government.

Provided further that every applicant, who has made an application under this section for allotment of a Director Identification Number, may be appointed as a director in a company, or, hold office as director in a company till such time such applicant has been allotted the Director Identification Number.

266-B. *Allotment of Director Identification Number.*—The Central Government shall, within one month from the receipt of the application under Section 266-A, allot a Director Identification Number to an applicant, in such manner as may be prescribed.

266-C. *Prohibition to obtain more than one Director Identification Number.*—No individual, who had already been allotted a Director Identification Number under Section 266-B, shall apply, obtain or possess another Director Identification Number.

266-D. *Obligation of director to intimate Director Identification Number of concerned company or companies.*—Every existing director shall, within one month of the receipt of Director Identification Number from the Central Government, intimate his Director Identification Number to the company or all companies wherein he is a director.

266-E. *Obligation of company to inform Director Identification Number to Registrar.*—(1) Every company shall, within one week of the receipt of intimation under Section 266-D, furnish the Director Identification Number of all its directors to the Registrar or any other officer or authority as may be specified by the Central Government.

(2) Every intimation under sub-section (1) shall be furnished in such form and manner as may be prescribed.

266-F. *Obligation to indicate Director Identification Number.*— Every person or company, while furnishing any return, information or particulars as are required to be furnished under this Act, shall quote the Director Identification Number in such return, information or particulars in case return, information or particulars relate to the director or contain any reference of the director.

266-G. *Penalty for contravention of provisions of Section 266-A or Section 266-C or Section 266-D or Section 266-E.*—If any individual or director, referred to in Section 266-A or Section 266-C or Section 266-D or a company referred to in Section 266-E, contravenes any of the provisions of those sections, every such individual or director or the company, as the case may be, who or which, is in default, shall be punishable with fine which may extend to five thousand rupees and where the contravention is a continuing one, with a further fine which may extend to five hundred rupees for every day after the first during which the contravention continues.

Explanation.—For the purposes of Sections 266-A, 266-B, 266-C, 266-D, 266-E, 266-F, the Director Identification Number means an identification number which the Central Government may allot to any individual, intending to be appointed as director or any existing directors of a company, for the purpose of his identification as such.''

Insertion of new Section 610-B, 610-C, 610-D and 610-E.— After Section 610-A principal Act, the following sections shall be *inserted*, namely:

''610-B. *Provisions relating to filing of applications, documents, inspection, etc., through electronic form.*—(1) Notwithstanding anything contained in this Act, and without prejudice to the provisions contained in Section 6 of the Information Technology Act, 2000 (21 of 2000), the Central Government may, by notification in the Official

Gazette, make rules so as to require from such date as may be specified in the rules, that—

(*a*) such applications, balance-sheet, prospectus, return, declaration, memorandum of association, articles of association, particulars of charges, or any other particulars or documents as may be required to be filed or delivered under this Act or rules made thereunder, shall be filed through the electronic form and authenticated in such manner as may be specified in the rules;

(*b*) such document, notice, any communication or intimation, required to be served or delivered under this Act, shall be served or delivered under this Act through the electronic form and authenticated in such manner as be specified in the rules;

(*c*) such applications, balance-sheet, prospectus, return, register, memorandum of association, articles of association, particulars of charges, or any other document and return field under this Act or rules made thereunder shall be maintained by the Registrar in the electronic form and registered or authenticated, as the case may be, in such manner as may be specified in the rules;

(*d*) such inspections of the memorandum of association, articles of association, register, index, balance-sheet, return or any other document maintained in the electronic form, which is otherwise available for such inspection under this Act or rules made thereunder, may be made by any person through the electronic form as may be specified in the rules;

(*e*) such fees, charges or other sums payable under this Act or rules made thereunder shall be paid through the electronic form and in such manner as may be specified in the rules;

(*f*) the Registrar shall, register change of registered office, alteration of memorandum of association or articles of association prospectus, issue certificate of incorporation or certificate of commencement of business, register such document, issue such certificate, record notice, receive such communication as may be required to be registered or issued or recorded or received, as the case may be, under this Act or rules made thereunder or perform duties or discharge functions or exercise powers under this Act or rules made thereunder or do any act which is by this Act directed to be performed or discharged or exercised or done by the Registrar, by the electronic form, in such manner as may be specified in the rules.

(2) The Central Government may, by notification in the Official Gazette, frame a scheme to carry out the provisions specified under sub-section (1) through the electronic form:

Provided that the Central Government may appoint different dates in respect of different Registrar of Companies or Regional Directors from which such scheme shall come into force.

610-C.—*Power to modify Act in relation to electronic records (including the manner and form in which electronic records shall be filed.*—(1) The Central Government may, by notification in the Official Gazette, direct that any of the provisions of this Act, so far as it is required for the purpose of electronic record specified under Section 610-B in the electronic form,—

(*a*) shall not apply, in relation to the matters specified under clauses (*a*) to (*f*) of sub-section (1) of Section 610-B, as may be specified in the notification; or

(*b*) shall apply, in relation to the matters specified under clauses (*a*) to (*f*) of sub-section (1) of Section 610-B only with such consequential exceptions, modifications or adoptions as may be specified in the notification:

Provided that no such notification which relates to imposition of fines or other pecuniary penalties or demand or payment of fees or contravention of any of the provisions of this Act or offence shall be issued under this sub-section.

(2) A copy of every notification proposed to be issued under sub-section (1), shall be laid in draft before each House of Parliament, while it is in session, for a total period of thirty days which may be comprised in one session or in two or more successive sessions, and if, before the expiry of the session immediately following the session or the successive sessions aforesaid, both Houses agree in disapproving the issue of the notification or both Houses agree in making any modification in the notification, the notification shall not be issued or, as the case may be, shall be issued only in such modified form as may be agreed upon by both the Houses.

610-D. *Providing of value added services through electronic form.*—The Central Government may provide such value added services through the electronic form and levy such fees as may be prescribed.

610-E. *Application of provisions of Act 21 of 2000.*—All the provisions of the Information Technology Act, 2000 relating to the electronic records (including the manner and format in which the electronic records shall be filed), insofar as they are not inconsistent with this Act, shall apply, or in relation, to the records in electronic form under Section 610-B.''

SUBJECT INDEX